MAGILL'S SURVEY OF AMERICAN LITERATURE

Revised Edition

MAGILL'S SURVEY OF AMERICAN LITERATURE

Revised Edition

Volume 5

Odets—Stein

Edited by

Steven G. Kellman
University of Texas, San Antonio

SALEM PRESS, INC.
Pasadena, California   Hackensack, New Jersey

Editor in Chief: Dawn P. Dawson

Editorial Director: Christina J. Moose	*Production Editor:* Joyce I. Buchea
Project Editor: Tracy Irons-Georges	*Acquisitions Editor:* Mark Rehn
Copy Editors: Sarah M. Hilbert	*Research Supervisor:* Jeffry Jensen
Elizabeth Ferry Slocum	*Research Assistant:* Rebecca Kuzins
Editorial Assistant: Dana Garey	*Graphics and Design:* James Hutson
Photo Editor: Cynthia Breslin Beres	*Layout:* William Zimmerman

Cover photo: Edgar Allan Poe (The Granger Collection, New York)

Library of Congress Cataloging-in-Publication Data

Magill's survey of American literature / edited by Steven G. Kellman. — [Rev. ed.].
    p. cm.
    Includes bibliographical references and index.
    ISBN-10: 1-58765-285-4 (set : alk. paper)
    ISBN-13: 978-1-58765-285-1 (set : alk. paper)
    ISBN-10: 1-58765-290-0 (vol. 5 : alk. paper)
    ISBN-13: 978-1-58765-290-5 (vol. 5 : alk. paper)
  1. American literature—Dictionaries. 2. American literature—Bio-bibliography. 3. Authors, American—Biography—Dictionaries. I. Kellman, Steven G., 1947- II. Magill, Frank Northen, 1907-1997. III. Title: Survey of American literature.
  PS21.M34 2006
  810.9′0003—dc22

                                                  2006016503

First Printing

PRINTED IN THE UNITED STATES OF AMERICA

Contents

COMPLETE LIST OF CONTENTS

Volume 1

Volume 3

Volume 4

Volume 5

Volume 6

Complete List of Contents

MAGILL'S SURVEY OF
AMERICAN LITERATURE

Revised Edition

CLIFFORD ODETS

Born: Philadelphia, Pennsylvania
July 18, 1906
Died: Los Angeles, California
August 14, 1963

In his first six plays, Odets established himself as the leading proletarian playwright of the 1930's.

Carl Van Vechten/Library of Congress

BIOGRAPHY

Clifford Odets's banner year was 1935, when he catapulted from the obscurity of acting with the Group Theatre to being the toast of Broadway. Odets became a founding member of the newly formed Group Theatre in 1931 after brief acting stints elsewhere.

His rise to fame began in 1935 with *Waiting for Lefty*, an agitprop play he wrote in three days late in 1934, rushing to enable its entrance in a *New Masses* contest. It was presented the following January at a *New Masses* benefit. *Waiting for Lefty* consisted of six vignettes around a central theme: a strike by taxicab drivers.

The play transfixed audiences. At the end, with the revelation that Lefty, the union organizer, has been killed, the audience is asked what the cab drivers should do. There is a collective cry of "Strike, Strike, Strike." Few plays have caught the public imagination as quickly as *Waiting for Lefty*. Within two months, it played all over the Western world, and it won Yale University's George Pierce Baker Drama Cup.

Meanwhile, the Group Theatre, seeking to capitalize on Odets's celebrity, quickly staged *Awake and Sing!* (pr. 1935) , an adaptation of his *910 Eden Street*, which had never been produced. Meanwhile Odets dashed off a short play, *Till the Day I Die* (pr. 1935), to create a double bill with *Waiting for Lefty*, whose running time of less than one hour

made it too short to be staged singly. By March, Odets had three plays on Broadway and a commitment for a Broadway production of his *Paradise Lost* for the 1935-1936 theater season.

Clifford Odets was born to twenty-year-old Lithuanian immigrant Louis J. Odets and his nineteen-year-old wife, Pearl Geisinger Odets. Louis Odets, a feeder in a print shop, hotly pursued the American dream of affluence. He moved his family from Philadelphia to the Bronx and bought his own print shop there.

Louis was upper middle class by the time Clifford was a teenager. The son, however, deplored both the bourgeois values his father embraced and his father's contempt for anything artistic, especially his son's interests in writing and theater. He smashed Clifford's typewriter to keep him from writing so much. Odets was closer to his aunt and uncle, Esther and Israel Rossman, than to his parents. They spoke in the Jewish American cadences that Odets later incorporated into his plays.

In 1923, Clifford dropped out of high school and worked with the Drawing Room Players, Harry Kemp's Poets' Theatre, and Mae Desmond's stock company. In 1929, he joined the Theatre Guild, but he left in 1931, going to the Group Theatre as a founding member.

Although Odets longed to be part of a family, he felt little closeness to his parents or his two sisters, Florence and Genevieve. The Group became his surrogate family. Members of the company lived together and cared about one another.

The success of Odets's first four plays posed a difficult problem for him. Whereas he had been living, as he once said, on ten cents a day, Hollywood studios now offered him tempting financial incentives to become a script writer. He capitulated in 1936, going West to write the script for *The General Died at Dawn* (1936). Odets felt guilty for having succumbed to Hollywood's enticements, thereby tacitly acceding to the bourgeois standards he deplored in his own father. In Hollywood, Odets met Austrian actress Luise Rainer, whom he married in 1937.

Golden Boy, produced in 1937, resulted from the anguish he felt at selling out. He wrote this new play specifically for the Group. It focuses on a Golden Gloves boxer who is forced to abandon his aspirations. Odets faced a personal choice similar to that facing golden boy Joe Bonaparte. This play helped rescue the Group Theatre from almost certain financial collapse, enabling it to stay afloat for a few more years. Odets's next play, *Rocket to the Moon* (pr. 1938), about an amorous dentist, disappointed critics as well as audiences.

At the onset of World War II, the U.S. economy recovered and unemployment was virtually eliminated. The social problems that enraged Odets in the 1930's faded. However, his life was beginning to fall apart. The Group Theatre was on the brink of dissolution. His marriage ended in divorce in 1941. People pondered the question posed by Frank Nugent on viewing Odets's first film: "Odets, where is thy sting?"

Odets's next play, *Night Music* (pr. 1940), did not succeed, and several of his Hollywood film scripts remained unproduced, as did his film script for *Night Music*. His final play during this period, *Clash by Night* (pr. 1941), had a disappointing run. Meanwhile, Odets met actress Betty Grayson, whom he married in 1943 and with whom he had two children, Nora and Walt. In 1951, three years before Grayson's death, she divorced Odets.

In 1952, the House Committee on Un-American Activities summoned Odets because he was suspected of having communist ties. During its inquisition, he gave the committee the names of associates who perhaps had communist affiliations, as many intellectuals in the 1930's did. Odets never forgave himself for buckling under the pressure of the congressional inquiry.

Between 1949 and 1954, he had three plays produced, of which *The Country Girl* (pr. 1950) was the most successful. It was turned into a film that brought its star, Grace Kelly, an Academy Award for best actress. In his final decade, Odets wrote less, although when he died of cancer in 1963, he had completed four new scripts for *The Richard Boone Show* and was under contract to write nine more. The year after his death, a musical version of *Golden Boy*, a collaboration with William Gibson, was produced on Broadway.

ANALYSIS

Critics are beginning to reconsider the full body of Clifford Odets's writing. Because he was initially viewed as a proletarian playwright, many critics expected him to write proletarian plays forever. When this expectation was not met, they were disappointed. The overt anger, vigor, and vitality of the early plays was lacking in the later ones, largely because a changing society had robbed Odets of the topic he was most effective in writing about, the exploitation of working-class people by capitalists.

Odets might have redirected his anger to other topics in the 1940's and 1950's—the House Committee on Un-American Activities hearings (by which he was personally affected), the Joseph McCarthy witch hunts, U.S. involvement in the Korean War, government waste, women's rights, racial discrimination, and anti-Semitism. A number of contemporary playwrights have taken on such topics.

Had Odets followed such a course, his anger might not have been viewed as genuine. Odets had moved into a new socioeconomic sphere, but doing so did not preclude his writing important and meaningful plays. Critics argue that Odets did not do his most effective writing in *Rocket to the Moon*, *Night Music*, or *Clash by Night*. He wrote these plays during a period of considerable personal upheaval, but even in them, he shows considerable concern for working people.

A seven-year gap followed the production of *Clash by Night*. During this time, Odets continued to write for Hollywood film companies, but many of his scripts were shelved. His disenchantment with the film industry grew and finally found expression in 1949 with the production of *The Big Knife* (pr. 1949), a pointed indictment of some of the practices of film corporations.

Just as taxicab drivers had been exploited in *Waiting for Lefty* and a promising boxer-violinist had been exploited by commercial forces in *Golden Boy*, Charlie Castle is being exploited by a Hollywood studio pressuring him to sign a fourteen-year, four-million-dollar film contract. Charlie resists selling himself to the studios, but he then becomes responsible for a fatal hit-and-run automobile accident. The studio has finagled a deal for Buddy Bliss, Charlie's publicist, to accept responsibility for tragedy. The bill for their corrupt involvement falls due: Charlie must sign with the studio or be outed and brought to justice.

Audiences and critics found it difficult to sympathize with someone whose problem was that he was being blackmailed into signing a contract that would bring him four million dollars. Charlie is not like the taxicab drivers in *Lefty*. He is, however, not unlike Joe Bonaparte in *Golden Boy*, and in indirect ways he bears a striking resemblance to the Clifford Odets who left the Group Theatre and, in his own eyes, sold out to Hollywood. Even though *The Big Knife* was not successful on stage in 1949, the play is well structured and filled with bristling dialogue. It appeared therapeutic for Odets to vent his feelings in such a play.

His next play, *The Country Girl*, despite a limited stage run in 1950, was successful as a film. The play marks a departure for Odets because it essentially has just two people in the cast, although there are minor characters in it as well. This action focuses on Frank Elgin, a down-and-out actor—an alcoholic who is being given one more chance to salvage himself and his career. His wife, Georgie, having assumed a maternal role in Frank's life, vows to help him overcome his alcoholism and regain his status as an actor.

The play afforded actors two extremely challenging roles, one for Frank, who must come across as a weak character and deceptive, mendacious, and unsure of himself. In opposition to him is the long-suffering wife-mother whose marriage is about to collapse because of Frank's problem but who makes one final, monumental effort to redeem him. Odets succeeded in building such incredible tensions between his two major characters that the action throughout remains taut almost to the breaking point. In that respect, the play is masterful.

In the last of Odets's plays, *The Flowering Peach*, produced and published in 1954, the author returns to the kinds of roots that made *Awake and Sing!* the hit it was in 1935. *The Flowering Peach* is Odets's version of the parable of Noah and the Ark.

Noah and his family bear a resemblance to the three generations living in Bessie Berger's respectable household. The kind of gentle wit one finds in *Awake and Sing!* is repeated by a Noah whose son Japheth is a confirmed skeptic and whose son Ham is a materialist with an eye to making business even as the world teeters on the brink of destruction. The Yiddish American vernacular in this last Odets play marks a welcome return to the authentic dialogue that characterizes plays such as *Awake and Sing!* and *Paradise Lost*.

One finds definite influences from the Group Theatre in many of Odets's plays. Because the Group discouraged the star system that such organizations as the Theater Guild promoted, its directors—Cheryl Crawford, Lee Strasberg, and Harold Clurman—favored ensemble plays in which six or eight characters play roughly equivalent parts. Odets certainly had this preference in mind when he wrote *Waiting for Lefty*, *Awake and Sing!*, and *Paradise Lost*, and he returns to it in his final production, *The Flowering Peach*.

WAITING FOR LEFTY

First produced: 1935 (first published, 1935)
Type of work: Play

In discrete vignettes, six taxicab drivers tell their stories and consider how to protect their interests.

In *Waiting for Lefty*, Odets captures fully the folk idiom of the six people on whom his play focuses. Each is a taxicab driver. Each has a story to tell. The six characters come from several walks of life but have one thing in common: They are forced by economic necessity to become cab drivers. Each exemplifies the antagonism that exists between the values of the business community and the human values of the play's protagonists.

In the six vignettes, connected only by the job that the actors have in common, Odets explores such matters as collective bargaining, anti-Semitism, environmental irresponsibility, family cohesiveness, and the exploitation of the masses. The big question the play poses concerns the extent to which workers should control their own destinies. A union organizer, who does not appear on stage, is scheduled to meet with them to discuss means by which workers can deal with big business. Lefty never arrives because he has been murdered on his way to the meeting. When his death is re-vealed, the audience, already at fever pitch, is drawn into the action of the play with the cry to "Strike, Strike, Strike."

Waiting for Lefty was premiered on January 14, 1935, and was staged innovatively, played on a blacked-out stage with the characters projected as shadows created by directional lighting. From the standpoint of play production, *Waiting for Lefty* was just what amateur groups were looking for. It had the simplest of sets, and its very structure lent it a versatility and flexibility that made it appealing to producers and directors. News of this play quickly spread across the country and throughout Europe, where *Waiting for Lefty* was performed extensively.

The dialogue in this play is rapid-fire. One critic referred to its short, jabbing scenes and commented on how well Odets captured the speech rhythms of the characters who told their stories in their highly charged vignettes. Nevertheless, the play, which was so right for its time, lacks the timely appeal of some of Odets's other plays. Michael Mendelsohn in *Clifford Odets: Humane Dramatist* (1969) muses that *Waiting for Lefty* has become dated, as dead as yesterday's newspaper, which is probably an apt assessment.

AWAKE AND SING!

First produced: 1935 (first published, 1935)
Type of work: Play

Three generations of a Jewish American family in the Bronx cope with the economic upheaval of the Great Depression.

Three generations of the Berger family live under one roof. The mother, Bessie, is the glue that has held the family together during difficult times. She is fearful that she, like an old woman on nearby Dawson Street, will be evicted from her home, her belongings put out on the street around her.

Odets has a well-balanced cast in *Awake and Sing!*. Bessie, whose father, Jakob, a left-leaning idealist, lives in her house, has a subdued husband, Myron, and two children, Ralph and Hennie. She has also taken in a boarder to enhance her slim budget. Appearances mean everything to Bessie, who wants little more from life than respectability. Her decent existence is severely threatened. She has already coped with one assault on her family's respectability, her daughter Hennie's pregnancy out of wedlock, but she forces Hennie into a loveless marriage to the boarder to whom she rents a room.

The son, Ralph, is appalled by the shotgun union his mother has engineered. An unemployed idealist, Ralph sides philosophically with his grandfather. Jakob rails against families, saying, "This is a house? Marx said it—abolish such families." Ralph complains that life should not be printed on dollar bills. The vernacular Odets achieves in this play is precisely the vernacular of the kinds of people around whom he grew up and whose speech patterns imprinted themselves indelibly on his mind.

In this play, Odets claimed that he was writing not about individuals so much as about a whole social class being sundered by economic problems beyond their control. One solution he offers is particularly chilling and ironic. Jakob, the idealist, disenchanted with the society in which he lives, goes to the roof of the building in which the Bergers reside and throws himself into the street below. Before he does this, however, he makes Ralph the beneficiary on his five-thousand-dollar life insurance policy, expecting this will give Ralph new hope. In creating this ending, Odets shows the confusion of value systems under which some of his characters were living. Jakob, who would abolish families, gives Ralph the wherewithal to marry and create a family. Ralph, who does not want life printed on dollar bills, ironically is saved by five thousand such bills that will assure his future, at least for a while.

PARADISE LOST

First produced: 1935 (first published, 1936)
Type of work: Play

A middle-class family, the Gordons, becomes increasingly pressured by the Great Depression and by the dishonesty of the father's business partner.

Odets thought better of *Paradise Lost* than most Broadway critics did. The play, although disappointing in many respects, is significant for its almost flawless development of the character of Sam Katz, the dishonest business partner of Leo Gordon, the head of the Gordon household. Odets considered *Paradise Lost* the most profound of his four dramatic productions to that time. Joseph Wood Krutch, a leading critic of the 1930's, on the other hand, called the play a mere burlesque on *Awake and Sing!*, although that criticism was probably more harsh than the play deserved.

Odets, in this play, attempted to deal with the same problems of the Great Depression that had afflicted the Bergers in *Awake and Sing!*, but he chose to examine these problems from the perspective of a family of higher social standing than the Bergers. His differentiation is between the lower and upper middle class.

Whereas the Bergers could not afford to pay to have their son's teeth fixed, the Gordons had grown used to a relatively comfortable existence and had managed to acquire a few luxuries, such as an expensive piano, in the years before the economic chaos of the early 1930's. As in *Awake and Sing!*, Odets's major focus in *Paradise Lost* encompasses a class of people. He writes about their aspirations, thwarted by forces outside their control. They essentially seem like pawns in a great malevolent chess game.

The most compelling characters in *Paradise Lost* are Sam Katz and his wife, Bertha, who are prototypes for Frank Elgin and Georgie in *The Country Girl*. Sam has been Leo Gordon's partner for several years, but unbeknownst to Leo, Sam is basically dishonest and has embezzled from the company. Sam's problem is impotence, which he cannot admit to. He blames Bertha for their not having children. Like Georgie, Bertha is long-suffering and

sympathetic. She nurtures Sam, calling him a good boy and allowing him to live with his delusions. Like Georgie, she is the wife-mother that a man as insecure as Sam needs.

The list of problems facing the Gordon family is so daunting that it plunges *Paradise Lost* in the category of melodrama. Not only does Leo lose his business and uncover the duplicity of his trusted partner, but his son is dying of encephalitis. His other son, Ben, once an Olympic runner, turns to crime and is felled by a policeman's bullets. The daughter Pearl, who seemingly can succeed at nothing, becomes a recluse, after which Leo is forced into bankruptcy and the family is evicted from their home.

GOLDEN BOY

First produced: 1937 (first published, 1937)
Type of work: Play

Joe Bonaparte, a promising violinist, is also a boxer who, by following this avocation, injures his hands and destroys his musical possibilities.

The first of Odets's plays since *Waiting for Lefty* not to employ the Yiddish American vernacular at which Odets was so adept, *Golden Boy* is also the first play he wrote after going to California to write film scripts. In this play, Joe Bonaparte, a poor youth from humble circumstances, is faced with the agonizing decision of whether to continue in boxing, which will bring him substantial material rewards but will compromise his wish to have a career as a violinist. At the time he wrote this play, Odets was facing a personal crisis not unlike Joe's, but he sought to assuage his pain at leaving the Group Theatre by writing a play for them that might relieve some of the financial pressures that threatened to force the Group to disband.

In *Awake and Sing!*, Moe Axelrod, the cynic, speaks of "One thing to get another." Making choices is what life is all about. Joe Bonaparte opts for the comfort and security that boxing will afford him. He enjoys the outward manifestations of his success, particularly his supercharged Duesenberg roadster, but, as Gerard Weales has observed, he suffers from "the disintegration brought on by success." The very sensitivity that a good musician needs is antithetical to the qualities that good fighters need. It is too late for Joe to turn back. His hands are damaged beyond repair, and now he faces failure as a boxer. His end comes when he crashes his Duesenberg and dies from the impact.

SUMMARY

Clifford Odets essentially became a rebel without a cause. His considerable talents as a playwright were not lost, as his last three plays attest, but the anger that he played out with such conviction in his plays of the 1930's had cooled by the end of the decade. When the economic crisis against which he had railed had played out, Odets could find little left to replace it. Despite that, he remains one of the most inventive American dramatists of the twentieth century.

R. Baird Shuman

BIBLIOGRAPHY

By the Author

DRAMA:

Waiting for Lefty, pr., pb. 1935 (one act)
Till the Day I Die, pr., pb. 1935
Awake and Sing!, pr., pb. 1935
Paradise Lost, pr. 1935, pb. 1936
I Can't Sleep, pr. 1935, pb. 1936
Golden Boy, pr., pb. 1937
Rocket to the Moon, pr. 1938, pb. 1939
Six Plays of Clifford Odets, pb. 1939, revised pb. 1993 (as *Waiting for Lefty, and Other Plays*)
Night Music, pr., pb. 1940
Clash by Night, pr. 1941, pb. 1942
The Russian People, pr. 1942, pb. 1946 (adaptation of Konstantin Simonov's play *The Russians*)
The Big Knife, pr., pb. 1949
The Country Girl, pr. 1950, pb. 1951
The Flowering Peach, pr., pb. 1954

SCREENPLAYS:

The General Died at Dawn, 1936 (adaptation of Charles G. Booth's novel)
Blockade, 1938
None but the Lonely Heart, 1944 (adaptation of Richard Llewellyn's novel)
Deadline at Dawn, 1946 (adaptation of William Irish's novel)
Humoresque, 1946 (with Zachary Gold; adaptation of Fannie Hurst's story)
The Sweet Smell of Success, 1957 (with Ernest Lehman; adaptation of Lehman's novel)
The Story on Page One, 1960 (directed by Odets)
Wild in the Country, 1961 (adaptation of J. R. Salamanca's novel *The Lost Country*)

DISCUSSION TOPICS

- In an interview, Clifford Odets said that the secret to writing plays was less about knowing how to write than knowing how to connect with oneself. In what ways do you think Odets connects with himself in the plays you have read?

- Anti-Semitism was rife during the 1930's. To what extent is this reflected in the plays you have read by Odets?

- To what extent do you think young, aspiring playwrights today can find productive venues in which to work, as Odets did in the Group Theatre?

- Do the plays you have read by Odets tell you much about the status of women?

- Odets admits that he was writing about social classes rather than individuals. Do you think he did this at the expense of effective characterization?

NONFICTION:
The Time Is Ripe: The 1940 Journal of Clifford Odets, 1988

About the Author

Brenman-Gibson, Margaret. *Clifford Odets—American Playwright: The Years from 1906 to 1940.* New York: Atheneum, 1981.

Cantor, Harold. *Clifford Odets: Playwright-Poet.* Lanham, Md.: Scarecrow Press, 2000.

Herr, Christopher J. *Clifford Odets and American Political Theatre.* Westport, Conn.: Praeger, 2003.

Mendelsohn, Michael J. *Clifford Odets: Humane Dramatist.* Deland, Fla.: Everett/Edwards, 1969.

Miller, Gabriel, ed. *Critical Essays on Clifford Odets.* Boston: G. K. Hall, 1991.

Murray, Edward. *Clifford Odets: The Thirties and After.* New York: Ungar, 1968.

Odets, Clifford. *The Time Is Ripe: The 1940 Journal of Clifford Odets.* New York: Grove Press, 1988.

Shuman, R. Baird. "Clifford Odets and the Jewish Context." In *From Hester Street to Hollywood: The Jewish-American Stage and Screen,* edited by Sarah Blacher Cohen. Bloomington: Indiana University Press, 1983.

Weales, Gerard. *Clifford Odets: Playwright.* New York: Pegasus, 1971.

FRANK O'HARA

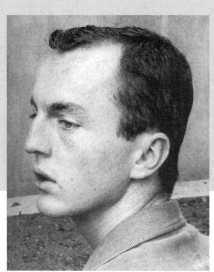

Born: Baltimore, Maryland
June 27, 1926
Died: Mastic Beach, New York
July 25, 1966

O'Hara renewed American poetry by his use of direct language, surreal imagery, humor, and personal subject matter.

Worcester Polytechnic Institute, Archives and
Special Collections/George C. Gordon Library/
Courtesy, George Montgomery

BIOGRAPHY

Francis Russell O'Hara was born in Baltimore, Maryland, on June 27, 1926. He grew up in central Massachusetts in Grafton, a suburb of Worcester. He attended local Catholic schools and graduated from St. John's High School in Worcester in 1944. After graduation he enlisted in the Navy and served as a sonar operator on a destroyer until his discharge in 1946. During his World War II service he did not see combat, although he was in the Pacific theater.

After military service, O'Hara entered Harvard University as an undergraduate, majoring first in music and later in English. He graduated from Harvard in 1950. While at Harvard, O'Hara was already writing poetry, and he was one of the founders of the Poet's Theatre in Cambridge. His play *Try! Try!* was produced at the Poets' Theatre in 1951. During the Harvard years, he met John Ashbery and Kenneth Koch, who were to become lifelong friends and subjects of a number of his poems. In 1950, O'Hara entered Michigan University to do graduate work in English, and in 1951 he was awarded the prestigious Avery Hopwood Major Award in Poetry. After a year at Michigan, he moved to New York City, which was to become his home until his death in 1966.

O'Hara was deeply involved in the New York art world during these years; he worked as an editor of *Art News* and as a special assistant and later as an associate curator of the Museum of Modern Art. Painting is very often the subject of his poems, and his technique has often been compared to that of modern painting. O'Hara was a friend of many of the most important modern painters, including Jasper Johns, Willem de Kooning, and Larry Rivers. They respected him as a fellow artist and appreciated his immediate and intelligent response to their paintings. O'Hara put together a number of exhibitions of such painters as Robert Motherwell, Franz Kline, and Arshile Gorky for the Museum of Modern Art. In 1959 he published *Jackson Pollock*, one of the earliest important studies of the painter. O'Hara was also well informed about modern music and wrote poems about Sergei Rachmaninoff and John Cage. For O'Hara, the arts were truly one and indivisible.

O'Hara wrote poetry at odd moments while he worked at the Museum of Modern Art. Some of these were circulated to friends or appeared in letters. He saw his poems as works designed to please friends or for special occasions rather than as monuments. Later, some of these poems were collected and published with the help of such friends as Ashbery, Koch, and James Schuyler. O'Hara did, however, publish several volumes during his life. His first book of poems, *A City Winter, and Other Poems*, was published in 1952, and was followed by *Oranges* in 1953. *Meditations in an Emergency* appeared in 1957, and many of his poems were included in *The New American Poetry 1945-1960*. One of his most typical volumes was *Lunch Poems*, which was published in 1964. Another important volume,

Love Poems (Tentative Title), was published in 1965. *The Collected Poems of Frank O'Hara* was published posthumously in 1971; many were amazed that the casual and occasional poems of O'Hara filled a volume of more than five hundred pages.

O'Hara was homosexual. His life was marked by intense friendships and love affairs, many of which became subjects for his poetry. There is a strong sense of the shared perspective of a small group in the poems. The intensity of the most casual experience and the significance of personal relationships is captured forcefully in O'Hara's poems, especially *Lunch Poems* and *Love Poems.* In July of 1966, O'Hara was fatally injured on Fire Island when a jeep struck him as he was waiting for a beach taxi. He died a few days later in Bayview Hospital at Mastic Beach, New York.

ANALYSIS

O'Hara's style and subject matter are very different from the dominant poetic tradition of the period. O'Hara disliked the complex modernism of T. S. Eliot, and he was displeased about Eliot's influence upon the most important critical school of the period, the New Criticism. He described Eliot's influence on modern poetry as "deadening." In contrast, he called his critical view "Personism"; this was a rejection of nearly all the formal aspects of poetry—such as rhyme, meter, assonance, even logical structure—while substituting for these elements the immediacy and presence of the individual speaking voice. Often, in some of O'Hara's most interesting and amusing poems, that personal voice is captured in conversation with friends about the seemingly trivial events of the day. There is no attempt to create symbolic or mythic depth out of these ordinary events; the emphasis is on the intensity and wit revealed in these exchanges and descriptions.

O'Hara did not, however, reject all poetic influence. He preferred the simplicity of diction of William Carlos Williams and the surrealistic imagery of the French Symbolists, especially Arthur Rimbaud, to the high modernism of poets who followed the lead of Eliot. Another important influence was the poetry of the Russian Formalist Vladimir Mayakovsky, whose riddling lines concentrated on making the literary device reveal itself. O'Hara never seeks to hide the fact that what he is creating is a work of art.

O'Hara also has a Walt Whitman-like openness to experience that is manifested in lists of people and places. The long list in "Second Avenue" is a good example of the technique. "And must I express the science of legendary elegies/ consummate on the Clarissas of puma and gnu, and wildebeest?" There is an exuberance in the production of witty lists. O'Hara has the same inclusiveness as Whitman, although O'Hara does not usually reach out to embrace all America. His world is bounded by Manhattan and the Hamptons. It is a particularly urban art that has little use for nature or the rural world.

Proper names, especially the names of friends, appear in nearly every one of his poems, and names dominate some of them. "At the Old Place" is a good example of O'Hara's insistence on naming. "Through the street we skip like swallows./ Howard malingers. (Come on Howard.) Ashes/ malingers. (Come on, J.A.) Dick malingers./ (Come on, Dick.) Alvin darts ahead. (Wait up,/ Alvin.) Jack, Earl, and Someone don't come." Naming seems to have a special value for O'Hara, although O'Hara's poetry seems, at times, to be addressed to those who know or can recognize the names that are invoked. Yet it is not necessary to know the names of places to which O'Hara refers, as the effect is to reveal the delight the speaker has about the world in which he lives.

O'Hara often mixes the real with the surreal in his poems to create what John Ashbery called "home-grown surrealism." A typical example can be found in the first stanza of "Je Voudrais Voir."

an immense plain full of nudes
and roses falling on them from the green air
a smile of utter simplicity speaking to the soldiers
of the camel corps, so brief and smelly

The effect is created by the precision of the detail and the strange mixture of roses and nudes, of a smile and the camel corps. O'Hara's version of Surrealism involves the connection of a conventional poetic image—the rose—to some esoteric imagery.

O'Hara once described some of his work as his "I do this, I do that poems." The most random and trivial events are related with a breathless excitement. Such a description can be found in "John Button Birthday":

And in 1984 I trust we'll still
be high together. I'll say "Let's go to a bar"
and you'll say "Let's go to a movie" and we'll go to
   both;
like two old Chinese drunkards arguing about
   their
favorite mountain and the million reasons for
   them both.

For O'Hara, every experience, even the most trivial, can become a poetic element. Poetry for O'Hara was made up not of grand moments but of small ones, especially those with friends, which the poet's voice singles out and exults over. Critic Marjorie Perloff has noted that O'Hara's "poetic world is one of immanence rather than transcendence."

Painters and painting were often the subjects of O'Hara's poems, and at times he used the structure of modern art in this poems. "Why I Am Not a Painter," paradoxically, is a good example of O'Hara's use of painting as subject and form. He describes a painter's process of inclusion and exclusion and contrasts it to his own method. Both the poet's and the painter's methods, however, are strikingly similar, as are the results. Both works are generated by an early impulse that may not exist in the completed work except as a remnant in the title. Neither art relies on logical form but rather on the path the work itself seems to take. Above all, the creation of a work of art—a painting or a poem—is something that cannot be consciously explained; some mystery about how it is brought about remains.

O'Hara's word choice is interesting. One of his favorite techniques is the use of exotic and strange words, which are often strung together: "Oh! kangaroos, sequins, chocolate sodas!/ You really are beautiful! Pearls,/ harmonicas, jujubes, aspirins!" O'Hara loves the sound of words for their own sake and for their strangeness. There is no attempt to transform such an amusing pattern of words into symbolic meaning; the pattern exists for its own sake.

O'Hara uses meter or rhyme only for effect, as in such lines as "At night Chinamen jump/ on Asia with a thump." The effect is comic rather than formal. The poetic line, however, is an important structural unit in O'Hara's poetry. Most of the lines run on, creating the effect of breathless conversation or suggesting the exuberance of a speaker as exulting over the wonder of life in all of its variety. O'Hara makes no attempt to keep his lines to similar metrical lengths, although he does attempt at times to create a visual design out of a series of lines.

"TO THE FILM INDUSTRY IN CRISIS"

First published: 1957 (collected in *The Collected Poems of Frank O'Hara*, 1971, 1995)

Type of work: Poem

A humorous celebration of the populist and mythic values of American films.

"To the Film Industry in Crisis" is a love letter from O'Hara to the most popular and accessible of the arts: motion pictures. The poem begins by excluding serious and pompous arts such as "experimental theatre" and "Grand Opera." The speaker rejects also "lean quarterlies and swarthy periodicals," because they, too, are for the elite, not the masses. The speaker does not merely approve of the "Motion Picture Industry" but declares his love and devotion to it. The title's emphasis on Hollywood as an industry effectively distinguishes the filmmaking world from the realm of art by defining it as a factory producing for the masses.

The second verse paragraph places O'Hara's preferences in a context. "In time of crisis, we must all decide again and again whom we love./ And give credit where it's due." O'Hara never makes clear what the "crisis" is, and the reference seems to be used as a comical provocation to inflate the reader's response to the subject.

The speaker rejects a few more candidates for his affection, such as the Catholic Church and the American Legion, and finally begins to discuss his true love: "glorious Silver Screen, tragic Technicolor, amorous Cinemascope,/ stretching Vistavision and startling Stereophonic Sound, with all/ your heavenly dimensions and reverberations and iconoclasms!" The technical innovations of the "industry" are greeted with the same hyperbole that went into their advertisement and promotion. Each of these has its own adjective; some of the adjectives are wildly inappropriate, such as "tragic Technicolor." The ironic point that O'Hara is making is that there can be no tragedy in the gaudy world of Technicolor.

The next section of the poem contains an even longer list of actors and their famous roles. The list ends with a reaffirmation of the devotion of the speaker: "yes, to you/ and to all you others, the great, the near-great, the featured, the extras/ . . . / my love!"

O'Hara often refers to the popular arts in his poems, and "To the Film Industry in Crisis" is his fullest and wittiest attempt to account for the power that motion pictures have over the public imagination. The poem first shows what films are not—high art—and then shows what they really are—magic. O'Hara does echo the hyperbole of his subject in his own style and reveal its essential function as providing myths by which to live.

"THE DAY LADY DIED"

First published: 1964 (collected in *The Collected Poems of Frank O'Hara*, 1971, 1995)
Type of work: Poem

The news of blues singer Billie Holiday's death turns the poet's trivial world into a tragic one.

"The Day Lady Died" is one of O'Hara's "I do this, I do that" poems, until the sudden reversal of the last few lines. The poem begins with the O'Hara speaker recording the details of the day. "It is 12:20 in New York a Friday/ three days after Bastille day, yes/ it is 1959. . . ." The casual description is an effective way of establishing the date and time in which a surprising and momentous event will be recognized.

The speaker switches to describing his own activities, which include getting a shoeshine and planning a train itinerary. He eats, and he buys "an ugly NEW WORLD WRITING to see what the poets/ in Ghana are doing these days." The preparations for the journey continue, as the speaker gets money at the bank and buys gifts for the people he is going to visit. There is a humorous aside about the bank teller, "Miss Stillwagon," who for once does not

look up the poet's bank balance; the poet also records his agitation about selecting the proper gifts.

Suddenly, in the midst of these mundane activities, the speaker experiences a moment of deep personal significance. The speaker buys a newspaper and sees "her" face on it. The poem's title, which refers to Holiday by her nickname, indicates who "her" is, although Holiday is not explicitly named in the poem. The news changes the poet's physical being ("I am sweating a lot by now," he remarks). He is then taken from the present moment back to a time when he had heard Holiday sing; he remembers "leaning on the john door in the 5 SPOT/ while she whispered a song along the keyboard/ to Mal Waldron and everyone and I stopped breathing."

The poem sets up its literally breathless moment by its cataloging of the trivial activities of the day. At other times, O'Hara seems to be using lists and names for their own sake, but in this poem there is a clear utility to these techniques, as the revelation transforms the ordinary into something memorable. It is interesting to note that the art of Billie Holiday is seen here as turning a public moment into a private one (she "whispers" a song in public), while O'Hara's art is to make private moments and experiences public.

"IN MEMORY OF MY FEELINGS"

First published: 1958 (collected in *The Collected Poems of Frank O'Hara*, 1971, 1995)
Type of work: Poem

The poem explores some of the different selves that live in the poet in order to sort out his authentic self, the artist.

"In Memory of My Feelings" is a surreal poem that attempts to find an authentic self amid the many selves that can be discerned within the speaker. The poet seems to relate these selves to the different feelings he has. For example, in the first section of the poem, he identifies both a "transparent" self that "carries me quietly, like a gondola, through the streets" as well as a number of "naked selves" that use "pistols" to protect themselves. The division continues as "One of me rushes/ to window #13 and one of me raises his whip. . . ." The speaker is also being hunted by some malign force.

The only unifying element in these contrasting selves is "love of the serpent." At first, this seems to be a phallic symbol; in the context of the poem, however, the serpent image operates as a symbol for the artist self, which the poet must acknowledge and privilege over all of his other selves. At the end of the poem's first section, the "transparent selves" are together "like vipers in a pail, writhing and hissing/ without panic, with a certain justice of response. . . ." The section's final line, in which "the aquiline serpent comes to resemble the Medusa," unites the various selves by the central symbol of the serpent. The Medusa, therefore, is not a threatening but a positive image.

The second section is a regressive movement dominated by references to those who have sacrificed their lives for the poet. "My father, my uncle,/ my grand-uncle and the several aunts. My/ grand-aunt dying for me. . . ." While this carnage of sacrifice is going on, the speaker is in a suite "in the Grand Hotel/ where mail arrives for my incognito." The cool facade is sometimes amusing in O'Hara's poems, but this one is clearly selfish, cruel, and isolated.

The next section begins to reverse the negatives, as the poet writes, "The most arid stretch is often richest." The speaker adopts the role of a war hero during the French Revolution or under Lord Nelson; however, he "wraps himself" in memories now "against the heat of life." The hero pose, finally, cannot be sustained, as it is an avoidance of life.

The following section deals with a real incident, a visit to Chicago. The poet begins to see some positive value in multiple selves: "Grace/ to be born

and live as variously as possible. The conception/ of the masque barely suggests the sordid identifications." There is, in contrast to section 3, an acceptance of life in its diversity that includes multiple selves. He then becomes a Hittite, a Chinese man, and a Native American who has "just caught sight of the *Niña,* the *Pinta,* and the *Santa Maria.*" He then asks "What land is this? so free?" That freedom consists of accepting the "whitemen" and their gift of "the horse I fell in love with on the frieze." The horse he is given is, as Marjorie Perloff suggests, a work of art. That acceptance of art as central to his existence serves as a transition to the last section of the poem.

The last section of the poem returns to the serpent, which is "coiled around the central figure." After briefly summarizing the different roles that have been assayed in the poem, the poet realizes what is needed. All the selves "I myself and singly must now kill/ and save the serpent in their midst." His essential being is as a serpent-artist, so the loss of the other selves becomes a gain that will enable him to live the fullest and truest life.

SUMMARY

O'Hara's poetry altered the range and possibilities of poetry in the middle of the twentieth century. He rejected complex modernism for a poetry of direct speech that dealt with everyday events. O'Hara showed other poets that a poem could be about any subject. It could be a description of the poet's daily actions or his changing relationships. There was no need for poetry to be profound; it needed only to delight. That delight and wit can be found in the details of nearly all of O'Hara's poems. O'Hara also expanded the range of poetic structures and subjects by his references to modern painting and French Surrealism. His poetry was at first criticized for being incoherent or trivial; however, later critics have confirmed that his poetry is grounded in an American literary tradition that includes such major figures as Walt Whitman and William Carlos Williams.

James Sullivan

BIBLIOGRAPHY

By the Author

POETRY:
A City Winter, and Other Poems, 1952
Oranges, 1953
Meditations in an Emergency, 1957
Odes, 1960
Lunch Poems, 1964
Love Poems (Tentative Title), 1965
In Memory of My Feelings: A Selection of Poems, 1967
    (Bill Berkson, editor)
The Collected Poems of Frank O'Hara, 1971, 1995
    (Donald Allen, editor)
Selected Poems, 1974
Early Poems, 1946-1951, 1976
Poems Retrieved, 1951-1966, 1977, revised and en-
    larged 1996

DRAMA:
The General Returns from One Place to Another, pr. 1964
Selected Plays, pb. 1978

NONFICTION:
Jackson Pollock, 1959
New Spanish Painting and Sculpture, 1960
Robert Motherwell, with Selections from the Artist's Writings, 1965
Standing Still and Walking in New York, 1975

MISCELLANEOUS:
Early Writing, 1977

About the Author

Altieri, Charles. "The Significance of Frank O'Hara." *Iowa Review* 4 (Winter, 1973): 90-104.
Breslin, James E. B. "Frank O'Hara." In *From Modern to Contemporary: American Poetry, 1945-1965*. Chicago: University of Chicago Press, 1984.
Feldman, Alan. *Frank O'Hara*. Boston: Twayne, 1979.
Gooch, Brad. *City Poet: The Life and Times of Frank O'Hara*. New York: HarperPerennial, 1994.
LeSueur, Joe. *Digressions on Some Poems by Frank O'Hara*. New York: Farrar, Straus and Giroux, 2003.
Perloff, Marjorie. *Frank O'Hara: Poet Among Painters*. New York: George Braziller, 1977.
Smith, Hazel. *Hyperscapes in the Poetry of Frank O'Hara: Difference, Homosexuality, Topography*. Liverpool, England: Liverpool University Press, 2000.
Vendler, Helen. "The Virtues of the Alterable." *Parnassus: Poetry in Review* 1 (Fall/Winter, 1972): 5-20.
Ward, Geoff. *Statutes of Liberty: The New York School of Poets*. New York: Palgrave, 2001.

DISCUSSION TOPICS

- What is painterly about Frank O'Hara's poems?
- Is Walt Whitman's influence on O'Hara greater in techniques or themes?
- Does the fact that people are much more important than external nature in O'Hara's poetry reflect his poetic theory or his temperament?
- Does O'Hara's rejection of traditional notions of poetic form liberate or limit his work?
- Do O'Hara's poems reflect craftsmanship—the quality that he tends to scorn in his pronouncements about poetry?

Courtesy, Pennsylvania State University Libraries

JOHN O'HARA

Born: Pottsville, Pennsylvania
January 31, 1905
Died: Princeton, New Jersey
April 11, 1970

O'Hara was one of the foremost realists of the twentieth century; his huge body of work is marked by its incisive examination of social behavior and richness of detail.

BIOGRAPHY

John Henry O'Hara was born in Pottsville, Pennsylvania, on January 31, 1905, the son of Patrick Henry O'Hara, a well-known doctor, and Katherine Elizabeth Delaney O'Hara. He was the eldest of eight children in a Catholic family. O'Hara attended Fordham Preparatory School and the Keystone State Normal School, and he graduated from Niagara Preparatory School in 1924, after which he worked at odd jobs—a great variety of them—before finally settling into journalism. He had passed the required examinations to enroll at Yale University, but his father's death precluded his attending college.

O'Hara worked as a reporter for two newspapers in Pennsylvania, then for three in New York. His journalistic experience was as varied as his previous work had been: He covered sports, news, politics, and religion. He served as film critic on the *Morning Telegraph*, football editor at *The New Yorker*, and editor-in-chief of the Pittsburgh *Bulletin-Index*. He was employed by *Time* magazine and would eventually write columns for the Trenton *Times-Advertiser*, *Collier's*, *Newsweek*, and *Holiday*. Some sources list Franey Delaney as an O'Hara pseudonym because he once wrote a radio column under that name. After the publication of his first novel, *Appointment in Samarra* (1934), he became a writer for motion pictures, working in turn for four of the largest studios in Hollywood.

Appointment in Samarra was such an extraordinarily successful first novel that immediately after its publication O'Hara was considered a major American writer. He went on to publish more than two dozen novels, volumes of short stories, plays, essays, and sketches. Of his more than three hundred short stories, many first appeared in *The New Yorker*.

Most of O'Hara's novels were best sellers, and a number were adapted as motion pictures. Among the most popular novels, in terms of both sales and critical reception, were *Butterfield 8* (1935), *Ten North Frederick* (1955), and *From the Terrace* (1958). For *Ten North Frederick*, O'Hara received the National Book Award in 1956. It became a successful film, as did both *From the Terrace* and *Butterfield 8*. Major film stars—such as Gary Cooper, Paul Newman, and Elizabeth Taylor—were cast in adaptations of O'Hara novels.

Among O'Hara's collections of short stories are *The Doctor's Son, and Other Stories*, (1935), *Pipe Night* (1945), *Hellbox* (1947), *Assembly* (1961), *The Cape Cod Lighter* (1962), *The Horse Knows the Way* (1964), *Waiting for Winter* (1966), and *Good Samaritan, and Other Stories* (1974). He also published collections of his essays and newspaper articles. He adapted some of his sketches about nightclubs and their habitués into a successful musical comedy, *Pal Joey* (1940), later a motion picture starring Frank Sinatra. O'Hara frequented nightclubs himself, once taking an apartment close to his favorite, "21," in New York City. In 1964, the American Academy of Arts and Letters presented O'Hara with the Gold Medal Award of Merit.

1934

In 1931, O'Hara married Helen Ritchie Petit, from whom he was divorced in 1933. On December 3, 1937, he married to Belle Mulford Wylie, who died in January, 1954. With Belle he had his only child, Wylie Delaney. His third marriage was to Katherine Barnes Bryan on January 31, 1955.

O'Hara was a blond, blunt-featured man, often described as tough and cynical. He was independent and impatient by nature—he was expelled from his first two schools, and he abandoned the Roman Catholicism in which he had been raised. When O'Hara left Pottsville in 1927 to seek work first in Montana, later in Chicago, and still later in New York and Hollywood, his travels and the many jobs he briefly held—steward on a boat, steel mill worker, soda jerk, guard at an amusement park, gas meter reader, press agent for Warner Bros., even actor in one scene of a 1936 film—gave him rich material and a wealth of details for the realistic fiction he would write.

He affected no interest in his reputation with the critics, and he laid no claims to being a great artist. Rather, he characterized himself as an honest and ordinary person who was a professional. He said that he knew what the "ordinary guy" liked and how to write it. Disparaged by some critics during the first half of his career as a writer of merely popular fiction, he was accused during the last half of his career of being old-fashioned and irrelevant. His answer to all criticism, favorable and unfavorable, was more stories. He once told an interviewer that he would like to fill the world up with his books. Although critics have generally argued that he is at his best in the short-story genre, he is probably remembered most for his many best-selling novels. O'Hara died at his home in Princeton, New Jersey, on April 11, 1970.

ANALYSIS

Critical opinion of O'Hara's work has long been divided. His receipt of the National Book Award in 1956 and the Gold Medal Award of Merit from the American Academy of Arts and Letters in 1964 indicates that the literary establishment considered him an important writer. The academic community, however, has largely ignored him. He is seldom found in the anthologies used on college campuses. One reason for this neglect, and the most obvious one, is that O'Hara's fiction gives the professor little to discuss in a literature class. O'Hara

avoids figurative language and rhetorical richness. His style was permanently influenced by his newspaper training. He is very traditional in his narrative technique, eschewing all trends toward experimentation with chronology, point of view, or dialogue.

Perhaps it is this spareness of style which led the eminent American critic Edmund Wilson to comment that O'Hara's long works always seemed like first drafts of what might eventually have become nice little novels. (Wilson did, though, praise O'Hara highly as a short-story writer.) Another adverse criticism often leveled against the novels is that they lack a moral center. The argument is that the narrative voice is so detached, so like the ideally objective journalist, that it is unclear how the author feels about his characters. O'Hara's fictional world is a very dangerous place; his characters are never secure. Their lives may be blighted at any moment by financial reversals, social missteps, even violent death. As is true in life (but often unsatisfying in fiction), what happens to the characters may have little to do with their behavior. As is also often true in real life, some characters appear to have no good reason for being in the story. They seem to result more from the protagonist's randomness of experience than from any necessity of the plot.

It has also been observed that O'Hara is America's foremost out-of-date novelist. As this argument goes, he took little note of the immense changes wrought by World War II and the nuclear age, continuing to write the same kind of stories he had written throughout the 1930's. In fact, say some critics, O'Hara continued to retell the same story in endless variety right up until his death. A substantial body of opinion holds that *Appointment in Samarra* is O'Hara's best novel. As a rule, novelists do not welcome being told that their first novel is their best, because the implication is that they have shown no improvement in all the work that followed. Perhaps this is why O'Hara stated that *Appointment in Samarra* was his second favorite novel.

On the credit side of the critical ledger, O'Hara has been called one of the finest social commentators in American literature. He has been favorably compared to Honoré de Balzac, Anthony Trollope, and William Faulkner—authors who take a society, or some segment of a society, and examine it from every possible angle in one work after another. O'Hara is especially effective in revealing the workings of class in a society that gives lip service to its democratic character. Because Americans are uncomfortable with the idea of a class structure, O'Hara seems to say, they disguise their class consciousness and make snobbery even more cruel.

O'Hara's ear for dialogue is almost unfailing. He also has the ability to characterize quickly and deftly with a snatch of dialogue or a few well-chosen details. O'Hara is justly famed for his accuracy of observation; his characters do not merely climb into a car, they climb into a particular make and model of car. A man is not merely wearing a blue suit, he is wearing a blue suit of a certain shade, made from a specific material, and cut in a particular style. Someone once made the point in this way: When O'Hara introduced into a story the schedule for trains running between two eastern cities, the contemporary commuter could have relied upon O'Hara's schedule every bit as much as upon the one issued by the railroad. O'Hara, the old newsman, always did his research and would not allow himself to be caught in a discrepancy or an anachronism. It has been argued that the myriad details sometimes overwhelm the story, that O'Hara's fiction is in danger of becoming more artifact than art. It is probably true that his books will serve future generations as valuable social histories of the first half of the twentieth century.

O'Hara revealed that he wrote quickly and revised little. He attributed this tendency to his early work as a rewrite man, when he was constantly getting pieces to rework just before deadline. The English novelist John Braine, who admired O'Hara very much, observes, of *Appointment in Samarra* particularly, that this rapid writing may account for the brisk pace and the energy of the narrative. He also praises O'Hara for not making judgments in his fiction, asserting that the proper role of the fiction writer is observer, not judge.

APPOINTMENT IN SAMARRA

First published: 1934
Type of work: Novel

The pointless life of a young country clubber drives him to destruction.

Appointment in Samarra was O'Hara's first published novel. For a 1953 Modern Library edition of the book, O'Hara wrote a foreword recounting how he had composed it. He wrote it over the period from September, 1933, to March, 1934, in a small hotel room in New York City. He worked five nights a week—he had developed a preference for nighttime writing during his early years in newspaper work. After completing the first twenty-five thousand words, O'Hara submitted the manuscript to Harcourt, Brace & Company. Alfred Harcourt was impressed with what he read and subsequently gave the young author a subsidy of fifty dollars a week until the novel was finished.

O'Hara credits Dorothy Parker with giving him, indirectly, the title of the novel. He had been using "The Infernal Grove" as a working title until the day Parker showed him a copy of W. Somerset Maugham's play *Sheppy* (1933). It contained Maugham's rendering of the Samarra legend: A servant meets Death, in the form of a woman, in the marketplace at Baghdad. He imagines that she makes a threatening gesture. Terrified, he borrows his master's horse and flees to Samarra. Death later tells the master that she was startled rather than threatening when she came upon the servant in the marketplace: She was surprised to see him in Baghdad, for she had an appointment to meet him that night in Samarra. O'Hara believed that *Appointment in Samarra* was the perfect title for the story of his doomed protagonist, Julian English. Parker disapproved of the title, as did O'Hara's editor and publisher, but he stubbornly insisted upon it and, in the end, had his way.

The setting is Gibbsville, Pennsylvania, in 1930. Many of O'Hara's stories would be set in Gibbsville, which was no doubt modeled upon his own hometown of Pottsville. He uses Gibbsville as a study of American society in microcosm and is, therefore, often compared to Balzac and Faulkner. In fact, he referred to Gibbsville on at least one occasion as his version of Faulkner's Yoknapatawpha County.

Julian English is thirty years of age. He sells automobiles, and he and his wife, Caroline, are well accepted in Gibbsville society. The Great Depression has just to begun, and F. Scott Fitzgerald's world of the roaring twenties has come to its apocalyptic end. For this reason, and because of certain stylistic similarities, O'Hara has been called Fitzgerald's successor as a chronicler of American society. The novel is also reminiscent of Sinclair Lewis in its depiction of small-town businessmen—their shallowness, superficiality, and class consciousness. Some critics see the influence of Ernest Hemingway as well in the taut construction and spare language of the novel. In the foreword to the 1953 edition, O'Hara acknowledges his debt to Fitzgerald and Lewis but says that, unlike the case with his early short stories, he sees no Hemingway influence in *Appointment in Samarra*.

Very much like a Fitzgerald hero, Julian English drinks too much. He is subject to compulsions which threaten his marriage, his financial well-being, and his social status. He is not a stupid man. He has some insight into his self-destructive nature, but he lacks the values that might save him from himself. He can see his life only in terms of money and social standing. It is not farfetched to compare Julian's story to a Greek tragedy. In his own mind, he lives under a curse: His paternal grandfather committed suicide after embezzling a considerable amount of money. Julian's father, a successful and straitlaced surgeon, fears that the character flaw has been passed down to his son. Also as in a Greek tragedy, the novel recounts the final catastrophic events in a situation which has been building for many years.

Over several days at Christmastime, 1930, Julian suffers a series of social disasters. Harry Reilly is a rich acquaintance of Julian and Caroline who is constantly attempting to overcome his Irish-Catholic background and ascend Gibbsville's social ladder. The previous summer, he lent Julian twenty thousand dollars when Julian's Cadillac agency was in straitened circumstances. He now believes—or so Julian believes—that this gives him the right to make advances toward Caroline. At a Christmas party at the country club, Julian has again drunk too much. He snaps and throws a drink in Reilly's face; Reilly is given a black eye by a big piece of ice. On the way home, Julian and Caroline have a terrible quarrel.

On Christmas Day, Julian falls out with another benefactor. Ed Charney is the local bootlegger. He has been a good customer and has helped Julian's agency sell cars to other bootleggers. Charney owns a roadhouse called the Stage Coach, where his mistress, Helene Holman, sings. Hung over, unhappy, and drinking again, Julian goes to the Stage Coach. He dances with Helene and eventually leaves with her but passes out in the backseat of a car. Charney is furious, as is Caroline. The next day, she and Julian quarrel on the street. She cancels the big party they were to have given that evening. She leaves him, determined to end their four-year-old marriage. Julian has lost his wife, has alienated the man who holds the mortgage on his agency and has a strong influence over potential Irish-Catholic customers, and has angered his powerful bootlegger.

Julian tries to work but cannot. He goes to his club for lunch in a foul mood. He ends up in an altercation with some elderly lawyers from another table. He hits one of them in the mouth and knocks out his false teeth. He goes home, where later he experiences his final fiasco. A society reporter calls at his door, wanting a story about the canceled party. Julian invites her in and begins drinking again. He makes a futile and humiliating attempt to seduce her. After her departure, he closes himself up in the garage and starts the engine of his car, keeping his appointment in Samarra. In the final pages of the book, others discuss Julian's death but have apparently learned nothing from it.

O'Hara is rightly labeled a literary realist, but the heavily deterministic nature of this novel causes it to be classified as naturalistic. Although the author concentrates primarily on the rich and the upper middle class of Gibbsville, other strata of society are represented by Ed Charney, Helene Holman, and Al Grecco, Charney's ex-convict handyman. O'Hara wrote that *Appointment in Samarra* was his second-favorite novel; he did not reveal which he ranked ahead of it.

FROM THE TERRACE

First published: 1958
Type of work: Novel

This long novel charts the protagonist's rise to a position of power and status and his subsequent fall.

From the Terrace is representative of O'Hara's later novels. The narrative covers a period from the protagonist's birth in 1897 to the postwar 1940's. *From the Terrace* is much longer than O'Hara's first novel and presents power struggles at the highest levels of business and government against a background of sexual intrigue and violent death. Thus, it provided excellent material for a motion picture and eventually became a successful vehicle for the actor Paul Newman.

Some similarities between *From the Terrace* and *Appointment in Samarra* are discernible. Raymond Alfred Eaton, called Alfred, is, like Julian English, born into the upper economic and social stratum of a small Pennsylvania town, Port Johnson. Alfred's father, Samuel Eaton, owns the local steel mill. Like Julian English, Alfred Eaton is deeply suspicious of himself, largely because of an occurrence during his boyhood over which he had no control. His elder brother, William, was the favorite

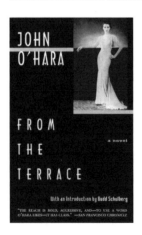

son and was destined to succeed his father as the first citizen of Port Johnson until he died of meningitis at fourteen. Alfred's father can never bring himself to show his surviving son the same attention he lavished upon William.

Two later events reinforce Alfred's sense of himself as a sort of jinx to others. He quarrels with his first love, sixteen-year-old Victoria Dockwiler, forbidding her to go riding in a borrowed Stutz Bearcat. She defies him and is killed in a car crash. Alfred then begins an affair with a family friend, Norma Budd, seven years older than he. Norma is later the victim of a mar-

ried lover, who kills first her and then himself. Although it is irrational for Alfred to think that he corrupted Norma, he feels vaguely responsible later for her death.

Alfred attends Princeton University until the United States enters World War I. He serves with distinction as a naval officer and does not return to Princeton after the war. He also chooses to decline his father's tepid offer of a job at the mill. Instead, he and Lex Thornton, a friend from Princeton, start an aircraft company together. Alfred meets eighteen-year-old Mary St. John at a party, and here begins the sort of sexual triangle typically found in O'Hara's later novels.

Mary is engaged to Jim Roper, a pre-medical student. Alfred is strongly attracted to Mary, more sexually than romantically, and he succeeds in winning her away from Roper. Their marriage in the spring of 1920 corresponds exactly with the death of Alfred's father. The marriage is not a happy one. Mary has never completely broken her ties with Roper, and Alfred will later learn that she has resumed her relationship with her former fiancé. Mary's adultery is especially sordid because Roper, who has become a psychiatrist, is also a declared homosexual who introduces her to a variety of deviant sexual practices.

Meanwhile, Alfred has happened upon a young boy who has fallen through the ice into a pond. Alfred saves the child from drowning, thus earning the gratitude of the boy's grandfather, James MacHardie. MacHardie is a rich and powerful Wall Street banker. He offers Alfred a job in New York, and the protagonist decides to leave his struggling company and take it. Alfred is an immediate success in banking, but he soon learns that he has relinquished his freedom of action. The image of MacHardie and Company is not to be tarnished by the divorce of any of its executives, so Alfred must stay married to Mary.

On a business trip back to Pennsylvania, Alfred meets and falls in love with Natalie Benziger. She becomes his mistress, but only after having suffered through a failed marriage of her own. Alfred and Mary's adulterous marriage of convenience continues for more than twenty years but is finally destroyed by the dislocations of World War II. Alfred takes a leave from MacHardie and Company to become an assistant secretary of the Navy in Washington, D.C. Mary's behavior becomes even more outrageous, and the couple's elder son, Rowland, is killed while in training as a naval aviator. Alfred feels compelled to resign his government post because of the questionable practices of some of his former business associates. In his absence, Alfred's enemies have forced him out of the company. Foremost among these enemies is Creighton Duffy, a prominent lawyer, who is James MacHardie's son-in-law and the father of the boy whose life Alfred saved. The Eatons are finally divorced.

Like Julian English in the earlier novel, Alfred Eaton is destined to fall. His neglected boyhood taught him to rely upon himself, and the resulting independence and individuality accounted for his early success; however, it failed to teach him how to connect with and cultivate others. He won Mary's heart but earned the undying enmity of his rival. He saved the boy, Sandy Duffy, but in later years neither Sandy nor his father like the man to whom they owe so much. Creighton Duffy has been waiting for the right moment to bring Alfred down.

As the novel ends, Alfred is recovering from an illness brought on by the travails of his public and private life. He is unable to find another position, having cut himself off from the business and government arenas in which he previously thrived. He is financially secure, but he is not yet fifty and is restive at the prospect of a future of enforced idleness. He is now married to Natalie, but even their happiness is marred by her loss of the child she was carrying. Natalie is thirty-eight and is unlikely to conceive again.

Other members of the large cast of characters are Jack Tom Smith, a Texas oilman and Alfred's temporary ally, and Tom Rothermel, a union organizer. (O'Hara often balances his privileged protagonist with a working-class character.) As usual in O'Hara's fiction, the physical details are flawless. The clothing, architecture, technology, and language of the novel's succeeding decades are authentic down to the minutest point.

"CHRISTMAS POEM"

First published: 1964 (collected in *Good Samaritan, and Other Stories,* 1974)
Type of work: Short story

A young man, home from college for Christmas vacation, has dinner with his family and spends an evening with friends.

O'Hara is an acclaimed master of the short-story genre. His numerous stories of the 1930's and 1940's were, as a rule, very short. In the 1950's and 1960's, pieces he wrote became longer and less numerous (he did, however, still average more than one short story per month during the last ten years of his life). "Christmas Poem" is one of the later, longer stories. It was first published on December 19, 1964, in *The New Yorker.*

Billy Warden has just arrived home from Dartmouth College for the Christmas vacation. The setting is Gibbsville, Pennsylvania, during some period earlier than the time of publication. No dates are given, but one character drives a new Marmon (not a Dort, his girlfriend insists), Billy orders a lemon phosphate at the drugstore soda fountain, and there is a discussion of getting a couple of pints of whiskey on credit, a suggestion of the Prohibition era. The Stage Coach Inn, featured so prominently in *Appointment in Samarra,* is mentioned in passing, though now spelled "Stagecoach."

For the first six pages, the story is almost exclusively dialogue as the Warden family chats at the dinner table. Clearly, Billy is loved and valued by his parents and his older sister, Barbara (Bobby). For the period between Christmas and New Year's Eve, he has been invited for skiing and a house party at Montrose, Pennsylvania, above Scranton. The hostess will be Henrietta (Henny) Cooper, who comes from a very wealthy family.

Billy excuses himself from dinner, although he really enjoys being with his family, and goes downtown in search of his friends. Billy spends an aimless evening. He fails to get a date with Irma Hipple, a young woman nicknamed "the Nipple" and rumored to go "all the way," even though none of the local boys has actually made the trip. In a crap game, he loses the ten dollars his father gave him, and he spends his loose change in a game of pool. He hopes to pick up a girl when the cinema lets out, but no appropriate target appears.

A familiar O'Hara motif is introduced when Teddy Choate asserts the superiority of his family's Yale University connections over Billy's matriculation at Dartmouth and, in turn, Billy lords it over Andy Phillips, a student at State. When Billy returns home, he learns he has had a long-distance call from the Scranton operator, suggesting that perhaps his relationship with Henny Cooper is more than casual. He also finds his father writing a Christmas poem to his mother. Mr. Warden has written such a poem every Christmas for twenty-six years, but Billy has learned of the practice only tonight. He goes to bed wondering if Henny's father has ever written a poem to her mother.

The reader is reminded of the opening chapter of *Appointment in Samarra*. That novel begins not with the desperately unhappy Julian English, but with one of his salesmen, Luther L. Fliegler. Julian's crumbling marriage stands in stark contrast to the stable, happy relationship of Luther and his wife, Irma. A critic has remarked that going to Hell in style is O'Hara's one and only theme. The reader wonders if Billy Warden will forsake the loving environment of his home and family for a world of house parties and skiing excursions among the rich—and concludes that probably he will.

"GOOD SAMARITAN"

First published: 1968 (collected in *Good Samaritan, and Other Stories*, 1974)
Type of work: Short story

After hosting a lunch, a woman is driven by a friend to the sheriff's station to get her husband, who has been missing for two days.

"Good Samaritan" first appeared in *The Saturday Evening Post* of November 30, 1968. As the story begins, Mary Wood is hosting twenty people for a buffet lunch. Her party may be associated with a golf tournament that is being held that weekend.

The setting is not identified specifically, but it is an affluent community of suburban or summer homes in the present day. When the Reeds—George and Carrie—arrive, they ask where Willoughby Wood is. Mary confides to them that her husband has been missing for two days, but she tells the other guests that he has been suddenly called away to Washington. Because it is Sunday, Mary's story is unconvincing. Only one of her guests, however, is sufficiently interested in the whereabouts of Willoughby Wood to challenge her. After all the other guests have left, Agatha Surtees, a "notorious stayer," attempts to intrude upon the private conversation Mary has been waiting to have with the Reeds. Mary practically expels Agatha with physical force, and the latter goes huffing off to her hired limousine. Agatha's age is given as fifty-two, Willoughby's as fifty-nine, so the reader infers that the other characters are in their fifties as well.

Mary receives a call from Lieutenant Hackenschmidt of the sheriff's patrol. Willoughby has been found wandering aimlessly in East Quantuck, unshaven, disheveled, and without money, watch, or identification. When picked up, he was not intoxicated—he appeared to have suffered some sort of nervous breakdown. The Reeds set out to take Mary to the substation where her husband is being held, but it is soon decided that George will drop Carrie off at their home. As George and Mary drive on alone, the reader is furnished with much exposition.

Willoughby Wood quit working about ten years earlier when he inherited his father's money, and the Woods' marriage has been in a precipitous decline ever since that time. Willoughby is estranged from their daughter, Marietta, because he insists that her husband and the father of her two children is a homosexual. Years before, Mary and George Reed were romantically involved to some unspecified degree, and Mary proposes that they become lovers now. George is receptive to the idea, but he tells her that he already has a mistress in Detroit. Mary also confesses, for the first time, to a sexual indiscretion with another member of their set only a week before serving as a bridesmaid in his wedding.

At the sheriff's substation, Lieutenant Hackenschmidt is very deferential to George, whom he recognizes as the president of the hospital. Hackenschmidt believes that Willoughby has been "rolled," although he bears no bruises or other signs of having been attacked. Another possibility, suggested though never stated, is that the missing identification and personal possessions represent Willoughby's temporary rejection of his identity.

Willoughby is released, but on the way home he becomes boorish toward his wife almost immediately. He is obsessed with the idea that Mary had an affair while visiting Marietta in California (which, in fact, she did), and he begins to accuse her again. George, the contemporary Good Samaritan, becomes exasperated and puts Willoughby out of the car a half a mile from home. Mary declines to join her husband on the side of the road, and the story ends. The narrative is carried forward almost exclusively by means of dialogue.

"THE JOURNEY TO MOUNT CLEMENS"

First published: 1974 (collected in *Gibbsville, PA: The Classic Stories*, 1992)
Type of work: Short story

On a drive through the snow, squabbling erupts between two members of an electric company engineering crew.

"The Journey to Mount Clemens" was written in 1966 or earlier, but *The Saturday Evening Post* did not accept it for publication until 1974. It was reprinted that same year in *Good Samaritan, and Other Stories.* "The Journey to Mount Clemens" is narrated in the first-person voice and contains a number of autobiographical elements.

The time period of the story is never stated outright, but all the details point to the 1920's. The narrator is eighteen years old, is Catholic, has just been expelled from prep school, and has recently acquired a job through the influence of his physician father. Despite not having an engineering degree, he is working with an engineering crew from an electric power corporation. All the preceding biographical details apply to the young John O'Hara as much as to his narrator. Further, the narrator is more or less an objective observer, not the protagonist.

The scene is eastern Pennsylvania in winter. The narrator's crew is making a tour of power plants, putting a valuation on the entire physical property of each. They have just finished their work at plant number 4 and are having their supper at Dugan's Hotel before heading to their next assignment, a new substation at Mount Clemens. Carmichael, the chief of their party, has driven them relentlessly during the two weeks at number 4, and the men dislike him heartily. He wants to end the tour quickly so that he can return to the main office in New York, then join a dam-building project in the Sudan. No one in the crew dares to challenge the austere Carmichael except King, a man who has worked all over the world for the company and who once was Carmichael's superior. The narrator observes that the company has gotten everything out of King that he had to give and has shunted him off to finish his career in a minor job. The narrator speculates that Carmichael will eventually suffer the same fate. When the conversation turns to Carmichael's upcoming trip to North Africa, he and King have words.

It has been snowing heavily for two hours. The crew starts the hazardous twenty-eight-mile trip to Mount Clemens in two cars. Carmichael, King, and Thompson go first in the Paige; the narrator and Edmunds follow in the Studebaker. The company has furnished drivers—Carney for the Paige and Ed Stone (Stoney) for the Studebaker. The journey is slow, uncomfortable, and dangerous. Either of the cars may stall, leaving its passengers stranded in below-zero weather, or, worse still, may plunge three or four hundred feet down the embankment into the timber. As in other O'Hara stories, the working-class characters (here, Carney and Stoney) are less interesting than their economic and social superiors but are also more stable, clear-headed, and dependable.

The drivers handle their automobiles admirably in the snow, and, when the bickering between King and Carmichael erupts into fisticuffs, with the former giving the latter a bloody nose, "Sergeant" Carney is the man who restores order. He sends King back to ride the rest of the way in the Studebaker. Amid Edmunds's repeated assertions that King has finally ruined himself with the company, King wraps a blanket about himself and goes to sleep. When the little caravan finally reaches Mount Clemens, Edmunds tries to rouse King but discovers that he is dead.

Again, O'Hara has traced the decline of the once powerful (or rich or prominent) to its ultimate conclusion. King's regal name adds an ironic touch to the story.

SUMMARY

O'Hara has been likened to F. Scott Fitzgerald for interpreting the United States of the 1930's through fiction as Fitzgerald had the United States of the 1920's. He has been likened to Ernest Hemingway in the cleanness and spareness of his style. He has been likened to the great naturalistic writers because of his trapped, doomed characters. The implication of the several comparisons is that he reminds the reader of these writers but fails to reach their level of achievement. What can be said with certainty is that he was a master craftsman, a prolific creator of works which have demonstrably pleased the reading public for many years.

Patrick Adcock

BIBLIOGRAPHY

By the Author

LONG FICTION:
Appointment in Samarra, 1934
Butterfield 8, 1935
A Rage to Live, 1949
The Farmer's Hotel, 1951
Ten North Frederick, 1955
A Family Party, 1956
From the Terrace, 1958
Ourselves to Know, 1960
Sermons and Soda Water, 1960
The Big Laugh, 1962
Elizabeth Appleton, 1963
The Lockwood Concern, 1965
The Instrument, 1967
Lovey Childs: A Philadelphian's Story, 1969
The Ewings, 1972

SHORT FICTION:
The Doctor's Son, and Other Stories, 1935
Hope of Heaven, 1938
Files on Parade, 1939
Pipe Night, 1945
Hellbox, 1947
Assembly, 1961
The Cape Cod Lighter, 1962
The Hat on the Bed, 1963
The Horse Knows the Way, 1964
Waiting for Winter, 1966
And Other Stories, 1968

DISCUSSION TOPICS

- What merits and what defects of John O'Hara's fiction can be traced to his journalistic training?

- Snobbery is far less often a theme of the American novel than it is of the European novel. How do you account for its being a prominent theme in O'Hara's works?

- What characteristic of Gibbsville makes it a microcosm of American society?

- Why was the title *Appointment in Samarra* so important to O'Hara?

- What is distinctive about O'Hara's dialogue in his short stories? What part does it play in O'Hara's success in that form?

- O'Hara's works are little studied in American colleges. Should they be studied more?

The O'Hara Generation, 1969
The Time Element, and Other Stories, 1972
Good Samaritan, and Other Stories, 1974
Gibbsville, PA: The Classic Stories, 1992

DRAMA:
Pal Joey, 1940
Five Plays, pb. 1961
Two by O'Hara, pb. 1979 (includes *Far from Heaven,* 1962, and the screenplay *The Man Who Could Not Lose,* 1959)

SCREENPLAY:
Moontide, 1942

NONFICTION:
Sweet and Sour, 1954
My Turn, 1966
A Cub Tells His Story, 1974
An Artist Is His Own Fault, 1977

About the Author

Bruccoli, Matthew. *John O'Hara: A Descriptive Bibliography.* Pittsburgh: University of Pittsburgh Press, 1978.
_____. *The O'Hara Concern.* New York: Random House, 1975.
Eppard, Philip B. *Critical Essays on John O'Hara.* New York: G. K. Hall, 1994.
Goldleaf, Steven. *John O'Hara: A Study of the Short Fiction.* New York: Twayne, 1999.
Grimes, William. "The John O'Hara Cult, at Least, Is Faithful." *The New York Times,* November 9, 1996, p. 17.
MacShane, Frank. *The Life of John O'Hara.* New York: E. P. Dutton, 1980.
_____, ed. *Collected Stories of John O'Hara.* New York: Random House, 1984.
Wolfe, Geoffrey. *The Art of Burning Bridges: A Life of John O'Hara.* New York: Knopf, 2003.

SHARON OLDS

Born: San Francisco, California
November 19, 1942

Olds's accessibility and her concern with family and human relationships give her work a general appeal.

BIOGRAPHY

Sharon Olds was born in San Francisco on November 19, 1942. She has said that her literal-minded approach to the world surfaced when, at the age of two, she tried to eat a book of ration stamps, having been told that they were to be the family's source of food during the war.

The family lived near a school for the blind, and Olds sang in an Episcopal church choir with some of the blind girls, an experience that became the subject for a later poem, "The Indispensability of the Eyes," in which she recalls her fear of the blind eyes and the unearthly things they saw. She also recalls that, as a child at Girl Scout camp, she began to recite her homemade verses aloud, hidden behind a tree. During that time, she also began to sense a relationship between her physical self and the earth, a perception that appears in her poetry.

Olds grew up in a troubled household; her poems refer to her grandfather's cruelties toward her and her sister, to her grandmother's anger, to her father's alcoholism, which led to her parents' divorce, and to her abusive sister. When Olds was fifteen, she was sent to a boarding school near Boston. There, she came to love Eastern landscapes and New York City. A poem from her adulthood ("Infinite Bliss") records her desire never to live where it does not snow.

Also during that time, Olds began to read a substantial amount of poetry and to write it as well, using conventional poetic forms for most of her early work. She has stated that it took her a long time to learn to balance a poem's need for exceptional language with the need to establish a voice of her own. She has said that she accomplished that discovery partly through dance, once more underscoring the relationship between her physical world and her writing.

Olds received a B.A. with distinction from Stanford University in 1964. She studied languages (French, Italian, German, Greek, and Middle English) as an undergraduate. In 1972, she earned a Ph.D. in American literature from Columbia University; her dissertation examined the prosody of Ralph Waldo Emerson.

Her first collection of poems, *Satan Says*, was published in 1980. Reviews were mixed but generally positive; reviewers attributed some of the collection's faults to Olds's inexperience. *Satan Says* was followed by *The Dead and the Living* (1984), which won the Lamont Poetry Prize and the National Book Critics Circle award. *The Gold Cell* was published in 1987, and *The Father* (a series of poems about her father's death from cancer) appeared in 1992. Her later volumes *The Wellspring* (1995), *Blood, Tin, Straw* (1999), and *The Unswept Room* (2002) continue her earlier themes, now in the retrospective voice of later middle age.

Olds has spent her adult life living in New York City. Although family life forms a major theme in her writing (she has described herself as a full-time mother and full-time poet), she has also made an active career of teaching and lecturing. She has taught at Sarah Lawrence, the Theodor Herzl Institute, Columbia University, New York University, and Brandeis University. She has conducted a poetry workshop at Goldwater Hospital for the severely physically handicapped and has worked with the PEN Freedom-to-Write committee. Olds's social concerns can also be recognized in her work with PEN's Silenced Voices subcommittee (which deals with censorship) and Helsinki Watch. In 1989, she became director of New York University's Graduate School of Arts and Science creative writing program. In 2002, she received an Academy Fellowship from the Academy of American Poets for her poetic achievement in mid-career; in 2004, she received a Barnes and Noble Writers for Writers Award. She was named New York State Poet Laureate for 1998 to 2000.

ANALYSIS

Olds has said that poetry has several wellsprings. It functions as the artist's release for personal emotion and satisfies the human desire to create beauty. It also establishes human interconnectedness by revealing writer to reader in an especially intimate way, and it bears witness for life and for the parts of the world that have no voice. That statement serves well as an introduction to Olds's work, for it implies much about her subjects, her themes, and her language.

Olds's poetry is, first of all, accessible. Without sacrificing poetic power, she nevertheless is careful to ground her reader in the poems. (Some early reviewers faulted her, in fact, for being too explicit, for explaining too much.) Settings and characters are from daily life—men, women, lovers, children. Her topics range from Chinese food to the atrocities recorded in the newspapers to the death of her estranged father.

Olds's language is as accessible as her subject matter; her syntax is usually composed of the direct structures of the speaking voice. Her diction is from daily life as well, with a strong presence of blunt sexual words. Commenting on her first book, *Satan Says*, some reviewers condemned her for overusing vulgarities and suggested that she was merely trying for shock effects. Yet sexual awareness is a significant element of Olds's work, and clinical euphemisms would seem out of place in her diction and her often angry tone. In the title poem of *Satan Says*, for example, the speaker makes quite clear that the curses Satan encourages her to utter against her parents are only part of her "freedom"; the other part is her admission that she loves them, too, with a love that both traps and warms her.

Sexuality holds an important place in Olds's view of the world. She writes unflinchingly about her sexual experiences, and she is strongly conscious of others' sexuality, including that of her parents and children. It is part of how she understands herself and them.

Anger and violence are also elements in this understanding. The abuses of Olds's childhood join with her awareness of the world as a place where the weak and helpless are routinely tortured and brutalized. The nature of Olds's imagery is such that violence and sexuality often merge in her poems in a way that some reviews have labeled sensationalism. The images of blood, the violent overtone of the sexual act, and the vulnerability of sexuality all seem to allow such connections, however, and Olds makes full use of those relationships. In "Monarchs," for example, she links the red wings of the monarch butterfly with the blood she shed during her first sexual experience and the dark red of her lover's "butcher's hands."

That Olds's poems offer the reader an intimate view of their creator is almost understatement, so willing is she to refuse readers nothing in her experience. She describes sitting out a family fight, crouched beside her sister in an upstairs hall; she records her sudden perception of her father as a potential killer while he is driving drunk; she pictures her five-year-old son abstractedly urinating on the front door, his mind on other things. She details the agonizing events of her father's death. The anger that some of these events call up in her has led some readers to compare Olds with Sylvia Plath, but Olds's work has themes that counterbalance her anger.

The most powerful of these themes is Olds's insistent emphasis on nurturing and caregiving. Those themes appear in her first volume and continue to appear steadily in her later poems as well, recording her awareness of what her commitments are by virtue of her sex—the fostering of life and growth wherever it seems possible.

The series of poems called "Young Mothers" from *Satan Says* makes a good example of the complex relationship between a mother and her infant. To Olds, nurture is far from a sentimental picturing of parental love. The infant is part of the mother herself; it depends on her for everything it receives. She loves and protects it more fiercely than anything else in her life, and at the same time she feels trapped by its dependence, its demands, and its vulnerability.

The Father, Olds's volume of poems about her father's death, demonstrates clearly the ironic tension that such nurture can create. In these poems, the reader at first sees a grown daughter returning home to help nurse her dying father. Typically, Olds spares the reader nothing in describing the mouth tumor that is devouring the old man; she pictures his daughter helping him drink, helping him spit and wipe his mouth. Gradually, the reader recognizes the special pain that attends this relationship. This is the cold, rejecting alcoholic father who made the daughter's life hell and who finally left his family. The wife in the poems is his second wife, not the daughter's mother. Yet during the horrors of tending him (as well as in the months that follow his death), Olds comes to terms with the hurt he has caused her and at last is freed to state her love for him and to recognize his for her, damaged though those loves must be.

One other quality of Olds's work demands notice: her ironic wit, which often helps to mitigate the pain of her subjects. In "The Indispensability of the Eyes," for example, she describes the discomfort she feels in the presence of blind girls; she cites as part of the reason for this discomfort the fact that the girls cannot tell when others are looking at them. She laughs at the sexual stereotyping done by an assistant fire commissioner on a television talk show ("The Housewives Watching Morning TV"). She describes her small children as puppies tangled around her ankles ("Seventh Birthday of the First Child"). Even Olds's angriest and most powerful poems retain her ability to see similarities, to recognize irony and to use it to soften the harsh realities about which she often writes.

"TIME-TRAVEL"

First published: 1980 (collected in *Satan Says*, 1980)
Type of work: Poem

The speaker journeys back in time to find her childhood self in her troubled family.

"Time-Travel" is a good introduction to Olds's use of themes concerning her painful past. The title and the poem's first sentence explain what is hap-

pening. The speaker says she has learned to return to the past in order to find doors and windows. The meaning of those apertures is made clear at the poem's end, but the reader recognizes them already as typical means of enlarging one's view or of escaping.

The next lines place the poem in time—a hot summer day in 1955. The setting seems to be a lake house, perhaps a vacation cabin, for it has pine walls and a splintery pine floor. The speaker says that she is looking for her father in this time travel, and her slow, deliberate tracing of her steps from small room to big (she even notes the doorway she passes through) suggests the elaborate care, perhaps because of fear or uncertainty, that she is using in this search. When she finds him, it is as if she stumbles over something inert lying on a chair.

The second stanza explains that the father is asleep, sleeping off a drinking bout. Once again, Olds leads the reader carefully through the picture, suggesting reasons for her care. She can somehow own her father, possess him, in this state. She shows him as he sleeps, newspaper comics on his stomach, plaid shirt, hands folded across his body. He looks almost dead. She describes his looks in some detail, but all of his physical characteristics are dependent on the central thing she has explained—that this "solid secret body" is "where he puts the bourbon." The care with which she has searched for him is partly caused by fear of waking him. The stanza ends with the information that this is the family's last summer together and that the speaker has learned to walk very quietly that summer, so that no one will be aware of her. The second stanza is enjambed into the third so that a stanza break occurs in the middle of the sentence after the word "walk," which hangs at the line's end like a careful footstep.

The third stanza locates the other members of this unhappy family. The mother is weeping upstairs. The brother, like the other children in the family, has escaped to the outdoors. He is in a tent, reading the speaker's diary. The older sister is "changing boyfriends somewhere in a car." Only the father seems really at peace; ironically, he is described as a baby, suggesting a sort of infantile quality in his relationship with his family.

The stanza ends with a reference to a twelve-year-old girl who is down by the lake, watching its waves. The speaker approaches her, and the girl turns to face her; the child is the speaker's young self, who looks up toward the house as if she does not see the speaker but must concentrate on the pain going on in her family. The adult speaker identifies her as the one she was seeking. She looks into the girl's eyes and sees waves that are somehow a cross between the lake's water and the air of hell. The poem concludes by explaining what the young girl cannot know: that this pain will have an end and that, of all of her family, she will be the survivor. Once again at the poem's end, Olds makes special use of a line break, ending the next-to-last line after "one" so that "survivor" rests all alone—like the girl herself—in its line. The line break also creates a sort of pun in the next-to-last line, which says that the girl does not know that "she is the one"—as if, in addition to being the "one" survivor, she has been singled out for some other special gift, a gift she will not recognize until much later.

"THE ONE GIRL AT THE BOYS PARTY"

First published: 1984 (collected in *The Dead and the Living*, 1984)
Type of work: Poem

A mother sees her daughter's imminent sexual maturity, even though the girl is still surrounded by childhood's images.

In the slender action of the twenty-one lines that make up "The One Girl at the Boys Party," Olds combines three patterns of imagery that underscore the speaker's recognition of her daughter's approaching maturity. In the poem, the speaker (that this is the mother is never explicitly stated) takes the girl, a superior math student, to a swimming party where boys immediately surround her. The speaker sees the young people dive into the pool and imagines her daughter working math problems in her head to calculate her relationship to the diving board and the gallons of water in the pool. The girl's suit has a pattern of hamburgers and french fries printed on it, and when she climbs from the pool, her ponytail will hang wet down her back. The speaker knows that as the girl looks at the

boys, she will be recognizing the appeal of their masculinity.

One element of the poem's language concerns the childishness of the young girl. The speaker calls her "my girl," as if she is a small child, and places her at the pool party as if she were an infant. Although she will soon become a woman, her appearance is childish, too. The hamburger-and-fries pattern of her bathing suit, her ponytail, and the sweetness of her face all suggest a very young child.

This girl, however, is no fool, as her mother knows. Humorously, the speaker imagines the girl's math scores unfolding around her in the air, and mathematics makes up the second significant element of the poem's language. Not only do her math scores follow her to the party, but her quick mind can also make calculations about the pool at the same time she is diving into it. Moreover, she can calculate the interesting qualities of the young men around her. At this point, the poem's mathematical diction merges with the sexual.

Early in the poem, the speaker compared the girl's sleek, hard body to a prime number. Now she sees the girl's face as a factor of one, as the girl evaluates the boys in numerical terms—eyes and legs, two each; the "curves of their sexes, one each." The speaker knows that this recognition will lead the girl to more interesting calculations, "wild multiplying."

The language of male and female has been present from the poem's start. The boys are early described as "bristling"; the girl is "sleek." So it is no surprise that the end of the poem reveals the girl's latent sexual power, which is about to appear. It will be considerable, as the concluding image suggests: Many droplets of water, which seem sexually energized by their contact with the girl's body, fall "to the power of a thousand."

The tone of the poem is both amused and admiring. Clearly, the speaker respects the girl's intellect as well as her right to grow into sexual maturity.

"THE LIFTING"

First published: 1992 (collected in *The Father*, 1992)
Type of work: Poem

The sight of her dying father's naked body makes a daughter aware of the depth of their relationship.

The collection from which this poem comes concerns the death of Olds's father from cancer, and it details her evolving relationship with the cold, alcoholic man who so hurt her and her family when she was a child. The father's death occurs about halfway through the collection; the poems following his death describe how their relationship continues to grow and deepen even after he has died. "The Lifting" is set not long before he dies, and it incorporates elements that are typical of Olds's work, particularly in her awareness of her father's sexuality and her linkage of that awareness to her own being and that of her daughter.

The poem begins with the shocking statement that her father suddenly lifts his nightgown, exposing himself to her. In this action, he violates a powerful taboo between fathers and daughters, and the tension of that taboo permeates the entire poem. The action is made still more complex by the poet's use of the word "nightie," a word for a woman's garment, and a rather playful word at that. Soon, the reader realizes that the setting is a hospital and the nightie is a hospital gown.

The speaker looks away when her father lifts the gown, but he calls her name to make her look. He wants to show her how much weight he has lost. The folds of loose skin tell her how near he is to death. Immediately, she goes beyond the shock of his gesture to notice that his hips look like hers and that his pelvis resembles her daughter's. When she looks at the smile on his face, she recognizes that he had done this not to offend her but because he knows she will be interested. In a strange way, perhaps because, despite the "thick bud of his penis," he resembles her and her daughter, he expects her to find him appealing. Despite the strangeness of the situation, she does, and she feels affection as well as "uneasy wonder." The mystery he seems to evoke is the mystery of generation; the sexual or-

gans she is viewing caused her to exist, and her sex has, in turn, created another person. The three of them are related in a way that somehow transcends the awful pain of their relationship. That pain plays little part in this poem and is not referred to explicitly.

The poem concludes with another reference to the title, this time extending its meaning. Olds describes the hospital gown lifting, rising as if on its own, as if it were the father's soul rising at death to approach the final mysteries.

"THE EXACT MOMENT OF HIS DEATH"

First published: 1992 (collected in *The Father*, 1992)
Type of work: Poem

The poet records the details of her father's last minutes.

"The Exact Moment of His Death" is another poem from the narratives of *The Father*; in it, Olds examines the strange mystery of the dividing line between living and not-living. At what point, she seems to ask, does the dying man change from being father into being mere inert flesh?

The poem opens with a series of painful details about the physical state of the dying man; he has been so changed by his illness that no one would recognize him. Nevertheless, it is still the man himself, the man with whom the family has come "so far," the speaker says, suggesting both the journey of the illness and even more the whole difficult journey of the man's life with them. When he has exhaled his last breath, "light as a milkweed seed," and the nurse has listened to his heart to confirm his death, for a moment he remains the speaker's father. Then, in an instant, he seems to change, "as if the purely physical were claiming him," and in that instant, he ceases to be the father and becomes part of the "unliving . . . matter of this world."

"ONCE"

First published: 1999 (collected in *Blood, Tin, Straw,* 1999)

Type of work: Poem

The speaker records a moment from her youth when she saw her father naked.

As in "The Lifting," in "Once" Olds recalls a moment in which taboos are violated and she sees her

Sharon Olds

Strike Sparks
Selected Poems, 1980-2002

father naked. In this case, she has opened the unlocked bathroom door to discover him sitting on the toilet where she sees that "all of him was skin." The bathroom is blue, the color of sky and innocence, and innocence made her open the door, knowing that if it was unlocked the bathroom was empty. Her father has neglected to lock it, however, and she sees him, observes him carefully from toes to nape of neck. She seems surprised that he appears unprotected and shy, even girlish, and she recognizes a sort of common humanity between them and all creatures that go through the rituals of elimination. She calls it a "human peace."

The speaker apologizes and backs out of the room, but she adds two surprising images for what she has seen. Her father was like a shorn lamb, she says, and like a cloud in the blue sky of the room, thus linking him to ideas of innocence. Now she adds that he is like a mountain road, and her eye has traveled all "hairpin mountain road of the naked male." She has seen his "unguarded flank," a phrase that reminds the reader that he is a man who shields himself against his own emotions and those of others, and she has seen the "border of the pelvic cradle," suggesting the link between his sex and her own existence. She is a product of that cradle, grown in the pelvic cradle of her mother, and, in that moment of vision, she seems to recognize her relationship to both of her parents.

SUMMARY

Olds's use of her family's past, her willingness to discuss delicate and painful subjects, and her lack of squeamishness about sex all place her in the tradition of confessional poetry. Additionally, her subjects are those that have often been associated with feminist writers. Her language, her ferocious honesty, and her equally fierce maternalism, which demands recognition of the rights of all living things to grow into what they were meant to be, constitute her special contribution to this sort of poetry.

Ann D. Garbett

BIBLIOGRAPHY

By the Author

POETRY:
Satan Says, 1980
The Dead and the Living, 1984
The Gold Cell, 1987
The Sign of Saturn: Poems, 1980-1987, 1991
The Father, 1992
The Wellspring, 1995
Blood, Tin, Straw, 1999
The Unswept Room, 2002
Strike Sparks: Selected Poems, 1980-2002, 2004

About the Author

Dillon, Brian. "'Never Having Had You, I Cannot Let You Go.'" *The Literary Review* 37 (Fall, 1993): 108-119.
Kirsch, Adam. "The Exhibitionist." *The New Republic* 221 (December 27, 1999): 38.

Lesser, Rika. "Knows Father Best." *The Nation* 255 (December 14, 1992): 748-750.

McGiveron, Rafeeq. "Olds's 'Sex Without Love.'" *The Explicator* 58 (Fall, 1999): 60.

"Sharon Olds." *The Writer* 114 (April, 2001): 66.

Swiontkowski, Gale. *Imagining Incest: Sexton, Plath, Rich, and Olds on Life with Daddy.* Selinsgrove, Pa.: Susquehanna University Press, 2003.

Tucker, Ken. "Family Ties." *The New York Times Book Review* 104 (November 14, 1999): 29.

Wineapple, Brenda. "I Have Done This Thing." *Poetry* 185 (December, 2004): 232-237.

Zeider, Lisa. Review of *The Father,* by Sharon Olds. *The New York Times Book Review,* March 21, 1993, 14.

DISCUSSION TOPICS

- Define some of the attitudes that Sharon Olds indicates concerning her father and children.

- How is sexual awareness related to her attitudes toward her family?

- How does Olds communicate her painful relationship with her father?

- What allows Olds to reconcile with the memories of her father?

- Can you find justification for her frank treatment of sexual themes in her work?

- What evidence do you find in Olds's work that family relationships are extremely important to her?

TILLIE OLSEN

Leonda Fiske

Born: Omaha, Nebraska
January 14, 1913

Olsen's fiction affirms the individuality and complexity of women; it led to a wider recognition of the contributions of women writers in literary history.

BIOGRAPHY

Tillie Olsen, the second of six children, was the daughter of Samuel and Ida Lerner. Her parents, Russian Jews, immigrated to America after the 1905 rebellion. Her father was a laborer, and he served for many years as secretary to Nebraska's Socialist Party.

Olsen knew she wanted to become a writer when she was fifteen. She bought a number of issues of *The Atlantic Monthly* in an Omaha junk shop. In those volumes she read in serialized form the novel *Life in the Iron Mills*. At that time *The Atlantic Monthly* did not publish the names of contributors. For many years Olsen d id not realize that the author of the novel was a woman, Rebecca Harding Davis. Olsen was impressed by the realism of this story and realized that literature could be made from the lives of ordinary people who struggled to eke out a living and raise a family. Olsen left high school during her senior year in order to find work and help her family. Shortly thereafter she was jailed after helping to organize packinghouse workers in Kansas City. That experience inspired her to begin a novel, *Yonnondio: From the Thirties* (1974), about the experiences of a working-class family whose hopes for a better life are dashed by a cruel capitalist economic system.

Olsen began to write this novel in 1932. Despite a battle with pleurisy, she continued to work on the manuscript. She moved to California and settled in San Francisco, where she worked closely with labor unions, was arrested for organizing, and was an active member of the Young Communist League. She published two poems and "The Iron Throat," a small section of the manuscript of the novel in progress, in *Partisan Review* in 1934.

In later issues of *Partisan Review* in 1934, she contributed an essay on the warehouse strike in San Francisco called "The Strike," and she wrote a first-person account of being arrested and brutally questioned with other communist sympathizers in "The Thousand Dollar Vagrant." "The Iron Throat" was enthusiastically received by critics. Bennett Cerf and Donald Klopfer, editors with Random House, offered her a monthly stipend if she would complete a chapter each month. She signed a contract and moved to Los Angeles to begin the project, but she was unable to concentrate on the writing. After canceling the contract, she returned to San Francisco. She never finished *Yonnondio: From the Thirties*.

In 1936, she married Jack Olsen, a union printer. They had four daughters: Karla, Julie, Katherine, and Laurie. She contributed no further stories, poems, or essays to *Partisan Review*. Instead, she worked as a transcriber in a dairy equipment company and worked at various part-time jobs; she produced no further published writings for twenty years.

Between 1953 and 1954, she composed "Help Her to Believe," a short story about a mother's reminiscences of her daughter. This story was published in 1956 in the *Pacific Spectator* and reprinted in 1961 under the title "I Stand Here Ironing" in her collection of four stories, *Tell Me a Riddle*. The other stories in the collection were "O Yes," the title story, and "Hey Sailor, What Ship?" With the publication of this book, Olsen broke her silence. The stories in the collection have been anthologized more than fifty times, and the book has been translated into several languages. Critical response to the book was enthusiastic, and her reputation as a writer and a spokesperson for the feminist literary tradition was assured with its publication.

Between 1961 and 1972, Olsen published three articles that arose from her involvement in grants and fellowships received after publication of *Tell Me a Riddle*. "Silences: When Writers Don't Write" appeared in *Harper's* in 1965. It was based on a 1964 seminar, "Death of the Creative Process." A second article, "One Out of Twelve: Writers Who Are Women in Our Century" (1972), was developed from notes from a 1971 address to the Modern Language Association Forum on Women Writers. In 1972, Olsen contributed the afterword to the Feminist Press reprint of Rebecca Harding Davis's 1861 classic novel, *Life in the Iron Mills*. This substantial essay was important both professionally and personally to Olsen. The fifteen-year-old girl who had read the novel in *The Atlantic Monthly* was now a highly regarded author. Having the opportunity to write the afterword to this novel closed an important circle in her life.

Another closing of a circle was the 1974 publication of her unfinished novel *Yonnondio: From the Thirties*. Her husband had discovered the manuscript while looking for other papers. Rather than try to add to the manuscript or revise it, she organized it from many drafts and versions of the text. After eight chapters the text ends suddenly, and the author adds a note commenting on its incomplete state. Critics hailed this unfinished novel as a great work of fiction.

During the 1970's, Olsen taught courses in literature and in women's studies at several universities in the United States and abroad, and she became well known as a lecturer to women's groups, university students, and writers organizations. In 1978, her book *Silences* was published. The book includes the two previously published essays noted above, the afterword from *Life in the Iron Mills*, and a compendium of quotations, excerpts, and comments by and about famous men and women writers who were "silenced" at some time in their creative lives.

Olsen became a mentor for young writers and a spokesperson for feminist concerns. She developed reading lists of works by women, and she promoted the reprinting of significant literary classics written by women. In 1979, she was awarded an honorary doctorate from the University of Nebraska. Olsen's *Mother to Daughter, Daughter to Mother: Mothers on Mothering* was published in 1984. The text includes a calendar of months, a series of excerpts from women's writings arranged according to topic based on mother-daughter relationships, and a list of titles of works by women.

ANALYSIS

Readers of Tillie Olsen's fiction may come away with a heightened understanding of the complexities inherent in being a woman in a society that values predominantly the male perspective on things. Olsen challenges readers to empathize with the woman's point of view. Whether she is speaking through a character in her fiction or speaking directly to teachers, writers, or readers of fiction, Olsen always seeks to redress the balance between the male and the female points of view.

What does Olsen want her reader to know about women? She invites readers to consider their various strengths, the history of their being an oppressed class of people, the limited roles they were offered in Western society, the abusive relationships they were forced to suffer, the powerful alliances they made with other women, the tolerance and patience they exhibited toward their husbands, the silences and solitudes they experienced at different times of their lives, their being expected to live "for" others instead of "with" others, and their capacity for insight and wisdom into the heart of life. In short, Olsen wants readers to know of the richness, depths, and diversity of the inner lives of women. She wants readers to view life through a woman's eyes—and see women as individuals.

Whether she tells a story from the point of view of the child Mazie in *Yonnondio: From the Thirties* or from the point of view of an old woman in "Tell Me a Riddle" (1961), Olsen uses the technique of interior monologue to great advantage. Olsen organizes the thoughts of the character directly on the page; readers, in effect, overhear what the character is thinking. This approach requires close reading and active participation on the part of the reader. It is impossible to skim these sections. Another aspect of style in Olsen's writing is her use of lengthy descriptive passages within the narrative. At times, her writing in *Yonnondio: From the Thirties* appears to be as lyrical as the poems of Walt Whitman or E. E. Cummings. At other times, the writing is graphic and detailed in its realism, with the density of phrasing similar to the fiction of William Faulkner. What stands out in all of her writings, however, is that Olsen's voice and style are unique. That she found her own voice and expressed themes of importance to her own life matters most in any assessment of her contributions as a writer.

Although her fiction emphasizes a woman's point of view, her characters and plots are universal ones, of importance to the lives of both men and women. Olsen's fiction is committed to the lives of the poor, the uneducated, the despised, and the downtrodden. Her mother's resistance against oppression in czarist Russia and her father's long membership in the Socialist Party contributed to her own commitment to socialist ideals in the 1930's. To some extent, Olsen sees herself as a spokesperson for those who do not have speech—for those who are silenced by governments, by societal attitudes, by economic systems. "The Strike" is a protest against unfair labor practices. *Yonnondio: From the Thirties* is a novel of protest about the evils of the capitalist economic system. "Tell Me a Riddle" is a protest about American society's tendency to patronize the elderly. *Silences* is largely a protest against a literary tradition in America that excludes an equal representation of women.

Since Olsen's fiction emphasizes the woman's point of view, it necessarily depicts women's roles within the family and women's place in generational conflicts. Her fiction contains stories that reveal dimensions of mother-daughter relationships, father-daughter relationships, and sibling relationships. "Tell Me a Riddle" is one of the few honest portrayals of a relationship between an old couple, married forty-seven years. That story also realistically depicts three generations in conflict. In her portrayal of women's experience, Olsen seeks to communicate the importance of choice in a woman's life. Without choices, women are reduced to stereotypes and offered few viable roles in life. With choices, women become equal to men, able to articulate individual goals, fully capable of a wide range of emotions and ideas.

Olsen's contributions as a writer are matched by her contributions as a spokesperson for the feminist literary tradition and as a role model for women (and men) who are writers. *Silences* is a rallying cry for teachers and critics to study at length the contributions of women writers. It is also an appeal for understanding how and why women writers, including Olsen herself, have been silenced through history. Olsen's own life and writings have inspired writers to sustain themselves through hard times and not yield to pressures or circumstances that would silence them.

YONNONDIO: FROM THE THIRTIES

First published: 1974
Type of work: Novel

A family in the 1920's barely survives a series of financial and family crises as the father ekes out a living as a common laborer.

The manuscript of *Yonnondio: From the Thirties* was lost to Tillie Olsen for more than thirty years before being accidentally discovered by her husband, who was looking for other papers. A portion of the novel had been published in 1934 in *The Partisan Review*, a journal devoted to socialist writing. Although the story was well received by critics, Olsen never completed the novel. Instead, she reared a family of four children and worked at part-time jobs for most of her adult life until the 1961 publication of *Tell Me a Riddle*. This collection of stories led to the discovery of Tillie Olsen as a major literary talent, and it made the publication of *Yonnondio* an important addition to her works. Olsen decided not to add to or substantially revise the manuscript. At the conclusion of the eight chapters of this unfinished novel, Olsen adds the following note: "Reader, it was not to have ended here, but it is nearly forty years since this book had to be set aside, never to come to completion."

The title is taken from a poem by Walt Whitman called "Yonnondio." In the poem, Whitman laments the passing of the great American Indian nations in the face of the white man's advance. After recalling the contributions of these peoples, Whitman concludes the poem, "Then blank and gone and still, and utterly lost." That line could serve as a description of the middle years of Olsen's career: Although she began to develop her art in the 1930's, circumstances led to her being silenced as a writer for more than twenty years.

The novel depicts the experiences of Jim and Anna Holbrook and their family. Jim is an itinerant laborer who struggles to find a decent job, first in a coal mine in Wyoming, then on a tenant farm in North Dakota, and finally in a meatpacking house in Omaha, Nebraska. No matter where Jim works, he never earns enough to make ends meet. He feels trapped in a recurring cycle of poverty and desperation. He loves his wife and children but feels trapped by them because they represent a limit to his freedom as a man and an insurmountable financial burden. He begins to drink excessively, abuses his wife, and neglects his children.

Anna tries to be responsive to his misery, but she is overwhelmed with the duties of homemaking and child care, and she often faces bouts of depression. She suffers from physical exhaustion and experiences a miscarriage. Anna wants her children to have a better life than Jim and she have had, and she values education as one way the children might improve their lot in life. The children, however, have few opportunities for education. Anna often experiences stress over the narrow limitations of her role as a woman. An old man in the novel characterizes her as a woman who "has had everything to grind out life and yet has kept life." Anna experiences a major victory in the novel when she asserts her independence in the face of Jim's restrictive attitudes.

The politics of the novel are clearly on the side of the proletariat, that class of people who have the lowest status—the working class in an industrialist society. Everyone who hires Jim Holbrook takes advantage of him. The coal mining company compels him to do work that is physically demanding and dangerous. The wage he earns is insufficient for his family's basic needs. After working one season on a tenant farm in North Dakota, Jim is deeper in debt than when he started at the beginning of the season. When he works as a laborer in Omaha, his wage never keeps pace with the family's expenses. Jim's plight underscores a common theme in Marxist-socialist politics: The worker has "nothing to sell but his labor power."

Consequently, the worker is stripped of his identity and becomes a tool of the economic forces that control his destiny. At one point, Olsen explains that if workers were to revolt, they "could wipe out the whole thing, the whole god-damn thing, and a human could be a human for the first time on earth." Both Jim and Anna, then, are victims of complex economic forces that exclude a number of people from the opportunities of attaining the American Dream.

Olsen portrays this economic exploitation symbolically throughout the novel. The coal becomes a symbol of the domination of the workers' lives: "Earth sucks you in, to spew out the coal, to make a few fat bellies fatter." The stench of the meatpacking houses in Omaha also dominated the landscape of the people who lived there. Olsen writes, "That is a reminder—a proclamation—*I rule here.*" Wherever the family turns, they are rendered powerless by a harsh and unsympathetic economic system.

At times Olsen's writing style appears to be a combination of the graphic realism of Upton Sinclair's *The Jungle* (1906) and John Steinbeck's *The Grapes of Wrath* (1939) with the lyrical poetry of Walt Whitman's *Song of Myself* (1855). The latter style is most evident in Olsen's emulation of the lengthy descriptive passages common to Whitman's poetry. In one scene, she summarizes what is lost when an individual realizes his lot in life: "the little things gone: shoeshine and tailormades, tickets to a baseball game, and a girl, a girl to love up, whiskey down your gullet, and laughter, the happy belch of a full stomach, and walking with your shoulders back, tall and proud." Such passages reveal both an eye for detail and a sensitivity to the suffering of impoverished human beings.

Most of the story is told from the point of view of Mazie, Jim and Anna Holbrook's oldest child. Mazie is in a position to witness the terrible deprivation experienced by the family and the growing sense of desperation felt by her parents. In some scenes Mazie is called upon to become a "parent" to her parents as well as to her siblings. Readers gain insights into Mazie's character directly, through the technique of interior monologues; they portray the thoughts of a character in richly descriptive passages. This technique helps readers identify with Mazie's experiences.

In other cases, Olsen introduces the points of

view of the parents and many minor characters. Late in the novel, Anna's point of view begins to predominate as she recovers a sense of purpose in her life and asserts herself in her relationship with Jim. On several occasions, Olsen directly addresses the readers in order to involve them in the political messages inherent in her work and in the lives of the characters she portrays. More than anything, Olsen wants readers to know that people such as Mazie and her parents suffer; she wants to give voice to the silent and the oppressed so that others can listen to what they have to say.

"I Stand Here Ironing"

First published: 1956 (as "Help Her to Believe"; collected in *Tell Me a Riddle*, 1961)

Type of work: Short story

Prompted by a counselor's inquiry, a mother reviews her nineteen-year-old daughter's childhood and examines the basis of their relationship.

The first sentence in "I Stand Here Ironing" sets the tone and establishes the mood of the entire story: "I stand here ironing, and what you asked me moves tormented back and forth with the iron." Prompted by the counselor's concern for her daughter's future development, the mother responds with a tone of resignation, even despair, as she tries to explain to her visitor the nature of her circumscribed life and the nature of her daughter's desperate attempts to find her own identity within a self-limiting environment. Like the iron to which she refers, her daughter's life has moved in a cycle of progression and retrogression, between moments of joy and satisfaction and moments of isolation and despair. Ironing is also a perfect metaphor for the limited roles imposed upon women—of wife, homemaker, and mother—and all that is lost to women because of those narrow roles.

The mother tells a story of self-denial, deprivation, and loss. Emily, the subject of the counselor's inquiry, is the oldest of five children. The mother recalls a special memory of Emily as a baby—

beautiful, joyous, full of life. "She was a miracle to me." After eight months of bliss, however, her husband leaves them suddenly, and she is forced to find work to rear her child. She is even compelled to leave the child with her former husband's family for a year. The mother remarries and soon is pregnant with her second child. For a time, she has to send Emily to a convalescent home because of her ill health. The effect of these separations on Emily is devastating: She becomes a remote, isolated girl who has few friends and does poorly in school. The mother concludes, "I was working, there were four smaller ones now, there was not time for her."

Somehow Emily survives these deprivations and develops a talent for mimicry. Although her mother is encouraged to help Emily refine that gift, she contends, "but without money or knowing how, what does one do? We have left it all to her, and the fight has as often eddied inside, clogged and clotted, as been used and growing."

One of the central themes in the story is that Emily's individuality and uniqueness of character are realized through her mother's reminiscences. The mother does not view Emily with the same limited perspective that society applied to her as a young woman. In fact, one of the ironies of the story is that Emily, who is nineteen, was born when her mother was nineteen. It is clear that the mother's reminiscences of Emily's childhood are meant as a comparison between constraints placed upon the mother's life when she was nineteen and the possibilities open to her daughter's life at the same age. In effect, Emily has choices, whereas her mother had none.

Another important aspect of the story is that readers gain insights into the complexities of mother-daughter relationships. Although the mother may have made mistakes in rearing her daughter, she refuses to accept all the responsibility for what her child has become. The details of her reminiscences help readers become sensitive to all that was lost, and yet all that was preserved, in this relationship. At the end of the story, the mother concludes, "Let her be. So all that is in her will not bloom—but in how many does it? There is still enough left to live by." Despite having grown up under harsh and impoverished living conditions, this young woman is a survivor and has the capacity to meet life on her own terms.

TELL ME A RIDDLE

First published: 1961
Type of work: Novella

> *An old woman defies her domineering husband's retirement plans and then undertakes a personal struggle against cancer.*

Tell Me a Riddle is Tillie Olsen's greatest achievement as a writer of fiction. This novella expands upon themes that Olsen developed in her earlier stories and adds new insights into relationships between married couples and the experiences of women.

The initial conflict in the novella is between Eva and her husband, David. Now that they have reared their family and all the children have established their own homes all over the country, their forty-seven-year marriage reaches a point of crisis. Eva's husband wants to sell the house and move into a retirement home, the Haven (a particularly appropriate metaphor for his need for a safe harbor from the lifetime of poverty and crushed expectations). His desire for freedom is really a desire for security. Eva seeks freedom too, but she defines freedom as *"never again to be forced to move to the rhythms of others."* She wishes "at last to live within." She perceives her husband's plan to sell the house as another in a long list of decisions that will continue her subservience to his will. Now, in old age, she makes a final stand against that form of bondage.

Their children are shocked at the dispute, and they have little sympathy for Eva's need to develop her inner life. When she becomes ill, they attribute it to lethargy and psychosomatic causes; then her illness is diagnosed as a malignant cancer, and she is given only a year to live. Her children rally around her and suggest that David take her to visit the various children and grandchildren. Although he is dismayed at the expenses required by these travels, he acquiesces and tries to be a cheerful and helpful companion.

Eva wants more than anything to find the solitude that will reconcile her to the deprivations of the past. She finds that inner peace partly through her interactions with a granddaughter, Jeannie, who is to some extent Eva's alter ego; that is, she is a young woman who believes that she has the power of choice in her life. Her self-fulfillment will not be thwarted by submission to male choices. She is the perfect attendant for Eva's last days. She takes care of Eva's physical needs, records the old woman's beauty through a series of sketches, and assists David in staying with his wife to the end.

Eva's truest inner peace and most perfect expression of solitude, however, comes as her mind returns to her roots as a child and young woman in Russia during the turbulent years at the turn of the century, when czarist oppression was felt by the peasant classes. She has two key memories that sustain her: One is of herself as a young woman. At that time she was a member of the resistance, fighting the czarists. She shared a cell with Lisa, who was a patriot for the anticzarist forces. Lisa killed an informer in order to save the lives of many of her comrades, even though that action led to her own death. Lisa was Eva's hero; she inspired Eva to consider larger social and political issues. To Eva, Jeannie is a modern-day version of Lisa.

Eva's other memory which sustains her in the face of death is a memory of being a child in Russia and dancing joyously at a country wedding. That image of a dancing child suggests a moment of perfect freedom before the girl child becomes a woman and is compelled to submit to social forces that require her to fulfill narrow roles. In a sense, then, Eva goes back to her childhood in order to reconcile the lifelong compromises she made with her own needs of identity and self-fulfillment. The novella ends with a hopeful tone, because even in death there is an affirmation of the beauty and timelessness of that inner peace that Eva sought so courageously in the last year of her life.

At one point in the novella, Eva notes that when her husband played with the grandchildren he "knew how to tickle, chuck, lift, toss, do tricks, tell secrets, make jokes, match riddle for riddle." When the children asked Eva, "Tell me a riddle," however, her answer was always, "I know no riddles, child." To some extent her response reinforces the difference—the conflict—between Eva and her husband, between all men and women. On another level, Eva's response is ironic, for her life has been a mystery to which she cannot give voice. So much is inside, and she seeks the answer to the riddle of her own life.

One of the main themes in the novella is that a woman's life must be her own, and not the lives of her children or of her husband. It is inappropriate for a woman to live her life "for" others. instead, she needs to find the same measure of self-fulfillment that men expect to find in their lives. Another theme is that women have as many insights into the human condition as men do. The woman in *Tell Me a Riddle* has a profound capacity for courage, an empathy for those who are impoverished and oppressed, and insights into the social and political ills that foster human oppression.

SILENCES

First published: 1978
Type of work: Essays

In this collection of essays, Olsen writes of the circumstances that can block writers' (especially women writers') abilities to create.

Written to "re-dedicate and encourage" writers, *Silences* is a compendium of essays, quotations, and commentaries devoted to the reasons various writers either have not written more or have not written at all. It includes two essays written by Tillie Olsen, her afterword to a reprinting of Rebecca Harding Davis's 1861 novel *Life in the Iron Mills*, and more than 150 pages of commentary and original source material relating to the "silences" of many well-known authors, such as Thomas Hardy, Gerard Manley Hopkins, Virginia Woolf, and Herman Melville. Olsen calls this long section "Acerbs, Asides, Amulets, Exhumations, Sources, Deepenings, Roundings, Expansions." Each entry is keyed to the two essays that begin the text.

Of major importance in *Silences* are the two essays that begin the text. The first, "Silences in Literature," was first published in 1965. In this essay Olsen decries the silences that have stopped great literary talents from producing to their full potential. Olsen assigns the term "silences" various categories: "some the silences for years by our acknowledged great; some silences hidden; some the ceasing to publish after one work appears; some the never coming to book form at all." Other silences are caused by censorship, restrictive governments, or narrow societal roles. She concludes, "Where the gifted among women (*and men*) have

remained mute, or have never attained full capacity, it is because of circumstances, inner or outer, which oppose the needs of creation." Her central example is her own story. For twenty years (from 1934 to 1954) she did not publish. She writes, "The simplest circumstances for creation did not exist." Although she kept alive in herself her love for writing, she was unable to bring any work to fruition. This essay is a lament for what she and other great writers have lost by not fulfilling their artistic potential.

The second essay, "One Out of Twelve: Writers Who Are Women in Our Century," was first published in 1972. Olsen contends that of all writers cited in anthologies, listed on syllabi of modern literature courses, noted in the year's best (or decade's best) collections, listed on required reading lists, or considered in book review sections, only one in twelve writers is a woman. Beginning with this simple but devastating statistic, Olsen goes on to cite many of the ways in which women have been rendered secondary or inferior to men in many cultures. She lists stereotypes, taboos, religious characterizations, and narrow and confining roles. She also places her own experience in the context of other women who were "silenced" and devalued. She concludes, "You who teach, read writers who are women. There is a whole literature to be re-estimated, revalued. . . . Read, listen to, living women writers. . . . Not to have audience is a kind of death." Both essays are an appeal for understanding that writers fail to create because of the "unnatural silences" that plague them.

SUMMARY

It is unusual for readers to look upon a writer as a role model, but that is the case for many readers of the works of Tillie Olsen. They have been inspired by this woman's long and difficult struggle to sustain her writing, and they have been moved by her commitment to the realization of women as individuals in her writing. Olsen's literary reputation is based primarily on an unfinished novel and a book of four stories, but her gifts as a writer have encouraged other writers and stimulated a new interest in feminist literary classics.

Robert E. Yahnke

BIBLIOGRAPHY

By the Author

LONG FICTION:
Yonnondio: From the Thirties, 1974

SHORT FICTION:
Tell Me a Riddle, 1961

NONFICTION:
"A Biographical Interpretation," 1972
Silences, 1978

EDITED TEXTS:
Life in the Iron Mills, 1972, revised 1984
Mother to Daughter, Daughter to Mother: Mothers on Mothering—A Daybook and Reader, 1984
Mothers and Daughters: That Special Quality—An Exploration in Photographs, 1987 (with others)

DISCUSSION TOPICS

- Tillie Olsen became a regularly practicing writer only in her forties. What factors account for this delay?

- What unusual demands does Olsen make on readers?

- What is the significance of the title of Olsen's story "I Stand Here Ironing"?

- In the novella *Tell Me a Riddle*, how does the riddle symbolize Eva's life and relationships?

- What structural principles unify Olsen's book *Silences*?

- To what causes other than feminism has Olsen contributed?

About the Author

Boucher, Sandy. "Tillie Olsen: The Weight of Things Unsaid." *Ms.* 3 (September, 1974): 26-30.

Cuneen, Sally. "Tillie Olsen: Storyteller of Working America." *The Christian Century* 21 (May, 1980): 570-574.

McElheny, Annette Bennington. "Alternative Responses to Life in Tillie Olsen's Work." *Frontiers* 2 (Spring, 1977): 76-91.

Martin, Abigail. *Tillie Olsen.* Boise, Idaho: Boise State University Press, 1984.

Orr, Elaine Neil. *Tillie Olsen and a Feminist Spiritual Vision.* Jackson: University Press of Mississippi, 1987.

Schwartz, Helen J. "Tillie Olsen." In *American Women Writers.* Vol. 3, edited by Lina Mainiero and Langdon Lynne Faust. New York: Frederick Ungar, 1981.

Shulman, Alix Kates. "Overcoming Silences: Teaching Writing to Women." *Harvard Educational Review* 49 (November, 1979): 527-533.

CHARLES OLSON

Born: Worcester, Massachusetts
December 27, 1910
Died: New York, New York
January 10, 1970

Olson was an influential poet and essayist during the post-World War II period; his long work, The Maximus Poems, *develops and experiments with the form of the long poem.*

BIOGRAPHY

Charles Olson was born on December 27, 1910, in Worcester, Massachusetts. His father, Charles Joseph Olson, was a letter carrier of Swedish descent, and his mother, Mary Theresa Hines, came from an Irish American background. The family was poor and lived in a lower-middle-class neighborhood in Worcester. Although the young Charles had the usual father-son conflicts during his youth, he greatly admired his father for the force of his personality and his fortitude in standing up to the high-handed political scheming of his supervisors in the postal service. Olson's relationship with his mother was extremely close, and a number of his finest poems are laments and elegies over her death in 1950. Both Olson and his father stood more than 6 feet, 7 inches tall and towered over Mrs. Olson, as family photographs show.

Olson's career as a student was earmarked by success at every step. He qualified for entrance into the Worcester Classical High School, where he earned the highest grades. He also began winning prestigious awards in oratorical contests, taking third place in a national oratory contest in Washington, D.C., in 1928. His prize was a ten-week tour of Europe, where he began his first personal contact with world history, especially Greek and Roman history. Returning from Europe, he entered Wesleyan University as a scholarship student, quali-

fying as a member of Phi Beta Kappa. During his years at Wesleyan, he participated in many theatrical productions, wrote for the school newspaper, played soccer (as a goalie), and became a candidate for a Rhodes Scholarship. During his summers, he performed in little theater productions in and around Gloucester, Massachusetts, his family's permanent summer residence during most of his younger years. Gloucester became the central subject matter and focus for Charles Olson's major long poem, *The Maximus Poems* (1960), which he began writing in 1947.

After graduation from Wesleyan, Olson attended Yale University on an Olin Scholarship and began work on a master's degree, but he decided to return to his undergraduate school instead. He earned his M.A. at Wesleyan in 1932 with a thesis on nineteenth century American novelist Herman Melville. After some intense research in the papers and books of Melville's personal library, Olson began teaching at Clark University in Worcester. At this time he met a writer who became for him a mentor and close friend, Edward Dahlberg. Dahlberg's commitment to scholarship and his standards of excellence influenced Olson to pursue further graduate studies at Harvard University, where he became one of the first three candidates for the newly formed Ph.D. program in American civilization.

After some intermittent sailing trips on a schooner and a hitchhiking trip across the United States, Olson took a variety of interdisciplinary courses at Harvard and started a dissertation comparing William Shakespeare's *King Lear* (1605) to Melville's

Moby Dick (1851), to be supervised by the renowned scholar of American literature F. O. Matthiessen.

For a variety of complex reasons, Olson decided not to finish his Ph.D. dissertation. He received a Guggenheim Fellowship and finished his book on Melville, which Edward Dahlberg advised him not to publish. Olson then worked in a variety of jobs in the Franklin D. Roosevelt administration and for the Democratic Party. He resigned after Roosevelt's death in 1945, even though he had been offered the job of assistant secretary of the treasury and the position of postmaster general. He had become thoroughly disillusioned by his experience in politics and began a series of visits to his poetic mentor, American poet Ezra Pound, at St. Elizabeths Hospital, where Pound had been confined for mental incompetence.

It was during this transitional period that Olson began writing poems and publishing them in such journals as *The Atlantic Monthly, Harper's,* and *Harper's Bazaar.* It was with the help and encouragement of Pound that Olson published his first book, called *Call Me Ishmael* (1947), which had come out of a major re-visioning of his earlier work on Melville. After a trip to the West Coast, where he met the poet Robert Duncan and the geographer Carl Sauer, he was invited to Black Mountain College in North Carolina by its rector, Josef Albers, to lecture. Olson so impressed the faculty and staff there that he was invited to become its new rector; he remained until the school closed in 1956. He also began a friendship there with the poet Robert Creeley that continued throughout his life and was perhaps his most crucial poetic and spiritual contact.

Two major works were published in 1950 that eventually made Olson well known and led to him being considered the leader of a school of writers called the Black Mountain poets. They included a number of Black Mountain faculty and students: Robert Creeley, Robert Duncan, Edward Dorn, Jonathan Williams, Denise Levertov, Joel Oppenheimer, and the fiction writers Fielding Dawson and Michael Rumaker. The first work for which Olson became famous was his revolutionary essay titled "Projective Verse" (1950), published in *Poetry New York,* and a poem called "I, Maximus of Gloucester, to You." This poem became the first of a long series of poems which would eventually become *The Maximus Poems.*

In 1952, Olson received a grant to study Mayan culture in the Yucatán peninsula, the results of which were later published as *Mayan Letters* (1953). In 1960, two other major publications emerged besides *The Maximus Poems.* Donald Allen edited and published an anthology that included Olson's famous essay "Projective Verse" and several of his notable poems, such as "In Cold Hell, in Thicket," "As the Dead Prey upon Us," and his response to T. S. Eliot's *The Waste Land* (1922), "The Kingfishers." Olson's first collection of shorter poems was also published, under the title *The Distances* (1960).

With the demise of Black Mountain College in 1956, Olson returned to Gloucester and worked steadily on the next major section of Maximus poems, called *The Maximus Poems, IV, V, VI* (1968). Although he taught periodically at the State University of New York at Buffalo and the University of Connecticut, he also lectured and gave poetry readings throughout the United States and Europe. He published a collection of his essays called *Human Universe, and Other Essays* in 1965. The title essay is the most comprehensive summary of his poetic and philosophical beliefs and is a vivid demonstration of his piercing intellectual insights. Olson's career ended prematurely when he became terminally ill with cancer of the liver; he died in New York City on January 10, 1970.

ANALYSIS

One of the important keys to understanding Olson's highly complex prose and poetry is the fact that he was also one of the greatest and most effective teachers in the history of American pedagogy. The success of his students as writers and artists attests his powerful classroom presence. His essays and poetry also consistently teach his readers the most important lesson: learning how to learn on their own. His advice to the young poet Edward Dorn at Black Mountain College in 1955 is a case in point. Dorn had asked Olson for a list of required readings, and Olson showed him how to use it: "Best thing to do is *to dig one thing or place or man* until you yourself know more about that than is possible to any other man. It doesn't matter whether it's Barbed Wire or Pemmican or Paterson or Iowa. But *exhaust* it. Saturate it. Beat it. And then U KNOW everything else very fast: one saturation job (it might take 14 years). And you're in, forever."

Edward Dorn did exactly that after leaving Black

Mountain: He devoted years of research to the American West and specifically to the Shoshone Indian tribe. Olson had taken his own advice and began gathering information of all kinds on his own hometown, Gloucester, Massachusetts, which eventually became the subject matter for his monumental *Maximus* poems.

Olson had published a radically new book on Melville's *Moby Dick* in 1947 called *Call Me Ishmael*, which he had abstracted from his proposed doctoral dissertation at Harvard on the affinities between Shakespeare's *King Lear* and *Moby Dick*. He had submitted the original to his mentor, Edward Dahlberg, who deleted half the text and urged him to rewrite it completely. Not only did Olson follow his teacher's advice, but he also refocused his entire thesis. *Call Me Ishmael* departs from the usual symbolic interpretations of *Moby Dick* in terms of "good versus evil" or viewing the sea as the existential void. Olson reinterprets *Moby Dick* as an economic blueprint of the relationship of various classes in society; that is, economic factors lie beneath everything and are the key to understanding the real themes of the novel and the history of that period. He viewed *Moby Dick* as one of the most compelling documents to date of America's perennial attempt to conquer nature by the sheer force of its will as expressed in destructive patterns of industrialization and mechanization.

Human attempts to control the powers of nature and the resulting chaos that such self-destructive behavior produces became one of Olson's principal themes throughout his poetry and prose. Olson perpetually used various versions of the mythic motif of the Fall, disengaging it from any specifically Christian contexts. He traced it back to humankind's fatal separation from a condition of oneness with nature that resulted from the fall into consciousness. In Olson's next prose work, "Projective Verse" (1950), he addressed humanity's fallen condition as it manifests itself in the kind of overly self-conscious, totally subjective poetry that practitioners of the poetics of the New Criticism were writing during the 1930's and 1940 s. Such anti-Romantic poets often described their mental anguish in traditional rhyme and meter and lamented a world completely cut off from anything but a subjective reality. Olson proposed that the spirit of Romanticism reassert itself in what he called "objectism" (a term he created) as a more radical alternative to William Carlos Williams and Ezra Pound's "objectivism":

> Objectism is the getting rid of the lyrical interference of the individual as ego, of the "subject" and his soul, that peculiar presumption by which western man has interposed himself between what he is as a creature of nature (with certain instructions to carry out) and those other creatures of nature which we may, with no derogation, call objects. For man is himself an object.

Olson further exhorts people to recognize themselves as objects among the other objects in nature and to do so with an attitude of humility. Only when one becomes conscious of one's proper position within nature's laws will one be able to stop destroying nature as well as oneself; one may even become of use.

Part of Olson's project to reenergize American poetry was very much connected to a humble recognition of humanity's place in nature, which, Olson hoped, would constitute a radical modification in the human stance toward reality. Because reality, as viewed from a Romantic perspective, is always a "process," then poetry must engage in that process. For Olson, poetry was not the "mirror held up to nature" that the pre-Romantics had proposed but a physical engagement with life's very energies and, therefore, an enactment of life itself. Olson redefines what poetry is in "Projective Verse": "A poem is energy transferred from where the poet got it . . . by way of the poem itself to, all the way over to, the reader. Okay."

For many modern artists and philosophers in the early twentieth century, knowledge had become an open field in which an observer recognizes patterns rather than creating them. Olson believed that the poet must follow suit and must work in the open; he must avoid the old rules of the iambic pentameter line, regular rhythm, and rhyme. "He can go by no track other than the one the poem under hand declares, for itself . . . FORM IS NEVER MORE THAN AN EXTENSION OF CONTENT." The rhythm should be established by the "musical phrase" that Pound exhorted and not by the stultifying regularity of the metronome that traditionalists follow. The length of the line should be determined "from the breath, from the breathing of the man who writes, at the moment that he writes." His evidence for what more conservative critics saw as an outrageous oversimplification of the rules of prosody was to go back to the etymological root of the word "is" and point out that the Aryan root "as" meant "to breathe."

Olson, true to his philosophical belief that "things" precede theory, had written one of his greatest poems the previous year, "The Kingfishers" (1949), from which he had derived the principles of his new poetics. This poem's form is indeed an extension of its content, thereby fulfilling the major requirement of an open-field composition. The poem refocuses T. S. Eliot's "wasteland" motif by including natural cyclicity as redemptive rather than relentlessly mechanistic. It also proposes a major reorientation away from the despair and ennui of the last stages of the Austro-Hungarian Empire, which Eliot's *The Waste Land* documents, toward a revaluation of the ancient civilizations of the West as Olson explores the Mayan ruins of Yucatán.

Olson consciously moved away from his Greco-Roman academic orientation and found a more viable path in pre-Socratic ideas, particularly in Heraclitus's proposition that reality is in constant flux and that any attempt to categorize or systematize flux is doomed from its inception. Olson visited the great Mayan ruins to see for himself the destruction that the "civilized" Europeans had brought with them. Olson embraced change in all its fluidity and found his vocation as a poet and archaeologist in his commitment to hunting among its stones. Although Olson was disturbed by the Mayan ruins, he perceived himself as an object among other objects within nature, and he dug even deeper into nature's endless change. Salvation consists of probing more deeply into the actual earth rather than resorting to Eliot's retreat into the comfort and security of English history and the Anglo-Catholic Church.

Olson published many poems and essays during the 1950's, the most notable of which were *In Cold Hell, in Thicket* (1953), *Mayan Letters*, "As the Dead Prey upon Us" (1956), and *The Maximus Poems 11-12* (1956). "As the Dead Prey upon Us" expresses his anguish over the death of his mother as she appeared to him in recurring dreams. The ultimate fear that a soul must face in a demythologized world is the necessary descent into Hell: "What a man has to do, he has to do, he has to/ meet his

mother in hell." Olson demonstrates exactly how projective verse works by using the raw material of his own dreams and then juxtaposing images of his broken-down car with a next-door neighbor and a mysterious "Blue Deer." He lyricizes all these disparate elements, thereby fusing them into his own surrealist but lucid narrative.

Two major volumes of poetry appeared in 1960: *The Maximus Poems* and *The Distances*. Olson's collected essays, titled *Human Universe, and Other Essays*, were published in 1965. *The Distances* encapsulates perfectly in its title the themes that Olson addressed throughout the remainder of his writing career: the sense of loss of a common consciousness and the disengagement of humankind from a direct experience of reality. Many of the poems in this volume lament humankind's fall into consciousness, a condition that automatically induces feelings of isolation and alienation from a primordial center. The poet alone possesses the power to enact a consciousness that can rediscover what "science has run away with . . . discovering this discarded thing nature."

Olson's enemy is the same one that troubled Ezra Pound, the penchant of the mind to abstract itself from the body, to systemize and categorize the essential wholeness of experience into endless classifications which people then mistake for life itself. Olson's definition of "the absolute" in "Human Universe" is uncompromisingly existential: "If there is any absolute, it is never more than this one, you, this instant, in action."

It is this very disengagement of people from the direct experience of reality that becomes the principal subject for the massive work Olson began to publish in 1960, *The Maximus Poems*. Only a restoration of humankind to the energies of the local could begin to mend the split, the "iron-dealt cleavage" that Hart Crane hoped to heal in his long poem *The Bridge* (1930). There is little doubt that Olson saw his epic poem as a timely successor not only to Crane's huge work but also to other large efforts, such as Pound's *Cantos* (1917-1970) and Walt Whitman's *Leaves of Grass* (1855). Most important, perhaps, he saw it standing beside William Carlos Williams's *Paterson* (1946-1958).

THE MAXIMUS POEMS

First published: 1960
Type of work: Long poem

The voice of "Maximus" awakens the citizens of Gloucester, Massachusetts, to their own potential.

The first volume of what eventually became a three-volume, six-hundred-page poem was called *The Maximus Poems.* It was published by the Jargon Society, a press which had been created by poet (and former student of Olson) Jonathan Williams. The keys to an understanding of the entire Maximus project are the specific maps that Olson placed on the covers of the first two volumes. A U.S. Coast and Geodetic Survey map of Gloucester, Massachusetts, appears on the cover of the first volume, immediately grounding the reader in the specific geography of the place where Olson spent his childhood summers and was to live the last ten years of his life.

Olson's major models for *The Maximus Poems* were Whitman's *Leaves of Grass,* Pound's *Cantos,* and (especially) Williams's *Paterson.* Williams's poem was an unequivocal reaction to the gloomy abstractions of Eliot's apocalyptic *The Waste Land,* which lamented, by means of literary fragments, the fractured consciousness of a European civilization that had lost its religious center. Williams proposed his own hometown, Paterson, New Jersey, as the subject of his epic poem, insisting that an authentic American poet, following the lead of Whitman, must begin with an activation of the energies of the local. Olson thoroughly agreed, and though both poets admired Pound's *Cantos,* they found them, Williams said, "too perversely individual to achieve the universal understanding required."

Williams, however, envisioned the American epic as a kind of newspaper: "It must be a concise sharp-shooting epic style. Machine gun style. Facts, facts, facts, tearing into us to blast away our stinking flesh of news. Bullets." Nothing could describe Olson's style more precisely than Williams's words. If the theme of much of Olson's poetry in *The Distances* concerns what Heraclitus described as "man's estrangement from that with which he is most familiar"—his own body—then *The Maximus Poems,* by the sheer weight of its geographical and histori-cal information, puts one back into contact with one's origins: nature as manifested in the literal ground upon which one stands. Olson was an authentic Romantic in that he believed redemption would come not from some remote, quasi-mystical center but from a proper introduction to nature itself on the most specific level.

Much of this first Maximus volume is organized in the form of letters from a fictive persona which Olson borrowed from ancient Greek literature. Maximus of Tyre was a philosopher and a dialectician who wandered about Mediterranean communities continually lecturing on Homer's *Odyssey* (c. 725 B.C.E.). The figure is also a version of psychologist Carl Jung's archetypal "homo maximus" or "greatest man." Olson begins by identifying himself with the figure of Maximus in the title of the first poem, which is also the first line of the poem: "I, Maximus of Gloucester, to you . . . a metal hot from boiling water, tell you/ what is a lance, who obeys the figures of the present dance." The reference to the dance is a direct connection with one of the principal metaphors that Williams used throughout *Paterson* to signify humanity's total physical and spiritual involvement with the energies of life itself.

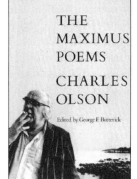

Olson, therefore, locates his task in awakening the citizens of Gloucester to the experience of natural life in spite of being cut off from its healing powers: "when all is become billboards, when, all, even silence, is spray-gunned?" Maximus continues to exhort his citizens to take drastic action against the commercialization and modernization of their soil: "o kill kill kill kill kill/ those/ who advertise you/ out." Much of this first volume laments the loss of traditional local values, beliefs, and practices that are being destroyed by a nation corrupted by blatant materialism. He renames Muzak "mu-sick" and decries the damage done to humankind's instinctual life: "No eyes or ears left/ to their own doings (all invaded, appropriated, outraged, all senses/ including the mind . . . lulled."

The Maximus Poems, then, can be viewed as an extended meditation of the ruins of the poet's own origins by a civilization whose arrogance has blinded it to its obligations to both the physical and spiritual ecology. Much of the remainder of this first volume is a painstaking reconstruction of the actual history of Gloucester, using information from archival documents and early historical sources and juxtaposing its data to reveal the subtexts of greed and power that drove the original European settlers to America. Olson refuses to create fictive structures of "versions" of history and strives more than any other American poet to permit the "facts" to speak for themselves. He wants, as far as possible, an unmediated vision whose primary content consists of historical and anecdotal records and even statistical facts. He demands an empirical myth whose origins and energies are grounded in a specific locale.

Olson's task is to arrange and organize these unconnected fragments of history in such a way that a continuity between the past and the present will become evident. His readers will, he hopes, learn from the past and improve their future. Olson firmly believed in his redemptive role as a historian when he declaimed: "My memory is/ the history of time," for without memory, there remains nothing but the disconnected segments of an exhausted civilization that Eliot documented in *The Waste Land*.

THE MAXIMUS POEMS, IV, V, VI

First published: 1968
Type of work: Long poem

This volume deepens and extends Olson's attentions beyond the local and into the mythic origins of Western civilization.

The key to this second volume of *The Maximus Poems*, sometimes called *Maximus II*, is the map that Olson placed on the cover. It is a map of Gondwanaland, the name by which many geographers call the primordial or unified continent that existed before, as Olson put it, "Earth started to come apart at the seams, some 125 million years awhile back and India took off from Africa & migrated to Asia." In this volume, Olson continues to probe the specific historical information of Gloucester but also moves inland to explore the history and ori-

gins of a section of Gloucester called Dogtown. Working, however, in an "open field" forced Olson to delve even more deeply into what preceded history, and he found himself confronting the nature and function of prehistorical forms of consciousness called myth. Much of this volume examines systems of mythic consciousness and attempts to understand how myths are encoded with essential human information and become permanent forms of human experience. Olson, an avowed believer in the theories of Jung, also viewed myths as archetypes of the collective unconscious.

Olson's advice to Edward Dorn to "exhaust" or "saturate" one place until he knew more about it than anyone else ever could became Olson's directive to himself in his years of examining Gloucester. It also, however, necessitated a rearrangement of the rest of the world in the light of what he learned about his origins. Immediately after declaring that his memory is "the history of time" in *The Maximus Poems IV, V, VI* he locates another, more onerous task: "I am making a mappemunde [a map of the world]. It is to include my being." Such an obligation demanded that Olson explore not only history and myth but also other associated subfields such as archaeology, paleontology, geography, geology, and anthropology.

What *The Maximus Poems, IV, V, VI* became, then, was a recapitulation of the origin and development of human consciousness, a task so demanding that the structure of the poem almost collapses beneath the burden. Few literary conventions are observed as the language becomes more dense and private. Transitions between sections are either nonexistent or so personal that understanding it is impossible. The influence of Alfred North Whitehead's *Process and Reality* (1929) is evident throughout, particularly in the in-process appearance of many of the poems. Olson suggested that the arrangement of the material was closer to that of a mosaic taking shape than to any kind of finished narrative product.

Many of the earlier characteristics of the fictive voice of Maximus are missing from this volume because Olson, following his own advice in "Projective Verse," removed "the lyrical interference of the individual as ego." This volume can be viewed as a prime example of what he called "objectism," as his control and arrangement of the mythological, historical, and geographical data are virtually undetectable. The "facts" do, indeed, "speak for themselves," and the structure suffers accordingly. What Olson was rigorously trying to avoid, however, was the appearance of any kind of tidy synthesis of myth and history, such as that which Joseph Campbell proposed in *The Hero with a Thousand Faces* (1949). Olson adamantly opposed any synthesizing structure that even remotely resembled an imaginative or fictive arrangement of "facts." Although he read and heavily annotated all of the fourteen volumes of Jung's works in his personal library, Olson refused to impose any kind of limiting interpretive structure on the materials of history and was much closer to the structuralism of French anthropologist Claude Levi-Strauss than to Campbell's Jungian archetypes.

Olson defined an American as "a complex of occasions,/ themselves a geometry/ of spatial nature" and added that this definition explained his feeling of oneness with the world: "I have this sense,/ that I am one/ with my skin." He kept coming back to the geographical, the local, and feared involvement with intellectual classifications of any kind. His grounding in Gloucester became a position from which he could measure the world.

THE MAXIMUS POEMS, VOLUME 3

First published: 1975
Type of work: Long poem

The Maximus Poems, Volume 3 *continues with the omniscient voice of "Maximus," but the personal crises of Olson himself are evident throughout.*

Volume 3 of *The Maximus Poems* was never completed by Olson, who died in 1970, but among the mass of material left after his death were indications of certain directions that later scholars followed in gathering the material and organizing it into a coherent form. University of Connecticut professors George Butterick and Charles Boer devoted many years to a thoughtful arrangement of the materials for volume 3. Olson had determined the first and last poems in the collection, and Butterick and Boer followed the same order that Olson

had used in the first two volumes—essentially chronological—in their edition. Many of the poems included were left in an unrevised form.

Olson's attentions had changed dramatically in this volume, and many of the poems became quite personal, reflecting the private crises that he was undergoing, specifically the tragic death of his wife in an automobile crash in 1964. The "Maximus" of this volume continues to dig into the local history and geological data of Gloucester, but he finds himself repeatedly confronting the bare earth itself. Unlike Wallace Stevens and Robert Duncan, whose imaginations found satisfaction in fictive certainties, Olson's inability to trust the powers of the imagination drove him to search for the divine in the physical. He stated it quite directly: "I believe in God/ as fully physical." In poem 143, "The Festival Aspects," he rehearses the various stages of humanity's Fall and division from sacred consciousness, but Maximus suggests that the continued force of human attentions would eventually redeem the fallen world and unify it by the almost telekinetic power of his consciousness.

Though Olson still rages against the dehumanizing encroachments of progress, he comes closer to a deeper understanding and acceptance of the essential mystery at the heart of existence. "Praise the mystery/ of creation, that in matter alone." By the conclusion of the volume, his concerns have become completely personal. He knows that he is dying of cancer of the liver and imagines that he is a stone. He also locates himself, finally, in both his origin and destiny in the next-to-last poem of the book, "Mother Earth Alone." The very last Maximus poem consists of only eight words that brutally summarize the attenuated range of his awareness in the final days of his illness: "my wife my car my color and myself." Haunted by the death of his wife and jaundiced by cancer, he returned to the source of his life as a poet—his own personal consciousness, from which an entire mythic world had emerged.

SUMMARY

In many ways *The Maximus Poems* constitute the postmodern equivalent of Williams's *Paterson* and Pound's *Cantos*. Olson saw his own effort as an attempt to find a middle ground between Pound's overinflated "EGO AS BEAK" and its disastrous results in the *Cantos*, and Williams's inability to forge a mythic persona powerful enough to keep *Paterson* from collapsing under the weight of its own historical data. Olson's "Maximus" is a hero of consciousness who recognizes the poem as the one area in which man may be totally himself. The poem as both art and historical document, which *The Maximus Poems* purports to synthesize, also makes the voice of the poet immortal. Olson combined the consciousness of the individual with the mythic energies of the local and became, as Maximus, a spokesman for the earth itself.

Patrick Meanor

BIBLIOGRAPHY

By the Author

POETRY:
Y & X, 1948
Letter for Melville 1951, 1951
This, 1952
In Cold Hell, in Thicket, 1953
The Maximus Poems 1-10, 1953
The Maximus Poems 11-22, 1956
O'Ryan 2 4 6 8 10, 1958, expanded 1965 (as *O'Ryan 12345678910*)
The Maximus Poems, 1960
The Distances, 1960
Charles Olson: Reading at Berkeley, 1966 (transcription)
The Maximus Poems, IV, V, VI, 1968
Archaeologist of Morning: The Collected Poems Outside the Maximus Series, 1970
The Maximus Poems, Volume 3, 1975
The Horses of the Sea, 1976
The Maximus Poems, 1983
The Collected Poems of Charles Olson: Excluding "The Maximus Poems," 1987
A Nation of Nothing but Poetry: Supplementary Poems, 1989

SHORT FICTION:
Stocking Cap: A Story, 1966

DRAMA:
The Fiery Hunt, and Other Plays, pb. 1977

NONFICTION:
Call Me Ishmael: A Study of Melville, 1947
"Projective Verse," 1950
Mayan Letters, 1953
Human Universe, and Other Essays, 1965
Proprioception, 1965
Selected Writings of Charles Olson, 1966
Pleistocene Man, 1968
Causal Mythology, 1969

DISCUSSION TOPICS

- Discuss the importance of the sense of place in Charles Olson's *The Maximus Poems*.

- What does Olson mean by "objectism"? What trends in poetry does it oppose?

- What were the results of Olson's application of his "projective" theory to the later Maximus poems?

- Trace the development of Olson's study of Herman Melville.

- What were Olson's principal achievements at Black Mountain College?

- Olson taught his students to become expert in knowledge of one subject. What benefit, aside from the mastery of that subject, did he believe could thus be achieved?

Letters for "Origin," 1950-1956, 1969 (Albert Glover, editor)
The Special View of History, 1970
On Black Mountain, 1971
Additional Prose: A Bibliography on America, Proprioception, and Other Notes and Essays, 1974
Charles Olson and Ezra Pound: An Encounter at St. Elizabeths, 1975
The Post Office, 1975
Muthologos: The Collected Lectures and Interviews, 1978-1979 (2 volumes)
Charles Olson and Robert Creeley: The Complete Correspondence, 1980-1996 (10 volumes; George F. Butterick, editor)
Charles Olson and Cid Corman: Complete Correspondence, 1950-1964, 1987-1991 (2 volumes; George Evans, editor)
In Love, in Sorrow: The Complete Correspondence of Charles Olson and Edward Dahlberg, 1990 (Paul Christensen, editor)
Selected Letters, Charles Olson, 2000 (Ralph Maud, editor)

MISCELLANEOUS:
Selected Writings of Charles Olson, 1966
Poetry and Truth: The Beloit Lectures and Poems, 1971
Collected Prose, 1997 (Donald Allen and Benjamin Friedlander, editors)

About the Author

Bollobás, Eniko. *Charles Olson.* New York: Twayne, 1992.

Cech, John. *Charles Olson and Edward Dahlberg: A Portrait of a Friendship.* Victoria, B.C.: English Literary Studies, University of Victoria, 1982.

Maud, Ralph. *Charles Olson's Reading: A Biography.* Carbondale: Southern Illinois University Press, 1996.

Olson, Charles, and Cid Corman. *Charles Olson and Cid Corman: Complete Correspondence, 1950-1964.* Edited by George Evans. 2 vols. Orono, Maine: National Poetry Foundation, 1987.

Rifkin, Libbie. *Career Moves: Olson, Creeley, Zukofsky, Berrigan, and the American Avant-Garde.* Madison: University of Wisconsin Press, 2000.

Rumaker, Michael. *Black Mountain Days.* Asheville, N.C.: Black Mountain Press, 2003.

MICHAEL ONDAATJE

Courtesy, Picador Publicity
Department, London

Born: Colombo, Ceylon (now Sri Lanka)
September 12, 1943

Blending historical fact with imaginary incidents, Ondaatje uses the building of Toronto, World War II, and the civil wars in Sri Lanka as the postcolonial contexts in which his characters struggle to find their cultural identities.

BIOGRAPHY

(Phillip) Michael Ondaatje was born in Colombo, Sri Lanka (then called Ceylon), on September 12, 1943. Ondaatje grew up surrounded by his extended family on an estate in Kegalle owned by his paternal grandfather, a wealthy tea planter. In 1952, four years after his parents' divorce, Ondaatje moved to England with his mother, sister, and brother to attend Dulwich College, a public school with a strong academic program and a long literary tradition.

At the age of nineteen, Ondaatje followed his brother, Christopher, to Montreal, Canada, then moved to Lennoxville in eastern Quebec, where he attended Bishop's University, majoring in English and history; it was there that he first began to write. In 1964, Ondaatje married the artist Kim Jones, with whom he has two children, and transferred from Bishop's University to the University of Toronto, where he earned his B.A. in 1965. That same year he was awarded the Ralph Gustafson Poetry Award, the first of many awards recognizing his work. In 1967, Ondaatje received an M.A. from Queen's University, published his first collection of poetry, *The Dainty Monsters*, and began teaching English at the University of Western Ontario.

In 1969, Ondaatje's second volume of poetry, *The Man with Seven Toes*, was published, followed a year later by the short critical work *Leonard Cohen* and *The Collected Works of Billy the Kid: Left Handed Poems*. During this time, he also became an editor at Coach House Press, the publisher of much of his early work, and directed a small film, *Sons of Captain Poetry*. In 1971, after declining to pursue a Ph.D., Ondaatje left the University of Western Toronto for Glendon College, York University, where he began his long teaching career.

From 1971 to 1981, Ondaatje published *Rat Jelly* (1973), *Coming Through Slaughter* (1976), *There's a Trick with a Knife I'm Learning to Do* (1979), and *Elimination Dance* (1978; rev. ed., 1980). During this period he received several awards, including two Governor-General's Awards, the Canada-Australia Literary Prize, and the *Books in Canada* First Novel Award, and he was selected as a Chalmer's Award finalist. After several years of strain, he separated from his wife in 1980 and spent 1981 as a visiting professor at the University of Hawaii. He then returned to Glendon College to become a full professor of English and published the semiautobiographical novel *Running in the Family* (1982), based on his experiences in Sri Lanka.

In 1984, Ondaatje published *Secular Love*, an exploration of the sadness of divorce and the excitement of new love. *In the Skin of a Lion*, which followed in 1987, won the City of Toronto Book Award and the Trillium Book Award, and it was a finalist for the Ritz Paris Hemingway Award. Ondaatje then received the prestigious Order of Canada in 1988. *The Cinnamon Peeler: Selected Poems* was first published in 1989. In 1990, Ondaatje edited *From Ink Lake: Canadian Stories*, a collection of short fiction praised for both its content and its organization, and taught at Brown University as a visiting professor.

Ondaatje's best-known work, *The English Patient*, for which he received the Booker Prize, the British Book Trust, and a third Governor-General's Award, was published in 1992, and it was in this work that he developed the postcolonial themes with which he is identified. It was adapted as a motion picture in 1996. *Anil's Ghost*, published in 2000, earned him the Giller Prize and the Prix Medicis, and was short-listed for the *Irish Times* Literature Prize.

Generous in his support of young Canadian writers, Ondaatje is also an accomplished scholar who has authored several critical volumes and numerous articles, edited several collections and anthologies, and directed five films.

ANALYSIS

Although he initially gained recognition for his poetry, Ondaatje came to be known for his novels, which are always based on historical events, whether the building of Toronto in the 1920's, the dropping of atomic bombs at the end of World War II, or the civil war in Sri Lanka in the 1980's. Ondaatje describes these events from a postcolonial perspective, meaning that he is interested in revealing resistance to colonial oppression. Redefining the status of historical truth in what has been called in Canada the New History, Ondaatje also challenges the traditional equation and confusion of past historical events with the events themselves. He implies that history has been rewritten in every generation according to the angle of vision of the historian. He suggests that this vision is determined by whether the historian belongs to the victorious or the vanquished. Because the political point of view of the observer must be taken into account, Ondaatje always addresses history from a fictional perspective. As a writer, he sees himself as performing an essential task: reevaluating official history that has been dominated by the perspective of the colonizers through providing a voice for the colonized, who have usually been left out of history books.

Specifically, Ondaatje studies the ideological forces that move the colonized to adopt the culture of the colonialist, a merger which also empowers the colonized to resist. Examining the double-consciousness of the colonized in their awareness of the conflict between indigenous and colonial culture, Ondaatje returns again and again to his central theme of the search for identity.

In the novel *In the Skin of a Lion*, Ondaatje describes this search as fraught with adventure and danger. Patrick Lewis, born in the backwoods, feels isolated from the dominant Canadian culture. He moves to Toronto, finds a job tunneling beneath Lake Ontario, and, searching for someone to blame for his own otherness, joins a revolutionary movement. Although he finds solace in his relationships with two female actors, these love affairs do not last, ended on one hand by death and on the other by his lover's return to her fiancé. After setting fire to a hotel and blowing up a dock, Patrick is imprisoned. Finally, his lover finds her way back to him, fulfilling his need for identity and community.

The English Patient also treats this same theme. Set in the ruins of an Italian villa at the end of World War II, the novel initially points to the tenuousness of both memory and nationality as clues to identity. The English patient has amnesia and lies upstairs in the villa with burns over his entire body, cared for by a Canadian nurse, Hana. He cannot remember whether he is British or Hungarian or even what his name is. Kirpal Singh arrives at the villa, attracted by the sound of Hana playing the piano; as a sapper (bomb detonator), he knows of the German habit of setting mines inside pianos. Kirpal is an Indian who has accepted the culture of the colonialist and enlisted in the British war effort. While at the villa, he falls in love with Hana. A few months later, when atomic bombs are dropped on Japan in 1945, he recognizes his true identity in allegiance to Asia. He tears off his insignia, leaves Hana, and returns to his roots in India. Like Patrick's love relationships in the novel *In the Skin of a Lion*, Kirpal's relationship with Hana is provisional; based on self-interest, it ends once that interest is served.

Although *Anil's Ghost* shares many qualities with Ondaatje's previous works, it redefines issues of identity and nationality. *In the Skin of a Lion* and *The English Patient* describe a struggle taking place between the culture of the oppressors and that of the indigenous people. This time, however, the oppressor is embodied in someone who was once one of the oppressed.

Reinforcing Ondaatje's sense of the provisionality of all relationships, the heroine, Anil Tissera, has married—and divorced—a traditional Sri Lankan while they were both in London. Now that she is returning to her native country as part of a U.N. commission investigating possible civil war atrocities, in an effort to evaluate her allegiance to Sri Lanka, she is trying to forget her marriage ever existed.

Two brothers helping her in her work, Sarath and Gamini Diyasena, offer a stark contrast to Tissera. Whereas Tissera has forgotten how to speak Sinhala in the fifteen years since she left, the two brothers never left Sri Lanka. Fondly believing she is objective and impartial, Tissera suspects Sarath of disloyalty to the work of the commission. Ultimately, however, he will give his life to save hers. Blurring the difference between barbarian and civilized, Tissera, the Western "civilized" one, becomes the barbarian. Naïvely expecting that her discovery of government corruption will be rewarded, instead she is forced to flee Sri Lanka, leaving Sarath to be murdered in her stead. In contrast to Tissera's broken personal relationships and her conflicted desire for the freedom of exile and nostalgia for the Sri Lanka of her childhood, Gamini's love for his brother persists even after death. Cradling Sarath's dead body in his arms as he tapes up a chest wound, he is thankful that at least Sarath's face has not been disfigured.

In this novel, although the language is less singular than in previous works, Ondaatje's poetic prose gives the clue to meaning: It is filled with sensory imagery ranging from the startling to the mundane. Its flexibility, along with Ondaatje's growing skill at connecting with the reader, despite temporal shifts and multiple story lines, communicates a new, unconventional understanding of historical events. Identity and nationality become fluid and provisional, whereas community and human relationships are stable. Survival depends not on official leaders but on a few traditionally marginal, unknown individuals whose single-minded dedication and persistence works against brutality, dehumanization, and oppression.

Ondaatje's reputation continues to grow, resting on the constant refinement of his understanding of nationality and identity as cultural constructs. His highly individualized use of recent events to develop understanding of world history through the use of characters who are not typically part of traditional historical accounts enables him to span many fields and makes him unique among writers today.

IN THE SKIN OF A LION

First published: 1987
Type of work: Novel

Three interconnected stories tell of early twentieth century Toronto set against a backdrop of immigrant workers and union politics.

In the Skin of a Lion opens on a young Patrick growing up in the wilds of the Canadian wilderness. Patrick lives outside a logging camp with his father, Hazen, a logger and self-taught explosives expert. Hazen, described as "taciturn," is withdrawn from both Canadian society and his son, instilling in Patrick the sense of being "other" within one's own culture. One winter night, Patrick is called to the frozen river by a vision of sparkling lights he takes to be fireflies. He finds the immigrant loggers ice skating while holding fistfuls of burning rushes. This is Patrick's first glimpse of community, and he watches with longing and fascination yet is unable to overcome his own isolation to join them. The men remain remote and anonymous figures representing an ideal of which Patrick is barely cognizant. Only later does Patrick discover that the skaters were Finns. In this way Ondaatje weaves the past, the present, and the future into a temporal labyrinth that connects characters to themselves and to one another.

Chapter 2, "The Bridge," focuses on Nicholas Temelcoff. Nicholas, a Macedonian immigrant, works the most dangerous job on the construction of the Prince Edward Bridge over the Don River. Suspended in mid-air, he is separated from his fellow workers by twin barriers of language and empty space. Nicholas's isolation is broken one night when he catches a nun who has been swept off the unfinished bridge by wind. The emotional intimacy engendered by the rescue causes Nicholas to perceive Toronto differently, as if the city has been imbued with the nun's spirit and beauty. One year later, Nicholas leaves the bridge and opens a bakery, the decisive move that makes him a part of his community.

As book 1 continues, Ondaatje returns to Patrick, now twenty-one and newly arrived in Toronto. In a city filled with life, Patrick finds himself isolated. He takes a job searching for a reclusive millionaire who has disappeared. While searching, he meets Clara and begins a short but passionate affair. When Clara breaks off the affair to return to her millionaire boyfriend, Patrick is again alone and returns to Toronto to seek solace in isolation and physical labor. In book 2, Patrick moves into an immigrant neighborhood and joins a work crew digging and blasting a waterworks tunnel beneath Lake Ontario. One night Patrick attends an illegal meeting of activists in the tunnel and is reintroduced to Clara's friend, Alice.

Alice is the catalyst that brings Patrick out of his isolation. He becomes a part of the immigrant community in which they live, forms a close bond with Alice's daughter, Hana, and even participates in a leftist political movement. When Alice is killed in an accident, Patrick, again lost to alienation, blames wealthy WASP society. He seeks revenge by blowing up a dock at a regatta and is sent to prison, where he meets another immigrant from his neighborhood, Caravaggio the thief.

Patrick reconnects to humanity through his contact with Caravaggio. He warns Caravaggio before he is attacked in his cell one night, and after Caravaggio's escape and Patrick's release, the two men meet again in their immigrant neighborhood. Upon his release, Patrick first goes to Nicholas Temelcoff's bakery, where Hana waits for him. Then, still bent on avenging the death of Alice, he enlists Caravaggio's help in a plan to blow up the waterworks facility. The plan goes well, but at the last moment, Patrick turns away from his rage. Hana becomes Patrick's anchor to community and connectedness—the final catalyst in his journey from isolation and otherness. The closing pages of the book find Patrick embarking on another journey. A call from Clara sparks a trip with Hana, whom Patrick now acknowledges as his daughter, to rescue Clara from the same isolation from which Patrick suffered. As the journey begins, Patrick begins telling Hana his own story, the event that brings the reader full circle and back to the preface of the novel.

THE ENGLISH PATIENT

First published: 1992
Type of work: Novel

Four survivors of World War II attempt to come to terms with war-shattered identities within the ruins of an Italian villa.

Revisiting characters from *In the Skin of a Lion, The English Patient* opens with Hana, a Canadian nurse, newly arrived with her English patient at the ruined Villa San Girolamo. The patient, Almasy, once a desert explorer, has been burned over his entire body. Soon the two are joined by Caravaggio, a Canadian thief conscripted as a spy, and Kirpal "Kip" Singh, an Indian bomb-detonator.

Ondaatje immediately reveals the intensity of recent suffering in the group's sharpened perceptions. Indeed, the entire book is expressed in the striking imagery characteristic of poetry. Hana drops a peeled plum into the mouth of Almasy, whom she calls her "despairing saint" with the "hipbones of Christ." Emphasizing the crucial role of imagination in shaping identity, the Christ-like patient becomes the blank tablet on which the villa inhabitants begin to carve their new selves. Kip and Almasy develop a bond based on their mutual knowledge of explosives and weapons. For Hana, mourning her father, baby, and lover, Almasy represents someone to nurture. Caravaggio, in contrast, blames Almasy for the mutilation of his thumbs on grounds that Almasy was once a German spy; he increases his morphine to make him talk.

The novel relies heavily on punning—Kip is a pun on Kim, the hero of Rudyard Kipling's story and a mutilation of his actual name, Kirpal. In fact, mutilation becomes a key theme as the characters' mutilated identities are healed through allegiance to nationality. Leading the way, the English patient at first rejects nationality altogether. Still, his fate has already demonstrated the folly of renouncing official allegiances. In love with Katherine, his friend's wife, Almasy becomes a victim of her husband's attempt to kill all three of them in a suicide-murder. When Almasy tries to get help for the wounded Katherine from British officials in Cairo, they label him German and imprison him. Later, he enlists Nazi aid and flies off in a "rotted plane" which immediately ignites and crashes. Almasy, himself afire, descends like a comet.

As he begins to piece together his own story, Almasy reveals that his desire to be rid of national allegiances stems from his admiration for the nomadic Bedouins who tend him after the crash, also suggesting that although some might consider them uncivilized, the Bedouins are well versed in medicinal remedies. Later, though, Almasy acknowledges that barbarism occurs in all groups and that his own self-interest may have caused him to behave savagely. He comes to accept, for example, that his willful independence has brought about the death of others, particularly Katherine. In a similar move toward reconciliation, Hana reaches out in a letter to her father's companion, Clara, saying her father "died in a comforting place." Moreover, linking mind with body, Caravaggio finally identifies his own story in the mutilated flesh and fractured memory of the English patient.

The greatest awakening, however, occurs within Kirpal Singh, a former colonial subject whose struggles official history has ignored. Even though Almasy may not be English, and the 1945 atomic bombs are dropped by Americans on the Japanese, Kirpal identifies the behavior as English. He rages to Almasy, "When you start bombing the brown races of the world, you're an Englishman." Declaring that the Allies, not the Germans or Japanese, are the real barbarians, he returns to India, where he becomes a doctor. Hana returns to Canada.

Questions remain. Does the author finally endorse hybridism or reject it? That is, do Kirpal's and Hana's returns to their native countries in fact affirm their freedom or merely represent new imprisonment? What is to be made of the quasi-mystical connection that still exists between Hana and Kirpal, despite their separation? Ondaatje is content to leave such questions to the reader.

ANIL'S GHOST

First published: 2000
Type of work: Novel

A forensic pathologist returns abruptly to the United States after investigating possible war crimes in her native Sri Lanka.

Anil's Ghost takes place during a gruesome civil war during the 1980's in Sri Lanka. It explores the legacy left by colonialism, represented through the actions of Anil Tissera, a forensic pathologist revisiting the country after a fifteen-year absence as part of a U.N. commission investigating human rights abuses. Alienated from Sri Lankan culture, Tissera blinds herself to the mortal danger in which her investigations place her fellow archaeologist, Sarath Diyasena, affiliated with the government.

Although the delicacy of language describing mental and physical wounds becomes "balm" to war's brutality, in *Anil's Ghost* Ondaatje most often reflects brutality directly, replacing the lushness of his earlier work with spare, straight narrative. Indeed, as seventy thousand citizens are quietly spirited away and murdered, silence replaces words as a reaction to repression. Characters find release in extreme acts: For example, Sarath's brother, Dr. Gamini Diyasena, lives like a beggar, snatching sleep at the hospital and taking drugs to continue performing round-the-clock surgery on civil war victims. When Anil discovers scientific evidence implicating the government in war crimes, Sarath tells her to abandon her notes and equipment and to leave the country. Her departure means that she is also abandoning those she has tried to help. Indeed, Ondaatje shows that Tissera, with her Western need to uncover "Truth," causes the suppression of the very truth she seeks.

Soon, Gamini discovers Sarath's dead body on a gurney. The novel concludes with Gamini pondering his surrender of his emotional and mate-

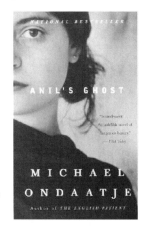

rial existence to others. For both Anil and Sarath, science and politics intersect disastrously; for Gamini, deeply attuned to his community, they work together to offer a protective camouflage enabling him to live to feel the "sweet touch of the world."

SUMMARY

As a postcolonial author, Michael Ondaatje has risked being misunderstood by compatriots as well as those from other former colonies who have accused him of a preoccupation with technique and aesthetics at the expense of involvement in politics. What is certain, however, is that many of Ondaatje's novels show that he remains unafraid to explore unapproved versions of history and reveal an increasing ability to merge aesthetics with politics as he describes the ways formerly colonized peoples construct a viable cultural identity of their own.

Susan Tetlow Harrington and Rebecca Curtiss-Floyd

BIBLIOGRAPHY

By the Author

LONG FICTION:
Coming Through Slaughter, 1976
In the Skin of a Lion, 1987
The English Patient, 1992
Anil's Ghost, 2000

DRAMA:
The Collected Works of Billy the Kid, pr. 1973 (adaptation of his poetry)
In the Skin of a Lion, pr. 1987 (adaptation of his novel)

POETRY:
The Dainty Monsters, 1967
The Man with Seven Toes, 1969
The Collected Works of Billy the Kid: Left Handed Poems, 1970
Rat Jelly, 1973
Elimination Dance, 1978, revised 1980
There's a Trick with a Knife I'm Learning to Do: Poems, 1963-1978, 1979
Secular Love, 1984
The Cinnamon Peeler: Selected Poems, 1989
Handwriting, 1998

NONFICTION:
Leonard Cohen, 1970
Claude Glass, 1979
Running in the Family, 1982

EDITED TEXTS:
The Long Poem Anthology, 1979
The Faber Book of Contemporary Canadian Short Stories, 1990
From Ink Lake: Canadian Stories, 1990
The Brick Reader, 1991 (with Linda Spalding)

DISCUSSION TOPICS

- In what ways does Anil demonstrate postcolonial "double-consciousness"?

- How do each of the main characters in Michael Ondaatje's *The English Patient*— Hana, Kip, Caravaggio, and Almasy—manifest alienation?

- Do you judge Kip's assertion of his Indian identity at the end of *The English Patient* as an advance toward or a retreat from his personal search for identity, and why?

- Why is Patrick emotionally isolated? How do the events of *In the Skin of a Lion* motivate him to overcome isolation and connect with community and family?

- Why, at the end of *In the Skin of a Lion,* does Patrick go to Clara's rescue after not having had any contact with her for many years?

- What political themes found in his novels define Ondaatje as a postcolonial writer?

- Ondaatje's prose has been recognized as being particularly lyrical and emotive. Select several passages and discuss devices he uses to achieve his poetic effects. Is his figurative language successful in his novels, or should it be confined to poetry?

Michael Ondaatje

An H in the Heart, 1994 (of bp Nichol's work; with George Bowering)
The Conversations: Walter Murch and the Art of Editing Film, 2002

EDITED TEXTS:
Lost Classics, 2000
Lost Classics, 2001

MISCELLANEOUS:
Vintage Ondaatje, 2004

About the Author

Barbour, Douglas. *Michael Ondaatje.* New York: Twain, 1993.

Bolland, John. *Michael Ondaatje's "The English Patient."* New York: Continuum, 2002.

Jaggi, Maya. "Michael Ondaatje with Maya Jaggi." In *Writing Across Worlds: Contemporary Writers Talk,* edited by Sushelia Nasta. New York: Routledge, 2004.

Jewinski, Ed. *Michael Ondaatje: Express Yourself Beautifully.* Toronto: ECW Press, 1994.

Mundwiler, Leslie. *Michael Ondaatje: Word, Image, Imagination.* Vancouver: Talon, 1984.

Ondaatje, Michael. *Running in the Family.* New York: Norton, 1982.

Soleki, Sam. *Ragas of Longing: The Poetry of Michael Ondaatje.* Toronto: University of Toronto Press, 2003.

_____. *Spider Blues: Essays on Michael Ondaatje.* Montreal: Véhicule Press, 1985.

EUGENE O'NEILL

Born: New York, New York
October 16, 1888
Died: Boston, Massachusetts
November 27, 1953

Often considered the greatest American dramatist of the twentieth century, O'Neill transformed the American theater from artifice into art through ceaseless experimentation and uncompromising psychological realism.

© The Nobel Foundation

BIOGRAPHY

Eugene Gladstone O'Neill was born in the Barrett Hotel in New York City in 1888, son of James O'Neill, an actor celebrated for his portrayal of the count of Monte Cristo, and Ella Quinlan O'Neill, a sensitive woman who became a narcotics addict shortly after Eugene's birth. His older brother Jamie was Eugene's early idol; another brother, Edmund, had died in infancy, evoking a great guilt in his mother. As a child, Eugene toured much of the year with his parents and spent the summers in New London, Connecticut. At the age of seven, partly to protect him from knowledge of his mother's drug addiction, he was sent to a boarding school outside New York City. Lonely and frightened, he retreated to his imagination and into the world of books. The discovery of his mother's addiction, when he was almost fifteen, was traumatic; it resulted in his rejection of the Catholic faith and infused his life thereafter with grief for her suffering and guilt for his part in it.

After a year at Princeton University, O'Neill prospected for gold in Honduras, leaving behind a pregnant wife, Kathleen Jenkins, who named their son Eugene, Jr. Shortly after O'Neill's return, he shipped out to Buenos Aires on the *Charles Racine*, one of the last sailing ships. The two-month voyage was a high point in his life, and the sea figures prominently in many of his plays, from *Bound East for Cardiff* (1916) to *Long Day's Journey into Night* (1956). Back in New York, he drifted aimlessly, drinking and loafing in saloons such as Jimmy-the-Priest's, which became the setting for *Anna Christie* (1921) and *The Iceman Cometh* (1946). Eventually, after cooperatively providing Kathleen with grounds for a divorce, he fell into a deep depression, culminating in a suicide attempt.

When he recovered, his father found him a job as a reporter on the New London *Telegraph*, but after a few months O'Neill contracted tuberculosis and spent the first half of 1913 at Gaylord Farm Sanatorium in Wallingford, Connecticut. Perhaps it was this confrontation with mortality that encouraged him to focus his literary talents. He wrote several one-act plays and in the fall of 1914 enrolled in George Pierce Baker's famous playwriting course at Harvard University, a serious step for a young man now determined to be "an artist or nothing."

When financial concerns made a second year with Baker impossible, O'Neill became acquainted with a group of Greenwich Village artists and intellectuals who, in the summer of 1915, had founded the Provincetown Players. Recognizing O'Neill's talent, they were happy to produce his *Bound East for Cardiff* and a number of his plays thereafter, both in Provincetown and in New York.

O'Neill's first Broadway production, *Beyond the Horizon* (1920), was a starkly realistic drama set in rural New England, in which two brothers live out each other's dreams. The play earned for him a Pulitzer Prize and critical recognition as a serious dramatist. The 1920's were productive years for

O'Neill. He wrote constantly, saw productions on and off Broadway of eighteen of his plays, and was awarded two more Pulitzer Prizes: for *Anna Christie,* a somewhat romantic play about a prostitute who is reformed by the sea and the love of a good man, and for *Strange Interlude* (1928), an experimental effort using stream-of-consciousness techniques. During his second marriage, to Agnes Boulton, he had two children, Shane and Oona. The marriage was not a happy one, and as the decade ended, O'Neill divorced Agnes and took a third wife, Carlotta Monterey. Theirs was a stormy and passionate relationship, which endured until his death.

The 1930's began with successful productions of the monumental *Mourning Becomes Electra* (1931) and *Ah, Wilderness!* (1933), the only lighthearted comedy O'Neill ever wrote. *Days Without End* (1934), a somewhat autobiographical story of a struggle with faith, was harshly criticized, and twelve years passed before another O'Neill play was seen on Broadway. In 1935, O'Neill began working on a cycle of eleven plays that would follow the history of an American family from the Revolution to the twentieth century. Titled *A Tale of Possessors Self-Dispossessed,* the plays were to focus on American materialism and greed through the generations, played against a background of national events. Unfortunately, only *A Touch of the Poet* (produced posthumously in 1957) was completed.

When the Nobel Prize in Literature was awarded him in 1936, O'Neill was already in the grip of a degenerative nerve disease. As he was accustomed to writing his plays in a minuscule longhand, the tremors of the progressive disease made him increasingly unable to hold a pencil, and thus to pursue his profession. Forced to abandon the cycle, from 1939 to 1941 he struggled with the creation of several plays, among them his two masterpieces, *The Iceman Cometh* and *Long Day's Journey into Night* (produced and published posthumously in 1956 and awarded a fourth Pulitzer Prize). When the Broadway production of *The Iceman Cometh* was not particularly successful, O'Neill retired into seclusion; his final days were spent under the care of his wife in Boston's Hotel Shelton. Shortly before he died, he noted, "Born in a hotel room—and God damn it—died in a hotel room!" Death came on November 27, 1953.

In tribute, *The New York Times* critic Brooks Atkinson wrote, "A great spirit and our greatest dramatist have left us, and our theater world is now a smaller, more ordinary place."

ANALYSIS

Like William Shakespeare, O'Neill was a man of the theater: He was born into it, grew up in it, worked in it, and wrote for it. He knew his craft, and he hated the artificiality and pretense of the commercial theater. He said, "The theatre to me *is* life—the substance and interpretation of life. . . . [And] life is struggle, often, if not usually, unsuccessful struggle." O'Neill was an artist of integrity and courage; he was constantly exploring, expanding, experimenting. He tended toward realism in his work, rejecting material that could not be verified by the senses.

At times, however, he played with nonrealistic, expressionistic devices, externalizing the interior state of a character with sound or light or language: the throbbing tom-toms in *The Emperor Jones* (1920), to signify Jones's increasing hysteria; the masks in *The Great God Brown* (1926), to portray the multifaceted nature of the characters; the foghorn in *Long Day's Journey into Night,* to parallel Mary's increasing confusion. At other times, his characters seem to have sprung from a Darwinian naturalism, helpless in the grip of forces beyond their control.

O'Neill also experimented with content and structure. When Eugene, Jr., became a classical scholar, the playwright sought to share these interests and grew fascinated by the powerful material of Greek tragedy: incest, infanticide, matricide, and the accompanying burden of guilt and atonement. He shared the Greeks' view of the individual in conflict with the universe and with whatever God or gods inhabit it, and he was further concerned with the dearth of tragedy in the modern theater. *Desire Under the Elms* (1924), which includes infanticide, and *Mourning Becomes Electra,* which derives from Aeschylus's *Oresteia* (fifth century B.C.E.), were efforts to create modern tragedies exploring the agonies suffered by those who behave against law and conscience.

The structure varies from play to play. O'Neill could use a traditional brief one-act structure, as in the early sea plays, but both *The Hairy Ape* (1922) and *The Emperor Jones* are long one-acts with a number of scenes. *Desire Under the Elms* is a traditional-length three-act play, but *Strange Interlude* is a very long play in two parts with fourteen scenes and a break for dinner. *Mourning Becomes Electra* is perhaps the longest, essentially consisting of three full-length plays, with a total of thirteen acts. *The Iceman Cometh* and *Long Day's Journey into Night*, with four acts each, run between four and five hours in the theater. At times both audiences and critics complained, but O'Neill insisted that the length was appropriate and necessary for his ideas.

Even at his most experimental, there is an unerring psychological validity to his characters. The ideas of Freudian psychoanalysis were contemporary throughout O'Neill's career, and the power of the unconscious suited his characters well. They may openly express a longing for the sea or for a farm or for a place in the universe, but the conflict with the father or the longing for love from the mother rages not far below the surface. Working from his own unconscious, O'Neill created plays that were disguised attempts to work through his personal conflicts with his mother, father, and brother, and with his own quest for identity. Travis Bogard claims that "the sum of his work comprises an autobiography."

Although O'Neill's view of humanity was despairing and nearly tragic, there are no moral messages in his plays. He does not preach or promote causes. There are few villains in his works; instead there are characters of enormous energy, driven by huge passions—lust, greed, ambition, and love. A major thematic concern with O'Neill is obsessive love, love that drives a person without reason and beyond conscience, love that does not heal but smothers and destroys. Although Christine and Lavinia Mannon in *Mourning Becomes Electra* are prime examples of this obsession, characters in *Beyond the Horizon*, *The Great God Brown*, *Desire Under the Elms*, and *Strange Interlude* are also consumed by their passions.

O'Neill explored the notion that there are many facets of personality and that people rarely reveal themselves unmasked to others—or even to themselves. When they do, they discover that others are presenting only masks in return, a response that can be disappointing and even frightening. While Shakespeare could use asides and soliloquies, O'Neill sought other methods to reveal the psyche. In *The Great God Brown*, he uses actual masks, which actors don and remove; in *Strange Interlude*, he uses interior monologues. Somewhat controversial,

these theatrical devices underscore the theme of the evasive nature of humanity.

A corollary theme concerns the need for illusion. O'Neill states that human beings often behave from a network of illusions that they have created about themselves and about others. In *Anna Christie*, Chris Christopherson believes that he hates "dat ole davil, sea"; his daughter Anna insists that all men are worthless. These illusions are shattered by events in the play and replaced by a better reality.

In *The Iceman Cometh*, written twenty years later, O'Neill draws characters surviving upon their "pipe dreams": They believe that they will leave Harry Hope's saloon in the near future and lead productive lives. When they are forced to face their illusions, they seek death.

As might be expected, O'Neill is not universally admired. His principal detractors find his style crude, his language clumsy, and his plays in need of editing. Concerning style, one must remember that O'Neill was blazing a path separate from the contrivances of the romantic "well-made play." Aside from the early *The Hairy Ape*, there are few overheard or misinterpreted conversations and few traditional happy endings with all threads resolved. As for language, on the printed page the dialogue may look stilted and unbelievable, but in the mouths of talented stage professionals, it rings true. Finally, as with the works of Shakespeare, judicious editing may be desirable, but the powerful experience provided by the plays in performance is undeniable.

THE EMPEROR JONES

First produced: 1920 (first published, 1921)
Type of work: Play

A greedy, materialistic ruler is stripped of his pretensions and pursued to his death.

The Emperor Jones, which ran for 204 performances at the Provincetown Playhouse in Greenwich Village, represented the first major success by a black actor on the American stage; it also made O'Neill famous.

Almost medieval in structure, this long one-act

play in eight scenes details the fall from power of a corrupt ruler, former Pullman porter Brutus

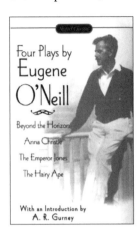

Four Plays by
Eugene
O'Neill

Beyond the Horizon
Anna Christie
The Emperor Jones
The Hairy Ape

With an Introduction by
A. R. Gurney

Jones, who has made himself emperor of a West Indian island and greedily exploited the natives. As the play opens, the populace has revolted, and Jones realizes he must flee. In his egocentricity, he believes that the legend he has created—that he can be killed only with a silver bullet—will protect him and that his planned escape route through the forest will take him to a waiting ship and safety with the riches intact that he has extorted from the people.

As Jones travels through the forest, he is stripped physically, mentally, and emotionally of the trappings of civilization and forced back through his racial memory to a tribal past, where, naked and hysterical before the Crocodile God, he uses his silver bullet to reject the possessive god as the natives approach to kill him, ironically, with their own silver bullets. The play permits several levels of interpretation. Socially, a proud, greedy, corrupt ruler is deposed by the downtrodden people. Psychologically, a person regresses through individual memory to his racial unconscious. Philosophically, a human being fights the inevitable losing battle with the forces of the universe. Theologically, one denies a possessive god and is sacrificed to it.

Equally significant are the expressionistic devices that O'Neill has incorporated. In the middle of the first scene a tom-tom "exactly corresponding to normal pulse beat—72—to the minute—[begins] and continues at a gradually accelerating rate from this point uninterruptedly to the very end of the play." Realistically, the drumbeats represent the natives communicating with one another as they pursue Jones. On the nonrealistic expressionistic level, they represent Jones's heartbeats as his anxiety increases and he regresses to a tribal past. When the drums stop, the audience knows that Jones is dead.

Another device is the gradual stripping of clothes, which is both physical and psychological: Jones begins in his emperor's robes and ends in

a tattered loincloth, as he regresses from a civilized to a savage state. Finally, daylight contrasts with moonlight (a device O'Neill also uses in *Long Day's Journey into Night* and *The Iceman Cometh*). Day represents harsh reality, where no illusions can survive; moonlight is illusion. The play begins at 3:30 in the afternoon, when the sun "still blazes yellowly."

The scenes pass through nightfall into darkness, at nine, eleven, one, three, and five o'clock, ending at dawn, and they parallel Jones's progress through the increasing darkness of his mind to his death in the bright light of day.

The play prefigures the basic theme of O'Neill's last plays, which is that one cannot live without illusions. Jones believes that he has manipulated and outwitted the natives' superstitions for his own ends. His great illusion is that he can deny his illusionary past, his humanity, and his need for a god force stronger than himself.

DESIRE UNDER THE ELMS

First produced: 1924 (first published, 1925)
Type of work: Play

The passionate desires of father, stepmother, and son result in a triangle of tragedy and retribution.

Banned in Boston and England, narrowly escaping a ban in New York, and its Los Angeles cast arrested for obscenity, *Desire Under the Elms*, with incest, adultery, and infanticide openly treated, brought O'Neill into conflict with various censors and brought much of the public to the box office. It ran for 208 performances on and off Broadway and may be the first important American tragedy.

The play demonstrates O'Neill's exploration of Greek theater. It does not derive directly from any particular play, but its material echoes *Hippolytus* and *Medea*, which contain incest and infanticide. The inhibited, puritanical society of New England in 1850 seemed to O'Neill appropriate for the epic Greek quality he sought. A further debt to the Greeks occurs in the sense of an inevitable fate awaiting the participants, Ephraim Cabot, his son Eben, and Ephraim's new wife, Abby Putnam.

The desire of Eben and Abby for each other is apparent from the moment she steps into the house, although it is masked by Eben's antagonism and her caution. He is loyal to the memory of his dead mother, whom he feels was robbed of her land and worked to death by Ephraim. The farm is his, he believes, and Abby is an intruder, seeking to steal his inheritance. She, in turn, has learned to fight for what she wants, and now she seeks security and a place of her own.

If Eben were not there, quite likely Abby would have made a good wife for Ephraim as long as he lived; however, the mutual physical attraction of Abby and Eben cannot be resisted. In a powerful scene in which Abby lures Eben into the parlor and declares her love, promising that she will take the dead mother's place, "with a horribly frank mixture of lust and mother love," the adultery is consummated.

One psychoanalytic critic noted that the play seems to have been written by someone in "intense mourning for his mother" (O'Neill had lost both his mother and brother in the previous two years). Certainly the yearning for the nurturing, protective mother permeates the work, not only in Eben's speeches about his love for his mother and in his incestuous love for the wife of his father, but also in Abby's speeches about her willingness to substitute for the mother. Further, both Abby and Eben strongly desire the land, which belonged to the mother, and which represents the same nurturing, protective qualities. This motif is further emphasized in O'Neill's specific directions for the visual effects of the setting, in which he calls for two elm trees on each side of the house with "a sinister maternity . . . like exhausted women resting their sagging breasts and hands and hair on its roof."

The Oedipal conflict of father and son for superiority, through possession of the woman, underlies the action of the play. Ephraim's superior maleness will be demonstrated unequivocally with the birth of a son by Abby. Eben's secret knowledge that Abby's son is his secures his male superiority as well as his claim to the farm. When Eben becomes jealous of Ephraim's possessiveness of the baby, Abby, literally accepting his cry that he wishes the baby had never been born, murders the child to prove her love. She readily acknowledges her crime, Eben accepts his responsibility, and both resign themselves to punishment. Ephraim must remain on the farm. "God's hard," he says, believing that a force beyond himself has guided events.

The structure of the play is one of O'Neill's tightest; its three acts are economical and swiftly moving. O'Neill's innovative set design of the original production made use of a house exterior and interior: When a scene occurred in one room, the exterior wall could be removed, and scenes set in different rooms could be viewed simultaneously. This allowed for an easy flow from one scene to another. The lighting also contributed, providing a contrast between the brightly lit exterior and the dim, shadowy interior.

O'Neill's use of language is masterful; the Yankee words and phrases such as "Ayeh," "purty," and "I love ye, Abby," and the biblical passages recited by Ephraim, arise naturally but effectively from the characters. The character of Eben is the key to the essence of the play. Of a sensitive nature, like the author himself, the weak, questing son is a figure O'Neill used many times. Here his love of the land, his awareness of its beauty, and his need for love infuse the play with poetry and elevate it above the level of simple realism into poignant tragedy.

THE GREAT GOD BROWN

First produced: 1926 (first published, 1926)
Type of work: Play

The rivalry of the artist in conflict with himself and a materialistic society results in his self-destruction.

"I love that play," O'Neill declared of *The Great God Brown*, which remained one of his favorites. Perhaps his fondness derived from the subjective, autobiographical nature of Dion Anthony, one of the characters, who expresses O'Neill's search for spiritual certainty, as well as his physical qualities and his bitterness. Perhaps O'Neill's liking sprang from the expressionistic device of the masks, which makes the play one of his strangest and most experimental. Although the critics did not share O'Neill's feeling, the public was fascinated by the play, which ran for more than 280 performances.

The plot, which is somewhat obscure, involves two young men, friendly rivals from childhood,

Dion Anthony and Billy Brown. Dion, an artist, should become a painter, but his father refuses to send him to college. Billy, the stereotypical ideal American boy, goes to college, becomes an architect, and joins his father's firm. It is Dion who wins the girl, Margaret, despite Billy's love for her.

Seven years pass. The marriage of Dion and Margaret is unsuccessful: "We communicate in code—when neither has the other's key!" says Dion, drinking and gambling his inheritance away. Billy, now successful, employs Dion at Margaret's request, and uses Dion's creativity to enhance his own designs. Their career rivalry extends to Dion's friend, the prostitute Cybel, whom Billy keeps as a mistress. The play's events are understandable, almost banal, until the end of act 2, when Dion suddenly accuses Billy of being unable to love and trying to steal Margaret and Cybel out of envy. Billy admits his love for Margaret; Dion replies, "with a terrible composure": "No! . . . [Billy] loves me! He loves me because I have always possessed the power he needed for love, because I am love!"

Dion then dies of his alcoholism, but his final wish is for Billy to assume the Dion Anthony identity through the device of the mask. Billy accedes, even playing husband to Margaret. The masquerade cannot be maintained, however, and he is shot as the supposed murderer of Dion.

The interest of the play lies not in the plot outline but in the way O'Neill has developed the characters and themes. The principal device is the use of the mask, a legacy from the Greek theater, which forcefully makes the statement that humans present images to one another, that they rarely expose the truth of themselves. Characters don and remove masks at significant moments: When Dion, in desperation, drops his mask before Margaret to beg for her love, she is so frightened she faints. Billy also drops his mask before Margaret to declare his love for her; she remains masked and rejects him. The expression of the masks changes as the characters alter, age, and experience emotion. The only relationship presented in which the participants are unmasked is that of Dion and Cybel. They are honest together. A masked drama is valuable, according to O'Neill, because it provides "a fresh insight into the inner forces motivating the actions and reactions of men and women."

The statement of the play, however, is not clear. As representative of American greed and material-

ism, Billy Brown is an unusually sympathetic character. He is a "good loser" with Margaret, and his success has fallen upon him without aggression on his part. Billy's assumption of Dion's identity in the third act, which apparently O'Neill intended to demonstrate the isolation and torment of the artistic psyche, leads to a confusing, almost farcical switching of masks. At one moment Billy, in his own mask, speaks to his employees as "Mr. Brown," then he runs offstage, returning almost immediately in Dion's mask to encounter Margaret.

Finally, the interest of the audience lies not with Billy, who hardly seems the "great god" of the title, but with Dion, O'Neill's artist surrogate, whose dark passion is sometimes narcissistic and self-pitying, sometimes poetic and touching. His torment results from his inability to be an artist and to win the approval of God. Instead, he must relinquish his creative ideas to another man and remain anonymous. Those familiar with O'Neill's history will recognize both the determined "I want to be an artist or nothing" that informs much of his work and the pain accompanying that desire. *The Great God Brown* is a flawed play, infrequently revived, but it merits study for its use of the masks and for its exploration of identity.

MOURNING BECOMES ELECTRA

First produced: 1931 (first published, 1931)
Type of work: Play

The Mannon family, seemingly cursed in its relationships of love and hate, commits adultery, murder, and incest through three generations.

O'Neill conceived of creating a modern psychological drama rooted in Greek legend in the spring of 1926, but *Mourning Becomes Electra* was not completed until the spring of 1931. Actually a trilogy of three full-length plays, it opened in October and was deemed a masterpiece by more than one critic. O'Neill said: "By the title *Mourning Becomes Electra* I sought to convey that mourning befits Electra; it becomes Electra to mourn; it is her fate; black is becoming to her and it is the color that becomes her destiny."

The Greek source for O'Neill was the *Oresteia* of Aeschylus, from the fifth century B.C.E., the trilogy detailing the relationships of the house of Atreus. In the first play, after the siege of Troy, Clytemnestra murders her husband, the victorious Agamemnon; in the second, their son Orestes, with his sister Electra, murders his mother and her lover Aegisthus; in the third, Orestes is hounded by the Furies for matricide but is eventually freed from his guilt and acquitted of the crime. O'Neill reworked much of this story; he also drew upon the versions of *Electra* by Sophocles and Euripides, which focus upon the daughter, a haunted woman, torn by hate and love and never at peace.

The Mannon family (the name may be associated with "mammon" and the family's materialism) is the center of O'Neill's play, which is set in New England immediately after the Civil War. The house is described in the stage directions as resembling a white Greek temple, with six columns across the front porch. In the first play, *The Homecoming*, Christine Mannon (Clytemnestra) has taken a lover, Adam Brant (Aegisthus), while her husband, Ezra (Agamemnon), has been fighting in the war. Daughter Lavinia (Electra) is jealously aware of the affair and threatens her mother with exposure. In this section, mother and daughter are rivals for the love of Ezra and Adam.

When Ezra returns, Lavinia desperately tries to win his love and attention from her mother, as Ezra makes an impassioned effort to communicate with Christine, begging her to love him. Thinking only of her lover, she rejects him, and when he has a heart attack, she administers poison rather than medicine. In his death throes, he reveals Christine's crime to Lavinia.

The triangular structure of the second play, *The Hunted*, includes Lavinia, Christine, and the newly returned battle-scarred Orin (Orestes). Each woman is seductive and persuasive with him, but Lavinia is victorious in convincing him that Christine killed Ezra and that he should avenge their father's murder by killing Adam Brant. He accomplishes the act, which drives Christine to commit suicide and leads to Orin's mental deterioration through his burden of guilt. In the final play, *The Haunted*, both Lavinia and Orin struggle to transcend their past crimes, first through incestuous love of each other, then through relationships outside the family. When this is impossible, Orin commits suicide, and Lavinia secludes herself in the Mannon mansion.

Although the plot represents another reworking of the O'Neill family drama, with the author infusing autobiography into both Lavinia and Orin, it is also faithful to the Greek legend. In addition, O'Neill borrowed other elements from the Greeks. He adopted the form of the trilogy, and he created the character of Seth to function as the leader of the chorus. The townspeople act as that chorus. Most important, O'Neill sought to find an equivalent to the Greek sense of fate, the inescapable destiny toward which the characters rush, which the Greeks achieved through their culture's belief in gods and goddesses and in their shared morality.

Such a climate was difficult to approximate in a modern culture that does not believe in such external forces. To solve the problem, O'Neill set the play in a Puritan-derived New England culture, similar to that of *Desire Under the Elms*, a culture which insisted upon personal responsibility and which offered no easy absolution or forgiveness. The sense of fate surrounds the past, present, and future of the family, as the past sins of the father (and mother) are redressed by the children with greater sins, for which they in turn must suffer in the future. "I'm the last Mannon," says Lavinia as she imprisons herself in the mansion. "I've got to punish myself." The tragic destiny of the Mannon family is oblivion.

The sense of fate is further reinforced by the use of the mask concept. O'Neill, still fascinated by the device, wrote one draft of the play with characters donning and removing masks, as in *The Great God Brown*; he soon rejected the device, although not its significance. Instead, he enlisted the actors' skills to create expressions on the faces of the Mannon family like "life-like masks." These emphasize the family similarity and the ties of blood that bind them together. In the final section, both Lavinia and Orin are altered in appearance and resemble their parents even more closely, a reminder that despite all resistance, heredity is destiny.

This view corresponds to that of the Darwinian naturalists, who describe humanity as the product of heredity and environment; thus, human beings are victims of forces beyond their control. Indeed, the play has links with the naturalistic theater. Where the naturalists claim that because of these forces people are not responsible for their actions, however, the Puritan mind claims that people should suffer guilt and be punished. Perhaps it is significant that in the Greek play Orestes is forgiven by the Eumenides and Electra is married to Pylades, a prince of Phocis, but in O'Neill's puritanical play there is no such mercy.

Once again, in *Mourning Becomes Electra* there is no moral message, only intense experience. The family is depicted in a tortured web of dependencies, jealousies, hatreds, and loves, which O'Neill describes without judgment. Reading the play later, he declared himself satisfied with its "strange quality of unreal reality." Finally, if *Mourning Becomes Electra* is not the artistic equivalent of the *Oresteia*, it is the closest example that twenty-five hundred years of theater have produced.

THE ICEMAN COMETH

First produced: 1946 (first published, 1946)
Type of work: Play

The salesman Hickey tries to shatter the "pipe dreams" of his friends in Harry Hope's saloon, but he succeeds only in proving that pipe dreams are necessary, even for himself.

With *The Iceman Cometh*, O'Neill discarded the literary sources and devices with which he had been experimenting for so long, as if they were pipe dreams of his own that protected him from the pain of reality, to concentrate upon realistic material and characters whom he had known firsthand. He set the action of the play in 1912, probably the most important year of his life, when he returned from South America, penniless and despondent, and landed at Jimmy-the-Priest's in New York.

In the play, Jimmy-the-Priest's becomes Harry Hope's saloon, where whiskey costs five cents a shot and where a month's room and board, including a cup of soup, is three dollars. Of the nineteen characters O'Neill shapes—bartenders, pimps, whores, ne'er-do-wells, retirees—most are based on the assorted derelicts and homeless people O'Neill encountered at that low period of his life. *The Iceman Cometh* is a naturalistic drama of "the lower depths," a genre displaying life at the extremities as more real, elemental, and meaningful than that of the pretentious, artificial middle class. Thus, the characters are the dregs of society, with few resources

and fewer opportunities. Their heredity and the environment have victimized them.

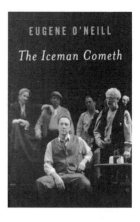

Almost classical in its adherence to the unities of time and place, the play is structured like a musical theme and variations. Each character seeks an escape through alcohol from the pain of living. Each maintains an existence through a "pipe dream" he or she has created, an illusion surrounding the self that allows a continuance of the lifestyle cultivated at Harry Hope's. This motif is announced early in Larry Slade's response to Rocky's joking remarks that Harry is going to demand payment from everyone—tomorrow. Larry says:

> I'll be glad to pay up—tomorrow. And I know my fellow inmates will promise the same. They've all a touching credulity concerning tomorrows. Their ships will come in, loaded to the gunwales with cancelled regrets and promises fulfilled and clean slates and new leases!

The theme is developed through repetition by each character of a particular dream—some comic, some serious, but all illusory.

Into this milieu of fantasy comes Hickey, the charismatic drummer (salesman), on his annual birthday visit. He is eagerly awaited by Harry's denizens, but this year he is somehow different; instead of settling down to his customary binge, he refuses alcohol, and he talks strangely about ridding himself of pipe dreams and helping Harry's regulars to rid themselves of theirs and find peace.

At first they think he is joking, that he is initiating a new game, but as he continues to goad, taunt, and ridicule, they become uneasy, irritated, and finally hostile. One by one he forces them to act upon their pipe dreams, to leave the comfort and security of their womblike existence, and to face their fantasies in the world beyond. These encounters with reality do not bring peace. As the fourth act begins, the characters have returned to their former places and seek oblivion in alcohol with even greater determination. The atmosphere is funereal, and O'Neill's principal statement, that human beings cannot survive without illusions, is underscored.

The only two characters who remain in the saloon are Larry Slade, who manages to withstand Hickey's campaign, and his young acquaintance Don Parritt, a newcomer from the West Coast, whose illusion is that he betrayed his anarchist mother to the police out of patriotism and love. Hickey recognizes that somehow he and Parritt are "members of the same lodge." Their similarities become evident as the play progresses.

The climax of the play is reached not only through action but also through revelation, as each act brings new information about Hickey: the first, that he wants to bring peace to his friends; the second, that his wife, Evelyn, is dead; the third, that she was murdered; and the fourth, that he is her murderer. Hickey's illusion parallels Parritt's, that he killed out of love—to bring his wife peace—but Parritt interrupts Hickey's confession to blurt out the truth about the betrayal of his mother. "It was because I hated her." Hickey, reliving his speech to the body of Evelyn, virtually echoes him: "Well, you know what you can do with your pipe dream now, you damned bitch!" Evelyn's pipe dream was a faith in Hickey's reform, a faith which resulted in his guilt and resentment. The reality of his hatred of Evelyn can be faced only for an instant; Hickey immediately insists that because he loved Evelyn, he must have been insane when he killed her. This is a new illusion, and it reinforces the illusions of the others: If Hickey is insane, all his urgings of their finding peace through discarding their pipe dreams must be false. They can comfortably return to their fantasy lives.

For Parritt, however, a return to fantasy is not possible; the guilt that his confession evoked cannot be denied, and he seeks punishment. Led away by officers Lieb and Moran, whose names bring associations with love and death, Hickey also seeks punishment. Parritt, with Larry's encouragement, commits suicide, and Larry is left without illusion, resigned to his humanity and his sympathy for both Hickey and Parritt, awaiting death.

A complex and disturbing play that runs about four and a half hours in performance, its greatness lies not in theatrical innovation but in psychological truth. Sharing the tedium and pain of this existence, the audience is also forced to face the neces-

sity for illusion in their own lives. Although the play was not successful in its original Broadway production in 1946, the Off-Broadway revival at the Circle-in-the-Square ten years later drew audiences for almost two years and sparked renewed interest in the O'Neill canon.

LONG DAY'S JOURNEY INTO NIGHT

First produced: 1956 (first published, 1956)
Type of work: Play

The Tyrone family struggles to cope with the mother's drug addiction, the father's miserliness, one son's tuberculosis, the other's profligacy, and, above all, the complexity of their feelings for one another.

By 1940, O'Neill had won three Pulitzer Prizes and the Nobel Prize in Literature, but the work for which he is remembered and praised and revered as America's foremost dramatist is *Long Day's Journey into Night*, his autobiographical work dealing with the torment of his own family. It earned for him a final Pulitzer Prize posthumously in 1956. In the dedication of the play to his wife Carlotta, O'Neill says:

> I mean it as a tribute to your love and tenderness which gave me the faith in love that enabled me to face my dead at last and write this play—write it with deep pity and understanding and forgiveness for all the four haunted Tyrones.

O'Neill was fascinated with the family unit and with the effects of heredity as well as relationships upon the generations. If one generation is poor, the second becomes miserly, and the third contemptuous, what remains for the fourth generation? O'Neill's outlined cycle of plays, which he was never to complete, explored the past and future of a single family through three hundred years and many generations. *Long Day's Journey into Night* also expresses the idea that bonds of blood are inextricable. Each of the characters is in conflict over the role of the independent self and the role of dependent family member. In their ambivalence, feelings of love and hate surface and clash. The family unit is confined, a self-contained universe, and beyond is only the void.

In this family drama the O'Neills become the Tyrones: father James, a famous actor known for his role as the count of Monte Cristo; mother Mary, a thinly disguised portrait of Ellen Quinlan O'Neill; and the two sons Jamie and Edmund, mirrors of Eugene's brother Jamie and the playwright himself. Set in New London, Connecticut, the time is 1912, the year of O'Neill's suicide attempt and his brush with tuberculosis.

Like *The Iceman Cometh*, the structure is classical; the events are compressed into one August day. The first act occurs in the morning, the second before and after lunch, the third at 6:30 P.M., and the fourth at midnight. There are five characters (including the maid Cathleen), a shared past, and individual guilt. The action unfolds through psychological revelation. The past is revealed through the dialogue, the guilt through the relationships of the four family members.

The catalytic agent is Mary's morphine addiction, which she believes occurred after Edmund's birth when James hired a "quack doctor" to treat her, a belief that arouses guilt in both Edmund and James and encourages resentment in Jamie. In the first act she is supposedly "well" again, and the facade of a happy family can be maintained. Edmund is ill, however, probably with tuberculosis (in that period usually fatal), and concern for him provides Mary an excuse to return to her habit.

The first to perceive that her latest cure is not successful is Jamie, who reveals his suspicions to Edmund. Soon all three men recognize that Mary's rambling complaints about their home, the servants, James's frugality, and Edmund's drinking are signs of her addiction. Each tries to persuade her not to succumb. Tyrone pleads brokenly, "Dear Mary! For the love of God, for my sake and the boys' sake and your own, won't you stop now?" She responds vaguely that they should not "try to understand what we cannot understand, or help things that cannot be helped—the things life has done to us we cannot excuse or explain."

After lunch, the men escape into town, leaving Mary alone. She begins to return to the past, or the past returns to her. With Cathleen imbibing Ty-

rone's liquor freely, Mary recalls her early days in the convent, her first meeting with James Tyrone, and her lost faith. When Edmund returns with confirmation of his tuberculosis, Mary refuses to listen and angrily cries, "I hate you when you become gloomy and morbid." Edmund bitterly retorts, "It's pretty hard to take at times, having a dope fiend for a mother!"

The last act unites the three men at midnight in drunken misery around the dining room table. First, James and Edmund alternate between bickering over the use of electricity and accusations of each other's culpability in Mary's addiction. Then each reveals a part of his real self: Tyrone's regrets about his wasted career and Edmund's love of the sea. Jamie arrives home, extremely drunk, to express in a moment of truth his hatred of Edmund. In the final moments, with the foghorn sounding in the background and the men in a drunken fog, Mary descends the stairs, in the deepest fog of all, trailing her wedding dress, and remembering how happy she had once been. Little hope remains.

The play is not totally autobiographical. O'Neill has exaggerated some aspects of his situations and omitted others. His father was not so miserly, nor his mother so emotionally dependent, nor he quite so blameless. Nevertheless, the skill with which complex relationships are developed and projected is masterful, and the truth of the family's conflicts is shattering.

SUMMARY

In both his personal relationships and his work, O'Neill embodies the flawed American character: alienated, isolated, guilty, and unable to separate from the family. Although he expresses concern with American greed, materialism, extravagance, and hypocrisy, he also probes deep into his own family romance. By revealing himself, he reveals theatergoers to themselves.

Sometimes called the father of American drama, O'Neill demonstrated to the world that the American theater could be serious, moving, artistic, and truthful. Many critics believe that the O'Neill canon towers above that of all other twentieth century dramatists.

Joyce E. Henry

BIBLIOGRAPHY

By the Author

DRAMA:

Bound East for Cardiff, wr. 1913-1914, pr. 1916, pb. 1919

Thirst, and Other One-Act Plays, pb. 1914

Chris Christophersen, wr. 1919, pb. 1982 (revised as *Anna Christie*)

Beyond the Horizon, pr., pb. 1920

The Emperor Jones, pr. 1920, pb. 1921

Anna Christie, pr. 1921, pb. 1923

The Hairy Ape, pr., pb. 1922

All God's Chillun Got Wings, pr., pb. 1924

Complete Works, pb. 1924 (2 volumes)

Desire Under the Elms, pr. 1924, pb. 1925

The Great God Brown, pr., pb. 1926

Lazarus Laughed, pb. 1927, pr. 1928

Strange Interlude, pr., pb. 1928

Mourning Becomes Electra, pr., pb. 1931 (includes *Homecoming, The Hunted*, and *The Haunted*)

Nine Plays, pb. 1932

Ah, Wilderness!, pr., pb. 1933

Days Without End, pr. 1933, pb. 1934

Plays, pb. 1955 (3 volumes)

The Iceman Cometh, pr., pb. 1946

A Moon for the Misbegotten, pr. 1947, pb. 1952

Long Day's Journey into Night, pr., pb. 1956

A Touch of the Poet, pr., pb. 1957

Later Plays, pb. 1967

The Calms of Capricorn, pb. 1981 (with Donald Gallup)

The Complete Plays, pb. 1988 (3 volumes)

Ten "Lost" Plays, pb. 1995

Early Plays, pb. 2001 (Jeffrey H. Richards, editor)

POETRY:

Poems, 1912-1944, 1979 (Donald Gallup, editor)

NONFICTION:

"The Theatre We Worked For": The Letters of Eugene O'Neill to Kenneth MacGowan, 1982 (Jackson R. Bryer and Ruth M. Alvarez, editors)

"Love and Admiration and Respect": The O'Neill-Commins Correspondence, 1986 (Dorothy Commins, editor)

"As Ever, Gene": The Letters of Eugene O'Neill to George Jean Nathan, 1987 (Nancy L. Roberts and Arthur W. Roberts, editors)

Selected Letters of Eugene O'Neill, 1988 (Travis Bogard and Bryer, editors)

A Wind Is Rising: The Correspondence of Agnes Boulton and Eugene O'Neill, 2000 (William Davies King, editor)

MISCELLANEOUS:

The Unknown O'Neill: Unpublished or Unfamiliar Writings of Eugene O'Neill, 1988 (Travis Bogard, editor)

DISCUSSION TOPICS

- In what respects do the family relationships in *Long Day's Journey into Night* and other Eugene O'Neill plays mirror those of his early life?

- What was the state of the American theater when O'Neill began writing?

- How did the Provincetown Players contribute to O'Neill's success?

- Does O'Neill's *Mourning Becomes Electra* differ thematically from Aeschylus's *Oresteia* (458 B.C.E.)?

- What is the significance of the masks in *The Great God Brown*?

- How does the setting of *The Iceman Cometh* facilitate the realization of the play's theme?

- Plays depend for their success on audiences. Would O'Neill's long plays have been more effective if he had shortened them substantially?

About the Author

Alexander, Doris. *Eugene O'Neill's Last Plays: Separating Art from Autobiography*. Athens: University of Georgia Press, 2005.

Bloom, Harold, ed. *Eugene O'Neill*. New York: Chelsea House, 1987.

Brietzke, Zander. *The Aesthetics of Failure: Dynamic Structure in the Plays of Eugene O'Neill*. Jefferson, N.C.: McFarland, 2001.

Manheim, Michael, ed. *The Cambridge Companion to Eugene O'Neill*. New York: Cambridge University Press, 1998.

Moorton, Richard F., Jr., ed. *Eugene O'Neill's Century*. New York: Greenwood Press, 1991.

Ranald, Margaret Loftus. *The Eugene O'Neill Companion*. Westport, Conn.: Greenwood Press, 1984.

Robinson, James A. *Eugene O'Neill and Oriental Thought: A Divided Vision*. Carbondale: Southern Illinois University Press, 1982.

Sheaffer, Louis. *O'Neill*. 2 vols. Boston: Little, Brown, 1968-1973.

_____. *O'Neill, Son and Playwright*. 2 vols. New York: Cooper Square Press, 2002-2003.

Törnqvist, Egil. *Eugene O'Neill: A Playwright's Theatre*. Jefferson, N.C.: McFarland, 2004.

Wainscott, Ronald H. *Staging O'Neill: The Experimental Years, 1920-1934*. New Haven, Conn.: Yale University Press, 1988.

GEORGE OPPEN

Born: New Rochelle, New York
April 24, 1908
Died: Sunnyvale, California
July 7, 1984

Oppen was one of the central figures in defining and developing the poetry movement known as Objectivism.

Ann Resor Laughlin/Courtesy,
New Directions Publishing

BIOGRAPHY

George Oppen was born in New Rochelle, New York, on April 24, 1908, the son of George August Oppenheimer (who changed the family name in 1927) and Elsie Rothfeld. When Oppen was four and his older sister Elizabeth was seven, their mother had a nervous breakdown and committed suicide, an unsettling event compounded by his father's marriage in March, 1917, to Seville Shainwald, a woman from a very wealthy family whose relationship with Oppen was difficult and abusive. Oppen developed a warm, supportive relationship with his half sister June Frances, who was born in 1918, the year the family moved to San Francisco.

In accordance with his family's social expectations, Oppen attended a military academy, but he was expelled six weeks before graduation for his drunken involvement in a fatal automobile crash. After traveling in the British Isles, he completed his secondary education at a small preparatory school and followed a friend to Corvallis to enroll at Oregon State College (later Oregon State University). There he met Mary Colby, an independent, literate young woman, and fell deeply in love. When the two were punished for violating a curfew, they both left school in 1926, pledging to form a pact to live together as artists. Oppen and Colby hitchhiked across the West in 1927, marrying in Dallas, Texas. The couple drove to the Great Lakes in 1928, sailed

down the Erie Canal to New York City, and settled there when Oppen took a position as a switchboard operator in a brokerage house. Oppen had been writing poetry during their travels, and in New York he met Louis Zukovsky, a young poet and teacher, and Charles Reznikoff, a lawyer and friend of Zukovsky.

When Oppen turned twenty-one, he received a substantial legacy. He and Mary moved to France in 1929, and he began the composition of *Discrete Series* (1934), his first collection of poems. In 1931, he and Zukovsky, who functioned as editor, began the press To Publishers, which issued important modernist texts by William Carlos Williams, Ezra Pound, and Zukovsky. The Oppens returned to the United States in 1933, and Oppen was instrumental in establishing the cooperative The Objectivist Press. The Oppens joined the Communist Party in 1935 to work for social change. In response to the controlled, propagandistic manipulation of artists by the party, and in response to the realization that he had no real experience from which to write, Oppen began an almost quarter-century of poetic silence. Oppen describes this period as "a poetic exploration at the same time it was an act of conscience."

Oppen maintained an active membership in Communist Party activities from 1936 to 1941. In 1942, after the birth of his daughter Linda Jean, he gave up a military exemption to provoke his induction into the armed services. He was driven by anger at the Adolf Hitler-Joseph Stalin pact, which nearly forced him out of the party, and perhaps by guilt that he had not volunteered to fight against fascism in the Spanish Civil War. Oppen saw active duty in Europe in 1944 and 1945 in an antitank company, fighting in the Battle of the Bulge and later suffering a severe wound. He won numerous decorations, including the Purple Heart and two Bronze Stars.

After the war, the Oppens settled in California, where George worked as a carpenter. Following four years of federal harassment during the Joseph McCarthy era, the Oppens moved into exile in Mexico in 1950; there, Oppen worked briefly for General Electric and did no writing. In 1958, Oppen was granted a U.S. passport, signaling the end of McCarthy's persecution. Following a session with a therapist, Oppen had a revelatory dream that, in a sense, unblocked his artistic inclinations. In May, 1958, he wrote the poem "Blood from the Stone" to initiate his new writing life. For the following two decades, Oppen worked diligently at both poetry and an extensive literary correspondence.

The Oppens returned to the United States in 1960; that same year, Oppen's sister Elizabeth committed suicide. In 1961, he worked closely with Reznikoff on a volume of selected poems, and in 1962 he published *The Materials*, his first book of poetry in thirty years. That volume was followed by *This in Which* (1965) and *Of Being Numerous* (1968), which won him a Pulitzer Prize in 1969. His *Collected Poems* was published in England in 1972, and an American edition followed in 1975.

In 1977, Oppen completed his final book, *Primitive* (1978), but he required his wife's assistance, as his health had begun to decline. He accumulated further honors in the early 1980's (including the PEN/West Rediscovery Award in 1982), but when he was diagnosed with Alzheimer's disease, he entered a nursing home in January, 1984. He died in July of that year.

ANALYSIS

Oppen's decision to stop writing poetry—literally in midpoem, as he wrote in a letter in 1972—stemmed from his belief that he was not prepared, either experimentally or technically, to satisfy his vision of what a poem could be. As the critic Rachel Blau De Plessis has pointed out, however, this act was not a negation of his career as a poet but a self-chosen silence that helped Oppen to prepare himself for the moment when he would feel ready to begin again. He was able to recommence his craft

with such verve in 1958 because of changing factors in his life, but he was still essentially dependent on the solid conception of a poem that he had developed during the relatively brief but intense time from 1928 to 1934, when he was in close association with Zukovsky, Williams, Reznikoff, and Pound.

The term "Objectivist" has been applied to this group—with Pound regarded as an allied member and mentor and Carl Rakosi and Lorine Niedecker as a part of the loose affiliation—but the association was never a conscious movement or a part of a strategy for gaining attention. What these poets shared was a group of assumptions—with individual variations. What drew them together was a mutual interest in a poetics that was at a distinct remove from many of the conventional or traditional ideas about what constituted a poem. The Objectivists were working in a near void as far as a general audience was concerned, and they needed one another's responses as well as a strong sense of their craft to work at all. Even the most prominent figures, Pound and Williams, were almost invisible for the early decades of the twentieth century. Oppen and the others wrote sporadically, with great gaps between volumes, and relied on their personal visions to sustain them.

As Oppen saw it, the term "Objectivist" had nothing to do with an objective viewpoint but expressed the idea that the poem itself was an important object—an entity recording not merely reality but a distinct and separate aspect of reality. For Oppen, the act of writing was not primarily a means of ordering the world (as critic Paul Auster has put it) but a discovery of it. As Oppen remarked, one has to "write one's perceptions, not argue one's beliefs," and the process of composition was one way to engage the perceptual apparatus.

This led Oppen to the revolutionary position that familiar poetic forms were not the only ways to arrange a poem. Oppen contended that the poet "learns from the poem, his poem: the poem's structure, image, language." This is one of the first statements of the distinction between "closed" (or traditional) and "open" (or original) form, and Oppen argued that "the danger is that as the poem forms, the doors close." In other words, as Robert Creeley, one of Oppen's most accomplished poetic successors, has phrased it, "there is an appropriate way of saying something inherent in the thing to be said."

Oppen also observed, "the poet does not write what he already knows."

The effect of these striking and radically new assertions was to make Oppen's poetry, even his work from the early 1930's, so unusual that it has not dated at all; in fact, the tremendous changes in poetry initiated by Oppen and his colleagues have made his work more accessible in the decades since. On the other hand, this treatment of poetry as a record of the poet's mind in action tends to make poetry narrowly specific, so that Oppen's style still may not be immediately accessible for a reader who has not moved beyond more conventional approaches to poetry.

Although there are interesting rhythmic patterns in Oppen's work, he has essentially eschewed the most magnetic kind of song that often makes poetry initially compelling. His use of elliptic, often austere word groupings and suggestions of images tends to produce a compression that is resistant to immediate emotional responses. As Oppen pointed out, "the weakest work . . . occurs where the poet attempts to drive his mind in pursuit of emotion for its own sake . . . I would hold that the mere autonomy of the mind or the emotions is mendacity." Oppen is not suggesting that emotion or feeling is inappropriate but rather that an easy evocation of an emotional response will prevent the more significant and hard-won kind of deep feeling he hopes to achieve. Therefore, the position of the poet with respect to the world is a function, in Oppen's work, of the totality of the poem rather than of any particularly dynamic line or image, and the effect of the poem depends on the entire piece, or in some cases on a grouping of poems that are linked, if not directly interconnected.

Hugh Kenner has called Oppen a "geometer of minima" and has rightly pointed out how effectively Oppen has used Williams's oft-quoted dictum "no ideas but in things." While this makes Oppen's poetry almost "unanthologizable" (as critic John Taggart has remarked), the difficulties of his style may eventually yield to an understanding of and appreciation for an original conception of how a poem works to connect a person and the world.

"O WESTERN WIND"

First published: 1962 (collected in *The Materials*, 1962)
Type of work: Poem

The poet regards the woman he loves, and his reflections on her beauty are deepened by his sense of her vital place in his life.

Oppen's determination to avoid what he considered a sort of easy emotionalism or cheap sentimentality restricted his production of poems that reached for a mood of intense feeling. Yet the absence of conventional protestations of desire and the austerity that is a signature of his style made his lyric moments glow with a special quality that he called "emotional clarity." He hoped to capture the moment "when the world stops, but lights up," as he put it.

The importance of love for his wife, Mary, is evident in his frequent comments in his letters. When she was the energizing figure for a poem, he wrote, "You will see that I have not exaggerated Mary's beauty, total beauty, confidence, strength of beauty." These attributes presented a challenge for Oppen, who did not want to resort to familiar styles of praise but who was aware of the power of the literature of romance. "O Western Wind" is an attempt to evoke the impact of the myriad moments when he looked at his wife and felt, afresh but with the memory of similar instances, the mystery and pleasures of her being.

The poem begins with an image that is construed in metaphysical terms. "A world around her like a shadow" is Oppen's first statement, suggesting both the tangible and the evanescent. The woman is presented in motion ("She moves a chair"), and her action implies a purposeful or useful endeavor ("Something is being made—/ Prepared/ Clear in front of her as open air"). There is no punctuation at the end of the first stanza, carrying the poem toward Oppen's familiar shift to a reflective mode. "The space a woman makes and fills," he says, reemphasizing the tangible and the theoretical. He then assumes an unusually direct position, his typically distant, sharply observant poetic consciousness transformed by the very personal phrase "I write again." The poet is fully involved, "Naturally," because he is concentrating on what is most familiar, his wife's face.

The third stanza is a direct continuance of the previous one. "Beautiful and wide/ Blue eyes/ Across all my vision," Oppen observes. He once explained that "the noun 'eyes' directly above 'across all my vision' gives immediacy to the poem—gives reality to the poem." In this stanza, the lyric impulse charges the poem with an indelible impression of a profound love that remains undiminished by custom and routine, alive still in the power of the poet's vision.

"THE BUILDING OF THE SKYSCRAPER"

First published: 1965 (collected in *This in Which*, 1965)
Type of work: Poem

The creative artist is compared to a steelworker on a girder, and the process of creation is considered in terms of a person's life.

Oppen's fascination with the meaning latent in an individual word, and his interest in the manner in which meaning is established and explored through the arrangement or construction of the words in a poem, led him in many works to compare the artist to an artisan or builder. In "The Building of the Skyscraper," Oppen begins with a rather specific image, a steelworker who has "learned not to look down," suggesting a kind of focus or concentration on the task at hand. Then, in a characteristic shift in vision, Oppen moves directly to his philosophic position, extending the poem beyond the steelworker by saying, "And there are words we have learned/ Not to look at,/ Not to look for substance/ Below them." He thus opens the poem to include a broader human reliance on the materials available for building an artifice of understanding—materials that might not bear the weight of too much close scrutiny.

In a letter, Oppen explained that, for him, the word "building" carried connotations of creation and "the building of one's life." He explained further that he felt the word "skyscraper" had a kind of "homeliness" that grounded the poem in the fun-

damental flow of life. This grounding permits a turn toward the reflective that brings the poet to "the verge/ Of vertigo." The balance between the skills required to continue a person's daily tasks and the curiosity that draws a person to inquire into areas that reveal no real or final answer carries the poem onward into the second stanza, in which the question of words is directly addressed.

After asserting that "there are words that mean nothing," Oppen states one of his basic tenets: "But there is something to mean." It is "the business of the poet" to struggle amid the "things of the world" and "to speak them and himself out." This is Oppen's central goal as a poet. He explained that "to speak them out" conveys both a sense of exhausting the possibilities of meaning in a situation and the ambition of the poet to speak "*out*-wards," or toward a greater meaning or larger audience.

The final stanza introduces the natural world in a heartfelt paean: "O, the tree, growing from the sidewalk," Oppen declares, contrasting its "green buds" with the human-made, perplexing uncertainty of "the culture of the streets." He concludes by reintroducing the vertigo of the initial stanza in a final image of a nation stretching back three hundred years toward an origin that is so open to construction—its "bare land" like a blank page—that the importance of finding amid the vastness "a thing/ Which is" offers ample compensation for the vertigo, the suffering, that the poet/builder must experience.

"OF BEING NUMEROUS 14"

First published: 1968 (collected in *Of Being Numerous*, 1968)
Type of work: Poem

The poet recollects his experiences in World War II and tries to reconcile his wartime feelings with his present ones.

Oppen thought of his fourth collection of poems, *Of Being Numerous*, as poetry written from the perspective of "the language of New York"—an expression of the forces and energies available in a huge city. He described the poems as "intellectual and philosophic," in contrast to those of his collection that followed, *Seascape: Needle's Eye* (1972), which concentrated on the terrain around San Francisco and which he thought of as "atmospheric." Consequently, the poems in *Of Being Numerous* tend to be introspective, probing the poet's

responses to various phenomena. The poem that begins, "I cannot even now/ Altogether disengage myself," characteristically is set in the poet's mind, the opening "I" and the reinforcing "myself" locating the poem in the realm of immediate consciousness.

Oppen's meditations here have been triggered by recurring thoughts of his experiences on the battlefields of World War II. Yet the nature of combat, however, is less his subject matter than are his comrades, people he knew only briefly but with the emotional fusion possible under very intense experiences. The most vivid image of the poem follows Oppen's declaration of his condition of mind, as he recalls men in "emplacements, in mess tents,/ In hospitals and sheds" who "hid in the gullies/ Of blasted roads in a ruined country."

In the second section of the poem, Oppen considers the philosophic consequences of the action he has recalled. Placing his thoughts in an interrogatory mode to show how he has been permanently shaped by his participation and by his continuing reflection on it, Oppen asks, "How forget that?" and moves into the present. His eye on the streets of the city has led him to group the anonymous crowds into something distant he calls "The People." His curiosity about individuals prohibits him from distancing himself from humanity, even when he is confronted with a mass of cars moving down "walled avenues." The crucial issue is that it is the individual whose actions "echo like history," but the nature of anonymous singularity—only rarely broken by some intense circumstance—places the poet in a position, as the last line states, "in which one cannot speak." The lack of resolution, the open-ended quality of the conclusion, carries the poem onward into time, its queries unresolved but ever-present.

SUMMARY

In his time, Oppen was largely ignored except by those poets who knew and valued his distinct and original approach. While he still remains largely unknown, his work has not become dated and will reward the serious student of literature who is prepared to look beyond the familiar.

Leon Lewis

BIBLIOGRAPHY

By the Author

POETRY:
Discrete Series, 1934
The Materials, 1962
This in Which, 1965
Of Being Numerous, 1968
Alpine, 1969
Seascape: Needle's Eye, 1972
The Collected Poems of George Oppen, 1972, 1975
Primitive, 1978
New Collected Poems, 2002 (Michael Davidson, editor)

NONFICTION:
"The Mind's Own Place," 1963
"A Letter," 1973
The Selected Letters of George Oppen, 1990

About the Author

Duplessis, Rachel Blau, ed. *The Selected Letters of George Oppen.* Durham, N.C.: Duke University Press, 1990.

Hatlen, Burton, ed. *George Oppen, Man and Poet.* Orono, Maine: National Poetry Foundation, 1981.

Ironwood 5 (1975).

Ironwood 13 (Fall, 1985).

Nicholls, Peter. "Of Being Ethical: Reflections on George Oppen." *Journal of American Studies* 31 (August, 1997): 153-170.

Oppen, Mary. *Meaning a Life: An Autobiography.* Santa Barbara, Calif.: Black Sparrow Press, 1978.

Paideuma 10 (Spring, 1981).

Thackrey, Susan. *George Oppen: A Radical Practice.* San Francisco: O Books and the Poetry Center & American Poetry Archives, 2001.

DISCUSSION TOPICS

- What is objectivism, and what is George Oppen's particular slant on it?

- Does Oppen's long "preparation," comprising the years when many poets are at their peak, make sense?

- What is Oppen's conception of the relationship between emotion and poetry?

- Building as a metaphor is fairly common in poetry. What makes the skyscraper a particularly useful one in Oppen's "The Building of the Skyscraper"?

- What is most original in Oppen's poetry?

JUDITH ORTIZ COFER

Born: Hormingueros, Puerto Rico
February 24, 1952

Judith Ortiz Cofer, in her poetry and prose, captures the essence of what it is to be a sensitive child growing up partly in Puerto Rico, partly in New Jersey.

John Cofer

BIOGRAPHY

When she was three or four, Judith Ortiz Cofer, born in Hormigueros, Puerto Rico, in 1952, began the routine that was to define her existence for a number of years. Because her father, J. M. Ortiz Lugo, was a career Navy man stationed on a ship from the Brooklyn Naval Yard in New York, Judith and her brother came with their mother, Fanny Morot Ortiz, to Paterson, New Jersey, where the family lived in "El Building," a vertical barrio. When the father went on long cruises, the family returned to Hormigueros in the southwestern corner of Puerto Rico and stayed with Judith's grandmother.

When she was nineteen, Judith Ortiz married Charles John Cofer, a businessman. The couple has a daughter, Tanya. Following her marriage, Ortiz Cofer continued her education at Augusta College, from which she received a B.A. in 1974. Three years later, she earned an M.A. from Florida Atlantic University. Ortiz Cofer attended Oxford University for part of 1977 on a scholarship from the English Speaking Union.

Fluent in English and Spanish, Ortiz Cofer worked as a bilingual teacher in the public schools of Palm Beach County, Florida, during the 1974-1975 school year. In 1978, master's degree in hand, she was named an adjunct instructor in English at Broward Community College in Fort Lauderdale,

Florida. The following year, she was appointed an instructor in Spanish at the same institution. During this period, 1978-1980, she was also an adjunct instructor in English at Palm Beach Community College.

In 1980, having published her first collection of poems, *Latin Women Pray* (1980), as a chapbook, Ortiz Cofer became a lecturer in English at the University of Miami at Coral Gables, staying there until 1984, when she joined the Department of English at the University of Georgia as an instructor. Her three-act play, *Latin Women Pray*, was performed at Georgia State University in 1984. Her poetry began to appear in anthologies. Having served as a regular staff member of the International Conference on the Fantastic in Literature from 1979 until 1982, Ortiz Cofer became a member of the Florida Fine Arts Council in 1982. During the summers of 1983 and 1984, she joined the administrative staff of the Bread Loaf Writers Conference in Ripton, Vermont, which she attended as a student in 1981 and as a John Atherton Scholar in Poetry in 1982.

The Bread Loaf experience did much to help Ortiz Cofer fix her sights on publishing her poetry. *Peregrina* (1986) and *Terms of Survival* (1987) owe a substantial debt to the extensive critiquing sessions that characterize Bread Loaf, as does Ortiz Cofer's fifty-seven-page contribution to *Triple Crown: Chicano, Puerto Rican, and Cuban American Poetry* (1987), for which she provided the section titled "Reaching for the Mainland." This essay was an initial step toward her expanded work on writing, *Woman in Front of the Sun: On Becoming a Writer* (2000).

These early collections and the Bread Loaf experience brought Ortiz Cofer a Witter Brynner Foundation Award for Poetry in 1988. There followed in 1989 a fellowship in poetry from the National Endowment for the Arts. She used these grants to complete her novel, *The Line of the Sun* (1989), and a collection of essays and stories, *Silent Dancing* (1990). In 1995, *An Island Like You* became the first work of fiction to be published by the University of Georgia Press.

Ortiz Cofer spent the 1987-1988 academic year as an instructor in the Georgia Center for Continuing Education, moving the following year to Macon College as an instructor in English. In 1990, she was the coordinator of special programs at Mercer University. Subsequently, she returned to the University of Georgia to teach writing. In 1992, she gained tenure there as an associate professor of English and Creative Writing.

Most of Ortiz Cofer's work relates to her early experience, focusing both on her home area of Puerto Rico and on Paterson, New Jersey. The life of Marisol, the narrator in *The Line of the Sun*, parallels Ortiz Cofer's life. The book examines the conflict a young girl feels when her father urges her to forsake her heritage and integrate into mainland culture, while her mother presses her to hold onto her true heritage.

Marisol is aided by her black-sheep uncle, Guzman, whose story Marisol tells. Guzman comes to stay with the family in Paterson, and with his help, Marisol attempts an accommodation that will satisfy both parents. Worlds apart in thinking and social outlook from both of Marisol's parents, Guzman makes the impressionable Marisol aware of possibilities she had never considered.

ANALYSIS

Judith Ortiz Cofer's writing is precisely right for its time. Latino American consciousness in the United States, already raised by such writers as Jesús Colón, Nicholasa Mohr, Rolando Hinojosa, Pedro Pietri, Piri Thomas, Tomás Rivera, and others, has been elevated to a new plane in Ortiz Cofer's work.

Her own life provided Ortiz Cofer with the built-in conflict between two cultures that her writing successfully depicts. She has managed to place the two major elements of this conflict into the kind of symmetrical juxtaposition that permits her work to bristle with dramatic tension.

Her novel *The Line of the Sun* is equally divided between the stories of her family in southwestern Puerto Rico and in Paterson, New Jersey; the first half of the book is set in Puerto Rico, the second half on the U.S. mainland. In *Silent Dancing*, Ortiz Cofer achieves an even greater contrast by intermixing stories of her island home with stories of her mainland home. Each story in this book has elements of both worlds in it.

The contrasts Ortiz Cofer builds are sharp and apparent. Puerto Rico is warm, both thermally and in terms of its people, whereas Paterson, New Jersey, is cold in the same terms. The autobiographical character in *Silent Dancing* is ever aware of Paterson's grayness, of its long, drab winters; the father is aware of Paterson's coldness to foreigners. To shield his family from this coldness and to avoid open hostility, he demands that his family members keep to themselves, realizing the near hysteria that the influx of Puerto Ricans into a formerly middle-class Jewish neighborhood has generated among the Anglos who remain.

The father, able to pass for an Anglo, contrasts strikingly to his wife and children, who are clearly Latino and cannot pass. The father has been assimilated; the mother never will be. Each has different aspirations for the children. The father hopes they will gracefully, inconspicuously become typical Americans; the mother that they will preserve and reflect their Puerto Rican heritage.

The basic tensions in Ortiz Cofer's work are heightened both by the obvious contrasts between two cultures and by the contrasts between the perceptions of children and adults. Ortiz Cofer handles these perceptions with disciplined consistency, revealing what she needs to reveal, never allowing a child to have adult perceptions or an adult to have those of a child. She draws her lines clearly as she shapes her characters; she resolutely keeps them from intruding upon one another's turf.

Ortiz Cofer acknowledges her great admiration of Virginia Woolf, who dealt with problems of personal isolation and alienation similar to those found in much of Ortiz Cofer's work. Ortiz Cofer, fortunately, had Puerto Rico to fall back on when her isolation and alienation threatened her equanimity; Woolf was less fortunate.

Ortiz Cofer possesses the same sort of eye for physical detail that characterizes Woolf's writing.

She presents her stories with an unencumbered sharpness of focus reminiscent of Woolf's best descriptive passages, yet with the sort of delicacy and decorum that Woolf attained in her most successful novels.

Ortiz Cofer's poetry deals with the same dualities found in her short stories and in her play *Latin Women Pray*. The conflict that most engages her attention cannot be viewed only as Puerto Rican culture versus mainstream American culture. In a sense, this surface conflict provides the pretext Ortiz Cofer requires to frame her deeply felt, sweeping questions about humankind.

Much of Ortiz Cofer's poetry is written in irregular lines of varied metrical schemes and lengths. Despite, or perhaps because of, this irregularity, Ortiz Cofer's verse achieves a relaxed rhythm that suggests easy, free-flowing conversation.

Her poetic lines are wholly appropriate to the atmosphere she seeks to build. Ortiz Cofer's ear for language is as good as her eye for detail, and the two combine happily in most of her poetry. Typical of the easy meter she achieves is a bitter yet matter-of-fact poem, "The Woman Who Was Left at the Altar." The spurned, now fleshy woman makes her unused wedding gown into curtains for her room and makes doilies from her wedding veil. She roves the streets, chickens dangling from her waist; in her mind, their yellow eyes mirror the face of the man who shunned her. She takes satisfaction in killing the chickens she sells, because in that act, she is killing him, annihilating troubled memories that haunt her.

This narrative poem, gaining much power from what is left unsaid, achieves its major metrical impact by moving at its exact center from two anapestic feet to trochaic and iambic feet, all in one line; the next line is iambic dimeter:

> Since her old mother died, buried in black,
> she lives alone.

Ortiz Cofer continues in the next lines with two dactylic feet, followed in the same line by two trochaic feet, and continuing to two lines equally varied metrically:

> Out of the lace she made curtains for her room,
> doilies out of the veil. They are now
> yellow as malaria.

These metrical irregularities are a fundamental part of Ortiz Cofer's narrative poetic style. Her poems never seem strained or unnatural, despite their somewhat bewildering metrical scheme.

In her prose writing, as in her poetry, moreover, Ortiz Cofer is ever aware that words, whether written or spoken, have sound. She has an inherent sense of the cadences of human speech, capturing those cadences with extraordinary verisimilitude.

THE LINE OF THE SUN

First published: 1989
Type of work: Novel

Marisol Vivente struggles between loyalty to her native Puerto Rico and loyalty to the United States.

Marisol San Luz Vivente, the protagonist in *The Line of the Sun*, Ortiz Cofer's first novel, is an autobiographical character. Like Ortiz Cofer, Marisol was born in southwestern Puerto Rico but, from an early age, spent much of her life in Paterson, New Jersey. The novel encompasses three decades, beginning in the late 1930's and ending in the 1960's, and traces the impact these decades have on three generations of a family.

Marisol's father, Rafael, works near New York City and lives with his wife and children. Marisol, through stories she hears from her mother, has enough direct and immediate contact with her heritage that she feels strongly impelled to cling to it—as her mother, who wants her to retain the values and culture of her forbears, thinks she should.

Her Puerto Rican father, having struggled successfully to become assimilated, wants Marisol and her brother to adopt the manners and customs of the United States so that they can blend in inconspicuously, thereby improving their economic opportunities. Marisol, at a highly impressionable age, has to deal with an inner conflict between her two cultures and, in doing so, has to consider the impact that the resolution of her dilemma will have on her relationship with her parents and on her future.

Into this situation, Ortiz Cofer, writing vividly and poetically about the family, introduces Uncle

Guzman, a relative about whom the parents have talked quite darkly. During the Korean War, Guzman's brother, Carmelo, was killed in combat. At about the same time, Guzman, fifteen and the wilder of the two brothers, was involved in a scandal in his native Salud, where he lived with a prostitute known as La Cabra. He fled his island for New York, going there as a migrant farmworker. Years later, he appears on the Viventes' doorstep in Paterson one Christmas Eve and stays with his relatives for several months. During part of this time, he is confined to bed after he is attacked by a neighborhood thug.

The introduction of Guzman, her father's best friend during adolescence, is necessary to the resolution of Marisol's conflict. She had known this uncle largely through reputation; the family talked about him in hushed tones. Guzman, quite unwittingly, enables Marisol to see in sharp focus the two major forces in her life and to balance them. He also finds peace by returning to Puerto Rico, where he marries La Cabra's daughter, Sarita, a saintly woman who takes satisfaction in redeeming Guzman.

Marisol's conclusion is that although she always carries her island heritage on her back like a snail, she belongs in the world of telephones, offices, concrete buildings, and the English language. This is essentially the decision Ortiz Cofer reached for herself during her own adolescence.

SILENT DANCING: A PARTIAL REMEMBRANCE OF A PUERTO RICAN CHILDHOOD

First published: 1990
Type of work: Autobiography

This personal narrative of growing up includes autobiographical tales set in Puerto Rico and New Jersey, with relevant poetry following each tale.

Early in *Silent Dancing*, which in 1991 won the PEN/Martha Albrand Special Citation for Nonfiction and was included in New York Public Library's 1991 Best Books for Teens, Ortiz Cofer warns her readers that she is not interested in "canning"

memories. Rather, like Woolf in *Moments of Being* (1976), she writes autobiographically to connect with "the threads of lives that have touched mine and at some point converged into the tapestry that is my memory of childhood."

Silent Dancing is not an autobiography as such; it does not progress linearly from the moment of birth to the day before the final revision is done. It is instead a collection of thirteen stories and a preface, with eighteen poems scattered amid the stories. The book's elements are interconnected but are also discrete. The sequence in which they are read need not be Ortiz Cofer's sequence, although she obviously spent considerable thought on arranging the book's disparate components as she moved toward publication.

"Casa," the lead story, explains elements of the book's genesis. The family has gathered, as it does every day between three and four in the afternoon, for *café con leche* with Mama, the term everyone uses in referring to Ortiz Cofer's grandmother. In the comfortable parlor that Mama's husband built to her exact specifications, drinking coffee together provides the adults with the pretext for spinning yarns, ostensibly for one another but covertly for the edification of the children present.

Young Judith was an attentive listener; Ortiz Cofer suggests that her desire to write stems from these sessions in her grandmother's inviting house in Puerto Rico. This story, like much of Ortiz Cofer's writing, is exact in detail, warm and tactile in depicting human relationships. Mama is voluble, but as she talks, her hands work steadily on braiding her granddaughter's hair.

In sharp contrast to "Casa" and stories such as "Primary Lessons" or "Marina," set in rural Puerto Rico, are the stories about the author's life in a dark, crowded apartment in Paterson. There, rather than being outdoors in a gentle climate, the children spend their winters huddled in a cramped living room around a television set. Despite its grayness, the New Jersey part of Ortiz Cofer's existence has its compensations in both comforts and educational opportunities.

The conflict between two cultures often at odds provides the basic conflict for *Silent Dancing*. Ortiz Cofer personalizes the conflict, yet she lends it a universality that exceeds the two specific cultures about which she writes.

THE LATIN DELI

First published: 1993
Type of work: Prose and poetry

Throughout this volume that intermixes poetry and prose, Ortiz Cofer deals with personal problems faced by Latino women.

Readers of *Silent Dancing* and *The Line of the Sun* will encounter in *The Latin Deli* many of the personalities and situations familiar from Ortiz Cofer's two earlier books. The delicatessen of the title is a *bodega* in Paterson where residents of El Building shop for such Puerto Rican comestibles as plantains and Bustelo coffee.

Most of the stories and poems in *The Latin Deli* are told from the perspective of a young girl torn between two worlds. The father, English-speaking and light-complected, is a working-class man who constrains a daughter in whom sexual desire is awakening. The mother is temporarily resident in El Building, ever longing for Puerto Rico and refusing to learn English.

El Building is a vertical barrio, an attempt to preserve in Paterson some sense of the community its inhabitants have traded for the economic opportunities the mainland offers. The girl in most of Ortiz Cofer's stories speaks English well, yet she endures discrimination directed against Puerto Ricans.

In "American History," the narrator, bright and more fluent in English than Spanish, is barred from classes for the gifted because English is not her native language. She develops a crush on Eugene, a boy from Georgia who is taking classes for the gifted. On the day of John F. Kennedy's assassination, she accepts Eugene's invitation to go to his house to study with him; Eugene's mother, however, asks her whether she comes from El Building, which is next door. When the narrator admits that she does, the mother bars her entry.

In "The Paterson Public Library," Ortiz Cofer deals sensitively with a complex social problem: the tensions between black people and Puerto Ricans. She explains that when Puerto Ricans fill jobs or move into vacant apartments, black people often feel that those are jobs they might have gotten or apartments they might have occupied.

The narrator is terrorized by a black girl, Lorraine, whom she is forced to tutor at school. Even though Lorraine beats her up, the narrator understands the frustrations that motivate Lorraine's violence. The narrator, who resents being treated like a mental deficient because her accent is different, understands how Lorraine's brand of English also causes her to be misjudged by racist teachers.

In "The Myth of the Latin Woman: I Just Met a Girl Named Maria," Ortiz Cofer focuses on what intelligent, well-educated women who are judged by ethnic stereotypes must endure. This piece, more sorrowful than bitter, speaks to members of any minority group.

The forty poems and fifteen stories in *The Latin Deli* are sensitive and searching. They demonstrate the depth of an author who has spent her adult life exploring the impact of her early years poised between two cultures.

WOMAN IN FRONT OF THE SUN: ON BECOMING A WRITER

First published: 2000
Type of work: Essays and poetry

In a combination of essays and poems, Ortiz Cofer offers her views of how one becomes a writer.

In this potpourri of essays and poetry, Ortiz Cofer reveals what it means to be a writer. It is obvious from her exquisite use of language that she is intoxicated with the wonder of words and with their emotive potential. She is also intrigued by the role memory plays in writing. Writers drift mentally through the full accumulation of experience and pluck from it the elements from which they construct stories.

For Ortiz Cofer, this revisiting of memory involved two distinct cultures, three or more generations, and the equilibrium that she was forced to reach as she moved from her childhood in Puerto Rico to her childhood in Paterson, New Jersey.

Hers was not a single adjustment. She and her family left Paterson and returned to Puerto Rico whenever her father was at sea for an extended period, then returned when he returned.

Ortiz Cofer also delves into her later life when, married to an Anglo and raising a daughter, she went to school in quest of two degrees and held various jobs—all of this while she continued to write. For Ortiz Cofer, the excuse "I cannot find time to write" does not hold up. Writers always find time to write because they have something that desperately needs saying; not to say it is the greatest hardship any writer can endure.

Born into a family that loved telling *cuentos* (stories), Ortiz Cofer began at an early age to construct her own realities through the magic of words. Her story "The Woman Who Slept with One Eye Open," which resulted in her collaboration with Marilyn Kallet titled *Sleeping with One Eye Open: Women Writers and the Art of Survival* (1999), reveals the measures that a would-be writer must take to avoid being sidetracked by other responsibilities. In essence, what she talks about in many of the essays in this book is time management, a concept drawn more from the vocabularies of efficiency experts than from the vocabularies of writing instructors.

Both by her advice and by her example, Ortiz Cofer emphasizes the importance of listening, of absorbing not only what people say but also how they say it, and of paying close attention to the small details that create believable worlds for readers. Her own cadences are those of natural speech. She adjusts them from character to character so that much of her characterization evolves from how people say what they say. She also builds atmospheres alive with details that shape them into credible realities.

In this book, as in several of her other publications, the author intermixes genres, using in this case both essays and poems. By doing this, she cre-

ates a microcosm that communicates the basic nature of what writing means to her. She does not chalk off some areas as prose, some as poetry. She combines them because she sees genres both as separate entities and as parts of a larger, all-important entity.

THE MEANING OF CONSUELO

First published: 2003
Type of work: Novel

This young adult novel focuses on the growing up of its protagonist and of the social changes that mark her native Puerto Rico in the last half of the twentieth century.

Ortiz Cofer ventured into writing books for young people in the early twenty-first century, notably *Riding Low on the Streets of Gold* in 2003 and *Call Me Maria* in 2004. *The Meaning of Consuelo* is directed toward a similar audience. This is the story of a young Puerto Rican woman whose name means "consolation." The story is not only an account of the gradual growth and maturing of Consuelo but also of the growth and changes that take place in the world around her.

Consuelo is the more stable of two sisters. The other, Mili, short for Milagros, which means "miracle," is called "Mill" in the story. She is often frivolous and light-hearted but is intermittently disrupted by her emotional problems that stem from schizophrenia. Unlike Mill, Consuelo tends to have a brooding personality, one in keeping with her feeling that she must be responsible and dependable.

The father of the family, who is fascinated by modern mechanical devices and loves anything American, is a maintenance engineer in a San Juan hotel. His humor substantially lightens the more serious elements in the story. He encourages his daughters to be modern, more like Americans, while his wife takes an opposite stand, urging her daughters to value their culture and observe the mores of the strictly structured older society gradually disappearing from modern Puerto Rico.

Ortiz Cofer raises many controversial questions in this novel, but she does so with taste and decorum. She feels the necessity to air for young people such matters as premarital sex and homosexuality, both of which she treats well in *The Meaning of Consuelo*. Although this emphasis might result in the book's being banned from libraries in some conservative venues, it deals forthrightly with questions that are much on the minds of her target audience.

Consuelo finds her own consolation in an understanding cousin, Patricio, who eventually leaves Puerto Rico for the freer atmosphere of New York City. Patricio, ever understanding and supportive of Consuelo, is a homosexual. He represents the new generation, but Consuelo thinks back to the 1950's when a transvestite lived in her neighborhood. He is tolerated, but barely so. He must come to their house through the back door to give Consuelo's mother a manicure, but the sisters are cautioned to treat him like a *fulano* (stranger) when they encounter him in public.

Consuelo is quietly rebellious. She thinks her own thoughts but seldom shares them. She has sex with a boy who then brags to his friends of his conquest. Consuelo, rather than dissolving in tears or withdrawing from society, has the self-confidence to declare that she is not like her mother, who had to seek permission from her relatives before she made any important decisions. Patricio has helped Consuelo reach this point, as has her classmate Lucila, a product of San Juan's slums who wholly rejects the strict social order by which Consuelo's mother and much of her family have always lived.

SUMMARY

Ortiz Cofer is no ideologue. She is a skilled teller of tales, a credible shaper of characters. Her writing never pontificates. Instead, it leads readers to form their own ideologies about the tensions that living as a part of two cultures, one cold, the other warm, engenders. Ortiz Cofer writes with intense realism, softened only slightly by the high level of poetic insight that she brings to her prose and that sustains her poetry.

R. Baird Shuman

BIBLIOGRAPHY

By the Author

LONG FICTION:
The Line of the Sun, 1989
The Meaning of Consuelo, 2003

SHORT FICTION:
Latin Women Pray, 1980
The Native Dancer, 1981
Among the Ancestors, 1981
An Island Like You: Stories of the Barrio, 1995

DRAMA:
Latin Women Pray, pr. 1984

POETRY:
Peregrina, 1986
Reaching for the Mainland, 1987
Terms of Survival, 1987
Reaching for the Mainland, and Selected New Poems, 1995

NONFICTION:
Silent Dancing: A Partial Remembrance of a Puerto Rican Childhood, 1990
Woman in Front of the Sun: On Becoming a Writer, 2000

EDITED TEXTS:
Letters from a Caribbean Island, 1989

Sleeping with One Eye Open: Women Writers and the Art of Survival, 1999 (with Marilyn Kallet)
Riding Low on the Streets of Gold: Latino Literature for Young Adults, 2003

CHILDREN'S LITERATURE:
Call Me Maria, 2004

MISCELLANEOUS:
The Latin Deli: Prose and Poetry, 1993
The Year of Our Revolution: New and Selected Stories and Poems, 1998

About the Author

Bruce-Novoa, Juan. "Judith Ortiz Cofer's Rituals of Movement." *The Americas Review* 19 (Winter, 1991): 88-99.

Davis, Rocio G. "Metanarrative in Ethnic Autobiography for Children: Laurence Yep's *The Garden* and Judith Ortiz Cofer's *Silent Dancing*." *MELUS* 27 (Summer, 2002): 139-158.

Faymonville, Carmen. "New Transnational Identities in Judith Ortiz Cofer's Autobiographical Fiction." *MELUS* 26 (Summer, 2001): 129-160.

Kallet, Marilyn. "The Art of Not Forgetting: An Interview with Judith Ortiz Cofer." *Prairie Schooner* 68 (Winter, 1994): 68-76.

Ocasio, Rafael. "The Infinite Variety of Puerto Rican Reality: An Interview with Judith Ortiz Cofer." *Callaloo* 17 (Summer, 1994): 730-743.

_____. "Puerto Rican Literature in Georgia? An Interview with Judith Ortiz Cofer." *Kenyon Review* 14 (Fall, 1992): 56-61.

Wilhelmus, Tom. "Various Pairs." *Hudson Review* 43 (Spring, 1990): 151-152.

DISCUSSION TOPICS

- To what purposes does Judith Ortiz Cofer use climate in her works?

- Discuss the contrasting personalities of Marisol's parents in *The Line of the Sun*. Does this contrast point to more than the differences between two people?

- How do the people who live in El Building view the members of the Jewish population who lived in the neighborhood before the Puerto Ricans arrived?

- What are the most salient generational differences present in Ortiz Cofer's writing?

- What are the most significant gender differences that you detect in her writing?

- Discuss the role personal isolation plays in what you have read by Ortiz Cofer.

- How does Ortiz Cofer use humor in her writing both to depict character and to control tension?

- Discuss the attitudes toward education that she reveals in characters from different generations.

Julius Ozick

CYNTHIA OZICK

Born: New York, New York
April 17, 1928

Ozick, a highly acclaimed author, is best known for her concern with Jewish culture and morals in a secular, post-Holocaust society.

BIOGRAPHY

Cynthia Ozick was born in New York City on April 17, 1928, the second child of pharmacist William Ozick and Celia Regelson Ozick. She was raised in the Pelham Bay section of the Bronx, a middle-class neighborhood, where she attended Public School 71. "At P.S. 71," Ozick once remarked in an interview, "I was dumb, cross-eyed, and couldn't do arithmetic." Remembering encounters with anti-Semitic teachers and peers, she vividly recalls "teachers who hurt me, who made me believe I was stupid and inferior."

Regardless of her negative early educational experiences, Ozick emerged as a gifted academic. Her youth was spent devouring books, sometimes for eighteen hours a day. She attended Hunter College High School in Manhattan and New York University, where she was inducted into Phi Beta Kappa and graduated cum laude with a bachelor's degree in English. She then taught from 1949 to 1951 at Ohio State University, where she earned an M.A. Her thesis, "Parable in the Later Novels of Henry James," revealed an early reverence for that late nineteenth and early twentieth century American novelist. In fact, throughout much of Ozick's early fiction rings a distinctive Jamesian tone.

Although she knew her destiny was to be a novelist, Ozick began her literary career by composing poetry, a pursuit she interspersed with fiction and essay writing until age thirty-six but then dropped.

Her primary goal, writing a great modern novel, she began immediately after acquiring her graduate degree and marrying Bernard Hollote, a lawyer. She ambitiously began writing a "philosophical" novel, taking seven years to compose some 300,000 words of an incomplete tome. "Mippel," as she calls the unfinished work, in reference to mythical poet and visionary William Blake's "Mercy, Pity, Peace, and Love" (1789), is a typically erudite allusion.

Seven years into writing "Mippel," Ozick entered herself in a novella contest of sorts, assuming that she could complete a short piece of fiction in six weeks, then return to her novel. The novella project grew longer, however, consuming another seven years of her life, and eventually evolved into Ozick's first published work, *Trust* (1966). Coinciding with its publication, Ozick gave birth to her only child, Rachel, at the age of thirty-seven. Although Ozick continued to read and write, activities she believes she does out of necessity, raising her daughter was distracting enough that she had little time to enjoy her new status as a published author.

Having always suffered from what she calls "age-sorrow," Ozick has measured the scale of her achievements on a chronological basis. Because she assumed that she would have published something of "literary merit" by the time she was twenty-five, and because she is highly self-critical, Ozick was not then unduly impressed with her literary achievement, and she has continued to doubt the mass appeal of her writing. Although her first novel met with widespread acclaim, it occurred twelve years later than she expected, thus diminishing her personal satisfaction.

After producing only one published work after fourteen years of novel writing, Ozick turned to short stories and novellas. In 1971, she published a volume of well-received short fiction, *The Pagan Rabbi, and Other Stories*, in which she illustrated the fact that profound subject matter can exist in the shorter fiction genres. Five years later, Ozick followed with more short fiction, *Bloodshed and Three Novellas* (1976). She did not attempt another novel until the mid-1980's, when she published two novels, both considerably shorter than *Trust*. These were *The Cannibal Galaxy* (1983) and *The Messiah of Stockholm* (1987). In 1989, she published *The Shawl*, which includes the novella *Rosa*. The play *Blue Light*, based on *The Shawl*, was produced in 1994 and renamed *The Shawl* when it opened in New York in 1996. In 1997, Ozick published the novel *The Puttermesser Papers*, and, in 2004, the novel *Heir to the Glimmering World* appeared.

In 1983, Ozick published her first collection of essays, *Art and Ardor*; it was followed in 1989 by *Metaphor and Memory*. She next published two collections of essays on writers: *What Henry James Knew, and Other Essays on Writers* (1993) and *Fame and Folly* (1996). *Quarrel and Quandry* was published in 2000. She is considered one of the best essayists writing in English. Ozick is a frequent contributor of essays, poems, reviews, and translations of Yiddish poetry to many periodicals, including *The New York Times Book Review, The New Yorker,* and *American Poetry Review.*

Ozick's numerous awards and grants, received over several decades, give testimony to her acknowledgment as a significant literary figure. In 1966, she taught at the Chautauqua Writers' Conference; two years later, she was one of two novelists awarded a fellowship by the National Endowment for the Arts (NEA). She was selected as a lecturer in the American-Israel Dialogue on Culture and the Arts at the Weizmann Institute in Israel in 1970, and in 1973, she served as O'Connor Professor at Colgate University. In 1975 and again in 1981, 1984, and 1992, she won the prestigious O. Henry Prize. She won the Epstein Fiction Award in 1977 and was a Guggenheim Fellow in 1982. In 1983, Ozick was chosen by the American Academy and Institute of Arts and Letters to receive one of the Mildred and Harold Strauss Living Awards, an annual tax-free award of $35,000 for a minimum of five years. She received the PEN/Spiegel-Diamonstein Award for the Art of the Essay in 1997, the John Cheever Award in 1999, and a National Book Critics' Circle Award nomination for criticism in 2000. Ozick has received honorary degrees from numerous institutions, including Yeshiva University (1984), Williams College (1986), Jewish Theological Seminary (1988), Adelphi University (1988) Brandeis University (1990), Bard College (1991), and Skidmore College (1992).

ANALYSIS

In her essays, as well as her fiction, Ozick has repeatedly returned to a handful of themes connected with problems created by being Jewish in a secular society. In the earlier works *Trust* and *The Pagan Rabbi, and Other Stories*, the Jewish connection is most obvious. In later works, the moral burden placed on post-Holocaust Jewish generations, while it might be less pronounced, remains indigenous to the characters' psyches. Ozick's work serves as a reminder that it is impossible to separate modern Judaism from the devastation that Jewish culture endured during World War II, because Judaism in a vast majority of the civilized world was directly affected. As a result of Adolf Hitler's "final solution" (his attempted extermination of the Jews), the Jewish community in the United States burgeoned, the state of Israel was formed, and European Jewish culture, developed over centuries, was decimated.

Ozick chose a career as a storyteller, yet she has remained unsure of the morality of telling stories. Whether the creativity that inspires storytelling is in conflict with the biblical Second Commandment prohibiting idol worship, and whether the human creativity required to enter an author's make-believe world competes with the world of the Creator of the Universe are common themes in Ozick's fiction. Yet her assertion that people become what they most desire to contend with is how Ozick has justified the apparent moral conflict with her career choice. "Usurpation (Other People's Stories)" warns against this bending of the Mosaic rule, while "The Pagan Rabbi" illustrates the dangerous results when the creative imagination is allowed to overtake the Jewish mind-set.

Another of her interests that recurs in several Ozick works is the nature of language and its influence upon human culture. Because Ozick is a highly articulate writer who manipulates language with enormous precision and artistry, this latter curiosity is not surprising. Not only is Ozick a master of English, the secular language, she also reveals her deep affection for Yiddish, the *mamaloshen*, or mother tongue, in stories such as "Envy: Or, Yiddish in America."

This interest in language has fueled Ozick's desire to plow through her vast and ever-growing reading list. Although she has read widely and broadly, Ozick has "collected" twentieth century writers, most of whom are either Jewish or women (Bernard Malamud and Virginia Woolf, to name two). Ozick has used reading to prime herself for writing, and much of her fiction has been inspired by writers whose work she has read. In an interview, she commented, "I read in order to write." *The Messiah of Stockholm* illustrates what Ozick meant by this. This title is borrowed from Polish writer Bruno Schulz's lost manuscript "The Messiah," and the plot is about the pursuit of the vanished masterwork. "Envy: Or, Yiddish in America" incorporates a caricature of another Jewish writer, Nobel laureate Isaac Bashevis Singer.

Other than reading, a main source of Ozick's inspiration has been her well-grounded Jewish knowledge. Her familiarity with the Talmud (the authoritative body of Jewish tradition and laws) and Kabbala (Jewish mysticism) has often been the foundation upon which Ozick has built her prose. In *The Puttermesser Papers*, the protagonist, using ancient rituals, creates a golem out of the earth of her houseplants. Ozick writes about Jewish matters with authority and authenticity, whether her characters be observant or assimilated Jews.

One drawback with being an intellectual and a writer of ideas is that Ozick's characterizations tend to lack warmth, often making it difficult for the average reader to identify with her characters. Protagonists such as Lars Andemening in *The Messiah of Stockholm* contribute to this perception of Ozick as a writer of ideas rather than as a window on the human condition. Lars, although an interesting character, has no ability to form lasting relationships and has all but cut himself off from society, even to the point of sleeping while everyone else is at work and working while everyone else is asleep. Edelshtein, the protagonist in "Envy: Or, Yiddish in America," is characterized as pitiable but basically unlikable—he, too, is unable to have a successful marriage or trust even his closest

friends. Rabbi Kornfeld in "The Pagan Rabbi," a character the reader knows only posthumously, lives in a world completely removed from reality. In *Heir to the Glimmering World*, Professor Mitwisser has become almost a recluse in his study of the Karaites, a medieval Jewish movement.

Ozick, opposing the generally accepted rule that writers should write about that with which they already are familiar, has taught that writers should write about what they do not know, thereby removing the tendency toward insulation and forcing them to broaden their imaginations. Ozick has followed her own rule, especially when choosing settings for much of her fiction. A native New Yorker who has lived almost her entire life in that state, Ozick has written novels and short stories set in places as varied as Paris, Sweden, Canada, the Midwestern United States, Jerusalem, and Germany.

Ozick embraces her designation as part of the Jewish intellectual establishment. Jewish myths, traditions, speech patterns, religious practices and customs, and historical experiences find their place in her fiction. She has offered her audience prose for thought. Often complex, her writing, with its carefully constructed sentences and rich description, rewards the reader in equal measure to the effort spent reading it.

THE CANNIBAL GALAXY

First published: 1983
Type of work: Novel

A middle-aged school principal who has spent his life seeking out a child prodigy is blind to the brilliance of one of his own pupils.

In a story rich with metaphor, even the title of Cynthia Ozick's first novel in seventeen years, *The Cannibal Galaxy*, is pregnant with meaning. An astronomical term, a cannibal galaxy is a huge galaxy that swallows another until the smaller becomes an insignificant component of the larger; Western culture is the cannibal galaxy that devours Jewish culture. This story is about the struggle against having Judaism devoured by the modern world, yet the characters' particularly Jewish struggles parallel and reflect the struggles of many people, regardless of religious or cultural background. Many unique cultures, while they attempt to emulate the West, paradoxically fear the loss of identity in becoming Westernized.

The protagonist, Principal Brill, is caught between two worlds—his native Parisian Jewish ghetto, where he studied the centuries-old traditions of his ancestors, and modern-day Paris, complete with arguably the world's best museum, the Louvre, and the world-renowned university, the Sorbonne. In order to fulfill his destiny, Brill founds an American school based upon what he considers to be his unique inspiration, a dual curriculum. He theorizes that this combined method of learning will bridge the gap between the secular and the Jewish, thereby improving both teaching methodologies. As in numerous Jewish day schools, Brill plans that students will learn traditional Hebraic subjects, the Talmud and Gemara, half the day, and modern secular subjects, science and mathematics, during the other half.

Brill devotes his adult life to this pedagogical pursuit, waiting for an exceptional child to work through his dual curriculum and to prove the worth of his life's work. Brill, however, is so fully absorbed in his preconception of the exceptional child that he overlooks her when she emerges. It is not until the child, Beulah Lilt, reaches adulthood and makes her significant contribution to society that Brill is at last able to see her brilliance, which has been discovered by others. Not surprising to the reader, but an agonizing shock to Brill, Beulah never mentions her childhood education except to note its lack of exception.

The way in which Ozick belittles Brill's entire life's work is severe, but her point, that compromise merely encourages mediocrity, is well taken. Rather than combining the best of both the traditional and modern worlds, Brill is left with a mediocre mixture of the two, which produces neither Jewish nor secular scholars of merit. Everything in middle-aged Brill's life is middling. Even his school is geographically located in the middle of the United States.

For much of his life, Brill sees himself as a creator and an original thinker. Yet when he meets the linguist Hester Lilt, a true intellectual, he cannot even hold a conversation with her without constantly being reminded of his ineptitude. Hester does not accept Brill's compliment that she is an original thinker. Rather, by way of his compliment, Hester forces Brill to realize how incredibly ordinary he is. Principal Brill acts as a reminder to many who think of themselves as original, creative, and maybe even brilliant. True brilliance is rare, and the last original thinking, Hester Lilt humblingly reminds him, occurred with Plato.

THE MESSIAH OF STOCKHOLM

First published: 1987
Type of work: Novel

An adult orphan pursues a lost masterpiece manuscript written by the man he imagines to have been his father.

The Messiah of Stockholm has a dual purpose: It is Ozick's tribute to Bruno Schulz, the legendary Polish author of *Sklepy Cynamonowe* (1934; *Cinnamon Shops, and Other Stories*, 1963) killed by the Nazis in a mass slaying. *The Messiah of Stockholm* also focuses on the aspect of human nature that craves knowledge of the past in order to have a basis upon which to mold a perception of the present. The deeply human need to have a personal, as well as a cultural, history is one theme winding through this complex novel; this need for a self-history directs the path that orphaned Lars Andemening's life follows.

Ozick's third novel, set in the frigid city of Stockholm, Sweden, is a chilling story of one man's desperate search and struggle to create a rational past for himself. Lars, who selected his name from a dictionary, seeks help from a cast of other World War II refugees who also have public identities of their own choosing. Not all the secondary characters are refugees, however; those in Lars's world fall into two distinct categories: colleagues with factual pasts from the "stewpot" where he works, and refugees from the bookstore with fictional histories. Lars seeks out members of the latter group to help him discover his own indeterminable origins. Obsessed with his search for verification of something impossible to verify, Lars is incapable of establishing lasting relationships with anyone from either category.

His lack of any family history is considered cause, at least by one of his former mothers-in-law, for Lars's lack of success in both his personal and professional life. His daughter lives in America; a dried-up childhood paint set is Lars's only remaining connection with her. He only chose to keep the paints because of Schulz, who had been an art teacher as well as a writer; Lars hoped to see some of his "father's" talent genetically passed on to his daughter.

Lars's obsession with Schulz invades his consciousness awake or asleep, the latter being when Lars sees "as if he lets me have his [Schulz's] own eye to look through." In his fixation with discovering his past, he searches relentlessly for photographs, letters, reviews—any tangible connection with the dead author.

Reading Ozick's intricate fiction, one wonders where history ends and invention begins. Ozick's deep interest in World War II refugees underlies the plot of *The Messiah of Stockholm*, whereas Judaism plays a far less direct role than in her previous fictional works. Lars presumes himself to be the son of Schulz, a Jew, but he never acknowledges any connection with Judaism, probably because Schulz wrote in Polish rather than in Yiddish. Lars chooses to connect with Schulz by becoming extraordinarily literary, hoping to establish his paternity by sheer force of intellectual achievement.

Lars's made-up world of presumed identities and a lost masterpiece is bound to crumble. His tangible connection with his "father" has been primarily through the findings of obscure Schulz memorabilia that Mrs. Eklund imports from Poland to Sweden on his behalf. After she delivers what she claims to be the missing manuscript, Lars does some of his most profound thinking and realizes the absurdity of his pursuit: He cannot prove the unprovable. In a sudden metamorphosis, Lars leaves behind his belles lettres and becomes not merely part of the stewpot but a success in his everyday world.

THE PUTTERMESSER PAPERS

First published: 1997
Type of work: Short stories

Ruth Puttermesser—a lawyer, a bureaucrat in a city department, and finally the mayor of New York City—searches for satisfaction in her career and in her personal life.

The Puttermesser Papers is composed of two short stories and three novellas that appeared in periodicals over the previous fifteen years. All center on Ruth Puttermesser and are loosely organized around the various decades of her life.

In the first section, Ruth, a lawyer in her midthirties, leaves one job because she faces discrimination as a woman and as a Jew and takes another with the city's Department of Receipts and Disbursement. Although her days are spent in the monotony of a bureaucracy, her evenings are enriched by her imagination. She envisions being in Paradise, indulging her desire to study everything from anthropology to chemistry to Roman law. She studies Hebrew with her Uncle Zindel who, as the reader discovers, died many years ago. Living alone in the Bronx apartment of her youth, she invents a world more to her liking.

The second chapter begins with loss: Her love affair with Morris Rappoport ends and at work she is replaced by her boss's inept college crony. She envisions a city where merit is the basis of appointment and promotion and where employees are educated, prepared, and diligent. In the novel, Ozick paints a bleak picture of late twentieth century New York. The city is overrun by vandals, arsonists, and rapists. Yet even with this dark outlook, the novel is often humorous, as seen in the portrayal of the workings of the city administration or of the foibles of the deftly drawn characters.

The chapter takes on the quality of a traditional Jewish fable when Ruth, in her sleep, cre-

ates a golem. Using the dirt from her flowerpots and performing ancient rituals, Ruth fashions the creature, who, although newly formed, knows all that Ruth does. Named Xanthippe, the golem types up Ruth's thoughts on revitalizing New York, which forms the basis of her bid for mayor. With Xanthippe's help, she wins the election, and the period that ensues represents a golden age for New York: The gangs are disbanded, venereal disease disappears, and robberies are nonexistent—all achieved with the guidance of the golem. When the golem discovers sex, however, all is lost. Xanthippe no longer advises Ruth and instead searches out lovers in the administration, who, exhausted, quit their jobs. The city returns to its former squalor, and Ruth, as the mayor, is ruined. Realizing that she must destroy the golem, Ruth recruits Rappoport, who lures Xanthippe to bed, and there Ruth reverses the rituals that bestowed life on Xanthippe.

The next two chapters depict Ruth in her fifties and sixties. Ruth, now unemployed, lives her life vicariously in literature. She longs for a relationship similar to that of the Victorian novelist George Eliot. Though she does meet an artist, the resulting affair ends in disappointment for her. Also disappointing is her encounter with Lidia, the granddaughter of her father's sister. Ruth imagines her to be politically and religiously oppressed in Russia and offers to sponsor her. For Lidia, however, America is a business opportunity. Eager for dollars, she cleans apartments, cares for children, and peddles Lenin medals and other Russian trinkets. After amassing several thousand dollars, she returns to Russia and her boyfriend.

The final section, "Puttermesser in Paradise," mixes the surreal with the realistic. Ruth, now almost seventy, is thinking of Paradise moments before she is brutally murdered and then raped by a robber angered over her lack of valuable possessions. In life, Ruth found no happiness or delight in family, friends, mythical creatures, or employment. In death, Paradise is another disappointment. She had imagined that she would be able to read and study at her leisure. In Paradise, however, all is already known. She could re-create the past, but that would be transitory. She concludes bitterly that it is better never to have loved than to suffer the loss of that love.

HEIR TO THE GLIMMERING WORLD

First published: 2004
Type of work: Novel

An eighteen-year-old orphan is employed as a typist, nanny, and companion in the household of a Jewish immigrant family headed by a scholar of an old Jewish sect.

In *Heir to the Glimmering World*, Cynthia Ozick examines what it means to be an exile or a refugee. The first refugee whom the reader encounters is Rose Meadows, who escapes from the unsettling world of her prevaricating father. Her mother died in childbirth, if she believes her father, or died when Rose was about three, if she trusts her own faint memories. Sent to live with Bertram, a distant cousin, she reluctantly attends a teachers' college in Albany; she would much prefer to study literature. When Bertram begins an affair with the radical Ninel (Lenin spelled backward), Rose must leave. With no other options, she accepts a position with the Mitwisser family, even though it is unclear exactly what she will be doing, and moves to the Bronx with them.

The Mitwissers are also refugees. They have recently fled Nazi Germany, leaving their language, culture, and careers. The family has trouble coping with the New World. Rudolf, the father, is no longer esteemed as a scholar of the Karaites, a Jewish community who rejected rabbinical interpretation and accepted the Scriptures literally. Rudolf attains a position at a college with the help of Quakers, but it is with a mistaken understanding of his speciality. His wife, Elsa, previously a physicist who studied elementary particles, now takes 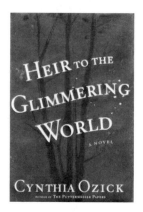 to her bed and is possibly insane. With different degrees of success, their five children are dealing with the displacement. Anneliese, the oldest, assumes the responsibility of running the household. The three sons have embraced the willfulness of American children, and the young girl Waltraut regresses emotionally. The family acquires a benefactor of sorts in James A'Bair, a mysterious character who, in his own way, is also a refugee.

James's father authored an immensely popular series of children's books with James as the hero (loosely based on A. A. Milne's Winnie-the-Pooh books about Christopher Robin). James's childhood was controlled by this fictional character, and now he struggles to escape his past. With a fortune from royalties, he should be free to pursue any goal. He first encounters the Mitwissers in Albany and pretends to be a tutor. Later, he tries acting and then travels with Anneliese as his companion. He finds no solace, however, and eventually commits suicide, leaving Anneliese, pregnant, to return to her family.

Bertram enters into the mix. Once financially stable, he has been brought low by his association with Ninel and, using his acquaintance with Rose, moves in with the Mitwissers. He soon becomes indispensable, even marrying Anneliese in order to provide a father for her child.

While the novel seems to be centered on Rose, she is more of an observer of the Mitwisser world, rather than a participant in her own world. At the novel's end, she leaves, but it is uncertain what she is going toward.

"THE PAGAN RABBI"

First published: 1966 (collected in *The Pagan Rabbi, and Other Stories*, 1971)
Type of work: Short story

A modern rabbi struggles between the religion he teaches and a forbidden world for which he yearns.

"The Pagan Rabbi" explores a modern Jewish problem, the overwhelming appeal of things non-Jewish, or "pagan." The title piece in Ozick's first short-story collection, "The Pagan Rabbi" is a mythical tale set in the modern world. There are three voices in the story: the intense dialogue controlled by the widow, the information provided by the narrator, and the reading of the deceased's suicide note.

Rabbi Isaac Kornfeld, a gifted and renowned intellectual, teacher, and writer, has hanged himself in the public park. The narrator, a childhood friend of the deceased. seeks to discover why a pious man, about to reach his intellectual peak at age thirty-six, would choose to end his life. Ozick was thirty-six years of age two years before "The Pagan Rabbi" was first published; she created a character similar to herself in age and talent. Kornfeld's mythical world exists in a modern city filled with parks bisected by filthy rivers rather than in an idyllic, nonpopulated nature reserve. In this unlikely setting, with his unique vision, Rabbi Kornfeld dares to experience the excruciating beauty, as well as the horrifying ugliness, of the pagan world forbidden to him.

In trying to unravel the mystery of his friend's death, the unnamed narrator pays condolences to Kornfeld's widow, Sheindel, a very clever mother of seven daughters, who as an infant miraculously survived a Nazi concentration camp. The widow reveals a letter left in her husband's coat to explain his fatal action posthumously. Sheindel describes it as a "love letter," but it does not confess any earthly infidelity. Kornfeld confesses that he has fallen in love with a free-spirited dryad. As a result of being unable to release what must be free, Kornfeld loses his own soul—revealed, to Kornfeld's horror, as an ugly, old man oblivious to anything of natural beauty around him, aware only of the worn Tractate of Mishna he is intently studying.

The three characters—the narrator, the widow, and the Rabbi—all approach Judaism differently. The narrator attempts to assimilate—he married out of the religion to a tall, blond, frigid Puritan named Jane. His approach does not work because he is secretly in love with Sheindel, who, with her seven female offspring, represents the survival of Judaism, a maternal religion. Sheindel stays within her Jewish world, accepting that she is different from those outside it. The third approach, a purely intellectual one, is Kornfeld's path. He questions and challenges everything, which has the paradoxical effect of strengthening his faith, while he becomes enamored of all that is forbidden by it. His duplicity, living publicly as a Jew and privately as a Hellenist, leaves the Rabbi no alternative to suicide.

"ENVY: OR, YIDDISH IN AMERICA"

First published: 1969 (collected in *The Pagan Rabbi, and Other Stories*, 1971)
Type of work: Short story

An unknown Yiddish poet envies a fellow Yiddish writer's success and blames his own failure on his lack of a translator.

"Envy: Or, Yiddish in America" first appeared in *Commentary*, then was published as part of Ozick's first short-story collection two years later. The connection between language and culture is explored as an aging Yiddish poet, a fictionalized Joseph Glatstein, centers his life on his all-encompassing jealousy of Yankel Ostrover, a thinly disguised Isaac Bashevis Singer.

True to Ozick's belief that large themes can be explored in short fiction, she expresses her concern with the nature of language while entertaining her audience with a comically wry story. It takes place in New York City, where Hershele Edelshtein, son of a Polish Hebraic tutor, has lived for forty years. Edelshtein writes Yiddish poetry for an obscure publication edited by his friend, fellow Yiddish poet and Ostrover envier Baumzweig. Baumzweig and Edelshtein are "secret enemies" (a concept that recurs in "The Pagan Rabbi" as well as in "The Shawl"). Their shared obsessive hatred of Ostrover, however, is the force that binds their tenuous friendship.

Ozick's treatment of the demise of Yiddish, the mother tongue of European Jews, reveals her fondness for the language of her forebears. Yet the death of Yiddish lacks sentimentality; in fact, it faces a brutal rejection from an educated young Jewish writer, Hannah. She represents the first generation of English-speaking secularized American Jews, those who have reduced the richness of Yiddish to a smattering of commonly used exclamations and insults.

Ironically, Edelshtein earns his meager living lecturing—in English—on the death of Yiddish. He is also forced to reduce Yiddish to a medium for telling jokes in order to hold the interest of his waning audiences. Edelshtein tells two of his jokes to the reader, one about a funeral. Then Edelshtein,

never able to read people well enough to mesh with current trends, realizes too late that the jokes "were not the right kind." Envy has kept Edelshtein in the pitiable position of being on the outside looking in since his boyhood in Minsk. In his dotage, Edelshtein daydreams about the past, when he was taken as a boy to Kiev, where his father taught the wealthy young boy with the beautiful face and the intricate German toys with whom Edelshtein could never play.

Several decades later, Edelshtein remains outside, watching his Yiddish universe modernize without him. He makes a fool of himself by sending pathetic letters that display his desperation, then blames his utter failure on everything he can think of: lack of a translator, the Nazi extermination of six million Yiddish speakers, and anti-Semitism. Edelshtein blames everyone but himself. His fury is twofold: He sees his beloved culture dying and he craves Ostrover's success.

Ozick endows her fictionalized Isaac Bashevis Singer with popular appeal and a quick wit. Ostrover goes so far as to use Edelshtein's failure as the basis for his latest successful fable, told as a story within the novella. Years earlier, Ostrover had done the same thing; after Ostrover's affair with Edelshtein's wife, he had written another successful story inspired by yet another of Edelshtein's failures.

"Envy: Or, Yiddish in America," while about a petty, narrow man with frustrated ambitions, also depicts, with a feeling of great loss, the deterioration of a culture as it disappears into the melting pot. While some, Ozick seems to say, can adapt and be translated, others, who are less flexible, can only look in from the outside, knowing the obscurity of death is imminent.

"THE SHAWL"

First published: 1980 (collected in *The Shawl*, 1989)
Type of work: Short story

A magical shawl sustains the life of a hidden infant in a Nazi concentration camp.

"The Shawl" is a brief story that has a lasting impact upon its reader. Ozick's most anthologized work condenses within seven pages the horrors of the infamous Nazi concentration camps. This prizewinning fiction reverberates with images and themes common in Ozick's work: the Holocaust, World War II refugees, and secret enmity. Chilling imagery leaves the reader's senses buzzing like the electrified fence against which Rosa's fifteen-month-old child, Magda, is thrown. Through Ozick's powerful, yet uncharacteristically simple language, the reader shares the spiritually elevating love that Rosa, a young mother, has for her infant daughter as well as her forbidden despair over Magda's barbaric murder.

Initially, the shawl provides warmth and protection as it hides the secret child. When Rosa can no longer suckle, the shawl magically nourishes Magda with the "milk of linen." In its third life-giving role, the shawl provides companionship, as Magda silently laughs with it as if it were the sister she never had. Without the shawl, Magda, separated from her source of life, is completely vulnerable. Her secret existence is instantly discovered, and her brief life brutally extinguished.

The central metaphor, the shawl, wraps baby Magda and the story in many layers of interpretation. Ozick has crafted her three characters in the fashion of a fifteenth century morality play. In a morality play, each character represents moral qualities or abstractions. Similarly, Ozick's characters represent three states of existence. Magda, wound in the magical shawl, is Life, full of warmth and imagination. Rosa, who no longer experiences hunger, "a floating angel," is Spirit. Stella, always so cold that it has seeped into her hardened heart, is Death.

Metaphorically, when Spirit looks away, Death, jealous of the warmth of Life, takes the life-source away, thus killing Life. The secret hatred that Stella harbors toward Magda is only surpassed by the disturbing images Rosa has of starving Stella cannibalizing the delicious-looking infant.

A powerful story, whether read literally or interpreted metaphorically, "The Shawl" offers a private insight into the chillingly painful world created by World War II Germany. Rosa's loss is humankind's loss, and the gut-wrenching pain she experiences as she sucks out what little taste of Magda's life remains in the shawl is the pain of the modern world, gagged and left speechless by inhumanity.

SUMMARY

Among her contemporaries, Ozick has been distinguished by her devotion to literature; she does not go on to the next sentence until she has perfected the first. Although her fiction has universal relevance, Ozick's stories are rooted in her Jewish conscience, along with the moral, ethical, and cultural questions accompanying that often burdensome state of mind.

A recipient of numerous literary awards, Ozick's toughest critic is herself. A shy individual who is deeply concerned with Jewish culture and morals, Ozick's true personality can only be discovered through careful reading of her work.

Leslie Pearl; updated by Barbara Wiedemann

BIBLIOGRAPHY

By the Author

SHORT FICTION:
The Pagan Rabbi, and Other Stories, 1971
Bloodshed and Three Novellas, 1976
Levitation: Five Fictions, 1982
The Shawl, 1989
The Puttermesser Papers, 1997

LONG FICTION:
Trust, 1966
The Cannibal Galaxy, 1983
The Messiah of Stockholm, 1987
Heir to the Glimmering World, 2004

POETRY:
Epodes: First Poems, 1992

DRAMA:
Blue Light, pr. 1994 (adaptation of her short story "The Shawl")

NONFICTION:
Art and Ardor, 1983
Metaphor and Memory: Essays, 1989
What Henry James Knew, and Other Essays on Writers, 1993
Portrait of the Artist as a Bad Character, and Other Essays on Writing, 1996
Fame and Folly: Essays, 1996
Quarrel and Quandry: Essays, 2000

EDITED TEXT:
The Best American Essays, 1998, 1998
Complete Works of Isaac Bable, 2001

MISCELLANEOUS:
A Cynthia Ozick Reader, 1996

DISCUSSION TOPICS

- How do historical events such as World War II or the Holocaust influence Cynthia Ozick's fiction?

- What points does Ozick make about the immigrant experience?

- Discuss how Ozick shows the corrupting influence of power, whether acquired through political patronage or through money.

- What effect does the secular society of the United States have on the Jewish community?

- Why does Ozick often people her fiction with adult orphans and exiles?

About the Author

Bloom, Harold, ed. *Cynthia Ozick: Modern Critical Views.* New York: Chelsea House, 1986.
Cohen, Sarah Blacher. *Cynthia Ozick's Comic Art: From Levity to Liturgy.* Bloomington: Indiana University Press, 1994.
Friedman, Lawrence S. *Understanding Cynthia Ozick.* Columbia: University of South Carolina Press, 1991.
Kauver, Elaine M. *Cynthia Ozick's Fiction: Tradition and Invention.* Bloomington: Indiana University Press, 1993.
Lowin, Joseph. *Cynthia Ozick.* Boston: Twayne, 1988.
Pinsker, Sanford. *The Uncompromising Fictions of Cynthia Ozick.* Columbia: University of Missouri Press, 1987.
Rainwater, Catherine, and William J. Scheick, eds. *Three Contemporary Women Novelists: Hazzard, Ozick, and Redmon,* Austin: University of Texas Press, 1983.
Strandberg, Victor H. *Greek Mind/Jewish Soul: The Conflicted Art of Cynthia Ozick.* Madison: University of Wisconsin Press, 1991.
Walden, Daniel, ed. *The Changing Mosaic: From Cahan to Malamud, Roth, and Ozick.* Albany: State University of New York Press, 1993.
_____. *The World of Cynthia Ozick: Studies in American Jewish Literature.* Kent, Ohio: Kent State University Press, 1987.

GRACE PALEY

Born: New York, New York
December 11, 1922

Through the unique and very personal voice of her short stories, Paley has vividly, humorously, and empathetically depicted the characters and social concerns of her time.

Courtesy, New York State Writers Institute,
State University of New York

BIOGRAPHY

Grace Paley was born in the Bronx, New York, on December 11, 1922. Her parents, Isaac and Manya (Ridnyk) Goodside, were Ukrainian-born Jews. As outspoken opponents of Russia's Czar Nicholas II, they had been sentenced to exile—he to Siberia and she to Germany—before being released from imprisonment and emigrating to New York in 1905. Isaac learned English quickly and became a physician, and the Goodsides lived first on Manhattan's Lower East Side and then in the East Bronx.

Listening to the stories of the old country and the struggles endured there, told in Russian and Yiddish as well as English, their daughter Grace inherited an interest in political issues, a progressive belief system, and a willingness to speak her mind. A good student, she graduated from high school at the age of fifteen. In 1938, she entered Hunter College in New York City, but she was expelled for poor attendance. She also enrolled at New York University but left without a degree. She loved and wrote poetry on her own, and in the early 1940's studied with poet W. H. Auden at New York's New School for Social Research.

In 1942, Grace Goodside married Jess Paley, a motion picture cameraman, with whom she had two children, Nora and Daniel. The Paleys lived in Greenwich Village in New York City, where the young mother did occasional office work and became involved in community activism, including Parent-Teacher Association demonstrations against civil defense and opposition to disruptive redevelopment of Washington Square Park.

Into the mid-1950's, Paley continued writing poetry, mostly traditional and literary in style, but gradually recognizing the limits of the genre for expression of social and political concerns, she turned to prose. Her first collection of stories, *The Little Disturbances of Man,* appeared in 1959 to enthusiastic response. Following the book's success, at the urging of friends and colleagues, Paley set out to write a novel; though never completed, sections of it appeared in *The Noble Savage* and *New American Review.*

In the early 1960's, Paley began teaching courses in writing at Columbia and Syracuse Universities, and in 1966 she became a member of the faculty of Sarah Lawrence College, outside New York City, where she taught for eighteen years. Still living in Greenwich Village and writing stories for occasional publication in magazines, Paley gained visibility speaking out on political issues. A fervent opponent of the American war effort in Vietnam, she went in 1968 on a fact-finding mission to visit draft dodgers in France and Sweden and the following year was among a group of pacifists that traveled to Hanoi, Vietnam, for the liberation of three American prisoners of war. Her account of the Asian trip, "Report from the Democratic Republic of Vietnam," appeared in *WIN,* the newspaper of the War Resister's League.

Having divorced her first husband in the early 1960's, she married Robert Nichols, a writer and landscape architect, in 1972. Paley's second volume of stories, *Enormous Changes at the Last Minute*, was published in 1974, the same year she traveled to Moscow as a delegate of the War Resisters' League at the World Peace Congress. With the end of the Vietnam conflict, her activism focused on other issues, including women's rights, prison reform, the environment, and nuclear weapons. Her activities ranged from distributing leaflets on street corners to unfurling an antinuclear banner on the White House lawn in December of 1978, for which she and the other "White House Eleven" were arrested, convicted, fined one hundred dollars, and given six-month suspended jail terms.

In 1980, Paley was elected to the American Academy and Institute of Arts and Letters. A film version of *Enormous Changes at the Last Minute*, adapted by filmmaker John Sayles, was shown at the Film Forum in New York in the spring of 1985. Also that year, Paley published her third collection of stories, *Later the Same Day*, and her first collection of poems, *Leaning Forward*, and her opposition to American policies in Central America led to a trip to Nicaragua and El Salvador.

Paley lived in Greenwich Village for most of her life, but by the early 1990's, she was dividing her time between New York and Thetford, Vermont. In her political years, the humanitarian stayed active in social movements that opposed war, that challenged nuclear plant installment and activity, and that perpetuated the feminist movement. Such activism had taken her to the 1961 cofounding of the Greenwich Village Peace Center and to the 1973 World Peace Congress in Moscow, where she challenged the Soviet Union's silencing of political dissidents.

From 1986 to 1988, Paley was elected New York State Author. In 1987, she was recognized for her lifetime literary contributions and awarded a Senior Fellowship by the National Endowment for the Arts (NEA). While supporting the causes most important to her, the author also continued to write. She published her third collection of short stories in 1985, entitled *Later the Same Day*. By 1998, Paley had crafted seven more works of poetry and short prose. Her collected works have earned nominations for a National Book Award and awards such as the 1983 Edith Wharton Award, the 1993 Rea Award for Short Story, and the Vermont Governor's Award for Excellence in the Arts, also in 1993.

In 2003, Paley was the fifth person to be named Vermont's State Poet. Under unanimous recommendation, she was honored by the State Poet Advisory Panel, composed of former State Poets Ellen Bryant Voigt, Louise Glück, and Galway Kinnell; Peter Gilbert, executive director of the Vermont Humanities Council; and Carol Milkuhn, vice president of the Vermont Poetry Society.

It is clear that, through the decades, as a devoted humanitarian who engaged in everything from membership in the Women's Pentagon Action to antiwar protests that landed her in jail, Grace Paley has shown an awareness of the plights of others and the needs of society as a whole. This attitude has informed her teaching, political sensibilities, and writing oeuvre and has earned her, besides numerous accolades, a devoted following.

ANALYSIS

On the dust jacket of *Enormous Changes at the Last Minute* appears Paley's comment that she "writes stories because art is too long and life is too short." Hers is an unusual accomplishment, for though the short story has earned its position as a respectable genre, few authors have achieved repute without venturing beyond its limits. The acclaimed masters of the short story—James Joyce, Ernest Hemingway, Honoré de Balzac, and Anton Chekhov—all wrote novels or plays as well. Paley's reputation is based on three relatively slim collections. Nevertheless, the first, *The Little Disturbances of Man*, was reissued by a different publisher nine years after its original appearance, a rare event in the history of the short story.

Paley's early interest in poetry inculcated in her art the values of verbal economy and the layering of meaning; her prose style is highly poetic—compact, full of imagery, and less reasoned than sensed or felt. Some of the pieces in *Later the Same Day*, such as "Mother," "This Is a Story About My Friend George, the Toy Inventor," and "In This Country, but in Another Language, My Aunt Refuses to Marry the Men Everyone Wants Her To," are so brief that they seem less stories than sketches or impressions.

Even in structuring her longer stories, Paley rarely accepts conventional formulae, choosing instead an often meandering movement with loose shifts in time, tone, or for the point of view. A glimpse into Paley's technique may be found in "A

Conversation with My Father" (1974), where the narrator, a writer, is asked by her father to compose a traditional story but finds it impossible to write that type of "plot, the absolute line between two points. . . . [B]ecause it takes all hope away. Everyone, real or imagined, deserves the open destiny of life." Such apparent plotlessness demands an equal openness of the reader, for very few standard expectations will be fulfilled. Occasionally she ventures into more fantastic or artificially stylized ground, as in the seemingly absurdist "The Floating Truth" (1959) or the whimsically postured "At That Time: Or, The History of a Joke" (1985).

For the most part, Paley's stories, like poems, ask to be read aloud. They have a conversational tone, and the often awkward precision of meaning, jarring usages, and odd logic create an immediacy of communication. This very particular language traces back to a polyglot family tradition. Paley's immigrant parents and relatives spoke Russian, Yiddish, and English, and her own Bronx vernacular was influenced by their very different syntax and rhythms. Certain of her stories, such as "Goodbye and Good Luck" (1959) and "Faith in the Afternoon" (1960), delightfully convey distinct voices from the Jewish American immigrant community.

Though seldom explicitly autobiographical, Paley's stories contain elements of her personal history. They often focus on Jews, mothers, and activists, and are generally set in New York City. A number of them are connected by common characters, centered around Faith, a wryly self-mocking divorcé, her parents, her friends Ruth and Edie, her sons Richard and Tonto, and her husbands and neighbors. Faith (the name suggests Grace) is generally considered Paley's fictional alter ego; her presence gives the individual stories personal reverberations and gives the collections overall a sense of unity.

Faith, like Paley, is a single mother concerned equally with the quality of life in Greenwich Village and in the future of the human race. Progressive social and political issues, though never completely eclipsing the portrayal of character and relationship, are important to Paley. Her treatment of women, their problems, their ambitions, and their relations with men has earned her the admiration of feminist readers. Some stories feature immigrants, minorities, and the poor—such as the Puerto Rican family in "In the Garden" (1985) or the black mother in "Lavinia: An Old Story" (1985)—or candidly portray the brutality of city life, as in "Samuel" (1968) and "Little Girl" (1974). In the light of the poverty, violence, and disease that Paley's characters witness and endure, there is no choice but to have opinions, to voice them shamelessly, and to act upon them with courage.

Paley's writing, though political, is very rarely didactic, pessimistic, or angry. As a writer, she is attuned to the subtle signals and meanings of human emotion and communication, whatever the situation or backdrop, and this sensitivity provides a foundation of warmth and humor. Her satire, applied to old gossips or overzealous activists, is never malicious, and her overriding concern is ultimately to amuse, to touch, and to remind her reader of the wonderful joy and variety of being alive.

"THE LOUDEST VOICE"

First published: 1959 (collected in *The Little Disturbances of Man*, 1959)
Type of work: Short story

An outspoken and strong-willed little Jewish girl is chosen to narrate her school's Christmas play.

"The Loudest Voice" is the first-person-voice recollection of Shirley Abramowitz, who remembers her childhood as a place where "every window is a mother's mouth bidding the street shut up" and where her "voice is the loudest." Shirley is the daughter of Jewish immigrants, a bright and uninhibited child who talks loudly and incessantly and, like her father, fearlessly speaks her mind.

On a cold November morning, Shirley is summoned by the teacher organizing the school's Christmas play. Knowing that she has a loud and clear voice, he asks her to be his narrator. The Christmas play, and the involvement in it of Jewish children such as Shirley, occasions debate and commentary throughout the Jewish community, where some embrace assimilation into primarily Christian America, while others firmly safeguard the integrity of ethnic and religious identity. In the

Abramowitz home, Shirley's mother disapproves, but her father counters with the argument, "In Palestine the Arabs would be eating you alive. Europe you had pogroms. Argentina is full of Indians. Here you got Christmas."

Shirley herself is proud of her voice and eager to perform; during the month of rehearsals her excitement focuses her usually dispersed energies, and she becomes the director's efficient and trusted assistant. The day of the play arrives; Shirley narrates sensitively and admirably, giving an objective and amusing account of her classmates' earnest presentation. The story concludes later that night as the Abramowitzes and a neighbor discuss the day's events in their characteristically opinionated fashion, and Shirley, lying in bed, silently says her prayers and then loudly yells to quiet her parents' arguments.

In "The Loudest Voice," Paley creates a delightful and very immediate protagonist. Shirley's personality is defined by her comments—her perception of the loneliness of unpopular people, her innocent fusion of the Christmas play with the very Jewish world in which it is performed, and the overheard conversations and repartee that have remained in her memory. The story's title signals an affirmation of personal freedom, for Shirley, who is constantly being silenced in her day-to-day life, proudly believes that a voice worthy of the Christmas play must also have the power to make both its opinions and prayers heard. The story contrasts loud voices with the silence of death, memory, and contemplation, and implicit in Shirley's pride is Paley's own valuation of the freedom of self-expression.

As she tells her story, Shirley makes a few simple comments that establish the distance of passed time, the death of her parents, and the warmth with which she views the past. The incident of the Christmas play, though simple and basically undramatic, is like a prism reflecting many facets of her childhood and the life of that remembered community. Her father's assertion, "What belongs to history, belongs to all men," informs Shirley's own generous feeling toward the municipal Christmas tree which, like the Jews, "was a stranger in Egypt," and defines her open attitude toward life. Through many such touches, Paley portrays with empathetic lightness the ghetto mentality as it makes the transition to acceptance and comfort, and, in a larger view, distills centuries of Jewish exile and accommodation into the experience of a single child.

"AN INTEREST IN LIFE"

First published: 1959 (collected in *The Little Disturbances of Man*, 1959)
Type of work: Short story

A young woman, deserted by her husband to raise four children alone, learns to find happiness in her simple life.

"An Interest in Life" holds nothing of the bizarre or extraordinary: It is a story about an ordinary woman named Virginia, her ordinary children, and the ordinary problems she faces making ends meet and finding happiness and love in an imperfect world.

The story begins as Virginia's husband deserts her, ostensibly to join the Army, after giving her a broom and dustpan for Christmas. The gift is not a kind one; the relations between Virginia and her husband have been bitter and sarcastic. Once he departs, Virginia begins adjusting to the life of a single twenty-six-year-old woman raising four young children—dealing not only with social service agencies, schools, and bills, but also with loneliness, anger, and the lingering mystery of where her husband went and whether he will ever return.

Into Virginia's misery and bitterness comes John Raftery, the married son of her widowed neighbor, as if, it seems, to "rescue" her. John offers her his devotion and comfort, but Virginia is hesitant to accept it fully. Still, he comes to see her faithfully every Thursday night, and his openheartedness and lightness of spirit bring life into her home, effecting subtle changes in the children's and Virginia's outlooks. In the comfort of John's  undemanding affection, she recalls the wildness of her passion for her husband and their tumultuous marriage, poisoned by his arrogance and cruelty, culminating in the broom and the desertion.

Then one Thursday, suddenly, without explanation, John stops coming. After two weeks' absence, Virginia abandons hope of his return. Dejected, she decides to go on a television game show called "Strike it Rich" and makes the requisite list of personal troubles. "The list when complete could have brought tears to the eye of God if He had a minute." It somehow cheers her up, however, and she realizes that all a person really needs "is an interest in life, good, bad, or peculiar."

Once she realizes this, the doorbell rings. It is John, returning to say goodbye forever, but Virginia's list and John's mocking response to her troubles—"They'd laugh you out of the studio. Those people really suffer"—impels her to act on another decision, and she finally accepts John as her lover. They settle into a steady situation that brings Virginia happiness and emotional stability and in which she still sometimes imagines, at the story's end, her husband's late-night return and a rediscovery of their lost passion.

"An Interest in Life" is told in the first-person voice, so Paley brings the reader into Virginia's mind and perceptions. A sharp and economical use of language potently portrays the character's emotional life, as when she remembers a domestic climate where "[f]ire may break out from a nasty remark" or says that after her husband's desertion "sadness was stretched world wide across my face." The story's recurring images are of burning, shriveling, consumption, and deterioration. These images express the volatility of Virginia's marriage as well as her own protective, even paranoid, attitude toward other people and new experiences.

Rather than be honest with her children, she feels the need to keep the truth from them and responds to their queries with evasive proverbs. In fact, she is generally critical of them, sardonic about her neighbors, and pessimistic about the system and her survival within it. Only when John enters her life does she begin to open up to the possibilities of change in herself and others and to accept life without suspicion or fear. The progress of the story is a movement toward a more positive perception of life.

Characteristically, Paley employs comedy to achieve a balance in what would otherwise be a rather depressing tale. Virginia's bitterness does not nullify the comic elements in the portraits she creates of her children or Mrs. Raftery; the devices of the gift broom and the television game show, full as they are with the power of "sweeping clean" and "Striking it Rich," infuse the critical moments of Virginia's life with a clumsy domesticity. In the ordinary world, Paley seems to be saying, there is little that is truly profound or timeless, yet there is always the potential for happiness, for meaning, and for love.

"FAITH IN A TREE"

First published: 1974 (collected in *Enormous Changes at the Last Minute*, 1974)
Type of work: Short story

During an afternoon in the park, a woman's detachment and cynicism are converted into a commitment to action.

"Faith in a Tree," as the title suggests, is about a woman named Faith, the protagonist of many a Paley story, sitting in a tree. It is a Saturday afternoon, and Faith has brought her two young sons, Richard and Tonto, to their New York neighborhood park to play and pass the time, among other parents and children and passersby doing the same.

Unlike those around her, however, Faith feels subtly trapped in her life as a single mother; she senses an unidentifiable longing, both carnal and intellectual, to make a more meaningful connection with the world. Bored with the mundane pretensions of the park's social scene, she withdraws, retreats into herself, and climbs into a sycamore to establish the distance and detachment she needs. From her post, she muses flippantly on the scene below her and its position in the universe—"What a place in democratic time!"

She answers the queries of casual acquaintances passionately, but her cryptic answers are enigmatic and senseless; she describes and lampoons the other mothers, such as the self-righteous Mrs. Junius Finn, who "always is more in charge of word meanings than I am" and "is especially in charge of Good and Bad." She responds to the various stimuli of passersby, such as a pair of men listening to

Bach on a transistor radio; she alternately ignores and wrangles with her clever and disapproving older son, Richard; she jumps down from the tree for some competitive flirtation with a likable and considerate man named Phillip Mazzano. She later considers climbing back up for oxygen when another woman seems to be prevailing in the contest for his attention. These and other comments and encounters are reported through Faith's ironic and imaginative eyes.

After flowing timelessly and haphazardly in a manner thus reflective of Faith's inner diffuseness, the story ends with a twist reminiscent of an O. Henry tale—and not at all typical of Paley's style. A group of parents and children approach, wielding signs and clanging pots in protest against the American use of napalm in Vietnam, and they are dispersed by a local conservative-minded policeman. In the aftermath of the incident, Richard chastises Faith and her friends for their failure to confront the policeman and impulsively emblazons the protesters' message—"WOULD YOU BURN A CHILD? and under it, a little taller, the red reply, WHEN NECESSARY"—across the sidewalk. The apathy and restraint of the afternoon combine with the sudden excitement of the protesters' expulsion and Richard's spontaneous anger to affect Faith's view of her life dramatically, and, in the story's final paragraph, she traces to that specific moment her subsequent changes in appearance, employment, social life, communication, and awareness of and involvement in the world.

The impact of "Faith in a Tree" derives from the care and leisure with which Paley establishes Faith's sense of detachment. This is accomplished not only through the imagery—for example, comparing the other mothers to naval vessels—and acutely facetious tone but also through Faith's attitude toward the reader, for she acknowledges the subjective posture she has taken to the world around her and on two occasions even includes footnotes that acknowledge the physical manifestation of her storytelling—the page—and refer beyond the internal context of the story to the reader's world as well.

The detachment, mentally and stylistically, is thus complete; it is its completeness which lulls the reader into an equal complacency, only to disrupt it again with Faith's sudden emergence from spiri-

tual withdrawal into an active participation in the world. Paley is rarely didactic, but in "Faith in a Tree" her purpose is not only to entertain but also to motivate. Just as Faith is somehow tricked by circumstance into a meaningful new awareness and acceptance of responsibility, so is the reader (by implication) left, seemingly alone at the conclusion, to ponder the nature of complacency and determination and the small ways in which an individual may be driven to action.

"ZAGROWSKY TELLS"

First published: 1985 (as "Telling"; collected in *Later the Same Day*, 1985)
Type of work: Short story

In an encounter with a former customer and antagonist, an old Jewish man recounts the ordeals that forced him to confront his racism.

In "Zagrowsky Tells," Paley's recurring character Faith appears again but in a secondary and not necessarily flattering role. The focus is on Zagrowsky, a retired Jewish pharmacist, as he sits in the park with his grandson, a black child named Emanuel.

Faith, a former customer whom Zagrowsky has not seen in years, approaches him and asks him about the boy. He begins to explain how he has come to have a black grandson, and as they reminisce about their shared past in the community he confronts her for having led a protest against him for supposedly racist practices. He denies having been racist, but Faith insists that he subtly mistreated his black customers. Faith then presses him to talk about Emanuel, and he tells the story: His daughter Cissy became mentally unbalanced, suffering attacks and even protesting his racism herself; she was committed to an institution north of the city where she became pregnant by a black gardener. Now she lives at home, still nervous and dependent, and Zagrowsky and his wife raise her son, Emanuel.

Having heard his story, Faith begins to offer advice about providing for the child's racial identity, but Zagrowsky interrupts and angrily sends her off. Now confused and frustrated, he vents his anger on another stranger, an innocent man who approaches him to praise and ask about Emanuel. Faith quickly returns with a group of her friends and saves Zagrowsky from the bothersome stranger, then they warmly say goodbye, leaving Zagrowsky alone with Emanuel and uncertain as to what exactly has transpired.

"Zagrowsky Tells" really concerns two separate stories told by Zagrowsky. One is the story of his and Emanuel's history, a sad tale in which much of the pain and the meaning is left between the lines. Zagrowsky is a proud and bitter man who must work hard to face the difficult truths of his life: his bigotry, his failures as a father and husband, his inability to trust or communicate with others. Thus, his story is easiest told when he relies on facts.

The other story, however, is the story he tells the reader. This account, given in the immediate first-person present, weaves together the external reality of the encounters in the park with the internal monologue of Zagrowsky's mind. As he talks to Faith and looks after Emanuel, he is constantly digressing—observing, judging, evaluating, speculating, anticipating, imagining, and above all, remembering—and it is through his observations, thoughts, and memories that a true view of his life and his personality emerges. Paley thus portrays from within the fears, anxieties, and longing of a confused and repressed old man upon whom life has played an ironic joke.

As in so many of her stories, Paley's prevalent attitude toward her subject is one of generosity. The case against Zagrowsky is not a clear one, for his bigotry is subtle and not malicious; he elicits empathy, comparing the histories of the black and Jewish peoples, communicating his desire to act fairly and honestly, and acknowledging, in spite of the accumulated years of guilt and shame, the incontrovertibility of the past and the life-affirming value of expressing oneself. "Tell!" he says, "That opens up the congestion a little—the lungs are for breathing, not secrets."

The ultimate redemption, however, as well as the story's emotional power, lies not in a reasoned defense of past bigotry but in the compassionate reality of Zagrowsky's present situation, as intimated throughout the story. Given Cissy's illness and Mrs. Zagrowsky's limitations, Zagrowsky has willingly become Emanuel's primary parent, teacher, and friend. The two are constant companions, and the old man's devotion to the boy is abso-

lute. Thus, during the course of the story the reader develops compassion—the same compassion that in the end motivates Faith to protect Zagrowsky—by recognizing the miraculous transformation that has been achieved in the heart of a bitter old man by the presence of an innocent little black boy.

Paley's stories may remind the reader of someone familiar. As A. S. Byatt, who has written introductions to Paley's stories, puts it, "She reminds me . . . of my mother at her best, who told terrible stories deadpan, ironing out the awful and the banal into one string of story." The cherished author, then, delivers her pieces from the *vox populi*, from the voice of mother, father, grandpa, grandma, and the next-door neighbor. The stories are told with a candor that strips all pretense—even when the speaker is pretending or posturing. The stories intrigue, even when they are important only to the common denominator of one—the speaker.

As with most of Paley's stories, "Zagrowsky Tells" engenders immediate intimacy between speaker (narrator) and listener (or reader), even if the speaker is socially challenged, bigoted, and egocentric to a fault. Izzy Zagrowsky is all of these to a certain degree, and yet the reader must rely on him for the story. It is the tale of his mentally and emotionally challenged daughter, who gives birth to a child out of wedlock and out of their "color" range. The child, he tells readers, is an intermediate color.

The story (within the story) begins in mid-conversation, but rather than alienate the reader by withholding information, Paley's narrator points out "that tree" and a group of women, as if speaking to a reader who is standing in that park with him—as is Faith, in close enough proximity to see whatever Zagrowsky points out. The intimacy is not lost on the reader, for Paley includes that natural beat of asides, the timbre and tenor shifts appropriate to the range of emotions that Zagrowsky expresses, and also incorporates an objective detailing of third-party accounting. These remarks, combined with the weighty narcissism and personal epiphanies displayed by the xenophobic teller, make the story work on multiple levels.

"THE EXPENSIVE MOMENT"

First published: 1985 (collected in *Later the Same Day*, 1985)
Type of work: Short story

An activist, in her later years, meditates on the choices she has made and on the political legacy left by her generation.

"The Expensive Moment" is a complex and textured fabric of moments, observations, encounters, emotions, and ideas in a particular period of Faith's life. Presumably the same character of Paley's other stories, she here inhabits a world of overtly political discussions and deeper, mellower wisdom.

The people in Faith's life are all vigorously engaged in political and emotional pursuits. Her sons are grown: Tonto is in love, and Richard is an active member of the League for Revolutionary Youth. Faith is in a solid but stale marriage to a furniture store salesman named Jack and is having an intellectually and sexually stimulating affair with an attractive, mercurial China scholar named Nick. Her best friend, Ruth, meets her for lunch at the Art Foods Deli and laments the absence and uncertain future of her daughter Rachel, an errant political revolutionary. Faith reminisces about her own activist past and debates trade and political theory with her son Richard. Along with Ruth and Nick, she attends meetings and dinners where she meets exiled Chinese artists and writers.

At such a meeting, Faith meets Xie Fing, a Chinese poet, "a woman from half the world away who'd lived a life beyond foreignness and had experienced extreme history." The two women become acquainted, and Xie Fing invites herself to see Faith's home, a request that delights and flatters Faith. They spend the next day drinking tea in Faith's kitchen, touring the house and the neighborhood, discussing themselves, their children, their political activities, and the future. The story ends simply on a shared note of wistful regret, both women acknowledging in retrospect how little they knew about preparing their children for the real world.

Throughout the story are a variety of interrelated themes: the disparity between the depth of the individual's concern and his or her limited power to affect the world, the passage of time and the wisdom that comes with it, the burdensome responsibility of raising children and then the painful necessity of letting them go, the contrast between the social and political ideals of the mind and the emotional and physical needs of the body.

These themes come together at various moments; one of the most potent is when Faith thinks back on her anti-draft activities in the 1960's and contemplates the sacrifices that young people sometimes must make for their country or their ideals. Thinking about such sacrifices in the context of Rachel's revolutionary activities, and about the possibility that Richard, too, could someday disappear and never be heard from again, Faith recognizes that there sometimes comes "a moment in history, the expensive moment when everyone his age is called but just a few are chosen by conscience or passion. . . . Then you think sadly, I could have worked harder at raising that child, the one that was once mine."

"The Expensive Moment" is a very thoughtful story that, in examining the difficult choices that history forces an individual to make, by extension examines the cost of all choices. The tone, though relentlessly questioning and sometimes regretful, is never maudlin or angry—those do not seem to be colors on Paley's emotional palette. Rather, she gently mocks political convictions—mentioning the "L.R.Y.'s regular beep-the-horn-if-you-support-Mao meeting" and envisioning John Keats writing verses in a rice paddy in provincial China—even as she portrays a world in which ideas have weight and magnetism. In such a world, convictions—or, for that matter, a healthy and reasoned cynicism—are dramatic and sensual. They establish the connections between people and help Faith and those around her to make sense of their complex lives and find things to value as they travel across the ugly map of contemporary political reality. Such a world is not to be dismissed and avoided; rather, like Faith and Xie Fing, one can only earnestly strive to do one's best and forgive, though never forget, the past.

SUMMARY

In proclaiming herself "a somewhat combative pacifist and cooperative anarchist," Paley brings together the intelligence, awareness, empathy, and self-mockery that illuminate her writing. The saying goes, "actions speak louder than words," and Paley's decades of involvement in social and political issues fill the silences between the infrequent publication of her stories. On their own as well, the stories stand as a delightful, provocative, and moving vision of a segment of society, a collection of unique individuals striving to improve their lives and their world.

Barry Mann; updated by Roxanne McDonald

BIBLIOGRAPHY

By the Author

SHORT FICTION:
The Little Disturbances of Man: Stories of Men and Women in Love, 1959
Enormous Changes at the Last Minute, 1974
Later the Same Day, 1985
The Collected Stories, 1994

POETRY:
Leaning Forward, 1985
New and Collected Poems, 1992
Begin Again: Collected Poems, 2000

NONFICTION:
Peace Calendar, 1988 (with Vera B. Williams)
Conversations with Grace Paley, 1997 (Gerhard Bach and Blaine H. Hall, editors)
Just as I Thought, 1998

MISCELLANEOUS:
Long Walks and Intimate Talks: Stories and Poems, 1991 (with paintings by Vera Williams)

About the Author

Cevoli, Cathy. "These Four Women Could Save Your Life." *Mademoiselle* 89 (January, 1983): 104-107.
DeKoven, Marianne. "Mrs. Hegel-Shtein's Tears." *Partisan Review* 48, no. 2 (1981): 217-223.
Gelfant, Blanche H. "Grace Paley: Fragments for a Portrait in Collage." *New England Review* 3, no. 2 (Winter, 1980): 276-293.
Harrington, Stephanie. "The Passionate Rebels." *Vogue* 153 (May, 1969): 151.
Iannone, Carol. "A Dissent on Grace Paley." *Commentary* 80 (August, 1985): 54-58.
Klinkowitz, Jerome. "Grace Paley: The Sociology of Metafiction." In *Literary Subversions.* Carbondale: Southern Illinois University Press, 1985.

DISCUSSION TOPICS

- In Grace Paley's "The Loudest Voice," Shirley defines Christians as "lonesome." Why?

- In "An Interest in Life," John Raftery claims that Virginia's problems—which he refers to as a "list of troubles"—only add up to "the little disturbances of man . . . ." What significance does this comment have not only in defining his and Virginia's characters but in shaping the underlying theme of the story and the collection of the same title? What does his comment say about his attitude toward women, considering that he deems Virginia's troubles not "real"?

- In the same respect, Virginia comments that "noisy signs of life" are "so much trouble to a man." What does this comment (and the above comment by Raftery) say about gender attitudes?

- Of her many stories, Paley's "The Loudest Voice" is often anthologized and quite popular. What makes the story so accessible, so universal?

- Consider the ambiguousness of the title "Faith in a Tree." What significant meanings do you find attached to the title and present in the story?

- What is the tone of "Faith in a Tree"? How is it conveyed by the author?

- Consider the stories with neighborhood settings. How do these settings reflect the attitude of the narrator? How does each alienate or embrace the narrator?

- As an author, Paley incorporates part of her familial, writing, and political life in her works. Which stories are clearly centered on family and the importance of family? Which are more political in tone or theme? Does the authorial inclusion interfere with the story? In the same respect, do you find her motherly themes an interruption of feminism?

McMurran, Kristin. "Even Admiring Peers Worry That Grace Paley Writes Too Little and Protests Too Much." *People* 11 (February 26, 1979): 22-23.

Paley, Grace. "The Seneca Stories: Tales from the Women's Peace Encampment." *Ms.* 12 (December, 1983): 54-58.

Park, Clara Claiborne. "Faith, Grace, and Love." *The Hudson Review* 38, no. 3 (Autumn, 1985): 481-488.

Scheifer, Ronald. "Grace Paley: Chaste Compactness." In *Contemporary American Women Writers: Narrative Strategies*, edited by Catherine Rainwater and William J. Scheik. Lexington: University Press of Kentucky, 1985.

Smith, Wendy. "Grace Paley." *Publishers Weekly* 227 (April 5, 1985): 71-72.

Sorkin, Adam J. "Grace Paley." In *Twentieth-Century American-Jewish Writers*, edited by Daniel Walden. Vol. 28 in *Dictionary of Literary Biography*. Detroit: Gale Research, 1984.

_____. "What Are We, Animals? Grace Paley's World of Talk and Laughter." *Studies in American Jewish Literature* 2 (1982): 144-154.

DOROTHY PARKER

Born: West End, New Jersey
　　　　August 22, 1893
Died: New York, New York
　　　　June 7, 1967

In her works, Parker displayed an unrivaled wit and irony which revealed a penetrating look at gender roles, failed love, and the absurdities, emptiness, and despair of modern society and romantic relationships.

Library of Congress

BIOGRAPHY

Dorothy Rothschild was born to J. Henry Rothschild, a rich, well-known Jewish clothing merchant, and Eliza A. Rothschild, a schoolteacher of Scottish descent who died a few years after Dorothy's birth. Dorothy's unhappy, lonely childhood was further saddened by the death of her stepmother a couple of years later and eventually the deaths of her brother in 1912 and her father in 1913. She was expelled from Blessed Sacrament Convent School after insisting that the Immaculate Conception was "spontaneous combustion," and was then sent to Miss Dana's finishing school in New Jersey. There she studied and imitated Latin writers such as Horace and Martial, whose epigrams influenced her early poems and witticisms.

After the death of her father, Dorothy lived in a Manhattan boarding house, supporting herself by working in a bookstore and playing piano in a dance school. She published her first poem in *Vanity Fair* magazine and soon after wrote captions ("Brevity is the soul of lingerie") in *Vogue* magazine for fashion ads. She was then hired as dramatic critic for *Vanity Fair.* There she met lifelong friends Robert Benchley and Robert Sherwood. In 1917 she married stockbroker Edwin Parker. Edwin, already a heavy drinker, came back from his military service in World War I and became an alcoholic.

Dorothy, too, became an alcoholic, from both his influence and that of the writers associated with the Algonquin Hotel. She separated from her husband a few years later and eventually divorced in 1928, retaining thereafter the name of "Mrs. Parker."

Together with Benchley and Sherwood, Parker was one of the founding members of the entity called the Algonquin Round Table at the hotel of the same name, where famous literary figures such as Franklin Pierce Adams, Alexander Woolcott, George S. Kaufman, James Thurber, Harold Ross, and others ate lunch and engaged in witty repartee which sometimes found its way into newspaper and magazine columns. Parker was one of the very few major women writers of this inner circle (sometimes called the "vicious circle" for its caustic sarcasm) and the only woman of the founding group who regularly attended. In later years, Parker dismissed the years of the 1920's that she spent at the Algonquin Round Table, saying that she was just "a little Jewish girl trying to be cute."

Nonetheless, at these gatherings Parker honed her razor-sharp sarcasm and became well known for her scathing wisecracks. For example, told that the taciturn President Calvin Coolidge was dead, she quipped, "How can you tell?" When asked to use the word "horticulture" in a sentence, she replied, "You can lead a horticulture but you can't make her think." Her short couplet "Men seldom make passes/ At girls who wear glasses" became a catchphrase of the time. In one of Parker's reviews of actress Katharine Hepburn in a lackluster play, she said, "Miss Hepburn ran the gamut of emotions—from A to B." In fact, one such disparaging comment about an actress who happened to be married to an influential financial backer caused Parker to be fired from her job as a *Vanity Fair* drama critic for being too severe. In sympathy with her, both Sherwood and Benchley quit their positions at the magazine in protest.

After a brief stint as an independent writer sharing with Benchley a cubbyhole office which was so small that "one cubic foot less would have constituted adultery," she found another reviewing job at *Ainslee's Life* magazine. She also contributed freelance verse and criticism to *Life, The Saturday Evening Post,* and the *Ladies' Home Journal* and published her first short story in *The Smart Set* in 1922. Outwardly, Parker's prospects looked bright in this Jazz Age of parties, speakeasies, and sexually liberated flappers. Inwardly, her ruined marriage and separation, her drinking, and the procrastinating, continuous party atmosphere was taking a toll.

After having a devastating romantic affair with playwright and screenwriter Charles McArthur and being abandoned, she had an abortion. The despair, emptiness, and alienation caused her in 1923 to attempt suicide by slashing her wrists. She was found in her hotel by the elevator operator; she recovered after a few days. In the hospital while visiting with her, Benchley said she had to snap out of it and that "you might as well live," a line Parker used at the end of her poem "Resumé." The drinking and series of abortive affairs continued. After another suicide attempt in 1925 using an overdose of sleeping tablets, Benchley tried to shock and shame her by saying that this second attempt was considered by the group a "bloody bore" and that she looked repulsive lying in the bed when he found her—a drooling mess. It was an image Parker would use in describing the character Hazel Morse after her unsuccessful suicide attempt by sleeping pills in the 1929 story "Big Blonde."

Parker's three volumes of poems, *Enough Rope* (1926), *Sunset Gun* (1928), and *Death and Taxes* (1931) were critically acclaimed and commercial best sellers. She began to publish both stories and her acerbic book reviews in *The New Yorker* in 1925. Her collections of stories, *Laments for the Living* (1930) and *After Such Pleasures* (1933), also garnered critical attention, and she won the O. Henry Award in 1929 for "Big Blonde." In about 1934 she married bisexual writer and actor Alan Campbell,

and they moved to Hollywood to cowrite screenplays, most notably *A Star Is Born* (1937) and Hitchcock's *Saboteur* (1942). They divorced in 1947 and remarried in 1950, staying together, off and on, until Campbell died in 1963. Always an outspoken leftist and communist sympathizer, in 1949 Parker was subpoened to testify before the House Committee on Un-American Activities, and she defiantly pleaded the Fifth Amendment. From 1963 she lived in a hotel in New York City, where she died of a heart attack in 1967. She willed her estate to Martin Luther King, Jr., which then, after his assassination, passed to the National Association for the Advancement of Colored People (NAACP).

ANALYSIS

Lost love, love's fleetingness, heartache, and disappointment, are Parker's central themes. Romantic clichés, attitudes, and language are satirically attacked as relationships are exposed as self-serving, pretentious, hypocritical, and founded on miscommunication and people's mistaken perceptions of one another. Society's rules and codes are also ironically critiqued as enforcing these hypocrisies and misperceptions and causing alienation. As critic Arthur Kinney puts it, Parker's women are "self-absorbed snobs, her men philanderers, scoundrels, or subservient husbands." Injustice, insensitivity, and hollowness—whether in the rich upper class (as in "Arrangement in Black and White") or in demanding, fickle male lovers who abandon or ignore the women grown dependent on them (as in "Mr. Durant")—often form the emotional center of the story or poem as it affects the oppressed or rejected woman protagonist. Parker's sympathies always lie with the outcast figures, those who are marginalized because of gender, race, or class. These same figures, however, are sometimes ironized and satirized as delusional, self-absorbed, and responsible for creating their own problems.

Often the wit, humor, and ludicrousness of a given protagonist or speaker or situation masks an underlying despair, loneliness, isolation, and lack of communication. Sometimes Parker openly uses modernist devices to explore these themes—fragmentation, alienation, divided selves, or inner monologues. Sometimes she twists or parodies a romantic convention or form to undercut it ironically. The debate between the inner and outer voice, private and social identity, fun party girl or "dizzy" dame and the melancholy loner mirrors the breakdown and disintegration of the Jazz Age culture: the "boozing," sexually liberated flapper on one side of the coin, and the abandoned, discarded housewife or aging lover on the other. The powerful and rich continue their insensitivity to the oppression of such women, or those people of color or of the underclass—and society not only condones but enforces it.

Parker's poems and stories are marked by their characters' speech. As Parker once explained to Marion Capron in a 1956 interview for *The Paris Review*, her stories told themselves "through what people say." She continued: "I haven't got a visual mind. I hear things." In her poems the speaker normally sets up a meditative, romantic tone of voice, extremely conventional or cliché, often with highbrow diction, which sets up a parallel pattern of a list of characteristics or items. Then, as a joke in a punch line or an epigram from classical Latin authors, the end stanza will have a twist, a line that will reverse all expectations, drastically alter the tone, often associated with a popular saying, lowbrow diction, or a slangy expression, and thus reveal a second tone of voice antithetical to the first.

Sometimes, as with "One Perfect Rose," the line is actually a repetition seen in a new context; other times, it will simply be a drastic reversal of tone and reader expectations, as in "Résumé." The images enumerated usually seem secondary to what the speaker says and how she says it.

In Parker's fiction, there is often a reliance on dialogue rather than plot, usually the conversation of lovers or a young pair who are miscommunicating (as in "Here We Are"), or else an interior monologue of a distraught or despairing woman agonizing over her romance, failed or failing. Characters are usually types or stereotypes (rich, pretentious socialites, young naïve couples, abandoned lovers), and the sketches depend on a tiny slice of time and a key moment of unraveling. The end of the story normally involves a repetition of an image, line, or scene which suggests a closing of the vicious circle in which the protagonist is trapped, or else an extension or continuation of the same private hell in which the character has already resided. For example, the nameless protagonist in "The Waltz," after suffering through a dance with a clumsy partner, agrees to another dance with the same man.

In such monologue stories (of which there are many, including Parker's famous work "A Telephone Call"), there is scarcely any description or setting, and the split between the public, social voice and persona dependent on approval (especially male approval) and the private, personal voice and persona that yearns for independence and escape is the source of the ironic discrepancy and humor. In other stories written from the third-person omniscient perspective, such as "Big Blonde," the narration is detached, cool, and ironic toward the situations and the protagonist, but the same type of divided self and repetition signaling a vicious circle of hell for the main character is nearly always present. In both types of stories, the protagonists are usually seen as self-destructive, passive, and self-absorbed, yet they simultaneously become the victims of society's expectations or male desires. The protagonists' hypocrisy, delusions, and pretensions are ironically exposed, sometimes making them, as with "Big Blonde," both pathetic and tragic.

"Résumé"

First published: 1926 (collected in *Enough Rope*, 1926)
Type of work: Poem

The speaker addresses a "you"—either herself or the reader—listing problems with various ways of killing oneself and in the end deciding to live.

This little eight-line poem, rhyming *ababcdcd*, is one of Parker's most famous, based on her first experience in attempting suicide when she cut her wrists in 1923. The last line ("You might as well live") is exactly what her friend Benchley said to her at the time. It serves as the punch line or the reversal "point" of the classical epigram, with a switch to a resigned or unconcerned tone of voice which contrasts with the methodical catalog of suicide methods. Addressing a "you" which may be herself or the reader, the speaker casually lists various methods she has tried in committing suicide.

The list is grammatically parallel, so that with the exception of the fourth line ("And drugs cause cramp"), each method is named first, as a noun. Then the problem or obstacle with each method is given. The catalog, objectively stated, appears to be a summary of the person's qualifications or achievements—as the title indicates—as if she were applying for a job. The title also puns on the word "resume," which may underscore the end line as a resigned sense that trying to commit suicide is too much trouble in all these ways already tried, and the speaker might as well "resume" her life. This switch in the last line is also highlighted as different by its shift to a five-syllable line, with an accent on the second and fifth syllable—in contrast to all but one of the other lines, which have four syllables and virtually all with an accent on the beginning word.

"ONE PERFECT ROSE"

First published: 1926 (collected in *Enough Rope,* 1926)
Type of work: Poem

In romantic, flowery language, the speaker describes "one perfect rose" which her lover has sent. She wonders why she has never received "one perfect limosine."

"One Perfect Rose" is written in three stanzas of four lines each, rhyming *abab*. The title is also the refrain repeated as the last line of each stanza, having four syllables instead of the iambic pentameter in each of the other lines. The opening two stanzas describe the "one perfect rose" the speaker's love has sent with all the standard romantic clichés and attitudes: He sent it "tenderly" and is "deep-hearted" and uses the poetic language of the flower shop in its note to express his love. In the context of the last stanza, in which the speaker wonders why she has never received "one perfect limosine" as a token of love, the refrain of "one perfect rose" changes from a thing initially desired—an object or "charm" symbolizing her lover's heart in a romantic personification and using slightly archaic and formal language ("single flow'r")—to an undesirable thing, an impractical, nonmaterial, disdained thing. The sarcasm and sigh ("Ah no, it's always just my luck") and the mocking repetition of the "one perfect" formula indicate the switch to the hidden attitude of the last stanza, in direct contrast to that of the opening romantic haze, which is

also underscored by the colloquial language ("do you suppose" and "just my luck").

"SYMPTOM RECITAL"

First published: 1926 (collected in *Enough Rope,* 1926)
Type of work: Poem

The speaker lists her unpleasant symptoms, physical, mental, and emotional, culminating in her realization that she is about to fall in love again.

"Symptom Recital" proceeds, again, to list a series of unpleasant traits or characteristics which the speaker is feeling in a parallel grammatical form and in ten couplets rhyming *aa, bb, cc,* and so on. The rhythm is virtually all iambic tretrameter in four accents per line. The speaker enumerates her bitter mind, her dislike of her legs and hands, her sneering at "simple folks," and her inability to take jokes or find peace. She sees the world and herself as "tripe" and empty, hates herself, senses her "soul" is crushed, and she "shudders" at the thought of men. At the penultimate line, an ellipsis after "men" indicates the pause before the joke, or "turn," as she realizes "I'm due to fall in love again."

Again, the hidden attitude and tone of voice is in conflict with the parade of "symptoms" of disease she recites, which turn out to be those of being in love. Love is not an ecstatic state (the romantic cliché) but a raging disease, a self-torture she will again endure. She is

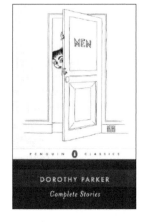

about to go back into hell, a repetition that is also a cycle, a repetition mirrored in the line structures. Each line (with the exception of three that begin with "My" and one with "For") starts out exactly the same: "I" plus a simple verb that shows her "diseased" symptoms. Her recital is also a public artistic rendering, like a piano recital.

"BIG BLONDE"

First published: 1929 (collected in *Laments for the Living*, 1930)
Type of work: Short story

After party girl Hazel Morse marries and shows her melancholy self, she loses her husband, then a series of lovers, until she unsuccessfully commits suicide.

"Big Blonde" is generally considered Parker's best and most serious story. Unlike her usual comic satire, this story opts for a third-person omniscient narrator, dispassionately yet ironically showing the decline of a "dumb blonde," a "party girl." The protagonist's public persona is that of the fun-loving "good sport," a big-busted, peroxide blonde who grows dependent on men's attention. After she marries Herbie, she tries to be her inner melancholy self, crying much of the time. Herbie insists she play the role of the "good sport" and gets her to drink. Eventually Herbie leaves her, toasting her with one last drink, "Here's mud in your eye." "Haze" remains in a drunken haze and hooks up with Ed at a neighbor's house because she feels financially and emotionally dependent. Eventually Ed leaves for Florida because Haze is always sad, and she then enters a series of affairs with a number of men. After her last lover, Art, tells her to cheer up by the time he gets back to town, she takes some sleeping tablets, saying, "Here's mud in your eye." The maid Nettie finds her and calls an elevator boy to get a doctor, and Mrs. Morse is saved. She shares a drink with Nettie, repeating, "Here's mud in your eye." Nettie tells her to cheer up, and Mrs. Morse replies, "Yeah. . . . Sure." The last repetition of the toast and the idea of "cheering up" signal that Mrs. Morse will enter her vicious circle of hell again.

SUMMARY

Though her reputation declined sharply after the 1920's and 1930's, Dorothy Parker has been rediscovered by biographers, feminist writers, and literary critics who more fully appreciate the social and political sides of her works. Her experiments in fictional form and voice especially have garnered her renewed critical interest. One could argue that of all the Algonquin Table members, Parker's literary reputation is now among the highest. In any case, general readers continue to enjoy her writings.

Joseph Francavilla

BIBLIOGRAPHY

By the Author

SHORT FICTION:
"Big Blonde," 1929
Laments for the Living, 1930
After Such Pleasures, 1933
Here Lies: The Collected Stories, 1939
The Portable Dorothy Parker, 1944
The Penguin Dorothy Parker, 1977
Complete Stories, 1995

DRAMA:
Nero, pr. 1922 (with Robert Benchley)
Close Harmony: Or, The Lady Next Door, pr. 1924 (with Elmer Rice)
The Coast of Illyria, pr. 1949 (with Ross Evans)
The Ladies of the Corridor, pr., pb. 1953 (with Arnaud d'Usseau)

SCREENPLAYS:
Business Is Business, 1925 (with George S. Kaufman)
Here Is My Heart, 1934 (with Alan Campbell)

One Hour Late, 1935 (with Campbell)
Mary Burns, Fugitive, 1935
Hands Across the Table, 1935
Paris in Spring, 1935
Big Broadcast of 1936, 1935 (with Campbell)
Three Married Men, 1936 (with Campbell)
Lady Be Careful, 1936 (with Campbell and Harry Ruskin)
The Moon's Our Home, 1936
Suzy, 1936 (with Campbell, Horace Jackson, and Lenore Coffee)
A Star Is Born, 1937 (with Campbell and Robert Carson)
Woman Chases Man, 1937 (with Joe Bigelow)
Sweethearts, 1938 (with Campbell)
Crime Takes a Holiday, 1938
Trade Winds, 1938 (with Campbell and Frank R. Adams)
Flight into Nowhere, 1938
Weekend for Three, 1941 (with Campbell)
The Little Foxes, 1941
Saboteur, 1942 (with Campbell, Peter Viertel, and Joan Harrison)
A Gentle Gangster, 1943
Mr. Skeffington, 1944
Smash-Up: The Story of a Woman, 1947 (with Frank Cavett)
The Fan, 1949 (with Walter Reisch and Ross Evans)
Queen for a Day, 1951
A Star Is Born, 1954

POETRY:
Enough Rope, 1926
Sunset Gun, 1928
Death and Taxes, 1931
Not So Deep as a Well, 1936
Not Much Fun, 1996
Complete Poems, 1999

DISCUSSION TOPICS

- How does Dorothy Parker create the sardonic humor and wit in her works?

- What is the role of the repetition of lines, images, and events in Parker's works?

- To what extent do social forces oppress or victimize the speaker or female protagonist? To what extent do these speakers or protagonists set themselves up for destruction or make themselves victims?

- How do the end stanzas, lines, or scenes demonstrate a reversal of what came before?

- How does the tone of voice change or shift in Parker's poetry and fiction?

- What are Parker's attitudes toward romantic love in her poems and stories?

About the Author

Capron, Marion. "Dorothy Parker." In *Writers at Work: The "Paris Review" Interviews*, edited by Malcolm Cowley. Reprint. New York: Viking Press, 1979.

Frewin, Leslie. *The Late Mrs. Dorothy Parker*. New York: Macmillan, 1986.

Gill, Brendan. Introduction to *The Portable Dorothy Parker*. Rev. and enlarged ed. New York: Viking Press, 1973.

Keats, John. *You Might as Well Live: The Life and Times of Dorothy Parker*. New York: Simon & Schuster, 1970.

Kinney, Arthur. *Dorothy Parker*. Boston: Twayne, 1978.

Meade, Marion. *Dorothy Parker, A Biography: What Fresh Hell Is This?* New York: Villard Books, 1988.

Melzer, Sondra. *The Rhetoric of Rage: Women in Dorothy Parker*. New York: Peter Lang, 1997.

Pettit, Rhonda S. *A Gendered Collision: Sentimentalism and Modernism in Dorothy Parker's Poetry and Fiction*. Madison, N.J.: Fairleigh Dickinson University Press, 2000.

SUZAN-LORI PARKS

Stephanie Diani

Born: Fort Knox, Kentucky
May 10, 1963 (some sources say 1964)

In her plays, screenplays, and novel, Parks revisits history and previously existing literary works in an effort to update them with contemporary issues and characters, creating plays, films, and novels that echo a life that once was while providing insight into life as it is today.

BIOGRAPHY

Suzan-Lori Parks was born in Fort Knox, Kentucky, in 1963 (or by some accounts, 1964), the daughter of Donald and Frances Parks. Donald was a career army officer, and Frances was a university administrator and storyteller. Upon retirement from the service, Donald earned a doctorate and began a second career as a college professor.

The young Parks began writing novels at the age of five. The Parks family moved a great deal during her childhood as a result of her father's army career. She lived in six states before the family was transferred to an army base in Germany. Regarding her life as "an army brat," she says: "I've heard horrible stories about twelve-step groups for army people. But I had a great childhood. My parents were really into experiencing the places we lived." She graduated high school in Germany, choosing to attend a traditional German school rather than the base high school provided by the American government. "In Germany," she remarked during a 1993 interview, "I wasn't a black person, strictly speaking. I was an American who didn't speak the language. I was a foreigner." Parks notes that spending time in a different country had an impact on her as a writer. In a 1996 essay in *Grand Street* magazine, she wrote, "Places far away like Timbuktu, like France, like Africa, they draw us out like dreams. The far-away provides a necessary distance, a new point of reference, a place for perspective." In a

way, spending her adolescent years abroad helped prepare her for a United States, which, during the 1990's and beyond, has become both intrigued and confused by the concepts of multiculturalism.

In 1985, she received her undergraduate degree from Mount Holyoke College with majors in English and German. While at Mount Holyoke, she wrote a short story called "The Wedding Pig" for a class she was taking with author James Baldwin. While preparing the story for class, she realized that the people from the story were with her, "not telling the story, but acting it out—doing it. It was not me, not the voice of confidence or the voice of doubt. It was *outside of me*. And all the stories I wrote for this class were like that." She "performed" the characters as part of the workshop, and Baldwin, who recognized her talent for dialogue and the dramatic, suggested that she try her hand at writing for the stage. She paid attention to his suggestion.

With his advice in mind, she completed her first play, *The Sinner's Place* (pr. 1984), during her senior year at Mount Holyoke. Even though *The Sinner's Place* earned her honors within the department of English, the theater department refused to stage it partly because the play required actual digging on stage, the directors saying, "You can't put dirt on stage! That's not a play!" In a 1996 interview, Parks referred to her initial effort as "only a first try at writing" and that the play "had all the things in it that I'm obsessed with now. Like memory and family and history and the past . . . a lot of dirt on stage which was being dug at." The Mount Holyoke experience was modified a bit when Mary McHenry of the English department gave the budding playwright a copy of Adrienne Kennedy's *Funnyhouse of a Negro* (pr. 1962). This play, along with the work of Ntozake Shange, informed Parks of the possibilities of the stage to tell the kinds of stories that she held in her head. With Kennedy, Shange, and Samuel Beckett informing her work, along with fiction writers William Faulkner, Virginia Woolf, and James Joyce, she determined that she could do anything she wanted with language, character, and plot. In a 1995 interview, she said, "I'm fascinated with what they were allowed to do, I guess. What Joyce allowed himself to do, what Beckett allowed himself to do, and Woolf . . . what they got away with." Following her Mount Holyoke undergraduate training, Parks traveled to London, where she studied acting for a year, and returned to the United States to study briefly at the Yale School of Drama.

While at Yale, Parks met Liz Diamond, a director who has since worked as a close collaborator. At age twenty-eight, her second play, *Imperceptible Mutabilities in the Third Kingdom*, was produced in 1989 in Brooklyn by BACA Downtown and not only received an Obie Award but also drew the attention of theater critic Mel Gussow of *The New York Times*; he called her "the year's most promising playwright." Following this success, she worked briefly at the Yale Repertory, which produced three of her plays, before she moved on to the New York Shakespeare Festival/Public Theatre, which produced her Pulitzer Prize-winning drama *Topdog/Underdog* in 2001.

From the stage, she turned her attention to film, writing *Girl 6* (1996) for Spike Lee and an adaptation of Toni Morrison's 1998 novel *Paradise* for Harpo, Oprah Winfrey's production company. In 2003, she published her first novel, *Getting Mother's Body*, adding yet another phase to her developing career. In 2001, she received a MacArthur Foundation "genius" award, firmly establishing her as one of the premier American writers. Before his death in 1987, Baldwin referred to Parks as "an utterly astounding and beautiful creature who may become one of the most valuable artists of our time."

In 2005, she lived in Venice Beach, California, with her husband, musician Paul Oscher, and taught at the California Institute for the Arts.

ANALYSIS

Parks has written an essay titled "Elements of Style," which contains her personal concept for developing plays for the stage. In this essay, she refers to her "characters" as "figures which take up residence inside me," figures that do not fit inside the more traditional forms or "the naturalism of, say, Lorraine Hansberry." Regarding her style, she writes, "As a playwright, I try to do many things: explore the form, ask questions, make a good show, tell a good story, ask more questions, take nothing for granted." She bases her new form on repetition and revision.

> Repetition: we accept it in poetry and call it "incremental refrain." For the most part, incremental refrain creates a weight and rhythm. In dramatic writing it does the same . . . it's not just repetition but repetition and *revision*. And in drama change, revision, is the thing.

As an author's note to her published plays, Parks provides a schematic to assist the reader in understanding her methodologies. The following is taken from the published version of *Venus*:

> In *Venus* I'm continuing the use of my slightly unconventional theatrical elements. Here's a road map.

- *(Rest)*
  Take a little time, a pause, a breather; make a transition.

- A Spell
  An elongated and heightened *(Rest)*. Denoted by repetition of figures' names with no dialogue. Has sort of an architectural look:

  The Venus
  The Baron Docteur
  The Venus
  The Baron Docteur

  This is a place where the figures experience their pure true simple state. While no action or stage business is necessary, directors should fill this moment as they best see fit.

- [Brackets in the text indicate optional cuts for production.]

- (Parentheses around dialogue indicate softly spoken passages (asides; sotto voce).)

Add to these characteristics Parks's unusual approach to writing dialogue (many critics refer to her accomplishment as poetry) and it is clear that she is revolutionizing the theater of the future.

Not all of her critics have viewed Parks favorably. Several African American reviewers have taken issue with her perceived skewed vision of the black experience. Even though Parks has dealt in her work with such African American issues as the middle passage, mistreatment in and by Western culture, and contemporary ghetto life, she has been chastened by a number of African American scholars. In her essay "The Re-objectification and Re-commodification of Saartjie Baartman in Suzan-Lori Parks's *Venus*" that appeared in the Winter, 1997, issue of *African American Review,* Jean Young writes, "Parks's slippery interpretation of the historical record surrounding the tragedy of *Venus* (Baartman) is in and of itself a tragedy." Parks responded to such criticism in a postperformance discussion led by Alisa Solomon. She said:

> It's insulting when people say my plays are about what it's about to be black—as if that's all we think about, as if our life is not about race. It's about being alive . . . Why does everyone think that white artists make art and black artists make statements?

In her essay, "An Equation for Black People Onstage," Parks writes,

> There is no such thing as THE Black Experience; that is, there are many experiences of being Black which are included under the rubric. Just think of all the different kinds of African peoples.

IMPERCEPTIBLE MUTABILITIES IN THE THIRD KINGDOM

First produced: 1989 (first published, 1995)
Type of work: Play

Winner of the Obie Award as best Off-Broadway play in 1989, this work employs poetry, indirection, metaphor, and persistent repetition to convey the horror of the slave trade. The play makes the loss of more than nine million African lives unaccounted for during the slave trade era immediate and personal.

Imperceptible Mutabilities in the Third Kingdom won for Parks her first Obie Award as the best Off-Broadway play of 1989 and led theater critic Robert Brustein to call her "a most unusual addition to the growing ranks of female playwrights."

Filled with "figures" rather than characters, the play deals obliquely with the slave trade when more than nine million Africans went missing. Written in what director Liz Diamond calls wonderful poetry, *Imperceptible Mutabilities in the Third Kingdom* defines contemporary and traditional dramaturgical methods while using indirection, metaphor, and persistent repetition to convey the horror of the slave trade and its impact on the lives of those who either experienced it or followed it. Shawn-Marie Garrett in her essay "The Possession of Suzan-Lori Parks" writes:

> Parks has dramatized some of the most painful aspects of the black experience . . . . Yet even as her plays summon up the brutality of the past, they do so in a manner that is, paradoxically, both horrific and comic—irresistibly or disrespectfully so, depending on your point of view.

Parks's opening question and answer provide a ringing tribute to the nature of what is to follow:

> CHARLENE: How dja get through it?
> MOLLY: Mm not through it.

As the first of her four plays which "re-member" history, Parks is exploring her love of language in a fashion that reflects her profound influences provided by Gertrude Stein, Woolf, Joyce, and most especially Beckett. Diamond, her long-time collaborator, stated in a Fall, 1995, interview published in *TDR:*

> The first time I read a Suzan-Lori Parks play, I flashed to Wittgenstein, not Gertrude Stein. There seemed to be a utilitarian focus to Parks' words—a surgical intensity—that belied her play's surface impression of hypnotic languor. Surely this is what Wittgenstein meant when he spoke of language games, I thought, and the contingencies of various meanings in languages' various contexts, words having uses and not mere definitions, family resemblances of certain words, etc. Wittgenstein believed that the philosopher's task was to bring words back from their metaphysical usage

to their everyday usage, and Parks' drama seems to play between the boundaries of both.

As Diamond notes, Parks's drama has more in common with jazz than with the dramaturgy which preceded it.

VENUS

First produced: 1996 (first published, 1997)
Type of work: Play

With eighteenth century Europe as backdrop and racial stereotyping as subject, Venus *relates the story of Saartjie Baartman, an African woman known throughout Europe as "The Hottentot Venus." Baartman is offered in public display because of her "abnormal" body parts in a play which won for Parks her second Obie Award for best Off-Broadway play of the year.*

With a cast of four and a chorus of five, thirty-one scenes, and a number of original songs, *Venus*—the true-life story of Saartjie Baartman, the Venus Hottentot—is brought to life by Parks; she received her second Obie Award as the best Off-Broadway play of the year in 1996 for it. In 1810, Baartman, a member of the Khoi-San peoples of South Africa, was transported to London and Paris, where she was dubbed "The Hottentot Venus" and put on public display in near nude conditions. Her "act" generated a thriving business: the display of her genitalia and buttocks, determined to be "abnormal" by European standards, was not only the source of the attraction but also became the model for black female uniqueness during the Victorian era. These facts provide Parks with the opportunity to fashion a drama that concerns itself less with history than with the quirkiness of society. *Venus* follows Baartman's experience in Europe from her departure from Africa to her untimely death in Paris and finds fascination with the relationship between this "Venus" and her sponsor, the Baron Docteur, thereby becoming a most unusual love story.

As in her other historical dramas, *Venus* pays more attention to paradox, humor, irony, and personal tragedy than to the facts. Parks takes advantage of the unusual situation surrounding the life

and times of Saartjie Baartman to bring contemporary racial clichés and stereotypes into clear focus. Using her unique style of dialogue and relying on Brechtian techniques, she develops a situation of the side-show carnival where exhibitions of the strange and exotic were common. In her own words, Parks saw Baartman as "vain, beautiful, intelligent, and yes, complicit. I write about the world of my experience."

IN THE BLOOD

First produced: 1999 (first published, 2000)
Type of work: Play

A play modeled on Nathaniel Hawthorne's The Scarlet Letter *(1850), Parks's remarkable dramatic transposition is a heartbreaking saga of a woman condemned to live beneath an urban bridge with her five children, each the product of different fathers. Combining comedy, social commentary, and confessions, Parks has taken the Hawthorne classic into new and unexpected terrain.*

One of two plays by Parks coming from Hawthorne's classic novel *The Scarlet Letter, In the Blood* introduces us to Hester, a woman of the street who has five children by five different fathers. Hester lives in a state of illiteracy while claiming as home for herself and her children the underside of a bridge. She is offered ineffectual help by her closest friend, Amiga Gringa, by a social worker, by a roaming medical doctor, and by an evangelical street preacher. Help is seemingly at hand when Chili, the father of her first "treasure," Jabber, appears and offers her a chance for rescue. However, when he learns of her four other children, he quickly withdraws, never to return. Her friend's offer of help is for Hester to pose with her in a series of pornographic opportunities. The social worker has a job readied for the mother, a job that would necessitate her children being taken over by the state. The doctor desires to remove Hester's reproductive organs to prevent her from having additional children. Finally, the minister refuses to acknowledge any responsibility for Hester or for the child he gave her. The only letter of the alphabet that her literate son, Jabber, has taught her is "A," a clear reference to the Hawthorne original in which Hester Prine must wear the scarlet "A." When vandals etch the word "slut" on the walls of the bridge, Jabber refuses to read it for her. However, in the end, when the same word is used by the evangelist, Jabber cannot contain himself over the smear leveled at his mother, resulting in a tragic ending and Hester's scrawling the letter "A" on the ground using her son's spilled blood as ink. In *The New York Times*, Margo Jefferson wrote,

> Suzan-Lori Parks's extraordinary new play, *In the Blood*, is about the way we live now, and it is truly harrowing. Ms. Parks's writing has grown leaner and hungrier, and you will leave this play feeling pity and terror. We cannot turn away, and we do not want to, and because it is a work of art, you will leave thrilled, even comforted, by its mastery.

During the writing of *In the Blood*, Parks began a second play on the same basic theme. In *Fucking A* (pr. 2000), again her lead character is named Hester, only in this instance the red "A" has been branded on her chest and stands for "abortionist." Written in nineteen scenes and punctuated with music of her own composition, *Fucking A* represents a departure from the Hawthorne original and invites comparison to Bertolt Brecht's classic *Mutter Courage und ihre Kinder* (pr. 1941, pb. 1949; *Mother Courage and Her Children*, 1941).

TOPDOG/UNDERDOG

First produced: 2001 (first published, 2001)
Type of work: Play

Two brothers, Booth and Lincoln, strive to bring meaning into their lives: one is a street hustler, the other an impersonator of President Abraham Lincoln on the night of his murder. Both want more than the limitations that life offers them at the moment. Topdog/Underdog *is a drama of passion which deals obliquely with class distinctions and racism without asking for judgment.*

In *Topdog/Underdog*, Parks returns to a motif that she introduced in *The America Play* (pr. 1993). In this work, set in "A great hole. In the middle of nowhere. The hole is an exact replica of The Great Hole of History," Parks introduces a black character called simply "The Foundling Father" who portrays a white-faced Abraham Lincoln in an arcade.

The Foundling Father is shot repeatedly by "A Variety of Visitors" playing John Wilkes Booth. A cap pistol is placed to the back of the Foundling Father's head, he is shot, he tumbles forward to the floor, and the Visitor proclaims a statement of his or her choice, some actually opting to ejaculate Booth's famous quotation taken from William Shakespeare's *Julius Caesar*.

Topdog/Underdog, which received the Pulitzer Prize in 2002, requires a single interior set. In this play, Parks introduces two of her most realistic characters (a graduation of sorts from her previously identified "figures") in the form of two brothers: Lincoln and Booth. The two share an apartment as well as their histories, aspirations, money, and women in what emerges as a tragic explosion of failed dreams. Lincoln at the beginning of the play is "The Foundling Father" from *The America Play*: He portrays President Lincoln at an arcade and is shot repeatedly for the sport and entertainment of paying patrons. The situation calls to mind Parks's statements regarding repetition and revision. Even though Lincoln loses his job at the arcade (as a result, he is told, of the owner's need to downsize his operation), the action of Booth shooting Lincoln continues, only this time it is for real.

Booth, the younger of the two brothers, is discontented with his station in life and attempts to master the street con-game of three-card monte by changing his name to "3 Card." Lincoln has forfeited the con-game for the more legitimate work of portraying Lincoln, but he has not forgotten the special and all-important secrets of the con as he practices his skills on an ill-prepared Booth. The con-game is an action found in several of Parks's plays and forms an important plot point in her novel *Getting Mother's Body*.

Topdog/Underdog is recognizably Parks's most accessible play to date. In it, she manifests her own words when she wrote in "Elements of Style": "We should understand that realism, like other movements in other artforms, is a specific response to a certain historical fact." In addition, she accomplishes another tenet of her dramaturgy by removing the white character from her drama. To her, as expounded upon in her essay "An Equation for Black People Onstage," drama about black oppression at the hands of white people is ridiculous. According to her definition, black drama has historically been drama about black oppression. She writes:

> Black presence on stage is more than a sign or messenger of some political point . . . I write plays because I love Black people. As there is no single "Black Experience," there is no single "Black Aesthetic" and there is no one way to write or think or feel or dream or interpret or to be interpreted.

Topdog/Underdog finds widespread success because it does not require that the audience, regardless of its ethnic makeup, pass judgment on the notion of black oppression.

GETTING MOTHER'S BODY

First published: 2003
Type of work: Novel

In the tradition of William Faulkner's classic As I Lay Dying *(1930), Parks turned to multiple narrators for her first novel,* Getting Mother's Body. *The passion which informs Parks's comic traipse across west Texas of the 1960's is greed: Billy Beede's mother was buried behind a motel in Arizona and now that the plot of land is being developed to house a shopping mall, the body must be removed and with it, the jewels that accompanied her burial.*

Parks admits to being captivated by Faulkner's novel *As I Lay Dying*, a work told through multiple points of view. *Getting Mother's Body* uses a similar technique as well as some of Faulkner's other structural and plot devices. Just as Faulkner's tale is one of travel (the family is returning mother's dead body to Jefferson County for burial), so is Parks's (Billy Beede, with the help of her friends and relatives, must travel to Arizona to exhume her mother's body before her burial site is destroyed by a new shopping center complex). In Faulkner's book, the mother speaks from her coffin; the same is true in Parks's novel, only in this instance, the mother, Willa Mae Beede, sings her thoughts since she had been a blues singer in life. As in the Faulkner original, the voices of the characters

in Parks's novel are clear and distinct, capturing the essence and variability of multiple narrations that Faulkner introduced.

In 1963, when Billy Beede, the sixteen-year-old pregnant heroine, learns that her mother's body is to be moved before the shopping-center developers begin clearing the land where she is buried, she determines to make the trip from West Texas where she lives to Arizona, not to rescue her mother's body but to secure the "treasures" that had been buried with her: a pearl necklace and a diamond ring. She is joined by a remarkably diverse cadre of relatives, all on the quest for varying reasons, most being of a money-grubbing nature. Billy's journey and her motivations for making it shift the closer she gets to her destination as well, as her true feelings not only for her mother but also for all those around her become apparent. The trek is filled with unexpected occurrences and humorous developments. The final resolution is rare for Ms. Parks in that it is satisfying and complete within itself.

SUMMARY

One of Suzan-Lori Parks's distinguishing features is her unique approach to capturing "black English." Brustein, in his essay "What Do Women Playwrights Want?" writes,

> Parks deconstructs language as a means of establishing the place of blacks in recorded history . . . It is refreshing indeed to come upon an African American play that values poetry over realism.

The compilation of an impressive body of work before her fortieth birthday speaks well for the future not only of Suzan-Lori Parks but for the American theatrical scene as a whole. This writer and many others await with great anticipation Parks's next spurt of creativity, whether it be for stage, page, or screen.

Kenneth Robbins

BIBLIOGRAPHY

By the Author

DRAMA:
The Sinner's Place, pr. 1984, pb. 1995
Betting on the Dust Commander, pr. 1987, pb. 1995
Imperceptible Mutabilities in the Third Kingdom, pr. 1989, pb. 1995
The Death of the Last Black Man in the Whole Entire World, pr. 1990, pb. 1995
Devotees in the Garden of Love, pr. 1991, pb. 1995
The America Play, pr. 1993, pb. 1995
The America Play, and Other Works, pb. 1995
Venus, pr. 1996, pb. 1997
In the Blood, pr. 1999, pb. 2000
Fucking A, pr. 2000, pb. 2001
The Red Letter Plays, pb. 2001 (includes *In the Blood* and *Fucking A*)
Topdog/Underdog, pr., pb. 2001

LONG FICTION:
Getting Mother's Body, 2003

SCREENPLAYS:
Anemone Me, 1990
Girl 6, 1996

RADIO PLAYS:
Pickling, 1990
The Third Kingdom, 1990
Locomotive, 1991

About the Author
Bernard, Louise. "The Musicality of Language: Redefining History in Suzan-Lori Parks's *The Death of the Last Black Man in the Whole Entire World." African American Review* 31, no. 4 (Winter, 1997): 687-699.
Brown, Rosellen. "Stumbling from Stage to Page." *New Leader* 86, no. 3 (May/June, 2003): 37-39.
Brustein, Robert. "The Element of Surprise." *New Republic* 222, no. 4 (January 24, 2000): 31-35.
_____. "What Do Women Playwrights Want?" *New Republic* 206, no. 15 (April 13, 1992): 28-31.
Bryant, Aaron. "Broadway, Her Way." *Crisis (The New)* 109, no. 2 (March/April, 2002): 43-46.
Drukman, Steven. "A Show Business Tale/Tail." *American Theatre* 13, no. 5 (May/June, 1996): 4-6.
_____. "Suzan-Lori Parks and Liz Diamond." *TDR* 39, no. 3 (Fall, 1995): 56-76.
Elam, Harry J., Jr. "The Postmulticultural: A Tale of Mothers and Sons." In *Crucible of Cultures: Anglophone Drama at the Dawn of the New Millennium*, edited by Marc Maufort and Franca Bellarsi. Brussels: Peter Lang, 2002.

DISCUSSION TOPICS

- What elements of Nathaniel Hawthorne's novel *The Scarlet Letter* (1850) does Suzan-Lori Parks incorporate in her drama *In the Blood*?
- Elaborate on the "truth" (or lack thereof) of Parks's statement that white artists create art while black artists make statements.
- What are the differences between what Parks calls "figures" and more traditional dramatists call "characters"?
- Compare Parks's novel *Getting Mother's Body* to William Faulkner's *As I Lay Dying* (1930).
- Who was Saartjie Baartman and how did Parks use or abuse her real-life story in her play *Venus*?
- Explain Parks's fascination with Abraham Lincoln.

Garrett, Shawn-Marie. "The Possession of Suzan-Lori Parks." *American Theatre* 17, no. 8 (October, 2000).

Graham, Don. "Not-So-Great Plains." *Texas Monthly* 31, no. 10 (October, 2003): 74-78.

Rayner, Alice, and Harry J. Elam, Jr. "Unfinished Business: Reconfiguring History in Suzan-Lori Parks's *The Death of the Last Black Man in the Whole Entire World.*" *Theatre Journal* 46, no. 4 (December, 1994): 447-461.

Roach, Joseph. "The Great Hole of History: Liturgical Silence in Beckett, Osofisan, and Parks." *The South Atlantic Quarterly* 100, no. 1 (Winter, 2001): 307-316.

Ryan, Katy. "'No Less Human': Making History in Suzan-Lori Parks's *The America Play.*" *Journal of Dramatic Theory and Criticism* 13, no. 2 (Spring, 1999): 81-94.

Smith, Wendy. "Words as Crossroads: Suzan-Lori Parks." *Publishers Weekly* 250, no. 19 (May 12, 2003): 37-39.

Sova, Kathy. "A Better Mirror." *American Theatre* 17, no. 3 (March, 2000): 32.

Wood, Jacqueline. "Sambo Subjects: 'Declining the Stereotype' in Suzan-Lori Parks's *The Death of the Last Black Man in the Whole Entire World.*" *Studies in the Humanities* 28, nos. 1/2 (June-December, 2001): 109-120.

Young, Jean. "The Re-objectification and Re-commodification of Saartjie Baartman in Suzan-Lori Parks's *Venus.*" *African American Review* 31, no. 4 (Winter, 1997): 699-709.

GARY PAULSEN

Born: Minneapolis, Minnesota
May 17, 1939

Telling stories of survival without romanticism or sentiment, Paulsen's young adult fiction defines the enormity of the natural world and surrounds his central figures within it. Whether or not these characters possess the imagination, adaptability, and willingness to suffer through their hardships becomes crucial to their success and survival.

BIOGRAPHY

Upon first glance, Gary Paulsen bears strong resemblance to his oft-compared-to literary antecedent Ernest Hemingway. Ubiquitous with a grayed beard, worn denims, and a fishing cap, Paulsen appears to be a surviving vestige of one of his own stories. Born May 17, 1939, in Minneapolis to Oscar, a military officer, and Eunice, a factory worker in a munitions plant, Paulsen led a nomadic life in his early years as a self-proclaimed army brat.

The constant uprooting caused by his father's military career placed stress on the Paulsen household. In fact, Paulsen claims not to have even met his father until he was seven when the family was stationed in the Philippines. Even then, Paulsen recalls spending most of his time wandering the streets of Manila alone looking for adventure because of his parents' strained relationship. This tension in his family played havoc with the young Paulsen. He remembers his mother as a promiscuous, if not adulterous, wife who constantly abandoned her commitment to both her husband, who himself was struggling with alcoholism, and her son. Paulsen found security, though, in his early teens when he left his parents to live stateside with more stable relatives—his grandmother and various aunts.

It was during this transition period that Paulsen, somewhat serendipitously, fell into his future career as a writer. Though never a dedicated academic—he barely graduated high school and only completed parcels of time at Bemidji College in 1957-1958 and the University of Colorado in 1976—Paulsen was a reader. He became so only by chance when, on a frigid winter day during his youth, he entered a public library to warm himself. When the librarian offered him a library card and introduced him to westerns, science fiction, and the occasional classic, Paulsen recalls having a great thirst in his life finally slaked. He became a steady and omnivorous reader.

That hunger for reading would be one of the few constants in Paulsen's early and multifaceted career; he became a renaissance man of sorts by virtue of necessity. To pay for his first college experience, he became a hunter and trapper for the state of Minnesota; he would later return to that line of work in the late 1970's aided by a team of sled dogs donated by a friend. Between that time, Paulsen served with the Army from 1959 to 1962, became a field engineer, falsified his own resume in order to pursue writing as an editor of a magazine in California, and somewhere along the way took the time to teach, act, sing, and farm, among myriad other vocations.

While writing prolifically during that time, his children's writing career only came to full bloom as result of an obviating circumstance: In 1977, his novel *Winterkill* (1976) had a libel lawsuit brought against it. Paulsen eventually won the suit, but he was left marred by the experience and felt a call to quit publishing and return to trapping. He recalls the intensity of working his dog team along a 60-mile stretch of Minnesota during this period as so invigorating and spiritually motivating that he felt reborn within the moment. He resolved to quit trapping as a profession and pursued a determined hobby racing in two Alaskan Iditarods in 1983 and 1985. The angina he suffered as a result of this experience ended his hobby and helped to refocus his energies into writing *Dogsong* (1985).

Since that time, Paulsen continued to write at an assiduous clip, publishing more than 175 books and 200 articles. By 2005, he resided with his wife, Ruth Ellen Wright, an artist and occasional illustrator of his books, in New Mexico.

ANALYSIS

Anyone choosing to familiarize oneself with the stories of Paulsen might acknowledge his debt to his literary predecessor, Jack London (Paulsen has written an introduction to an edition of London's 1903 *Call of the Wild*). Paulsen's work might be best recognized within the literary movement that London, himself, is most readily identified with: American naturalism. Paulsen's naturalism asks the reader to study the characters objectively within his fictions working in or out of concert with capricious nature. Paulsen's characters thereby often operate by instinct and self-governed passion. Their success or failure is largely outside of their control and given to the whim of an indifferent nature, but often they can survive if youth, imagination, and adaptability is on their side.

In connection with this viewpoint, Paulsen often writes of youthful men from a third-person omniscient perspective. This approach allows for tension to heighten in his plots by distancing the reader from the security of the protagonist's thoughts and illustrating them as alone with only their wits to aid them against their isolation. In some cases, Brian in *Hatchet* (1987) and Russel in *Dogsong*, for example, this concept can be seen as obvious within their situation: Brian's plane crash leaves him alone to survive in the woods, and Russel specifically takes his spiritual journey by himself as he feels that all who surround him have been corrupted by civilization. Other times, however, the feeling of isolation is more subtle. For example, in *Soldier's Heart* (1998), the Union Army surrounds Charley Goddard—he is never alone—but within his own mind he can neither find nor appreciate any offered companionship or bond. When the possibility of a connection with another soldier seems likely, the nature of the war intervenes with that soldier's untimely death.

With this isolation, Paulsen's writing is characterized by a terse, limited dialogue and a very clean prose style often critically compared to Hemingway. His narratives are often constructed upon the observation and reporting of the characters' situation with scant glances into their minds. This reporter's stance offers the reader a powerful, never-retreating and often unforgiving view of the world in all its glory and infamy; Paulsen spares the reader no detail, no matter how visceral, in order to preserve the reality of the situation. For example, when the medics must operate out in the chilly cold of the Civil War in winter, a lead surgeon instructs Charley to create a barrier out of the corpses of fallen soldiers to cut the wind. Exhausted both mentally and physically after doing do, he falls asleep next to the wall to keep warm.

Survival, as such, proves to be Paulsen's most dominant theme. In many instances, in order to survive, Paulsen's characters arguably revert to a feral state that they were not aware existed within them, as when Brian eats innumerable raw turtle eggs in order to stave off starvation or when Charley discovers an insatiable bloodlust to kill Confederate soldiers when he feels that his survival is predicated upon either killing or being killed. Likewise, the incursion of civilization upon nature, the apparent facade of humanity's belief that it can domesticate the wild, frequents Paulsen's stories and is vilified. More often than not, characters who do survive his stories quickly discover that nature will tame them before they will tame it. Thus, Paulsen's figures often undergo a transformation: Brian, Russel, and Charley all regard it as a form of rebirth where their old selves dissolve and fall away under the weight of their new circumstances.

DOGSONG

First published: 1985
Type of work: Novel

Fearing the loss of his cultural mores, a young boy takes a dog team on a quest to reclaim his traditions and find himself.

At times almost impressionistic in its narrative, *Dogsong* tells the story of Russel Susskit, a young Inuit living in the shadows of what he perceives as

Western society's incursion upon his Eskimo culture. Partially inspired by a seven-day-run Paulsen himself took in Minnesota during his trapping days and his two runs of the nearly twelve-hundred-mile Iditarod, the plot approaches the idea that to know oneself is to know nature and reject civilization and all its trappings.

Western civilization, for Russel, brings about the destruction of tradition, whether that comes in the form of his father's abandonment of tribal religion in lieu of accepting the missionary's Jesus Christ or the disintegration of his people's songs—the oral history which they no longer sing. His father notices Russel's discontent and acquiesces to him finding himself through the old ways. There is almost a resigned desperation to Russel's father since he has become so far separated from his own culture that he cannot teach Russel of the old traditions—he can only point him to a surrogate who can: the elder Oogruk.

Even to Russel, the idea is somewhat preposterous: While the community venerates and respects Oogruk's role in their society, he is blind and therefore considered invalid and he is also considered wildly eccentric and completely out of touch with the contemporary mores encroaching upon his people. Oogruk, however, becomes the panacea for Russel's angst when he sets him off on a path with no direction except self-fulfillment. He teaches Russel the traditional ways and values of the hunter, and he teaches him about the value of his pack dogs.

The dogs themselves are possibly the most complex element of *Dogsong*. Both his property and his custodians, the dogs are an invaluable part of Russel's mission and survival. Oogruk intuits that Russel must drive the dogs north to come to a rite of passage where he will become a man. In this process, Russel comes to discover the dogs as idiosyncratically as he does the world around him. They become characters within their own right with their own personalities, particularly the lead dog who becomes, in many ways, Russel's copilot and confidant.

Russel's run, like the parentage of the wolf/dogs themselves, is hybrid, part waking dream, part reality—the further Russel journeys into it, the more he begins to lose distinction between the two until his narrative loses its borders and becomes a "dreamrun" of indistinguishable qualities. The dream itself seems to bring Russel closer to the traditions that he seeks. By the same token, it is

marked with insidious portents pointing to his death, the death of others, and the death of great beasts—all of which seem to come at his hands. As the dual narratives of dream and reality continue to blur, these potentially grim omens come to fruition when he discovers an outcast Eskimo girl nearly frozen to death in a storm. Arguably, Russel discovers his purpose when he determines to overcome the death that haunts his dreams by saving the life of the girl and her unborn child. The resultant events become the song eponymous with the novel's title.

HATCHET

First published: 1987
Type of work: Novel

Stranded alone in the Canadian wilderness after a plane crash, a young boy must adapt to his new environment in order to survive until help arrives.

In many ways, *Hatchet* manifests as a contemporary take on the *Robinson Crusoe* plot. Paulsen recalls an incident during his stay in the Philippines where he saw an airplane crash, with military personnel unable to save the victims; it has been speculated that these youthful memories partially influenced the plot of *Hatchet*. The story's thirteen-year-old protagonist, Brian Robeson, finds himself at the mercy of the Canadian woods after the Cessna 406

taking him up to oil fields where his father works as a mechanical engineer crash lands into a lake.

While the plot focuses on the survival narrative, a conflict of Brian versus nature, a large internal conflict echoes throughout *Hatchet*. The entire reason Brian flies out to see his father in Canada is the result of his parent's divorce; in flashback, the reader learns that Brian discovers his mother during an extramarital affair. That Brian retains that information as a secret, constantly reiterated throughout the story as he ponders his predicament, compels the reader to wonder how much blame he places on his mother for his situation of being stranded. Had Brian disclosed the secret to his father, the assumption is made that his father might have gained different visitation rights rather than flying out for summer visits, which in turn has caused Brian's predicament. This inherent causality within *Hatchet* becomes a point of disgust and self-loathing for Brian as he discovers that perhaps he is most at blame for not speaking up when he had the opportunity.

The hatchet, itself, given to him as a parting gift from his mother, becomes a complicated symbol within the story. As Brian's only real tool, it comes to symbolize his survival as he uses it to fashion other tools: spears, arrows, fire, and shelter. By the same token, it also comes to symbolize death through its connection to his mother and its penultimate use in Brian's eventual escape as he hollows through the plane's fuselage in his attempt to get to its emergency survival pack. When he comes upon it, he discovers the pilot's remains still sitting in the cockpit. The body has been eaten away to the bare skeleton by the same fish he has been eating to survive in the wild.

In these scenarios, Brian begins to understand himself and his place within the world anew after having faced his own imminent mortality and defeated it. As nature throws what the cloistered urban Brian would have seen as impossible scenario after impossible scenario, this new Brian finds ways to adapt and survive, growing leaner and stronger by the process. Where at one point he considers using his hatchet to commit suicide after not lighting his signal fire in time to alert a passing search plane, the isolation-hardened Brian grows from berry-forager to meat-hunter and finally to confronting nature, itself, by novel's end as one of its own inhabitants.

The novel, itself, is somewhat episodic—time for Brian exists through a series of developmental firsts: first shelter, first fire, or first meat. In this manner, Paulsen shows Brian evolving from a boy who acclimates what he knows about survival and living in the wilderness from his own culture's eyes (most often through television shows and films) to the gradual relearning process of seeing his new world on its own terms. It is only when Brian abandons hope of returning to his old life and accepts his new world as his home that he grows to the extent that he can survive as a member of it.

SOLDIER'S HEART

First published: 1998
Type of work: Novella

A young Minnesota boy's romantic misconceptions about the Civil War are quickly dispelled when he lies about his age and enlists to fight.

Soldier's Heart deviates from Paulsen's other work as it does not directly have autobiographical analogues to his own life. However, it is partially modeled on the real-life exploits of Charley Goddard, a Minnesota farm boy who decides to enlist in the Union Army during an earlier point in the Civil War.

Therein, the story itself does have biographical tenets, but the narrative distances itself from Charley (as Charley does from others during the war) by unabashedly looking at his naïveté and romanticism surrounding the conflict. He enlists thinking that this shooting war, as he calls it, will be more exciting than a circus, even though he has never been to a circus either. Paulsen continues with his trend toward family dissolution by having Charley leave his mother behind in Minnesota for the war under the auspices that he can occupy his dead father's position as a provider for the family. Knowing that he is driven to the war, Charley's mother relents.

His romantic delusions, though, are quickly shattered. Couched within Paulsen's laconic narrative is an exhaustive history lesson of the Civil War from Charley's perspective. The longer he remains within the conflict, the more the battles, deaths, and disturbing sensory impressions he receives change his perspective from boy to man in a matter of months. Age no longer becomes a determinate factor of maturity for Charley; though possibly younger than Nelson, a new recruit to his unit, he

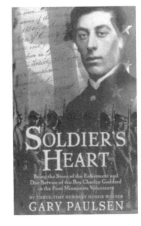

is not nearly as green as Nelson, and that becomes a determining factor of life and death.

Death itself surrounds Charley. He quickly determines that his own is imminent and that there is nothing that can stop it. Just as quickly, Charley begins to covet death, not for himself necessarily but for that of his enemy, the rebel Confederate army. This does not come without complexity either. In one of the more complex exchanges of the entire work, Charley and an unnamed rebel discuss trading supplies while both are stationed in a hot zone. Charley comes to discover that these people he is fighting and killing are people very similar to himself: young farmers with families back at home. When the war ends and he finally returns home, it becomes difficult for Charley to separate himself from the atrocities that he has seen and has committed from the civility that now surrounds him. Survival, at this point, becomes one of reintegra-tion into a world he tried to protect but does not understand anymore.

Summary

A terse and versatile writer, Gary Paulsen muddies the waters of later nineteenth and early twentieth century American naturalism by writing survival narratives of young children who beat the odds against them. Consequently, though, these children only overcome by abandoning their modern world in lieu of a more primitive existence in communion with the nature that could just as easily destroy them. Never afraid to illuminate the harsh realities of the decisions his characters make, Paulsen stares headlong into the face of mortality without diminishing the consequences or complexities of the subject matter.

Joseph Michael Sommers

Bibliography

By the Author

children's literature:
Winterkill, 1976
The Foxman, 1977
The Night the White Deer Died, 1978
The Spitball Gang, 1980
Dancing Carl, 1983
Popcorn Days, 1983
Tracker, 1984
Dogsong, 1985
Sentries, 1986
The Crossing, 1987
Hatchet, 1987
The Island, 1988
The Winter Room, 1989
The Voyage of the Frog, 1989
Canyons, 1990
The Boy Who Owned the School, 1990
The Cookcamp, 1991
The Monument, 1991
The River, 1991
The Haymeadow, 1992
Harris and Me, 1993
Nightjohn, 1993
Mr. Tucket, 1994
The Tent, 1995
Call Me Francis Tucket, 1995

The Rifle, 1995
Brian's Winter, 1996
Sarny, 1997
The Schernoff Discoveries, 1997
Amos Binder, Secret Agent, 1997
Soldier's Heart, 1998
The Transall Saga, 1998
Brian's Return, 1999
Alida's Song, 1999
Tucket's Gold, 1999
The White Fox Chronicles, 2000
Tucket's Home, 2000
The Beet Fields: Memories of a Sixteenth Summer, 2000
The Glass Café, 2003
How Angel Peterson Got His Name, 2003
Brian's Hunt, 2003
The Glass Cafe: Or, The Stripper and the State—How My Mother Started a War with the System That Made Us Kind of Rich and a Little Bit Famous, 2003
The Quilt, 2004
Molly McGinty Has a Really Good Day, 2004
The Time Hackers, 2005

SHORT FICTION:
The Madonna Stories, 1989

NONFICTION:
Eastern Sun, Western Moon: An Autobiographical Odyssey, 1993
Father Water, Mother Woods: Essays on Fishing and Hunting in the North Woods, 1994
Winterdance: The Fine Madness of Running the Iditarod, 1994
Puppies, Dogs, and Blue Northers: Reflections on Being Raised by a Pack of Sled Dogs, 1996
Pilgrimage on a Steel Ride: A Memoir About Men and Motorcycles, 1997
Guts: The True Stories Behind "Hatchet" and the Brian Books, 2001
Caught by the Sea: My Life on Boats, 2001

EDITED TEXT:
Shelf Life: Stories by the Book, 2003

DISCUSSION TOPICS

- Typically, Gary Paulsen's protagonists grow through necessity. How does nature operate as an ally to the characters? A hindrance? As ambivalent?

- Even though the protagonists in each story are pitted against incredible odds and must rise above overwhelming adversity, are these adventure stories or something more complex?

- In Paulsen's fiction, family bonds tend to be broken. How does the dissolution of family operate in his stories, and what does it tell a reader about the nature of the family unit?

- What does each protagonist gain from his isolation?

- Does Brian's "rebirth" in *Hatchet* revert him to a feral state or does he learn to civilize nature?

- How does the tone of Paulsen's realism affect a reader's sympathy toward the main characters?

- How does "civilization" pose a threat to the Inuit culture in *Dogsong*?

About the Author

Jones, J. Sydney. "Paulsen, Gary." In *Something About the Author,* edited by Alan Hedblad. Farmington Hills, Mich.: Gale, 2000.

Moore, John Noell. "Archetypes: The Monomyth in *Dogsong.*" In *Interpreting Young Adult Literature.* Portsmouth, N.H.: Boynton/Cook, 1997.

Paulsen, Gary. *Father Water, Mother Woods: Essays on Fishing and Hunting in the North Woods.* New York: Delacorte Press, 1994.

_____. *Guts: The True Stories Behind "Hatchet" and the Brian Books.* New York: Delacorte Press, 2001.

Salvner, Gary. *Presenting Gary Paulsen.* Boston: Twayne, 1996.

Wood, Susan. "Bringing Us the Way to Know: The Novels of Gary Paulsen." *English Journal* 90, no. 3 (January, 2001): 67-72.

WALKER PERCY

Born: Birmingham, Alabama
     May 28, 1916
Died: Covington, Louisiana
     May 10, 1990

Widely recognized as the preeminent Christian "novelist of ideas" in the second half of the twentieth century, Percy created the American existentialist novel.

© Jerry Bauer

BIOGRAPHY

Walker Percy was born in Birmingham, Alabama, on May 28, 1916, living a basically idyllic southern childhood until the suicide of his father, who was eloquently portrayed in the character of Will Barrett, protagonist of Percy's 1980 novel, *The Second Coming*. After his mother's death, the teenage Percy and his two brothers moved to Greenville, Mississippi, where they were raised by their father's first cousin, William Alexander "Uncle Will" Percy, a lifelong bachelor, whose autobiography, *Lanterns on the Levee* (1942), was itself a southern classic, portraying the proud South emerging from the ravages of the Civil War.

Walker Percy had no intention of becoming a writer, making his way instead to New York's Columbia College of Physicians and Surgeons in 1938 to become a psychiatrist after finishing his B.A. in chemistry at the University of North Carolina at Chapel Hill. During this time, Percy himself underwent psychoanalysis, whiling away his little free time as a medical student going to films and observing the behavior of other filmgoers, a habit that would profoundly influence his literary career.

After earning an M.D. degree in 1941, he attempted to complete his internship at Bellevue Hospital in New York City, and there contracted tu-

berculosis while performing autopsies on cadavers. This illness became pivotal in his career and in his life. While recovering in a sanatorium in upstate New York, he read voraciously, particularly existentialist philosophy, including the works of Swedish philosopher Søren Kierkegaard. The result was an improbable conversion to Christianity in 1943 and a decision to abandon medicine as a career and seek a vocation as a full-time writer.

Between 1943 and 1946, Percy attempted two forgettable novels, and he eventually turned instead to studying language acquisition theory and linguistics, developing themes that would later undergird the thematic concerns of his novels. After he married Mary Townsend in 1946, they both converted to Catholicism and relocated to Covington, Louisiana, near the quintessential southern city of New Orleans. There they subsisted on Percy's inheritance from his uncle's estate. During the 1950's, Percy published a number of learned essays in scholarly journals on linguistics and its connections with psychology, and he continued to dabble in fiction.

When he finally settled on a set of characters and an appropriate theme, he deliberately steered his narrative craft away from that of the towering figure of William Faulkner and his convoluted regionalism toward a more direct, post-southern genre of fiction. The result was Percy, at the age of forty-five, publishing his first novel, *The Moviegoer* (1961), a National Book Award winner clearly patterned after the intense, philosophical "novel of ideas" written by Jean-Paul Sartre and Albert Camus, which Percy had discovered during his convalescence from tuberculosis. In essence, Percy created a peculiarly American genre of existential fiction but with this difference: Percy wrote as a Christian whose characters were haunted as much by the presence as the absence of God in the modern world.

Percy followed *The Moviegoer* with a longer, even more philosophical novel in 1966, *The Last Gentleman*, whose plot introduces Will Barrett, a troubled, confused young man in search of himself. Barrett eventually finds meaning in laying down his life for others. As Percy's reputation as a formidable novelist of ideas grew, he upset expectations with his third novel, published in 1971, *Love in the Ruins*. It is a hilarious satire of modern technological life and the sham of modern psychiatry. Its protagonist, Dr. Tom More, is a thinly disguised evocation of Sir Thomas More who dutifully skewers the false utopias of Eastern religion, consumer capitalism, and errant liberal Catholicism.

As Percy continued to reap critical plaudits for his fiction, his nonfiction essays were collected and published in *The Message in the Bottle* in 1975, astonishing his readers with their variety and their expertise in arcane linguistic and psychological theory. Percy's fourth novel, the dark, disturbing *Lancelot* (1977), is the story of a vengeful husband who murders his wife and her lover.

Attempting to write his first "nonalienated," or optimistic, novel, Percy revived the character of Will Barrett for his 1980 book, *The Second Coming*. The now widowed Barrett finds true love—and God—in a densely plotted, comic work that revealed a new emphasis of affirmation in Percy that earned him back the critical respect he seemed to have lost with *Lancelot*. Percy's publisher rewarded the critical and financial success of *The Second Coming* by bringing out Percy's quirky nonfiction book, *Lost in the Cosmos: The Last Self-Help Book*, in 1983. *Lost in the Cosmos* was at once a satire of television talk-show hosts, a serious monograph on language and semiotics, and a brief for Christianity—delighting some critics and readers and confusing others.

In 1987, Percy published what many regard as his greatest achievement, *The Thanatos Syndrome*, This novel also revives a past Percy character, Dr. Tom More. Fresh from a prison sentence for selling drugs to truck drivers, More discovers and thwarts a fiendish plot—engineered by a coterie of prominent and respectable lawyers and doctors—to anesthetize the populace by drugging the drinking water of Feliciana Parish in Louisiana.

Percy died on May 10, 1990, after a battle with cancer. He will long be remembered for his poignant warnings against a potential holocaust in Western culture because of its creeping acceptance of situational ethics at the expense of an eternal moral standard.

ANALYSIS

Like fellow southern Catholic writer Flannery O'Connor before him, Percy saw through the pious pretensions of an irreligious age. His southernness may have cleared his vision, but it was his sweeping grasp of Western civilization and its foundations that gave his fiction its substance.

The twentieth century, Percy declared in the words of Father Smith, hero of *The Thanatos Syndrome*, is that period of history in which God "has agreed to let the Great Prince Satan have his way with men for a hundred years—this one hundred years." Percy's protagonists—from Binx Bolling in *The Moviegoer* and Tom More in *Love in the Ruins* to Will Barrett in *The Second Coming*—are all, in their unique ways, refugees from that century, one in which, Percy notes, "more people have been killed . . . by tender-hearted souls than by cruel barbarians in all other centuries put together."

Percy found the roots of the twentieth century's sentimental nihilism in science's bastard son, "scientism," by which he meant the pathological attempt to objectify humanity as simply one more organism trapped in its environment. He concluded:

> [T]he modern objective consciousness will go to any length to prove that it is not unique in the Cosmos, and by this very effort establishes its own uniqueness. Name another entity in the Cosmos which tries to prove it is not unique.

The offense of humankind's uniqueness in the universe bemused Percy, and it became a predominant theme not only in his fiction but also in his engaging excursions into the philosophy of language. How humankind and language are each informed by the other, how neither people nor language can be understood apart from the other—these primary questions provoked Percy to challenge the "official version" of how humans acquire language skills promulgated by linguists, scientists, and philosophers such as Noam Chomsky, B. F. Skinner, and Jacques Derrida.

In Percy's hands, fiction and linguistics both became a subtle brand of apologetics, an inquiry into the nature of humans, God, and the Cosmos that yielded an exhilarating (although indirect) defense of the Christian faith.

From his improbable base in Covington, Louisiana, Percy conducted anthropological safaris into the human psyche. His credentials as a navigator were impeccable, possessing as he did the single most important trait such a guide can have: He recognized a clue when he saw one. Each fact about human communication, its successes and its failures, pointed Percy to a transcendent order of meaning, a transcendence that could be explained only by reference to an Eternal Logos who made creatures in his own image and thus made them capable of responding to him with language.

A traditionalist who lamented the twentieth century's loss of the perception of sin and its need for grace, Percy created protagonists who search for the source of their alienation and melancholy in the most prosperous country on earth. The typical Percy protagonist is a roughly middle-aged man, comfortable financially but plagued by a vague sense of disorientation and depression. This cerebral main character communicates his sense of disorientation through paradox and oxymoron. His story is always one of "coming to oneself," of suddenly discovering the extraordinary in the ordinary, of the transcendent in the mundane. To Percy, a person is neither "a beast nor an angel but a wayfaring creature somewhere between." The ultimate challenge is to seize one's own destiny and act on one's own or some other's behalf against the status quo.

As a narrator, Percy often came to readers in the guise of the island "castaway" desperately awaiting news from home. The "message in the bottle" (the title of his profound nonfiction study of language) found by Percy was language itself. Humankind is wallowing, Percy posited, in a spiritual malaise, a post-pagan, post-Christian identity crisis. Men and women, intended by their Creator to become full persons, settle for existence as ghostly personas— bifurcated creatures propped up by a pseudoscience all too ready to ratify humankind's soulless state.

Percy saw himself as a castaway with news even more newsworthy than a few tidbits from home. The "authorized version" of humankind's story is, according to Percy, a myth, yet a true myth, one that actually happened: a story of wickedness in high places, of a fall from grace, of a scandalous redemption achieved by a dying God. Percy's diagnosis of humankind's malaise at the end of the modern age will thus be his lasting legacy.

Set in the then-future 1990's, his last novel, *The Thanatos Syndrome*, represents Percy's "final warning" to an age that seems to regard a death wish as the epitome of mature adulthood. Homeless, nostalgic, twentieth century people face extinction, Percy believed, from a new gnosticism manifested in various permutations as deconstructionism, radical feminism, and overt racialism. This latest gnostic faith drives one further inside one's own head and tribe, creating a cerebrating creature who nevertheless participates in the real, public cosmos only as a brute consumer. There is no "outside," no transcendent reference point that might give one direction or purpose.

Percy knew that the apologist must be careful, however; what he has to say must be heard as news and not mere gossip. His compatriots must connect the message in the bottle with the longings deep within their own hearts:

> What if the news the newsbearer bears is the very news the castaway had been waiting for, news of where he came from and who he is and what he must do, and what if the newsbearer brought with him the means by which the castaway may do what he must do? Well then, the castaway will, by the grace of God, believe him.

THE MOVIEGOER

First published: 1961
Type of work: Novel

The story of a young man alienated from modern life who finds more meaning in the quest for God than in its resolution.

The Moviegoer won the 1962 National Book Award for fiction for Percy when he was forty-five; it launched his career as a novelist. As a novel of ideas, *The Moviegoer* consistently raises the largest questions of human life. Is there a God? If so, what is mankind's relationship to him and to the quest of knowledge of him? As became Percy's trademark handling of plot, much of the action of *The Moviegoer* takes place within the mind of the protagonist, Binx Bolling, who, nearing his thirtieth birthday, retreats to a mentalist existence, "sunk in the everydayness of life," unequipped to live life to the fullest and baffled by its ambiguities and contradictions.

A successful broker in New Orleans and a war veteran, Binx nevertheless has few friends. Although he has had a number of affairs with his secretaries, he knows neither what friendship or love truly is nor how to find a purpose for living. Binx is stuck in the mundaneness of life, which saps his strength for caring and believing in others. Immersed in the ordinariness of his social life, family, and job, he is a "wayfarer" who feels homeless and abandoned.

Binx thus embarks on a quest for meaning that evolves into a veiled search for God. As a seeker he is discouraged, because "as everyone knows, the polls report that 98 percent of Americans believe in God and the remaining 2 percent are atheists and agnostics—which leaves not a single percentage point for a seeker." He wants to be "onto something," to feel authenticated as a human being, because "to become aware of the possibility of the search is to be onto something." In launching a search that takes him away from the consumerism and aestheticism of his environment, Bolling rebels against the mundanities of life: family heritage, job status, material good. Binx seeks a different kind of authentication and becomes obsessed with motion pictures. "The movies are onto the search," he says, but they always end in the same everydayness which brings him despair: The hero "takes up with the local librarian" and "settles down with a vengeance."

Ultimately his cinematic excursions bring him no closer to a solution, but when he is drawn into the life of Kate Cutrer, the stepdaughter of his great-aunt Emily, he finds both the courage and the determination to confront life as it is. When Kate's fiancé is killed in an automobile crash, she lapses into despair, secretly drinking heavily and contemplating suicide. After Kate jilts a willing suitor, Emily Cutrer enlists Binx as an aide and confidant in helping Kate through her emotional trauma.

During the Mardi Gras season, Binx is sent on a business trip; impulsively, Kate requests that he let her join him. In the aftermath of their trip and the growing empathy with which Binx perceives Kate's malady, he discovers his own humanity and worth. In his compassion and risk-taking on Kate's behalf, he has transcended the ordinariness in which he was trapped and has conquered his malaise.

In the novel's climax, Binx is lectured severely by his aunt for his failure to meet the standards of southern gentlemanliness. Paradoxically, this liberates Binx: He and Kate marry, free of the facade of gentility in which they were both bred. In the epilogue, Binx reveals that his aunt has learned to understand and forgive him for what he is; "the Bolling family had gone to seed and . . . I was not one of her heroes but a very ordinary fellow."

In bringing Kate through her crisis, Binx resolves his own and discovers both humanity and purposefulness. Binx and Kate together discover that being is made meaningful through mutual trust and authentic, individual commitment. Consequently, Percy's characterization in *The Moviegoer* underscores the fact that in the modern South—indeed, in the world at large—this is the very kind of commitment that family, tradition, job, and the usual mundane social concerns can never engender or replenish. If anyone is to become a "person," he or she must step out of the security of established roles and stations and take the awful risk of individuality.

The same culture that detaches Binx from himself also permits his eventual return as a "reborn" southerner and human being, equipped both to critique and to coexist peacefully with his heritage. This can only occur, however, if Binx will act rather than merely contemplate the possibilities. In reaching out to Kate he finds the impulse he needs to free himself from the past and face the future with integrity and hope.

THE LAST GENTLEMAN

First published: 1966
Type of work: Novel

A young man relocated to New York from his native South finds release from his empty pondering of the meaning of existence by befriending a dying young man.

The Last Gentleman is Percy's most ambitious and overtly philosophical novel, one whose "ideas" take precedence over character, plot, or theme. It is as if Percy's long years of cogitation about language, humankind, and the cosmos and the alienation evident in American culture suddenly coalesced and compelled him to write a series of interesting, though convoluted, monologues to be placed in the mouths of the brooding searchers populating his narrative. Here the reader finds a compendium of Percy's personal indictments against crass "Christian America," modeled on the work of his existentialist mentor, Søren Kierkegaard, in nineteenth century Denmark.

The protagonist in his second novel, Will Barrett, has spent five years in psychoanalysis; he is a native southerner serving as a "humidification engineer" at Macy's department store in New York City. An introspective, educated man vaguely aware of his own despair, Barrett is "dislocated in the universe." Percy's opening description of Barrett succinctly circumscribes his character: "He had to know everything before he could do anything."

Paralyzed by his commitment to abstract knowledge before making decisions, Barrett lives in a world pervaded by ordinariness. He despairs of clear answers to his nagging questions about the purpose of life—both for himself and others—but he has some dim hopes that his quest will eventually bear fruit. One day, as he contemplates his station in life while at Central Park, he opts to become, as Binx Bolling had in *The Moviegoer,* an observer and not merely the observed. He spots a beautiful young woman, Kitty Vaught, through his newly purchased telescope and sets out to meet her. Smitten, Barrett traces her to a New York hospital, where he discovers that she and the Vaught family are comforting her younger brother, Jamie, who is dying.

In an improbable sequence of events, Will Barrett's southern charm and gentlemanly pose win over each of the Vaught family members, and he is invited to accompany them back home to Atlanta, mostly as companion and confidant to Jamie as he lives out his remaining days. Barrett agrees, interested as he is in staying as close to Kitty Vaught as possible. During his stay, Kitty's sister, Valentine, who has joined a Catholic order of nuns that takes care of indigent children, enters Barrett's life and coerces him to seek Jamie's conversion, believing that she alone can ensure that Jamie enters eternity as a "saved" person.

Soon thereafter, Sutter Vaught, Jamie's brother, arrives on the scene. Barrett finds in him a curious but appealing sense of daring and courage. He seems to be someone who has lived life and not merely hypothesized about it. Sutter and Jamie disappear, and it becomes Barrett's duty to track them down and return Jamie home—a task made all the more alarming and tenuous when Barrett discovers in Sutter's New Mexico apartment, along with some helpful maps, a stenographic notebook recording Sutter's jaded outlook on life and community in the United States.

Barrett familiarizes himself with the notebook during his subsequent trek, as Percy interweaves excerpts from Sutter's painful explorations with Barrett's unfolding search for the two brothers. Percy pushes the reader to diagnose the debilitating malady from which both Sutter and Barrett suffer: an utter sense of homelessness in the world that seems to make errant materialism or suicide the only options for the thoughtful individual. Barrett quickly sees that while he shares Sutter's disaffection with the new paganism and its philosophical implications, "in fact my problem is how to live from one ordinary minute to the next on a Wednesday afternoon."

When Barrett catches up with Sutter, Jamie has been placed in a hospital, dying of a pulmonary edema, and Sutter is working at a Santa Fe guest ranch. Barrett brings calm to both Jamie and Sutter, and their independent friendships deepen. Barrett also discovers a passage in Sutter's notebook that indicates a previous suicide attempt and begins to recognize signs that he may try it again. Determined to forestall Sutter's suicide and to fulfill his commitment to bringing Jamie to faith, Barrett steels in himself the fortitude to act apart from exhaustive knowledge of the way the world works or what the consequences of his actions will be.

Before his death, Jamie is led to offer halting words of faith in the presence of Barrett and the hospital chaplain. Moments later, Barrett chases after the departing Sutter, hoping to assure him of his worth in the world, confident that he can and will convince him of that fact.

LOVE IN THE RUINS

First published: 1971
Type of work: Novel

A comic anti-utopian novel that satirizes liberal civil religion and oversexed American culture through the exploits of dissident psychologist Dr. Tom More.

Offered as a tongue-in-cheek, pre-holocaust tale, *Love in the Ruins* is subtitled *The Adventures of a Bad Catholic at a Time Near the End of the World*. Its protagonist and narrator, Dr. Tom More, is named for the famous sixteenth century saint who authored *Utopia* (1516). More is a rueful psychologist who has developed an instrument for research which he calls the "lapsometer." The lapsometer is a device that measures certain psychic forces in the brain

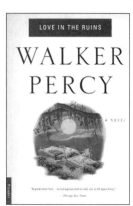

and thereby makes it possible to determine the source of irrationality, which for Percy is characterized by one of two extremes.

In Percy's view, the two most evident maladies of modern life are angelism, the tendency to abstract oneself from the ordinary circumstances of life and attempt to live above them in aloof intellectualism, and bestialism, the tendency to live as a brute consumer with an unrestrained, animal-like preoccupation with sex without procreation. This protracted indictment of modern culture surfaces frequently in Percy's later fiction, most prominently in *Lancelot* and in *The Thanatos Syndrome*.

The narrative is bracketed into five main sections, followed by an epilogue that delineates what has happened in the five years subsequent to the July 4 climax. It is an apocalyptic time in which the social institutions that are supposed to provide stability and continuity have broken down or become ridiculous parodies of themselves. The halls of academe, the medical profession, civil government, and a host of venerable religious institutions, particularly the Catholic Church, are all satirized as ineffectual and compromised, each having sold out to the spirit of modernism and therefore being contemptible to Percy.

Racial tensions have erupted into violent confrontations as the very fabric of American society is about to unravel. Under the accumulated weight of centuries of guilt and alienation, "ordinary folk" find their self-image slowly disintegrating, their sex lives impotent, and their digestion failing; they seek help from two main sources, proctologists and psychologists.

The reader discovers Dr. More in the midst of a personal and professional crisis made all the more difficult by heightened racial tensions across the United States but particularly in his region of the South. He looks out over an interstate cloverleaf and describes the four quadrants of his city. One quarter is occupied by conservative Christian businessmen. Another is the federal complex, where government funding has produced a hospital where More works, a NASA facility, a Geriatrics Center, and the Love Clinic. A third quarter encompasses Paradise Estates, the suburb where More lives in his deceased wife's house. The fourth is the Honey Island swamp, where assorted antisocial derelicts, castoffs, and the ferocious Bantus, a group of militant black guerrillas seeking social justice, reside. As he speaks, More is awaiting the end of civilization, surrounded, nevertheless, by three attractive women—two erstwhile girlfriends and his loyal nurse, Ellen.

More's financial and professional situation is precarious, and he makes a dubious, Faustian bargain with the diabolical Art Immelmann, who promises to market More's invention and help him earn favor with foundations to fund further research. More soon realizes that Immelmann is not to be trusted—he alters More's device so that it not only detects but also remediates the psychic imbalances, then distributes lapsometers to ill-trained students who misuse the instruments with sometimes hilarious consequences.

A racial uprising of Bantus, planned for July 4, provides the comic backdrop for the novel's ambiguous ending. Praying to his sainted ancestor, Sir Thomas More, Tom More succeeds in thwarting Immelmann's evil plans. The social upheaval proceeds apace, however, and in the epilogue, More intimates that black people have displaced white people as the ruling class but have acquired the same social pathologies that had plagued black-white relations in the first place. More, on the other hand, has settled peacefully into the "slave quarters" of a large apartment complex down by the bayou. Here he is safely ensconced in a new middle-class life, having married his faithful nurse, Ellen, content to live out his natural life in a new, though obviously imperfect, Eden.

Tom More serves Percy's satire of modern sensibilities toward spirituality and social decorum in two ways. First, as a "bad Catholic," More exhibits a healthy skepticism toward what Percy believed was an unwelcome shift away from tradition and authority in the American Catholic Church. More holds no quarter for liberal scavenging of Christian doctrine. Second, More is heroic in standing against the excesses and the megalomania of the medical profession. Percy mercilessly skewers his own compatriots in the practice of psychology for their preoccupation with relatively trivial or peripheral matters while ignoring the major sources of human foibles and sin.

Percy revived the character of Dr. More seventeen years later for an even more devastating sequel, *The Thanatos Syndrome*, in which the disintegration of the morality in the modern world is laid at the feet of the medical profession in its advocacy of abortion rights, euthanasia, and genetic engineering.

The Second Coming

First published: 1980
Type of work: Novel

A middle-aged man, contemplating suicide, finds redemption when he asks for and receives a sign that God exists.

Will Barrett of *The Last Gentleman* returns in this sequel as a wealthy middle-aged man, recently widowed, suffering both from inexplicable blackouts in which he loses consciousness and from his faltering sense of a calling in life. Also resurrected are Sutter Vaught, whom Will counseled out of suicide, and Sutter's sister Kitty, whom Will once courted. The three are brought together again in a most unusual circumstance as Will encounters Kitty's purportedly schizophrenic daughter, Allison, during a "scientific experiment" to determine whether God exists.

Worn down by the affluence and religiosity—particularly his own daughter's rigid fundamentalism—that surrounds him in southern suburbia in Linwood, North Carolina, Will Barrett is convinced that the only question left for him to answer about humankind is whether life has any transcendent meaning—that is, whether God exists. His wife, when alive, had heavily invested herself and her family fortune in "do-gooding." Will spends his days, when well, playing golf and more golf and obsessively recovering the lurid details of his relationship with his father, who committed suicide.

In his emptiness, Will makes a vow of ending his life if he cannot ascertain there is a God who exists—and cares. He vouchsafes his "experiment's" details and its consequences in a letter to Sutter Vaught. Will's plan is implausible yet inspired: He will hide in a nearby cave and fast until God gives him a sign of his existence. If God calls, Will shall emerge wiser and more secure in his footing for the future; if God remains silent, Will shall embrace the heritage bequeathed him by his father. Ironically, all that Will receives is an excruciating toothache whose pain sends him stumbling toward the cave's exit.

On his way out he plunges into an uncharted shaft and from there directly into an abandoned greenhouse in which Allison, Kitty Vaught's daughter, is hiding, having escaped from a mental institution. She, like Will, is searching for stability and hope in an ambiguous world. Subjected to electroshock treatments after exhibiting extreme withdrawal and forgetfulness, Allison is determined to prove she can live without psychologists or her meddling parents. As she nurses Will back to health, Will has found God, and she has found a spiritual benefactor and protector of her own who understands her alienation and inner heart.

As the narrative ends, the resourceful couple outwit their various pursuers, rescuing other social outcasts along the way, and they plan a marriage. Both Will and Allison are "reborn," but in an unconventional fashion—a fashion utterly spiritual but apart from and oblivious to the normal routes exemplified by the thoroughly religious town in which they have found each other. Once again, Percy offers a strong rebuke to the easy belief of conservative Christianity, with its pat answers to deep questions, and also to the secular abandonment of spiritual values that, if understood, might enrich and give substance to the pursuits of the good life.

SUMMARY

Percy once commented that his major novelistic concern was to depict "what it means to be a man living in the world who must die." In his work, the modern South—the last authentic refuge of American religious faith—is the typical setting for protagonists beset by alienation and the conflicting demands of community and tradition in a hostile modernity. Only a recognition of a transcendent order may provide the basis for recovery of self and a unified vision of the world.

At the center of this recovery, Percy places the mystery of humankind's origin and the clues provided by language in solving it—specifically, the human ability to make symbol and metaphor. What separates Percy from other, more pretentious writers of philosophical fiction is his keen sense of everydayness, the vivid capturing of the details of modern life.

Bruce L. Edwards

DISCUSSION TOPICS

- How did Walker Percy's linguistic studies enrich his fiction?

- Does Percy, a consciously southern writer, repudiate values—such as tradition, the family, and religious conservatism—often considered distinctively southern ones?

- Is Binx Bolling of *The Moviegoer* an authentic Everyman?

- How does Percy's existentialist fiction differ from that of earlier writers in this mode, such as Jean-Paul Sartre and Albert Camus?

- Is Percy more Christian apologist than artist?

BIBLIOGRAPHY

By the Author

LONG FICTION:
The Moviegoer, 1961
The Last Gentleman, 1966
Love in the Ruins: The Adventures of a Bad Catholic at a Time Near the End of the World, 1971
Lancelot, 1977
The Second Coming, 1980
The Thanatos Syndrome, 1987

NONFICTION:
The Message in the Bottle, 1975
Lost in the Cosmos: The Last Self-Help Book, 1983

Conversations with Walker Percy, 1985 (Lewis A. Lawson and Victor A. Kramer, editors)
The State of the Novel: Dying Art or New Science?, 1987
Signposts in a Strange Land, 1991 (Patrick Samway, editor)
More Conversations with Walker Percy, 1993 (Lawson and Kramer, editors)
A Thief of Peirce: The Letters of Kenneth Laine Ketner and Walker Percy, 1995 (Samway, editor)
The Correspondence of Shelby Foote and Walker Percy, 1997 (Jay Tolson, editor)

About the Author

Allen, William Rodney. *Walker Percy: A Southern Wayfarer.* Jackson: University Press of Mississippi, 1986.

Coles, Robert. *Walker Percy: An American Search.* Boston: Little, Brown, 1978.

Desmond, John F. *At the Crossroads: Ethical and Religious Themes in the Writings of Walker Percy.* Troy, N.Y.: Whitston, 1997.

Dupuy, Edward J. *Autobiography in Walker Percy: Repetition, Recovery, and Redemption.* Baton Rouge: Louisiana State University Press, 1996.

Hardy, John Edward. *The Fiction of Walker Percy.* Urbana: University of Illinois Press, 1987.

Kobre, Michael. *Walker Percy's Voices.* Athens: University of Georgia Press, 2000.

Lawson, Lewis A. *Following Percy: Essays on Walker Percy's Work.* Troy, N.Y.: Whitston, 1988.

O'Gorman, Farrell. *Peculiar Crossroads: Flannery O'Connor, Walker Percy, and Catholic Vision in Postwar Southern Fiction.* Baton Rouge: Louisiana State University Press, 2004.

Pridgen, Allen. *Walker Percy's Sacramental Landscapes: The Search in the Desert.* Selingsgrove, Pa.: Susquehanna University Press, 2000.

Quinlan, Kieran. *Walker Percy: The Last Catholic Novelist.* Baton Rouge: Louisiana State University Press, 1996.

Sheppard, Beth M., ed. *Signs of the Giver: The Collected Papers of the 2002 Southwestern College Walker Percy Seminar.* New York: Writers Club Press, 2003.

Tharpe, Jac. *Walker Percy.* Boston: Twayne, 1983.

ANN PETRY

Born: Old Saybrook, Connecticut
October 12, 1908
Died: Old Saybrook, Connecticut
April 28, 1997

Petry's fiction broke new ground for African American women writers by exploring the deterministic impacts of race, gender, and class.

AP/Wide World Photos

BIOGRAPHY

Ann Lane Petry was born to Peter Clarke Lane and Bertha James Lane on October 12, 1908, joining a family that had lived for several generations as the only black citizens of Old Saybook, Connecticut. The descendant of a runaway Virginian slave, Petry never felt herself to be a true New Englander; her cultural legacy was not that of the typical Yankee, and as a small child she came to know the effects of racism upon being stoned by white children on her first day of school.

Nevertheless, her family distinguished itself within the community and boasted numerous professionals: Her grandfather became a licensed chemist, her father, aunt, and uncle became pharmacists, and her mother became a chiropodist. Inspired by the examples of independent women relatives, Ann pursued a degree in pharmacology from the University of Connecticut and graduated as the only black student in the class of 1931. She worked in family-owned pharmacies until 1938, when she married George D. Petry and moved to New York City.

There, Petry began her writing career and quickly secured jobs with various newspapers. Participation in a creative writing seminar at Columbia University greatly influenced her during this period. Her first published short story, "On Saturday the Siren Sounds at Noon," appeared in a 1943 is-

sue of *The Crisis* and led to Petry's receipt of the 1945 Houghton Mifflin Literary Fellowship. With that financial support, she completed *The Street* (1946), which was to earn her widespread critical acclaim and make her the first African American woman to sell more than a million copies of her fiction.

Over the following thirty years, she published stories and essays in numerous magazines, wrote two more adult novels, *Country Place* (1947) and *The Narrows* (1953), and issued a collection of her short fiction, *Miss Muriel, and Other Stories* (1971). Petry also began writing for children and produced such classics as *The Drugstore Cat* (1949), *Harriet Tubman: Conductor on the Underground Railroad* (1955), and *Tituba of Salem Village* (1964); the latter two books deal with historical figures and reflect Petry's desire to give the United States an honest picture of its racial history.

Disconcerted by the fame brought by the success of *The Street*, in 1948 Petry returned with her husband to the obscurity of Old Saybook, where the couple raised a daughter, Elizabeth Ann. Petry held a visiting professorship at the University of Hawaii in 1974-1975, and in 1977 she received a National Endowment for the Arts grant. Boston's Suffolk University awarded her a D. Litt. degree in 1983.

ANALYSIS

While Petry's fiction typically involves African Americans struggling against the crippling impact of racism, her overarching theme involves a more broadly defined notion of prejudice that targets class and gender as well as race. That vision explains what might otherwise seem to be inconsistencies of direction in Petry's career: her decision, for example, following the potent racial protest of *The Street*, to focus her next novel, *Country Place* (1947), on a white community's postwar crises of adjustment, or her movement into the realm of children's literature. Uniting these diverse efforts is Petry's critique of oppressive social hierarchies and her admiration for those whose moral epiphanies lead them to more inclusive, life-affirming conceptions of human community.

Petry's dissection of cultural hypocrisies exists alongside her willingness to allow her characters their own moments of narrative self-revelation through alternating interior monologues. The chorus of voices thus created avoids privileging any single character and infuses Petry's fiction with compassion. Petry delineates time and again how the American society has proved cruelly adept at building walls that deny some of its citizens real participation in its prosperity.

Rather than celebrating the American ideal of self-making with which her native New England is so closely associated, Petry exposes the illusions it has fostered and depicts their graphic costs to those relegated to the periphery of American possibility. Racism invites Petry's most scathing attacks, not only for the material hardship it forces upon people of color but also for the psychological and cultural distortions it produces. At her most biting, Petry lampoons the absurdist systems of human classification into which racist societies ultimately fall. Generally, her perspective is more tragic than comic, however, and includes the recognition that confronting racism necessitates confronting history itself.

That class distinctions pervade American culture becomes one of Petry's most insistent indictments of the egalitarian myths of American opportunity. In quest of the material security, comfort, and status that propel middle-class striving, Americans, she suggests, acquiesce to a soul-numbing view of labor and retreat into a moral inflexibility that blindly sanctions aggressive self-interest. A novel such as *Country Place* shares with Petry's other work an interest in how the American class structure produces venal, grasping have-nots at the bottom whose ambitions mimic the ruthless acquisitiveness of those at the top.

Petry's most important characters are those who reject the fallacy of the self-made individual existing independent of the world or the continuing legacy of the past. Though that perspective assumes certain mechanistic dimensions in her work, she does not concede full authority to deterministic necessity; the dice may be loaded against her protagonists, but the game is not inexorably mandated to play itself out to any single predetermined end. Her characters sometimes prove capable of personal growth that moves them toward a common humanity. At its most compelling, such discovery may fuel real and far-reaching change in the social order itself. Petry's narratives often grow from characters' chance movements across rigid cultural boundaries; the resulting crises test the spiritual flexibility of many others besides her protagonists.

Overlooked by academic critics, Petry's children's books offer tantalizing clues to her larger agenda as a writer. Their emphasis upon personal fearlessness in rethinking assumptions and disengaging from systems invites comparison to figures from her adult fiction such as Abbie Crunch of *The Narrows* or Mrs. Gramby of *Country Place*, both of whom escape the prejudices that have constrained their humanity. Moreover, in applying their new insights, these characters take subtly revolutionary actions that defy the cultural boundaries that previously defined their lives. It takes a saint, perhaps, to challenge a predatory universe with an alternative vision of love, but having told children in *Legends of the Saints* (1970) that true sanctity is a function of bravery, Petry seems willing to evaluate her "serious" fictional characters on their receptivity to grace as an antidote to hate.

THE STREET

First published: 1946
Type of work: Novel

Inspired by the American Dream, a young black mother discovers the inhibiting power of racism, sexism, and poverty.

When *The Street* appeared in 1946, earning Alain Locke's praise as "the artistic success" of the year, it was immediately identified with the literature of social protest that had become the primary vehicle for African American fiction of the period. Petry's novel tells the story of a young African American mother in New York City whose ambitions have been fed by her early reading of Benjamin Franklin and her domestic service in the household of wealthy white suburbanites.

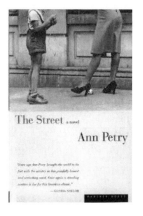

Lutie Johnson's goals are the stuff of the American Dream itself and on the surface appear eminently worthy: Although recently abandoned by her husband, she eschews defeat and is convinced that she will obtain a white-collar job that will foster her personal dignity and provide a comfortable life, a good education, and promising social opportunities for her eight-year-old son, Bub. As Petry makes evident, however, Lutie fails to recognize the incongruity of applying the credo of upward mobility to her own circumstances, which reflect a social system organized to benefit the dominant white community and dismiss the claims of the marginal. Nor has Lutie registered the spiritual bankruptcy that accompanies the success she so covets.

Lutie pays dearly for her unexamined adherence to white bourgeois myths. While emphasizing the crippling impact of poverty, sexuality, and race upon individual striving, *The Street* is also a thoughtful examination of a complex character whose education and class aspiration lead to self-conscious choices and allegiances that demand as much scrutiny as the sociological obstacles she confronts.

Not that those obstacles are minimized. Lutie's circumstances reveal the interplay between the economic disenfranchisement of black men, the exploitative employment options imposed on black women, the fragmentation of the black family, and the terrifying vulnerability of black youth. To offset his humiliation at being unable to support his family, Lutie's husband Jim takes up with another woman. Forced by her restricted means to move in with her father and his string of mistresses, Lutie chafes at having to leave Bub each day among the vulgar underclass she so desperately seeks to escape. She painstakingly masters secretarial skills to secure a civil-service appointment with better pay, only to find that her access to better neighborhoods is still constrained by the exorbitant rents charged the poor.

Lutie reluctantly takes an apartment on morally dissolute 116th Street, the kind of area she describes as "the method the big cities used to keep Negroes in their place." For all her concern about Bub, she cannot alter the fact that at the end of a school day soured by the bigotry of his white teacher, Bub must manage alone for hours until his mother returns home. Finally, Lutie discovers that as a black woman she is made most vulnerable by her sexuality, which arouses virulent male passions she can neither predict nor control.

Ironically, Lutie's beauty baits the trap that crushes her dreams when it sparks the lust of three men, each of whom attempts to deflect her life to his own ends. Jones, the janitor of her apartment building, is a man psychologically deformed by years of diminishment in grinding jobs. Lutie's appearance in his life crystallizes his dissatisfactions, making him determined to possess her from the moment he meets her. He makes a devious alliance with the lonely Bub that later allows him to dupe the boy into criminal activity when Jones's rape attempt against Lutie fails.

Boots Smith, although far more glamorous a figure than Jones, proves just as venal: A jazz-band leader who discovers Lutie's singing ability, he cynically tries to turn her ambition to his own sexual benefit. The most far-reaching figure of male control in the novel, however, is Junto, the white entrepreneur whose businesses dominate the neighborhood. Not coincidentally, he employs the two black men and sees to it that his desire for Lutie effectively cancels out theirs. He is responsible for rescuing her from Jones's stalking, only to preserve her for himself; he insists that Boots deny Lutie a real salary for singing with his band, so as to ensure the economic vulnerability on which he will prey.

As Lutie discovers that she has become a pawn in a larger sexual competition among these men, she becomes increasingly frantic and self-destructive. When Jones's vengeful scheme against Bub lands the boy in jail and threatens him with reform school, Lutie desperately seeks an attorney, unaware that she could handle the legal proceedings herself. The quest for money that has defined her character from the first thus assumes a heightened urgency that leads her back to Boots, who in turn plays procurer for Junto. Lutie resists explicitly selling herself for personal gain, although she does attempt to manipulate Boots's interest to her own advantage. She learns how unskilled she is at such games when Boots tries to beat and rape her; in retaliation, she kills him with a candlestick. Convinced that the white justice system does not believe in black female virtue, she boards a Chicago-bound train and becomes a fugitive. The novel ends with Lutie's having implicitly consigned her son to a reformatory and herself to the life of moral degradation she had resisted for so long.

In *The Street*, Petry conveys the monstrous distortions of the human spirit effected by racism and privation, but she does so through interior monologues that illuminate the complex psychological history explaining each monster. Similarly, the rich musicality of the text, with its insistent evocation of blues and jazz, offers yet another measure of the interior struggles between dehumanization and survival waged in the souls of the oppressed. Petry's first novel remains her most potent enunciation of the tragedies wrought by urban blight even in the lives of those determined to transcend it.

THE NARROWS

First published: 1953
Type of work: Novel

An interracial love affair exposes the murderous hostilities that lie beneath the surface of a New England town.

The Narrows combines the racial protest of *The Street* with the exposé of small-town America in *Country Place*. It depicts the steady march toward disaster of the Dartmouth-educated veteran Lincoln Williams (or Link), who has returned from four years at war with little faith in the opportunities for a satisfying life he has theoretically earned by his various accomplishments. Link grew up as the foster son of a black middle-class couple living on a street now overtaken by the rougher elements of African American urban life. Throughout the novel, he

functions as a bridge figure, connecting radically alien worlds whose citizens abjure contact with one another.

Link's attraction to antithetical worlds deprives him of a true home anywhere, while his boundary-jumping earns him an enmity on all sides that eventually assumes lethal proportions. Link is also full of a misogynistic rage; such suspicion of women fills Petry's fiction and suggests the deadliness of the gender dialectic operating within a patriarchal power structure.

Link's gender biases are complicated by race when chance introduces him to Camilo Treadway Sheffield, a beautiful Barnard graduate whose boredom prompts her to take a late-night walk on the African American side of town. Fleeing in dense fog from a grotesque street figure, she is rescued by Link, who does not realize that Camilo is white until he later takes her into a bar (when she discovers with a jolt that he is black). Not until much later does he learn that she is both married and the heir to the Treadway family fortune, a fortune derived from the munitions works that is the town's major employer.

The animus aroused by their pairing erupts first within the black community. Abbie Crunch, Link's prim adoptive mother, and Bill Hod, his earthy street-life mentor, find themselves unlikely partners in sabotaging the couple. Abbie throws Camilo into the street as a trollop, and Bill humiliates Link by exposing Camilo's deceits.

Nor are the lovers themselves free from prejudice. Camilo reveals a tendency to see Link as something of an exotic toy on whom she lavishes her money and affection in return for sexual and intellectual excitement. Link's fascination stems in no little part from Camilo's iconographic status as the proverbial white goddess, an obsession that reveals its sinister underside when he feels emasculated by the news of her betrayal. With both psyches deteriorating under the pressure of their desire for each other, the accusations become more virulent, until Camilo finally uses the most deadly charge at her command to punish Link for repudiating her. She accuses him of rape and thereby sets in motion the machinery of the larger social order, which will not tolerate Link's iconoclastic threat.

If the black community proves resistant to Link's attempted move across boundaries, the white power structure responds with even more malice. No one believes the rape charge, but that does not exonerate Link, as the truth is in fact far more dangerous: The white woman has actually fallen in love with the black man. To the powers that be, Camilo's mental breakdown embodies the damage to family reputation and social hierarchies she has wreaked, and the man responsible for her lapse must be eliminated. The old order, though, is beyond recovery, a point made through Petry's grim version of the lynch mob to whom she subjects her hero: Link's murderers are a genteel dowager and her effete son-in-law, who pursue their victim in a limousine. More important, their insular privilege is shattered forever as the retributive power of the justice system now turns against them.

The novel comes to rest, finally, with Link's adoptive mother, Abbie Crunch. Over the course of the novel, Abbie moves beyond the internal class divisions that have guided her life, preparing her for the even more startling decision to challenge the racial antimonies that kill her son. Given evidence that Bill Hod is plotting against Camilo to avenge Link, Abbie chooses to free herself from the expanding waves of hatred, and she warns the police of the threat. Abbie's quiet gesture is at heart a revolutionary one, for it bespeaks her attentiveness to the real lesson of Link's martyrdom—his effort, however flawed, to move beyond the crippling polarities of race and class.

MISS MURIEL, AND OTHER STORIES

First published: 1971
Type of work: Short stories

The wide-ranging consequences of a cultural obsession with racial difference create a community of lost souls seeking some clearer vision of human relationship.

The pieces in this volume range over several decades of Petry's career and provide a compact introduction to her imaginative concerns, chief among them racism's psychological consequences. In the prize-winning story "Like a Winding Sheet," a husband's impotence before the racist assaults he sees all around him makes him respond to his

wife's affectionate teasing with the beating he is forbidden to direct at his real oppressors. His actions lay bare the starkness of the struggle between male and female in Petry's world and the sobering betrayals that occur in it.

"In Darkness and Confusion," a meditation on the Harlem riot of 1943, fictionalizes a historical event. The story's protagonist, William Jones, a man who has worked hard to secure a better life for his son, witnesses the killing of a black soldier and erupts into a violence that expresses his grief and rage; Petry assigns Jones responsibility for leading the first mobs.

In "Miss Muriel" and "The New Mirror," Petry creates a black family much like her own—the Layens are professionals who own the pharmacy in a small New England town. The adolescent girl who narrates these tales speaks of "the training in issues of race" she has received over the years, not only through casual bigotries but also through the painful self-consciousness of respectable people like her parents, whose behavior is a continual refutation of cultural stereotypes. The child learns to use the codes by which the black middle class shields itself from white contempt, and she learns as well the burden of always acting with an eye on the reputation of "the Race": "all of us people with this dark skin must help hold the black island inviolate."

Against the most aggressive forms of white hatred, however, there is no defense except a temporary erasure of one's humanity. "The Witness" presents the case of a retired black college professor who takes a high school teaching position in a northern white community. Called upon to assist the local pastor in counseling delinquent adolescents, he finds himself their prey out in the world as they kidnap him and force him to watch their sexual abuse of a young white woman. Having at one point coerced him to place his hand on the girl, they effectively blackmail him into complicit silence about their crime. His exemplary life and professional stature cannot protect him, and he bitterly describes himself as "another poor scared black bastard who was a witness."

In "The Necessary Knocking on the Door," a participant at a conference about Christianity finds herself unable to master her dislike for a white woman dying in the hotel room across the hall from hers—a woman who had earlier in the day refused to be seated next to a "nigger." In these stories, Petry vividly captures the spiritual anguish of discovering that one's own grievances can weaken, rather than strengthen, one's moral courage.

Petry's handling of white perspectives on racism is more unyielding. For example, the absurdities into which segregationist practices lead multiracial societies are lampooned in "The Bones of Louella Brown," wherein the most prestigious family in Massachusetts finds its plans to build a chapel for its deceased members compromised when an undertaker's assistant confuses the bones of an African American maid and the sole noblewoman in the clan.

Other stories in the collection evoke the mysterious private centers of grief hidden in the human heart: "Olaf and His Girl Friend" and "Solo on the Drums" show Petry's interest in African American music as an exquisite, untranslatable evocation of pain. "Mother Africa" introduces Emanuel Turner, a junk dealer who acquires the huge sculpture of a female nude that a wealthy white woman is discarding. Convinced that the figure is a mythic evocation of Africa itself, he resents the prudish efforts of others to clothe it, just as missionaries had once insulted his ancestors. Thus he is stunned to learn that this dark madonna is not a black woman at all but a white woman—the oxidation of the metal had misled him. By parodying the assumed black male obsession with white women, Petry implies that the real hunger at work in the story is for authentic enunciation of the African American experience, a hunger left unmet as Turner hurriedly rushes to sell the piece for scrap.

DISCUSSION TOPICS

- What did Ann Petry learn about "rigid cultural boundaries" in her childhood, and how does she apply it in her fiction?

- What function do Petry's interior monologues serve?

- For Petry, what is the relationship between class and race?

- Discuss the theme of racial misidentification in Petry's fiction.

- Are the themes in Petry's children's books similar to those in her books for adults?

SUMMARY

Petry analyzes the American scene from a variety of angles, always exposing the debilitating impact of its hierarchical social systems and capitalistic materialism. Like her contemporaries, she recorded the daunting obstacles to human fulfillment facing those on the margins of American prosperity, and yet hers is finally a Christian existentialist vision celebrating the individual's potential for spiritual liberation through which an entire culture might relinquish its crippling prejudices. Her examination of gender as another locus of oppression laid important groundwork for the writings of African American women since the 1960's.

Barbara Kitt Seidman

BIBLIOGRAPHY

By the Author

LONG FICTION:
The Street, 1946
Country Place, 1947
The Narrows, 1953

SHORT FICTION:
Miss Muriel, and Other Stories, 1971

CHILDREN'S LITERATURE:
The Drugstore Cat, 1949
Harriet Tubman: Conductor on the Underground Railroad, 1955

Tituba of Salem Village, 1964
Legends of the Saints, 1970

About the Author

Bell, Bernard. "Ann Petry's Demythologizing of American Culture and Afro-American Character." In *Conjuring: Black Women, Fiction, and Literary Tradition,* edited by Marjorie Pryse and Hortense J. Spillers. Bloomington: Indiana University Press, 1985.

Clark, Keith. "A Distaff Dream Deferred? Ann Petry and the Art of Subversion." *African-American Review* 26 (Fall, 1992): 495-505.

Ervin, Hazel Arnett, and Hilary Holladay, eds. *Ann Petry's Short Fiction: Critical Essays.* Westport, Conn.: Praeger, 2004.

Gross, Theodore. "Ann Petry: The Novelist as Social Critic." In *Black Fiction: New Studies in the Afro-American Novel Since 1945,* edited by A. Robert Lee. New York: Barnes & Noble, 1980.

Hernton, Calvin. "The Significance of Ann Petry." In *The Sexual Mountain and Black Women Writers.* New York: Doubleday, 1987.

Holladay, Hilary. *Ann Petry.* New York: Twayne, 1996.

Petry, Ann. "A *MELUS* Interview: Ann Petry—The New England Connection." Interview by Mark Wilson. *MELUS* 15 (Summer, 1988): 71-84.

Washington, Gladys. "A World Made Cunningly: A Closer Look at Ann Petry's Short Fiction." *College Language Association Journal* 30 (September, 1986): 14-29.

JAYNE ANNE PHILLIPS

Born: Buckhannon, West Virginia
July 19, 1952

Phillips, recognized as one of the most gifted writers of her generation, portrays the changes occurring in family relationships as reflections of a changing society.

© Jerry Bauer

BIOGRAPHY

Jayne Anne Phillips was born in Buckhannon, West Virginia, a pleasant middle-class town, on July 19, 1952, the middle child, between brothers, of Russell R. Phillips, a contractor, and Martha Jane Thornhill, a teacher. Phillips attended West Virginia University, where she earned a B.A. degree, and graduated in 1974 magna cum laude. Four years later, she earned a master of fine arts degree from the University of Iowa's renowned writer's program. Phillips taught briefly at Humboldt State University and then held the Fanny Howe Chair of Letters at Brandeis University and the post of adjunct associate professor of English at Boston University. In 1985, she married Mark Brian Stockman, a physician.

Phillips began writing poetry in high school. Her childhood ended abruptly in the early 1970's, when her parents were divorced and she moved away from her hometown to begin college nearby. Her poetry was published while she still attended the University of West Virginia as an undergraduate. Only after graduation did she begin writing fiction, creating highly compressed stories in which her poetic discipline shone through. Phillips has continued in this vein, using carefully chosen words and images to their potential. She has tended to write not from an outline, as novelists often do, but line by line, as do poets.

In 1978, Phillips made the most of an opportunity when she gave Delacorte editor Seymour Lawrence a copy of *Sweethearts* (1976), one of her early chapbooks. Lawrence, within weeks, wrote Phillips a postcard with the career-launching message, "Bring your stories to Boston." This contact led to Phillips's first publication, *Black Tickets* (1979), which met with widespread praise and critical acclaim. In this collection of twenty-seven works, ranging in length from single-paragraph vignettes to well-developed short stories, Phillips displayed her talent at giving characters from all walks of life, including the unsavory, an empathetic voice, while managing to avoid any traces of sentimentality.

Phillips gathered much of her sharp insight into the underworld in 1972, when she and a girlfriend hitchhiked from Cape Cod, Massachusetts, to California and back again. The writer once remarked in an interview how during that odyssey she "learned what it meant to be afraid," as the twenty-year-old girls narrowly escaped physical violence several times.

In the novel *Machine Dreams* (1984), her second major publication, Phillips continued to create empathetic characters and again received largely favorable criticism. The film rights to her novel were purchased by actress Jessica Lange.

Phillips has won numerous awards for both her trade publications and chapbook stories. In 1977, 1979, and 1983, she was awarded the Pushcart Prize for four short stories. The Coordinating Council of Literary Magazines gave Phillips the Fels Award in fiction in 1978; she received National Endowment for the Arts fellowships in 1978 and 1985, and in 1979, she was awarded the St. Lawrence Award for fiction. A milestone was reached in her career in 1980 when she received the Sue Kaufman Prize for First Fiction from the American Academy and Institute of Arts and Letters, followed in that same year by the O. Henry Award. In 1981, Phillips won a Bunting Institute fellowship from Radcliffe College. Upon publication of her first novel, *Machine Dreams*, in 1984, Phillips won a National Book Critics Circle Award nomination, an American Library Association Notable Book citation, and *The New York Times* Best Books of 1984 citation. *Shelter*, her 1994 novel, won an Academy Award in Literature by the American Academy and Institute of Arts and Letters and was chosen one of the Best Books of the Year by *Publishers Weekly*.

ANALYSIS

The long list of awards with which Phillips has been honored indicates how favorable the critics have been from the onset of her career. *Black Tickets* was released with advance praise from nine writers emblazoned on the back cover, a prophesy of what was to come, even from well-known critics, such as popular contemporary novelist John Irving. Irving noted that Phillips is "especially effective with sex and drugs."

Black Tickets contains three distinct subgenres: brief (as short as a single paragraph) literary exercises, more developed interior monologues of desperate or deranged individuals, and fully developed short stories about ordinary people struggling with family relationships. Irving, along with the majority of Phillips's critics, believed that, although her shocking shorter pieces and interior monologues were evidence of Phillips's extraordinary talent, her best work was done in the longer stories that explored the nature of the modern American family.

Phillips's preoccupation with generations of families and changing gender roles emerged as major themes in her first novel, *Machine Dreams*. This work displayed her talent at giving a range of characters unique and believable voices, which matured appropriately as the characters lost their youthful innocence and their world changed around them, inexplicably, yet permanently. During another interview, Phillips explained that her source for such honest, first-person prose "has to do with ear, with listening in a particular way to how

people talk and being able to expand on fragments of heard talk, staying with the sound and then enlarging it."

Because her main subject matter has been either social outcasts or the decay of American societal values, Phillips could not have avoided planting political messages within her fiction. Her concern with the differences between the 1960's and the successive decades remains evident in her work. She has contrasted the community-oriented 1960's with the 1970's, when young people no longer rallied around unifying causes such as civil rights and lacked national heroes such as Martin Luther King, Jr. During an interview, she capsulized her perspective on changes between two decades in this example: "Kids dropping acid [in the 1970's] did it to obliterate themselves, not to have a religious experience." In a technologically advanced, mechanized world, Phillips has witnessed a decline in the richness of life. With more mechanization having pervaded Americans' lives during the 1980's, Phillips does not predict improvement over time. In the same interview, she continued: "In the '70's there was still enough security so that people felt they could be floaters. Now things are too shaky for that."

Phillips's ominous perspective on modern times accounts for the shocking images of sexual deviation and drug abuse that she portrays in much of her short fiction. "Gemcrack," for example, is about a mass murderer, and even the title of "Lechery" indicates its unsavoriness. This focus on the most negative aspects of contemporary society contrasts sharply with Phillips's loving portrayal of a nostalgic past in *Machine Dreams*, complete with drive-in hamburger joints and the post-World War II American love affair with luxurious automobiles.

Phillips has been classed as a regional writer after the fashion of distinguished southern storytellers Flannery O'Connor and Eudora Welty, whom she has claimed as two of her influences. While Phillips has objected to the term "regional," claiming that she, as well as her role models, have far more universal appeal than the classification "regional writer" would indicate, she has accepted the high praise of being grouped with these masters of fiction.

"Home"

First published: 1975 (collected in *Black Tickets*, 1979)
Type of work: Short story

A young woman's return home makes her divorced mother confront her daughter's and her own sexuality.

Phillips's only story in the *Black Tickets* collection with any degree of humor, "Home" was considered by many critics to be the best work in the book. In reference to "Home," John Irving noted that Phillips "shows us the good instinct to tell stories in which something that matters takes place."

What matters to Irving, then, is telling the story of the ordinary American family. "Home" has all the typical elements of one of three distinct story types appearing in *Black Tickets*. It is of conventional short-story length, and the plot depicts the tragedies that occur in ordinary family relationships. There is the typical protagonist in her middle twenties, a divorced parent, and strained conversation revealing unresolved conflict. These elements reveal Phillips's interest in the psychological connections and gaps found in generations of families.

With this well-crafted first-person narrative, Phillips brings her reader into an average American living room where an ordinary, uncelebrated homecoming takes place. The mother watches the evening news and worries about Walter Cronkite getting cancer while she warns her neglectful daughter that she "will be sorry when she is gone." Guilt plays a vital role in this mother-daughter relationship. The narrator's divorced mother reminisces about how devoted she was to the care of her own invalid mother, expressing, but never actually admitting, her hurt at being neglected by her own daughter. Unfulfilled needs for affection and for sex, nonexistent in her life for years, are interwoven inseparably with this guilt.

The conflict occurs when the narrator invites a former lover to visit. The mother overhears their lovemaking, which brings forth a cornucopia of negative emotions—embarrassment, guilt, shame, possibly even jealousy—to the surface. Confronting her daughter, she reveals the complexity of her mixed-up emotions: "I don't know what to do about anything."

Phillips's tendency to politicize is found even in this short story. The narrator's lover and mother both have visible scars, his from a botched napalm attack and hers from a bungled breast surgery. These healing physical scars foil the festering wounds lying below the surface. They are the result of divorce, or of the Vietnam War, hidden wounds hinting at the general deterioration of family life in the post-1960's era. Phillips's exploration of her generation's rootlessness and the difficulty of going "home" reflects modern times with the visual and aural acuity typically found in her work.

"Lechery"

First published: 1975 (collected in *Black Tickets*, 1979)
Type of work: Short story

A teenage prostitute who entices virginal young boys offers a glimpse into her life.

"Lechery" lends the reader insight into the gritty "urban underbelly" that Phillips encountered as she hitchhiked across the United States in the early 1970's. Several works in *Black Tickets* fall into this genre of disturbing stories in which the cruel side of life is examined, where people are denied unconditional love and beauty.

Combining an acute ear and eye for the most sordid details with her creative imagination, Phillips wrote a fully believable and horrifying narrative. She employed the first-person voice to enable the reader to identify with the wretched narrator, thus instilling the fear that this grotesque could have been the reader under similar circumstances.

In this and in similar stories, Phillips has given a voice to the inarticulate. In this narrative, told by a fourteen-year-old prostitute who molests little boys, the narrator recounts how, two years before, she was purchased by two sexually perverse drug addicts for thirty dollars. The simple, powerful prose overflows with sensually shocking images of the narrator's early life in the orphanage with her friend Natalie and of her current life as a peddler of pornography, a sexual toy for deranged adult drug addicts, and a seductress of virginal, pre-adolescent schoolboys. "I get them before they get pimples, I get them those first few times the eyes flutter and get strange," the narrator tells the reader, without a hint of shame or embarrassment.

The narrator lacks any reason to feel guilt or shame because of her lifestyle. She opens with the following justification: "Though I have no money I must give myself what I need." Because it is for her own survival that she lives as she does, one of her final comments, "I'm pure, driven snow," is understandable, and even a relief to the reader, who has been pulled into her desperate world so quickly and has, by Phillips's design, identified with the narrator so strongly.

MACHINE DREAMS

First published: 1984
Type of work: Novel

A forty-year portrait of the Hampson family explores changes in the fabric of American society from the pre-World War II era to the years of the Vietnam War.

Phillips's first novel, *Machine Dreams*, focused on one very ordinary West Virginia family, the Hampsons. Phillips chose to write her first novel about the less shocking of her preoccupations in *Black Tickets*: generations of families and the changing roles of men and women. Written from many perspectives, the novel combines first-person narrative (each family member is given a chance to speak) and third-person narrative and includes two chapters of letters sent home from soldiers at war.

The letters are an effective tool that Phillips uses to reveal her interest in generations. First, one reads Mitch Hampson's letters written from boot camp, then from various stations in the Pacific during World War II, where he operates heavy machinery to bulldoze airstrips and sometimes to bury corpses. Later, one reads a modernized version of those same letters, this time written by Billy, Mitch's son. These letters are written from boot camp, then from South Vietnam, where he is a helicopter machine gunner.

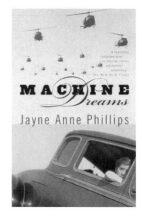

The lives of the female generations also reflect, mirrorlike, upon one another. Jean Hampson, who, emotionally and financially, holds her family together until the children are grown, inherited her mother's strength, which she then passes on to Danner, her daughter. "I always assumed I'd have my own daughter," Jean tells Danner in the opening chapter. "I picked out your name when I was twelve, and saved it. In a funny way, you were already real. I never felt that way about your brother." The mother-daughter bond, regardless of the generation gap, is strong indeed.

Although both play a role, generation gaps have less impact than do gender gaps in the Hampson family. Billy inherits his father's fascination with machines as well as his selective telling of events from the war zone to female family members. "Of course you will not say anything about this to the family," writes Mitch to a male friend in the early 1940's. Billy follows in his father's footsteps as, from Vietnam, he writes pleasantries to his mother. He breaks out of his father's mold, however, when he depicts the brutal truth in letters to his sister. This departure from machismo also testifies to the strength of the siblings' relationship, made stronger by their parents' unhappy marriage.

While Phillips tells the story of the Hampsons' decline, she also tells the story of changing American lifestyles and values from the Depression to the early 1970's. Jean contrasts her early life with Danner's as she explains that "Life wasn't like it is now. . . . all this I hear about drugs. We had the Depression and then the war; we didn't have to go looking for something to happen."

Phillips intended *Machine Dreams* to carry a political undercurrent, one of the novel's only facets that met with criticism in several reviews. Yet Phillips believes that all good writing is political, whether intentionally so or not. She imbued her novel with the nostalgia—parking dates, a dance at the community swimming pool, a summer waitressing job carrying heavy trays, heaving petting in the front seat of a car—that makes the Hampsons a family that is representative of middle America. Even if readers' families do not resemble the Hampsons in the least, the family of that era as represented in television and motion pictures makes it possible for everyone to identify with the shattered dreams of the Hampson family.

SUMMARY

A poet become short-story writer become novelist, Phillips has combined the disciplines of all three fields to create compact prose filled with imagery and with sometimes familiar, sometimes strange, yet always distinctive voices. Her stories of family life smell of Americana, while her tales of the deprived and depraved reek of the America that is ignored.

Phillips offers the reader an honest look at how contemporary issues have negatively affected the core of American society, the family. Her stories, while not cheerful, explore sensitive issues in an age of mechanization.

Leslie Pearl

DISCUSSION TOPICS

- How does the lack of sentimentality in Jayne Anne Phillips's fiction affect the presentation of its themes?

- How is Phillips's fiction a portrait of the cruelty, desperation, and violence of contemporary American life?

- How is Phillips's fiction an analysis of the mechanization of American life?

- Can a case be made that Phillips is essentially a southern writer? Is she part of the southern grotesque tradition?

- What does Phillips's fiction say about the conflicts within families?

- How has the Vietnam War influenced Phillips's characters and themes?

BIBLIOGRAPHY

By the Author

SHORT FICTION:
Black Tickets, 1979
How Mickey Made It, 1981
Fast Lanes, 1984

LONG FICTION:
Sweethearts, 1976
Counting, 1978
Machine Dreams, 1984
Shelter, 1994
MotherKind, 2000

About the Author

Disheroon-Green, Suzanne. "Jayne Anne Phillips." In *The History of Southern Women's Literature*, edited by Carolyn Perry and Mary Louise Weaks. Baton Rouge: Louisiana State University Press, 2002.

Godden, Richard. "No End to the Work?: Jayne Anne Phillips and the Exquisite Corpse of Southern Labor." *Journal of American Studies* 36 (August, 2002): 249-279.

Jarvis, Brian. "How Dirty Is Jayne Anne Phillips?" *Yearbook of English Studies* 31 (2001): 192-204.

Phillips, Jayne Anne. "The Writer as Outlaw." In *The Writing Life: Writers on How They Think and Work*, edited by Marie Arana. New York: PublicAffairs, 2003.

Rhodes, Kate. "Interview with Jayne Anne Phillips." *Women's Studies: An Interdisciplinary Journal* 31 (July/August, 2002): 517-520.

Robertson, Sarah. "Dislocations: Retracing the Erased in Jayne Anne Phillips' *Shelter*." *Mississippi Quarterly: The Journal of Southern Cultures* 57 (Spring, 2004): 289-311.

ROBERT PINSKY

Born: Long Branch, New Jersey
October 20, 1940

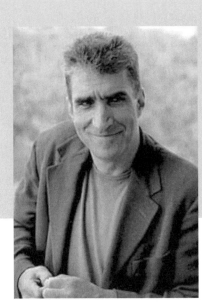

N. Alicia Byers

In his poems, Pinsky portrays a certain human interconnected-ness of all people and from all times in this world. Through his poems and poet laureateship, he has given the United States and the world a substantial vision of the past for the United States to prevail in the new millennium.

BIOGRAPHY

Robert Pinsky was born in Long Branch, New Jersey, on October 20, 1940. His father was an optician, and his parents were Orthodox Jews. Though influenced by keeping kosher and going to Hebrew school, his parents went to synagogue only on High Holidays.

Pinsky attended Long Branch High School in New Jersey, and while growing up, he fell in love with music. Childhood impressions of everyday sounds gave Pinsky his first desire to explore the mysterious rhythms of life. He began as a saxophonist and with writing songs. He eventually started writing poetry. This became not only his outlet for rhythm, voice, and sound, but also for ideas and a connection to humanity. He earned his B.A. from Rutger's University and then his M.A. and Ph.D. from Stanford University. At Stanford, he held the Stegner Fellowship for creative writing. He then taught at Berkeley University in California and Wellesley College in Massachusetts. He eventually moved to Boston, where he continued to teach creative writing at Boston University into the twenty-first century.

After publishing a collection of essays, *Landor's Poetry*, in 1968, he received a National Endowment for the Humanities Fellowship in 1974. In 1975, he published a collection of poetry titled *Sadness and Happiness*. In 1976, Pinsky published another col-lection of essays titled *The Situation of Poetry*. In 1980, his second collection of poems, titled *An Explanation of America* (1979), received the Saxifrage Prize. He was awarded the William Carlos Williams award of the Poetry Society of America in 1984 for his publication of *History of My Heart* (1984). He published a third collection of essays, *Poetry and the World*, in 1988, which was followed in 1990 with a collection of poems titled *The Want Bone*. In 1996, he published *The Figured Wheel: New and Collected Poems, 1966-1996.* This collection of poetry became the definite book for Pinsky's poetic lifetime, encompassing his life's work of poetry. It was awarded the Pulitzer Prize in Poetry, the Ambassador Book Award in Poetry of the English Speaking Union, and the Lenore Marshall Award.

Pinsky translated into English *The Inferno of Dante* in 1994, keeping the original style of terza rima and giving English readers a living vocal poetic version of the book. His translation received the Los Angeles Times Book Prize and the Harold Morton Landon Translation Award. He also translated *The Separate Notebooks* by Czesław Miłosz (1983) with Renata Gorczynski and Robert Hass.

Pinsky claimed in a 1998 interview with Ted Genoways for *Meridian* that he "grew up with the idea that to practice an art was to be involved in every part of it and to try to involve art in every part of life." Pinsky first associated this through music, and one can see the roots of what would later become Pinsky's love of the spoken word and the voice of poetry. Parallel to his love for music and the sound of life, at a young age, he came to respect the common worker and the person who could do something: the carpenter, builder, and painter. When one combines these two threads, the sensitivity to sound and rhythm as well as the understanding of practical knowledge, practical people, and artisans, one may see how Pinsky came to write the poems that would come to enhance the knowledge of the interconnectedness of the United States with the greater world.

Because of Pinsky's ability to incorporate the various histories, places, and times of the United States and the past in his poems, he was named the thirty-ninth United States Poet Laureate and Consultant in Poetry of the United States. He held this position from 1997 to 2000.

His major proposal for the nation and poetry was the Favorite Poem Project in which Pinsky compiled fifty short video documentaries of people saying their favorite poem. The recordings were then housed in the Library of Congress. The project encompasses America and the voice of its people, and through this voice, poetry is resurrected and still powerful on the tongues of the contemporary world. Poetry to Pinsky is not merely ancient and classical. It is a living form of art, and throughout his poet laureateship, Pinsky kept this art alive and strong.

ANALYSIS

Pinsky continually confronts the major contemporary issue of human interconnectedness and every person's involvement in one another's lives: ethnically, socially, politically, historically, religiously, temporally, and through place. Though raised in a Jewish household, he seems to express an ambiguity or inner conflict of calling himself Jewish in his poems and dismisses a labeling of himself as only a Jewish author. His poetry encompasses far more than one religion or one place. In the closing notes of *The Figured Wheel*, Robert Pinsky states: "Religion concerns me . . . as a vivid, charged example of the passion to create." His affinity for religion then may be a religion of art itself.

Pinsky's poetry is known for reverberating and echoing the past in each present moment and image. For example, in "Shirt," one finds a circling back and forth in time and place between a shirt the speaker is wearing, the people who made this shirt, a fire in 1911 at the Triangle Shirtwaist factory in New York City, and the English poet George

Herbert. This poem acts like a photograph album where each image is like a depiction of different scenes but all of the same book, all somehow of similar fate and destiny.

For Pinsky, it became art that could translate the complexities of the world and its people into an understandable language. This language is best understood through hearing poetry spoken by a living human being. Pinsky often claims that a person's actual voice in poetry is necessary to the art of poetry.

Pinsky's poetry is also known for its sharp contrasting images and juxtapositions. For instance, in "The Figured Wheel," an imaginary wheel of fate rolls through several scenes set in contrast with one another: In the first line, for example, the wheel rolls through "shopping malls and prisons." By setting up this contrast within the same line, Pinsky forces the reader to reexamine all that is viewed as generally good and bad. In the closing lines, the wheel rolls by Pinsky himself and his family, and this is where Pinsky's major theme of human interconnectedness, a theme that reverberates throughout his life's work, becomes explicit.

On a smaller scale, the poem "The Unseen" takes a specific scene and concentrates on the immediate effects of one place while broadening itself to the effects years later on tourists going through the Nazi death camp in Krakow, Poland. The poem begins with a general visual description of Krakow and its surroundings. The dream vision in the poem brings the reader back to a hypothetical historical account of the death camp in action during World War II. In this way, it acts as a striking contrast to the tourists roaming around an empty death camp like a museum. Once again, Pinsky echoes the past through each present moment, and as each moment unfolds, the reader may understand more about where he or she has come from rather than where he or she is going.

In poems such as "The Want Bone," Pinsky is less specific about a certain place with a particular history. Instead, the poem's scene is a beach with a shark's dried mouthbone opened like a gaping hole, and the speaker in the poem is describing the bone and his reaction to the bone. The poem still uses a specific object as a vehicle to a universal idea. In this way, it is similar to "Shirt" but leaves the reader craving something more, because there are less specific details about this bone's history. It is a universal bone, some object that desires or wants or instills desire in the person seeing the bone.

Furthermore, a sense of desire lurks throughout Pinsky's poems, and sometimes it is a desire to know the reasons for history's outcome and humanity's fate. Pinsky's use of the wheel is appropriate in his cyclical analysis and descriptions of generation after generation being faced with the same problems. In "The City Dark," from *The Figured Wheel*, one may use the line "the mathematical veil of generation" to describe this unknowingness which the mysterious figured wheel rolls through. There are an infinite amount of possibilities and poems to describe another aspect of this mystery. It is a mystery that plays on human interconnectedness as in "An Explanation of America" from *An Explanation of America*: on the death and life cycle, the learning and forgetting of each generation in one nation, and particularly, the negative things of the past. "An Explanation of America" is a poem written for Pinsky's daughter, and therefore one must notice the poem's contrasting grievous and joyous moments. For instance, in the section titled, "IV Epilogue: Endings," his daughter (and the reader) is presented with hope and fear as the poet describes children that "bind us to the future." In the following scenes, there are more hopeful descriptions, such as "In the Sierras,/ Where Winter's never far, the country is clear,/ A stage of granite swept for mediation." It may be hope and fear then, that accurately describe Pinsky's poetry, a fear of the figured wheel and the cycles of the past continuing through each generation, committing the same atrocities, yet somewhere, there is a hope for the future.

reader a specific image that acts as a device to carry the reader through each scene.

The images and actions of the poem are set in contrast within each line throughout the poem. In a single line, snow and sand are separated and then recombined, and the wheel rolls through fresh water and salt water as well as flecks of tar and molten rock. There is a constant separating and combining through each image as the reader passes through the pantheons of gods, demigods, gargoyles, and dryads. An inescapable terror also

exists in this "cold, cyclical dark, turning and returning," an undeniable guilt that is in both the scorched and the frozen parts of this world.

These images and scenes through which the figured wheel rolls are collected by the wheel and eventually include the life of Pinsky and his family. Because the poet is also a part of this figuration, the reader may get a sense of himself or herself as a part of this wheel's accretion, and thus one is led to a vision of complicity. In the final line, three versions of this figuration are presented: figured, which may represent a present state; prefigured as in a past figuration; and transfiguring, something that will continue to change. This suggests that in all three states—past, present, and future—Pinsky, his family, and the reader exist on this wheel.

"THE FIGURED WHEEL"

First published: 1984 (collected in *History of My Heart*, 1984)
Type of work: Poem

A poem depicts an imaginary collective wheel that rolls through the human condition.

"The Figured Wheel" is a poem that reports the condition of humanity. The first line describes the wheel as rolling, which immediately gives the

"THE UNSEEN"

First published: 1984 (collected in *History of My Heart*, 1984)
Type of work: Poem

The reader is given an image of Krakow, an empty World War II concentration camp, and the dream vision of a man's inner conflict about the past and its burden.

"The Unseen" is set in a specific town in Poland with a particular historical burden. Immediately, the reader knows the setting: the rain, the stone arcade, and smoky air of one "penetrating color." This color is gray, setting a particular empty tone to the poem. The people in the poem are on a tour and the speaker in the poem provides the images for the reader, including the audience to tour the death camp.

Pinsky presents a list: toothbrushes, hair, shoes, photographs. These are all human ordinary materials, which adds irony to this tour of a death camp, since a death camp seems unordinary and horrific. The speaker even remarks, "We felt bored," but then, with the use of enjambment, Pinsky juxtaposes boredom with the next line, "And at the same time like screaming Biblical phrases: *I am poured out like water.*" It is necessary to grasp this allusion to Psalm 22:14 in order to understand the poem's underlying theme. Psalm 22 is the prophecy of the Messiah, of Christ, and begins with the words "Why Hast Thou Forsaken Me," Christ's final words when dying on the cross. Though Pinsky is Jewish and is walking through a death camp where Jews were tortured and killed, he still includes the suffering of Christ, who was a Jewish man, with the suffering of all the Jews killed in these death camps. This brings the poem a more universal theme of suffering and loss.

All this is suddenly altered with the dream vision of the speaker in the poem, invisible, unseen, walking the camp, and killing the Nazi soldiers and officers. The reader may identify with this desire to do justice unto those who have done evil, but the speaker in the poem comes out of the dream and humbles himself. The speaker confronts the "discredited Lord" as a "servant" gaping obediently, accepting all that has been in the face of a much greater being whose mysteriousness is inexplicable.

The easy interpretation of this poem would be to accept that Pinsky is giving his readers a nihilistic outlook of this world, but the textual evidence reads with more humility and acceptance of a powerful unknowable being. When the speaker states, "but still/ We try to take in what won't be turned from in despair," the reader must recognize that the speaker in the poem will not despair and believe in nothing, but rather, like Job, the speaker will trust those mysterious secrets of the day and night to be something greater.

"SHIRT"

First published: 1990 (collected in *The Want Bone*, 1990)
Type of work: Poem

The complex history of one shirt is expanded to portray the interconnectedness of humanity.

"Shirt" is an example of Pinsky using historical occurrences and translating the effects of these occurrences into present-day situations. The first scenes are in sweatshops in Korea and Malaysia, where Pinsky portrays the everyday workers, gossiping over tea or talking politics.

Pinsky uses the language of the factory, mentioning the presser, the cutter, the wringer, the mangle, the needle, the union, the treadle, and the bobbin. What changes this rhythm of listing is a sole phrase: "The Code." The reader's attention is drawn back and is set up for the next scene: "The infamous blaze/ At the Triangle Shirtwaist factory in nineteen-eleven." This allusion is to the Triangle Shirtwaist factory in Manhattan, a sweatshop where, in 1911, a fire broke out and killed more than one hundred immigrant workers. The conditions of sweatshops were difficult to work in, with low wages, long hours, dangerous conditions, and, as Pinsky points out ironically, they were unsafe in the case of fire because the fire "Code" might be dismissed.

The next scene in the poem displays a vision of martyrs from the Triangle Shirtwaist factory falling to their death and is juxtaposed with a reference to Hart Crane's poem "To Brooklyn Bridge." This image brings the reader back to the subject of the poem: the shirt. Pinsky makes a more complex list of designs and patterns and shirt-making history and of Scottish and Calico patterns. Then there is George Herbert, the seventeenth century British poet who becomes an ancestor to Irma, a woman in South Carolina who inspected Pinsky's shirt. Thus, Pinsky returns to himself in the poem as a part of this history, a part of the effects of the Triangle Shirtwaist factory and Herbert, a part of the loss and the gain over time.

"A WOMAN"

First published: 1984 (collected in *History of My Heart*, 1984)
Type of work: Poem

"A Woman" is a poem of memory, looking back at childhood scenes of restriction.

"A Woman" begins by looking back thirty years ago. The speaker in the poem describes a scene and a "fearful" woman taking a child for a walk. The word "fearful" is the reader's first indication of tone. The poet lists the specific particularities of his location, recreating the place as in a memory. Once Pinsky has established his composition of place, the woman's character becomes apparent. She is a woman who is superstitious, warning the child in every sentence, dreaming of "horror and catastrophe—/ Mourners, hospitals."

Following this is a detailed scene that the woman dreams of where she finds a family in her own room with their throats cut. Then the reader is brought back to the New Jersey shore where the child and woman have walked out to Port-au-Peck. They pass the "ineffectual sea wall," something that tries to hold the sea back from spilling onto land but is described as "ineffectual." Then the speaker in the poem describes the violence of the ocean meeting the river, the "exhilaration of water." All this energy is suppressed into the next image of froth from a milk shake poured from a steel shaker into a glass. No energy or violence in the milk shake exists. It is another precaution, a holding back.

The poem ends with a final vision of restriction as the boy remembers a previous Halloween and the woman holding him back from going up the street with the other children in their cowboy gear. The irony is in the boy's costume. A cowboy is known as a solitary man, living under no rules or restrictions, able to go off and return whenever he wants. One may ask then, does the speaker in the poem who vowed never to forgive this woman forgive her thirty years later?

"AT PLEASURE BAY"

First published: 1990 (collected in *The Want Bone*, 1990)
Type of work: Poem

The poem serves as an exploration of place through the effects of time at Pleasure Bay.

"At Pleasure Bay" is a place poem, but unlike many other poems by Pinsky, it lacks a formal structure. This gives the reader a more fluid exploration of place and captures the spirit of place through Pleasure Bay's historical context and landscape.

In the second line of "At Pleasure Bay," Pinsky employs the catbird as singing "never the same phrase twice." This line reverberates throughout the poem in various scenes with the catbird at Pleasure Bay and from the music issuing from Price's Hotel near the landing. A catbird is a small gray bird in the same family as mockingbirds and thrashers. It is known for its irregular succession of notes and its catlike meowing phrase. The catbird may act as the poet of this poem. This is observable when Pinsky, melding and changing the sounds and images of Pleasure Bay, writes of "the catbird filling/ The humid August evening near the inlet/ With borrowed music that he melds and changes." The contrast of a piano's music across the river, "the same phrase twice and again," and the catbird carry the reader through "the same place. But never the same way twice." This is the outline structure of the poem within which people live and die, boats run whiskey, and cars cross the bridge. That this is Pleasure Bay, one may wonder what is pleasurable about it. Does one choose the catbird's phrase or the piano as one's pleasure? Or, one may simply lay down with the spirit of place and become another presence, a part of the spirit at Pleasure Bay.

"THE WANT BONE"

First published: 1990 (collected in *The Want Bone*, 1990)
Type of work: Poem

"The Want Bone" is a meditation poem about a shark's mouth bone on the beach and desire.

"The Want Bone" begins with a paradoxical image: "The tongue of the waves tolled in the earth's bell." "Tongue" and "wave" are both words that imply fluidity and change, whereas the Earth suggests solidity. A tolling of bells often connotes death. Then there is "the dried mouthbone of a shark." The mouth bone gapes but cannot close on anything.

The image of the gaping mouth, dead and dried, but still gaping, even as the tongues of the sea waves and the Earth toll death, suggests an image of the action of desire. Whatever the desire is, the poem acts as a meditation on wanting. Pinsky also employs the letter *O* as a poetic visual and audible device to give the impression of openness, a gaping hole or something empty to be filled.

The act of desire, when one wants something, cannot be expressed except by a reaching out for the desirable thing, a gaping toward the thing wanted. Because the dried mouth bone of a shark is in the sand on a beach under the hot sun, one may imagine the shark's flesh that wrapped around the bones. If one imagines further back in time to the shark alive, one may imagine the shark's desire to return to the water, to its home where it could continue living. This desire then may be a desire for life.

"The Want Bone" may be a monumental poem for Pinsky. It exemplifies the desire to create life, to give through poetry and emotion, voice and rhythm, the common experience of humanity, that of wanting and yearning to be alive.

SUMMARY

In all of Robert Pinsky's poems, one sees the poet as actor in each scene. He is a part of the history of humanity. Through manifesting interconnectedness, Pinsky carries the burden of the past. It is only through Pinsky's recognition of the past that his poems begin to live in the present moment. His poetry is about living and life. To Pinsky, life is the chief concern of the poet, and the poet, through creation, gives life to history, time, and ghosts. The poet gives the forgotten past a voice for the people of the contemporary world by which to remember the past.

Matthew Nickel

BIBLIOGRAPHY

By the Author

POETRY:
Sadness and Happiness, 1975
An Explanation of America, 1979
History of My Heart, 1984
The Want Bone, 1990
The Figured Wheel: New and Collected Poems, 1966-1996, 1996
Jersey Rain, 2000

LONG FICTION:
Mindwheel, 1984 (computerized novel)

NONFICTION:
Landor's Poetry, 1968 (dissertation)
The Situation of Poetry, 1976
Poetry and the World, 1988
Image and Text: A Dialogue with Robert Pinsky and Michael Mazur, 1994
The Sounds of Poetry: A Brief Guide, 1998
Democracy, Culture, and the Voice of Poetry, 2002

Robert Pinsky

TRANSLATIONS:
The Separate Notebooks, 1983 (of Czesław Miłosz)
The Inferno of Dante, 1994

EDITED TEXTS:
The Handbook of Heartbreak: 101 Poems of Lost Love and Sorrow, 1998
Americans' Favorite Poems: The Favorite Poem Anthology, 2000 (with Maggie Dietz)
Poems to Read: A New Favorite Poem Project Anthology, 2002 (with Dietz)
Selected Poems: William Carlos Williams, 2004
An Invitation to Poetry: A New Favorite Poem Project Anthology, 2004 (with Dietz)

About the Author

Dietz, Maggie, and Robert Pinsky, eds. *An Invitation to Poetry: A New Favorite Poem Project Anthology.* New York: W. W. Norton, 2004.
Downing, Ben, and Daniel Kunitz. "The Art of Poetry: LXXVI." *Paris Review* 144 (Fall, 1997): 180-213.
Pinsky, Robert. *Democracy Culture and the Voice of Poetry.* Princeton, N.J.: Princeton University Press, 2002.
_____. *The Figured Wheel: New and Collected Poems, 1966-1996.* New York: Farrar, Straus and Giroux, 1996.
_____. *Poetry and the World.* New York: Ecco Press, 1988.

DISCUSSION TOPICS

- In what ways does Robert Pinsky use contrasting images in poems such as "The Figured Wheel"?

- How does Pinsky use allusion in "The Figured Wheel"?

- Is the catbird a necessary image in "At Pleasure Bay"? Why?

- Why is the history of Krakow or the history of the Triangle Shirtwaist factory important in order to understand "The Unseen" or "Shirt"?

- When Pinsky held the Poet Laureate position, he created the Favorite Poem Project. How does this project exemplify Pinsky's themes of humanity in his poems?

Courtesy Sophia Smith Collection, Smith College

SYLVIA PLATH

Born: Boston, Massachusetts
October 27, 1932
Died: London, England
February 11, 1963

A leader in the "confessional school of poetry" that reigned in the 1960's and 1970's, Plath erased the barriers between poetry and one's most private life.

BIOGRAPHY

Sylvia Plath was born in Boston, Massachusetts, to Otto and Aurelia Plath on October 27, 1932. Her father, whose distorted and terrifying image dominates so much of her work, was a Polish German who taught at Boston University and whose beekeeping provided another central symbol for his daughter's poetry. Her mother, of Austrian descent, was an educated woman who later taught at the college level. Warren Plath, Sylvia's only sibling, was born on April 27, 1935.

For most of Plath's early childhood her family lived in Winthrop, a seaside town near Boston, and as a child Plath spent much of her time exploring, collecting shells, and examining marine life. In her thinly veiled autobiographical novel, *The Bell Jar* (1963), she was to have her heroine, Esther Greenwood, reminisce about the happiness she had felt "running along the hot white beaches with my father the summer before he died."

The major event in Plath's life was the death of her father, which occurred as a result of pulmonary embolism following an injury complicated by diabetes. His death occurred in November, 1940, when she was eight. The picture she paints of him throughout her work is not usually the idyllic memory of *The Bell Jar*, however, but a bitter assault. He becomes a Nazi, a demon, a devil—even a demon lover calling her to the grave. After her father's death, Plath distinguished herself as a student and

a precociously talented writer. She won numerous school and local prizes and managed to publish her first short story, "And Summer Will Not Come Again," in the August, 1950, issue of *Seventeen*, just as she was entering college.

Plath went to Smith College on two scholarships, one from the Wellesley Smith Club and the other a private fund endowed by Olive Higgins Prouty, the author of *Stella Dallas* (1922), who was later to help pay for Plath's medical treatment and was uncharitably caricatured in *The Bell Jar*. In August, 1951, Plath's short story "Sunday at the Mintons" won *Mademoiselle*'s fiction contest. Plath also won great recognition at Smith for her poetry and her scholarship. In 1952, she won a guest editorship in *Mademoiselle*'s College Board Contest, giving her the experience in New York that she later recorded in *The Bell Jar*, and she had poems accepted by *Mademoiselle* and *Harper's*. From the outside, things seemed to be going perfectly.

Pressures were building up, however, and to Plath the few disappointments (such as not being received into a writing class she wanted) outweighed her many achievements. She sank into a serious depression and, after ineffective psychiatric treatment, attempted suicide in the summer of 1953 by hiding herself away in a womb-like hole in her mother's cellar and taking an overdose of sleeping pills. This confusion of birth and death is a major theme in her novel and poems. Discovered and hospitalized, Plath was given electroshock treatments and psychotherapy and was discharged as cured. She returned to Smith for a triumphant final year, a year studded with prizes and publications and crowned by a scholarship to the University of Cambridge.

At Cambridge, Sylvia met the English poet Ted Hughes; she married him in London on June 16, 1956. The couple lived in Cambridge, England, until the spring of 1957, when they moved to Boston. Plath became an instructor at Smith. She really wanted to be a writer and not an academic, however; she quit her post to spend her time revising and resubmitting her much-rejected poetry book. In December, 1959, they moved back to England. Their first child, Frieda, was born there in April, 1960.

To her great satisfaction, her book of poetry, *The Colossus, and Other Poems* (1960), was accepted by William Heinemann for publication. In addition, she received a Eugene F. Faxton Fellowship to complete the novel she had begun about her nervous breakdown; the family was then living in rural Croton, Devon. By the time her son, Nicholas, was born in January of 1962, Plath was well at work on *The Bell Jar.*

Plath and Hughes decided to separate in the fall of 1962. She moved to London with her children and was overjoyed to find free an apartment in what had once been W. B. Yeats's house. Always a believer in signs and portents, she felt that this was surely an indication of coming good fortune. Although *The Bell Jar* was published in January of 1963, however, the reviews were not what she had wished, and the physical conditions of Yeats's house were not conducive to optimism. The apartment was cold and drafty, pipes froze, and Plath could not get a telephone installed.

Ironically, at this time when she was despairing and often ill, she was driven to write almost furiously—she scribbled intense, desperate poems each morning before the children woke up. "The blood jet is poetry," she said in one of these poems, "There's no stopping it." She did find a way to stop the blood jet. On February 11, 1963, she placed towels on the floor to prevent seepage into the other room where the children were sleeping, and she turned on the gas oven. She died at thirty, leaving her most acutely painful autobiographical poems to be published posthumously in *Ariel* (1965), *Winter Trees* (1971), and *Crossing the Water* (1971).

ANALYSIS

Plath's poetry has a two-level audience—some readers are drawn to her work for its sensational-

ism, its willingness to share details of nervous breakdowns, sexual embarrassments, and attempts at suicide. This aspect of her work has resulted in many imitators. On another level, her poems and stories, by showing the reactions of a raw-nerved, hyperaware individual to an indifferent, if not hostile, environment, provide a sensitive interpretation of universal vulnerabilities. Plath's strongest poems invoke archetypal figures and stories in a way that reenergizes early childhood images of the evil parent, the human sacrifice, and all forms of death-bringers.

The subject of Plath's poetry is Plath. Her feelings for her loved and hated father, her suicide attempts, her anger at the world, and her existential loneliness are described in sharp detail. The poems rage or speak up faintly from a well of despair. Occasionally they scream a furious triumph over the forces that oppress her. These outcries are direct and unmediated by art, as the final lines of the devastating poem "Daddy" illustrate:

> There's a stake in your fat black heart
> And the villagers never liked you.
> They are dancing and stamping on you.
> They always *knew* it was you.
> Daddy, daddy, you bastard, I'm through.

Many of the poems express the need for purification—for a death followed by a rebirth. "Lady Lazarus" touches on her suicide attempt at twenty and looks toward her third, successful attempt at thirty; including a near-drowning at ten, the poem ritualizes suicide as an act of purification. The work is cited by those who argue that Plath did not intend her third attempt to be successful but wanted to be found just in time and revived, as she had been before. "Dying," she says, "Is an art, like everything else./ I do it exceptionally well." It could be said that Plath's basic subject is the art of dying.

Stylistically, the poems changed as her emotional intensity increased. Her first poems were carefully structured, delicately rhymed pieces, but she soon learned to do violence to form to produce tough, forceful poems that were spare and cutting. Her early poems were characterized by sharply detailed nature imagery, with verbs carrying much of the burden of description.

"Point Shirley," essentially an elegy for her grandmother, begins

From Water-Tower Hill to the brick prison
The shingle booms, bickering under
The sea's collapse.
Snowcakes break and welter.

Later on, after the grandmother's absence is noted, the poet returns to the natural scene with more verb-dominated detail:

The waves'
Spewed relics clicker masses in the wind,

Grey waves the stub-necked eiders ride.

The rhymes are almost-rhymes (collapse/ leaps/ chips; against/ danced/ lanced). The off-rhymes and the alternating long and short lines suggest the rhythm of the sea, a movement that provides a subtle counterpoint to the argument of the poem.

The later poems are more direct, more personal, and far less pictorial. Nature images are pressed casually into the service of an emotional immediacy:

I am incapable of more knowledge.
What is this, this face
So murderous in its strangle of branches?

The last poems are dominated by images of wounds and mutilations, surgical operations, Holocaust victims, and illness. The final poems become incandescent in their suffering; Jew and Nazi become a metaphor for the relationship between Plath and her dead father and in fact the whole male, oppressive society. The natural world that was at first Plath's delight and absorption now becomes permeated with human pain, as in "Poppies in October":

Even the sun-clouds this morning cannot manage
    such skirts,
Nor the woman in the ambulance
Whose red heart blooms through her coat so
    astoundingly.

All barriers between the metaphoric and the real, the interior and exterior world, blur as Plath approaches her final act of self-deliverance.

Her autobiographical novel, *The Bell Jar*, shows the same confrontation between its hypersensitive woman persona, Esther Greenwood, and a hostile world. Written in England during the period after the birth of Plath's children, the novel describes the events that led up to her breakdown in 1953. Particularly vivid in her novel is the growing feeling of detachment from herself that she must have shared with her protagonist: Esther pictures herself as "a hole in the ground," "a small black dot," a vacancy. When she looks at herself in mirrors, she does not recognize herself but sees the image as someone else.

Like the poetry, *The Bell Jar* is dominated by death and the oppressive male world that pulls Esther deathward. Esther's deterioration is chronicled from her New York experience, which Plath experienced when she won the *Mademoiselle* contest, back to Boston, where she sank deeper and deeper into depression, through her institutionalization and treatment, up to her release from the asylum as cured. The style reflects the content, as scenes become shorter and more disconnected to reflect Esther's progressive loss of contact with reality. The poems' preoccupation with purification and their confounding of life with death are also present in the novel. These recurrent, even obsessive themes are perhaps most directly described when Esther tells what happened when she tried to commit suicide, as Plath herself had done at twenty, by climbing into a hole in the cellar:

Cobwebs touched my face with the softness of moths. Wrapping my black coat around me like my own sweet shadow, I unscrewed the bottle of pills and started taking them. . . .
The silence drew off, baring the pebbles and shells and all the tatty wreckage of my life. Then, at the rim of vision, it gathered itself, and in one sweeping tide, rushed me to sleep.

THE BELL JAR

First published: 1963
Type of work: Novel

An individualistic and egalitarian-minded young woman struggles with the suffocating conformism of the 1950's.

In *The Bell Jar*, the veil of fiction over the story of Plath's own life is so thin that her mother fought its publication in the United States, writing to Harper & Row that "practically every character represents someone—often in caricature—whom Sylvia loved; each person had given freely of time, thought, affection, and, in one case, financial help during those agonizing six months of breakdown in 1953." Nevertheless, the story has the appeal of the novel, and it uses the conventions of fiction in the structuring of the experience it narrates.

The heroine, Esther Greenwood, is looking back (like Holden Caulfield, J. D. Salinger's even more famous misfit) on the events leading up to her mental collapse. As in Salinger's *The Catcher in the Rye* (1951), readers will be split as to what is to blame for the breakdown—the self or the world. Through Esther's eyes are recorded the events of the early 1950's: McCarthyism, "I Like Ike,"

the electrocution of the Rosenbergs, the relative tameness of 1950's New York City. To the eyes of Esther, come to New York as the winner of a magazine contest to be guest editor of *Ladies' Day*, the real world is exclusively male and has no place for her.

Women writers create fluffy fashion articles. Women English majors should learn shorthand. The only other option readily available, wifehood, is little more than death-in-life, a self-obliteration as certain as the fate of the rug her boyfriend's mother made out of pretty scraps, then put on the floor to become "soiled and dull and indistinguishable from any mat you would buy for a dollar in the five and ten."

The richness of detail re-creates the 1950's in their patriotism and naïveté. The standard female responses to the time period are represented in Esther's fellow contest winners, such as the innocent optimist Betsey, and Hilda, the right-wing zealot with a flair for housewifely economies. At least partly because Esther believes that there is no use for her talents, which are not in one of the standard female lines, she goes into a decline. Her inability to embrace any accepted woman's role is demonstrated in a symbolic scene in which she throws her new clothes, one by one, out the hotel window, so

that "flutteringly, like a loved one's ashes, the grey scraps were ferried off, to settle here, there, exactly where I would never know, in the dark heart of New York."

Back at her home in Boston, the depression deepens, and flashbacks to her experiences with her boyfriend and her college years give more insight into the nature of her alienation. She is unable to accept that there is a double standard for sexual behavior—that her boyfriend Buddy is expected to be sexually experienced and she is not. In all the relationships she sees or participates in, the woman appears to be a puppet or plaything for the man. Yet Esther does not want to give up her sexuality for her art, either. Unable to choose between mutually exclusive options, she is paralyzed. Trying to write a novel about someone trying to write a novel, she creates one paragraph. She investigates far-fetched career and education possibilities and gives up. She never changes her clothes. She is in a state of clinical depression, just as Plath was after her trip to New York for *Mademoiselle*. Her thoughts turn to suicide.

As the protagonist becomes more and more fragmented, the novel begins to mirror her inner world, its scenes becoming shorter and transitions being suppressed so that scenes are juxtaposed as they are in Esther's mind. The jumps in time and space are a key to Esther's inner world, a world in which birth is death, death is birth, and the ultimate loss of self is both the greatest fear and greatest desire. The association of death with freedom occurs again and again. Headlong speed, careening wildly down a hill on skis, is the only thing that makes Esther happy. The chance of getting out of herself, away from the prison of self that is represented by the bell jar of the title, comes with this speed; the mad flight is followed by a crash and pain—a small death.

More and more obsessed with death, Esther collects news clipping about suicides and reacts to only that part of any conversation that could possibly be related to suicide. An important element of the whole novel, the humor of the self-deprecating narrator, is ever-present in the descriptions of the events leading up to the major suicide attempt, such as a discussion at a beach picnic in which Esther tries to get her blind date to tell her how to get at a gun:

I rolled onto my back again and made my voice casual. "If you were going to kill yourself, how would you do it?"

Cal seemed pleased. "I've often thought of that. I'd blow my brains out with a gun."

I was disappointed. It was just like a man to do it with a gun . . .

"What kind of gun?"

"My father's shotgun. He keeps it loaded."

"Does your father happen to live near Boston?" I asked idly.

After the conversation, Esther does swim out and try (most ineffectively) to drown herself. The scene is followed by the flashback to an attempt to hang herself that morning—an attempt that left her "walking about with the silk cord hanging from my neck like a yellow cat's tail and finding no place to fasten it."

The true attempt, however, is described as a serious, almost mystical event: This death is a return to the womblike hole in the cellar where, after taking the pills, she is swept away into darkness. She is then reborn: "The chisel struck again, and the light leapt into my head, and through the thick, warm, furry dark, a voice cried, 'Mother!'"

The rest of the novel explores her treatment at the state hospital and then at the private hospital that her novelist patroness sends her to, and it is perhaps less believable that Esther recovers from the illness. Her recovery is signaled by various events: She learns to admit her dislike of her mother and her mother's role, and she loses her virginity, therefore making her equal to Buddy. She feels that the bell jar that had been stifling her has, at least for a time, lifted. The final scene is the reconciliation ritual with the world. She is about to be interviewed by the doctors and dismissed from the hospital as cured. Many readers, however, will find her as lost and alienated as she was at the beginning.

The Bell Jar is striking in its appeal. It is a Salingeresque tale of a young woman who does not accept things as they are and will not compromise. The events and realities of the 1950's are seen in sharp, grotesque detail through the curved glass of Esther's bell jar.

"BLACK ROOK IN RAINY WEATHER"

First published: 1960 (collected in *The Collected Poems*, 1981)
Type of work: Poem

Unexpected, startling beauty is the gift of self-renewal that may be called miraculous.

An early work that is one of the few life-affirming Plath poems is "Black Rook in Rainy Weather," a description of a bird in a tree that uses terms of the heavenly ("angels," "radiance," and "miracles") to describe things of this earth. One of the most frequently anthologized early poems, it demonstrates the gift of the visual. Like many of the poems in *The Colossus*, it is formally controlled. It uses a unique stanza form of five-line stanzas with repeating rhymes of *Abcde* throughout the poem; off-rhymes are common. (For example, the *a*-rhymes are "there," "fire," "desire," "chair," "honor," "flare," "fear," and "occur" from the beginning to the end of the poem.) This pattern helps to convey the impression that this is a diminished world with haphazard arrangements.

Seeing a "wet black rook/ Arranging and rearranging its feathers in the rain," the observer reflects that she no longer looks for intention in nature. She no longer believes that there is some kind of "design" in the world, that natural phenomena bear God's signature. She admits to wanting some kind of communication with the Other: "I desire,/ Occasionally, some backtalk/ From the mute sky." Yet she is willing to accept the physical delight of the occasional natural revelation in its place, the "minor light" that may transform an ordinary object into a vision: "As if a celestial burning took/ Possession of the most obtuse objects now and then."

It is these unexpected transformations, these "hallowing[s]" of the daily, that redeem time "by bestowing largesse, honor,/ One might say love." The rook, with its shining feathers, may be reminiscent of Gerard Manley Hopkins's windhover, whose beauty expresses God's grandeur, but the rook's transcendence is less clearly attributed. Still, it is a redemption for the watcher, who hopes to be relieved from boredom and despair by beauty.

The poem concludes that, despite the dullness of the ordinary, miracles do occur "If you care to call those spasmodic/ Tricks of radiance miracles." The observer realizes that it is her part to be observant, to endure "the long wait for the angel,/ For that rare, random descent." Even this poem is not overly optimistic: The scene is rainy, the weather "desultory," and the season one "of fatigue." The miracles of transformation can be neither predicted nor controlled. Nevertheless, they do occur, and they redeem time from emptiness, filling it with purpose, even love. Within this limited affirmation, the poem becomes one of Plath's more positive statements.

"THE DISQUIETING MUSES"

First published: 1960 (collected in *The Collected Poems*, 1981)
Type of work: Poem

The poet is graced not by the traditional figures of inspiration but by the bizarre, distorted visitors of a surrealist painting.

Written in 1957, when most of Plath's work was still in formal verse, "The Disquieting Muses" is an unnerving explanation of alienation and otherness. The title, as Plath explained, refers to a painting by the artist Georgio de Chirico—a painting of three faceless dressmaker's dummies with elongated heads who cast eerie shadows in a strange half-light. "The dummies suggest a twentieth century version of other sinister trios of women—the Three Fates, the witches in *Macbeth*, [Thomas] De Quincey's sisters of madness," she commented. The equation suggests that the poet associates women, distortions, inspiration, magic, and poetry.

The poem is written in eight-line stanzas containing roughly four stresses per line and some rhyme, notably rhyme of the fifth and seventh line in each stanza. The poem is addressed to "Mother," who tried to teach her daughter a limited and accepted art, telling her stories of witches who "always/ Got baked into gingerbread" and praising her piano and ballet exercises. The mother, too, tried to teach her children how to keep irrational

forces at bay, chanting at the hurricane winds that threatened to blow in the windows. The power of unreason is too strong, however; the art it engenders too compelling.

Like Plath's other parent poems, this one blames the parent, at least in part, for the situation of the poet. Mother failed to invite some "illbred aunt" or "unsightly cousin" to her christening, thus provoking the anger of the uninvited. The daughter is thus set apart, unable to continue the mother-daughter tradition of benign, trivial art. She could not dance with the other schoolgirls in the "twinkle-dress" but "heavy-footed, stood aside/ In the shadow cast by my dismal-headed/ Godmothers, and you cried and cried."

The conclusion of the poem indicates that the girl is still surrounded by her otherworldly company, the distorted muses, who are witches, fates, visitors from the world of madness. She indicates that she has learned not to betray her difference:

"No frown of mine/ Will betray the company I keep." The surrealist painting is reminiscent of Salvador Dali's deathscapes, although not so explicit as they in its message. The poem suggests that to be an artist is to look at eternities and infinities, and that this gift—in the speaker's case, caused in part by her mother's oversight—is a curse rather than a blessing.

"STINGS"

First published: 1965 (collected in *The Collected Poems*, 1981)
Type of work: Poem

The bees sting a bystander in the transfer of a hive; this shakeup in the bee world facilitates the renewal of the queenship, a renewal in which the speaker participates.

One of a series of poems based on her father's (and subsequently her own) knowledge of beekeeping, "Stings" uses the behavior of bees within their hive as an allegory for her own obsession with death and renewal. A free-verse poem, "Stings" describes the transfer of the bees to the woman who is their new owner. During this transfer, the bees sting a third person, a scapegoat figure; the stinging of the scapegoat enables the hive to renew itself and re-place or awaken its sleeping queen.

In this hive there are drudges, "unmiraculous women" who are only interested in things of the household/hive, and there is a sleeping queen. The speaker refuses to identify with the drudges: "I am no drudge/ Though for years I have eaten dust/ And dried plates with my dense hair." She identifies with the queen, old and worn out, or more accurately with the queenship: The queen dies and is replaced by another queen, but the queenship is immortal, going through generation after generation.

When the bystander is stung, he takes away the pain and exorcises the male at once. The bees that stung him—they are presumably a part of her, too—"thought death was worth it"; their sacrifice was needed to exorcise the male. The rebirth, or re-covery, follows: "I/ Have a self to recover, a queen." Now that the scapegoat is gone, the queenship, glo-rious, can revive, with power and dominance and nothing of the drudge:

> More terrible than she ever was, red
> Scar in the sky, red comet
> Over the engine that killed her—
> The mausoleum, the wax house.

This poem, written a year before "Daddy," expresses much of the same theme, but here the theme is presented through the metaphor of the hive. The hive expends part of itself to expel the male and free the queen. The queen, liberated by the re-moval of the male, is triumphantly empowered.

"DADDY"

First published: 1965 (collected in *The Collected Poems*, 1981)
Type of work: Poem

The dead father who has suffocated his daughter for thirty years of her life is exorcised.

"Daddy" has an ironically affectionate title, for this poem is a violent, discordant attack on the dead parent. One of the poems Plath wrote in the fever-ishly active last six months of her life, "Daddy" is a reworking of the evil-father theme so prominent in

her poems. Because her father died when he still had mythic power to the child, the woman must de-flate and exorcise the father figure somehow. She must go through a symbolic killing of the powerful ghost in order to be free.

In contrast to the subtle rhythms of her earlier work, this poem's movement is direct and obvious. It uses harsh, insistent rhyme to hammer its mes-sage home. Its banging, jangling rhythms unnerve the reader and lodge in the mind. It relies on one repeated rhyme, an "oo" sound that becomes a cry of pain. Read aloud, the poem sounds like a chant, a ritual chant of exorcism and purification. In this poem and some others, Plath seems to be using words for their apotropaic value—as charms to ward off evil.

A series of metaphors presents the relationship between father and daughter in graphically nega-tive terms. Progressively throughout the poem, he is a "black shoe" in which she has "lived like a foot" for thirty years; he is a Nazi and she a Jew; he is a devil and she his victim; he is a vampire who drinks her blood. The vampire and the victim are perhaps the most telling images, for she sees him as a dead man draining her living blood, calling from the grave for her to join him. When she believes that she has broken his thrall, she announces victori-ously, "The black telephone's off at the root,/ the voices just can't worm through," mingling images of telephone and grave.

The poem telescopes the events of Plath's life in her recurrent pattern of contamination and purifi-cation. The father was unreachable when alive; she could not talk to him: "The tongue stuck in my jaw," the speaker says. "It stuck in a barb wire snare./ Ich, ich, ich, ich." The repetition of the German word for "I" expresses that she could not articulate her-self and establish her individuality, and it rein-forces the German-Jew image while sounding like something flapping, painfully ensnared.

"I was ten when they buried you," she says. (Plath was eight when her father died.) "At twenty I tried to die/ And get back, back, back to you," she continues. Unable to find and escape him simulta-neously that way, she tried a kind of voodoo: She married a man like her father and separated from him, thus "killing" both the husband and the fa-ther. The end of the poem is a triumphant asser-tion of rejection and freedom: "Daddy, daddy, you bastard, I'm through."

Like the ending of *The Bell Jar*, this triumph seems to be contradicted by Plath's suicide four months later. Perhaps more accurate in reflecting her state of mind is the ambivalence in an earlier stanza:

No God but a swastika
So black no sky could squeak through.
Every woman adores a Fascist,
The boot in the face, the brute
Brute heart of a brute like you.

"MEDUSA"

First published: 1965 (collected in *The Collected Poems*, 1981)
Type of work: Poem

The monstrous, distorted mother-figure is rejected so that the self may find freedom.

As "Daddy" exorcises the powerful father, the companion poem "Medusa," written four days later, casts off the engulfing mother in order to free the emergent self. Medusa is a genus of jellyfish, and Judith Kroll has pointed out that Plath's mother's name, Aurelia, is a synonym for medusa. In this poem the scene suggests a delayed birth, a watery womb-world where the jellyfish's tentacles continue to enwind and stifle the speaker, despite her desire for separation. Picturing herself as a ship chased by the medusa, she asks, "Did I escape, I wonder?" The medusa is compelling: "My mind winds to you/ Old barnacled umbilicus, Atlantic cable."

If the father is cold and distant in "Daddy" but sharply outlined and precise, in "Medusa" the mother is a blob without definition. She is "Fat and red, a placenta/ Paralysing the kicking lovers." She complains of suffocation and renounces the mother as she has the father in her desire to be herself. With the epithet "Blubbery Mary," the image slides from sea to church: "I shall take no bite of your body,/ Bottle in which I live,/ Ghastly Vatican."

The mother-medusa is swollen and grotesque; she presents a model of martyrdom and negativity whose attraction must be denied if the speaker is to be potent as an individual. Thus the poem concludes with a demand for the medusa's withdrawal:

Green as eunuchs, your wishes
Hiss at my sins.
Off, off, eely tentacle!

There is nothing between us.

For Plath, reaching selfhood does not involve the introjection of the parent figures but necessitates their rejection. This is the message of both "Daddy" and "Medusa."

"EDGE"

First published: 1965 (collected in *The Collected Poems*, 1981)
Type of work: Poem

Perfection, for the woman who has accomplished her fate, is death.

"Edge" is dated February 5, 1963; a week after it was written, the poet was dead. It is possible to consider the poem a suicide note. The often-anthologized poem is not only a statement that the writer will commit suicide; it also contains subtle suggestions about the relationship between art and life and death.

"Edge" is a free-verse poem that maintains a formal appearance through its use of twenty paired lines. "The woman is perfected," begins its description of the dead woman. The reader is reminded of the "perfection" in the early poem "Medallion," in which the snake is translated by death into art: "The yardman's/ Flung brick perfected his laugh." The dead woman of "Edge," too, is a sort of artifact; endowed with the paraphernalia of tragedy, she has transcended life and become something else:

The illusion of a Greek necessity

Flows in the scrolls of her toga,
Her bare

Feet seem to be saying:
We have come so far, it is over.

The dead children are there with her: "Each dead child coiled, a white serpent." Death is the work of art she has made of her life. Yet the poem represents a splitting of consciousness. The moon, her muse, seems to be a symbol of mind that is detached from the individual self, and the moon "has nothing to be sad about." The poem seems to see the individual life as realized through death and turned into art through death. Yet the moon, symbol of inspiration (and of the female mind), continues to shine.

Nevertheless, although the poem may suggest some kind of immortality or transcendence through its personified moon, the image that remains with the reader from this final poem is of a deathlike stillness.

SUMMARY

Plath's art is a desperate dance between order and chaos, control and abandon. In its emphasis on death and rebirth, pollution and purification, it touches strings common to many readers. Her images are memorable for their violence and eerie appropriateness. Her exact, verb-dominated descriptions of the natural world and her use of the formal devices of poetry to communicate personal pain mark her work as unique. None of her many followers in the so-called confessional school of poetry achieved her intensity.

Janet McCann

BIBLIOGRAPHY

By the Author

POETRY:
The Colossus, and Other Poems, 1960
Three Women, 1962
Ariel, 1965
Uncollected Poems, 1965
Crossing the Water, 1971
Winter Trees, 1971
Fiesta Melons, 1971
Crystal Gazer, 1971
Lyonesse, 1971
Pursuit, 1973
The Collected Poems, 1981
Selected Poems, 1985
Ariel: The Restored Edition—A Facsimile of Plath's Manuscript, Reinstating Her Original Selection and Arrangement, 2004

LONG FICTION:
The Bell Jar, 1963

SHORT FICTION:
Johnny Panic and the Bible of Dreams, 1977, 1979 (prose sketches)

NONFICTION:
Letters Home, 1975

DISCUSSION TOPICS

- Discuss Sylvia Plath's ambiguous attitude toward father figures.

- Plath was her own chief subject matter. Does she get outside herself in poems of external nature such as "Black Rook in Rainy Weather," "Stings," and "Blackberrying"?

- In what respects is Esther Greenwood of *The Bell Jar* decidedly not like Plath herself?

- What generalizations can you make about the length and arrangement of Plath's lines and stanzas?

- The poem "Edge" begins with the statement "The woman is perfected." What does this mean? Is there any definition of "perfected" other than the most usual one that applies?

- How does Plath's confessional poetry differ in tone from that of Robert Lowell and Anne Sexton?

The Journals of Sylvia Plath, 1982 (Ted Hughes and Frances McCullough, editors)
The Unabridged Journals of Sylvia Plath, 1950-1962, 2000 (Karen V. Kukil, editor)

CHILDREN'S LITERATURE:
The Bed Book, 1976

About the Author

Anderson, Robert. *Little Fugue*. New York: Ballantine Books, 2005.

Axelrod, Steven Gould. *Sylvia Plath: The Wound and the Cure of Words*. Baltimore: Johns Hopkins University Press, 1990.

Bassnett, Susan. *Sylvia Plath: An Introduction to the Poetry*. New York: Palgrave Macmillan, 2005.

Brain, Tracy. *The Other Sylvia Plath*. New York: Longman, 2001.

Bundtzen, Lynda. *Plath's Incarnations: Woman and the Creative Process*. Ann Arbor: University of Michigan Press, 1983.

Butscher, Edward. *Sylvia Plath: Method and Madness*. New York: Seabury Press, 1976.

_____, ed. *Sylvia Plath: The Woman and the Work*. New York: Dodd, Mead, 1977.

Hall, Caroline King Barnard. *Sylvia Plath*. New York: Twayne, 1998.

Hughes, Frieda. Foreword to *Ariel: The Restored Edition*, by Sylvia Plath. New York: HarperCollins, 2004.

Hughes, Ted. *Birthday Letters*. New York: Farrar, Straus and Giroux, 1998.

Kirk, Connie Ann. *Sylvia Plath: A Biography*. Westport, Conn.: Greenwood Press, 2004.

Malcolm, Janet. *The Silent Woman: Sylvia Plath and Ted Hughes*. New York: Alfred A. Knopf, 1994.

Middlebrook, Diane. *Her Husband: Hughes and Plath—a Marriage*. New York: Viking, 2003.

Stevenson, Anne. *Bitter Fame: A Life of Sylvia Plath*. Boston: Houghton Mifflin, 1989.

Wagner, Erica. *Ariel's Gift*. New York: W. W. Norton, 2001.

Wagner-Martin, Linda. *Sylvia Plath: A Biography*. New York: St. Martin's Press, 1987.

EDGAR ALLAN POE

Born: Boston, Massachusetts
January 19, 1809
Died: Baltimore, Maryland
October 7, 1849

Although best known as the author of gothic tales, Poe's most important achievement was to provide a theoretical basis for short fiction and a critical foundation for American literature.

Library of Congress

BIOGRAPHY

Edgar Allan Poe was born on January 19, 1809, in Boston, Massachusetts. His parents, David Poe, Jr., and Elizabeth Arnold Poe, were struggling actors who died while Poe was a small child. The young Edgar was taken in by a wealthy Scottish tobacco exporter, John Allan, from whom he took his middle name.

For most of his early life, Poe lived in Richmond, Virginia, with the exception of a five-year period between 1815 and 1820 when the Allan family lived in England. Back in the United States, Poe attended an academy until 1826, when he entered the University of Virginia. He withdrew less than a year later because of various debts, many of them from gambling, which his foster father refused to help him pay. After quarreling with Allan about these debts, Poe left for Boston in the spring of 1827, where he enlisted in the Army under the name Edgar A. Perry.

In the summer of 1827, Poe's first book, *Tamerlane, and Other Poems*, signed anonymously as "A Bostonian," appeared, but neither the reading public nor the critics paid much attention to it. In January, 1829, Poe was promoted to the rank of sergeant major and was honorably discharged at his own request three months later. Near the end of 1829, Poe's second book, *Al Aaraaf, Tamerlane, and Minor Poems*, was published and was well received by the critics.

Shortly thereafter, Poe entered West Point Academy. After less than a year, however, either because he tired of the academy or because John Allan refused to pay his bills any longer, Poe got himself discharged from West Point by purposely neglecting his military duties. He then went to New York, where, with the help of some money raised by his West Point friends, he published *Poems* in 1831. After moving to Baltimore, where he lived at the home of his aunt, Mrs. Clemm, and his cousin Virginia, Poe entered five short stories in a contest sponsored by the *Philadelphia Saturday Courier.* Although he did not win the prize, the newspaper published all five of the pieces. In June, 1833, he entered another contest sponsored by the *Baltimore Saturday Visiter* and this time won the prize of fifty dollars for his story "MS. Found in a Bottle."

During the following two years, Poe continued to write stories and to try to get them published. Even with the help of a new and influential friend, lawyer and writer John Pendleton Kennedy, Poe was mostly unsuccessful. His hopes for financial security became even more desperate in 1834 when John Allan died, leaving him out of his will. Kennedy finally succeeded in getting the *Southern Literary Messenger* to publish several of Poe's stories and to offer Poe the job of editor, a position that he kept from 1835 to 1837. During this time, Poe published stories and poems in the *Southern Literary Messenger.* It was, however, with his extensive publication of criticism that he began to make his mark in American letters.

In 1836, Poe married his cousin, Virginia Clemm, a decision that, because of her young age and her relationship to Poe, has made him the subject of much adverse criticism and psychological speculation. In 1837, after disagreements with the owner of the *Southern Literary Messenger,* Poe moved to New York to look for editorial work. Here he completed the writing of *The Narrative of Arthur Gordon Pym* (1838), his only long fiction, a novella-length metaphysical adventure. Unable to find work in New York, Poe moved to Philadelphia and published his first important story, a Platonic romance titled "Ligeia." In 1839, he joined the editorial staff of *Burton's Gentlemen's Magazine,* in which he published two of his greatest stories, "The Fall of the House of Usher" and "William Wilson."

In 1840, Poe left the magazine and tried to establish his own literary magazine, which did not meet with success. He did, however, publish a collection of his stories, *Tales of the Grotesque and Arabesque* (1840). He became an editor of *Graham's Magazine,* where he published "The Murders in the Rue Morgue," in which he created the detective Auguste Dupin, the forerunner of Sherlock Holmes and numerous other private detectives in literature and film. In 1842, Poe left *Graham's Magazine* to try once again to establish a literary magazine but not before publishing two important pieces of criticism concerning other nineteenth century American writers: a long review of Henry Wadsworth Longfellow, in which Poe established his definition of poetry as being the "rhythmical creation of Beauty," and a review of Nathaniel Hawthorne, in which Poe proposed his definition of the short tale as being the creation of a unified effect.

Between 1842 and 1844, after Poe moved to New York to join the editorial staff of the *New York Mirror,* he published many of his most important stories, such as "The Masque of the Red Death," "The Pit and the Pendulum," "The Black Cat," and two more ratiocinative stories, "The Mystery of Marie Roget" and "The Gold Bug." It was with the publication of his most famous poem, "The Raven," in 1845 that he finally achieved popular success.

Poe left the *New York Mirror* to join a weekly periodical, the *Broadway Journal,* in February, 1845, where he continued a literary war against the poet Longfellow, begun in a review he had written earlier for the *New York Mirror.* The series of accusations, attacks, and counterattacks that ensued damaged Poe's reputation as a critic at the very point in his career when he had established his critical ge-

nius. Poe's collection of stories, *Tales,* was published in July, 1845, to good reviews. Soon after, Poe became the sole editor of the *Broadway Journal.* In November, 1845, he published his collection *The Raven, and Other Poems.*

The year 1846 marked the beginning of Poe's decline. In January, the *Broadway Journal* ceased publication, and soon after Poe was involved in both a personal scandal with two female literary "groupies" and a bitter battle with the literary establishment. Moreover, Poe's wife was quite ill, a fact that necessitated Poe's moving his family some thirteen miles outside the city to a rural cottage at Fordham. When Virginia Poe died on January 30, 1847, Poe collapsed. Although he never fully recovered from this series of assaults on his already nervous condition, in the following year he published what he considered to be the capstone of his career, *Eureka,* subtitled, *A Prose Poem,* which he presented as an examination of the origin of all things.

In the summer of 1849, Poe returned to Richmond, once more in the hope of starting a literary magazine. On September 24, he delivered a lecture on "The Poetic Principle" at Richmond in what was to be his last public appearance. From this time until he was found semiconscious on the streets of Baltimore, Maryland, little is known of his activities. He never recovered and died on Sunday morning, October 7, in Washington College Hospital.

ANALYSIS

Poe is best known as the author of numerous spine-tingling stories of horror and suspense. He should also be remembered, however, as the author who helped to establish and develop America's one real contribution to the world of literature—the short-story form. Poe was the first writer to recognize that the short story was a different kind of fiction than the novel and the first to insist that, for a story to have a powerful effect on the reader, every single detail in the story should contribute to that effect. His stories and criticism have been models and guides for writers in this characteristically American genre up to the present time. No one who is interested in the short-story form can afford to ignore his ideas or his fiction.

Poe was influential in making American literature more philosophical and metaphysical than it had been heretofore, especially in terms of the dark Romanticism of Germany rather than the sometimes sentimentalized romanticism of New England Transcendentalists. Poe also helped to make periodical publishing more important in American literary culture. American writing in the mid-nineteenth century was often discouraged by the easy accessibility of English novels. Lack of copyright laws made the works of the great English writers cheaply available; thus, American writers could not compete in this genre. Periodical publishing, and the short story as the favored genre of this medium, was America's way of fighting back. Poe was an important figure in this battle to make the United States a literary force in world culture.

Although much of his early criticism is routine review work, he began in his reviews to consider the basic nature of poetry and short fiction and to develop theoretical analyses of these two genres, drawing upon both the German criticism of A. W. Schlegel and the English criticism of Samuel Taylor Coleridge. Poe's most important contribution to criticism is his discussion of the particular generic characteristics of short fiction in his famous review of Nathaniel Hawthorne's *Twice-Told Tales* (1837). Poe makes such a convincing case for the organic unity of short fiction, argues so strongly for its dependence on a unified effect, and so clearly shows how it is more closely aligned to the poem than to the novel, that his ideas on the short tale have influenced short-story writers and literary critics ever since.

In his theories of the short story, Poe argues that, whereas in long works one may be pleased with particular passages, in short pieces the pleasure results from the perception of the oneness, the uniqueness, and the overall unity of the piece. Poe emphasizes that by "plot" he means pattern and design, not simply the temporal progression of events. It is pattern that makes the separate elements of the work meaningful, not mere realistic cause and effect. Moreover, Poe insists that only when the reader has an awareness of the "end" of the work—that is, its overall purpose—will seemingly trivial elements of the story become meaningful in its total pattern.

Poe is too often judged as being simply the author of some horror stories that many people remember vividly from their adolescent days but that few adult readers take very seriously. Moreover, Poe is often judged on the basis of errors and misunderstandings about his personality. He has been called an alcoholic, a drug addict, a hack, and a sex pervert. As a result of these errors, myths, and oversimplifications, serious readers are often reluctant to look closely at his work. There is little doubt that Poe, however, both in his criticism and in his dark, metaphysically mysterious stories, helped create a literature that made American writing a serious cultural force.

"THE FALL OF THE HOUSE OF USHER"

First published: 1839 (collected in *The Complete Works of Edgar Allan Poe*, 1902)
Type of work: Short story

A young nobleman, haunted by a family curse, buries his twin sister alive after she falls into a cataleptic trance.

"The Fall of the House of Usher" is Poe's best-known and most admired story, and rightfully so: It expertly combines in a powerful and economical way all of his most obsessive themes, and it brilliantly reflects his aesthetic theory that all the elements of a literary work must contribute to the single unified effect or pattern of the work itself. The central mystery on which the thematic structure of the story depends is the nature of Roderick Usher's illness. Although its symptoms consist of an extreme sensitivity to all sensory stimuli and a powerful unmotivated fear, nowhere does Poe suggest its cause except to hint at some dark family curse or hereditary illness.

The actual subject of the story, as is the case with most of Poe's work, is the nature of the idealized artwork and the precarious situation of the artist. Roderick, with his paintings, his musical compositions, and his poetry, is, above all, an artist. It is the particular nature of his art that is inextricably tied up with his illness.

Roderick has no contact with the external world that might serve as the subject matter of his art. Not only does he never leave the house, but he also cannot tolerate light, sound, touch, odor, or taste. In effect, having shut down all of his senses, he has no source for his art but his own subjectivity. The narrator says that if anyone has ever painted pure idea, then Roderick is that person. As a result, Roderick has nothing metaphorically to feed upon but himself.

The house in which Roderick lives is like an artwork—an edifice that exists by dint of its unique structure. When the narrator first sees it, he observes that it is the combination of elements that constitutes its mystery and that a different arrangement of its particulars would be sufficient to modify its capacity for sorrowful impression. Moreover, Usher feels that it is the form and substance of his family mansion that affects his morale. He believes that, as a result of the arrangement of the stones, the house has taken on life. All these factors suggest Poe's own aesthetic theory, that the "life" of any artwork results not from its imitation of external reality but rather from its structure or pattern.

The only hold Roderick has on the external world at all is his twin sister, who is less a real person in the story than the last manifestation of Roderick's physical nature. By burying her, he splits himself off from actual life. Physical life is not so easily suppressed, however, and Madeline returns from her underground tomb to unite her dying body with Roderick's idealized spirit. As the story nears its horrifying climax, art and reality become even more intertwined. As the narrator reads to Roderick from a gothic romance, sounds referred to in the story are echoed in actuality as the entombed Madeline breaks out of her vault and stalks up the steps to confront her twin brother. Madeline, Roderick, and the house all fall into the dark tarn, the abyss of nothingness, and become as if they had never been. In Poe's aesthetic universe, the price the artist must pay for cutting himself off from the external world is annihilation.

"THE MURDERS IN THE RUE MORGUE"

First published: 1841 (collected in *The Complete Works of Edgar Allan Poe*, 1902)
Type of work: Short story

Dupin, the great amateur detective created by Poe in this story, solves his first and most unusual case.

Experimenting with many different fictional forms, such as the gothic tale, science fiction, occult fantasies, and satire, Poe gained great recognition in the early 1840's for his creation of a genre that has grown in popularity ever since: the so-called tale of ratiocination, or detective story, which features an amateur sleuth who, by superior deductive abilities, outsmarts criminals and outclasses the police. Such stories as "The Murders in the Rue Morgue" and "The Mystery of Marie Roget" created a small sensation in the United States when they were first published. "The Purloined Letter," the third and final story in the Dupin series, has been the subject of much critical analysis as a model of ironic and tightly structured plot.

"The Murders in the Rue Morgue" is the most popular of the three because it combines horrifying, inexplicable events with astonishing feats of deductive reasoning. The narrator, the forerunner of Dr. Watson of the Sherlock Holmes stories, meets Auguste Dupin in this story and very early recognizes that he has a double personality, a bipart soul, for he is both wildly imaginative and coldly analytical. The reader's first encounter with Dupin's deductive ability takes place when Dupin seems to read his companion's mind, responding to something that the narrator has only been thinking. Dupin, as he explains the elaborate method whereby he followed the narrator's thought processes by noticing small details and associating them, is the first of a long history of fictional detectives who take great pleasure in recounting the means by which they solved a hidden mystery.

The heart of the story, as it was to become the heart of practically every traditional detective story since, is not the action of the crime but rather Dupin's extended explanation of how he solved it. The points about the murder that baffle the police are precisely those that enable Dupin to master the case: the contradiction of several neighbors who describe hearing a voice in several different foreign languages and the fact that there seems no possible means of entering or exiting the room where the murders took place. Dupin accounts for the first contradiction by deducing that the criminal must have been an animal; the second he explains by following a mode of reasoning based on a process of elimination to determine that apparent impossibilities are, in reality, possible after all. When Dupin reveals that an escaped orangutan did the killing, the Paris Prefect of Police complains that Dupin should mind his own business. Dupin is content to have outwitted the prefect in his own realm; descendants of Dupin have been outwitting police inspectors ever since.

"THE TELL-TALE HEART"

First published: 1843 (collected in *The Complete Works of Edgar Allan Poe*, 1902)
Type of work: Short story

A young man kills the old man he lives with because of the old man's eye; he then feels compelled to confess.

Poe is often thought to be the author of stories about mad persons and murders, but attention is seldom given to the psychological nature of the madness in his stories. "The Tell-Tale Heart," one of his best-known stories about murderous madness, is also one of his most psychologically complex works. The story is told in the first-person voice by the killer, who has obviously been locked up in a prison or in an insane asylum for his crime. He begins by arguing that he is not mad and that the calm way he committed the crime and can now tell about it testify to his sanity.

The central problem of the story is the narrator's motivation for killing the old man. He begins by assuring his listeners (and readers) that he loved the old man, that he did not want his gold, and that the old man had not abused him or insulted him. There was neither object nor passion for his crime; instead, it was the old man's eye. He says that when the eye fell on him, his blood ran cold and that he

made up his mind to kill the old man and rid himself of the eye forever. Because the narrator provides no explanation for his extreme aversion to the eye, the reader must try to understand the motivation for the crime, and thus for the story itself, in the only way possible—by paying careful attention to the details of the story and trying to determine what thematic relationship they have to one another.

To understand a Poe story, one must accept Poe's central dictum that every element in the work must contribute to its central effect. The determination of those elements that have most relevance to the central effect of the story, and are thus true clues rather than mere irrelevant details, is the principle that governs the communication of all information—the principle of redundancy or repetition. Because the narrator who tells the story is a man obsessed, those things that obsess him are repeated throughout the story.

In addition to the motif or theme of the eye, which lies at the center of his obsession and thus is repeated throughout, another central theme of the story is the narrator's identification with the old man. As he plots his crime by nightly placing his head inside the old man's bedroom door, he says the old man sits up in his bed listening, just as he himself has done night after night. Moreover, he says that the old man's groan is a sound he knows well, for many a night at midnight he has felt it rise up within himself. "I knew what the old man felt," he says, "and pitied him."

If the reader ties these two ideas together and listens to the sound of "eye" rather than sees it, it is possible to understand the narrator's desire to rid himself of the "eye" as his desire to rid himself of "I"—that is, his own self or ego. Such a displacement of the image of an "eye" for that which it sounds like—the "I"—is not an uncommon "mistake" for the dreamlike nature of the narrator's madness. In order to understand why the narrator might wish to destroy himself by destroying the old man—which he does succeed in doing by the end of the story—one can turn back to the motifs of time and the tell-tale heart, which also dominate the story.

Throughout the story, the narrator notes that the beat of the old man's heart is like the ticking of a watch. Moreover, he says, he and the old man have both listened to the "death watches" (a kind of beetle that makes a ticking sound) in the wall at night. Finally, there is the theme of the tell-tale heart itself—a heart that tells a tale. Although in the surface plot of the story, the narrator thinks that it is the old man's heart that "tells a tale" on him when the police come to check on a scream that has been reported to them, it is clear that it is his own heart he hears beating. On the psychological level of the story, however, the tale that the heart tells that so obsesses the narrator is the tale that every heart tells. That tale links the beating of the heart to the ticking of a clock, for every beat is a moment of time that brings one closer to death.

Once the narrator becomes obsessed with this inevitability, he becomes obsessed with the only way one can defeat the tale of time—that is, by destroying the self, or "I," that is susceptible to time and thus death. Because the narrator cannot very well escape the time-bound death of self by killing the self, he must displace his desire to destroy the "I" by projecting it onto the "eye" of the old man with whom he identifies. Thus by destroying the "eye" he does, indirectly, succeed in destroying the "I."

"The Tell-Tale Heart," like many of Poe's other tales, seems at first to be a simple story of madness; however, as Poe well knew, there is no such thing as "meaningless madness" in the short story. The madness of the narrator in this story is similar to the madness of other Poe characters who long to escape the curse of time and mortality but find they can do so only by a corresponding loss of the self— a goal they both seek with eagerness and try to avoid with terror.

"THE CASK OF AMONTILLADO"

First published: 1846 (collected in *The Complete Works of Edgar Allan Poe*, 1902)
Type of work: Short story

In this sardonic revenge story, Poe undermines the plot with irony.

"The Cask of Amontillado" is one of the clearest examples of Poe's theory of the unity of the short story, for every detail in the story contributes to the overall ironic effect. The plot is relatively simple. Montresor seeks revenge on Fortunato for some

unspecified insult by luring him down into his family vaults to inspect some wine he has purchased. However, Montresor's plot to maneuver Fortunato to where he can wall him up alive is anything but straightforward. In fact, from the very beginning, every action and bit of dialogue is characterized as being just the opposite of what is explicitly stated.

The action takes place during carnival season, a sort of Mardi Gras when everyone is in masquerade and thus appearing as something they are not. Montresor makes sure that his servants will not be at home to hinder his plot by giving them explicit orders not to leave, and he makes sure that Fortunato will follow him into the wine cellar by playing on his pride and by urging him not to go. Every time Montresor urges Fortunato to turn back for his health's sake, he succeeds in drawing him further into the snares of his revenge plot.

Moreover, the fact that Montresor knows how his plot is going to end makes it possible for him to play little ironic tricks on Fortunato. For example, when Fortunato says he will not die of a cough, Montresor knowingly replies, "True, true." When Fortunato drinks a toast to the dead lying in the catacombs around them, Montresor ironically drinks to Fortunato's long life. When Fortunato makes a gesture indicating that he is a member of the secret society of Masons, Montresor claims that he is also and proves it by revealing a trowel, the sign of his plot to wall up Fortunato.

The irony of the story cuts much deeper than this, however. At the beginning, Montresor makes much of the fact that there are two criteria for a successful revenge—that the avenger must punish without being punished in return and that he must make himself known as an avenger to the one who has done him the wrong. Nowhere in the story, however, does Montresor tell Fortunato that he is walling him up to fulfill his need for revenge; in fact, Fortunato seems to have no idea why he is being punished at all. Furthermore, the very fact that Montresor is telling the story of his crime some fifty years after it was committed to one who, he says, "so well know[s] the nature of my soul," suggests that Montresor is now himself dying and confessing his crime to a priest, his final confessor.

That Montresor's crime against Fortunato has had its hold on him for the past fifty years is supported by another detail in the story, the Montresor coat of arms—a huge human foot crushing a serpent, whose fangs are embedded in the heel; the accompanying motto translates as "No one harms me with impunity." If the foot is a metonymic representation of Montresor crushing the metaphoric serpent Fortunato for his bite, then it is clear that, even though Montresor gets his revenge, the serpent continues to hold on.

The ultimate irony of the story then, is that, although Montresor has tried to fulfill his two criteria for a successful revenge, Fortunato has fulfilled them better than he has. Moreover, although Montresor now tells the story as a final confession to save his soul, the gleeful tone with which he tells it—a tone that suggests he is enjoying the telling of it in the present as much as he enjoyed committing the act in the past—means that it is not a good confession. Thus, although the story ends with the Latin phrase "rest in peace," even after fifty years Montresor will not be able to rest in peace, for his gleeful confession of his story damns him to Hell for all eternity.

Although "The Cask of Amontillado" seems on the surface a relatively simple revenge story, it is, in fact, a highly complex story riddled with ironic reversals. Every detail in the story contributes to this central effect, and it is the overall design of the story that communicates its meaning—not some simple moral embedded within it or tacked on to the end.

"THE RAVEN"

First published: 1845 (collected in *The Raven, and Other Poems*, 1845)
Type of work: Poem

A young student is visited by a raven that can only utter one ominous word.

"The Raven" is unquestionably Poe's most famous poem. After its publication, it became so well known that its refrain "nevermore" became a catchphrase repeated by people on the street. Poe, who told one friend that he thought the poem was the greatest poem ever written, was delighted one night at the theater when an actor interpolated the word into his speech, and almost everyone in the audience seemed to recognize the allusion.

The work remains Poe's best-known poem today partly because, in his "Philosophy of Composition," Poe describes what he claims was the method by which he composed the poem. Whether or not that description is an accurate account of how the work was composed, it is surely a description of how Poe wished the poem to be read. Thus, Poe himself was the first, and is perhaps still the best, critic and interpreter of his own poem.

As Poe makes clear in "The Philosophy of Composition," he wished to create an effect of beauty associated with melancholy in the poem; he decided that the refrain "nevermore," uttered to a young man whose mistress has recently died, was perfectly calculated to achieve that effect. According to Poe, the basic situation, the central character, and the plot of the poem were all created as a pretext or excuse for setting up the "nevermore" refrain, to be repeated with a variation of meaning and impact each time.

The plot is a simple one: A young student is reading one stormy night in his chamber, half-dreaming about his beloved deceased mistress. He hears a tapping at his window and opens it to admit a raven, obviously someone's pet which has escaped its master, seeking shelter from the storm. The raven can speak only one word, "nevermore." When the student, amused by this incident, asks the raven questions, its reply of "nevermore" strikes a melancholic echo in his heart. Although he knows that the raven can only speak this one word, he is compelled by what Poe calls the universal human need for self-torture to ask the bird questions to which the response "nevermore" will cause his suffering to be even more intense. When this self-torture reaches its most extreme level, Poe says, the poem then naturally ends.

The sorrow of the young student and the stormy midnight hour contribute to the overall effect of the poem, but the most important feature is the sound of the refrain—a sound that is established even before the raven appears by the dead mistress's name "Lenore." The echo of the word "Lenore" by "nevermore" is further emphasized in stanza 5, when the student peers into the darkness and whispers "Lenore?" only to have the word echoed back, "Merely this and nothing more."

Once the lost Lenore is projected as the source of the student's sorrow, the appearance of the raven as a sort of objectification of this sorrow seems poetically justified. When he asks the raven its name and hears the ominous word, "nevermore," the student marvels at the bird's ability to utter the word but realizes that the word has no inherent meaning or relevance. The relevance of the bird's answer depends solely on the nature of the questions or remarks the student puts to it. For example, when he says that the bird will leave tomorrow, like all his "hopes have flown before," he is startled by the seemingly relevant reply, "nevermore."

The student begins to wonder what the ominous bird "means" by repeating "nevermore." When he cries that perhaps his god has sent him respite from his sorrow and memory of Lenore, the bird's response of "nevermore" makes him call the bird "prophet" and compels him to ask it if, after death, he will clasp the sainted maiden whom the angels call Lenore; to this question he knows he will receive the reply, "nevermore." Obsessively pushing his need for self-torture to its ultimate extreme, the young man calls for the bird to take its beak from its heart and its form from his door, once again knowing what response he will receive. Although the poem is often dismissed as a cold-blooded contrivance, it is actually a carefully designed embodiment of the human need to torture the self and to find meaning in meaninglessness.

"ULALUME"

First published: 1847 (collected in *The Complete Works of Edgar Allan Poe*, 1902)
Type of work: Poem

A young man visits the tomb of his deceased lover on the anniversary of her death.

"Ulalume" is a striking example of what Aldous Huxley characterized as the "vulgarity" of Poe's poetry when he was trying too hard to make his work poetical. It is also an example of what made critic Yvor Winters, in the most severe attack ever launched against Poe, call him an "explicit obscurantist." Winters's distaste for the poem begins with its use of unidentified places such as Weir, Auber, and ghoul-haunted woodlands, which he says are introduced merely to evoke emotion at small cost. He also claims that the violent emotion suggested by the references to Mount Yaanek and the Boreal

Pole in the second stanza are not adequately accounted for or motivated. Finally, Winters argues that the subject of grief in the poem is used as a general excuse for obscure and only vaguely related emotion.

Such criticism, however, ignores Poe's critical theory that a poem should be the "rhythmical creation of Beauty" derived from those techniques that communicate the melancholy feeling of the loss of a loved one. "Ulalume" shares many characteristics with "The Raven," for the basic situation is the same. Instead of a repetition of a refrain as in "The Raven," however, the important repetition here is a dramatic one: the speaker's return to the place where he buried Ulalume exactly one year before—a return he seems to make in a dreamlike and hallucinatory trance.

The subtitle of the poem, "A ballad," justifies the rhythmic repetition of references to "crispéd and sere" leaves; the leaves serve as an objectification of the treacherous and sere memories that haunt the speaker and bring him unwittingly down by the dim lake of Auber, in the ghoul-haunted woodland of Weir. The narrator roams here with Psyche, his Soul, with whom he carries on an interior dialogue. When the narrator and his Soul see the planet Venus, the goddess of love, the narrator is enthusiastic about her, but the Soul says she distrusts the star and wishes to flee. The narrator pacifies Psyche and soothes her, however, and they travel on until stopped by the door of a tomb. When the narrator asks his Soul what is written on the tomb, Psyche replies, "'Tis the vault of thy lost Ulalume!" At this point the narrator remembers that it was last October at this same time that he brought the body of Ulalume to the tomb. In the last stanzas of the poem, the narrator asks whether the spirits of the dead have thrown up the "sinfully scintillant planet" in front of them to hide the secret that lies in the wood.

Although "Ulalume" is indeed lush in rhythm, rhyme, and sonorous words, its actual subject—the thematic motivation for the repetitions and rhythms that hold the poem together—is Poe's notion that the ideal of love (as objectified by the goddess of love, Venus) can only momentarily obscure the fact that the physical beauty that arouses love ultimately leads to the dark secret of the ghoul-haunted woodlands—the ultimate secret of death itself. Thus, although what is most obvious about the poem is its dark music, its theme of the transitory nature of physical beauty is what makes it a typical Poe poem.

"THE PHILOSOPHY OF COMPOSITION"

First published: 1846 (collected in *The Complete Works of Edgar Allan Poe*, 1902)
Type of work: Essay

Poe explains his theory of aesthetic unity and describes how he wrote "The Raven."

From the beginning of his career as a poet, short-story writer, and critic and reviewer, Poe was developing a body of critical doctrine about the nature of literature. Basically, the doctrine assumes that, whereas the lowest forms of literary art are realistic works and works created to illustrate a didactic moral lesson, the highest form of literary art is the aesthetic creation of beauty. Bits and pieces of this theory can be found developing from Poe's earliest reviews and prefaces. The theory comes together in a unified fashion in Poe's most extended and famous theoretical statement, "The Philosophy of Composition."

Poe begins his discussion by asserting that literary works should start with the conclusion or denouement and then work back to the motivation or causes that lead to the "end." Only in this way, Poe insists, can the writer give the plot an indispensable air of consequence by making both the incidents and the tone contribute to the development of the overall intention. Poe says he always begins with an "effect," preferably a novel and a vivid one; then he determines what combination of incidents and tone will best aid him in the construction of that effect.

Poe then launches into an extended discussion of "The Raven," his best-known poem, to illustrate this procedure. The first consideration in the writing of the poem, Poe asserts, was the issue of the length and scope of the work. Poe always argued that a long poem was a contradiction in terms—a long poem is actually a succession of brief ones. His first criterion for the length of a work is that it can be read at a single sitting. If the work is too long to be read at a single sitting, it loses the important effect derivable from unity of impression. Thus, Poe arbitrarily decided to limit his poem to about one hundred lines; "The Raven" is actually 108 lines.

Second, Poe decided on the "impression" or "effect" that he wished to convey. Because for Poe the sole province of all poetry is beauty, he decided that his poem should focus on this universally appreciable effect. Once making that decision, he had to decide on the "tone" of the poem. Because beauty always excites tears in the sensitive person, he concluded that his tone should be one of sadness and melancholy. Having made these decisions about the effect he wished to achieve, Poe then made decisions about what techniques would best bring about these effects. His first decision about method was to make use of the refrain, for it is universally appreciated in poetry, and its impression depends on repetition and a monotone of sound. Although the sound would remain the same, however, the thought conveyed by the sound should constantly vary. Deciding that the best refrain would be a single word, Poe claims that the first word that came to his mind to suggest the melancholy tone he had chosen was the word "nevermore."

After he made those decisions, Poe says he then decided on a "pretext" for the use of this word in such a manner. This is an important point, for Poe does not begin with the plot, theme, or the so-called personal dilemma of his primary character. Rather, the character and the plot—what one often thinks are the most important elements—are really only a pretext or an excuse for using the techniques that will create the effect that he wants.

Realizing that the monotonous repetition of the word "nevermore" would belie any reasoning person, Poe decided to have an unreasoning creature utter the word; the raven, a bird of ill omen, was the natural choice. Next, Poe decided on the subject of the poem. After admitting that the most melancholy subject is death, Poe then, in one of his famous pronouncements, asserts that the most melancholy subject occurs when death is associated with beauty: "the death, then, of a beautiful woman is, unquestionably, the most poetical topic in the world."

Readers and critics have often criticized Poe for this essay, arguing that it makes the creation of a poem sound cold-blooded and rational, rather than the stroke of inspiration some would prefer to credit. Poe's central theoretical assumption, however, is that poetry is the careful creation of beauty and should create pleasure in the reader. Above all, Poe is a formalist for whom the technique and pattern of a poem, not its so-called theme or human interest, is its sole reason for being.

SUMMARY

Because of critical bias against the short story in general and the gothic horror story in particular, Poe's works have not often received the serious attention they deserve. Once one sees that all Poe's fiction, poetry, and criticism revolve around his central aesthetic ideas about the self-contained pattern of the artwork, however, it becomes clear that Poe is the United States' single most important nineteenth century precursor to what is now often called postmodernism. Reality, for Poe, is constantly created in an aesthetic process. If it is the task of the artist to reflect true reality, then the artist must be concerned with the fiction-making process itself. Art is not a reflector of reality; reality is a function of art.

Charles E. May

BIBLIOGRAPHY

By the Author

SHORT FICTION:
Tales of the Grotesque and Arabesque, 1840
The Prose Romances of Edgar Allan Poe, 1843
Tales, 1845
The Short Fiction of Edgar Allan Poe, 1976 (Stuart Levine and Susan Levine, editors)

LONG FICTION:
The Narrative of Arthur Gordon Pym, 1838

DRAMA:
Politian, pb. 1835-1836

POETRY:
Tamerlane, and Other Poems, 1827
Al Aaraaf, Tamerlane, and Minor Poems, 1829
Poems, 1831
The Raven, and Other Poems, 1845
Eureka: A Prose Poem, 1848
Poe: Complete Poems, 1959
Poems, 1969 (volume 1 of *Collected Works*)

NONFICTION:
The Letters of Edgar Allan Poe, 1948
Literary Criticism of Edgar Allan Poe, 1965
Essays and Reviews, 1984

DISCUSSION TOPICS

- "The Philosophy of Composition" purports to explain the process of Edgar Allan Poe's construction of "The Raven." What thematic or imagistic elements in the poem does this essay entirely fail to account for?

- How does Poe's deliberately vague description of the House of Usher contribute to the effect of the story?

- Is Yvor Winters's criticism of "Ulalume" unfair?

- For what famous detectives in fiction did Poe's Auguste Dupin establish the precedent?

- What are the strengths and weaknesses of a critical theory that emphasizes inducing or accommodating the reader?

- For Poe, what is the relationship between art and reality?

MISCELLANEOUS:

The Complete Works of Edgar Allan Poe, 1902 (17 volumes)
Collected Works of Edgar Allan Poe, 1969, 1978 (3 volumes)

About the Author

Burluck, Michael L. *Grim Phantasms: Fear in Poe's Short Fiction.* New York: Garland, 1993.

Hoffman, Daniel. *Poe Poe Poe Poe Poe Poe Poe.* Baton Rouge: Louisiana State University Press, 1998.

Hutchisson, James M. *Poe.* Jackson: University Press of Mississippi, 2005.

Irwin, John T. *The Mystery to a Solution: Poe, Borges, and the Analytical Detective Story.* Baltimore: Johns Hopkins University Press, 1994.

Kennedy, J. Gerald. *A Historical Guide to Edgar Allan Poe.* New York: Oxford University Press, 2001.

May, Charles E. *Edgar Allan Poe: A Study of the Short Fiction.* Boston: Twayne, 1991.

Peeples, Scott. *Edgar Allan Poe Revisited.* New York: Twayne, 1998.

Quinn, Arthur Hobson. *Edgar Allan Poe: A Critical Biography.* Baltimore: Johns Hopkins University Press, 1998.

Silverman, Kenneth. *Edgar A. Poe: Mournful and Never-Ending Remembrance.* New York: HarperCollins, 1991.

Sova, Dawn B. *Edgar Allan Poe, A to Z.* New York: Facts On File, 2001.

Whalen, Terence. *Edgar Allan Poe and the Masses: The Political Economy of Literature in Antebellum America.* Princeton, N.J.: Princeton University Press, 1999.

KATHERINE ANNE PORTER

Born: Indian Creek, Texas
        May 15, 1890
Died: Silver Spring, Maryland
        September 18, 1980

Porter's fiction is generally regarded as being of the highest quality; her short fiction is lauded for its distinctiveness and is considered a model of conciseness, subtlety, and elegance.

Courtesy, Special Collections, University
of Maryland Libraries

BIOGRAPHY

Katherine Anne Porter was born in Indian Creek, Texas, on May 15, 1890, the daughter of Harrison and Mary Alice Jones Porter. Porter was proud of her descent from Daniel Boone, the brother of her great-great-grandfather. Her mother died in 1892, and the family moved to Kyle, Texas, where she was raised by her grandmother.

She early showed her independent and intrepid spirit. Educated at home and in several convent schools in the South, Porter eloped at sixteen and was divorced at nineteen. The name of her first husband is not known. Her apprenticeship as a writer began with a newspaper job in Chicago, where she also acted small parts in films. In Denver, Colorado, she worked for the *Rocky Mountain News* and, it is generally believed, contracted tuberculosis and influenza. She continued hack writing in New York, studied art in Mexico, and wrote her first story to be published in a large national magazine: "Maria Concepción" appeared in *Century Magazine* in 1922. It was followed by the publication of "He," in *New Masses* in 1927; "Rope," in *The Second American Caravan*, an annual of new writing, in 1928; and "The Jilting of Granny Weatherall," in *Transition*, 1929.

In 1930, her first book appeared: *Flowering Judas, and Other Stories*, which included (in addition to the title story) the four stories mentioned above and six others. The following year, she received a Guggenheim Fellowship and returned to Mexico, where she formed a close relationship with the writer Hart Crane. After a bitter quarrel, Porter sailed for Europe in August, 1931. Crane committed suicide in 1932. The following year Porter married Eugene Pressley, a member of the U.S. Foreign Service; they were divorced in 1938. Afterward Porter married Albert Russell Erskine, Jr., a member of the faculty at Louisiana State University; they were divorced in 1942.

Despite the confusion and unsettled nature of her personal life—the many moves, disappointments, illnesses, and occasional poverty—Porter produced some of her most distinguished work in the decade of the 1930's. The stories in *Flowering Judas* are all set in the South, the Southwest, or Mexico except for one; "Theft" is set in New York. Although the author denied that they were autobiographical, she did admit that many of them were based on episodes that she had experienced or observed and insisted that everything she ever wrote was solidly based on something in real life.

A Book-of-the-Month-Club Award was given to Porter in 1937, and two years later, a collection of three long stories appeared under the title of one of them: *Pale Horse, Pale Rider: Three Short Novels* (1939), which also contains *Noon Wine* and *Old Mortality*. Colorado, where Porter nearly died from influenza, is the setting of the title story; *Noon Wine* and *Old Mortality* take place in the Southwest. There followed another award, the first annual gold medal for literature from the Society of Libraries of New York University in 1940. Porter was elected to the National Institute of Arts and Letters in 1943, and the following year saw the publication of *The Leaning Tower, and Other Stories*, which contained a collection of seven stories titled "The Old Order," set in the South, and two others set in the Southwest. "A Day's Work" takes place in New York, and the title story uses Berlin as its setting.

From 1949 to 1962, Porter was a lecturer and teacher at writers' conferences in more than two hundred universities and colleges in the United States and Europe and was a member of the faculties of English at Olivet College, Stanford University, the University of Michigan, the University of Virginia, and Washington and Lee University.

Her long-expected and only novel, *Ship of Fools*, was published in 1962; Porter, then aged seventy-one, claimed that she had been working on it since the age of five. It is generally thought to have taken about twenty years to write. This book again suggests possible sources in her experiences in Mexico and Germany. Although critical responses to the novel were not unanimously favorable, it was a success, and further recognition followed: election to the American Academy of Arts and Letters, the Gold Medal for Fiction, the National Book Award for fiction, and the Pulitzer Prize in fiction. *The Collected Stories of Katherine Anne Porter*, including four not previously published in book form, appeared in 1965, and *The Collected Essays and Occasional Writings* in 1970. Porter also published critical essays, reminiscences, and poems. Her last place of residence was Silver Spring, Maryland, where she died on September 18, 1980, at the age of ninety.

ANALYSIS

Compared to many other successful and renowned writers, Porter published a rather small amount of writing. Among the reasons were that, by her own account, she burned many of her manuscripts and made no attempt to publish anything at all until she was thirty years old. Her fiction comprised twenty-three short stories, four short novels, and one long novel. Perhaps another reason for this rather small amount of published fiction is that Porter had to earn her living in ways other than writing, primarily as a teacher and lecturer.

Her fiction is closely related to her firsthand experiences, thus avoiding generalizations in favor of close observation, deeply felt emotions, and careful craft. Although the work is not obviously autobiographical, it is clearly based on places and people that she knew. Three distinct groups constitute Porter's fiction: working-class or middle-class families, situations and persons in Mexico or Germany (including a ship voyaging between the two countries), and various relationships explored against a background of the South and the Southwest.

Porter lacks what could be called "vulgar appeal," but her meticulous devotion to clear, plain writing and her conviction that human life has meaning, even in the chaos of world catastrophe, made her a writer whose themes—love, marriage, other relationships, and alien cultures—appeal to readers who value serious subjects treated seriously and language that is precise and pure.

In a foreword to *Flowering Judas*, Porter wrote about her craft and asserted her faith in "the voice of the individual artist" and in the unchanging survival of the arts, which, she said, are indestructible because "they represent the substance of faith and the only reality." It is this conviction and this spirit that informs in some way everything Porter wrote.

With her own credo in mind, Porter's fiction can be seen to have a meaning that is related to her views of human nature and her ideas about the human spirit. For example, *Ship of Fools*, her only novel and her most ambitious work, explores the ways that human beings reveal themselves—in all their meanness, self-centeredness, vanity, lust, and greed. In the foreword mentioned above, Porter indicated the connection between her fiction and her effort to "grasp the meaning" of threatened world catastrophe and to "understand the logic of this majestic and terrible failure of the life of man in the Western world." Her attempts to deal with this large question are found primarily in *Ship of Fools*, but her faith in the larger human spirit of love, generosity, and tenderness is present only by implication as she exposes without pity that side of human nature which is least admirable, least lovable.

In her shorter fiction as well, Porter presents the same ambiguity. For example, *Noon Wine*, "Theft," and "Magic" are only three stories that portray human nature at its worst—weak, dishonest, and cruel. By contrast, the stories set in the familiar world of her girlhood, the seven stories included under the heading "The Old Order" (such as "The Source," "The Last Leaf," and "The Grave"), are tender, gently humorous, and poignant evocations of people and situations that were part of Porter's past. These stories and others portray a view of humanity that is in strong contrast to the harsher realities of *Ship of Fools*.

A notable quality of the fiction that depicts people in friendly, loving, close relationships, such as *Old Mortality, Pale Horse, Pale Rider,* and "The Fig Tree," is that of timelessness. These works are not dated in the way that *Ship of Fools* is. Thus Porter seems to be asserting the faith that is mentioned in the foreword to *Flowering Judas,* though the title story seems to belie it.

It is these contradictory elements that make Porter's work ambiguous, not easy to summarize or categorize. Within individual works, Porter uses counterpoint to underline the ironies of life.

In "Holiday," for example, she contrasts the busy, matter-of-fact lives of the Müllers with the lonely, strenuous life of the crippled mute who is a member of the family yet totally ignored by them. Another counterpoint is that of the narrator, a young woman who may well be Miranda, though she is not named. (Several of Porter's stories have as their main character a girl or young woman named Miranda or someone like her; she is a kind of stand-in for the author.)

Porter's relatively small body of work encompasses a notable variety of characters, situations, and settings. In itself, that is not a remarkable achievement, but when one also notes the skill with which Porter selects her details, the concentration of effect, the way that the impact of the story is sometimes felt only after one has finished it and put it aside, and perhaps most especially, the transcendent beauty of the style, one understands why Porter's work is so admired by critics, academicians, other writers, and readers.

"FLOWERING JUDAS"

First published: 1930 (collected in *Flowering Judas, and Other Stories*, 1930)
Type of work: Short story

A young woman works so diligently and selflessly to help Mexican revolutionaries and children that she seems untouched in her secret inner self.

Laura, the principal character in "Flowering Judas," is a young woman who spends her days teaching English to Mexican Indian children, attending union meetings, and visiting political prisoners, for whom she runs errands and brings messages. Despite all this activity, Laura appears emotionally uninvolved, doing her work, listening to the children and the prisoners, and particularly, listening courteously to the wretched singing almost nightly of Braggioni, a revolutionary leader. Egotistical and cruel, Braggioni appears unaware of Laura's unspoken revulsion and anger at him.

Laura does feel betrayed by the discrepancy between the way she lives and what she feels life should be. She also feels fear—of Braggioni, who symbolizes her disillusionment, of danger, of death. She is caught between her commitment to her present life and her rejection of her life before she came to Mexico.

Laura has been courted by a young captain in the army, but she rejects him, making her horse shy when the soldier tries to take her in his arms. Another young man has serenaded her as he stood under the blossoms of the Judas tree on her patio, but again she is only disturbed by him; she feels nothing more for him than she does for her pupils, who she realizes are strangers to her.

Wearing a nunlike dress with a lace-edged collar, Laura strives to attain stoicism, drawing strength from a single word which epitomizes her aloofness and fear: no. Using that word as a talisman, she can practice denial, fearlessness, detachment.

Eugenio, the third young man in Laura's life, is not a suitor; he is a prisoner to whom she brought the narcotics he had requested.

When she tells Braggioni that Eugenio has taken all the tablets at once and has gone into a stupor, Braggioni is unmoved, calling him a fool. He then departs, and Laura senses that he will not return for a while. She realizes that she is free and that she should run, but she does not leave. She goes to bed; in her sleep, Eugenio appears and takes her to "a new country," which he calls death. He makes her eat of the flowers of the Judas tree, calling her a murderer and cannibal. The sound of her voice crying "No!" awakens her, and she is afraid to go back to sleep.

The theme of betrayal is first suggested by the title of the story, the red blossoms of the Judas tree being a well-known symbol of the betrayal of Jesus Christ by one of his disciples. Laura feels that she has been betrayed by the separation between her past life and her present one. She does not seem to realize fully that she has also betrayed herself by closing herself off from commitment and love. This is an ambiguous story which, like so many of Porter's stories, places the burden of interpretation upon the reader. Porter offers only subtle hints and clues to what she might mean.

"The Grave"

First published: 1935 (collected in *The Leaning Tower, and Other Stories*, 1944)
Type of work: Short story

Two children hunt rabbits and explore the emptied graves in their family cemetery.

"The Grave" is the final story in a collection titled "The Old Order," which was included in *The Leaning Tower, and Other Stories*. The seven stories in the collection are commonly called "the Miranda stories," as the principal character in each one is named Miranda; she also appears in *Old Mortality* and *Pale Horse, Pale Rider*. It is generally thought that Miranda is the author herself at different points in her life.

In "The Grave," Miranda is nine and her brother, Paul, twelve. While hunting rabbits, they come upon the family cemetery, which has been emptied because the land has been sold. The children explore the pits where the graves had been and discover two small objects: a gold ring and a tiny silver dove. Miranda persuades Paul to give her the ring he has found, and Paul is pleased with the dove,

which he guesses was once the screw head for a coffin.

Feeling like trespassers, they then continue to look for small game, and Paul shoots a rabbit. Skinning it, he discovers that the rabbit was pregnant and carefully slits the womb, exposing the tiny creatures within. At first Miranda is filled with wonder (not by chance is she named Miranda), but then she becomes agitated without understanding what it is that disturbs her. Paul cautions her not to tell a living soul what they have seen.

Miranda never does tell their secret, which sinks into her mind, where it lies buried for nearly twenty years. One day, wandering in the market of a foreign city, the episode returns to her consciousness as she looks with horror at a tray of candy in the shapes of small animals and birds. The heat of the day and the market smells remind her of the day that she and her brother found their treasures.

The theme of death and birth is expressed in several ways. The family graves and the body of the dead rabbit are related; perhaps most important, however, is the image of Miranda's mind as a burial place. For many years, she has not thought of her brother's face as a child, but it is that sudden recollection of him, smiling, pleased, sober, as he turned "the silver dove over and over in his hands" that wipes out the horror and disgust at the sight of the candied creatures and the long-forgotten feeling of agitation at the sight of the unborn rabbits.

Noon Wine

First published: 1937 (collected in *Pale Horse, Pale Rider*, 1939)
Type of work: Short novel

An encounter between a poor, shiftless farmer and a stranger seeking a hired man ends in murder.

Noon Wine is the second of a trilogy of short novels, as Porter preferred to call them (instead of novelettes or novellas, as many critics and commentators have insisted on designating those pieces of her fiction that are longer than a short story but shorter than a conventional novel). *Noon Wine* appeared in book form with *Pale Horse, Pale Rider*, from which the book took its title, and *Old Mortality*. In an essay, "'Noon Wine': The Sources," published in her *Collected Essays* in 1970, Porter explained how she shaped a work of fiction out of her memories of disparate incidents, persons, and impressions.

The setting of this short novel is a small farm in south Texas; it begins in 1896 and moves swiftly to 1905. As befits the concentrated form of a short novel, there are only three major characters in *Noon Wine*: Royal Earl Thompson, a proud and slothful man; Ellie, his weak-eyed, ailing wife; and Olaf Helton, a taciturn Swede from North Dakota, who appears one day in search of a job as a hired hand and who, through untiring industry, transforms the farm from a run-down, subsistence-level operation into a profitable concern.

Helton does not endear himself to the family, however, which includes two small boys, Arthur and Herbert, whose growth over the next nine years marks the passage of time. One day there arrives the last person to take a prominent part in the story, Homer T. Hatch, to whom Thompson takes an immediate dislike even before he has reason to do so. Hatch is seeking Helton, who escaped years ago from a lunatic asylum to which he had been committed after killing his brother for losing one of his harmonicas, the only possessions he seems to have or care about.

Hatch admits that he earns handsome rewards for rounding up escaped lunatics and convicts. In a confused burst of actions by Thompson, Hatch, and Helton, Thompson kills the stranger, believing that he was attacking the hired man. In court, Thompson is exonerated, but he still feels a need to justify his act, and he and his wife go from farm to farm as he tries to explain himself and to understand what happened. Finally, when his two sons turn on him, he realizes that he cannot continue. He writes a short note, and the story ends as he figures out how to work his shotgun with his big toe, the barrel of the gun under his chin.

The story takes its title from a drinking song that the hired man played endlessly on one of his harmonicas. As Hatch explained to Thompson when they heard Helton's tune, it is about feeling so good in the morning that all the wine intended for the midday break is drunk before noon. It is typical of Porter to choose such a passing reference for her title; the reader may comment on the significance of such a title, but Porter does not. Thus she main-tains her impersonal, detached position and forces the reader to confront the story without hindrance or help from the author, except in the matter of a tightly constructed, unembellished tale with an impact that has its source in the tale itself.

SHIP OF FOOLS

First published: 1962
Type of work: Novel

On a ship traveling in 1931 from Veracruz, Mexico, to Bremerhaven, Germany, more than thirty passengers of various nationalities reveal themselves as they interact with one another.

Porter derived the title of her only novel, *Ship of Fools*, from a fifteenth century moral allegory by Sebastian Brant. In her brief introduction, Porter states that she had read a German translation of the work while she still vividly recalled her impressions of her first trip to Europe in 1931. The thirty-odd important characters include men and women of various ages and classes from the United States, Germany, Switzerland, Spain, Cuba, Mexico, and Sweden. The novel opens as the passengers embark on August 22, 1931, from Veracruz, Mexico. (Part 1 is titled "Embarkation," the middle section is named "High Sea," and the third and final section is "The Harbors.") The novel ends on September 17, 1931, when the ship, having stopped at several ports to allow all the passengers except the Germans and three Americans to disembark, finally reaches the last port, Bremerhaven, Germany.

The ancient and familiar image of the world as a ship on its journey to eternity provides the frame-work of the novel. Temporarily isolated from their normal, ordinary lives, the travelers include people of all kinds and conditions as well as the ship's officers at one end of the ship's social scale and 876 passengers in steerage at the other end. Thus Porter can examine a large number of her many characters in highly

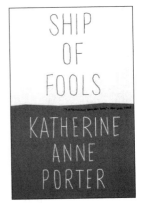

concentrated and revealing detail—their personalities, their principal relationships of varying duration and quality, and, by implication, her own attitudes toward the people she has collected and brought together in association with one another for a brief time.

There is no one protagonist, but two characters are notable for their singularity: Dr. Schumann, the ship's physician, and La Condesa (the countess), a fallen noblewoman being deported for revolutionary activities from Cuba to exile in Tenerife. Addicted to drugs and adored by a group of six noisy Cuban medical students, La Condesa becomes a patient of Dr. Schumann, who falls despairingly and futilely in love with her. The physician is also suffering from a weak heart and a sense of alienation and depression.

Two American women are especially distinguishable from the crowd because of the apparent sympathy felt for them by the author, a feeling that she does not show for the other characters. The latter are pitilessly exposed in all their unlikable natures and habits, such as the elderly couple who lavish inordinate amounts of attention on their white bulldog, the alcoholic hypochondriac, the lecherous publisher of a ladies' garment trade magazine, the abusive mother of a sickly little boy, two psychopathic children, and the company of singers and dancers who prey upon the ostensibly respectable passengers.

Instead of a plot in the usual sense, the novel consists of a series of anecdotes or scenes in which the characters appear in groups, usually as a family or a couple, with a few solitary figures. Porter's skill as a writer of stories is evident; the novel is a collection of scenes that reveal the weaknesses, if not vices, of a large number of repellent people who can only be characterized, because of the way Porter portrays them, as hateful, destructive, and evil.

Porter presents a portrait of humanity that is characterized by a large assortment of follies and sins, unrelieved, for the most part, by any redeeming qualities. The general situation of the book is that of Western civilization heading toward Fascism and on the brink of another world war. Lacking a narrative structure that builds on developing action, conflict, and resolution, the novel instead depends for its interest on the author's apparent theme of Western civilization's failure. This theme must be inferred from the unattractive, even despicable characters, not from any direct or clear statement by the author, who tells her tales, as usual, with dramatic intensity, vivid characterization, and plain, direct language.

When *Ship of Fools* appeared, the large majority of critics were enthusiastic, if not ecstatic, in their praise, but a small percentage found the book dull, repetitive, indiscriminate, and harsh—redeemed by neither humor nor compassion. As the immediate responses to the book were followed by more considered and objective evaluations, it seemed clear that Porter's reputation as a distinguished woman of American letters would rest on her short fiction, not her novel.

SUMMARY

The critic Edmund Wilson called Porter's stories baffling and elusive. These are apt descriptive terms, for Porter's stories and her single novel do not yield their meaning easily. Yet the experiences narrated are intense, the characters are undeniably human and real, and their feelings are clear and strong. The human spirit is presented in all its variety, and this spirit is not easily described. In her own words, as well as in the comments of many critics, it is just this spirit that Porter's works are all about, however difficult it is to identify and define.

Natalie Harper

BIBLIOGRAPHY

By the Author

LONG FICTION:
Ship of Fools, 1962

SHORT FICTION:
Flowering Judas, and Other Stories, 1930
Hacienda, 1934

Katherine Anne Porter

Noon Wine, 1937
Pale Horse, Pale Rider: Three Short Novels, 1939
The Leaning Tower, and Other Stories, 1944
The Old Order, 1944
The Collected Stories of Katherine Anne Porter, 1965

POETRY:

Katherine Anne Porter's Poetry, 1996 (Darlene
   Harbour Unrue, editor)

NONFICTION:

My Chinese Marriage, 1921
Outline of Mexican Popular Arts and Crafts, 1922
What Price Marriage, 1927
The Days Before, 1952
A Defence of Circe, 1954
A Christmas Story, 1967
The Collected Essays and Occasional Writings, 1970
The Selected Letters of Katherine Anne Porter, 1970
The Never-Ending Wrong, 1977
Letters of Katherine Anne Porter, 1990

About the Author

Austenfeld, Thomas Carl. *American Women Writers
   and the Nazis: Ethics and Politics in Boyle, Porter,
   Stafford, and Hellman.* Charlottesville: University Press of Virginia, 2001.
Bloom, Harold, ed. *Katherine Anne Porter: Modern Critical Views.* New York: Chelsea House, 1986.
Brinkmeyer, Robert H. *Katherine Anne Porter's Artistic Development: Primitivism, Traditionalism, and Totalitarian-
   ism.* Baton Rouge: Louisiana State University Press, 1993.
Busby, Mark, and Dick Heaberlin, eds. *From Texas to the World and Back: Essays on the Journeys of Katherine Anne
   Porter.* Fort Worth: TCU Press, 2001.
Fornataro-Neil, M. K. "Constructed Narratives and Writing Identity in the Fiction of Katherine Anne Por-
   ter." *Twentieth Century Literature* 44 (Fall, 1998): 349-361.
Givner, Joan. *Katherine Anne Porter: A Life.* New York: Simon and Schuster, 1982.
Hartley, Lodwick, and George Core, eds. *Katherine Anne Porter: A Critical Symposium.* Athens: University of
   Georgia Press, 1969.
Spencer, Virginia, ed. *"Flowering Judas": Katherine Anne Porter.* New Brunswick, N.J.: Rutgers University Press,
   1993.
Stout, Janis. *Katherine Anne Porter: A Sense of the Times.* Charlottesville: University Press of Virginia, 1995.
Walsh, Thomas F. *Katherine Anne Porter and Mexico.* Austin: University of Texas Press, 1992.

DISCUSSION TOPICS

- What typically southern values predominate in Katherine Anne Porter's short stories?
- Discuss the theme of betrayal in "Flowering Judas."
- What "old order" do the stories of *The Old Order* reflect?
- Discuss the tension between the demands of civil law and individual conscience in *Noon Wine.*
- Is Porter's *Ship of Fools* in effect a "moral allegory" similar to that of Sebastian Brant?
- By what techniques does Porter seek to unify the novel *Ship of Fools* with its many diverse minor characters? Is she successful in the attempt?

Jonathan Portis

CHARLES PORTIS

Born: El Dorado, Arkansas
December 28, 1933

Portis carries on the proud tradition of the southwestern humorists, while writing novels that are highly humorous without being frivolous.

BIOGRAPHY

Charles McColl Portis was born in El Dorado, Arkansas, on December 28, 1933, the son of Samuel Palmer and Alice Waddell Portis. His father was a school superintendent, and his mother was a woman of strong literary inclinations. He grew up and went through public schools in Hamburg, Arkansas, located in the southeastern corner of the state. There the Old South plantation culture of neighboring Mississippi gradually gives way to the frontier culture which characterizes most of Arkansas. Portis graduated from high school in 1951. In 1952, he left Arkansas for the first time to join the United States Marine Corps. He served during the latter part of the Korean War and was discharged in 1955, having attained the rank of sergeant.

Portis returned to his home state and entered the University of Arkansas, where he studied journalism. He earned a B.A. in 1958. Upon graduation, he pursued a career in journalism. He had worked for the *Northwest Arkansas Times* and during 1958 was a reporter for the *Commercial Appeal* of Memphis, Tennessee. The next year, he moved to Little Rock, Arkansas, as a reporter on the *Arkansas Gazette*. In 1960, he left Arkansas again, this time to take a reporting job with the *New York Herald Tribune*. He remained there until 1964, eventually becoming the newspaper's London correspondent. In that year, he quit his job and began a career as a full-time writer. He returned to Little Rock, Arkansas, where he still resides.

Portis's four-year sojourn at the *New York Herald Tribune* was very successful. He became a feature writer as well as a reporter, and his feature stories were so effective that at least one of them appeared in a college composition text as a model for student writing. His job as London correspondent was one of the most attractive the newspaper had to offer. Also, he came into close contact with Tom Wolfe and other architects of the "new journalism." Portis's desire to devote all of his time to fiction, however, was so strong that he resigned abruptly from the newspaper and returned to Arkansas.

He moved into a fishing shack and began to write. His long article "The New Sound from Nashville" appeared in *The Saturday Evening Post* for February 12, 1966. (It is an interesting coincidence that the career of another regional humorist was launched a few years later when Garrison Keillor also published a long article on Nashville's country music scene in *The New Yorker.*) This was the first piece by Portis to reach a national audience, and more important, it led to the serialization of his first two novels. "Traveling Light" appeared in two numbers of *The Saturday Evening Post*, those for June 18 and July 2, 1966. A considerably altered version of that short novel was published in the same year under the title *Norwood*. A condensed version of *True Grit* appeared in *The Saturday Evening Post* on May 18, June 1, and June 15, 1968. The full text appeared in book form that same year.

True Grit was both a critical success and a best seller. It was subsequently adapted for the screen in 1969; the veteran film star John Wayne played the role of Deputy Marshal Rooster Cogburn. Wayne was such a success in the part that he won an Academy Award and went on to reprise the role in *Rooster Cogburn* (1975). The latter film simply borrowed the character from Portis's novel; Portis was not involved in the preparation of either screenplay. In 1970, *Norwood* also became a film, with two of the principal players from *True Grit* acting the leading roles. Again, Portis took no hand in writing the screen version.

So commercially successful were his first ventures into fiction—especially *True Grit* and its irascible Rooster Cogburn—that Portis was able to spend eleven years on the preparation of his next novel. *The Dog of the South* was published in 1979. It was brought out by a different publishing house and did not prove nearly as successful as its predecessors, although it has won a coterie of devoted admirers. His fourth novel, *Masters of Atlantis*, appeared in 1985, his fifth, *Gringos*, in 1991. Late in his career, he began to experiment in writing for the theater. With his ear for dialogue, drama should be a natural genre for him.

ANALYSIS

Portis is a regional writer whose works occupy an honored place in the line of descent from the "Old Southwestern" humorists of the 1840's and 1850's. He has been compared to Mark Twain and, even though any humorist emerging from the South or West is likely to be compared to Twain, in Portis's case the comparison is appropriate. Like the best of the regional writers (Twain, William Faulkner, Eudora Welty, Flannery O'Connor, and Larry McMurtry, for example), his work has a much broader than regional appeal, as the commercial success of his first two novels attests. Still, his home state of Arkansas is always his center of consciousness.

Portis takes the cliché of the Arkansas Traveler and stands it on its head. In the old folktale/song, the Traveler is an outsider, and the lazy Arkansawyer is content to sit and fiddle at his cabin door. Portis takes his Arkansas protagonists and sets them on the move, launching them into a bewildering, and sometimes dangerous, world. Norwood Pratt (technically a Texan but living only a few miles beyond the border city of Texarkana) sets off to collect a debt owed him. Ray Midge of Little Rock, Arkansas, is trailing his runaway wife and his stolen car. Mattie Ross, the most determined traveler of them all, is pursuing her father's killer. Jimmy

Burns, of Shreveport, Louisiana—a city quite near the Arkansas state line—is searching for two missing persons in the Mexican jungle.

Portis's motif of the odyssey is well grounded in his home state's past. In the Dust Bowl days of the 1930's, many of the so-called Arkies went west, especially to California, seeking better economic opportunities. Many returned to Arkansas after having accumulated a little capital. Many others continued to regard their emigration, even after it had stretched into a period of many years, as temporary. Among Arkansas natives, it became proverbial that the wandering Arky would eventually return. Portis, who gave up an excellent job in eastern journalism to come home and write, always brings his peripatetic protagonists full circle, back to Arkansas. Rooster Cogburn, a central character in *True Grit*, roams for the last twenty years of his life, but he returns to die and be buried in Arkansas.

Arkansas, along with Texas and Louisiana, is westernmost among the states of the Old Confederacy. Throughout most of the nineteenth century, the western border of Arkansas was the frontier where the West began. The frontier quality of Arkansas is treated explicitly in Portis's "Western," *True Grit*, but it is also treated implicitly elsewhere. Norwood Pratt and Ray Midge might seem unlikely frontiersmen at first glance, but they share several of the frontiersman's traits. They are disposed to leave a settled life and see where the road will lead them. Neither is much attached to material possessions. Norwood is supposedly seeking repayment of a debt, but as soon as he gets his money he lends it right out again. Midge trails his stolen car through several countries, but when he finds that it has been destroyed he shrugs off the loss. The objects of these searches were merely calls to exploration and adventure. Both Norwood and Midge are uncomplicated and inner-directed. Both hold to a simple moral code that grows out of life experiences rather than religious or philosophical theory.

There is a kindliness and an affirmative quality in Portis's novels that sets them apart from most comic fiction of the period. Norwood takes a pregnant woman, abandoned by another man, as his wife. Midge takes his errant wife back, only to have her desert him yet again. The first impulse of Norwood and Midge is to care for anyone who needs caring for. The fourteen-year-old Mattie Ross and the grizzled bounty hunter Cogburn develop a chaste love that is totally convincing, never cloying or contrived. The eccentrics who abound in Portis's novels are not the southern gothic horrors encountered elsewhere; they are objects of gentle mockery. Although *True Grit* is a novel containing fine scenes of comedy and action, it is essentially a story of courage, honor, and fidelity.

Portis is not an experimenter in fiction. His narratives, though often loose, are constructed along traditional lines. He writes with precision and economy. His pacing is effective, even when his plots turn episodic and erratic. His finest achievement is his dialogue and his flawless representation of idiomatic language. He is a master of the dialects of Arkansas, Texas, and the Southwest. In fact, his dialogue rings so true when read aloud that huge chunks of it were used verbatim in the film version of *True Grit*.

Although he has so far elicited little interest from the scholarly community, Portis is a major comic writer. Indeed, the chief complaint that critics have made about his work is that he has chosen to publish so little of it over the years.

NORWOOD

First published: 1966
Type of work: Novel

The title character undertakes a comic quest, encountering eccentrics and zany situations every step of the way.

Norwood contains the autobiographical elements so often found in a first novel. Norwood Pratt served in the Marine Corps, as did his creator. Norwood lives in Ralph, a little town in the northeastern corner of Texas, only a few miles from the Arkansas line. The protagonist travels to New York City, then returns home, completely unaltered by the many adventures he has had during his odyssey. The novel is set in the late 1950's.

There are many suggestions of Voltaire's *Candide* (1759) in the story line. Norwood is a lovable, optimistic innocent. He works at a gas station for which unpretentious would be the most charitable characterization. Like Candide with his Pangloss, Nor-

wood lives in the same house as his mentor. His brother-in-law lives on disability checks from the Veterans Administration and spends his many hours of leisure spouting crack-brained philosophy. Norwood is a simple young man, both intellectually and in the sense that he is unaffected in the extreme. His ambitions are modest. He loves country music, and his life's dream is to sing on the *Louisiana Hayride* in Shreveport—he does not even aspire to the Grand Ole Opry.

Norwood's motivation for leaving Ralph is modest as well. A buddy from Marine Corps days owes him seventy dollars. He believes his friend to be living in New York City, and he heads east to collect his money. At this point, the novel becomes picaresque. As he meanders around the country on a Trailways bus, he has a series of encounters with grotesque characters. Foremost among them are Edmund B. Ratner, a "wonder hen," and Rita Lee. Edmund B. Ratner is a midget with a philosophical turn of mind. When Norwood finally gets his money, he immediately lends it to the midget. The wonder hen is a version of the performing animal with amazing powers familiar from so many off-color jokes. Rita Lee is a hapless, jilted, and pregnant young woman, who will eventually become Norwood's bride.

The part of the novel that Portis fleshes out the least is the New York segment. His former colleagues on the *New York Herald Tribune* recall that throughout his tenure there he remained the droll southerner, unchanged by the New York environment. Norwood is similarly unscathed by his big-city adventures. Ironically, the trail of the elusive seventy dollars leads finally to Old Carthage in southwestern Arkansas, only a few miles up the highway from Norwood's hometown. There both Norwood and his creator seem most comfortable.

It is the tone of the novel which causes the analogy with *Candide* to break down. Whereas Voltaire's satire is sharp and often bitter, Portis makes good-natured fun of virtually everyone and everything in the novel. The mood is genial. Portis seems to have no particular satirical target. Everyone's character traits verge upon the ridiculous, he suggests—they are merely more pronounced and exaggerated in the novel's eccentrics. This lack of focus has been criticized, but it does give the novel that buoyant comic tone which lifts it lightly over the rough spots in the episodic plot.

The author's journalistic background can be seen in the crisp, straightforward prose and the sharply delineated characters and scenes. The real strength of *Norwood*, however, lies in its dialogue, in the authenticity of the characters' vernacular speech, and—especially—in the portrayal of southern dialect.

TRUE GRIT

First published: 1968
Type of work: Novel

Two characters who appear to be opposites but are really kindred spirits undertake an exciting and hazardous mission.

True Grit is a first-person narrative that exploits the tradition of the "innocent eye"—a story seen through the eyes of an unsophisticated adolescent—a tradition going back at least to Mark Twain's *Adventures of Huckleberry Finn* (1884). The narrator-protagonist, Mattie Ross, is fourteen, the same age Huck was when he experienced his adventures on the mighty Mississippi. Mattie's narration, however, strikes a very different tone from Huck's for two reasons. First, Mattie is looking back over a period of fifty years on the events she recounts. Second, Mattie was much the same at fourteen as she is in her sixties—the kind of girl who is an adult from birth.

The setting is Arkansas and the Indian Territory in the late 1870's. Mattie lives on a farm in Yell County, Arkansas, located near Dardanelle, an Old South settlement on the banks of the Arkansas River. Mattie's father, Frank Ross, travels on business to Fort Smith—where the West begins—and there he is shot down and robbed by Tom Chaney, one of his farmhands. Chaney flees into the Indian Territory and joins a band of outlaws led by Lucky Ned Pepper. Mattie leaves her mother, sister, and brother at home and travels to Fort Smith, ostensibly to claim her father's effects but in reality to bring Tom Chaney to justice.

Portis utilizes his Presbyterian background and the cultural geography of his home state to their fullest effect. Mattie is a girl of the Old South. She is self-confident and self-righteous in her flinty Prot-

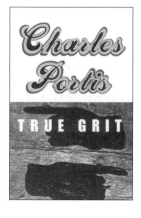

estantism, prim, proper, absolutely single-minded, and totally lacking in patience for the follies of others. She is also cool-headed, dogged, and courageous. She habitually speaks in the elevated prose of genteel Victorian literature. To her, Dardanelle and Yell County represent civilization, and she repeatedly threatens the frontier barbarians of Fort Smith with her family lawyer, J. Noble Daggett. These are the days of Judge Isaac Parker, the notorious "hanging judge," and Mattie witnesses the public hanging of three outlaws on her first day in Fort Smith.

To bring in Chaney, Mattie turns to Reuben J. "Rooster" Cogburn, U.S. deputy marshal for the Western District of Arkansas. Cogburn is approaching middle age, has lost an eye, is growing fat, and drinks too much. Mattie is looking for someone with grit, however, and Cogburn has killed twenty-three men in the past four years; he appears to possess the desired commodity. Rooster is unwilling to accept the commission without some payment in advance, and Mattie's machinations in getting the needed money produce a series of wonderful comic scenes.

A horse trader named Stonehill had sold Frank Ross four cow ponies just before the farmer was killed. Mattie insists that Stonehill buy the ponies back, in addition to paying for her father's horse, stolen by Chaney. Stonehill begins by haughtily declaring that he does not conduct business with children but eventually crumples beneath Mattie's onslaught. After he has bought back the ponies, he is even forced to sell the best one of them to Mattie at a price greatly advantageous to her (this is Little Blackie, who will play a crucial role in the climactic scenes of the novel). Mattie leaves Stonehill huddled and shivering beneath a blanket, as much the victim of her indomitable will as of his recurring malaria.

The pursuit of Chaney is complicated by the appearance of a Texas Ranger named LaBoeuf. He announces that Chaney is really Theron Chelmsford, who murdered a state senator in Waco, Texas. LaBoeuf is on detached service, working for the senator's family, and plans to take Chaney back to Texas. Naturally, Mattie wants Chaney to hang in Arkansas for the murder of her father. When Mattie, Rooster, and LaBoeuf finally cross the Arkansas River into the Indian Territory, they form an uneasy alliance.

Portis skillfully plays upon the rivalries existing among the states of his native region and incorporates the resulting raillery into the novel. To Mattie the Arkansas girl, the Indian Territory (one day to become the state of Oklahoma) is the end of the world, a savage and lawless robbers' roost. Both she and Rooster are irritated by the young Texan, whom they take to be representative of his state. LaBoeuf is flashy, conceited, and condescending. Yet, in the moment of crisis, all three—the priggish Mattie, the brash LaBoeuf, and the drunken Rooster—will prove their mettle, for they share the one crucial quality, true grit.

Pepper's gang is finally run to ground. Mattie shoots and wounds Chaney (whom Rooster later kills) with her father's service revolver. Rooster singlehandedly destroys half the gang in an exciting shoot-out on horseback, and LaBoeuf kills Lucky Ned Pepper with a magnificent 600-yard rifle shot. In the course of this action, Mattie falls into a pit of rattlesnakes, where she breaks her left arm and is eventually bitten. Rooster makes manifest his growing affection for the girl; he pulls her from the pit and races the many miles back toward Fort Smith and medical attention. Rooster's horse, Bo, has been shot from under him, so he takes Mattie's Little Blackie. The pony gallantly carries the big man and the girl at full gallop until he falls dead. Rooster then carries Mattie on his back as far as the Poteau River, where he commandeers a wagon and a team of mules at gunpoint. As a result of the wild ride, Mattie survives, although she loses the injured arm just above the elbow.

In the final pages, Mattie summarizes Rooster's fading career. As the frontier has disappeared, men like Rooster Cogburn have become increasingly anomalous. By the turn of the century, he is traveling with Cole Younger and Frank James in a Wild West show. Rooster dies suddenly while the show is at Jonesboro, Arkansas. Mattie has Rooster's body exhumed from the Confederate cemetery in Memphis and re-buried in the Ross family plot at Dardanelle. She knows that her neighbors consider this the act of an old maid going funny in the head,

but Mattie is still Mattie and will be ruled by no judgment other than her own. The crisp prose and the nineteenth century flavor of the dialogue make Mattie's narrative seem plausible from the first page to the last.

THE DOG OF THE SOUTH

First published: 1979
Type of work: Novel

An Arkansan sets out on a quest for a stolen car and a stolen wife.

By the time Portis's third novel, *The Dog of the South*, was published, his central fictional motif, the quest, was well established. *The Dog of the South* is slightly longer than his first two novels and is more whimsical even than *Norwood*. This novel, like *True Grit*, is a first-person narrative told by the protagonist. As the story begins, Ray Midge, a twenty-six-year-old resident of Little Rock, Arkansas, has just made a startling discovery. His wife, Norma, has run away with her loathsome first husband, Guy Dupree, a would-be radical. Even more distressing is the discovery that the pair has fled in Midge's new Ford Torino. In its place, they have left Dupree's compact, a 1963 Buick Special with 74,000 miles on the odometer and slack in the steering wheel.

Like *Norwood*, Ray Midge is innocent, placid, long-suffering, and optimistic. He holds no grudges and wishes no one ill, but he does want that Ford Torino back. Norma and Dupree have also taken Midge's American Express and Texaco cards. As the bills start coming in, Midge is able to follow their paper trail. Norwood's quest for his seventy dollars led him north and east; Midge's leads south and west. He follows the lovers to Texas, from there into Mexico, and finally to a remote 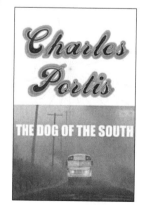 plantation in Honduras. The trip is the best part of the novel, as it allows Midge to meet the sorts of misfits and oddballs about which Portis writes so well.

Dr. Reo Symes travels with Midge. He is a "defrocked" old M.D. from Texas who is constantly pursuing the American Dream in his own fashion, through a series of harebrained get-rich-quick schemes. He drives a broken-down bus, the Dog of the South. Dr. Symes emulates the super salesmanship of John Selmer Dix, M.A., whom he knows through the latter's self-help books. The Doc considers Dix the world's greatest author. His most enduring dream, or delusion, of a great financial coup centers upon Jean's Island. The "island" is a Mississippi sandbar the Doc hopes to inherit from his mother. While he waits for it to come into his possession, he lays innumerable absurd and grandiose plans for its development. With the publication of *True Grit*, much critical commentary placed Portis in the tradition of Mark Twain, and as Ray Midge travels southward with the scheming Doc, the reader is reminded of Huckleberry Finn's journey in the company of the two confidence men, the King and the Duke. Some critics consider Dr. Symes to be Portis's finest comic creation.

Midge encounters a number of other slightly loony characters as well: Norma, who wishes to be known as Staci or Pam; Symes's mother and another perky old lady who operate an ineffectual nondenominational mission in Central America; Dupree's chow, who wears plastic bags on his paws; a pugnacious artist whose specialty is overpriced rabbits. Midge faces a number of obstacles—the first husband, jail, a hurricane—but none of them is truly threatening in Portis's comic world. It is a formless and haphazard world, which the structure of the novel mimics.

Midge wants to recover his Ford because he feels that his cuckolding will thus be lessened somehow. When he finally catches up with Dupree, he learns that the car has been ruined and sold for junk. Instead, he gets Norma back and takes her home. At the end of the novel, she runs off again. In an objective sense, the quest has been fruitless; now the car and the wife are gone for good. Yet Midge accepts these vicissitudes with relative equanimity. After all, in the Portis novels (even *True Grit*) it is the quest rather than the outcome that is important.

MASTERS OF ATLANTIS

First published: 1985
Type of work: Novel

A good-natured spoof of the cult phenomenon in twentieth century America.

Masters of Atlantis is perhaps Portis's most curious novel. It deals humorously with a fictional cult not unlike many that flowered and then wilted in twentieth century America. The story begins in 1917. Lamar Jimmerson—an American soldier and, like so many of Portis's characters, an innocent—is in France with the American Expeditionary Force. For two hundred dollars, a gypsy sells Jimmerson a handwritten Greek manuscript. It is a copy of a book written in legendary Atlantis many thousands of years ago. When the destruction of the city was imminent, the book was sealed in an ivory casket and committed to the waves. This book is the *Codex Pappus*. After floating at sea for nine hundred years, it washed ashore in Egypt and was found by Hermes Trismegistus. After nine years of diligently studying the book, Hermes is able to read the text. Only after another nine years is he fully able to understand it, thus becoming the first modern Master of the Gnomon Society.

Jimmerson vainly searches on Malta for Pletho Pappus, the Master of Gnomonry, and the Gnomon Temple; however, he does find his first convert, Sidney Hen, a young Englishman. Jimmerson marries Hen's crippled sister Fanny and returns to the United States. He has fifty copies of an English translation of the *Codex* printed and sets out to win more converts. Gnomonry languishes during the prosperous and high-spirited 1920's (Jimmerson wonders if he will ever get the fifty copies off his hands), but it begins to flourish during the bleaker days of the 1930's. On April 10, 1936, the Gnomon Temple is dedicated in Burnette, Indiana—characterized as Gary's most fashionable suburb.

Through twenty-four chapters, the novel traces the rise and fall of Gnomonry. It chronicles the mystical careers of Jimmerson, Hen, and the other Masters of Atlantis. During the sixty years of the pseudo-religion's existence, the Gnomon leaders must face the competition of Rosicrucians, alchemists, and charlatans and loonies of every stripe.

The Masters must watch the decline of their sect from the glory days of the limestone temple in Indiana to the final housing of the sacred artifacts in a polystyrene mobile home in Texas. Portis has traced another odyssey—this time it is the journey of a harmlessly and charmingly insane idea rather than an individual.

Masters of Atlantis is certainly a satire on the tendency of many Americans to take up, briefly, the latest guru to claim a knowledge of the secrets of the universe. As the *Codex Pappus* is a jumble of non sequiturs (aphorisms, riddles, and puzzles, which combine to mean nothing or anything), the novel is also a satire on the popular books of psychic enlightenment that expound the appealing thesis that there is more to be learned from feelings and intuitions than from a rigorous study of the traditional arts and sciences. In fact, in the novel, the *Codex Pappus* spawns a hilarious brood of just such books. *Masters of Atlantis* is a gentle satire, however. Portis has Gnomonry come into being in the period of H. L. Mencken's virulent attacks upon what he considered the invincible arrogance of southern fundamentalists and Sinclair Lewis's exposé of fraudulent evangelists in *Elmer Gantry* (1927). There is no such sense of outrage in Portis's novel.

It has been noted that Portis is sometimes compared to Mark Twain, but he is assuredly not like Twain in his equanimity, geniality, and tolerance. Even in his earliest books, Twain was often angered almost to the point of madness by the perfidy and stupidity of humankind. Portis is, in this respect, much closer to the great medieval poet Geoffrey Chaucer. He finds humanity infinitely fascinating, curious, and entertaining—and most entertaining of all when combining extravagance with wrongheadedness.

GRINGOS

First published: 1991
Type of work: Novel

A typical gaggle of Portis eccentrics suffer misperceptions and misadventures, some dangerous, on the Yucatán Peninsula in Mexico.

Jimmy Burns, the protagonist and narrator, is a native of Shreveport, Louisiana, a former Marine military policeman, and a veteran of combat in Korea. He resides at the Posada Fausto in Mérida, capital of the state of Yucatán. Other expatriates living there are Doc Richard Flandin, a self-styled expert on Mayan culture, and Frau Alma Kobold, the invalid widow of a photographer. Doc Flandin affects Frenchness but grew up in Los Angeles. Frau Kobold is bitter, wheelchair-ridden, and chain-smoking. She has for many years been sending Jimmy anonymous hate letters. She sets the incidents in motion which comprise the most tightly woven of Portis's plots. She writes a letter—again, anonymous—to a flying-saucer newsletter prophesying the appearance of a mysterious El Mago at Likí'n (the City of Dawn), a hilltop ruin across the river in Guatemala.

The predicted event draws Rudy Kurle, an investigator of extraterrestrial visitations, to Mérida. Kurle believes the City of Dawn to be a landing site for visitors from outer space. He is accompanied by Louise Kurle, supposedly Rudy's wife, a young woman with a degree in human dynamics. She eventually reveals that she is not his wife but his sister. Kurle wanders off down the river and disappears. Jimmy, who earns his living as a freelance teamster, is also an occasional tracer of lost persons. He and his friend Refugio Bautista Osorio go in search of Kurle and the mystical City of Dawn. Portis sends each of his protagonists on a quest. The City of Dawn is fabricated from a ruin which Frau Kobold and her husband photographed many years earlier.

Jimmy's jungle quest leads him into a confrontation with the Jumping Jacks, a gang of dangerous hippies. The Jumping Jacks, led by Dan, an aging biker and white supremacist, are seeking the mystical leader El Mago at the City of Dawn. On the way south, Dan has picked up a girl runaway called Red and kidnapped a Mexican boy. Red is actually LaJoye Mishell Teeter of Perry, Florida, for whom a two thousand dollar reward has been offered. Jimmy characterizes Red as a girl who too easily gets into cars with strangers. Beany Girl, another Jumping Jack, is a tall, slovenly woman who horrifies Jimmy by urinating before his eyes only moments after they meet. Dan has two lieutenants, toughs with shaved heads and vacant eyes.

At the climax of the novel, the characters converge at the City of Dawn. In a desperate battle atop a Mayan temple, Jimmy and Refugio shoot Dan and his two lieutenants dead. Afterward, all ends well. Red is returned to her father. Doc Flandin has announced early in the novel that he is dying of prostate cancer. However, after acquiring a young female admirer, he seems no longer to have any inclination to die or even to be ill. Also, Jimmy's life undergoes a profound change.

Louise pretended to be Rudy's wife in order to avoid unwanted advances from the gringos of Mérida, but she finds that advances from Jimmy would be very welcome indeed. She persuades marriage-shy Jimmy to take the plunge, and they are man and wife by the end of the novel. In a final scene, Jimmy meets Beany Girl again. She has cleaned up and is now using the name Freda. She has become the live-in girlfriend of one of his old temple-robbing colleagues. Gallantly, Jimmy—

a typically decent Portis protagonist—does not expose her.

SUMMARY

Without any exaggeration of his abilities, Portis can be compared to several literary masters. Like Mark Twain, he has perfected the fictional representation of the dialect of the Upper South and the Mississippi River Valley. Like Charles Dickens, he delights in the eccentric and the absurd and depicts them wonderfully well. Finally, like Geoffrey Chaucer, he portrays his fellow humans, no matter how outrageous their behavior, with sympathy and tolerance. His books are more than funny, but if they were only funny, they would still be valuable.

Patrick Adcock

BIBLIOGRAPHY

By the Author

LONG FICTION:
Norwood, 1966
True Grit, 1968
The Dog of the South, 1979
Masters of Atlantis, 1985
Gringos, 1991

About the Author

Blackburn, Sara. Review of *True Grit. The Nation* 207 (August 5, 1968): 92.

Blount, Roy. "745 Boylston Street." *The Atlantic Monthly* 270 (December, 1992): 6.

Clemons, Walter. Review of *The Dog of the South. Newsweek* 94 (July 9, 1979): 12.

Disch, Thomas M. "Cultcrazy." *The Nation* 241 (November 30, 1985): 593-594.

Garfield, Brian. Review of *True Grit. Saturday Review* 51 (June 29, 1968): 25.

Houston, Robert. Review of *Gringos. The New York Times Book Review,* January 20, 1991, 7.

Jones, Malcolm. Review of *Gringos. Newsweek* 107 (February 11, 1991): 60.

King, L. L. Review of *The Dog of the South. The New York Times Book Review,* July 29, 1979, p. 12.

Marcus, James. Review of *Gringos. Voice Literary Supplement* 93 (March, 1991): 7.

The New Yorker. Review of *Masters of Atlantis.* 61 (November 25, 1985): 163.

Shuman, R. Baird. "Portis' *True Grit*: Adventure or Entwicklungsroman?" *English Journal* 59 (March, 1970): 367-370.

DISCUSSION TOPICS

- All of Charles Portis's protagonists are similar in a number of ways. However, what character traits contrast Norwood Pratt and Mattie Ross? What character traits contrast Ray Midge and Jimmy Burns?

- Portis is said to be a regional writer. What universal elements, if any, can be found in his work?

- How does *Masters of Atlantis* differ markedly from Portis's other four novels?

- In what ways can the quests of Mattie Ross and Jimmy Burns be compared?

- Many American novelists have treated expatriates in their work. What common characteristics do Portis's expatriates in Mexico and Central America share?

© Jerry Bauer

CHAIM POTOK

Born: New York, New York
February 17, 1929
Died: Merion, Pennsylvania
July 23, 2002

In his insightful and sympathetic portrayals of Orthodox and ultra-Orthodox Jewish communities, Potok has given dramatic form to the confrontation between religious tradition and modern secularism.

BIOGRAPHY

Chaim Tzvi Potok was born in the Bronx, New York, in 1929, the son of Benjamin Max Potok (a businessman and Belzer Hasid) and Mollie (Friedman) Potok, a descendant of a Hasidic family. Though Potok was raised in Jewish Orthodoxy and was sent to Orthodox parochial schools, by the age of ten he became interested in drawing and painting, something both his father and his teachers frowned upon.

For the Orthodox Jew, art is at best considered a waste of time and at worst a violation of the commandment forbidding graven images. Potok was told that it was better to study the Hebrew Bible and the commentaries on it (the Talmud) than to engage in such "foolishness." Writing, however, had a more ambiguous place among the Orthodox. In 1945, Potok's reading of Evelyn Waugh's *Brideshead Revisited* (1945) convinced him to become a writer.

Potok's father was a Polish émigré whose stories of the suffering of the Jews in the Eastern European pogroms taught the young Potok that Orthodoxy must be preserved in the face of a world bent on destroying both it and the Jews. He was convinced that one day the suffering of his people would play a part in the world's redemption. Much later, Potok would stand at the Hiroshima memorial in Japan, contemplating the atomic destruction unleashed upon the world and his own place in such a world. As he told an interviewer in 1981,

all of his novels would flow from that moment in Japan.

Potok's Orthodox childhood brought him into contact with the ultra-Orthodox, the Hasids ("pious ones"). Within the wide range of Judaism, from Liberal and Reform to Conservative, Orthodox, and Hasidic, the Hasids are the most rigorously fundamentalistic. Originating in Poland in the eighteenth century as a reaction against an over-intellectualized faith controlled by the rabbis, Hasidism at first emphasized the mystical elements of Judaism, though it, too, emphasized the study and interpretation of the Talmud.

Central to the Hasidic movement was the *tzaddik* ("righteous one"), a powerful leader who, it was believed, embodied the essence of the Jewish community and whose word was law. Various Hasidic sects followed different *tzaddiks*, each sect claiming to be the true faith. What was common to all was their separation from the world and even from other Jewish groups, their tightly knit communities, and the immense persecution visited upon them. Potok's novels express an ambivalence about the Hasids and thus reveal a tension within his own life.

The movement had enabled Judaism to survive despite the European pogroms and had stood in the way of tendencies toward assimilation that would have diluted and eventually purged the faith of its uniqueness. Nevertheless, in its unyielding demand for obedience to "the rebbe" and its suspicion of modern scientific and literary studies, Hasidism, he felt, was in danger of making Judaism irrelevant in the twentieth century. For Potok, the world of the Hasidim was narrow and confining, as was his own Orthodoxy. In 1950, after taking his graduate degree in English literature from Yeshiva University, he began his studies for the Conservative rabbinate.

Ordained as a Conservative rabbi in 1954, Potok became national director for the Conservative youth organization, the Leaders Training Fellowship. In 1955, as a chaplain in the United States Army, he served in Korea during the Korean War. His overseas experience proved to be formative for his writing career. In *Wanderings: Chaim Potok's History of the Jews* (1978), his nonfiction account of Jewish history, Potok explains:

> My early decades had prepared me for everything—except the two encounters I in fact experienced: a meeting with a vast complex of cultures perfectly at ease without Jews and Judaism, and a confrontation with the beautiful and the horrible in the world of oriental human beings . . . Jewish history began in a world of pagans: my own Judaism was transformed in another such world.

Though his first novel, based on his Korean experiences, was repeatedly rejected, a second novel, *The Chosen* (1967), became a popular success. In the intervening years, Potok had married a psychiatric social worker, Adena Mosevitzky (their daughter Rena was born in 1962, Naama in 1965, and son, Akiva, in 1968), and had become managing editor of the New York-based *Conservative Judaism*.

In 1965, Potok received the doctorate in philosophy from the University of Pennsylvania and became associate editor of the Jewish Publication Society of America. A year later, he was named editor in chief and appointed to the society's Bible Translation Committee. *The Promise*, a sequel to *The Chosen*, followed in 1969; *My Name Is Asher Lev* was published in 1972 (its sequel, *The Gift of Asher Lev*, appeared in 1990). Then in 1975, followed *In the Beginning*. *The Book of Lights*, which gave literary form to Potok's Korean chaplaincy, followed in 1981, and *Davita's Harp* in 1985. Potok published *The Gift of Asher Lev* in 1990, *I Am the Clay* in 1992, and *Old Men at Midnight* in 2001.

After living for some four years in Jerusalem in the mid-1970's, the family settled in Pennsylvania, where Potok taught courses in the philosophy of literature at the University of Pennsylvania. He also taught occasionally at Bryn Mawr College and at the Johns Hopkins University.

Diagnosed with cancer in 2000, Potok remained as active as his health permitted. He was coeditor with David Lieber and Harold Kushner of *Etz Hayim*, a new commentary on the Torah aimed at Conservative Jews that was published in 2001. He finally succumbed to his cancer on July 23, 2002, at the age of seventy-three.

ANALYSIS

In his first attempt at dramatizing his experiences as a chaplain during the Korean War, Potok had planned a series of flashbacks to the protagonist's Jewish boyhood that would show the stark contrast between the ingrown world of the ultra-Orthodox Hasidim and the secular, non-Jewish world that he encountered as a chaplain. A crisis of faith would find the chaplain rejecting strict Jewish fundamentalism but adhering to the Commandments with a degree of openness toward the science and literary methodology produced by other cultures.

That original unpublished novel became instead a series of books thematically linked, each exploring some aspect of the nature of a strict orthodox religious community in its confrontation with the world of secular learning and values. Rather than speak from an assimilationist or modernist position, as do the creations of such Jewish American writers as Saul Bellow and Philip Roth, Potok's characters must choose between two versions of the same living faith: the world of the Hasidim, closed yet immensely resilient in the face of suffering, and the world of Jewish Orthodoxy, reverent to the Commandments but open to the insights of modern science, psychology, and literary criticism, and whose adherents are thus tempted to forsake the One True God.

In his published novels, Potok returns again and again to the *Bildungsroman*, the developmental novel, to show the intellectual and spiritual development of his main characters and to assess how they wrestle with the main questions each book poses. In *The Chosen* and *The Promise*, for example, Danny Saunders, genius son of a Hasidic rabbi, must reconcile his strict upbringing in Talmud studies with his growing appreciation of Freudian psychology. *In the Beginning* traces the intellectual growth of young David Lurie, who decides to confront anti-Semitism and show the relevance of Judaism to the modern world by using tools of textual analysis developed in Germany. *Davita's Harp* considers the place of women in Jewish Orthodoxy, and *My Name Is Asher Lev* and *The Gift of Asher Lev* view the plight of the artist whose work wounds those dearest to him.

Potok pits good against good. His sympathies for the Hasidic community and the importance of Jewish practice mean that his characters cannot simply abandon their childhood nests without a deep struggle to keep what is of value and to add from the outside world what is also of value. It is a male-dominated society (Potok's usual first-person narrator is almost always a young man, always a genius), and fathers and sons form the core of most of the novels. Some fathers, such as David Malter in *The Chosen*, are veritable saints in their compassion and understanding; others, like Asher Lev's father, Aryeh, cannot understand their son's preoccupation with the world.

Potok's stories develop in diary-like fashion, full of everyday experiences revealed in simple diction. It is a conscious style, one patterned after such American writers as Stephen Crane and Ernest Hemingway, the short, simple declarative sentences achieving a kind of "flattening" effect as incident follows incident. This simple style belies the careful construction of each novel, and Potok has acknowledged the influence of Irish writer James Joyce, especially Joyce's *Ulysses* (1922), which is a modernist parallel of the ancient Homeric epic.

In *The Promise*, Potok has Rachel Gordon write a paper on the "Ithaca" section of the Joyce novel, in which the artistic young Stephen Daedalus is contrasted to the earthbound Leopold Bloom. Potok's references to Joyce are far from subtle. He drives home the point that Rachel, in love with literature and raised by secular Jewish parents, must come to terms with her love for Danny Saunders, raised by a Hasidic rebbe. Danny's passion is psychology.

In the Beginning is patterned after the biblical book of Genesis, in which David Lurie's many illnesses parallel the rise and fall of the Jewish people. Lurie as a child is literally dropped by his mother in an accident that shapes the rest of his life. *The Book of Lights*, with its references to the mystical Jewish Kabbala, is divided into ten chapters corresponding to the ten emanations of God.

Protagonist Gershon Loran's Kabbala teacher is named Jakob Keter; "keter" is the name for the primary emanation.

Each novel unfolds chronologically against the background of world events. *In the Beginning* takes the reader from the Great Depression of the 1930's into the World War II era, *Davita's Harp* from the 1930's through the Spanish Civil War (1936-1939) and into World War II, and *The Chosen* and *The Promise* from 1944 to the mid-1950's. *The Book of Lights* takes its story to the late 1950's, and the two Asher Lev books encompass the 1940's through the 1980's.

Throughout the novels, a radio station or newspaper headline reminds readers that the story of the central characters mirrors the struggles in the wider world: anti-Semitism in the United States during the Depression, the attraction of communism to partisans in the Spanish Civil War, the confrontation of Jewish Orthodoxy with alien cultures, the Hasidic and Orthodox conflict over whether Israel should be formed as a political state, and the question of the Holocaust and how the Master of the Universe could have allowed it. In each novel, Potok reworked his own experiences to provide tentative solutions to the problems he has set for himself.

Controlling images shape his works. The baseball game in *The Chosen* is symbolic of the competition between Hasidic and Orthodox Jewish communities; the funeral of his uncle in *The Gift of Asher Lev* speaks of the sacrifice Asher must make for the sake of his art and his Hasidic community; the vision of the pups being born in the rundown Brooklyn neighborhood in *The Book of Lights* represents the fertile, mystical Jewish experience which, Potok believed, can enrich the intellectually sterile study of Jewish law.

Potok found such mysticism useful in crafting his novels. From *In the Beginning* onward, dreams, visions, and mystical visitations haunt most of Potok's main characters. The ability of the artistic imagination to fashion some resolution to the novel's questions reflects Potok's position that Jewish fundamentalism can be enriched by its painters and writers, once they are permitted the freedom to work out their gift within the community.

In the final years of his life, Potok remained committed to exposing the irrationality and destructive potential of anti-Semitism. Like Simon

Weisenthal, he exposed the cancer of racial and religious discrimination wherever he found it.

In *I Am the Clay*, although he departed from his usual focus on subjects related to Judaism, he offers hope that human hearts can be changed. The old man in this story does not want to help the child he and his wife find lying near death in a drainage ditch, but his wife insists that they save the boy. In time, as the boy matures and shows his mettle, the old man comes to value and respect him.

Potok was convinced that without stories, history would disappear. Throughout his life, he presented the stories that would preserve many elements of history, most notably the history of the Holocaust.

THE CHOSEN

First published: 1967
Type of work: Novel

THE PROMISE

First published: 1969
Type of work: Novel

Jewish cultures conflict in the lives of two brilliant young men who must unite in their efforts to help a young friend.

The Chosen met with popular success upon publication, despite its being concerned with a small and narrow Hasidic Jewish community in the Williamsburg section of Brooklyn. The story of Danny Saunders, son of the imperious and strictly Orthodox Reb Saunders, and Danny's friend Reuvan Malter, son of a teacher at a Jewish yeshiva (parochial school), has universal implications: Can the culture of one's early years be transcended without being denied?

Danny has been chosen by his father to be the next leader of the Hasidic sect, but Danny feels trapped. His father, in an effort to impart a compassionate soul to his genius son, has raised him in silence; all the while, however, Danny has been exploring secular psychology at the library under the guidance of David Malter, Reuvan's father.

After the two boys clash at a baseball game, their friendship gradually develops, though when David

Malter becomes active in the project of building a new Jewish homeland in Palestine after the revelations from the German concentration camps, Reb Saunders imposes silence upon Danny's friendship with Reuvan. The rebbe is saddened by the news of the Holocaust, but he believes that a new state of Israel can be built only by the Messiah, not by human politics.

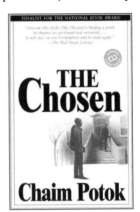

Following the creation of Israel as a state in 1948, the ban between Danny and Reuvan is lifted; the two must now explain to Reb Saunders that Danny will not wear the rebbe's mantle but will instead pursue his study of psychology. In a climactic conversation, Reb explains to Danny (through Reuvan) that the silence he had experienced will allow him to hear the cries of the world. The rebbe himself cries and finally speaks directly to his son, this time as a father, not as a teacher. Reb Saunders accepts Danny's decision; Levi, Danny's younger brother, will assume the mantle as the leader of the Hasids.

Danny's own freedom is mirrored in news reports of the Israeli war of liberation. Ironically, Reuvan, raised by his father to be a keeper of the Commandments yet open to the world's learning, becomes a rabbi after studying, as Potok himself did, at an Orthodox seminary. Danny, who has removed his distinctive Hasidic adornments of earlocks and beard, receives his degree from Columbia University.

The Promise continues the story of the two men, now in their twenties, and intertwines their lives with those of Professor Abraham Gordon and his family. Gordon has earned the disdain of Orthodox Jews for his unorthodox questioning of Jewish verities, such as the literal truth of the Hebrew Bible. When Gordon's fourteen-year-old son, Michael, explodes in a violent denunciation of Orthodoxy for its excommunication of his father, Michael is taken to a psychological treatment center to be helped by Danny Saunders.

Reuvan's father, David, has also published a book, one criticizing the reliability of certain texts of the Talmud. This book has earned him the wrath of Reuvan's teacher Rev Kalman. The Holocaust survivor fears that modernism will make deadly inroads into Orthodoxy. Reuvan can thus understand Michael's feelings, though David Malter has taught his own son about the value of Hasidic Orthodoxy in preserving Judaism in the midst of terrible suffering.

Michael refuses to talk until Danny isolates him with silence. Broken at last, Michael voices hatred for his father, whose condemnation Michael himself is forced to share. Once having expressed his true feelings, Michael can begin to heal. Meanwhile, Gordon's daughter Rachel, at first Reuvan's date, falls in love with Danny, and the two are soon married, a union of the deeply religious psychologist with the cosmopolitan secularist.

The Chosen and *The Promise* share in their cores a profound love of learning, and if both Reuvan and Danny perhaps seem too perfect, they express well the ideas of silence and its power, the varying forms of love of fathers for sons, and the journey of two young men seeking to reconcile their faiths with the wider world of knowledge. David Malter had told his son Reuvan in *The Chosen* that a person must create his own meaning: Both Reuvan and Danny chose meaning that encompassed the past as well as the present, though each in his own way. Such choices, the novel suggests, are the stuff of heroism.

MY NAME IS ASHER LEV

First published: 1972
Type of work: Novel

THE GIFT OF ASHER LEV

First published: 1990
Type of work: Novel

A gifted artist faces self-imposed exile in order to pursue his work; in middle age, he finds that the price he must pay for his creativity includes his only son.

A perennial theme in Potok's work considers the place of the artist (painter or writer) within the Hasidic community. In *My Name Is Asher Lev,* the controversy is over representational art. Asher is born in Crown Heights in Brooklyn in 1943, and as he grows it is evident that he has a gift for drawing and painting. Asher's father is frequently away on trips for the rebbe as the Ladover Hasid community (patterned perhaps on Lubavitch Hasidism) seeks to expand throughout Europe. While Aryeh Lev is arranging help for Jewish families emigrating to the United States, Asher and his mother spend long nights in loneliness. (Asher had refused to join his own father in Europe.)

When his mother's brother is killed on a mission for the rebbe, Rivkeh Lev suffers a breakdown. Later, taking up her brother's uncompleted work, she surrounds herself with her Russian studies to help her forget her heartache. Images of work completed and uncompleted pervade the novel, and Asher finds as he develops his gift that he must complete his understanding of the world by painting not only what he sees with his eyes but also what his inner vision shows him.

The pictures he paints often depict the reality of evil. At the end of the novel, Asher has revealed two crucifixion paintings to his parents. In both, the face of his mother stares from the cross, looking in abstract fashion at the ever-traveling husband on one side and at Asher the stranger on the other. Asher's parents are horrified, and the rebbe tells Asher that the artist has passed a boundary beyond which even the rebbe is powerless to be of help.

Earlier, sensing Asher's talent, the rebbe had turned him over to painter Jacob Kahn, a nonobservant Jew, who introduces Asher to the work of Pablo Picasso, especially *Guernica* (1937), the painting of the horror of the German bombing of the Basque capital during the Spanish Civil War.

In time, Asher will leave for France to work with Kahn, who tells Asher that the young man's genius is the only justification for all the hurt his paintings will cause. Yet in his exile Asher will not cease to be a keeper of the Commandments (though the commandment to obey one's parents must be reinterpreted); Potok is saying that the genuine artist must—perhaps inevitably—leave the Orthodox community but not necessarily Orthodoxy.

Asher frequently dreams of his "mythic ancestor" (a Jew who served a nobleman only to have the nobleman visit evil upon the world) and realizes that just as the ancestor might travel the world to redress the wrongs done by the nobleman, so the artist, as he reshapes the images of a world of suffering, himself can impart a kind of balance to that world as a sort of completion.

The Gift of Asher Lev begins many years later; Asher, now in his forties, is married to Devorah and has a daughter, Rocheleh, eleven, and a son, Avrumel, five. The family has returned from France to the home of Asher's parents for the funeral of Asher's uncle Yitzchok. The old rebbe convinces Asher to stay past the week of mourning, and soon it becomes clear that the rebbe, who had once put a blessing on Asher's talent, is now blessing him for another of his gifts: his son.

Asher's father will become the new rebbe someday soon, but to ensure continuity to the Ladover community, some successor must be guaranteed. Normally that would be Asher's position; but, as Danny Saunders did in *The Chosen*, Asher removes himself from consideration. It falls upon Avrumel, the father's grandson, to be next in the line of succession.

In the end, visited by visions of the dead (Picasso, Jacob Kahn), Asher returns to France alone to paint, promising a return trip to the United States to see his wife and their children. Death enfolds the story, with the funeral of Uncle Yitzchok and the "loss" of Asher's son to the Ladover community framing the novel.

Asher is convinced that his painting gift is from the Master of the Universe, yet he cannot understand why that same God would exact such a price for that gift. Avrumel will be raised in the Hasidic tradition, but, though not an artist, he will also know art.

Potok seems to suggest that the child may one day bring a new appreciation of creative talents to the Ladover. As Asher lifts Avrumel over his head and hands him to Aryeh Lev, his father, Asher hears the voice of his mythic ancestor shouting something. In some way the artist has atoned for his gift, the gift that brings both blessings and curses upon the earth.

IN THE BEGINNING

First published: 1975
Type of work: Novel

In the Bronx section of New York City, a young boy struggles against anti-Semitism.

In the Beginning, Potok's fourth published book, marked a stylistic advance in his art. In its extensive use of flashbacks and impressionistic language, Potok moved forward and backward in time creating concrete worlds suffused with the stuff of dreams, preparing the reader for the final vision of the climax. The novel is David Lurie's story. Now a teacher, Lurie's reminiscences transport him to his sixth year. At the close of the novel, Lurie has become a graduate student at the University of Chicago.

The Luries, an Orthodox Jewish family, emigrated from Poland and settled in the Bronx. David's father, Max, founded the Am Kedoshim (Holy Nation) Society to bring fellow Jews to the United States and away from the bloody pogroms that plagued their homeland. Max Lurie is full of rage at the Gentiles who perpetrate such violence. David himself falls victim to anti-Semitism after he accidentally runs over the hand of a neighbor boy with his tricycle.

Eddie Kulansky torments the sickly David, who struggles in his thoughts against the bullies of the world. David dreams of the Golem of Prague, similar to Frankenstein's monster, and imagines his putting to rest all those who would persecute the Jews.

Though he is frequently ill, David is (as are all Potok's narrators) a prodigy, making adults uncomfortable with his questions and picking up attitudes of anger against the Gentiles. With the failure of Max Lurie's real estate business during the Depression and the financial ruin of the Am Kedoshim Society, the family must face Max's own depression. Max's wife, Ruth, the widow of Max's brother David (Max married her according to the Law of Moses) is frail and superstitious. Ruth reads to her son in German, and the young David begins a study of the Torah, the Five Books of Moses, with businessman Shmuel Bader.

It is Bader and David's Hebrew Bible teacher,

Ray Sharfman, who encourage the boy to use his intellect to argue against the traditional Jewish commentators. For David, the study of the Bible texts is infused with life. His father's watch repair business prospers, and the family is able to move to a larger apartment house, but Max Lurie is burdened by his older son's interest in the new science of textual criticism, developed in Germany. There is still much rage in him, for his brother David had died in a pogrom, and his son's study seems to be bringing the Jewish tradition into question. Max's younger son, Alex, has taken up the study of modern novels and Sigmund Freud. David tries to explain that his intention is to use the learning of the secular world as a weapon against that world.

A visionary reconciliation occurs at the end of the novel, during David's visit, years later, to the site of the Bergen-Belsen concentration camp. David is joined by the spirit of his father, now dead, and by Max's brother David, who tells Max that there has been no betrayal, that Orthodoxy must be enriched by outside knowledge.

Rage will not overcome anti-Semitism; only a deep penetration of pagan culture with the insights of Orthodoxy, tempered by modern science, can ever succeed. In this vision, Potok draws upon the principles of argumentation and consolidation in Orthodoxy itself. Orthodoxy is not one generation's interpretation but the whole tradition of interpretation, wherein one rabbinical argument is countered with a second, reconciled by a third, and so on down through the centuries. David's explorations of new knowledge outside the tradition may well return to enrich the tradition itself and enable it better to penetrate the modern consciousness.

As in Potok's other *Bildungsromane*, the most fascinating scenes in the novel involve David's challenge of his instructors, and the ancient rabbinical commentators as well, on points of Scripture. The conflict here is that of good against good; the ultra-Orthodox tradition is drawn with sympathy and care, for these are the people of Potok's past. Yet, as the author's break with the Hasidim came, so David Lurie must strike out on his own, the burden of his people still in his heart. David will fight the anti-Semitic words with words of his own, not with guns, as his father had. He will make a new beginning.

DAVITA'S HARP

First published: 1985
Type of work: Novel

A young girl, spurned by the very Jewish community she hoped to embrace, finds that her time of innocence is over.

Ilana Davita Chandal, Potok's precocious narrator of *Davita's Harp*, is in sharp contrast to David Lurie of *In the Beginning*. Davita is Potok's first female protagonist, but she is also the first main character in Potok's novels to seek to join Orthodoxy from pagan society. She is rebuffed by that Orthodoxy, and in the end expresses the rage that David Lurie hoped to overcome by his mediation of secular learning and Orthodox tradition.

Davita's mother is a nonbelieving Jew, her father a nonbelieving Christian. Growing up in the New York area before World War II, Davita is accustomed to frequent moves. Her parents are involved in the Communist Party in its attempts to fight fascism in Spain and in the United States.

Davita's early life is full of stories. Aunt Sara, a devout Episcopalian, tells Davita tales from the Bible. Jakob Daw, an old family friend, aging and infirm after having been gassed in World War I, tells Davita the story of a little bird and its futile efforts to stop the beautiful and deceitful music that lulls the world into accepting the horrors of war.

Davita's father, a writer for *New Masses*, is killed in the bombing of Guernica during the Spanish Civil War. In *My Name Is Asher Lev*, the artist protagonist was introduced to Picasso's famous painting; now, in *Davita's Harp*, Potok provides a dramatic account of the event that inspired it.

Soon both Davita's mother and Jakob Daw have rejected the communists because that group had also committed atrocities. Spiritually homeless, Davita begins attending a Jewish high school, where she excels. Her mother marries an Orthodox Jew who had loved her years before, and though Jakob Daw dies in Europe, his last story remains in Davita's heart.

The little bird ceased its search for the music of the world, Jakob told her, and instead made itself very small to fit inside Davita's harp to bask in the music of innocence. Hers is a small door harp with little balls that strike piano wires whenever the door is opened. Davita's time of innocence has ceased as well.

Though the most brilliant student in her yeshiva, in 1942, Davita is passed over for the Akiva Prize because she is a woman; another student, Reuvan Malter (first introduced in *The Chosen*) refuses to accept the award after he learns the truth. Davita feels betrayed by her adopted community and her lack of opportunity to speak a few parting words on behalf of all those who suffered in the twentieth century.

Potok provides Davita with a vision of a meeting inside the harp, where Jakob Daw, Davita's father, and Aunt Sara appear. Davita says she does not understand a world that kills its own, its best. The harp sings in memoriam to all the Davitas who would never be able to speak their own few words.

Aunt Sara offers parting advice that Davita be angry with the world but always respectful. Davita would go on to public school, but the betrayal would change her life. The conflict between Orthodoxy and feminism was a new exploration for Potok, but the theme of the artist making a reconciliation with the world through art is reaffirmed.

I Am the Clay

First published: 1992
Type of work: Novel

Unlike most of Potok's writing, this book departs from his usual focus on Jewish life and, instead, is a product of the years he served as a military chaplain during the Korean War of the 1950's.

I Am the Clay is a most touching story that should have particular appeal to young readers. This novel chronicles the arduous departure of an old Korean peasant couple who are forced from their village because the Chinese and people they identify as friends from the north are invading their territory and will unquestionably deal harshly with any civilians left behind.

As their precipitate flight continues, they find a boy near death in a drainage ditch. Although the old man wants to abandon the child, his wife will not hear of doing so. She nurses the boy back to health and takes him into her family as one of her own. The boy, as it turns out, is able to reciprocate their care in remarkable ways. First he saves the couple from an attack by a pack of wild dogs. Next he finds fish for them to eat when they are desperately hungry and on the brink of starvation. Eventually, he manages to obtain an ox for them.

Finally the old man is won over by the boy and accepts him as a surrogate member of the family. He is convinced that the boy has brought him and his wife luck. As these three disparate characters move toward evolving into a family, each of the three has to deal with ghosts from their pasts.

The old man has to fight his overwhelming appetite for meat, developed when he was young and strong enough to hunt for his food. His insatiable cravings are difficult for him to control. His wife, on the other hand, has to deal with her sad, lingering memories of having lost her own child in infancy. The boy in many ways becomes a surrogate for the child the old woman has lost.

This boy, however, probably has the most difficult demons to fight in his past as he reflects on how his entire family has been killed and on how his village has been leveled. He has a new life and hope for a future, but his past will always haunt him. Potok once said that without stories we lose the past, and this is a typical example of how stories keep the past alive and serve as cautionary memories of the brutality of human conflict.

Despite the harsh events of the Korean conflict, Potok seems to suggest that there is always hope for the future. Possibly he believes in the perfectibility of humans, although he certainly suggests that they move toward perfection at a snail's pace and that they experience incredible setbacks along the way.

THE GATES OF NOVEMBER: CHRONICLES OF THE SLEPAK FAMILY

First published: 1996
Type of work: Nonfiction

Potok had followed the misadventures of the Slepak (also rendered Slaypek) family for several years before he and his wife flew to the Soviet Union in January, 1985, and finally were able to meet Vilotja and Masha in their apartment in Mongolia, where, after their five-year confinement in Siberia, they now lived in exile.

The Gates of November, whose title is derived from a line in a poem by Aleksandr Pushkin, recounts the experiences and ordeals of Solomon Slepak and his son, Volodya. Solomon, born in 1893 in a remote Russian village, was a faithful communist whose loyalty enabled him to rise quickly within the communist bureaucracy that controlled the Soviet Union after 1918. Solomon served in the military before assuming a diplomatic post in the government. Finally, he became a propagandist for the Russian news agency, Tass.

Solomon led a charmed life. When Josef Stalin set about cleansing the communist ruling class of Jews, Solomon was not eliminated. During this time, he maintained his unswerving allegiance to Bolshevism and managed to make his Jewishness inconspicuous. He went so far as to cease to have anything to do with his son when Volodya announced his desire to leave Russia and to relocate in Israel.

Volodya and his wife endured nightmarish reverses because of their decision to leave the Soviet Union. They were not only denied exit visas for eighteen years, but during this period they also were dismissed from their jobs, forced to divorce each other, and exiled to Siberia before being released after serving five years of confinement there and sent to external exile on the Mongolian border. It was in this situation that the Potoks found the couple when they visited them for one memorable evening in 1985.

When the Potoks took their leave of the Slepaks, they thought that they would never see them again, and they were convinced that the couple would

never be permitted to leave Russia. Shortly after the Potok's visit, however, the Slepeks were granted the exit visa they needed for their flight to Israel.

The Gates of November is an important documentary. It demonstrates how a corrupt political system can turn ordinary people into dissidents who can be controlled only by the most punitive measures. Corrupt governments can exist only through reducing the populace into a group of easily controlled conformists, and this state is achieved through constant intimidation.

OLD MEN AT MIDNIGHT

First published: 2001
Type of work: Novellas

In Potok's ninth and final work of fiction, the author pieces together three interconnected novellas that, when taken as a whole, might be viewed as a novel. Published in the year before his death, this book deals with a topic near to Potok's heart: the horrors of war.

The narrator for all three stories is Iania Davita Dinn, newly graduated from high school in Brooklyn when the first novella, *The Ark Builder,* unfolds. As interesting as the story is, it is perhaps unfortunate that it is told from the standpoint of the young girl who, as Potok's mouthpiece, is less than convincing. Potok's shadow casts itself over her dialogue and action in this story.

Be that as it may, Noah Stremin, a sixteen year old in 1947, to whom Davita gives English lessons, is at first quite reticent and reserved, but as the summer wears on, he eventually tells his tale to Davita. Noah, it turns out, is the only Jew from his Polish village to escape the Holocaust. As he becomes more comfortable with Davita, he tells her of his close friendship with Reb Binyomin, who looks after his village's synagogue.

Davita next appears as a graduate student, in which role she makes a more convincing narrator than she did in *The Ark Builder.* In this second novella, *The War Doctor,* Davita urges a visiting lecturer, Leon Shertov, to record in writing his experiences in Josef Stalin's Soviet Union. In his youth, when he served in the Russian army during World War I, a

Jewish doctor saved his life. Eventually Leon became a KBG interrogator, and as such, he again meets the doctor who saved his life. This time, the doctor is a prisoner, jailed in Stalin's campaign against physicians and, especially, Jewish physicians.

In the third novella, *The Trope Teacher,* Davita has matured into an accomplished woman, an author of some repute, who becomes friends with the renowned historian Benjamin Walter, who needs expert help in writing his memoirs. Davita piques him into dredging the memories of events from his adolescence, when Mr. Zapiski, who served in World War I with Benjamin's father, tutored him. She leads Walter to resurrect long-forgotten memories of his own experiences in World War II, and in so doing, she presents a convincing antiwar argument that borders on pacifism.

The War Doctor is at once the most artistically executed and most disturbing of the stories in this group that, when taken together, present a coherent case for banishing war from the universe. The depths of feeling that Potok brought to his final literary effort is clearly apparent in its execution.

SUMMARY

The novels of Potok represent both a personal quest and an artistic achievement. The quest is that of finding a viable faith that affirms ancient beliefs yet is open to the best thinking of modern times. The artistic achievement is in the working and reworking of personal experience into the stuff of human transformation, an invitation to readers to learn from their own pasts and draw on the strength of their communities even as they move beyond or away from the traditions that nurtured them.

Potok's quiet tales of small Jewish sects in New York are poignant in their simplicity and powerful in their evocation of the mending that art can accomplish in one burdened by suffering, anger, and betrayal.

Dan Barnett; updated by R. Baird Shuman

DISCUSSION TOPICS

- Is the Judaism that Chaim Potok presents essentially inclusive or exclusive?

- What roles do ancestry and tradition play in Potok's writing? How does Potok use ancestry and tradition to advance his stories thematically?

- What would you identify as the main conflict with which Potok's principal characters are usually forced to deal? Are these conflicts generational, or do they have some other origins? Provide examples.

- What role does the concept of guilt play in his stories?

- What specific historical events overshadow much of Potok's writing?

- Discuss the roles of women in the writings by Potok that you have read.

BIBLIOGRAPHY

By the Author

LONG FICTION:
The Chosen, 1967
The Promise, 1969
My Name Is Asher Lev, 1972
In the Beginning, 1975
The Book of Lights, 1981
Davita's Harp, 1985
The Gift of Asher Lev, 1990
I Am the Clay, 1992
Old Men at Midnight, 2001 (three novellas)

NONFICTION:
Wanderings: Chaim Potok's History of the Jews, 1978
Tobiasse: Artist in Exile, 1986
The Gates of November: Chronicles of the Slepak Family, 1996
My First Seventy-nine Years, 1999 (with Isaac Stern)
Conversations with Chaim Potok, 2001 (Daniel Walden, editor)

CHILDREN'S LITERATURE:
The Tree of Here, 1993
The Sky of Now, 1995

About the Author

Abramson, Edward A. *Chaim Potok.* Boston: Twayne, 1986.

Greenstein, Stephen J. *"The Chosen": Notes.* Lincoln, Nebr.: Cliff Notes, 1999.

Kauvar, Elaine M. "An Interview with Chaim Potok." *Contemporary Literature* 28 (Fall, 1986): 290-317.

Potok, Chaim. "A Reply to a Semi-Sympathetic Critic." *Studies in American Jewish Literature* 2 (Spring, 1976): 30-34.

Sternlicht, Sanford V. *Chaim Potok: A Critical Companion.* Westport, Conn.: Greenwood Press, 2000.

Studies in American Jewish Literature 4 (1985). Special Potok issue.

Walden, Daniel, ed. *Conversations with Chaim Potok.* Jackson: University of Mississippi Press, 2001.

EZRA POUND

Born: Hailey, Idaho
October 30, 1885
Died: Venice, Italy
November 1, 1972

One of the most innovative and accomplished of twentieth century writers, Pound determined the standards and direction of much of modern literature, especially poetry.

BIOGRAPHY

Ezra Loomis Pound, one of the most influential and controversial figures in modern literature, was born in the mining town of Hailey, Idaho, in 1885. When Pound was only eighteen months old the family moved to Philadelphia, where his father, Homer, became an official with the United States mint—an occupation that perhaps influenced Pound's later interest in economic and monetary matters. Pound made his first trip to Europe in 1898 with his great aunt; he would later live most of his adult life on the Continent, becoming a virtual exile from his native country. To some he would be more than that: He would be a traitor.

In 1901, Pound began college at the University of Pennsylvania, then completed his undergraduate degree at Hamilton College, in Clinton, New York, in 1905. He received an M.A. in Romance languages from Hamilton the following year, then a fellowship to travel in Spain, Italy, and the Provence region of France, where he gathered material for a book on the troubadours—the poets of courtly love who flourished during the late middle ages.

Returning to the United States, Pound was briefly an instructor in French and Spanish at Wabash College in Crawfordsville, Indiana. He was dismissed after he allowed a stranded young actress to share his room in a boardinghouse.

Having determined, at age fifteen, to become a poet, Pound considered his dismissal a release, and

he returned to Europe, writing and traveling, mainly in Italy. In 1908, he published his first books, a slim volume titled *A Lume Spento* ("with candles extinguished") and *A Quinzaine for This Yule.* Both were heavily influenced by the troubadour poets and by the highly elaborate and artificial diction of late nineteenth century verse.

In 1908, Pound moved to London, where he remained until the end of World War I, establishing himself as a flamboyant personality as well as an aspiring poet. He affected earrings, flowing capes, and a dramatic red beard; his antics were wild and outrageous. Partially he sought to mask his own social insecurities, but he also wished to draw attention to his commitment to art. He became known by the major writers of the time, including Ford Madox Ford, Wyndham Lewis, and William Butler Yeats, and he continued to publish poems, translations, reviews, and essays.

Around 1912, Pound developed a poetic doctrine which he termed Imagism, which put emphasis upon clear, specific language and poems stripped of excess ornament and useless words: The particular image was to be the new focus of verse. Within two years Pound had moved in another direction, that of "vorticism," which was based on the concept of energy as symbolized by the vortex, a whirlpool or spiral form. Although Pound soon abandoned the formal aspects of these theories, their central tenets would remain part of his poetry for the rest of his life.

A third enduring influence from this time was that of Chinese poetic and philosophical thought. Believing that Chinese poets had used their language to reach the very essence of meanings naturally inherent in words, Pound eagerly translated their writings, adapting them in his volume *Cathay* (1915). Later he would incorporate Chinese ideograms, without translation, into *The Cantos* (1917 through 1970).

After World War I, Pound believed that London was exhausted as an intellectual center. He moved to Paris, first publishing *Hugh Selwyn Mauberley* (1920) as a scornful, satirical farewell. Established in France, he continued to write, but much of his energies were taken up with assisting fellow artists: Pound was unique among moderns in being an untiring champion of others. He secured grants and patrons for James Joyce, assisted T. S. Eliot in being able to leave his work at Lloyd's Bank (and then helped edit *The Waste Land*, 1922, into its final shape), and generally used every opportunity to advance the careers of any artist he believed talented and worth notice.

After four years Pound moved from Paris to Rapallo, Italy, which was to be his home for most of his life. In 1914, he had married Dorothy Shakespear, but he had since met the musician Olga Rudge. In Rapallo, Pound established two separate households for himself and the women. On July 9, 1925, Pound and Olga Rudge had a daughter, Mary; on September 10 of that year Pound and Dorothy became the parents of a son, Omar Shakespear Pound. The dual arrangement would continue throughout Pound's life.

Pound had early conceived the notion of writing an epic poem based on history. The first parts were published in 1917, and in 1925 a substantial portion appeared with the title *A Draft of XVI Cantos*; it has become known simply as the *Cantos*. Pound continued to work on it for the rest of his life; it was never completed, only abandoned. The work is one of the most important of twentieth century literature. Ironically, it is more influential than read, more discussed than known.

Disgusted by the senseless slaughter of World War I and insulted by the degradation of culture that followed, Pound was convinced that social and economic matters needed reform. Artists, he believed, had an obligation to lead in this effort.

Unfortunately, his path led to unsound fiscal theories such as "social credit" and to the also dangerous political doctrines of Fascism. Believing that Italian Fascist leader Benito Mussolini was an authentic heir to Confucian ideals of the enlightened ruler, and infected by the anti-Semitism of the times, Pound began to make broadcasts over Italian radio when World War II began. He continued these even after the United States entered the conflict. His talks were too rambling and bizarre to be effective propaganda, but they did get him indicted for treason, in absentia, in 1943. In 1945, U.S. troops arrested Pound in northern Italy.

Held as a prisoner for six months in the Army disciplinary center at Pisa, Pound was returned to the United States, but he was declared mentally unfit to stand trial in 1946. Committed to St. Elizabeths Hospital in Washington, D.C., he remained there until 1958, receiving visitors, reading, and continuing to write and publish, including new sections of the *Cantos*. One of these, *The Pisan Cantos* (1948), won the Bolligen Prize for Poetry in 1949, causing an immense literary and political furor. Ironically, Pound's imprisonment was a period of great productivity, and he brought out a major work almost every year while in St. Elizabeths.

Through an arrangement devised between such noted literary figures as Ernest Hemingway and Archibald MacLeish on one hand and the United States government on the other, Pound's indictment for treason was dismissed in 1958, and he was freed to return to Italy. During the last years of his life Pound, once so voluble and self-confident, subsided into silence. His writing became less frequent, and his doubts about himself and his work seemed to increase. He despaired over completing the *Cantos*, and the great work trailed off into fragments as its author concluded, "I cannot make it cohere." In 1970, he published *The Cantos of Ezra Pound I-CXVII*: It is not the "finished" version, because Pound had come to realize there could be no such thing. After so many years, his life's work still remained a draft.

Refusing to speak and brooding over the past, Pound made his final visit to the United States in 1969. He had already attended the funeral rites of many of his friends and companions from the earlier days; when he died in Venice on November 1, 1972, Ezra Pound was the last of a generation that had changed modern writing.

ANALYSIS

Pound's influence on twentieth century literature was felt in three ways: through his life, his theories, and his poetic practice. It can be argued that the first two were of greater impact than the third, and while this may seem unusual for a writer, Pound's career made this result almost inevitable.

Pound decided when he was only fifteen that, by the time he was thirty, he would know more about poetry than any person living.

Although this might seem at first the typical dream of a talented, ambitious adolescent, Pound obviously meant it, and his dedication to his art was so intense that he largely fulfilled his pledge. His knowledge of verse form, meter, rhythm, and poetic devices and traditions was unrivaled among his contemporaries. In pursuit of his goal, Pound became the image of the modern poet: He dressed the part, acted the role, and subordinated almost everything in his personal life to his poetry.

Pound the character could be dismissed were it not for his interaction with other writers of his time. He was a generous friend, securing funds for men such as Joyce, tutoring aspiring poets such as Hilda Doolittle (whom he renamed H. D., by which she is now known to literary history), and assisting T. S. Eliot in editing *The Waste Land* into final form. Pound was concerned with promoting true talent wherever he discovered it, and it is likely that many modern classics would have been unwritten—or written less well—without Ezra Pound.

In his theories, Pound exerted a similar influence. He found English poetry to be verse that was largely content with outworn techniques, sentimental vision, and an inability to distinguish excellence from mediocrity. Although Pound despaired over his lack of influence, he actually succeeded remarkably well in establishing higher poetic standards and forcing modern poets to abide by them. Pound brought renewed attention to the key elements of poetry: precise word choice, attention to rhythm, and creation of poems that were organic wholes rather than vaguely pleasing collections of soothing sounds.

Some complained, and still complain, that this made modern poetry difficult, even incomprehensible. These objections do have a certain merit, because Pound articulated theories that led to poetry which made greater demands on the reader. If at times modern poetry cries out more for translation than simple reading, this is the legacy of Pound. Because it focuses more attention on the poem itself, however, and causes the reader to become a partici-

pant in the work of art, this is a legacy which has strengthened true poetry while giving the attentive reader more worthwhile pleasure.

Pound's own poetry, as contrasted to his theories, has not had a comparable effect, at least among the poetry-reading public. He is a difficult poet—although not intentionally so—and his work requires a level of knowledge and sensitivity which some readers cannot bring to the page and which others do not believe worth the effort. It is among fellow poets that Pound's verse has been most important. Although he founded no real school and established no specific tradition—other than a general "modernism" which was only partially his and is impossible to define narrowly—Pound created an atmosphere which expanded the horizons of modern poetry.

The *Cantos* have been called the great unread poem of the twentieth century. Along with Joyce's *Finnegans Wake* (1939), they mark the outer boundaries of modern literature, perched on that edge where creativity and incomprehensibility come dangerously close. Pound may have been right when he concluded that he could not make the *Cantos* cohere. Still, in their individual sections they offer breathtaking vistas of language and thought, a collection of shining images that radically redefine what poetry can be and what it can do. Perhaps it was inevitable that Pound's practice should fall short of his own stringent standards, but by having the standards and attempting to fulfill them, Pound once again made poetry matter.

His was a paradoxical, perhaps pyhrric victory, because Pound's poetry could never be truly popular poetry—certainly not in the sense that Walter Scott or George Gordon, Lord Byron, once had the poetic equivalent of best sellers. Without intending to do so, Pound's theories led to a poetry that could be understood only by a relatively limited, elite audience. To his credit, Pound recognized this and sought a solution. No ivory tower intellectual, but a socially committed writer, he wanted to include, rather than exclude, and he consistently advocated education, true education, as essential for a fully human society. In a sense, Pound wanted a society where anyone had the opportunity and the ability to read the *Cantos*. It was only a vision, perhaps, but a worthy one.

"PORTRAIT D'UNE FEMME"

First published: 1912 (collected in *Collected Early Poems*, 1976)
Type of work: Poem

Pound presents a satirical yet ambiguously affectionate depiction of a literary hostess.

The literal translation of Pound's title "Portrait d'une Femme" is "portrait of a lady," which has inevitable associations with the novel *The Portrait of a Lady* by Henry James, published in 1881. Pound greatly admired James's book, especially for its keen psychological insights, and in this poem he attempts to re-create the same sort of description, outlining the character of a person by detailing her surroundings.

The woman is a London literary hostess who rules over a conventional, if slightly boring, salon where writers and artists have come for "this score years," amusing the lady and themselves with clever but, it would seem, inconsequential conversation. Nothing really important is said here, possibly because it would be wasted: "Great minds have sought you—lacking someone else," Pound writes.

The woman is compared to the Sargasso Sea, that area in the North Atlantic where floating seaweed from the Gulf Stream gathers and where tradition says that wrecked ships, lost hulks, and vanished vessels are mired forever. In much the same way, the lady of the title has gathered cast-off ideas, second-rate notions, and "fact that leads nowhere." In this respect the poem is in keeping with Pound's satirical verse on the English literary scene, a view that he expressed more forcibly and much more bitterly in *Hugh Selwyn Mauberley*. Thus, by extension, the woman in "Portrait d'une Femme" becomes an embodiment of an entire culture, one which is incapable, or at least unwilling, to recognize and appreciate true originality in art. Perhaps it would be threatened by it; perhaps it is simply not interested.

On the other hand, there is a certain affection for the character, and Pound's poem sounds wistful, almost elegiac, when it recounts the meager hoard the woman has gathered after twenty years of association with artists and writers. While she is compared to the Sargasso Sea, a stagnant backwash of the vital ocean, she is not explicitly condemned. Perhaps, the poem implies, she, like the artists of the time, has been a victim of the culture.

The style of the poem is notable for Pound's use of blank verse, a poetic form that he seldom employed and seems to have thought the refuge of second-rate writers of his time. It has become a critical commonplace to remark on Pound's ear for the music of English poetry, while at the same time maintaining that he could not discipline himself to write in conventional forms. "Portrait d'une Femme" shows that the first half of this commonplace is precisely right, the second half, decidedly wrong.

"IN A STATION OF THE METRO"

First published: 1913 (collected in *Collected Early Poems*, 1976)
Type of work: Poem

Pound uses a brief vivid image to express a profound aesthetic experience that occurred in everyday life.

The short poem "In a Station of the Metro" is an example of Pound's artistic theory of Imagism, which he advocated for a brief while in his career and which had a lasting impact on his writing and modern poetry. During his time in London, just before World War I, Pound developed a theory of poetry, which he termed Imagism, that stripped away the rhetorical excesses and vagueness that he believed obscured so much of contemporary poetry. In their places he advocated precise, careful presentation of specific images accurately rendered. Although Pound would later move beyond this rather limited concept, he retained the essential parts of it, and many of the passages in the *Cantos* are basically Imagist in their style.

An Imagist poem, by the very definition of the term, was brief. Seldom has the concision been carried so far as Pound's 1913 verse, "In a Station of the Metro," which consists of only two lines. The poem appears to be a translation of some Japanese haiku, and while Pound was undoubtably influenced by that tradition, his poem was completely original.

He has left a description of how he composed it. One evening, while coming out of the London subway (the "metro" of the title), Pound was struck by the sight of a beautiful face, then another and yet another. Seeking to express this experience, he began writing a poem which ran to thirty-two lines. After much paring and revision, he finally achieved the image and effect he sought: "The apparition of these faces in the crowd;/ petals on a wet, black bough."

Although at first reading the poem seems to be about very little (and even that little is mysterious), a second glance shows how well it fits into Pound's theory of imagism and just how Imagism works. To begin with, there is the single image, designed in this case to reproduce an experience not literally but emotionally and psychologically. Further, the image is presented in a specific literary form, the metaphor, recognized since ancient Greece as one of the most powerful devices of poetry. Aristotle, for example, termed the proper use of metaphor the supreme test of a writer. This use of metaphor is worth noting, because Pound is often considered a poet who rejected past conventions and techniques. Actually, he delighted in the poetic devices and scorned only their inferior use.

In keeping with Imagist theory, the words in the poem are, with one significant exception, concrete and specific: "faces," "crowd," "petals," and "bough" are all common English nouns, strung together in conventional English syntax. The two adjectives, "wet" and "black," are hardly unusual, and are just the sort of precise words to modify a noun such as "bough." Moreover, the metaphor is logical: Beautiful faces seen against a rainy London evening are like flower petals on a dark, wet branch. Through a careful selection of relevant images, Pound has re-created for the reader the effect impressed upon him that night.

The one word that is not a concrete noun is "apparition," and its unusual nature is highlighted by its placement at the beginning of the poem. By using this word, suggestive of ghostly sightings or supernatural experiences, and linking it with a string of commonplace nouns and modifiers, Pound is again re-creating what happened and what he experienced: a seemingly ordinary climb up a flight of subway stairs that turned into a vision.

In only two lines and fourteen words, Pound managed to re-create an entire experience by careful use of a specific image. A brief poem has been made to carry more emotional and psychological weight than Pound's contemporaries would have thought possible. His poetic successors would find the techniques used here essential in writing the poetry of the rest of the twentieth century.

HOMAGE TO SEXTUS PROPERTIUS

First published: 1919 (collected in *Personae: The Collected Poems of Ezra Pound*, 1926)
Type of work: Poetry

A re-creation, rather than a translation, of the work of a Roman poet, in which Pound comments upon contemporary society.

When Pound published *Homage to Sextus Propertius* in 1919, a surprisingly large number of readers apparently thought that the work was intended to be a literal, or at least close, translation of classical Roman poetry. This misperception came despite the obvious clue in the title: Pound was paying tribute to Sextus Propertius and attempting to capture the spirit of his verse rather than the word-by-word meaning.

Still, a number of classical scholars attacked Pound for his many supposed mistakes and errors in translation. One of the more intemperate attacks, by William Hale of the University of Chicago, stated flatly: "If Mr. Pound were a professor of Latin, there would be nothing left for him but suicide." Dr. Hale missed the point sublimely; Pound was not a professor of Latin but was a poet, paying homage to another poet.

Propertius was a Roman writer who lived during the first century B.C.E. He was a contemporary of poets better known today—Vergil, Ovid, and Horace—but during his time, Propertius was judged one of the finest elegiac poets in Latin. The elegy was a particular poetic genre, whose subject matter was most frequently lost love and whose tone was a mixture of wistfulness and sadness. Propertius gave the elegy a different twist, because his treatment of the form used language that was satirical, even bitter. He not only mocked the conventions of the traditional elegy but also used the form to mock the pretensions of imperial Rome. These qualities were the most congenial to Pound when he undertook his version of Propertius's work.

Pound wrote *Homage to Sextus Propertius* in 1917, when the slaughter of World War I was at its greatest; he had come to detest the war for its senseless destruction of life and culture, and his re-creation of another anti-imperial poet was an expression of that disgust. There was a connection, Pound noted, because the ancient Roman poems presented "certain emotions as vital to me in 1917, faced with the infinite and ineffable imbecility of the British Empire, as they were to Propertius some centuries earlier, when faced with the infinite and ineffable imbecility of the Roman Empire."

Pound constructs his poem by rearranging Propertius's verse into a twelve-part structure, sometimes combining different elegies, sometimes taking passages or even single lines from several different poems and linking them together. The twelve parts of the poem fall into two major categories: despair over the poet's love affair with Cynthia, who is certainly unkind to him and probably unfaithful as well; and his mocking commentary on the accepted poetry of the time (heroic verse celebrating the glories of empire) contrasted to his own intense, highly personal, and ultimately more honest writing. Even the poems that supposedly have Cynthia as their theme manage to include the comparison between epic verse and love poetry, clearly favoring the latter.

In adapting Propertius, Pound retained much of the original: The references to Roman history, mythology, and literature are frequent and require the reader's ability to catch the full range of allusions and their meanings. By contrast, however, even someone ignorant of Latin history and poetry should be able to respond to the poetic force and power that Pound retained from Propertius.

To achieve this, and to make Propertius once more a contemporary poet, Pound deliberately employed a number of anachronisms—terms or references that are after Propertius's time. In one passage, for example, he calls the ancient Greek poet Hesiod a "respected Wordsworthian," and in another section he parodies the style of W. B. Yeats. In his most celebrated anachronism, Pound even brings in a twentieth century kitchen appliance:

My cellar does not date from Numa Pompilius,
Nor bristle with wine jars,
Nor is it equipped with a frigidaire patent.

The impact of these jarring references is to heighten the satirical nature of the poems, and that seems to have been Pound's major intention. What he was doing with *Homage to Sextus Propertius* was not only re-creating a dead poet's work but also reanimating the dead poet himself. In a sense, Sextus Propertius, the actual poet, becomes "Sextus Propertius," a literary mask (or persona, to use one of Pound's favorite words) for the modern poet, Ezra Pound.

Pound was clearly fascinated by the concept of the persona. He used the Latin plural of the noun, *Personae*, twice as a title: in 1909, for a slender volume of his early verse, and again in 1926, for a much more extensive book, *Personae: The Collected Poems of Ezra Pound*. His masterwork, the *Cantos*, is a series of masks or personae through which Pound enters the personalities of figures from all times and places in human history. *Homage to Sextus Propertius* is more limited than that. In this work, Pound is concerned with linking an ancient Roman's vision of true, personal poetry with his own and with showing that poets, no matter how separated by time or language, share essential qualities. These qualities may be, perhaps must be, in conflict with the values of emperors or empires—but in the end it is Propertius, not Caesar, who will prevail.

HUGH SELWYN MAUBERLEY

First published: 1920
Type of work: Poetry

A bitter, satirical farewell to English society and its corruption of the values of life and art.

In the poems of *Hugh Selwyn Mauberley*, Pound expressed the disgust and rejection of British society which had been building in him during World War I. Increasingly at odds with a culture that had embraced sordid economic gain at the expense of art and lives—ten million people died in the war, and for nothing, in Pound's view—Pound used *Hugh Selwyn Mauberley* to pen a sharp, critical farewell to England and to his own poetic theories and practices. The book is thus a dual break: with his society and with his own poetic style.

The book is in two parts, and it comprises eighteen short poems. In the first part, Pound gives a general survey of contemporary England, attacking the low value it places on true art, especially poetry. There is much trenchant social criticism in these brief poems, and Pound makes direct attacks on a corrupted civilization whose marketplace ethics debase everything, especially human life and art. The second part of the book focuses on the career of a representative poet of the time, the fictitious Hugh Selwyn Mauberley, and his gradual descent into a sterile and isolated aestheticism, an artistic philosophy that Pound once shared, at least in part, but which he found artistically and morally untenable after the cataclysm of the war.

The work opens with one of Pound's best-known and most often anthologized poems, "E. P. Ode pour l'Election de son Sepulchre" ("E. P. ode for carving upon his tomb"). In this introductory poem, Pound, the E. P. of the title, gives an ironic, mocking farewell to his own artistic efforts in England: In an artistic sense, he is dead, and this brief work is his epitaph. The poem is satirical, but its satire is double, aimed at both Pound and his society. He was, Pound writes, "wrong from the start" in his attempts to bring a new renaissance into such indifferent, even hostile surroundings.

The rest of the poems in the first part show just how indifferent and hostile that culture was to poetry. In succeeding poems, Pound turns to the baleful effects of artistic philistinism, unjust economics, social indifference, and, inevitably following, a senseless war whose only real result was the death of millions—as Pound puts it: "Quick eyes gone under earth's lid." Although he mentions no names, Pound was undoubtably thinking especially of his friend, the brilliant young sculptor Henri Gaudier-Brzeska, killed in the trenches of France. Much of Pound's fury in *Hugh Selwyn Mauberley* is fueled by intense personal anger and anguish.

Having renounced his society, Pound next renounced much of the artistic credo he had embraced during his stay in England. The poem "Yeux Glauques" (gray eyes) is the occasion for this renunciation. It refers to a painting by the Pre-Raphaelist artist Edward Burne-Jones which was

itself an attack upon the crass materialism and hypocrisy of English culture. Pound rejects both the culture and the artistic responses of the Pre-Raphaelites and the aesthetic movement, because both were ultimately inimical to true art: the first because it placed no value on such creations, the second because they neglected the duty of artists to improve their society. From this point on in his poetic career, Pound was increasingly outspoken about social and economic matters. Though he may often have been wrong, he was seldom silent.

Part 1 of *Hugh Selwyn Mauberley* ends with a poem called "Envoi," based on the verse "Go, Lovely Rose," by the seventeenth century English writer Edmund Waller. By using Waller's poem, Pound is being subtly but severely ironic, for he believed Waller to have been one of the greatest of English lyric poets. In modern England, Pound is intimating, Waller would be rejected and unhonored—just as Pound is.

Part 2 gives the fictional case history of a modern English poet, Hugh Selwyn Mauberley, who is in many ways a mask, or persona, of Pound himself. Attempting to write true, rather than merely popular, poems, Mauberley is battered by life, ignored by the public, and tempted by the cynical advice of more successful writers. Mr. Nixon—perhaps based on well-known author Arnold Bennett—is one such character, a thorough materialist who has prostituted his talent for monetary reward and a "steam yacht." Other literary figures encountered by Mauberley are equally spurious as guides, having abandoned art for the momentary success of the marketplace world.

Pound, however, lets the reader understand that Mauberley's way is ultimately no more correct than Mr. Nixon's. The poem that ends the book, "Medallion," seems to be a typical piece by Mauberley, although critics have debated this point. At any rate the poem, while technically proficient, is limited. It employs many of the poetic devices that Pound advocated—close attention to detail, the creation of a sharp visual image, the juxtaposition of elements—but it employs them in a way that limits, rather than expands, the reader's comprehension. In a sense, "Medallion" bids farewell to an aspect of Pound's career, just as *Hugh Selwyn Mauberley* does: After this, Pound would write on a larger scale.

The Cantos

First published: 1917-1970
Type of work: Long poem

Pound's ambitious masterwork, this sprawling epic attempts to include all human history and culture.

Pound began writing the *Cantos* in 1915, published the first ones in 1917, published his first collection in 1925, and continued on them for most of the rest of his long life. He finally abandoned them after fifty-three years of effort. The *Cantos* are his most notable work, crammed with allusions, learning, splendid poetry, musical notations, Chinese ideograms, bitter invective and insults, baffling transitions and private jokes, and characters from Pound's personal life as well as from world history. They form an immensely long work, and the *Cantos* have caused despair in ordinary readers and produced an entire Pound industry among literary scholars.

Although it is not immediately apparent, there is a loose but definite structure to the poem. Crucial concepts reappear throughout the work, embodied in specific actors who are either actual historical figures or characters from literature or mythology. These concepts can also be expressed by reference to images from the natural world or by artistic creations—specific examples of music, architecture, poetry—which Pound thought significant.

In this way, the nineteenth century American president Martin van Buren appears to underscore the idea of economic justice, while a single column in a cathedral, signed by its carver, represents the ideal of true art as opposed to mass-produced imitations. Because Pound presents these images in quick flashes without overt connections, the reader must rely on juxtaposition rather than narration to discover the meanings. Despite their expansive nature, and although they were composed over a period of half a century, the *Cantos* contain only a few major subjects: the importance of knowledge and art, the power of nature, the need for economic justice, and the necessity to order human society in accord with natural rhythms and cycles.

As befits a work that attempts to survey all human history, the *Cantos* contain many changes—metamorphoses, or shifts from one form to another. It was a concept pervasive in Greek mythology, and a continual fascination for Pound. These metamorphoses can be for good or evil; the first lead to harmony, while the second cause decay in society and culture. The chief villain for Pound was economic injustice, which inevitably changed societies for the worse. Usury, the lending of money at excessive rates of interest, was Pound's primary economic concern, and he railed against it powerfully in his famous "Usury Canto," XLV:

> With usura hath no man a house of good stone
> each block cut smooth and well fitting
> that design might cover their face,
> with usura
> hath no man a painted paradise on his church wall

This concern with economics appears throughout the poem, sometimes expressed openly, as here, sometimes implied. The same is true of the other concepts which interested—some might say obsessed—Pound. They weave throughout the *Cantos*, changing form and shape, presenting themselves in many disguises, literally embodying the theme of metamorphoses.

As Pound worked on the *Cantos*, his emphasis on history gradually shifted. In the earlier sections he presented events largely from an outside point of view, sometimes commenting upon them directly but generally using persons beyond his contemporary world. Cantos VIII through XI, for example, are known as the "Malatesta Cantos," because they concern the fifteenth century Italian soldier and ruler Sigismundo Malatesta, who becomes a figure of the enlightened ruler. In later cantos, Pound draws more on his own times and injects himself more personally into the poem (although he had never been completely absent, even from the very start).

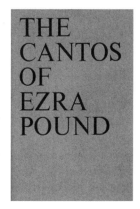

THE CANTOS OF EZRA POUND

The major break comes with the section of the poem known as the "Pisan Cantos." These were written while Pound was imprisoned in the U.S. Army Disciplinary Center at Pisa, awaiting return to the United States for his treason trial. Allowed access to writing materials but denied books or notes, Pound was forced to rely solely on his memory; from this point on, memory itself becomes a key motif in the *Cantos*. Pound turned inward, examining his own life and actions, trying to strip away all that was dross and retain only the essentials. A note of uncertainty and self-doubt appears; as Pound worked on in his later years, this tone becomes stronger.

Pound did not doubt the underlying validity of his themes, merely his ability to express them adequately. Faced with the task of pulling together the work of half a century, he wondered if he could accomplish it. Toward the end he decided that he could not: "I cannot make it cohere," he announced in one of the last fragments. Pound overstated the case. True, he was unable to conclude the *Cantos* in a well-rounded finale. His ambition to compose a long poem equal to Homer's *Odyssey* (c. 725 B.C.E.) or Dante's *La divina commedia* (c. 1320; *The Divine Comedy*, 1802) proved beyond his reach. The fault, however, was not solely with Pound: His era lacked the underlying unity and intellectual harmony required for such an undertaking.

Because of the diversity and complexity of modern life. Pound's method was probably the only one he could have used. He termed it the "ideogrammic method," by which he meant the juxtaposition of significant details which would fuse together in the mind of the reader to express more than was openly stated. For this method to work, the reader must either have Pound's knowledge of all the details and allusions found in the *Cantos* or must accept moments of confusion to arrive at some sort of total understanding. It is only when readers try to track down every reference, understand each cryptic comment, that the *Cantos* become confused and incomprehensible; the proper method is to plunge on, trusting that the poem will, despite Pound's doubts, cohere.

After a contentious lifetime, Pound came to realize that he had made many mistakes. He admits this in the *Cantos:*

> Pull down thy vanity, it is not man
> Made courage, or made order, or made grace,
>   Pull down thy vanity, I say pull down.
> Learn of the green world what can be thy place
> In scaled invention or true artistry,
> Pull down thy vanity.

Yet, having admitted this, Pound also realized that his vision and goal of true art had been valid ones and that the *Cantos*, flawed though they are, cohere though they did not, were a worthy effort: "To have gathered from the air a live tradition/ or from a fine old eye the unconquered flame/ This is not vanity."

SUMMARY

Pound's impact on twentieth century literature and culture was twofold. First, he largely reestablished the artist as a figure of important, and often provocative, influence in contemporary events. Calling artists "the antennae of the race," Pound implied that they not only anticipate society's direction but also influence its course. Second, he provided poetic techniques that are able to accept and incorporate all that is vital of past art into the art of the present and future. All artists can draw upon and use the same themes, images, and words, so long as they revitalize them; in Pound's words, as long as they "make it new."

Pound articulated and demonstrated literary theories; he also assisted other writers. In the end, he staked his own reputation upon an immensely long and wide-ranging work, the *Cantos*, which has become the supreme example of modernism in twentieth century literature.

Michael Witkoski

BIBLIOGRAPHY

By the Author

POETRY:
A Lume Spento, 1908
A Quinzaine for This Yule, 1908

Personae, 1909
Exultations, 1909
Provença, 1910
Canzoni, 1911
Ripostes, 1912
Lustra, 1916
Quia Pauper Amavi, 1919
Hugh Selwyn Mauberley, 1920
Umbra, 1920
Poems, 1918-1921, 1921
Indiscretions, 1923
A Draft of XVI Cantos, 1925
Personae: The Collected Poems of Ezra Pound, 1926
A Draft of the Cantos XVII-XXVII, 1928
Selected Poems, 1928
A Draft of XXX Cantos, 1930
Eleven New Cantos XXXI-XLI, 1934
Alfred Venison's Poems: Social Credit Themes, 1935
The Fifth Decade of Cantos, 1937
Cantos LII-LXXI, 1940
A Selection of Poems, 1940
The Pisan Cantos, 1948
The Cantos of Ezra Pound, 1948
Selected Poems, 1949
The Translations of Ezra Pound, 1953
Section: Rock-Drill 85-95 de los cantares, 1955
Thrones: 96-109 de los cantares, 1959
Drafts and Fragments of Cantos CX-CXVII, 1968
Selected Cantos, 1970
The Cantos of Ezra Pound I-CXVII, 1970
Selected Poems, 1908-1959, 1975
Collected Early Poems, 1976 (Michael J. King, editor)

NONFICTION:
The Spirit of Romance, 1910
Gaudier-Brzeska: A Memoir, 1916
Instigations of Ezra Pound, Together with an Essay on the Chinese Written Character by Ernest Fenollosa, 1920
Antheil and the Treatise on Harmony, 1924
Imaginary Letters, 1930
How to Read, 1931
ABC of Economics, 1933
ABC of Reading, 1934
Make It New, 1934
Social Credit: An Impact, 1935
Jefferson and/or Mussolini, 1935
Polite Essays, 1937
Guide to Kulchur, 1938
Orientamenti, 1938
What Is Money For?, 1939
Carta da Visita, 1942 (*A Visiting Card*, 1952)

DISCUSSION TOPICS

- What are the characteristics of Ezra Pound's most successful Imagist poems?

- In what ways does *Hugh Selwyn Mauberley*, published shortly after World War I, adumbrate the posture Pound adopted in World War II?

- How has *Homage to Sextus Propertius* influenced later students and translators of classical Greek and Latin poetry?

- Does Pound's poetic practice contradict his poetic theories, or was he simply unable to carry out his theories in his poetry?

- In what ways do Pound's *Cantos* mirror the twentieth century world in which they were written?

- Pound assisted many other writers. What does the diversity of their talent and accomplishments say for Pound's literary judgment and tutorial skills?

Introduzione alla natura economica degli S.U.A., 1944 (*An Introduction to the Economic Nature of the United States*, 1950)

L'America, Roosevelt, e le cause della guerra presente, 1944 (*America, Roosevelt, and the Causes of the Present War*, 1951)

Orro e lavoro, 1944 (*Gold and Work*, 1952)

"If This Be Treason . . . ," 1948

The Letters of Ezra Pound, 1907-1941, 1950

Lavoro ed usura, 1954

Literary Essays, 1954

Impact: Essays on Ignorance and the Decline of American Civilization, 1960

Nuova economia editoriale, 1962

Patria Mia and the Treatise on Harmony, 1962

Pound/Joyce: The Letters of Ezra Pound to James Joyce, 1967

Selected Prose, 1909-1965, 1973

Ezra Pound and Music: The Complete Criticism, 1977

"Ezra Pound Speaking": Radio Speeches of World War II, 1978

Letters to Ibbotson, 1935-1952, 1979

Ezra Pound and the Visual Arts, 1980

From Syria: The Worksheets, Proofs, and Text, 1981

Pound/Ford: The Story of a Literary Friendship, 1982

Ezra Pound and Dorothy Shakespear: Their Letters, 1909-1914, 1984

The Letters of Ezra Pound and Wyndham Lewis, 1985

Pound/Williams: Selected Letters of Ezra Pound and William Carlos Williams, 1996 (Hugh Witemeyer, editor)

Ezra and Dorothy Pound: Letters in Captivity, 1999 (Omar Pound and Robert Spoo, editors)

TRANSLATIONS:

The Sonnets and Ballate of Guido Cavalcanti, 1912

Cathay: Translations by Ezra Pound for the Most Part from the Chinese of Rihaku, from the Notes of the Late Ernest Fenollosa and the Decipherings of the Professors Mori and Ariga, 1915

"Noh"; or Accomplishment, 1916 (with Ernest Fenollosa)

The Natural Philosophy of Love, 1922 (of Remy de Gourmont's work)

The Testament of François Villon, 1926 (translation into opera)

Rime, 1932 (of Guido Cavalcanti's poetry)

Homage to Sextus Propertius, 1934 (poetry)

Digest of the Analects, 1937 (of Confucius's work)

Italy's Policy of Social Economics, 1930-1940, 1941 (of Odon Por's work)

Confucius: The Unwobbling Pivot and the Great Digest, 1947

The Translations of Ezra Pound, 1953

The Classic Anthology Defined by Confucius, 1954 (also known as *The Confucian Odes*)

Women of Trachis, 1956 (of Sophocles' play)

Love Poems of Ancient Egypt, 1964

Confucius, 1969

EDITED TEXTS:

Des Imagistes: An Anthology, 1914

Catholic Anthology 1914-1915, 1915

Active Anthology, 1933

Confucius to Cummings: An Anthology of Poetry, 1964 (with Marcella Spann)

About the Author

Froula, Christine. *A Guide to Ezra Pound's Selected Poems.* New York: New Directions, 1983.

Heymann, David. *Ezra Pound: The Last Rower.* New York: Viking Press, 1976.

Kenner, Hugh. *The Poetry of Ezra Pound.* London: Faber & Faber, 1951. Rev. ed. Lincoln: University of Nebraska Press, 1985.

Knapp, James F. *Ezra Pound.* Boston: Twayne, 1979.

Laughlin, James. *Pound as Wuz: Essays and Lectures on Ezra Pound.* St. Paul, Minn.: Graywolf Press, 1987.

Nadel, Ira Bruce. *Ezra Pound: A Literary Life.* New York: Palgrave Macmillan, 2004.

Stock, Noel. *The Life of Ezra Pound.* 1970. Rev. ed. San Francisco: North Point Press, 1982.

Surette, Leon. *Pound in Purgatory: From Economic Radicalism to Anti-Semitism.* Urbana: University of Illinois Press, 1999.

Tryphonopoulos, Demetres P., and Stephen J. Adams, eds. *The Ezra Pound Encyclopedia.* Westport, Conn.: Greenwood Press, 2005.

Hugh Powers

J. F. POWERS

Born: Jacksonville, Illinois
July 8, 1917
Died: Collegeville, Minnesota
June 12, 1999

Known as a writer's writer, Powers was acclaimed as one of the finest storytellers of his day, his talent revealed in his meticulously crafted and understated short stories and novels.

BIOGRAPHY

Born on July 8, 1917, in Jacksonville, Illinois, James Farl Powers was one of three children of James Ansbury and Zella Routzong Powers. His father was the dairy and poultry manager for Swift and Company, and his mother an amateur painter. Powers grew up in a comfortable, middle-class environment in which he played the usual sports and read Tom Swift adventures, the Arthurian legends, and Charles Dickens's *Oliver Twist* (1837-1839). What set Powers apart from his neighbors was that he and his family were Catholics in a predominantly Protestant town.

In 1931, his family moved to Quincy, Illinois. During his four years at Quincy Academy, taught by the Franciscans, Powers was more skilled as a basketball player than as a student. Upon graduation in 1935, he returned to live with his parents and took on various jobs during the following several years, including being the chauffeur for a wealthy investor in the South, an editor with Chicago Historical Records Survey, and a clerk at Brentano's bookstore. While working at Brentano's in 1942, he wrote his first short story, "He Don't Plant Cotton."

He was dismissed from his job in the bookstore for refusing to buy war bonds. During the early years of American involvement in World War II, Powers associated with various radical groups in Chicago such as the Catholic Worker movement, political exiles from Europe, and jazz musicians from the South. During this time he became a pacifist and turned to his writing to develop his sense of the clash between spiritual ideas and American materialist values.

In 1945 he married Betty Wahl, and they set up house in Avon, Minnesota. In 1947, he was briefly a resident at Yaddo, a writer's conference, where he completed his collection of short stories *Prince of Darkness, and Other Stories* (1947). "The Valiant Woman" earned Powers an O. Henry Award in that year. While teaching classes at St. John's College, Minnesota, and Marquette University in Milwaukee, he began publishing his stories in such magazines as *Collier's, The New Yorker,* and *Partisan Review.*

In 1951, Powers moved with his family to Greystones, Ireland, where they lived for two years. In 1952, they returned to the United States and took up residence in St. Cloud, Minnesota, for the following five years. In 1956, he published his second collection of short fiction, titled *The Presence of Grace.* He and his family again lived in Ireland (in Dublin) for a year and then returned to St. Cloud in 1958, where they remained until 1963. It was during these last years at St. Cloud that Powers worked on his first novel, *Morte d'Urban;* when published in 1962, it was awarded the National Book Award.

Many of Powers's short stories appeared over the years in *The New Yorker,* a magazine well suited to his subtle, ironic style and to his satiric portrait gallery of fallible and quietly heroic priests. Although a few of his stories focus upon such social issues as the plight of black people and Jews, most of Powers's tales, including his third collection of short fiction, *Look How the Fish Live* (1975), dwell upon the clergy. Powers's second novel, *Wheat That Springeth Green* (1988), reverts to the theme of *Morte d'Urban*, as his new hero attempts to balance priestly spiritual values against the forces of American secular life. Not the same critical success as *Morte d'Urban*—some reviewers found the spiritual rebirth of the hero in the last chapter to be unconvincing—*Wheat That Springeth Green* nevertheless offers a perceptive insight into the character of the American priesthood and the need to rethink accepted middle-class American values.

Powers taught writing at St. John's University in Collegeville, Minnesota. *Wheat That Springeth Green* was nominated for both the National Book Award and the National Book Critics Circle Award in 1988. The following year Powers was honored by the Wetherfield Foundation in New York City. He died in 1999, at the age of eighty-one, leaving five children.

ANALYSIS

The focus of all Powers's major stories and two novels is upon the clash between the secular values of American society and the spiritual ideals of the Catholic Church. Breaking away from the tradition of sentimental portraits of the religious life that characterized popular Catholic literature and film (Bing Crosby and Barry Fitzgerald as idealized priests, for example), Powers depicts his priests with a satiric and yet compassionate eye. He poses the question: How is one to model his or her life after Jesus Christ and yet survive in an attractive, materialistic society that demands success? In answering, Powers created some of the most memorable characters in recent literature: Fathers Didymus, Urban, and Hackett.

Powers's failure to become a popular writer may have rested in his singular focus upon the psychological and spiritual struggles of priests to discover themselves and the meaning of their vocations. This is not the stuff of popular literature, especially as his books are notably devoid of overt sex and violence. While it is true that he lacks the scope of Catholic writers such as Graham Greene, Evelyn Waugh, and François Mauriac, Powers's intense and perceptive analysis of the priestly mind has no equal. Despite the simple surfaces of his stories, he draws upon a rich tradition within and without his church to develop his characters.

His works are filled with allusions to medieval Christianity, Arthurian legends, and arcane theological writings, and he skillfully blends the bountiful texture of Catholic tradition with the most mundane affairs of modern life. A Trappist monk watches the Minnesota Twins on television. A priest, loosely drawn after Sir Lancelot, constructs a golf course to increase the number of retreatants for his order.

Although Powers's fiction can be comic, it also confronts and examines serious issues, ranging from the mistreatment of black people and Jews to his more familiar subject of the inner struggles of clerics to achieve a balance between physical and spiritual values. Powers's pacifism and critical attitude toward American superficiality underlies many of his stories. One does not need to be a Catholic to appreciate his portrayal of young men, who happen to be priests, doing battle with the symbols of corporate America while sometimes falling prey to its seductive attractions. Powers, in short, was fascinated with a fallen humanity that has not abandoned its dreams and ideals. Despite all the irony and satire, his writings attest the obsessive desire all people share to make their lives worthy of memory.

Powers is noted for his crisp dialogue and transparent narrative. There is not an abundance of action or painterly passages in his works. Rather, he establishes a believable setting—usually in small-town America—in which he develops his characters. Even when he is not writing from the first-person point of view, he stages his dialogue and narrative so as to reveal the minds and characters of his heroes. Careful not to moralize or judge his characters, Powers presents to the reader a series of characters who are neither villains nor saints but complex amalgams of good and evil, innocence, and experience. Through the use of irony, he provides a comic perspective from which to view his characters, careful always of maintaining a detached and frequently compassionate attitude toward them.

Finally, it is important to note Powers's uniquely American priests. Like the author, they are devoted to such national sports as football and baseball, enjoy such things as drinking (sometimes too much), golf, flashy automobiles, television, and entering into the competitive fray (like any good American businessperson) in order to satisfy their ambitions for power, prestige, and the material symbols of success. This tradition of American materialism, however, frequently clashes with the Roman Catholic tradition of asceticism and the Puritan values of early America. Powers has no peer when it comes to capturing this cultural duality in the Catholic Church poignantly.

MORTE D'URBAN

First published: 1962
Type of work: Novel

An assertive priest attempts to revitalize the stagnant Order of St. Clement by applying the methods of corporate America.

In the epigraph to *Morte d'Urban,* a quotation from J. M. Barrie, Powers sets forth the central ironic theme of his novel: "The life of every man is a diary in which he means to write one story, and writes another." Father Urban (Harvey Roche), a clever, manipulative speaker and organizer dedicated to making the Church a prospering and efficient social institution, comes to discover in the eleventh hour that what really counts in the religious life is one's spiritual well-being.

Acknowledged by many critics as Powers's best book, *Morte d'Urban* was originally written from the point of view of its hero, Father Urban. Powers recast his novel, employing a third-person narrative while skillfully retaining Father Urban as the central intelligence of the story. This shift in point of view enabled Powers to develop the important ironic perspective that shapes the entire novel. Funny, ironic, satiric, and compassionate, Powers brings a Chaucerian tone to the modern novel.

A middle-aged member of the fictitious Order of St. Clement, Father Urban travels out of Chicago, raising money, preaching dynamic sermons to standing-room-only crowds of admiring listeners. His charm, energy, and go-getting spirit would have made him an outstanding success in business, but the Clementines are run by and constituted of priests who are largely conservative, fumbling, and doddering fellows. As far as religious orders go, the Clementines are losers: Their vocations are down, some of their houses have been taken over by more aggressive diocesan priests, and none of

their members but Father Urban seems to understand their problem.

By wooing a wealthy benefactor named Billy Cosgrove, an egotistical son of Mammon, Father Urban manages to obtain new quarters for the Clementines. Instead of nurturing Father Urban's enterprising spirit, however, the provincial sends him, along with Father John (Jack), to the order's failing retreat center in the remote community of Duesterhaus (meaning "house of gloom"). Father Wilfrid, the rector, obsessed with the petty details of maintaining the retreat house and with asserting his dominance over Father Urban, sets Fathers John and Urban to the task of painting walls and varnishing floors (with the cheapest materials) in order to make the house more attractive to retreatants.

Having spent more than a month wasting his talents at St. Clement's Hill (so named by Father Urban), Father Urban is sent by Father Wilfrid to replace a vacationing pastor at St. Monica's Church. During the next month and a half, Father Urban manages to convince the cautious and ailing pastor, Father Phil Smith, to build a new church. When he later discovers that Father Smith has died during his vacation, Father Urban thinks that he may be chosen to be the new pastor. The bishop, however, offers him an Indian mission, which he rejects in favor of returning to St. Clement's Hill.

Father Urban persuades Billy Cosgrove to buy a tract of land adjoining St. Clement's Hill, have it developed as a golf course, and donate it to the order. Hearing that the Bishop is interested in taking over the Hill as the site for a new seminary, Father Urban invites the bishop to play a round of golf with him in the hope of convincing him of the Hill's productive future. During the course of the game, however, the bishop's ball strikes Father Urban in the head, sending him to the hospital. After he regains consciousness at the hospital, Father Urban learns that the bishop, feeling guilty for striking him in the head with his golf ball, has decided not to take over St. Clement's Hill.

Nevertheless, after being struck by the ball, Father Urban moves into a series of adventures that totally changes his life. He goes to live at the estate of the wealthy benefactor of St. Clement's, Mrs. Thwaites, in order to recuperate from his trauma. While there, he attempts to help out Mrs. Thwaites's servant, a young Irish woman named Katie, who has lost most of her earnings playing dominoes with Mrs. Thwaites. Father Urban learns later that his intervention has proved fruitless.

Later, Father Urban goes on a fishing trip with Billy Cosgrove and again rebels against the wealthy establishment by undermining Billy's attempt to drown a deer. As Billy struggles to drown the animal, Father Urban revs the engine of the boat, causing Billy to fall into the lake. Angered by his humiliation, Billy gets into the boat and drives away, leaving Father Urban to fend for himself. On his return to St. Clement's Hill, Father Urban is picked up by Sally Thwaites Hopwood, the married daughter of Mrs. Thwaites. She drives him to an island tower, where she attempts to seduce him by stripping nude for a swim. He resists the temptation. Furious, she drives away from the island in her boat, leaving Father Urban stranded.

Plagued by headaches and aging rapidly, Father Urban attempts to carry out his work at St. Clement's Hill. Beaten down by his recent trials, he no longer attempts to challenge the plans of Father Wilfrid. During a conference at the Hill, however, he receives the news that he has been appointed the new provincial of the Order of St. Clement. Ironically, he no longer possesses the energy and will to develop the order's material well-being. He gains a reputation as a pious priest who finds himself comfortable in his home at St. Clement's Hill.

Has Father Urban become more spiritual and saintly, or has he simply been beaten down by the unexpected turns of the economic forces that he had formerly mastered? Like Lancelot, Father Urban has chosen earthly desires over heavenly bliss and thus failed to discover the Holy Grail. Having withstood the temptations of Mrs. Thwaites, Billy Cosgrove, and Sally Thwaites, however, he, like Lancelot, may have achieved his sanctity by becoming a true priest—one devoted to spiritual rather than material values.

As in so many of Powers's stories, he develops the tension between action and contemplation and suggests that only a balance between the two

forces may bring about inner peace and salvation. "Should be two kinds of men in every busy parish," Father Smith says, "priest-priests and priest-promoters." Father Urban replies, "I'd say a man *has* to be both. At least a man can try. Sometimes that's the most a man can do." Up until the time he is hospitalized, however, Father Urban is almost exclusively the priest-promoter. He is a regular guy who is at his best when raising money, shaking hands with congregants who have been dazzled by his sermons, and persuading wealthy parishioners to contribute to the Church.

All these activities, to be sure, seem necessary if the Church is to compete in a United States that prizes new construction, growth, numbers, and other visible signs of achievement. On the other hand, if the Church models itself after successful corporate America, how is it to model itself after Christ? The seemingly simple admonition of Christ to render unto Caesar the things that are Caesar's and to God the things that are God's proves to be a very difficult and complex task, especially if one is an American who is bent upon being a winner.

Father Urban's getting struck in the head by a golf ball proves to be the ironic turning point in his life (and in the novel). Hoping to bring into St. Clement's Hill a better class of retreatants by constructing an attractive golf course on the adjoining grounds, Father Urban—at the top of his game as a promoter—is physically stopped in his tracks by a golf ball, the very emblem of his new enterprise. As Powers himself has said, "the hit on the head is a real factor. It is not psychological. It's physical. Nothing else could have slowed up a man like Urban, but he is also a wiser and a better man. He has lost this aggressive 'be a winner' kind of thing, which in an American, I think is not a bad thing."

Although the last chapter of the novel is titled "Dirge," Father Urban's "death" proves to be metaphorical. His former self has died, and he is resurrected from his previous life as a go-getter to accept the spiritual values of the Church. It no longer matters to him that the incompetent Father Wilfrid continues to run St. Clement's Hill, that the order has lost its building on the North Side of Chicago, and that its weekly radio program had been canceled in favor of news and music. Many of the younger Clementines cannot understand why their new provincial is allowing their order to slide back into its dilatory and unproductive ways. Father Urban thus finds himself in the position of the previous provincial when he (Father Urban) had rebelled against him for the very same reasons.

Morte d'Urban may, then, simply be read as a Catholic novel in which an aggressive, worldly wise priest discovers spiritual values after he is chastened by a physical disability, sexual temptation, and betrayal by his wealthy sponsors. The novel, however, has broader implications. It may also be read as the story of the hollow success of the American Dream. Although a priest, Father Urban has most of the characteristics of the successful American businessman: He is smooth, glib, manipulative, on the move, and desperate to be in the center of new development, new ideas, new growth. He believes in going first class or not at all. The nearly fatal blow to his action and head, however, makes it clear to him that the world will go on without him and that his previous bravado, based in part upon his childlike denial of mortality, has left him with an empty, worrisome world.

WHEAT THAT SPRINGETH GREEN

First published: 1988
Type of work: Novel

In developing his suburban parish and in working with his new curate, a middle-aged diocesan priest rediscovers his true vocation and turns to working with the poor.

Taking its title from a medieval French carol, *Wheat That Springeth Green*, like *Morte d'Urban*, develops the great Christian theme of the resurrection from the dead. The novel tells the story of Joe Hackett, a midwestern Catholic diocesan priest. At age forty-four, he is pastor of a comfortable suburban church in Inglenook, Minnesota. Despite his successful building campaign, he is an unhappy man who begins drinking; he is headed for despair until his curate, Father Bill, arrives. A priest of the 1960's, immature and idealistic, Father Bill unwittingly elicits Joe's paternal and pastoral instincts. In his struggle to shape Father Bill into a solid, responsible priest, Joe regains his sense of vocation, abandons his suburban parish, and dedicates his life to working with the poor in a slum parish.

Although writing from a third-person point of view, Powers frequently interjects dialogue and comment within parentheses to reflect Joe's inner thoughts or to pick up talk that he hears going on around him. For example, when Joe is discussing his building plans with the archbishop, Powers projects within parentheses Joe's imagined interpretation of his remarks:

So Joe, then living in a room in the school and quite prepared to go on living under such conditions if advised to build a new church but dearly wishing, as he'd told the Arch and his reverend consultors, to keep the best wine till last (*"Wine, Archbishop? Did he say wine?"*—"Means a new *church*, you dummy"), had got his rectory.

After briefly tracing some of Joe's tribulations and humiliations as a boy, Powers develops his character's growing spiritual idealism as a seminarian. Convinced that the only ambition worthy of the priest was holiness—getting to know God and growing more like him—Joe begins to wear a hair shirt, like the saints of old, in order to subdue the flesh. He is determined to become a contemplative—otherwise, as he says, "our life . . . becomes one of sheer activity—the occupational disease of the diocesan clergy."

Joe's initiation into the practical world comes with his assignment as curate in Holy Faith Church, the pastor of which, Father Van Slaag, is the only known contemplative in the diocese. As he gradually learns, Van Slaag's detachment from worldly matters means that he, Joe, must take on most of the duties to keep the parish going. After five years at Holy Faith he openly admits, in what seems like an act of betrayal not only of Father Van Slaag but also of his own high spiritual standards, that Father Van Slaag is not doing his job.

Joe finally obtains his own parish in the upper-middle-class suburbs of Inglenook, Minnesota. Having put his priestly idealism (the hair shirt, the life of contemplation, Father Van Slaag) behind him, Joe quickly establishes one of the finest rectories, schools, and convents in the diocese. Joe has become a go-getter, much like Father Urban, and is proud of his accomplishments.

In the process of developing his parish and educating his new curate, however, Joe becomes increasingly disillusioned about the values embodied in this upper-middle-class world. Although taking to drink as a means of escape, he continues to battle materialist corruption, as embodied in one of his wealthy parishioners, who uses his wealth and influence with the archbishop to get his children into the parish school, over Joe's objections. His growing radicalism can also be seen in his moral support of a young parishioner who flees to Canada to avoid fighting in the Vietnam War.

Tempered with the wisdom that comes from experience, Joe's youthful idealism returns with renewed vigor. Believing that "the separation of Church and Dreck was a matter of life and death for the world, that the Church was the one force in the world with a chance to save it," Joe abandons his suburban parish for one in the slums, appropriately named Holy Cross.

"THE FORKS"

First published: 1947 (collected in *The Stories of J. F. Powers*, 2000)
Type of work: Short story

The opposition between a worldly pastor and his idealistic young curate leads to a series of comic confrontations.

In "The Forks," Powers depicts two very different kinds of priests. On one hand is Monsignor, a snobbish man very much at home with the things of this world. He wears a Panama hat, uses Steeple cologne, and drives a long black car. Doomed to remain a monsignor now that all his intercessors are dead, he determines to live as comfortably as he can. He orders for himself the luxury of a medieval garden with a spouting whale jostling with Neptune in the waters of the fountain. He has no intellectual pretensions and maintains his mental calm by either ignoring or condemning innovations and controversy: "His mind was made up on every-

thing, excessively so." In his eyes, communism and organized labor are the chief dangers to society.

The status quo has been kind to Monsignor, and he wants no interference with tradition now. His curate, Father Eudex, on the other hand, reads the radical *Catholic Worker*, neglects to shave under his armpits, contemplates buying a Model A in opposition to Monsignor's contention that a shabby car is unbefitting a priest, works in his undershirt with Monsignor's gardener, and sympathizes with labor unions.

In short, Powers has placed in one rectory an old, worldly traditionalist and a young, idealistic radical, and the drama that unfolds from their interaction is what the story is about. On the surface, Powers seems to be satirizing the worldly monsignor and lauding the saintly and socially conscious curate, but upon closer reading one discovers that Father Eudex, with his blinkered vision and unyielding idealism, is also the object of Powers's satire.

Assuming Christlike motives in his concern for social justice, Father Eudex (his name in Latin means "judge") actually appears to be driven by perversity. If Monsignor enjoys his prestigious automobile, Father Eudex rejoices in its humble counterpart, the Model A. When the monsignor accepts a check from the Rival Tractor Company, Father Eudex, to show his support for labor, destroys his. The monsignor condemns communism; Father Eudex reads *The Catholic Worker*.

The very title of the story suggests the opposition between the two priests. After dinner, Monsignor notices that his curate has failed to use all the silverware provided at his plate and declares that "Father Eudex did not know the forks." The implication is that the young man's idealism is naïve and a little foolhardy, that it has blinded him to the religious, social, and political exigencies of parish life. The ideal priest, one might assume, would be one who could balance the experience and wisdom of the monsignor with the idealism and energy of his curate.

Powers implies a judgment of Father Eudex not only through Eudex's series of negative judgments of his superior but through an allusion to the parable of the talents. In order to solve its excess-profits problem, the Rival Tractor Company annually sent checks to local clergymen. Father Eudex is the only character in the story reluctant to accept the money, which he views as Rival's dishonest attempt to win away sympathy from its union workers who have frequently struck the company. On the surface, Father Eudex seems to have acted nobly by destroying his check. In the parable of the talents, however, Eudex's biblical counterpart is described as foolishly burying his one talent and is declared wanting in his stewardship.

Paradox and irony keep the reader from being too harsh a judge of either character. Perverse, idealistic, naïve, Father Eudex is not a bad priest nor is he a saintly one. Rather, like his superior, he is a flawed human being. Although the parable of the talents clearly implies a judgment upon Father Eudex, the Rival Tractor Company is not truly analogous to the just Master in the Bible; consequently, one's final judgment of Father Eudex is tempered with mercy and compassion.

"LIONS, HARTS, LEAPING DOES"

First published: 1943 (collected in *Lions, Harts, Leaping Does, and Other Stories,* 1963)

Type of work: Short story

An aged, saintly Franciscan friar seeking spiritual perfection believes, shortly before his death, that he has failed God.

The setting for "Lions, Harts, Leaping Does" is a Franciscan monastery during a bleak, snowy winter. Father Didymus, an aged priest, is being read to by his friend, Brother Titus, a simple, holy, and rather forgetful old man. As this elegiac story opens, Titus reads from Bishop Bale's critical *Lives of the Popes,* which reminds Didymus of the foibles of even great church leaders.

As the two friars go for a walk in the cold snow, Didymus meditates upon his own spiritual lapses. He is especially distressed with his decision not to visit his ninety-two-year-old brother, Seraphin, also a priest, recently returned from Rome after twenty-five years. Didymus feels that by adhering to the letter of his vows as a cloistered priest in not visiting his brother he has exhibited spiritual pride and has hurt his brother. Upon returning from his walk, he

receives a telegram informing him that his brother has died.

Later, during the Vespers ceremony, Didymus collapses and wakes to find himself confined to a wheelchair. Titus brings a caged canary to his room for companionship and continues to read to him. This time, however, he reads from the writings of the mystic saint and poet Saint John of the Cross. One of Saint John's paradoxical tenets is that one may be closest to God during the moments one believes oneself to be abandoned by him. Powers clearly implies that Didymus, despite his religious scruples and his sense of failure, achieves a heightened sanctity through his present suffering.

Projecting his own sense of imprisonment unto the canary, Didymus releases the bird from its cage, and it flies out the window and disappears into the snowy trees, "the snowy arms of God." Didymus will die without discovering a sign of God's presence within himself. Knowing he still has to look outside himself for such a sign, he turns to Titus. "God still chose to manifest Himself most in sanctity," he thinks. Didymus's denial of a sign, however, is paradoxically the very sign he is seeking. Like the canary that vanishes among the dark, cold trees, the soul of Didymus blends into the bleak landscape that occupied so much of his attention during his last days. His soul has become "lost in the snowy arms of God"; his soul was saved without his ever being conscious of the spiritual climax.

"Lions, Harts, Leaping Does" was Powers's first clerical story. Unlike his subsequent fiction, this story eschews satire and comedy for a compassionate, sensitive, and theologically rich portrait of a priest's quest for sanctity. Temptation here is not of the usual, dramatic kind—that of sex, money, or ambition—but of a subtle, almost unrecognizable variety that stems from doing the right thing for the wrong reason—in this case, obeying the rules of the cloister out of pride. Didymus's suffering is quiet and internal, and Powers attempts to portray it by describing Didymus's dreams and by using such symbols as the caged canary.

SUMMARY

J. F. Powers stands as one of the most accomplished Catholic authors of the twentieth century. Unlike James Joyce or Graham Greene, he lacks breadth and variety in his writing, but his perceptive, ironic, and compassionate probing of the clerical mind has no equal. Like Jane Austen, he worked on a small scale, but within that framework he proved himself a master chronicler of American Catholicism by exploring life in the rectory, parish, and diocese.

Some critics believe that his short stories are his true metier. His two novels, however, which grew out of his short fiction, contain complex characters and exhibit an ample, Chaucerian humor that requires a larger canvas to develop. The crisp dialogue that captures the comic human voices of the time can be heard in their eloquence in both the short fiction and the novels.

Richard Kelly

BIBLIOGRAPHY

By the Author

SHORT FICTION:
Prince of Darkness, and Other Stories, 1947
The Presence of Grace, 1956
Lions, Harts, Leaping Does, and Other Stories, 1963
Look How the Fish Live, 1975
The Old Bird: A Love Story, 1991 (a short story, originally pb. in *Prince of Darkness, and Other Stories*)
The Stories of J. F. Powers, 2000

LONG FICTION:
Morte d'Urban, 1962
Wheat That Springeth Green, 1988

About the Author

Evans, Fallon, comp. *J. F. Powers*. St. Louis: Herder, 1968.
Gussow, Mel. "J. F. Powers, 81, Dies." *The New York Times*, June 17, 1999, p. C23.
Hagopian, John V. *J. F. Powers*. New York: Twayne, 1968.
Long, J. V. "Clerical Character(s)." *Commonweal*, May 8, 1998, 11-14.
McInerny, Ralph. "The Darkness of J. F. Powers." *Crisis*, March, 1989, 44-46.
Merton, Thomas. "*Morte D'Urban:* Two Celebrations." *Worship* 36 (November, 1962): 645-650.
Meyers, Jeffrey. "J. F. Powers: Uncollected Stories, Essays and Interviews, 1943-1979." *Bulletin of Bibliography* 44 (March, 1987): 38-39.
Powers, Katherine A. "Reflections of J. F. Powers: Author, Father, Clear-Eyed Observer." *The Boston Globe*, July 18, 1999, p. K4.
Preston, Thomas R. "Christian Folly in the Fiction of J. F. Powers." *Critique: Studies in Modern Fiction* 16, no. 2 (1974): 91-107.

DISCUSSION TOPICS

- What aspects of priests' lives make them appropriate characters in J. F. Powers's stories of the clash of materialistic and spiritual values?

- How closely does the range of priests in Powers's stories resemble that found in modern society?

- Why is humor such an important ingredient in Powers's typical short stories about priests?

- What accommodations to a materialistic world does Father Urban make in *Morte d'Urban?*

- How does Powers avoid preachiness?

RICHARD POWERS

Born: Evanston, Illinois
June 18, 1957

Functioning on a uniquely high intellectual plane, Powers's stylistically complex novels intermix science, music, photography, history, and human psychology in strikingly original ways.

BIOGRAPHY

Richard Powers has been called reclusive, but the term is misleading. Although he struggles to maintain a low profile, fearing that celebrity will make inordinate demands on the time he needs to write, he is outgoing. Interviewers find him cooperative but firm in his refusal to share the personal information around which interviews with notables often revolve.

This reluctance is not a pose Powers has adopted to project some calculated public image. He firmly believes, however, that one's writing must stand on its merits, that details about the life of an author or an author's autograph on the flyleaf of a book should affect neither the public perception of what authors produce nor the value of their books.

Powers's novels display an easy command of specific information about an amazing range of subjects, from literature to art to photography to science to music to history to astronomy to folklore. His knowledge in this daunting array of subjects is not superficial: He has a thorough understanding of the subjects he chooses to explore and he absorbs complex information quickly.

An encompassing influence on Powers's literary structure is the music of Johann Sebastian Bach, stemming from his exposure to Bach's music as a cellist. Elements of Bach's harmony and, particularly, Bach's counterpoint underlie the structure of *Three Farmers on Their Way to a Dance* (1985) and *Prisoner's Dilemma* (1988). *The Gold Bug Variations* (1991) draws its title in part from Bach's *The Goldberg Variations*; its structure stems from Powers's comprehensive understanding of Bach's inventions.

There are thirty Goldberg variations; Powers's novel has thirty chapters. Bach's *Variations* were based upon four notes or musical phrases; the number four, a controlling element in Powers's novel, is fundamental to an understanding of deoxyribonucleic acid (DNA), the mysteries of which play a central role in *The Gold Bug Variations*. Powers's title alludes both to Bach's musical masterpiece and to Edgar Allan Poe's short story "The Gold Bug." The latter correspondence alerts readers to the cryptograms and veiled allusions that pervade the novel.

An interchapter toward the end of *Prisoner's Dilemma* provides a rare bit of autobiographical information about Powers. Major elements of *Prisoner's Dilemma* are autobiographical, although not dependably so. In the autobiographical interchapter, for example, Powers reveals that although his fictional family consists of the Hobsons and their four children, his actual family consisted of his parents, Richard Franklin and Donna Powers, and five children. Major elements of this book, set in De Kalb, Illinois, where Powers lived during his high school years, draw upon details surrounding his father's final illness.

Much of *Operation Wandering Soul* (1993) is based upon experiences that the author's older brother, a surgeon, had when he completed a rotation as a resident in pediatric surgery in a large California hospital. In this novel, the protagonist is named Richard Kraft. *Kraft* is German for *power*, the plural form of which is the author's name. In his other novels, Powers plays with his surname, dedicating *Prisoner's Dilemma* to "the powers."

Powers, a physics major for his first two years at the University of Illinois at Urbana-Champaign, graduated in 1978 with a bachelor's degree in rhetoric, completing his university studies with a perfect A average. The following fall, he entered Illinois's master's degree program in English, receiving the M.A. in 1980. For three semesters, he held teaching assistantships in composition and literature. Upon completing the master's degree, Powers lived for nearly three years in the Boston area before returning to Champaign in 1983.

Powers, honored in 1986 by the American Academy of Arts and Sciences, was named a MacArthur Fellow in 1989. *Three Farmers on Their Way to a Dance* and *The Gold Bug Variations* were both among the five finalists for the National Book Critics Circle Award; *The Gold Bug Variations* was *Time* magazine's 1991 book of the year. *Operation Wandering Soul* was among five finalists for the 1993 National Book Award in fiction.

From 1987 until 1992, Powers lived in Heerlen, a coal-mining town in the southern tip of the Netherlands, within biking distance of Germany and Belgium. In the spring of 1992, he was artist-in-residence at Sidney Sussex College at Cambridge University in England. After he returned to the United States, he was appointed writer-in-residence in the Department of English at the University of Illinois at Urbana-Champaign.

In 1998, he became the first occupant of an all-university endowed professorship, the Swanlund Chair, a position he occupied until 2005 as a member of the department of English and the fledgling Program in Creative Writing. He retired from that position and was appointed writer-in-residence of the College of Liberal Arts and Sciences with no teaching duties. On May 18, 2001, he married Jane Kuntz.

ANALYSIS

Powers has a consuming need to understand his world. He has been driven by the necessity to define—for himself and for those who read his novels—his own century, its shift from agrarianism to industrialism to modernism. His books, demonstrating the unique range of his knowledge and reflecting his experimentation with literary style and structure, consistently pose barbed questions that lead readers to serious contemplation and eventually, perhaps, to deepened understandings.

Powers's first published novel, *Three Farmers on Their Way to a Dance*, illustrates the complexity of his literary structure. The book's twenty-seven chapters are arranged in triplets. One chapter of each triplet carries and sustains the story lines of the book. Another chapter is essentially a philosophical essay relating to the times and their intellectual and historical underpinnings. Yet another chapter presents a historical vignette that helps to relate the basic story to a broader sociopolitical perspective, enabling readers to understand each interlocking plot in its historical context.

Three Farmers on Their Way to a Dance, a multiplot novel, ambitiously—and deftly—sustains the three basic stories developing outside the interchapters while simultaneously interweaving them ingeniously into the whole. The first-person narration, introduced in the first chapter and used elsewhere, lends immediacy and credibility to the stories Powers unfolds.

Powers's subsequent novels use interchapters to place their stories outside the confined milieux within which most storytelling occurs and to key the stories to their broader reference points in Western culture. Powers's ability to relate the plot structure of his novels to what philosophers have called the "Great Chain of Being" distinguishes his work and enhances its artistic impact.

For Powers, such historical events as Henry Ford's organization of a "Peace Ship" to convey well-known Americans to Europe at the height of World War I in his effort to negotiate a peace, or the World War II internment of Japanese Americans, or the evacuation of children from London to Canterbury during World War II are secondary but telling dollops of history that help to explain the confounding century upon which he focuses. They also enable Powers to relate his stories to the broader contexts in which they occur.

Some of Powers's historical vignettes reach to the thirteenth century (the children's Army of the Crusades, to which a chapter of *Operation Wandering Soul* is devoted); others extend beyond a single chapter to create a fuller impression of their subjects than could be gleaned from a single chapter (the Henry Ford vignettes in *Three Farmers on Their Way to a Dance*, for example).

Prisoner's Dilemma's vignette about the internment of Japanese Americans during World War II enables Powers to develop a continuing subplot. From this vignette emerges the fanciful story of an interned Walt Disney, who is released from his internment, spirited off to De Kalb, Illinois, and commissioned by the government to create a scale model of the entire United States along the lines of a theme park. Powers invents a Japanese mother for Disney to justify his internment.

Interchapters are the underlying mechanisms that allow Powers to construct his complex, multitext narratives; the interchapters provide much of the intricate counterpoint underlying the structure of his novels. This counterpoint distinguishes Powers's writing and permits the author to employ the closely interconnected intellectual crosscurrents that mark his work.

Powers's novels are novels of ideas. They rely on a carefully crafted and extremely calculated style to deliver the essence of what their author seeks to communicate. Powers's chief concerns are philosophical; characters concern him secondarily, even though he has created some touching and memorable ones.

For example, the beguiling Joy Stepaneevong in *Operation Wandering Soul*, who remains innocent and trusting in the face of the severe dislocations she has experienced throughout her twelve years of existence, both touches the hearts and engages the emotions of those who encounter her. Joy quickly becomes a burr in readers' social consciences.

Anyone approaching Powers's work for the first time will be dismayed by the broad range of vocabulary upon which it draws. Technical words and terms from many fields of science and other specialized areas proliferate as the complexity of each novel grows. The scientific background of a book such as *The Gold Bug Variations* is extensive and reflects Powers's scientific training, but the author reveals a sufficient understanding of the mysteries of the DNA molecule to enable him to relate the unraveling of its mysteries to such other intellectual currents as Bach's counterpoint.

In his search for answers to the questions of existence, Powers uncovers suggestions of the interconnectedness of many human accomplishments and events. This author's artistic quest is, simply put, to understand the universe, to try to unlock the meaning of human existence—indeed, of all existence.

Having embarked on this ambitious course, Powers works steadily, resolutely, eyes fixed unflinchingly on achieving his intellectually ambitious ends. These ends, often much clearer to him than to some of his critics, determine the direction his work takes. He permits himself no detours, no time-outs to write the occasional potboilers or television scripts that some authors use to replenish shrinking coffers. Instead he remains in the shadows, focused always on his far-reaching, long-term, self-imposed artistic and philosophical ends.

Judging from asides Powers makes in all of his books, he views authors as artists who create situations that will entice readers into interacting with ideas, dredging up from within themselves memories of experiences that will shape their interpretations of what they read. His obeisance to readers aligns Powers with reader-response enthusiasts.

THREE FARMERS ON THEIR WAY TO A DANCE

First published: 1985
Type of work: Novel

> *This novel uses the lives of three rural farmers who are captured in a photograph to present a striking exploration into twentieth century modernism.*

In the first chapter of *Three Farmers on Their Way to a Dance*, the first-person narrator happens upon a haunting August Sander photograph in the Detroit Institute of Arts while passing some hours between trains. The photograph captures three youthful peasants resplendent in weekend finery. The picture, bearing the same title as Powers's book, is dated 1914. Given that date, the narrator reads his own meaning into the title: The dance these rural Americans are destined for is World War I.

The first narrative frame of the novel recounts the narrator's search for basic information about the picture and, once he has gained it, about the people Sander's lens captured. It turns out that all three—Hubert, Adolphe, and Peter—died in the war.

Yet *Three Farmers on Their Way to a Dance* is about much more than three peasants united in an obscure photograph. The book recounts in some detail the birth of twentieth century modernism and the virtually unbelievable interconnectedness of all human events. In order to fix the story historically, Powers provides readers with recurring interchapters, all related in some way to his skillful development of the book's three major plots.

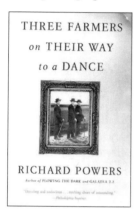

Several historical interchapters deal with the impact Henry Ford had upon American life and culture. Powers includes an interchapter on Ford's unofficial diplomatic efforts to end World War I by chartering an ocean liner and sailing it to Norway with as many prominent people as he could cudgel into joining his midwinter voyage, hoping that this cadre of celebrities might negotiate a peace treaty. Other historical chapters treat such figures as the renowned nineteenth century actress Sarah Bernhardt, the essayist Walter Benjamin, and others whose lives impinge upon the three main stories.

The narrator's account of his quest for information about the photograph constitutes the first narrative frame, which is related closely to the other two narrative frames and to the interchapters. The second frame is concerned with the three subjects in the picture and their simultaneously independent and historically interdependent existences. The third frame, a modern romance, concerns Peter Mays, a computer editor in Boston who pursues a haunting redheaded woman on the street, only to discover that she is an actress playing Sarah Bernhardt in a one-woman show.

Peter Mays, it turns out, has immigrated to the United States from the area that was home to Sander's three farmers. Peter, indeed, is the son of the brightest of these, also named Peter. When the younger Peter gave his full name—Peter Hubertus Kinder Schreck Langerson van Maasricht—to im-

migration officials at Ellis Island, he became "Peter Mays," the name he subsequently carries.

Sarah Bernhardt is subtly woven into each plot. Henry Ford figures in the Peter Mays story because Peter, scavenging in his mother's attic, discovers a picture that leads him to the discovery that he might be due a $250,000 legacy from Ford's estate. He also discovers among his mother's possessions a print of Sander's photograph of the three farmers, one of whom is Peter's father.

The narrator is last seen at an office Christmas party, where he talks with Mrs. Schreck, the aging immigrant who cleans his office. She has a motherly interest in him, regularly leaving chocolate bonbons on his desk. Mrs. Schreck knows Sander's picture and something about its subjects. She does not, however, have the answers the narrator seeks. A clandestine meeting with her in her home reveals only that the three subjects in the Sander picture "had led lives as verifiable, if not as well documented, as any of those Great Personalities I had poured over."

THE GOLD BUG VARIATIONS

First published: 1991
Type of work: Novel

A double love story provides Powers's pretext for this novel about genetics, DNA, music, computers, information theory, metaphysics— and, ultimately, the meaning of life.

On the surface, *The Gold Bug Variations* consists of two intertwined love stories, those of former DNA scientist Stuart Ressler and Jeanette Koss, Ressler's married lover, and of reference librarian Jan O'Deigh, thirty-four, and art historian Franklin Todd, thirty. Powers's title gives readers the initial wink. This book has something to do with Johann Sebastian Bach, the eighteenth century composer of *The Goldberg Variations*, and with Edgar Allan Poe, the nineteenth century author of "The Gold Bug." Poe's short story is cryptic; from the outset, Powers's novel is equally cryptic.

Arcane meanings lurk in unexpected places throughout *The Gold Bug Variations*, making rereading the book perhaps more pleasurable than the initial reading. The novel overflows with word games and puzzles relating to numbers and to science; this is the sort of book that makes for challenging group reading and discussion.

Stuart Ressler, once a member of the University of Illinois team that cracked the code of the DNA molecule, has faded from public view. Franklin Todd knows him, however; Ressler works with Todd, a part-time computer hacker working nights. He fascinates Franklin. It is clear that Ressler, who now—apparently by choice—lives at the subsistence level, once experienced a little more than the fifteen minutes of public recognition that Andy Warhol suggested was every American's due.

Eager to know more about Ressler, Todd enlists the aid of Jan O'Deigh, the reference librarian at the Brooklyn Branch of the New York Public Library. Tracking down information about Ressler (including his picture in a back issue of *Life*), Jan and Franklin become romantically entangled.

The plot of *The Gold Bug Variations* is told largely through Jan's eyes, in a flood of recollections set loose when, during her lunch hour one day, she finds in her mail a brief note from Franklin announcing Ressler's death. Through Franklin, Jan had met and come to know Ressler. Memories consume her. She quits her library job so that she can devote herself fully to ferreting out the meaning of Ressler's life and, more broadly, of life in general.

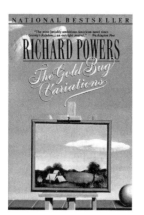

Ressler's work on DNA contained so many mysteries about the origins of existence that he, the accomplished scientist, suspected that anything able to create consciousness (life) was too complex for that consciousness to fathom. This suspicion caused Ressler to become an adult dropout from society, to live obscurely and ascetically, working of his own volition at a level considerably below his potential.

As in all of Powers's writing, the plot is not the novel. The novel plays with ideas so profound and so complex that they defy brief or simplified presentation. *The Gold Bug Variations* richly rewards frequent rereading, spirited discussion, and imaginative interpretation.

OPERATION WANDERING SOUL

First published: 1993
Type of work: Novel

Set in a large California hospital's pediatric surgical ward, this novel explores the evil that society visits upon children.

The most pessimistic of Powers's novels, *Operation Wandering Soul* uses a pediatric surgical ward as the microcosm that exposes what modern American society does to its children. At the same time, the book provides Powers the opportunity to discuss the status of children in society through the ages and to highlight many of the societal dangers of the late twentieth century. Carver Hospital is located in California, near Los Angeles, where many contemporary social and ecological problems are so exaggerated that they erupt there before middle America notices them.

Richard Kraft, thirty-three, is serving a rotation at Carver as part of his surgical residency. A former musician who, at twenty, traded the conservatory for college and then medical school, Kraft passed a peripatetic youth as his family followed its father from one overseas assignment to another.

Readers encounter the sensitive youth as he is being transformed into a ward-savvy physician. He struggles against his deepest human instincts to insulate himself from the horrors he witnesses in his patients. He strives consciously to wall off his emotions so that they will not be torn to shreds by the medical realities that daily assail him.

The children on Kraft's surgical ward are a badly afflicted lot: Joy, a twelve-year-old Asian girl with a malignant growth above her right ankle, will lose her leg; Nicolino suffers from progeria and, at puberty, is already an old man; Chuck, a preadolescent, has no face; Tony the Tuff, an adolescent, had his ear lopped off; Ben, also an adolescent, is a double amputee. Visiting this ward is not calculated to lift the spirits.

Into this mix, Powers brings Linda Espera, part physical therapist, mostly saint. She loves these children and learns as much about each of them as she can. Kraft remains aloof. Linda, however, will not countenance his professional detachment. After Kraft snares Linda sexually, she changes his outlook, adding him to her list of those she must save.

Linda plans to compose a year's worth of historical tales relating to the lives of children through the ages; 365 tales in all. Some of these tales provide the fodder for Powers's riveting interchapters, which deal with such stories as the Children's Army during the Crusades, the Peter Pan story, Herod's slaughter of the Innocents, and, as the artistic high point of the novel, the story of the Pied Piper of Hamlin.

These stories add to Powers's tale the historical perspective that makes his story frightening. They ask, "Has humankind learned anything from history?" while Powers's contemporary account inquires, "Will humankind ever learn anything from history?" The answers readers inevitably reach are bound to be discouraging, which makes *Operation Wandering Soul* essentially pessimistic, although Powers suggests, however faintly, that hope ultimately may reside in one-on-one human relationships, in human understanding and perseverance.

GALATEA 2.2

First published: 1995
Type of work: Novel

This novel offers two overlapping stories, one of which features a fictional protagonist named Richard Powers.

If Richard Powers is less than forthcoming in providing interviewers with autobiographical information, one had only to turn to two of his novels, *Prisoner's Dilemma* and *Galatea 2.2*, to find a great deal of such information. Indeed, in *Galatea 2.2*, Powers goes so far as to name the novel's fictional protagonist Richard Powers. This novel is one of Powers's more accessible novels. The characters he creates in it, particularly Richard Powers and C., the girlfriend he followed to the Netherlands where he lived with her for several years, are better rounded and more human than any characters he created previously.

In this novel, Powers pursues two distinct but overlapping story lines—the Richard Powers/C. story and the Lentz/Powers story. Powers, who in the novel works at the Center for Advanced Sciences (Powers's fictional name for the Beckman Center of the University of Illinois), first comes into contact with Philip Lentz at the Center. Lentz looks with disdain on the humanities. Familiar with Powers's work, he dubs him "Marcel," likening him to Marcel Proust, whose sprawling multiplot novels bear broad similarities to Powers's writing.

One night, out boozing with friends, Lentz stumbles on Powers and asks what one has to do to qualify for a master's degree in literature. When he learns that the degree is granted after successful completion of the prescribed course work, familiarity with the literary works on a six-page reading list, and a passing grade on a comprehensive examination that occupies two days, Lentz boasts that he could program a computer to master such a reading list and pass the requisite examination. He suggests that he and Powers embark on a project to create such a computer program within a ten-month time period. It is the story of this project that occupies the novel's second story line.

In the course of the novel, one learns not only of the relationship that developed between the fictional Powers and C., a student in his freshman English class, but also about the devastating effect his father's death has upon him at a crucial time in his life. Readers also learn of the profound effect that Professor Taylor, in actuality the late Professor Robert Schneider ("Schneider" is German for "tailor"), had on Powers in a seminar he took with him early in his college career. So profound an effect did this seminar have upon him that Powers switched majors from physics to English. Taylor, indeed, changed the course of Powers's life.

The Lentz/Powers part of the story unfolds after Powers has separated from C. and has returned to the United States. Powers is shocked to learn that during the years of his relationship with C., she has been almost paralyzed emotionally through the awe in which she held him. She ends up marrying an instructor in the translating school where she is taking a four-year course, interestingly an authoritarian teacher who often reduces his students to tears.

The Lentz/Powers collaboration moves from Computer A to Computer B and continues to Computer H, when, like the robots in Karel Capek's *R. U. R.* (1921), it is humanized. Its creators give it a human name, Helen, and now have only to go through the mechanics of programming it to complete their task.

PLOWING THE DARK

First published: 2000
Type of work: Novel

Powers intertwines two story lines, one that focuses on an American held hostage in Beirut by Muslim extremists and the other about a team effort to create a virtual world generated by computers.

Readers of *Prisoner's Dilemma* will recall that in his earlier novel, Powers brought Walt Disney to De Kalb, Illinois, to create a virtual world, a scale reproduction of the entire United States, but Disney's projected world is not computer-generated. The virtual reality portion of *Plowing the Dark* is related to the Microsoft Corporation, although the company is never named. The setting is Seattle, the home of Microsoft. Many of the concerns are ones that suggest Microsoft. Stevie Spiegel, involved in a project to turn a room, "The Cavern," through computer engineering into anything one wishes—the Sistine Chapel, the pyramids of Egypt, Michelangelo's *David*—calls upon a friend from his college days to help him, but he cannot reveal to her exactly what it is that he is attempting to achieve. Adie Klarpol, a disenchanted New York artist, has blind faith in what Stevie is doing, although she is not aware fully of the dimensions of his work. Her talent in art is vital to Stevie's project with the TeraSys virtual reality team. She is to re-create past artistic events and to trace the lineage of art history to such artifacts as the Lescaux Cave paintings.

Meanwhile, Taimur Martin, thirty-three, has arrived in Beirut to teach English. He leaves a pregnant girlfriend behind in the United States. Shortly after getting to Beirut, he is kidnapped by Muslim fundamentalists, thrust into holding facilities, and chained to the wall. As his confinement drags on, he creates his own virtual realities to preserve his sanity, dredging up memories from the past and shaping them into realities in his mind. At one point, after months of being held hostage and seeing no hope of escape, he attempts suicide.

Powers explores the origins of being in this novel and at one point comments, "All those old dead-end ontological undergrad conundrums? They've now become questions of engineering." One cannot reasonably argue that virtual reality will not change human existence perceptibly, but Powers tempers this conclusion with the virtual realities that Martin creates as a means of his own transformation during his imprisonment. His virtual realities have nothing to do with engineering.

THE TIME OF OUR SINGING

First published: 2003
Type of work: Novel

A German Jewish refugee, a musically talented African American woman, and their children face challenges in a racially divided nation.

On the Easter Sunday of 1939 when David Strom, a German and a nonpracticing Jew who has fled from Nazi Germany, met Delia Daley, a gifted black gospel singer from Philadelphia, the two were drawn irresistibly to each other. Delia, a physician's daughter, and David, a physicist teaching at Columbia University, were well aware of the complications that their marriage would ignite both in Delia's family and in their own lives. Nevertheless, they married and had three children, one of whom, Joey Strom, is Powers's narrator. Each of the children, Joey, Jonah, and Ruth (nicknamed Rootie), is gifted musically, but Jonah is a world-class tenor, who eventually flees to Europe to pursue his career in an atmosphere where he will be identified as a singer rather than as a "black singer."

David and Delia do everything they can to protect their children from the racial difficulties that mixed-race children faced in New York—indeed, in most of the United States—at that time. They home-schooled the children, and music became the center of their lives, the unifying force that enabled them to create their own exclusive realities. It is a combination of music and physics that causes Albert Einstein to make a cameo appearance in the novel.

When the children are of an age to leave home, their parents attempt to find the most compatible situations for them, but even in racially tolerant educational institutions in Boston, they are subjected to racial discrimination on a social if not professional level. The story, which encompasses three generations, takes its characters through World War II, Hiroshima, the Korean War, the Kennedy brothers' assassinations, and up to such contemporary debacles as the Rodney King beating in Los Angeles and the race riots in 1992 that ensued.

By the time of these riots, Rootie has become a civil rights activist. After her activist husband is killed by police, Rootie opens an alternative primary school in Oakland. Joey, who has tried various musical pursuits, now settles down to teaching music in his sister's school. Jonah, who attempts to be apolitical, became involved nevertheless in the Watts Riot on one of his return trips to the United States and was injured.

Now home again on tour, he visits with Joey in Berkeley before continuing his tour in Southern California. There be becomes involved in the riots following the King beating, is struck in the face by a police officer's baton, and the next morning is found dead in his hotel room.

The one hope for the family now seems to be in Rootie's bright, musically gifted son, Robert, whose life may be less scarred by racial prejudice than were the lives of his parents and uncles. It appears that Robert's closest associations, however, will be with the black rather than with the white community.

BIBLIOGRAPHY

By the Author

LONG FICTION:
Three Farmers on Their Way to a Dance, 1985
Prisoner's Dilemma, 1988
The Gold Bug Variations, 1991
Operation Wandering Soul, 1993
Galatea 2.2, 1995
Gain, 1998
Plowing the Dark, 2000
The Time of Our Singing, 2003

NONFICTION:
"Losing Our Souls, Bit by Bit," 1998
"Life by Design: Too Many Breakthroughs," 1998

SUMMARY

Powers is among the most intellectually complex novelists to appear since James Joyce and Thomas Pynchon. His novels are the fruits of a Renaissance mentality. Powers's encompassing grasp of abstract ideas is impressive; more impressive still is his ability to link them to the compelling central reference points his fiction creates and to do so with a literary style consistently and dependably excellent.

R. Baird Shuman

DISCUSSION TOPICS

- What roles do events from history play in the writings that you have read by Richard Powers?

- In the Powers novels that you have read, do you find much affirmation in the role that humans play in the universe?

- Powers writes about a world that has become increasingly mechanized and stereotyped. Comment briefly on how human beings in his novels cope with this situation.

- Powers is a great believer in the role that communication and articulation have in determining human beings' position in the universal scheme of things. Comment on how he deals consciously with questions of communication and articulation in his novels.

- Powers is a cellist and knowledgeable about music. What role do music and other arts play in the novels that you have read by him?

- With what major social issues does Powers's writing seem to be most concerned?

- Cite some specific instances in which Powers introduces current events and popular culture into his writing. What artistic aim does he achieve by including such references?

"Eyes Wide Open," 1999
"American Dreaming: The Limitless Absurdity of Our Belief in an Infinitely Transformable Future," 2000

About the Author

Baker, John F. "Richard Powers." *Publishers Weekly* 238 (August 16, 1991): 37-38.

Dewey, Joseph. *Understanding Richard Powers.* Columbia: University of South Carolina Press, 2002.

Howard, Maureen. "Facing the Footage." *The Nation* 251 (May 14, 1988): 680-684.

_____. "Semi-Samizdat and Other Matters." *Yale Review* 77 (Winter, 1988): 243-258.

Hurt, James. "Narrative Powers: Richard Powers as Storyteller." *Review of Contemporary Fiction* 18 (1998): 24-41.

LeClair, Tom. "The Systems Novel." *The New Republic* 198 (April 25, 1988): 40-42.

Powers, Richard. "State and Vine." *Yale Review* 79 (Summer, 1990): 690-698.

Stites, Janet. "Bordercrossings: A Conversation in Cyberspace." *Omni* 16 (November, 1993): 38-48, 105-113.

Margaret Sartor

REYNOLDS PRICE

Born: Macon, North Carolina
February 1, 1933

Price has transformed the people living in the border area between Virginia and North Carolina, where he was born, into universal types.

BIOGRAPHY

Reynolds Price was born during the Great Depression in the small town of Macon on the North Carolina side of the Virginia-North Carolina border. His birth was difficult and almost killed both him and his mother, Elizabeth Rodwell Price. Price's father, William Solomon Price, a salesman with a taste for liquor, vowed that if his wife's life was spared, he would stop drinking. After a prolonged labor, Reynolds, the first of the Prices' two children, was born. Will, whose twenty-seven-year marriage to Elizabeth was happy and passionate, struggled to keep his vow.

A second son, William, was not born until eight years later, so Reynolds was raised as an only child for nearly a decade, doted on by a gallery of aunts and uncles, most of whom appear in one form or another in his writing. Money was tight, and the Prices moved from town to town. They lost their house when Will fell short of an overdue fifty-dollar mortgage payment.

Reynolds, having few playmates and being brought up among adults with the penchant for storytelling common to people from small southern towns, depended upon his imagination for company. Besides being good storytellers, Price's relatives were readers, so, following their examples, he developed an early enthusiasm for books. He was a good enough listener that he learned early the rhythms, cadences, vocabulary, and syntax of southern speech, which he was later to reproduce authentically in his writing.

The adolescent Price wrote poetry as well as some plays. Reynolds grew close to his mother's sister, Ida Drake, who was forty-six when he was born. Price's early school experiences were positive. Jane Alston (called Miss Jennie) and Crichton Thorne Davis, his seventh-grade and eighth-grade teachers at the John Graham School in Warrenton, were exceptional motivators who recognized the young Price's potential. The family moved to Raleigh when Reynolds entered high school. There Phyllis Peacock, head of the English department at Needham-Broughton Senior High School, a demanding taskmistress, taught Reynolds how to write prose.

Price entered Duke University as an English major in 1951, beginning an association that has continued throughout his professional life. When, at the invitation of Professor William Blackburn, Eudora Welty came to Duke University early in the 1950's to work with undergraduates interested in creative writing and to comment on some of their work, Price's submission rose above the rest. A decade later, Price was back at Duke, having completed a residence at Merton College, Oxford University, which he had attended as a Rhodes scholar and from which he received a bachelor of letters degree in 1958. A fledgling assistant professor of English, he was pushing hard to finish his first novel.

Welty not only gave Price perceptive critiques of his early writing but also had a hand in helping him to place *A Long and Happy Life*, which was published in 1962. It was through her interest and intervention that *Harper's* agreed to publish this first novel in its totality in its April, 1962, issue. The novel won the William Faulkner Foundation Award for a first novel. Following a return to England in 1963, Price published a collection of short stories, *The Names and Faces of Heroes* (1963). His early story that Welty had praised during her visit to Duke a decade earlier, "Thomas Egerton," is included in this collection.

Price's second novel, *A Generous Man*, was published in 1966. Although it was not artistically up to *A Long and Happy Life*, it is, nevertheless, interesting for its frank phallic symbolism as represented by a python named Death that is suspected of having hydrophobia and has recently escaped from a traveling circus. The novel is humorous if heavy-handed in its symbolism.

Price's next novel, *Love and Work*, published in 1968, is an academic novel, but Price remains close to his southern roots: Town in this book is more pervasive than gown. Even though the protagonist, Thomas Eborn, is a thirty-four-year-old college professor, he cannot legitimately be viewed as a completely autobiographical character. The book received mixed reviews. Some of what Price experimented with in *Love and Work*, the intermixing of autobiographical fact with fiction, continued in his next book, *Permanent Errors* (1970). In that year, Price received an award from the American Academy and National Institute of Arts and Letters.

As the 1970's began, Price had started work on a more ambitious novel than he had yet undertaken, *The Surface of Earth*, which was finally published in 1975 and was followed by its sequel, *The Source of Light*, in 1981. A collection of essays, *Things Themselves: Essays and Scenes* (1972), was his only other book in the early 1970's. The critics were divided in their reception of the two novels.

In 1977, *Early Dark*, a play based on *A Long and Happy Life*, was published. At about the same time, Price published *A Palpable God: Thirty Stories Translated from the Bible with an Essay on the Origins and Life of Narrative* (1978), which brought him considerable critical praise. A collection of poetry, *Vital Provisions*, followed in 1982. *Mustian*, a collection that includes Price's first two novels and "A Chain of Love," was released in 1983.

A turning point came in Price's creative life in 1984, when an operation for spinal cancer left him a paraplegic. To help control the pain that he was suffering, Price underwent hypnosis, and this course of treatments resulted in unlocking for him much of his distant past, putting him in touch with information that helped him produce a flood of books in the next few years.

Another volume of poetry, *The Laws of Ice*, appeared in 1986, as did the immensely popular novel *Kate Vaiden*. A collection of Price's essays, *A Common Room: Essays 1954-1987*, was published in 1987. In 1988, another novel, *Good Hearts*, appeared, and in the next year his extensive autobiography, *Clear Pictures: First Loves, First Guides*, was published, followed by the novels *The Tongues of Angels* (1990), *Blue Calhoun* (1992), *The Promise of Rest* (1995), and *Roxanna Slade* (1998), as well as the autobiographical *A Whole New Life: An Illness and a Healing* in 1994. His amazing productivity continued into the twenty-first century with the children's book *A Perfect Friend* (2000) and the novels *Noble Norfleet* (2002) and *The Good Priest's Son* (2005). During this period, he also published various collections of his stories, poetry, and plays; wrote a number of religious books; and oversaw the publication of *A Great Circle: The Mayfield Trilogy* in 2001, consisting of *The Surface of Earth*, *The Source of Light*, and *The Promise of Rest*.

In 1988, Price was elected to membership in the American Academy and National Institute of Arts and Letters. He continues to teach at Duke University, where he was named James B. Duke Professor of English in 1977.

ANALYSIS

Reynolds Price has consistently written of human affirmation, and his depiction of the South and his presentation of race relations there have been authentic and commendable. Superficially, one might compare Price to William Faulkner. Both write about the South, and both focus on a limited geographical region. Also, as Price's work continued, particularly in *The Surface of Earth* and *The Source of Light*, his style became increasingly complicated, and some critics thought that it had been directly influenced by Faulkner. Before leaping to such conclusions, however, one must remember that Price is a John Milton scholar who regularly teaches a course on that seventeenth century English poet. Close examination is likely to reveal that Miltonic elements are more evident, particularly in Price's later work, than Faulknerian influences.

Price has acknowledged his debt to Milton as well as to Russian novelist Leo Tolstoy and to the Bible. His association with Eudora Welty provided another significant influence, as has the work of Flannery O'Connor. Price, who is unusually open in discussing his own approach to writing, has admitted in *Things Themselves* the impact that Ernest Hemingway's writing has had upon him stylistically. He also writes about his craft in some detail in *Learning a Trade: A Craftsman's Notebooks, 1955-1997*, published in 1998.

Price has never denied that his works are strongly autobiographical. He contends that although a writer's imagination is fundamental to any significant piece of fiction writing, writers cannot write from anything but their experience. He cautions, however, that art reshapes that experience so that few one-to-one correlations exist between writers' experience and their lives. Therefore, it is risky to draw conclusions about authors from characters that resemble them in their novels.

Two of Price's books with the strongest correlations to his own life are *Love and Work* and *Permanent Errors*, but the protagonists in these books do not exist within the limited context of one person's life; rather, they function symbolically and metaphorically as types. *Kate Vaiden* also has strong elements that make Kate resemble Price's mother, of whom he admittedly was trying to reach deeper understandings when he wrote the book, but Kate clearly is not Elizabeth Rodwell.

The nexus Price uses to relate his stories to society on a universal level is the family, which he considers the quintessential element in human existence, the fundamental organism within which society functions. This emphasis on the family is a particular emphasis in southern literature, although it pervades the works of many other major writers as well. Certainly it was the central force in John Steinbeck's *The Grapes of Wrath* (1939) and later in his less successful *East of Eden* (1952). It is the driving force behind most of Faulkner's novels and certainly motivates the action in such Eugene O'Neill plays as *Desire Under the Elms* (1924), *Mourning Becomes Electra* (1931), *Long Day's Journey into Night* (1956), and *A Moon for the Misbegotten* (1947).

The first fictional family Price examined closely was the Mustians, who are central to *A Long and Happy Life*, *A Generous Man*, "A Chain of Love," and to his play, *Early Dark*, based upon *A Long and Happy Life*. This examination was essentially of the Mustian characters who are alive at the time of the story. In his examination of the Kendal-Mayfield family in the trilogy *A Great Circle*, however, Price undertakes something much more ambitious: He seeks to understand four generations of a family.

In his examination of both families, Price is much concerned with questions of heredity. His conclusion is that no matter how hard people try to be different from their progenitors, they are, inevitably, like them. He postulates this as an axiom that cannot be overturned in the course of human existence. Price is much concerned with the concept that the sins of the father are visited upon the children, and all these novels are concerned directly and overtly with the biblical question of Original Sin. Even though people are born with the burden of sin, Price implies, they have free will, and in its exercise lies some hope of salvation.

In *The Tongues of Angels*, the protagonist, Bridge Boatner, an adult, has spent the past thirty-four years living with the burden placed upon him in the summer before his senior year at the University of North Carolina in Chapel Hill. Then struggling to come to grips with the recent death of his father, Bridge grew close to one of the fourteen-year-old campers in his charge. The boy, Raphael Noren, was talented beyond any of the other boys at the camp. His accidental death has haunted Bridge, particularly because he fears that in some way he may have caused it. In this book, Bridge is trying to cope not only with Original Sin but also with a great guilt and emotional upheaval relating to Raphael's death.

The "permanent errors" of which Price speaks in his book by that title are the sins of the fathers. For Price, they persist, generation after generation. The determinism of heredity is inexorable for Price, as it was for O'Neill, Faulkner, and Steinbeck before him. In much of his work, Price deals with the tensions created by the paradoxes in the Christian mystique. He sees these paradoxes in the whole of southern culture and finds them personified in family relationships.

A LONG AND HAPPY LIFE

First published: 1962
Type of work: Novel

A novel about small town southerners whose hope for a long and happy life is constantly overshadowed by the specter of death.

Few authors have the good fortune to have a whole issue of a major, high-circulation magazine devoted to the publication of their first novel at about the time the hardcover edition is released. Such fortune was Price's, however, when *Harper's* published *A Long and Happy Life* in its April, 1962, issue. The book went on to win a William Faulkner Foundation Award for a first novel, and the critical reception of this first book was singularly favorable.

A Long and Happy Life presents Rosacoke Mustian to the reading public, as well as her erstwhile boyfriend, Wesley Beavers, who gets the innocent girl pregnant. Although he condescends to marry her, he then pretty much leaves her on her own. The book is alive with local color. In one of the early, most memorable scenes, Rosacoke needs to attend a funeral at a black church on a sizzling day in summer. Her friend Mildred Sutton has died in childbirth and is to be eulogized. Wesley Beavers drives his noisy motorcycle up to deliver Rosacoke to the funeral, but he does not go inside. Instead, he lingers outside and polishes his motorcycle, which is an extension of his being. Before the services are over, he leaves precipitously to get ready for the church picnic that he and Rosacoke are to attend that afternoon. As he screeches away from the church, he raises a trail of red dust behind him that one can almost taste, so vivid is Price's description.

The book is divided into three long chapters, each with appropriate subdivisions. The action takes place between July and Christmas, and each section marks a visit from Wesley, who three times comes the 130 miles from the naval base in Norfolk to see Rosacoke, his girlfriend. They have known each other for six years. Rosacoke is now twenty, Wesley twenty-two. Wesley is sexually experienced; Rosacoke is not.

Price supplies necessary details unobtrusively, partly through Rosacoke's interior monologues, partly through the letters she exchanges with Wesley, and partly through flashbacks, most of them part of her interior monologues. He also introduces his readers to an amusing, warm-hearted cast of small-town characters who are far removed from the world outside their own community.

At the church picnic, Wesley tries to seduce Rosacoke, but she resists his advances. It is not until his next visit in November that he succeeds in deflowering Rosacoke, for whom the sexual experience is especially threatening because the death of her friend Mildred is still in the forefront of her mind. Rosacoke realizes that her long and happy life could be cut short by a pregnancy if it were to be a difficult one.

Death is very much a part of the novel. Rosacoke's brother, Milo, suffers the loss of his first child, a baby meant to carry on the family name, but who, dying at birth, takes the name Horatio Mustian III to the grave with him. Mildred's baby, Sledge, has survived, and Rosacoke visits him, doing her duty and being calmed by her visits, although they constantly remind her of what could happen to her, because she soon knows that Wesley's child is growing within her.

Through a series of mischances, Rosacoke is forced to play the Virgin Mary in the annual Christmas pageant that her mother is directing at the Delight Baptist Church. The baby Jesus is an overgrown eight-month-old child, Frederick Gupton, who has been drugged with paregoric so that he will not disrupt the pageant. Rosacoke realizes what her lot will be with Wesley, but she comes to an acceptance of it, partly through her participation in the pageant.

Price chose his microcosm well and constructed it with an authenticity that gained the respect of most of the critics. His dialogue is easy and believable. His humor is irrepressible, as in the scene in which Uncle Simon misplaces his false teeth at the church picnic and in the scene in which the preacher who can walk on water sinks.

The isolation of his characters from the world, being drawn as they are into the social and religious web of their own community, encapsulates them and insulates them from outside influences. Some outside influences—although not very desirable ones—intrude upon the story by means of Wesley's periodic visits.

Within the limited confines in which he works, Price has been able to find universal significance in his characters and has been able to deal intricately with questions of life and death, with the dream of a long and happy life, and with the fact of quick death for infants and other relatively young people within the story.

A GENEROUS MAN

First published: 1966
Type of work: Novel

A southern posse's search for a hydrophobic python echoes the meaning of life and death.

The story of the Mustians that Price initiated in *A Long and Happy Life* is also the focus in *A Generous Man*, his second novel. The cast of characters is not identical, but enough of them overlap that readers of the first novel will have a sense of identity with the main characters in the second.

The action of *A Generous Man* takes place nine years before the action of *A Long and Happy Life*. Wesley Beavers is not a part of the narrative because Rosacoke, now only eleven years old, has not yet met him. Milo, married and a father in *A Long and Happy Life*, is a fifteen-year-old boy in *A Generous Man*.

The book revolves around an unlikely event that imposes a light, sometimes hilarious tone upon a story that deals with matters of enduring importance with universal meaning. As the story opens, Milo Mustian, fifteen, has just lost his virginity to Lois Provo—a girl who, significantly, works with the snake show at the Warren County fair. Milo, waking the next morning, finds that the family dog, Phillip, is sick. In typical southern fashion, the whole family must go with Phillip to the veterinarian, a drunkard who quickly misdiagnoses Phillip's ailment as rabies, although Rato, the retarded son, later discovers it is only worms.

His dire diagnosis does not cause the doctor to confine or destroy the dog. Rather, he provides a muzzle, and Phillip goes off to the fair with the family. Rato takes Phillip's muzzle off, and before long, the dog gets into a fight with the eighteen-foot python, Death, that Lois's father gave to her pregnant, unmarried mother as a parting gift before he deserted her years before.

Rato, the python named Death, and Phillip all disappear into the woods. Realizing that they might have a hydrophobic python on their hands, the townsmen form a posse to save the town from impending disaster—their real motive, however, is to bring a little excitement into their flat lives. The men in the posse quickly become drunk and comradely. Price's symbol, of course, is completely outrageous, his basic premise patently absurd. Yet that does not matter; it is clear that he is carefully constructing an allegory whose wit and good nature entice readers.

Sheriff Rooster Pomeroy leads the posse, leaving his wife, Kate, to her own devices. Kate seeks sexual fulfillment wherever she can find it; her husband is impotent. As the posse scours the woods, Milo, now one of its more intoxicated members, stumbles from the woods into the Pomeroy house, where the eager Kate whisks him into her bed. Their pillow talk includes Kate's reminiscence about her first sexual encounter with, of all people, Milo's cousin, the very cousin who had left Lois's mother pregnant and in possession of Death, the eighteen-foot python.

Milo is not to have complete satisfaction with Kate. The doorbell rings, and the terrified Milo is out the window, clutching his clothing in his hands. He goes back into the woods and finds the python. He wrestles with Death and is on the verge of defeat when Sheriff Pomeroy shoots and kills (defeats) Death, enabling Milo to escape. When Milo next meets Lois, he is eager for another tussle in bed, but Lois rejects him, accusing him of being uncaring and insensitive. Milo, having bungled their first encounter through his inexperience, asks for and receives another chance. He has now learned to give as well as to take; he is both generous and a man.

LOVE AND WORK

First published: 1968
Type of work: Novel

An academic novel in which the protagonist deals with the death of his parents and learns a lesson about sharing.

Thomas Eborn, *Love and Work*'s protagonist, is a writer and a professor. Although he is largely an autobiographical reflection of Price, one would be mistaken to presume that he is completely so. He is partially a fiction, so one cannot reach conclusions about Price's life and personality on the basis of what he tells about this character who is, admittedly, quite like him.

Many writers try to understand their own problems and personalities through writing about situations that have eaten away at them for years. *Love and Work* is obviously an example of a work by an author who is wrestling with his own past. The past, in Price's case, became much clearer to him after hypnosis in 1984 (a decade and a half after the appearance of this novel) released from his unconscious mind many details about his past.

Much that Price could not present clearly in *Love and Work*, because he did not yet have enough information to understand it, he was able to present in clearer perspective in his autobiography, *Clear Pictures: First Loves, First Guides*, published twenty-three years after *Love and Work*, when he had come to grips with a past that was lost to him until his hypnosis.

Thomas Eborn is a dutiful son, but his sense of duty sometimes precludes warmth and love. He believes that work frees a person. He becomes so devoted to work that he allows it to intrude upon his life, which becomes increasingly mechanistic and impersonal. In the final hours before his mother's unexpected death, she, perhaps having a premonition of what lies ahead, tries to reach out to Eborn, but he is busy with his work and will not talk with her on the telephone. It is interesting to compare this account with Price's account of his last telephone call from his own mother as he recounts it in *Clear Pictures*.

Much of *Love and Work* takes place after Eborn's mother has died. He is clearing out her house, disposing of the past. He comes upon papers that enable him to reconstruct his parents' relationship with each other and with society. In the course of this activity, Eborn realizes that his mother's death, which frees him of a pressing responsibility, really does not free him at all, because he imposes his own type of personal bondage upon himself.

Eborn maintains his own house, and its inner sanctum, his study, is surrounded by an invisible moat that makes it inviolable to everyone. He has tried to put all of his human relationships into pigeonholes, to file them away, to prevent them from intruding upon his work. In so doing, he has also kept himself from having any genuine human relationships, even within the closeness of his immediate family.

In this book, Price's sense of place is strong; place, however, becomes the constraint that stands in the way of one's having personal relationships.

KATE VAIDEN

First published: 1986
Type of work: Novel

Kate Vaiden reflects on the death and desperation in her past and emerges an admirable woman who has learned how to be strong.

Kate Vaiden is an unusual book in that it has its base in a sensationalism that is almost melodramatic, yet its author has the skill to elevate the narrative above the level of sheer sensationalism into the realm of serious literature that deals with and presents universal truths. Before she was eighteen, Kate Vaiden, now a fifty-seven-year-old woman, had survived the murder of her mother by her father and his suicide, the accidental death of her favorite lover, the suicides of two of her lovers, the illegitimate birth of a son, and the anguish of giving him up. The basic story has the makings of a cheap, tawdry novel, but Price imbues it with dignity and shows nobility in its protagonist, Kate.

The telling of the narrative occurs in 1984, when Kate—like Price himself—was recuperating from cancer surgery. Her brush with death has made her determined to find the son she bore some forty years before. Facing pressures with which she was quite unequipped to deal, she had abandoned him when he was four months old. Her story unfolds as a justification, an explanation that will possibly help her child, Lee, to understand, possibly even to love, his natural mother. The story is also a step in Price's quest to

understand his own mother, a quest that is prevalent in *Love and Work* and that he deals with more overtly in *Clear Pictures*, his autobiography.

In the first scene of the novel, Kate has accompanied her mother, Frances, to the funeral of her cousin, Taswell Porter, who has been killed in a motorcycle crash. Dan, Kate's father, does not want Frances to go to the funeral, and he stays home in Greensboro in a rage. The day afterward, however, he goes to Macon, the rural community in Warren County where the funeral took place, and follows his wife to the grave, where she has gone with her cousin, Swift, to check the flowers placed there. Later Frances's sister, Caroline, who had virtually raised Frances, comes to Kate with Swift, whom she forces to tell the eleven-year-old the news: Both of her parents are dead.

An oppressive burden of guilt is placed upon Kate. She muses that had she gone with her father to look for her mother, the killing might have been avoided. She inherits fully, as many Price protagonists do, the sins of the father.

Kate, even before her parents' deaths, was distrustful. Now that she is faced with the abandonment that their deaths imply, she is still more distrustful. People reach out to her with love. She returns their love in some measure but never fully; she cannot trust enough to abandon her emotions to another person. Kate is not Price's own mother, Elizabeth, but certain correspondences—Elizabeth was an orphan raised by an older sister—suggest that in Kate, Price was certainly trying to understand some of his mother's personality traits and conflicts.

Left to be raised by Frances's sister, Kate at thirteen has a rewarding love relationship with Gaston Stegall, a sixteen-year-old, who eventually joins the Marines and is killed. Kate's adolescent happiness is snatched from her by death, just as her childhood happiness was destroyed by the death of her parents. She learns early that she cannot depend upon anyone, that, as the slogan in her penny-show garden proclaimed, people will leave you. If they do not leave voluntarily, death will take them away.

Kate's life is filled with sorrow and disappointment. She finally tracks down Douglas Lee, the father of her son, who had lived with her cousin Walter in Norfolk. Walter had taken Douglas from an orphanage and had exploited him sexually. In retaliation, the young Douglas seduced Kate, resulting in her pregnancy. Now, after all these years, Kate reestablishes contact with Douglas, who works as a chauffeur in Raleigh. Before long, however, Douglas commits suicide.

Price does not provide the outcome of Kate's reunion with her son after so many years. That is left to the reader's imagination. Lee will hear the story that the reader has just read; what he makes of it, one can only surmise.

"THE FORESEEABLE FUTURE"

First published: 1991 (collected in *The Foreseeable Future*, 1991)
Type of work: Short story

This story follows a man who returns from fighting World War II to life as a traveling insurance adjuster.

The title story in *The Foreseeable Future*, a collection of three long stories, tells the tale of Whit Wade, a soldier technically dead on the field of battle in World War II who is resuscitated. He has now returned to his wife and daughter in North Carolina. His family loves Wade quite genuinely, and he has always loved them, but his close encounter with death has left him with the feeling that he is not really alive. The thought of his death and that of many of his comrades on the battlefield nags him. He functions almost as a ghost.

Wade's occupation as an insurance adjuster is ironic. He spends his days dealing with people who want compensation for their accidents or for the death of their loved ones. Wade himself feels the need for compensation because he has lost something ineffable through his near death in combat. He is convinced that God has given him a second chance at life for some reason, but he does not know what that reason is. He does the best he can by providing for his family, giving them a secure house in which to live, but something vital is missing in his life. He realizes that he cannot allow himself to die a second time without salvation.

As he travels the back roads of North Carolina for his job, he stops one day for lunch and stumbles on Juanita, a medium who lives with her dogs and conducts her business in a trailer. Juanita worms

information out of Wade, finally asking how he knows that he was dead. He responds that he saw God either as a boy or as a tall young angel. Juanita counters, "Had to be dead." Juanita is somehow relieved by this revelation. She smiles a smile of "what looked like fifty gold teeth" and seems younger.

In time, Wade finds that relating his story to everyone who will listen helps him enormously. Through revealing his feelings to friends, relatives, and absolute strangers, he reconnects with the human race and finally begins to live again. He helps another former soldier who is haunted by his memories of the war. By reaching out to others in this way, he begins to come to grips with his own future and to be reconstituted as a contributing member of society.

THE PROMISE OF REST

First published: 1995
Type of work: Novel

This novel focuses on a bisexual man whose homosexual son is dying.

This last work in Price's trilogy *A Great Circle*, of which *The Surface of Earth* and *The Source of Light* are the other components, is easily understood by those who have not read the first two novels in the trilogy. The characters in these three novels consist of four generations of the Mayfield family. In *The Promise of Rest*, the family is in deep trouble.

Hutch Mayfield is a bisexual English professor at Duke University. His wife has left him, and he is now living through the final days of his son's life. Wade Mayfield is dying from acquired immunodeficiency syndrome (AIDS), which he contracted from Wyatt Bondurant, his lover of several years. Wade has conceived a child with Wyatt's sister, Ivory. Wyatt is black. He scorned Wade's family and eventually committed suicide. Hutch's own homosexual experience makes him sympathetic toward

his son and especially toward Wade's condition, although he has a very different take on homosexual relations than Wade has had. Hutch cannot envision a gay relationship lasting as long as his son's lasted. The rest that the book's title promises is not Wade's death, as one might superficially expect, but the rest that Hutch works toward achieving as he tries to make amends for his former bigoted racial attitudes and tries to pursue his own sexual activities with zeal, fervor, and a sense of self-acceptance.

Wade's illness has brought into the open a subject that had lurked in the shadows through much of Hutch's life. Now that the subject of homosexuality and the complicating factors that it can involve, including the danger of infection with human immunodeficiency virus (HIV) and the resulting progression to AIDS, is on the table for discussion, Hutch discovers the magnanimity of many people whom he has known for years but really never known because he could not, until now, be wholly honest with them.

Price presents an almost clinical account of Wade's illness, but he does so with a consummate compassion and with full recognition of Wade's strength of character. Price's own emotional involvement in his writing comes through in his account of the memorial service held for Wade. He follows this with Hutch's public utterances defending homosexuality, which are really somewhat detached from the rest of the story. One has the distinct sense that Price is fighting a conflict within himself, not a conflict about whether homosexuality is right or wrong—he has long passed beyond that pointless argument—but a conflict that involves his own emotions, one that suggests that he has suffered this sort of loss.

Although Price is recognized as one of the best writers of female characters, his portrayal of Wade's mother, Hutch's former wife, in *The Promise of Rest* is virtually without compassion. He does not demonstrate any hostility toward her, but he seems indifferent to her feelings, which are not delved into as deeply as they might have been. Perhaps Price tried to accomplish too much in this novel, which is beautifully written. The bifurcation of his characterization is at times distracting. The novel might have been more compelling had Price focused largely upon Wade rather than exploring Hutch's adjustments as well.

ROXANNA SLADE

First published: 1998
Type of work: Novel

This first-person narrative is related by a truly twentieth century southern woman.

This is Price's first novel since *Kate Vaiden* to be written from a female perspective. Roxanna Slade was born in 1900. Readers first meet her when she is twenty and living in a small North Carolina town, and they continue their relationship with her until she is ninety-four, the age at which she unfolds her long, complex story. Roxanna's life has been filled with trials, and, although at ninety-four she is quite removed from them in time, they molded the woman whom Price has created.

The novel's seven chapters are arranged chronologically. Some of them cover an act of such drama that the chapter is confined to one crucial day. Other chapters cover several years as Price telescopes Roxanna's experience. Price structures the chapters to reflect how Roxanna views the patterns of her life.

Some of Roxanna's trials will be familiar to readers of Price's short stories, in which a number of them had their genesis. Roxanna endured a horrible tragedy when the first man she truly loved drowned before her eyes. Having recovered from this catastrophe, Roxanna married, only to suffer the loss of a child. Then she was made aware of her husband's infidelities. While these events are relatively commonplace, and not unlike troubles that may have perplexed Price's readers in their own lives, Roxanna reveals her true strength of character and her fortitude through her rendition of these misfortunes. As the millennium approached, Price chose to comment on American society from the vantage point of a woman who lived through what might be called "the century of women." The suggestion is that in the upcoming century, women should come into their own quite fully, having made the initial gains they did in the 1900's.

Price makes it clear that Roxanna has learned to live with disappointment without being embittered by it. She frequently has had cause for anger, but in the wisdom of her years, she has learned to channel this anger to the point that it evaporates. She does not dwell on her regrets and, even at ninety-four, considers life a blessing rather than the curse that many people living through similar experiences might deem it to be. The pervasive theme that emerges from this book is that love is the counterbalancing force in a seemingly chaotic universe.

SUMMARY

Reynolds Price is more than merely the regional author that many people consider him to be. He is regional in the sense that William Faulkner was regional, but his concerns are also as broad as Faulkner's were. Fate plays a strong role in Price's work, and this fate is connected to heredity. Free will enables people to make choices, but in exercising their free will, Price's characters often make the same choices their parents made; therefore, the results are almost identical. Hereditary determinism is stronger in Price's work than in that of almost any other contemporary American author.

R. Baird Shuman

BIBLIOGRAPHY

By the Author

LONG FICTION:
A Long and Happy Life, 1962
A Generous Man, 1966
Love and Work, 1968
The Surface of Earth, 1975
The Source of Light, 1981
Mustian: Two Novels and a Story, Complete and Unabridged, 1983
Kate Vaiden, 1986
Good Hearts, 1988

Reynolds Price

The Tongues of Angels, 1990
Blue Calhoun, 1992
The Honest Account of a Memorable Life: An Apocryphal Gospel, 1994
The Promise of Rest, 1995
Roxanna Slade, 1998
A Great Circle: The Mayfield Trilogy, 2001 (contains *The Surface of Earth, The Source of Light,* and *The Promise of Rest*)
Noble Norfleet, 2002
The Good Priest's Son, 2005

SHORT FICTION:
The Names and Faces of Heroes, 1963
Permanent Errors, 1970
The Foreseeable Future: Three Long Stories, 1991
The Collected Stories, 1993

DRAMA:
Early Dark, pb. 1977
Private Contentment, pb. 1984
New Music: A Trilogy, pr. 1989, pb. 1990
Full Moon, and Other Plays, pb. 1993

TELEPLAY:
House Snake, 1986

POETRY:
Late Warning: Four Poems, 1968
Lessons Learned: Seven Poems, 1977
Nine Mysteries (Four Joyful, Four Sorrowful, One Glorious), 1979
Vital Provisions, 1982
The Laws of Ice, 1986
The Use of Fire, 1990
The Collected Poems, 1997

CHILDREN'S LITERATURE:
A Perfect Friend, 2000

NONFICTION:
Things Themselves: Essays and Scenes, 1972
A Common Room: Essays, 1954-1987, 1987
Clear Pictures: First Loves, First Guides, 1989
Conversations with Reynolds Price, 1991 (Jefferson Humphries, editor)
A Whole New Life: An Illness and a Healing, 1994
Three Gospels, 1996
Learning a Trade: A Craftsman's Notebooks, 1955-1997, 1998
Letter to a Man in the Fire: Does God Exist and Does He Care?, 1999
Feasting the Heart: Fifty-two Essays for the Air, 2000
A Serious Way of Wondering: The Ethics of Jesus Imagined, 2003

DISCUSSION TOPICS

- What role does guilt play in the writings of Reynolds Price?

- Is there evidence in any of Price's works that he believes in the concept of Original Sin?

- Much of Price's writing has been called "a dialogue between love and solitude." Do you agree or disagree with this characterization?

- Present some examples of how Price uses language, especially dialects, to depict his characters authentically.

- Price has written several religious books. Do you find specific elements of religion in his fiction?

- Price called the Great Depression his generation's Civil War. Do you find in his fiction evidence to support such a statement?

- To what extent is Price dependent on symbolism to drive home the essence of his stories?

TRANSLATIONS:

Presence and Absence: Versions from the Bible, 1973
Oracles: Six Versions from the Bible, 1977
A Palpable God: Thirty Stories Translated from the Bible with an Essay on the Origins and Life of Narrative, 1978

About the Author

Drake, Robert, ed. *The Writer and His Tradition.* Knoxville: University of Tennessee Press, 1969.

Humphries, Jefferson, ed. *Conversations with Reynolds Price.* Jackson: University of Mississippi Press, 1991.

Kaufman, Wallace. "A Conversation with Reynolds Price." *Shenandoah* 17 (Spring, 1966): 3-25.

Price, Reynolds. *Learning a Trade: A Craftman's Notebooks, 1955-1997.* Durham, N.C.: Duke University Press, 1998.

Rooke, Constance. *Reynolds Price.* Boston: Twayne, 1983.

Schiff, James A., ed. *Critical Essays on Reynolds Price.* New York: G. K. Hall, 1998.

_____. *Understanding Reynolds Price.* Columbia: University of South Carolina Press, 1996.

Shuman, R. Baird. "Reynolds Price." In *Encyclopedia of American Literature,* edited by Steven R. Serafin. New York: Continuum, 1999.

Woiwode, Larry. "Pursuits of the Flesh, Adventures of the Spirit." *The Washington Post Book World,* April 26, 1981, p. 5.

Wright, Stuart, and James L. West III. *Reynolds Price: A Bibliography, 1949-1984.* Charlottesville: University Press of Virginia, 1986.

THOMAS PYNCHON

Born: Glen Cove, New York
May 8, 1937

Pynchon is recognized as one of the leading practitioners of metafiction, the dominant avant-garde style in novels of the 1960's and 1970's.

BIOGRAPHY

Thomas Ruggles Pynchon, Jr., descendant of an early New England Puritan family, was born and raised in a middle-class Long Island suburb. His first known literary works were satiric essays published in the literary magazine of Oyster Bay High School, from which he graduated in 1953. He enrolled at Cornell University in that year, majoring in engineering physics. His college career was interrupted by a two-year hitch in the U.S. Navy; he returned to Cornell and graduated in 1959. While at Cornell, he took writing courses from the novelist Vladimir Nabokov, who was evidently impressed by the younger man's abilities but who had little direct influence on Pynchon's style or themes. Pynchon may have been married briefly during the 1950's, but careful investigations have produced no concrete evidence of this.

In 1959, he published two stories, one in the Cornell literary magazine, the other in *Epoch* 9; he published four more stories in 1960 and 1961. Most of these stories were eventually collected in *Slow Learner: Early Stories* (1984). Also in 1959, he began work on his first novel, *V.*, while living in New York's Greenwich Village; during 1960 and 1961, he worked as a technical writer for the Boeing Company in Seattle, Washington.

Virtually nothing is known about Pynchon's life after 1961. *V.* was published in 1963 and received the William Faulkner Foundation Award for the best first novel of that year. Pynchon's second novel, *The Crying of Lot 49*, appeared in 1966. He published *Gravity's Rainbow* in 1973; it has attracted what amounts to a cult of readers and massive critical attention.

Pynchon has chosen to live in obscurity, and his family and friends have cooperated in his wish to live outside the glare of publicity. In the years since 1961, he has supposedly spent most of his time in California and Mexico (his novels tend to confirm this speculation), but he later moved with his family to New York. He has given no interviews and made no public appearances; no photographs of Pynchon since he graduated from high school are known to exist. Apart from a few endorsements of other writers' fictions, the introduction to his own collection *Slow Learner*, an introduction to a friend's book, and two book reviews, he published nothing between the appearance of *Gravity's Rainbow* and *Vineland* (1989). Almost another decade elapsed before he published his *Mason and Dixon* (1997), which was critically acclaimed.

He took no part in the controversy over the 1974 Pulitzer Prize in fiction; the prize committee voted to present the award to *Gravity's Rainbow*, but the decision was overruled by the board that governs the Pulitzer awards. In 1975, Pynchon declined to accept the Howells Medal (named for William Dean Howells, nineteenth century American editor and novelist) from the American Academy of Arts and Letters. In 1989, he was awarded a fellowship by the MacArthur Foundation, which paid him $310,000 over a five-year period.

ANALYSIS

Pynchon is among the best known of the writers who came to prominence in the 1960's and 1970's with a new kind of fiction. At first this movement was called "black humor" because the novels and stories written by such authors as Pynchon, John Barth, Joseph Heller, Bruce Jay Friedman, and Gilbert Sorrentino, among others, tended to present events that were grim and terrifying but to deal with them in a wildly humorous manner. This style was also called "fabulation," a term coined by the critic Robert Scholes to reflect the idea that these writers rejected realism and deliberately called attention to the fabulous nature of their stories and novels. More recently, most critics have taken to using the term "metafiction" to describe the works of these writers. The term is intended to suggest that these writers have gone beyond conventional fiction and are creating works that make no pretense of representing reality.

Pynchon occupies a special place among this group of writers. All of them attempt to create distinctive styles, as style is an essential element in a fiction that does not try to represent human reality, but Pynchon commands a wider and wilder variety of styles than any of his contemporaries. He moves readily from wisecracking informality to obscenity to elegiac prose to fast-paced narrative. He employs humor ranging from high-comedy word play to pie-throwing and outrageous puns. From the beginning, he gives his characters names which are significant or simply silly (Jessica Swanlake, Benny Profane, Herbert Stencil, Mucho Maas, Stanley Kotecks, Dr. Hilarius the psychiatrist).

More important, Pynchon's novels, especially *Gravity's Rainbow,* generally acknowledged to be his masterpiece, deserve to be called "encyclopedic," a critical term used to describe huge novels which contain vast amounts of information about the writer's culture. In Pynchon's work, this means that the reader is presented with obscure lore about films, technical data from physics and mathematics, folklore from a number of cultures, new readings of historical events, informed references to popular and classical music, and various other types of knowledge. No other contemporary writer commands such a wide range of information.

Pynchon's stories and novels, at least until the publication of *Vineland,* have been dominated by two themes. The first is the concept of entropy (the second law of thermodynamics), which states that particles in any closed system tend to become increasingly agitated and their movements increasingly random as the system decays until they reach a stage ("heat death") in which no energy is exchanged, no further motion is possible, and the system dies. Pynchon owes to Henry Adams, the nineteenth century American novelist, historian, and autobiographer, the idea of applying this principle from physics to human organizations, especially to political entities. One of Pynchon's first stories is titled "Entropy" and tries to spell out how the idea can be used in fiction.

The other dominant concept in Pynchon's fiction is paranoia, the psychological condition which has been popularly called a persecution complex: the idea that the individual is the target of the unmotivated hatred of almost everyone and everything. As the fourth of Pynchon's "Proverbs for Paranoids" states in *Gravity's Rainbow,* "You hide. They seek." For Pynchon's characters, the idea that they live in a world in which everything is connected and everything is hostile to them is basic; a few of these characters, however, find themselves even more terrified by antiparanoia—the idea that nothing is connected, that everything is totally random.

The paranoid concern is certainly present in Pynchon's first novel, *V.,* where hints of an all-encompassing plot disturb the lives of most of the characters, but it becomes more dominant in *The Crying of Lot 49,* whose central figure keeps stumbling across indications of an ancient conspiracy whose manifestations include mass murders which are sometimes fictitious, sometimes apparently real. Pynchon's preoccupation with paranoia reaches a climax in *Gravity's Rainbow,* which includes the five Proverbs for Paranoids, a song titled "Paranoia," and discussions of the phenomenon by the narrator and by the characters. The problem is less noticeable in *Vineland,* Pynchon's fourth novel, but it clearly affects a number of the characters.

The concerns with entropy and paranoia are developed, in all his novels, through plots that detail quests. The important characters in all these books are in search of something. Although in *Gravity's Rainbow* Pynchon relates his characters' questing to the ancient search for the Holy Grail, these fictional quests are often for vaguely defined goals, and in Pynchon's hands they almost always fail or end ambiguously.

Benny Profane, the nearest thing to a protagonist in *V.,* is looking for something he cannot define, something that would give a meaning to life, but many of the other characters are involved in a search for the mysterious woman known by several names, all beginning with the letter "V." This woman, or one of her manifestations, appears at places and times where violence is imminent. The violence may or may not occur, but the mysterious woman—becoming less and less human—may be the cause of it, or she may be attracted to it. The truth of this is never made clear, but the characters are no less determined in their quest for V.

Oedipa Maas, the central figure in *The Crying of Lot 49*, is on a more clearly defined quest. She finds that she has been made the executor of the will of a former lover, a tycoon whose estate she must try to discover and define. Oedipa falls into a nightmarish California world, stretching from Silicon Valley to San Francisco, where she encounters hints of a secret organization called Tristero and what seems to be a subversive postal system called WASTE. She pursues her quest through encounters with human wreckage and scientific puzzles, never knowing with any certainty whether the tycoon is really dead or whether she is deliberately being led through a maze which has no solution.

The object of the quest involving almost every character in *Gravity's Rainbow* is an advanced German rocket, fired in the final days of World War II. In more or less elaborate ways, each of the characters searches for evidence of the rocket. For the British, American, and Russian officials, the search is for technology that will be useful in trying to gain a military advantage in the postwar world. For the survivors of an African tribe which has been living in Germany, locating the rocket would provide a means to regain their tribal unity and character. For Tyrone Slothrop, the American lieutenant who is the central character in the novel's early sections, the search is a compulsion forced on him by the manipulation of his subconscious mind. For other characters, the search for the rocket is an end in itself, something that gives form and meaning to otherwise pointless lives.

In *Vineland*, the quest is diffuse. Zoyd Wheeler is hiding out, looking for security, while his daughter Prairie searches for her mother, Frenesi Gates, who left husband and daughter years before, fatally attracted to Brock Vond, a menacing federal prosecutor. Prairie, whose search is the nearest thing in this novel to a genuine quest, is also trying to find the truth about her mother and the reasons for her departure. Frenesi seems to have disappeared; Vond is also looking for Frenesi and, incidentally, for Prairie. Other characters have their own searches; as in other Pynchon works, many of these have no real goal but serve to provide a shape for otherwise formless lives.

"ENTROPY"

First published: 1960 (collected in *Slow Learner: Early Stories*, 1984)
Type of work: Short story

Dwellers in two separate apartments provide a lesson in the workings of entropy.

"Entropy" was the second professional story published by Pynchon, and this comic but grim tale established one of the dominant themes of his entire body of work. The setting is an apartment building in Washington, D.C., on a rainy day early in 1957. In a third-floor apartment, Meatball Mulligan and a strange group of friends and interlopers are in the fortieth hour of a break-the-lease party. Some of Mulligan's friends are listening to rock music played on a huge speaker bolted to a metal wastebasket; when the music ends they carry on a hip discussion of the jazz music of the time, centering on Gerry Mulligan's piano-less quartet. The Duke di Angelis quartet, as they call themselves, carry on an experiment, playing music without any instruments and without any sounds, a kind of telepathic nonmusic. Women guests are passed out in various places in the apartment, including the bathroom sink.

As the party continues, more people arrive. One man comes because he and his wife have had a fight about communication theory and she has left him. A group of coeds from Georgetown University arrives to join the party. So does a group of five sailors, who have been told that Mulligan's apartment is a brothel. They refuse to leave, latch onto the unattached women, and continue the party. At one point a fight almost breaks out between the sailors and the musical group, but Mulligan decides to intervene and calm people down. At the end of the story, the party is continuing.

On the floor above, a man named Callisto and his girlfriend, Aubade, live in a closed environment. Over seven years, Callisto has created a sealed space, complete with vegetation and birds, cut off from the world outside. The temperature inside and outside is holding steady at 37 degrees. Callisto is holding a sick bird, trying to make it well with the warmth of his body, but in the end the bird dies. They have reached the moment of stasis predicted by the theory of entropy: There is no longer any heat exchange. Aubade breaks the window, and they wait together for all life to end.

The story intends to illustrate Pynchon's understanding of the theory of entropy as it might be applied to human beings and their activities. He acknowledges that the idea came from Henry Adams, who first applied the physical law to society, but Pynchon sets up the contrasting apartments as a means to demonstrate the differences between open and closed systems. Callisto's system is totally closed, and in a relatively short time loses all motion based on the exchange of heat; when everything is the same temperature, nothing moves. The bird's death prefigures the death of the entire system.

Mulligan's apartment, on the other hand, is for the time being an open system. People come and go. The Duke di Angelis quartet can play its silent music, and the sailors can get drunk and flirt with the women. Choice is still possible, so Mulligan can choose to defuse the fight rather than allow the party to degenerate into total chaos. The laws of thermodynamics apply here as well as in Callisto's apartment, however; the party verges on chaos because, as a system heats up, motion within it becomes increasingly random and violent. The system in this apartment will continue to function as long as fresh energy can enter from outside, but once external stimuli cease to arrive, this system, too, will reach a point of stasis.

"THE SECRET INTEGRATION"

First published: 1964 (collected in *Slow Learner: Early Stories*, 1984)
Type of work: Short story

Three boys and an imaginary playmate try to subvert the world of their prejudiced parents.

"The Secret Integration" is the longest and most interesting of Pynchon's early stories. Set in Mingeboro, a small town in the Berkshire Hills of western Massachusetts, it concerns a group of teenage boys who have hatched a plot to disrupt the adult community and eventually to assume control of the town themselves. At the time of the story they are preparing their second annual trial run, pretending to attack the school and considering what other steps they might take.

The four boys most deeply involved are Grover Snodd, a kind of genius, an inventor whose inventions rarely work but who has convinced his parents and the school board to let him leave the local school to study at the nearby college; Tim Santora, a typical teenager; Étienne Cherdlu, a compulsive joker (his name is a pun on the old printers' fill-in line, etaoin shrdlu); and Carl Barrington, son of a black family that has just moved into a new housing development. The mothers of Grover and Tim make anonymous obscene phone calls to the Barringtons' home, trying to force them to leave town.

The story depends on misdirection. The four boys seem to be cast in the mold of Booth Tarkington's Penrod and Sam or Mark Twain's Tom Sawyer—mischievous but good-hearted, involved in boys' games that cannot harm anyone. (Tarkington was a twentieth century novelist who wrote about boys' games in a small Indiana town; Twain was a nineteenth century American novelist, some of whose works dealt with boys' adventures.) It seems to be merely a joke that one of their other friends, Hogan Slothrop, son of the town doctor, has been an alcoholic at age eight and a member of Alcoholics Anonymous (A.A.) since age nine. The boys even have a secret hideout where they do most of their planning, a basement room in an abandoned mansion. The mansion seems to be haunted, and it has to be approached in a leaky boat—classic conditions from adventure tales for boys.

Their plot has been going on for three years and seems to be running out of steam as they leave their hideout, but then the story seems to lurch into a long digression on events that had occurred previously. It concerns Hogan Slothrop, who a year earlier was supposed to infiltrate a PTA meeting and set off a smoke bomb but was called by the local A.A. to go to the local hotel and sit with a fellow alcoholic who is under stress. Tim accompanies Hogan, and Grover and Étienne soon appear at the hotel as well. They try to help the black musician, Carl McAfee, who has somehow wandered into Mingeboro, broke and miserable. They are let in on McAfee's life and his misery. They try unsuccessfully to help a man who is beyond any help they can provide. Eventually they witness his removal by the local police.

After this episode, the boys' lives return to normal; they even have a successful adventure, using small children and a kind of stage set to terrify the crew and passengers of a railroad train one night. Then, the following summer, the Barringtons move into the new development, and the boys find Carl and make him their friend. As the climax of the story makes clear, however, Carl is a fantasy, made up by the three other boys to compensate for their parents' prejudice and hatred. When the boys visit the new development and find definite evidence that their parents have been involved in dumping garbage on the Barringtons' lawn, they try to clean up the mess, only to be sent away by Mrs. Barrington. Carl then departs; they send him away, because they cannot bear to give up their need for their parents and the comforts of their homes. They are becoming adults.

V.

First published: 1963
Type of work: Novel

Characters either wander aimlessly in postwar America or search for a woman who may provide a clue to the violent nature of the modern world.

Pynchon's first extended work of fiction focuses on two disparate plots. At the center of the first of these is Benny Profane, a self-styled schlemiel, a veteran of the Navy who spends his time going up and down the East Coast (in the novel his movement is called "yo-yoing") between New York City and the naval base at Norfolk, Virginia. Profane's life has no real purpose, and he has no deep attachments to anyone; his parents are never mentioned, and his girlfriends come and go. He takes only jobs that are by their nature temporary. At one point he is a night watchman in a crazy kind of computer laboratory; at another he is part of a crew that roams New York's sewers at night, shooting the alligators that have been flushed down when they grew too big to be pets. His friends are a group who call themselves the Whole Sick Crew; like him, they have no sustaining purpose in life.

The other continuing thread running through *V.* has to do with a mysterious woman who began appearing around the time of a crisis in East Africa before World War I, known in history as the Fashoda affair, which seemed likely to bring about an armed conflict between Great Britain and France. The woman has many names (Veronica, Victoria, Vera), all beginning with the letter V. She appears in other places, as well, first in German Southwest Africa at a time of native rebellion, living among a besieged group of Europeans in a fortified farmhouse. She is present when a group of South Americans in Italy is planning a revolution in their homeland, and still later she is the lover of a young ballerina in Paris between the two world wars. Finally she appears on the Mediterranean island of Malta during World War II, at a time when the island is subject to intense bombing by the Italian and German air forces.

V. metamorphoses from a seemingly innocent English girl with a fascination for violence into a cosmopolite whose ethnic origins are obscure and who seems to feed on violence done to herself as well as to others. In the German redoubt she is German herself, but in her later manifestations her origins and her real nature are unclear; one mad priest in New York even believes that she manifests herself as a rat living in the sewers beneath the city. Over the years she becomes less and less human, as mechanical devices are substituted for parts of her body. By the 1940's she is almost entirely a machine.

The connection between Benny Profane and the Whole Sick Crew on one hand and V. on the other hand is an Englishman who associates with them named Herbert Stencil. Stencil's father, a British agent, had known and been fascinated by V. since the Fashoda affair. There is also a link through a young woman, Paola Maijstral, who is a friend of Benny and a member of the Whole Sick Crew. Paola is Maltese by birth; her parents had married during the war and had endured the air raids together. Paola's father, Fausto Maijstral, has written a diary (it occupies a long chapter of *V.*) which provides important information about the character V. Paola finally convinces Benny to visit Malta in the 1960's.

In general terms, the different plot lines represent the two different themes of *V.* Benny and the Whole Sick Crew represent the forces of entropy; their activities become increasingly frenzied and random as the novel progresses and as the system of which they are a part becomes more closed. The searchers for V. are subject to strong forces of para-noia, believing that there is a gigantic plot they can uncover if only they can find the key. The mysteri-ous land called Vheissu, a kind of fantasy British colony of which no one knows anything real, rein-forces their belief. At the same time, it is evident that the characters in Benny's world are subject to paranoid fears; moreover, the world of the spies and agents is also a closed system, increasingly fre-netic and destructive, likely to either explode or end in an inertial balance.

Despite all the humor and wild improbability it involves, *V.* is finally a grim book. Benny Profane is loved by several women but is unable to return their love in a meaningful way. When last seen, he is standing on the shore in Valletta, the capital of Malta, in total darkness, no happier and no wiser than he was in the beginning. The epilogue to the book shows that the older Stencil, having located V. on Malta in 1919, disappeared when a waterspout suddenly appeared on a calm day and destroyed the boat on which he was leaving the island.

V. is not, however, a hopeless book. The very viv-idness of its writing, the inventiveness of many of its characters in the face of potential disaster, and the humaneness some of them exhibit show that some of these strange creatures, at least, are capable of a sort of redemption. Pynchon in *V.*, as in other sto-ries and novels, suggests that art, in its many forms, can provide potential alternatives to chaos or to en-tropy. He puts in the mind of a black jazz musician named McClintock Sphere the palliative words: "The only way clear of the cool/crazy flipflop was obviously slow, frustrating and hard work. Love with your mouth shut, help without breaking your ass or publicizing it: keep cool, but care."

THE CRYING OF LOT 49

First published: 1966
Type of work: Novel

A California housewife embarks on a quest for the real nature of a secret organization called Tristero and its underground postal system called WASTE.

The Crying of Lot 49 is Pynchon's briefest book and the one with the least complicated plot, although it contains plenty of twists and turns. Oedipa Maas, a bored California housewife, is informed that she is the executor of the estate of Pierce Inverarity, a for-mer lover. Oedipa is plunged into an increasingly complicated and increasingly sinister search for the estate, which becomes a search for meaning.

Oedipa uncovers what seems to be a vast under-ground conspiracy with ancient origins. Its present manifestation is an illegal communications system whose origins go back to the Middle Ages, when the private European postal service operated by Thurn and Taxis (this is historically accurate, as is so much in Pynchon's work) gained a monopoly on mail delivery in Europe. In the novel, a rival group calling itself Tristero began a bitter and violent at-tempt to take business away from Thurn and Taxis. Remnants of the subversive group found their way to the New World and tried to subvert the U.S. Postal Service. Their system is called WASTE, which may mean that the alternative system is a waste of time and effort (some of their mail drops are garbage cans), but which may be an acronym and slogan: "We Await Silent Tristero's Empire."

Oedipa first finds the system operating among employees at a Silicon Valley electronics company called Yoyodyne, located in a town called San Narcisco, which, seen from a hill, looks like a printed computer circuit. She follows clues to a housing development in the area, where she is told a story about an American detachment in World War II that was wiped out by Nazis on the shores of an Italian lake. Later she attends a play, "The Cou-rier's Tragedy," supposedly written by a contempo-rary of William Shakespeare, in which a similar massacre took place at the same spot as the climax of an Elizabethan tragedy of revenge. There are suggestions that Tristero was somehow responsible for both events, but Oedipa is unable to track down the original version of the play. The man who staged and acted in it mysteriously dies.

Oedipa's search continues through encounters with strange people, including a crazy psychiatrist; a scientist who is trying to prove the existence of a puzzle in physics called Maxwell's Demon, named for the famous British physicist Clark Maxwell; her increasingly deranged husband, Mucho; and a conference of deaf people who dance in perfect rhythm to music they cannot hear. At the end of the novel she is waiting for the opening of a stamp auc-tion (the title, *The Crying of Lot 49*, refers to the opening of bidding for one item or group of items at an auction) which may reveal the meaning of Tristero, if indeed it has a meaning.

All of this sounds somewhat grim, but like Pynchon's other works, *The Crying of Lot 49* is lightened by the style, by high and low comedy, and by Pynchon's verbal gymnastics. The characters' names include Mike Fallopian, Stanley Koteks, Randolph Driblette, Bloody Chiclitz, and Arnold Snarb, among many others. There is a rock group calling themselves the Paranoids, who imitate the Beatles in every possible way. There is a law firm called Warpe, Wistfull, Kubitschek and McMingus. The canned music in Oedipa's local supermarket plays a nonexistent Vivaldi Kazoo Concerto, performed by the Fort Wayne Settecento Ensemble (also nonexistent). "The Courier's Tragedy," summarized at considerable length, is an accurate parody of the Elizabethan tragedy of revenge, exemplified by Thomas Kyd's *The Spanish Tragedy* (pr. c. 1585-1589, pb. 1594?) or by Shakespeare's *Titus Andronicus* (1594).

More clearly than *V.*, *The Crying of Lot 49* focuses on questions of behavioral psychology and free will. It is never clear to Oedipa whether Pierce Inverarity has really died; she becomes uncomfortably aware that if he has not, all of her investigations may be part of a complicated game in which Inverarity maneuvers her every move. If she is little more than a robot, the possibility exists that American culture has eliminated most possibilities for diversity. If Tristero exists (and even this is never certain), it may be only a feeble final protest against a society that is as carefully organized as a computer chip. It is also possible that Oedipa is hallucinating the whole thing. Yet there is the chance that a genuine resistance to an overly controlled society is really functioning. *The Crying of Lot 49* raises these issues but leaves them unresolved.

GRAVITY'S RAINBOW

First published: 1973
Type of work: Novel

A huge cast of characters searches through post-World War II Europe for a super rocket invented by the Nazis.

The questions of free will and determinism in a universe which may be subject to entropy are most sharply defined by Pynchon in his longest and most complete novel, *Gravity's Rainbow*. Set in the closing days of World War II and the months immediately following the end of the war, this novel takes the themes and techniques of the two earlier novels to higher levels. *Gravity's Rainbow*—in part because many regard it as a masterpiece and in part because it is so complex, involves so many strands of action, and poses so many unanswered questions—has been the subject of more critical attention than any novel in English since James Joyce's *Ulysses* (1922).

The central symbol of *Gravity's Rainbow* is a new type of rocket developed by the Germans at the end of World War II, designated the A-4. The first rocket designed to carry a human being into space, it is a triumph of technology. It suggests the possibility that humankind may have found a way to transcend its earthly origins, but it is much more likely that it carries beyond previous limits—beyond any limits—people's ability to destroy themselves. Technology, in Pynchon's view, has a capacity for destruction that threatens to overwhelm its capacity for construction. At the beginning of the novel, a screaming in the sky seems to indicate that a rocket is on the way; at the very end, the reader sits in a theater with a descending rocket poised just overhead.

The action of *Gravity's Rainbow* centers on attempts to trace the A-4 rocket and its components, especially an advanced form of plastic called Imipolex-G. The British, the Americans, and the

Russians, nominal allies in the war against Adolf Hitler's Germany, are rivals in trying to find the rocket and its makers in order to gain an advantage in the postwar world. One part of the British effort is managed by a behavioral scientist named Ned Pointsman.

Pointsman is the spokesman in the novel for the Pavlovian idea (named for the Russian psychologist Ivan Pavlov) that people, like all other animals, act in response to stimuli. Pointsman believes that if the correct stimuli are applied, anyone can be trained to undertake any action his or her controller directs. He makes use of the fact that an American lieutenant named Tyrone Slothrop (he is, incidentally, the younger brother of Hogan Slothrop in "The Secret Integration") was the subject of an early experiment in conditioning a young baby. The experimenter, a mysterious figure named Lazslo Jamf, who also invented Imipolex G, supposedly removed "Baby Tyrone's" early conditioning, although remnants of it apparently remain.

Using a variety of behavioral methods, Pointsman sets Slothrop on the track of the A-4 rocket, and for much of the first half of *Gravity's Rainbow*, Slothrop is the center of the action. He moves from London to the French Riviera to Switzerland. When the war ends he moves into the "Zone," an area geographically similar to the British, American, French, and Russian zones of occupied Germany but much larger, symbolically encompassing all the postwar world. Slothrop has a variety of adventures, some frightening, some hilarious.

Other characters are involved in their own quests for the rocket. The Hereros, remnants of a tribe transplanted to Germany years before from what was (before World War I) German Southwest Africa, have assisted in work on the rocket and now search for leftover parts to construct a rocket for themselves. Their leader, Enzian, is convinced that the rocket will provide a new center for the tribe, without which it will wither away. Enzian's path crosses Slothrop's from time to time. So does that of the chief American searcher, Major Marvy, a gross and vicious scout not only for the American armed forces but for American industrial interests as well. All of them, at one time or another, encounter the Soviet agent, Tchitcherine, who happens to be Enzian's half brother.

There are dozens of other characters and other plots involved in the novel. Countering Pointsman is a British officer named Roger Mexico, a mathematician who rejects Pointsman's determinism and argues that traditional Western ideas of cause and effect are too limited. In his view, new scientific ideas about chance and indeterminacy are more important. Mexico's affair with a member of the British WAAF (Women's Auxiliary Air Force) named Jessica Swanlake is the nearest thing the novel contains to a love story. It ends when the war is over and Jessica chooses a more conventional man. A British secret agent called Pirate Prentice is also involved, along with one of his spies, a Dutch woman named Katje Borgesius.

While these characters (and many others) are engaged in their quests, the novel also recounts the story of the German characters who built and launched the rocket. Chief among these is the sinister Captain Weissman (also known as Blicero), who was responsible for assembling the men with the special skills needed to create and build the rocket. Once the rocket was launched, he evidently died. He has been Enzian's lover. One of his aides is a scientist named Franz Pokler, who is forced to keep working on the project because his wife, a radical, and his daughter are being held in a prison camp; if he fails to cooperate, they will presumably be killed.

Entropy is less important in *Gravity's Rainbow* than in Pynchon's earlier work; it still operates, but it seems to be less an immediate threat than the nuclear weapons that could destroy the known world in a few minutes. Paranoia, however, is more important than ever. The novel includes many episodes in which characters' suspicions that they are involved in some gigantic plot are supported by all the available evidence. The most perceptive characters have frequent intimations that there is a group called only "They," which is international in scope and which intends to gain control over everything: people, resources, and ideas. At one point, for example, Enzian experiences a revelation that all the destruction caused by bombing and shelling in World War II has been specifically planned to wipe out the old industrial establishment in order to make way for a new and more efficient physical plant.

There are small rays of hope. Art provides an alternative to the regimentation of modern society. Rebellion is still possible; when Slothrop disappears, his friends and supporters form a group called the "Counterforce" to oppose "They." The Counterforce inevitably becomes bureaucratic and public relations-oriented, but members are capable of individual acts of defiance which can provide hope. The style of the novel, varied and spectacular, is itself the strongest denial of the grayness and blandness that result from the control of society by those who use technology for their own ends. At the end of the novel, however, destruction seems to be inevitable.

VINELAND

First published: 1989
Type of work: Novel

In 1984, a teenage girl searches the past and present-day California for information about her mother, who disappeared around 1970.

Vineland is Pynchon's most accessible novel, the one in which he makes his most direct statements about politics and repression in the United States, and the one in which the "good guys" and "bad guys" are most clearly distinguished. It is also, paradoxically, the one in which he makes use of the most indirect narrative methods.

There has always been an element of indirection in Pynchon's fiction, a technique related to sleight-of-hand in which the author seems to be pointing in one direction, only to shift to something unforeseen. There have also been elements of surprise in the depiction of many of Pynchon's characters. In *Vineland*, however, indirection becomes a basic technique. For example, an important chapter that will lead Prairie Wheeler, the central figure, to essential information about her mother begins with an extended depiction of a mobster, Ralph Wayvone, Sr.

At the outset, *Vineland* centers on a former hippie named Zoyd Wheeler. He lives in Northern California with his daughter, Prairie, a teenager who works in a "New Age" pizza parlor. Zoyd has a small business and receives a government allotment for engaging in one crazy act a year, usually leaping through a plate-glass window in a local restaurant. He is harried by drug enforcement agents and, early in the novel, by a federal prosecutor who is

trying to find Zoyd's ex-wife, Frenesi. It seems clear that Zoyd will be the central character in the novel.

The fact is, however, that Zoyd virtually disappears from the action for a long period once Prairie leaves with her boyfriend and his punk band, Billy Barf and the Vomitones.

The real quest in the novel is Prairie's search for her mother, Frenesi Gates, and for the truth about Frenesi. Her father and grandmother, Frenesi's radical mother, have always told her that Frenesi offended the establishment and was forced to go underground. Through a series of improbable coincidences (another common element in Pynchon's fiction), Prairie meets DL Chastain, a woman martial arts expert who was a close friend of Frenesi when both were involved with radical politics during the Vietnam War era. DL takes Prairie to a women's colony, the Sisterhood of Kunoichi Attentives, where women learn Ninja, and where she finds records that begin to reveal the truth about Frenesi.

What Prairie learns, over a period of time, is that her mother had been part of a radical film collective which had, at the height of the protests against the Vietnam War in the late 1960's, been filming a student uprising on a college campus in Southern California. Her friends did not realize that Frenesi had been seduced by Brock Vond, the federal prosecutor and the blackest of all Pynchon's villains. Just as the troops and police were about to move in to break up the students' rebellion, Frenesi betrayed her friends by acting as the agent for the murder of a professor, the leader of the student movement (and incidentally one of Frenesi's lovers). When the troops moved in, Frenesi was taken to a detention center, from which DL Chastain rescued her. She then married Zoyd and gave birth to Prairie before Brock reclaimed her. Since then she has lived as a protected government informer, with a fellow informer named Flash and their son, Justin.

As the novel nears its end, the characters gather in Vineland, a fictional town and county in Northern California. Zoyd, Frenesi, Prairie, DL, her partner Takeshi, and some others attend a reunion of the large extended family of Sasha, Frenesi's mother. Brock Vond is on hand as the leader of what is supposed to be a huge government operation aimed at the marijuana crop but which is, in fact, intended to be more generally repressive; on a personal level, it is his opportunity to kidnap Frenesi and Prairie, whom he believes is his daughter. Hector Zuniga, a drug enforcement agent, is trying to arrange a motion picture based on Frenesi's life.

It is clear in *Vineland* that Pynchon's sympathies are with anyone and anything that represents resistance to what he regards as an increasingly repressive government. The use of drugs such as marijuana, LSD, and even cocaine is seen as part of such resistance; any harm they might do is harm only to the user, while a character such as Vond, in his lust for power, harms everyone he touches. Government installations built in recent years to house potential resisters in a time of national emergency are used by Pynchon to suggest the lengths to which the government is prepared to go in stamping out resistance to its policies. Raids on marijuana growers are seen as exertions of power aimed at controlling everyone.

Despite the power wielded by Vond and his agents, the ending of *Vineland* is more hopeful than that of any of Pynchon's other novels. At the very moment when Vond is about to abduct Prairie, her sharpness and a sudden cutting off of his funding by Ronald Reagan-era reductions in government spending frustrate him; he is then carted off and destroyed. Prairie, although she has felt the power and attraction that seduced and nearly destroyed her mother, is safe. In the final lines, her dog, Desmond, who had disappeared when Zoyd's house was occupied by government agents, reappears. At least for a time, she has escaped from danger.

Vineland includes elements of fantasy, most important among them the creatures called "Thanatoids," who are spirits of the unquiet dead, and there are plenty of coincidences and improbabilities. For the most part, however, this novel attempts to depict what Pynchon sees as the important realities in the world of the 1980's and 1990's. Paranoia is clearly present, but the emphasis on entropy has largely disappeared, replaced by concern about the effect on individual freedoms of these recent developments. Pynchon finds these frightening, but not yet clearly triumphant.

MASON AND DIXON

First published: 1997
Type of work: Novel

Pynchon's account of the lives of Mason and Dixon and their creation of the Mason-Dixon line is metafiction, a blending of the historical and fictional, and a satiric look at the nature of colonialism and science.

Thomas Pynchon's *Mason and Dixon* is narrated by the Reverend Wicks Cherrycoke, whose protracted stay at his sister's home in Philadelphia depends upon his entertaining his two nephews, Pliny and Pitt. The entertainment consists of his account of the adventures of Mason and Dixon, the surveyors who created the line dividing Pennsylvania from Delaware and Maryland. Although he knew the two surveyors, he was not privy to all the information, factual and otherwise, with which he regales his audience. His embellished account is occasionally interrupted by the nephews and other members of his audience.

The novel is divided into three parts, the first of which concerns the backgrounds of the two surveyors; their first meeting; their travels to South Africa and St. Helena to conduct transit of Venus observations; their meeting with Nevil Maskelyne, a rival astronomer who wins the post of Royal Astronomer that Mason seeks; and their encounters with the fictitious Vroom family. The first part of the novel also introduces three themes that permeate the novel. First, Mason and Dixon are part of the Age of Reason, which stressed science, but that science was imperfect at best and is subject to Pynchon's satire. Second, slavery, with its necessary "engine," the gallows, is seen as a means by which white people become more "savage" than the indigenous people they exploit. Third, Mason's inability to escape the guilt he feels about the death of Rebekah, his wife, and his subsequent abandonment of his sons.

The "meat" of the novel's "sandwich" structure is ostensibly the actual creation of the Mason-Dixon line in the United States, but the second part not only continues the first part's focus on drinking in taverns and uttering bombastic speeches, but also introduces some historical figures and several lengthy digressions. In Philadelphia, Mason and Dixon meet Ben Franklin, who entertains them with his electrical experiments and his buxom assistants, Molly and Dolly, and gives them the sage advice to "never pay the Retail Price." George Washington is portrayed as a land speculator and a hemp addict, and Martha Washington resembles Barbara Bush as she presents the surveyors with a plate of home-baked cookies. Perhaps the most humorous character is Gersom, a black Jewish servant who is cooking hog jowls. The digressions include a story about a mechanical duck capable of defecation and intent on pursuing a cook, and the account of Eliza Field's kidnapping by Indians and her captivity in Quebec. The melding of fact and fiction, fictional characters and historical personages, history and fiction—these are all characteristics of metafiction.

Part Three, "The Last Transit," is a short wrap-up of the material. Mason remarries, brings his children to America, and then returns to England.

Despite his scientific contributions, he is never admitted to the Royal Society, but Maskelyne, his rival with political connections, is. While in London, Mason meets Samuel Johnson and James Boswell, his biographer; the meeting is appropriate because Pynchon's novel is itself a biography of sorts, one told by the Boswell-like Cherrycoke, as well as being a satiric look at colonialism with its attendant evils and the nature of science and progress.

SUMMARY

Pynchon's stories and novels depict a wild modern world in which motion pictures, rock music, and drugs provide an outlaw alternative to an increasingly repressive society. His characters inhabit a landscape of their own which nevertheless bears eerie resemblances to everyday life. Pynchon uses a wide range of styles, employing slang, obscenity, vivid narrative, and poetic prose to convey his sense of the hazards and possibilities of the second half of the twentieth century, in which the forces of repression have all the power but in which creative art and occasional joy are still possible.

John M. Muste; updated by Thomas L. Erskine

BIBLIOGRAPHY

By the Author

LONG FICTION:
V., 1963
The Crying of Lot 49, 1966
Gravity's Rainbow, 1973
Vineland, 1989
Mason and Dixon, 1997

SHORT FICTION:
"Mortality and Mercy in Vienna," 1959
"The Small Rain," 1959
"Entropy," 1960
"Low-Lands," 1960
"Under the Rose," 1961
"The Secret Integration," 1964
Slow Learner: Early Stories, 1984

NONFICTION:
Deadly Sins, 1993

About the Author

Chambers, Judith. *Thomas Pynchon.* New York: Twayne, 1992.

Clerc, Charles. *"Mason and Dixon" and Pynchon.* New York: University Press of America, 2000.

Copestake, Ian D. *American Postmodernity: Essays on the Recent Fiction of Thomas Pynchon.* New York: Peter Lang, 2003.

Grant, J. Kerry. *A Companion to "V."* Athens: University of Georgia Press, 2001.

Hite, Molly. *Ideas of Order in the Novels of Thomas Pynchon.* Columbus: Ohio State University Press, 1983.

Madsen, Deborah L. *The Postmodern Allegories of Thomas Pynchon.* New York: Palgrave Macmillan, 1991.

Mead, Clifford. *Thomas Pynchon: A Bibliography of Primary and Secondary Materials.* Elmwood Park, Ill.: Dalkey Archive Press, 1989.

Patell, Cyrus R. K. *Negative Liberties: Morrison, Pynchon, and the Problem of Liberal Ideology.* Durham: Duke University Press, 2001.

Seed, David. *The Fictional Labyrinths of Thomas Pynchon.* Iowa City: University of Iowa Press, 1988.

Walhead, Celia M. "Mason and Dixon: Pynchon's Bickering Heroes." *Pynchon Notes* 46-49 (Spring-Fall, 2000-2001): 178-199.

DISCUSSION TOPICS

- Thomas Pynchon is critical of authority, whether it is parental or political. In his fiction, how successful are attempts to subvert authority?

- Of the many characters in Pynchon's fiction, which character or characters seem most like Pynchon in outlook and behavior?

- What is the nature of the loss in *Gravity's Rainbow*?

- Discuss the nature of paranoia in *Vineland* and how it affects the plot.

- *Mason and Dixon* contains, like most of Pynchon's fiction, a quest. Identify the quest or quests and to what extent they are successful.

- Most literary digressions are at least tangentially related to the main plot. Discuss the relevance of the digressions in *Mason and Dixon*.

- What environmental concerns surface in *Mason and Dixon*?

AYN RAND

Born: St. Petersburg, Russia
February 2, 1905
Died: New York, New York
March 6, 1982

Rand demonstrated that the novel can present a challenging philosophy to a wide public and at the same time have the entertainment value of a best seller.

Library of Congress

BIOGRAPHY

Ayn Rand was born Alissa Rosenbaum, the child of Zinovy and Anna Rosenbaum, in St. Petersburg, Russia, on February 2, 1905. From an early age Rand decided to become a writer. Her early influences included adventure fiction and American movies. The Russian Revolution of 1917 caused her father, a successful chemist, to lose much of his wealth. Communism's intellectual constraints gave Rand a loathing of Communism and all related doctrines. Nevertheless, Rand completed her schooling in Russia, majoring in history at the University of Petrograd, and then took courses at the State Institute of Cinematic Arts. Her knowledge of history and her background in the cinema would serve her well as a writer.

Rand eventually left the Soviet Union in 1926 and went to Chicago, staying briefly with her cousins the Portnoys before moving to Hollywood. During this time, she changed her name from Alissa Rosenbaum to Ayn Rand. In Hollywood, she worked as a film extra, then moved to scriptwriting. She met and fell in love with actor Frank O'Connor, whom she claimed inspired her fictional heroes. The two were married in 1929. Though their marriage was often strained, it lasted until O'Connor died in 1979. Gradually Rand gained modest literary success. Her earliest works were *We the Living* (1936), a novel of the Russian Revo-

lution, the courtroom drama *Night of January 16th* (1936), and the futuristic short novel *Anthem* (1938). She and O'Connor eventually moved to New York to work on *The Fountainhead* (1943).

The Fountainhead received some favorable reviews and slowly climbed onto the best-seller list. Following its publication, Rand returned to Hollywood to work again as a screenwriter. After receiving a fan letter from a young man named Nathaniel Branden, Rand and he formed a close personal and professional relationship. Branden, his wife Barbara, and others joined Rand for discussions of her philosophy. During the 1940's and 1950's, Rand worked on several screenplays, including the screenplay for *The Fountainhead*. Her main project, however, was an expansion of the themes expressed in *The Fountainhead*. The new novel was *Atlas Shrugged* (1957)—Rand dedicated it to Frank O'Connor and Nathaniel Branden.

After the publication of *Atlas Shrugged*, Rand devoted her time to producing nonfiction works expounding on her philosophy of Objectivism, including *For the New Intellectual* (1961), *The Virtue of Selfishness* (1964), *Capitalism: The Unknown Ideal* (1966), and *The Romantic Manifesto* (1969). Much of the material for these books came from the journals she was producing: *The Objectivist Newsletter* (1962-1965), *The Objectivist* (1966-1971), and *The Ayn Rand Letter* (1971-1976). Other contributors to these journals included Nathaniel and Barbara Branden, Leonard Peikoff, and Alan Greenspan, the future head of the Federal Reserve System. Rand also took part in the Nathaniel Branden Institute and taught classes in Objectivist philosophy.

Revelations about Rand's extramarital affair with Nathaniel Branden damaged her image, and in 1968 she and Branden dissolved their partnership. Overall, though, she became a fixture on the intellectual scene, sometimes discussing public issues on television. Rand died in New York in 1982. Following her death, Peikoff, Rand's intellectual heir, edited *The Early Ayn Rand: A Selection from Her Unpublished Fiction* (1984), containing some early stories and discarded sections from her novels. Other posthumous works include *Letters of Ayn Rand* (1995) and *Journals of Ayn Rand* (1997).

ANALYSIS

Rand's fiction embodies the philosophy of Objectivism. She wants to provoke a philosophical response from her readers, to make each one choose a side. Objectivism asserts an uncompromising individualism, in which human beings' rights to life, liberty, and the pursuit of happiness are paramount, and their primary social obligation is to respect the rights of others. Rand believed that in modern times, the greatest threat to freedom is collectivism, the belief that the state, whether Communist, Fascist, or democratic, can control humans, especially by infringing on the right to hold property and to buy and trade freely. She supported capitalism as an expression of the highest freedom and loved the United States for its commitment to individual rights.

In keeping with this philosophy, all of Rand's heroes and sympathetic characters are self-reliant and self-starting. They are frequently tall, lean and hard with strong, craggy names like Howard Roark, Dagny Taggart, and John Galt. They are makers and builders: architects, inventors, and industrialists. They love their work and respect competence above all. Rand's villains, often referred to as second-handers or looters, tend to be pudgy, formless, and weak with names such as Wesley Mouch or Ellsworth Toohey. They live parasitically off the labor or ideas of others, to which they feel entitled. Frequently they support government programs to redistribute wealth from the producers to weak people like themselves. Their moral standards lie in what others think. As one villain says, "Give your soul. To a lie? Yes, if others believe it. To deceit? Yes, if others need it." The conflicts in Rand's stories, therefore, are between different sets of values.

Rand uses several techniques to develop her themes. One of the best-known is having her characters make long speeches expounding their philosophies. Rand often excerpts these passages into her nonfiction, further reinforcing the connection between fiction and philosophy in her writing. More compelling are the brief, one-line passages which sum up an entire philosophy, like the venomous Ellsworth Toohey's remark, "Genius is an exaggeration of dimension. So is elephantiasis. Both may be only a disease." Rand also allows physical details to advertise her characters' inner natures, as when a minor villain is said to carry a gun in one pocket and a rabbit's foot in the other, demonstrating his brutality and irrationality.

Rand adheres to a romantic theory of art which holds that art should make moral ideals concrete. She rejects naturalism, preferring to portray people as she thinks they should be. Her characters do not sound, look, or act like people in the real world, even when they are taken from real-life models. This belief violates some tenets of modern literature. If modern literature stresses ambiguity in characterization, Rand has clear-cut heroes and villains. If modern tastes favor the downbeat and question happy endings, Rand never loses faith in her heroes' ability to triumph. Rand took her cue from the great Romantic nineteenth century novelists like Victor Hugo, who wrote about highly charged historical events and larger-than-life characters.

Rand also uses the techniques of popular fiction. Her long novels have the strong drive and pace of the best thrillers. Some have the futuristic settings of science fiction. Like a mystery writer, she often teases her readers with questions and puzzles, such as the riddling catchphrase of *Atlas Shrugged*, "Who is John Galt?" Rand's literary works also all have love-story plots or subplots. Her heroes and heroines love each other passionately because they see value in each other. Her novels, though tame by today's standards, were considered very sexy in their day.

Although sex in Rand's work sometimes resembles conquest or even rape, she asserted that sex is a joyous act between consenting adults. Certainly, her strong female protagonists expect and even demand the best from their men. Rand's popularity continues long after her death, though critics and scholars have often ignored or dismissed her work. Recent academic studies, such as Mimi Reisel

Gladstein's books, suggest that Rand is getting serious attention and respect. Perhaps Rand will belatedly receive the literary recognition she often sought.

THE FOUNTAINHEAD

First published: 1943
Type of work: Novel

Architect Howard Roark fights against nearly overwhelming odds to build according to his own vision.

The Fountainhead's major theme is the need for integrity and independence as exemplified in the career of Howard Roark. Roark is the fountainhead, or productive force, in the novel. To develop this theme, Rand places Roark in contrast with three other men, Peter Keating, Ellsworth Toohey, and Gail Wynand.

The novel begins with a jarring contrast. Howard Roark is expelled from the Stanton Academy on the same day that Peter Keating graduates with honors. Roark is the true architect, making a building's design fit its purpose, while Keating's practice of architecture seeks to please other people. In New York, Roark works for Henry Cameron, a brilliant, unconventional architect whose career and body are in decline. Cameron becomes Roark's mentor, but he is also a foreboding image of how the world may destroy Roark.

After Cameron retires, Roark begins working for a series of architects but keeps getting fired because he will not bend to mediocrity. Roark designs in one style—his own—and ignores architectural fashions and traditions. Keating, meanwhile, advances in his career. Every time he has to design a building on his own, however, he turns to Roark for help. In this way Rand dramatizes the nature of the "second-hander." Keating cannot produce because he worries about how his buildings will be received, while Roark, the fountainhead, can think on his own.

While working at one firm, Roark meets the intellectual Austen Heller, who appreciates the young architect's work. Heller gives Roark his first commission and the money to open his own architectural firm. A string of commissions comes in but

then peters out. Roark eventually closes his offices and finds works cutting stones in a quarry in Connecticut.

There Roark meets Dominique Francon, a beautiful, intelligent woman, who despises the world for its worship of mediocrity. Rand once described Dominique as "myself in a bad mood." Dominique destroys the beautiful art objects she loves in order to keep the world from ruining them. Roark and Dominique come to love each other deeply, but their acts of love are savage. In New York Roark and Dominique develop a unique romance. Dominique believes that the world will destroy Roark as it destroys every person or thing of integrity. Rather than see him end up like Cameron, she tries to ruin his career before it starts. Her charm and wit, as well as the newspaper column she writes, turn potential clients away from Roark.

Dominique's campaign against Roark brings him to the attention of architectural critic Ellsworth M. Toohey, a selfless human-itarian. As one would expect from Rand, Toohey is the novel's villain. He and Dominique collaborate against Roark but for different reasons. Toohey hates Roark because he is great, and greatness is an affront to the average man.

Despairing of any personal happiness, Dominique enters into two loveless marriages, one to Peter Keating and the other to newspaper publisher Gail Wynand. Wynand is a might-have-been Rand hero—a slum boy who became a self-made millionaire. Wynand has Roark's brains and drive but not his independence. Wynand's tabloid newspapers control mass opinion by selling news to the lowest common denominator. Despite their differences, Wynand and Roark eventually become friends.

Peter Keating receives a commission for the Cortland Building, a public housing project. Roark actually designs it, demanding only that Keating ensure that the building follows Roark's plans exactly. Keating fails in this, and the resulting building travesties Roark's design. Roark, having no legal recourse, dynamites the Cortland building.

Following Roark's arrest, Wynand puts all his power behind Roark, and his power evaporates. Wynand's control over public opinion is a sham—the public listened to him only when his papers preached what they wanted to hear. Wynand thought he had the world on a leash, but "a leash is a rope with a noose at both ends."

At his trial, Roark defends himself with a speech expressing the novel's intellectual core. The man who invented fire, it begins, "was probably burned at the stake he had taught his brothers to light." Civilization was built by a few creative minds—always facing public disapproval. Roark argues that he blew up a housing project which only he could have created. The jurors acquit Roark, who marries Dominique at last. Wynand gives him a commission to design the greatest skyscraper in the world.

ATLAS SHRUGGED

First published: 1957
Type of work: Novel

In a near-future world, John Galt and his cohorts remove themselves from the world and destroy a collectivist society.

Atlas Shrugged is the fullest expression in fiction of Rand's philosophy of Objectivism. The novel begins sometime in the near future. Technology and fashion are close to what they were when Rand wrote the novel, but private property has been abolished in most countries, now called "People's States." Shortages, delays, and excuses are commonplace. The United States still maintains some freedom, but the government increasingly dictates terms to producers through planning boards and economic directives. A few notice that gifted people in business, the sciences, and the arts are vanishing.

The novel's opening line, "Who is John Galt?" introduces Rand's theme: the value of the productive individual. John Galt institutes a strike by the world's best minds against a collectivist social order. While Galt is the book's spirit, the main plot line focuses on Dagny Taggart, the vice president of Taggart Transcontinental, whom reviewer Mimi Reisel Gladstein has called "probably the most ad-

mirable and successful heroine in American fiction." Another important character is Hank Rearden, a self-made steel magnate. The novel's villains ruin the world by confiscating the wealth of the productive.

Dagny, aided by Hank Rearden and his new company Rearden Metal, tries to save her foundering railroads by rebuilding one of the company's abandoned lines (which she renames the John Galt line) into Colorado, one of the few states with a growing economy. Rand shows the joy of achievement through a thrilling account of the line's construction. Dagny and Hank persevere and triumph. Hopes for an economic turnaround in Colorado are dashed, however, by a series of new laws crippling the state's businesses. Rand's heroes can control nature but not politics.

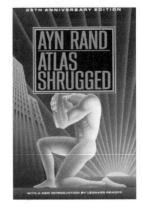

While on a trip, Dagny and Rearden—now lovers, though Hank is married—find in a ruined factory a new, revolutionary type of motor. Dagny dedicates herself to finding the motor's inventor, a quest giving the novel a mystery-story appeal. The motor also develops the novel's main themes. The abandoned factory was once owned by the significantly named Twentieth Century Motors. The company's failure suggests the failure of the entire twentieth century, while the motor symbolizes the driving intellect, which the looters ignore or abuse.

Meanwhile, the United States starts turning into a "People's State." Hank Rearden succumbs to government directives rather than have his affair with Dagny be made public knowledge. Rand demonstrates how Rearden's shame gave his enemies their power over him. Dagny's search for the motor's creator fails. She hopes that the bright young engineer Quentin Daniels may discover the motor's principles. Daniels, like so many talented people, then goes missing. Dagny flies after him in her plane but crash-lands in a hidden valley.

The valley is called Galt's Gulch. Here Dagny finally meets John Galt and hears his story. Galt had created the motor, but when Twentieth Century

Motors became a collectivist enterprise, he started his strike of the productive and gifted against the looters. His old friends and teachers, Francisco d'Anconia, Ragnar Danneskjöld, and Hugh Akston, retired to the valley, later joined by others, or fought the looters in their own ways. Like Atlas, the mythical giant, they held up the world, and now they are shrugging off their burden.

Dagny falls in love with Galt, but she remains a "scab." Eventually America's economy collapses as resources are allocated to the politically savvy. Among Rand's telling examples is the loss of the Minnesota wheat crop, which rots because the trains that might have carried it to a starving nation instead transport a Florida soybean crop, the pet project of a Washington string-puller.

The novel's climax comes when Galt takes control of radio broadcasting and gives a long speech, which may be encapsulated in the motto "I swear by my life and my love of it that I will never live for the sake of another man, nor ask another man to live for mine." Eventually Galt is captured and tortured, while the novel's villains show their absurdity by ordering Galt to give orders, in order to make the world run. Galt's friends fly out from the hidden valley to rescue him. They return, bringing Dagny Taggart, while the lights of New York City go out, the final image of a bankrupt society. With the looters purged, Galt and his friends return to the world.

SUMMARY

Rand is an American phenomenon. Her few literary works have endured and remained influential. These works, despite their flaws, have much to say about individualism, the role of government in personal and economic life, and artistic independence. Rand takes her place among those American writers who "march to a different drummer."

Anthony Bernardo, Jr.

BIBLIOGRAPHY

By the Author

LONG FICTION:
We the Living, 1936
Anthem, 1938, revised edition 1946
The Fountainhead, 1943
Atlas Shrugged, 1957
The Early Ayn Rand: A Selection from Her Unpublished Fiction, 1984 (Leonard Peikoff, editor)

DRAMA:
Night of January 16th, pr. 1934, pb. 1936 (also titled *Woman on Trial* and *Penthouse Legend*)
The Unconquered, pr. 1940 (adaptation of *We the Living*)

SCREENPLAY:
The Fountainhead, 1949

NONFICTION:
For the New Intellectual: The Philosophy of Ayn Rand, 1961
The Virtue of Selfishness: A New Concept of Egoism, 1964
Capitalism: The Unknown Ideal, 1966
Introduction to Objectivist Epistemology, 1967, second enlarged edition, 1990 (Harry Binswanger and Leonard Peikoff, editors)
The Romantic Manifesto, 1969

DISCUSSION TOPICS

- What are the physical and other characteristics, such as names and professions, of Ayn Rand's sympathetic and unsympathetic characters? What purpose does she have in giving them these particular features?

- How does Rand's admiration for human beings as builders and creators show up in her fiction?

- Rand's novels often have long speeches by the characters justifying their actions. What purpose is served by these speeches?

- Rand said that her purpose in fiction is to set forth a moral ideal. How do her heroes and their actions reflect a moral ideal?

- How does Rand use her novels to contrast the values of individualism and collectivism?

- How does Rand criticize prevalent social trends?

The New Left: The Anti-Industrial Revolution, 1971
Philosophy: Who Needs It?, 1982
The Ayn Rand Lexicon: Objectivism from A to Z, 1984 (Peikoff, editor)
The Voice of Reason: Essays in Objectivist Thought, 1988 (Peikoff, editor)
The Ayn Rand Column, 1991
Letters of Ayn Rand, 1995 (Michael S. Berliner, editor)
Journals of Ayn Rand, 1997 (David Harriman, editor)
The Art of Fiction: A Guide for Writers and Readers, 2000 (Tore Boeckmann, editor)
The Art of Nonfiction: A Guide for Writers and Readers, 2001 (Robert Mayhew, editor)

MISCELLANEOUS:

The Objectivist Newsletter, 1962-1965 (later *The Objectivist,* 1966-1971; edited by Rand)
The Ayn Rand Letter, 1971-1976 (published by Rand)

About the Author

Baker, James T. *Ayn Rand.* Boston: Twayne, 1987.
Branden, Barbara. *The Passion of Ayn Rand.* Garden City, N.Y.: Doubleday, 1986.
Gladstein, Mimi Reisel. *The New Ayn Rand Companion.* Westport, Conn.: Greenwood Press, 1999.
Gladstein, Mimi Reisel, and Chris Matthew Sciabarra, eds. *Feminist Interpretations of Ayn Rand.* University
    Park: Pennsylvania State University Press, 1999.
Yang, Michael B. *Reconsidering Ayn Rand.* Enumclaw, Wash.: WinePress, 2000.

JOHN CROWE RANSOM

Born: Pulaski, Tennessee
April 30, 1888
Died: Gambier, Ohio
July 3, 1974

Ransom achieved fame as poet, editor, literary critic, and mentor for younger writers; his approach, New Criticism, dominated literary analysis for thirty years.

BIOGRAPHY

Born April 30, 1888, in Pulaski, Tennessee, John Crowe Ransom was the third child of John James Ransom and Ella Crowe. From his mother, an English teacher, he absorbed an interest in ballads and myth, especially the Cavalier myth. From his father, a Methodist minister and district superintendent, he inherited a love of poetry, eloquence with language, lifelong interest in metaphysical questions, and facility in languages.

Admitted to Vanderbilt University at age fifteen, Ransom chose a course of study emphasizing Latin and Greek classics, philosophy, and history. After his graduation in 1909, Vanderbilt professors nominated him for a Rhodes Scholarship, and in 1910, he entered Oxford University, choosing again to focus on philosophy and the classics. His three years there reinforced his classicism, and discussions with fellow Rhodes Scholars increased his interest in British and American literature.

In 1914, Ransom returned to Vanderbilt as a member of the English faculty, leaving briefly to serve in World War I. Again returning to Vanderbilt, he joined a group of young intellectuals who met weekly to discuss philosophy and poetry. Soon this group began critiquing one another's poetry, eventually publishing *The Fugitive* (1922-1925), a journal devoted to poetry, criticism, and poetic theory. *The Fugitive* was widely read and highly respected in literary circles.

Becoming convinced of a need to defend the agrarian South of small farms and subsistence farming, several Fugitives published a collection of essays titled *I'll Take My Stand: The South and the Agrarian Tradition* (1930). Unfortunate timing of the publication led readers to consider the essays a literal plan to end the Great Depression, rather than a metaphorical statement about art's central position in human life.

Ransom continued to teach English at Vanderbilt, but his growing literary reputation increased his salary very little. He supplemented his income with summer teaching, especially after his marriage to Robb Reavil in 1920 and the births of their three children. Despite several offers of larger salaries and smaller teaching loads at other universities, Ransom remained in Nashville to care for his aging parents. Finally, Ransom accepted an offer from Kenyon College; a major incentive was the promise to establish a journal reminiscent of *The Fugitive* but emphasizing both critical theory and poetry. Moving to Gambier, Ohio, in 1937, Ransom began *The Kenyon Review.*

Until his retirement in 1959, Ransom's academic responsibilities were teaching, editing *The Kenyon Review,* and establishing the Kenyon School of English, which he hoped would provide a forum for writers, critics, and students to discuss theories of literary criticism. Although he published no new poems after 1945, he received the Bollingen Prize for Poetry in 1951, and his 1963 edition of *Selected Poems* received the 1964 National Book Award. After retirement, Ransom continued to lecture and write essays about criticism and poetry. His health gradually deteriorated, and on July 3, 1974, he died at his home on the Kenyon College campus.

ANALYSIS

Ransom is best known for the persona, or mask, he establishes in his poems: a courtly, somewhat old-fashioned gentleman, viewing the world with ironic detachment. He accepts the inextricable mix of death and life in human existence. His poetic stance is always aloof. For example, in "Dead Boy" (1927), the persona is almost an outsider, part of "the world of outer dark," but refers to the boy as "the little cousin," establishing both kinship with the family and distance from the boy himself and emphasizing the dual perspectives of family and community.

An underlying theme is the disparity between human desires and human destinies. The young girl of "Piazza Piece" (1924) dreams of a fairy-tale lover, but the gray old man is her future. "Blue Girls" (1924) stroll happily, chattering like birds, but Ransom's persona warns that soon their beauty will fade. Even children are not exempt; for Janet ("Janet Waking," 1927) a seemingly normal morning holds the lesson that death is an essential part of human experience. "Dead Boy" concludes with unsatisfactory attempts to explain his death, but the speaker turns to one incontrovertible fact: Vitality and an essential life force have been removed from the family tree's "sapless limbs," leaving them "shorn and shaken."

Amid constant mutability, one's only defense is the sustaining force of sensibility, yet sensibility seems besieged in a world that prefers abstractions. Reason and scientific discourse cannot supply all necessary knowledge; one needs knowledge derived from imagination, myth, and poetry in order to accept the dualism inherent in human experience. "Painted Head" (1945) illustrates Ransom's "fury against abstraction," the source of the conflict between science and art. This poem focuses on the interdependence of head (analytical reason, which is capable of knowing) and body (sensibility, which can use beauty to develop a way of perceiving and knowing). Properly joined, head and body create a nurturing home for beauty, myth, and the truths they provide.

Generally, Ransom does not experiment with poetic forms or meter, restricting incongruities to diction and tone. The reader's emotional distance is established by the diction. In "Dead Boy," for example, the death is referred to as a "transaction" (a term from commerce) and also as "foul subtraction." "Foul" suggests extravagant emotion, but its drama is undercut by "subtraction," which reduces the death to a mathematical process. The speaker further separates event and emotional response by developing the conventional symbol of the family tree into a conceit (a pattern of symbolism which uses domestic images and actions to clarify a serious philosophical concept). Initially the tender young branch has been subtracted; in the final stanza, however, it has been "wrenched away"—a much more violent action, with a much more destructive effect on the tree.

Another distancing device is Ransom's "habitual ironic humor," but the irony's tone is sympathetic. Understatement is frequently used for comic relief, and even Ransom's most serious poems reveal his fascination with language (especially archaic and regional words). Puns and other types of word play that demonstrate keen wit are found throughout his poems. In "Philomela" (1923), he playfully exploits the tendency to create verbs from almost any noun or adjective, by adding the suffix "-ize." Thus, Philomela has been successfully "apostrophized" by the Romans and "gallicized" by the French but never "baptized" by Protestant Americans.

Ransom writes minor, domestic poems that deal with ultimate subjects, but he uses community ritual (ceremony) to balance the emotions that these subjects arouse. Ceremony provides a way to transcend the immediate situation because it asserts the most vital human values. Ransom's decision to write domestic poetry provided the impetus for his most productive period. In fifteen years, he wrote an astonishing number of excellent poems in which ironic wit and understatement allow him to deal successfully with harsh realities of the human condition: Communities cope with the deaths of children ("Bells for John Whiteside's Daughter" and "Dead Boy"); a young girl learns about mortality ("Janet Waking"); old men take up arms to defend an aging tradition ("Antique Harvesters," 1927); and young girls are forced to recognize the fate awaiting all beauty ("Blue Girls"). Ransom draws upon the chivalric romance to portray the fate of the epic hero in the modern age: Every attempt at noble action by "Captain Carpenter"

(1924) results in destructive violence, yet Ransom's understatement and archaic diction provide an aesthetic distance that mutes the effect of essentially gory actions.

For Ransom, domestic poetry is a deliberate choice based on self-knowledge. Robert Crocodile ("The Amphibious Crocodile," 1925) experiences the cosmopolitan lifestyle and wins acceptance by the intellectual elite, but plagued by homesickness, he abruptly discards all the trappings of sophistication and contentedly retreats to the mud of the family bayou, where he chooses to remain.

"PHILOMELA"

First published: 1923 (collected in *Chills and Fever,* 1924)
Type of work: Poem

Discovering that he cannot appreciate Philomela's song, an American intellectual wonders if the United States can become worthy of the classical aesthetic.

"Philomela" opens by naming the players in the classical myth of the nightingale's origin. To the American speaker, despite the violence of the story, the sound of their names is pleasing, but the power of myth has waned; the speaker finds the tale "improbable." Philomela's song of continuing sorrow is not in harmony with modern American poetry.

Elsewhere, the nightingale has found satisfactory homes, but her myth is at odds with the Puritanism that Ransom considers the most influential force in American culture. Ancient Greeks would consider America "barbarous"; though the speaker never explicitly agrees, he separates himself from overall American culture, conceding that Philomela is unlikely to survive in his "cloudless, boundless, public" democracy. At Oxford, the speaker seeks and finally hears the nightingale but declares her song, supposedly the most beautiful of all songs, a bit flat. Disappointed, the speaker leaves her presence.

In the final stanza, the mature speaker addresses Philomela, questioning whether Americans can become worthy of her. A society where bantering has replaced wit and minute analysis has replaced

appreciation of the aesthetic whole seems unsuitable for myths; the nightingale belongs in societies where fables seem possible. "Philomela" can be read as an indictment of American aesthetic, but it also deplores the loss of innocence that has led to "post-scientific poetry" and resulted in humans' limited knowledge of the world, as they ignore what Ransom calls "the world's body" and substance.

"BELLS FOR JOHN WHITESIDE'S DAUGHTER"

First published: 1924 (collected in *Chills and Fever,* 1924)
Type of work: Poem

Family and neighbors react with astonishment to the unexpected death of a lively little girl.

"Bells for John Whiteside's Daughter" shows Ransom's pattern of addressing ultimate metaphysical issues and using the conventional quatrain form to impose order that distances speaker and reader from the emotions involved. The occasion for the bells is the funeral of John Whiteside's daughter. This poem is her elegy, and the speaker represents the community, describing everyone's astonishment at her unexpected death.

The poem refuses to dwell on the present and the girl's death, focusing instead on the past and her active life. The first line establishes the contrast between the child's speed then and her stillness now. Except for the neighbors' reaction in the first stanza, the first four stanzas are written in past tense, and each implies a contrast with the present. The neighbors are "astonished" at the contrast between the "lightness" they remember and her uncharacteristic "brown study," an appearance of deep contemplation.

While discussing the death, the speaker appears to digress into a whimsical description of her using a rod to rouse lazy geese from "their noon apple-dreams." Another contrast is set up, however. Ironically, the girl's "tireless heart" has stopped, and no external force (rod) can make her rise. Her "brown study" is very different from the pleasant "noon apple-dreams" of her geese, and her position (lying "primly propped") is the antithesis of their "scuttling goose fashion." The speaker's statement that the geese "cried in goose, Alas" gains significance when closer examination suggests that the overblown language can have two meanings: The geese may be extravagantly lamenting their own condition, but "Alas" is followed by a comma, usually a signal that the meaning extends to the next line—in this case, "For the tireless heart within the little/ Lady. . . . " Thus, the passage can be read as implying that the geese also grieve.

The final stanza, in present tense, describes the neighbors' reactions just before the funeral. The bells sound, calling them to the service, and they believe they are prepared for the funeral, but all such thoughts are "sternly stopped" when they enter the house (possibly a house of worship). They are "vexed" to see the child's body "lying so primly propped." Balancing the word "astonished" in the first stanza, the word "vexed" downplays the neighbors' emotional reaction, carrying the dual connotations of being "annoyed" by the fact of the girl's death and being "puzzled" about its explanation.

"DEAD BOY"

First published: 1924 (collected in *Two Gentlemen in Bonds*, 1927)
Type of work: Poem

"Dead Boy" describes the significance of a young boy's death to his family and community.

"Dead Boy" deals with the intrusion of death into a rural community. The poem's form is conventional: quatrains rhyming *abab* or *cdcd*. The relatively prosaic title, "Dead Boy," sets the no-nonsense tone. The speaker breaks with the sentimental tradition, using understatement to distance both speaker and reader from emotional involvement in the death of this unnamed child. No attempt is made to describe the grief of the boy's extended family (county kin) and neighbors; instead, the reader learns that they "do not like" what has happened. Thus, the reader is led to examine this death with detachment, and the full emotional impact is saved for the final stanza and the speaker's conclusions about this "deep dynastic wound."

The speaker ironically undercuts any tendency toward sentimentality, describing a boy not heroic, talented, or beloved by the community; his disposition seems more "stormy" than sunny. At times his mother called him a sword beneath her heart, but her bitter weeping shows deep love for him.

Having approached raw emotion in describing the mother's grief, however, the speaker immediately retreats to ironic discussion of changed attitudes toward the child; death has transformed a squealing, pasty-faced pig into a "little man," and in his face, the speaker professes to see family resemblance.

The speaker shifts from this little man to focus on the "elder men" of the community, who represent age and its accompanying loss of vitality. Uncomfortable remaining in the house, these men congregate outside, exchanging rumors in an unsuccessful attempt to deal with their deep dynastic wound, the loss of a male heir to carry on the family name.

"JANET WAKING"

First published: 1925 (collected in *Two Gentlemen in Bonds*, 1927)
Type of work: Poem

A young girl first experiences death and loss when her pet hen dies.

"Janet Waking" is a metaphor for her initiation into knowledge of grief, loss, and the irreversibility of death. After a pleasant sleep, nothing seems amiss in Janet's world, but her true awakening begins when she decides to see how Chucky (a "dainty-feathered hen") has "kept" (a colloquial expression referring to its well-being). As she pauses to give each parent a dutiful morning kiss, it is obvious that she usually gets her way. Next Janet runs "across the world upon the grass" to Chucky's house. In running from her home (where she is in control) to Chucky's house, she figuratively runs "across the world" because her world is about to be completely changed, as she moves from innocence to knowledge. (The speaker may also be punning with the Southern colloquialism of 'run across' meaning 'inadvertently discover.')

Janet discovers that "alas" Chucky has died. "Alas" both suggests the depth of her shock and loss and, by its very extravagance, creates a mock serious tone that undercuts and balances her grief. Chucky has died from a bee sting on its bald head. The "venom" (a term usually associated with evil) has caused a large purple knot on Chucky's head and rigor throughout the hen's body. The speaker observes that now Chucky's "poor comb" stands straight but Chucky does not. This flippant understatement seems intended to distance the speaker from Janet's emotions and remind the reader that a pet hen's death may not be taken very seriously by adults.

This initiation poem, which begins with literal sleep, ends with death (a sleep from which Chucky cannot be awakened). Janet attempts to "wake" Chucky, but the hen is "translated" beyond the reach of earthly power. Weeping so hard that her sobs seem inseparable from her breathing, Janet then turns to the adults, begging them to intervene. When they try to explain the concept of death, Janet simply rejects this idea that she is not ready to comprehend.

"PIAZZA PIECE"

First published: 1925 (collected in *Two Gentlemen in Bonds*, 1927)
Type of work: Poem

An old man attempts to make a beautiful young lady aware of universal mortality.

Written as a Petrarchan sonnet (fourteen lines of iambic pentameter rhyming *abbaacca deeffd*), "Piazza Piece" illustrates Ransom's skill with traditional forms. The octave (first eight lines) and sestet (remaining six lines) are an attempted dialogue between age (an elderly man) and youth (a young lady). Their differing attitudes make "Piazza Piece" essentially a debate poem (two characters argue the merits of diametrically opposite philosophical positions).

The old man's message is human decline and eventual death. He tries to attract the lady's attention and point out that decay is a law of nature, seen in the "dying" roses on her trellis and the "spectral" (ghostlike) moon above them. He introduces possible sexual tension when he insists that he is destined to "have" her soon (to possess her, possibly with violence). The final line of the octave repeats the first but with a period, a full stop, at the end. This line therefore becomes a pun on the two meanings of "trying": The gentleman is attempting to communicate with the lady, but his behavior is very 'trying' (exasperating, even frightening) to her.

Likewise, in the first and last lines of her stanza, the lady describes herself as "a lady young in beauty waiting." The placement of the adjective 'young' after the noun 'lady'—characteristic of chivalric tales, not colloquial speech—removes the lady from the sphere of everyday life. Filled with romantic dreams, she waits for her "truelove" and his awakening kiss; however, her reverie is interrupted by the appearance of a "gray" (old, colorless) man at the foot of her trellis. She knows he is speaking to her, but she cannot understand his "dry," "faint" words. Still, aware of menace in him, she orders him away, threatening to scream if he does not leave. Her final line indicates that her romantic atmosphere has been restored: She is once again the "lady young," and she remains in the midst of beauty (her own and that of her dreams) still awaiting her truelove.

"PAINTED HEAD"

First published: 1934 (collected in *Selected Poems*, 1945)
Type of work: Poem

A portrait suggests to the speaker the separation of head (reason) from body (sensibility).

"Painted Head" involves an issue central to Ransom: the separation between reason and sensibility. The head's separation from the body is described as "dark severance"—a sinister act of violence that makes this head appear ghostlike. The speaker believes this head illustrates the instinct of heads (reason) to cut themselves off from the "body bush" (sensibility), which they consider inferior.

The happiest heads are those remaining "married" to their bodies. In this typical Ransom conceit, these heads represent individuals able to maintain a balance of reason and sensibility (in Ransom's terms, science and beauty). Having remained unknown, these "housekeeping heads" are not tracked by "historian headhunters" (a typical play on words). More highly developed ironic sense and puckish pleasure in punning are seen as the speaker returns to the painted head. The "capital" irony is that an artist (not comprehending the head's treasonous ambitions) has "abstracted" this head from its body. The action is "capital" in two senses: It is the height of irony, and the artist has decapitated the portrait's subject, "unhoused" this head from its body. (For Ransom, abstraction is the worst effect of science's increasing dominance over art.) The conceit is carried to its logical conclusion: Cut off from its body, the head becomes a skull, sometimes called a death's head. Separation brings the head, not immortality, but death.

"Painted Head" explores the theme of interdependence between head and body. The speaker insists that their separation leads to a terrible outcome (punning with the colloquial meaning of something extremely bad, and the literal meaning, something that causes terror among onlookers). In the proper relationship, the body bears (supports, tolerates), even feeds and obeys the head, but its ultimate goal is not to achieve glory for the head but to increase (strengthen, expand) itself. Beauty (the aesthetic) is resident in the body (the sensibility); the head (reason) is metaphorically a rock garden because its limited flesh cannot display beauty. Thus, the head must accept its need for the body because the body enables it to see the color in the surrounding world and prepares it to absorb myths and ideas; without access to the body (sensibility), art is impossible.

SUMMARY

Most of Ransom's poetry was written before the 1930's. However, his best poetry remains timeless because he employs the greatest of human resources—outstanding intellect, a sympathetic heart, superb classical training, and a personality grounded in the balance of head (intellect) and sensibility (soul, aesthetic imagination)—to lessen the alienation and hopelessness that seem poised to overwhelm humanity. Ransom realizes that, especially in the modern age, poets must provide aesthetic and spiritual guidance for society because poetry best prepares humankind to wrestle with age-old ambiguities of mortality and fate.

Ransom seeks a code to provide meaning for individuals attempting to cope with an apparently meaningless universe. For Ransom, that code seems most accessible through deliberately minor poetry. Though he continued to revise a few early poems, his emphasis turns to the sustaining sense of community in the small towns of his youth. There, social tradition, religious ritual, and personal philosophy combined to keep the world's violence at bay.

Throughout his career, Ransom attempted to define in essay format what he was achieving in poetry. The results, though impressive, never totally satisfied him. His essays of social and aesthetic philosophy define the nature of poetry, establish the role of the poet, and assert poetry's significant relationship with modern society. Thomas Daniel Young's title for the definitive Ransom biography describes him as *Gentleman in a Dustcoat* (trying to be heard).

Charmaine Allmon Mosby

BIBLIOGRAPHY

By the Author

POETRY:
Poems About God, 1919
Armageddon, 1923
Chills and Fever, 1924
Grace After Meat, 1924

Two Gentlemen in Bonds, 1927
Selected Poems, 1945, revised and enlarged 1963, 1969
Poems and Essays, 1955

NONFICTION:

I'll Take My Stand: The South and the Agrarian Tradition, by Twelve Southerners, 1930 (with others)
God Without Thunder: An Unorthodox Defense of Orthodoxy, 1930
Topics for Freshman Writing, 1935
The World's Body, 1938 (criticism)
The New Criticism, 1941 (criticism)
American Poetry at Mid-century, 1958 (with Delmore Schwartz and John Hall Wheelock)
Symposium on Formalist Criticism, 1967 (with others)
Beating the Bushes: Selected Essays, 1941-1970, 1972
Selected Letters of John Crowe Ransom, 1985 (Thomas Daniel Young and George Core, editors)

EDITED TEXTS:

Studies in Modern Criticism from the "Kenyon Review," 1951
The Kenyon Critics, 1967

About the Author

Brooks, Cleanth. "John Crowe Ransom: As I Remember Him." *American Scholar* 58, no. 2 (Spring, 1989): 211-233.

Cowan, Louise. *The Fugitive Group: A Literary History.* Baton Rouge: Louisiana State University Press, 1959.

Howard, Maureen. "There Are Many Wonderful Owls in Gambier." *Yale Review* 77 (Summer, 1988): 521-527.

Malvasi, Mark G. *The Unregenerate South: The Agrarian Thought of John Crowe Ransom, Allen Tate, and Donald Davidson.* Baton Rouge: Louisiana State University Press, 1997.

Modern American Poetry Web site. "John Crowe Ransom." http://www.english.uiuc.edu/maps/poets/m_r/ransom/life.htm.

Quinlan, Kieran. *John Crowe Ransom's Secular Faith.* Baton Rouge: Louisiana State University Press, 1989.

Rubin, Louis D., Jr. "The Wary Fugitive: John Crowe Ransom." *Sewanee Review* 82 (1974): 583-618.

Young, Thomas Daniel. *Gentleman in a Dustcoat: A Biography of John Crowe Ransom.* Baton Rouge: Louisiana State University Press, 1976.

DISCUSSION TOPICS

- What parts of John Crowe Ransom's academic and personal background explain his tastes in English poetry?

- Ransom was well acquainted with the King James Bible, and his poems frequently echo the Scriptures in diction, syntax, and metaphysical issues. Examine three or four of his poems and point out examples of direct and indirect influence.

- Ransom repeatedly was associated with groups of writers and intellectuals. In what ways were his poetry and criticism changed by association with these critics and writers? In what ways was their work changed by association with Ransom?

- Critics have sometimes considered Ransom's poetry cold and detached. Explain why this criticism is or is not justified. What elements in his poetic philosophy explain the persona he created?

- According to Ransom, poetry possesses a dual nature, a logical sequence of meanings and an objective pattern of sounds. How do his choices of metrical forms and diction affect tone in his poems?

- Although contemporary poets speak admiringly of Ransom, none has emulated his style, especially in diction and tone. What factors in his background and experiences probably are unavailable to contemporary poets?

- Many Ransom poems deal with death, decay or loss. Does his emphasis on these subjects make Ransom's poems morbid? How does he avoid this problem?

ISHMAEL REED

Born: Chattanooga, Tennessee
February 22, 1938

Reed integrates African aesthetics and religion into American popular culture in what he calls "Neo-HooDoo" fiction and poetry.

James Lerager

BIOGRAPHY

Ishmael Scott Reed was born in Chattanooga, Tennessee, on February 22, 1938, the son of Henry Lenoir and Thelma Coleman. A year later, his mother married Bennie Stephen Reed, and the infant Ishmael assumed his stepfather's name.

When World War II began, Reed's mother moved north to find work in factories depopulated by the draft, and young Ishmael went with her. They settled in Buffalo, New York, where Reed would spend the following twenty years. Reed's first encouragement in his writing came from his mother: When he was a boy, she asked him to write a poem for the birthday of one of her coworkers. He remembers writing another poem for Christmas, 1952, but did not return to poetry until after college. He spent his first two years of secondary school at Buffalo Technical High School but finished at East High, from which he graduated in 1956.

Finding employment as a clerk in the Buffalo public library system, Reed attended night classes at the State University of New York, Buffalo. In an English class at the university, he received further encouragement for his writing. Feeling alienated from the university's predominantly white, middle-class student body, however, Reed withdrew in 1960 and moved to a government housing project. In September of 1960 he married Priscilla Rose.

Reed began writing professionally at this time for a Buffalo-based African American newspaper, *Empire State Weekly.* Through the paper, and a weekly community affairs show he cohosted on a Buffalo radio station, Reed became increasingly involved in civil rights activism. He also became active in Buffalo's growing theater groups; learning roles in such classics as Edward Albee's *The Death of Bessie Smith* (1960) and Lorraine Hansberry's *A Raisin in the Sun* (1959) helped Reed to develop his ear for dialogue.

In 1962, the birth of his daughter Timothy Brett Reed (for whom he wrote the poem "instructions to a princess") was, he says "the only friendly event." Separated from his wife, he left Buffalo to seek better literary opportunities in New York City, and he found them. He became a member of the Umbra Workshop, a seminal black writers group on the Lower East Side, whose magazine, *Umbra,* published his poetry.

On the trip from Buffalo to New York, Reed had lost all of his early poems, but he immediately began writing more. "The Ghost in Birmingham," published in 1963, shows the influence, Reed admits, of the white poets he read in college. "The Jackal-Headed Cowboy," written only a year later, shows some of the amalgamation of African myths and American popular culture that would result in his later "Neo-HooDoo" novels.

In 1965, Reed founded a newspaper for the black community in Newark, New Jersey, called *Advance,* which gave first publication to many young writers, black and white. A landmark underground newspaper, *The East Village Other,* was influenced by *Advance* and was named by Reed, who was involved in its creation. In the same year, Reed and three other black writers organized the American Festi-

2181

val of Negro Art, and Reed began writing his first novel, *The Free-Lance Pallbearers* (1967). The immediate critical success of this novel assured Reed's reputation, and, riding the crest of this success, he moved to Berkeley, California, to teach at the University of California.

Another purpose for the move was to get a feel for the American West for his second novel, *Yellow Back Radio Broke-Down* (1969). This book, a "Neo-HooDoo western," was another public and critical success. By the end of the 1960's, Reed enjoyed wide recognition. One acknowledgment of his position as an authority on American dialects came in the first edition of the *American Heritage Dictionary* (1969), which employed Reed on its "usage panel" as a contributor of informed opinions on contemporary American usage. The banner year 1969 also saw the second American Festival of Negro Art.

Now established as a major African American writer, Reed used his experience as an editor to help other minority writers get their works published. His anthology *19 Necromancers from Now* (1970) brought together the works of many new black writers and included his own piece, "Cab Calloway Stands In for the Moon," which featured the first appearance of his detective character Papa La Bas. A year later, he and *Umbra* editor Steve Cannon founded Yardbird Publishing Company, dedicated to publishing writers of all ethnic backgrounds who could not get into print elsewhere.

In 1970, Reed was divorced from his first wife and married modern dancer and choreographer Carla Blank. His early poems were published as a *Catechism of D Neoamerican Hoodoo Church* (1970) in London and later as *Conjure: Selected Poems, 1963-1970* (1972) in the United States. Two Neo-Hoo-Doo detective novels followed, *Mumbo Jumbo* (1972) and *The Last Days of Louisiana Red* (1974), both featuring Papa La Bas. Reed's next novels, *Flight to Canada* (1976) and *The Terrible Twos* (1982), no longer emphasized the Neo-HooDoo aesthetic but continued to mix dream-fantasy with contemporary reality and to combine historical periods. Reed continued to teach at Berkeley, despite being denied tenure in 1977. The story of his tenure battle is told in an essay in *Shrovetide in Old New Orleans* (1978). He has held visiting professorships at the University of Washington (1969), his alma mater at Buffalo (1975), Yale University (1979), and Dartmouth College (1980).

Reed has continued to write poetry, fiction, and essays and to help other writers into print. He brought together his first quarter-century of poetry in *New and Collected Poems* (1988). His work has influenced contemporary writers and established him as one of the foremost satirists of the late twentieth and early twenty-first centuries.

ANALYSIS

An understanding of Reed's fiction must begin with his concept of "Neo-HooDoo." The term "hoo doo," sometimes spelled and pronounced "voodoo," is derived from the East African religion of *vodun*. In his fiction and poetry, Reed traces the influence of this religion, brought to America by the slave trade, in American popular culture. Reed's Neo-HooDoo seeks to capture the spirit of this African religion and integrate it with the concerns of modern America.

Reed's first expression of his theory was "Neo-HooDoo Manifesto," published in the *Los Angeles Free Press* on September 18-24, 1970, and reprinted several times. "Neo-HooDoo is a 'Lost American Church' updated," the manifesto begins. Reed describes the integration of African and Western cultures in Neo-HooDoo:

> Africa is the home of the loa (Spirits) of Neo-Hoo-Doo although we are building our own American "pantheon." Thousands of "Spirits" (Ka) who would laugh at Jehovah's fury concerning "false idols" (translated everybody else's religion) or "fetishes." Moses, Jehovah's messenger and zombie swiped the secrets of VooDoo from old Jethro but nevertheless ended up with a curse.

Western culture's "swiping" of African culture through Judaism during the Egyptian exile is a common theme in Reed's fiction, which is an important vehicle for popularizing the discoveries of anthropologists in this area.

Reed's fiction is sharp-edged satire, and the gift for it seems to have found him early. In his junior year at East High, he was sent to the principal for writing a lampoon about his teacher called "A Strange Profession." In his first college English class, he wrote a satire called "Something Pure," in which Christ returns to earth as an advertising agent. The focus of his satires is wide: All the follies of American culture, right or left, black or white, are ridiculed in his fiction.

Just as important as the cultural criticism in his books is the formal criticism: His novels parody various forms of writing. His first novel, *The Free-Lance Pallbearers*, parodies African American "confessional" novels; critic Henry Louis Gates identifies Ralph Ellison and James Baldwin as particular targets, although the content is drawn mostly from Reed's own experience. His second novel, *Yellow Back Radio Broke-Down*, parodies the Western, pulp fiction, and old radio adventures. *Mumbo Jumbo* and *The Last Days of Louisiana Red* lampoon the detective story and *Flight to Canada*, the slave narrative.

Time in Reed's fiction is fluid; while set in another time (the Jefferson era in *Yellow Back Radio Broke-Down*, the 1920's in *Mumbo Jumbo*, the Civil War in *Flight to Canada*, and the near future in *The Terrible Twos* and the 1989 novel *The Terrible Threes*), his novels refer to all points in American history, especially the second half of the twentieth century. In a 1974 interview in *Black World*, he called this process "necromancy": "I wanted to write about a time like the present or to use the past to prophesy about the future—a process our ancestors called necromancy."

Necromancy is an important word for Reed. He titled his first anthology of black poets *19 Necromancers from Now* and called the reader's attention to the word's etymology in the preface. It means "black magic," and writing is magic for Reed.

"A man's story is his gris-gris," he says in the first chapter of *Flight to Canada*, using another black magic term. In Haitian voodoo, a gris-gris is a sacred object, a charm that gives a magician power as long as it is kept. Creole voodoo terms are never used to obscure or decorate Reed's fiction. They are always precisely the right words, and the meaning can usually be found in context.

If writing is magic, it is also a way to strike back, to define one's self against oppressors. In the opening of his 1974 interview in *Black World*, Reed quotes Muhammad Ali's dictum, "writing is fighting," and he made that phrase the title of his book about boxing literature. Reed does not limit his sparring to his critical essays: It shows up in his fiction as well. His novels usually have at least one scene of confrontation between two literary points of view.

In *Yellow Back Radio Broke-Down*, the scene is Bo Shmo's meeting with Loop Garoo in the desert, where Shmo tries to get Loop to conform to Marxist realist ideas of what the African American novel should be. The scene is repeated in *Mumbo Jumbo*, in which the Marxist realist is Abdul Sufi Hamid, and Reed's point-of-view character is PaPa LaBas. In *The Last Days of Louisiana Red*, the conflict is embedded in the character of Chorus, who objects to her disappearance in modern literature. Reed's appearance in a Buffalo production of Jean Anouilh's *Antigone* (1944) in 1960 may have led to his interest in the Antigone myth in which Chorus appears in his novel.

In *Flight to Canada*, Raven Quickskill has literary arguments with his lover Qua Qua and presents post-Civil War literature as a continuation of the struggle: "What the American Arthurians couldn't win on the battlefield will now be fought out on the poetry field." In *Reckless Eyeballing*, Ian Ball objects not only to feminist attacks on his writing but also to the critiques of fellow black playwright Jack Brashford.

The feminist critique reflects attacks on Reed's own works, as do the other literary arguments in his fiction. Reed has been labeled sexist by feminist critics for his portrayal of women and for what is perceived as his ratification of black "macho" stereotypes. In a 1981 essay in *Playgirl*, Reed reiterated a thesis that the black male was victimized by feminist gains in the 1970's and that popular images of middle-aged males, black or white, are invariably villainous. The thesis is central to *Reckless Eyeballing*, where it is developed more fully. The biggest irony of Reed's status in American letters is that this radical black writer seems to have more enemies on the Left (Marxist and feminist) than on the Right.

YELLOW BACK RADIO BROKE-DOWN

First published: 1969
Type of work: Novel

The Loop Garoo Kid, a HooDoo cowboy, fights the powers of evil in their current manifestation: a powerful Old West rancher.

In a self-interview in the journal *Black World*, Reed explained the title of *Yellow Back Radio Broke-Down* word by word. "Yellow back" refers to the pulp-novel fiction that created the myth of the Old West at the end of the nineteenth century; "radio" continued it; "broke-down" means stripped to its essence. The novel, then, is a dissection of the popular culture images of the Old West and an indictment of the way they portray minorities.

Reed's first HooDoo hero, the Loop Garoo Kid, is the black cowboy who runs the circus at the opening of the novel; clues to a larger identity begin to accumulate as the novel progresses, and Loop is revealed as an eternal, the trickster figure from African myth, mistakenly identified by Western rationalists as the power of evil. Loop Garoo (whose name means "werewolf" in Haitian Creole) is the eternal good guy of Western fantasy.

The bad guy is Drag Gibson, a powerful rancher who jealously protects his way of life by trying to kill Loop and his circus people. He is hired by the people of Yellow Back Radio to return their town to them; it has been taken over by their children—an allegory of what seemed to be happening to the United States when the novel was written in 1969. Drag's men attack and defeat the circus train, and Loop is stranded in the desert. He is picked up, however, by Chief Showcase, "the only surviving injun," in a high-technology helicopter, one of the many examples of anachronism in the novel. Show-

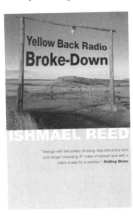

case, as another exploited minority, identifies with Loop and offers clandestine aid. Loop returns to haunt Drag's men on the desert.

When Loop continues on the loose, the secretary of defense, General Theda Doompussy Blackwell, is called in. With Congressman Pete the Peek providing military appropriations, Blackwell hires the scientists Harold Rateater and Dr. Coult to develop weapons to subdue Loop. Here the satire is aimed at the military development of the Vietnam War era, contemporary with the novel.

In the final section of the novel, Pope Innocent arrives from Europe, giving an idea of the cosmic scope the conflict is about to assume. The pope, representing Western orthodoxy and authority, is

upset that his American minions, the likes of Blackwell and Gibson, have been unable to subdue Loop Garoo. He has not always been Loop's foe, however: His discussion with Drag reveals that Loop had originally been a member of the divine family of the Christian mythos. Put off by Jehovah's demand of exclusive worship, Loop left him. Jehovah, however, now dominated by the feminine principle represented by Mary, needs Loop's help. Only Loop could keep the feminine force under control: He knew her as his lover, Black Diane (the Greek Artemis). One of her followers appears as Mustache Sal, another former lover of Loop, now Drag's wife.

Yellow Back Radio Broke-Down may be enjoyed on a number of levels. A parody of Western thrillers, it is as exciting and quick-paced as any of the horse operas it parodies. One index of its success as a story is a laudatory review in *Western Roundup*, a rodeo magazine written by and for modern-day cowboys. On another level, the novel functions, as does all Reed's fiction, as a critique of American culture. Because the Western as a genre illustrates the errors of American culture—looking on the resources of the American West, including the human resources of its aboriginal people, as sources of wealth to be exploited—Reed uses the genre to exorcise those errors.

On a third level, the novel attacks critical presuppositions about what constitutes African American fiction. Instead of limiting himself to the black urban experience, Reed takes the popular forms of the majority culture and skews them to his own comic vision. The reaction of the literary establishment, black and white, to Reed's choice of form is embedded in the novel itself. The Marxist "neorealists" who have claimed black fiction for their own political uses show up as a posse seeking to hang Loop Garoo. They are led by a spokesman, Bo Shmo, who delivers a hilarious parody of the leading arguments of Reed's literary enemies. Loop's reply to Bo is such a succinct summary of Reed's poetics that it is often quoted: "What if I write circuses? No one says a novel has to be one thing. It can be anything it wants to be, a vaudeville show, the six o'clock news, the mumblings of wild men saddled by demons."

Reed has certainly let his novels be anything they want to be, and they are never the same thing twice. *Yellow Back Radio Broke-Down* delivers his now-familiar Neo-HooDoo picture of the United States, and it is appropriate that his first use of the HooDoo aesthetic was in a Western.

MUMBO JUMBO

First published: 1972
Type of work: Novel

HooDoo detective Papa LaBas seeks the origins of the disease "Jes Grew" while pursued by agents of the mysterious Wallflower Order.

Reed's characteristic use of fluid time, effective in other novels, is particularly apt in *Mumbo Jumbo*. The Harlem Renaissance, the setting of the novel, has striking parallels to the African American experience of the late 1960's and early 1970's. The fact that the 1920's were called "the jazz age" indicates how much black culture was affecting the white majority. *Mumbo Jumbo* traces that influence; the rhythms, the dances, sometimes the words of ragtime and jazz songs came from rituals of the African *vodun* religion, transplanted to America by the slave trade. Reed documents those connections by footnotes and a partial bibliography at the end of the novel.

The novel is not a documentary, however. The quick-spreading influence of African culture in America is represented as an epidemic, "Jes Grew" (a phrase from Harriet Beecher Stowe's 1852 novel *Uncle Tom's Cabin* referring to the character Topsy, whose origins were unknown). The Wallflower Order, a secret society dedicated to maintaining the power of white Western rationalism, seeks to stop the disease. Unlike other plagues, however, instead of harming the hosts, Jes Grew makes them feel better. Thus, the Wallflower Order shows itself to be an enemy of pleasure.

Yet Jes Grew has powerful friends as well as powerful enemies. PaPa LaBas, the HooDoo detective in Harlem, tracks down Jes Grew in order to find it a sacred text and to protect it from the Wallflower Order. The Wallflowers, under the leadership of Hinckle Von Vampton (after they kidnap him), seek to contain Jes Grew by sponsoring black poets, thereby limiting and defining what black literature is. To some extent, that happened in the Har-

lem Renaissance of the 1920s, though the motives may not have been so overt. Von Vampton is modeled after Carl Van Vechten, among others, who brought the Harlem poets into prominence in white literary circles.

LaBas is joined by T Malice and Black Herman, who, though of a younger generation, share LaBas's views about black culture. One of their circle who does not is Abdul Sufi Hamid, the Muslim who wants to coopt the entire Harlem culture into the leftist politics he sees as the only means to black liberation. Von Vampton's young black protégé, Woodrow Wilson Jefferson (W. W.), is a fan of Abdul who also wants Jes Grew stamped out. W. W. is hired as "The Negro Viewpoint": By trying to define African American art, limiting it to one point of view, von Vampton feels he can control it.

A subplot in *Mumbo Jumbo* involves the Mútafikah, a multiracial group dedicated to returning non-Western art objects that came to New York after World War I. To the Mútafikah, these were stolen under cover of the war, and they represent an irony: The majority culture that denies any value to non-Western art objects steals them and puts them into museums (or "Centers for Art Detention," as Reed calls them, lampooning the Western "curator" mentality).

Fighting the Mútafikah directly is Biff Musclewhite, a parody of the white strong-arm hero. Former Police Commissioner of New York, now charged with guarding the Center for Art Detention (C.A.D.), he is kidnapped by three Mútafikah in the process of raiding the C.A.D. (a telling acronym). Representing three races—the African Berbelang, the Asian Yellow Jack, and the Nordic Thor—they are in solidarity against the suppression of non-Western culture, though Thor is of Western origin himself. In fact, that proves his undoing. Left alone with the bound Biff Musclewhite, Thor succumbs to his accusations of being a traitor to the white race and lets Musclewhite go.

All threads of the plot come together when von Vampton, seeking writers for his periodical *The Be-*

nign *Monster,* discovers the dead body of Abdul. The corpse clutches a rejection slip, which gives LaBas a clue: Apparently Abdul had found the text Jes Grew was seeking and tried to publish it as his own. All the pieces are put together in a parody of the final explanation scene of detective fiction.

LaBas's explanation is the longest chapter in the book and takes in thousands of years of history. The battle between Jes Grew and the Wallflowers turns out to be a recent outgrowth of an eternal struggle between followers of the Egyptian gods Osiris and Aton. The Wallflowers are Atonists, worshipers of the cruel god who forbade them to follow any other. Moses introduced his worship to the Israelites, and thence to the West, when he lived in Egypt, transferring Aton's qualities to Jahweh. The chapter acts as a fitting punch line to Reed's most popular satire.

FLIGHT TO CANADA

First published: 1976
Type of work: Novel

The money from his published poem about escape allows a slave to escape a Virginia plantation and flee to Canada during the American Civil War.

Although *Flight to Canada* is Reed's Civil War novel, all ages of American history are squeezed into this satire. As in all Reed's novels, time is fluid. It opens with Reed's poem "Flight to Canada," followed by a present-day reflection on the ways in which Josiah Henson's escaped slave narrative and Harriet Beecher Stowe's more celebrated version of it helped create the history of the war.

Thus, the time-consciousness of this novel is always double, referring to the events, real and fictitious, of the 1860's and the 1970's simultaneously. Deliberate anachronisms are commonplace; when Abraham Lincoln first meets the Virginia aristocrat Arthur Swille, Swille is talking on the telephone. The play at Ford's Theatre at which Lincoln is assassinated is carried on public television.

There is a tinge of autobiography in the novel's protagonist, Raven Quickskill. Quickskill is a poet, and it is his writing that helps him to escape slavery

on a Virginia plantation. The Civil War ends before Quickskill actually leaves, but his master, Arthur Swille, pursues him anyway. Swille is a seductive villain. A powerful international businessman and financier, he deals with both sides in the war, and treats President Lincoln, Jefferson Davis, and Generals Lee and Grant like toadies. The scenes with Lincoln produce some of Reed's most enjoyable satire. Reed's Lincoln is a bit of a hick, and his assistance to the slaves is shown to be political expediency. Nevertheless, Reed makes him likable: He defends his wife against cruel attacks by Swille, and though he takes Swille's money, he does not trust him. Lincoln's assassination is presented as Swille's revenge for freeing the slaves.

Flight to Canada gains additional meaning when read against *Uncle Tom's Cabin.* Reed's Uncle Tom (there are references to him and the "Legree plantation") is Uncle Robin, an old compliant black slave who has so capitulated to the machinery of slavery that he keeps Swille's records. Robin's fawning is only apparent, however; by juggling the books, he is able to cover for escaped slaves, and he always destroys the invoices so that Swille will have no proof of "ownership." His final bit of forgery tops them all: He doctors Swille's will so that Robin inherits the plantation.

As in Reed's other novels, the supporting characters carry much of the satire. Raven's lover, Princess Qua Qua Tralaralara, is an American Indian dancer and tightrope walker. He wins her away from Yankee Jack, whom Raven exposes as a pirate who killed Qua Qua's father. Mammy Barracuda, as her name suggests, is the secretly ruthless plantation mammy; Reed suggests that it is her conversion to Christianity that makes her so nasty. Swallowing whole the value system of her oppressors, she turns oppressor herself, of such poor creatures as the slave girl Bangalang (a version of Stowe's "Topsy") and even her master's wife, beating her until she becomes the model of a southern belle. Cato the Graffado, Swille's white servant, is so self-abasing that he is indistinguishable from the slaves, who laugh at him.

While much of the book is social satire, a major theme is the power of literature itself to emancipate. Reed, like Raven, has freed himself with his words, despite the ridicule of white and black enemies and misunderstanding friends. For a black artist, however, there is a further barrier: the dominant white culture that suppresses black art by ridicule, theft, and denial. Part of what Reed has achieved in *Flight to Canada* is returning the story of the escaped slave to its rightful owners, the former slaves themselves. Josiah Henson's autobiography foundered in obscurity; Harriet Beecher Stowe made it famous but by whitewashing it into sensationalism aimed at a white audience. *Flight to Canada* corrects Stowe's distortion, not by re-creating the clinical facts but by skewing it in another direction, providing the slave's-eye view through one hundred years of history.

RECKLESS EYEBALLING

First published: 1986
Type of work: Novel

A black southern male playwright fights white people, northerners, and feminists to get his new play produced.

As in *Flight to Canada*, the title of *Reckless Eyeballing* is the name of a work within the novel, written by the main character. Ian Ball, a southern black playwright, has been "sex-listed"—that is, blacklisted as sexist—by the feminist critics who control New York theater. In an attempt to redeem himself, he has written a play called *Reckless Eyeballing*, which caters to feminist views.

Ian Ball bears some resemblance to Reed, who dabbled in playwriting in the 1980's, though he is clearly not Reed's point-of-view character. In a carefully controlled ironic narration, Reed makes it clear that Ball has sold out his real beliefs in order to be popular, yet neither Ball nor the narrator ever says so explicitly. In fact, Ball himself is guilty of "reckless eyeballing"—that is, looking at women lasciviously, "undressing them with his eyes." Even while he argues with the feminists who oppose him, he is thinking about them sexually. Further, his very name is "I. Ball."

Like Reed's other novels, *Reckless Eyeballing* coalesces several simultaneous plots. While Ball is trying to get his play produced, Detective Lawrence O'Reedy, a parody of Clint Eastwood's Dirty Harry Callahan (whom Reed mentions several times in the novel), is chasing the "Flower Phantom," who

accosts feminists who have denigrated black men, shaves their hair, and leaves them with a chrysanthemum. In a third plot, Jim Minsk, the powerful director who stands up to the feminist bullies Tremonisha Smarts (playwright and director) and Becky French (producer), is murdered in an anti-Semite conspiracy that is never explained.

Jim's murder puts Ian at the mercy of his enemies, Tremonisha, who takes over as director, and Becky, who moves the play to a smaller, less prestigious "workshop" theater. During the course of their collaboration, however, Ian has his consciousness raised, and Tremonisha begins to see some truth in his point of view, which she had previously discarded as sexist. Ian beings to think of women as more than sex objects, and Tremonisha begins to realize that men are not monsters.

If Reed had left the plot there, it would not be much more than a trendy situation comedy. The last chapter, however, provides an ironic subtext to the whole novel. In an interior monologue, Ian's mother, Martha, recalls a hex placed on him at birth, making him "a two-head, of two minds, the one not knowing what the other was up to." This revelation is foreshadowed in Ball's reaction to the "Flower Phantom" in chapter 11: "Ian's head told him that this man was a lunatic who should be put away for a long time, but his gut was cheering the man on. His head was Dr. Jekyll, but his gut was Mr. Hyde." In the final paragraph of the novel, it is revealed than Ian, unknown to himself, is actually the Flower Phantom.

A fourth interwoven plot counterbalances the main story of Ball's struggle to mount his play. The lush theater originally scheduled to house his play is now running *Eva's Honeymoon*, a feminist romp presenting Eva Braun, Adolf Hitler's lover, as a victim. Mysterious scenes in the novel with an old lady who mumbles about leaving Hitler in a bunker forty years earlier make the reader realize that the play is, in fact, written and subsidized by Eva Braun herself, still alive and hiding in New York.

Stylistically, *Reckless Eyeballing* is more conservative than any of Reed's previous novels. The only remotely HooDoo character is Ian's mother, a Caribbean peasant with "second sight," a fortune teller very powerful in the politics of New Oyo, Ian's island birthplace. Yet none of the scenes are given a surreal or otherworldly point of view, with the possible exception of O'Reedy's hallucinations of the ghosts of innocent minorities he killed while on duty. There is no use of unusual spelling and punctuation to reproduce dialect, as in Reed's previous novels. The novel is uncharacteristically realistic.

Reckless Eyeballing is a portrait of every conceivable type of hatred in contemporary America—racism, sexism, anti-Semitism, regionalism, classism, and infighting among factions of every group. Yet the attitude that Reed projects in the novel is not hatred but ridicule. By exposing every type of extremism—racial, gender-related, cultural—Reed has made many enemies, but he has also helped American readers see their demons and, it is hoped, exorcise them.

SUMMARY

Reed is an innovative black satirist. His Neo-HooDoo style, a mixture of African religion and art with American popular culture, created fiction that is popular, yet educates the reader about the African roots of American culture. Defining the African American artist as a "necromancer," or magician, Reed sees his art as a form of conjuring, calling up the spirits of his African ancestors to comment on the past, present, and future of America. Reed's heroes are underdogs fighting oppression in many forms, usually by turning the system upside down.

John R. Holmes

BIBLIOGRAPHY

By the Author

LONG FICTION:
The Free-Lance Pallbearers, 1967
Yellow Back Radio Broke-Down, 1969
Mumbo Jumbo, 1972
The Last Days of Louisiana Red, 1974
Flight to Canada, 1976
The Terrible Twos, 1982
Reckless Eyeballing, 1986
The Terrible Threes, 1989
Japanese by Spring, 1993

POETRY:
Catechism of D Neoamerican Hoodoo Church, 1970
Conjure: Selected Poems, 1963-1970, 1972
Chattanooga, 1973
A Secretary to the Spirits, 1977
Cab Calloway Stands In for the Moon, 1986
New and Collected Poems, 1988

NONFICTION:
Shrovetide in Old New Orleans, 1978
God Made Alaska for the Indians, 1982
Writin' Is Fightin': Thirty-seven Years of Boxing on Paper, 1988
Airing Dirty Laundry, 1993
Conversations with Ishmael Reed, 1995
Another Day at the Front: Dispatches from the Race War, 2002 (essays)
Blues City: A Walk in Oakland, 2003

DISCUSSION TOPICS

- Does Ishmael Reed's poetry deal with the same themes as his fiction? Are the styles of the two genres similar?

- How is the concept of Neo-HooDoo central to Reed's fiction?

- How is *Yellow Back Radio Broke-Down* a parody of the Western genre? How is it a satire of the Vietnam War era?

- How effective is Reed's manipulation of time in *Flight to Canada* in supporting his themes?

- Compare *Flight to Canada* to *Uncle Tom's Cabin* (1852). How is Reed commenting on Harriet Beecher Stowe's novel?

- How valid are feminist attacks on Reed for his portrayal of women?

- How do the attacks on racism in Reed's novels differ from those by other African American writers?

EDITED TEXTS:

19 Necromancers from Now, 1970

Yardbird Lives!, 1978 (with Al Young)

Calafia: An Anthology of California Poets, 1979 (with Young and Shawn Hsu Wong)

The Before Columbus Foundation Fiction Anthology: Selections from the American Book Awards, 1980-1990, 1992 (with Kathryn Trueblood and Wong)

MultiAmerica: Essays on Cultural Wars and Cultural Peace, 1997

From Totems to Hip-Hop, 2003

MISCELLANEOUS:

The Reed Reader, 2000

About the Author

Beauford, Fred. "A Conversation with Ishmael Reed." *Black Creation 4* (1973): 12-15.

Bryant, Jerry H. "Old Gods and New Demons: Ishmael Reed and His Fiction." *The Review of Contemporary Fiction 4* (1984): 195-202.

Chaney, Michael A. "Slave Cyborgs and the Black Infovirus: Ishmael Reed's Cybernetic Aesthetics." *MFS: Modern Fiction Studies* 49 (Summer, 2003): 261-283.

Dick, Bruce Allen, ed. *The Critical Response to Ishmael Reed*. Westport, Conn.: Greenwood Press, 1999.

Dick, Bruce, and Amritjit Singh, eds. *Conversations with Ishmael Reed*. Jackson: University Press of Mississippi, 1995.

Gates, Henry Louis. "Ishmael Reed." In *Afro-American Writers After 1955*, edited by Thadious M. Davis and Trudier Harris. Detroit: Gale Research, 1984.

Harde, Roxanne. "'We Will Make Our Own Future Text': Allegory, Iconoclasm, and Reverence in Ishmael Reed's *Mumbo Jumbo*." *Critique: Studies in Contemporary Fiction* 43 (Summer, 2002): 361-377.

McGee, Patrick. *Ishmael Reed and the Ends of Race*. New York: St. Martin's Press, 1997.

Martin, Reginald. *Ishmael Reed and the New Black Aesthetic Critics*. New York: St. Martin's Press, 1988.

Mvuyekure, Pierre-Damien. "American Neo-HooDooism: The Novels of Ishmael Reed." In *The Cambridge Companion to the African American Novel*, edited by Maryemma Graham. New York: Cambridge University Press, 2004.

_____, ed. *A Casebook Study of Ishmael Reed's "Yellow Back Radio Broke-Down."* Normal, Ill.: Dalkey Archive, 2003.

Nicholls, David G. "Ishmael Reed." In *Postmodernism: The Key Figures*, edited by Hans Bertens and Joseph Natoii. Malden, Mass.: Blackwell, 2002.

O'Brien, John. "Ishmael Reed." In *The New Fiction*, edited by Joe David Bellamy. Urbana: University of Illinois Press, 1974.

Schmitz, Neil. "Neo-HooDoo: The Experimental Fiction of Ishmael Reed." *Twentieth Century Literature* 20 (April, 1974): 126-140.

ADRIENNE RICH

Born: Baltimore, Maryland
May 16, 1929

Rich's poetry and essays take a multifaceted approach to expressing American culture and taking aim at one's assumptions of private versus public life.

Library of Congress

BIOGRAPHY

Adrienne Cecile Rich was born in Baltimore, Maryland, on May 16, 1929, the elder of two daughters. Her father, Dr. Arnold Rich, was a medical professor at John Hopkins University, and her mother, Helen Jones, was trained as a concert pianist though she abandoned this career to devote herself to her domestic responsibilities and to teach. Rich's father, a man of science, was extremely well versed in the humanities and steeped Rich in the tradition of his favorite English poets, such as Alfred, Lord Tennyson, and John Keats. Her relationship with her father dominated both her upbringing and her subsequent poetic career.

While she was in her senior year at Radcliffe College, Rich's first collection of poems, *A Change of World* (1951), was selected by W. H. Auden for the Yale Younger Poets Award. These early poems reflect tight formalist lyrics and, as Auden notes, the poems focus more on modest and discretionary content than her later poems.

After graduation, Rich was awarded a Guggenheim Fellowship, which enabled her to travel in Europe. In 1953, she married Alfred Haskell Conrad, a Harvard economist six years her senior. They lived in Cambridge, Massachusetts, where their first son, David, was born in 1955. Rich published her second book of poetry, *The Diamond Cutters, and Other Poems*, the same year. This collection,

which contains a number of travel poems based on her experiences in Europe, continued the formalism denoted in *A Change of World*. Rich bore two more sons, Paul in 1957 and Jacob in 1959. During this time, Rich devoted herself to fulfilling the socially prescribed roles of wife and mother and allocated little energy to writing. (She describes the problems of this period of her life in "When We Dead Awaken" in *On Lies, Secrets, and Silence: Selected Prose 1966-1978*, a collection of essays published in 1979.) Rich found these roles at odds with her aspirations, and this tension became a productive force in her later work.

After eight years, Rich broke her silence with *Snapshots of a Daughter-in-Law* (1963), a more personal work, in which she began to explore her identity as a woman, marking a significant new direction in her work. However, the book received much criticism for its focus on women, so in *Necessities of Life* (1966), Rich retreated to the more "universal" and traditional themes present in some of her earlier work.

In 1966, Rich moved to New York City, where she became involved in the Civil Rights movement, the antiwar movement, and the women's movement. Her presence in the literary arena was more pronounced, as she focused on teaching, giving lectures, and offering poetry readings. Rich's father died in early 1968 after a long illness, and in *Leaflets* (1969), she confronted both the personal changes taking place in her own life and the problems of American society as a whole as she grappled with the need to break with the past. Rich excelled early as a technical virtuoso in her poetry, but now she abandoned that formal expertise and experimented with fragmentation, pushing at the limits of coherence to express new poetic ideas. This experimentation resulted in *The Will to Change* in 1971.

This period of experimentation was interrupted by a personal loss. Rich's marriage had deteriorated during the 1960's, and, after the couple separated in 1970, Alfred Conrad committed suicide. Rich has seldom referred to this event publicly (one important exception is "From a Survivor" in *Diving into the Wreck*, 1973), consistently refusing to use the event as "a theme for poetry or tragic musings." The impact of the loss, therefore, remains difficult to trace in her work, but it clearly precipitated many changes. It forced Rich to explore a new way of writing and allowed a different side of her identity to emerge in the early 1970's. In 1973, she published *Diving into the Wreck*, one of her most important collections. Rich was again criticized for the personal and even militant tone of her poetry; nevertheless, *Diving into the Wreck* won the National Book Award in 1974.

As a token of her newfound sense of shared identity with other women, Rich accepted the award on behalf of Audre Lorde and Alice Walker, who were also nominated. In *Poems: Selected and New, 1950-1974* (1975), a retrospective selection of her previously published works as well as a number of new poems, Rich summarized her poetic career.

In the 1970's, Rich began the process of embracing and publicizing her lesbianism. This involved not only taking a personal stand but also developing the theme of sexuality to explore broader political issues, connections that became increasingly evident in her work. An example is *Twenty-one Love Poems* (1976), which was reprinted as part of the important collection *The Dream of a Common Language* (1978), a work that contributed significantly to Rich's poetic reputation. In this collection, Rich continued her formal experimentation while developing the theme of women's love and commitment as a source of power. Rich also began publishing her most important prose works in the 1970's, including *Of Woman Born: Motherhood as Experience and Institution* (1976) and *On Lies, Secrets, and Silence.*

In *A Wild Patience Has Taken Me This Far* (1981), Rich reached an acceptance of anger and shifted her focus to a reverence for everyday life, in which she was able to perceive the connections with all forms of life. This reconciliation with the present

allowed Rich to take up the unfinished business of her past. In *Sources* (1983), she undertook an investigation of her repressed roots as a southern Jew, another source of personal power. Rich's mother was not Jewish, but her father was, and yet through internalized anti-Semitism, he was proud of his ability to become assimilated into non-Jewish society, leaving a complex legacy for Rich to unravel.

In 1984, Rich left the East Coast for California. A second retrospective of her work appeared that year, titled *The Fact of a Doorframe*, and *Sources* was reprinted as part of *Your Native Land, Your Life* in 1986. Rich extended her investigation of the continued relevance of the past in *Time's Power* (1989). She also published her collected prose writings: *Blood, Bread, and Poetry* (1986), a collection of essays and speeches, testifies to the importance of her role as spokeswoman for the women's movement. It contains important essays (for example, on the role of memory) that inform the reading of her poetry.

Rich experienced increased popularity in the 1990's. *An Atlas of the Difficult World* was published in 1991 and is considered one of her best collections. *What Is Found There: Notebooks on Poetry and Politics* (1993) is a work of nonfiction that focuses on the materialistic fascination that became widespread in the late 1980's and 1990's. For Rich, this is a disease of the mind which she asserts cannot be ignored. *Dark Fields of the Republic* (1995) revisits the theme started in *An Atlas of the Difficult World* of the disappointment and pain that can be associated with identifying with one's country. Rich is demanding that her readers become politically and culturally aware. Rich also published two compilations of old and new poetry during this period: *Collected Early Poems, 1950-1970* (1993) and *Selected Poems, 1950-1995* (1996). In *Midnight Salvage* (1999), Rich revisited her cutting-edge tone, collecting poems that critically examine and interweave the malicious nature of history, one's search for self, human longing, love, and beauty. She incorporated factual people into this compilation of longer poems, often to explore the politics of war.

Rich's nonfiction prose collection *Arts of the Possible: Essays and Conversations* (2001) once again reaffirmed her commitment to the country's confused notions of culture. She sees American culture as desecrated by materialism, greedy politics, and social injustice. Rich's *Fox* (2001) probed deeper into one's understanding of history and its relationship with self. In this poetry collection, Rich was searching, longing at times, for something, and the reader senses that only she knows the answer; yet Rich highlights the fallibility of utopian ideals. Rich won the National Book Critics Circle Award in Poetry for her collection *The School Among the Ruins* (2004). These poems are inherently political in nature, critiquing the social and political culture of the first four years of the twenty-first century with vengeance. War, greed, lies, imperialism, and technology's destruction of common courtesy all find a place in the pages of this book. It is perhaps Rich's finest example of the power of language.

Rich's literary merit is well documented. She has been awarded two Guggenheim Fellowships, the first Ruth Lilly Poetry Prize, the Brandeis Creative Arts Medal, the Common Wealth Award, the William Whitehead Award for Lifetime Achievement, the National Poetry Association Award for Distinguished Service to the Art of Poetry, a MacArthur Fellowship, an Academy of American Poets Fellowship, a Lifetime Achievement Award from the Lannan Foundation, and the Lenore Marshall Poetry Prize. In 1997, she declined the National Medal for the Arts, unable to back down from her political agenda: "I could not accept such an award from President Clinton or this White House because the very meaning of art, as I understand it, is incompatible with the cynical politics of this administration."

ANALYSIS

In the ghazal (a verse form borrowed from Middle Eastern poetry) "7/14/68: ii," published in *Leaflets*, Rich rhetorically asks: "Did you think I was talking about my life?/ I was trying to drive a tradition up against the wall." This couplet summarizes her poetic career: Autobiography is used to examine universal issues in order to effect change. *Snapshots of a Daughter-in-Law* was the first volume in which this important aspect of Rich's work was apparent. Starting with this collection, Rich began to write more personal and experimental poetry in which meaning was not subordinate to form. Rich assumed a more personal voice, addressing more directly the issues she faces as a woman and allowing herself more formal innovations. Although Rich did not yet allow herself to speak directly (the

daughter-in-law of the snapshots, an important autobiographical sequence, is referred to as "she," not "I"), these were her first feminist poems, and she drew inspiration from the work of Simone de Beauvoir and Mary Wollstonecraft.

Rich's mature work is intensely biographical, not merely for the sake of pure honesty and personal expression, but because by describing her own struggles, she wishes to stimulate what she calls "the will to change" and thereby bring about political transformation in others. The "will to change" is created by the rigorous examination of one's own inner self as well as by "diving into the wreck" of past tradition. As Rich states in "Tear Gas" (in *Poems: Selected and New*), "the will to change begins in the body not in the mind," thereby linking biography to larger issues. In pursuing this rigorous self-examination, one is carried by a kind of visionary anger best described as "a wild patience," which provides the energy to create the dreamed-of community that speaks "a common language." In this way, Rich is interested in the real world and is concerned with the way poetry can affect daily life. She is not a poet interested only in form, the purely abstract, or the self-referential aspects of writing; she strives to intermingle all of these within the current social context.

That the personal is political was a slogan of the 1960's and 1970's, and Rich's poetry examines and exemplifies this connection. As she states in "The Blue Ghazals: 5/4/69" (in *The Will to Change*): "*The moment when a feeling enters the body/* is political. This touch is political." The feeling, the touch, could be caused by pain (the context of this poem suggests torture) or by love (as in "Twenty-one Love Poems"), but what matters to Rich is that such personal interactions are conditioned by larger, political structures. As Rich states in "The Phenomenology of Anger" (in *Diving into the Wreck*), "every act of becoming conscious// is an unnatural act." Thus, for Rich, the lesbian theme in her poetry not only is a personal statement but also becomes a metaphor for all the "unnatural acts" of becoming conscious of oppression and making a choice to resist.

Rich finds the energy to personally evolve in anger, an important and powerful emotion in her work, although alienating to some readers. She explores this theme explicitly in "The Phenomenology of Anger," in which she allows herself to explore her fantasies of murder, which result in "a changed man." She describes anger as a kind of "wild patience" and, in "Natural Resources" (in *The Dream of a Common Language*), as "impatience—my own—/ the passion to make and make again! where such unmaking reigns/ the refusal to be a victim." It is thanks to such fuel that she is able to sustain her poetic explorations, and she speaks positively of the potential of "visionary anger" as a force that others, too, can draw upon. In *A Wild Patience Has Taken Me This Far*, she even describes her anger as an "angel," a striking and suggestive image for the role it comes to assume in her work.

Rich found her insights increasingly hard to express, however, as she became aware of the ways in which language reflects the assumptions and values of dominant culture. In *The Will to Change*, she is aware of the limitations of what she calls "the oppressor's language" and later allows herself to "dream of a common language," the title of one of her most important collections. She explores, too, the visionary potential of poetry as she imagines a world in which women are not divided against one another but where their shared community is a source of transformative power. The idealism of this vision is tempered, however, by the recognition that, in the real world, language can be distorted and taken out of context ("North American Time").

Having once defined her vision, Rich realizes that it requires continual effort to maintain it. This daily struggle incorporates the past, which is far more than a mere "husk" (as Rich suggests in *A Wild Patience Has Taken Me This Far*), and leads her to the personal interrogations of her own past, best represented by *Sources*. The recognition that ideals such as freedom depend on the prosaic, everyday act of remembering also leads Rich to be more attentive to the ordinary routines of her daily life. Her descriptions of New England landscapes are the occasion for striking and beautiful imagery, such as the description of beet roots in "Culture and Anarchy" (from *A Wild Patience Has Taken Me This Far*). This element of her work places her firmly in the tradition of poets she admired and was influenced by, such as Robert Frost.

The attempts to break with poetic tradition and forge something entirely new (yet that will incorporate the past) result in what Rich calls "a whole new poetry beginning here" ("Transcendental Ètude" in *The Dream of a Common Language*). It is this origi-

nality, which transforms the most intensely personal material into statements that reflect a wider truth, that has compelled respect and admiration for Rich's work. Although Rich has been criticized for her anger, unremitting seriousness, and occasional self-righteousness, her work is favorably compared to that of major poets such as Anne Bradstreet, Emily Dickinson, Robert Frost, Robert Lowell, Sylvia Plath, and Anne Sexton.

"AUNT JENNIFER'S TIGERS"

First published: 1951 (collected in *A Change of World*, 1951)
Type of work: Poem

Aunt Jennifer creates a work of art that lasts beyond her death.

"Aunt Jennifer's Tigers," which appeared in Rich's first collection of poems, is typical of her early work, illustrating the modest poetic ambitions for which she was praised by Auden. Technically, the work displays flawless craftsmanship, with a carefully regulated meter and rhyming couplets. Only later did Rich recognize how formalism functioned as she writes, "asbestos gloves," enabling her to grasp potentially dangerous materials without putting herself at risk, as in this poem.

The formalism of "Aunt Jennifer's Tigers" hides the more disturbing aspects of the poem and subordinates the theme of Aunt Jennifer's "ordeals" in marriage to the more "poetic" theme of the transcendence of art. The first verse of the poem describes the fearless tigers Aunt Jennifer creates in needlepoint. Their freedom and dignity is contrasted in the second verse to the restrictions of marriage, symbolized by the wedding band that weighs down Aunt Jennifer's fingers as she sews. The themes are resolved in the final, third, verse: Even death will not free Aunt Jennifer from her "ordeals," but the tigers she has created will continue to appear "proud and unafraid."

While the poem is technically brilliant, the themes that art endures beyond human life and that suffering may be redeemed through art are hardly original. Rich, however, uses an inventive image to recast these conventional themes in a new way and even hints, in the image of Aunt Jennifer weighed down by an oppressive marriage, at the feminism that would permeate her later work. Yet the poem remains quite impersonal; the reader sees Aunt Jennifer but is scarcely aware of the voice of the poem's narrator. For the reader, it is as though the picture is framed by an invisible hand, in contrast to Rich's later work, where the reader cannot help being aware of the poet's personal presence.

"The Burning of Paper Instead of Children"

First published: 1971 (collected in *The Will to Change*, 1971)

Type of work: Poem

A comparison between the burning of books and physical human sufferings and an observation of the inadequacy of language to convey pain.

"The Burning of Paper Instead of Children" is a good example of Rich's developing experimental style. Between 1968 and 1970, Rich confronted in her poetry the inability of the language that she had inherited to express the pain both of her own life and of society as it underwent turbulent social change. The results of this experimentation can be seen in *Leaflets* but are also evident in this collection, *The Will to Change*. Whereas in her early work, exemplified by "Aunt Jennifer's Tigers," Rich encapsulated a certain experience, in this experimental vein the poem itself is the experience. As Rich allows the unconscious to speak through her poetry, the poem contributes to the creation of new experiences for both poet and reader. The poem consists of five interrelated sections, which vary in form from fragmented free verse to prose poetry.

The starting point for the poem is autobiographical—a neighbor calls to complain about the poet's son burning a textbook—and the poet does not hesitate to use the first-person voice, thus illustrating the role of personal memory as the key to political connections as well as Rich's assumption of personal presence in her work. The poet juxta-

poses this incident with a picture of Joan of Arc being burned at the stake, a memory from her privileged childhood in which she had access to books and education though they failed to teach about the reality of suffering. This memory also serves as the occasion for Rich to explore the difficult relationship of "love and fear" she experienced with her father, a relationship she now begins to perceive as oppressive. The relationship with her father is another recurrent theme in Rich's work, and some critics have gone so far as to suggest that it is the dominant theme.

In the second section, the poet records her frustration that language is necessary, yet inadequate, to communicate. The third section lists different forms of suffering and concludes with the observation that, in order to overcome suffering, the language must be repaired. Rich thereby links the themes of the first two sections and illustrates the connection, for her, between language and politics. Once Rich broke away from the formalism that conveniently shielded her from the power of raw language, she became increasingly preoccupied with this subject.

The fourth section again explores frustration in a personal relationship and the uselessness of written texts to describe and understand experience (suggesting that burning books is a reasonable response). The final section further investigates the problems described above in a stream-of-consciousness list that strives to capture the poet's own feeling of burning with impotence to solve the different yet related problems that range from poverty in the United States to the burning of children by napalm in Vietnam.

The experimental form of the poem forces the reader to confront a complexity that resists easy summary. This is in marked contrast to Rich's earlier work, where the theme of the poem was more easily extracted. Rich abandons conventional form and attempts to put into language thoughts that were not previously considered poetic, to push at the limits of what is considered "poetry." Along with the exploration of form, Rich allows a more personal voice to be heard in the poem, blending autobiographical scenes and reminiscences with only minimal clues for the reader as to their context and significance. Rich does not pretend to maintain traditional poetic language and integrates black dialect into the poem as a means of illustrating the inadequacy of Standard English to capture some forms of experience. This incorporation of different voices also symbolizes the connections Rich perceives between different struggles for change and justice.

"ORIGINS AND HISTORY OF CONSCIOUSNESS"

First published: 1978 (collected in *The Dream of a Common Language*, 1978)
Type of work: Poem

The poet tries to explain the connection between the true nature of poetry and life.

"Origins and History of Consciousness," as the title suggests, is an account of the poet's search for what poetry means to her and how it is connected to personal issues in her life. Appearing in *The Dream of a Common Language*, one of Rich's most critically acclaimed works, it represents an important summary of themes and concerns at the center of her work.

The first section consists of what appears to be a relatively straightforward description of a room, but it rapidly becomes clear that this description incorporates many symbolic layers. The blank walls, for example, represent the erasure of women writers from history, an absence of tradition that the woman poet must confront. The search for origins, and foremothers, that the poet undertakes also recalls the archaeological explorations of *Diving into the Wreck*. The social change movements of the 1960's and 1970's helped to create an atmosphere in which questioning the past and the need for change—both personal and political—were widely accepted.

Rich's work echoed these concerns and gave poetic expression to ideas that many were struggling to articulate, both in *Diving into the Wreck* and in *The Dream of a Common Language*. In the latter collection, Rich understands that sexuality is only one of the ways women express a commitment to each other. (These ideas were later developed in her influential essay "Compulsory Heterosexuality and Lesbian Existence," first published in 1980.) The theme of a community of women began to figure more prominently in her work, along with peace, feminism, and antiracism. The three sections of the book, focusing on power, love, and the need to confront the immediate context, explore the dream, or ideal, of a community based on values of nurturance and care and mirror the concerns of the burgeoning women's movement.

In "Origins and History of Consciousness," from the first part, titled "Power," the poet acknowledges that for her, the "true nature of poetry" is "the drive/ to connect/ The dream of a common language." In the second section, the poet contrasts the simplicity of falling in love with the difficulty of integrating this private life into the public world of the surrounding city, an example of how Rich uses personal situations such as sexual orientation to draw larger connections. She continually emphasizes that various aspects of life cannot be kept separate but overflow into one another, just as the lines of her poem run on into one another.

In the third and final section, the poet names the problem as one of trust. Using an image of lowering herself on a rope, a reflection reminiscent of her earlier work "Diving into the Wreck," the poet describes how she gradually explores the problem. Having gained an understanding of the situation (having explored its "origins and history"), the poet ends by stressing the need for public acknowledgment of those connections in order to reconcile the splits and forge a more holistic vision of life.

The poem uses experimental forms such as incomplete sentences and fragmented phrases to capture the difficulty of formulating the message. The descriptions of the room at the beginning of the poem retain a certain even structure; the punctuation, though minimal, lends coherence. As the poet delves further into her inner consciousness, however, the poem becomes more fragmented. The lines are more varied in length, greater use is made of italics and dashes (the characteristic punctuation of Emily Dickinson, who figures so frequently in Rich's work), and imagery is accumulated without an attempt to impose order as a means of conveying the dreamlike state of the poet. Rich uses both striking poetic imagery and prosaic language inspired by her surroundings in New York City to blend a dreamlike poetic vision with the everyday reality, a fusion that represents in the poem the integration she seeks in life.

Adrienne Rich

"NORTH AMERICAN TIME"

First published: 1986 (collected in *Your Native Land, Your Life*, 1986)

Type of work: Poem

A meditation on the power and responsibility of words.

While continuing to explore themes taken up in other poems (such as the power of language), "North American Time" places these concerns in the context not of new discoveries but of continued struggle. As in *A Wild Patience Has Taken Me This Far*, Rich rejects the Romantic emphasis on certain peaks of perception and, instead, focuses on the daily struggle to change the world through quiet strength and resistance. In *Your Native Land, Your Life*, Rich continues to explore the ways that common experience, especially the natural and indigenous scenes of her "native land," provides the raw material of art that becomes the artist's life.

The phrase that gives the title to the collection occurs in a poem titled "Emily Carr," about the Canadian artist who paints totem poles of the Northwest Coast Indians. It encapsulates the importance of art rooted both in landscape and in traditions, especially those of minorities. Rich continues to incorporate the past, on a personal level by analyzing the powerful relationship with her father and the role of her background, and on a general level by attending to the indigenous history of the United States and its connections to the rest of the world.

The collection echoes the tripartite structure of *The Dream of a Common Language*, with sections titled "Sources," "North American Time," and "Contradictions: Tracking Poems." The poem "North American Time" is part of the second section. In this poem in nine parts, Rich takes stock of her accomplishments as a poet and discusses the connection of poetry to history. She begins to wonder about these matters in the first verse, when she fears that her poetry has become circumscribed and predictable. As she explains in subsequent verses, the issue not only is one of personal importance but also has wider ramifications because, once words become part of the world, they take on a life of their own; they escape the speaker's control and can be used in a way the speaker never intended.

Attempts to deny political responsibility are futile, Rich maintains, and she goes on to sketch connections between "North American Time" and other world events, figures, and places that are routinely denied or ignored because of ethnocentrism. This attention to lost or muted voices becomes an increasingly important theme in Rich's work, as her sensitivity to the suppression of women's culture makes her aware also of the erasure of American Indian, black, and other minority experiences.

Rich views herself as a kind of messenger, a prophet or seer, called upon to engage the reader with these issues, and uses this image, which she admits is rather grandiose, as an incentive to continue writing and speaking out. She concludes by characteristically incorporating the words of another woman writer, the Puerto Rican poet Julia de Burgos, and, as she watches the moon rise over New York City, an image that portends change, she shifts from introspection to action—that is, speech.

The attention to the lives of other women (artists, writers, explorers, and scientists) is one of Rich's enduring concerns. In this poem, Rich both quotes de Burgos and refers to other women whose names have been erased from the "almanac" of North American time. In this collection, as in her previous work, such allusions are pervasive and telling. Such "re-visions" (a central concern of literature, as Rich explained in *On Lies, Secrets, and Silence*), are an inspiration to Rich, a celebration of the buried traditions of women's writings she has excavated elsewhere, and a benchmark for women's experience.

"XIII. (DEDICATIONS)"

First published: 1991 (collected in *An Atlas of the Difficult World*, 1991)

Type of work: Poem

Rich works to invade the reader's personal space, challenging the assumptions of the accessibility and tangibility of poetry.

Rich boldly proclaims "I know you" to twelve types of readers in "XIII. (Dedications)." She strives to isolate the reader as a way of asserting her intense connection with the authentic readers who approach her work. She is acutely aware that the idyllic poetry readers—the single guy in the coffee shop or group of girls in the basement of the dorm—are not real. She goes even further to imply that even if these readers do exist, they are not the ones to whom she is writing. She does not include in her catalog of readership anyone that would seem typical.

She invades the reader's personal space, making it impossible for him or her to dismiss the work as nothing more than words on a page. According to Rich, all readers are "stripped" and "listening for something." She speaks to those who are trapped by life, those living "where the bedclothes lie in stagnant coils on the bed/ and the open valise speaks of flight/ but you cannot leave yet." Immediately following this characterization of entrapment is one of intense freedom—readers full of dare and blithe who are "running up the stairs/ toward a new kind of love/ your life has never allowed." She pulls at the heartstrings of a woman searching for the life that she has lost amid "warming milk, a crying child on your shoulder, a book in your hand/ because life is short and you too are thirsty." Rich reminds her readers that, as literate beings, they all are empty without words. She wants to know what it is that readers find within and between her inconsistent stanza styles, asking to know with which words they struggle and with which words they identify.

The theme of the poem is the natural misreading of language. As a reader, she states you are "turning back once again to the task you cannot refuse," not daring to dismiss her words yet striving for self-assuredness that you can stand without them. She poignantly warns the reader that though "there is nothing else left to read/ there where you have landed, stripped as you are" you may find solace in the fact that you share this space with those surrounding you who work to find meaning and work to dismiss it as quickly as it is found.

"SEVEN SKINS"

First published: 1999 (collected in *Midnight Salvage*, 1999)
Type of work: Poem

Rich explores the path that one's search for knowledge may take and how incapacitating such intangible searches can be.

Midnight Salvage explores a unique path of poetry for Rich. In it, she uses real people to tell her stories of war, memory, history, and the violence of power. These are all themes with which Rich's readers are familiar, but in this collection she requires her readers to question the social context, as well as what is accepted as truth.

"Seven Skins" portrays a young woman's quest for knowledge in 1952. It begins in the library, where Rich makes a symbolic reference to elevation. A graduate student, Vic Greenberg, who is a "paraplegic GI-Bill of Rights Jew" rolls into the elevator and goes "up into the great stacks where all knowledge should and is and shall be stored like sacred grain," while the rest of the world remains outside the library "stuck amid so many smiles." Those outside the library are "lonely" for knowledge too but choose not to permeate the invisible barriers set forth because of the war; they remain "aground."

Rich uses the limitations of one's handicap, whether it be physical or mental, to point to the larger limitations of postwar society, including the inaccuracy of memory and one's inability to re-create events with factual detail. She argues that part of remembering is re-creating what is lost in translation: "And this is only memory, no more/ so this is how you remember." When one is outlining history, especially the history of a war society, remembering becomes entrenched in forgetting certain things.

Rich references Vic's difficult mobility throughout the poem. He chooses a restaurant "which happens to have no stairs" and showers in a tub with "suction-cupped rubber mats." Vic embraces his life and accepts his fate. He is confident and self-aware. He is everything that the young woman is not. She is a girl "ready for breaking open like a lobster" and "a mass of swimmy legs." When Vic asks "the usual question" of whether she will join him for a postdinner drink in his room, she answers the way in which she believes any woman "has to an-swer/ you don't even think." Though the woman wants to go, and imagines the kind of night that she and Vic might have experienced between his "linen-service/ sheets," she declines his offer, un-able to defy the woman whom society judges she should be.

"Fox"

First published: 2001 (collected in *Fox*, 2001)

Type of work: Poem

Fox symbolizes rebirth and the key to recognition and recollection, both necessary ideals for happiness and self-awareness.

Rich's signature themes spring up throughout *Fox*. The collection's title poem reflects a longing for

recognition and recollec-tion. To have the latter, she must acquire the for-mer. Recognition of self and identity, Rich has taught her readers, can be ascertained through his-tory and self-exploration. She warns her reader, "I needed history of fox" and moves into the sym-bolic nature of birth to emphasize how formative recollection can be to self-awareness: Go "back far enough it blurts into the

birth-yell of the yet-to-be human child/ pushed out of a female the yet-to-be woman." Though Rich has discovered the secret to attaining her recognition, and thus recollection, it is lost—born into the world, but lost nevertheless. It is important to note that the "fox" is not an animal, but symbolic of the animal-like nature of human beings.

In this poem, Rich revisits the promises of birth set forth in *Of Woman Born*, yet she finds herself un-able to fulfill them without the fox. However, "Fox" conveys an optimistic tone not shared by the poems surrounding it because it is written in the past tense: "I needed fox." This signifies that she has does find the lost symbol, fox, enabling her to de-pict accurately the "tearing and torn endless and sudden" haunting effects of memory.

SUMMARY

Taken in its entirety, Rich's work may be viewed as what Albert Gelpi has called "a poetics of change," a systematic attempt to explore and un-derstand change through poetry. Rich gradually developed a poetic voice that is both personal and universal.

Her consummate works of poetry, *The Will to Change*, *Diving into the Wreck*, and *The Dream of a Common Language*, along with some of her prose works, are frequently quoted because they seem to express the essence of a female consciousness; many of her phrases articulate important human experiences in novel ways. Rich's use of poetry to link abstract metaphysical questions to concrete daily life revitalizes poetry, facilitates understand-ing, and offers relevance to some of the unanswer-able cultural questions of our time.

Melanie Hawthorne; updated by Amanda B. Wray

BIBLIOGRAPHY

By the Author

POETRY:
A Change of World, 1951
The Diamond Cutters, and Other Poems, 1955
Snapshots of a Daughter-in-Law, 1963
Necessities of Life, 1966
Selected Poems, 1967
Leaflets, 1969
The Will to Change, 1971
Diving into the Wreck, 1973

Poems: Selected and New, 1950-1974, 1975
Twenty-one Love Poems, 1976
The Dream of a Common Language, 1978
A Wild Patience Has Taken Me This Far, 1981
Sources, 1983
The Fact of a Doorframe: Poems Selected and New, 1950-1984, 1984
Your Native Land, Your Life, 1986
Time's Power: Poems, 1985-1988, 1989
An Atlas of the Difficult World: Poems, 1988-1991, 1991
Collected Early Poems, 1950-1970, 1993
Dark Fields of the Republic: Poems, 1991-1995, 1995
Selected Poems, 1950-1995, 1996
Midnight Salvage: Poems, 1995-1998, 1999
Fox: Poems, 1998-2000, 2001
The School Among the Ruins: Poems, 2000-2004, 2004

NONFICTION:
Of Woman Born: Motherhood as Experience and Institution, 1976
On Lies, Secrets, and Silence: Selected Prose, 1966-1978, 1979
Blood, Bread, and Poetry: Selected Prose, 1979-1985, 1986
What Is Found There: Notebooks on Poetry and Politics, 1993
Arts of the Possible: Essays and Conversations, 2001

MISCELLANEOUS:
Adrienne Rich's Poetry and Prose: Poems, Prose, Reviews, and Criticism, 1993 (Barbara Chartesworth Gelpi and Albert Gelpi, editors)

EDITED TEXTS:
The Best American Poetry, 1996, 1996
Selected Poems / Muriel Rukeyser, 2004

About the Author

Dickie, Margaret. *Stein, Bishop, and Rich: Lyrics of Love, War, and Peace.* Chapel Hill: University of North Carolina Press, 1997.

Gwiazda, Piotr. "'Nothing Else Left to Read': Poetry and Audience in Adrienne Rich's 'An Atlas of the Difficult World.'" *Journal of Modern Literature* 28, no. 2 (Winter, 2005): 165-188.

Halpern, Nick. *Everyday and Prophetic: The Poetry of Lowell, Ammons, Merrill, and Rich.* Madison: University of Wisconsin Press, 2003.

Keyes, Claire. *The Aesthetics of Power: The Poetry of Adrienne Rich.* Athens: University of Georgia Press, 1986.

O'Reilly, Andrea. *From Motherhood and Mothering: The Legacy of Adrienne Rich's "Of Woman Born."* New York: State University of New York Press, 2004.

Ostriker, Alice. *Writing Like a Woman.* Ann Arbor: University of Michigan Press, 1983.

Spencer, Luke. "That Light of Outrage: The Historicism of Adrienne Rich." *English: Journal of the English Association* 51, no. 200 (Summer, 2002): 145-160.

Yorke, Liz. *Adrienne Rich: Passion, Politics, and the Body.* Thousand Oaks, Calif.: Sage Publications, 1998.

DISCUSSION TOPICS

- Compare the more formal style of writing present in Adrienne Rich's early poetry, "Aunt Jennifer's Tigers" for example, to the experimental stylistic elements that mark her later works. Does the lack of uniformity in her later works encourage meaning or distract the reader?

- Rich's poetry is said to mimic themes of Emily Dickinson and, at times, her somber tone. What could Rich, as a twentieth century American woman, have in common with a woman born nearly one hundred years before her?

- One theme that permeates much of Rich's poetry is where and how one's private life intersects with one's public life. Where does this theme emerge in her poetry? Why might Rich be so focused on this relationship?

- Rich incorporates the limitations of language into much of her poetry, showing that while words are necessary, they almost always fall short of reflecting emotions accurately. Analyze this theme in the light of her role as a poet. What is to be gained by a writer calling attention to the restrictions of language?

- Rich is the mother of three sons. Where in her poetry are images of motherhood? What are Rich's opinions of motherhood in the light of her feminist rhetoric?

CONRAD RICHTER

Born: Pine Grove, Pennsylvania
October 13, 1890
Died: Pottsville, Pennsylvania
October 30, 1968

Best known for his fiction about pioneer life in Pennsylvania, Ohio, and the Southwest, Richter contributed significantly to the development of the realistic historical novel of American westward expansion.

BIOGRAPHY

Conrad Richter was born on October 13, 1890, in Pine Grove, Pennsylvania, the first of three sons of John Absalom and Charlotte Henry Richter. His ancestors were tradesmen, soldiers, blacksmiths, farmers, and ministers. As a boy accompanying his clergyman father on pastoral calls among the farm settlements and coal-mining regions of Pennsylvania, Richter carefully observed the manners and behavior of the people, developing a keen ear for their idiomatic language. He took note of their strength of character and sturdy fortitude in the face of hardships, values derived from their pioneer forebears.

Richter's family expected him to follow in his father's footsteps and become a clergyman. Accepting the assumptions of science with as much faith as his grandfather and father had accepted the assumptions of Christianity, however, he found himself doubting Christian beliefs. At the age of thirteen he declined a scholarship that would have taken him through preparatory school, college, and seminary on condition that he become a Lutheran minister.

Graduated from high school at the age of fifteen, Richter continued to educate himself, reading widely and working at various jobs as a teamster, mechanic, farm laborer, coal breaker, timberman, and bank clerk. Inspired by a series of articles about newspaper writers, he decided to become a journalist, reporting for and editing small-town newspapers and eventually working for *The Pittsburgh Dispatch*. Moving to Ohio in 1910, he wrote

for the *Johnstown Leader.* In 1913 he began to write short stories, and a year later *Forum* published his "Brothers of No Kin," a widely acclaimed work of fiction that Edward J. O'Brien selected for *The Best Short Stories of 1915.*

Disappointed by the low payment he received for his first serious fiction, Richter decided to concentrate his main energies on journalism and business, devoting his spare time to writing the kind of stories that brought a fair price. He married Harvena Achenbach of Pine Grove in 1915 and started a small publishing company and a juvenile periodical, *Junior Magazine Book.* Turning his hand to juvenile fiction, he wrote children's stories for his own periodical and other magazines. His daughter, Harvena, was born on March 13, 1917, and five years later Richter moved his family to a farm in Clark's Valley, Pennsylvania, where he continued his publishing work and the writing of fiction. In 1924, he had collected enough of his previously published stories to make up a volume titled *Brothers of No Kin, and Other Stories.*

While establishing himself as a journalist, publisher, and writer of fiction, Richter sought a scientific and factual explanation of the eternal enigmas. His desire to seek answers to questions about human nature and destiny led to his interest in widely discussed notions of evolution, psychology, and related aspects of physical and biological science. In 1925 he published a book-length essay, *Human Vibration: The Mechanics of Life and Mind;* this was followed by *Principles in Bio-Physics* (1927). Both books are serious, if amateurish, attempts to understand first causes, human vitality, the relationship of mind and body, and creative evolution. Their limited reception convinced Richter that he would do better to dramatize his ideas through fiction.

Because of his wife's failing health, Richter sold his business and moved his family to Albuquerque, New Mexico, in 1928. His philosophical ideas and growing discontent with the modern drift toward an industrial, urban civilization kindled his interest in the frontier, and Richter decided in 1933 to become a writer of serious fiction, devoting himself to painstaking research in diaries, journals, and old newspaper accounts of frontier life in the Southwest. The short stories that grew out of this research were collected in *Early Americana, and Other Stories* (1936), marking the beginning of a distinguished career as a writer of fiction using American backgrounds. His first novel, *The Sea of Grass* (1936), was well received and was later made into a first-rate film.

In the decade from 1940 to 1950, Richter published six novels, including the Ohio trilogy—*The Trees* (1940), *The Fields* (1946), and *The Town* (1950)—and became widely recognized as an important historical novelist. The Society of Libraries of New York University awarded him the gold medal for literature for *The Sea of Grass* and *The Trees*. In 1944 he received an honorary doctoral degree from Susquehanna University, and three years later the Ohioana Library Medal Award for Literature. Although the historical trilogy was clearly at the center of Richter's attention during these years, he published another novel about the early Southwest, *Tacey Cromwell* (1942), and two less successful novels, *The Free Man* (1943) and *Always Young and Fair* (1947). At the end of the decade, he moved his family back to Pine Grove, the town of his birth. The following year (1951), he was awarded the Pulitzer Prize in fiction for *The Town*.

In the last fifteen years of his life Richter continued to publish impressive novels of American backgrounds and to gain recognition for his achievement. He explored complex racial relationships in *The Light in the Forest* (1953) and *A Country of Strangers* (1966), companion novels about the forcible repatriation of white people from Indian captivity. His third book-length essay, *The Mountain on the Desert* (1955), revealed his continuing interest in the psychological and mystical ideas that had always informed his fiction. After publishing his last southwestern novel, *The Lady* (1957), Richter received an honorary doctoral degree from the University of New Mexico (1958).

In 1960, he won the National Book Award for *The Waters of Kronos*, the first novel of a projected autobiographical trilogy, which was followed by *A Simple Honorable Man* (1962). Although Richter did not complete this trilogy, he published three more novels, *The Grandfathers* (1964), *Over the Blue Mountain* (1967), and *The Aristocrat* (1968). The Ohio trilogy was republished as *The Awakening Land* (1966) and later dramatized on television. Richter died of heart disease in Pottsville, Pennsylvania, on October 30, 1968. *The Rawhide Knot, and Other Stories*, a collection of his short stories, was published posthumously in 1978.

ANALYSIS

Richter's literary reputation rests chiefly on his achievement in writing the historical novel. In his fictional recovery of the past, he avoided the weaknesses and limitations inherent in the genre of historical fiction. He shunned the costume romance, with its emphasis on action, exciting narratives of adventure and love, and sensational events. He had no interest in the novel of recognizable events or personages or in the fictionalized biography of important men and women. At the same time, he eschewed the period novel, which is more concerned with background details than with the whole of life.

Richter knew that his strength as a writer lay in his ability to keep in touch with the living muscle and tissue of actual experience, to keep the destiny of common people central to his vision. He believed that the greatest influence on historical events was the broader stuff of reality lived by the majority of men and women who led quiet, obscure lives but who found life endlessly resourceful and inexhaustible. To recapture the spirit and flavor of an age as revealed in the everyday relations of people, Richter steeped himself in the documents of social history—diaries, journals, letters, newspapers, and oral histories.

The desire to give fictional form to the experience of American westering derived in large part from Richter's homespun theories of human behavior and destiny. Although his speculative theories, which he named "psycho-energies," are too complex and esoteric to consider in detail, it is important to see their relationship to his major themes. According to Michael, the rug-weaving philosopher in Richter's *The Mountain on the Desert*, the distinguishing feature of life is limited energy, and the basic primal motive is energy hunger. Creative growth, which requires the body and mind to expend energy, is the purpose of being. This growth is always accompanied by pain or discomfort; to remove all occasions of disharmony or suffering results in the stifling of creative growth. Moreover, human attempts to avoid hardship and suffering are inevitably thwarted by a mystical force that Richter calls fate or destiny. Natural adversity will ensure creative growth, and people can cooperate with this cosmic plan by practicing self-discipline and embracing a lifestyle that values hardihood.

Richter's fiction invariably reflects his belief that the universe uses hardship and discipline to ensure human progress. The implications he draws from this life pattern account for most recurring themes in his fiction: adversity and hardship as a means of growth, the development of higher intelligence wrought by experience, the intuition of a cosmic destiny ordering human affairs, the stoic conception of *amor fati* (love of the order of God), and the superiority of the primitive and natural over the civilized and artificial.

All of Richter's narratives are implicitly concerned with the relationship of the past to the present. His knowledge of the American past provided him with a well-defined historical image of a change in the human condition attended by cultural loss. This accounts for the persistent lyrical and elegiac tone of his fiction; there is undeniable nostalgia, but Richter stops short of sentimentality by revealing the human weaknesses and failings as well as the courage and strength that emerge under the pressure of harsh reality. In *The Sea of Grass*, for example, he tells the story of a people and land ravaged by years of conflict and change as the cattleman resists the homesteader in the battle for the ranges of Texas and New Mexico.

The focus of the story, however, is not on sensational events (violence is normally muted and off-stage) but on certain distinguishing traits in the major characters brought out by the conflict—Colonel Brewton's practical intelligence, hardiness, and self-discipline, in contrast to the shrewd opportunist Chamberlin, who relies on political influence and the collective will to impose an agricultural economy on a fragile range environment suited only to stock raising.

The Ohio trilogy similarly offers an interpretation and judgment of the cultural loss that accompanied the change from a harsh frontier to a settled civilization. Richter's sense of the continuity of past and present enabled him to weave into a meaningful whole the epic strands of the archetypal American experience: the nomadic penetration into primeval wilderness in *The Trees*, the clearing and cultivation of the land in *The Fields*, and in *The Town*, the growth of community from the soil and the inevitable emergence of an industrial civilization and mode of life that threaten to erode something vital in the human spirit.

The narrative is objectified in the experiences of a pioneer family through four generations. The heroine, Sayward Luckett Wheeler, one of Richter's most memorable characters, is strong, elemental, and determined to survive. The surface narrative of Sayward's life is effectively connected with a background meaning: the cosmic role of hardship and adversity as a means of growth. The theme of cosmic order and individual destiny thus gives unity to the three novels by providing a principle for selecting those details and episodes that enable Richter to coordinate structure and meaning.

As useful as Richter's theories are in understanding the design of his work, however, it is his artistic transmutation of historical materials into realistic narratives that gives his novels enduring appeal. From the beginning, Richter's aim was to give the sensation of living in the past by re-creating the details and authenticities of early life in a style suggestive of the times. Richter defines a story as the record of human achievement; he thus reveals his meanings in terms of characterization. He conveys habits of mind, indigenous patterns of speech, and characteristic actions—all embedded in authentic folk traditions—in a simple, colloquial style, rich in feeling and precise in the rendering of effect. The form of his fiction, rooted in the novella, is essentially episodic, concentrating on central situations that reveal character. Striking an artistic balance in blending fact and fiction, he effectively integrates character, setting, and action. The overall effect is of careful artistry, classical condensation, and emotional restraint.

THE LIGHT IN THE FOREST

First published: 1953
Type of work: Novel

When a white boy raised by Indians is repatriated to his family, he cannot readjust to civilization or reconcile the claims of blood and loyalty.

In *The Light in the Forest*, Richter presents the Indians' point of view toward the settlement of the wilderness, putting an unusual twist on the traditional captivity tale: He tells the story of a white boy who resents being returned to his natural parents. John Butler was only four years old when Delaware Indians captured him during a raid on his father's farm in western Pennsylvania. Adopted by a tribal chief and renamed True Son, he lived for more than a decade in the Ohio wilderness until Colonel Bouquet's treaty with the Delaware Indians called for the repatriation of all white captives. On True Son's reluctant journey to the Paxton settlement, he sees an ancient sycamore that symbolizes his predicament. A dead limb points toward the white settlement, while a live branch points back toward his beloved Indian culture. The conflict in the story turns on these two claims to his loyalty.

Stubbornly insisting on his Indian identity, True Son refuses all efforts to reinstate him into the life of family and community. His invalid mother seems ineffectual, and his father preoccupied with business ledgers and property. Only his little brother, Gordon, provides comfort and companionship. True Son reserves his greatest hostility for his uncle, Wilse Owens, an Indian-hater and one of the Paxton Boys, who had massacred Indian women and children in an earlier reprisal against the Conestoga.

True Son's smoldering resentment at his "captivity" in the white settlement reaches a crisis when Half Arrow, his adopted Indian cousin, visits one night to show True Son the body of Little Crane, slain when he tried to visit his repatriated white wife. True Son confronts his uncle, accusing him of the murder. In the ensuing struggle, Half Arrow wounds Owens, and the two boys flee after failing to get Owens's scalp as a trophy.

True Son's reunion with his Indian family is joyful but short-lived. Joining Cuyloga, his Indian fa-

ther, and a group of braves in a war party to avenge Little Crane's death, True Son is appalled to see one of the warriors massacre and scalp little children. The warriors compel him to serve as a decoy to lure white settlers into an ambush and thereby prove his loyalty, but he cannot repudiate his blood ties to white people, and he warns the intended victims. This betrayal causes Cuyloga to reject his adopted son, declaring him an enemy and banishing him from the tribe. Adrift between two cultures, True Son cries in despair, "Then who is my father?"

The details, anecdotes, and incidents Richter derived from his historical sources enabled him to provide an authentic sensation of life on the Pennsylvania-Ohio frontier without the distortions of sensationalism or sentimentality. Although objective in his portrayal of both the Delaware Indians and the white settlers, Richter carefully controls the narrative point of view, rendering most of the experience through True Son's consciousness. This allows Richter to convey the poetic imagery and idioms of Indian thought and language as True Son expresses delight in the wild, joyous free-

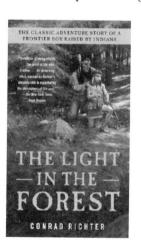

dom of the natural world and disgust at the white people's thoughtless destruction of the forest; their building of fences, walls, and roofs to shut out nature; and their relentless accumulation of material wealth. One of Richter's aims in writing the novel was "to point out that in the pride of our American liberties, we're apt to forget that already we've lost a good many to civilization."

True Son's predicament objectifies the theme of the organic unity of humans and nature inevitably giving way to the restrictions of civilization in the historical process of westering. It also dramatizes the archetypal experience of youth who must give up an idyllic and secure child's world and take on the responsibilities of adulthood, with its painful moral choices. His discovery that hateful racial prejudice exists in both Indian and white culture and his costly moral choice at the climax of the

Conrad Richter

story reflect his spiritual maturation and intuitive understanding of the need for brotherhood. The novel's conclusion is a concession to harsh reality: True Son must accommodate his alienation and work out his own identity without the guidance of an earthly father or the comfort of a sustaining cultural community.

SUMMARY

One of the values of literature is that it gives form to life so that it may be analyzed and understood—a particularly formidable task when that life must be reconstructed from the past. Richter's fictional recovery of the past and celebration of traditional values will strike some as old-fashioned, especially those who equate progress with comfort and values with expediency. Yet no American writer has more successfully re-created in fiction that early American quality of strength and hardihood. Richter truly enables his readers to understand, feel, and sense what it was like to live in earlier times.

Clifford Edwards

DISCUSSION TOPICS

- Conrad Richter's fiction has received very little critical attention in recent years. What qualities in his works can account for this neglect?

- What do *The Light in the Forest* and *A Country of Strangers* say about racial relations in the United States?

- How do the ideas explored in *The Mountain on the Desert* help in understanding Richter's fiction?

- What is Richter's fiction saying about the relationship of the past to the present?

- How is the Ohio trilogy unified thematically?

- One of Richter's major strengths is said to be his skill at characterization. Analyze the complexities of one of his protagonists.

BIBLIOGRAPHY

By the Author

LONG FICTION:
The Sea of Grass, 1936
The Trees, 1940
Tacey Cromwell, 1942
The Free Man, 1943
The Fields, 1946
Always Young and Fair, 1947
The Town, 1950
The Light in the Forest, 1953
The Lady, 1957
The Waters of Kronos, 1960
A Simple Honorable Man, 1962
The Grandfathers, 1964
The Awakening Land, 1966 (includes *The Trees*, *The Fields*, and *The Town*)
A Country of Strangers, 1966
The Aristocrat, 1968

SHORT FICTION:
Brothers of No Kin, and Other Stories, 1924
Early Americana, and Other Stories, 1936
The Rawhide Knot, and Other Stories, 1978

NONFICTION:
Human Vibration: The Mechanics of Life and Mind, 1925
Principles in Bio-Physics, 1927
The Mountain on the Desert, 1955
A Philosophical Journey, 1955

CHILDREN'S LITERATURE:
Over the Blue Mountain, 1967

About the Author

Barnes, Robert J. *Conrad Richter.* Austin, Tex.: Steck-Vaughn, 1968.

Carpenter, Frederic I. "Conrad Richter's Pioneers: Reality and Myth." *College English* 12 (1950): 77-84.

Cowan, William. "Delaware Vocabulary in the Works of Conrad Richter." In *Papers of the Twenty-ninth Algonquian Conference,* edited by David H. Pentland. Winnipeg: University of Manitoba Press, 1998.

Edwards, Clifford D. *Conrad Richter's Ohio Trilogy.* The Hague, Netherlands: Mouton, 1970.

Flanagan, John T. "Conrad Richter: Romancer of the Southwest." *Southwest Review* 43 (1958): 189-196.

Gaston, Edwin W., Jr. *Conrad Richter.* Rev. ed. Boston: G. K. Hall, 1989.

Johnson, David R. *Conrad Richter: A Writer's Life.* University Park: Pennsylvania State University Press, 2001.

Kohler, Dayton. "Conrad Richter's Early Americana." *College English* 7 (1947): 221-228.

Courtesy, Oberlin College Special Collections

EDWIN ARLINGTON ROBINSON

Born: Head Tide, Maine
December 22, 1869
Died: New York, New York
April 6, 1935

In his poems, Robinson created lonely characters and unusual situations to hint at the uncomfortable mysteriousness of human existence. Without providing answers, his writings encourage readers to wonder why things happen as they do (causality) and especially why humans behave as they do (motive).

BIOGRAPHY

The son of Mary Elizabeth Palmer and Edward Robinson, Edwin Arlington Robinson was born on December 22, 1869, in Head Tide, Maine. Although he grew up in the small-town environment of Gardiner, Maine, fortunate childhood friends led to the cultivation of his taste for poetry and the classics. Robinson fell in love with Emma Shepherd in 1887 but encouraged her to marry his brother in 1890 in part because he felt that his devotion to writing would be unfair to her.

While Robinson attended Harvard University between 1891 and 1893, his father's death in 1892 and a worldwide economic depression in 1893 took a heavy toll on his family's timber business. Financial hardship forced Robinson to return home, where both his morphine-addicted brother and his mortally ill mother needed care. In 1896, the year his mother died, Robinson self-published *The Torrent and the Night Before*, which he revised the following year and self-published as *The Children of the Night*. Fleeing his lingering feelings for Emma and evidence of her unhappy marriage, Robinson moved in 1897 to New York City, where he steadily sank into poverty.

After President Theodore Roosevelt's favorable review of *The Children of the Night*, Scribner's re-released the book in 1905. This volume introduced readers to Tilbury Town, Robinson's fictional small community of lonely dreamers and enigmatic ec-

centrics battered by life. The book included poems that later would be frequently anthologized: "Luke Havergal," "Reuben Bright," "Cliff Klingenhagen," and especially "Richard Cory." Such popularity was slow to arrive, however, because critics generally ignored or dismissed *The Children of the Night* and also his next book, *Captain Craig* (1902). Robinson languished in poverty until Roosevelt assigned him to a customs house, where, until 1909, his unofficial job was to write poetry.

The Town Down the River (1910), Robinson's next book, was dedicated to Roosevelt and earned some positive critical attention. His reputation also received a boost from *The Man Against the Sky* (1916), which was particularly praised by the influential poet Amy Lowell. After four more books, Robinson's *Collected Poems* (1921) was published and won a Pulitzer Prize. His *The Man Who Died Twice* (1924) won another Pulitzer, and *Tristram* (1927) took a third Pulitzer, after which Robinson was financially comfortable until the end of his life. He died of stomach cancer on April 6, 1935, in New York City.

ANALYSIS

Although during his lifetime Robinson's long narrative poems, particularly *Tristram*, stirred admiration, his short poems set in Tilbury Town became much more popular in subsequent decades. Since these short poems follow established verse patterns (such as the sonnet form), their familiar structures at first seem old-fashioned. These poems, however, are hardly time-locked. Instead, they are thoroughly modern in attitude because their stories stress how difficult it is to detect cause or motive in a basically mysterious world. The poems also emphasize how people cannot escape a sense of personal isolation. In Robinson's Tilbury Town, people feel lonely because of the limitations of their individual ways of making sense of human experience. As a result, Robinson's readers are left with shifting truths and unclear explanations about the meaning of life.

Beneath the deceptive, smooth surfaces of the technically precise poetic forms, Robinson's poems are disturbing, cheerless stories of people living far from their youthful hopes and dreams. The old-fashioned structures of these works, then, are misleading. These familiar verse forms contribute to the poet's theme that the reassuring appearances which humans tend to trust in life are deceptive. Some deeper meaning lies beneath such ordinary appearances, but unfortunately, this deeper meaning behind people's unavoidable disillusionment always remains beyond their understanding.

Sometimes Robinson pinpoints specific factors that contribute to human unhappiness. The detrimental impact of industrialism on individual lives, for example, is featured in "The Mill." "The Clerks" highlights the loss of cultural values in a commerce-driven world, the same world where the narrator of "Karma" has lost his human values. In "Richard Cory," economic circumstances and class boundaries take a dreadful toll. Gender disparities and social expectations concerning men and women figure in "The Tree in Pamela's Garden" and "Eros Turannos." "Miniver Cheevy" and "Flammonde" dramatize the gap between dreamy hopes and uncontrollable circumstances, while "Ben Trovato" raises questions about truth when people try to see the best in others. Time's erosion of the human spirit is dramatized in "Mr. Flood's Party," while the limits of what anyone, even a doctor, can do for another person are assessed in "How Annandale Went Out."

However, for Robinson, such specific issues always point to some much larger and unknowable explanation for the general sadness haunting humanity. That larger something is hinted at in "The Haunted House," in which a married couple suddenly sense the scary possibility that they might not really know each other. Robinson's work suggests that loneliness, a sense of separation from one an-

other, and also from ultimate meanings, is an inescapable human condition. The best humans or art such as Robinson's can do is sympathetically acknowledge the tragedy of unfilled longing, even though this compassion makes little or no difference in the tragic outcome of human hopes.

"RICHARD CORY"

First published: 1897 (collected in *Collected Poems*, 1937)
Type of work: Poem

The impoverished citizens of Tilbury Town admire wealthy Richard Cory and are baffled by his suicide.

"Richard Cory," which first appeared in *The Children of the Night* and remains one of Robinson's most popular poems, recalls the economic depression of 1893. At that time, people could not afford meat and had a diet mainly of bread, often day-old bread selling for less than freshly baked goods. This hard-times experience made the townspeople even more aware of Richard's difference from them, so much so that they treated him as royalty.

Although the people were surprised that Richard came to town dressed "quietly" and that he was "always human when he talked" (that is, he did not act superior), they nonetheless distanced themselves from him. This distance is suggested by the narrator's words "crown," "imperially," "grace," "fluttered pulses," and "glittered." The townspeople never stopped to consider why Richard dressed and spoke the way he did, why he came to town when everyone else was there, or even why he tried to make contact with them by saying "good morning."

Richard was wealthy, but (as his name hints) he was not rich at the life-core of himself. Despite his efforts at communal connection, Richard's wealth isolated him from others. He was alone. If the townspeople wished they were in his place because of his wealth, he in turn wished he were one of them because they were rich in one another's company. The townspeople failed to appreciate the value of their mutual support of one another, their nurturing communal togetherness. So one hot, breezeless summer night (before the availability of electric fans or air conditioners), Richard lay awake, unable to sleep or to stop painful thoughts. Depressingly lonely, he ended his friendless life. The poem's reader is supposed to understand what the townspeople did not understand about Richard's suicide: that there was a price, in a human rather than in a monetary sense, that he paid for being perceived to be "richer than a king."

"MINIVER CHEEVY"

First published: 1907 (collected in *Collected Poems*, 1937)

Type of work: Poem

Miniver Cheevy, an alcoholic who has accomplished nothing in his life, believes that he would have been successful if he had been born centuries earlier.

"Miniver Cheevy," which first appeared in *Scribner's Magazine* and later in *The Town Down the River*, presents a character whose name suits him. His name sounds as if it belongs to the medieval past that he wishes still existed. His name also satirically hints at his minimal achievements in life. Miniver maintains that he was born too late, that he should have lived many centuries ago. He childishly romanticizes the Greeks' siege of Troy, Alexander the Great's attack on Thebes, and King Arthur's combat near Camelot, as if such battles were fun. Such mistaken fantasies of past warfare inform his rejection of the khaki military uniform of his own time as too deficient in grandeur. When Miniver speaks of the gracefulness of medieval armor, the outlandishness of his claim is evident because medieval body armor was not graceful.

Besides modern warfare, Miniver finds fault with contemporary politics, which he says fails in comparison to the Renaissance rule of the passionate Medicis in Florence, Italy. Believing he should have been born rich, Miniver will not work and looks down on people who succeed financially. The more readers hear about Miniver, the angrier he seems to become until he curses the change of seasons. This moment, like his notion of graceful body armor, undercuts Miniver's credibility. It is senseless to rail at something so natural and inevitable as the change of the seasons or the passage of time.

When in the last stanza Miniver coughs and "call[s] it fate," for him the word "it" refers to his ill-timed life. However, the immediate referent of that word is "cough," and by joining of two meanings around "it," the narrator suggests that Miniver's life is finally no more significant than a mere cough. Notable, too, are the rhymed stanza lines ending in two syllables. The second "weak" syllable of each of these rhymes is not stressed, a limp-ending effect that conveys a sense of Miniver's lack of personal courage.

The satiric tone of this poem makes clear that the narrator disapproves of Miniver's outlandish excuses, his self-serving thoughts, and his drinking to drown his discontents. However, Miniver's interior self is unavailable to readers, leaving an unanswered question: Is he only a dreamer whose experience of disappointments has led him to drink, or is he merely a drunk who speaks of disappointments only to justify himself? Since readers are unable to answer these questions for sure, their moral judgment of Miniver is hampered by what they do not know about him.

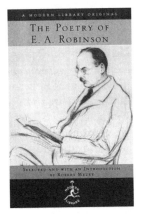

"FLAMMONDE"

First published: 1915 (collected in *Collected Poems*, 1937)

Type of work: Poem

A man who hints that he is descended from royalty charms various Tilbury Town residents into paying for his upkeep.

"Flammonde," which first appeared in the magazine *The Outlook* and later in *The Man Against the Sky* (1916), depicts a con-artist loner with a secret background who one day suddenly appeared in Tilbury

Town and then just as suddenly disappeared. Aged fifty and bearing a French name, Flammonde encouraged people to compare him to royalty. He represented himself as "the Prince of Castaways" as if some European event well before World War I had "banished him from better days." Although most likely his background was actually disreputable (tarnished), he nonetheless succeeded in conning people. A surprising number of sympathetic townsfolk aided him financially. "What he needed for his fee/ To live, he borrowed graciously." These so-called loans would never be repaid.

A fraud, one normally thinks, would have a negative impact on people. Oddly, Flammonde had a positive influence. He revised the community's image of a woman with a "scarlet" reputation. He also productively tutored a boy whom others thought was uneducable. He ended a long-standing feud between two townsfolk, among other notable good effects in Tilbury Town. In short, Flammonde was able to help people prosper, although paradoxically he was never able to help himself succeed in life. After he vanished from town, he left people wondering about who he really was and what inner secrets were hidden behind the protective "shield" of his charming personality. Flammonde (whose name translates into "flame of humanity") represents the unpredictable successes and failures, as well as the unexplainable gap between surface impressions and inner self, that generally dominate human experience.

sees underscores his situation. Harvested crops have a use at the end of their cycle, whereas Eben has outlived the late-autumn stage of his life and is of no use to anyone, not even to himself. The townspeople do not welcome him, probably because they think he is a mere drunk. He is so lonely that, tipsy with drink on the way to his empty hilltop house, he talks to himself as if he were two people celebrating together.

There is, however, more to Eben Flood than meets the townspeople's eye. Despite his name's close sound to "ebb and flow," they do not think about what ups and downs he may have experienced in his life. Unlike the townsfolk, readers overhear Eben and learn that he believes everyone leads "uncertain lives" in a hard world where precious "things break" all too easily. When he says this, he is remembering the loss of his family and his many long-gone friends.

In his younger years, Eben apparently possessed an appreciation of the arts, especially poetry. He still quotes from folk poet Robert Burns ("For auld lang syne") and Edward FitzGerald's famous translation of *The Rubáiyát of Omar Khayyám* ("the bird is on the wing"). Now his birdlike inner spirit lifts up with drink instead of verse. However, it is a sorry substitute, "like Roland's ghost winding a silent horn." In the epic poem *The Song of Roland*, young Roland blew his ivory horn to summon help from his king; in contrast, old Eben's raised jug in the night far from town is a hopeless gesture silently summoning only cheerless memories.

"MR. FLOOD'S PARTY"

First published: 1920 (collected in *Collected Poems*, 1937)
Type of work: Poem

During an autumn night, Eben Flood, old and friendless, slowly walks toward his empty home while drinking and talking to himself about the sorry outcome of time's passage.

"Mr. Flood's Party," which first appeared in *The Nation* and later in *Avon's Harvest* (1921), is a sad portrait of a friendless man who has witnessed "many a change" and has now outlived his time. Eben feels that he has lived too long. The harvest moon he

"DEMOS AND DIONYSUS"

First published: 1925 (collected in *Collected Poems*, 1937)
Type of work: Poem

In a conversation, Dionysus defends the independence of the human spirit while Demos insists on a rational end to the disorder that comes from such freedom.

"Demos and Dionysus," which first appeared in *Theatre Arts Monthly* and later in *Dionysus in Doubt* (1925), is a heated dialogue between two characters: Dionysus, whose name recalls the ancient

Greek wine god associated with the resurrection of new life each spring, and Demos, whose name derives from the word for ancient Greek administrative districts that governed local citizens. Together they represent competing impulses within humanity. Dionysus defends human freedom, an independence of inner spirit that fosters love and art. Demos dismisses love and art as merely frivolous "playing" with "feeling and with unprofitable fancy." Disgusted by "the insurgent individual/ With his free fancy and his free this and that," Demos wants people to be controlled by a more economically productive rationality.

Dionysus speaks for Robinson, who viewed forced social conformity, including the eighteenth constitutional amendment prohibiting the sale of alcohol in 1919, as a threat to human happiness and creativity as well as to American democracy. Dionysus calls Demos's version of utopia a prison of "amiable automatons" (robots) and "compliant slaves." He also contends that Demos hides a secret desire behind his efforts to convert the world into a beehive of worker drones. He accuses Demos of deceitfully wearing a "suave and benevolent mask" to conceal his real motives, which he "dare not show" to his followers. His secret is the wish to be the king over subdued humanity, though Dionysus substitutes the word "tyrant" for "king."

Demos's impulse to order the self only toward productive ends derives from within humans just as does Dionysus's love of unruly, creative freedom. The Demos side of humanity has a legitimate claim, and so does the Dionysus side. Humans experience a tug-of-war between both inclinations. However, Robinson maintains that trouble develops when one side gets out of balance. Robinson remains hopeful despite the problems he sees in the 1920's. Demos may win for now, Robinson suggests, but not forever because the joyous and free Dionysian spirit in humanity always returns like the season of spring.

SUMMARY

Edwin Arlington Robinson does not conclude his poems with explanations for the situations depicted in them. The reader must carefully look for clues in the wording of the poetry in order to piece together each story's puzzle. Still, there are many missing pieces, and this poet-managed insufficiency of detail always prevents the reader from putting together the whole story. So many missing pieces likewise tend to prevent the reader from making easy moral judgments about Richard Cory, Miniver Cheevy, Flammonde, Eben Flood, or even Demos.

William J. Scheick

BIBLIOGRAPHY

By the Author

POETRY:
The Torrent and the Night Before, 1896
The Children of the Night, 1897
Captain Craig, 1902, 1915
The Town Down the River, 1910
The Man Against the Sky, 1916
Merlin, 1917
Lancelot, 1920
The Three Taverns, 1920
Avon's Harvest, 1921
Collected Poems, 1921, 1927, 1929, 1937
Roman Bartholow, 1923
The Man Who Died Twice, 1924
Dionysus in Doubt, 1925
Tristram, 1927
Sonnets, 1889-1927, 1928

Cavender's House, 1929
The Glory of the Nightingales, 1930
Matthias at the Door, 1931
Nicodemus, 1932
Talifer, 1933
Amaranth, 1934
King Jasper, 1935

DRAMA:
Van Zorn, pb. 1914
The Porcupine, pb. 1915

NONFICTION:
Selected Letters of Edwin Arlington Robinson, 1940
Untriangulated Stars: Letters of Edwin Arlington Robinson to Harry de Forest Smith, 1890-1905, 1947
Edwin Arlington Robinson's Letters to Edith Brower, 1968

MISCELLANEOUS:
Uncollected Poems and Prose of Edwin Arlington Robinson, 1975

About the Author

Anderson, Wallace L. *Edwin Arlington Robinson: A Critical Introduction.* Boston: Houghton Mifflin, 1968.

Bloom, Harold, ed. *Edwin Arlington Robinson.* New York: Chelsea House, 1988.

Coxe, Louis. *Edwin Arlington Robinson: The Life of Poetry.* New York: Pegasus, 1969.

Franchere, Hoyt C. *Edwin Arlington Robinson.* New York: Twayne, 1968.

Joyner, Nancy Carol. *Edwin Arlington Robinson: A Reference Guide.* Boston: G. K. Hall, 1978.

Murphy, Francis, ed. *Edwin Arlington Robinson: A Collection of Critical Essays.* Englewood Cliffs, N.J.: Prentice-Hall, 1970.

Smith, Chard Powers. *Where the Light Falls: A Portrait of Edwin Arlington Robinson.* New York: Macmillan, 1965.

DISCUSSION TOPICS

- In Edwin Arlington Robinson's "Richard Cory," if the townspeople had guessed Cory's need for their companionship, would they have been able to rescue him from his loneliness?

- Would Miniver Cheevy have behaved differently if he had actually been born in an earlier time period?

- In "Mr. Flood's Party," why is Eben Flood said to wear an "armor of scarred hopes outworn"?

- Just how good was Flammonde at winning people over to voluntarily finance his stay in Tilbury Town?

- What is suggested about human nature when Dionysus accuses Demos of wearing a mask to cover up his true motives?

THEODORE ROETHKE

Courtesy, University of Michigan

Born: Saginaw, Michigan
    May 25, 1908
Died: Bainbridge Island, Washington
    August 1, 1963

Roethke was one of the leading personal, confessional, and nature poets of the twentieth century, reaffirming the principles of the Romantic movement for the modern period.

BIOGRAPHY

The circumstances of Theodore Roethke's birth and childhood were very important for his development as a poet. Roethke was born in 1908 in Saginaw, Michigan, to a family of gardeners and florists. His father and uncle built and maintained a huge greenhouse complex, considered one of the best in the United States and used primarily to grow roses, orchids, and other ornamental plants. Roethke grew up in the midst of this fecundity, and in later years he returned to it in memory and spirit as the source of inspiration and power in his poetry.

Although Roethke's father loved his son, and that love was returned, there was conflict between them. Otto Roethke was an outdoorsman and wanted his son to be a "man's man" and a lawyer. Young Ted was clumsy at sports and outdoor activities, and he preferred books and the life of the mind and imagination. The Roethke brothers sold the greenhouse in 1922, and the next year, when Theodore was only fourteen, his father died, dealing his son a wound and a sense of unfulfillment that the poet was able to relieve only near the end of his life. Subconsciously, Roethke felt that his father had betrayed and abandoned him by dying; consciously, he believed that he had a debt to his father which he had to repay.

After Roethke graduated from high school in Saginaw, he attended the University of Michigan, receiving a bachelor of arts degree in 1929. He then attended graduate school at Harvard University but did not take a degree, returning to the University of Michigan for a master of arts diploma in 1936. Although Roethke had always been interested in literature (he subscribed to *The Dial* when he was in the seventh grade), at Harvard he began to write poetry seriously and was encouraged to publish it. From that time on, it was clear to him that it was his destiny to be a poet, and he devoted as much of his time as possible to studying the poets of the past, writing notes and lines, and trying to improve his craft. He published in journals and magazines throughout the 1930's and produced his first volume of poems, *Open House*, in 1941.

Meanwhile, Roethke earned a living through a series of teaching jobs, which was the way he was to sustain himself for the rest of his life. His first appointment was at what was then Michigan State College in 1935, and there began another feature of Roethke's life which was both disturbing and, finally, transforming. Roethke lost his job at Michigan State after only one semester because of a mental breakdown which required hospitalization. The nature and cause of his illness were never determined; he was diagnosed with familiar catch-all designations—paranoid schizophrenia and manic depression—and several times again he became unable to deal with everyday life and had to be institutionalized.

It is unknown whether Roethke's mental problems were based on something in his upbringing (perhaps his strained relationship with his father) or were congenital. Whatever their cause, Roethke was quite insecure, demanding the constant approval of those around him and finding it difficult even to maintain a public personality. This affliction caused great pain and humiliation for Roethke and much sorrow and discomfort for his friends. He was refused service in World War II because of his condition, and when courting his future wife, he did not tell her of his mental problems. Later in life Roethke began to see his illness as a gateway to new imaginative and spiritual realms, and he allied himself proudly with other "mad" poets such as Christopher Smart and William Blake.

In spite of his inner turmoil, Roethke found his life as a poet and academician continuing to grow. In 1936 he obtained a position at Pennsylvania State University, where he also coached the tennis team, and he remained there until 1943, when he moved to Bennington College. There he had the good fortune to meet a brilliant group of faculty members, including literary critic and semanticist Kenneth Burke, who admired Roethke's poetry and urged him to continue to develop his own style and outlook. The result of this stimulation from Burke and others, along with Roethke's hard work, was the breakthrough volume *The Lost Son, and Other Poems* (1948). In this volume Roethke produced the emotionally strongest poems he had yet written in a manner that was his alone. He was now a significant poet with a message and voice of his own.

After his appointment at Bennington ended in 1946, he returned to Pennsylvania State for one semester in 1947 and then moved to the University of Washington the same year. He would remain in Seattle, except for occasional trips abroad (such as when he won two Guggenheim Fellowships and a Ford Foundation Fellowship), for the rest of his life. Poems and collections continued to come, and with them increasing critical recognition. *Praise to the End!* appeared in 1951; *The Waking, Poems, 1933-1953*, for which he won the Pulitzer Prize, in 1953; and *Words for the Wind*, a collection of previous work and new material for which he won both the Bollingen Prize and the National Book Award, in 1958. Roethke also wrote two books for children, *I Am! Says the Lamb* (1961) and *Party at the Zoo* (1963). While on a visit to New York in 1952, he happened to meet one of his former students at Bennington,

Beatrice O'Connell, and the two were married early in 1953. She was both an inspiration and a helpmate to him for the rest of his life.

In 1962, Roethke was awarded the title Poet in Residence at the University of Washington, but his physical health had begun to decline. On August 1, 1963, while he was swimming, he was stricken with a massive heart attack and died. The volume of poems he had been preparing, *The Far Field*, was published posthumously in 1964; it, too, won the National Book Award. Some critics have said that many of the poems in that book suggest that their author knew that his days were short. *The Collected Poems of Theodore Roethke*, containing most of his published work, appeared in 1966. Roethke's reputation has continued to grow since his death. He is recognized as one of the major American poets of the twentieth century, influencing not only a younger group of poets who were his students, such as James Wright and David Wagoner, but also previously established writers such as Robert Lowell and Sylvia Plath.

ANALYSIS

As Roethke used the world of nature as his primary source of inspiration and imagery, one can easily use an organic metaphor to describe the nature and growth of his poetry. Roethke believed, like the Romantics, that ultimate meaning grew from the encounter of the sensitive individual with nature in an attempt to determine personally the relationship between humankind and all existence. In his first volume, *Open House*, the seeds of Roethke's poetic thought have taken hold and are beginning to poke above the soil. They burst into full flower in the next volume, *The Lost Son, and Other Poems*; and in the succeeding volumes, *Praise to the End!*, *The Waking*, and *Words for the Wind*, the reader discovers not only blossoms and fruit but also the root system and nutrients (the subconscious mind) from which the poems spring. Finally, in the last volume, *The Far Field*, the poet's mind and his creation are seen not only close up but also in panorama as they assume their place in the entire biosphere—that is, the world wider than the life of one individual.

Open House, despite its expansive title, contains poems that are rather guarded in their expression. This was Roethke's first collection, and rather than hosting a party he is really knocking at the door, asking to be admitted to the company of poets. Roethke shows that he can manage traditional forms such as the sonnet and the Spenserian stanza, so that the emphasis is more on pleasing the assumed academic audience rather than saying what he himself wants to say in a manner that is unmistakably his. Nevertheless, a great artist finds his themes early, and the reader familiar with Roethke's career can easily recognize the preoccupations of his later work appearing like tendrils in a garden in early spring.

In the first and title poem, Roethke states that he will tell all his secrets and withhold nothing from the reader, but the poem remains on a general level, and the secrets are not named. The last two lines, however, produce a shudder: "Rage warps my clearest cry/ To witless agony." Roethke's mental illness had already asserted itself, and here the poet recognizes that this "secret" will be both a barrier to communication and a source of emotion for the rest of his life.

In "The Premonition," Roethke remembers trying to keep up with the wide strides of his father as they walked through the fields and the older man's dipping his hand into a stream so that his reflection was shattered. The poem suggests simultaneously the importance of nature in Roethke's life and poetry, Roethke's difficult relationship with his father, and Otto Roethke's death, which was to trouble the poet until late in his career. In "The Signals," Roethke maintains, "Sometimes the blood is privileged to guess/ The things the eye or hand cannot possess," indicating that he relies on intuition and nonrational knowledge more than most poets. In "For an Amorous Lady," he compares his lover to the snake, which enjoys giving as well as receiving caresses, in a poem which combines sensuality and humor in the manner of his best later love poems.

Roethke abandoned his attempt to please an audience of older, accepted poets in the poems collected in his next book, *The Lost Son, and Other Poems*. This volume contains the "greenhouse poems," which, his critics agree, mark the beginning of his career as an independent craftsman and which some think are his best work. In this series, Roethke returns in his imagination to the world of his childhood, finding there not only pleasant memories (such as in "Big Wind," which describes how everyone worked to save the roses in the green-

house during a bitterly cold and stormy night), but also scenes of horror and fright. "Root Cellar" tells of how the discarded bulbs, manure, and other greenhouse trash continued to put out roots and stems, stinking up the area but refusing to die: "Nothing would give up life:/ Even the dirt kept breathing a small breath."

In "Weed Puller," young Roethke is himself plunged into this dirty womb. As a child, he was small enough to get under the benches where the roses and other flowers grew in order to cut and pull away the roots and undergrowth that were not wanted. "Tugging all day at perverse life," young Roethke considered this work an "indignity," and describes it in such terms that it is almost revolting: "Me down in that fetor of weeds,/ Crawling on all fours,/ Alive, in a slippery grave." The word "fetor" suggests "fetus," combining both birth and death images. Although the emphasis in this poem is on the horror and fright of the young boy thrust into the grimy scene, later Roethke would use the union of life and death as a central theme of his poetry. Life both feeds upon death and arises from death; it is impossible to separate the two, which are part of the same process.

In this volume, Roethke sees nature not only as overwhelmingly powerful but also as a comforting friend. Here he comes closest to his Romantic predecessors, such as William Wordsworth and Samuel Taylor Coleridge, but there is a difference. While Wordsworth drew comfort from the quiet splendor of the English lake country and Coleridge admired the grandeur of the vale of Chamouni, in "The Minimal," Roethke examines the barely visible insects on a leaf, little beetles and lice. He finally comments on bacteria, which can be seen only with a microscope; each organism has its role to play in the cycle of life. Roethke is the poet of small nature: Toads, slugs, sparrows, and minnows are the heroes of his poems. They are the inspirers of his life, with their reminders that the nameless and the small are no less important than the large and famous, that—as another of Roethke's Romantic poetic models, William Blake, said—"Everything that lives is Holy."

Another theme with which Roethke grapples appears in the title poem of the volume, "The Lost Son." In this long, multipart, and multistyle poem, Roethke attempts to come to terms with his grief and guilt over the loss of his father and with his own mental illness. He dips into his unconscious to find a way out of his depression and confusion and regresses to childhood, using the meter and subject of nursery rhymes and childish taunts to gain some understanding of the roots of his problem. At the end of the poem, he has not attained understanding but at least finds solace.

The psychological investigation continues through the major poems in Roethke's next collection, *Praise to the End!*, the title of which is a quotation from Wordsworth. This volume contains more poems in the manner of "The Lost Son," poems in which Roethke dives into the subconscious, a psychic adventure expressed in the form of extremely short lines reminiscent of the thoughts and sensations of a child. These poems include the title poem, the remarkable "Where Knock Is Open Wide," "I Need, I Need," "Sensibility! O La!," and "Unfold! Unfold!" In some of these poems Roethke may be trying to hit a high note that no one else can hear, for many critics think that they plumb the subconscious so deeply that their meaning becomes lost in obscurity or in purely personal reference. To others, these poems present Roethke as most himself and provide a deep well from which interpretations and insights may be continually drawn.

In *The Waking*, Roethke continues the long confessional and personal poems but also begins to write poems of a more traditional form and content in which he acknowledges his kinship with and debt to other poets, chief among them W. B. Yeats (mentioned in "Four for Sir John Davies") and T. S. Eliot. From Yeats, Roethke borrowed the metaphor of the dance as a symbol for the totality and interaction of all life, as well as certain stylistic approaches to poetry: "I take this cadence from a man named Yeats;/ I take it, and I give it back again." (Roethke later said that it was not really the meter but the manner of writing poetry that he took from Yeats.) From Eliot, he took the bitter, almost conversational line reflecting the staleness and disappointment of modern life (as seen in "Old Lady's Winter Words"). The two earlier poets had also reacted to modern life by finding comfort in religion, and in this area Roethke shied away from Eliot's Anglo-Catholicism and favored the mysticism of Yeats.

In his earlier collections, Roethke had firmly established his own style and approach; now he could move back to the world of traditional poetry and not feel as if he were intruding. This new nimbleness produced poems that both pleased more traditional readers with their mastery of familiar and difficult poetic forms and satisfied Roethke's established audience with their presentation of his particular themes, such as the villanelle which provides the title of the book, "The Waking:" "I wake to sleep, and take my waking slow./ I learn by going where I have to go." This volume contains Roethke's most famous and frequently anthologized poem, "Elegy for Jane," a tribute to one of his students who died young.

Words for the Wind collected much of the previous work and also added some beautiful love poems which Roethke wrote after his marriage, such as "I Knew a Woman." The collection also contains another tribute to Yeats, "The Dying Man," and another multipart poem in which Roethke considers death by separating himself from the event by adopting the persona of his mother, "Meditations of an Old Woman." In his last book, the posthumous *The Far Field*, Roethke presents his most powerful expression of the mystic union with all life that sometimes resulted from his struggles with insanity, "In a Dark Time." The volume also includes a more conventional poem (in the manner of "Meditations of an Old Woman"), "North American Sequence," in which he describes his whole life as a journey across the northern United States from east to west, ending with a vision of a rose growing from the rocks on the Pacific Coast. The flower reminds him of his own childhood and life with his father, whose life and death he can now accept, as his own death approaches.

"CUTTINGS (LATER)"

First published: 1948 (collected in *The Collected Poems of Theodore Roethke*, 1966)
Type of work: Poem

The poet identifies with vegetable life reasserting itself in the face of death.

This poem, one of the most frequently reprinted of the "greenhouse" series, shows Roethke's close attention to the plant world and his identification with it. His sense of unity with the rest of life transcends the ordinary and becomes a spiritual experience, while at the same time remaining grounded in everyday reality. The highly emotional poem is also written using a style and themes that could only be Roethke's.

As in "Root Cellar," the discarded cuttings from the greenhouse refuse to die, putting forth new shoots and roots although they are only the mutilated parts of other plants. When Roethke compares the "struggling" plants to tortured saints trying to return to their religious battles, the spiritual connection between the human and vegetable world is established. It is made more definite in the second verse paragraph, in which the poet himself identifies with the chopped up, but still living, plants. He implies that his growth also comes as a result of a long struggle, for it has come "at last." The last two lines introduce a familiar motif, fish, with which Roethke was fascinated for a number of reasons (one of which was their ability to thrive in a mysterious other world which humans can only visit), and a familiar theme, birth ("sheath-wet") combined with fear ("I quail"). Birth, the inevitable result of the struggle for life, must happen, but it is terrifying for the new creature to be thrust into the living world.

"THE LOST SON"

First published: 1948 (collected in *The Lost Son, and Other Poems*, 1948)
Type of work: Poem

A son, grieving for his father, returns to the world of his childhood in an attempt to comprehend and assuage his loss.

"The Lost Son" has five parts—"The Flight," "The Pit," "The Gibber," "The Return," and "'It Was Beginning Winter'"—each of which describes a stage in the grief of the poetic persona (in this case, surely Roethke himself). The poet works through the various stages of his feelings of sorrow and desolation to reach a conclusion which is not really a relief of his feelings but a hope for future solace.

Part 1, "The Flight," begins with a reference to a cemetery ("Woodlawn"), and it is from this place and the fact of death that the flight occurs. From other references later in the poem, one can deduce that the death which has so shocked the poet is that of his father. Although the poet hopes to find some comfort in the little creatures of nature and specifically asks them to help him, he receives no such comfort: "Nothing nibbled my line,/ Not even the minnows came."

He feels alone and isolated and specifically asks for help, praying not to God but to the creatures of nature to tell him something and give him some sign. They only answer him in riddles ("The moon said, back of an eel") and in negatives: "You will find no comfort here,/ In the kingdom of bang and blab." As if in response to this comment, the section ends with a riddle posed by the poet which describes a strange creature, part land animal and part amphibian. Critics have suggested that the creature is an unborn child, and this answer compels the poet to delve deeper into his unconscious mind, back even further than childhood, to find the relief for his fear and depression.

Accordingly, the next section, "The Pit," which is the shortest, describes a literal hole in the ground filled with roots, moss, and small animals such as moles. This section contains a warning that the unconscious may be a dangerous place, a trap wherein waits the death that must finally take all: "Beware Mother Mildew." Thus, in trying to understand the death of his father, the poet finds an even more terrifying truth: The death which has touched another will also come for him.

"The Gibber" is an aptly named segment of apparently disconnected lines and elements through which the poet appears to be wandering without plan, merely in the hope of finding some help. His old friends in nature are not only unhelpful but also actively hostile: "The cows and briars/ Said to me: Die." The poet also examines his own life in society and finds it empty of spiritual and emotional value: "I run, I run to the whistle of money."

The poet begins to find his way back to order and stability in "The Return," which is a memory of his childhood and his life with his father. He sees and describes the life of the greenhouse, describing in particular the morning coming, the steam knocking its way through the radiator pipes, and frost slowly melting from the panes of glass, suggesting the return of order, meaning, clarity, and peace: "Ordnung! ordnung!! Papa is coming!"

The last section, "'It Was Beginning Winter,'" reveals that although a kind of peace has been reached, there is still no understanding; after such emotional turmoil, however, mere rest is a great comfort. The poet first describes a quiet winter scene, then tries to evaluate it, without success. The lines "Was it light within light?/ Stillness becoming alive,/ Yet still?" suggest that the speaker is searching for a unity that would resolve opposites by containing and transcending them. Significantly, this analysis is not an answer but another question. The poem ends with a kind of emotional blessing, its origin unclear:

> A lively understandable spirit
> Once entertained you.
> It will come again.
> Be still.
> Wait.

This section, with each line becoming shorter and simpler than the previous one until the last, which is only one syllable, reminds the poet (and the reader) that life is a cycle and that—even if there are no final answers to one's problems—happiness and joy will come again. One needs the intelligence and the courage not to act, but to wait.

"IN A DARK TIME"

First published: 1960 (collected in *The Collected Poems of Theodore Roethke*, 1966)
Type of work: Poem

The poet confronts his own fear and triumphs over it in a mystic vision.

Several of the elements of Roethke's mind, personality, and poetic skill combine to assert themselves in "In a Dark Time," one of his most personal and most powerful works. The poem begins with a violent description of a psychic breakdown, a comment on Roethke's own mental illness, and ends by invoking the vocabulary of religious mysticism. Underlying the whole poem is the startling assumption that such a collapse may be necessary in order for a person to reach truth and achieve integration of the personality and unity with the rest of nature. Roethke certainly thought this theory true for himself; the end of the poem is stated in the first line,

for in Roethke's view, it is only "in a [psychically] dark time" that "the [inner] eye begins to see."

The natural imagery in the poem does not refer to the neat, ordered, and humanly understandable world of the greenhouse, where growth takes place in regular, ordered patterns. Roethke knew that the greenhouse was an artificial place sustained by rational activity; the world outside was a far different place, teeming with wild and threatening life and unexplainable creatures and events. In this poem there are no beautiful roses but instead "beasts of the hill," "serpents of the den," and "a ragged moon." The natural world is not a comforting place but instead is an index of madness, as outer reality reflects the inner turmoil of the poet. The last natural image in the poem, the fly which buzzes at the window sill, seeing the world it desires but unable to reach it, frequently appears in Roethke's writing as a symbol of mental illness.

Roethke's presentation of this condition is clinically accurate; it is common; for example, for the psychotic person to think that everything is obviously related to everything else ("a steady storm of correspondences") but also to think that knowledge of these relationships is useless or uncommunicable: "The edge is what I have." At the same time that thoughts and ideas may occur with unusual clarity, sense impressions may mirror the lack of a frame of reference for these ideas or may defy common sense: "I meet my shadow in the deepening shade," "all natural shapes blazing unnatural light." Another such discordant image, "in broad day the midnight come again," may be a description of a sudden dislocation of the senses, but it may also describe how the sufferer is plunged without warning into meaningless confusion. The poetic images shift back and forth from the physical to the mental, both indicating the welter within the mind of the poet and perplexing the reader and thus forcing him or her to join and endure the poet's wild ride.

In the last stanza, there is a resolution of these contradictions, but not a peaceful resolution. After touching bottom, plumbing the depths of disaster, the poet is finally free of his fear, presumably because he has experienced what he was afraid of and survived, and therefore need fear no longer, but that is only a presumption. Roethke does not offer a logical explanation for the change, nor did he feel that one was necessary, for he thought that human life was based on much more than cogitation. As he had written in "The Waking:" "We think by feeling. What is there to know?" Whatever the reason, the poet finds himself united with God but still in the midst of a maelstrom: "free in the tearing wind."

The most pregnant lines in the poem are "What's madness but nobility of soul/ at odds with circumstance?," Roethke's answer to those who would dismiss his more difficult poetry as mere babble. The "mentally ill" person may very well be the one who can see life more clearly than others precisely because he or she has not abandoned his or her personal vision for a utilitarian view. That is a large and perhaps unfair claim, but at the end of the poem, Roethke is clearly a twentieth century Romantic, for unlike his fellow "mad" poet and mentor, William Blake, Roethke did not insist that the vision of mystic union with God should be true for all people. He merely described it happening to himself, recognizing the twentieth century belief that there are many paths to truth. In so doing, he also reaffirmed the Romantic principle that each person must find his or her own role in life and that salvation is finally an individual matter.

SUMMARY

Roethke provides a link with the poetic tradition of the past while remaining very much a poet of the twentieth century and one with his own unique vision. He demonstrates that the Romantic philosophy of imaginative, transcendent, and fulfilling unity with nature is not a relic of the dead past but an approach to life that is still valid today. His invocation of more recent poetic tradition shows that he was aware of the problems of his own time, and his use of poetry to grapple with his emotional and psychic distress reaffirms the role of poetry as a regenerative and healing agent.

James Baird

DISCUSSION TOPICS

- Theodore Roethke wrote poems celebrating both wild and cultivated plants. Are there any significant differences in his attitudes toward the two groups?
- Roethke has a line referring to "All things innocent, hapless, forsaken." Discuss this theme in his poetry.
- What is elegiac poetry? Which Roethke poems can be so classified?
- What poetic forms does Roethke favor? How well do they suit the content of his poems?
- In what poems besides "Cuttings" does Roethke identify with greenhouse plants?
- Mental illness can hardly be called an advantage for anyone, but did Roethke's awareness of his precarious mental health ever lend strength to his poems?

BIBLIOGRAPHY

By the Author

POETRY:
Open House, 1941
The Lost Son, and Other Poems, 1948
Praise to the End!, 1951
The Waking: Poems, 1933-1953, 1953
Words for the Wind, 1958
Sequence, Sometimes Metaphysical, 1963
The Far Field, 1964
The Collected Poems of Theodore Roethke, 1966

NONFICTION:

On the Poet and His Craft: Selected Prose of Theodore Roethke, 1965 (Ralph J. Mills, Jr., editor)
The Selected Letters of Theodore Roethke, 1968 (Mills, editor)
Straw for the Fire: From the Notebooks of Theodore Roethke, 1943-1963, 1972 (David Wagoner, editor)
On Poetry and Craft: Selected Prose of Theodore Roethke, 2001

CHILDREN'S LITERATURE:

I Am! Says the Lamb, 1961
Party at the Zoo, 1963

About the Author

Bloom, Harold, ed. *Theodore Roethke.* New York: Chelsea House, 1988.

Bogen, Don. *Theodore Roethke and the Writing Process.* Athens: Ohio University Press, 1991.

Bowers, Neal. *Theodore Roethke: The Journey from I to Otherwise.* Columbia: University of Missouri Press, 1982.

Kalaidjian, Walter B. *Understanding Theodore Roethke.* Columbia: University of South Carolina Press, 1987.

Kusch, Robert. *My Toughest Mentor: Theodore Roethke and William Carlos Williams (1940-1948).* Lewisburg, Pa.: Bucknell University Press, 1999.

Malkoff, Karl. *Theodore Roethke: An Introduction to the Poetry.* New York: Columbia University Press, 1966.

Seager, Allan. *The Glass House: The Life of Theodore Roethke.* New York: McGraw-Hill, 1968.

Stiffler, Randall. *Theodore Roethke: The Poet and His Critics.* Chicago: American Library Association, 1986.

Wolff, George. *Theodore Roethke.* Boston: Twayne, 1981.

PHILIP ROTH

Born: Newark, New Jersey
March 19, 1933

Roth is recognized, along with Saul Bellow and Bernard Mala-mud, as one of the foremost Jewish American novelists.

© Nancy Crampton

BIOGRAPHY

Philip Roth was born in Newark, New Jersey, on March 19, 1933, and grew up in a section of Newark that was then predominantly middle-class Jewish. Roth graduated from Weequahic High School in 1951 and attended Newark College at Rutgers University for a year before transferring to Bucknell University in Pennsylvania. Though the family could scarcely afford the expensive private college, Roth's father was determined to make the sacrifices necessary to let his son get the education he wanted.

At Bucknell, Roth wrote for the literary magazine, in which he published his earliest stories. He made Phi Beta Kappa and graduated with an A.B., magna cum laude, in 1954, after which he went to the University of Chicago as a graduate student and instructor in English literature. He received his M.A. in 1955 and then served in the United States Army in 1955 and 1956. By this time, his stories had begun appearing in literary magazines such as *The Chicago Review* and *Epoch*; in 1955, one of them was selected for Martha Foley's anthology *Best American Short Stories*. While in the Army Roth continued writing, and in 1959 his first collection, *Goodbye, Columbus, and Five Short Stories*, was published. It won the National Book Award for fiction in 1960. Roth was only twenty-six.

Much of his early life is presented in *The Facts: A Novelist's Autobiography* (1988), in which he de-

scribes in detail what it was like growing up in Newark in the 1930's and 1940's among lower-middle-class Jews. Family life was close and intense; whatever internal friction or strife there might be, everyone recognized that "family indivisibility" was "the first commandment."

Although Roth modeled the life of Alexander Portnoy in *Portnoy's Complaint* (1969) somewhat upon his own experiences, the reader must be careful not to make exact identifications between the real Roth and his fictional counterpart—a major concern especially in his later fiction. Roth idolized his mother, who from all accounts was vastly different from Sophie Portnoy, just as his hard-working, devoted father differed from harried, constipated Jack Portnoy, Alex's father. Although both were employed by large insurance companies and were discriminated against for being Jewish, their personalities are scarcely identical. Unlike Alex Portnoy, but like Nathan Zuckerman in "Salad Days" (one of the "useful fictions" in *My Life as a Man*, published in 1974), Roth has an older brother, Sandy, who studied art at the Pratt Institute in New York after serving in the Navy. It was through his brother that Roth began reading works such as Sherwood Anderson's *Winesburg, Ohio* (1919) and James Joyce's *A Portrait of the Artist as a Young Man* (1916) while still in high school.

Like other boys of his social class and religion, Roth attended Hebrew School after public school and received at least a rudimentary training in Judaism. That aspect of his life may be glimpsed in stories such as "The Conversion of the Jews" and "'I Always Wanted You to Admire My Fasting': Or, Looking at Kafka." The energy, vitality, and iconoclasm of his schoolmates contrasted vigorously with the biblical stories of Jews living in tents or building the pyramids, and in his later life Roth admitted to missing that kind of person when he moved for a while to London. (He has since returned to the United States.) Young Roth was also an avid baseball fan and loved to play the sport. His powerful interest in baseball appears in several of his novels, but in *The Great American Novel* (1973) it takes over the scene and situation completely.

College confirmed Roth's interest in literature. His stories written while still an undergraduate were not at all about Jews or Newark, and they were not humorous. He admits to the influence of Thomas Wolfe, J. D. Salinger, and Truman Capote. With several of his fraternity brothers, he helped to found *Et Cetera*, the campus literary magazine, which he edited in 1952-1953.

At the University of Chicago, Roth was a popular graduate student; his gift for mimicry made him the hit of many parties. In Chicago he met and became friends with Theodore Solotaroff, later an editor for *Commentary* and subsequently of *The New American Review*, and an important literary critic. At this time, Roth was seriously interested in the work of Henry James, whose influence on Roth's first full-length novel, *Letting Go* (1962), is profound. Returning to Chicago after his Army service to work on a Ph.D. in English, Roth began dating Margaret Martinson, a divorcée with two children. They were married in 1959 after a tumultuous relationship. Far from a happy marriage, theirs was fraught with quarrels and antagonism, which Roth fictionalized in *My Life as a Man* (the trick that Margaret's counterpart uses to get her lover to marry her is factual).

Encouraged by the success of *Goodbye, Columbus*, Roth had by then abandoned his doctoral studies and was writing *Letting Go*, set largely in Chicago. From 1960 to 1962, he was visiting writer at the University of Iowa. In 1962, Roth won a legal separation from Margaret and went to Princeton University as writer-in-residence. Afterward, he lived in New York City and continued writing full time. Margaret refused to grant him a divorce, and the stringent laws of New York State then made it impossible for him to obtain one in any other way.

Roth lived in a small apartment, where he studiously wrote his next novels and had a long romance with someone he calls May Aldridge in *The Facts*. Margaret was killed in an automobile crash in 1968, leaving Roth free to marry, yet he did not wed

Aldridge. From 1967 to 1980, he was a popular part-time lecturer at the University of Pennsylvania, where he taught the works of Franz Kafka, Fyodor Dostoevski, and other great novelists. He became interested in contemporary Eastern European writers and edited a series for Penguin Books called "Writers from the Other Europe," in which books by such authors as Milan Kundera appeared in English translations.

When he began sharing his life with the British actress Claire Bloom, Roth divided his time between London, where he kept a flat and a studio for working, and his home in rural Connecticut. He married Bloom in 1990 and then lived mostly in the United States. In 1993, he and Bloom were divorced, and Roth settled permanently into his home in Connecticut, where he enjoyed his solitude and being able to write without distraction every day for many hours. He became reclusive and seldom ventured out for interviews, public readings, or social events.

Many of his novels have won major awards since his first National Book Award in 1959. In 1992, his memoir of his father, *Patrimony*, won the National Book Critics Circle Award; in 1993, his novel *Operation Shylock* won the PEN/Faulkner Award; in 1995, *Sabbath's Theater* won his second National Book Award; in 1997 *American Pastoral* was given the prestigious Pulitzer Prize in fiction; and in 2000 *The Human Stain* won another PEN/Faulkner Award. In 1998, Roth received the National Medal of Arts from President Bill Clinton at a ceremony in the White House. Roth has been a member of the American Academy since 1970.

ANALYSIS

Often called a psychological realist by literary critics, Roth uses a variety of techniques in his fiction that make it difficult to classify his work under only one category. His early stories and novels, including *Goodbye, Columbus, Letting Go*, and *When She Was Good* (1967), were heavily influenced by the great nineteenth century psychological realists such as Henry James and Gustave Flaubert and by later ones such as Theodore Dreiser and Sherwood Anderson. *Portnoy's Complaint*, however, while drawing for its themes and structure upon therapeutic psychoanalysis, represents a breakthrough to new forms of fiction. Since then, Roth has written satire, such as *Our Gang (Starring Tricky and His Friends)*

(1971), fantasy (*The Great American Novel*), *Bildungs-roman* (the *Zuckerman Bound* trilogy, 1985), and other types of fiction that demonstrate his versatility and originality as a writer.

Roth has also been called a social critic, and he has definitely earned the title. Taking on the conservative Jewish establishment in both his fiction and nonfiction, he exposes the foibles, coarseness, hypocrisies, and materialism of middle-class Jewish families, as in his portrayal of the Patimkin clan in *Goodbye, Columbus*. At the same time, he shows the intensity, closeness, and warmth that are also part of their lives. Attacked for his story "Epstein," in which a decent, hardworking Jewish businessman gets caught in the trammels of an adulterous relationship, Roth has defended himself against rabbis and others who feel he has defamed the Jewish people. He presents his views in essays such as "Writing About Jews" (1963) and "Imagining Jews" (1974), collected in *Reading Myself and Others* (1975), where he argues on the behalf of the writer's freedom and the autonomy of the imagination against those who insist on greater discretion and diplomacy.

Where formerly he brilliantly portrayed middle-class Jewish life as it was in the neighborhoods where he grew up, Roth subsequently moved on to other aspects of Jewish life, as in his vivid descriptions of kibbutz life and the controversy over West Bank settlements in Israel in *The Counterlife* (1986) and the problems of anti-Semitism he encountered while living in England in *Deception* (1990).

Above all, Roth is an amusing and witty writer, with a good ear for the cadences and inflections of actual speech and a stand-up comedian's sense of timing. His humor has been attributed to influences such as comedians Lenny Bruce and Henny Youngman, but Roth also acknowledges the influence of the "sit-down" comedy of Franz Kafka, about whom he writes in "'I Always Wanted You to Admire My Fasting': Or, Looking at Kafka" (collected in *Reading Myself and Others*). He modeled his novella *The Breast* (1972; revised, 1980) partly on Kafka's story "Metamorphosis." The humor and tall tales that grew out of the great American Southwest inform *The Great American Novel*, which also indulges in send-ups of famed American writers Ernest Hemingway, Nathaniel Hawthorne, Herman Melville, and others.

In *Portnoy's Complaint*, Roth has said, he tried to bring obscenity to the level of a subject. He may or

may not have succeeded, but it is true that in that novel, as in his later works, he has taken full advantage of the current freedom to explore sexual involvements in an open and direct way. Yet, for all his apparent licentiousness, as in his stunning take-off on Irving Howe as the pornography king, Milton Appel, in *The Anatomy Lesson* (1983), Roth remains what he always was, a serious writer with a strong moral strain that remains under even the wildest humor or most grotesque fantasy.

For all of his extravagant sexual exploits, Portnoy is a pathetic creature, a man desperately trying to become whole with the help of a psychiatrist. For all of his craziness in getting involved with Maureen Ketterer, Peter Tarnopol is someone who goes through countless agonies trying to determine the noblest courses of action he should take. The jokes are there in Roth's novels, but it would be a mistake to read them for their humor alone. Like the best of the humorists who have preceded him, Roth writes with a more serious agenda underlying the comedic elements in his fiction.

GOODBYE, COLUMBUS

First published: 1959
Type of work: Novella

A young Newark man falls in love with a Radcliffe student from a nouveau riche Jewish family in suburban New Jersey and discovers how spoiled she is.

In *Goodbye, Columbus*, Neil Klugman meets and falls in love with Brenda Patimkin, the spoiled, attractive daughter of a middle-class Jewish family. The family has recently moved from Newark to the suburbs in Short Hills, New Jersey, where they have a large, comfortable home, typical of the nouveau riche class to which they belong. For Neil, however, Brenda and Short Hills represent an enticing version of a pastoral ideal. When he met her for the first time at a country club swimming pool, she was for him "like a sailor's dream of a Polynesian maiden, albeit one with prescription sun glasses and the last name of Patimkin." She has an older brother, Ron, a basketball star just graduating from Ohio State University, whose favorite record,

"Goodbye, Columbus," gives the story its title. She also has a kid sister, Julie, a younger version of Brenda, equally as smart and equally as spoiled.

By contrast, Neil's more humble family consists of parents, permanently absent in Arizona because of their asthma, and his Aunt Gladys, with whom he lives and who cooks his meals as well as her husband's, her daughter's, and her own—all different and all served at different times. Aunt Gladys is modeled on the stereotyped Jewish mama and has a funny accent, but she also demonstrates the most common sense and genuine humanity of any of the characters in the novella.

As their affair progresses, Neil and Brenda spend more and more time together at her family's home in Short Hills, where at the end of the summer Neil is invited to spend a week of his vacation. They have sex clandestinely in her room every night. The family is suddenly plunged into a frenzy of activity when Ron announces his engagement to Harriet, his Ohio State sweetheart, and they decide to get married over Labor Day weekend. In all the turmoil that ensues, Brenda gets Neil an extension on his visit as well as an invitation to Ron's wedding.

Neil is not sure whether he feels more love or lust for Brenda, and he debates with himself whether to ask her to marry him. Fearing rejection, he proposes instead that she get a diaphragm. At first, she demurs, but Neil argues that their lovemaking will be not only safer but also more enjoyable, at least for him. Still she demurs, and it becomes a contest of wills, like many of the other games played in the story. Finally, under Neil's insistence, Brenda capitulates, and they go to New York together for her to be fitted with the device. While she is in the doctor's office, Neil enters St. Patrick's cathedral and questions himself and his feelings. He recognizes his carnality, his acquisitiveness, and his foolishness in coveting all that Brenda is and represents: "Gold dinnerware, sporting-goods trees, nectarines, garbage disposal, bumpless noses"—and the list goes on.

Ron's wedding is a typical Jewish celebration, with too much food and champagne. The occasion provides Roth with further opportunities for satire,

as Neil meets the rest of the family and Ron's college friends. He gets considerable free advice from Leo Patimkin, one of Brenda's uncles, who tells Neil that he has a good thing going with Brenda and he should not louse things up. Actually, in demanding that she get the diaphragm to please him, he already has begun to louse things up.

The sad end of the story comes when Brenda asks Neil to come to Boston for the Jewish holidays in the fall. Although he is not an observant Jew and has difficulty getting time off from his work at the Newark Public Library, Neil goes to the hotel that Brenda has booked for them. When he arrives, however, Brenda is deeply distressed. She has foolishly left her diaphragm at home, where her mother has found it and thereby discovered the affair. Her parents each write separate letters to her, telling her in their different ways of their shame and unhappiness. When Neil learns all this, he is shocked at Brenda's carelessness but then realizes that leaving the device where it could be found may have been the result of an unconscious desire on her part to end the affair. As she has invited Neil to Boston ostensibly to continue their lovemaking and insists that he make every effort to get there, she obviously has some ambivalence (or perhaps Roth does) toward Neil. He finds it impossible now to go on with her, and he takes the train back to Newark, where he arrives just in time to begin work on the Jewish New Year.

Neil Klugman, whose surname translated from Yiddish means "clever man," is typical of Roth's early heroes. Sophisticated, bright, and educated, he is nevertheless a schlemiel, a loser, someone who bungles golden opportunities that come his way. He is the prototype for Gabe Wallach in *Letting Go*, another loser, whose divided self prevents him from having satisfying and permanent relationships with others. Both have the knack, as Neil puts it, of turning winning into losing, so that the name "Klugman" comes to have an ironic implication. Nevertheless, Roth is hardly an advocate for the values represented by the Patimkin family, who are the principal and most obvious targets for his ridicule.

"THE DEFENDER OF THE FAITH"

First published: 1959 (collected in *Goodbye, Columbus, and Five Short Stories*, 1959)
Type of work: Short story

Sergeant Nathan Marx, a World War II combat veteran, struggles with his conscience over the favors demanded from him by a new Jewish recruit.

After the Allies are victorious in the battle against the Axis in Europe, Sergeant Nathan Marx, in "The Defender of the Faith," is rotated back to the States, to Camp Crowder, Missouri. A veteran and a war hero with medals to prove it, Sergeant Marx is modest enough—and totally unprepared for confrontations with Private Sheldon Grossbart from the Bronx, whom he is assigned to train along with other recruits for the continuing war against Japan. Quickly recognizing in Marx a "landsman"— that is, a fellow Jew from New York—Grossbart begins to play on the sergeant's hidden sympathies. Although he is far from an observant Jew himself, Marx cannot bring himself to reject totally the pleas for special favors that Grossbart repeatedly brings to him, such as being excused from a "G.I. Party" (that is, a barracks cleaning) on Friday nights (the start of the Jewish Sabbath). Marx is uncomfortable about this, but Grossbart is persuasive, not only on his own behalf, but also on behalf of Fishbein and Halpern, two other Jewish men in the company.

One success leads to another, as Grossbart wheedles favor after favor from Marx. He apparently goes too far when he complains about the non-kosher food and writes a letter to his congressman over his father's signature. When the commanding officer of his company finds out, he questions Grossbart in front of Marx, holding the sergeant up to him as a model. At this point, Grossbart backs off, and another letter arrives, again purportedly from Grossbart's father to his congressman, praising Sergeant Marx for helping his son over the hurdles he has to face in the Army. In a note attached to the letter, passed down through the chain of Army command to Marx, the congressman also praises the sergeant as "a credit to the U.S. Army and the Jewish people." After that, Grossbart seems to disappear from his life for a while, and Marx is relieved.

The reprieve, however, is short-lived. Grossbart turns up one day in Marx's office with two matters on his mind. The first concerns their eventual assignment; Marx surmises, rightly, that it will probably be in the Pacific region. Grossbart hopes it might be New York so he could be near his immigrant parents. The other matter concerns a pass for Passover dinner with relatives in St. Louis. Marx reminds him that passes are not possible during basic training, but Grossbart perseveres, using a variety of ploys and tactics, until he gets passes for himself and his two friends as well. When they return from St. Louis, they bring Marx a gift—Chinese egg rolls, not Passover fare.

Marx is disgusted, and his fury mounts; he calls Grossbart a liar, a schemer, and a crook. When he discovers soon afterward that Grossbart has manipulated another Jewish noncommissioned officer in order to get himself sent to Fort Monmouth, New Jersey, instead of the Pacific with the rest of the company, Marx decides to use Grossbart's tactics against him. He asks a friend in Classification and Assignment to alter the orders, sending another man to Fort Monmouth in place of Grossbart. He invents a story about Grossbart's longing to fight against the enemy because his brother was killed and he would feel like a coward staying stateside. Marx explains that Grossbart is Jewish and that he would like to do him this favor.

A final confrontation ends the story, as Grossbart accuses Marx of anti-Semitism, of really wanting to see him dead. At first, Marx ignores him, but a bitter, fruitless argument ensues. Both of them know, however, that Grossbart will be all right, and so will Fishbein and Halpern, as long as Grossbart can continue to find ways to use them for his own advantage. Weeping, Grossbart eventually accepts his fate, as Marx accepts his, rejecting the strong impulse to turn and ask Grossbart's pardon for his vindictiveness.

The story shows Roth's ability early in his career to develop vivid and convincing characters and use themes not designed to be popular with Jewish audiences. Other stories in the collection *Goodbye, Columbus*, such as "The Conversion of the Jews" and "Eli the Fanatic," develop similar themes and characters with the kind of irony that Roth uses here. In those stories, Roth shows realistically what makes people behave in the ways they do—self-interest may be an irresistible motive, as it is in Grossbart's case. The motives are not always admirable and, as Marx demonstrates, not always simple. When conflict occurs, resolution is seldom easy, and it always comes at a cost.

PORTNOY'S COMPLAINT

First published: 1969
Type of work: Novel

A man seeks help from his psychiatrist for the anxieties and other difficulties he attributes to the conflict between his Jewish upbringing and his strong sexual urges.

Portnoy's Complaint is not only the title of this novel, it is also the illness defined in an epigraph that precedes the book: "A disorder in which strongly-felt ethical and altruistic impulses are perpetually warring with extreme sexual longings, often of a perverse nature." Alexander Portnoy, after whom the disease is named, is a young Jewish professional, the Assistant Commissioner for Human Opportunity in New York City. After a recent trip to Israel in which he discovers, to his dismay, that he has become impotent, he seeks the help of a psychiatrist, Dr. Otto Spielvogel. The novel, in fact, is in the form of a long monologue, or a series of psychiatric sessions, in which Portnoy describes his past life, beginning with his earliest years, growing up in Newark as the son of Sophie and Jack Portnoy, to his present life as an important official in the New York bureaucracy. The monologue is punctuated by much dialogue, as he recalls conversations, quarrels, and arguments with his family and a number of lovers, culminating in his disastrous sexual experience in Israel.

The dominant figure in his early life is his mother, whose behavior as a stereotyped Jewish mother is the subject of much satire and humor. Little Alex is astonished at her omnipotence and her apparent omnipresence. A good little boy, he is nevertheless punished at times for faults he cannot understand how—or if—he committed. His rebellions are futile, and his perplexity is immense. His

mother's threats puzzle him, as does his poor, constipated father's reluctance to stop her. As Alex enters puberty, he finds solace in masturbation, which, like everything else in this novel, becomes excessive. In a whimsical allusion to the amoral protagonist of Dostoevski's *Prestupleniye i nakazaniye* (1866; *Crime and Punishment*, 1886), Portnoy calls himself at one point the Raskolnikov of "whacking off."

Ashamed of his parents and, to some extent, of his Jewishness, Portnoy yearns for a more typical American family life. From an early age he tries to woo Gentile girls, disguising himself when he can as a non-Jew. His nose is his greatest impediment, he believes; hence, he imagines excuses and explanations for it and for his name (saying that it is from the French, *porte-noir*). A hilarious episode occurs when he joins two of his friends to visit the notorious Bubbles Girardi, known to have sex with boys, and he wins the chance to be the only one on that occasion whom she will see. Like so much else in his life, however, the event turns into disaster. At first he cannot even get an erection, and later he climaxes too quickly and ejaculates directly into his own eye. Thinking he has gone blind, he fantasizes returning home with a seeing-eye dog, much to the horror of his parents—especially his mother, who becomes upset because she has just cleaned the house and her son has brought home a dog.

Other sexual escapades include the romance with his college sweetheart, Kay Campbell, nicknamed "The Pumpkin," who invites him to spend Thanksgiving in Iowa with her and her family. He is amazed at his reception and the civility he witnesses; it is so different from the outlandish melodramas that daily characterize his family life. The romance cools when, half-jokingly, Alex suggests her conversion to Judaism after they are married, and Kay responds indifferently. Another Gentile lover several years later is "The Pilgrim," Sarah Abbott Maulsby, the daughter of a New England family. Alex realizes that his desire for her is fueled as much by his determination to wreak vengeance against her family, typical of those anti-Semites who discriminate against his hardworking father, as by any other appeal she may have for him.

Portnoy apparently finds everything his hedonistic heart desires in Mary Jane Reed, "The Monkey," a sexually adept sometime model, who is trying to overcome her hillbilly childhood. Mary Jane does everything that Portnoy wants, but unfortunately in the process falls in love with him—unfortunately because he is far from ready to accept marriage with anyone, least of all her. Another shiksa (non-Jewish woman), she has too checkered a career, although for a brief moment while they impersonate a married couple on a weekend holiday in Connecticut, he almost believes that it might be possible. Portnoy's sexual adventures end in Israel where, after abandoning Mary Jane in Greece, he meets his match in Naomi, a six-foot-tall Israeli woman whom he tries to seduce and even rape, only to discover that he is unable to get an erection.

Throughout the novel, Portnoy's "extreme sexual longings" conflict with his "ethical and altruistic impulses," invariably to comic effect. For example, he wants to educate The Monkey and tries hard to do so, with ludicrous results. He complains to his psychiatrist that he is the Jewish son in a Jewish joke and wants to find a way out of it, because to him it is not funny; it "hoits." His expression is funny, however, partly through its excessive diction, his inherited tendency to melodrama, and the ridiculous plight that he himself describes. He concludes his monologue with what amounts to a long primal scream, after which Dr. Spielvogel delivers his famous punch line: "So. Now vee may perhaps to begin. Yes?"

MY LIFE AS A MAN

First published: 1974
Type of work: Novel

Peter Tarnopol struggles to write a novel about his traumatic marriage, introducing fictitious character Nathan Zuckerman as his alter ego.

In *My Life as a Man*, Roth invents a fictitious character, Peter Tarnopol, whose life closely parallels his own, just as the life of Tarnopol's fictitious character, Nathan Zuckerman, closely parallels his. The result is what Roth calls a "useful fiction." Such fictions help the writer explore alternative ideas of one's fate—in this instance, alternative versions of Roth's early years and particularly of his marriage to Margaret Martinson.

The novel begins with two such "useful fictions." The first, "Salad Days," recounts Zuckerman's early

childhood, not unlike Portnoy's, although here it is the father who dominates rather than the mother. Lighthearted and funny, especially in Zuckerman's seduction of Sharon Shatzky, it is different in tone from the darker humor of "Courting Disaster," the "useful fiction" that follows it, in which Tarnopol describes his strange courtship and unhappy marriage to Maureen Ketterer.

In "My True Story," Tarnopol drops his alter ego, Zuckerman, and attempts to tell what really happened. He writes while secluded in Quahsay, an artists' colony similar to Yaddo, Roth's favorite retreat. He describes meeting Maureen while an instructor at the University of Chicago. Not her beauty so much as her prior experience, especially with men who had mistreated and abused her, is her main attraction. Eventually, although their affair has been anything but tranquil, Maureen tricks Tarnopol into marrying her, and when the marriage proves to be bad, she will not let him go. She is determined, she says, to make a man of him, to force him to accept his responsibilities. Several years later, Tarnopol gets a legal separation and flees to New York City to try to develop his career as a writer.

Maureen follows and even attempts to compete with him as a writer. Meanwhile, Tarnopol meets and falls in love with Susan Seabury McCall, a charming, rich, and devoted young woman. From the storms and stresses of his marriage to Maureen, Susan provides a calm and welcome shelter. Tarnopol eventually gives her up, however, knowing that she wants children and believes she should have them; he does not want marriage and a family. She attempts suicide. Tempted to return to her, Tarnopol resists the urge. Meanwhile, he has sought help from a therapist, none other than Dr. Otto Spielvogel, and Maureen is killed in an automobile wreck.

The novel ends where it began, with nothing resolved, except that Tarnopol is now freed at last from his marriage. He has also been able to write the story of his life with Maureen—the novel with which Roth struggled for years after his own wife's death in a similar accident. After five years, he has given up therapy, partly as the result of an article Spielvogel wrote, titled "Creativity: The Narcissism of the Artist," in which Tarnopol appears, very thinly disguised as an Italian American poet. Like *Portnoy's Complaint*, *My Life as a Man* uses interesting and original fictive devices and techniques, eschewing straight linear narrative for more discursive, nonchronological accounts that are not, however, at all confusing. On the contrary, Roth's juxtapositions are witty and meaningful, pointing up many aspects of the absurdity of human existence.

ZUCKERMAN BOUND

First published: *The Ghost Writer,* 1979; *Zuckerman Unbound,* 1981; *The Anatomy Lesson,* 1983; *Epilogue: The Prague Orgy,* 1985

Type of work: Novels

The series of novels traces the development of Nathan Zuckerman as a young writer through the successful publication of his notorious novel, "Carnovsky," and its aftermath.

The Ghost Writer opens as young Nathan Zuckerman comes to visit the distinguished stylist E. I. Lonoff at his home in the Berkshires. Zuckerman is filled with admiration and awe for the older writer, with whom he enjoys discussing literature. He is struck, moreover, by the young woman, Amy Bellette, a former student of Lonoff, who is helping Lonoff assemble his papers for deposit in the Harvard library where she works. He is also struck by Lonoff's wife, Hope, the descendant of New England families different from Lonoff's Russian-Jewish heritage. At several points, she expresses extreme frustration with the life her husband leads and asks him to "chuck her out" in favor of Amy Bellette, who is obviously in love with him. Lonoff has no intentions of doing any such thing; although he recognizes the young woman's attractions and devotion to him, he is loyal to his wife and rejects all of her exhortations to the contrary.

Amazed by the situation he finds, but flattered by Lonoff's praise of his work so far—four published short stories—Zuckerman is easily persuaded to spend the night on a daybed in Lonoff's study. While trying to write a letter to his father, he finds and reads *The Middle Years* by Henry James. Lonoff has excerpted an intriguing passage from it about the "madness of art" and pinned it to a bulle-

tin board near his desk. Later, after Amy returns for the evening, Zuckerman hears an argument in the bedroom above him, in which Amy tries to persuade Lonoff to leave Hope and go off with her to a villa in Florence. Lonoff refuses, and afterward Zuckerman has a long fantasy in which he imagines that Amy Bellette is in reality Anne Frank, miraculously saved from the Nazi death camps.

The next morning, all illusions disappear after another scene between Lonoff and Hope, when Zuckerman can find no trace of a tattooed number on Amy's forearm. As he returns to the artists' colony at Quahsay, Zuckerman receives some words of advice from Lonoff, who also anticipates with interest what Zuckerman will make in his fiction of everything he has seen and heard during his visit.

In *Zuckerman Unbound*, Nathan is no longer a young, somewhat callow writer, anxious about making his way in the world, but an accomplished novelist whose fourth book, *Carnovsky*, has become notorious (just as *Portnoy's Complaint* became notorious in Roth's own life and career). By this time it is apparent that the trilogy is a *Bildungsroman*, or portrait novel, based, like *My Life as a Man*, on Roth's own experiences. It thus presents another "idea of one's fate," but without the mediation of Peter Tarnopol. The reader must be constantly careful, however, not to draw exact equivalences between Roth and his surrogates. For example, Zuckerman's father becomes very upset by his treatment of the family in *Carnovsky*, quite unlike Roth's own father, who took pride in everything his son wrote. Roth fictionalizes his experiences to see how they might otherwise have come out, to explore alternative, imaginative versions of them, and thereby gain further insights.

In *Zuckerman Unbound*, Nathan is beset by people, such as Alvin Pepler, the Jewish Marine, who recognizes him as the author of *Carnovsky* and believes that the book is autobiographical. A mysterious caller telephones and tries to extort money from him, threatening to kidnap his mother in Miami if he does not pay up. When Zuckerman gets a message from his aunt in Florida, be is sure that his mother has been abducted, but it is his father who is in trouble. He has had a serious heart attack, which proves fatal soon after Zuckerman arrives with his brother Henry.

His father's last word is ambiguous. Nathan believes that he said "bastard," but Henry reassures him on the flight home after the funeral that he said "batter," referring to the days when they all played baseball together. When they get to the Newark airport, after exchanging some further confidences on the plane, Henry suddenly turns on Nathan, and they become estranged. Nathan is left to drive alone through the neighborhood he once knew so well but which has now changed drastically. He feels like he is no one—no man's son, no woman's husband, no longer his brother's brother. He does not come from anywhere any longer, either. He is utterly alone.

He is not quite alone, however, in *The Anatomy Lesson*. Afflicted by a strange pain in the neck and back that no doctor has been able to diagnose, let alone treat successfully, Zuckerman is attended by four women who look after his various needs, including his sexual needs. Among them are his financial adviser's wife, the most sexually adroit of them all; a young college student from nearby Finch College, who also works as his secretary; another young woman who lives in Vermont and occasionally comes to town to visit and encourage Zuckerman to come and live in the mountains with her; and finally, Jaga, the Polish émigré who works at the trichologist's clinic where Zuckerman goes to have his increasing baldness treated.

Nothing works, so Zuckerman decides to give up writing, which he has not been able to do anyway, and return to the University of Chicago, his alma mater, and become a doctor. His college friend, Bobby Freytag, now a prominent anesthesiologist, tries to talk him out of it, but disaster strikes from an unexpected direction. Zuckerman takes Bobby's father to the cemetery where his wife has recently been buried, and while there Zuckerman goes berserk. Having taken too much Percodan and drunk too much vodka for the pain in his neck, and feeling antagonized by the old man's sentimentalism, he attacks him, then falls on a tombstone and fractures his jaw. Learning what pain is really like now, in the hospital after surgery, Zuckerman spends his days recuperating and helping patients more unfortunate than he is.

The theme of fathers and sons, pervasive in the trilogy, takes a different twist in *The Prague Orgy*, which forms the epilogue. Zuckerman is persuaded by a Czech émigré and writer to rescue his father's short stories, written in Yiddish, from the writer's sex-crazy wife. In Prague, Zuckerman meets other

writers and intellectuals, as well as Olga Sisovsky, who finally turns over the stories to him. Although well known as the author of *Carnovsky* to some who admire his work, he is not allowed to leave the country with the stories, which are confiscated. Instead, he is escorted to the airport by Novak, the minister of culture, who delivers a lecture to him on the values of socialism, particularly as they pertain to cultural deviance and filial respect. The patriotism of Novak's father, however, is little more than political expediency, and the cultural deviance is simply a code word for divergence from the party line. Zuckerman realizes this and realizes, too, that it apparently was not his fate to become a "cultural eminence" or hero by performing extraordinary literary deeds such as rescuing the Sisovsky manuscripts.

THE COUNTERLIFE

First published: 1986
Type of work: Novel

In a series of contrasting episodes, Nathan and Henry Zuckerman trade places as victims of serious heart disease, ending in their deaths.

In *The Counterlife*, Roth more forthrightly and ingeniously than ever before exploits the technique of developing alternative versions of one's fate. Thus, in the first section, "Basel," Henry Zuckerman, a successful dentist, husband, and father of three children, suffers from a serious heart ailment that is properly treated by use of a beta-blocker, which renders him impotent. Finding his sex life reduced to nothing and desperate to resume an extramarital affair with his dental assistant, he decides to undergo surgery, and dies. Before the surgery, feeling the need to talk to someone, he confides in his brother, Nathan, from whom he has been long estranged. At Henry's funeral, however, Nathan is unable to deliver the eulogy, as the three thousand words he has written are hardly suitable for the occasion. Always the novelist, he knows that they are more suitable to his craft than for his brother's funeral.

In the next section, "Judea," Henry has not died but is alive and well and living in Israel. The surgery, while successful, left him deeply depressed, and he experiences a kind of ethnic conversion during a visit to the Orthodox quarter in Jerusalem. His wife asks Nathan, now married to an Englishwoman, Maria, and living in London, to find Henry and try to get him to come home to his family. More interested in what has happened to his brother than in actually returning him to New Jersey, Nathan agrees. He finds Henry in a kibbutz on the West Bank under the influence of an extreme right-winger, Mordecai Lippman. During his visit, Nathan is several times put on the spot, not only by Henry but also by others, who question his politics, his loyalty to Israel, and his Jewishness.

In "Aloft," he returns to London without Henry and becomes comically implicated in an abortive hijack attempt by a crazy young man from West Orange, New Jersey.

The fourth section, "Gloucestershire," is the most complex. Now Nathan is afflicted with the heart ailment and wants to get off the beta-blocker so that he can marry Maria and have children. She is his upstairs neighbor, married to a man who fails to appreciate her. She tries to talk Nathan out of the operation, but he goes ahead with it, and he dies. At his funeral, Henry is unable to give the eulogy, which is delivered by Nathan's editor and is mostly about *Carnovsky* and the role of the novelist. Henry is outraged by everything he says. When he goes to Nathan's apartment, he finds "Draft #2," including chapters of *The Counterlife* that the reader has read as well as an additional chapter, "Christendom," which follows. Henry is further outraged by his brother's fictionalizing—his "lies." Henry has never had an affair with his dental assistant or gone to Israel. To avoid any possible embarrassment to himself or his family, he takes 250 pages of the manuscript and destroys them on his way home.

Maria also enters the apartment and finds "Christendom," which she criticizes, as Henry had done the earlier chapters. She does not destroy the manuscript, however compromising it appears (it includes passages about their love affair); instead she determines to brazen her way out of whatever problems may arise with her husband. When the reader comes to "Christendom," he or she finds that it is about Nathan and Maria's imagined married life together, their happiness (Maria is pregnant), and their problems (Maria is from an anti-Semitic family). The novel ends with a quarrel over

English attitudes toward Jews, and Nathan imagines a farewell letter that Maria has written to him.

The Counterlife is a postmodernist tour de force. Despite the convolutions of its plot and the ways the novel loops back upon itself and alters events, characters, and impressions, the reader is never confused for long as to what is happening. Roth exercises to the fullest his novelistic imagination, juxtaposing counterlives upon counterlives with wit, humor, and excellent technical skills.

OPERATION SHYLOCK: A CONFESSION

First published: 1993
Type of work: Novel

The author learns that someone in Israel is posing as Philip Roth, so he goes there to confront him and attend the Demjanjuk trial.

Over his English wife's objections, Philip Roth goes to Israel in 1988 ostensibly to interview his friend Israeli novelist Aharon Appelfeld and to attend the trial of John Demjanjuk, the man accused of being one of the sadistic guards at Treblinka, a Nazi death camp during World War II. Roth interviews Appelfeld and attends the trial, but he is even more interested in a man who is posing as him, calling himself Philip Roth. He not only looks like Roth but also dresses exactly like him. He goes around arguing for a reverse diaspora—that is, for all the Ashkenazi Jews in Israel to leave the country in order to avoid what he is sure will become another Holocaust if they remain. He calls his project "Diasporism." This, along with everything else that the man represents—including his organization called Anti-Semites Anonymous—infuriates the real Philip Roth, who nicknames his imposter "Moishe Pipik."

While in Israel, Roth not only meets Appelfeld, who gives him his views on current Israeli politics, but also meets another old friend, George Ziad, a wealthy Palestinian who has espoused Diasporism because of the Israeli occupation of Palestinian lands and the Israelis' treatment of his people. Roth listens to his friends as they engage in lengthy monologues, much as Nathan Zuckerman does in *The Counterlife*. The major incident occurs in the novel, however, when Roth is abducted by Mossad agents under the direction of one Smilesburger, who wants Roth to engage as a spy in some espionage on behalf of Israel. Under considerable duress, Roth agrees to engage in what is then called Operation Shylock (hence the book's title). It involves a secret mission in Athens, but what that mission is, readers never learn. Roth says that he wrote it up in "Chapter Eleven" of this book, but under Smilesburger's persuasion, he has deleted it. No "Chapter Eleven" appears in the book; instead, Roth presents himself and a now retired Smilesburger having brunch together in New York, where Smilesburger offers some comments on the book that he has just read and prevailed on Roth to allow him to censor.

When *Operation Shylock* first appeared, Roth wrote articles for *The New York Times* insisting that everything in the book was true, that it all really happened. This was a piece of "Jewish mischief," he later admitted, for the novel is pure fiction, except for the trial of Demjanjuk and the interview with Appelfeld, which actually occurred.

AMERICAN PASTORAL

First published: 1997
Type of work: Novel

In the 1960's, a successful businessman married to a former Miss New Jersey seems to have it made, but then his world comes crashing down.

Seymour "Swede" Levov, the older brother of Nathan Zuckerman's classmate at Weequahic High School, embodies the American Dream. An outstanding Jewish athlete, he becomes a U.S. Marine and a graduate of Upsala College, where he meets and falls in love with Mary Dawn Dwyer, Miss New Jersey of 1949 and a contestant in the Miss America Pageant. Although her beauty, talent, and intelligence did not win her the crown, she does manage to win some concessions from Swede's father, who reluctantly agrees to his son's wedding to this daughter of an Irish American working-class family.

From then on, one success seems to lead to another, as Swede takes over his father's flourishing glove-making business in the 1960's; settles his wife and daughter, Meredith ("Merry"), in a 150-year-old house in suburban Morris County; and helps his wife get started raising cattle. The only cloud on their horizon is Merry's terrible stutter, which defies the best efforts of her therapist, Sheila Salzman. Whatever it is that underlies Merry's stutter apparently also motivates her rebellious teenage behavior, which culminates in 1968 when she bombs the village store and post office. A much-loved physician, Dr. Fred Conlon, dies as a result of the bombing, and Meredith becomes a fugitive, going underground for five years.

During this period, Merry is responsible for more bombings and the deaths of three more people, as she tells her shocked and disconsolate father when he finally finds her living in a derelict section of Newark. By now, she has become a Jain, wearing a stocking veil over her face, eating little, and washing never. Meanwhile, the idyllic life that Swede had tried to establish for his family is further shattered by his wife's breakdowns, the infidelities of which both she and Swede are guilty, the sale of the cattle business, and Dawn's desire to move into a new house that her lover, Orcutt, the scion of 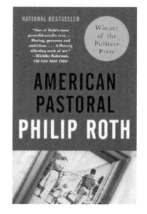 a family dating from colonial days, has designed for her. Much of this information Swede learns when he finds Merry, who refuses to return home with him, where he and Dawn are having a dinner party for Swede's aged parents, the Orcutts, and two other couples. While Swede is racked with questions about what he should have done or should do now, the dinner conversation turns to the decline of American morality, as evidenced by the acclaim that Linda Lovelace has won for her performance in the pornographic film *Deep Throat*.

Roth narrates Levov's story through his favorite alter ego, Nathan Zuckerman, who encounters Swede's brother Jerry at a high school reunion. The story that Nathan tells is largely his imagined reconstruction of events. At the same time, it is a political satire, as the ironic title of the book suggests. How and why could the events of Swede's life have happened? he asks at the end of the novel. What insidious disease so infected the American middle-class culture—of which the Levov family tragedy is representative—that it could cause such terrible destruction? Roth provides no answers to these questions, although some critics suggest that Vietnam and Watergate destroyed the spirit engendered by the victory over fascism. Others see Swede's story as a parallel to the biblical story of Job. Still others see *American Pastoral* as Roth's further attempt to portray the problems of being a Jew and raising a family in a predominantly gentile America.

THE HUMAN STAIN

First published: 2000
Type of work: Novel

Coleman Silk, a fair-skinned African American, rejects his family, marries, and becomes a professor of classics at Athena College, until his use of an unintended ambiguity ruins everything.

Apparently inspired by the life and career of Anatole Broyard, the late, well-known literary critic of *The New York Times*, *The Human Stain* is the story of Coleman Silk, a Newark-born African American whose fair complexion allows him in his adult life to pass as a white man. Determined not to be held back by his black heritage, Coleman renounces his family after the disastrous occasion when he brings his blond sweetheart to meet his mother and she decides to break off their relationship. They had met at college in New York, where he is studying classics after serving in the Navy during World War II. Silk later marries Iris Gittelman, the daughter of atheistic Russian American Jews, and declares himself to be a secular Jew as well. Neither Iris nor any of their children ever learn the secret that Coleman harbors for the rest of his life.

While Silk manages to keep his secret from everyone else, Roth reveals it to the reader by chapter 2 as a means of developing some of the many ironies that pervade the novel. The most significant irony occurs when Silk is accused of bigotry: One day while lecturing, he quite innocently asks his class about the identity of two students who have never shown up, wondering if they are real or "spooks." He does not know that the two students in question are black, and they accuse him of racism for using a derogatory term. Enraged by the accusation and even more by his colleagues' refusal to support him against the charge, he resigns in high dudgeon. He is especially offended when one of his colleagues, himself an African American— the first one ever to be hired at Athena College and by none other than Coleman Silk when he became dean—refuses to stand by him. The turmoil that the controversy occasions becomes too much for Iris Silk, who soon dies of a heart attack, which Coleman blames on the college.

Two years later, Coleman Silk visits the writer Nathan Zuckerman, who lives and works nearby. They scarcely know each other but become close friends when Coleman asks Nathan to write the book about the affair that he has been unable to write himself. In the months that follow, they spend a good deal of time together, until Silk begins his affair with Faunia Farley, a thirty-four-year-old woman who works as a janitor at the college and pretends to be ignorant and illiterate. She is divorced from Les Farley, a half-crazed Vietnam veteran who haunts her and blames her for the death of their two small children when their house caught fire.

The passionate affair in which Coleman and Faunia engage is based firmly but not exclusively on sex, and it affronts not only Les Farley but the college community as well. It especially infuriates Delphine Roux, the young Frenchwoman and Yale Ph.D. who was Coleman's department chair at the time of his resignation. An ardent feminist and an ambitious academic, Delphine nevertheless is lonely and wants a man. When she tries to write an ad for the personals in *The New York Review of Books*, she has problems with both her biography and the description of the kind of man she wants. She realizes only too late—after she accidentally hits the "send" key instead of the "delete" key on her computer—that the man whom she has been describing closely resembles none other than Coleman Silk, and that the message she has been composing has gone out to her entire department and eventually to the entire community.

In this manner, Roth manages to inject some farce into what is otherwise a very serious novel that attacks the kinds of political correctness that had taken over college campuses and much else in American life in the 1990's, when many Americans seem to be obsessed with the scandal caused by Monica Lewinsky's affair with President Clinton. The "stain" in the title may, in fact, allude to the notorious stain on Lewinsky's blue dress, although it has deeper significance—alluding for example, among other possible interpretations, to the stain of racism that marks human nature.

Only after Silk is killed together with Faunia, deliberately driven off the road by Les Farley in his pickup truck, does Nathan learn the secret that his friend has so carefully guarded all those years. Only then, too, is he able to begin writing the book that Coleman had earlier asked him to write. In the process, he portrays both the racial intolerance that led Coleman Silk to pass as a white man and the pious hypocrisies that culminated in President Clinton's impeachment. Throughout the novel, which brings to a fitting conclusion Roth's "American Trilogy" of *American Pastoral, I Married a Communist* (1998), and *The Human Stain,* Roth offers a portrait of post-World War II life, with a startling mixture of successes and failures that encourages readers to examine closely who and what the United States truly has become.

THE PLOT AGAINST AMERICA

First published: 2004
Type of work: Novel

Roth reimagines American history in the early 1940's, with Charles A. Lindbergh running against Franklin D. Roosevelt and winning the election, depriving the latter of an unprecedented third term.

In the 1940 of Philip Roth's reimagined history, many Americans are so afraid that President Franklin D. Roosevelt is leading the country into the war in Europe that the Republican Party nominates not Wendell Wilkie but Charles A. Lindbergh, the hero who was the first to fly across the Atlantic Ocean solo. To the great consternation of American Jews, Lindbergh wins the election. Jews are concerned because Lindbergh not only has admired the German *Luftwaffe* but also has accepted a medal from Adolf Hitler himself, a clear sign of his pro-German sympathies.

As nine-year-old Philip Roth narrates events, the Roth family—including Philip's father and mother, Herman and Besse, and his older brother, Sandy—and their friends in the Jewish section of Newark, New Jersey, are terribly upset by this turn of events and fear the worst. They suspect that the kinds of anti-Semitism that Hitler has propounded and is rapidly carrying out in Germany and in the parts of Europe that he has conquered will, under Lindbergh's administration, begin to happen in the United States. The first experience that they have of this intolerance comes during a trip to Washington, D.C., where they are expelled from their hotel despite their confirmed reservations. This outrage is followed by a scene in a cafeteria where the family experiences anti-Semitic slurs. Worse events are still to follow.

Not all Jews believe as Herman Roth believes. A rabbi, Lionel Bengelsdorf, supports the new administration and soon becomes head of the Office of American Absorption. This new office is established to promote Lindbergh's plan to disperse Jews from enclaves, such as the one in which the Roths live in Newark, to other parts of the country, thereby promoting their assimilation into the American mainstream. After years of working for an insurance company, Herman Roth is reassigned to Louisville under this plan, but rather than accept the assignment, he resigns and goes to work instead for his brother's produce business. Sandy Roth, meanwhile, is enticed into a program called "Just Folks," another attempt to foster Jewish assimilation, and spends the summer on a farm in Kentucky with a typical "American" family. He comes back with a southern accent and views quite opposed to those of his father. A neighbor's family, the Wishnows, is forced to accept the reassignment and goes to Danville, Kentucky, a town near Louisville. Later, Mrs. Wishnow is killed in a violent attack against Jews as she tries to drive home one night.

Roth brings in many historical characters: Father Coughlin, the extremist Catholic priest who fulminates against Jews; Walter Winchell, the Jewish newspaper reporter whose Sunday night radio broadcasts the Roth family and their friends dutifully listen to each week, and who at one point runs for president against Lindbergh, only to be assassinated for his efforts; the German foreign minister Joachim von Ribbentrop, who is honored by a state dinner at the White House by President and Mrs. Lindbergh; Fiorello La Guardia, the mayor of New York City, who is an eloquent spokesperson and a champion of civil rights; and many others. The picture of the United States under the Lindbergh administration is a very grim, even terrifying one. Although Roth insists he intended no allusion to politics in the twenty-first century, his novel clearly posts a warning for what might happen should American civil liberties suffer increased depredations, using the Iraq War as a pretext or an excuse.

Roth even brings into *The Plot Against America* the notorious kidnapping case of the 1930's, in which the Lindberghs' infant son was stolen. In this imagined reconstruction of events, the baby is not killed (as he was in actual fact) but taken by the Nazis and brought up in Germany as a good member of the *Hitler Jugend*. Events at the end of the novel culminate with the disappearance of Lindbergh himself and subsequent anti-Jewish riots in many cities across the United States in which 122 Jews lose their lives. Lindbergh, however, has not been kidnapped but has fled to Germany, using the *Spirit of St. Louis* for his escape, and is never seen again. Eventually, law and order are restored (thanks in part to the efforts of Mrs. Lindbergh), the Democrats take over Congress, and Roosevelt wins his unprecedented third term as president.

SUMMARY

Roth's development as a novelist shows both a deepening of his comedy and an expanding range of skills. Preoccupied by the idea of "counter-lives," or variations upon self-portraits, he examines various versions of his experience with telling effect and enormous insights. His preoccupation notwithstanding, he rarely repeats himself. Instead, he constantly attempts to expand the boundaries of his comic art, whose depths he tirelessly and wittily explores, with bountiful rewards.

Jay L. Halio

BIBLIOGRAPHY

By the Author

LONG FICTION:
Letting Go, 1962
When She Was Good, 1967
Portnoy's Complaint, 1969
Our Gang (Starring Tricky and His Friends), 1971
The Breast, 1972, revised 1980
The Great American Novel, 1973
My Life as a Man, 1974
The Professor of Desire, 1977
The Ghost Writer, 1979
Zuckerman Unbound, 1981
The Anatomy Lesson, 1983
Zuckerman Bound, 1985 (includes *The Ghost Writer, Zuckerman Unbound, The Anatomy Lesson*, and *Epilogue: The Prague Orgy*)
The Counterlife, 1986
Deception, 1990
Operation Shylock: A Confession, 1993
Sabbath's Theater, 1995
American Pastoral, 1997

I Married a Communist, 1998
The Human Stain, 2000
The Dying Animal, 2001
The Plot Against America, 2004

SHORT FICTION:
Goodbye, Columbus, and Five Short Stories, 1959
"Novotny's Pain," 1962, revised 1980
"The Psychoanalytic Special," 1963
"On the Air," 1970
"'I Always Wanted You to Admire My Fasting': Or, Looking at Kafka," 1973

NONFICTION:
Reading Myself and Others, 1975, expanded 1985
The Facts: A Novelist's Autobiography, 1988
Patrimony: A True Story, 1991
Shop Talk: A Writer and His Colleagues and Their Work, 2001

About the Author

Halio, Jay L. *Philip Roth Revisited.* New York: Twayne, 1992.

Halio, Jay L., and Ben Siegel, eds. *"Turning Up the Flame": Philip Roth's Later Novels.* Newark: University of Delaware Press, 2004.

Lee, Hermione. *Philip Roth.* London: Methuen, 1982.

Milbauer, Asher Z., ed. *Reading Philip Roth.* New York: St. Martin's Press, 1988.

Pinsker, Sanford. *The Comedy That "Hoits": An Essay on the Fiction of Philip Roth.* Columbia: University of Missouri Press, 1975.

_____, ed. *Critical Essays on Philip Roth.* Boston: G. K. Hall, 1982.

Rodgers, Bernard F., Jr. *Philip Roth.* Boston: Twayne, 1978.

Schechner, Mark. *After the Revolution: Studies in the Contemporary Jewish American Imagination.* Bloomington: Indiana University Press, 1987.

_____. *"Up Society's Ass, Copper": Rereading Philip Roth.* Madison: University of Wisconsin Press, 2003.

Shostak, Debra. *Philip Roth—Countertexts, Counterlives.* Columbia: University of South Carolina Press, 2004.

DISCUSSION TOPICS

- What aspects of Philip Roth's early fiction could have caused such a vigorous opposition to it by the conservative Jewish community?

- Is the charge against Roth of being a self-hating Jew credible?

- What is the basis for much of Philip Roth's humor?

- How accurate is Roth's portrayal of the United States in the post-World War II period in his "American Trilogy"?

- In some of his novels, Roth introduces himself as a character. How effective is this device?

- Roth has sometimes been criticized as an antifeminist because of his portraits of women. Is the charge justified? If so, how?

GABRIELLE ROY

Courtesy, McGill University

Born: St. Boniface, Manitoba, Canada
March 22, 1909
Died: Quebec City, Quebec, Canada
July 13, 1983

Roy's first book was a pioneering social realist novel depicting urban poverty in Montreal. It contrasted sharply with previous French Canadian fiction celebrating peasant life in rural Quebec.

BIOGRAPHY

Gabrielle Roy was the youngest of eleven children of Leon and Melina Roy, eight of whom survived to maturity. For eighteen years, her father had been a federal Department of Colonization agent, helping immigrants settle in the Prairie Provinces. He was dismissed in 1915 by newly elected Conservatives shortly before becoming eligible for a pension. Gabrielle grew up in poverty in St. Boniface, a largely French-speaking suburb of Winnipeg. Despite winning best-in-province medals in high school, university education was unattainable. She attended Winnipeg Normal Institute, graduating in 1929, and worked at several schools before being hired in 1930 to teach first grade at Winnipeg's prestigious Catholic boys' academy.

In September, 1937, having obtained a leave of absence, Roy sailed for Europe. Brief attendance at a London theater school ended dreams of becoming a professional actress. Three articles accepted by a Paris weekly convinced her that she could succeed as a French writer. Roy returned to Canada in April, 1939. Despite objections of her mother, who could not understand abandoning a secure, well-paying job during the Great Depression, as well as the anger of her sisters who thought she was selfishly evading contributing to family finances, Roy settled in Montreal as a freelance journalist.

Roy's work pleased editors of *Le Bulletin des agriculteurs*, a general-interest monthly magazine circulating mainly in rural Quebec. During the next five years, they regularly commissioned articles. In 1941, to celebrate the three hundredth anniversary of the founding of Montreal, *Le Bulletin des agriculteurs* published four essays in which Roy toured the city. She did not focus on poverty, but neither did she ignore it when visiting slums along Montreal's waterfront.

Hoping that the drama and tragedy she sensed in slum life could be turned into literature, Roy began a short story in 1941 that grew into an eight-hundred-page manuscript. Published in French as *Bonheur d'occasion* in Montreal in 1945 and in English as *The Tin Flute* in New York and Toronto in 1947, Roy's novel became a financial and public relations success previously unheard of in Canada.

Montreal critics praised the novel's thematic freshness. Readers responded enthusiastically, requiring three new printings in the next twelve months. A New York publisher commissioned an English translation. The Literary Guild book club choose *The Tin Flute* as its May, 1947, Book of the Month, an unprecedented honor for a Canadian novel, guaranteeing unexpectedly large monetary returns. Hollywood signed a contract for a film, which was never made. In 1947, the novel received the Governor-General's Award for fiction.

Roy visited Winnipeg in the summer of 1947 where friends celebrated her amazing success. While there she met, fell in love with, and married Marcel Carbotte, a gynecologist. They lived in

France for three years. After 1951, they settled in Quebec City, where Carbotte established a successful practice. They had no children.

Publication in France followed the American triumph. Reviewers praised her depiction of urban life and found her use of Quebec colloquialisms fascinating. The climax of Roy's success came with the award of the Prix Fémina in December, 1947, the first time a Canadian novel won a major French prize. Montreal literary circles were delighted to see France honor a Canadian book. Quebec nationalists disagreed, protesting that her portrait of slum life presented a negative image of French Canada to the world. With one book, Roy established herself as a major Canadian writer. *The Tin Flute* rapidly achieved the status of a classic of Canadian literature and became a favorite for academic analysis—the first M.A. thesis on the book appeared in 1949.

Roy found it difficult to produce the second novel that her publishers expected and shelved early efforts in favor of stories drawing on her experiences teaching French Canadian pupils in northern Manitoba. Literary critics in Montreal and Paris expressed disappointment with *La Petite poule d'eau* (1950; *Where Nests the Water Hen*, 1950), but the book proved popular with English-language readers who considered it a celebration of Canada's pioneer heritage. With notes in English added, schools adopted it as a French-language text for English-speaking students.

Nine years after publication of her first novel, the French version of *Alexandre Chenevert* (1955; *The Cashier*, 1955) appeared in Paris and Montreal in 1955. Reviewers unfavorably compared this realistic study of urban middle-class anxieties to *The Tin Flute*. Quebec critics were harshest, yet the book sold better there than elsewhere. Her final urban novel became another favorite text for academic analysts.

More popular with Canadian readers were two collections of semiautobiographical stories describing a young French Canadian girl growing up in Manitoba—*Rue Deschambault* (1955; *Street of Riches*, 1957), which won Roy a second Governor-General's Award in 1957, and *La Route d'Altamont* (1966; *The Road Past Altamont*, 1966). However critics and book buyers in the United States and France showed little interest, and after 1966, her New York publisher rejected later books.

Growing Canadian cultural nationalism helped boost Roy's popularity, since her stories exemplified multiculturalism and the ethnic mosaic view of nationality that Canadians preferred to the "melting pot" image. *La Montagne secrète* (1961; *The Hidden Mountain*, 1962) and *La Rivière sans repos* (1970; *Windflower*, 1970) were situated in arctic Quebec, the latter narrating the tribulations of an Inuit woman raped by an American soldier as she struggled to raise her son. *Un Jardin au bout du monde* (1975; *Garden in the Wind*, 1977) featured four different minorities; the title story described efforts of a Ukrainian housewife to grow flowers on the Great Plains.

Roy's fictional work *Ces enfants de ma vie* (1977; *Children of My Heart*, 1979), which went back in time to her experiences teaching children in Manitoba, was a complete triumph, a best seller hailed by critics as a significant contribution to Canadian literature. The novel won for Roy an unprecedented third Governor-General's Award.

ANALYSIS

The scene of *The Tin Flute* lay almost literally at the feet of Montreal's literary establishment, many of whom lived in affluent Westmount directly above Saint-Henri, on higher ground with less polluted air. However, no one before Roy grasped the dramatic and tragic possibilities of life in that area, and her book generated a sense of both shock and of belated recognition among its first reviewers.

The contrast between *The Tin Flute* and traditional French-Canadian fiction made Roy's work seem especially fresh and original. Such novels stressed the rural roots and Catholic faith of French Canadians. Fur traders and lumbermen exploring the new world of North America loomed large as heroes. Even more omnipresent were bucolic images of pious peasants living self-sufficient lives on the land, obediently following the injunctions of their priests to raise large families whose growth would ensure the persistence of French culture and Roman Catholicism in North America.

Roy's subject matter was very different. Her depiction of poverty was unsparing. Roy's training as a journalist showed in the precise language with which she described the sights, sounds, and smells of the slum. The reader could see the miasma of pollution rising from the Lachine Canal, feel trains on the nearby railroad shake the houses, and smell the odor of stale cooking and unwashed bodies that permeated the tenements of Saint-Henri. The reportorial precision of Roy's descriptive prose was enhanced by careful use of colloquial French Canadian speech in dialogues, which Parisian critics found fascinating. Although unique to Quebec, the dialect of the book was comprehensible to readers of standard French and has been successfully translated into eight languages.

The author refused to sentimentalize the impact of poverty upon her characters. Roy wanted the reader to sympathize with the two heroines in *The Tin Flute,* but she never suggested that they were ennobled by poverty. Azarius's inability to earn money eroded Rose-Anna's love for him; she could be mean and calculating when defending her brood. Florentine used sex to try winning Jean and was willing to deceive Emmanuel about who fathered her child when he became her escape out of poverty.

Roy made extensive use of irony in the French and English titles of her first novel, in the names of her characters, and throughout her body of work. For example, the French title *Bonheur d'occasion* suggests that the poor must settle for "bargain-basement happiness"; the slum child gets the tin flute he desires only after being hospitalized with a fatal illness. Alexandre Chenevert's name deliberately suggests characteristics he does not share— Alexander is a warrior king and chenevert is a type of oak tree, but Chenevert is not a warrior, nor does he have the strength of an oak. The major irony running through *The Tin Flute* is that only war and death will bring the people of Saint-Henri out of poverty.

Both urban novels present direct oppositions of city to country, of artificial to natural, of urban-industrial civilization to rural-agricultural life. Each book has a middle section—one chapter in *The Tin Flute* and seven in *Alexandre Chenevert*—in which the characters move to a rural locale. However, Roy is ambivalent about the polar opposition. Natural locales are always more attractive than artificial urban ones, yet they are ultimately disappointing; they do not provide a solution to problems of city life. Rose-Anna looked forward to revisiting the farm where she grew up, but the trip left her de-

pressed. Chenevert viewed the farm as paradise, but paradise was ultimately boring, and he returned to the city before his vacation ended. Roy portrayed the bus trip back to Montreal as almost a descent into hell; houses got closer together, heavy traffic slowed movement, noise and foul odors wafted through the bus. In the city, he was nearly run over crossing the street; when he looked up at the sky, the heavens urged: Drink Pepsi-Cola.

Although Roy avoided direct comments on political or controversial issues and never engaged in feminist polemics, her work has been praised by feminist critics impressed by her clear presentation of the iniquities of women's position and her nuanced dramatization of mother-daughter relationships in *The Tin Flute* and her Manitoba stories. She never discussed Catholic views on birth control, but descriptions of the deleterious effects of unlimited childbearing on women clearly convey her feelings to the reader.

Roy disliked proposals for Quebec independence, and her belief in Canadian federalism informs all her books. Sympathetic stories about native peoples and immigrants openly support the idea of a multicultural, bilingual Canada. Her books celebrating French Canadians on the Great Plains were clear rebukes to those who believed that interests of French speakers in Canada ended at the border with Ontario.

Her major novels consider universal themes. The struggles of characters in *The Tin Flute* are those of poor families in every industrial country during the Great Depression. Alexandre Chenevert is a prototype of middle-class employees living in an urban-industrial environment that bombards them with more information than they can adequately assimilate. The Manitoba novels explore difficulties that immigrants face everywhere. However, after the first flurries of international interest, Roy's appeal was primarily to Canadians, who celebrated her as perhaps the most quintessentially Canadian of authors, one whose appeal successfully transcended the language barrier. She remains one of the very few writers read and admired as much in English- as in French-speaking circles decades after her death.

THE TIN FLUTE

First published: 1945
Type of work: Novel

A mother and daughter, Rose-Anna and Florentine Lacasse, struggle to survive in a Montreal slum during World War II.

Roy's original French title of *Bonheur d'occasion* has no precise English equivalent—critics have suggested "chance happiness," "bargain-basement happiness," and "second-hand happiness" as approximate translations. *The Tin Flute* is a toy that young Daniel Lacasse only gets when dying with a fatal illness.

The scene is the Saint-Henri district of Montreal, a slum adjoining factories along the Lachine Canal, from which noxious odors permeate the district. The time is early 1940; news of triumphant German armies forms an ominous background to the novel.

Young Florentine Lacasse, a waitress at a five-and-dime lunch counter, supports her family financially. Her father, Azarius, a carpenter by trade and an idealistic daydreamer, cannot hold a job. Florentine flirts with Jean Lévesque, an ambitious young machinist who realizes that war work is his road out of poverty.

Rose-Anna Lacasse, pregnant with her twelfth child, worries about spending her family's meager funds. They will shortly need to move, probably to even worse conditions. Her son Eugène proudly tells his mother that he has enlisted and the army will send her twenty dollars a month. When Rose-Anna visits the five-and-dime, Florentine treats her to a meal. As Rose-Anna leaves, she examines a toy tin flute that her sick young son Daniel would like but cannot justify the expense and puts it back.

Emmanuel Létourneau, in uniform on leave after enlisting in the army, meets old buddies who complain of long-lasting unemployment. He falls in love with Florentine, but she is only interested in Jean. When Rose-Anna desires to visit the farm where she grew up, Azarius drives the family there, but the contrast between her healthy nieces and nephews and her own sickly brood saddens Rose-Anna. Azarius had taken a truck without his employer's knowledge and is fired.

Florentine chose not to go on the trip and instead invited Jean to her home, where the two have sex and she becomes pregnant. Jean is repulsed by her house, which smells of the poverty that he is desperate to escape. He moves to a distant armaments factory without leaving a forwarding address. Florentine reluctantly accepts Emmanuel's marriage proposal and begins to convince herself that her child is really his.

Young Daniel is hospitalized with leukemia. The nurses surround him with toys, including his long-desired tin flute. As his life ebbs away, he is happier in the hospital than he had ever been at home.

News of the fall of France stimulates Azarius to deliver a rousing oration expressing the love of French Canadians for a country that they have never seen but still consider their homeland. He and his listeners enlist to fight with the English to free France. The army will send Rose-Anna ninety-seven dollars a month, more than Azarius ever earned. The war becomes salvation for men of Saint-Henri who will earn steady money for the first time in their lives.

THE CASHIER

First published: 1955
Type of work: Novel

A bank teller living a sterile life isolated in his glass cage deplores the state of the world, discovers he has cancer, and dies.

Alexandre Chenevert, the cashier, wakes up at night worrying about world affairs. Longshoremen are on strike, and food rots on the docks while poverty-stricken children suffer from malnutrition. It is 1947, Germany has surrendered, the war is over, yet fighting still continues in Greece. Chenevert visualizes Jewish refugees, refused admission by the

British mandate government, drowning off the coast of Palestine, and decides he hates England. His stomach hurts, but medicines in his bathroom cabinet offer no relief. He falls asleep shortly before the alarm rings and awakes befuddled and unrefreshed.

At the bank in his glass teller's cage, Chenevert tries being impassive and working in a mechanical manner but becomes irritable and scolds customers who fail to fill out deposit or withdrawal slips properly. He quarrels with a coworker who does not share his worries about world affairs. When closing his accounts for the day, he discovers a one-hundred-dollar error, which he must repay in small installments.

Chenevert consults a doctor, but tests fail to show objective causes for stomach pains. The doctor thinks he worries unnecessarily and suggests he take a vacation. Chenevert decides to rent a lakeside cabin and recruit his strength in the countryside while his wife visits their daughter.

Roy inserts a pastoral episode as the middle third of the novel, occupying seven of the book's twenty-two chapters. Chenevert sleeps well in his cabin and enjoys the beauty of the landscape. The farmer tells him that his family is self-sufficient in food, raising crops, getting fish from the lake, and meat from moose he hunts in the fall. Chenevert views the farm as paradise but cannot find adequate words when he tries to write down his ideas. Growing bored with the country, he returns early,

enduring a nightmarish bus ride that gets snarled in heavy traffic as he approaches Montreal.

The concluding four chapters chronicle Chenevert's decline and death. Although he claims to feel better after his vacation, he grows thinner and uses many medications for stomach pain. He frets over news of the Nuremberg trials and has to be dissuaded from fasting to protest Mahatma Gandhi's assassination.

Chenevert believes that he has cancer but avoids seeing a doctor, hoping medical advances will soon produce a cure. When hospitalized, he is diagnosed with prostate cancer, not the stomach cancer he feared. By then it is too late for surgery. He comes down with pneumonia and a kidney infection. Chenevert and his wife realize they love each other. When employees and clients of the bank come to visit, he discovers that he has many friends. Morphine soon ceases to work, and Chenevert and the priest who hears his confession pray for his death.

SUMMARY

Gabrielle Roy's first novel established her enduring reputation as a major Canadian author. Her books exerted a powerful influence on later Canadian writers, encouraging them to deal realistically with Canadian life. The novels continued in print in both French and English editions into the twenty-first century, and her readers remained enthusiastic. Roy's childhood home was turned into a museum, and an admirer leads walking tours of the places in Montreal described in her novels. When the Bank of Canada in 2004 introduced a new twenty-dollar bill designed to honor arts and culture, it included a quotation from Roy on the back of the bank note.

Milton Berman

BIBLIOGRAPHY

By the Author

SHORT FICTION:
Rue Deschambault, 1955 (18 linked stories; *Street of Riches*, 1957)
La Route d'Altamont, 1966 (4 linked stories; *The Road Past Altamont*, 1966)
La Rivière sans repos, 1970 (*Windflower*, 1970)
Cet été qui chantait, 1972 (*Enchanted Summer*, 1976)
Un Jardin au bout du monde, 1975 (*Garden in the Wind*, 1977)

Ces enfants de ma vie, 1977 (*Children of My Heart*, 1979)

De quoi t'ennuies-tu, Éveline?, 1982

LONG FICTION:

Bonheur d'occasion, 1945 (*The Tin Flute*, 1947)

La Petite poule d'eau, 1950 (*Where Nests the Water Hen*, 1950)

Alexandre Chenevert, 1955 (*The Cashier*, 1955)

La Montagne secrète, 1961 (*The Hidden Mountain*, 1962)

NONFICTION:

Fragiles lumières de la terre, 1978 (*The Fragile Lights of Earth*, 1982)

La Détresse et l'enchantement, 1984 (*Enchantment and Sorrow*, 1987)

Ma chère petite soeur: Lettres à Bernadette, 1943-1970, 1988 (*My Dearest Sister: Letters to Bernadette, 1943-1970*, 1990)

CHILDREN'S LITERATURE:

Ma vache Bossie, 1976 (*My Cow Bossie*, 1980)

Courte-Queue, 1979 (*Cliptail*, 1980)

L'Espagnole et la pekinoise, 1986 (*The Tortoiseshelle and the Pekinese*, 1989)

DISCUSSION TOPICS

- Does the city of Montreal itself serve as a powerful character in Gabrielle Roy's urban fiction? How or how not?

- Since Roy never discusses feminism in her written work, why would some call her a feminist?

- In what ways does the title of *The Tin Flute* symbolize Roy's central themes in that novel?

- Do you think Alexandre Chenevert can be considered a universal type? In what ways? How not?

- Are Roy's negative images of urban, industrial cities still valid? Why or why not?

About the Author

Clemente, Linda M., and William A. Clemente. *Gabrielle Roy: Creation and Memory*. Toronto: ECW Press, 1997.

Hesse, M. G. *Gabrielle Roy*. Boston: Twayne, 1984.

Lewis, Paula Gilbert. *The Literary Vision of Gabrielle Roy: An Analysis of Her Works*. Birmingham, Ala.: Summa, 1984.

Mitcham, Allison. *The Literary Achievement of Gabrielle Roy*. Fredericton, New Brunswick: York Press, 1983.

Ricard, Francois. *Gabrielle Roy: A Life*. Translated by Patricia Claxton. Toronto: McClelland & Stewart, 1999.

Roy, Gabrielle. *Enchantment and Sorrow: The Autobiography of Gabrielle Roy*. Translated by Patricia Claxton. Toronto: Lester & Orpen Dennys, 1987.

MURIEL RUKEYSER

Born: New York, New York
December 15, 1913
Died: New York, New York
February 12, 1980

Rukeyser, primarily noted for her poems of social protest, also wrote some of the twentieth century's most moving and lyrical love poetry.

Library of Congress

BIOGRAPHY

Muriel Rukeyser was born on December 15, 1913, in New York City to Lawrence B. and Myra (Lyons) Rukeyser. Her father was from Milwaukee, Wisconsin, and cofounded a building business. Her mother was from Yonkers, New York. Muriel Rukeyser was brought up as the sheltered daughter of her affluent parents, spending time at yacht clubs, camps, and symphonies. Despite her privileged childhood, she grew up with a sense of the larger world: Her toddler years coincided with World War I, and she was a teenager when the stock market crashed in 1929. The activism of Rukeyser's adult years was a complete rejection of her former protected existence.

Even as a child, Rukeyser wrote poems, although the only people she knew who read any poetry were servants. Rukeyser continued writing poetry during her high-school years, attempting to reconcile normal adolescent troubles with her feelings about the outrages in the newspaper headlines. The executions of Nicola Sacco and Bartolomeo Vanzetti (two Italian immigrant anarchists convicted of murder and theft) in August, 1927, even after worldwide protest on their behalf, made a powerful impression on the adolescent Rukeyser.

After high school, Rukeyser attended Vassar College, Columbia University, and Roosevelt Aviation School. As she wrote in *The Life of Poetry* (1949), her "first day at college ended childhood." She began to write the poems that would be published in her first book while cofounding (with Elizabeth Bishop, Mary McCarthy, and Eleanor Clark) a literary magazine called *Student Review* to protest the policies of the established *Vassar Review.*

Rukeyser frequently contributed to *Student Review*; as part of this work, she drove to Alabama in 1932 to report on the trial of the Scottsboro Boys, nine young black men who were accused of raping two white girls during the spring of 1931. Rukeyser viewed the resulting death sentence as evidence of a dual system of American justice, which discriminated against the poor and the nonwhite. While in Alabama, Rukeyser was arrested by police after she and her friends were discovered talking to black reporters; she was carrying thirty posters advertising a black student conference at Columbia University. In the Alabama jail, Rukeyser contracted typhoid.

In 1935, Rukeyser's first book of poetry, *Theory of Flight*, was published and won the Yale Younger Poets Prize. In 1936, Rukeyser traveled to Barcelona, Spain, to cover the Anti-Fascist Olympics for *Life and Letters Today*. While there, she witnessed the outbreak and first fighting of the Spanish Civil War. She lobbied for the cause of the Spanish Loyalists and incorporated the images she witnessed into her poetic work.

Rukeyser's second volume of poems, *U.S. 1* (1938), was based on her investigation into the death by silicosis of miners in West Virginia, a notorious scandal of the mid-1930's. Her three following volumes, *Mediterranean* (1938), *A Turning Wind: Poems* (1939), and *The Soul and Body of John Brown* (1940), continued Rukeyser's emphasis on social injustice in America. Upon the outbreak of World War II, she became passionately involved in portraying the atrocities visited upon the Jewish people by the Nazis, a subject of great personal interest because of her Jewish heritage and her earlier opposition to fascism in the Spanish Civil War.

In 1945, Rukeyser moved to California, where she was briefly married to painter Glynn Collins. A few years later, she gave birth to an illegitimate son, for which her father disowned her. She incorporated these experiences into her later work, often using the image of giving birth to combat the horrors of the modern world. During this time, Rukeyser was helped by an anonymous benefactor (later known to be the wealthy Californian Henriette Durham) who provided funds to support Rukeyser until her return to New York in 1954, when she began teaching part time at Sarah Lawrence College.

For the rest of her life, Rukeyser continued to write, to teach part time (leading poetry workshops at various institutions), and to protest against injustice. In 1972, she flew to Hanoi, Vietnam, to participate in a peace demonstration, and later that year she was arrested on the steps of the U.S. Capitol in Washington, D.C., for protesting the Vietnam War. In 1974, as president of the international writers organization PEN, she traveled to South Korea to protest the imprisonment and death sentence of the radical Catholic poet Kim Chi-Ha.

Though Rukeyser was often characterized as a poet of political or social protest, many of her poems were very personal, exploring her experiences as a mother and a daughter, discussing her opinions on creativity and sexuality, and describing her slow recovery after a debilitating stroke. Rukeyser's work is often compared to Walt Whitman's in its imagery and optimism. Yet her work was distinctly individual and always created strong impressions in the minds of her readers.

As the writer and poet Kenneth Rexroth wrote, "Muriel Rukeyser is not a poet of Marxism, but a poet who has written directly about the tragedies of the working class. She is a poet of liberty, civil liberty, woman's liberty, and all the other liberties that so many people think they themselves just invented." Rukeyser died in New York on February 12, 1980.

ANALYSIS

While writing *The Life of Poetry*, Rukeyser was able to look back at her childhood and pinpoint moments that opened her eyes to the world. Once she began really to see the world, she wrote, she never stopped paying attention to and writing about what she saw.

"Breathe-in experience, breathe-out poetry." So begins "Poem out of Childhood," the first poem in Rukeyser's first book, *Theory of Flight*. The phrase expresses her fundamental belief that poetry is based on experience: Life, feelings, and reactions are the source of poetry. Further, for Rukeyser, the personal, the political, and the poetical are inextricably woven together. As she frequently acted on this belief, some critics have called her the poet of the downtrodden.

Her poetry, however, contains more than social commentary, slogans, or expressions of outrage over injustice. Rukeyser's poems embody optimism, a belief in the noble aspirations of humanity, and a sense of wonder at the beauty of the world, all expressed in a powerfully lyrical voice. Rukeyser used her lyrical writing to express her social and political awareness and to encourage (even, at times, to exhort) the reader to action or, at least, to awareness. For example, in "Poem out of Childhood," she expresses astonishment at being taught about the ancient Greeks in high school while being taught nothing about current events: "Not Sappho, Sacco," she complains.

Rukeyser's poem "Theory of Flight" is representative of her early work. It is written as a cluster of short verses under seven subheadings; the first section, "Preamble," begins with an appeal to the opposites of the earth and the sky: "Earth, bind us close, and time ; nor, sky, deride/ how violate we experiment again." Near the section's end, the poet writes that the sky is the "meeting of sky and no-sky" and that "flight, thus, is meeting of flight and non-flight." These images present one of Rukeyser's themes, the reconciliation of opposites. As critic David Barber has noted, Rukeyser's goal was to resolve the conflicts in herself; her means was "to deal completely with the self," and her specific tool was poetry. One aspect of this reconciliation is found in her later work, which included poems exploring her relations with her parents, making peace with her dead mother, and dealing with her failing health. Another aspect of the reconciliation

Rukeyser desired was the resolution of conflict between the upper, middle, and lower classes.

Rukeyser's concern with themes of class oppression, death, and justice in America is most clearly visible in "The Trial," a part of "Theory of Flight" that discusses the trial of the Scottsboro Boys in Alabama. This section could have been written with bitterness and anger, but although it describes lynchings and other terrible injustices, the passage ends with a powerful affirmation of life and human striving as represented by an airplane. The last phrase of the section is the shout "FLY," expressing precisely the sort of optimism in the midst of horrors that led critics to view Rukeyser's work in the same light as Whitman's. This aspect of her work, however, has often been ignored by scholars more interested in her frequently strident social commentary and philosophizing.

While Rukeyser was primarily known for being outspoken and courageous, her language changed over the course of her early career. She moved from an oratorical, prophetic tone to a meditative, spiritual one based more directly on her immediate experience; she also moved away from forming most of her poems out of clusters of verses and toward a more compact style. These changes in form did not, however, affect her passion or lyricism. To the end of her career, Rukeyser remained bardic, romantic, and compassionate.

"POEM OUT OF CHILDHOOD"

First published: 1935 (collected in *Theory of Flight*, 1935)
Type of work: Poem

This work presents contrasting images of the poet's sheltered youth and societal injustices, which she eventually resolves.

Part 1 of "Poem out of Childhood" opens with Rukeyser's famous declaration "Breathe-in experience, breathe-out poetry" and continues with images of high-school students being affected by the outside world: a girl whose father and brother have just died, for example, and the image of the "mouldered face" of a "syphilitic woman" that intrudes upon a school orchestra's playing. The poet is hit with image after image that, like bandages,

wrap her head: "when I put my hand up I hardly feel the wounds."

The poet continues, protesting against those "who manipulated and misused our youth, / smearing those centuries upon our hands," by focusing the students' attention on the past and ignoring present-day horrors. Part 1 ends with the proclamation, "Rebellion pioneered among our lives, / viewing from far-off many-branching deltas, / innumerable seas."

During part 2 of "Poem out of Childhood," Rukeyser is still thinking about world events: "Prinzip's year bore us : see us turning at breast/ quietly while the air throbs over Sarajevo/ after the mechanic laugh of that bullet." The reference is to Gavrilo Princip, the Serbian student whose assassination of the Austrian Archduke Ferdinand at Sarajevo on June 28, 1914, triggered World War I. The aftermath of the assassination is the throbbing pain accompanying the birth of Rukeyser's modern world, and the children born into that world are shown as innocent and ineffective. The early days of the modern world are viewed through a kaleidoscope of Rukeyser's memories, including an abandoned factory at which "the kids throw stones." The empty factory seems to represent the old social structures, abandoned during the war.

Part 3 begins with the poet's decision to

Organize the full results of that rich past
open the windows : potent catalyst,
harsh theory of knowledge, running down the
  aisles
crying out in the classrooms, March ravening on
  the plain,
inexorable sun and wind and natural thought.

As critic Louise Kertesz has explained, this is how Rukeyser will deal with her memories of suffering and conflict, by creating "an organizing vision which is intensely personal and hard-won." The youth now will not throw stones at the abandoned factory but will knock at its walls, questioning its meaning and determining its place in her life. Here is Rukeyser's reconciliation of the opposites of her innocent, sheltered youth and her memories of the awful events that took place during that youth. Part 3 of "Poem out of Childhood" ends with the positive image of young people trying on different roles and exploring their significance by "summoning fact from abandoned machines of trade," ready "for the affirmative clap of truth."

"AJANTA"

First published: 1944 (collected in *The Collected Poems of Muriel Rukeyser,* 1978)
Type of work: Poem

"Ajanta" chronicles Rukeyser's inner journey to free herself from the bonds of society and to resolve her conflict between personal and political values.

"Ajanta" has been hailed as the finest poem of Rukeyser's first decade of work and is one of her most famous writings. The name Ajanta refers to a number of ancient cave temples and monasteries in India that are famous for their wall paintings. The poem is written in Rukeyser's characteristic cluster form and is made up of five parts, titled "The Journey," "The Cave," "Les Tendresses Bestiales," "Black Blood," and "Broken World."

"The Journey" explains the significance of "Ajanta": The poem will describe Rukeyser's solitary youthful journey through the stormy world to that moment of peace that is the cave. Although she blessed her heart's ability to suffer (and to empathize), she was torn between youth's natural desire to cherish the values it had been taught and the activism that her conscience demanded at the sight of injustice. In other words, "Ajanta" will tell the story of her synthesis of personal and political concerns.

"The Cave" represents the peacefulness the poet will feel when she finally accepts the world's condition and her place in that world. In this section, Rukeyser describes the nature of the cave: It is both a space in the mind and a space in the body, yet it "is not a womb," for "nothing but good emerges" from the cave. (This contrasts with the mixture of good and evil in all humans.) Rukeyser's journey, then, is to be an internal one. In the cave, "the walls are the world," and "the space of these walls is the body's living space." She senses that the "spaces of the body/ Are suddenly limitless," that once she reconciles her inner conflicts she will have her freedom.

In the third section of "Ajanta," "Les Tendresses Bestiales," it becomes apparent that Rukeyser has

not yet reached the cave but is still held in the outside world. This world suddenly changes from a world of beauty into a world of savagery and tumult, paralleling the change in Rukeyser from a peaceful, sheltered child into a torn, lost being. She writes, "I am plunged deep. Must find the midnight cave."

"Black Blood," the fourth section of "Ajanta," conveys all the anger, fear, greed, and turmoil of real life. As the poet runs, lost in this welter of blood and viciousness, she is found by a bit of hope: "—As I ran I heard/ A black voice beating among all that blood:/ 'Try to live as if there were a God.'"

In the fifth section, "The Broken World," Rukeyser has reached the Ajanta cave, "The real world where everything is complete./ There are no shadows, the forms of incompleteness." Here, the conflicts within her have been resolved, and she has no doubts. She experiences not merely freedom from conflict but also happiness, and she writes, "Here all may stand/ On summer earth."

Even as she has achieved unity and contentment, however, "Crawls from the door,/ Black at my two feet/ The shadow of the world." This shadow reminds Rukeyser of the disunity and trouble in the world outside the cave and will not let her withdraw into herself. By writing "Ajanta," she has not only united the differences within herself but also accepted the task of speaking out against worldly injustices.

"SEARCHING/NOT SEARCHING"

First published: 1972 (collected in *The Collected Poems of Muriel Rukeyser,* 1978)
Type of work: Poem

The poet bears witness to truth while in the midst of social crises and tries to transcend the barriers between people.

The poem "Searching/Not Searching" carries an epigraph attributed to the poet Robert Duncan: "Responsibility is to use the power to respond." This might almost be taken as Rukeyser's motto, as her entire adult life and most of her poems responded sharply to the world events that she witnessed.

The first of the fourteen sections of "Searching/ Not Searching" asks, "What kind of woman goes searching and searching?/ . . . or what man? for what magic?" The answer is that Rukeyser's kind does. Throughout the world, she "searched for that Elizabethan man,/ the lost discoverer, the servant of time." This reference is to the latter part of the sixteenth century, when classical humanism (providing a noble vision of the dignity of humanity) and the medieval tragic sense of life (providing an awareness of death) were united into a heroic picture of humanity that was circumscribed by the sense of human mortality. This unification parallels Rukeyser's unification of the personal and the political; in the light of her unflagging optimism and her sense of reality, Rukeyser might almost be called Elizabethan.

Rukeyser's commitment to speaking out (or bearing witness) is renewed in the poem's second section, "Miriam : The Red Sea." The section's title refers to a prophet of the Old Testament, the elder sister of Moses and Aaron who led the celebration of the Hebrew women after the crossing of the Red Sea. Rukeyser, as Miriam, says "I along stand here/ ankle-deep/ and I sing, I sing,/ until the lands/ sing to each other."

As critic Louise Kertesz explains, each section of "Searching/Not Searching" is "another witness to wholeness and unity, despite the discouragement of silence and unresponsiveness." Further, each section provides a particular image, either of inspiration or of outrage, which gives the poet strength to continue her quest. For example, in the third section, "For Dolci," in Kertesz's words, "the direct vision and speech of children will help the poet in her search to speak the truth." In section 4, "Concrete," Rukeyser's poems are poured down as concrete is poured, both forming the foundation for the future, helping to alleviate the poet's sense of futility.

Inspiration also comes from a Vietnamese epic heroine who sells herself to save her father, from the Sistine Chapel, and from Rukeyser's dying friend Hallie Flanagan (the director of the Works Progress Administration Federal Theatre Project), who taught Rukeyser the most important element of a theatrical production: "The audience the response." Outrage is felt in the tenth section, "The President and the Laser Bomb," in which a politician's proclamation of peace is juxtaposed with an image of destructive technology.

The poem, however, closes with a declaration of hope in the power of communication. What the poet has found in her quest for truth is that communication between people "was the truth." Through their words and deeds, everyone is "trying to make, to let our closeness be made,/ not torn apart tonight by our dead skills."

SUMMARY

Rukeyser merged her personal vision with her political vision and wrote poems of remarkable intensity. Her work was so linked to current events that one critic claimed that the whole of twentieth century history could be learned by reading Rukeyser's work. Though noted for her poems of social protest, Rukeyser also wrote deeply personal poems, incorporating such diverse elements as scientific language and mysticism, all in a unique lyrical, demanding style. One of her most unique traits was her optimism: While describing the injustices and the horrors of her times, Rukeyser usually was able to express faith in the potential of civilization, wonder at the beauty of the world, and love for humanity.

Katherine Socha

BIBLIOGRAPHY

By the Author

POETRY:
Theory of Flight, 1935
U.S. 1, 1938
Mediterranean, 1938
A Turning Wind: Poems, 1939
The Soul and Body of John Brown, 1940
Wake Island, 1942
Beast in View, 1944

The Green Wave, 1948
Elegies, 1949
Orpheus, 1949
Selected Poems, 1951
Body of Waking, 1958
Waterlily Fire: Poems, 1935-1962, 1962
The Outer Banks, 1967
The Speed of Darkness, 1968
Twenty-nine Poems, 1972
Breaking Open: New Poems, 1973
The Gates: Poems, 1976
The Collected Poems of Muriel Rukeyser, 1978
Out of Silence: Selected Poems, 1992

TRANSLATIONS:
Selected Poems, 1963 (of Octavio Paz's poems)
Sun Stone, 1963 (of Paz's poems)
Selected Poems, 1967 (of Gunnar Ekelöf's poems; with Leif Sjoberg)
Three Poems, 1967 (of Ekelöf's poems)
Early Poems, 1935-1955, 1973 (of Paz's poems)
Uncle Eddie's Moustache, 1974 (of Bertolt Brecht's poems)
A Mölna Elegy, 1984 (of Ekelöf's poem)

LONG FICTION:
The Orgy, 1965

DRAMA:
The Colors of the Day: A Celebration for the Vassar Centennial, June 10, 1961, pr. 1961
Houdini, pr. 1973, pb. 2002

NONFICTION:
Willard Gibbs, 1942
The Life of Poetry, 1949
One Life, 1957
Poetry and the Unverifiable Fact: The Clark Lectures, 1968
The Traces of Thomas Hariot, 1971

CHILDREN'S LITERATURE:
Come Back, Paul, 1955
I Go Out, 1961
Bubbles, 1967
Mayes, 1970
More Night, 1981

MISCELLANEOUS:
A Muriel Rukeyser Reader, 1994

DISCUSSION TOPICS

- What experiences of Muriel Rukeyser's early life help explain her reactions to the political and economic turbulence of the 1930's?

- What unusually mature childhood perceptions are evident in her "Poem out of Childhood"?

- Discuss Rukeyser as a poet of civil liberty.

- What pattern can you discern in the imagery of "Searching/Not Searching"?

- What structural principles does Rukeyser regularly employ in her longer poems?

About the Author

Ciardi, John. *Mid-Century American Poets*. New York: Twayne, 1950.

Herzog, Anne F., and Janet E. Kaufman, eds. *How Shall We Tell Each Other of the Poet? The Life and Writing of Muriel Rukeyser*. New York: St. Martin's Press, 1999.

Kertesz, Louise. *The Poetic Vision of Muriel Rukeyser*. Baton Rouge: Louisiana State University Press, 1980.

Moss, Howard. *The Poet's Story*. New York: Macmillan, 1973.

J. D. SALINGER

Born: New York, New York
January 1, 1919

National Archives

Although primarily a writer of short stories, Salinger is best known for his novel The Catcher in the Rye, *which had an enormous influence on young readers of the 1950's and succeeding generations.*

BIOGRAPHY

Because of Salinger's insistence on preserving his privacy, and the willingness of his family and friends to assist him in doing so, little biographical information on Salinger is available, especially regarding his later life. Moreover, his habit of deliberately misleading would-be biographers with false information further complicates the picture; nevertheless, some elements of Salinger's biography are generally accepted as true.

Jerome David Salinger was born in New York City on January 1, 1919, to a Jewish father, Sol Salinger, a successful importer of hams and cheeses, and a Christian mother, Miriam Jillich Salinger. He was the second of two children; his sister, Doris, was eight years his senior. Salinger attended public schools on the upper West Side of Manhattan and seems to have been an average student.

At age thirteen, Salinger was enrolled in the prestigious McBurney School in Manhattan, but he was dismissed with failing grades after a year. He was then sent to Valley Forge Military Academy in Pennsylvania, which was to become the model for Pencey Prep in *The Catcher in the Rye* (1951). At Valley Forge, Salinger was the literary editor of the school yearbook, and there he wrote his first stories.

After he graduated from Valley Forge, Salinger attended the summer session at New York University, then accompanied his father to Vienna to learn the Polish ham business. He soon returned to the United States, however, and entered college again, this time at Ursinus College in Pennsylvania. He wrote a column called "The Skipped Diploma" for the *Ursinus Weekly*, but he dropped out in the middle of his first semester there. He then enrolled in a story-writing class at Columbia University taught by Whit Burnett, editor of *Story* magazine. Salinger's first published story, "The Young Folks," appeared in the March/April, 1940, issue of *Story*.

Salinger subsequently published stories in *Collier's* and *Esquire* magazines, and more stories in *Story*, before being drafted into the Army in 1942. He attended officer training school, achieved the rank of staff sergeant, and was sent to Devonshire, England, for counterintelligence training. On D day, June 6, 1944, Salinger landed on Utah Beach in Normandy with the Fourth Army Division. As a security officer, he was assigned to interrogate captured Germans and French civilians to identify Gestapo agents. While in France, Salinger met Ernest Hemingway, to whom he later wrote an admiring letter.

After the war ended, Salinger was hospitalized for psychiatric treatment in Nuremberg, Germany, but continued to write and publish stories, as he had done throughout the war. He returned to New York in 1947 and signed a contract to write stories for *The New Yorker.* In 1950, Salinger's story "For Esmé—with Love and Squalor" was designated one of the distinguished American stories of the year. Salinger spent much of this period in Greenwich Village, where he associated with other young writers and artists, and reportedly dated a wide variety of women in order to collect dialogue for his stories. He also began to exhibit a keen interest in religion—particularly Zen Buddhism, which would greatly influence his work.

Another Salinger characteristic that began to manifest itself at this time was a desire for isolation. Salinger left Greenwich Village for a cottage in Tarrytown, New York (although he is said to have finished writing *The Catcher in the Rye* in a room near the Third Avenue El in New York City). When *The Catcher in the Rye* was published in 1951, Salinger went to Europe to avoid publicity and the following year traveled to Mexico. In 1953, he bought ninety acres of land on the Connecticut River in Cornish, New Hampshire. During that year, he agreed for the first and last time to be interviewed by a reporter—a sixteen-year-old high school girl writing for a local newspaper.

After marrying and divorcing a French doctor named Sylvia, in 1955 Salinger married Claire Douglas, an English-born graduate of Radcliffe College. Salinger is said to have written the story "Franny" (1955) as a wedding present for Claire, and the heroine of the story is supposed to be based on her. The couple had two children before divorcing in 1967. In 1972, Salinger began an affair with Joyce Maynard, who, at age nineteen, was just a few years older than his daughter at that time. Maynard is a writer whose memoir of life with Salinger, *At Home in the World*, was published in 1998. In the 1980's, Salinger married a woman named Colleen.

Though his wife is reportedly active in the community where they live in Connecticut, Salinger continues to be extremely reclusive. Despite frequent fan mail and attempts to contact him, Salinger has refused all requests for interviews and declined all correspondence. His daughter, Margaret Salinger, against her father's will, went public with their family life with the publication of her book *Dream Catcher: A Memoir* in 2000. Salinger also continues to refuse commentary on his published work, saying, "The stuff's all there in the stories; there's no use talking about it."

ANALYSIS

Several characteristic themes are evident throughout Salinger's work: the innocence of childhood versus the corruption of adulthood; honesty versus phoniness; estrangement, isolation, and alien-

ation; and the quest for enlightenment and understanding of such fundamental issues as love, suffering, and the problem of evil.

Characteristic techniques recur as well. They include the use of dialogue, gesture, and personal objects to reveal character and relationships; the repetition of characters from one story to another; the reliance on puzzles, paradoxes, and riddles in a way similar to that used by teachers of Zen Buddhism; and frequent allusions to religious teachers and texts, philosophers, and authors and their works.

The importance of children to Salinger becomes obvious upon reading even a few of his stories: Sybil in "A Perfect Day for Bananafish," Esmé in "For Esmé—with Love and Squalor," and Phoebe and several other children in *The Catcher in the Rye* are examples of a certain wise innocence which the older protagonists of the stories seem to have lost and struggle to recapture. It is also noteworthy that many of these children are extremely precocious; indeed, *Franny and Zooey* (1961), as well as *"Raise High the Roof Beam, Carpenters"* and *"Seymour: An Introduction"* (1963), deals with a whole family of precocious "whiz kids" who have been regular contestants on a radio quiz program called *It's a Wise Child*. The use of precocious children and the title of the program itself reflect Salinger's sense that children possess some kind of innate understanding only rarely and with great difficulty retained in growing up.

Such an idea is closely linked to the theme of honesty versus phoniness. "Phony" is Holden Caulfield's favorite epithet for any kind of behavior that strikes him as insincere (in *The Catcher in the Rye*), and phoniness appears to Holden as one of the chief evils of the world. Thus the attraction children have for Holden and other Salinger spokesmen: They are rarely, if ever, "phony." Sincerity, honesty, and innocence are the features of the ideal state to which Salinger's characters aspire and whose absence, scarcity, or remoteness causes them such pain.

The quest for these lost qualities is ultimately a religious quest for Salinger, and his writing relies heavily on terms and concepts taken from a wide variety of religious teachings to describe this quest. Christian references are frequent in *The Catcher in the Rye*. Another religious tradition that is equally important to an understanding of Salinger's work but less familiar to most readers is the tradition of Zen Buddhism.

Zen is a branch of Buddhist philosophy that emphasizes the impossibility of arriving at enlightenment by logical means. For this reason, teachers of Zen make use of paradoxes and riddles (called koans) to illustrate the futility of logic as a means of acquiring religious understanding. One of the best known of these koans serves as the epigraph for Salinger's *Nine Stories* (1953): "We know the sound of two hands clapping/ But what is the sound of one hand clapping?" Just as this question has no rational answer, so many of Salinger's stories seem to have no rational explanation—particularly "A Perfect Day for Bananafish," which ends with the unexpected and unexplained suicide of the main character. By using such Zen techniques, Salinger may be adopting the role of a Zen teacher in inviting (or forcing) the reader into a nonrational mode of experiencing the story. If each reader experiences the story in a unique way, it then becomes impossible to establish an agreed-upon "meaning" or "message" for the story, but this may be just what Salinger intended. In Zen, enlightenment can never be imparted to one person by another— each seeker must arrive there on his or her own.

As important as Zen may be as a means toward enlightenment, it makes no attempt to answer the profound questions troubling many of Salinger's characters: how to deal with the problems of evil, suffering, estrangement, and alienation. Esmé is obsessed with "squalor"; Holden is haunted by the inevitability of change and loss. Few of Salinger's characters can speak directly with those to whom they are supposed to be closely related, those whom they are supposed to love. They talk over the telephone, through bathroom doors, or by means of letters, but rarely look one another in the eye; they are afflicted with the essential estrangement and alienation that plagues modern life. The task of Salinger's characters is to overcome these barriers through love, but it is a task infrequently and imperfectly achieved.

The most widely admired of Salinger's writing techniques is his ability to create convincing dialogue, especially for Holden Caulfield in *The Catcher in the Rye*. Holden's speech is slangy enough to be believable, yet eloquent enough to make profound and intellectually challenging observations. Salinger also shows a particular gift for creating re-

alistic telephone conversations in several stories, as well as minutely detailed descriptions of revealing personal gestures, such as Muriel's painting of her fingernails in "A Perfect Day for Bananafish." Salinger describes significant personal objects with the same effect: Allie's baseball glove, covered with poems written in green ink, in *The Catcher in the Rye* is a good example. Critics sometimes fault Salinger for excessive attention to dialogue and seemingly trivial details (particularly in *Franny and Zooey*), but Salinger consistently prefers to let his characters reveal themselves through their words and actions, rather than perform that operation for them.

Many of Salinger's characters are introduced in abbreviated form in his earlier stories, only to reappear for fuller development later on. Holden Caulfield appears several times (although sometimes called by other names) in stories published before *The Catcher in the Rye*, and Seymour, Walt, and Boo Boo Glass are first introduced in three separate stories published in *Nine Stories*, written well before the Glass family was first presented in its entirety in *Franny and Zooey*. This repetition of characters could be explained as merely the fondness authors often feel for the products of their imaginations or as representing various facets of Salinger himself, but their effect is one of further uniting Salinger's work, as if it were one long story composed of a number of distinct but interrelated chapters.

Finally, there are Salinger's frequent and wide-ranging references to religious, philosophical, and literary figures and works: Christ, Buddha, Lao-tzu, Chuang-tzu, Epictetus, Sri Ramakrishna, the *Bhagavadgītā*, T. S. Eliot's *The Waste Land* (1922), Fyodor Dostoevski, F. Scott Fitzgerald's *The Great Gatsby* (1925), and Ring Lardner are only a few. Some of these, particularly the religious and philosophical references, may be intended to point to the universality of the quest for enlightenment in which Salinger's characters are engaged. The literary references sometimes seem to be a form of literary criticism put by Salinger into the mouths of his characters, and other times merely examples of the honesty and sincerity for which his characters yearn. It is impossible to say just what expectations Salinger may have had for his audience, because he has never said, but if he had any intention of directing his readers on their own quests for enlightenment, he may have left these references as signposts of a sort.

THE CATCHER IN THE RYE

First published: 1951
Type of work: Novel

Having been kicked out of a prestigious prep school, a sensitive adolescent makes a disturbing odyssey through New York City.

The Catcher in the Rye, Salinger's only full-length novel, is the work that made him famous and for which he is remembered by high school and college students throughout America and much of the world. It has been translated into nearly every major language and continues to be assigned reading in many high school and college classrooms (though it has also been banned from many high school classrooms for allegedly obscene language and sexual situations). Its utterly convincing portrayal of the thoughts, words, and feelings of a troubled adolescent has permanently influenced entire generations of young people, as well as writers throughout the world.

The book opens with these words from Holden:

If you really want to hear about it, the first thing you'll probably want to know is where I was born, and what my lousy childhood was like . . . and all that David Copperfield kind of crap, but I don't feel like going into it, if you want to know the truth. . . . I'll just tell you about this madman stuff that happened to me around Christmas just before I got pretty run-down and had to come out here and take it easy.

The opening paragraph is emblematic of the book in several ways. First, it introduces the reader immediately to Holden's essential character—his cynicism, irreverence, and complicated mixture of frankness and evasiveness. Eventually the reader comes to learn that "out here" is actually a psychiatric hospital in California and that Holden has been sent there for observation and treatment, not merely to "take it easy." Second, the language Holden uses to begin his story gives further insight into his character. Several phrases appear here which will serve as refrains for the novel: "If you really want to hear about it," "I don't feel like . . . ," "if you want to know the truth," and "madman." Holden's language is both representative of the typical ado-

lescent of his time and place and indicative of his personal fears and frustrations. "If you really want to hear about it" and "if you want to know the truth" reflect Holden's despair that most people really do not want to know the truth. "I don't feel like . . ." demonstrates the emotional paralysis that contributes to Holden's breakdown, and "madman" expresses his fear of going crazy, not only going crazy himself, but the world going crazy as well. "This madman stuff" is everything that led up to Holden's collapse, beginning with his ejection from Pencey for "failing everything but English."

Holden begins his account with a description of the school and the "phonies" in it: administrators, teachers, and students. Phoniness is one of the many things that Holden says "drive me crazy" or "make me puke," another example of a slang expression pointing to an underlying truth—that the corruption of the world makes him physically ill. Holden despises his fellow students for being physically repulsive, like Ackley, the pimply boy with bad teeth in the room next door, or for being too attractive, like Stradlater, Holden's "handsome, charm-

ing bastard" of a roommate. Strangely enough, Holden ends up missing these same people, and practically everyone he has met, by the end of the book—typical of the mixture of attraction and repulsion life holds for him. Following a fight with Stradlater about a girl both boys have dated, Holden decides to leave Pencey in the middle of the night and, after shouting "Sleep tight, ya morons!" by way of farewell, walks to the station to catch a train to New York City.

Once in the city, Holden is unsure what to do. He is afraid to go home and let his parents know he has been kicked out of school, so he ends up taking a room at the sleazy Edmont Hotel. He spends the night watching "perverts" in the opposite wing of the hotel, thinking about calling up old girlfriends (but deciding he's "not in the mood"), and going to bars seeking companionship. In the bars he finds only pitiful, boring, or "phony" people, so he eventually returns to the hotel, where an encounter with a teenage prostitute and her pimp gets him beaten up. He then leaves the hotel and goes to Grand Central Station to eat breakfast, where he meets a pair of nuns on their way to teach school and discusses *Romeo and Juliet* with one of them. (Religion and literature are frequent subjects for Holden's commentary.)

Holden spends the rest of the day wandering along Broadway and around Central Park. It is on Broadway that he observes the scene which gives the book its title: A family is walking home from church: "a father, a mother, and a little kid about six years old." The boy is walking in the street, next to the curb, singing a song that Holden hears as "if a body catch a body coming through the rye": "The cars zoomed by, brakes screeched all over the place, his parents paid no attention to him, and he kept on walking next to the curb and singing 'If a body catch a body coming through the rye.'" It is not until Holden sneaks home to visit his sister Phoebe, near the end of the book, that he explains the significance of the scene:

> I keep picturing all these little kids playing some game in this big field of rye and all. Thousands of little kids, and nobody's around—nobody big, I mean—except me. And I'm standing on the edge of some crazy cliff. What I have to do, I have to catch everybody if they start to go over the cliff—I mean if they're running and they don't look where they're going I have to come out from somewhere and *catch* them. That's all I'd do all day. I'd just be the catcher in the rye and all. I know it's crazy, but that's the only thing I'd really like to be. I know it's crazy.

It is here that Holden expresses most clearly what is bothering him: the inevitable loss of innocence involved in growing up. Other than children, the only people Holden respects completely (outside books) are the two nuns, who have managed to remain unstained by the world. Holden realizes that it is nearly impossible for a child to grow up in the world and remain innocent, so his greatest wish is somehow to protect all children from the danger of going over the "crazy cliff" of adulthood. For Holden, the passage to adulthood proves to be a crazy cliff indeed.

FRANNY AND ZOOEY

First published: 1961
Type of work: Novella

In this introduction to the Glass family, the youngest member recovers from an emotional breakdown with the help of her brother's explication of love.

Franny and Zooey is actually a compilation of two long stories first published separately in *The New Yorker*, and it indicates an increasing tendency of Salinger to create stories more as vehicles for the expression of religious and philosophical ideas than as pieces of dramatic fiction. The first story, "Franny," describes the emotional collapse of the youngest member of the Glass family, several other members of which appear repeatedly in Salinger's work.

Franny Glass, an honors student in English and drama at a New England women's college, goes to visit her boyfriend Lane at his Ivy League school on the weekend of the Yale game. Lane takes Franny to a fashionable restaurant for lunch, but as soon as they sit down she begins criticizing English professors, poets, actors, and almost everyone she and Lane know. When Lane seeks an explanation for her sudden peevishness, Franny begins talking about a book she has been reading called *The Way of a Pilgrim*, in which a nineteenth century Russian peasant learns to "pray without ceasing" by discovering the secret of the "Jesus Prayer." Lane dismisses the story as "mumbo jumbo," whereupon Franny leaves the table and collapses in the middle of the restaurant floor. At the end of the story, Franny is lying in the manager's office staring at the ceiling, "her lips . . . forming soundless words"—evidently practicing the Jesus Prayer.

"Zooey" picks up Franny's story at the Glass family home, where she has been brought to recuperate in the care of her mother, Bessie, and brother Zooey. Zooey is five years older than Franny, and both he and Franny, as well as their five older siblings, were regular contestants as children on a radio quiz show called *It's a Wise Child*. Both were also influenced by their older brothers Seymour and Buddy to study a wide variety of religious and philosophical literature at a very early age. Zooey is now a successful television actor, however, and is convinced that Seymour's and Buddy's program of education has ruined him and Franny for the purposes of living in the actual world. (Franny got *The Way of a Pilgrim* from Seymour's old desk, which has remained undisturbed in the Glass apartment since his suicide.)

In contrast to Franny, Zooey, Buddy, and Seymour, Bessie Glass is every bit a creature of the actual world. She always appears in the story dressed in an old kimono with pockets sewn on front to serve as "the repository for the paraphernalia of a very heavy cigarette smoker and an amateur handyman." These pockets are stocked with a hammer and screwdriver "plus an assortment of screws, nails, hinges, and ball-bearing casters—all of which tended to make Mrs. Glass chink faintly as she moved about." Bessie's idea of a cure for Franny's breakdown is chicken broth. Zooey responds to Bessie's suggestions with sarcasm and ridicule, but, in her plodding way, Bessie gets to the root of Franny's and Zooey's problem: They do not "know how to talk to people you don't like. . . . Don't love, really." Though Zooey fails to acknowledge Bessie's insight here, at the end of the book he confirms Bessie's diagnosis with a prescription of an all-encompassing love as the solution to Franny's cynicism and despair.

Zooey leads up to his prescription by relating how Seymour used to tell him to shine his shoes "for the Fat Lady" before going on *It's a Wise Child*. Zooey had formed a mental picture of the Fat Lady "sitting on the porch all day, swatting flies, with her radio going full-blast from morning till night." Franny remembers that Seymour had told her to "be funny for the Fat Lady" and she had formed an almost identical mental picture. Zooey then proclaims, "I'll tell you a terrible secret—Are you listening to me? *There isn't anyone out there who isn't Seymour's Fat Lady. . . .* And don't you know—*listen* to me, now—*don't you know who that Fat Lady really is?. . .* It's Christ himself. Christ himself, buddy."

Zooey is here rephrasing Seymour's advice to him in a letter written years earlier to "Act . . . when and where you want to, since you feel you must, but do it with all your might," with the added thought that any act must be done out of love to be worthwhile and that any act done out of love toward a human being is an act of worship, an act offered up to Christ. Franny's response to Zooey's message is to lie quietly "smiling at the ceiling," before falling into a "deep, dreamless sleep," a sure sign, in Salinger, that a cure has been effected.

"A PERFECT DAY FOR BANANAFISH"

First published: 1948 (collected in *Nine Stories*, 1953)
Type of work: Short story

While vacationing with his wife at a Florida resort, a disturbed World War II veteran commits suicide after an enigmatic conversation with a little girl.

"A Perfect Day for Bananafish," published first in *The New Yorker* and later in the collection *Nine Stories*, is one of Salinger's best-known and most puzzling stories. Although a few generally accepted themes can be identified, critics are widely divided as to the significance of the title, symbolism, and climax of the story.

The story opens with Muriel Glass, the wife of Seymour, oldest of the Glass children, waiting for a telephone call to be put through to New York. When the phone rings, the party on the other end of the line is Muriel's mother, who is extremely concerned about Seymour's state of mind and Muriel's safety. Muriel's mother is afraid that Seymour will "lose control of himself"—evidently with good reason. Seymour has recently driven a car into a tree, among other alarming acts that Muriel's mother relates: "That business with the window. Those horrible things he said to Granny about her plans for passing away. What he did with all those lovely pictures from Bermuda . . . what he tried to do with Granny's chair." During the course of the conversation the reader learns that Seymour was in Europe during the war and afterward was placed in an Army hospital, presumably as a psychiatric case. The Army apparently decided that Seymour was well enough for release, but his behavior remains erratic, at least by Muriel's mother's account. Muriel herself does not seem overly concerned, but she promises to call her mother "the *instant* he does, or *says*, anything at all funny," as her mother puts it, before Muriel hangs up.

The scene then shifts to the beach outside the hotel, where Seymour is lying on his back in his bathrobe. Sybil Carpenter, a little girl Seymour has befriended, approaches him and says, "Are you going in the water, see more glass?" Sybil is fascinated with Seymour's name, and she keeps repeating it like some kind of incantation: "Did you see more glass?" After some seemingly disconnected banter about the color of Sybil's bathing suit and the lack of air in Seymour's rubber float, Seymour takes Sybil down to the water. As they begin to wade in, Seymour tells Sybil, "You just keep your eyes open for any bananafish. This is a *perfect* day for bananafish." Bananafish, explains Seymour,

> lead a very tragic life. . . . They swim into a hole where there's a lot of bananas. They're very ordinary looking fish when they swim *in*. But once they get in, they behave like pigs. Why, I've known some bananafish to swim into a banana hole and eat as many as seventy-eight bananas. . . . Naturally, after that they're so fat they can't get out of the hole again. Can't fit through the door.

Sybil asks what happens to the bananafish after that. "Well, I hate to tell you, Sybil. They die . . . they get banana fever. It's a terrible disease." Just then a wave passes, and Sybil says, "I just saw one." "My God, no!" Seymour exclaims, "Did he have any bananas in his mouth?" Yes, says Sybil: "Six." Delighted with Sybil's answer, Seymour kisses her foot. He then returns her to the beach, goes back to his room where Muriel is sleeping, pulls "an Ortiges calibre 7.65 automatic" from his suitcase, and "fire[s] a bullet through his right temple." There the story ends.

As previously mentioned, critics have suggested a wide range of interpretations of "A Perfect Day for Bananafish." Some of the most convincing look at the story in its relationship to Zen Buddhism. The epigraph to *Nine Stories* is the Zen koan, "We know the sound of two hands clapping. But what is the sound of one hand clapping?" There are numerous allusions in the story to the Buddhist concept of the "wheel of life," the ceaseless round of daily existence from which it is the goal of Buddhism to escape. During Seymour's conversation with Sybil, the girl asks him if he has read the story "Little Black Sambo," in which six tigers chase one another around a tree until they melt into butter;

Sybil also informs Seymour that she lives in "Whirly Wood, Connecticut," another possible reference to the wheel of life. Sybil's reading of Seymour's name as "see more glass" may reflect the Zen emphasis on self-knowledge and insight. The bananafish themselves, whatever else they represent, seem to symbolize the danger of being trapped in the world of physical appetite, from which the only escape appears to be death.

Seymour's death is the most puzzling element of the story, coming as it does immediately after what appears to be a moment of great joy. This paradox has caused some critics to see Seymour's suicide as a moment of triumph, of having finally escaped from the wheel of life to some sort of nirvana. Others see it as an act of surrender, in which Seymour is destroyed by the oppressiveness of daily existence, a victim of "banana fever." Salinger has left no definitive clues by which either interpretation can be proved or disproved—in this sense the entire story may be seen as a Zen koan, intended to aid the reader in approaching truth, rather than to present the truth itself. In Zen, truth cannot be imparted by one person to another; one must achieve enlightenment on one's own. Whether or not Seymour achieved it Salinger leaves to the individual reader to decide.

"FOR ESMÉ—WITH LOVE AND SQUALOR"

First published: 1950 (collected in *Nine Stories*, 1953)
Type of work: Short story

In England during World War II, am American soldier has an encounter with a girl that leaves a lasting impression.

"For Esmé—with Love and Squalor" was first published in *The New Yorker*, to critical acclaim. The story opens with a man receiving an invitation to a wedding that he would like to attend but cannot. He then proceeds to reminisce about being a soldier in England in 1944, taking a training course in Devon, England. Out walking at the end of the course, before shipping out to battle, he wanders the town and stumbles upon a children's choir rehearsal. He is enchanted by the singing in general and in particular by a thirteen-year-old girl in the choir. He leaves the rehearsal and retreats to a tea shop. As he sits, the girl from the choir practice enters, accompanied by her younger brother, Charles, and their governess. The girl, the Esmé of the story, notices the narrator and comes over to sit with him.

They have a conversation that has a profound effect on the narrator. Esmé confides to him that both parents are dead—their father was slain in Northern Africa, and their mother has recently died. The narrator, who remains unnamed throughout this section of the story, notices a watch on Esmé's wrist that is much too large for her; she confides that it was her father's, given to her before his death. On discovering that the soldier is a writer, Esmé requests that he write a story for her, saying, "I prefer stories about squalor." The soldier agrees to write her a story and pens his address for her. Esmé wishes him a safe journey and hopes that he comes back from the war "with all your faculties intact."

The next section of the story, the "squalid, or moving, part of the story" takes place in Bavaria, where the narrator, now named Sergeant X, is quartered with other American soldiers. It is just after V-E Day, and readers find that Sergeant X has been traumatized by his wartime experiences and is suffering a breakdown. He is unable to concentrate, hostile, and depressed. The violence that he has encountered—encapsulated in an anecdote about a cat that one of his fellow soldiers senselessly kills—has rendered him unable to perform the simplest tasks or to conduct the tamest of social interactions.

Sergeant X tries to write a letter, but he cannot complete it and turns his attention to the letters and packages that have piled up on his desk. One stands out in particular—a small package in green paper, readdressed several times over. He opens the package without looking at the return address and inside finds a letter from Esmé. She has written to him fondly and has enclosed her father's wristwatch as a lucky talisman, saying that it is "extremely water-proof and shock-proof." Sergeant X finds that the watch's crystal has been broken en route. He holds it, and the letter, in his hands for a long time and finally feels himself grow sleepy—a sign of returning normalcy. As he states, "You take a really sleepy man, Esmé, and he always stands a

DISCUSSION TOPICS

- How does J. D. Salinger's use of detail and description aid in characterization? In the development of themes?

- Salinger typically uses dialogue and everyday speech in his works. What is the effect of this language? How does it further his themes and ideas?

- Where do religious concepts and ideas appear in the stories? Why?

- In what ways does Salinger explore human isolation and loneliness?

chance of again becoming a man with all his fac— with all his f-a-c-u-l-t-i-e-s intact."

Drawing, as he has, on the experience of war and subsequent trauma, Salinger explores the destructive force of violence. The isolation felt by the soldier throughout the piece—and isolation felt even in the presence of his brothers-in-arms—is typical of Salinger's other works in which loneliness and depression are characteristics of the protagonist. The hopefulness of the scene with Esmé, and the redemptive, optimistic closing moment of the story, speak to the hunger for human connection. Esmé's loss of her parents speaks to Sergeant X's experience of loss through violence; her diminished, yet still resilient innocence, and that of her brother Charles (who includes an affectionate addendum in the letter) provide healing for him, demonstrating the redemptive power of love and caring.

SUMMARY

The stories of Salinger present complex characters—brilliant, sensitive, and prone to nervous breakdowns and suicide—struggling to retain a belief in innocence, goodness. and truth in an increasingly corrupt and artificial world. Through a combination of vividly realistic dialogue and meticulous description of personal characteristics and mannerisms, the characters in Salinger's stories take on lives of their own and occupy permanent places in the minds of readers who come to know them.

Alan Blackstock; updated by Adrienne Pilon

BIBLIOGRAPHY

By the Author

LONG FICTION:
The Catcher in the Rye, 1951

SHORT FICTION:
Nine Stories, 1953
Franny and Zooey, 1961
"Raise High the Roof Beam, Carpenters" and *"Seymour: An Introduction,"* 1963

About the Author

Alexander, Paul. *Salinger: A Biography*. Los Angeles: Renaissance Books, 1999.

Alsen, Eberhard. *A Reader's Guide to J. D. Salinger*. Westport, Conn.: Greenwood Press, 2002.

Belcher, William F., and James W. Lee, eds. *J. D. Salinger and the Critics*. Belmont, Calif.: Wadsworth, 1962.

French, Warren T. *J. D. Salinger*. Rev. ed. Indianapolis: Bobbs-Merrill, 1976.

Hamilton, Ian. *In Search of J. D. Salinger*. New York: Random House, 1988.

Kotzen, Kip, and Thomas Beller, eds. *With Love and Squalor: Fourteen Writers Respond to the Work of J. D. Salinger*. New York: Broadway Books, 2001.

Lundquist, James. *J. D. Salinger*. New York: Frederick Ungar, 1979.

Steinle, Pamela Hunt. *In Cold Fear: "The Catcher in the Rye" Censorship Controversies and Postwar American Character*. Columbus: Ohio State University Press, 2000.

Sublette, Jack R. *J. D. Salinger: An Annotated Bibliography, 1938-1981*. New York: Garland, 1984.

CARL SANDBURG

Born: Galesburg, Illinois
January 6, 1878
Died: Flat Rock, North Carolina
July 22, 1967

Sandburg celebrated democracy and the common person using the idiom of the American Midwest. Although he also wrote fiction and biography, he is revered for capturing the essence of America in poetry.

BIOGRAPHY

Charles August Sandburg was born in a modest clapboard cottage on January 6, 1878, in Galesburg, Illinois, to Swedish immigrants August Sandburg and Clara Anderson Sandburg. August worked for the Chicago, Burlington, and Quincy Railroad; Clara Anderson had been a hotel chambermaid before she was married. August Sandburg could read a Swedish Bible, but that was all. He signed his name with an X. Clara Sandburg could write in colloquial Swedish and could phonetically spell English and encouraged her son's learning.

Charles, or Carl, as he was later to call himself, enjoyed school but deviated from the prescribed curriculum. He quit school after the eighth grade to help his father support the family. Sandburg stated that his true education began then, when he learned that crime and politics mixed and that justice belonged to the rich. At eighteen, Sandburg left home, working odd jobs and living with hoboes. When the Spanish-American War broke out, he enlisted. By the time his regiment was ready for action, however, the war was nearly over, so Sandburg saw no fighting.

Because he was a considered a war veteran, Sandburg was admitted to Lombard College without a high school degree. There the distinguished professor Philip Green Wright encouraged his writing. Sandburg was active in academics and extracurricular activities but left college without a degree, probably because he failed to take some required courses. Despite this, Sandburg experienced the satisfaction of seeing his words in print: Professor Wright privately printed Sandburg's first three books of poetry.

Sandburg wandered from Galesburg from time to time, supporting himself by peddling and by writing for a Chicago magazine. While in Chicago, he became associate editor of another Chicago magazine and active in the Social Democratic Party. His loyalties to the poor, the oppressed, and the exploited, which found voice in his writings, became a permanent part of his psyche while he campaigned for Populist and Socialist causes. In fact, it was at the Milwaukee Socialist headquarters that Sandburg met his future wife, Lillian Steichen, sister of Edward Steichen (who became a world-famous photographer). They were married after several months' courtship; it was a union that proved happy and lasted until Sandburg's death. With Lillian, Sandburg had three daughters, one of whom, Helga, became a novelist.

Sandburg broke with the Socialist Party after the outbreak of World War I, but still he wrote articles and editorials for socialist magazines. Despite his busy involvement in newspaper work, he also still wrote poetry. *Chicago Poems* (1916) began his reputation. The key poem "Chicago" launched his literary fame, and some critics believe that "Chicago" is Sandburg's finest poem. From *Chicago Poems* followed two other volumes of poetry, *Cornhuskers* (1918) and *Smoke and Steel* (1920). These books illustrate Sandburg's concern for the working class; the first book is sometimes considered raw, the second more mellow.

His next book was not poetry but a collection of children's stories, *Rootabaga Stories* (1922). Afterward, he contracted with Harcourt and Holt to write a biography of Abraham Lincoln for teenagers. This modest project grew into an obsession for Sandburg, who adored Lincoln. Sandburg produced a two-volume work titled *Abraham Lincoln: The Prairie Years* (1926). This biography was financially successful, and its popular acclaim encouraged him to continue Lincoln's biography through his presidency. At last financially secure, Sandburg could concentrate on his goal of writing a complete Lincoln biography.

Because Sandburg's future was assured, he was unaffected, except by his constant sympathies with the poor, by the Great Depression. During this time he published *The People, Yes* (1936), which asserted his faith in the people. In 1939, Sandburg published his four-volume continuing biography of Lincoln, *Abraham Lincoln: The War Years*. This was well received both by critics and by lay readers. It won the Pulitzer Prize in 1940 and may well be considered his most lasting work.

Ironically, Sandburg's wholehearted commitment to America resulted in one of his most flawed books. As a gesture of support for the United States efforts in World War II, Sandburg wrote the novel *Remembrance Rock* (1948), a too-obvious symbolic representation of heroic people and heroic action. Critics agree that whereas his intentions are noble, the book fails as art because of its patriotic overzealousness. The year the war ended, 1945, Sandburg and his family moved from his beloved Midwest to Flat Rock, North Carolina, where he would live until his death in 1967 at eighty-nine years of age.

Sandburg's *Complete Poems* (1950) earned another Pulitzer Prize but received mixed critical reviews. The new poems in this volume were often overlooked by critics who had stereotyped him as too "folksy" and too popular to be literary. Sandburg's public success, however, had increased steadily since his later volumes of poetry. This was, in part, attributable to his talent as a public performer, both as a reader and as a folk singer. His po-

etry, performances, and Lincoln biographies combined to make him an American institution. In 1953, Sandburg published his autobiography, *Always the Young Strangers*. This was widely acclaimed as a sensitive, unpretentious portrait of a boy's growth in the Midwest.

ANALYSIS

Sandburg wrote of the American common people; his work glorified both the everyday person and everyday life. "Moonlight and mittens," he believed, were the stuff of art. In addition, he made poetry of the harsh realities of immigrant urban life. Like nineteenth century American poet Walt Whitman, Sandburg broke with poetic convention by addressing "unpoetic" subjects, such as butchering and railroads. Also like Whitman, he broke with conventional rhyme schemes and forms; his verse is often called "prosy" in that he uses much dialogue and employs long lines.

Sandburg defended free verse by quoting Oliver Wendell Holmes: "Rhythm alone is a tether, and not a very long one. But rhymes are iron fetters." Sandburg had an excellent ear for speech rhythms and the musical cadences of words. His form grew naturally out of his content, not only because of his skill in hearing the musical connotations of words but also because of his ability to balance and counterbalance phrases and clauses.

Critics sometimes regarded Sandburg as "subliterary." The polished literary fashion of his time considered form, structure, imagery, tension, and irony more important than content.

Sandburg's poetry was a vehicle for his message of faith in "the people." He did not brood over poetry and what constitutes art but instead had an almost irreverent attitude toward aesthetic theories. The question remains, however, whether Sandburg invented adequate poetic structures to replace those he spurned. Sandburg was not without poetic theory, but his definitions of poetry were impressionistic ("poetry is a shuffling of boxes of illusion buckled with a strap of facts") more than analytical. He wanted to synthesize the ethereal and the concrete, "hyacinths and biscuits," by juxtaposing one with the other. His poetry itself, however, reveals more care than his vague definitions would indicate.

William Carlos Williams made a classic case against Sandburg by charging that he had no unifying imaginative vision; as he had no formal poetic theory, he could write no coherent poetry. His poetry simply cataloged realistic detail in a sprawl of words. Other critics, however, found this uniting vision in the very inclusiveness of Sandburg's work and in his faith in the people, a faith that the slang and hardships of the people were the materials as well as the subjects of art.

Sandburg's poetry touched on the variety of American life, particularly that of the working class. Although he made his reputation on the brassy poem "Chicago," he also wrote of simple moments of joy, poignancy, and despair. A Jewish fishmonger has "a joy identical with that of [Anna] Pavlova dancing"; a runaway girl is "Gone with her little chin." His populist views appear in countless images of struggle, such as a woman so worn out from making mittens that she sees evergreens by moonlight as a pair of mittens. That Sandburg should be obsessed with Abraham Lincoln is no surprise. Lincoln exemplified the worker who made good, the American Dream, the practical one who retained Midwest ideals in the face of one of America's most complex periods.

Sandburg has been faulted for not dealing with the evils of life, but this is a superficial criticism at best. True, there are no villains or monsters either in his poetry or in his children's tales, but evil exists, usually in the form of poverty, despair, and recurring defeats. The individual is saved not by circumstances, but by one's resilience, humor, and common sense.

Although Sandburg has often been linked with Whitman, they differ in major respects, such as their attitudes toward death. Whitman celebrates death as undergirding and completing life; Sandburg views it merely as a terminus. Whereas Whitman believes in a pantheistic kind of immortality, Sandburg asks the eternal questions throughout his work but fails to find answers. Only in his last volume does he think he sees something of a "purpose" in life's randomness.

A typical Sandburg poem, however, does employ literary devices that are similar to those of Whitman. Like Whitman, Sandburg is a master of the long, "prosaic" line, and he catalogs, glorifies, and repeats details from daily life. Sandburg's repetitions, however, also owe much in style to the Bible. He makes heavy use of dialogue in his work, and the verse is so free that it would be almost form-

less were it not for Sandburg's keen ear for the musical sequence of words. Sandburg's best work combines colloquial speech and homely imagery with an energy and force which come from unconventional line lengths. His long lines are saved from being prose by his handling of the sounds of words and his skill in paralleling words, phrases, and clauses, thus creating rhetorical rhythm.

Sandburg takes his images from the rural and urban Midwest, grounding them in physical reality. There are no fairy kingdoms or mystical revelations; instead, his work tells of strawberries, lattice shadows of doorways, cornhuskers, and men with their shirts off. Often he piles detail upon detail until the effect is kaleidoscopic.

Although Sandburg is noted for his celebration of exuberance and unthinking animal spirits, he has a melancholy side that mourns the transience of life. His better-known poems, such as "Chicago," are optimistic, but he also wrote meditative, weary lyrics that question life's meaning. His long poem *The People, Yes* achieves something of a balance between these two facets of Sandburg's personality.

"CHICAGO"

First published: 1916 (collected in *Chicago Poems*, 1916)
Type of work: Poem

In sprawling Chicago, one sees young America, a vital people who can laugh at their destiny through sheer exuberance.

"Chicago" started Sandburg's literary rise, and many critics consider it one of his best poems. Certainly it is one of the most anthologized. "Chicago" contains most of the characteristics that made Sandburg famous: It breaks with conventional poetic versification, deals with the "unpoetic," and expresses his lifelong faith in the American people's resilience.

The opening verse imperatively addresses the city with brutal imagery and staccato lines. Sandburg personifies Chicago as a laborer by calling it "Hog Butcher for the World" and "City of the Big Shoulders." The following long and prosy lines challenge the city on its reported evils, cataloging instances of cruelty and injustice. The speaker then defends Chicago for its pride, strength, and energy, implying that the aforementioned evils are by-products of its heartiness. Unconventional images describe the city's vitality: a dog eager for action, an ignorant, undefeated prizefighter.

In "Chicago," Sandburg demonstrates his love affair with the United States and its working class. This is evident in the image of Chicago as a brash prizefighter. The images of corruption of farm boys by prostitutes and of hunger on the faces of women and children also affiliate the city with the worker and the poor. Nowhere in its salute to Chicago's vitality does it refer to its rich or elite.

Supporting the themes of raw energy in America's working class is free verse and the use of

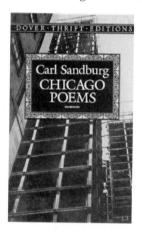

several literary devices. Sandburg not only uses his excellent ear for words but also builds his lines as if constructing a skyscraper to achieve the effect of a bustling, amoral city. The first verse has short lines of salutation, then long-lined accusations followed by a rebuttal in the same form. The next statement abruptly lists the city's qualities. Parallelism speeds a tempo which has been slowed by long-lined accusations and defense. The following long lines reflect the lazy insolence of a braggart, Sandburg's central image of the city. The one-word verse "Laughing!" expresses shock at Chicago's daring, and the final long descriptive lines express grudging approval.

"Chicago" shocked a public used to pretty poems. Some critics still refer to it as shrill and abrasive. Others consider it Sandburg's most brilliant poem. It captures like no other Sandburg poem the author's respect for his country's brawling nature. Sandburg's work is sometimes unfairly stereotyped by "Chicago," however; he is seen as the versemaker of the lower classes, the poet who honors unthinking animal exuberance. He is much more.

"GRASS"

First published: 1918 (collected in *Cornhuskers*, 1918)
Type of work: Poem

In this poem on the war dead, Sandburg links America with the rest of the world in resignation over death's inevitability and nature's indifference to humankind.

"Grass," first published in *Cornhuskers*, presents a side of Sandburg often overlooked: his melancholy in the face of death. Unlike "Chicago," "Grass" is conventional in subject, language, and tone. It is a "typical" Sandburg poem in its reference to train passengers and conductors in the Midwest and its stress upon the American war dead, but the link between Americans and people of other nations in the first line suggests a common fate.

"Grass" opens with the imperative to pile bodies high at Austerlitz and Waterloo, then to bury them so that the grass can get on with its work of covering the ground. The second verse calls for the same procedure at American Civil War battle sites: Bury the dead so the grass can grow, and after two years train passengers will ask the conductor where they are. Because of the grass's work, all who fell in battle will be forgotten. It is the grass's destiny to express nature's indifference by obliterating memories of the war dead.

This poem achieves its melancholy by simple words and images, conventional diction, and repetition. Words such as "pile," "shovel," "bodies," and "under" connote death, as do the names of specific battle sites. Graveyards, trains, and conductors provide homely images, but there are no colorful colloquialisms. Instead, simple but standard English provides a formality similar to a chant or funeral dirge. The long lines are instructions to pile the bodies and shovel them under; the short lines are thematically significant, repeating that the passengers' questions and the relentless work of the grass prove that all is forgotten.

Even though it exhibits Sandburg's penchant for repetition, "Grass" is understated and concise. Unlike his better-known poems, "Grass" does not express faith in the people's ability to transcend life's difficulties. Its matter-of-fact tone is more reminiscent of Emily Dickinson than Walt Whitman, as it faces a mournful but unchangeable fact of life. In his mention of American battles and trains and conductors, Sandburg implies that even brash Americans with their outrageous democratic ideals are not exempt from war, death, and the silence of an unresponsive nature.

Although not given as much publicity, Sandburg's somber side is almost as prevalent in his work as his buoyant optimism toward "the people." He continued to ask large spiritual questions but never found solace in conventional religions. Although Sandburg has been accused of being nonpoetic, his preoccupation with loss and melancholy place him in the tradition of English meditative verse, particularly the English graveyard poets.

SUMMARY

Sandburg was the first modern poet to use the language of the American people extensively in his work. For this reason alone, he deserves a place in American literary history. Although his work is not always polished, he achieved at times an enduring art. His best poems convey the vigor and brokenness of industrialization, the quaintness of small towns, and the transience of nature and love. His vision encompassed both the light and the dark. His best poems captured a part of the essence of his time and enlarged the potentials of language and subjects for other modern poets.

Mary H. Barnes

BIBLIOGRAPHY

By the Author

POETRY:
In Restless Ecstasy, 1904 (as Charles A. Sandburg)
Chicago Poems, 1916
Cornhuskers, 1918
Smoke and Steel, 1920
Slabs of the Sunburnt West, 1922
Selected Poems of Carl Sandburg, 1926
Good Morning, America, 1928
Early Moon, 1930
The People, Yes, 1936
Home Front Memo, 1943 (verse and prose)
Chicago Poems: Poems of the Midwest, 1946
Complete Poems, 1950
Wind Song, 1960
Harvest Poems, 1910-1960, 1960
Honey and Salt, 1963
Breathing Tokens, 1978 (Margaret Sandburg, editor)
Ever the Winds of Chance, 1983 (Margaret Sandburg and George Hendrick, editors)

LONG FICTION:
Remembrance Rock, 1948

NONFICTION:
The Chicago Race Riots, 1919
Abraham Lincoln: The Prairie Years, 1926 (2 volumes)
Steichen the Photographer, 1929
Mary Lincoln: Wife and Widow, 1932 (with Paul M. Angle)
A Lincoln and Whitman Miscellany, 1938
Abraham Lincoln: The War Years, 1939 (4 volumes)

Storm over the Land: A Profile of the Civil War, 1942

The Photographs of Abraham Lincoln, 1944

Lincoln Collector: The Story of Oliver R. Barrett's Great Private Collection, 1949

Always the Young Strangers, 1953

Abraham Lincoln: The Prairie Years and the War Years, 1954

The Sandburg Range, 1957

"Address Before a Joint Session of Congress, February 12, 1959," 1959

The Letters of Carl Sandburg, 1968 (Herbert Mitgang, editor)

CHILDREN'S LITERATURE:

Rootabaga Stories, 1922

Rootabaga Pigeons, 1923

Abe Lincoln Grows Up, 1928

Potato Face, 1930

Prairie-Town Boy, 1955

The Wedding Procession of the Rag Doll and the Broom Handle and Who Was in It, 1967

EDITED TEXTS:

The American Songbag, 1927

The New American Songbag, 1950

DISCUSSION TOPICS

- The popular American poetry of 1916 tended to be sentimental and cliché-ridden. What contrasting qualities in Carl Sandburg's poem "Chicago" would have been much appreciated by perceptive readers of the time?

- In Sandburg's poem "Grass," how does his imaginative handling of grass differ from Walt Whitman's in *Song of Myself* (1855)?

- Which poet, Sandburg or Robert Frost, deserves more credit for using "the language of the American people" effectively in poetry?

- What qualifications did Sandburg bring to his biographies of Abraham Lincoln?

- Is William Carlos Williams's charge that Sandburg had no unifying imaginative vision a just one?

About the Author

Allen, Gay Wilson. *Carl Sandburg.* Minneapolis: University of Minnesota Press, 1972.

Callahan, North. *Carl Sandburg: His Life and Works.* University Park: State University of Pennsylvania Press, 1987.

Crowder, Richard. *Carl Sandburg.* New York: Twayne, 1964.

Durnell, Hazel. *The America of Carl Sandburg.* Washington, D.C.: University Press of Washington, D.C., 1965.

Hallwas, John E., and Dennis J. Reader, eds. *The Vision of This Land: Studies of Vachel Lindsay, Edgar Lee Masters, and Carl Sandburg.* Macomb: Western Illinois University Press, 1976.

Niven, Penelope. *Carl Sandburg.* New York: Charles Scribner's Sons, 1991.

Yannella, Philip. *The Other Carl Sandburg.* Jackson: University Press of Mississippi, 1996.

WILLIAM SAROYAN

Born: Fresno, California
August 31, 1908
Died: Fresno, California
May 18, 1981

Briefly in the front rank of American dramatists, Saroyan is mostly valued for his pre-World War II plays and fictional sketches that espoused an infectious optimism and sanguine view of humankind during a period of great social and economic turmoil.

Courtesy, D.C. Public Library

BIOGRAPHY

William Saroyan was born in Fresno, California, on August 31, 1908, the son of Armenak and Takoohi Saroyan, poor Armenian immigrants. In 1911, when his father died, Saroyan was put into an Oakland orphanage with his brother, Henry, and his two sisters, Cosette and Zabel, but in 1915 he returned to Fresno with his family. Over the following decade, Saroyan attended school in Fresno and held various after-school jobs, including work as a telegraph messenger boy, an experience which he would later re-create in his fiction.

In 1926, after repeated expulsions from school for disciplinary reasons, Saroyan left Fresno without a high school diploma, first going to Los Angeles, where he served briefly in the California National Guard, then to San Francisco, where, after working as a telegraph operator, he eventually became manager at a branch office of the Postal Telegraph Company. By 1928, when he made his first trip to New York, Saroyan had made up his mind to make writing his career. Soon depressed, homesick, and discouraged, he returned to San Francisco, taking a series of brief jobs and spending most of his time learning his craft at the library and the typewriter.

Recognition and success first came to Saroyan in 1934, when *Story* magazine published two pieces

that would also appear in his first collection of sketches, *The Daring Young Man on the Flying Trapeze, and Other Stories* (1934). Once discovered, Saroyan quickly found markets for his backlog of pieces as well as his new works. In 1936, after travels abroad, Saroyan began work as a screenwriter in Hollywood. There he continued to write stories and sketches, published in several collections.

Three years later, in 1939, he made his first serious venture into dramatic form with *My Heart's in the Highlands*, which opened in New York as a Group Theatre project. It was soon followed by his best-known play, *The Time of Your Life* (1939), for which, in 1940, Saroyan won both the New York Drama Critics Circle Award and the Pulitzer Prize, which, with characteristic obstinacy, he refused to accept. In 1940, frustrated by conditions imposed by Broadway entrepreneurs, Saroyan directed and produced his own play, *The Beautiful People*, and he did the same for two of his one-acts, *Across the Board on Tomorrow Morning* (1941) and *Talking to You* (1942), establishing, as an impresario, a reputation for his unconventional methods of casting and directing. His best-known one-act play, *Hello Out There*, was staged on Broadway in 1942, the year that marked the end of his most vital development as a dramatist.

Success brought Saroyan his share of problems. In fact, soon after the enthusiastic reception of *My Name Is Aram* (1940), fictionalized sketches based on his boyhood, Saroyan began to experience serious financial reversals, in part because of his addiction to gambling. Needing money, he agreed to write a screenplay for Metro-Goldwyn-Mayer, turning out *The Human Comedy*, which he would later rewrite as a novel under the same title. Published in 1943, *The Human Comedy* remains Saroyan's most reputable fictional work.

Drafted into the Army in 1942, Saroyan served to the end of World War II and, in the interval, married Carol Marcus, whom he would later divorce, remarry, and then divorce again. Upon his release from service, Saroyan attempted to reestablish himself as a premier playwright and writer of fiction, but with only partial success. His propaganda novel, *The Adventures of Wesley Jackson* (1946), was met with hostile reviews that even questioned his patriotism. The film version of *The Time of Your Life*, released in 1948, proved to be a financial disaster. Gambling losses continued to plague him and contributed to his marital difficulties. With the publication of *The Assyrian, and Other Stories* (1950), however, critics pronounced that he had returned to form. He also gained some popularity as a lyricist when his song "Come on-a My House," coauthored with his cousin, topped the Hit Parade in 1951.

From 1952 to 1958, after his second divorce from Marcus, Saroyan lived in Malibu, California. During that period, in addition to other works, he wrote his first nonfictional autobiographical work, *The Bicycle Rider in Beverly Hills* (1952); a bitter novel based in part on his troubled marriage, *The Laughing Matter* (1953); and his first play to be staged in New York in fourteen years, *The Cave Dwellers* (1957).

In 1959, proclaiming himself a tax exile, Saroyan left the United States for Europe, producing plays in London before returning to teach at Purdue University in 1961. Thereafter, Saroyan met with little success as a playwright and turned almost exclusively to fiction and autobiography. He did author a teleplay, "The Unstoppable Gray Fox" (1962), which was broadcast on *The General Electric Theater*, but over the last twenty years of his life Saroyan concentrated on personal memoirs. The most important works of this period include an autobiography, *Here Comes, There Goes, You Know Who* (1961); a novelized memoir, *Boys and Girls Together* (1963); an anthology of occasional pieces, *I Used to Believe I Had Forever: Now I'm Not So Sure* (1968); and several memoirs, including *Obituaries* (1979), for which, in 1980, he was nominated for the Ameri-

can Book Award. Another autobiographical work, *My Name Is Saroyan*, was published posthumously in 1983, two years after he died of cancer.

ANALYSIS

From 1934, when *The Daring Young Man on the Flying Trapeze* appeared, to the wartime era of the early 1940's, Saroyan enjoyed a literary reputation rivaling those of William Faulkner and Ernest Hemingway. After the war, however, he was unable to achieve enough critical recognition and popularity to regain it. To later generations of readers, the vigor and originality that marked his writing in the 1930's and early 1940's was gone, and, with some exceptions, his successive works seemed too familiar, self-centered, and routine. As a result, his postwar era audience steadily dwindled.

Ironically, it was partly Saroyan's success that accounted for his ebbing popularity. The literary voice he fashioned was well suited to the bad times of the Great Depression and the anxious situation of the prewar era, but conditions changed, and, like many other writers, Saroyan was unable to make a full adjustment to either his fame or the changing times. His later literary career seems largely spent in self-justification.

The solipsistic self-centeredness of Saroyan's later work is, to some measure, foreshadowed by the earlier work on which his reputation rests. His first collection of stories, *The Daring Young Man on the Flying Trapeze*, contains several pieces in which the narrative voice is unabashedly the author's own, despite the narrator's fictional identification as a character of a different ethnic or national origin from Saroyan's.

Although some critics demurred, the conspicuous presence of the author did not repel Saroyan's early readers. What they found in his work was a freshness in style and theme offering a welcome tonic for the harshness of the times. Breaking with the tradition of the "well-made" or formulaic story, Saroyan presented a series of stories centered on character rather than plot. Some of them seem to be little more than transliterations of notebook observations, without conflict, plot, or theme, more rightly considered sketches than stories. Still, despite a rather sophomoric audacity that marks the preface, and the authorial intrusions in some pieces, the work has an engaging, highly individual, lyrical style.

To a nation standing in bread lines, Saroyan (himself poor but optimistic) offered an affirmation of life in his insistence that, even in starvation, people have a dignity and grace of which no external conditions can deprive them. This idea infuses all of Saroyan's early work, including the two works for which he is best known: *The Time of Your Life* and *The Human Comedy*.

Throughout these and his shorter fiction, Saroyan insists that there is an irrepressible joy in living and hope even in death. Within that general thematic frame, Saroyan focuses mostly on have-not characters who struggle against bad odds with simple faith and compassion. Saroyan's best-delineated characters are males, many undergoing an internal rite of passage from adolescence to adulthood with a self-consciousness that is, itself, the story. In nine pieces of *The Daring Young Man on the Flying Trapeze*, the central character is a writer who is, in fact, Saroyan, rallying his lust for life under a thin fictional veil.

Although full of ironic contradictions, *The Daring Young Man on the Flying Trapeze* iterates Saroyan's notion that fiction should not be contrived and artificially plotted but should be an expression of the writer's inner self, presented free of dogmatic principles of composition. The lyric and impressionistic quality of much of Saroyan's prose derives from this artistic credo. In a narrow, less all-consuming way, Saroyan shares the involvement in humankind that is the focus of Walt Whitman's poetry. He repeatedly confirms his determination, through himself, to investigate humans, to reveal their inner core, to understand and honor them.

In his more mature work, especially *The Time of Your Life* and *The Human Comedy*, Saroyan achieves greater objectivity, but the dominant themes remain. In the exchange of ideas and in their thoughts, Saroyan's wholly sympathetic characters explore most of the essential notions advanced in his first stories. Perhaps a bit facile and naïve, the characters are nevertheless warm and engaging. Saroyan's world is one in which the poor and the weak can find riches in human love and compassion and strength in hope and simple decency. It is also a world in which innocence can be restored to the fallen, and human greatness has nothing to do with the public recognition of it.

Although even Saroyan's best works have been faulted for their lack of a principal conflict and a corresponding lack of a strong plot line, many of his episodes and vignettes are memorable. Saroyan, of course, explicitly rejected plot as a vital concern in his fiction. Many of his short pieces are sketches, even personal essays and letters, rather than stories, and his plays, including *The Time of Your Life*, tend to be diffuse and lacking in dramatic urgency. As a result, Saroyan's characters are more memorable than their contexts.

At his best, Saroyan creates highly original, atypical, and occasionally quixotic characters. For example, he floods *The Time of Your Life* with a variety of genial and zany losers and misfits, all of whom are highly individualized. Particular character poignancy is achieved in motifs that occur in several works, especially in the spiritual bonding of male characters. Saroyan's better characters tend to transcend their simple, humdrum lives in their basic goodwill and kindness, and it is principally for these, his beautiful people, that Saroyan will be remembered.

THE HUMAN COMEDY

First published: 1943
Type of work: Novel

A lad of fourteen in wartime America learns to accept death through the affirmation of life.

The Human Comedy, dedicated to Takoohi Saroyan, was first written as a screenplay under a contractual arrangement with Metro-Goldwyn-Mayer, but in 1943, with the film version in production, Saroyan used the script scenario as the basis of his first and most popular novel. Set in Ithaca, a fictional name for Fresno, the work is based on some of Saroyan's boyhood experiences and familiar reminiscences. In fact, the Macauley family, central in the plot, has parallels to Saroyan's real family, without, however, a similar heritage.

The novel's main character, Homer Macauley, is a fourteen-year-old adolescent with a job and some experiences that relate to actual events in the author's life. With his father deceased and his older brother in the Army, Homer must assume adult responsibilities beyond his years. He is a surrogate father to his younger brother, Ulysses, and the provider for his whole family. At the outset of the novel, he has secured a part-time job as a telegraph messenger boy, which takes him into a variety of homes and businesses to encounter the richly delineated and variegated characters that people the novel.

Apart from Homer, the most engaging characters are Mr. Grogan, the old, rummy telegraph operator; Spangler, the telegraph office manager; Homer's mother, Kate Macauley; Miss Hicks, Homer's teacher; and Ulysses, his younger brother. These and a few others, such as Marcus, Homer's older brother, are rather representative of the vintage Saroyan character who, though well enough individualized, shares with the rest a simple faith, love for life, and inherent goodness.

Although there is a central, persistent concern with the disruptive impact of World War II on the lives of these characters, the novel, like Saroyan's early sketches, provides a series of vignettes that are only loosely connected. Some have no inherent connection to the central focus of the novel or causal relationship to scenes juxtaposed to them. Nevertheless, most offer charming, human-interest interludes and comic leavening to the novel's more serious themes and maudlin moments. Two examples are the episodes in which Ulysses gets caught in the trap in Covington's Sporting Goods Store and his later confrontation with Mr. Mechano, a mechanical man on display in a drug-store window.

Despite the thematic similarities and use of characters who seem familiar from Saroyan's earlier stories, *The Human Comedy* departs from his earlier work both in style and in technique. The novel is basically more objective, the style more direct and less effusive. The point of view is that of an omniscient and unidentified third person, and although there are incursions into the thoughts of some characters, the impressionistic reverie that marks several of the sketches is virtually gone. Saroyan's earlier concern with his travails as artist is totally obliterated, and his authorial presence is largely masked and mute.

Perhaps the result of writing for the stage, Saroyan also makes very effective use of dialogue in the novel, something sparingly used in his very first sketches. In focusing on character interaction, Saroyan may sacrifice the lyricism of his internal monologues, but he in turn gains an admirable economy and tough simplicity of expression reminiscent of Hemingway's prose.

Despite its convoluted development, the novel prepares the reader for its final, inevitable revelation: the death of Marcus and its impact on Homer and the rest of the Macauleys. From the outset, it is clear that death is never far away for the Macauley family.

The much-beloved deceased father is frequently alluded to, with an insistence that his spirit lives in those who remain alive. It is Homer, though, who most often confronts the fact of death throughout the novel. As a telegraph messenger, he bears the burden of delivering the War Department telegrams to the surviving families of those killed at war. Homer does not know the families, but it is a hateful duty which he comes to dread. Near the

novel's end, death suddenly becomes more personal for Homer, first with the death of Mr. Grogan, then with the death of Marcus. Homer, death's envoy and bringer of pain, finally has the devastating duty of carrying home to his mother the telegram informing her of her oldest son's death.

What Homer learns is that death, if accepted as a necessary part of life, is largely an illusion, as Mrs. Macauley had earlier explained to Ulysses. The spirit of Marcus lives in the remaining family members; it also lives in his special friend and fellow soldier, Tobey George, who coincidentally appears in Ithaca on the very day the War Department telegram announcing the death of Marcus arrives. In an earlier episode, Marcus and Tobey engage in a ritual of spiritual bonding that prepares the reader for the novel's conclusion. Tobey is accepted into the Macauley family and welcomed home as if he were, in truth, Marcus himself. Although it strains credibility, it is a touching scene that evades sentimentality through its terse, direct, and unadorned style. It is also a good example of Saroyan's ebullient view of human beings and his ability to evince a zest for life under the most devastating circumstances.

William Saroyan

THE TIME OF YOUR LIFE

First produced: 1939 (first published, 1939)
Type of work: Play

A group of destitute drifters and misfits invades a waterfront dive in San Francisco and discovers the fundamental goodness of humanity in others and themselves.

The Time of Your Life, Saroyan's most critically acclaimed play, was received with warm praise for its great originality. As in his early fiction, Saroyan seemed determined to break with tradition, developing the comedy in his own, inimitable fashion and playing havoc with standard theatrical conventions. Set in Nick's, a San Francisco waterfront honky-tonk, the play focuses on Joe, his friend Tom, and an engaging prostitute named Kitty Duval. There are a host of other destitute but benign characters who drift in and out. Nick's offers a haven of hope for all who enter, unless, like Blick, an abrasive detective, they are persecutors of the downtrodden.

Nick's is also a sort of microcosm of Saroyan's ideal of America. It is clearly a melting pot, for among its denizens are a melancholy Arab, a starving young black man, an Irish cop, the gruff Italian proprietor, a prostitute of Polish ancestry, a Greek newsboy, and a crusty old mule skinner who seems to embody an offbeat variety of every trait ascribed to the legendary frontiersman.

More important, Nick's is a place of great tolerance and freedom, bordering more on fantasy than reality. It is a place where the dreams of the characters begin to come true, where the starving find sustenance, the deprived get a break, and the lonely and disheartened find love and hope.

Other than Nick, only Joe has any money. Throughout the play, as if he possesses a magic pocket, Joe pulls out whatever cash is needed to fulfill his momentary whim. Surely one of Saroyan's most enigmatic characters, Joe is merely evasive and mysterious about his money's origin. He has no job and seems simply to reside at Nick's, seldom even rising from his chair. At most, he hints that the money is somehow tainted because his possession of it has entailed grief for others. About him, too, there is the aura of the Hollywood gangster. He is taciturn, shrewd, steady, and impassive, in obvious contrast to his errand runner, Tom, who is eager, effusive, and earnest in a tongue-tied sort of way. Yet, except in his penchant for bossing Tom around, there is no meanness in Joe. As he himself claims, he is simply trying to see if it is possible to live in such a way as to bring no harm to anyone. At worst, he is somehow trying to expiate past sins.

Detached from the welter of activity in Nick's, Joe sits and steadily drinks, almost mechanically, until, without apparent forethought, he sends Tom off on what seems another trivial errand—to fetch him magazines, gum, and toys, things to keep him amused. It is, however, other humans that really interest and amuse Joe, especially Kitty Duval, the whore, in whom Joe sees an innocence and beauty despite her profession.

In Nick's, Saroyan's happy place, the characters who find refuge provide a human carnival in their various chaotic activities. If Joe is impassive and at times remote, most of the others are irrepressible and ardent. The monologues of Kit Carson, encapsuling his eccentric life, gush forth breathlessly. Harry, the self-styled comedian, breaks into his sadly unfunny comic stories with little prodding, then whirls away in a dance routine when another character drops a coin in the jukebox. Willie, the pinball addict, drops nickel after nickel in the machine, beating away on it until he finally wins.

Nick, the animated owner of the bistro, is loud and brassy, though hiding, through his gruffness, a golden heart. Wesley, once discovering the piano, plays the blues incessantly, providing a counterpoint to the more joyous, upbeat mood generated by the others. Only the sullen, gloomy, nearly silent Arab sits at the bar unaffected by anything.

Like the idealized green worlds of Shakespearean comedy, Saroyan's honky-tonk is a place where the wonderful becomes the possible. It is a place of realized dreams, a place where instant love is possible, where a prostitute can regain her lost innocence, where bullies are destroyed, where the machine bends to human will and repeatedly registers, with whistles and waving flags, one's victory over it.

In mood and technique, *The Time of Your Life* is surrealistic. Many of the characters, like Joe, seem detached from any sort of past; they appear from the dark world outside as if from a void. Kit Carson is more an anachronistic figure from a tall tale than a valid character, needed to kill the dastardly Blick as a sort of heroic ringer for Joe. He shoots Blick offstage, as if to confirm that in Saroyan's happy world violent death is really not allowed. Character motivation, so carefully investigated in the drama of psychological realism, is often lacking. Joe seems to aid and abet Tom's love for Kitty with the same capriciousness with which he buys the newsboy's remaining papers.

There is a tumultuous quality to the play. Several actions go on simultaneously, like several vaudeville routines all being staged at once, and focus in the play keeps shifting from one character to another, with no particular rationale. It is a three-ring technique that could easily become distracting, but Saroyan's skillful control makes it all work. For sheer ingenuity of design and experimental method, the play ranks with pieces such as Thornton Wilder's *The Skin of Our Teeth* (1942) as a classic of the American theater.

"THE DARING YOUNG MAN ON THE FLYING TRAPEZE"

First published: 1934 (collected in *The Daring Young Man on the Flying Trapeze, and Other Stories,* 1934)
Type of work: Short story

A destitute writer, unable to find work, starves to death.

"The Daring Young Man on the Flying Trapeze," the story giving Saroyan's first collection of stories and sketches its title, initially appeared in *Story* magazine. The piece is basically an impressionistic reverie. Although told in the third-person voice, it works through the recording consciousness of the unnamed protagonist, an impoverished writer who is literally starving to death. The writer's thoughts are disjointed and incoherent, as is characteristic of the stream-of-consciousness technique used by French novelist Marcel Proust, whose work the writer reads in the story.

The hunger gnawing at the writer's body presumably accounts for the randomness of his thoughts. Aware that his strength is slipping away, he sets out to look for work, fortified, as on many previous days, with only coffee and cigarettes. Little actually happens during his sojourn outside. He finds a penny in a gutter and speculates on its possible use, moves through the city (looking at his reflection in the window glass of stores and restaurants), and goes for an interview at an employment agency. He goes to the YMCA and to the library to read Proust before returning to his room, where, at last, he falls face down on his bed and dies a peaceful, almost welcomed death.

During these mostly mechanical actions, his mind races through a welter of disconnected ideas. The song of the title keeps humming in his brain, as do thoughts about public figures, writers, food, places, and his plan to write *An Application for Permission to Live.* His only interaction with another character occurs in his interview with the cold and efficient woman at the employment agency.

Saroyan's style in the story is poetic in its lyric statement and rich allusions to people and things. Like images of a life going quickly by, the names cascade through the character's mind, seemingly out of his control to shape them into a logical pattern. His desperation at times directs his thoughts to food and shelter, but his weakness does not allow him to hold or develop any singular thought for long. At the last, his thoughts drift up, away from his body, with his life, in death, becoming "dreamless, unalive, perfect." That dissolving of life into nothingness offers a quiet, dignified apotheosis of the human spirit that Saroyan makes almost enviable.

"THE MAN WITH THE HEART IN THE HIGHLANDS"

First published: 1936 (collected in *The Man with the Heart in the Highlands, and Other Early Stories,* 1989)
Type of work: Short story

An old drifter is fed by a poor family and returns their kindness by winning food from others with his enchanted bugle.

"The Man with the Heart in the Highlands," later to evolve into the full-length play *My Heart's in the Highlands,* first appeared in a collection of Saroyan's short fiction titled *Three Times Three,* issued in 1936. It is a charming fantasy focusing on an old vagabond actor named Jasper MacGregor and his magical bugle, the use of which results in a minor miracle.

The narrator, Johnny, recalls the story as an experience he had in 1914, when he was six years old. Old MacGregor appears in front of Johnny's house on San Benito Avenue, presumably in Fresno, playing his bugle. In the exchange that follows, MacGregor insists that his heart is in the highlands of Scotland, where it grieves, though for what remains a mystery. The thirsty bugler begs for water, and Johnny takes him inside to give him some. When MacGregor asks for food, Johnny's father, a poet, sends Johnny to a local grocer, Mr. Kosak, to get cheese and bread on credit. At first adamant in his refusal, Kosak finally relents and sends Johnny home with the requested items and advice that the boy's father find work. The trio quickly down the food, but MacGregor remains unsatisfied. He begins searching the house for more to eat.

When Johnny refuses to allow him to stew up a pet gopher snake, MacGregor resorts to using his bugle. His blowing is so loud that people from miles around gather by the house to listen. In exchange for playing music for each of them, MacGregor asks them to go and return with food. All comply, and the family and its guest feast grandly on the food from the newly stocked larder. MacGregor remains with Johnny and his father for more than two weeks, but he is then asked to go to an old people's home to serve as lead actor in an entertainment for the inmates. He complies, whereupon the poet once more sends his son to Kosak's store to get food on credit. Johnny returns with birdseed and some maple syrup, which makes his father ponder his chances of writing great poetry fed on such fare.

The tale is fablelike and otherwise typical of Saroyan in its cheerfulness and buoyancy. Yet in its style and technique, it departs sharply from the earlier impressionistic sketch "The Daring Young Man on the Flying Trapeze." It develops largely through dialogue, with its narrative description held to an essential minimum, at times serving no other purpose than to identify the speaker of a line of the dialogue. It was this dramatic method that prompted the editor of *The One-Act Play Magazine* to suggest that Saroyan turn the piece into a one-act play, which became, in fact, the first form that the play *My Heart's in the Highlands* took.

The first portion of the story has Johnny functioning as an insistent inquisitor, interrogating MacGregor almost unmercifully. The staccato exchange of one-liners is direct and abrupt and is interrupted only when Johnny's father comes out to the porch. Then there is a similar exchange between father and son. Many of the lines, like theatrical dialogue, are elliptical sentence fragments. Questions and commands are dominant, with simple, monosyllabic words like "get" and "go" beginning the speeches and being repeated in tight patterns. Similar dialogue, though modified by more description as the story progresses, is used throughout the piece, notably in the exchanges between Johnny and Mr. Kosak. Coupled with diction that is very simple, the style is tough, brusque, and brittle. Furthermore, there is no probing of any character's thoughts, so the narrative point of view is wholly objective.

The relationship between Johnny and his father is particularly amusing. The father is crusty and demanding, cursing freely as he orders Johnny about, but Johnny more than holds his own, talking back and arguing with his father spiritedly. The father's cantankerousness is being visited on the son, but in an entirely humorous and harmless way. Neither the father nor the son is anything other than a Saroyan good guy in a gruff disguise.

SUMMARY

In his 1966 critical study of William Saroyan, Howard Floan claims that the writer's reputation would ultimately rest on the plays and fiction that he wrote prior to World War II. That view, issued when Saroyan was still actively writing, has since been validated.

The quintessential Saroyan pieces are unquestionably his early works. It is they that bear his peculiar stamp—the charm, goodwill, and delight in experimentation for which he will be remembered. Perhaps it was the war that robbed him of his youthful, wide-eyed acceptance and love of life that is the hallmark of his best work; perhaps it was the misfortune of success and his stormy marriage. In any case, from the war's end to his death, except for brief flashes of his former brilliance, Saroyan never again achieved the high critical esteem he once enjoyed.

John W. Fiero

BIBLIOGRAPHY

By the Author

LONG FICTION:
The Human Comedy, 1943
The Adventures of Wesley Jackson, 1946
Rock Wagram, 1951
Tracy's Tiger, 1951
The Laughing Matter, 1953 (reprinted as *The Secret Story*, 1954)
Mama I Love You, 1956
Papa You're Crazy, 1957
Boys and Girls Together, 1963
One Day in the Afternoon of the World, 1964

SHORT FICTION:
The Daring Young Man on the Flying Trapeze, and Other Stories, 1934
Inhale and Exhale, 1936
Three Times Three, 1936
The Gay and Melancholy Flux: Short Stories, 1937
Little Children, 1937
Love, Here Is My Hat, and Other Short Romances, 1938
The Trouble with Tigers, 1938
Three Fragments and a Story, 1939
Peace, It's Wonderful, 1939
My Name Is Aram, 1940
Saroyan's Fables, 1941
The Insurance Salesman, and Other Stories, 1941
Forty-eight Saroyan Stories, 1942
Some Day I'll Be a Millionaire: Thirty-four More Great Stories, 1944
Dear Baby, 1944
The Saroyan Special: Selected Stories, 1948
The Fiscal Hoboes, 1949
The Assyrian, and Other Stories, 1950
The Whole Voyald, and Other Stories, 1956
William Saroyan Reader, 1958
Love, 1959
After Thirty Years: The Daring Young Man on the Flying Trapeze, 1964
Best Stories of William Saroyan, 1964
The Tooth and My Father, 1974
The Man with the His Heart in the Highlands, and Other Early Stories, 1989

DRAMA:
The Hungerers: A Short Play, pb. 1939, pr. 1945
My Heart's in the Highlands, pr., pb. 1939
The Time of Your Life, pr., pb. 1939
Love's Old Sweet Song, pr., pb. 1940
Three Plays: My Heart's in the Highlands, The Time of Your Life, Love's Old Sweet Song, pb. 1940
Subway Circus, pb. 1940

DISCUSSION TOPICS

- In what ways does William Saroyan take advantage of his California roots in his writings?

- How does Saroyan avoid sentimentality in *The Human Comedy*?

- What techniques does Saroyan employ to unify his play *The Time of Your Life*?

- Saroyan's period of success coincided with the Great Depression. What qualities of temperament and what literary virtues of Saroyan might account for this fact?

- Is Saroyan's lack of success in his post-World War II writing better explained by changes in the reading and play-going public or by changes in Saroyan himself?

The Ping-Pong Game, pb. 1940 (one act)
The Beautiful People, pr. 1940, pb. 1941
The Great American Goof, pr. 1940, pb. 1942
Across the Board on Tomorrow Morning, pr., pb. 1941
Three Plays: The Beautiful People, Sweeney in the Trees, Across the Board on Tomorrow Morning, pb. 1941
Hello Out There, pr. 1941, pb. 1942 (one act)
Jim Dandy, pr., pb. 1941
Talking to You, pr. 1942
Razzle Dazzle, pb. 1942 (collection)
Talking to You, pr., pb. 1942
Get Away Old Man, pr. 1943, pb. 1944
Sam Ego's House, pr. 1947, pb. 1949
A Decent Birth, a Happy Funeral, pb. 1949
Don't Go Away Mad, pr., pb. 1949
The Slaughter of the Innocents, pb. 1952, pr. 1957
The Cave Dwellers, pr. 1957, pb. 1958
Once Around the Block, pb. 1959
Sam the Highest Jumper of Them All: Or, The London Comedy, pr. 1960, pb. 1961
Settled Out of Court, pr. 1960, pb. 1962
The Dogs: Or, The Paris Comedy, and Two Other Plays, pb. 1969
An Armenian Trilogy, pb. 1986 (includes *Armenians, Bitlis,* and *Haratch*)
Warsaw Visitor and Tales from the Vienna Streets: The Last Two Plays of William Saroyan, pb. 1991

SCREENPLAY:
The Human Comedy, 1943

NONFICTION:
Harlem as Seen by Hirschfield, 1941
Hilltop Russians in San Francisco, 1941
Why Abstract?, 1945 (with Henry Miller and Hilaire Hiler)
The Twin Adventures: The Adventures of William Saroyan, 1950
The Bicycle Rider in Beverly Hills, 1952
Here Comes, There Goes, You Know Who, 1961
A Note on Hilaire Hiler, 1962
Not Dying, 1963
Short Drive, Sweet Chariot, 1966
Look at Us, 1967
I Used to Believe I Had Forever: Now I'm Not So Sure, 1968
Letters from 74 Rue Taitbout, 1969
Days of Life and Death and Escape to the Moon, 1970
Places Where I've Done Time, 1972
Sons Come and Go, Mothers Hang in Forever, 1976
Chance Meetings, 1978
Obituaries, 1979
Births, 1983

CHILDREN'S LITERATURE:
Me, 1963
Horsey Gorsey and the Frog, 1968
The Circus, 1986

MISCELLANEOUS:
My Name Is Saroyan, 1983 (stories, verse, play fragments, and memoirs)
The New Saroyan Reader, 1984 (Brian Darwent, editor)

About the Author

Balakian, Nona. *The World of William Saroyan.* Lewisburg, Pa.: Bucknell University Press, 1998.

Calonne, David Stephen. *William Saroyan: My Real Work Is Being.* Chapel Hill: University of North Carolina Press, 1983.

Floan, Howard R. *William Saroyan.* New York: Twayne, 1966.

Foard, Elisabeth C. *William Saroyan: A Reference Guide.* Boston: G. K. Hall, 1989.

Foster, Edward Halsey. *William Saroyan.* Boise, Idaho: Boise State University Press, 1984.

_____. *William Saroyan: A Study of the Short Fiction.* New York: Twayne, 1991.

Hamalian, Leo, ed. *William Saroyan: The Man and Writer Remembered.* Rutherford, N.J.: Fairleigh Dickinson University Press, 1987.

Haslam, Gerald W. "William Saroyan." In *A Literary History of the American West,* edited by Thomas J. Lyon et al. Fort Worth: Texas Christian University Press, 1987.

Keyishian, Harry, ed. *Critical Essays on William Saroyan.* New York: G. K. Hall, 1995.

Lee, Lawrence, and Barry Gifford. *Saroyan: A Biography.* 1984. Reprint. Berkeley: University of California Press, 1998.

Leggett, John. *A Daring Young Man: A Biography of William Saroyan.* New York: Alfred A. Knopf, 2002.

Saroyan, Aram. *William Saroyan.* San Diego: Harcourt Brace Jovanovich, 1983.

Whitmore, Jon. *William Saroyan: A Research and Production Sourcebook.* Westport, Conn.: Greenwood Press, 1994.

© Gabriel Amadeus Cooney/Courtesy,
W. W. Norton and Company

MAY SARTON

Born: Wondelgem, Belgium
May 3, 1912
Died: York, Maine
July 16, 1995

Sarton has integrated aspects of her life and art through a variety of artistic forms and served as a role model to generations of readers.

BIOGRAPHY

May Sarton was born Eléanore Marie Sarton, the daughter of George Sarton, an eminent philosopher and author of a four-volume history of science, and Mabel Sarton, an artist and designer. Because she was born on May 3, she was called May. In 1916, her parents emigrated from Belgium to the United States because of the events of World War I. The Sartons settled in Cambridge, Massachusetts, where George taught part time at Harvard University.

May was a precocious child; she wrote poetry from the age of nine, and some of her poems were published when she was seventeen. She attended an innovative high school in Cambridge known as Shady Hill School. Her future path was set: She would attend Vassar College and then marry a prominent man. After seeing the renowned actress Eva La Gallienne star in Henrik Ibsen's *Hedda Gabler* (pb. 1890, pr. 1891; English translation, 1891) in 1928, however, Sarton became devoted to the theater. She became a member of the Civic Repertory Theater in New York City, then the founder and director of her own theater company in New York City from 1933 to 1935. Although her company failed, partly as a result of the Depression, she found a new direction in her life when she drew

upon one of her many strengths and reinvented herself as a writer.

Sarton's first book was a collection of poems, *Encounter in April* (1937), which explored themes related to the differences between physical passion and love. In order to support her career as a writer, she began a cycle of almost forty years devoted to teaching, lecturing, and reading from her works. She taught creative writing, was a poet-in-residence, and lectured at several colleges and universities over the next forty years, including Harvard University and Bryn Mawr College, and the prestigious Bread Loaf Writer's Conference. At her death, she was the author of more than fifty books—novels, books of poetry, nonfiction works—including her journals, children's books, essays, and other writings.

Her first novel, *The Single Hound*, was published in 1938, and her second book of poetry, *Inner Landscape*, was published in 1939. After World War II, she continued to write novels and poems. She was unusually close to her parents. She was an only child, and she never married. Her mother died in 1950, and her father died in 1956. Her move to Nelson, New Hampshire, in 1958 marked a turning point in her life. There she wrote the memoir *I Knew a Phoenix: Sketches for an Autobiography* (1959), which examined her childhood, parents, early education, work in theater, and early years as a writer. At her home in Nelson, May Sarton settled into middle age as a woman who lived alone, who no longer had family ties, and who had no part in the traditional roles of wife and mother.

Her record of her life from the ages of forty-five

to fifty-five is found in *Plant Dreaming Deep* (1968), a journal of her middle age. The book inspired numerous readers because it showed the possibilities of the solitary working woman's life. She balanced this enthusiastic response to her life alone in rural New England with the 1973 book *Journal of a Solitude*, which drew upon her frustrations with celebrity. By then, she was a world-famous author and literary personality. She often felt confounded by the pressures of fame and the tendency of people to expect her to live up to their ideal of "May Sarton."

As We Are Now, a novel about an old woman who suffers harsh treatment after she is placed in a rural nursing home, also appeared in 1973. That year, she moved again, this time to her house Wild Knoll in York, Maine. *Collected Poems, 1930-1973,* appeared in 1974, and a journal about her new home, *The House by the Sea,* appeared in 1977. Although she had reached retirement age, she gave little consideration to retiring from her writing. Twice she made use of experiences related to illness or disability and found a means of resolving her traumas through the process of writing journals. In 1980, she wrote *Recovering: A Journal,* after suffering from breast cancer, and in 1988 she wrote *After the Stroke,* a journal about her recovery from a debilitating stroke. Her achievements as a literary figure were celebrated by her receipt of honorary degrees from eight colleges and universities—a remarkable accomplishment for a woman who never attended a college or university.

In the 1980's, she also wrote two novels, *Anger* (1982) and *The Magnificent Spinster* (1985), the latter based upon the life of one of Sarton's former teachers; three books of poetry, *Halfway to Silence* (1980), *Letters from Maine* (1984), and *The Silence Now* (1989); and *At Seventy* (1984), a journal that examined the vitality of her old age. In the 1990's she wrote two other journals which explored her experiences as an older adult. In *Endgame: A Journal of the Seventy-ninth Year* (1992), Sarton shared the emotional and psychological pain associated with chronic illness and physical disabilities, but the following year, chronicled in *Encore: A Journal of the Eightieth Year* (1993), was more hopeful. Although she continued to experience recurring bouts of chronic pain and depression, Sarton found ways to overcome them by gardening, maintaining longtime friendships, and writing poetry. She died in 1995 at the age of eighty-three.

Additional works by Sarton have been published posthumously. They include *At Eighty-two* (1996) and several volumes of her letters, edited by Susan Sherman.

ANALYSIS

Although she wrote novels, journals, memoirs and literary criticism, May Sarton considered poetry to be the primary means by which she expressed her creativity and identity. She wrote poetry as a child, and it was to poetry that she turned when she left the theater. She published seventeen collections of poetry, the first, *Encounter in April,* in 1937 and the last, *Coming into Eighty,* in 1994. Several themes dominated her poetry, including love relationships, her passion for the natural world, her devotion to art and music, her interest in aging and death, the dynamics of growth and change, solitude, travel, and contemporary social issues.

Although she wrote in free verse, the majority of her poems used stricter formal structures such as the sonnet. Four of her major poems were collections of sonnets. The sonnets in *Encounter in April* portrayed the depth of passion between two lovers and their inevitable separation and sense of loss. This pattern of love found and love failed dominated in two other sonnet sequences: "A Divorce of Lovers," which recounted an emotionally painful separation, and "The Autumn Sonnet," where the agony of lost love led eventually to a healing process and an acceptance of renewal. In *Letters from Maine,* the poet affirmed the desire for love that is sustained in late life. In *Coming into Eighty,* Sarton examined some of the universal metaphors of old age, including wisdom, simplicity, and optimism.

Despite her lifelong devotion to writing poetry, most of her readers return time and again to May Sarton's memoirs and journals. In the memoir *I Knew a Phoenix,* Sarton recalled her childhood, the influence of her parents, and her experiences in the theater. In effect, this memoir ended at the point where May Sarton's career as a writer began, in 1937. As in her journals, Sarton recounted significant friendships that provided mentoring, inspiration, and education for the young woman. *Plant Dreaming Deep* opened Sarton's works to a wider audience. Sarton wrote about her middle age, the years between the ages of forty-five and fifty-five, when she began to live alone in rural New England. Many readers responded positively to the ideal life of a working woman living alone. Sarton's life alone enabled her to engage in a struggle with solitude and to find the means through which she could experience self-renewal and creativity.

Sarton continued to explore that struggle in eight later journals. These works are among the most accessible, and in some ways most enduring, contributions that she made as a writer. If *Plant Dreaming Deep* provided the model for the joys of solitude, then *Journal of a Solitude* provided a corrective by noting the negative effects of the solitary life. Sarton viewed solitude as a source of bliss and inspiration; at the same time, she felt—in that solitude—stricken by times of loneliness and despair.

In all of her journals, Sarton took great risks to expose her fears and insecurities, her bouts with depression, and her ambivalence toward fame. Another risk was to write about events that are part of the round of daily living, such as preparing meals, visiting the doctor, feeding the birds, or planting bulbs. Yet readers embraced Sarton's journals because they see in her struggle as a writer and as a woman the capacity to maintain a freshness and originality despite writing about mundane events. She maintained sufficient distance between the emotion of the moment and the creative act of recounting the effects of that emotion. Self-discipline, honesty, and objectivity were her strengths in her journals. In two of them, *Recovering: A Journal* and *After the Stroke*, Sarton shared her struggles with disease and physical disability. In two of her last three journals, *Endgame* and *Encore*, she exposed her feelings of vulnerability and hopelessness because of physical disabilities and chronic pain. In these journals, Sarton raged against the frailties and losses that she associated with her aging process.

The title of her novel *Crucial Conversations* (1975) provides a clue to a basic organizing principle that Sarton employed in most of her fiction. The dominant internal structure within her novels is the conversation between two characters. In fact, extended dialogue between characters is emphasized far more than the conventional use of external action and plot construction. In some respects, this technique may reflect Sarton's theatrical aptitude and skills. Perhaps, however, Sarton employs conversations because the action of most of the novels is internal rather than external. What matters is how characters change, not what characters

experience. The subject matter of her novels is the process of women (more often than men) coming to an understanding of their identity and values, the significance of relationships in their lives, the possibilities for change in their lives, and their strengths and autonomy. Unfortunately, the attendant thinness of plot distracts from the repeated use of the conversational structure.

Sarton used the novel form to celebrate important women in her own life (a character in *The Single Hound* is based on a teacher Sarton had in Belgium, and the main character in *The Magnificent Spinster* is modeled after her teacher Anne Thorp). *Mrs. Stevens Hears the Mermaids Calling* (1965) and *The Education of Harriet Hatfield* (1989) explore themes related to androgyny and homosexuality.

In all of Sarton's work, the integration of the self, and particularly the self of women, is of primary value. Working inward to discover self-knowledge, balance, wholeness, and creativity is the most important task of the individual.

JOURNAL OF A SOLITUDE

First published: 1973
Type of work: Journal

Sarton records and reflects upon her experiences, ever-changing moods, significant relationships, and strains in her personal and creative life.

In *Journal of a Solitude*, Sarton explores significant issues in her life through the creative form of the journal. To Sarton, the journal is not to be confused with the diary. In the journal, the writer reflects upon experiences and analyzes the details of daily living. To Sarton, writing a journal means examining her life, putting herself in touch with priorities in her life (friends, work, gardening), reflecting upon the imbalances in her personal and creative life, and, most important, clarifying and resolving aspects of her sense of self.

Entries in *Journal of a Solitude* begin September, 1970, and end September, 1971. At the beginning of the journal, she examines a dominant theme in her life: the conflict between the opposing forces of solitude and society. She acknowl-

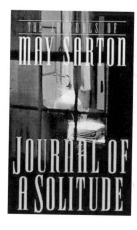

edges the strains of public appearances and social engagements and recalls the times she yielded to the onslaught of personal inquiries and unwanted visits. These, she declares, are not part of her "real life." For Sarton, who has always lived alone as an adult, real life means engaging in a process of reclaiming the self and finding a creative center from which new life can spring. In many respects she welcomes solitude, because in spite of its recurring loneliness, depression, and rage, solitude provides a source of energy and vitality to stimulate her creativity.

Sarton settles down in the fall of the year to renew herself in solitude. She realizes that after publication of *Plant Dreaming Deep* in 1968, she was "discovered" by many who viewed her as a seer or sage, someone who seemed "above" emotional frailty. She wrote *Journal of a Solitude* to reveal a May Sarton who faces daily the struggles between solitude and society, joy and despair, companionship and loneliness.

Love and creativity are closely allied in Sarton's life. She comments several times on the rejuvenating power of love in an affair with someone she refers to only as "X." This relationship spurs a creative breakthrough in her writing of poetry. Other high points in the year include the publication of her latest novel, *Kinds of Love* (1970); reunions with friends; several poetry readings; and her plans to publish a new book of poems, *A Durable Fire: New Poems*, to mark her sixtieth birthday in 1972. Low points include the death of a handyman, Perley Cole, who was the inspiration for a character in her 1973 novel *As We Are Now*; the death of one of her pets, a parrot named Punch; and the eventual ending of the relationship with her lover.

After a year of entries, Sarton realizes that it is time to end her journal. She marks the transition in her life with the decision to move away from Nelson, New Hampshire, to live in a house by the sea in Maine. For Sarton, writing the journal has been a process. She examines moods as they come, charts the high and low points of her days, and measures the gradual changes that occur within her sense of self. In this way, the changes in her life unfold, like the changes of the seasons. At the end of the journal, she is a different person, but that difference is not based upon one event or encounter. She has been changed through the process of living, thinking, interacting, surviving, and creating.

AS WE ARE NOW

First published: 1973
Type of work: Novel

An old woman, oppressed and abused by her caregivers after moving to a nursing home, strikes back with a desperate act.

The plot of *As We Are Now* is simple: An old woman, Caro Spencer, is placed in a rural nursing home, finds little stimulation in her relationships with other residents, experiences hostile and abusive treatment from the administrator and head nurse, communicates her distress to helpful acquaintances from the outside world, is frustrated and ridiculed by the head nurse after repeated attempts to improve conditions in the home, and decides finally to set fire to the nursing home and kill everyone inside, including herself.

Sarton tells this tragic story from Caro's point of view by means of a journal that she begins to write shortly after entering the nursing home. The journal reveals Caro as an intelligent, articulate, and sensitive older woman who is definitely out of place in this inadequate rural facility. Few residents share her intellectual background. Only one, Standish Flint, befriends her. He is a tough-minded old farmer who appreciates Caro's clarity of mind and sense of humor. He seems a potential ally of Caro, but his untimely death hastens the development of her desperate state of mind.

Sarton wants readers to feel the physical, psychological, and spiritual degradation the elderly experience at the hands of insensitive, controlling caretakers who treat them as invisible and useless. The journal format invites readers to empathize with Caro's feelings of helplessness and vulnerability and to appreciate the individuality and complexity of older adults. Caro begins her journal with the reference to the nursing home as "a concentration camp for the old, a place where people dump their parents or relatives exactly as though it were an ash can." Sarton aims to show that individuals (the old included) may strike back when they are made to feel abandoned, unproductive, and worthless. The only escape may be a cleansing holocaust that occurs when the old person, her identity and sense of well-being crushed by cruel and abusive treatment, believes there are no other options available to her.

Caro does meet others who understand the complexity of her character and the beauty of her spirit. A minister who visits residents befriends her, and his daughter joins him and soon comes to love and appreciate Caro. They do their best to assist Caro in her attempt to alleviate the degrading conditions in the nursing home, but their actions are undermined by the oppressive hand of Harriet Hatfield, the administrator. When Harriet goes on vacation, Caro experiences a brief respite from this woman's harsh treatment. Anna Close replaces Harriet and treats Caro as an individual. Anna's warmth and affection rejuvenate Caro, but when Harriet returns to work and Anna leaves, Caro becomes desperate and feels trapped.

Caro's last act before setting the fire is to place her journal inside an old refrigerator so that it will be spared and others can read about her experiences. Caro's creative act of writing the journal represents a victory over her oppressive caregivers and suggests a view of old age as a time of creativity and growth.

"GESTALT AT SIXTY"

First published: 1972 (collected in *A Durable Fire*, 1972)
Type of work: Poem

To mark her sixtieth birthday, Sarton reviews the forces that have contributed to her identity and to the meaning of her life.

"Gestalt at Sixty," a poem in May Sarton's *A Durable Fire* (1972), repeats many of the themes found in her earlier poems, journals, and novels. The poet reviews her ten years of living in Nelson, New

Hampshire, celebrates her sixtieth birthday, and explores the fabric of her life and the significance of her experiences. The gestalt of the title refers to the wholeness or totality of life experiences. In Gestalt psychology, the overall meaning of one's experience is greater than the sum of its parts (individual experiences, events, interactions). Thus, when Sarton analyzes her life on her sixtieth birthday, she tries to make sense of the underlying patterns that are the basis of her experiences. She examines the various forces that have contributed to the formation of her identity, her values, and her philosophy of life.

What does it mean to be sixty? Sarton divides her response to that question into three parts. In part 1, she affirms the importance of the natural world in her life. She refers to the lakes, mountains, flowers, and trees, all of which nurture her soul and stimulate her creativity. She addresses an important theme of the relationship between solitude and creativity. She maintains, "Solitude exposes the nerve." Solitude provides the greatest test for the artist, who has to face the limitations, fears, and shortcomings within herself in order to create. The pressures of solitude provoke passionate responses to life. Sarton admits to fits of weeping, loneliness, and panic, all of which constrain her and diminish her sense of well-being. In the face of these trials, she draws upon an inner resolve of courage and fortitude in order to find a sense of wholeness in herself. She survives by creating a world for herself the same way her garden grows; in order for creativity to bloom, she must clear away inner constraints and renew herself.

In part 2, she admits that sometimes she is overwhelmed by the fruits of her fame. She feels oppressed when the contacts with others become collisions, when she is plagued by the pressure of unwanted interactions. In this context solitude is a restorative, because she can be nourished by the joys of music and poetry and aloneness. For Sarton, there must be a balance between the forces of solitude and society. When she finds that balance, she is able to participate fully in human relationships and open herself to growth and change.

In part 3, Sarton integrates her response toward her aging with a synthesis of a variety of religious and philosophical perspectives, including Daoism, a Chinese philosophy; Buddhism; and Christianity. She characterizes herself with images reminiscent of the Daoist sage, the wise person who embraces change as the basis of all life. Her acceptance of her impending old age and her mortality reflects Buddhist thought in her references to "detachment" and "learning to let go." She ends the poem with a Christian prayer. There she accepts a God who is at once merciful and demanding. She acknowledges that on these various spiritual levels, creativity flows from the dynamic tension between life and death, youth and old age, light and dark, just as her creativity has flowed from the tension between solitude and society.

MRS. STEVENS HEARS THE MERMAIDS SINGING

First published: 1965
Type of work: Novel

Hilary Stevens, a poet in her seventies, spends a day remembering and reflecting upon the key moments in her life and the significant personal relationships that sparked her creativity.

This novel tells the story of Hilary Stevens, who reflects upon the various manifestations of the poetic muse throughout her life. She shares those reflections with two young interviewers from a literary magazine who visit her one day at her New England home. Mrs. Stevens, like May Sarton, lives alone in a house by the sea. She loves gardening, and she has made of her home a work of art. The title of Sarton's novel comes from a reference in T. S. Eliot's poem "The Love Song of J. Alfred Prufrock." Near the end of the poem, the narrator, a disenchanted middle-aged man, admits, "I have heard the mermaids singing, each to each/ I do not think that they will sing to me." In other words, he realizes that his life lacks meaning and purpose. Life has passed him by. Sarton employs Eliot's lines as a metaphor for the creative individual who hears the mermaids singing—in other words, the writer attuned to her muse, the source of her inspiration, her guiding genius in the creative process.

Before the interviewers arrive for their scheduled visit, Mrs. Stevens gardens, and she reflects upon Mars Hemmer, a young man and neighbor who has become, in some respects, her latest muse.

Mars is gay, and he shares with Mrs. Stevens a recent disappointment regarding his love for an older man. Hilary encourages Mars, a budding poet himself, to write about his pain as a way of objectifying it and filtering out his anger and self-pity. At the end of the novel, after the interviewers have left, Hilary meets Mars Hemmer again, and she realizes that Mars represents her masculine side, that part of her which confronted all aspects of her self in the struggle to create poetry. Even in her old age, then, Hilary Stevens uncovers more of the truth about the core of her identity through her friendship with Mars.

Most of the novel consists of conversations between Hilary and the interviewers and other scenes in which Hilary, alone, reflects upon her past. In the latter scenes, she relives the key moments in her life, including her relationships with her parents, her marriage and widowhood, and several key relationships—including love affairs—with both men and women. Her passionate attachments to women always precede the appearance of her muse—the engine for her creativity.

Hilary fell in love with her governess at fifteen and for the first time discovered the power of poetry in her life. Later, she married happily, but her concerns about how to balance domesticity and the creative process were short-circuited by his accidental death early in their marriage. In her grief, Hilary was attended by a physician named Holliwell. He recognized a dangerous pattern in her creative intensity and advised her to focus on her recovery, objectify her emotional pain, and pour her creative energies into writing poetry. Dr. Holliwell (note the name, "whole and well") represents the perfect male figure in Sarton's fiction— the sensitive man who has  integrated his feminine and masculine sides. His advice (similar to the advice that she gives Mars) speeds Hilary's recovery. Later, she admits that the struggle with the muse is multidimensional; it is at once inspiring and terrible, a balancing act between joy and pain, courage and fear, hope and despair. The struggle with the muse represents the poet's attempt to plumb the mysteries of the self.

One of her most tragic attachments is to a dear friend, Willa MacPherson. When Willa shares the pain of a broken relationship with a man, that sharing prompts another appearance of Hilary's muse. She can write again, and she is ecstatic. Now she desires the accompanying passionate attachment, but Willa rejects her at first. Finally, the two consummate their relationship in an unforgettable night of passion. Fate intervenes, however, and two days later Willa suffers a stroke and is severely disabled. In a few months, the muse withdraws, and although Hilary does see Willa again, their relationship is at an end.

A secondary theme in the novel is that women seeking the ideas of domesticity and creativity face extraordinary obstacles. This concern is reflected in the young female interviewer who wants to be married and raise a family—and yet also be a writer. Yet Hilary believes there is hope that this young woman can accomplish her goals. She characterizes the role of the creative woman as a "total gathering together where the most realistic and the most mystical can be joined in a celebration of life itself. Women's work is always toward wholeness."

ENCORE: A JOURNAL OF THE EIGHTIETH YEAR

First published: 1993
Type of work: Journal

Sarton takes the measure of her eightieth year, from 1991 to 1992, and feels rejuvenated by a flowering of friendship, honors, and creativity.

Much of this journal represents May Sarton's recovery and rejuvenation after a difficult year characterized by illness and frailty—as reflected in her previous journal, *Endgame: A Journal of the Seventy-ninth Year.* In that journal, Sarton lacked the energy to work in her beloved garden, and she tired after only an hour or two of creative activity. She suffered several losses, including the deaths of old friends and lovers, a loss of independence and autonomy, and a loss of identity. She felt that the May Sarton people had come to know was now a stranger,

someone very old and ill. She ended *Endgame* on her birthday, May 3, and she begins *Encore* two days later.

The first sign of Sarton's rejuvenation appears in her response to her garden in the late spring on Maine's coast. To Sarton, being able to work in the garden again is a major accomplishment after a year of frailty and medical concerns. Her garden represents an evolving, ever-changing work of art. She brings flowers in the house and is heartened by the blooms.

Sarton's journal reveals her strengths and values in her old age. She is committed to the ideals of friendship, and many of the peak times in her year are based upon renewing several friendships by visiting old friends. She is a dedicated letter writer and maintains other longtime friendships through her correspondence. She is a voracious reader of literature and includes numerous passages of prose and poetry that have moved her. She continues to evolve as a person and refines her points of views on key social and political concerns.

Throughout the journal, her deepest friendship is with Susan Sherman, a professor of English who lives in New York City and is writing a book titled *Among the Usual Days,* based on unpublished Sarton works. Sherman visits Sarton numerous times during the year, and each time that she arrives, she brings flowers and other gifts. Sherman is a calming, loving presence in Sarton's life, and she brings order out of chaos. She is an emotional anchor and confidant.

Unfortunately, Sarton's medical concerns persist throughout the year. Despite trying various homeopathic cures, she suffers chronic pain in her abdomen. At the onset of winter, and for the first few months of 1992, she suffers from diverticulitis, an inflammation of the bowels, and must take antibiotics. On good days, she is able to work for only two hours on her many projects. She becomes increasingly anxious about the difficulty of completing all the tasks before her, including writing this journal, maintaining the garden, and visiting her doctor. These and other requirements of daily living conspire to sap her emotional energy and precipitate feelings of depression.

Yet her year is also filled with several peak experiences that provide strong emotional release, as well as comfort in the context of her aging and frail physical condition. At the end of June, she celebrates her first lengthy outing in more than a year. In July, she spends a week on Cape Cod and visits an old friend recovering from a stroke. During the year, Sarton meets and approves of her biographer, Margot Peters.

Throughout the journal, Sarton is revealed as a prominent American literary figure. She receives an honorary Ph.D. (her sixteenth) from West-brook College in Maine. Her journal *Endgame* is published during the year, several of her new po-ems are published, and two new collections of her poetry are in process. After a rough winter and months of suffering severe chronic pain, she man-ages a two-week trip to England in March and visits one of her oldest friends, Juliette Huxley, aged ninety-five, and even some of her English cousins. In June, she gives a poetry reading on the final day of a three-day conference celebrating her work. She ends her year of journal writing feeling ful-filled, despite her continued ill health; feeling a sense of joy for her recognition as a significant liter-ary figure; and feeling a deep and abiding love for her good friend, Sherman. Most important to this writer is that she does not fail her friends and that she begins to write poetry again after her creativity lay fallow for more than a year.

SUMMARY

May Sarton's public and private lives were not separate and distinct, as is the case for most writers and celebrities. Through a lifetime of writing mem-oirs, journals, novels, and poems, Sarton shared the details of her childhood, her relationships to her parents, significant friendships, love affairs, and aspects of her daily living in the context of a solitary life. She triumphed as a writer because she maintained freshness and originality and avoided repeating narrow formulas. In her journals, she strove to discern a synthesis of her overall experi-ence by devoting herself to a rigorous examination of what all of her moods and experiences meant to her on a particular day, as well as in the larger context of her life's work. Readers—particularly women—have identified with her struggles to adapt to a life of solitude. In effect, she distilled the meaning of her own life through her writings and uncovered universal themes for her readers.

Robert E. Yahnke

BIBLIOGRAPHY

By the Author

POETRY:
Encounter in April, 1937
Inner Landscape, 1939
The Lion and the Rose, 1948
The Land of Silence, and Other Poems, 1953
In Time Like Air, 1958
Cloud, Stone, Sun, Vine: Poems, Selected and New, 1961
A Private Mythology, 1966
As Does New Hampshire, and Other Poems, 1967
A Grain of Mustard Seed: New Poems, 1971
A Durable Fire: New Poems, 1972
Collected Poems, 1930-1973, 1974
Selected Poems of May Sarton, 1978 (Serena Sue Hilsinger and Lois Byrnes, editors)
Halfway to Silence, 1980
Letters from Maine, 1984
The Silence Now: New and Uncollected Earlier Poems, 1989
Collected Poems, 1930-1993, 1993
Coming into Eighty, 1994

LONG FICTION:
The Single Hound, 1938
The Bridge of Years, 1946

Shadow of a Man, 1950
A Shower of Summer Days, 1952
Faithful Are the Wounds, 1955
The Birth of a Grandfather, 1957
The Fur Person: The Story of a Cat, 1957
The Small Room, 1961
Joanna and Ulysses, 1963
Mrs. Stevens Hears the Mermaids Singing, 1965
Miss Pickthorn and Mr. Hare: A Fable, 1966
The Poet and the Donkey, 1969
Kinds of Love, 1970
As We Are Now, 1973
Crucial Conversations, 1975
A Reckoning, 1978
Anger, 1982
The Magnificent Spinster, 1985
The Education of Harriet Hatfield, 1989

DRAMA:
The Underground River, pb. 1947

NONFICTION:
I Knew a Phoenix: Sketches for an Autobiography, 1959
Plant Dreaming Deep, 1968
Journal of a Solitude, 1973
A World of Light: Portraits and Celebrations, 1976
The House by the Sea, 1977
Recovering: A Journal, 1980
Writings on Writing, 1980
May Sarton: A Self-Portrait, 1982
At Seventy: A Journal, 1984
After the Stroke: A Journal, 1988
Honey in the Hive: Judith Matlack, 1898-1982, 1988
Endgame: A Journal of the Seventy-ninth Year, 1992
Encore: A Journal of the Eightieth Year, 1993
At Eighty-two, 1996
May Sarton: Selected Letters, 1916-1954, 1997 (Susan
    Sherman, editor)
Dear Juliette: Letters of May Sarton to Juliette Huxley,
    1999 (Sherman, editor)
May Sarton: Selected Letters, 1955-1995, 2000 (Sherman, editor)

CHILDREN'S LITERATURE:
Punch's Secret, 1974
A Walk Through the Woods, 1976

MISCELLANEOUS:
Sarton Selected: An Anthology of the Journals, Novels, and Poems of May Sarton, 1991 (Bradford Dudley Daziel,
    editor)
May Sarton: Among the Usual Days, 1993 (Susan Sherman, editor)
From May Sarton's Well: Writings of May Sarton, 1994 (Edith Royce Schade, editor)

DISCUSSION TOPICS

- How can women maintain a creative life in the context of the requirements of domesticity? May Sarton writes, "Women's work is always toward wholeness." Use this response as a starting point for a discussion of women and creativity.

- Examine some of the distinctions that one can make between loneliness and solitude. What are the relationships between solitude and creativity?

- Sarton wrote numerous journals in her career. What does the journal require of the writer? What are the possibilities of journal writing for all ages—young, middle-aged, and old?

- Sarton was interested in working out the gestalt of her life, the integration or structure of all the separate aspects of her experience and values. How is her goal—of finding an integrative self—relevant to people's lives today?

- Consider the garden as a metaphor for the creative individual's life. What does the garden require of the individual? How is gardening akin to the individual working to perfect the self throughout life?

- In what ways is Sarton a mentor or guide for individuals facing their old age? What evidence does she provide in her journals, novels, and poems to support others in their aging process?

About the Author

Berman, Harry J. "May Sarton and the Tensions of Attachment." In *Integrating the Aging Self: Personal Journals of Later Life*. New York: Springer, 1994.

Blouin, Lenora P. *May Sarton: A Bibliography*. 2d ed. Metuchen, N.J.: Scarecrow Press, 2000.

Braham, Jeanne. *Crucial Conversations: Interpreting Contemporary American Literary Autobiographies by Women*. New York: Teachers College Press, Columbia University, 1995.

Fulk, Mark. *Understanding May Sarton*. Columbia: University of South Carolina Press, 2001.

Ingersoll, Earl, ed. *Conversations with May Sarton*. Jackson: University Press of Mississippi, 1991.

Kallet, Marilyn, ed. *A House of Gathering: Poets on May Sarton's Poetry*. Knoxville: University of Tennessee Press, 1993.

Peters, Margot. *May Sarton: A Biography*. New York: Knopf, 1997.

Sherman, Susan, ed. *May Sarton: Selected Letters*. 2 vols. New York: Norton, 1997-2000.

Swartzlander, Susan, and Marilyn R. Mumford, eds. *That Great Sanity: Critical Essays on May Sarton*. Ann Arbor: University of Michigan Press, 1992.

Library of Congress

ANNE SEXTON

Born: Newton, Massachusetts
November 9, 1928
Died: Weston, Massachusetts
October 4, 1974

One of the most widely read and imitated of the confessional poets, Sexton wrote memorable poems exposing the most intimate aspects of her painful personal life.

BIOGRAPHY

Anne Sexton was born Anne Gray Harvey on November 9, 1928, in Newton, Massachusetts. The third child of wealthy wool manufacturer Ralph Churchill Harvey and his wife, Mary Gray Staples, Anne was surrounded by luxury. The four-story Harvey house contained living quarters for maids, a cook, and a butler. Anne, however, felt overlooked and unwanted, and even as a child she developed a reputation for doing daring and drastic things just to be noticed. Later, she would write of her economically comfortable childhood with bitterness rather than nostalgia.

Her years in the public schools of Wellesley, Massachusetts, and then at the boarding school Rogers Hall were marked by episodes of rebelliousness. After graduation, she enrolled in the Garland School, a Boston finishing school. In 1948, before her twentieth birthday, she eloped with Alfred Muller Sexton II, a sophomore at Colgate University.

Anne and "Kayo," as she called him, then led such a difficult life for five years or so that she must have at least at that time looked back with regret at her privileged childhood. The couple moved to Hamilton, New York, where Kayo attempted to finish his education, but financial pressures were extreme. Then Kayo joined the Naval Reserve and shipped out; Anne lived sometimes with her parents and sometimes with his, while she used her

dazzling good looks to support herself by working as a model between his leaves.

In 1953, she gave birth to Linda Gray Sexton, her first child; she found this experience shocking and devastating. It now became apparent that Anne suffered from serious emotional troubles. Her illness was triggered by the birth of her first child, but it continued to plague her for the rest of her life. She was treated for depression and attempted suicide but seemed to be making a recovery when she became pregnant again. Her second daughter, Joyce Ladd Sexton, was born in August, 1955. Six months later, Anne was admitted to a mental hospital for several months, and the second child was sent to live with Kayo's parents. Sexton's discharge from the hospital was followed by another suicide attempt, but this time she found a new psychiatrist, Dr. Martin Orne, who suggested she write about her problems as part of her therapy. Thus Sexton became a poet.

Sexton's realization that she could exorcise her own demons and provide a moving experience for others through poetry prompted her to enroll in John Holmes's poetry seminar at Boston University. There she met Maxine Kumin, a fellow poet who would inspire and encourage her and who would eventually coauthor children's stories with her. Sexton also learned much from W. D. Snodgrass and Robert Lowell, whose work was beginning to popularize the confessional mode of poetry. In 1960, her first collection of poetry, *To Bedlam and Part Way Back*, was published by Houghton Mifflin. The book's poems chart her experiences through the crisis of mental illness and back toward health.

Her work gained attention within the poetry establishment instantly; although some critics panned it, no one ignored it. Sexton's second book, *All My Pretty Ones*, appeared in 1962, again describing the mental illness but also focusing on the personal losses the author had suffered. The book was followed by prestigious awards and grants. Travel grants allowed Sexton to visit Europe and Africa, although her travels never seemed to provide satisfaction but instead left her depressed.

Her book *Live or Die* (1966) won for her the Pulitzer Prize in poetry in 1967. She received honorary degrees from a number of prestigious universities and a Guggenheim Fellowship; the woman who had dropped out of finishing school taught at Harvard and Radcliffe. Houghton Mifflin published *Love Poems* in 1969 and *Transformations* in 1971, and these books were widely reviewed. By then, it was clear that Sexton's career was an unqualified success.

Yet Sexton did not find peace within herself. She wrote several more books and prepared them for publication during the last four years of her life, and all these show a struggle between despair and religious belief. *The Book of Folly* appeared in 1972. *The Death Notebooks* came out in 1974, the last year of her life. *The Awful Rowing Toward God* (1975) and her 1969 play, *45 Mercy Street* (1976), were published posthumously, as was *Words for Dr. Y: Uncollected Poems with Three Stories* (1978). In these last books, Sexton's earlier themes are recapitulated, but the element of personal turmoil is often represented by a battle between herself and a dimly understood God.

During these last few years, Sexton became more difficult to live with, and it became harder for her to live with others. In 1973, she withdrew from her marriage, against her husband's will; she entered a hospital once more to be treated for depression. She refused most invitations, and her lifelong friendships dwindled. This time, no new outlet presented itself, as poetry had through the agency of Dr. Orne in 1956. On October 4, 1974, Sexton committed suicide by poisoning herself with carbon monoxide.

ANALYSIS

Sexton believed and frequently asserted that poetry should hurt. Her poetry deals with the most painful incidents in her life in a direct and uncompromising way; it is often excruciating to read. Although her style changed considerably over the approximately twenty years of her writing life, her subjects remained basically the same: madness, death, and God's silence. Although she had written some poetry as a student, she did not really begin her career as a poet until after her first mental breakdown, when her psychiatrist directed her to write down her feelings. Thus her work begins on a basis of breakdown and chaos. Her various books show her attempt to work back to some sense of wholeness.

The first collection, *To Bedlam and Part Way Back*, focuses on her mental illness and conveys to the reader the impressions of a patient in a mental ward. Written after the crisis that followed the birth of her first child, it shows Sexton's slow steps back to the rational world. Poems of her experiences in the asylum are interspersed with elegies for people she has known. Her second book, *All My Pretty Ones*, deals with the loss of her parents and other loved ones, as well as with other losses—lovers, faith, identity. In an interview, she explained that the first book described the nature of madness and the second explored the causes of it.

Sexton felt constantly aware of death and loss, and this awareness overwhelmed any other, more positive feelings. In her first two collections, she often uses formal patterns to contain and control her materials. This formality often distances the material somewhat and gives the work the tone of a dignified elegy. Patterns are part of the effect of "Elizabeth Gone" and "Some Foreign Letters," two poems in which Sexton commemorated the life and death of her aunt, Anna Ladd Dingley, who had lived with her. These poems are restrained but moving in their effort to show, through particulars of the woman's life, how much the speaker has lost through her death.

The fear of death and the sadness of loss are replaced, to a certain extent, in the Pulitzer Prize-winning *Live or Die* by a deep longing for death. When she hears of the death of poet Sylvia Plath, according to "Sylvia's Death," she is envious of Plath. In "Wanting to Die," she explains how the desire to end her life obsesses her, addressing those who are not afflicted by this visceral urge and do not understand it. Her tone is ironic, almost playfully so:

> But suicides have a special language.
> Like carpenters they want to know *which tools.*
> They never ask *why build.*

The collection ends with the poem "Live," which describes her decision not to kill the unwanted puppies her dog bore, and her choice to allow herself to live also. Although the book ends with this positive poem, darker tones outweigh any glimmers of hope throughout the collection.

The later Sexton is more unrestrained, wilder in her outpourings and yet not always directly confessional. *Transformations* is something of a diversion from her usual concerns. She puts her anger at the world's injustices into retellings of Grimm fairy tales. *Transformations* consists of feminist poetry that bears the mark of the 1970's. The fairy tales Sexton has twisted and retold are in themselves frightening; they are tales of Rapunzels and Cinderellas and Snow Whites, women who are abused and imprisoned but who are finally able to overcome all obstacles to win the ultimate joy of the happily-ever-after marriage with the prince. The 1970's feminist interrogated the fairy tales of her childhood to ask whether this desired ending was, after all, the ultimate joy—or if it was not, in fact, just more imprisonment and abuse.

Sexton retells these stories with dark humor and wicked irony, so that the reader can share her doubts about the tales and the values they imply. She stresses the unreality of the Cinderella ending, for example, when she concludes her tale that Cinderella and the prince lived "happily ever after,/ like two dolls in a museum case/ never bothered by diapers or dust,/ . . . their darling smiles pasted on for eternity./ Regular Bobbsey Twins." (The Bobbsey Twins are two sets of unrealistically upbeat twins in a popular children's series dating to Sexton's childhood.) The *Transformations* tales show a different Anne Sexton; they sparkle with wicked humor. In this one collection, she substitutes women's issues for her own torments, at least in part.

Sexton's later work, however, returns to her earlier preoccupations, this time without the use of form to shape them. The last few years of her life resulted in several books that express her desperate struggles to escape despair and find a reason for living. The search for God became an obsession, as the poet tried to find some way of approaching the deity that would make her feel validated and forgiven. "Rowing," a frequently anthologized poem from *The Awful Rowing Toward God,* shows the intensity of her desire for God and her energetic pursuit of grace. She begins the poem with a quick summary of her emotional life, presented as a tale: "A story, a story!/ (Let it go. Let it come.)" Rowing is her metaphor for her search: "God was there like an island I had not rowed to." The rest of the poem takes her on an exhausting trip toward this island: "I am rowing, I am rowing/ though the oarlocks stick and are rusty/ and the sea blinks and rolls/ like a worried eyeball." When she arrives, she says, God will "get rid of the rat inside"—the "gnawing pestilential rat" that has been eating her all of her life. "God will take it with his two hands/ and embrace it."

The rat is a presence throughout Sexton's poetry, and she even wanted to have it in her epitaph. She desired to have the sentence "RATS LIVE ON NO EVIL STAR," which she claimed to have found in an Irish churchyard, engraved on her tombstone. According to her daughter, the statement—which reads the same forward and backward—gave Sexton an odd kind of comfort. Yet if the last collections are not unremittingly grim, anything positive in them tends to be set in a hypothetical future—when she arrives at the island of God, when he plays cards with her. The present action in the poetry depicts only the ongoing struggle to arrive at a distant place of peace and forgiveness.

Sexton's poetry provides an unforgettable vision of one woman's search for healing. Moreover, it carries the reader along on his or her own quest.

"THE STARRY NIGHT"

First published: 1962 (collected in *All My Pretty Ones,* 1962)
Type of work: Poem

The speaker reflects on Vincent van Gogh's well-known painting and on her desire to dissolve into the infinite.

"The Starry Night" shows Sexton's identification with another tortured and suicidal artist, Vincent van Gogh. The short, free-verse poem begins with an epigraph from one of van Gogh's letters to his brother. "That does not keep me from having a terrible need of—shall I say the word—religion," van Gogh wrote. "Then I go out at night to paint the stars." Sexton used epigraphs from a variety of works to begin her poems, and the epigraphs are often of major importance, pointing to a main theme of the poem that might otherwise be overlooked. Here she is indicating that she shares not only the mental imbalance, suicidal tendencies, and artistic nature of the Dutch artist but also his unsatisfied desire for the spiritual.

When van Gogh wrote the letter to his brother, he was painting the masterpiece *Starry Night on the Rhone*, which is described in the poem. The painting captures the night sky in blues and blacks, with a swirl of violent orange representing the moon, and burning yellow-white stars. One would expect a peaceful scene from the title, but this painting is intensely disquieting. The movement seems to be a great rush skyward, the sleeping town beneath the sky unconscious of this spiraling of all nature toward infinity. Sexton sees this painting as a reflection of her own death wish. The dark tree at the edge of the painting is described as "black-haired"—Sexton was a brunette—and it "slips/ up like a drowned woman into the hot sky." To make her meaning clearer, she continues, "This is how/ I want to die."

The poem interprets the painting as presenting a nature that is animate and hostile. Nevertheless, the picture attracts the speaker, because nature's brute force promises death, release from the burden of self. Sexton sees the central moon image in the painting as a great dragon that will suck her up into its being. She desires, she says, "to split/ from my life with no flag,/ no belly,/ no cry"—to merge silently and painlessly with the infinite. The images may suggest not a rediscovery of religion but a terrifying substitute for it. Part of the appeal of this poem lies in the vivid interpretation of the painting and in the kinship the reader sees between Sexton and van Gogh.

"ALL MY PRETTY ONES"

First published: 1962 (collected in *All My Pretty Ones*, 1962)
Type of work: Poem

A daughter sorts through her father's belongings after his death and reviews their difficult relationship.

"All My Pretty Ones," the title poem of Sexton's second collection, expresses the grief and loss characterizing the entire volume. In this poem, Sexton uses formal, rhymed verse to reflect upon the shock and sorrow of losing both her parents within a few months. The title recalls the grief of William Shakespeare's character Macduff, when he is told that Macbeth has had his wife and children killed. Sexton quotes the relevant passage as an epigraph to the poem.

Sexton's poetry closely reflects her life and appears to represent her own voice. "All My Pretty Ones" follows her efforts to go through her father's effects after his death, which occurred shortly after her mother's. His business fortunes had suffered a reversal. Addressing her father directly, she tells of her attempts to "disencumber/ you from the residence you could not afford" and get rid of mementos that were meaningful to him but not to her: "boxes of pictures of people I do not know./ I touch their cardboard faces. They must go."

The father's life is woven into the dead reminders of him that are of another time period. The daughter finds news clippings in an old album and is taken back through history and through her father's history. The clippings describe the destruction of the *Hindenburg* and the election of U.S. president Herbert Hoover. The father's personal history is chronicled in photographs of formal dances, speedboat races, and horse shows, reflecting the wealth and luxury of the life he led.

As the poem progresses, however, it becomes clear that this is no ordinary elegy. The problems in the family become evident: The daughter calls the father "my drunkard, my navigator" and tells of the diary her mother kept, in which she did not speak of the father's alcoholism but only said that he "overslept." The daughter wonders if the alcoholic tendency has been passed on to her with the rest of her dubious inheritance: "each Christmas Day/ with your blood, will I drink down your glass/ of wine?" At the poem's conclusion, the daughter reflects on how brief a space love and memory endure.

The poem is often anthologized with "The Truth the Dead Know," another poem about her parents' deaths, written at approximately the same time. Both poems express a sense of loss complicated by resentment and feelings of isolation. "All My Pretty Ones" gives a memorable portrayal of a survivor who, not having resolved the difficulties with her father during his life, is forced to cope with his death.

"WITH MERCY FOR THE GREEDY"

First published: 1962 (collected in *The Complete Poems*, 1981)
Type of work: Poem

The speaker considers a crucifix that she received as a present and concludes that, for her, poetry must serve as confession.

"With Mercy for the Greedy" shows Sexton's need for religious faith and her inability to find it. The

poem also provides her explanation of how her art functions as therapy and, to some degree, takes the place of the religion that she cannot comfortably accept. Addressed to a friend "who urges me to make an appointment for the Sacrament of Confession," the poem explores the speaker's attempt to grasp faith. The friend, identified as "Ruth," has sent her a cross, which she has been wearing "hung with package string" around her neck. This cross, though, has nothing to say to her. It remains unresponsive to her desperate need. "I detest my sins and I try to believe/ in The Cross," she says. Yet she must conclude, finally, that "need is not quite belief."

Having determined that she cannot approach traditional religion through her friend's gift, she tells her friend what she does do: She writes poems, and these are her confession, her way of dealing with her sense of guilt. "I was born/ doing reference work in sin, and born/ confessing it. This is what poems are," she explains. Poems are the struggle with the self and the world that provide "mercy for the greedy"—they are "the tongue's wrangle,/ the world's pottage, the rat's star." Only through the difficult and painful process of creating poetry can she aspire to any kind of peace. The phrase "tongue's wrangle" suggests the awkwardness and difficulty of setting oneself straight through words.

The rat is Sexton's inner turmoil and torment. Later, in "Rowing," she would imagine the rat transformed and accepted. In "With Mercy for the Greedy," however, Sexton does not go so far as to imagine this acceptance, this forgiveness. The only means of confession for her is the poetry, the "rat's star." This poem is anthologized frequently, perhaps because it shows how literally the term "the confessional poet" may be understood when it is applied to Sexton. She is not only sharing intimate and painful experiences with her readers but also making a confession to her god.

SUMMARY

Sexton's direct and personal poetry forcefully imparts her obsession with loss, suicide, and the authoritarian male figure. Her recurrent images, bones and rats and other reminders of death and psychic torment, retain their ability to surprise and shock the reader, despite their repetition. She always has an original twist that violates expectations and leads the reader to question his or her assumptions. In her poetry Sexton seems to skim over experience like a magnet attracting iron filings, seeking out suicidal soulmates in literature, history, folklore, and her daily life. However, the intensity of Sexton's poetry makes up for the narrowness of its range. Her work serves to define and illustrate confessional poetry.

Janet McCann

BIBLIOGRAPHY

By the Author

POETRY:

To Bedlam and Part Way Back, 1960
All My Pretty Ones, 1962
Selected Poems, 1964
Live or Die, 1966
Poems, 1968 (with Thomas Kinsella and Douglas Livingston)
Love Poems, 1969
Transformations, 1971
The Book of Folly, 1972
The Death Notebooks, 1974
The Awful Rowing Toward God, 1975
Words for Dr. Y.: Uncollected Poems with Three Stories, 1978
The Complete Poems, 1981
Selected Poems of Anne Sexton, 1988

DRAMA:

45 Mercy Street, pr. 1969, pb. 1976

NONFICTION:

Anne Sexton: A Self-Portrait in Letters, 1977 (Linda Gray Sexton and Lois Ames, editors)
No Evil Star: Selected Essays, Interviews, and Prose, 1985

CHILDREN'S LITERATURE (WITH MAXINE KUMIN):

Eggs of Things, 1963
More Eggs of Things, 1964
Joey and the Birthday Present, 1971
The Wizard's Tears, 1975

About the Author

Furst, Arthur. *Anne Sexton: The Last Summer.* New York: St. Martin's Press, 2000.

Hall, Caroline King Barnard. *Anne Sexton.* Boston: Twayne, 1989.

McClatchy, J. D. *Anne Sexton: The Artist and Her Critics.* Bloomington: Indiana University Press, 1978.

McGowan, Philip. *Anne Sexton and Middle Generation Poetry: The Geography of Grief.* Westport, Conn.: Praeger, 2004.

Middlebrook, Diane Wood. *Anne Sexton: A Biography.* Boston: Houghton Mifflin, 1991.

Sexton, Linda Gray, and Lois Ames, eds. *Anne Sexton: A Self-Portrait in Letters.* Boston: Houghton Mifflin, 1977.

Swiontkowski, Gale. *Imagining Incest: Sexton, Plath, Rich, and Olds on Life with Daddy.* Selinsgrove, Pa.: Susquehanna University Press, 2003.

Wagner-Martin, Linda, ed. *Critical Essays on Anne Sexton.* Boston: G. K. Hall, 1989.

DISCUSSION TOPICS

- Contrast Anne Sexton's attitude toward her father in "All My Pretty Ones" with Sylvia Plath's in "Daddy."

- How is it possible that reading about painful struggles like Sexton's can give pleasure?

- How does one explain Sexton's rejection of confession as a religious exercise while practicing it as a poetic one?

- What do Sexton's epigraphs contribute to the poems that they introduce?

- Does Sexton avoid morbidity in her poems about death?

- What changes in poetic form marked Sexton's poetry as her writing career proceeded?

NTOZAKE SHANGE

Born: Trenton, New Jersey
October 18, 1948

Through her poetry, novels, and writing for the theater, Shange has given a distinctive voice to the experience of African American women.

Jules Allen

BIOGRAPHY

Ntozake Shange was born Paulette Williams in Trenton, New Jersey, on October 18, 1948, the eldest of four children. Her father, Paul T. Williams, was a surgeon, and her mother, Eloise Williams, was a psychiatric social worker and educator. During her childhood, her family moved from Trenton to upstate New York, then to St. Louis, Missouri.

Although many of the characters she writes about in her literary works are rural, poor, or members of the urban underclass, Shange grew up in a privileged, upper-middle-class environment. Her father was a musician and painter as well as a ringside surgeon, and the Williams household was frequently visited by well-known African American musicians, writers, and sports figures. Cultural and artistic achievement was emphasized within the family environment; the members of the Williams family would entertain one another on Sundays with readings, music, and dance.

Despite this protective environment, Shange was spared neither the experience of racial discrimination nor that of sexual discrimination. As a young teenager in St. Louis, she was bused, as part of a desegregation program, to a mostly white school, where she felt out of place and was mistreated by her fellow students. She was also told that her career goals (she wanted to be a war correspondent or a jazz musician) were not appropriate for a woman. Experiences of these kinds are the roots of the interest in feminism and African American issues that informs Shange's literary work.

Shange attended Barnard College in New York City, where she earned a bachelor's degree in American studies, emphasizing African American poetry and music, in 1970. She married a lawyer; depression over his leaving her prompted several suicide attempts. (A later marriage, to jazz musician David Murray, would also dissolve.) She became active in political and social movements, concluding later, however, that they were not receptive to women. She went on to graduate study in Los Angeles at the University of Southern California, where she earned a master's degree in American studies in 1973. She changed her name in 1971 as part of her effort to establish her African American identity. The name Ntozake means "she who comes with her own things," while Shange means "who walks like a lion." The new name clearly represents the strength and independence that Shange, like many of the characters in her writings, was seeking.

While living in Oakland, California, and teaching in the women's studies program of a nearby college, Shange began giving readings of the poems she had been writing, often collaborating with dancer Paula Moss, who would develop dances based on the poems. On occasion, Shange and Moss also collaborated with musicians. These experiments developed into the theatrical text *for colored girls who have considered suicide/ when the rainbow is enuf* (1975). Shange and Moss moved to New York City in 1975, where they performed the work in a variety of venues. Ultimately, their work attracted the attention of theatrical producers, first Woodie King, the preeminent producer of African American theater in New York, then the New York Shakespeare Festival's Joseph Papp. Papp first produced the play at the festival's Public Theatre, then transferred it to a commercial theater in 1976, where it enjoyed a two-year run.

For colored girls who have considered suicide/ when the rainbow is enuf, which received almost uniformly favorable reviews, was also criticized for some of its feminist sentiments and its depiction of African American men. The work catapulted Shange into the public eye. She continued to write plays, and Papp continued to produce them at the Public Theatre. Her next play was *A Photograph: Still Life with Shadows; A Photograph: A Study in Cruelty* (1977), published in 1981 as *A Photograph: Lovers in Motion.* Subsequent plays include *Boogie Woogie Landscapes* (first produced in 1979) and *Spell # 7: Geechee Jibara Quik Magic Trance Manual for Technologically Stressed Third World People* (1979). Her adaptation of Bertolt Brecht's *Mutter Courage und ihre Kinder* (1941; *Mother Courage and Her Children*) was produced at the Public Theatre in 1980. In 1985, she adapted her novel *Betsey Brown* (1985) for the musical stage in collaboration with playwright Emily Mann and composer Baikida Carroll; the musical premiered in 1989.

In addition to acting in *for colored girls who have considered suicide/ when the rainbow is enuf,* Shange continued to perform her poetry. Her first published collections of poems were *Nappy Edges* (1978) and *Natural Disasters and Other Festive Occasions* (1979). Shange's first effort at writing fiction was the novella *Sassafras* (1976), which she later expanded into the novel *Sassafras, Cypress, and Indigo* (1982). Her major publications of the 1980's include *A Daughter's Geography* (1983), a collection of poems, and *See No Evil: Prefaces, Essays, and Accounts, 1976-1983* (1984), a collection of prose pieces. Returning to an interest in the visual arts inspired by her father's activity as a painter, Shange collaborated with visual artist Wopo Holup for *From Okra to Greens* (1984), a collection of poems and illustrations based on a piece first performed in 1978, and wrote *Ridin' the Moon in Texas: Word Paintings* (1987), a collection of responses in prose and poetry to works of visual art by a variety of artists. Shange's poetry has received more consistently favorable critical response than her work in other forms.

Her writing does not fall easily into the traditional categories of drama, poetry, and fiction, however; it is noteworthy that she won the *Los Angeles Times* Book Prize for Poetry in 1981 for *Three*

Pieces (1981), actually a collection of plays in poetry. She has received a number of other prestigious literary and theatrical awards, including two Obie (Off-Broadway) awards and the Pushcart Prize. Although her recent work for the theater has not attracted the attention lavished on *for colored girls who have considered suicide/ when the rainbow is enuf,* Shange has continued to write plays and to direct her own plays and those of others, often in experimental theater spaces or outside New York. She serves on the faculty in the department of drama at the University of Houston and makes her permanent residence in Philadelphia.

ANALYSIS

Although Shange writes poetry, drama, essays, and fiction, she thinks of herself primarily as a poet. In an essay titled "Unrecovered Losses/ Black Theatre Traditions" (the foreword to *Three Pieces*), she writes: "I am interested solely in the poetry of a moment" rather than in traditional dramatic structure, which she rejects.

A Shange poem, play, or story typically is best understood as an accumulation of moments rather than as a sustained action or narrative. Many of her early works, especially, are structured as groupings of thematically related poems and lyric passages to be read or performed together. Her best-known play, *for colored girls who have considered suicide/ when the rainbow is enuf,* is a series of poems spoken by a group of women. *Spell No. 7* (first produced in 1979) begins as a minstrel show, a collection of individual acts and routines.

Shange is concerned primarily with the inner lives of her characters. Her work tends toward the lyrical exploration of those inner lives, even in the context of a realistic, autobiographical novel such as *Betsey Brown,* in which the main character's thoughts, imaginings, and reveries are as central to the impact of the story as her actions. The play *Boogie Woogie Landscapes* consists entirely of the thoughts of one central character, a young woman. Other figures who appear on the stage are her memories and dreams.

The episodic structure, lyricism, and intensely personal tone of Shange's work, however, do not exclude the expression of larger political and social concerns. Quite the contrary: Shange is concerned with the impact of political and social structures on the inner life of African Americans, particularly African American women. Her description of her characters in one play as "afflicted with the kinds of insecurities and delusions only available to those who learned themselves thru the traumas of racism" could apply to all of her characters. Thematically, Shange's work reflects an ongoing concern not only with the implications of being black in a white world and female in a male world but also with the forms of discrimination that exist within African American communities (based on skin color, cultural sophistication, urban or rural origins, and so forth) and the difficulties those pressures create for the individual attempting to arrive at a sense of self and a sense of racial identity.

Shange refers frequently to the folk culture of rural, southern African Americans. Although many of her more urbane characters look down upon that culture, it figures in Shange's work as a source of spirituality and a positive influence on the lives of the characters touched by it. Her works also contain frequent allusions to urban African American culture, especially jazz and rhythm-and-blues music, and to the African American literary heritage.

Important aspects of Shange's effort to find a distinctly African American voice that reflects the positive values of African American culture are her diction and orthography. She generally writes in a nonstandard English that reflects the grammatical characteristics of African American dialects (the use of "they" for "their," for example). She uses these dialects to individuate characters and also as narrator or authorial voices in her poems and stories. In this way, she posits so-called Black English as a valid and expressive literary language rather than simply as a nonstandard dialect.

Her early writings and most of her poems are rendered in lower case, using irregular spellings of some words and using both common and unusual abbreviations and symbols (the ampersand, for example) in place of others. In addition to asserting the nonstandard nature of her language, these devices make her writing a form of visual, as well as literary, art. For Shange, her orthography connects her writing with music and dance, which she considers the essential forms of African American culture. Her unconventional spelling and orthography make the visual aspect of her writing akin to dance and make reading her work a participatory act.

FOR COLORED GIRLS WHO HAVE CONSIDERED SUICIDE/ WHEN THE RAINBOW IS ENUF

First produced: 1975 (first published, 1975; revised, 1976)
Type of work: Play

Seven African American women describe the pains and joys particular to being black and female in the United States.

For colored girls who have considered suicide/ when the rainbow is enuf is Shange's first, and most acclaimed, theater piece. It is not really a play in that it has no continuous plot or conventional development; it consists, rather, of a series of poetic monologues to be accompanied by dance movements and music—a form Shange calls the "choreopoem." Shange originally wrote the monologues as separate poems in 1974, then began performing them in California with choreography and musical accompaniment under their collective title. After moving to New York City, she continued work on the piece, which opened on Broadway to an enthusiastic reception in 1976.

The play is performed by seven women, each dressed in a different color. In the introduction, the Lady in Brown describes the purpose of the piece as to "sing a black girl's song/ bring her out to know herself." The majority of the poetic monologues describe relationships between black women and black men. The Lady in Yellow describes her loss of virginity the night after her high school graduation; the Lady in Brown tells of the first boyfriend she had, at the age of eight. Harboring a secret crush on Toussaint Louverture, the eighteenth century Haitian patriot, the eight-year-old girl finds herself attracted to a young boy, also named Toussaint. The Lady in Red describes "the passion flower of southwest los angeles"—a woman who seduces men, then rejects them.

In a contrapuntal passage, three of the women describe the violence and abuse suffered by women who are raped by male acquaintances. Several speeches concern the women's feelings of having been rejected by men, despite their love for them. The last, and longest, story, recounted by the Lady in Red, is of Beau Willie, a Vietnam veteran, and Crystal, with whom he has two children. Crystal leaves Beau Willie because of his drug-induced violence and his inability to provide for the children; ultimately, he returns and threatens to kill the children if she will not marry him.

Although the poetic monologues in the play are unquestionably fueled by rage at the mistreatment of black women within their own community, the rage is balanced by compassion and joy. Even Beau Willie, illiterate and adrift after serving his country, is portrayed as a victim as well as a victimizer. Even as the women speak out against their mistreatment, they find pleasure in music, dance, love (when it succeeds), and African American history and heritage, the points of reference in all of Shange's work. Shange's diction and style are, as always, ripe and exuberant, themselves testimonies to the joys of creation and expression available to the women on stage.

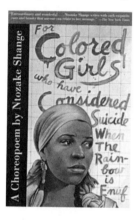

The ultimate point of the theater piece is that the African American woman must learn to accept herself and her ethnic identity and learn to find strength in herself through them, rather than depending on her relationship with a man for identity. The fact that there are only black women onstage, describing their experiences in the first-person voice, is an expression of Shange's thesis. In the final passage, the women talk of feeling that they are "missin somethin" even when in love. The Lady in Red describes an epiphany in which she finds the missing thing: "I found god in myself/ & i loved her." This line combines the sense of self, self-identity, and self-love that Shange's "choreopoem" is intended to create for black women. The image of the rainbow, enacted by the women dressed in different colors, derives from Shange's experience of seeing a rainbow and thinking that it represents for African American women "the possibility to start all over again with the power and the beauty of ourselves."

A PHOTOGRAPH: LOVERS IN MOTION

First produced: 1977 (first published, 1981)
Type of work: Play

Five young African American artists and professionals contend with the difficulty of achieving their aspirations and with changes in the relationships among them.

A Photograph: Lovers in Motion, first produced by the New York Shakespeare Festival in 1977, is a more conventionally structured play than *for colored girls who have considered suicide/ when the rainbow is enuf.* The characters exist as individually developed entities rather than as the storytellers of the earlier play: They interact through dialogue and action and advance a plot. Two of the characters, Sean and Michael, are struggling artists; he is a photographer, she is a dancer. Earl and Nevada are both attorneys; Earl is also a longtime friend of Sean. The fifth character, Claire, is a model who poses for Sean's photography.

The plot concerns Sean's relationships with the three women: Michael, Nevada, and Claire. All three are or have been his lovers; initially, he wants to maintain all these relationships, saying to Michael: "There are a number of women in my life/ who i plan to keep in my life." Nevada and Michael, however, each want an exclusive relationship with Sean, a situation that results in several confrontations among the characters, including a physical fight between Michael and Claire. Sean, who has decided he is most attracted to Michael, attempts to persuade Earl to take up with Nevada. The final scene is a confrontation among all five characters, from which three withdraw, leaving Sean and Michael together.

Although the emotional entanglements are played out fairly realistically, Shange retains her commitment to poetic drama. In addition to realistic exchanges among the characters, the characters speak in lyrical passages describing their feelings and aspirations. Some of these lyrical sections are performed by a single character, alone on stage. Even when placed in the context of dialogue, the passages seem more like solo expressions than genuine exchanges. In the first scene, Sean has a long lyrical passage on his artistic hero, the nineteenth century French novelist Alexandre Dumas, to which Michael responds with a long poem on the image of a man she had heard of that has governed the choices she has made in her own relationships with men.

Sean and Michael also have poetic speeches concerning their feelings about and ambitions for their respective art forms, photography and dance. They describe these two arts in similar terms, as activities that enable them to fix a moment in time. Michael describes dance as allowing her to "be free in time/ a moment is mine always." Sean says that "a photograph is like a fingerprint/ it stays & stays forever."

A Photograph touches on a number of Shange's major themes. The issues concerning relationships between African American women and men are addressed through the attitudes expressed by the characters, including Sean's view that he can be involved with as many women as he chooses, Nevada's desperate need for Sean, Claire's indiscriminate seductiveness, and Michael's attraction to a kind of man she knows to be dangerous. Shange raises racial issues through Nevada, who considers herself racially superior to the other characters, even though all are African Americans, because her slave ancestors were freed earlier than those of the other characters. She looks down on the others and refers to them in disparaging racial terms, yet she is attracted to the very qualities she disparages in Sean.

As artists, Sean and Michael must also address the issues confronted by Shange's creative characters. Sean views his art as a means of satisfying personal needs. He sees the story of Alexandre Dumas's rejection of his illegitimate son as an allegory for his own unsatisfying relationship with his father, and also for the position of the black man in American culture. He fantasizes that he will receive the Nobel Prize for photographs that reveal the truth of African American life. Michael questions his ambitions, suggesting that he is more interested in personal success than in the integrity of his art, or the lives of the human subjects he photographs.

The women in the play represent different options for Sean. Nevada is a snobbish, wealthy, professional woman who wants to support Sean's career but looks down on his artistic lifestyle. Claire, the model, represents the sensual side of Sean's

work. His photographs of her are provocative, but they lack the seriousness of purpose to which he aspires. By choosing Michael as his true love, Sean chooses the one woman who understands and shares in the nature of the creative artist and who challenges Sean to remain faithful to his higher aspirations.

SASSAFRASS, CYPRESS, AND INDIGO

First published: 1982
Type of work: Novel

Three sisters discover themselves through explorations of their ethnicity, sexuality, and creativity.

Sassafrass, Cypress, and Indigo incorporates Shange's earlier novella *Sassafras* (1976). Apparently set during the Vietnam War era, it tells the story of Hilda Effania and her three daughters, African American natives of Charleston, South Carolina, descendants of a family of weavers who did piecework for a wealthy white family. Hilda Effania has conventional aspirations for her daughters, hoping that each will marry well and happily, preferably to a doctor's son. She gives them the means to follow an upwardly mobile path: She sends Sassafrass to an exclusive northern prep school and Cypress to New York City to study ballet. She offers Indigo the opportunity to study the violin. Her daughters, however, are not content merely to follow the paths she suggests to them.

The daughters' stories are told separately. Indigo's story concerns her arrival at sexual maturity at the age of twelve and the resulting changes in her life. Her constant companions have been dolls she has made, and she sees herself as inhabiting a world of magical people and events. When she is on the verge of giving up her dolls, Uncle John the ragpicker, one of the mysterious figures she has befriended, gives her a violin. She becomes adept at improvising on the instrument, producing unconventional but compelling music. Initially resisting her mother's desire that she learn to play properly, she ultimately does learn to play conventionally.

For a while, Indigo uses the magical power of

her fiddle as part of a motorcycle gang, the Geechee Capitans. Her epiphany occurs when she is being chased during a misadventure through vaults where African slaves were once imprisoned. At that point, she renounces her flirtation with a life of violence: "Indigo knew her calling. The Colored had hurt enough already." Ultimately, she goes to live with her aunt on a coastal Carolina island, where she learns the aunt's trade of midwifery.

Despite her education, Sassafrass eschews college in favor of the artistic life. A weaver like her mother, she has turned the craft of weaving into an art form, weaving expressive hangings rather than utilitarian cloth. In Los Angeles, she becomes involved with Mitch, a tenor saxophonist and drug addict, with whom she has a tempestuous relationship. Mitch wants Sassafrass not to be a weaver but to express herself through writing. They finally move together to an artistic commune in Louisiana, where Sassafrass finds herself through religion and leaves Mitch behind definitively.

Sassafrass's story is interwoven to an extent with Cypress's—during a stormy episode with Mitch, Sassafrass goes to visit her sister in San Francisco. Cypress has become a dancer in an African American idiom rather than ballet, with a dance troupe called The Kushites Returned. She supports herself largely by selling drugs and surrounds herself with a bohemian entourage. She travels with The Kushites Returned to New York City. Disgusted with the behavior of the male dancers around her, she enters the orbit of Azure Bosom, a radical feminist dance company by which she feels comforted and protected for a time. Feeling betrayed by one of the dancers in Azure Bosom, however, she falls into a relationship with Leroy, an alto saxophonist, with whom she finds happiness.

Sassafrass, Cypress, and Indigo combines third-person narration with other literary forms: It includes letters, journal entries, even recipes and magical spells. Although each sister's story is told separately, they are punctuated by letters to the sisters from their mother which frame each story in terms of the mother's values and ambitions for them. This diversity mirrors the multiple pressures and issues the three women must face as they discover themselves. Each woman must, in her own way, reconcile the need for autonomy with her family and ethnic history, and with the urge to create.

Indigo negotiates her mother's disapproval of her interest in magic and desire to leave the mythological aspect of their heritage behind by immersing herself in Geechee culture, where she is accepted as a midwife and woman of magic, while simultaneously studying the violin. Her fiddle playing, spell casting, and desire to help her race fit comfortably into the folk culture of the island.

Through her immersion in non-Western religion, Sassafrass also finds a context that gives her natural creative outlet, weaving, a higher significance. Cypress explores several possibilities, expressing aspects of herself through her work with African American and feminist dance companies. Through her relationship with Leroy, she is freed from the attempts of others to define her creativity and also freed to express her rage at the historical mistreatment of African Americans. Ultimately, all three women return to Charleston to attend to the birth of Sassafrass's child. Each has found her own path and place in life, her own way of reconciling their common conflicts, and her own way of permitting her particular sense of personal and racial identity to create a context for her need to create.

BETSEY BROWN

First published: 1985
Type of work: Novel

Betsey Brown, a thirteen-year-old girl in St. Louis, negotiates the pressures of growing up in a racially charged atmosphere.

Although all of Shange's works contain elements of autobiography, *Betsey Brown* is the most overtly autobiographical, clearly deriving from Shange's own experiences as a young teenager in St. Louis during the 1950's. Like Shange, Betsey is a member of an upper-middle-class black family originally from the North. Her father, Greer, is a physician, while her mother, Jane, is a social worker. Many of the book's episodes describe universal adolescent experiences: Betsey contends with her physical maturation, her desire for a boyfriend, and her need for privacy and a sense of her own identity. She also, however, confronts issues that are specific to the African American experience.

Stylistically, *Betsey Brown* is more conventional than *Sassafrass, Cypress, and Indigo*. The narrative follows Betsey through a series of experiences from an omniscient third-person point of view that makes the reader privy to Betsey's thoughts and emotions in addition to her behavior. The point of view shifts periodically, so that the thoughts and motivations of the adults in Betsey's life (her parents and her grandmother, for example) are made available to the reader as well. In this way, the

reader is able to share Betsey's adolescent perspective on the world around her while also gaining some perspective on her through the thoughts of those responsible for her environment.

The Brown household is distinctive. Greer, who is intensely concerned that his children grow up with an appreciation of African American culture, wakes them each morning by beating on a conga drum (Shange's own father was a percussionist) and by playing jazz and rhythm and blues on the household radio. Jane is somewhat disapproving of this raucous behavior but accepts it out of her love for Greer. Greer's mother-in-law, Vida, looks down upon him as too overtly African for her tastes. This intraracial discrimination causes the major conflicts in the narrative.

Betsey identifies with her father's appreciation for the sensual side of African American culture. Her ambition is to sing with Ike and Tina Turner as an "Ikette." Her identification with African Americanism is only heightened by her being bused to a white school, where she feels alienated and out of place. Her mother's tacit disapproval of Betsey's particular sense of her race causes Betsey to attempt to run away to a place where she can be the kind of African American she wants to be, away from the pressures of white society and her own mother's desire for gentility. The tension between Greer's and Jane's respective senses of themselves

as black people also creates a rift between them, which causes Jane to leave her family for a period after Greer insists to her that he wants their children to participate in a demonstration against segregation.

Another set of events that address social issues within the African American community has to do with the Brown family's efforts to secure domestic help. The people they hire are other African Americans who have come to St. Louis from rural areas of the South and are somewhat looked down upon by the urbanites. After Betsey and her three siblings terrorize one such character, Betsey is made to feel ashamed by a friend of hers whose mother does domestic work. A subsequent domestic has better luck with the family, only to lose her job after committing a crime.

Although the tensions governing the story between an insular black community and the surrounding white world, between growing children and the adults trying to maintain order, and between different understandings of African American cultural and social aspirations are not fully resolved at the end of the story, they are sufficiently resolved to allow the family to continue as a unit and to permit Betsey some sense of having her own place in her world.

SUMMARY

Shange's effort to give expression to the African American experience, particularly the experience of African American women, has led her to innovation at every level of her writing, from her choices of subject matter to the unconventional forms of her plays and novels to her distinctive diction and orthography. Her interests in African American culture, both urban and rural, and in music, dance, and the visual arts are evident throughout her literary output. The dominant trend in her work has been toward a more personal kind of writing. In her earlier works, she embodies her concerns in those of archetypal characters; subsequently, she has acknowledged the basis of her work in her own experience and biography more directly.

Philip Auslander

BIBLIOGRAPHY

By the Author

DRAMA:

for colored girls who have considered suicide/ when the rainbow is enuf, pr., pb. 1975

A Photograph: Still Life with Shadows; A Photograph: A Study in Cruelty, pr. 1977, revised pr. 1979, pb. 1981 (as *A Photograph: Lovers in Motion*)

Where the Mississippi Meets the Amazon, pr. 1977 (with Thulani Nkabinde and Jessica Hagedorn)

From Okra to Greens: A Different Kinda Love Story, pr. 1978, pb. 1985

Spell # 7: Geechee Jibara Quik Magic Trance Manual for Technologically Stressed Third World People, pr. 1979, pb. 1981

Boogie Woogie Landscapes, pr. 1979, pb. 1981

Mother Courage and Her Children, pr. 1980 (adaptation of Bertolt Brecht's play)

Three Pieces, pb. 1981

Betsey Brown, pr. 1989 (adaptation of her novel)

The Love Space Demands: A Continuing Saga, pb. 1991, pr. 1992

Plays: One, pb. 1992

Three Pieces, pb. 1992

LONG FICTION:

Sassafras: A Novella, 1976

Sassafras, Cypress, and Indigo, 1982

Betsey Brown, 1985

Liliane: Resurrection of the Daughter, 1994

POETRY:

Nappy Edges, 1978

Natural Disasters and Other Festive Occasions, 1979

A Daughter's Geography, 1983, 1991

From Okra to Greens: Poems, 1984

Ridin' the Moon in Texas: Word Paintings, 1987

I Live in Music, 1994

The Sweet Breath of Life: A Poetic Narrative of the African American Family, 2004 (photos by the Kamoinge Workshop; photos edited by Frank Stewart)

NONFICTION:

See No Evil: Prefaces, Essays, and Accounts, 1976-1983, 1984

If I Can Cook, You Know God Can, 1998

CHILDREN'S LITERATURE:

Whitewash, 1997

Muhammad Ali: The Man Who Could Float Like a Butterfly and Sting Like a Bee, 2002

Daddy Says, 2003

Ellington Was Not a Street, 2004

DISCUSSION TOPICS

- What does the meaning of Ntozake Shange's name suggest about the themes of her works?

- What image of men is conveyed in *for colored girls who have considered suicide/ when the rainbow is enuf*?

- What role is played by visual images in Shange's poetry?

- How does Shange examine discrimination within African American communities?

- How does Shange blend the characteristics of urban and rural African American cultures?

- How does Shange employ Black English to support her themes and develop her characters?

- What is Shange saying about male-female relationships in *A Photograph: Lovers in Motion*?

- How is music central to Shange's works?

EDITED TEXT:
The Beacon Best of 1999: Creative Writing by Women and Men of All Colors, 2000

About the Author

Christ, Carol P. *Diving Deep and Surfacing: Women Writers on Spiritual Quest.* Boston: Beacon Press, 1980.

Effiong, Philip U. *In Search of a Model for African-American Drama: A Study of Selected Plays by Lorraine Hansberry, Amiri Baraka, and Ntozake Shange.* Lanham, Md.: University Press of America, 2000.

Flowers, Sandra Hollin. "'Colored Girls': Textbook for the Eighties." *Black American Literature Forum* 15 (Summer, 1981): 51-54.

Lester, Neal A. *Ntozake Shange: A Critical Study of the Plays.* New York: Garland, 1995.

Mullen, Harryette. "'Artistic Expression Was Flowering Everywhere': Alison Mills and Ntozake Shange, Black Bohemian Feminists in the 1970s." *Meridians: Feminism, Race, Transnationalism* 4 (2004): 205-235.

Olaniyan, Tejumola. *Scars of Conquest/Masks of Resistance: The Invention of Cultural Identities in African, African-American, and Caribbean Drama.* New York: Oxford University Press, 1995.

Palmeri, Jason. "A Laying On of Discourses: The Rhetoric(s) of Subjectivity in Shange's *for colored girls.*" *Text & Presentation: The Journal of the Comparative Drama Conference* 24 (April, 2003): 115-125.

Richards, S. L. "Conflicting Impulses in the Plays of Ntozake Shange." *Black American Literature Forum* 17 (Summer, 1983): 73-78.

Rushing, A. B. "For Colored Girls, Suicide or Struggle." *The Massachusetts Review* 22 (Autumn, 1981): 539-550.

Shange, Ntozake. "From Memory to the Imagination." In *The Writing Life: Writers on How They Think and Work,* edited by Marie Arana. New York: PublicAffairs, 2003.

Squier, Susan Merrill, ed. *Women Writers and the City: Essays in Feminist Literary Criticism.* Knoxville: University of Tennessee Press, 1984.

Timpane, John. "'The Poetry of a Moment': Politics and the Open Form in the Drama of Ntozake Shange." *Studies in American Drama, 1945-Present* 4 (1989): 91-101.

SAM SHEPARD

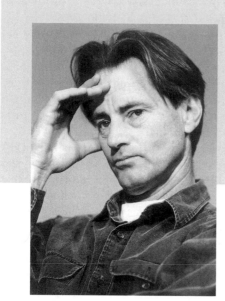

Martha Holmes

Born: Fort Sheridan, Illinois
November 5, 1943

Shepard's is one of the most individualistic voices on the American stage, and his work is considered the most enduring post-modern dramatic literature of the 1970's and 1980's.

BIOGRAPHY

Born Samuel Shepard Rogers on an Army base in 1943, growing up mainly on a California ranch, arriving in New York City in the 1960's, living for three years in London, gifted in timpani, devoted to sports, and an outdoorsman of the working kind, Sam Shepard is almost a living example of the kind of characters he puts on the stage. After high school graduation (in Duarte, California, in 1960), Shepard experimented with several lifestyles and occupations, including ranch hand, sheep shearer, and rock-and-roll musician. The early successes of one-act plays such as *Cowboys* (1964) and *The Rock Garden* (1964, and 1969, as part of Kenneth Tynan's Broadway revue *Oh! Calcutta!*), especially in the Off-Off-Broadway theaters of New York in the 1960's, gave him the incentive to continue in drama (other genres, as well as music and art, drew him and still invest his plays with variety and a unique creative signature).

Shepard moved to New York at nineteen and changed his name to Sam Shepard. Waiting tables at Village Gate allowed him to pursue his interests in theater, which he did by writing several one-act plays which were produced Off-Off Broadway at such venues as La Mama, the Open Theatre, and the American Place Theatre and with such works as the now familiar *Cowboys*. By the time of the 1965-1966 theater season, the up-and-coming playwright

with the mixed reviews had won Obie Awards (granted by *The Village Voice*) for *Chicago* (1965), *Icarus's Mother* (1965), and *Red Cross* (1966).

An avant-garde comedy, *La Turista*, was produced in 1967 in New York and in 1969 in London. His first full-length success, *Operation Sidewinder* (1969), was performed as part of the inaugural season of the new producer/directors of Lincoln Center, Jules Irving and Herbert Blau. The play, combining American Indian folklore with high-technology weaponry, drew strong critical response in both directions, but it clearly marked Shepard's debut as an important new writer of the American cultural present.

In 1971, with much acclaim came *The Mad Dog Blues*. With its success, Shepard took wing to England, where he lived for the next three years, writing numerous international hits, such as *The Tooth of Crime* (1972) and *Geography of a Horse Dreamer* 1974). By the late 1970's, Shepard would have a substantial bibliography, one that included *Buried Child* (1978), which won the Pulitzer Prize. By the mid- to late 1980's, he would pen such notable plays as the disturbing and yet undeniably stunning and provocative *True West* (1980) and the equally explorative and evocative *A Lie of the Mind* (1985), which won the prestigious New York Drama Critics Circle Award. In 1986, Shepard was elected into the American Academy of Arts and Letters.

His long canon of plays from that time is attributable in part to his prolific imagination and in part to his indifference about editing or polishing his work, preferring to get it produced and letting it stand or fall in its original form. He once remarked, "I like to start with as little information about where I'm going as possible." Some critics have found fault with this tendency on his part, noting that his plays lack the cohesion and sense of closure usually found in successful stage work.

Shepard's artistic skills are not limited to writing for the stage, however. His gifted presence is his essence behind the scenes of the film industry as scriptwriter and in the scenes of numerous films as an actor playing his and others' characters as well. His screenplays are distinctly Shepard: visual, asymmetrical, and obtuse, full of creative bravado, not entirely interested in telling the story in a coherent way. He cowrote *Zabriskie Point* (1969) with Michelangelo Antonioni and traveled with Bob Dylan and the Rolling Thunder Review in 1975 to write, at Dylan's request, the screenplay for a film that would become *Renaldo and Clara* (1978). He has also received accolades as an actor in such films as *The Right Stuff* (1983); his 1985 adaptation of his play *Fool for Love* (1983), with Kim Basinger; *Steel Magnolias* (1989) as Dolly Parton's husband; *All the Pretty Horses* (2000); and dozens more. He has directed and written the films *Far North* (1988), starring Shepard's paramour Jessica Lange, and *Silent Tongue* (1994).

Shepard's personal relationships have been subject for discussion, tied as they were to his work and creativity. In 1969, he married O-Lan Johnson. Their union saw a son born six months later. In 1970, Shepard, twenty-six years old and dreaming of being a musician (despite, by this time, having twenty plays to his credit), was playing drums with a cult band from Vermont, the Holy Modal Rounders, at the Village Gate. There he met Patti Smith, legendary rocker and soon to be poet, who fell in love with Shepard. As biographer Patricia Morrisroe reports in *Mapplethorpe: A Biography* (1995), the two were exceptionally close (despite Smith commenting that she and O-Lan were still good friends). Shepard and Smith, writes Morrisroe, "regarded themselves as partners in crime, and often when they went to Max's [Kansas City] they would drink too much and start fights. 'Everything you heard about us in those days is true,' Smith admitted. 'We'd have a lot of rum and get into trouble. We were hell-raisers.'"

More than renegade partiers, Smith and Shepard were cowriters. He encouraged her to continue writing the poetry that she so wanted to and asked for her contributions to his play *The Mad Dog Blues*, for which Smith wrote the lyrics. They cowrote a rock opera, *Cowboy Mouth* (1971), and Shepard would dedicate *Hawk Moon* (1973) to his counterpart of the "emotionally packed" early 1970's. Yet because they were such emotionally packed times—inundated with drugs and drink and spotlighted acts and actions, as he would later tell his biographer, Don Shewey—Shepard extracted himself from the relationship, the scene, and New York, moving to London in 1971.

A little over a decade later, on the set of the 1982 motion picture *Francis*, Shepard met film star Lange. In 1983, he divorced O-Lan and began what would be a long-term relationship with Lange, with whom he has acted in films such as *Country* (1984) and *Don't Come Knocking* (2005), which he also wrote; whom he has directed; and with whom he has lived in New Mexico, Minnesota, Montana, Virginia, and New York. Together, they have two children.

Shepard continued to write for the stage despite his financial and artistic success as a screenwriter and actor. His *A Lie of the Mind*, another anguished examination of the disfigured family, brought to the stage once again the conflict among passion, family, and a strangely American sense of lost dignity. Most of his plays since 1976 have debuted at the Magic Theatre, in San Francisco, where he was playwright-in-residence in the 1970's. *The Late Henry Moss*, featuring Sean Penn and Nick Nolte, debuted at the Magic Theatre on November 7, 2000, the same year that Shepard was nominated for Broadway's Tony Award for *True West* (four years after he received a Tony nomination for *Buried Child*). In 1985, his screenplay for *Paris, Texas* won a Palme d'Or, the prestigious Cannes Film Festival prize.

ANALYSIS

Shepard has something of the American cowboy in him—the dreamer, the drifter, the outdoorsman, the individualist, the misfit. These traits are coupled with a deft linguistic touch, a visual imagination based on observation, and a sophisticated view of the value of myth in articulating the modern human condition. His works tend to be enigmatic; they seem almost right but somehow off the mark, as though too much reality would get in the way of Shepard's describing the chaos of actual day-to-day existence. Shepard is obsessed with a "loss" of some kind, often identified by critics as the failure of the American spirit, of "America in flames," or as the dilemma of the rugged individual consumed by high technology in a world too complex for individual achievement and success.

Shepard's heroes are, if not sociopaths, at least angry and isolated loners, always bordering on the violent; when this violence is turned against women, the plays get frighteningly sadistic. There is an edge of Old Testament righteousness gone sour, as though too strict an upbringing has evoked a rebel response—but with an underlying need for rules just under the dialogue.

The structure of the plays is imperfect. Superficially realistic in the later works, but stylized and theatrical in the earlier works, the plays move quickly into what has been called suprarealism, an enlarged version of realistic, detailed life that somehow transcends itself to speak, however vaguely, of larger orders and disorders in the playwright's universe. Robert Cohen, in his discussion of *Buried Child*, defines suprarealism as "a device that seeks patterns beneath the surface of everyday reality, and meanings in the silences that punctuate everyday speech." Far from being a symbolic writer or an allegorist, Shepard manages to speak of reality while at the same time tapping into universal combats with his specified opponents. For example, Hoss and Crow in *The Tooth of Crime*, besides fighting their own duel to the death, are fighting the eternal battle of the successful figure struggling to keep his reputation versus the newcomer, full of energy and undaunted by the reputation of the current champion. In this work, as in *Geography of a Horse Dreamer* (1974), the artist himself is the subject of the action.

The same Jack London or James Dean attitude that can make the male American seem romantic and inaccessible at the same time is present in Shepard's work. There is also a taint of incest, a hint of forbidden love, in the character studies as the plots unravel, never spoken directly but implied by the narrative voice (as in *Fool for Love*) or hinted at in the dialogue (as in *Buried Child*). If the work is autobiographical in any way, it is in Shepard's obsession with interfamily affections and emotions, both tender and violent.

While it would be too facile to say that Shepard is searching for his father, the characters in his work are all struggling with a father who fell under the demands of American individuality. The obsessive, often violent, attraction of male to female protagonists cannot be ignored when examining his work, but it would be a mistake to simplistically identify those themes with the playwright's own biography. The attraction takes on its violent stage form as a signal to the depth and importance of essential relationships such as male/female love or family ties. No social philosopher, Shepard stays well inside the personal worlds of his own experience, neither casting about for historically viable motifs nor seeking commercial success. His ideas and images are distinctly his own.

Shepard's plays are probably parts of a whole imaginative construction, as were the works of Eugene O'Neill, with whom Shepard is often compared, and whose family served as grist for his mill as well. The whole epic, whose parts will emerge as Shepard continues his work, develops the chaotic impulses that work within him. His single subject is an examination of what went wrong, somewhere, somehow, in his life as well as in the American Dream. His concentration on family distortions allows ready comparisons with other American playwrights, such as Arthur Miller and Clifford Odets, who also found their themes inside family life.

Shepard's major themes are the loss of the American Dream, the romance of the West, the artist's exploitation by commerce, the "musical" significance of contemporary dramatic rhythms, the breakdown of the family unit because of unspoken parental imperfections, and the ongoing search for place and identity in a fragmented world. In the final analysis, however, themes are not as important as lyrics for Shepard. Ruby Cohn names her chapter on Shepard "The Word is My Shepard," and Bonnie Marranca speaks at length of Shepard's poetic voice. In a sense, all his plays are songs, written to a rhythm and beat that is entirely his own. They make sense only in near-rhymes, and the parallels to myth are imperfect, sketched in, barely recognizable. Neither a thinking playwright nor an intellectual analyst, but an instinctive observer of human beings, Shepard is writing song lyrics for the stage, caring not so much about the content as the amorphous, yet distinctive, form and rhythm of human relationships.

LA TURISTA

First produced: 1967 (first published, 1968)
Type of work: Play

In mirrored acts, a pair of tourists fights the hallucinating effects of disease, assisted by a voodoo doctor and his son.

Shepard wrote his first two-act play while living in Mexico; the mirroring acts give him a structure for his ideas that would work in several subsequent plays, including *The Tooth of Crime, Geography of a Horse Dreamer,* and *Operation Sidewinder.* Shepard takes advantage of the automatic tendency on the part of the audience to compare and contrast the events of each act, thereby informing both parts in the examination.

Kent and Salem are traveling in Mexico (in act 1) when Kent becomes very sick with *la turista,* the Mexican slang name for diarrhea. In a crazed, fevered state, Kent is "treated" by a native doctor and his son. Salem interrupts the dialogue with long monologues of the past, a device that Shepard had employed in earlier, short plays. Salem's speeches add color and shadow to the bare plot. In act 2, which takes place earlier in time than act 1, Kent suffers from sleeping sickness (judging from the symptoms). Again, a doctor and his son are called in to help; Kent becomes violent in his hallucinations, eventually crashing through the wall of his room.

"La Turista" is both the tourist and his disease—a displacement of the artist, with concomitant suffering. Two figures, echoed in each act, on one level the doctor and his son, are on another level the appeal to the hero of a cosmic cure to a universal sickness. The two invade the privacy of the tourist with a curative, but at the expense of forcing Kent and Salem into the mythic structure of the alien place, transforming "tourist" mentalities (removed and temporary) into serious participating members of an old cult. The acts are reversed in time, the second act coming before the trip to Mexico of the first act.

The first act's disease is replaced in the second act by a kind of sleeping sickness, to counteract which Kent is walked up and down until he can find the strength to leave the theater entirely. His rambling, inchoate monologue, underscored by "Doc," tells the story of Doc himself, in the present tense, seeking "the beast" in a Western setting. In the second act, the "cult" participation involves the storytelling and the crying out of the fevered victim, a freeing of the soul from the body. The disease invading Kent is insidious, destructive from the inside, and one of its symptoms is delirium, here vocalized in ranting speeches whose content seems arbitrary, almost a jazz improvisation around a theme. As the monologue climaxes in pain and absurd sacrifice, Kent swings from a rope, crashing through the upstage wall, leaving his silhouette in the drywall, like a cartoon character in an absurdist universe.

Critics point out several important features of this play: the mirrored acts, each of which contains a reflection of the other; the Western pioneer motif, especially of Kent's final speeches; the enigmatic characters of the Mexicans; and the cold, almost brutal love relationship. Easy connections with cigarette brands, Kent and Salem, can be made, as an indictment of American myth, for example, but in this early work, any speculation as to real meaning takes more effort from the critic than the playwright put into the play's subcontext.

THE TOOTH OF CRIME

First produced: 1972 (first published, 1974)
Type of work: Play

Two rock-and-roll hoodlums duel with words and bravado for the commercial turf of musical stardom.

The Tooth of Crime is a large idea, a play imbued with the energy and chaos of jazz and rock, a 1960's look at the future alterations in the nature of the duel, and the challenge of sexual and power-oriented dominance as found in competitiveness. This play attempts to combine street-gang dueling traditions with the commercial competition of the rock-and-roll industry: Hoss ("Rip Torn only younger") opens the first act with a "flyting," or bragging of his superiority; Crow ("just like Keith Richard") opens the second act as the young upstart ready to duel the famous but aging Hoss.

The result, despite its shouting violence and rapacious arena, is a strangely touching portrait of the aging artist, torn between continuing popularity and an admission of his own mortality. The cycle of leadership and popular appeal drives the plot forward, from Hoss's early claims to superiority, through his moments of doubt (in which he is encouraged by his "moll" Becky and his gang of singing hoods), to the second-act duel, a stand-off. The finale, an imperfect and inconclusive scene in which Hoss kills himself, ostensibly to take Crow's victory from him by choosing to "lose to the big power," implies that the cycle will continue, with Crow eventually finding the same hollowness, only temporarily concealed by the "image" of his commercial and popular success.

Shepard adds songs to this piece, the lyrics in the country and western style, the music in the rock-and-roll idiom. Hoss's gang (called Four Guys when singing together) acts as commentary to the action, underscoring the violence and combativeness of the scenes. Taken alone, the combined western/rock musical numbers do not make much sense, but as background to the almost dancelike violence of the players, they serve as a kind of film score to the nonverbal combat: "We're fighting ourselves. . . . He's my brother and I gotta kill him."

The central act, a rock duel between Crow and Hoss, substitutes for physical violence a competition using language instead of weapons; the metaphor makes this play more a musical combat than a story with a through line. The dialogue, often a forced slang, part authentic and part fabricated, moves the play forward slowly. This is a futuristic world, where violence is delimited by power combats on "turf," and each player tries to get "kills" as a way of keeping score. In the process, the "duel" takes on thematic substance—the role of jazz in the emancipation of the slaves is one particularly artificial and awkward example of the intrusion of styles into the dramatic action.

Hoss's moll, Becky Sue, handles his weapons and serves as messenger to the other sinister participants in the game. In one scene she acts out roles both of sexual victim and sexual assailant, stripping herself with her own hands while protesting to an invisible assaulter, assumed to be Hoss. Difficult to cast and stage, *The Tooth of Crime* does not receive the same number of productions as other, more realistic, Shepard works. Nevertheless, it deserves

consideration as a rock-and-roll musical drama, along with such musicals as *Hair* (1968) and *Tommy* (1975).

GEOGRAPHY OF A HORSE DREAMER

First produced: 1974 (first published, 1974)
Type of work: Play

A prophetic dreamer of horse race results, kidnapped by hoodlums, changes his predictions to dog races and is rescued by his brothers.

In this portrait of the artist exploited by big business (a recurrent theme with Shepard, who nevertheless found a commercial outlet for his talents quite early in his career), the artist is a dreamer, and his dreams are his art. The hero, Cody, has been kidnapped by thugs, who cull race winners from his dreams, moving him from place to place. As in all Shepard's two-act plays, the two acts bear likenesses to each other that underscore their differences. In act 1, it is horse racing that Cody dreams about, but in act 2, he has switched to dog racing. Once the thugs understand the switch, they continue to let the dreamer do his work. Cody's brothers rescue him from the Doctor (a sinister figure representing cold-blooded murder) in a violent ending, which unfortunately seems almost tacked onto the mood of the rest of the piece.

A displacement from one's locale, another standard Shepard theme, is what makes the dreams so vivid and so destructive. When Cody is removed from his (Western) homeland, he suffers. Shepard is saying that the artist has been displaced from his "geography," in this case the American West, where much of Shepard's own youth was spent. From the play's opening, Cody has been dreaming of the past rather than the present (the opening act is called "The Slump"). The thugs will be in trouble with their boss, Fingers, if Cody ("Mr. Artistic here") does not come up with some winners soon. The whole operation has fallen on hard times since Cody's failures; they have gone from fancy hotels to this cheap motel, where even the wallpaper goes against the grain of dreaming.

The hero-artist, handcuffed to a bed, is a commodity in one of its sinister forms; when the dreams turn from horses to dogs, the artist is exploited even more. The disorientation caused by the boarded-up windows and the blindfolded travel have caused him to lose his sense of place. The fact that his brothers save him, rescuing him in the only really violent scene in the play, is important. The goons of society, milking and draining the artist, will eventually be overcome by the irresistible force of brotherly comradeship.

As in Shepard's other two-act plays, the mirror images of the two acts help the reader to understand each of the images themselves. Cody needs a sense of geography to keep his dreams intact; when he dreams of dog races, the implication is that he has been moved, possibly to Florida. (Shepard worked on this piece while in London; he raised and bred racing dogs during this period.)

If there is significance to the pair of hoodlums watching Cody, it lies in the contrast between them; there is the hard-shell Santee, against whom the more sympathetic Beaujo offers relief. They are there for exposition more than for plot, because neither character serves as more than an instrument; there are no significant changes in their personalities. The drama is not about them. Fingers, a sinister offstage figure until the end of the play, is the real antagonist, and Cody remains in his power until freed by his brothers. The Doctor, a symbol of death as much as an integral part of the crooked gang, has the real power, however, as shown by the deference paid to him by Fingers. Until the entrance of Fingers and the Doctor, the reader is led to believe that Fingers is the main force, but in fact it is the Doctor who figures as the main evil.

As ingenious as the basic plot idea is, the possibilities of the situation do not seem to be fully exploited; the piece remains stationary until the climax. It is essentially the staging of a large metaphor: The artist, who dreams of possibilities, is held captive by money interests, displaced and disoriented, until rescued by a return to his roots.

BURIED CHILD

First produced: 1978 (first published, 1979)
Type of work: Play

The return of grandson Vince to the family homestead churns up a past that has been buried for years in the cornfield.

A family drama, a strange parody of the warm families of many previous American plays, the three-act *Buried Child* is perhaps the best known of Shepard's work. From the striking images of the old man on the couch to the moment when his son carries in the buried child from the cornfield, the play embodies all that is best about Shepard's combining of realistic family drama with larger mythic patterns. Either as American gothic or as a modern-day version of Greek tragedy, the play invites examination on many levels.

The opening of the play sets the tone of the entire piece; Dodge is lying asleep or drunk on the couch, "a sedentary cougher solaced only by television and whiskey," as Ruby Cohn describes him. He holds the center of the stage while his family—wife Halie, an aging flirt in league with the local clergyman; half-wit son Tilden, silently returning again and again to the family secret; and vicious son Bradley, crippled but powerful, full of sexually destructive energy—lives a half life in the shattered family home.

When a young grandson, Vince, brings home his girlfriend to meet the family, the worst in them is called out, and one can see the decay of the American family in general, caused in part by the wanderlust of the previous generation (brought about by war) and in part by the avoidance of unhappy truths—family secrets hidden away in the cornfield.

Vince, traveling adventurously through the United States with his girlfriend, drops in on the family for some reminiscences; his father, Tilden, does not recognize him, nor do his grandparents. The prevailing sense of the awkward, unwelcome meeting is that the youth of the house—its promise, its reputation, its future—has been "buried" along with a real corpse, the buried child, the secret in the corn. Although far from explicit, the plot seems to suggest that the buried child is the result of an incestuous union of the mother and one of the sons.

As in all Shepard's "family cycle" plays, which also include *True West* (1980) and *Curse of the Starving Class* (1976), the ostensible battle of the family is enlarged by the oddly symbolic details. The most important of these is the buried child of the title (reminiscent of the absent child in Edward Albee's 1962 play, *Who's Afraid of Virginia Woolf?*), dug up from the corn rows and tragically reintroduced. The child is the buried secret of the family that must be dealt with in order for the family finally to find rest in the present.

The details of the play—such as Tilden pouring corn husks over Dodge, with the corn husks sticking in his hair and hat; Bradley, the older brother, his artificial leg a prop dominating the action as Bradley dominates Vince's girlfriend, forcing his finger into her mouth; the suggestion that Halie has spent the night with the minister (she comes home in a different dress from the one she wore when she left)—add up to a very dark family portrait indeed. The mother, cheating on the old man, is a shadow of the lust that once dominated the family. Tilden's simple madness, contrasted with his former football glory, transforms his character from the pathetic mold of Lenny in John Steinbeck's *Of Mice and Men* (1937) into a brooding, giantlike Tiresias (the seer in Sophocles' *Oedipus Tyrannus* from the fifth century B.C.E.). Bradley's artificial leg may remind one of the lame king in the Arthurian legends and the quest for the Holy Grail. Finally, the last image of the play leaves the entire story only partly told, perhaps hinting that Shepard will return to this destructive family in subsequent work.

This is not the chronicle of a real family, despite the play's realistic trappings, but of the struggle of every family to reconcile itself to the imperfections, the "humanness" of the parents, whose offspring, losing their youth day by day, have romanticized them beyond recognition. The play is not so much about revealing secrets as it is about forgiving or understanding the parents as people. However, Shepard allows no reconciliation or forgiveness to enter into the play's climactic scene.

The tone of *Buried Child* marks a turning point for Shepard. While still far from a realistic play, it depicts an actual family dwelling, with recognizable characters acting in a "real" world. It is a family gone wrong somewhere in its past. Critics have offered various explanations for the central symbol, the buried child—the secret that has disintegrated the family. Is the child a real one, possibly the product of an incestuous union? How did it die? Who was responsible for the burial itself; was it agreed upon by the family, or was it the act of an individual? (Tilden carries the little body wrapped in rags onstage at the end of the play.) And how does the return of Vince precipitate the play's action?

These and other questions will remain, but critics agree that a deeply mythic, symbolic death is implied in the action. Whether Shepard meant to depict a real child or was returning to his theme of a lost American spirit is a matter of theatrical interpretation. As a stage event, *Buried Child* is a powerful experience, full of tensions and puzzles, gripping as it unfolds. Such acts as Tilden slowly showering the sleeping figure of his father with corn husks linger in the viewer's mind long after the play is over. When the play is done carelessly, the flaws in its exposition get in the way of the theatrical experience, which turns into an exasperating and unfulfilling evening. When performed effectively, it never leaves the imagination.

TRUE WEST

First produced: 1980 (first published, 1981)
Type of work: Play

Two brothers, rivals in a writing contest, debate their views of the lost American West and compete for their mother's affection.

Part of a family trilogy, *True West* differs from Shepard's other plays in its almost lighthearted bantering dialogue between the two protagonists. Austin, one brother of a pair, is conservative and formal, fitting into society with reasonable comfort. Lee, the other brother, is the cowboy misfit character of the type that Shepard uses in virtually every drama. They are both writing a film scenario about the true West, and their conversation, wildly funny in the beginning of the play, deepening as the action moves forward, is actually a debate about what (if anything) made America great. Shepard is, in a way, having a conversation with himself in this play, taking the two sides in the form of the two brothers.

The kitchen setting is appropriate, especially in the light of the late arrival of the mother, the actual adjudicator between the two brothers and the person whose affection they both seek. The two brothers are central to Shepard's mythology. The brief appearance of the mother at the end of the play demonstrates what the competition was really about. The kitchen is her domain, despite the fact that the two brothers have temporarily claimed it for their lives and their debate. Again, the family in disarray, the siblings at odds and representing diverging lifestyles, the homage to a lost American tradition represented by the cowboy's life—all the trademarks of Shepard—are here.

What sets this play apart from the others is the humor with which Shepard deals with the subject. The dialogue, relatively realistic and conversational here, plays the two brothers off each other both in content and in linguistic style. The proliferation of physical objects, in the manner of Eugene Ionesco, underlines the immovability and intractability of the "real" world as opposed to the world of the imagination that both brothers are seeking to portray in their screenplays.

The two brothers here bear virtually no resemblance to Tilden and Bradley from the earlier *Buried Child*. Their articulation, their energy, and their obvious partnership (despite their differences) is antithetical to the family of Dodge and Halie; here is found a masculine bonding within the combat, a family unit despite all the superficial antagonisms.

FOOL FOR LOVE

First produced: 1983 (first published, 1983)
Type of work: Play

Eddie and May, lovers and half siblings, fight out their jealousies while their otherworldly absent father drinks and comments on their past.

Shepard begins the stage directions of *Fool for Love* with an admonition that could be applied to his whole artistic life: "This play is to be performed relentlessly without a break." Stepping aside from the

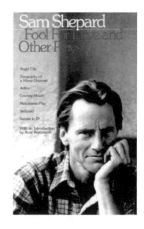

two-act form that worked in his previous few plays, but in no way retreating to the short sketches of his first Off-Off Broadway successes, *Fool for Love* is a long, single-minded battle. In dance terms, it is an "apache," or violent combat between lovers. Frank Rick refers to this play as "a western for our time," seeing Eddie and May as "gunslingers."

The scene is a seedy motel room "on the edge of the Mojave Desert," lit by neon from the window covered with Venetian blinds—a place of transition, flight, and homelessness. May, a beautiful woman in her late twenties, has fled here to escape her half brother, Eddie, whose pursuit has reduced itself to an obsessive search of the countryside for his lover and half sister.

This play is another of Shepard's combats between two related forces. The stylized and energetic choreography of the fights is distinctive, and it brings a kind of ritualistic dancelike universality to the piece. Eddie has tracked down his fleeing half sister, May, and tries, with words, memories, and physical force, to persuade her to come back home with him. Half brother and half sister, desperately and destructively in love, confront the impossibility of their situation in this seedy, transitory space, a metaphor for the inability of the two lovers to find a place for themselves in the world.

Again, the combat motif substitutes for a truly dramatic situation—the audience is not so much concerned with whether Eddie will win May as with whether May will survive the anger and vengeance of the jealous lover who has found her and will apparently do anything to force her to return with him. A mild-mannered suitor, Martin, acts as a foil for the powerful and destructive force of Eddie, a cowboy who ropes the bedposts during the whole show. At one point, Eddie stands against the wall, digging his heels into the woodwork, a kind of silhouette not unlike the final image in *La Turista*—man, flattened out, two-dimensional, a presence by the strength of his outline on the wall.

The extreme down-left stage is occupied by a rocking chair and an old man in gray and subdued tones; he is the father of both Eddie and May, telling his story in disjointed monologue, drinking and dreaming, neither in the world of the motel nor entirely out of it. On several occasions he shares the bottle of liquor with Eddie and May, either by placing it on the "real" table in the motel room or by pouring a drink into Eddie's cup.

The old man is the closest that Shepard gets to identifying and articulating the father figure that dominates his work. In the father's monologues, a sort of dream remembrance, one hears the father's side of the story, culminating in the realization that the father was a bigamist whose children are now in love with each other in a destructive way. Eddie was the son of one family that he maintained in one town; May was the daughter of another family. The moment of their meeting, which Eddie remembers vividly, was the moment their love was born.

The set, in one sense a simple, scaled-down motel room and in another sense a surreal fighting pit with amplified walls, puts the play into the supra-real category. As an ever-present counterbalance to the hyperrealism of the main scene, the old man is visible in a black, undefined space, suspended in time, talking as though from the shadows. He is neither in Eddie's head nor in May's head but is a presence representing the past.

The story proceeds by impassioned argument between Eddie and May, Eddie roping the bedposts in a vaguely sinister, threatening gesture, May preparing for her "date," moving in and out of the bathroom during the course of the argument. The only relief in the story is the introduction of Martin, a mild-mannered local suitor to May, representing not so much a real threat to the Eddie-May relationship as an example of the kind of safe, even timid, life May would face without the energy of Eddie's love. At his entrance, however, Martin tackles and overpowers Eddie, a temporary physical advantage quickly countered by the psychological advantage that Eddie has: He knows what his relationship is to May and his power over her.

Another complication, this time an offstage presence, is apparently a rich woman who follows Eddie from place to place; she arouses a jealousy that shows May to be equally obsessed by this destructive relationship, and she forms a menacing presence outside the temporally safe motel room. An offstage figure, signaled onstage by flashing and whirling headlights shining through the blinds

of the window, she actually shoots out Eddie's windshield in a moment of dangerous intrusion.

Far more than an incestuous love story, *Fool for Love* can be seen as a psychological examination of the duality in the human psyche. It is about the obsession of one part of a person trying to find the other part. The themes of search and pursuit of the separated ideal, and the combat between those halves, will be told again in the screenplay *Paris, Texas* and in Shepard's *A Lie of the Mind*, in which the female figure suffers such a severe beating that she requires hospitalization. Thus, Shepard takes to its extreme the question of whether the male/female split in every human being is a permanent and self-destructive schism or is a temporary separation to be eventually reconciled.

THE LATE HENRY MOSS

First produced: 2000 (first published, 2002)
Type of work: Play

Brothers Earl and Ray re-create the events of a fishing trip—events that precipitated their estranged father's death.

The Late Henry Moss is, as are numerous other Shepard works, ripe for Freudian brain-picking: The deistic father has spun his dysfunctional American family web and then disappeared, leaving the fractured unit members to replay the past with longing, with resentment, and with climactic and uncontrollable violent episodes. The post-traumatic stress is as acute for the offspring as it is for the survivors of battle. As Earl Moss tells the audience, he remembers the past and family life "like a war."

The brothers Moss relive the battle, however, in more than panoramic flashbacks: Where in *True West* the sibling rivalry and ultimate role reversal are depicted with an overkill of toast and beer contrasted against the homey desert dwelling and the vociferous crickets and wolves, *The Late Henry Moss* is represented by the warm and musty womb of the Mexican hovel as it is intruded upon by the living specters of their father's past few hours (the taxi driver who drove him to the piers, the father's Indian prostitute/girlfriend, the menudo-wielding friend), by the ever-constant flow of bourbon, and by foreshadowing and flashback-instigating family photographs.

While the character motivation shares a subliminal aim—brothers playing out parts as badly imprinted by a father who has abandoned them and who is dead (and whose death has brought the two disparate siblings back together after seven years)—that motivation is exacerbated by the exponents of a death which is the focus of the play. With the appearance of Henry Moss, the play departs from *True West* but piggybacks *Fool for Love*, in the style of *Hamlet*.

The Shepard signature language and landscape of *The Late Henry Moss* are consistent with the playwright's spectacular and yet understated American emotional iconography, blended with the dysfunction of a finally broken home: In the opening act, for example, the dialogue reveals the violence and chaos that was childhood for Earl and Ray, who refer to Mother as only "she" and Father as "he," in that detached and distancing way that broken adult children might. The conventions that Shepard produces so masterfully are the absurdist comedy-lovers' dreams come true: The comic relief at least temporarily takes the pressure off the cooking pot of volatility and the contradictions and suspicions (Ray suspecting that his older brother has more information on Henry's death than he

will give up, for instance) that keep audience members grinding their teeth for the rest of the play. All devices, as ever, are aligned perfectly for the psychoanalyst in Western residence: The obvious but slowly developed onstage hatred for the father, for each other, and seemingly for anyone involved is arguably some of the most abrasive and compelling in American theater today. Shepard has his finger not only on the pulse of working class, underclass, and überclass psychoses but also on the jugular of the sons who live (and grow to repeat) the war that is family life with womanizing, booze, and abuse.

SUMMARY

Sam Shepard, as much a poet as a playwright, prevails as a major literary and theatrical voice because his themes speak to a sense of lost dignity in American culture and society. What the American West means to Shepard and his characters is so successfully expressed in the plays that he will always be seen as a critic of the present day, despite his own natural abilities to survive in it. All of Shepard's plays are cries for another time, whether expressed in the ultramodern idiom of rock and roll or in the voices of lost American heroes misplaced on the concrete sidewalks of the big city.

Thomas J. Taylor; updated by Roxanne McDonald

BIBLIOGRAPHY

By the Author

DRAMA:
Cowboys, pr. 1964 (one act)
The Rock Garden, pr. 1964, pb. 1972 (one act)
Up to Thursday, pr. 1964
Chicago, pr. 1965
Dog, pr. 1965
Icarus's Mother, pr. 1965, pb. 1967
4-H Club, pr. 1965, pb. 1971
Rocking Chair, pr. 1965
Fourteen Hundred Thousand, pr. 1966, pb. 1967
Melodrama Play, pr. 1966, pb. 1967
Red Cross, pr. 1966, pb. 1967
La Turista, pr. 1967, pb. 1968
Cowboys #2, pr. 1967, pb. 1971
Forensic and the Navigators, pr. 1967, pb. 1969
The Unseen Hand, pr., pb. 1969

Operation Sidewinder, pb. 1969, pr. 1970
Shaved Splits, pr. 1969, pb. 1971
The Holy Ghostly, pr. 1970, pb. 1971
Back Bog Beast Bait, pr., pb. 1971
Cowboy Mouth, pr., pb. 1971 (with Patti Smith)
The Mad Dog Blues, pr. 1971, pb. 1972
The Tooth of Crime, pr. 1972, pb. 1974
Nightwalk, pr., pb. 1972 (with Megan Terry and Jean-Claude van Itallie)
Action, pr. 1974
Geography of a Horse Dreamer, pr., pb. 1974
Little Ocean, pr. 1974
Killer's Head, pr. 1975, pb. 1976
The Sad Lament of Pecos Bill on the Eve of Killing His Wife, pr. 1975, pb. 1983
Angel City, pr., pb. 1976
Curse of the Starving Class, pb. 1976, pr. 1977
Suicide in B Flat, pr. 1976, pb. 1979
Buried Child, pr. 1978, pb. 1979
Seduced, pr. 1978, pb. 1979
Tongues, pr. 1978, pb. 1981
Savage/Love, pr. 1979, pb. 1981
True West, pr. 1980, pb. 1981
Fool for Love, pr., pb. 1983
A Lie of the Mind, pr. 1985, pb. 1986
States of Shock, pr. 1991, pb. 1992
Simpatico, pr. 1994, pb. 1995
Plays, pb. 1996-1997 (3 volumes)
When the World Was Green, pr. 1996, pb. 2002 (with Joseph Chaikin)
Eyes for Consuela, pr. 1998, pb. 2002
The Late Henry Moss, pr. 2000, pb. 2002
The God of Hell, pr. 2004, pb. 2005

SHORT FICTION:
Cruising Paradise, 1996
Great Dream of Heaven, 2002

SCREENPLAYS:
Me and My Brother, 1967 (with Robert Frank)
Zabriskie Point, 1969 (with Michelangelo Antonioni)
Ringaleevio, 1971
Renaldo and Clara, 1978 (with Bob Dylan)
Paris, Texas, 1984 (with L. M. Kit Carson)
Far North, 1988
Silent Tongue, 1994
Don't Come Knocking, 2005

NONFICTION:
Rolling Thunder Logbook, 1977

DISCUSSION TOPICS

- In *Fool for Love,* how does Sam Shepard treat the theme of the American Dream?
- What role does the old man play in *Fool for Love*?
- How is the emphasis on the men's dead father significant in *True West*?
- What is the significance of the title *True West,* and how is that significance perpetuated throughout the play? What props, auditory elements, names, and stories define the setting and attitude that are used to further the "true west" theme?
- Consider the technique of the slow and subtle role reversal of the brothers in *True West.* Where does it begin to take shape? Where are the shifts, and how does Shepard use characterization to reveal them?
- Consider the secondary theme of writing and the writing business. How does it play out as a significant message throughout *True West*?
- What roles do the coyotes and crickets play in *True West*?
- Critics have drawn parallels between Austin and Lee and animals that they represent. Which animals are each likened to in *True West*?
- In Shepard's works, much emphasis is placed on American iconography. What symbols of popular culture are present in *True West,* and what might each suggest in the context of the play?
- Also relevant to many if not most of Shepard's plays is the dysfunctional family unit. Considering a work such as *The Late Henry Moss,* then, would you say the work is universal? If so, how? If not, why not?
- How do the characters in *The Late Henry Moss* express or show love?

MISCELLANEOUS:
Hawk Moon: A Book of Short Stories, Poems, and Monologues, 1973
Motel Chronicles, 1982 (journals, poetry, and short fiction)
Joseph Chaikin and Sam Shepard: Letters and Texts, 1972-1984, 1989

About the Author

Auerbach, Doris. *Sam Shepard, Arthur Kopit, and the Off-Broadway Theater.* Boston: Twayne, 1982.

Bottoms, Steven J., and Don B. Wilmeth. *The Theatre of Sam Shepard: States of Crisis.* Cambridge, England: Cambridge University Press, 1998.

Cohen, Robert. *Theatre.* Palo Alto, Calif.: Mayfleld, 1981.

Cohn, Ruby. *New American Dramatists: 1960-1980.* New York: Grove Press, 1982.

Hart, Lynda. *Sam Shepard's Metaphorical Stages.* Westport, Conn.: Greenwood Press. 1987.

Marranca, Bonnie, ed. *American Dreams: The Imagination of Sam Shepard.* New York: Performing Arts Journal, 1981.

Marranca, Bonnie, and Gautam Dasgupta. *American Playwrights: A Critical Survey.* New York: Drama Book Specialists, 1981.

Mottram, Ron. *Inner Landscapes: The Theater of Sam Shepard.* Columbia: University of Missouri Press, 1984.

Oumano, Ellen. *The Life and Work of an American Dreamer.* New York: St. Martin's Press, 1986.

Patraka, Vivian M., and Mark Siegel. *Sam Shepard.* Boise, Idaho: Boise State University Press, 1985.

Rosen, Carol. *Sam Shepard: A Poetic Rodeo.* New York: Palgrave Macmillan, 2005.

Roudané, Matthew, ed. *The Cambridge Companion to Sam Shepard.* Cambridge, England: Cambridge University Press, 2002.

Shewey, Don. *Sam Shepard.* New York: Da Capo Press, 1997.

Wilcox, Leonard, ed. *Re-reading Shepard: Contemporary Critical Essays on the Plays of Sam Shepard.* New York: St. Martin's Press, 1993.

CAROL SHIELDS

© Neil Graham

Born: Oak Park, Illinois
June 2, 1935
Died: Victoria, British Columbia, Canada
July 16, 2003

In her plays, poems, literary criticism, short stories, and novels such as the Pulitzer Prize-winning novel The Stone Diaries *(1993), Shields negotiates the complexity of the personal within the context of a larger social history.*

BIOGRAPHY

Carol Ann Warner Shields was born on June 2, 1935, in Oak Park, Illinois, a middle-class community on the outskirts of Chicago. After graduating from a local high school, she attended Hanover College. While there, she participated in an exchange program with Exeter University in England where, when traveling to Scotland, she met her future husband, Canadian civil engineer Donald Hugh Shields. In 1957, Carol graduated from Hanover with a B.A. in English. Soon afterward, she married Donald, and the two moved to Canada. There, the couple lived in Vancouver, Toronto, and finally Ottawa. Two of their five children were born during this time: John and Anne. The Shields family moved to England in 1960 so that Donald could complete a doctorate at Manchester University. When the family returned to Canada, they settled in Toronto, where Shields took a magazine writing course at the University of Toronto. Her teacher sold Shields's first short story to the Canadian Broadcast Company (CBC); she won CBC's Young Writers Competition in 1965.

Meanwhile, Shields's family continued to grow: Daughters Catherine, Margaret, and Sara were born. Carol enrolled in an M.A. program at the University of Ottawa and earned her degree in 1975 after writing a thesis on a nineteenth century Canadian writer, which became the basis for her critical book *Susanna Moodie: Voice and Vision* (1976).

During her time at the University of Ottawa, Shields became a Canadian citizen, though she maintained a dual citizenship with the United States. In addition, Shields worked as an editorial assistant and editor for the journal *Canadian Slavonic Papers* (1973-1975) and spent a year in France (1975-1976). She began teaching part time at the University of Ottawa in 1976, eventually teaching both creative writing and English. She also taught at the University of British Columbia and the University of Manitoba. She was named chancellor of the University of Winnipeg in 1996. She and her husband retired to Victoria, British Columbia, in 2000.

Shields's literary career began with the publication of *Small Ceremonies* (1976), which won the Canadian Authors' Association Award for the best novel of the year. She began writing novels to depict the women that she rarely saw in fiction—clever, politically conscious women who loved their homes and families. Yet, for much of the 1970's and early 1980's, her work was not known outside Canada.

After the publication of *Swann: A Mystery* (1987), however, Shields's audience widened to include both British and American readers. Shields's most successful novel, *The Stone Diaries* (1993), was short-listed for Britain's Booker Prize and won both the Governor-General's Award and the Pulitzer Prize in fiction. *Larry's Party* (1997) also maintained Shields's status by winning the Orange Prize.

In 1998, Shields was diagnosed with stage 3 breast cancer. After her diagnosis, Shields continued to write, publishing a collection of short stories as well as an award-winning biography of writer Jane Austen in 2001. Her last novel, *Unless* (2002), was short-listed for the Booker Prize.

Shields died from complications of breast cancer on July 16, 2003. Her collected short stories were published posthumously in 2004.

ANALYSIS

Shields wrote poetry, plays, biography, literary criticism, short stories, and novels but is probably best known for her novels. In all her work, Shields shows mastery in her attention to the minutiae of the human condition; her depictions of the quirky moments in her characters' lives provide much of the humor in these works. However, her texts often examine the problems inherent in uncovering a life and the impossibilities of complete understanding between two persons, be they lovers, spouses, or family members. Shields counters these complex themes of identity and recognition by creating characters with a persevering, often comic look at the world they inhabit.

These themes can be found in her first novel, *Small Ceremonies*. Shields's narrator, Judith Gill, a biographer and frustrated novelist, must examine the complexity of the literary life by uncovering the life of another writer. The follow-up to this novel, *The Box Garden* (1977), stays in the same family. Told from the perspective of Judith Gill's younger sister Charleen Forrest, this novel looks at the benefits and frustrations of family life.

Shields's third and fourth novels also work in tandem. Published first as *Happenstance* (1980) and *A Fairly Conventional Woman* (1982) in Canada, the two novels were joined together into one text, *Happenstance*, in 1993. They recount the same time period in the lives of a married couple, Jack and Brenda Bowman. Brenda tells one version of the events; Jack tells another. Neither has the self-consciousness of knowing about the other's version. Thus, the texts comment on each other in illuminating ways, illustrating one of Shields's overarching themes: the innate misunderstandings between family members, regardless of the intimacy of the relationship.

Happenstance also more solidly articulates a recurring feminist theme in Shields's work. In the novel, Brenda, a quilter, must decide whether she wants to maintain her art for herself or for a larger audience; in effect, she must decide what she gives up as a result of the decision. This idea of women's choices being narrowed and inhibited by society will be found in other Shields's texts as well.

Though many critics argued that Shields's early work lacked innovation, her more experimental short fiction in collections such as *Various Miracles* (1985) gave her the opportunity to vary narrative structures and find alternate methods of conveying point of view. These experiments assisted her as she put together *Swann*, the novel which catapulted Shields into international prominence. *Swann* is told from the viewpoints of multiple persons who want to uncover and then restructure the life of a rural Canadian poet named Mary Swann. In an ironic look at the academic industry that forces scholars to publish or perish, the novel also suggests that a person can be reconstructed after he or she has been deconstructed. The postmodern novel also contains at its end a screenplay in which all of the characters enact a kind of Beckettian play about the text's own fictionality. *Swann* was the winner of the Arthur Ellis First Mystery Novel Award (1988) and was short-listed for the Governor-General's Award (1988).

Shields's plays and poetry also display many of her themes. For example, her poems, such as those found in *Coming to Canada* (1992), reveal her changing sense of identity as she moved to her new country. Her plays such as *Fashion, Power, Guilt, and the Charity of Families* (1995), cowritten with her daughter Catherine Shields, often echo her writerly interests in the intersecting roles of family members.

In *The Republic of Love* (1992), perhaps Shields's most comic novel, she problematizes the love affair between academic researcher Fay McLeod and the disk jockey Tom Avery. Like other artists and professional women in Shields's work, Fay must make professional and personal decisions that balance a successful career with a fulfilling personal life. Part of the joy of this text is how Fay and Tom's relationship works, despite their differing lifestyles.

The Stone Diaries, which won a series of awards including the Pulitzer Prize in fiction, chronicles Daisy Goodwill Flett's life in a mock diary arrangement of lists, letters, pictures, dialogue, recipes, and other minutiae of her life. The novel illustrates

Shields's abiding interest in the work of biography and autobiography, even as it explores how Daisy's life belonged to others rather than herself.

Larry's Party depicts the life of a man who must find his way in the ever-changing demographics of the late twentieth century. The novel suggests the importance of those small, often insignificant moments in Larry's growth. A topiary maze-builder by trade, Larry must learn to traverse the maze of his own life to discover who he is.

Fittingly, Shields paid homage to one of her influential foremothers in her Penguin biography *Jane Austen*. This critical piece offered up her perceptions on the author but also allowed Shields to enact her theories concerning the biographical form. In 2002, *Jane Austen* won the Charles Taylor Prize for literary nonfiction.

Shields's collection of stories *Dressing Up for the Carnival* (2000) shows her return to narrative experimentation. One of the stories from this collection, "A Scarf," introduces the character Reta Winters who becomes the first-person narrator of Shields's last novel, *Unless*. In *Unless*, the main character Reta unravels the mystery of her daughter Norah, who has dropped out of college to become a homeless person. One of Shields's darkest works by far, *Unless* continues Shields's focus on family relationships and the mysteries which bring families together and drive them apart.

THE STONE DIARIES

First published: 1993
Type of Work: Novel

In this novel filled with the fragments of Daisy Goodwill Flett's life, Shields suggests that no one's life can ever be fully understood

---

In her Pulitzer Prize-winning novel, *The Stone Diaries*, Shields depicts the life of her fictional heroine, Daisy Goodwill Flett, by gathering the bits and pieces of that life into a form that resembles an autobiography or personal diary. This arrangement allows her to comment on the nature of autobiography and the fragmented ways in which one person must piece together his or her own life. The text is divided into sections reflecting the major events of Daisy's life: "birth," "childhood," "love," "marriage," "motherhood," "work," "sorrow," "ease," "illness and decline," and "death." The neatness of these descriptors, however, is overshadowed by the slipperiness of memory and consequence. As the narrator says at the beginning of the novel:

> The recounting of a life is a cheat, of course; I admit the truth of this; even our own stories are obscenely distorted; it is a wonder really that we keep faith with the simple container of our existence.

Throughout the retelling of Daisy's life, the reader may wonder how Daisy knows the information that she recalls. Furthermore, narrative shifts occur periodically throughout the novel, sometimes altering the point of view to another character's perspective. Other times, Daisy is clearly speaking as the first-person narrator. Other disruptions include newspaper articles inserted in the text, as well as letters, dialogue, lists, and even photos. These disruptions put the onus on the reader to piece together Daisy's life, even as Daisy proposes to be the person telling her story. Though in diary format, the reader has more information about Daisy than she has about herself.

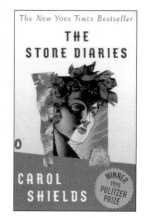

The novel opens with Daisy's unlikely retelling of her unusual birth. Her mother, Mercy Stone, an orphan whose last name becomes synonymous with the local industry—stonecutting—is immensely fat as well as naïve about the physiology of her own body. Thus, Mercy conceives and carries to term her daughter, Daisy, without anyone, including herself, knowing she was pregnant. As a result, Daisy is born to an unprepared mother who dies in childbirth. Her neighbor, Clarentine Flett, who has been feeling unloved by her husband, takes young Daisy with her to her son Barker's home in Winnipeg and the three create a family borne of necessity and mutual support.

Meanwhile, her father, Cuyler, mourns her mother's death, turns to religion, and builds a huge limestone memorial to her mother, a testament so grand that people make pilgrimages to see this monument to love. Eventually, other stonecutters hear of his expertise, and he receives a job offer at the Indiana Limestone Company in Bloomington, Indiana. At about the same time, Daisy's guardian, Clarentine, is killed in a freak bicycle accident, and Daisy goes with her father, whom she hardly knows, to Indiana. While there, Daisy marries an alcoholic member of a respectable family who dies in another freak accident during their honeymoon in England. Daisy spends nine years alone before she decides to visit Barker Flett, her onetime pseudo guardian, in Canada. The two marry, despite their more than twenty years age difference. These early chapters portray a woman who has things done to her life; she does not seem to be an active participant.

By the "motherhood" and "work" chapters, however, the narrative begins to twist around to give the reader others' perspectives on Daisy's life. For example, her children Alice, Warren, and Joan all present their narratives about their mother during their childhood. Her friends "Beans" Anthony and "Fraidy" Hoyt contribute their ideas about their friend's choices. These middle sections also contain pictures of the extended family, including portraits of Mercy Stone, as well as snapshots of Daisy's grandchildren. These bogus pictures coupled with the extended family tree at the beginning of the novel build the sensation of this being an authentic diary, even as the commentary within the text belies the possibility of the text revealing the authentic life.

This lack of vision becomes prominent during the "sorrow" chapter, when everyone close to Daisy tries to figure out her depression. Some give testimonials that deride each other with conscious self-referential nature. For example, Alice, Daisy's daughter, thinks her mother's sadness came from her lack of success at work, but Daisy's friend "Fraidy" mocks Alice's theory in favor of hers—that Daisy had a frustrated sex life. The theories eventually become farfetched, taking into account the random thoughts of those outside Daisy's immediate sphere.

The last section details Daisy's final hours and juxtaposes Daisy's poetic but often abstract thoughts about her own life with the mundane, mostly artificial self that she reveals to those visiting her as she dies. The novel slows down considerably, tak-

ing time to allow Daisy to try to articulate who she thinks she is, but more important, what she has missed. As she dies, she feels herself turning to stone, a symbol which pervades the novel from its beginning.

The Stone Diaries extends to include things found after her death—a recipe, a list of books, a copy of her memorial service, a list of things to do. This marginalia of Daisy's life serves as reminder of the inability of the diary to define Daisy's sense of self. The reader learns the most about Daisy after she dies.

LARRY'S PARTY

First published: 1997
Type of work: Novel

Larry Weller makes his way through the maze of his life toward self-revelation.

Following the success of her Pulitzer Prize-winning novel *The Stone Diaries*, Shields's *Larry's Party* uncovers the life of Larry Weller, an ordinary, slightly sensitive, topiary maze-builder. Winner of the Orange Prize for Fiction, *Larry's Party* follows its protagonist through a series of jobs, relationships, and travels as he attempts to uncover his potential as he learns about himself.

Larry's life is revealed through fifteen self-contained sketches detailing specific moments from or aspects of Larry's life. In some cases, the event does not seem particularly remarkable. For example, in the introductory vignette, Larry walks down a Winnipeg street when he realizes that he has picked up the wrong coat at his neighborhood coffeehouse. Aptly titled "Fifteen Minutes in the Life of Larry Weller, 1977," the sketch reveals that he works for a flower company, he lives at home, he is a bit indecisive, and he feels wrong wearing a jacket that does not reflect whom he thinks he is. He also realizes in a moment of clarity that he loves his girlfriend Dorrie as he walks to meet her.

These brief overviews of moments and their implications for the unveiling of a life and that life's journey are a part of this novel's charm. Shields has a unique strategy in *Larry's Party* of plopping the reader down at seemingly random moments in that life, then letting the narrative thread of the moment reveal the months or years since the previous chapter. For example, the second section of the book, "Larry's Love," begins with his getting a haircut. Only later does the reader find out that the haircut presages Larry and Dorrie's marriage. Even later, the reader learns that Dorrie is pregnant and their honeymoon is not as joyous as it first

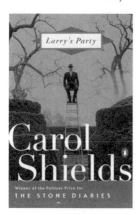

seems. Shields uses this leapfrog approach until the last section of the novel, which concludes with the party mentioned in the title.

Shields shows how the fragments and specific moments or single events are the things which, inevitably, destroy or uphold people. The simple events and small details of Larry's life such as the simple description of his clothes in "Larry's Threads" become the pieces of his life that give his character hope as he fumbles through two dissolved marriages, the deaths of his parents, a coma, and success in his maze-building career.

Larry's success as a maze-builder mirrors his relative success at life. Larry's life—his fickle movements and feeble misunderstandings but also his eventual self-discovery which allows him to move into satisfying work and, eventually, a satisfying relationship—disclose the misunderstandings, false starts, and difficulties of being a man in a world where the relationships between men and women take on a deepening complexity. Yet, like the maze-wanderer who is rewarded for his or her perseverance, Larry has his party at the end of the novel, a party which rewards him with continued hope in his resolve.

SUMMARY

Carol Shields's explorations of the struggles and frustrations of the ordinary man and woman reflect her notions about how personal history mirrors the larger history which surrounds it. Shields's attention to her characters' perseverance in spite of sometimes bleak situations makes them heroic in spite of their surface ordinariness. Furthermore, Shields's playfully postmodern use of narrative structure and point of view allows her to present these modern, middle-class characters in more innovative and fully realized manifestations.

Rebecca Hendrick Flannagan

BIBLIOGRAPHY

By the Author

LONG FICTION:
Small Ceremonies, 1976
The Box Garden, 1977
Happenstance, 1980
A Fairly Conventional Woman, 1982
Swann: A Mystery, 1987
A Celibate Season, 1991 (with Blanche Howard)
The Republic of Love, 1992
The Stone Diaries, 1993
Happenstance, 1993 (contains *Happenstance* and *A Fairly Conventional Woman*)
Larry's Party, 1997
Unless, 2002

SHORT FICTION:
Various Miracles, 1985
The Orange Fish, 1989
Dressing Up for the Carnival, 2000
Collected Stories, 2004 (pb. in U.S., 2005)

DRAMA:

Departures and Arrivals, pr., pb. 1990

Thirteen Hands, pr., pb. 1993

Fashion, Power, Guilt, and the Charity of Families, pr., pb. 1995 (with Catherine Shields)

Anniversary: A Comedy, pr., pb. 1998 (with Dave Williamson)

Thirteen Hands, and Other Plays, pb. 2002

POETRY:

Others, 1972

Intersect, 1974

Coming to Canada, 1992

NONFICTION:

Susanna Moodie: Voice and Vision, 1976

Jane Austen, 2001

EDITED TEXTS:

Dropped Threads: What We Aren't Told, 2001 (with Marjorie Anderson)

Dropped Threads Two: More of What We Aren't Told, 2003 (with Anderson and Catherine Shields)

About the Author

Besner, Neil K., ed. *Carol Shields: The Arts of a Writing Life*. Winnipeg: Prairie Fire Press, 2003.

Eden, Edward, ed. *Carol Shields, Narrative Hunger, and the Possibilities of Fiction*. Toronto: University of Toronto Press, 2003.

Hollenberg, Donna Krolik. "An Interview with Carol Shields." *Contemporary Literature* 39 (Fall, 1998): 339-355.

Werlock, Abby H. P. "Canadian Identity and Women's Voices: The Fiction of Sandra Birdsell and Carol Shields." In *Canadian Women Writing Fiction*, edited by Mickey Pearlman. Jackson: University Press of Mississippi, 1993.

DISCUSSION TOPICS

- In many of Carol Shields's works, the reader must become an investigator or biographer who tries to uncover the life of another person. How does Shields use artifacts such as lists, letters, and conversations as clues to learn more about Daisy Goodwill Flett in *The Stone Diaries*?

- Two of Shields's works, *The Stone Diaries* and *Larry's Party*, present the lives of Daisy Goodwill Flett and Larry Weller, respectively. In what ways does the gender of the two main characters alter the ways Shields structures and develops the themes of the novels?

- In *Unless*, Shields explores gaps in understanding, particularly within families. Discuss the trajectory of Reta Winters's quest to understand her daughter, Norah.

- Shields is a poet, biographer, novelist, short-story writer, literary critic, and dramatist, yet one could argue that elements of each of these genres appear in her longer works. Show how Shields's expertise in a number of forms manifests itself in longer works such as *Unless*.

- Many of Shields's characters find fulfillment by persevering. How does this perseverance contribute to the growth of Jack and Brenda Bowman's marriage in *Happenstance*?

LESLIE MARMON SILKO

Born: Albuquerque, New Mexico
March 5, 1948

Recognized initially as one of the leading female contributors to the renaissance in American Indian literature, Silko has established a place for herself in the accepted canon of contemporary American literature.

Courtesy, University Press of Mississippi

BIOGRAPHY

Leslie Marmon Silko was born with a diverse heritage derived from her mixed ancestry (Laguna Pueblo, Mexican, and white). Much of her work examines the culture of Native Americans as it conflicts and combines with those of Mexican Americans and Anglo-Americans in the Southwest. Her biography, mostly revealed through her stories, resonates with the pain of cultural collisions and racism. It also acknowledges, in a self-assured tone, the value of multiplicity, of perceiving things in more than one way as a method of surviving in the modern world.

Vital to Silko's upbringing was her great-grandmother, Marie Anaya. Married to Silko's paternal great-grandfather, Robert G. Marmon, a pioneer who moved from Ohio to settle in New Mexico, Marie was known to Silko as Grandma A'Mooh ("A'Mooh" is a Laguna expression of love). A'Mooh cared for Silko when she was a baby and lived into her eighties while Silko grew up. She told Silko many stories of earlier, difficult times, of the ancient traditions that had sustained the Laguna people.

Equally important are Silko's memories of her great-grandfather Stagner, his wife, Helen, and their daughter Lillie, who was Silko's grandmother. Helen, of the Romero family near Los Lunas, New Mexico, represents the Mexican influence on Silko's life and work, making Spanish as important to her as English and the Indian language of Laguna. Silko acknowledged the vital connections between generations of her family when she dedicated *Ceremony* (1977) to both her grandmothers, Jessie Goddard Leslie and Lillie Stagner Marmon, and her sons, Robert William Chapman and Cazimir Silko.

Perhaps the most significant contributor to Silko's early perceptions and later work was her father, Lee H. Marmon. A talented amateur photographer, he experienced racism as a young boy when he was denied entrance to an Albuquerque hotel while his light-skinned father was told he was welcome anytime (Hank Marmon, Silko's grandfather, refused to patronize the hotel for the rest of his life). Like the protagonist of *Ceremony*, Lee Marmon fought in World War II; his photographic records of the life to which he returned—the Laguna and Paguate villages, the Marmon Trading Post, his daughters, the deer hunts, the desert stretches of New Mexico and Arizona—contribute to the richly patterned texture of *Storyteller* (1981).

In addition to Silko's ethnic heritage, the landscapes of her life have profoundly influenced her writing. Most of her work incorporates the distinctive geography around Albuquerque, where she was born, and the Laguna Pueblo Reservation, where she grew up. In contrast to the mountains and mesas of her childhood, Silko, in some of her stories, beautifully describes the stark environment of Alaska, a landscape she became familiar with after spending 1974 as artist-in-residence at the Rosewater Foundation-on-Ketchikan Creek.

Silko has achieved much recognition for her work, publishing many stories and poems in numerous journals and widely read anthologies. She has garnered praise and support from other American Indian writers, notably N. Scott Momaday, whose novel *House Made of Dawn* (1968), followed by his tribal autobiography, *The Way to Rainy Mountain* (1969), helped to instigate what is now referred to as the Native American Renaissance in literature. Throughout *Storyteller,* Silko also acknowledges the influence of her Acoma Pueblo colleague Simon Ortiz, who included her story "Private Property" in his edited collection of Native American fiction, *Earth Power Coming* (1983). When the *Norton Anthology of American Literature* included Silko's short story "Lullaby," anthologized from *Storyteller,* she became the youngest woman ever to have a work published in that influential anthology.

A poet, short-story writer, novelist, and teacher (as a faculty member at the University of Arizona, Navajo Community College—now known as Dine College—and as artist-in-residence), Silko has received support from the National Endowment for the Arts (NEA) and was the recipient of a highly prestigious five-year MacArthur Foundation grant, from 1981 to 1986. Throughout the 1980's, however, Silko published little as she wrote and rewrote her long-awaited "Alaska novel," which has yet to see publication.

Instead, in 1991, she published *Almanac of the Dead,* a 768-page complex narrative with multiple narratives that culminate in a startling geopolitical development which apparently will occur just beyond the end of the novel, a violent overthrow of Euro-America by an indigenous, peripatetic army of *campisanos,* slowly walking north through the Americas. *Almanac of the Dead* includes long passages of Silko's compelling storytelling, but both scholarly and mainstream audiences have at times wondered whether to accept the text as, in part, a supernatural novel or a political diatribe. No ethnic or national group is spared from irony and critique as Silko describes various conspiracies—from exploitation by a mafioso of the ecosystem of southern Arizona to the grandiose and ultimately fatally, foolhardy plans of the Mexican warlord Menardo to Castro-sympathizing Mexican City College revolutionaries to drug-dealing and gun-running Americans using Tucson as a base of operations.

As *Almanac of the Dead* increasingly was categorized with such relatively inaccessible long novels

as Thomas Pynchon's *Gravity's Rainbow* (1974) and James Joyce's *Ulysses* (1922) and even *Finnegan's Wake* (1939), Silko was writing prose poems about the scarcity of water in the Southwest, which she compiled and privately published as *Sacred Water* (1993). The discursive "Author's Note" at the end of the collection describes her understanding of the relationship between the text and the visual images (photographs) that accompany each text. In the paired series of images and insights about water, Silko shows how not gold but water is the true treasure of the Southwest.

In *Gardens in the Dunes* (1999), Silko follows the developing story of Indigo, an adolescent Sand Lizard girl who gets separated from her Sister Salt and Grandmother Fleet. Indigo is temporarily adopted by Hattie, a disgraced scholar who has married Edward, an older scholar and botanist whose schemes to make a fortune in exotic plants miscarry horribly. Indigo is taken to Long Island and then does a version of the Grand Tour of Western Europe, a charming contemporary Native American version of what might have been a Henry James novel a century ago, with echoes especially of *The Portrait of a Lady* (1880-1881) and *The Ambassadors* (1903). In a karmic reversal of roles, Indigo ends up rescuing Hattie and helping her to reorient her perspective, even as the Ghost Dance is affecting Indian people and tribes of the Southwest. At the end of the novel, Grandma Fleet has died, but Indigo is inevitably reunited with her Sand Lizard people and especially with her sister. Hattie has learned that her spiritual salvation will likely not be near the Riverside Indian School or an orchid hothouse in South America; it will likely be nearer the Celtic baths and statuary of her own English background, and she is headed back in that direction as the novel concludes.

ANALYSIS

Silko is not a writer whose style is easily defined. Mixing the genres of fiction and poetry, and blurring the lines between reality and fantasy, Silko's works *Ceremony* and *Storyteller* portray a vision of rich complexity. Interested in cultural collision and the violence it sometimes engenders. Silko also explores the possibilities of cultural connectedness. Her primary artistic concern is to celebrate the power of storytelling and ceremony in human life. The forms of her poetry and fictions parallel, to a great extent, the oral traditions of her Indian ancestors.

Silko's work is also open to feminist interpretation. The opening story of *Ceremony* is about Ts'its'tsi'nako, or Thought-Woman, who has created the universe with her two sisters. Thought-Woman is the creator who names things; whatever she thinks about appears. Additionally, one of the characters who is most useful in bringing about the protagonist's healing is a mysterious woman who becomes his lover and warns him of evil he will encounter in his future. The strength of these mythic figures is echoed in many of the narratives related by human women that are part of *Storyteller*. In the title story, an Inuk girl not only lures her parents' killer to his death on an icy river (an occurrence that white lawyers want to define as an accident) but also takes over the tribal storytelling function of the old man who has raised her. This demonstration of her power gains her the respect of the villagers, who formerly scorned her.

The culture-bearing function of women is further apparent in the stories that Silko has heard from her own relatives. She received much of her practical and moral instruction through the tales told by her grandmother and aunts. Many of the heroines are women who accomplish exceptional tasks, often by accepting the possibility of the supernatural intervening in their lives.

In "Yellow Woman," and also in *Storyteller*, the heroine, an ordinary woman, is abducted by Silva, apparently an outlaw rancher but possibly a Pueblo deity in disguise. Uncertain, but willing to believe that she is living out the stories told to her in childhood by her grandfather, she becomes the beloved Yellow Woman and temporarily escapes her dull life as a housewife to lead a sensuous existence in the mountains. The important ability of women both to create and to accept the truth of storytelling is emphasized repeatedly in Silko's work, suggesting the valuable contributions Native American women make to the continuation of their cultures.

Silko's concerns are also modern and political. She examines racism and the violence it engenders and reveals the devastating consequences of war, both for the individuals who participate in it and for the earth itself. Her love and respect for the earth are evident in her many lyrical descriptions of the New Mexico landscape. Part of modern humans' plight, she suggests, is alienation from the earth that sustains them.

Racism is developed as the counterpart to the selfish misuse of the natural world; it is the force that alienates people from one another. Silko's primary concern is the racism that has allowed the systematic oppression of Native Americans by descendants of white Europeans, but in *Ceremony*, especially, she examines the way that racist attitudes can foster and prolong violence against any group or individual defined as different by the majority. Only by recognizing the essential connectedness of human beings and by choosing to refrain from violence can humans break the brutal cycles of hatred. Silko acknowledges that such recognition is not easy—it requires ceremonial, ritualistic healing, as if all suffer from a psychological illness.

That such healing is possible, however, suggests Silko's fundamentally positive view of human nature and its recuperative powers. In *Ceremony*, enough knowledge of the ancient ways remains to perform the necessary life-giving ceremonies. More ancient knowledge can be recovered and sustained through storytelling. Silko is trying to capture, in writing, the power and rhythms of oral tradition, a task that fulfills at least two functions. First, it makes accessible to people outside Indian culture the rich myths and beliefs that were fostered by the North American landscape. Second, it preserves those myths for future generations at a time when the integrity of Native American culture is threatened by assimilation into mainstream American society.

Already, many languages are lost; by writing primarily in English, with smatterings of Laguna and Spanish, Silko conveys the essential meaning of many of her tribal myths, while helping to preserve the tribal language. Working with three languages further suggests the strengths of assimilation; each culture can enhance and enrich the others. Such connectedness may be the only hope for a productive future; undivided by racism, less alienated from the natural world, the human community has a greater chance of survival, both physically and psychologically.

CEREMONY

First published: 1977
Type of work: Novel

Experiencing deep depression after fighting in World War II, a young man finds health and new meaning after his return to the Laguna reservation.

Ceremony, Silko's first published novel, won the attention of critics and other Native American writers, particularly N. Scott Momaday. Interestingly, the basic situation of Silko's novel parallels that of Momaday's *House Made of Dawn*. Both writers create protagonists who have been psychologically wounded by service in the Army during World War II and who encounter racism and brutality when they attempt to return to reservation life afterward. Although Momaday's character eventually experiences a partial return to health, Silko's main character, a "half-breed" named Tayo, fully overcomes his impulses toward violence by undergoing the traditional healing ceremonies of the past.

The novel continually pits the world of the white race against Indian culture, a contrast that is highlighted by Tayo's experience as a soldier. Seen only as an American when he is in uniform, Tayo is treated well by white women and store owners, who are eager to help the boys at the front. Out of uniform, Tayo is relegated to the position of second-class citizen, either ignored or insulted by the same people who had been kind previously.

Tayo's position is further complicated by the fact that he is not fully accepted in the Indian community either, because he has a Mexican father. The racism that contributes to his confused sense of identity also precipitates his breakdown: When he suddenly perceives a Japanese enemy to be no different from his Indian uncle, he collapses on the battlefield. His precarious mental condition is further jeopardized when his cousin Rocky, who has worked hard to assimilate himself into the mainstream culture, is killed in the war. Tayo returns to his aunt's home on the reservation, convinced that he, not Rocky, is the one who should have died.

Racism is also seen as a major contributor to the self-destructive behavior of other Indian veterans.

Tayo's friends retreat into alcoholism and repetitive recitations of their sexual exploits with white women; eventually they can feel good about themselves only when they commit violent acts of domination, reenacting the atrocities of war. Tayo himself falls victim to this temptation and stabs another veteran before embarking on his ceremonial journey toward psychological wholeness.

The process of healing provides another cultural juxtaposition: Tayo's illness originally is defined and treated by white doctors, who attempt psychological explanations and scientific cures. Tayo's stay in a mental hospital is described in images of whiteness; most tellingly, he feels immersed in a white fog. It is not until he goes through the ritual healing ceremonies of the Laguna that he realizes that his "craziness" may actually be a the result of special perception, the ability to realize the interconnectedness of seemingly unrelated events.

Through ceremony and story, Tayo comes to accept not only the power of traditional Indian ways

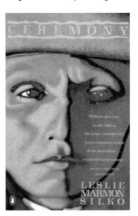

but also the truth of ancient beliefs. Embarking on a journey to find his uncle's stolen cattle, Tayo gradually senses his oneness with the earth and acknowledges that the earth gives of itself to humans out of love. Through this realization, he is able to overcome his hatred of humans—particularly the white people who are destroying the earth and one another—and his impulses toward violence.

Faced with the difficult test of stopping a brutal attack only by performing worse brutality himself, Tayo decides not to act and thus frees himself from the fear that he is as others have defined him: a drunken, lawless, incapable half-breed. With his choice, Tayo not only gains a sense of himself as an independent, strong individual but also recognizes the kinship among all peoples. His earlier confusion of the Japanese soldier with his uncle is transformed into the startling awareness that people are artificially divided and made to hate one another.

Symbolically, this recognition occurs near the site of played-out uranium mines in New Mexico; the weapon that defeated the Japanese had its origins on traditional Indian lands. Both Japanese and Native Americans have been victimized by the white race and have been deceived into fighting each other, but Tayo realizes that, ultimately, white people have injured the earth and themselves beyond repair or redemption. In realizing this, he affirms his Indian heritage and sees himself as the inheritor of Laguna traditions, traditions that teach him how to live fully after his dehumanizing military experience.

STORYTELLER

First published: 1981
Type of work: Short stories, poems, autobiographical sketches

This collection of narrative and poetic tales focuses on the author's Laguna heritage.

The unifying theme of the short stories and poems of *Storyteller* might be considered Silko's life itself. Punctuated with photographs of the Laguna reservation and surrounding landscape, often taken by her father, *Storyteller* seeks to assert the importance and vitality of an oral culture. Many of the tales included were told to Silko by her relatives; although not always understanding their import at the time, Silko came to realize that such stories include practical or moral instruction. Other tales and poems are imaginative reconstructions of ancient myths or are Silko's responses to her immediate environment. Throughout, the connective thread is Silko's experience of life as an American Indian woman.

Silko assumes many guises as a storyteller and becomes many narrators, each with an individual voice. With equal versatility, she is the Inuk girl who tricks her parents' killer to his death, the mythic Yellow Woman riding into the mountains with her lover, or herself as a child, tormenting her uncle's goat. As she demonstrates so forcefully in *Ceremony,* she capably creates male characters, catching the rougher resonances of their voices as well. Two striking stories narrated by male characters are "Tony's Story" and "Coyote Holds a Full House in His Hand."

In the first, Silko focuses on the killing of a New Mexico state patrol officer, seen from the point of view of one of the participants. Brutalized by the patrol officer, who seeks out Indians in order to beat them, Antonio Sousea kills the officer in front of his friend Leon and then sets fire to the body in the squad car. Leon, who has responded to an indiscriminate beating from the officer by talking about his civil rights and appealing to the Pueblo meeting, is appalled. Tony, however, has perceived the officer to be something worse than a violent racist; he believes the man to be a force of evil, the focal point of a bad spell that perpetuates the drought conditions on the reservation.

Tony believes that to exorcise the evil, the killing and burning are necessary and justified from the perspective of ancient beliefs. His view is in sharp contrast to Leon's, which has been affected by his service in the military and his desire to assimilate into the cultural mainstream.

"Coyote Holds a Full House in His Hand" is much more lighthearted. The final story in the collection is the tale of an old Laguna man who poses as a medicine man in order to take advantage of a gathering of Hopi women. Coyote is a traditional trickster of Laguna legend who is foiled by his own cleverness as often as he succeeds in getting what he wants. In this tale, however, he is victorious, securing for himself a photograph of the women, who have believed his lie and submitted to his cure, which involves caressing their thighs with juniper ashes. The humor of this tale, especially contrasted with the seriousness of "Tony's Story," demonstrates the versatility of Silko's art, not only in her creation of multiple voices but also in her treatment of diverse subject matters. *Storyteller* is a brilliant exhibition of her range and imaginative powers.

ALMANAC OF THE DEAD

First published: 1991
Type of work: Novel

Silko's pre-millennial jeremiad is structured by the Mayan codices that provide the novel with its title and one of its more compelling controlling metaphors.

Almanac of the Dead remains Silko's longest and most ambitious novel, with hundreds of characters populating multiple plot narratives with overlaying cultures. Structuring the book as nineteen books within six parts, Silko truly provides a "Five-Hundred Year Map," not only literally within the outside covers of the published book but also in the multiple narratives that describe a moral history of North America as individual characters reveal the ideas, the passions, and their own understandings of history. Tucson provides the geographic center of an intersection of cultures that brings together Mafia capo Sonny Blue from Cherry Hill, New Jersey; Pueblo gardener Sterling down from Laguna Pueblo; Wilson Weasel Tail the Barefoot Hopi down from Winslow, Arizona; and Seese from California, seeking her missing child and connecting with Lecha, the television psychic who may or may not be able to aid (or be interested in aiding) her, among sundry others.

Bartolomeo's Freedom School, a Cuban-influenced and -financed school of revolution in Mexico City, provides the setting for the beautiful, intellectual architecture student Alegria, who sells out by marrying wealthy Menardo and building an incongruous and doomed luxury retreat in the jungle outside Tuxtla Gutierrez. Silko shows how cocaine is smuggled northward across the border to Tucson by revolutionaries, who then use the money to finance the purchase of arms for their continuing insurrection in the state of Chiapas. Meanwhile, drunks in Tucson are being rolled, and their organs are being harvested for resale on a medical black market, while drugs and women are commodities provided for a price to people of all races who, like sundry others, have been drawn to Phoenix since the end of the Apache Wars: speculators, confidence men, embezzlers, lawyers, judges, "police and other criminals, as well as addicts and pushers."

The vision seems apocalyptic, but there is reason for individual and collective hope in some of the developments that occur later in the novel. Although from a Western perspective, the northward march from Central America of thousands of peo-

ple under the leadership of the Twin Brothers might seem frightening, the migration of peoples is seen as inevitable and natural, belying the artificiality of the imaginary lines of international borders. As well, the sixth and final part of the novel is titled "One World, Many Tribes." Although the greed and rapacity that has informed much of the westward expansion and colonization of the world continue, there is a karmic balance that allows, for example, Menardo to be killed in a failed bullet-proof vest test. In water-critical southern Arizona, careful husbandry of limited resources is a necessity, and Mafia-funded developers who seek to create green-grass golf courses in the desert will inevitably fail because the land will endure through any period of human use or misuse.

SACRED WATER

First published: 1993
Type of work: Prose poems and photography

This collection contains forty-two prose poems, each with an accompanying photograph, and concludes with an "Author's Note," all focusing in some way on the scarcity and sacredness of water in the American Southwest.

Leslie Marmon Silko's commitment to shared husbandry of the land of the Southwest is perhaps nowhere better and more simply articulated than in this privately published, limited edition collection of prose poems and photography. Silko incorporates her family traditions in photography to create a multimedia text. The black-and-white pictorial images of water, clouds, mountains, rocks, reptiles, and flora nicely accompany the written text, which shows Silko's understanding of the importance of water in terms of sustenance, ecological balance, and religious practice.

GARDENS IN THE DUNES

First published: 1999
Type of work: Novel

Set at the turn of the twentieth century, this novel follows Indigo, one of the last of the Sand Lizard people, as she leaves her ancestral hidden garden near the Colorado River to travel to New York and Europe before her return home.

Leslie Marmon Silko's *Gardens in the Dunes* received more acclaim that the lengthy *Almanac of the Dead*, and a number of critics, as well as professors and students in higher education, compared the text favorably to her earlier book-length works *Ceremony* and *Storyteller*, in terms of both the beauty of the prose and the ultimate positive resolution of the circumstances of the text.

Adolescent Indigo is separated from her Sand Lizard people in the hidden gardens near the Arizona-California border. She spends most of the balance of the novel engaging in compelling discussions of cultural conflict, principally with upper-class Hattie, who views herself initially as Indigo's savior and form of entrée into mainstream Western culture. Hattie herself is an iconoclastic figure in being a female scholar, in refusing to follow the protocols of academe, and then in marrying Edward, a much older scholar and botanist, but not becoming a mother.

Edward's defilement of the natural landscape through his foolhardy, greedy scheme concerning citron stock and illegal orchids ultimately destroys his life and his relationship with Hattie. The Grand Tour of Europe that the improbable threesome—Edward, Hattie, Indigo—undertake results in Edward's arrest in Livorno, Italy, and Indigo's increasing boredom with the trappings of Western culture. However, a visit to Bath, England, shows Hattie the ancient Celtic gardens that Aunt Bronwyn continues to maintain, and after Hattie later endures physical assault and abandonment in the Arizona desert, humiliation after her husband's arrest, and the disdain of an embarrassed family, her resolution at the end of the novel to return to Europe shows that she seems to have come to the realization that her spiritual sanctity will be achieved by a deeper understanding of her own cultural background rather than in ministering to others.

Gardens in the Dunes is especially concerned with how different human cultures manifest different presuppositions and belief systems concerning how to live on, and with, the earth. Even though Indigo is in her early teens and has had virtually no formal education beyond some brief interactions within the Riverside Indian School, her spiritual and subsistence understanding of human life on earth is modeled as a more reasonable mind-set than Edward's scientific and capitalistic approach or Hattie's alternately accepting and rejecting attitudes toward Western value systems and norms. As well, there is a recurrent and underlying theme of motherhood and nurturing in the text that is revealed in a number of ways and in multiple cultures. Hattie's return to Europe at the conclusion of the novel cannot therefore be understood as a failure on her part to understand and live in concert with the geography and spirituality of the New World; instead, it should be seen as her self-actualizing understanding of the manner in which each individual and each culture needs to know its sources of power and where to go for insight and renewal.

SUMMARY

Historically, Silko's significant contribution may be the retrieval and recording of stories that are part of an oral culture not accessible to many Americans. Aesthetically, her art provides much more: Politically and socially aware, Silko offers a critique of American culture that emphasizes the importance of Indian values to the mainstream population. Without the Native American ability to accept multiple points of view, to embrace ambiguity, American society becomes sterile and divisive. Further, without the Indian respect and love for the land, the very future of American society is threatened. Through her gift of storytelling, Silko offers her readers ways to embrace a holistic, healing perspective by understanding the import of ancient beliefs and ceremonies.

Gweneth A. Dunleavy; updated by Richard Sax

BIBLIOGRAPHY

By the Author

SHORT FICTION:
Yellow Woman, 1993

LONG FICTION:
Ceremony, 1977
Almanac of the Dead, 1991
Gardens in the Dunes, 1999

POETRY:
Laguna Woman: Poems, 1974

DRAMA:
Lullaby, pr. 1976 (with Frank Chin)

NONFICTION:
The Delicacy and Strength of Lace: Letters Between Leslie Marmon Silko and James Wright, 1986
Sacred Water: Narratives and Pictures, 1993
Yellow Woman and a Beauty of the Spirit: Essays on Native American Life Today, 1996
Conversations with Leslie Marmon Silko, 2000 (Ellen L. Arnold, editor)

MISCELLANEOUS:
Storyteller, 1981 (includes poetry and prose)

About the Author

Aithal, S. K. "American Ethnic Fiction in the Universal Context." *American Studies International* 21 (October, 1983): 61-66.

Antell, J. A. "Momaday, Welch, and Silko: Expressing the Feminine Principle Through Male Alienation." *American Indian Quarterly* 12 (Summer, 1988): 213-220.

Chavkin, Allan, ed. *Leslie Marmon Silko's "Ceremony": A Casebook*. New York: Oxford University Press, 2002.

Danielson, Linda. "The Storytellers in *Storyteller*." *Studies in American Indian Literatures* 5, no. 1 (1989): 21-31.

Dunsmore, Roger. "No Boundaries: On Silko's *Ceremony*." In *Earth's Mind: Essays in Native Literature*. Albuquerque: University of New Mexico Press, 1997.

Garcia, Reyes. "Senses of Place in *Ceremony*." *MELUS* 10 (Winter, 1983): 37-48.

DISCUSSION TOPICS

- Leslie Marmon Silko's Laguna Pueblo traditions involve oral narrative storytelling, but she writes in English and in multiple genre forms—novel, nonfiction prose, poetry. How effective have her genre choices been in conveying her meaning?

- A number of Laguna Pueblo myths are interpolated within the narrative structure of *Ceremony*. How do the traditional stories provide insight into the events of the novel, especially in an understanding of Tayo, the protagonist?

- Comment on the importance of Mt. Taylor in *Ceremony*. In Laguna Pueblo, the mountain is referred to as Tse-pi-na, the Woman Who Walks in the Clouds. Does the female character who identifies herself as "Ts'eh" to Tayo bear comparison to Ts'its'tsi'nako (Thought-Woman) or to Tse-pi-na (Mt. Taylor/Woman Who Walks in the Clouds) or to both?

- Should Hattie be understood as a caring and altruistic figure who seeks the betterment of Indigo in *Gardens in the Dunes*, or is she attempting to indoctrinate culturally a bereft young woman who has been separated from her family and tribe?

- Discuss how each of the following characters has an initial understanding of a personal relationship with the land and how that understanding is altered in the course of the work: Tayo in *Ceremony*, Sterling in *Almanac of the Dead*, Edward in *Gardens in the Dunes*, and Leon in "The Man to Send Rain Clouds," from *Storyteller*.

- How do the articles in *Yellow Woman and a Beauty of the Spirit* and even the letters in *The Delicacy and Strength of Lace* provide insight into some of the critical and thematic concerns that Silko describes in her imaginative fiction?

Hirsh, B. A. "The Telling Which Continues: Oral Tradition and the Written Word in Leslie Marmon Silko's *Storyteller.*" *American Indian Quarterly* 12 (Winter, 1988): 1-26.

Jahner, Elaine. "Leslie Marmon Silko." In *Handbook of Native American Literature,* edited by Andrew Wiget. New York: Garland, 1996.

Lincoln, Kenneth. "Grandmother Storyteller: Leslie Silko." In *Native American Renaissance.* Berkeley: University of California Press, 1985.

Nelson, Robert M. "Rewriting Ethnography: The Embedded Texts in Leslie Silko's *Ceremony.*" In *Telling the Stories: Essays on American Indian Literatures and Cultures.* New York: Peter Lang, 2001.

Sax, Richard. "One World, Many Tribes: Crosscultural Influences in Silko's *Almanac of the Dead.*" In *Celebration of Indigenous Thought and Expression.* Sault Ste. Marie, Mich.: Lake Superior State University Press, 1996.

NEIL SIMON

Born: Bronx, New York
July 4, 1927

Simon's humorous plays have made him the most commercially successful playwright in the history of theater.

Library of Congress

BIOGRAPHY

Born in the Bronx, New York, on July 4, 1927, Marvin Neil Simon was the second of two sons in a middle-class Jewish family. His father, Irving, was a garment salesman who abandoned the family several times before the Simons' marriage ended in divorce. Because of his parents' domestic difficulties, Simon's childhood was not particularly happy, but he nevertheless developed his affinity for comedy at an early age. As a schoolboy, he earned his nickname "Doc" for his ability to imitate the family doctor, and he reported in a *Life* magazine interview:

> When I was a kid, I climbed up on a stone ledge to watch an outdoor movie of Charlie Chaplin. I laughed so hard I fell off, cut my head open and was taken to the doctor, bleeding and laughing. I was constantly being dragged out of movies for laughing too loud. Now my idea of the ultimate achievement in a comedy is to make a whole audience fall onto the floor, writhing and laughing so hard that some of them pass out.

Simon's plays are often quite nearly that amusing, but his gift for provoking riotous laughter has ultimately been a burden, because it has prevented most critics from taking him seriously as a comic dramatist.

Simon demonstrated his ability to make people laugh even as a teenager, when he teamed with his older brother Danny to write material for stand-up comics and radio shows. After briefly attending New York University (he never graduated from college) and serving in the Army at the end of World War II, Neil teamed with Danny again as they began, in 1946, to create material for one of the radio era's most successful comedy writers, Goodman Ace.

The Simon brothers prospered as radio comedy writers but shifted in the early 1950's to television as the new medium developed. Writing for such television notables as Phil Silvers and Tallulah Bankhead, they were each earning huge weekly salaries of sixteen hundred dollars by the mid-1950's. During his television writing in the 1950's, Simon worked alongside many young writers who would later make successful careers of their own, most notably Mel Brooks and Woody Allen. Danny left the writing team in 1956 to pursue a career as a television director, but Neil continued writing for such stars as Sid Caesar, Garry Moore, Jackie Gleason, and Red Buttons, earning two Emmy Awards (in 1957 and 1959) for his comedy writing.

Simon believed that writing for television did not allow him enough independence, so while writing for *The Garry Moore Show*, he teamed with Danny to develop his first play, *Come Blow Your Horn* (1960), which eventually ran eighty-four weeks on Broadway. The success of this play encouraged Simon to leave television for good. Working solo this time, Simon first wrote the book for a musical comedy, *Little Me* (1962), and then wrote his second Broadway comedy, *Barefoot in the Park* (1963). The latter, starring a young actor named Robert Redford, was an enormous success, running for four years and 1,532 performances. As the first of many television and film offers followed, Simon soon became rich and famous. While *Barefoot in the Park* was still running on Broadway, Paramount bought the film rights to Simon's next play, *The Odd Couple* (1965), on the basis of a forty-word synopsis, and he soon sold the television rights to the American Broadcasting Company, although for only a small percentage of the millions of dollars the television series eventually earned.

By the mid-1960's, then, Neil Simon was already a household name, his popularity and wealth virtually assured. Although he experienced some setbacks (*The Star-Spangled Girl* in 1966 was not a Broadway hit), he recovered almost immediately with the successes of *Promises, Promises* (1968), *Plaza Suite* (1968), and *Last of the Red Hot Lovers* (1969). Simon has suffered occasional disappointments— for example, with *The Gingerbread Lady* (1970), *The Good Doctor* (1973), *God's Favorite* (1974), and *Fools* (1981)—but overall, his comedies have been very successful at the box office, his name on the marquee assuring a receptive audience.

In 1973, Simon's personal life was dealt a severe blow when his wife of twenty years, dancer Joan Bairn, died of cancer. He eventually recorded his grief in *Chapter Two* (1977), the story of a man who loses his wife and then immediately remarries, fending off the subsequent feelings of guilt. *Chapter Two* was hailed by some critics as a new kind of triumph for Simon, a comedy that could be taken seriously, that was more than a series of one-liners. Then, in 1983, the first of a trilogy of semiautobiographical plays confirmed this assessment in the eyes of even more critics. *Brighton Beach Memoirs* (1982), *Biloxi Blues* (1984), and *Broadway Bound* (1986) did not assure everyone that he was a serious playwright, but they convinced enough people for those plays to be considered a turning point in Simon's career. Respect for Simon's work reached its peak with the reception of *Lost in Yonkers* (1991), which garnered almost universal praise, winning the Tony Award for Best Play and earning Simon a Pulitzer Prize in drama, an award that he had predicted would never be given to a writer of comedies.

New plays by Simon continued to appear in the 1990's and into the twenty-first century. Some were farces, such as *Jake's Women* (1990). Others combined comedy with more serious themes; for example, *The Dinner Party* (2000) found laughs in marital disasters.

In addition to his comedies, Simon has written four musicals—*Little Me* (1962; revised, 1982), *Sweet Charity* (1966), *Promises, Promises* (1968), and *They're Playing Our Song* (1978). He has also written extensively, although not as successfully, for the screen. Starting with *After the Fox* in 1966, Simon's original film scripts include *The Heartbreak Kid* (1972), *Murder by Death* (1976), and *The Goodbye Girl* (1977). He has also adapted most of his own plays for the screen. Simon's habit is to write daily from 10:00 A.M. to 5:00 P.M. in either his Manhattan apartment or his Bel-Air, California, home. He usually starts ten or more plays for every one that he finishes. If he passes page thirty-five of a play, Simon usually completes it, although he reports that the revision process always lasts much longer than the original composition.

ANALYSIS

A natural gift for wit and humor and a decade's experience writing television comedy in the 1950's enabled Simon to create enormously amusing plays from the very beginning of his career. Even in *Come Blow Your Horn* and *Barefoot in the Park*, Simon had mastered the one-liner, the clever and witty reply that catches an audience by surprise and compels it into explosive laughter.

Take, for example, Victor Velasco's quip upon entering the nearly barren one-room apartment of Paul and Corie Bratter in *Barefoot in the Park*. Their furniture has not yet arrived, but Corie announces that "we just moved in"; looking around the barren room, Velasco replies, "Really? What are you, a folksinger?" Initially, the audience is surprised by the apparent incongruity of the remark; then, within milliseconds, they realize that there is a certain aptness in the reply, given the circumstances. The laughter is boisterous because surprise triggers it, and then the laughter is sustained because aptness justifies it. Simon had polished this technique in his early writing for such television comedians as Phil Silvers, Sid Caesar, and Jackie Gleason. In the introduction to volume 2 of *The Collected Plays of Neil Simon* (1979), Simon recalls that writing humorous dialogue for his film *The Goodbye Girl* was much easier than trying to write "a funny lead-in to Jo Stafford's next song" on the old *Garry Moore Show*.

Although his ability to create uproarious laughter endears Simon to the general populace, it has done little to impress many critics, who see comedy as a thought-provoking genre and who associate steady, boisterous laughter with mind-numbing television situation comedies. Simon himself has been sensitive to this critical disparagement of his work and has attempted throughout his career to make his comedies more "serious" without sacrificing the laughter that he loves to create and that his audiences pay to enjoy. As early as *The Odd Couple*, Simon was attempting to go beyond the gag-comedy, one-liner format of *Come Blow Your Horn* and *Barefoot in the Park*. As reported in a 1979 *Playboy* interview, Simon's original conception for his famous play about Oscar and Felix was to make it a black comedy.

Transcending his one-liner format and gaining more respect from the critics did not come easily. By 1979, Simon was secure in his commercial success, having turned out popular hits on Broadway and in Hollywood for nearly twenty years. Yet in the introduction to volume 2 of his *Collected Plays*, Simon admitted that he was still suffering from insecurity as a writer, and he openly confessed to neurosis, an ulcer, and envy over his good friend Woody Allen's success with the motion picture *Manhattan* (1979), which had led reviewers to call Allen "the most mature comic mind in America."

Simon acknowledged in that same introduction that people ranked his plays in terms of aesthetic extremes, judging them anywhere from "a delightful evening" to "worthy of Moliere." Those who ranked his plays as "a delightful evening" were essentially admitting that the plays, although very amusing, could only be considered entertainment. Those who ranked his plays as "worthy of Moliere" were asserting that his comedy should be taken as seriously as the plays of such classic comic writers as Aristophanes, William Shakespeare, and George Bernard Shaw.

Very few mature and responsible critics would go that far, and a much more fruitful comparison for Simon's work is with that of playwright Alan Ayckbourn, who is often referred to as the "English Neil Simon." Both are prolific, writing very amusing plays about conventional middle-class people. The chief value in the comparison is that Ayckbourn's work has received a far more positive reception from the serious-minded critics, which

may enable one to deduce what the critics find lacking in Simon.

The more positive critical assessment of Simon's work, however, which began with the response to *Chapter Two*, seems at least partially justifiable; his later, semi-autobiographical plays are indeed different from his earlier comedies. *Chapter Two* does not seem to depend so much on one-liners and boisterous laughter. Written as a response to the death of his first wife, *Chapter Two* finally turned the focus of Simon's plays toward dramatic narrative, toward the situations in which he put his characters. The play opens, quite typically, with a wise-cracking character named Leo Schneider, but when Leo's brother George is introduced, the pain that George feels over the loss of his wife Barbara begins to dominate the opening scene and create genuine pathos. The play does have sections where the one-liners predominate, but overall, the play focuses on the courtship of George and his new girlfriend, Jennie, and the portrayal in the last act of their posthoneymoon conflict is as genuine and moving as the pathos in the first scene. Those more serious qualities also appear prominently in *Lost in Yonkers* and in the plays of Simon's autobiographical trilogy: *Brighton Beach Memoirs*, *Biloxi Blues*, and *Broadway Bound*. As Simon entered the twenty-first century, he continued to bask in the increased critical respect generated by these plays.

Critical opinion, however, is seldom unanimous. Although the new plays were clearly different, critics such as the redoubtable John Simon of *New York* magazine suggested that Neil Simon had simply substituted one commercial formula for another—that the gag writer had merely been replaced by a sentimental writer. So, although the disparagement of Simon's work abated, not all voices were raised in praise.

BAREFOOT IN THE PARK

First produced: 1963 (first published, 1964)
Type of work: Play

A newly married couple irons out superficial differences and agrees to live happily ever after, finding happiness for the bride's mother in the bargain.

In *Barefoot in the Park*, newlyweds Corie and Paul Bratter have completed their six-day honeymoon and are moving into their first apartment. Corie is romantic, impulsive, and enthusiastic, while her husband is a proper, careful, even "stuffy" young attorney who is more concerned with his budding legal career than he is with helping to build their love nest and perpetuating the honeymoon atmosphere. Soon Corie and Paul quarrel, Paul questioning Corie's judgment and Corie questioning Paul's sense of romance and adventure. Complicating their discord is Corie's attempt to enliven the life of her widowed mother, Ethel. Against Paul's advice, Corie tricks her mother into a blind date with their eccentric neighbor, Victor Velasco, who skis, climbs mountains, and is known as "The Bluebeard of 48th Street."

By the end of act 2, the question of the blind date has precipitated such a conflict between Corie and Paul that they agree to divorce, and in act 3, they fight over the settlement before Paul stalks out. Ethel and Velasco, however, reveal that they have found romance. Ethel has rediscovered her vitality, while Velasco has decided that he must act his age and settle down. After the new lovers depart, Paul returns, outrageously drunk, having walked barefoot in the park in the middle of winter to prove that he is not a "fuddy-duddy." The newlyweds are reconciled and promise to live happily ever after.

Even in his first play, Simon had mastered the qualities that would make him enormously successful. First and foremost, *Barefoot in the Park* is clever and hilarious, filled with snappy dialogue and witty one-liners. One of the most famous of his "running gags" (a joke repeated for laughs) appears in this play. Because Paul and Corie's apartment is on the fifth floor of their building, nearly all the characters suffer extreme exhaustion in the climb. The joke is carried throughout the play but continues to elicit laughter because Simon always finds a different angle when he repeats it.

Nevertheless, the limitation that has haunted Simon throughout his career is present: The humor of the one-liners overwhelms the potentially literary elements of the play. There is a clear sense that the characters and plot are simply serving as framework for the funny lines. As a result, the dramatic conflicts in the play do not seem real or deeply felt.

In act 3, for example, when Paul and Corie are arguing about their divorce, Simon manages to maintain the rich humor of the play, but he is not able to create a convincing sense of conflict at the same time. Corie exclaims that she wants Paul to move out immediately, and as Paul angrily begins to pack his suitcase, Corie says, "My divorce. When do I get my divorce?" Paul replies, "How should I know? They didn't even send us our marriage license yet." The one-liner reestablishes the play's frivolous tone and creates the impression that there is really little at stake. There is no satiric attitude toward either point of view, no comic judgment of anyone's folly, and really no thought process, only the explosive laughter that comes from the line. The dominant tone created by the one-liners suggests that this marital discord is both trivial and temporary, a condition that will be resolved painlessly in a happy ending.

Simon does attempt to make a serious point in his play, asserting that moderation will make everyone happier and that marriage is too important an institution to take lightly, but his sentiments strike most critics as conventional and not thought-provoking. Ironically, Simon's penchant for safe sentiments traps him in this play. At a pivotal moment, when Corie's mother is counseling Corie about how to resolve the marital conflict and get Paul back, Simon gives the mother some marriage-saving "wisdom" that dates the play and made it seriously anachronistic within a decade. What seemed to Simon in the early 1960's to be conservative, conventional wisdom would soon become sexism in the 1970's:

> It's very simple. You've just got to give up a little of you for him. Don't make everything a game. Just late at night in that little room upstairs. But take care of him. And make him feel important. And if you can do that, you'll have a happy and wonderful marriage.

THE ODD COUPLE

First produced: 1965 (first published, 1966)
Type of work: Play

Two men, one divorced and sloppy, the other newly separated from his wife and very tidy, discover that they cannot live together.

The Odd Couple was not merely another Neil Simon hit: It might be considered the greatest hit of his career, if popularity is measured by the kind of impact a play has on American culture. *The Odd Couple* ran on Broadway for nearly one thousand performances, then was made into a film (1968), then into a very successful network television program (1970-1975), and then recast in a female version (1985), in which the two roommates are played by women. These facts alone would be significant indications of popularity, but Simon's play has had such an impact on American life that the phrase "odd couple" has become part of American folklore. Many may not remember the names of the two men or which was the messy one, but nearly every adult is familiar with the situation to which the phrase "odd couple" refers and can use the phrase to describe similar situations.

The Odd Couple refers to Oscar Madison and Felix Ungar. Oscar, the messy one, is divorced from his wife and lives alone in a spacious, eight-room apartment on Riverside Drive in New York City. Even when he entertains Felix and his other poker-playing buddies, Oscar's apartment is littered with dirty dishes, discarded clothes, and even garbage. When Felix's wife demands a trial separation, Felix comes to live with Oscar and soon wears out his welcome, even with their poker buddies, because he insists on keeping the apartment sparkling clean and tidy. Furthermore, Felix's despondency over his separation not only depresses Oscar but also ruins Oscar's plans to seduce the two British sisters, Cecily and Gwendolyn Pigeon, who live in the apartment above them. When Oscar can endure no more, he demands that Felix leave, and Felix moves upstairs temporarily with the Pigeon sisters, who find his sensitivity charming. Thus the play ends in an uncomplicated way, with Oscar and Felix agreeing to separate.

In many ways, Simon demonstrates more skill as a playwright in *The Odd Couple* than in earlier works. He does not depend on simple "running gags" such as the exhausting flights of stairs in *Barefoot in the Park*, and his one-liners are much more integrated into the play's action and characterization. As adept as Simon had been with theatrical gesture in *Barefoot in the Park*, it is clear in *The Odd Couple* that he has become even more expert at creating a captivating theatrical experience for his audience.

For example, in the opening lines of the play, the poker players have gathered at Oscar's apartment for a game, and the exasperated Speed is watching the painfully deliberate Murray shuffle the cards. This opening moment is spellbinding even before Speed's first word is spoken. The curtain rises on an arresting image, an obviously lavish apartment comically devastated by neglect, a diverse group of men engaged in a smoky masculine ritual around the poker table, and the group's focus immediately engaged on the comically slow Murray, shuffling the cards as if he were handling precious jewels. Speed then delivers the opening line and the first one-liner of the play:

> *Speed* (Cups his chin in his hand and looks at Murray) Tell me, Mr. Maverick, is this your first time on the riverboat?

Even in *The Odd Couple*, however, a masterpiece in many ways, Simon was still unable to achieve a convincing level of seriousness to accompany the rich laughter. This is most apparent at the end of the play, when it finally appears that there really has not been much of a point to the conflict between Oscar and Felix. Some critics claim that the play shows how incompatibility is as likely to occur between roommates as between spouses and that the spirit of compromise is necessary to partnership. Most critics argue, however, that this is not saying much beyond the painfully obvious.

The Odd Couple ends inconclusively without being thought-provoking; it ends ambiguously without being suggestive. Oscar and Felix part as friends, Oscar has become more neat and more responsible about paying his alimony, and Felix will spend a few days with the Pigeon sisters before facing some unknown future.

LAST OF THE RED HOT LOVERS

First produced: 1969 (first published, 1970)
Type of work: Play

A middle-aged man discovers that extramarital affairs are less satisfying than conventional matrimony.

Last of the Red Hot Lovers is one of the most amusing of Neil Simon's comedies. It focuses on Barney Cashman, a forty-seven-year-old owner of a seafood restaurant who is afraid that the sexual revolution of the 1960's is passing him by. Over the space of nine months, he invites three different women to his mother's Manhattan apartment in an attempt to have an afternoon of extramarital sex. None of the affairs is consummated, however, and Barney decides after the last one that he would prefer a romantic afternoon with his wife, Thelma.

Of the three women who meet Barney, the first two are caricatures of sexually liberated women from the 1960's. In act 1, Elaine Navazio comes to the afternoon tryst as a veteran of casual sex. In her late thirties and married, Elaine indulges frequently in extramarital affairs simply because they make her feel good. Flippant and irreverent, Elaine is openly contemptuous of Barney's maladroit, unsophisticated style (he is nervous, wanting the affair to be "meaningful") and bombards him with insults that hit like machine-gun fire. She is interested only in their sensual experience and is comically desperate for a cigarette throughout their meeting. When the encounter fails to produce sexual satisfaction, Elaine leaves, and Barney vows never to be tempted again. Yet eight months later, he repeats the experience with Bobbi Michele.

Bobbi is an uninhibited and adventurous twenty-seven-year-old woman who entices Barney into smoking his first marijuana and regales him with wild stories about her prospects in show business, about men attempting to have sex with her, and about the lesbian Nazi vocal coach with whom she lives. The totally bizarre Bobbi generates tremendous laughter as her high-energy, nonstop talk reduces Barney to bewilderment. The frenetic pace that was established in the first act with Elaine is maintained, and perhaps even topped, in this segment.

In act 3, less than a month later, Barney is attempting to seduce Jeanette Fisher, who is thirty-nine years old and the wife of a close friend. Unlike the promiscuous Elaine and Bobbi, Jeanette is a reluctant visitor, joining Barney only because she thinks her husband, Mel, is having an affair of his own. Depressed and guilt-ridden, an unwilling participant in the prevailing sexual climate, Jeanette lectures Barney on moral issues and challenges him to prove that there are decent people in the world. The comic energy in this segment is generated by the reversal of Barney's role. In this act Barney has become the aggressor, having gained savoir faire and confidence from his previous meetings. Rich laughter is generated by the conflict between Barney's new impatience and Jeanette's reticence. Barney finally sees the wisdom of not engaging in illicit sex, and when he and Jeanette part at the end of the play, Barney seems to be cured of his desire for promiscuity.

In addition to being a very funny play, *Last of the Red Hot Lovers* is a critique of the permissive 1960's from a conservative point of view. Simon's message is that the conventional values of marriage, home, and family are still sacrosanct, even though they seem old-fashioned in the prevailing cultural climate. Ironically, Simon's conservative thinking serves him well in this case. Looking back, one can see that the permissiveness of the 1960's was beginning to fade as Simon was writing this comedy. The increasingly moralistic climate of the 1980's would make this play look like an eloquent and prophetic swan song for an era. Thus, in *Last of the Red Hot Lovers*, Simon added, perhaps inadvertently, a serious quality to his comic writing. It was not, however, a seriousness that all the critics considered profound, subtle, or artistic.

BRIGHTON BEACH MEMOIRS

First produced: 1982 (first published, 1984)
Type of work: Play

Problems are caused by having too many relatives live under one roof, but they are resolved, and a young boy comes of age during the process.

Brighton Beach Memoirs is about the Jeromes, a Brooklyn family in the late Depression era (1937), and the financial difficulties they face when three relatives join the household. For three and one-half years, Kate Jerome's sister Blanche Morton and Blanche's two teenage daughters, Laurie and Nora, have lived with the middle-class Jeromes. Although the arrangement is basically amicable, new financial tensions culminate in hard words between Kate and Blanche. Fortunately, the argument teaches Blanche about independence, and the play ends happily, with Blanche making plans to move and with the two sisters closer than ever.

Brighton Beach Memoirs does not really focus on this story of sibling love, however; rather, it is what

Simon calls his first "tapestry play." In all of Simon's previous plays, he focused on two or three characters and made the other characters peripheral. Here, there is a sense that each character's story is told with similar emphasis.

Jack Jerome struggles to balance all of his familial roles, as husband, father, and surrogate parent for Laurie and Nora. Stanley Jerome, the eldest son, achieves adulthood by learning from his errors in judgment. Nora Morton, the eldest daughter, gives up illusions of easy fame and fortune as a Broadway showgirl, accepting a closer relationship with her mother and a more responsible familial role, while Laurie Morton, the sickly and highly pampered youngest daughter, will clearly profit from a less indulgent treatment of her illness. A slightly greater dramatic emphasis is perhaps given to fifteen-year-old Eugene Jerome, Simon's autobiographical alter ego, who serves as the play's charming narrator. Eugene comes of age in the play, leaving puberty behind as he confronts sexual feelings for his cousin Nora.

As the first play in Simon's autobiographical trilogy, *Brighton Beach Memoirs* decisively raised the critical opinion of Simon's comedies because the play was not at all dependent on one-liners. Its laughter was less boisterous and explosive, becoming warmer, more gentle, more related to character and situation, and more sentimental. Take, for example, one of the first big laughs in the play. Eu-

gene is banging an old softball against a wall, and his mother asks him to stop because Aunt Blanche is suffering from a headache. Eugene begs for a few more pitches because it is a crucial moment in his imaginary replaying of a Yankee World Series game.

When he finally has to give in, he "slams the ball into his glove angrily" but then "cups his hand, making a megaphone out of it and announces . . . 'Attention, ladeees and gentlemen! Today's game will be delayed because of my Aunt Blanche's headache'" This humor provokes a smile or chuckle rather than a guffaw; it directs warm and sentimental feelings back toward the character. While there are many one-liners in *Brighton Beach Memoirs*, they come after the tone of the play has been set and are absorbed by the play's emphasis on character development and narrative.

Building on the more delicate seriousness achieved in *Chapter Two*, *Brighton Beach Memoirs* displays a Simon capable of creating moments of genuine tenderness, as in the scene between Laurie and Nora that begins with "Oh, God, I wish Daddy were alive" and ends with the image of Nora searching the deceased father's coat pocket for her usual gift. Many critics responded appreciatively, lauding Simon's new direction. For others, however, the overall effect of the play was still sentimental rather than convincingly serious. Blanche's fear of intimacy after the death of her husband was easily resolved, for example, and Eugene's obsession with sex, although cute, was hardly profound.

BILOXI BLUES

First produced: 1984 (first published, 1986)
Type of work: Play

Eugene Jerome emerges from his time in the Army emotionally and sexually mature and already started on his writing career.

The second play in Simon's autobiographical trilogy, *Biloxi Blues* continues the saga of Eugene Jerome's coming-of-age as he survives ten weeks of Army basic training in 1943. The play opens in a railroad carriage as five draftees travel south toward the Army base in Biloxi. Eugene introduces each character to the audience by reading from the "memoir" in which he records his thoughts—throughout the play, Eugene comments on the action by speaking directly to the audience.

The scene shifts to a barracks, where a drill sergeant introduces the crew to military discipline by finding arbitrary reasons for ordering them to perform one hundred push-ups and forcing them to down every morsel of unappetizing food. Simon uses humor to make serious points. Admitting the need for strict discipline, he remarks: "If nobody obeys orders, I'll bet we wouldn't have more that twelve or thirteen soldiers fighting the war.... We'd have headlines like, 'Corporal Stanley Lieberman invades Sicily.'"

More than in previous plays, Simon explores significant themes. Eugene and his fellow Jew, Arnold Epstein, encounter prejudice and endure anti-Semitic remarks. When a fellow soldier is arrested for engaging in homosexual activity, the rest of the squad expresses compassion over his probable prison sentence (perhaps unrealistically, considering the prevalent homophobia of the 1940's). The soldiers at first believe that Epstein is the guilty homosexual, having read Eugene's memoir in which he speculated about Epstein's sexuality. Eugene is left feeling guilty for writing down his suspicions. He learns the difference between sex and love during a weekend leave at the close of his training. In one scene, he clumsily engages in sex for the first time with a prostitute. In another, he meets a beautiful, literate, and witty southern belle at a dance, falls in love, and decides that loveless sex is flavorless.

The central theme of the three autobiographical plays is Eugene's maturation into a successful writer. At the start of *Biloxi Blues*, he blithely records his observations and thoughts in his memoir, oblivious of the possible consequences of the act. The dismay of his barracks mates when they discover his notebook demonstrates that words have the power to hurt. The reaction of the squad to his suspicions about Epstein brings recognition that anything written down magically acquires an aura of reality. Epstein's rebuke, when Eugene tears up the offending page, that compromising one's beliefs is the road to mediocrity, reinforces the message—a responsible writer thinks and gets it right the first time.

In the closing scene of the play, the squad is once again in a railroad car, leaving Biloxi for war

service. Eugene's final remarks to the audience describe the later experience of the characters. He never saw battle. Injured in an accident in England, Eugene was assigned to the *Stars and Stripes* soldiers' newspaper. At war's end, he is well on his way to becoming a professional writer, aware of his career's ethical responsibilities.

LOST IN YONKERS

First produced: 1991 (first published, 1991)
Type of work: Play

Two young boys spend ten months in the care of a strict grandmother, who dominates a severely dysfunctional family.

The year is 1942; the scene is the living and dining rooms of Grandma Kurnitz's apartment above Kurnitz's Kandy Store in Yonkers, New York. Two young boys, Jay and Arty, wait in the living room while their father, Eddie, asks Grandma in her bedroom to take the boys for a year; he needs to travel to earn money and repay loan sharks from whom he borrowed to pay for his dead wife's cancer treatment.

The boys fear their grandmother, who walks with a limp, her foot having been crippled during an anti-Semitic demonstration in her native Germany. She is convinced that only hardness can succeed in the world, and her sternness in raising her four surviving children has psychologically damaged them. Eddie trembles in fear when he speaks to her. Another son, Louie, has become a small-time gangster and is hiding from his associates in his mother's apartment. Daughter Bella is mentally retarded. Gert gasps for breath when she talks to her mother.

The passage of time is indicated by blackouts during which Eddie reads letters to his sons describing his travels across the South dealing in scrap iron needed for the war effort. Act 1, after establishing the psychological problems of the characters, ends with a voice-over in which Eddie tells the boys how pleased he is that they are safe in the care of his family.

Simon mines humor from the play's grimness. Critic David Richards remarked that, "Were it not for his ready wit and his appreciation of life's incongruities, *Lost in Yonkers* could pass for a nightmare." Uncle Louie praises his mother's stoicism, noting that, although her injured foot aches constantly, she will not even take aspirin to ease the pain. Simon gets a surefire laugh when Arty later tells his brother, "I'm afraid of her, Jay. A horse fell on her when she was a kid and she hasn't taken an aspirin yet."

The dramatic center of the play is Bella's struggle to find emotional support and fashion a life of her own, despite opposition from her mother and the incomprehension of her siblings. Bella appears a comic figure as she tells her relatives around the dinner table that she has met a similarly retarded usher at a movie theater and that the two plan to marry and open a restaurant. Louie mockingly asks whether what the usher really wants is her money, but Simon abruptly stops the audience's laughter when Bella cries "He wants *me*! He wants to marry me!" Grandma does not deign to respond, but silently rises and goes to her bedroom.

Louie advances Bella money to open a restaurant, but her boyfriend proves too timid to leave the safety of his parents' home, and her plan fails. At play's end, when Eddie returns from his travels to reclaim the boys, Bella is still living with her mother, but she establishes some independence by inviting newfound friends to dinner.

Lost in Yonkers won a Tony Award for best play. Although Simon believed that his reputation as a comedy writer precluded his ever being given a Pulitzer Prize, the play also won the 1991 award for drama. Many critics consider this powerful dark comedy to be Simon's masterpiece.

SUMMARY

Simon has always been able to make audiences laugh, although it has been debated whether he is more than a gag writer, a creator of situation comedies for the stage. *Chapter Two*, the three plays of his Brighton Beach trilogy, and *Lost in Yonkers* have wrested additional respect from most, though not all, critics. Audiences, on the other hand, have been markedly less critical, usually flocking to Simon plays regardless of the level of seriousness he achieves. While it is not yet appropriate to place Simon in the company of Shakespeare, Moliere, or Shaw, his is no small achievement: to have become the most commercially successful playwright in the history of theater.

Terry Nienhuis; updated by Milton Berman

BIBLIOGRAPHY

By the Author

DRAMA:

Come Blow Your Horn, pr. 1960, pb. 1961
Little Me, pr. 1962, revised pr. 1982 (music by Cy Coleman, lyrics by Carol Leigh; adaptation of Patrick Dennis's novel)
Barefoot in the Park, pr. 1963, pb. 1964
The Odd Couple, pr. 1965, pb. 1966
Sweet Charity, pr., pb. 1966 (music and lyrics by Coleman and Dorothy Fields; adaptation of Federico Fellini's film *Nights of Cabiria*)
The Star-Spangled Girl, pr. 1966, pb. 1967
Plaza Suite, pr. 1968, pb. 1969
Promises, Promises, pr. 1968, pb. 1969 (music and lyrics by Hal David and Burt Bacharach; adaptation of Billy Wilder and I. A. L. Diamond's film *The Apartment*)
Last of the Red Hot Lovers, pr. 1969, pb. 1970
The Gingerbread Lady, pr. 1970, pb. 1971
The Comedy of Neil Simon, pb. 1971 (volume 1 in *The Collected Plays of Neil Simon*)
The Prisoner of Second Avenue, pr., pb. 1971
The Sunshine Boys, pr. 1972, pb. 1973
The Good Doctor, pr. 1973, pb. 1974 (adaptation of Anton Chekhov's short stories)

God's Favorite, pr. 1974, pb. 1975 (adaptation of the story of Job)
California Suite, pr. 1976, pb. 1977
Chapter Two, pr. 1977, pb. 1979
They're Playing Our Song, pr. 1978, pb. 1980 (music by Marvin Hamlisch, lyrics by Carole Bayer Sager; adaptation of Dennis's novel)
The Collected Plays of Neil Simon, pb. 1979 (volume 2)
I Ought to Be in Pictures, pr. 1980, pb. 1981
Fools, pr., pb. 1981
Brighton Beach Memoirs, pr. 1982, pb. 1984
Biloxi Blues, pr. 1984, pb. 1986
The Odd Couple, pr. 1985, pb. 1986 (female version)
Broadway Bound, pr. 1986, pb. 1987
Rumors, pr. 1988, pb. 1990
Jake's Women, pr. 1990, pb. 1991
Lost in Yonkers, pr., pb. 1991
The Collected Plays of Neil Simon, pb. 1991 (volume 3)
Laughter on the 23rd Floor, pr. 1993, pb. 1995
London Suite, pr. 1994, pb. 1996
Three from the Stage, pb. 1995
Proposals, pr. 1997, pb. 1998
The Collected Plays of Neil Simon, pb. 1998 (volume 4)
The Dinner Party, pr. 2000, pb. 2002
45 Seconds from Broadway, pr. 2001, pb. 2003
Oscar and Felix: A New Look at the Odd Couple, pr. 2002, pb. 2004
Rose's Dilemma, pr. 2003, pb. 2004

SCREENPLAYS:
After the Fox, 1966 (with Cesare Zavattini)
Barefoot in the Park, 1967
The Odd Couple, 1968
The Out-of-Towners, 1970
Plaza Suite, 1971
The Last of the Red Hot Lovers, 1972
The Heartbreak Kid, 1972
The Prisoner of Second Avenue, 1975
The Sunshine Boys, 1975
Murder by Death, 1976
The Goodbye Girl, 1977
California Suite, 1978
The Cheap Detective, 1978
Chapter Two, 1979
Seems Like Old Times, 1980
Only When I Laugh, 1981
I Ought to Be in Pictures, 1982
Max Dugan Returns, 1983
The Lonely Guy, 1984
The Slugger's Wife, 1985
Brighton Beach Memoirs, 1987

DISCUSSION TOPICS

- What characteristics distinguished Neil Simon's early plays?

- How did Simon become the most successful playwright in the history of the American theater?

- How did the Brighton Beach trilogy enhance Simon's reputation?

- Why do critics consider *Lost in Yonkers* to be superior to Simon's previous plays?

- Simon has speculated that some day his plays might be compared to the comedies of William Shakespeare and George Bernard Shaw. How do you think they compare?

- Compare Simon to other playwrights with whose works you are familiar.

Neil Simon

Biloxi Blues, 1988
The Marrying Man, 1991
Lost in Yonkers, 1993
The Odd Couple II, 1998

TELEPLAYS:
Broadway Bound, 1992
Jake's Women, 1996
London Suite, 1996
The Sunshine Boys, 1997
Laughter on the 23rd Floor, 2001
The Goodbye Girl, 2004

NONFICTION:
Rewrites: A Memoir, 1996
The Play Goes On: A Memoir, 1999

About the Author

Henry, William A., III. "Reliving a Poignant Past." *Time* 128 (December 15, 1986): 72-78.

Johnson, Robert K. *Neil Simon.* Boston: Twayne, 1983.

Konas, Gary, ed. *Neil Simon: A Casebook.* New York: Garland, 1997.

Koprince, Susan. *Understanding Neil Simon.* Columbia: University of South Carolina Press, 2002.

McGovern, Edythe M. *Neil Simon: A Critical Study.* New York: Frederick Ungar, 1979.

Meryman, Richard. "When the Funniest Writer in America Tried to Be Serious." *Life* 70 (May 7, 1971): 60-83.

Richards, David. "The Last of the Red Hot Playwrights." *The New York Times Magazine,* February 17, 1991, 30-32, 36, 57, 64.

UPTON SINCLAIR

Born: Baltimore, Maryland
September 20, 1878
Died: Bound Brook, New Jersey
November 25, 1968

One of the most prolific and socially engaged writers of the first half of the twentieth century, Sinclair is remembered as the chronicler of American conscience toward big business and the working class.

Library of Congress

BIOGRAPHY

Born in a boardinghouse in Baltimore, young Sinclair grew up in poverty. In compensation, he was sent to live for months with rich uncles. Their endless snobbery and flaunted wealth outraged Sinclair, who, at the end of his life, wrote in *The Autobiography of Upton Sinclair* (1962) that everything in his later life confirmed his resolve never to sell out to that class. Aided by phenomenal memory, at the age of five he taught himself to read, devouring whole libraries. Later he maintained that it was Charles Dickens and William Makepeace Thackeray who molded his instinct for social justice. At fourteen, he entered City College (now the City College of New York), reading all textbooks in the first few weeks, after which he stayed home and read that which really interested him. At that time he discovered Percy Bysshe Shelley, not the Romantic poet from the canonized literary history but the Romantic revolutionary and anarchist, a utopian rebel and nonconformist. The utopian ardor and idealism that characterize Sinclair's life and work would soon find the means to achieve his vision of universal social justice in socialism.

Learning that a classmate had a story published, young Sinclair immediately penned one of his own, selling it to *Argosy*, one of the United States' most prestigious magazines. At the age of fifteen, he found himself supporting his parents by writing ethnic jokes, short fiction, children's stories, and

sketches. By 1897, upon entering graduate studies in literature and philosophy at Columbia, Sinclair was already one of the most successful "hack" writers in history, contributing full time to magazines and writing prolifically seven days a week. It is estimated that in the first two years alone, he contributed magazine material in excess of two million words, all while writing a novel a week, taking graduate courses, and teaching himself German, French, and Italian.

In April, 1900, tired of writing potboilers, Sinclair felt ready to take on serious matters: not yet the oppression of the proletariat and political corruption but the literary establishment. He went to Canada and, in a small cabin in the woods, composed *Springtime and Harvest* (1901), rewriting it in his head until he was ready to put it to paper. It was at this point that Upton Beall Sinclair, Jr., became Upton Sinclair. In 1900, he also got married: Because he was sexually and emotionally inexperienced, he did not find happiness until his second and third marriages. His first "serious" novels were all flops, yet his zeal for literature and social reform never flagged, as documented in one of his key essays, "My Cause," published in 1903 by the *Independent*. "My Cause" was a declaration of literary independence and an attack on social conditions which prevented young writers from achieving artistic maturity. In 1906, the year of the book publication of *The Jungle*, the author—reflecting on his earlier essay "My Cause"—concluded that his error lay in supposing that it is literature that makes life, rather than the other way around.

At twenty-four, Sinclair became a dedicated socialist. His cheerful manner and all-American pragmatism belied the caricatures of bearded malcontents who made bombs and free love, anarchists bent on destroying the American way of life, lazy foreigners who infiltrated the workforce, or evil communists underneath the socialist veneer—all caricatures typical of contemporary press. At around that time, the leading "slick" magazine, *McClure*, set the muckraking (investigating journalism) precedent in a widely read editorial that defined its enemy as "The American Contempt of Law." Attuned to the pulse of contemporary life, Sinclair seized the opportunity offered him by the largest socialist newspaper, *The Appeal to Reason*. In 1904, it reported on a brutally crushed strike against meatpackers, and, because Sinclair wrote previously on slavery, the editors asked him to pen something about industrial wage slavery. Armed with a small advance, he went to Chicago for seven weeks in order to research the horrors of the stockyards. *The Jungle*, released in 1904 in serialized form and in 1906 as a significantly self-censored book, changed literary and social history.

Sinclair was always skinny, always a bookworm, and always beset by stomach problems, leading him to experiment with eccentric diets and causing derision by political foes during his 1934 EPIC (End Poverty in California) campaign for the governorship of California. Running as a Democrat, he came within inches of victory, losing only when President Franklin Delano Roosevelt betrayed him in order to boost his own New Deal. Already famous for a series of hard-hitting best sellers, including *King Coal* (1917), *Oil! A Novel* (1927), and *Boston* (1928, on the Sacco-Vanzetti case), Sinclair went back to fiction. In 1938, he released *Little Steel*, and in 1940, *World's End*, a novel that launched an immensely successful eleven-book cycle united by the protagonist Lanny Budd; the third book in the series, *Dragon's Teeth*, published in 1942, got the Pulitzer Prize in 1943. A tireless self-promoter, even though he had many opportunities to become rich, Sinclair was forever committed to improving the lot of common men and women. Leaving Pasadena in 1953, he moved to rural Arizona, from where, after another fifteen years of essayistic and social activism, he returned to New England, where he died at the age of ninety.

ANALYSIS

In the first half of the twentieth century, Upton Sinclair was the United States' most important writer. He was not necessarily the best, in the sense of leaving the most enduring and aesthetically accomplished body of literature. However, he was more responsible than most for changing the way in which Americans saw themselves, their lives, and their expectations of these lives.

When Sinclair was starting out, few basic rights existed for Americans: no minimum wage, no maximum working hours, no employer liability for accidents, no right to bargain collectively, no pure food and drug act, no strong unions, no voting rights for women, no birth control or venereal disease education, no health insurance, no unemployment compensation, no provisions against price fixing, and no supervision of financial institutions such as banks, stock exchanges, or insurance companies. These are only some of the domains in which Sinclair's writing and tireless public campaigning brought about reform. Despite initial fame and notoriety, Sinclair's reputation has declined since his heyday, although it was revived briefly in 1988 and again in 2003 with the release and then re-release of the lost first edition of *The Jungle*. A brief survey of the criticisms that have dogged his career helps cast them in proper light as well as illuminate his body of work.

The most common censure is that Sinclair is not a litterateur but rather a muckraking journalist or, at best, a social chronicler of American life. As if to make the point, his writings have been taught in literature as often as in sociology, history, political science, and economics. If anything, however, that merely testifies to his literary range and power. Journalistic and historical veracity are fitting companions for literature that aims to reflect and engage contemporary affairs. Even though the label "nonfiction novel" had to wait until Truman Capote's *In Cold Blood* (1965), Sinclair's prose proves simply that he was ahead of his time. Indeed, his journalistic and historical descriptions of the inner workings of social groups, the public arena, or industrial practices are often among his best prose (though their factual accuracy was occasionally called into question).

Much debate of Sinclair's literary merit has centered on socialism and whether it brands him as too ideologically foreign and immersed in revolutionary politics to be a good writer. On inspection, however, there is nothing foreign or revolutionary about the themes and issues in his novels. From *The Jungle* to *King Coal* to *Oil! A Novel*, Sinclair's brand of *litterature engagé* aims to refurbish the homegrown socioeconomic system, making his brand of socialism akin to Benjamin Franklin's homegrown, commonsense, liberal pragmatism. Indeed, Jurgis's can-do refrain from *The Jungle*, "I will work harder," is Horatio Alger and the rags-to-riches work ethic writ large, albeit cast in ironic light. Social and political activism, in fact, allows Sinclair to break away from the conventions of literary naturalism and, consequently, from the bleak negativity of Theodore Dreiser or Stephen Crane. Instead of existential and socioeconomic determinism (if not Darwinism), Sinclair dishes out solutions to well-defined social problems, often with a view to a broader and, ultimately, more complex picture of society.

Sinclair's prose has often been maligned as simplistic and repetitive. Indeed, next to high modernism that swept the United States following the 1913 New York Armory Show, his novels are linear and stylistically conservative, free of experiments in point of view or prosody characteristic of William Faulkner or John Dos Passos. Instead of self-reflexive modernistic high jinks, the narration is fast-paced and plot-oriented, with characterization playing second fiddle to an encyclopedia of background detail. Though in a 1951 letter to poet William Carlos Williams, Sinclair defended himself by saying that the goal of writing is never to make communication difficult, in truth, his style is at best uneven. He is capable of rich passages of camera-eye ethnographic detail, such as in the *veselija* (wedding) from the opening of *The Jungle*. He is capable of arresting minimalist impact, such as in the scenes from the working life in Packingtown. Yet, more often than not, these are interspersed with sentimental melodrama and overt commentary that threaten to overwhelm a work of literature with the ardor of a political pamphlet. This uneven quality owes much to his speed of composition and the almost superhuman volume of output (there are nine tons of papers in the Sinclair Collection at the University of Indiana alone, including a quarter million letters).

One of Sinclair's notable shortcomings is characterization. The writer who wanted to record the whole truth about the human condition frequently peopled his books with little attention to human depth and emotional development. Plot-driven and brimming with real-life issues, Sinclair's focus is clearly on ideas and principles and not on the nuances of people's inner lives. It is a different story, however, to indict his characters for being low and contemptible. True to Ralph Waldo Emerson's call for an artistic mirror to all aspects of American life, Sinclair's meat packers and oil-field roustabouts are wrought with the same loving detail and symbolic bravura as the democratic snapshots of America crafted by Walt Whitman.

Incited by his lifelong reformist zeal, Sinclair's writings have also been criticized as a species of social and cultural propaganda. Taking sides, for example by clearly identifying speakers for noble and progressivist ideas, his narratives return time and again to contrasts between classes, social iniquities, political corruption, and abuses of power by Big Business. His favorite structural device is to introduce characters from both social worlds, the rich and the poor, with plots contrived to carry the reader from one to the other. However, any common definition of propaganda subsumes most forms of art. Sinclair understood this point, arguing that all literature is propaganda in the sense of being written to affect what readers think. His critics would reply that good literature conveys ideological truths through the totality of the work and preferably through characters in action, rather than authorial remonstrations, however poignant.

THE JUNGLE

First published: 1906
Type of work: Novel

Jurgis Rudkos and his family of Lithuanian immigrants exchange the American Dream for a life-and-death struggle in the industrial jungle of Chicago stockyards.

The abuses in the meatpacking industry were known before the publication of *The Jungle*. In the 1898 intervention in Cuba, some three thousand American soldiers died from eating canned beef, and (soon to be President) Theodore Roosevelt himself testified against the Beef Trust. The Hearst newspapers brought about a Senate investigation, and there were several muckraking exposés, but little changed until Sinclair's fateful trip to Chicago to observe immigrant workers at work. Although he had little interest in them as immigrants, Sinclair's descriptions of their customs, mentality, and behavior are some of the best in American letters. Similarly, he had little interest as such in attacking the beef industry. He dedicated the novel "To the Workingmen of America," underscoring his goal of improving their overall conditions rather than exposing the filth prevailing in the country's slaughterhouses. After the sensational success of *The Jungle*—in London, Winston Churchill penned a glowing review article—Sinclair avowed that he aimed at the public's heart and accidentally hit it in the stomach.

Between the opening chapter of an ethnic wedding and the closing scenes of a political rally, the novel traces more than two years in the life of a newly arrived Lithuanian immigrant family. Lured by the advertising blitz that promised them the American Dream, they instead suffer almost unbearable exploitations and deprivations at the hands of unscrupulous lawyers, shysters, judges, police, and Packingtown bosses. Working their hands to the bone, they gradually lose their house, jobs, livelihood, and dignity to layoffs, malnutrition, industrial accidents, prostitution, and for some, even death.

Most of the story centers on the newlywed Jurgis. At the outset, he is healthy, optimistic, and fired up with confidence in his ability to earn a living and prove a model worker. Halfway through, having lost his job, health, family, and hope, in a poignant epiphany he sees himself as a squealing hog led to slaughter, one among thousands fed into the industrial machine on the conveyer belt of systematic exploitation. Toward the end, having gotten out of the Midwest and traveled as a hobo throughout the land like a character out of a Jack London story, Jurgis returns north to discover the precepts of socialism and the brotherhood of

working-class organizers. It is at this point that Sinclair's hard-hitting and starkly mesmerizing book loses much of its narrative momentum, getting bogged down in a series of ill-masked exhortations of socialism.

Although Sinclair had to tone down the book version in a number of ways, he preserved the material relating to the unhygienic and corrupt practices on the slaughterhouse floor, much as the telling alliteration of the meatpacking moguls (Anderson, Smith, and Morton stand for the real-life meatpacking firms of Armour, Swift, and Morris). Once released, the novel became widely popular; a nationwide scandal erupted overnight, so much so that a popular song changed into: "Mary had a little lamb/ And when she saw it sicken/ She shipped it off to Packingtown/ And now it's labeled chicken." Riding the wave of disgust and media-fanned protests, Sinclair ended up being invited to the White House, where the groundwork was laid for the 1906 Pure Food and Drug Act and Meat Inspection Act. By the early twenty-first century, *The Jungle* had almost eight hundred different editions in some fifty languages, cementing Sinclair's reputation as one of the most distinguished literary figures of the early twentieth century.

Oil! A Novel

First published: 1927
Type of work: Novel

Bunny Ross, son of an oil magnate, grows up to be a socialist millionaire while his childhood friend, Paul Watkins, becomes a labor strike leader.

Oil! was to the California oil boom what *The Jungle* was to the Chicago stockyards: a chance for Sinclair to present, as he quipped, human nature laid bare. The first major American novel on the oil industry, this minor epic is a hard-nosed, hard-hitting docket of corporate machinations, in striking ways describing the United States today as much as during the Jazz Age. The Harding administration and the Teapot Dome scandals were the direct catalysts for Sinclair's reformist passion, and his exposé of bribery, corruption, appalling industrial practices, and dog-eat-dog economic warfare had lost nothing of its edge decades later. However, unlike the unremitting squalor of Packingtown and its wage slaves, *Oil!* is set in sunny, breezy Southern California and narrated in a brisk and lively style punctuated up by the Roaring Twenties slang and jitterbug energy.

Through a coming-of-age (*Bildungsroman*) story of two boys (later young men), Sinclair contrasts the scorched-earth, laissez-faire capitalism with the romanticized universal panacea for proletarian suffrage—socialism. In an effort to eschew one-sidedness and stereotyping, the author not only focuses on the family of an oil magnate but also takes pains to develop members of the Ross household as full characters with their own principles, troubles, and even virtues. Although the novel was censured

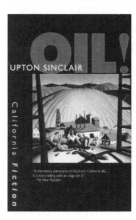

and even censored for references to birth control, its real focus is independent operators struggling against the oil monopoly. Against the background of the first two and one-half decades of the century, punctuated by the turmoil of World War I, the book climaxes with Paul's death, leaving Bunny a wiser, though not necessarily fully matured, hero.

Widely regarded as one of Sinclair's best works, *Oil!* contains many autobiographical elements, such as Bunny's failed efforts at establishing a socialist commune. Descriptions of corporate greed and venality of the media on one hand, and taboo subjects such as abortion and birth control on the other, give this racy and colorful work the sweep of a hot-off-the-press best seller. Between oil tycoons, bankers, independent developers, union and strike leaders, oilfield workers (not all of them admirable), Bolsheviks, silent-era Hollywood stars, characters from the automobile and youth culture, and even a fire-and-brimstone evangelist, *Oil!* has the kind of flair that would later land Sinclair Lewis the first American Nobel Prize in Literature in 1930.

SUMMARY

In 1932, writers and scholars from more than fifty countries signed a petition to nominate Upton Sinclair for the Nobel Prize in Literature. Although unsuccessful, the campaign reflected the international consensus that, at his prime, he was the voice of America. During his long career, literary and political luminaries such as Robert McNamara, Norman Mailer, Allen Ginsberg, Walter Cronkite, Bertolt Brecht, Theodore Roosevelt, Franklin Delano Roosevelt, John F. Kennedy, Leon Trotsky, George Bernard Shaw, Charlie Chaplin, Albert Einstein, Jack London, Sinclair Lewis, and scores of others cited him as a source of inspiration. His commitment to literature in the service of society was, perhaps, best summed up by McNamara, secretary of defense in the 1960's, who said that Sinclair influenced his thinking by identifying many of the problems which, unresolved even in modern times, continued to divide the nation.

Peter Swirski

BIBLIOGRAPHY

By the Author

LONG FICTION:
Springtime and Harvest, 1901
Prince Hagen, 1903
The Journal of Arthur Stirling, 1903
Manassas, 1904 (revised as *Theirs Be the Guilt,* 1959)
The Jungle, 1906
A Captain of Industry, 1906
The Overman, 1907
The Metropolis, 1908

The Moneychangers, 1908
Samuel the Seeker, 1910
Love's Pilgrimage, 1911
Sylvia, 1913
Sylvia's Marriage, 1914
King Coal, 1917
Jimmie Higgins, 1919
100%, 1920
They Call Me Carpenter, 1922
Oil! A Novel, 1927
Boston, 1928
Mountain City, 1930
Roman Holiday, 1931
The Wet Parade, 1931
Co-op, 1936
The Flivver King, 1937
No Pasaran!, 1937
Little Steel, 1938
Our Lady, 1938
World's End, 1940
Between Two Worlds, 1941
Dragon's Teeth, 1942
Wide Is the Gate, 1943
Presidential Agent, 1944
Dragon Harvest, 1945
A World to Win, 1946
Presidential Mission, 1947
One Clear Call, 1948
O Shepherd, Speak!, 1949
Another Pamela: Or, Virtue Still Rewarded, 1950
The Return of Lanny Budd, 1953
What Didymus Did, 1954
It Happened to Didymus, 1958
Affectionately Eve, 1961

DRAMA:
Plays of Protest, pb. 1912
Hell: A Verse Drama and Photo-Play, pb. 1923
The Millennium, pb. 1924
The Pot Boiler, pb. 1924
Singing Jailbirds, pb. 1924
Bill Porter, pb. 1925
Wally for Queen!, pb. 1936
Marie Antoinette, pb. 1939
A Giant's Strength, pr., pb. 1948

NONFICTION:
Our Bourgeois Literature, 1904
The Industrial Republic, 1907
The Fasting Cure, 1911
The Profits of Religion, 1918

DISCUSSION TOPICS

- Upton Sinclair dedicated *The Jungle* "To the Workingmen of America." How does this dedication reflect his attitudes in other novels?

- A fierce fighter for women's rights, Sinclair rarely created memorable female characters. Do you find that this detracts from his attempt to portray a full picture of society?

- What journalistic or muckraking (investigative) aspects are prominent in Sinclair's art?

- Sinclair is admired for his fine detail of ethnic customs, traditions, and other aspects of immigrant life. Can you identify such passages and analyze their literary technique?

- Does Sinclair aim to shock and scandalize or rather portray the people and events in a truthful, albeit unflinching, light?

- Some of Sinclair's fictions resulted in changes to American laws and customs. Can you think of other writers whose works had such impact on the country?

The Brass Check: A Study in American Journalism, 1919
The Book of Life, Mind, and Body, 1921
The Goose-Step: A Study of American Education, 1923
The Goslings: A Study of the American Schools, 1924
Mammonart, 1925
Letters to Judd, 1925
Money Writes!, 1927
Mental Radio, 1930
American Outpost: A Book of Reminiscences, 1932
I, Governor of California, and How I Ended Poverty, 1933
The Way Out—What Lies Ahead for America?, 1933
The EPIC Plan for California, 1934
I, Candidate for Governor, and How I Got Licked, 1935
What God Means to Me, 1936
Terror in Russia: Two Views, 1938
Expect No Peace!, 1939
A Personal Jesus, 1952
The Cup of Fury, 1956
My Lifetime in Letters, 1960
The Autobiography of Upton Sinclair, 1962

CHILDREN'S LITERATURE:
The Gnomobile: A Gnice Gnew Gnarrative with Gnonsense, but Gnothing Gnaughty, 1936

About the Author

Bloodworth, William A. *Upton Sinclair.* Boston: Twayne, 1977.

Bloom, Harold. *Upton Sinclair's "The Jungle."* Philadelphia: Chelsea House, 2002.

Harris, Leon. *Upton Sinclair: An American Rebel.* New York: Thomas Y. Crowell, 1975.

Mookerjee, Babindra Nath. *Art for Social Justice: The Major Novels of Upton Sinclair.* Metuchen, N.J.: Scarecrow, 1988.

Sinclair, Upton. *The Autobiography of Upton Sinclair.* New York: Harcourt, Brace and World, 1962.

_____. *I, Candidate for Governor and How I Got Licked.* 1935. Reprint. Berkeley: University of California Press, 1994.

_____. *The Jungle: The Uncensored Original Edition.* With an introduction by Kathleen De Grave. Tucson, Ariz.: Sharp Press, 2003.

Yoder, Jon A. *Upton Sinclair.* New York: Ungar, 1975.

JANE SMILEY

Born: Los Angeles, California
September 26, 1949

Smiley applies both tragic and comic lenses to dissect the impact of desire, egotism, and greed upon American middle-class domesticity and the attendant health of the larger social and natural order.

BIOGRAPHY

Jane Graves Smiley was born in Los Angeles on September 26, 1949, during her father's military tour of duty. Parents James La Verne Smiley and Frances Graves Nuelle soon returned to their Midwest origins, and although Jane did not grow up on a working farm, she claims deep "roots in rural country." After a childhood spent in St. Louis, Missouri, she attended Vassar College and in 1971 received a B.A. in English following completion of her first novel, done as a senior thesis. Subsequently she earned a master of fine arts degree (1976) as well as an M.A. and Ph.D. in medieval literature (1978), all from the University of Iowa. A Fulbright Fellowship to Iceland (1976-1977) enabled Smiley to transform her graduate study of Norse sagas into *The Greenlanders* (1988), an epic novel of fourteenth century Scandinavian pioneers. Grants from the National Endowment for the Arts (NEA) supported her writing in 1978 and 1987. From 1981 through 1996 she taught literature and creative writing at Iowa State University in Ames, with stints as a visiting professor at the University of Iowa in 1981 and 1987.

Having begun her publishing career in 1980 with *Barn Blind*, Smiley had seen two more novels to press (*At Paradise Gate* in 1981 and *Duplicate Keys* in 1984) by the time critical praise for her work intensified with the appearance of *The Age of Grief* (1987), a collection of short fiction nominated for the National Book Critics Circle Award. It was followed by an acclaimed pair of novellas published together as *"Ordinary Love" and "Good Will"* (1989). With the novel *A Thousand Acres* (1991), Smiley won the 1991 National Book Critics Circle Award and the 1992 Pulitzer Prize in fiction. The commercial success of that work, along with the sale of film rights (for an adaptation of the same title released in 1997) enabled Smiley to leave Iowa State in 1996 and establish a horse farm in Northern California, where she breeds and trains Thoroughbreds—a change in venue she subsequently mined as subject matter for two horse-centered texts, the novel *Horse Heaven* (2000) and the memoir *A Year at the Races* (2004).

Smiley has suggested that the dominant themes of her early work—"sex and apocalypse"—derived from a childhood shadowed by the atomic bomb and an adolescence informed by "the Pill." Her strong feminist convictions have fed a belief that, because "the personal is political. . . [e]ach household is a manifestation of a political, economic and cultural system" that becomes one's subtext in every fiction about family life. Accordingly, her own adult family history regularly feeds her published nonfictional ruminations on American cultural change. A first marriage, in 1970 to John Whiston, ended in 1975. Her second marriage, to William Silag, lasted from 1978 to 1986 and produced daughters Phoebe and Lucy. During a third marriage, to Stephen Mark Mortensen from 1987 to 1997, son A. J. was born.

Yet Smiley resists the diagnosis of cultural crisis

often accompanying laments about the "break-down of the traditional family." Rather, as she explains in "Why Marriage," consciously choosing to resist the lure of another marriage and "forswear fidelity [to a new lover] is to open yourself up to other ideas, other thoughts, about what love is, what desire is, what happiness is, and what commitment is." Such willingness to learn "by experience how to express love" and its attendant emotions—"Compassion, tenderness, patience, responsibility, kindness, and honesty"—actually sustains rather than subverts the quest for meaningful webs of human connection, whatever labels one gives them.

Clearly, Smiley regards her experiences as woman, lover, and mother as important influences on her literary imagination. Having begun her career as a "devoted modernist" infatuated with the nihilistic vision of early twentieth century literature, she found herself losing that alienated edge during her first pregnancy and took as a personal mission the challenge of answering the skeptics' question, "Can mothers think and write?" Smiley proudly joins other contemporary women writers who have documented the recesses of female subjectivity—including the paradoxes of sexual desire and maternity.

In the 1990's, her convictions about the social responsibility of the writer took on new urgency in the aftermath of the 1993 Oklahoma City bombing, where ideologically driven violence horrifically underscored escalating societal schisms and inequities. Taking her lead from "The great writers: Dickens, George Eliot, [Virginia] Woolf, Tolstoy, Dostoyevsky, Homer, not a single one [of whom] failed to engage," Smiley flatly asserts that "Every novel I write is political. . . . Your political views and your moral views connect you in a responsible way to other people, to society." This attitude explains the sharpening of her critique of capitalism in *Moo* (1995) and *Good Faith* (2003) as the driving compulsion of American institutions at the cost of the great good of the common people and the health both of individuals and of the physical world in which they are rooted.

ANALYSIS

Smiley's ambitions for her writing are vast, even when she enacts them on a small canvas. She wants to document, in the familiar mode of literary realists, the vagaries and turmoil of the contemporary middle class, particularly as evidenced in the crucible of the family. Yet she also shares her generation's belief in the social responsibility of the writer and has increasingly used her fiction to challenge the political, economic, and cultural presumptions of American capitalism and its deformations of individual aspiration. Even her entry into the world of horse racing in *Horse Heaven* and *A Year at the Races* explores her characteristic concern with the mysteries of personality—equine as well as human—caught in the uncompromising grip of the profit motive.

Smiley's fascination with the interplay of small-scale and large-scale stories of human endeavor has taken various forms over the course of her career, including a determination to produce fiction in the four primary literary modes of epic, tragedy, comedy, and romance. Each offers a different enactment of the struggle between individual and societal agendas grounded in the domestic spaces that promise a fragile refuge from the chaos of existence. Yet the coherence sought in those spaces rarely holds up under the pressure of personal desire and its disruptive impact on those around them.

In this regard, Smiley's medieval studies, given fictional expression in *The Greenlanders*, illuminate her distinctive perspective on the human condition. In that novel, characters pursue their lives within a tragic and incomprehensible universe. The steady turn of the wheel of fortune exposes the transitory nature of earthly pursuits—prosperity, power, fame, and pleasure all prove ephemeral under the yoke of human mortality. The violence, sexual betrayal, greed, and envy that human beings inflict upon themselves and others through weaknesses that they cannot conquer upend the most strenuous efforts to create social harmony, and even love proves as likely to destroy as to create.

In confronting such a world, Smiley's most admirable characters are those who, despite their limitations and failures, stumble toward a personal vision of moral responsibility and communal obligation that both enables their survival and dignifies their self-awareness. The medieval and the existential merge within characters who stoically confront their griefs—a trait that one discovers among Smiley's modern midwesterners as well, people whom she finds equally equipped to absorb disaster, commit themselves to the burdens of daily labor, and engage in serious moral examination of their lives even as they go about the epic task of building or sustaining new outposts of civilization. Not surprisingly, her signal foray into American historical fiction—*The All-True Travels and Adventures of Lidie Newton* (1998)—unfolds in "Bloody Kansas" at a critical national turning point: the eve of the Civil War, when the first armed skirmishes over the future of slavery set the terms not only for the catastrophe to come but also for the renewed democratic purpose of the nation to which it would give birth.

Yet it is also somewhat misleading to identify that work strictly in the epic vein, since Smiley herself regards it as her foray into the popular nineteenth century romance, with its picaresque expansiveness of plot and character. What one discovers in Smiley's work, in fact, is a consistent hybridity of forms where tonal complexities underscore the writer's mixed ambitions for any given narrative. The tragic underpinnings of so many of her family dramas crescendoed in *A Thousand Acres*, whose self-evident updating of William Shakespeare's *King Lear* (pr. c. 1605) in the heartland starkly distilled her well-established midwestern theme of "taking responsibility for what is going on around you." Much of her early fiction had already explored the tragic power of parents over children and the lifelong contortions that such influence can assume: The matriarchal rigidities of Kate Karlson in *Barn Blind* forecast the more terrible patriarchal violations of Larry Cook in *A Thousand Acres*, whose presumed ownership of his offspring feeds a will to power that underpins the primal transgression in Smiley's world. By linking the subordination of children and the conquest of nature quite openly in this novel, Smiley details the ecological as well as the human costs of overweening egotism and the tragic lust for dominance that it promotes. Perhaps this also clarifies her later—and far different—writings about horses, whose mysterious impenetrability defies possession of their inner lives by any "owner" and thereby puts the lie to the superiority of the human species altogether.

Moving in the mid-1990's from the grim mission of tragedy in *A Thousand Acres* to the carnivalesque tableau characterizing subsequent works such as *Moo* and *Good Faith* may seem a dramatic break from Smiley's earlier vision, but in fact it derives from that same medieval wheel of fortune, with its droll reminder of the vanity of all human wishes and the inevitability of the mighty's demise. In *Moo*, Smiley's highly popular burlesque of higher education, she sketches what reviewer Pico Iyer calls "a riotous assemblage of types as various as the Deadly Sins," language evoking medieval morality plays. In it, she set herself comedy's challenge to forge "a dagger so sharp the victim doesn't feel it going in at first, but also [remain both] acerbic and loving, [delivering] a criticism so kindly meant that the victim smiles and says, 'You're right. I must certainly change my ways.'"

Although Smiley's protagonists belong to both genders, range broadly in age (from the adolescent boys in *Barn Blind* to the Vietnam War veteran in *Good Will* to the septuagenarian grandmother in *At Paradise Gate*), and even occasionally cross the species barrier (as in *Moo* and *Horse Heaven*), the sensibility that most consistently colors her fiction is the middle-aged voice of adult experience ruefully taking stock of its shattered illusions and discovering its potential for compromise and negotiation. It is the absolutist who comes in for the harshest treatment in Smiley's work for refusing to admit that maturity demands a willingness to settle for less than one once imagined as one's due. As Rachel Kinsella, the fifty-two-year-old Iowan narrator of *Ordinary Love*, concedes, "I have learned over the last twenty years to embrace the possible and not mourn the rest."

Smiley's feminism explains her attention to the nature of power and the hierarchical valuations that it encourages within social structures ranging from the family to the state. Her novels are especially astute at capturing the inner lives of women whose subjectivity has often been assumed nonexistent simply because it has been hidden or obscured. In giving these women voice, Smiley dissects the platitudes about women's nature that obstruct their ability to see themselves clearly and live authentically. She also challenges sentimental equations of sexual desire and romantic love, creating decent women who learn, to their dismay, how easily the two may be separated.

Smiley's most significant feminist insight lies in her insistence that women take themselves seriously as moral beings responsible for their own self-definition. She exposes the attitudes and social structures that encourage women toward economic, emotional, and societal dependency and critiques the wider consequences of patriarchal assumptions: "Women, just like nature or the land, have been seen as something to be used. . . . Feminists insist that women have intrinsic value, just as environmentalists believe that nature has its own worth, independent of its use to man." Yet she does not create idealized feminist saints; her women characters include shrews, tyrants, obsessives, intellectuals, wallflowers, apologists, and airheads along with solid, matriarchal earth mothers. Moreover, she insists on the reality of women's lifelong polymorphous sexual appetites in contradiction to still-powerful models of asexualized bourgeois femininity. The result is that Smiley's work boasts as rich a collection of female personalities as exists in modern fiction.

Like her acknowledged literary model Charles Dickens, Smiley has devoted considerable ink in mapping the intricate social, economic, and political vectors shaping (and deforming) the culture around her. What unites her varied body of work is a sustained interest in the centripetal pull of the American Dream and its endlessly seductive and elusive promises: perhaps the only "good faith" (in keeping with the title of her 2003 novel) that holds the diffuse American fabric together, both in its most venal and its most transformational modes.

THE AGE OF GRIEF

First published: 1987
Type of work: Short stories

Young adults, confronting the impossible expectations surrounding love, marriage, and family, discover the compromises necessary to sustain those relationships.

The collection of short fiction entitled *The Age of Grief* presents a wide array of adults battling for and against emotional commitment. These five stories examine family life through characters on the periphery of domesticity. Because the women protagonists in "Lily" and "The Pleasure of Her Company" admire a marital realm they observe only from a distance, both prove unprepared for the disappointments that ensue. Their limited insight into human relationships results, in part, from the

absence of such entanglements in their own lives. Lily's emotional "virginity" permits her the freedom to write but also leads her to meddle unwittingly in a marriage whose compromises she has overlooked. In "The Pleasure of Her Company," Florence witnesses the dissolution of an "ideal" marriage but also rejects the cynic's dismissal of love as a delusion, pursuing her own blossoming love affair with the realist's admonition that "it's worth finding out for yourself."

Smiley also caricatures those who orchestrate their emotional lives with the same professional calculation they apply to their stock portfolios, as with the female letter-writer of "Jeffrey, Believe Me." Here the protagonist remains so intent on bearing a child before she is too old that she willfully seduces a gay male friend and callously rejects any personal responsibility for the other human beings she is exploiting. The male protagonist of "Long Distance" offers an alternative response to such narcissism: His Christmas odyssey to join his brothers for the holidays prompts a reassessment of his callousness toward a Japanese woman with whom he has had an affair. Never having acknowledged the continual negotiations at the heart of family life, he now sees the moral bankruptcy in his self-serving behavior.

In "Dynamite," a woman in early middle age juggles conflicting impulses about integrating her past lives. A radical political activist in the 1960's, Sandy has lived underground for the past twenty years. Even as she yearns to recover ties with a mother she has never truly known, she restlessly yearns "to do the most unthought-of thing, the itch to destroy what is made—the firm shape of life, whether unhappy, as it was, or happy, as it is now." Memory and fantasy weave an elaborate web of longing in her that prompts wild behavior swings and punctures the bourgeois stability that she seems, superficially, to covet. Sandy's paradoxes defy taming and make her representative of the struggle against self that is typical of Smiley's protagonists.

The volume's title novella depicts a family crisis in which a laboriously constructed normality gives way from within. The story is told in the first person by David Hurst, guardian of that normality. Father of three young daughters and a successful dentist, he sees his carefully balanced world collapse when his wife and professional partner, Dana, falls suddenly in love with another man. David struggles with how to handle his knowledge of the affair and chooses to remain silent even as it intrudes into every facet of his life. The family moves to the edge of dissolution as Dana's obsession keeps her away from home for twenty-four hours. When she finally reappears, she and David agree not to discuss what has led her to relinquish her lover and cautiously resume their marriage. With a generosity of spirit—or failure of will—steeped in profound sadness, David describes his midlife experiences as "the same cup of pain that every mortal drinks from."

"ORDINARY LOVE" AND "GOOD WILL"

First published: 1989
Type of work: Novellas

The loss of parental illusions about one's control over the family circle sparks the dubious consolation of witnessing one's children fall from innocence—and into humanity.

By placing a mother's story alongside a father's story in this volume, Smiley experiments with the differing narrative rhythms she associates with each gender. The first-person voice of *Ordinary Love* belongs to a fifty-two-year-old Iowan, a divorced mother of five grown children who typifies Smiley's clear-eyed defiance of sentimental pieties about the heartland matriarch. Rachel Kinsella's story, matter-of-factly told in a tone at once stoic and unrepentant, involves the jarring incompatibility of having proudly borne five babies in five years while married to a doting, ambitious doctor, then initiating an adulterous love affair that ruptured the family idyll so completely that even her identical twin sons were separated in ensuing custody battles. Rachel's history, an arc of emotional devastation and recovery, leads her in middle age to a maturity brought into being out of wildness, grief, and tenacity.

The novella's more immediate drama involves Rachel's effort to manage the return of one twin son, Michael, from a two-year stint in India as a teacher. In a family in which each separation reprises the traumatic earlier severance of mother from child, sibling from sibling, Michael's personal transformation overseas again exposes the instability of even the most basic human ties. Within this charged atmosphere, a series of confidences unfolds. Rachel tells her children for the first time about the love affair that disrupted their lives; her elder daughter Ellen retaliates with a description of their subsequent neglect by an irresponsible father, and Michael reveals his destructive liaison with a married woman. Meditating on these secrets, Rachel concedes that the real fruit of such knowledge lies not simply in one's own suffering but also in learning one's potential to inflict suffering on others, especially those one holds most dear. Rachel confronts the fact that she cannot spare her children the heart's perverse and unrelenting hunger for what it cannot have, a lesson she herself taught them years ago.

Good Will further demonstrates Smiley's insights into the daily struggles for psychological control underlying the surfaces of family life. Here the first-person narrative belongs to Vietnam War veteran Bob Miller, a man who has systematically created a world for his nuclear family meant to exist independently of mainstream society. The novella opens eighteen years into his counterculture experiment.

Bob's talents with his hands permit him an economic self-sufficiency meant to repudiate the empty materialism of American culture. Yet his virtues slip over into dogmatism, as he uses his ingenuity to enclose his loved ones within the range of his own authority. Ironically, the discord within Bob's self-willed paradise comes from the very people he believes to be his allies. In joining a fundamentalist religious congregation, his wife, Liz, betrays a spiritual longing that she cannot satisfy through marriage.

More sinister, and ultimately more disastrous, is the racist hostility conceived by their seven-year-old son, Tommy, for an African American schoolmate whose affluent home life focuses the boy's rage at his own marginality. His destructiveness forces his parents to confront their arrogance in assuming the right, much less the power, to control Tommy's responses to the world. To his surprise, Bob finds himself mimicking his son's emotional conflicts. Lydia Harris, the mother of Tommy's victim, proves a similar challenge to Bob's professed allegiances, with her university professorship, her elegant decorating sense, and her acceptance of life's ambiguities (her field of study is, suggestively, probability). Like Tommy, Bob struggles with the shock of seeing the limitations of his own meager existence so baldly exposed.

Bob is equally humbled by his inability to curtail Tommy's escalating violence. This failure compels ever tighter reliance on the community from which he has so aggressively distanced himself. The real target of Tommy's anger, of course, is the father who has isolated him from the world of his peers and has refused him his own choices. The boy sets in motion a grim social services machinery that slowly strips the Millers of their hard-won autonomy. Demands for reparations force the sale of their homestead and convert both adults into wage earners struggling to keep up with the expenses of apartment living. All three family members enter therapy, and the adults face the threat of further legal action for the "recklessness" that led them to cut themselves off from the networks that might have intervened to save Tommy.

As the story ends, Bob concedes the futility of his effort to keep the incoherence of human life at bay: "Let us have fragments, I say . . . and remember the vast, inhuman peace of the stars pouring across the night sky above the valley." Whether Bob will find the inner resources to withstand the future remains ambiguous, but he will no longer evade the grinding truth of Eden's evanescence or his own role as the worm at the heart of his own dreams.

A THOUSAND ACRES

First published: 1991
Type of work: Novel

The vagaries of a midwestern patriarch upend a tenuous familial equilibrium to destroy its material and spiritual moorings.

If Bob Miller must come to terms with his desire for control and the damage it wreaks, Larry Cook, the patriarch who sets in motion the tragedy of *A Thousand Acres*, reflects his opposite number: a man whose stunted interior life crashes in upon him as his family grapples with the emotional devastation he has wrought. The third-generation heir to a homestead begun in 1890 and steadily expanded to become the largest farm in the area, Cook decides suddenly to retire and to form a corporation, with his three daughters and sons-in-law as joint stockholders. Quickly bcoming a best seller, Smiley's novel secured both popular and critical acclaim; it also netted her the National Book Critics Circle Award and the 1992 Pulitzer Prize.

The obvious parallels to Shakespeare's *King Lear* contain an important difference. While the play explores the failure of filial responsibility resulting from its protagonist's moral blindness, it aligns itself ultimately with the sufferings of Lear and his youngest child, Cordelia; in contrast, Smiley emphasizes the parental betrayal of all three children and tells the tale through the first-person perspective of the eldest, Ginny. (The names of the Cook family principals echo those of the characters in the play: Larry/Lear; Ginny/Goneril; Rose/Regan; Caroline/Cordelia.) As Smiley explains, "I never bought the conventional interpretation that Goneril and Regan were completely evil. Unconsciously at first, I had reservations: this is not the whole story."

By setting her revisionist *King Lear* in the Midwest, she again brings together medieval notions of the rise and fall of kings with American assumptions of prosperity as the just reward for lifelong diligence and skill. The wheel of fortune thus meets the American Dream to produce a forceful indictment of the hubris underscoring American privilege. Larry's willful acquisition of land (in some cases through the business failures of neighbors) updates the frontier mission to conquer the wilderness and nature itself, a mission furthered into the twentieth century by aggressive farming methods meant to manage and exploit nature's force. Patriarchal egotism prompts a domination of children and landscape against which the narrative's violent backlash occurs. Ginny's retrospective commentary expresses her desire to learn exactly how the spring of tragic machinery in her family's history has been released, as well as what role she herself has played in the ensuing disaster.

Larry's decision about the farm elicits mixed responses from the extended family. For questioning his wisdom in the matter, Caroline is abruptly cut out of the picture, while her sisters' husbands leap at the chance to move into the forefront of the farm's management, and Rose sees herself as finally rewarded for years of unarticulated grievance. Ginny's usual efforts to placate and mediate fail under the pressure of her husband's excitement and her own surfacing resentments. For his part, Larry does not expect the disorientation he suffers upon relinquishing his primacy within the household and thus becomes increasingly eccentric and difficult. Following a confrontation with Rose and Ginny in which he erupts in loathing for both, he rushes off into a violent summer storm and suffers the consequences. Larry's deterioration prompts Caroline to return, but her self-righteous dismissal of her sisters' perspectives makes her appear far less noble than Shakespeare's Cordelia—at least when seen through Ginny's eyes.

Both Rose's and Ginny's marriages deteriorate, in part because of the disequilibrium introduced into their lives by Larry's action but also because of the sexually charged intrusion of a returning neighbor, Jess Clark. Based on the Gloucester subplot within *King Lear*, Harold Clark manipulates the filial loyalties of his two sons, one dutiful and dull, the other a daring rebel. Returning home to make his peace with his father and seduced by the possibility of applying his organic farming ideas to the family homestead, the prodigal son not only threatens his brother's expected patrimony but also exploits the emotional hungers of Ginny and Rose, becoming the lover of first one and then the other.

Like *King Lear*'s Edmund, Jess exacerbates the disorder set in motion by patriarchal tyranny and provides yet another locus of male exploitation within the novel. Jess's distrust of his father hardens when Harold publicly repudiates his younger son and mocks his ambitions, which he has cynically manipulated. He is, in turn, punished for his arrogance and cruelty with a blinding as gruesome as its Shakespearean model. Jess proves as destructive a presence as Larry himself, for he undermines both sisters' marriages, fuels the suicidal despair that kills one husband, and ruptures the bond between Ginny and Rose that has sustained each through a lifetime of crisis.

Rose eventually explains that her hatred of her father derives from his repeated sexual abuse of her years earlier; in response, Ginny too traumatically unearths memories of her own violation at Larry's hands. Ironically, it is Rose's determination to see Larry confront the magnitude of his sin that feeds a vindictiveness that accelerates the spectacle

of his descent—and escape—into madness. Forgiveness lies outside Rose's ken—grace evades her as it did her father, and before the book ends, her previous cancer recurs. She dies a wasting death and leaves two more motherless daughters for Ginny to raise. The homestead disappears, cannibalized by debt, the family enterprise played out.

Smiley does not, however, privilege the supposedly faithful daughter. Caroline's suit to restore her father's legal control of the farm fails, and the judge sternly rebukes her for bringing a case without legal merit. Having been preserved from the knowledge of her father's transgressions, her ignorance precludes her claims to wisdom. Nor can Caroline take comfort in her father's doting upon her; the whimsy of a madman, it exposes his confused inability to distinguish his three children from one another. He dies without even being able to recognize them.

Ginny is accorded the last word. She ends the novel living an almost anonymous life as a waitress in St. Paul and responding to the teenage angst of the nieces who now live with her—motherhood at last, but with its burdens far more real than its joys. Trying to heal and achieve some measure of self-respect, she hones a keener self-awareness than had been hers in the past. In this tragedy, then, it is not the patriarch who comes to wisdom but his orphaned eldest child, who finds herself not exactly capable of forgiveness but willing to imagine herself into the psyche of her victimizer. Such a leap of understanding appears the best that grace allows in a fallen world.

Moo

First published: 1995
Type of work: Novel

The fiscal struggles of a contemporary midwestern "multiversity" expose the competing and at times self-canceling priorities of American higher education, even as its diverse population of opportunists, idealists, and apparatchiks perform their own intricate dance of politics and personal vendettas.

Jane Smiley's exuberant satire of academe, *Moo*, showcases an antic side of her imagination that had been overshadowed by the melancholy series of family sagas that had catapulted her into literary fame over the preceding decade. With its publication, as reviewer Alison Lurie noted, Smiley cemented her stature as "the Balzac of the late twentieth century American Midwest" (though she herself might have preferred comparison to Charles Dickens, on whom she authored in 2002 a well-received critical essay for the Penguin Lives series).

Set in Iowa in academic year 1989-1990, the novel maps the personal and professional machinations of those associated with the fictional land-grant "Moo University." Smiley deftly captures the three-ring-circus quality of a large cast of characters exploiting, seducing, and sabotaging one another in a fin de siècle collision of agrarian traditionalism, postindustrial consumer capitalism, and postmodern intellectual contingency. The question "What is a university?" both literally and figuratively speaks the novel's central concern: How does disinterested and meaningful intellectual inquiry survive in a culture ever more devoted to a gospel of greed (the decade of the 1980's serving as Smiley's shorthand for that dramatic cooptation of democratic values)? Far from an ivory tower, at Smiley's Moo U the broader currents of American life—politics, economics, education, religion, and bureacracy—converge in ways that produce immediate impacts on the "real world" beyond its walls.

Smiley herself refers to the structure of *Moo*, with its myriad subplots and couplings, as "an ecosystem," a metaphor underscoring the interdependency of its various constituencies in a hivelike structure of intricate hierarchies and elaborately ritualized behaviors. The main plot complication of the narrative derives from a competing mechanistic metaphor—the hostile Governor Early's savaging of the university budget with the intent of redefining education's "investment" value in terms of its stock market variant: enhanced profit taking through maximized production, downsized efficiencies, and "customer satisfaction" replacing the "deconstructionist" anarchy that he believes to be running the show.

The resultant forced march into the lap of corporatization thus focuses the novel's most unambiguous critique. Economist Lionel Gift (Moo U's top-paid faculty member) leads the pack to this money trough, forging self-serving partnerships with shady Texas tycoon Arlen Martin, whose multinational empire employs Gift's expertise and contacts to further a plan to mine the last virgin rain forest in Costa Rica for the gold beneath its canopy.

Not far behind Gift are agricultural scientists such as Dean Jelinek, who is determined to breed milk cows tricked into endless production through endlessly induced false pregnancies. In the consummate fusion of intellectual passion and species-driven hubris, Professor Bo Jones pours considerable industry funding into the care and feeding of Earl Butz, a seven-hundred-pound pure white Landrace boar being raised to plumb the essence of "hogness": It is no coincidence that Earl is named for the Nixon-era agriculture secretary credited with escalating the calorie consumption of the American populace to keep up with skyrock-

eting farm output. Smiley shamelessly anthropomorphizes Earl, imbuing him with a subjectivity more complicated than even his devoted undergraduate keeper Bob Carlson suspects (a preview of the equine-centered storytelling of *Horse Heaven* and *A Year at the Races*). In his efforts to fathom his profoundly circumscribed world, Earl serves as a satiric embodiment of both the grotesque voracity of contemporary life (extolled elsewhere as the law of insatiability) and the poignant costs to the planet's other species of the human will to mastery.

Yet human will is not unidirectional in its ambitions. As many reviewers have noted, *Moo*'s depictions of human folly are generally tempered by compassion for the human neediness that spawns them and are countered by faith in the occasional capacity of the well intentioned to mobilize, albeit clumsily, against the worst injustices engulfing them. Smiley has called *Moo* the "most personal" of her fictions in the deliberateness of its plotted movement toward recovered ethical balance. Eventually, the loose chain of academic narcissists who learn about Gift's collusion with Martin find varying avenues to expose and ultimately stop it, offering a "model for how well-meaning people can act together for a larger interest."

Moreover, the university itself escapes its financial noose through the deus ex machina of a lone farmer-tinkerer, Loren Stroop, whose years of isolated invention produce a contraption he leaves to the agricultural extension office that for him had differentiated the university among all other modern bureaucracies, however badly the institution had made good on that potential. The obvious artifice of this resolution nonetheless underscores what critic Catherine Stimpson has noted as the true crisis of the modern multiversity: "it has made too many promises to too many constituencies."

Ultimately, however, *Moo* takes refuge from these weightier matters in a comic trajectory in which satiric deflation gives way to romantic restoration, updated for the late twentieth century: Two weddings of established middle-aged partners ensue, one involving the wildest remaining campus radical, "Chairman X" of the Horticultural Department, and his longtime mate (as well as mother of his four children) in the aftermath of his tempestuous intrafaculty affair; the other joining the staid bachelor Provost Ivar Harstad and the epicurean modern languages professor Helen Levy. All of this unfolds (as does Gift's demise) under the bemused and godlike eye of Mrs. Walker, assistant to the provost and true power broker of Moo U.

THE ALL-TRUE TRAVELS AND ADVENTURES OF LIDIE NEWTON

First published: 1998
Type of work: Novel

A feisty young heroine undertakes the twin challenges of marriage and frontier homesteading as an abolitionist in "Bloody Kansas" on the eve of the Civil War and discovers the moral ambiguities that compromise all ideological fervor.

Two distinct impulses—one political and one aesthetic—inspired *The All-True Travels and Adventures of Lidie Newton.* Timothy McVeigh's 1993 terrorist bombing of the Alfred P. Murrah Building in Okla-

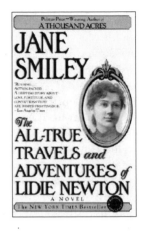

homa City awoke Smiley's interest in the legacy of ideologically driven violence scarring American history, while her desire to create fiction in each of the major narrative genres led her to cast her tale as a literary romance—in her words, "a story in which the protagonist sets out on a journey and sees many amazing things." Since the novel's publication, critics have also speculated that in it Smiley underscored what she saw as the racist failures of Mark Twain's classic boy's tale *Adventures of Huckleberry Finn* (1885), in contrast to the underappreciated *Uncle Tom's Cabin* (1852) of Harriet Beecher Stowe, which had offered nineteenth century readers a far more honest and artful treatment of the political and moral turmoil engulfing the antebellum world.

By her own admission, "the DNA" of both books suffuses her own novel, a first-person account of an unconventional twenty-year-old heroine who is rescued from impending spinsterhood in the summer of 1855, only to be quickly widowed and abruptly thrust into activist politics on her own, all within two years' time. Lydia (Lidie) Harkness meets and quickly marries the bookish idealist Thomas Newton on his way to join the abolitionist settlement of Lawrence in the still-contested Kansas Territory (or "K.T.") just as violence over the future of slavery in the region—and the nation—escalates. Initially ambivalent about Thomas's political passions, she joins him primarily because of her own restless spirit: Her truest soulmate in the staid world of Quincy, Illinois, is her twelve-year-old Tom Sawyer-ish cousin Frank, not the circle of demure older stepsisters who decry her unfeminine ways. Lidie craves a look for herself at the new frontier of the Great Plains, even as she welcomes the emotional and sexual mysteries of marriage itself.

Lidie does indeed find herself swept up in dynamic circumstances that relentlessly test her capacity for improvisation within a murkily complex moral landscape. Entrepreneurial river towns such as St. Louis and Kansas City stand in contrast to the moral citadel of Lawrence and volatile pro-slavery vigilante outposts. The unforgiving prairie winter of 1856 and the worsening political polarization of a nation entering the first phase of its pending civil war prevent the newlyweds from establishing their envisioned homestead, and Thomas becomes one of many martyrs to the abolitionist cause that spring.

Determined to avenge his murder, Lidie assumes the persona of a young male roustabout not unlike Huck Finn himself, and she pursues the possible killers into Missouri, regional logistics center for pro-slavery terrorism. Lidie's femininity, however, is not abandoned as easily as her bobbed hair and comfortable trousers had implied: When an unanticipated pregnancy ends in miscarriage, she becomes the guest of a Missouri plantation Days family and finds herself immersed in the slave milieu itself, its luxuries surprisingly seductive even though she recognizes the theft of human labor and liberty on which they rest. Here again she discovers that moral absolutism of any stripe not only provokes dangerously inaccurate pictures of one's antagonists but also pollutes one's own capacity for measured action and thus catalyzes the kind of worsening violence ripping apart the national fabric.

Yet as her vendetta dissolves, she cannot sidestep the hard choices of her historical moment, for the family's strong-willed house slave Lorna demands that Lidie take her along when she leaves Missouri. By agreeing, Lidie embraces the true message of her husband's life and finds a more constructive recompense for his death, even as she must accept the unease of betraying the Dayses' generosity alongside the considerable physical dangers of their undertaking. If Twain refused to present readers with the unhappy facts of the runaway slave's life-or-death circumstances, then Smiley commits no such mistake: When their escape plot fails, Lidie is imprisoned and Lorna is summarily dispatched "down river" and out of the novel altogether, an outcome as haunting to Lidie as her husband's murder—and far more guilt-provoking.

Saved from prosecution by her jailers' unease with her transgressive femininity, Lidie returns to where she began her odyssey, in Quincy, but not for long. Upon traveling to Massachusetts to meet her in-laws, she learns how to tell a truthful story of "Bloody Kansas" that conveys its paradoxical lessons. Thus she finds herself writing this "memoir" itself, having discovered the healing power of narrative not only politically but also personally—for Smiley, the real starting point of social transformation.

SUMMARY

Smiley's fiction of the 1980's and early 1990's explored the destructive nature of human desire and dissected the emotional power concentrated within the family, where middle-class faith in the future often succumbs to the paralyzing grip of the past and the terrible grief often attendant upon love. Her later career has ranged more widely and employed more comedy than elegy to expose the competing values of American life—self-fulfillment, material success, personal usefulness, and love.

Barbara Kitt Seidman

BIBLIOGRAPHY

By the Author

SHORT FICTION:
The Age of Grief: A Novella and Stories, 1987
"Ordinary Love" and "Good Will": Two Novellas, 1989

LONG FICTION:
Barn Blind, 1980
At Paradise Gate, 1981
Duplicate Keys, 1984
The Greenlanders, 1988
A Thousand Acres, 1991

Jane Smiley

Moo, 1995
The All-True Travels and Adventures of Lidie Newton, 1998
Horse Heaven, 2000
Good Faith, 2003

NONFICTION:
Catskill Crafts: Artisans of the Catskill Mountains, 1988
Charles Dickens, 2002
A Year at the Races: Reflections on Horses, Humans, Love, Money, and Luck, 2004

About the Author

"The Adventures of Jane Smiley." *Atlantic Unbound* 28 (May, 1998).

Bonetti, Kay. "An Interview with Jane Smiley." *Missouri Review* 21, no. 3 (1998): 89-108.

Fletcher, Ron. "Bringing a Timeless Humanity to Writing." *The Christian Science Monitor*, April 30, 1998, B2.

Frumkes, Lewis Burke. "A Conversation with . . . Jane Smiley." *Writer* 112 (May, 1999): 20+.

Kessel, Tyler. "Smiley's *A Thousand Acres*." *Explicator* 62, no. 4 (Summer, 2004): 242-245.

Nakadate, Neil. *Understanding Jane Smiley*. Columbia: University of South Carolina Press, 1999.

Simmons, Ryan. "The Problem of Politics in Feminist Literary Criticism: Contending Voices in Two Contemporary Novels." *Critique* 41, no. 4 (Summer, 2000): 319-336.

Strehle, Susan. "The Daughter's Subversion in Jane Smiley's *A Thousand Acres*." *Critique* 41, no. 3 (Spring, 2000): 211-217.

Urquhart, James. "Talking About a Revolution: Feminism, Horses, Sex, and Slavery—Jane Smiley's Novels Are a Potent Mixture of All of Them." *The Independent (London)*, October 16, 1998.

DISCUSSION TOPICS

- How does Jane Smiley depict the layered complexities and contradictions of the parent-child relationship? What are the special challenges of motherhood? Fatherhood? How do her child characters learn to negotiate the minefields that their parents lay, however unwittingly?

- What role do environmental themes play in Smiley's depiction of contemporary American life? What does the health of the physical world say about the lives of the individuals and institutions inhabiting it (for example in *A Thousand Acres* or *Moo*)?

- The 1980's has become a particular focal point in Smiley's fiction for its "greed is good" ethos. How does her concern with the raw appetite of consumer capitalism shape the stories that she tells in works such as *A Thousand Acres, Moo,* and *Good Faith*?

- Smiley's subjects have ranged widely over a variety of specific subcultures—the university, the real estate industry, the racetrack. How does she bring each of these worlds to life?

- Ideological intractability of any political stripe comes under scrutiny in Smiley's fiction. How does she make it the butt of comic deflation in *Moo*? In what ways do its tragic consequences become clear in *The All-True Travels and Adventures of Lidie Newton*?

- In what ways does *Moo*'s most celebrated character, the huge white boar Earl Butz, symbolize Smiley's greatest concerns for American life at the beginning of the twenty-first century?

- Smiley has explained her fascination with the world of horses and horse racing in terms of her predilections for the mysteries of personality. How does she render animal subjects along such lines, and to what effect? What is it in the dynamic between human and horse that fixes her attention?

GARY SNYDER

Born: San Francisco, California
May 8, 1930

A celebrated poet, essayist, and translator, Snyder weaves strands of American transcendentalism, American Indian culture, and Asian philosophy into writings that illuminate the spiritual and ecological connectedness of humans with the natural world.

Courtesy, Author

BIOGRAPHY

Although he was born in San Francisco, Gary Snyder moved to the Pacific Northwest before he was two, and he spent his youth and college years there. His parents, Harold and Lois Snyder, eked out a living on small family farms, first near Seattle, then near Portland. Snyder and his sister, Thea, enjoyed the plants and animals of these rural areas and learned the challenges and satisfactions of hard physical work. Snyder also traces his political orientation through family roots: His grandfather was a labor organizer for the Industrial Workers of the World, and Snyder often cites their motto of "forming the new society within the shell of the old"—of developing a healthy alternative culture rather than seeking to confront and destroy outmoded institutions.

During his high school years, and through college and several years after, Snyder worked at a variety of jobs. Some were cerebral (such as jobs in journalism, radio programming, and teaching), but more often they involved manual labor and craftsmanship in the outdoors—aspects of a lifestyle that Snyder has continued to embrace even after he could have supported himself solely as a writer. This physical work in his youth involved jobs as a ranger and fire lookout, logger, trail crew worker, and seaman. Snyder was refused reemployment as a lookout in 1954 as a result of his involvement with social and political activists, in spite of uniformly superior evaluations from coworkers and administrators.

In 1947, Snyder enrolled at Reed College, a progressive liberal arts institution in Portland, which he says taught him valuable research and writing skills and encouraged critical thinking from a wide range of viewpoints. He earned a B.A. in literature and anthropology in 1951, and his honors thesis, *He Who Hunted Birds in His Father's Village: The Dimensions of a Haida Myth*, was published in book form in 1979. This thesis, a research study of a Native American myth from British Columbia, is both a remarkably mature piece of scholarship and an extraordinary early statement of the principles linking poet, community, and nature that would come to guide Snyder's poetic practice throughout the coming decades.

Also while at Reed, he entered the first of his four marriages—to Alison Gass, a marriage that lasted less than one year. Snyder's first move toward an academic career was also short-lived: He began a graduate program in linguistics at Indiana University in 1951 but dropped out after a semester. Returning to the West Coast in the fall of 1952, Snyder lived in the San Francisco Bay Area for four years—a crucial period in his development as a poet. In 1953, he began a three-year stint in the graduate program in Oriental languages at the University of California at Berkeley.

Even as a child, Snyder's imagination had been drawn to Asia. When he first saw Chinese landscape paintings at age nine, he noted close similarities between the wet, heavily forested mountains of Washington and Chinese "mountains of the spirit."

Later he immersed himself in the poetry of China, which he viewed as "a high civilization that has managed to keep in tune with nature." Ezra Pound and Kenneth Rexroth served as models of older American poets who had also learned from the concentrated imagery of Asian poetry.

During these years in the Bay Area, Snyder also became part of the loosely knit community of writers who became known as the Beats. On October 13, 1955, a reading at Six Gallery in San Francisco publicly launched the Beat movement; though the event is best remembered for Allen Ginsberg's reading of *Howl*, Snyder also contributed a memorable reading of his poem "A Berry Feast" (later published in *The Back Country* in 1967). In the frequent public readings that were an important part of the Beat movement, Snyder found reinforcement for his belief (drawn from American Indian cultures) that poetry is primarily an oral art that energizes and binds a community. Snyder's poetry did not become nationally known until he began to publish it in book form in 1959, but his reputation as a charismatic oral poet and Asian scholar preceded him by way of the hyperbolic fictional portrait of him as Japhy Ryder in Jack Kerouac's novel *The Dharma Bums* (1958).

Just as the glare of national publicity and controversy began to bear down on the Beats in 1956, Snyder left for Japan, where he spent most of his time during the following dozen years. There he embarked on a challenging program of Zen Buddhist study and meditation with the *roshi* ("old teacher") Oda Sesso at the Daitoku-ji monastery in Kyoto. During these years, Snyder also traveled further into Asia, and he worked as a seaman on an oil tanker sailing to the Middle East. He returned repeatedly to the United States, to teach (at Berkeley in 1964) and to oversee the publication of seven books of poetry, journals, and essays—from *Riprap* (1959) through *Earth House Hold: Technical Notes and Queries to Fellow Dharma Revolutionaries* (1969).

Snyder married poet Joanne Kyger in 1960 and traveled with her to India during 1961 and 1962. They were divorced in 1964. In January of 1967, Snyder presided with Ginsberg over the Great Human Be-In in San Francisco—an event that proved to be a historic apex of that decade's American counterculture.

During the late 1960's, the focus of Snyder's life and poetry shifted slightly but significantly, from that of an individual soul adventuring in quest of spiritual truth to that of a man singing in praise and protection of the family and communities to which he had become committed. *Earth House Hold* is a pivotal work in this regard, for in it Snyder gives increased emphasis to the themes of tribal community and global ecological responsibility.

At the end of that book, he writes of his stay at the Banyan Ashram, an island commune in southern Japan, and of his marriage there to his third wife, Masa Uehara, in August, 1967. Snyder and his wife had two sons, Kai in 1968 and Gen in 1969, and in 1970 they moved into the Sierra Nevada foothills north of Sacramento. There they built a home: Kitkitdizze (from the local native language name for a plant called "Mountain Misery"), an eclectic, primitivist-New Age homestead. Kitkitdizze became the center for the Allegheny Star Route community, a group committed to living on the land and to supporting fundamental changes in society.

Snyder's life after 1970 took on a seasonal rhythm of work on his home and land during the spring and summer, and writing and travel for public readings and lectures during the fall and winter. He continued to publish books of prose and poetry; among the latter, *Turtle Island* (1974) won the 1975 Pulitzer Prize in poetry, selling more than 100,000 copies. Snyder generously contributed his talents as a writer, scholar, and engaging public speaker to the support of the social, religious, and literary viewpoints he espouses. He presented poetry readings and lectured as an advocate of greater environmental awareness and responsibility. In the late 1970's, he was appointed to the California Arts Council by Governor Jerry Brown and served as its first chairman. He gathered his ideas about the environment in a long essay *The Practice of the Wild* (1990), saw his life celebrated by friends and admirers in the Sierra Club publication *Gary Snyder: Dimensions of a Life* (1991), and completed his forty-year-long "poem of process" *Mountains and Rivers Without End* (1996), which led to the Bollingen Prize for Poetry in 1997. He was the featured poet in Bill Moyer's Public Broadcasting Service (PBS) series *The Language of Life* in 1997, became the first American writer to receive the Buddhism Transmission Award from the Bukkyo Dando Kyokai Foundation, and was made a chancellor of the Academy of American Poets in 2003.

He taught at the University of California at Davis, eventually joining the emeriti faculty.

Snyder's marriage to Masa Uehara ended in 1989, and in 1991, he and Carol Koda were married. They traveled extensively together while Snyder read poetry, taught, and lectured about his life's concerns into the twenty-first century. Snyder's *Danger on Peaks* (2004) joins descriptions of some of his earliest climbs on Mount St. Helens with recent sojourns "on the trail" with Carol, and even though he stated in "Waiting for a Ride" that "Most of my work,/ such as it is is done," the work that remains is likely to be as vital and interesting as all that Snyder has done before.

ANALYSIS

In his recurrent themes and various styles, Gary Snyder could be considered the first truly international Pacific Rim writer. That is, his poetry and prose take the westward impulse of American civilization and literature all the way west to Asia, and his work represents an original and exhilarating synthesis of the two cultures.

From the American West, Snyder derives his interest in American Indian tribal culture and in wilderness adventure. With his backwoods experience as a forest lookout, logger, mountain climber, and foothills homesteader, he is the contemporary equivalent of the American frontiersman—seeking now not to conquer nature, but rather to live in harmony with it. His roots in American literature reach from the New England transcendentalism of Ralph Waldo Emerson and Henry David Thoreau, to the trans-American proto-nationalism of Walt Whitman, to the West Coast celebrations of nature in the works of John Muir, Robinson Jeffers, and Kenneth Rexroth. Some of Snyder's poetry collections, such as *Myths and Texts* (1960) and *Mountains and Rivers Without End* (a four-decade sequence of poems based on the extended, unfolding screens of Asian painting), display the expansive ambitiousness to encompass America—or even all Western culture—that one finds in such classic American long poems as Whitman's *Leaves of Grass* (1855-1892), Ezra Pound's *Cantos* (1917-1970), and William Carlos Williams's *Paterson* (1948-1954).

On the other hand, Snyder's longtime commitment to Asian philosophy and aesthetics has led him to the mastery of a very different sort of poetry. He was drawn very early to Chinese verse as translated by Arthur Waley and Pound, and his study of Chinese and Japanese language and literature (and of Zen Buddhism) has helped him to create masterful short lyrics. This side of Snyder's poetry can be seen in his devotion to simple, direct images that resonate in their clarity and depth, sometimes akin to Japanese haiku.

This mystic Asian imagism is particularly characteristic of Snyder's early poetry, and the title of his first volume, *Riprap*, presents his controlling metaphor for this aesthetic. To "riprap," as a worker on a trail crew, is to embed rocks on a steep mountain trail to provide sure footing for horses. For Snyder, the placement of what he calls "tough, simple short words" establishes a necessary connection to natural facts—and to words felt as palpable objects—even as his mind and spirit expand through and beyond these objects to transcendent states of enlightenment. Though Snyder has published several major collections of poetry since *Riprap*, it is a testimony to the enduring appeal of these early short lyrics that several are still among the most anthologized and analyzed of Snyder's poems: "Riprap," "Piute Creek," "Milton by Firelight," "Above Pate Valley," and "Water."

Myths and Texts, Snyder's second collection, also employs this riprap approach to poetry, and it, in fact, makes explicit the intended spiritual resonances of this aesthetic when, toward the end of the book, Snyder includes a definition of poetry as "a riprap on the slick rock of metaphysics." Whereas *Riprap* is a collection of shorter lyrics that makes no direct attempt at overall coherence, in *Myths and Texts* Snyder groups forty-eight lyrics into three long, interrelated poems. The individual lyrics often display the anecdotal settings, concentrated imagery, and monosyllabic diction of the riprap style, but Snyder hopes through the course of the book to render not only isolated, disparate moments of enlightenment but also an overall critical perspective on Western civilization.

Thus "Logging," the first long sequence poem, adds up to a critique of American logging practices and the sometimes destructive alienation from nature that these practices reveal. "Hunting," the second poem, presents an alternative approach to gaining one's livelihood from nature: The poem dramatizes the attempts made by tribal hunters to enter the consciousness of their animal prey. "Burning," the final poem, presents a series of dark visions of fire and falling—visions that ultimately lead to a sense of renewal and rebirth. Some academic critics rate *Myths and Texts* as Snyder's best book of poetry, praising the precise craftsmanship of its individual sections, the expansive comprehensiveness of its overarching structure, and the wide range of its cultural allusions. The close correspondence of Snyder's perspective in these poems with American Indian thought has become increasingly clear as the work of American Indian poets began to reach print in the latter decades of the twentieth century. In addition, the global reach of Snyder's work is evident in the excellent translation of some of these poems by Ignacio Fernández in Spain.

The other collection of Snyder's poetry that academic critics often rate highly is *Mountains and Rivers Without End*, also a book of sequence poems but of a different type from *Myths and Texts*. Snyder sets forth the most useful terms for discussing the difference in a journal entry in "Tanker Notes," in *Earth House Hold*:

> *Poems* that spring out fully armed; and those that are the result of artisan care. The contrived poem, workmanship; a sense of achievement and pride of craft; but the pure inspiration flow leaves one with a sense of gratitude and wonder, and no sense of "I did it"—only the Muse.... [O]ne can see where it goes: to all things and in all things.

In these terms, Snyder's riprap lyrics would be the poems of "artisan care," "workmanship," and "craft," while what he later calls his "shaman poems" would be the poems of "pure inspiration flow" that go "to all things and in all things." *Mountains and Rivers Without End*, according to Snyder, explores the "close correspondence between the external and internal landscapes" of his life. It grew gradually as other books were published. Six sections were published in the 1965 volume, another was added in a 1970 edition, and the project concluded in 1996 in a book that surprised some commentators who felt Snyder would never be able to pull it all together. Critics have been particularly impressed by the additions "The Blue Sky" and "The Hump-Backed Flute Player," which aspire to the magical powers of a healing chant or mantra. Now complete, the work has been compared to Whitman's *Leaves of Grass* and Pound's *Cantos*, two

other cumulative poetic projects that occupied their authors over much of their lifetimes, although in his characteristic relaxed style, Snyder has not himself asked for comparisons with these masters even as his work evinces a tighter coherence and sense of completion than these works.

Snyder's shamanic style also informs the short poems of *Regarding Wave* (1970), but in a more compressed, less overtly allusive manner. The book was the first of Snyder's to bear a dedication, "For Masa"; the poems make clear how his third wife fulfilled his ideals, expressed in the essay "Poetry and the Primitive" in *Earth House Hold*, of how a loving and creative relationship between man and woman can reflect and become attuned to the larger creative processes of nature. The shamanic effect of these poems depends on their silences as well as their sounds, on their repetitions of sound and idea, and on the multiple references of words that express the reflexive unity of poetic, sexual, and ecological harmonies.

In the years since the publication of *Regarding Wave*, Snyder has tried to lead a life more centered on his family, home, and local community. At the same time, he has graciously (though with some reluctance) accepted the role increasingly thrust on him of international spokesman on environmental issues. This dual focus of his life is reflected in four volumes of his poetry published after 1970: *Turtle Island*, *Axe Handles* (1983), *Left Out in the Rain* (1986), and *Danger on Peaks*.

Each volume contains impressive, deeply felt, and highly knowledgeable celebrations of nature, like those found in *Regarding Wave*, along with two other types of poems. One type is the colloquial anecdote, often humorous, sketching incidents in Snyder's daily life and often involving his wife and children. An entertaining example in *Turtle Island* is "The Bath," although the vivid physicality of this poem moves toward some of Snyder's most strongly expressed ideas about the sheer power of the body. The other type is polemic, in which Snyder speaks in a more firmly didactic voice on environmental or political issues; examples in *Turtle Island* are "Front Lines" and "The Call of the Wild." Often, Snyder shifts among these three voices—anecdotal, polemic, and shamanic—in a single poem, addressing the reader on personal, political, and religious levels.

The directions that Snyder's style has taken in

his anecdotal and polemic voices has made his reputation as a poet—a matter of some contention among academic critics—more controversial than the power of his poetry might suggest, although the opening of the poetic field toward the turn of the twenty-first century has made conventional critical strictures less relevant for many readers. Yet rather than become anxious himself that his anecdotal voice is becoming too relaxed and prosaic or his polemical voice too strident and propagandistic, Snyder seems content to reach out to a wider audience and to express the political zeal that he feels is appropriate to specific occasions.

EARTH HOUSE HOLD

First published: 1969
Type of work: Journals, essays, and translations

Snyder's first volume of collected prose traces his transition from a life of individual exploration to a life of community responsibility.

Snyder derived the title for his first book of collected prose from wordplay on the root of the word "ecology." As he points out in the key essay in the book, "Poetry and the Primitive," "eco" comes from the Greek work *oikos*, meaning "house." Thus Snyder playfully renders "ecology" as "earth house hold"—as a perspective that compels humans to consider the entire "earth" as a "house" that they must "hold" with more tenderness and reverence.

The book gathers journals, essays, and translations from 1952 to 1969, a period of many changes in Snyder's life. Some of these pieces, such as reviews of two books of Native American folktales and a translation of the biography of a Buddhist master, are of interest mainly to serious Snyder scholars. For the general student and reader, however, the main interest of the book lies in the personal journals and the later essays, which show important transitions in Snyder's life, philosophy, and conception of poetry. In the course of *Earth House Hold*, Snyder evolves from a wandering, questing individualist to a man firmly rooted in specific commitments to wife, community, and a communal notion of poetry.

Three chapters drawn from Snyder's journals show his developing sense of commitment to family and community. In "Lookout's Journal" (1952), notes from his two summers as a ranger and forest lookout in the Washington Cascades, Snyder writes an entry that is surprisingly prophetic of his later marriage to Masa and their life at the Banyan Ashram. On the other hand, his prevailing attitude is expressed in a quotation from a friend: "'Should I marry? It would mean a house; and the next thirty years teaching school.' LOOKOUT!" Similarly, in "Tanker Notes" (1957), journals from his period as a merchant seaman, Snyder's references to women express the exploitative attitude of sailors. By contrast, in the final chapter of the book, "Suwa-no-se Island and the Banyan Ashram," Snyder treats his relationship with Masa, and his marriage to her, as part of a communal life in close connection with nature. Snyder includes no description of Masa, or of their meeting and courtship, but describes in considerable detail the setting and rituals of their marriage ceremony and the ensuing community celebration.

Snyder's journals and essays in *Earth House Hold* show his conceptions of religion and poetry also developing more of a community orientation. Snyder's 1951 undergraduate dissertation shows that he had long understood, on an intellectual level, the role that he believed a poet should ideally play in the aesthetic and religious life of a community. The writings in *Earth House Hold* show that before Snyder was able to enact such a role, he needed to work through other conceptions involving self, poetry, religion, and nature.

A 1952 entry from "Lookout's Journal" considers poetry as a solitary activity, with primary emphasis on the poet's attempt to express a mystical relationship with nature that is, in Asian religions, considered essentially inexpressible: "If one wished to write poetry of nature, where an audience? Must come from the very conflict of an attempt to articulate the vision." On the other hand, in the early 1960's essay "Buddhism and the Coming Revolution," Snyder argues that Buddhism must move beyond its traditional focus on "liberating a few dedicated individuals" through its schools of meditation. In Snyder's view, persons who hold Buddhist values should move through meditation and personal liberation to a larger purpose of liberating all societies and "moving toward the true community (sangha) of 'all beings.'"

In the culminating essay of *Earth House Hold*, "Poetry and the Primitive: Notes on Poetry as an Ecological Survival Technique," Snyder presents a highly sophisticated analysis of how poetry should become part of oral community ritual. Through "the skilled and inspired use of the voice and language," the poet sings of "rare and powerful states of mind" that are "common to all who listen" and that unify individuals on a deep level with their inner selves, with other people, and with "all beings" with whom they share the planet. In a section called "The Voice as a Girl," Snyder explores concepts—crucial to an understanding of his later poetry—of how his poet's relation to this deeper voice, called "the Muse" in Western culture and "Vak" in Hinduism, was analogous to his relationship with his wife Masa.

"RIPRAP"

First published: 1959 (collected in *Riprap*, 1959)

Type of work: Poem

The craft of embedding rocks on a steep trail serves as a metaphor for the poet's placement of words as footing for journeys of the spirit.

"Riprap," the title poem in Snyder's first collection of verse, is an accomplished example of the craftsmanlike yet transcendent nature of his early poetry. He begins with short, percussive words, mostly monosyllabic, which follow the rhythm of the trail work that he had done in the Sierra Nevada:

> Lay down these words
> Before your mind like rocks.
>   placed solid, by hands
>   In choice of place, set
> Before the body of the mind

> in space and time:
> Solidity of bark, leaf, or wall
>   riprap of things.

Snyder's goal is not merely to reproduce the experience of trail work but also to jolt the reader's mind into higher levels of consciousness through close attention to natural facts and to words experienced as palpable objects. In the practice of Zen religion, masters sometimes deliver unexpected physical blows to surprise their students into satori (enlightenment). Snyder stated in a 1960 interview that he wrote the *Riprap* poems under the influence of "the five-and-seven-character-line Chinese poems I'd been reading at the time, which work like sharp blows to the mind." From this foundation of hard physical facts and sharp, simple words, Snyder then launches the poem into cosmic realms:

> Cobble of milky way,
>   straying planets,
> These poems, people,
>   lost ponies with
> Dragging saddles—
>   and rocky sure-foot trails.
> The worlds like an endless
>   four-dimensional
> Game of *Go*.

In his playful references to the "milky way," "planets," "worlds," and the "game of *Go*," Snyder implies that the poet need not be limited to mundane physical facts for his or her choice of words, images, and concepts. Rather, through the placement of words, the poetic craftsman can embed seemingly ungraspable materials in the lines of a poem, just as nature can form into solid rock materials which once seemed too hot and fluid to control:

> Granite: ingrained
>   with torment of fire and weight
> Crystal and sediment linked hot
>   all change, in thoughts,
> As well as things.

Though "Riprap" is known as one of Snyder's carefully composed, craftsmanlike poems, in these concluding lines one can see Snyder prophesying other possibilities for his verse, affirming the heated and volatile flow of poetic imagination.

"Regarding Wave"

First published: 1969 (collected in
Regarding Wave, 1969)
Type of work: Poem

This poem sings of Snyder's love for his wife, for the processes of nature, and for the universal spirit of Dharma.

"Regarding Wave," the title poem in Snyder's remarkable 1969 collection of verse, contains references to Asian religion at the very beginning and end. The chief wonder of the poem, however, is more in the ways it performs, rather than alludes to, its religious and ecological ideas.

The title expresses in two simple words a large range of ideas that Snyder explores in the essay "Poetry and the Primitive" in *Earth House Hold*. According to that essay, in Indo-European etymology the word "yak" is the name of the Muse-like wife of the Hindu god Brahma, and it is also the common root of the words "voice," "wife," "wave," and "vibration." Snyder considers his shamanic act of allowing a voice to flow through his poems to be analogous both to the act of making love to his wife and to the waves (the myriad rhythms, breaths, pulses, and vibrations) of natural processes that are flowing through a healthy ecosystem. The phrase "regarding wave" refers to an act of reciprocal and simultaneous perception that involves poet, wife, and world.

The opening lines of the poem call the reader to attention—attention to the waves of physical and spiritual energy that are moving like music through every being and object at every moment. "Dharma" in this context means "divine law":

> The voice of the Dharma
> the voice
> *now*
>
> A shimmering bell
> through all.
> . . . .
> Every hill,   still.
> Every tree alive. Every leaf.
> All the slopes flow.
> old woods, new seedlings,
> . . . .

Dark hollows; peaks of light.
. . . .
Each leaf living.
All the hills.

The words are simple, but the rhythms are subtle and powerful. Snyder makes language sing through many musical repetitions of words and syntax (such as "the voice" and "every"), by approximate and exact rhymes ("bell" and "all," "hill" and "still," "all" and "hill"), by assonance and consonance ("slopes," "flow," and "old"; "alive" and "every"; "each leaf"), and by alliteration ("leaf living"). The imagery of landscape (of "hollows," "slopes," and "hills") also refers to the contours of his wife's body, and it ties into a circular movement back to a reference to the voice from the beginning of the poem: "The Voice/ is a wife/ to/ him still." "Regarding Wave" is a moving and profound lyric, a ringing poem near the center of one of Snyder's most resonant collections.

"The Bath"

First published: 1974 (collected in *Turtle Island*, 1974)
Type of work: Poem

A family bath becomes an expansive, joyous occasion that involves the interrelated "body" of the poet's family and the natural world.

"The Bath" illustrates how the experience of fatherhood has provided Snyder with new perspectives on the interrelationship between the bodies of humans and the ecological "body" of nature.

The poem begins with a vivid description of Snyder giving his older son, Kai, a bath in the sauna at their backwoods home. The poet's mood is relaxed, yet also attentive to details of his son's body and how that body relates to his own. When Snyder washes his son's penis, it surprises him by becoming erect. Yet rather than becoming embarrassed or anxious, Snyder is amused and delighted:

> Laughing and jumping, flinging arms around,
> I squat all naked too,
>
> *is this our body?*

These italicized words become a refrain throughout the poem: first *"is this our body?,"* then *"this is our body"* as Snyder's wife, Masa, and his younger son, Gen, also become involved in the scene.

In the second stanza, Masa joins Snyder and Kai in the bath, and the poet draws a loving analogy between her body and that of the landscape where they make their home: "The body of my lady, the winding valley spine." Snyder caresses and kisses his wife, acts which stimulate him to draw further imaginative connections among the sexual and nurturing powers of his family:

> Kai's little scrotum up close to his groin,
>   the seed still tucked away, that moved from
>   us to him
> In flows that lifted with the same joys forces
>   as his nursing Masa later,
>   playing with her breast,
> Or me within her,
> Or him emerging.

Coming out of the bath, and out of the sauna enclosure, Snyder, Masa, and Kai enjoy a variety of nature's sights, smells, and sounds. The poet's use of personification ("murmuring gossip of the grasses,/ talking firewood") further contributes to his theme that his family's interrelated body is part of the larger interrelated body of nature. At the end of the poem, as he and his wife play with their children, Snyder brings the refrain into his domestic narrative; this theme is now firmly grounded in reality and no longer needs to be treated as a separate "cosmic" thought.

> This is our body. Drawn up crosslegged by
>   the flames
>   drinking icy water
>   hugging babies, kissing bellies,
>
> Laughing on the Great Earth
>
> Come out from the bath.

In many other poems in *Turtle Island,* Snyder gives vent to righteous environmentalist anger. In "The Bath," however, he allows the reader to share in a joyous domestic scene that reflects a surrounding joyous spirit in the natural world. With its humor and love, "The Bath" reminds readers in a gentle way of some of the reasons that nature is worth fighting for.

AXE HANDLES

First published: 1983
Type of work: Poetry

The accumulated wisdom of a life devoted to literature, the environment, and his family and community is expressed with the humor, insight, and clarity that readers have come to expect from the poet.

Following the pattern of earlier collections, *Axe Handles* is a compilation of journal entries, evocations of the natural world in conjunction with bioethical declarations, lyrics in praise of the human spirit based on the sensual textures of the body, and philosophical insights grounded in the accumulated wisdom drawn from Snyder's experiences with "the real work" of writing, reading, and raising a family in a caring community intricately involved with the environment in its largest dimensions. The title poem is a summary of Snyder's core beliefs, using the metaphor of a tool that is both an extension of human power and potential and an instrumental illustration of artistic vision in action. Citing an illustrious poetic predecessor, Snyder proclaims, "the phrase/ First learned from Ezra Pound/ Rings in my ears!: 'When making an axe handle/ the pattern is not far off.'"

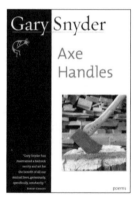

Snyder uses a pattern of recurrence to describe the way in which he shapes the handle for his son Kai, enthusiastically proclaiming "And he sees" to demonstrate the process of transmission of acquired knowledge, summarizing "Pound was an Axe,/ Chen was an axe, I am an axe/ And my son a handle," past, present, and future in a chain preserving the "craft of culture" that the poet holds dear.

The same kind of care for a craft and appreciation of a useful and beautiful instrument is expressed in the poem "Removing the Plate of the Pump/ on the Hydraulic System/ of the Backhoe," a title that functions as the first stanza, followed by:

Through mud, fouled nuts, black grime
it opens, a gleam of spotless steel
machined-fit perfect
swirl of intake and output
relentless clarity
at the heart
of work

in which Snyder fuses the lyric form with a philosophical proposition to shape a crisp, sharp image that conveys the essence of his feeling about the things that matter most to him.

These two poems set the direction and spirit of the collection, which includes many date-specific observations from Snyder's journal that evoke the natural world, such as his expansion of Matsuo Bashō's famous frog haiku ("Old Pond") or his always sharp-eyed re-creations of the moods of the terrain as he walks through mountain and river landscape, bringing places to life in poems such as "True Night," "So Old," or "Geese Gone Beyond." He sees the natural world as the home that supports and surrounds his family, which leads him toward observations of his family that generate meditative reflections on the place of family and friends in a social community.

Many of these poems are taken from his residence in Japan ("At the Ibaru Family Tomb/ Tagami village, great Loo Choo: Grandfather of my sons") and establish connections between his very American youth and his extensive involvement in the culture of Asia, and Japan in particular. There are also some political poems ("Talking Late with the Governor/ about the Budget," dedicated to Jerry Brown, then governor of California). In an exposition of the high-spirited, often exuberant, and primarily optimistic tenor of the collection, Snyder concludes the volume with a fond recasting of the familiar Pledge of Allegiance, "For All," in which he proposes an oath of responsibility and revitalization, a restated commitment to "Turtle Island," the ancestral home of his core values, the "ecosystem/ in diversity," which he treasures and hopes to protect and restore.

SUMMARY

As an American cultural figure, Snyder has gained the stature of a modern Thoreau while going beyond Thoreau's isolation to live as a wise elder, a sage whose affable, accessible, and inspirational qualities have not diminished the hard intelligence and rigorous poetic practice of his working life. He leads an exemplary life in accord with both the practical counsel and the visionary ideals that his writings express so eloquently. Snyder's place in the canon of great American poets is more problematic, primarily because some critics contend that much of his later poetry is more polemical or more relaxed than the most highly praised poems of his early career. Few would dispute, however, that Snyder's poetic voice often speaks with clarity, humor, and wisdom. Many would go further to insist that his poetry is powerful enough to transform the consciousness of those who read it, creating a shared vision that represents humanity's best chance to preserve the earth for future generations.

Terry L. Andrews; updated by Leon Lewis

BIBLIOGRAPHY

By the Author

POETRY:
Riprap, 1959
Myths and Texts, 1960
Hop, Skip, and Jump, 1964
Nanao Knows, 1964
The Firing, 1964
Riprap, and Cold Mountain Poems, 1965
Six Sections from Mountains and Rivers Without End, 1965
A Range of Poems, 1966
Three Worlds, Three Realms, Six Roads, 1966

The Back Country, 1967

The Blue Sky, 1969

Sours of the Hills, 1969

Regarding Wave, 1969, enlarged 1970

Manzanita, 1972

The Fudo Trilogy: Spel Against Demons, Smokey the Bear Sutra, The California Water Plan, 1973

Turtle Island, 1974

All in the Family, 1975

Axe Handles: Poems, 1983

Left Out in the Rain: New Poems, 1947-1986, 1986

No Nature: New and Selected Poems, 1992

Mountains and Rivers Without End, 1996

Danger on Peaks, 2004

NONFICTION:

Earth House Hold: Technical Notes and Queries to Fellow Dharma Revolutionaries, 1969

The Old Ways, 1977

He Who Hunted Birds in His Father's Village: The Dimensions of a Haida Myth, 1979

The Real Work: Interviews and Talks, 1964-1979, 1980

Passage Through India, 1983

The Practice of the Wild, 1990

Gary Snyder Papers, 1995

A Place in Space: Ethics, Aesthetics, and Watersheds, 1995

Look Out: A Selection of Writings, 2002

MISCELLANEOUS:

The Gary Snyder Reader: Prose, Poetry, and Translations, 1952-1998, 2000

The High Sierra of California, 2005 (with Tom Killion)

About the Author

Almon, Bert. *Gary Snyder*. Boise, Idaho: Boise State University Press, 1979.

Altieri, Charles. *Enlarging the Temple: New Directions in American Poetry During the 1960's*. Lewisburg, Pa.: Bucknell University Press, 1979.

Dean, Tim. *Gary Snyder and the American Unconscious*. New York: St. Martin's Press, 1991.

Halper, Jon. *Gary Snyder: Dimensions of a Life*. San Francisco: Sierra Club Books, 1991.

Molesworth, Charles. *Gary Snyder's Vision: Poetry and the Real Work*. Columbia: University of Missouri Press, 1983.

Steubing, Bob. *Gary Snyder*. Boston: Twayne, 1976.

Suiter, John. *Poets on the Peaks*. New York: Counterpoint, 2002.

DISCUSSION TOPICS

- Gary Snyder has stated that "As a poet I hold the most archaic values on earth. They go back to the late Paleolithic; the fertility of the soil, the magic of animals, the power-vision in solitude, the terrifying Initiation and rebirth; the love and ecstasy of the dance, the common work of the tribe." Consider how each of these concepts can be applied to a specific poem.

- Snyder believes that "the rhythms of my poems follow the rhythms of the physical work I'm doing." Discuss the ways in which the variety of rhythmic patterns in Snyder's poetry help to develop the mood and tone of a poem.

- Snyder has said that his intention in *Mountains and Rivers Without End* was to break down "the limit between the psychic and the physical." How does this inform individual sections of the poem?

- In "What You Should Know to Be a Poet," Snyder lists "all you can about animals as persons." Examine the ways in which he establishes a correspondence between human and animal nature in his work.

- In explaining his goals, Snyder has proclaimed, "In a visionary way, what we want poetry to do is guide lovers toward ecstasy, give witness to the dignity of old people, intensify human bonds, elevate the community and improve the public spirit." Identify poems that accomplish each of these tasks, and show how they do this.

CATHY SONG

Born: Honolulu, Territory of Hawaii (now in Hawaii)
August 20, 1955

The winner of the prestigious Yale Series of Younger Poets Award in 1982, Song has made a major breakthrough for Asian American poetry.

A. Michele Turner/Courtesy, University
of Pittsburgh Press

BIOGRAPHY

Cathy Song was born in 1955 to a Korean American airline pilot and a Chinese American seamstress in Honolulu. Until the age of seven, she was raised in Wahiawa, a small plantation town on the island of Oahu that serves as the setting for many of her poems. Because her ancestral roots can be traced to both China and Korea—the two countries where her maternal and paternal grandparents originated—and because she has spent most of her life in Hawaii, Song has at times been identified as a Hawaiian poet; at other times, she has been called either a Korean American or Chinese American poet, though in fact the three aspects of her heritage are essentially indivisible.

As a child, Song exercised her creative energy in what she later called the "pure fantasy" and "dream wishes" of fiction (her first story, written at the age of eleven, is a spy novel), romance (short stories about "beautiful blonde heroines on summer vacations"), and make-believe journalism ("imaginary interviews with movie stars"). Later, she also aspired to be a songwriter like Joan Baez and Joni Mitchell. After her schooling in Hawaii, when Song had left the University of Hawaii for Wellesley College in Massachusetts, her talent in poetry began to blossom. While attending Wellesley, she came across Georgia O'Keeffe's book *Georgia O'Keeffe* (1976), which so deeply impressed Song that it in-

spired her to write an entire sequence of poems (loosely known as the "O'Keeffe poems").

After receiving her B.A. from Wellesley in 1977, Song went on to study creative writing at Boston University, where she earned an M.A. in 1981. She also attended the Advanced Poetry Workshop conducted by Kathleen Spivak, who offered suggestions on the divisions and subtitles of Song's first book manuscript. The manuscript, *Picture Bride*, which collects poems formerly published in journals and anthologies such as *Bamboo Ridge*, *The Greenfield Review*, and *Hawaii Review*, was selected by the poet Richard Hugo from among 625 manuscripts as the winner of the 1982 Yale Series of Younger Poets competition and was published by Yale University Press as volume 78 of the series in 1983. The series, which had previously featured poets such as Adrienne Rich and John Ashbery, brought Song to prominence. The book was nominated for the National Book Critics Circle Award.

Song's second collection of poems, *Frameless Windows, Squares of Light*, was published by W. W. Norton in 1988. Her third collection of poems, *School Figures*, appeared in 1994, and her fourth, *The Land of Bliss*, in 2001, both published by the University of Pittsburgh Press. Song's poetry has been widely anthologized in such volumes as *Breaking the Silence: An Anthology of Contemporary American Poets* (1983), *The Norton Anthology of Modern Poetry* (2d edition, 1988), *The Norton Anthology of American Literature* (3d edition, 1989), *The Heath Anthology of American Literature* (1990), *The Open Boat: Poems from Asian America* (1993), *Unsettling America: An Anthology of Contemporary Multicultural Poetry* (1994), *Boomer Girls: Poems by Women from the Baby Boom Generation* (1999), and *The Norton Anthology of Modern and Contemporary Poetry* (2003). She is also the coeditor, with Juliet S. Kono, of *Sister Stew: Fiction and Poetry by Women* (1991).

Song's numerous prizes and awards include the Frederick Bock Prize from *Poetry* magazine, the Shelley Memorial Award from the Poetry Society of America, the Hawaii Award for Literature, the Elliot Cades Award for Literature, the Pushcart Prize, and a National Endowment for the Arts (NEA) grant.

Song has taught creative writing at various universities on the U.S. mainland and in Hawaii, where she maintains a permanent home in Honolulu and teaches mainly for the Poets in Schools program. She is married to Douglas Davenport, a doctor, and has three children.

ANALYSIS

Song's poetry generally deals with her personal experience as a woman with family roots in Hawaii and with ancestral and kinship ties to Korea and China. Although her subject matters revolve around regional, ethnic, and private experiences, they are expressed in idioms evidently inseparable from her formal training in Western culture. Her interest in art also comes through unmistakably in the visual qualities of her poems, especially in those inspired by family photographs, paintings by O'Keeffe, and prints by eighteenth century Japanese artist Kitagawa Utamaro. In her poetry, Song often affectionately thematizes about family ties by providing portraits of and stories about family members in language that is both contemplative and dramatic, retrospective and prospective, moving freely between past and present and between observation and speculation. Because her memory of the past often merges with the reality of the present as if the two were indivisible, there is a lively immediacy to her poems.

Many of her poems employ the second-person pronoun, thus simulating a conversational style, which in turn is characterized by frequent understatements. Deceptively prosaic at times, her language has in store delightful surprises of images and a variety of emotions ranging from sadness to humor. Initially, readers such as Richard Hugo tended to see Song's poems as "flowers—colorful, sensual and quiet—offered almost shyly as bouquets." In his 1986 review of *Picture Bride*, however, Stephen Sumida cautioned that "Song's poems

seem especially liable to being appreciated or criticized for the wrong reasons" and suggested that her work deserves an alternative approach.

Although Song is one of the most visible of Asian American poets, her poetry, curiously, has not generated critical attention and acclaim proportionate to her phenomenal emergence as a member of the Yale Series of Younger Poets and her inclusion in prestigious anthologies. *Picture Bride* attracted a handful of reviews, and her second book, *Frameless Windows, Squares of Light*, though published by a commercial publisher, received hardly more than a couple. Furthermore, the few reviews that did appear, though positive, are somewhat reserved about the merits of Song's work. The mixed reception of her poetry may have resulted from the small readership of poetry in general and of Asian American poetry in particular or from the fact that Song's output has been rather modest.

A significant factor affecting her reception, however, appears to be that Song, despite (and because of) her initial success, has been faced with the same predicament by which most Asian American writers are plagued: to explore their ethnicity explicitly often subjects them to risks of exoticism (if the ethnic experience is noticed) or marginality (when such experience is assumed to be beneath notice). As Song warily put it in a 1983 interview, "I'll have to try not to write about the Asian-American theme," although such a focus is "a way of exploring the past." Song's statement is essentially a reflection on the artificial dilemma, between ethnicity ("Asian") and the mainstream ("American") culture, that is deeply ingrained in the literature of the United States. As a poet, Song deserves special attention for her struggle to bridge the hiatus—not so much by circumventing ethnicity as by concentrating on her personal experience as a woman. This effort is reflected in the introduction to *Sister Stew*, where she and coeditor Kono proclaim the primacy of women's experience and assert the plenitude of women's voices. This introduction, in retrospect, could also serve as an introduction to Song as "a poet who happens to be Asian American."

The effort to bridge the hiatus discussed above is already evident in the textual history of Song's *Picture Bride*, a collection of thirty-one poems covering a range of topics including family history, life in Hawaii, childhood memories, sibling relationships, love, art, character studies, ethnic experience, and the quest of the self. The book is organized according to two interrelated frameworks or principles. To take the title poem as the focal text, the book is apparently a collection of poems structured around the immigration and assimilation experience of the Song family, beginning with the arrival of her Korean grandparents—her grandmother in particular. Seen from this perspective, the book is essentially autobiographical in nature, with the poems serving as miniature memoirs and chronicles of the family's history and as memories of parents, relatives, and siblings. It is important to note, however, that such an ethnicized principle of organization was not Song's idea but her publisher's.

Even as it stands, the book, which Song originally intended to title *From the White Place*, also incorporates another framework of organization. This framework is derived from a five-part sequence, "Blue and White Lines After O'Keeffe," a poem placed at the center of the collection. The subtitles of the volume's five divisions ("Black Iris," "Sunflower," "Orchids," "Red Poppy," and "The White Trumpet"), which were suggested to Song by Kathleen Spivak, in fact come from this strategically positioned text. Used as a structuring device, these subtitles imply that the book can be perceived as a poet's attempt, by way of visual art (the work of Georgia O'Keeffe and Kitagawa Utamaro), to fashion personal experience into esthetic experience and thereby define her vision as an artistic one.

Reading the book according to this framework tends to deemphasize the ethnic elements of the poems, but the risk of viewing the book as an ethnographic document is also reduced. Such an artist's framework is not without its problems, as it poses the danger of diminishing the peculiarity of Song's experience and her voice. Taken alone, neither of the two frameworks is entirely satisfactory, but as Fujita-Sato explains, "What results . . . from the interlocked frameworks provided by the book's title and sections titles, is a structure embodying synthesis." Corresponding to this synthesis, Fujita-Sato proposes, is the technique of "singing shapes" derived from O'Keeffe's paintings, by which two often dissimilar objects are juxtaposed and become mutually illuminated and transformed into "a fluid shaping and reshaping of energy."

The motivation toward synthesis in *Picture Bride* is further developed in *Frameless Windows, Squares of Light*, in which Song concentrates on personal experiences in various stages of her life as a daughter, sister, wife, mother, and Hawaiian and Asian American woman. In this collection, her voice as a poet who is not only a woman but also an artist also matures. The volume consists of twenty-six poems and is divided into four parts ("The Window and the Field," "A Small Light," "Shadow Figures," and "Frameless Windows, Squares of Light") that are named after the title poems of each section. The organization recalls but transcends that of *Picture Bride*; the aesthetic rendition of personal experience no longer relies on the appeal of ethnic elements or the authority of another artist but rather disseminates from the play and interplay of framed and frameless blocks and touches of light and shadow—vignettes of life as lived.

The higher level of unity in this second collection also stems from Song's technique—related to that of "singing shapes"—of juxtaposing and transposing (or compressing) different segments of time, in the manner a telescope is collapsed or expanded, so that memories of the past and realities of the present merge into one another. For example, she shows how what happened to herself and her brother as children in the past would recur, with variations, in the present when she looks upon her son and daughter growing up. This unique approach to experience, by which the personal is merged with the familial and the mundane is elevated to the aesthetic, suggests that Song's attempt to bridge the hiatus, and hence resolve the dilemma confronting Asian American writers, is, in fact, feasible.

Song continues with similar efforts in bridging the hiatus between the mundane and the aesthetic in her third collection, *School Figures*, in which she concentrates on the local world of Hawaii's Asian American communities, exploring personal experiences of family, history, ethnicity, and cultural conflicts. Such personal explorations further intensify in her fourth collection, *The Land of Bliss*, in which the poet embarks on extended narratives about the sickness and dying of her mother, and the pain and suffering of those affected by her, and about life itself in its many spectacular or quotidian ways; such moments, and their attendant memories of warmth and fondness, however, are invariably recollected for the purposes of transformation, through poetic mediation, resulting in their transcendence in the spiritual realm of bliss.

"PICTURE BRIDE"

First published: 1983 (collected in *Picture Bride*, 1983)
Type of work: Poem

A young woman leaves Korea to marry a sugarcane field laborer in Hawaii.

"Picture Bride," the title poem with which Song's volume begins, serves as the seminal text of the collection, in a way defining the thematic direction of the book. In this poem, the poetic persona, aged twenty-four, attempts to imagine what it was like for her maternal grandmother, at the age of twenty-three, to leave Korea for Hawaii to marry a laborer thirteen years her senior, a man she had never seen before. The entire poem, except for the first three lines, consists of a series of questions intended to re-create not only the scenes of the departure, the journey, and the arrival but also the psychology and emotions of the picture bride throughout the process. The concluding question, which speculates on how willing she might have been with regard to her conjugal obligation ("did she politely untie/ the silk bow of her jacket,/ her tent-shaped dress"), focuses an entire economic and sociohistorical phenomenon onto the question of sexuality, making the poem linger on a moment of truth in human terms. This ability to crystalize the general into the personal is characteristic of Song's poetry.

The figure of the picture bride serves as a muse of sorts for the poet, in part because the questions raised in "Picture Bride" are either answered or contextualized in the volume's other poems. For example, in "Untouched Photograph of Passenger," Song contemplates the picture of a man dressed in a poorly tailored suit who is gazing into the camera; she observes, "Rinsing through his eyes/ and dissolving all around him/ is sunlight on water." The portrait is probably of the speaker's grandfather, and the poem captures the optimism with which the emigrant embraces the promise of a foreign land.

The other poems in the volume, which loosely chronicle the proliferation of the first generation through two more generations, can be regarded as indirect answers to the question of sexuality raised in "Picture Bride." As an older woman, the bride jokes about her extraordinarily big breasts, which the poet describes as being like "walruses" and imagines to have been sucked by "six children and an old man"; certainly the breasts are symbolic of the bride's fecundity, but they are also realistically personal. Always keeping her focus on the personal dimension, when Song finally writes about the death of the grandmother in "Blue Lantern," she makes it clear that what matters in the picture bride phenomenon is, ultimately, the human element. Prearranged marriages and love are not mutually exclusive under certain circumstances, as is evident from the grandfather's mourning: "He played for her each night;/ her absence,/ the shape of his grief/ funneled through the bamboo flute."

"A PALE ARRANGEMENT OF HANDS"

First published: 1983 (collected in *Picture Bride*, 1983)
Type of work: Poem

The poet pays tribute to her mother by way of recollections of childhood.

"A Pale Arrangement of Hands," also from *Picture Bride*, begins with the poet sitting at the kitchen table listening to the all-night rain. Seeing her own hands on the table, she remembers her mother's hands, which always seemed nervous "except when they were busy cooking": "Her hands would assume a certain confidence/ then, as she rubbed and patted butter/ all over a turkey as though/ she were soaping and scrubbing up a baby." The poet further recalls that her mother used to describe the rain in Hawaii as "liquid sunshine" to her three children. Further associations bring back memories of the mother applying lipstick; the poet remembers the mother using her discarded tissues for a surprising purpose during rainy afternoons when the children were idle: She shows them "how to make artificial carnations . . . with a couple of hairpins." As the memory unfolds, many more mundane but fond episodes emerge.

By detours, the poet's memories begin to reel back to the present, concluding with one more memory—of the children's habitual refusal to take a nap in the afternoon, which for the mother was the longest part of the day: "Sleep meant pretending. Lying still/ but alert, I listened from the next room/ as my mother slipped out of her damp dress./ The cloth crumpling onto the bathroom floor/ made a light, sad sound."

Although the poem appears to be unstructured and plain, and although the moments captured are mundane, Song's ability to re-create the vivid and even noisy scenes of childhood is unmistakable. The poem also exemplifies Song's favorite device of bringing the past and the present together. More important, however, "A Pale Arrangement of Hands" is a good example of what Song and Juliet S. Kono have characterized as women writers' voices. The mother in the poem is not deified, but the poet, through negotiations between her subjectivity and her subject matter, has given an ordinary mother a voice—a tribute to women who have most of the time been silent. The poem "The Seamstress," from the same book, can also be interpreted from a similar perspective, as can "Humble Jar" from *Frameless Windows, Squares of Light*, a poem occasioned by the memory of an assortment of buttons that the mother kept in a jar.

"HEAVEN"

First published: 1988 (collected in *Frameless Windows, Squares of Light*, 1988)
Type of work: Poem

A mother ponders the significance of her son's childish ideas about an afterlife.

"Heaven" appears toward the end of *Frameless Windows, Squares of Light*. By this time, the poet has already married and is the mother of a son and a daughter. The son, who has blond hair (which comes from his father), "thinks when we die we'll go to China," causing the mother to pause at the thought of "a Chinese heaven." The poet further imagines how her son's hand "must span like a bridge/ to reach it." She continues to wonder how

such an idea could occur to her son, as she herself has never seen China. As the question of identity and ethnicity is pressed, the poet's thoughts are re-routed to a historical time when a boy in southern China started his long journey to the United States to make a living at the gold mines and the railroad, indefinitely prolonging his stay. Switching back to the present, the poet muses that "It must be in the blood,/ this notion of returning./ It skipped two generations, lay fallow,/ the garden an unmarked grave." This realization, triggered by the innocent thoughts of a child, leads the poet to call to the children to look to where "we can see the mountains/ shimmering blue above the air."

Although one of the themes in "Heaven" is innocence, this poem obviously contradicts Song's earlier statement that she would try not to write on the Asian American theme. Her observation that "it must be in the blood" can be seen as a bold correction of that earlier declaration. The question of returning to China is a symbolic rather than a practical concern, especially after an entire generation of Asian American writers has worked furiously to establish the legitimacy of Asian Americans as Americans. Yet the poem raises a fundamental issue about the nature of Song's poetry in particular and American literature in general: To what extent is it possible, or desirable, to purge the American experience of ethnicity? Song's return to this issue is an important signal because, unlike her earlier, mostly retrospective treatments of the Asian American experience, "Heaven" involves a future generation and is forward-looking. The fact that Song can raise such a controversial issue at all intimates the arrival of another stage in the Asian American writer's search for identity.

"SUNWORSHIPPERS"

First published: 1993 (collected in *School Figures*, 1994)
Type of work: Poem

A young woman reflects on the care of the body in different cultures and her experience of anorexia.

"Sunworshippers" is included in *School Figures*, a collection populated by various characters from

Song's family. As the idiosyncrasy of relatives often gets on her nerves, she cannot accept them at face value and must negotiate, with herself, for ways of coming to terms with her family heritage. "Sunworshippers," like Song's many other poems characterizing members of her family, exemplifies this position.

The poem begins with the poet's recollection of her mother's preachy lectures about sunbathers: "Who will marry you/ if your skin is sunbaked and dried up like beef jerky?" Raising her daughters by Old World precepts, the mother would make them wear hats and gloves when they went for a drive and would use an umbrella under the sun. Contemplating her mother's philosophy about the body now that she is a woman, the speaker relates how, in her struggles against those disagreeable preachings, she became anorexic. In a voice that is at once sarcastic, resentful, and perhaps mixing delight with regret, she satirizes the mother's view of the body. Taking a deliberately confrontational stance, she interprets the mother's cautions against exposure to the sun in terms of prohibitions against loving oneself "too much." As if to retaliate, she eats less and less.

Despite its alarming development as a health issue, anorexia also serves as a conceit for the speaker's construction of her identity. Akin to being a portrait of the artist as a young woman, the poem reaches some sort of epiphany by celebrating the speaker's hypersensitive and even mystical capabilities. As someone with a heightened awareness of self, she "devoured radiance,/ essential as chlorophyll." It is under these strange circumstances that she experiences an intellectual coming-of-age, so that she can finally claim that "Undetected, I slipped in and out of books,/ passages of music, brightly painted rooms// to weave one's self, ropes of it, whole/ and fully formed, was a way of shining/ out of this world." Since the context for this experience is anorexia, there is an implied irony that this moment of extreme brilliance may be a form of delusion induced by fasting. The tension between mother and daughter that started the poem remains unresolved. Paradoxically, this lack of resolution is what keeps the poet motivated to write.

"GHOST"

First published: 2001 (collected in *The Land of Bliss*, 2001)
Type of work: Poem

A Hawaiian Asian woman muses upon the issue of race, challenging preconceived stereotypes.

"Ghost" appears in *The Land of Bliss* as a critical reflection on the issue of racial difference in the multiethnic context of Hawaiian society, where, in 2000, Asians, Pacific Islanders, and native Hawaiians made up about 51 percent of the population and white people were a 24 percent minority. To understand this poem, it is useful to consider the fact that, historically, "ghost" (*gwai*) was a term often used among the Chinese to refer to people of other races (typically white Caucasians) perceived to be oppressive or repulsive. Although an epithet suggesting repugnance and contempt, "ghost" also signifies a sense of helpless subjugation, as racism against Asians had been rampant historically. Typical of the younger generation, the poet does not endorse the sentiments underlying the epithet.

In the first part of the poem, the speaker, a schoolteacher of Asian descent, refers to herself as a "yellow ghost" who flutters "like a moth/ invisible to these/ children of soldiers." Despite this invisibility and potential lack of authority and recognition, the speaker acknowledges that she occupies a position of power. However, rather than perpetuating the pattern of domination, the speaker attempts to restructure the interracial self-other relationship in nonconfrontational terms, offering to share with her pupils "a jeweled seeded fruit,/ a poem I pare and peel/ that has no flesh," a poem that "tastes like nothing/ they want to eat." Song, who has been involved in the Poets in Schools program, thus raises questions about the meaning of the prevalent epithet. The color of power can be white, and it can also be yellow, but, more important, it needs to be vested not in the form of racial hierarchies but rather, as the poet seems to suggest, in culture and education.

In the second part of the poem, the speaker challenges her mother's offhanded use of the term *bok gwai* (white ghost). The daughter does see the mother's point about white privilege, but she questions the mother's categorical myopia: "Bok gwai, white ghost,/ she chose to call them./ By choosing, she chose/ not to see/ them/ as she so surely saw/ she was not seen." Fortunately, this is a vicious circle that the daughter is able to short-circuit when she starts dating a white man. The mother recoils at his "odor/ of a meat eater," but eventually she is pleased enough with him to invite him back—thus paving way for the daughter's interracial romance and, perhaps metaphorically speaking, the construction of a sustainable relationship for people from different cultures and ethnicities.

"Ghost" is hence a poem that bridges racial gaps on personal terms. In the context of the main action of the collection—the deteriorating health of the mother, and how that dying process intimately leaves a deep impact on the feelings, memories, and anxieties of the daughter—"Ghost" also bridges existential gaps between the two women. The mother might have accepted the daughter's choice of a "round eye," but it appears as if it is the daughter who grants the terms of reconciliation: The mother will be remembered and honored, but her flaws stay on the record even as she is immortalized in the land of bliss created by the daughter's poetry.

SUMMARY

Song's struggle to be heard as a poet is tied to her experience as a woman with multiple cultural backgrounds. Her exploration of subject matter related to immigrants, family history, generational ties, Hawaiian culture, and personal visions of life and art is an integral part of the American experience. Confronted with the gulf between ethnic and mainstream cultures, Song has worked toward bridging the gap with creative means informed by her artistic sensibility. Her unfaltering interest in the primacy of the human and the personal, especially from the perspective of women without voices, is a distinct and dominant trait of her poetry.

Balance Chow

DISCUSSION TOPICS

- How does Cathy Song deal with family history in "Picture Bride" and related poems? What are some of the issues with which a young poet might have to grapple in her approach to this family history?

- Women and their activities recur frequently in Song's poetry. How does she portray these women, and what is the significance of their activities in Song's poems? Would you argue that she is a feminist poet?

- What is ethnicity, and what kind of impact does it have on Song's attempts to explore her personal experiences and transform them into works of art that appeal to a broad audience? In what ways can the poet deal with ethnicity differently and maintain her integrity as a person and an artist?

- What kind of conflicting values does "Sun-worshippers" exemplify? How does the poet resolve those conflicts? Is the resolution satisfactory?

- What does the term "ghost" refer to, and how does Song reshape the meaning of this term in the poem "Ghost"? What can Americans on the mainland learn from this poem?

- What role does the figure of the mother play in Song's poetry? Does she expand or does she limit the poet's literary imagination?

- What role does art play in Song's poetry?

- Without categorizing in facile terms such as "Asian American" or "Hawaiian," how would you characterize Song's lyrical voice?

BIBLIOGRAPHY

By the Author

POETRY:
Picture Bride, 1983
Frameless Windows, Squares of Light, 1988
School Figures, 1994
The Land of Bliss, 2001

EDITED TEXT:
Sister Stew: Fiction and Poetry by Women, 1991 (with Juliet S. Kono)

About the Author

Chang, Juliana. "Reading Asian American Poetry." *MELUS* 21, no. 1 (Spring, 1996): 81-98.
Chun, Gary. "Poet Sings of Journey of Life." *Honolulu Star-Bulletin*, January 11, 2002.
Cobb, Nora Okja. "Artistic and Cultural Mothering in the Poetics of Cathy Song." In *New Visions in Asian American Studies: Diversity, Community, Power*, edited by Franklin Ng et al. Pullman: Washington State University Press, 1994.
Fujita-Sato, Gayle K. "'Third World' as Place and Paradigm in Cathy Song's *Picture Bride*." *MELUS* 15, no. 1 (Spring, 1988): 49-72.
Hugo, Richard. Foreword to *Picture Bride*, by Cathy Song. New Haven, Conn.: Yale University Press, 1983.
Lim, Shirley. Review of *Picture Bride*, by Cathy Song. *MELUS* 10, no. 3 (Fall, 1983): 95-99.
Song, Cathy. "Cathy's Song: Interview with Cathy Song." Interview by David Choo. *Honolulu Weekly* 4 (June 15, 1994): 6-8.
Song, Cathy, and Juliet S. Kono. Introduction to *Sister Stew: Fiction and Poetry by Women*. Honolulu: Bamboo Ridge Press, 1991.
Sumida, Stephen. *And the View from the Shore: Literary Traditions of Hawaii*. Seattle: University of Washington Press, 1991.
Wallace, Patricia. "Divided Loyalties: Literal and Literary in the Poetry of Lorna Dee Cervantes, Cathy Song, and Rita Dove." *MELUS* 18, no. 3 (Fall, 1993): 3-19.
Zhou, Xiaojing. "Intercultural Strategies in Asian American Poetry." In *Re-placing America: Conversations and Contestations*, edited by Ruth Hsu et al. Honolulu: University of Hawaii Press, 2000.

SUSAN SONTAG

Born: New York, New York
January 16, 1933
Died: New York, New York
December 28, 2004

A controversial and influential critic of the arts and the author of several landmark essays, Sontag was also an innovative writer of fiction.

Annie Leibowitz/Courtesy, Farrar Straus Giroux

BIOGRAPHY

Susan Sontag was born Susan Rosenblatt in New York City. Her businessman father died in China when she was only five, and her mother moved the family to Arizona, where she hoped the climate would alleviate her daughter's asthma. Sontag and her sister Judith spent their early years in Tucson, where they were educated in the public schools. Already evincing signs of her formidable intellect, Sontag began school in the third grade.

She drew on memories of her early years in her short-story collection, *I, Etcetera* (1978), where she mourns the loss of her father and describes herself in her Tucson backyard trying to dig a hole to China. In "Project for a Trip to China," included in this volume, she imagines going to the land where her father died—a trip she later took after she wrote this autobiographical story, which reveals how as a young girl she tried to fill the emptiness and loneliness of her childhood through reading and an intense imagination. Sontag felt the need to draw deeply on her own resources because of what she described as an aloof and alcoholic mother.

Sontag's mother remarried Nathan Sontag when her daughter was twelve, and both Susan and Judith were given their stepfather's last name. The family moved to Canoga Park, California, where Sontag attended North Hollywood High School. A brilliant student who wrote for the student newspaper and was already developing an avid taste for music, art, and literature, Sontag was easily bored—as she recounts in her autobiographical essay "Pilgrimage," published in *The New Yorker* on December 21, 1987.

The precocious Sontag graduated from high school at the age of fifteen and spent a semester at the University of California, Berkeley, a compromise choice because her mother feared her daughter was too young to attend the University of Chicago, her daughter's first choice because of its radical reputation.

However, after only one semester, Sontag departed for Chicago, attracted to its intense intellectual atmosphere and the chance not only to enroll in philosophy and literature classes but also to audit as many other classes as she liked—including one in psychology taught by a brilliant sociology instructor, Philip Rieff, whom she married at the age of seventeen. Their intense relationship and their efforts to educate their son David are explored in "Baby," a story in *I, Etcetera*.

Sontag worked with her husband on a groundbreaking book, *Freud: The Mind of a Moralist* (1959), but her role in this important study was acknowledged only in the first edition and then omitted in subsequent printings of the book following the couple's divorce—a painful episode that Sontag alludes to in "Zero," the prelude to her novel *In America* (2000).

After receiving a master's degree in philosophy from Harvard and teaching at several colleges and universities, including Columbia University and

Sarah Lawrence College, Sontag embarked on a career as a freelance novelist and critic. Her first two novels, *The Benefactor* (1963) and *Death Kit* (1967), received respectable but mixed reviews. To many critics, this work seemed to slavishly imitate the French "new novel" pioneered by writers such as Natalie Sarraute and Alain Robbe-Grillet. Sontag's fiction tended toward the surrealistic, and her literary criticism rejected the social and psychological realism of contemporary American novelists.

Sontag made her reputation as a public intellectual with two collections of criticism, *Against Interpretation, and Other Essays* (1966) and *Styles of Radical Will* (1969). These two works summed up her aesthetic and political positions as an ardent advocate of avant-garde art and as an adversary of U.S. foreign policy in Vietnam, South America, and developing countries, where the United States, in her view, was attempting to enforce its hegemony and thwart the right of other countries to determine their own political systems.

In her later work, especially in her essay collection *Under the Sign of Saturn* (1980), Sontag seemed to temper her leftist politics and take a more conservative position politically and aesthetically, returning to a form of writing that reminded critics of nineteenth century men of letters such as Matthew Arnold who were concerned with preserving cultural values rather than challenging or overturning them. Other books, however, such as *On Photography* (1977) and her novel *The Volcano Lover* (1992) reflected her abiding affection for taking radical positions and for admiring radical thinkers and activists.

Although Sontag devoted most of the last two decades of her life to fiction, she continued to write essays on art and politics. She wrote another book about photography, *Regarding the Pain of Others* (2003), in which she took issue with some of her earlier opinions, and published editorial pieces in *The New York Times*, *The Guardian*, and *The Nation*, supporting U.S. intervention in the former Yugoslavia and opposing the Iraq war.

Sontag was diagnosed with a virulent form of breast cancer in the early 1970's and given only a 10 percent chance to survive. However, through heroic efforts to find new treatments, including experimental chemotherapy in France, she was able to overcome her disease and to write about cancer in *Illness as Metaphor* (1978).

A recurrence of cancer in the 1990's—this time in her uterus—led to drug treatments that damaged her immune system and led to the leukemia that caused her death.

ANALYSIS

Sontag wrote in a highly allusive style; that is, she was constantly referring to other writers and works of art. She assumed—as did Oscar Wilde, one of her great influences—that art of all kinds shaped the world. Writers and artists did not imitate nature—as Aristotle argued—but rather created their own world, so that the works of art are autonomous; they are independent entities that have to be judged in their own terms and not by any standard that society imposed on art or the artist.

Reading a Sontag essay is like taking a course in the history of the arts. Readers without a strong background in literature, art history, and philosophy confront a writer who concedes very little to their lack of knowledge. Even more daunting, she rarely focuses on one work of art or artist. Rather, she refers to many sources to illustrate her point, for example, about the surrealism of photography. In order to grasp her argument, some familiarity with the poet Walt Whitman, the critic Walter Benjamin, and photographers such as Alfred Stieglitz and Diane Arbus is necessary. Moreover, her books on photography contain no photographs—evidently because it is the style of the argument that is important rather than the explanation of any particular photograph.

One way to understand Sontag's difficulty as a writer is to realize that she is challenging her readers' opinions. She is taking issue, in other words, with the way people have been educated. Moreover, she is trying to shape and, in her early essays, to change public opinion. Her writing makes sense insofar as her readers have had the education and life experience to understand and to quarrel with Sontag.

Sontag expects, in other words, to have her ideas attacked. She writes as provocatively as possible to arouse public consciousness about certain issues. She also argues with herself, so that one book may well contradict or at least modify an earlier position she has taken. She called this approach "Thinking Against Oneself," the title she appended to her essay on the Romanian philosopher E. M. Cioran.

A classic example of Sontag's own thinking

against herself is the way that she changes positions on the work of German filmmaker Leni Riefenstahl. In *Against Interpretation,* Sontag defends films such as *Triumph des Willens* (1935; *Triumph of the Will*), a work that glamorized Adolf Hitler and the Nazi movement, because the documentary is a beautifully constructed work of art. Its message may be repugnant, and yet the beauty of its images and the director's supple grasp of the film medium call for the highest praise. However, in "Fascinating Fascism," included in *Under the Sign of Saturn,* Sontag reverses the argument and suggests that it is wrong to praise art apart from its political implications. In this case, she is keen to point out that the glorification of strength that pervades *Triumph of the Will* is part of a fascist aesthetic that suffuses all of Riefenstahl's work as an actress and director.

Sontag's thinking is Hegelian; that is, like the philosopher Hegel, she believes that learning is dialectical—one idea is challenged by its opposite, and eventually a synthesis of opposing ideas will occur. In Sontag's case, she does not so much reject her earlier praise of Riefenstahl's art as suggest it was one-sided and that aesthetics cannot be so easily divorced from politics and that all art has to be viewed not only for itself but also in its historical context.

Sontag's last two novels reflect her desire to see events, personalities, and ideas in a historical context. A novel can encompass the tensions between ideas, characters, and political movements in ways that essays, she believed, could not. Essays demanded a rigor of argument, whereas fiction, though it can be a form of argument, also has to be narrative. In other words, a story must be told.

By setting her stories in the past and writing historical novels, Sontag was able to gain some perspective on ideas that her role as an advocate of ideas in her essays did not allow. In novels, she could contemplate several opposing forces at once and not feel the need to be conclusive. Thus, in *The Volcano Lover* she can provide an empathetic account of Lord Nelson, the war hero who saved Britain from a French invasion, and his lover Emma Hamilton, while at the same time portraying the radical women of the Romantic period who opposed Nelson and the imperial politics of the age.

If Sontag's novels have received mixed reviews, however, it is because her attempt to combine narrative and analysis, history and an assessment of history, is troubling. Storytelling (narrating) and explication (explaining ideas and themes) are quite different modes of writing, and Sontag tried to incorporate both the critic and the creator in fiction.

Perhaps her most successful writing has been the biographical essay, in which she offers an appreciation of the writer's life and career. The best example is "Under the Sign of Saturn," the title essay of her 1980 collection, an essay which does not merely explain the work of critic Walter Benjamin but attempts to evoke his personality, not only by dwelling on certain episodes of his biography but also by lingering over photographs of him for what they reveal about his sensibility. This essay, like the first essay in the collection, "On Paul Goodman," defines Sontag's personal connection to her subject. This autobiographical thrust, reminiscent of some of her short stories in *I, Etcetera,* is perhaps her highest achievement.

AGAINST INTERPRETATION, AND OTHER ESSAYS

First published: 1966
Type of work: Essays

This work encompasses twenty-six essays revealing the impressive range of Sontag's interests—from literary theory to film and popular culture, to philosophy, art history, and the theater.

Sontag's signature essay, "Against Interpretation," like its companion piece, "On Style," highlights her concern with form. Sontag feels she is writing at a time when critics tend to discuss content, reducing works of art to their messages or themes. What art says is less important than how the art expresses itself, Sontag insists. In her view, to treat art as simply a conveyer of content is to negate the idea of art itself.

"Against Interpretation" provides an erudite summary of the history of literary criticism, in which Sontag takes issue with Aristotle's definition of art as mimetic; that is, art as an imitation of nature. To Sontag, this definition makes art beholden to standards outside itself.

The implications of Sontag's position are apparent when she attacks the idea that art can be judged by society's notions of morality. Since those notions change over time and differ from one society to another, art has to transcend the immediate circumstances of its production, and art should be judged by its own terms. In other words, Sontag is reiterating the "art for art's sake" argument advanced by Wilde in his famous essays "The Critic as Artist" and "The Decay of Lying."

Against Interpretation, and Other Essays contains many of Sontag's most famous essays, including "The Imagination of Disaster" (her anatomy of science-fiction films) and "Notes on 'Camp,'" the work that made her virtually an overnight sensation when *Time* magazine published a summary of it. The essay on camp is hardly an essay at all but rather a series of numbered pithy passages. Sontag defines camp in many different ways, but the essential point is that it is a sensibility that values style—works of art that are flamboyant, exaggerated, and even corny. A film such as *King Kong* is campy, for example, because it is so overdone, so self-consciously attempting to be a monster film meant to thrill its audience.

What made "Notes on 'Camp'" so startling is Sontag's willingness to discuss virtually in the same breath high culture (opera) and popular culture (film) as camp. She blurs the distinction between elite and mass cultural tastes, shocking certain critics and exciting others who see her work as revolutionary—a new way to unify disparate kinds of art.

ILLNESS AS METAPHOR

First published: 1978
Type of work: Essay

A probing essay on the nature of human reactions to illness, especially to cancer.

Sontag wrote this polemical book in the wake of her own arduous recovery from breast cancer. Although she nowhere mentions her own illness in the book, her own experience with a life-threatening disease (as she admitted in interviews) was the inspiration for her work.

Sontag's main concern is to refute the idea that there are psychological causes of disease. To her, disease is a physical problem that is best treated by securing the best possible medical diagnosis and therapy. She is particularly disturbed by the idea that cancer, for example, can be induced through the repressing of emotions. She likens this belief to earlier notions that tuberculosis was somehow associated with the artistic sensibility or with especially sensitive natures. In the end, the disease, scientists discovered, had nothing at all to do with personality but with a bacillus that could be treated with antibiotics.

Sontag argues that a mystique envelops diseases such as tuberculosis and cancer, which is only dispelled when the physical causes of these illnesses are revealed. In the nineteenth century, for example, a body of Romantic literature associated tuberculosis with the long-suffering artist, just as cancer in Sontag's own time was associated with certain inhibited personality types. Sontag draws on an impressive body of literature to demonstrate how art has shaped the public's reaction to illness.

The consequences of such Romantic thinking are that the ill person feels doomed—even feeling that he or she has in some mysterious way caused the sickness. This sense of fate works against the patient's efforts to secure the best medical treatment. It even prevents doctors from being honest with the patients for fear that the dreaded word "cancer" will sap the patient's desire to get well. Sontag argues vigorously against this tendency to succumb to fear and shame, urging her readers to take charge of their own medical care by aggressively seeking the best treatment.

THE VOLCANO LOVER

First published: 1992
Type of work: Novel

The Volcano Lover is an erudite historical novel about diplomat and art collector Sir William Hamilton, his wife, Emma, and her lover, Lord Nelson, the British hero who saved England from a Napoleonic invasion.

IN AMERICA

First published: 2000
Type of work: Novel

This historical novel describes the emigration of the great Polish actress Maryna Zalewska to Anaheim, California, where she tries to establish a utopian community.

A historical novel seems a radical departure for Sontag, whose critical work scorns realistic fiction and argues in favor of avant-garde styles that challenge conventional ideas about the self and society. However, on another level, *The Volcano Lover* is an experimental novel. The narrator writes what are, in effect, mini-essays about the nature of art, why people collect it and prize it, and why Sir William Hamilton, in particular, was drawn to the beautiful. The novel is, in other words, about the aesthetic view of life which is, nevertheless, attached to the world of politics and history. Sir William Hamilton is, after all, a British ambassador living in Naples. He is a volcano lover and traverses the hot surface of Mount Vesuvius, an obvious metaphor for the passion that he is able to express only intermittently in his political life and in his marriage to Emma.

Into this aesthetic world Nelson (called only "the hero") intrudes, enticing both Sir William and his wife to his side. Nelson's boldness, his attentiveness, and his single-minded devotion to England and to his destiny as a hero make him irresistible—except to the narrator, whose ironic tone questions the brutal consequences of Nelson's devotion to honor and patriotism.

Both a critical and popular success (the novel was a best seller), *The Volcano Lover* came at a unique moment in Sontag's career, justifying her shift away from the essay form to that which she regarded as a more creative, capacious, and spontaneous kind of writing. Her radical politics and her aesthetics remain an important ingredient in the novel, but in this new form of fiction, she is able to harness her ideas to a very romantic and appealing story.

For a writer often deeply critical and even dismissive of her native land in essays such as "What's Happening in America" (included in *Styles of Radical Will*), *In America* is another surprise. Setting her novel in nineteenth century America, however, allows her to gain some perspective on her ambivalent feelings toward her native land.

On one hand, Zalewska has unrealistic expectations, thinking that she can create and sustain a commune formed of those followers (most of them male) who have followed their charismatic leader to the new world. On the other hand, her mission reflects the grandeur of America, where no dream seems impossible to fulfill. The epigraph for Sontag's novel is poet Langston Hughes's ecstatic remark "America Will Be!"

This sense that the United States has an unlimited future is what draws emigrants to the new land, even though many of them, such as Maryna, fail to achieve their dreams. In her case, she abandons her commune for a return to the theater, providing Sontag with wonderful comic moments as Maryna tours the United States and is exposed to an amusing array of eccentric characters.

Sontag's last novel reflects her desire to write fiction that unifies her interests in art and politics. It also reflects her own self-dramatizing personality and her often-stated view that the United States, for all its faults, is a world in which individuals feel they can invent and reinvent themselves.

Critical opinion divides sharply on this novel, with a minority feeling it is Sontag's best work and the majority considering it rather static and lacking in the deft handling of narrative and characters exemplified by *The Volcano Lover.* Nevertheless, the novel won the National Book Award.

SUMMARY

Although Sontag's novels have earned considerable critical praise, her essays remains the most significant part of her work—not only for their intrinsic merits as dazzling dialogues of ideas but also for their historical importance, since they played a significant role in shaping the cultural discussions of her era. Sontag herself seemed aware of her special place, since, in spite of her avowed desire to write only fiction, she continued to produce provocative essays, collected in *Where the Stress Falls* (2001).

Carl Rollyson

BIBLIOGRAPHY

By the Author

NONFICTION:
Against Interpretation, and Other Essays, 1966
Trip to Hanoi, 1968 (journalism)
Styles of Radical Will, 1969
On Photography, 1977
Illness as Metaphor, 1978
Under the Sign of Saturn, 1980
AIDS and Its Metaphors, 1989
Conversations with Susan Sontag, 1995 (Leland Poague, editor)
Where the Stress Falls, 2001
Regarding the Pain of Others, 2003

LONG FICTION:
The Benefactor, 1963
Death Kit, 1967
The Volcano Lover, 1992
In America, 2000

SHORT FICTION:
I, Etcetera, 1978

DRAMA:
Alice in Bed: A Play in Eight Scenes, pb. 1993

SCREENPLAYS:
Duet for Cannibals, 1969
Brother Carl, 1972
Promised Lands, 1974
Unguided Tour, 1983

DISCUSSION TOPICS

- How is the idea of "camp" related to Susan Sontag's belief that style in art is what is most important?

- In what sense was Sontag "against interpretation"? To what kind of interpretation was she opposed?

- What happens when illness is made into a metaphor? Why is it dangerous to use a word such as cancer as a metaphor rather than as just the description of a disease?

- What ideas in *The Volcano Lover* correspond to the ideas Sontag wrote about in her essays?

- What is Sontag saying about America in her novel *In America*? What does it mean to be an American and to live in the United States?

EDITED TEXTS:
Selected Writings, 1976 (by Antonin Artaud)
A Barthes Reader, 1982
Homo Poeticus: Essays and Interviews, 1995 (by Danilo Kiš)

MISCELLANEOUS:
A Susan Sontag Reader, 1982

About the Author

Kennedy, Liam. *Susan Sontag: Mind as Passion.* Manchester, England: Manchester University Press, 1997.

Poague, Leland, ed. *Conversations with Susan Sontag.* Jackson: University Press of Mississippi, 1995.

Poague, Leland, and Kathy A. Parson, eds. *Susan Sontag: An Annotated Biography, 1948-1992.* New York: Garland, 2000.

Rollyson, Carl. *Female Icons: Marilyn Monroe to Susan Sontag.* New York: iUniverse, 2005.

_____. *Reading Susan Sontag.* Chicago: Ivan R. Dee, 2001.

Rollyson, Carl, and Lisa Paddock. *Susan Sontag: The Making of an Icon.* New York: W. W. Norton, 2000.

Sayres, Sohnya. *Susan Sontag: Elegiac Modernist.* New York: Routledge, 1990.

Seligman, Craig. *Sontag and Kael: Opposites Attract Me.* New York: Counterpoint, 2004.

GARY SOTO

Born: Fresno, California
April 12, 1952

Soto was one of the first writers to capture the life and labor of the impoverished Chicanos in the streets and fields of California.

M. L. Martinelle

BIOGRAPHY

Gary Soto was born on April 12, 1952, in Fresno, California. His parents were Mexican American, and Soto was born into not only a Chicano culture but also a culture of poverty. His father died in 1957, when Gary was only five years old; this created economic hardship for a family that was already having difficulties.

Soto went to school in the Fresno area, and he worked in the fields as an agricultural laborer and as a low-paid factory worker, the inevitable lot of so many in his situation. He entered Fresno City College in 1970; when he started college, he was a geography major, but he switched to English when he entered California State University, Fresno. At that institution, he studied under Philip Levine, a noted American poet. Levine taught him how to read a poem, and he helped Soto to form a style and develop his craft as a poet. Soto graduated magna cum laude from Fresno State in 1974, and he spent the next two years as a graduate student at the University of California, Irvine. He received an M.F.A. in creative writing from Irvine in 1976. He also published a number of poems in important journals and began making his reputation as a poet.

A poet needs to make a living, however, and Soto began to teach in the English and Chicano Studies departments at the University of California at Berkeley. In 1975, he married Carolyn Oda, whose father owned a small farm in the Fresno area. The couple had one daughter and settled in Northern California near the Berkeley campus, where Soto became an associate professor.

In 1974, Soto published his first book of poetry, *The Elements of San Joaquin.* It is an ambitious book that attempts to describe and classify the harsh world of migrant workers and other poor people in Central California. Those workers are portrayed as stoically enduring the hostility or indifference of the Anglo establishment. In 1975, Soto was awarded the Academy of American Poets Prize. In 1977, *Poetry* magazine, the most prestigious journal in the field of poetry, awarded Soto the Bess Hopkins Prize.

Soto's second book of poetry, *The Tale of Sunlight* (1978), represented an expansion of his subject matter and vision. In 1979, he received a Guggenheim Fellowship, and he spent 1979 and 1980 in Mexico City, observing the culture and writing.

In 1981, Soto published *Where Sparrows Work Hard.* These poems are, for the most part, autobiographical pieces that give some distance to pure memoir by the use of irony, especially in the resolution of the poems' structure.

Soto was granted a National Education Association Fellowship in 1981, and in 1984, he received the Levinson Award from *Poetry* magazine. Soto had become one of the most prolific and honored of the young poets of the period. In 1985, another book of his poems, *Black Hair,* was published. It again dealt with childhood experiences and male friendship, but it is filled with forebodings of death.

In 1988, Soto was named Elliston Poet at the University of Cincinnati, and he spent a year in residence there. In 1990, he published his fifth book of poetry, *A Fire in My Hands*, a compilation of poems from the earlier collections. *Who Will Know Us?* (1990) represented a new direction. Soto counterpoints his life as a professor with a wife and daughter in Northern California to his early life as a poor Mexican American child and worker. There are also a number of poems that deal with death, an important and recurrent theme in Soto's work. Soto's 1995 collection, *New and Selected Poems*, was a 1995 finalist for both the *Los Angeles Times* Book Prize and the National Book Award. In 1999, he won the Literature Award from the Hispanic Heritage Foundation, the Author-Illustrator Civil Rights Award from the National Education Association, and the PEN Center West Book Award for *Petty Crimes* (1998).

Soto wrote three collections of prose that portray the world of his childhood and adolescence. He won the American Book Award in 1985 for *Living up the Street: Narrative Recollections*. *Small Faces* (1986) is a book of short narratives that explore the world of the San Joaquin Valley in a less individual way than Soto's poems do; it focuses on community and friendship as well as on adolescence. *Lesser Evils* (1988), Soto's third collection of prose narratives, also deals with his early experiences. Soto saw his prose as having some of the same concentration and imagery as his poetry, but he said that his real achievement as a writer must be in poetry.

ANALYSIS

Soto is one of the most important voices in Chicano literature. He has memorably portrayed the life, work, and joys of the Mexican American agricultural laborer. Furthermore, he has done this with great poetic skill. He has an eye for the telling image in his poetry and prose, and he has the ability to create startling and structurally effective metaphors. Each of his poems has a design. One aspect of that design is his frequent use of an ironic reversal to resolve the poetic structure. His style is concrete and rooted in the language of the fields and the barrio.

There are many significant themes in Soto's poetry. One of the earliest and most persistent is his view of the natural world as a wasteland. Although he uses natural imagery, nature is never benign or pastoral. It is, instead, harsh and unrelenting. It scars those who are nakedly exposed to it from dawn to nightfall. A related theme is Soto's refusal to yield to the temptation to evoke a transcendental view of nature. His heroes are obliterated from that world; they cannot and do not transcend it.

Soto does, however, modulate his bleak view of the human condition when he writes about childhood. That state is filled with a quest for knowledge and experience. In the poem "Chuy," the young speaker may be naïve or mistaken in his idealized love; however, he does manage to pass through his experiences and gain some wisdom, and he does not give in to cynicism. In the later poems, Soto contrasts the bleak conditions of his childhood with the innocence and privilege of his own daughter. In "Small Town with One Street," for example, he shows his daughter a young boy in Fresno whom he says is an image of himself as a child. The daughter is shocked to see that poor and troubled image of her apparently powerful father. Soto did not alter his pessimistic view of the world as he grew older and prospered. In "The Way Things Work," the speaker inventories the expenses of the day and worries about meeting them. The culture of poverty cannot be overcome by relative affluence; it continues to mark Soto's view of the world, as the wind and dirt marked the workers in the field.

Soto's poetic style is marked by the use of short free-verse lines. There are seldom more than three stresses to a line, and the lines often run on, creating the effect of a rapid flow of images hurrying to reach a final resolving line. He uses occasional metaphors, but his primary poetic device is imagery. The poems are packed with images that follow one another, often creating a structural design. Because the poems deal with the Chicano experience in the field or in the street, the language is always concrete and dense in detail. Soto does not write many long poems; nearly all are short lyrics. If he does expand a poem, he does so by creating a longer poem that has many separate sections.

Soto uses irony consistently in his poems. He seems chary of ending a poem with a positive statement or image. The last few lines often reverse or sardonically comment on what went before. These ironic structures convey his bleak view of a world in which everything passes away, including any sign of the poor inhabitants. Soto is concerned not only with the fact of death but also with whether individuals can leave any sign of their presence on an indifferent universe.

Soto is the poet of the Chicano experience, but his view of that people is not hopeful. He shows their condition to be one of hard work with few rewards. There may be a few isolated moments of joy on the street or in the privacy of the home, but difficult economic conditions make such happiness short-lived. The one positive element in Soto's poetry is his portrayal of his own family, which has escaped the confined and limiting world of manual labor Soto had experienced in Fresno. That family is also a composite, as Soto's wife is Japanese American. The family scenes he creates are tender and hopeful.

Soto's prose has many similarities with his poetry. His subject in his prose books is primarily childhood and adolescence. He does not, of course, use the formal devices of poetry in these books, but he does use the same concrete detail and imagery. He often uses the same ironic reversal in many of the short pieces that make up each book. The prose narratives do have more humor than the poems, and they tend to deal more fully with relationships within the Chicano community than the poems do.

THE ELEMENTS OF SAN JOAQUIN

First published: 1977
Type of work: Long poem

This work catalogs the fierce natural forces that make the lives of workers difficult and unfruitful.

The Elements of San Joaquin is a long poem divided into seven sections that together make up the "Elements" of this agricultural workers' world. "Elements" is an interesting word choice, as it has connotations of scientific, objective discourse, while the poem is a direct personal statement. "Elements" may also refer to the four classical elements of the universe: earth, air, fire, and water.

The first section of the poem is titled "Field." The field is described in harsh, naturalistic terms; forces of nature impose their presence and will upon the impoverished workers who work the field. One of these forces, the wind, "sprays dirt into my mouth/ The small, almost invisible scars/ On my hands." The speaker is literally marked by these natural forces; this is not a pastoral communion but a painful union. In the second stanza, there are some positive suggestions, as the speaker's pores "have taken in a seed of dirt of their own." Yet the seed image is ironic because it is not a seed that will flower or produce anything that will sustain life.

The forces in the field continue making marks upon the speaker as they create "lines/ On my wrists and palms." The last stanza brings together the separate parts of the poem. The speaker is "becoming the valley"; humans and nature are, apparently, united. That unity, however, is ironically reversed in the last two lines, when the speaker realizes that the soil "sprouts nothing/ For any of us." The perspective has now widened to include all those who work this land. For them, there is no sustenance to be wrought from the land that they work.

The third section, "Wind," deals with the power of this natural force. The poem presents a human figure waking in the morning beneath a blazing sun. The sky darkens, and a cold wind begins "moving under your skin and already far/ From the small hives of your lungs." Once more, nature is a destructive force. It can burrow under the skin, but it will not bring its life-giving breath to the lungs that need it.

The last section of the poem, "Daybreak," portrays the workers entering an onion field at dawn. They are contrasted to the distant consumer who will literally feed on their labor: "And tears the onions raise/ Do not begin in your eyes but ours," the poet notes. The consumers will not know or see that other world, but the laborers "won't forget what you failed to see,/ And nothing will heal/ Under the rain's broken fingers." The rain does not give life but only shatters those who are vulnerable to its power. The poem ends with an image of rain that first suggests a flourishing world and then denies it. Soto's poems are rooted in actual experience and not in transcendence.

"Chuy"

First published: 1981 (collected in *Where Sparrows Work Hard*, 1981)
Type of work: Poem

A portrait of a poor boy who passes from early experiences through the exploration of his world to his oblivion.

"Chuy" is an autobiographical poem that portrays the earliest formative experiences of the speaker. The poem is divided into separate sections and moves from youthful initiation to oblivion.

The first section of "Chuy" presents the young speaker alone in the landscape announcing his presence and causing changes in his environment. For example, both birds' nests and "pocked fruit" drop into his arms. Such fruitfulness, however, contrasts with his poverty. His lunch bag contains only air from his lungs. Chuy then observes the stars, and a voice announces that he is "blessed/ In the name/ Of a violin."

At the end, however, what transforms him is not nature; it is, instead, a sexual initiation with his first "touch of breast." The fullness of this image reverses the emptiness of his impoverished life and the distance of the stars. He has been acted on by nature in the poem, but the touch is both a conscious act and a transforming one.

The fourth section of the poem further deals with a young man's experience with women. This time, however, it is not an actual sexual experience but an idealistic longing that is released by his vision of a "girl/ On a can of peas." He pictures her as the object of a knightly quest; in contrast, he portrays himself as a poor squire whose wrists are "shackled in sores." At the end of this section, Chuy gains what solace he can by using his knife to pop a pea into his mouth. The section thus ends with an ironic reversal: The ideal is driven out, and all that remains are the actual, all-too-literal peas and not the vision.

In the next section, Chuy is seen as an explorer who wonders about the nature of electricity. He unscrews the flashlight to search for answers; he notices that "light bends." He writes in his journal, "Light/ Is only so strong." For a moment, he is portrayed as a hero who seems to be developing into a scientific genius. The ending, however, brings him back to a reduced world: "Chuy wondered what/ He could do after lunch." The discovery that light bends is not sufficient to fill the emptiness of his days. It seems, instead, an isolated experience. There is no outlet to develop that curiosity about the world into the discipline of scientific inquiry.

In the last section, Chuy attempts to discover not only the nature of things but also "why/ He was there." He now sees nature in a poetic rather than a scientific manner; he sees the moon as "a lozenge/ Sucked before sleep." Both light and the moon are seen as natural elements that are vulnerable to change and decay. This foreshadows the end of the poem, in which Chuy buries a leaf and other signs of this existence on Earth so that extraterrestrial explorers will discover a sign of his presence among the ruins. The poem moves from the emergence of the hero to his destruction; in that destruction, Chuy attempts to leave some sign of his creative search for meaning.

"Black Hair"

First published: 1985 (in *Living up the Street*, 1985)
Type of work: Short story

This story describes a young man's early experiences as a laborer and his attempts to come to terms with that life.

"Black Hair" is a brief autobiographical story that deals with Soto's working experiences. The narrator introduces that theme in the first sentence: "There are two kinds of work: One uses the mind and the other uses muscle." The work that uses muscle is degrading, but it is the only choice the narrator has during the troubled period he is going through. Muscle work is also the only option for both the small group of workers with whom Soto comes into contact and the larger group who are condemned to such labor by their race or birth.

The main character is a seventeen-year-old runaway. He takes a romantic swim in the ocean at a Southern California beach, but he must then confront the world of work to survive. He sleeps in abandoned cars and houses and walks miles to Glendale to apply for a job in a tire factory.

The work is exhausting and dirty, and the character has no place to live until he receives his first paycheck. At the tire factory, he is isolated from the black workers by race and the Mexican workers because of his poor Spanish. He is alienated from everyone, without the support that a home supplies, and he must survive with his muscle and what wits he has.

In one scene, the narrator is united with the poor Mexican workers who had spurned him earlier. When immigration authorities make a raid, his boss thinks he is an alien, so he runs with the others. Afterward, those who fled make up outrageous stories about their exploits. For the only time, there is both joy and unity at work. The telling of tales suddenly changes the atmosphere of the factory; it seems to bring the world of the street into the world of work. The spinning of stories also points to the path that Soto would later take. The work of writing would use, of course, not muscle but mind; that type of work would be joyful and meaningful.

Soto portrays the lives of menial laborers at the tire factory as dismal and joyless. The work is monotonous and dirty and makes the workers' home lives just as empty. Soto asks why they had all arrived at this place but supplies no answer. He merely gives an image that defines this life: "When you picked up a tire, you were amazed at the black it could give off." The menial and unending work literally marks those caught in it, as the dirt of the San Joaquin Valley marks the farmworkers there. An alternative is suggested in the first sentence of the story: work that "uses the mind." Soto would take that way, although he continues to write of the life of manual labor that he has escaped. He does not, however, describe mental labor as an alternative in the story. He shows little solidarity with the poor working men; he asks only why these people have reached such a hopeless and degrading state. There is, of course, an understanding of their condition and an implicit sympathy, but Soto does not provide an answer to his own question.

SUMMARY

Soto has chosen as his subject the culture of poverty. He portrays that world without sentimentality; it is a hard and, at times, an inhuman one. Soto has described this world in detailed and memorable images and complex poetic structures. Of special importance to Soto are childhood and adolescence. In his view, childhood shapes people for good or ill. People who develop their imaginations may find a way out of a life of monotonous manual labor and find "the work that uses the mind," which may make for a fuller life.

James Sullivan

BIBLIOGRAPHY

By the Author

POETRY:
The Elements of San Joaquin, 1977
The Tale of Sunlight, 1978
Where Sparrows Work Hard, 1981
Black Hair, 1985
Who Will Know Us?, 1990
A Fire in My Hands, 1990
Home Course in Religion, 1991
New and Selected Poems, 1995
A Natural Man, 1999
One Kind of Faith, 2003

LONG FICTION:
Nickel and Dime, 2000
Poetry Lover, 2001
Amnesia in a Republican County, 2003

CHILDREN'S LITERATURE:
Baseball in April, and Other Stories, 1990
Taking Sides, 1991
Neighborhood Odes, 1992 (poetry)
Pacific Crossing, 1992
The Skirt, 1992
Too Many Tamales, 1993
Local News, 1993
Crazy Weekend, 1994
Jesse, 1994
Boys at Work, 1995
Canto Familiar, 1995 (poetry)
The Cat's Meow, 1995
Chato's Kitchen, 1995
Off and Running, 1996
Buried Onions, 1997
Novio Boy, 1997 (play)
Petty Crimes, 1998
Big Bushy Mustache, 1998
Chato Throws a Pachanga, 1999
Chato and the Party Animals, 1999
Nerdlania, 1999 (play)
Jesse De La Cruz: A Profile of a United Farm Worker, 2000
My Little Car, 2000
Body Parts in Rebellion: Hanging Out with Fernie and Me, 2002 (poetry)
If the Shoe Fits, 2002
The Afterlife, 2003
Chato Goes Cruisin', 2004

NONFICTION:
Living up the Street: Narrative Recollections, 1985
Small Faces, 1986
Lesser Evils: Ten Quartets, 1988
A Summer Life, 1990 (39 short vignettes based on his life)
The Effect of Knut Hamsun on a Fresno Boy, 2000

EDITED TEXTS:
California Childhood: Recollections and Stories of the Golden State, 1988
Pieces of the Heart: New Chicano Fiction, 1993

DISCUSSION TOPICS

- How is the theme of male friendship explored in Gary Soto's works?

- How is death a consistent theme in Soto's works?

- Describe the image of the Mexican American laborer as portrayed by Soto.

- Discuss Soto's use of natural imagery.

- How is irony central to Soto's works?

- Discuss Soto's theme of the individual in conflict with an indifferent universe.

- How do Soto's novels build upon the themes examined in his poetry?

About the Author

Blasingame, James. "Interview with Gary Soto." *Journal of Adolescent and Adult Literacy* 47 (November, 2003): 266-267.

Bruce-Novoa, Juan. "Patricide and Resurrection: Gary Soto." In *Chicano Poetry: A Response to Chaos*. Austin: University of Texas Press, 1982.

Candelaria, Cordelia. *Chicano Poetry.* Westport, Conn.: Greenwood Press, 1986.

Cooley, Peter. "I Can Hear You Now." *Parnassus* 8, no. 1 (1979): 297-311.

De la Fuentes, Patricia. "Mutability and Stasis: Images of Time in Gary Soto's *Black Hair.*" *American Review* 16 (1988): 188-197.

Murphy, Patricia. "Inventing Lunacy: An Interview with Gary Soto." *Hayden's Ferry Review* 18 (Spring/Summer, 1996): 29-37.

Olivares, Julián. "The Streets of Gary Soto." *Latin American Literary Review* 18 (January-June, 1990): 32-49.

Soto, Gary. "The Childhood Worries: Or, Why I Became a Writer." *Iowa Review* 25 (Spring/Summer, 1995): 104-115.

Williamson, Alan. "In a Middle Style." *Poetry* 135 (March, 1980): 348-354.

JEAN STAFFORD

Born: Covina, California
July 1, 1915
Died: White Plains, New York
March 26, 1979

The beautifully crafted fiction of Stafford contains sensitive portraits of characters, especially young women and children, who feel alienated from their worlds.

BIOGRAPHY

Jean Wilson Stafford was born in Covina, California, on July 1, 1915, to Ethel McKillop Stafford and John Richard Stafford, a writer of Westerns who had three years before moved out from Missouri. In 1920, John sold his Covina ranch, moved to San Diego, and began to play the stock exchange. Within a year, he had lost his life savings as well as a substantial inheritance from his wealthy father. John next took his family to Colorado, first settling in Colorado Springs, then in Boulder, only to find that the frontier he had imagined, with its limitless opportunities, was gone forever. Although John did occasionally sell a story, he was never again able to support his family. As she saw her beloved father retreating further and further into bitterness and eccentricity, and her mother seemingly becoming indifferent to everything except her money-making ventures, Jean Stafford developed the sense of alienation that permeates her work.

Although the small university town of "Adams," or Boulder, is shown in Stafford's fiction as a dull, provincial, and intellectually stifling place, it did at least provide Ethel with the economic opportunity she had so desperately sought. She kept the family afloat by running a boardinghouse for students, and though the family was poor, the children could live at home, work, and get college educations.

After she entered the University of Colorado in 1932, the beautiful and brilliant Jean Stafford found friends both among the professors and the student "barbarians," a group of intellectuals who, like Stafford, were too impoverished to join Greek-letter organizations. She also won her first recognition as a writer when her play about the German composer Ludwig van Beethoven won first place in a contest and was performed on campus. Nevertheless, Stafford's college years were not untroubled. A medical student broke off his engagement to her, saying he needed a wife with better social credentials. More important, when her flamboyant friend Lucy McKee committed suicide, Stafford was suspected of being somehow responsible. The resulting scandal probably cost her a Phi Beta Kappa key and caused her parents to leave Boulder for Oregon.

In 1936, after she was awarded both her bachelor's and her master's degrees, Stafford spent a fellowship year at the University of Heidelberg. When she returned to the United States, she went to a writers' conference in Boulder, where she met the young poet Robert Lowell, a member of the famous and wealthy Massachusetts family, who was obviously attracted to her. After a miserable year teaching at a girls' school, Stephens College in Missouri, which she satirized effectively in "Caveat Emptor" (1956), Stafford went to Cambridge, Massachusetts, to be near James Robert Hightower, a longtime friend to whom she had become engaged.

Lowell, however, continued to pursue her, and Stafford found him fascinating. In several ways, their relationship was to prove disastrous. In December, 1938, Lowell, who was drunk, caused a car crash in which Stafford was badly injured. Despite a long hospital stay and excruciatingly painful operations like the one graphically described in her short story "The Interior Castle" (1946), Stafford was never to look or feel the same again. During her recuperation, she formed the habit of drinking alcohol to alleviate her suffering; eventually, of course, this addiction would further damage her health and imperil her relationships. The marriage of Lowell and Stafford in 1940 produced still more problems. Stafford submitted to Lowell's religious obsessions and to his emotional and physical abuse; she also remained loyal to him when he was imprisoned for refusing to serve in the armed forces.

Stafford must have been annoyed by the fact that in the academic circles they frequented, she was expected to take a subordinate role because of her gender. Moreover, from the first, the poor girl from the West, who had her own distinguished ancestors, was infuriated by the snobbishness of the Lowell family. The great success of Stafford's first novel, *Boston Adventure* (1944), which satirized the society of which her husband was a part, must have been immensely satisfying to her.

By 1946, the marriage was over. During the next several years, Stafford drank heavily, threatened suicide, and spent time in mental hospitals. Nevertheless, in 1947, she published one of her best novels, *The Mountain Lion*, which was based on her memories of the West. During this period, too, she got to know Katherine White, the fiction editor of *The New Yorker*, who became her friend, her adviser, and her mentor. As a result of this association, over the next thirty years Stafford was to publish some twenty-two short stories in the highly respected magazine.

Although the early 1950's saw Stafford into and out of another marriage, this time to *Life* staff writer Oliver Jensen, they proved to be her most productive years. In 1952, she published an impressive novel, *The Catherine Wheel*, and in 1953 she brought out a collection of her short fiction. What ended this creative spurt has been much debated. Certainly Stafford had problems with alcoholism. She may also simply have been too contented to write. At last she had found the perfect man for her, the writer Abbott Joseph ("A. J." or "Joe") Liebling, whom she met in 1956, married in 1959, and lived with happily until his death in 1963. During those years, Stafford published only two children's books and a great many book and film reviews.

After Liebling's death, Stafford was again short of money, and although she disliked teaching, she was forced to accept visiting lectureships and speaking engagements. She also wrote feature articles, reviews, book introductions, and *A Mother in History* (1966), a journalistic account of an extended interview with Marguerite C. Oswald, the mother of Lee Harvey Oswald. In 1970, she was awarded a Pulitzer Prize for *The Collected Stories of Jean Stafford*, published the preceding year. However, her career as a fiction writer was over; she was never able to finish a projected autobiographical novel, to be titled "The Parliament of Women."

During her final years, Stafford waspishly alienated members of her family and even her most devoted friends. In 1976, after a stroke left her unable to talk or to write, she seems to have turned to her housekeeper for solace. When her final will was read, it was found that Stafford had made this uneducated woman her literary executor and had left her the bulk of her estate.

ANALYSIS

Stafford's fictional world is one of loneliness, isolation, and alienation. For one reason or another, her protagonists are separated from other individuals or from their society as a whole. Even though they are often powerless to transcend their situation, their detachment makes these characters excellent observers. It is through their eyes that Stafford tells her stories.

Some of Stafford's most appealing protagonists are imaginative, rebellious children. In "Bad Characters" (1954), Emily Vanderpool becomes fascinated by a young thief and, with her, embarks on a brief but exciting crime spree. In "A Reading Problem" (1956), the same protagonist gets involved with a traveling evangelist, again with hilarious results. In such stories, however, the protagonists face nothing worse than a scolding from their parents. There is no danger that society will actually expel them.

Some of Stafford's adults, too, manage to transcend the problem of alienation from society. In "Maggie Meriwether's Rich Experience" (1955), for example, an American girl who has been humiliated by a group of sophisticates at a French country house transcends her embarrassment by dramatizing it for American friends, thus making it truly "rich," or funny. Similarly, in "Polite Conversation" (1949), Margaret Heath and her husband, both of whom are working writers, risk losing only their time and their privacy when local organizers try to incorporate them into summer activities.

One suspects that the Heaths can find appropriate excuses.

In such comic and satirical stories, the protagonist-observer emerges triumphant. Stafford's tone, however, can be far gloomier. In "A Modest Proposal" (1949), for example, a dinner guest is confronted at once with the prevalence and the horror of colonial racism. On a more personal level, in "A Country Love Story" (1950), a wife comes to realize that what she had thought was a temporary estrangement between herself and her husband is, in fact, the kind of separate life that he desires. Sometimes, too, Stafford blends sadness with satire, as in the novel *Boston Adventure*, in which Stafford ridicules Boston society and yet sympathizes with the outsider who has exposed herself to it.

A similar mixture is evident in the autobiographical story "The Tea Time of Stouthearted Ladies" (1964), in which struggling boardinghouse keepers, like Stafford's own mother, engage in transparent attempts to convince themselves and one another that their daughters have wonderful lives, both as "Barbarians" excluded from college social life and as summertime waitresses serving the affluent. In this story, the eavesdropping daughter pities and yet despises the "ladies," while recognizing that their efforts will enable girls like her to escape.

It is interesting to note that the patterns and preoccupations of Stafford's works did not change in the course of her writing career, although her style did. While it has many virtues, *Boston Adventure* has the fault of Victorian wordiness. By the publication of *The Mountain Lion* just three years later, however, Stafford had transformed her style; her prose had become precise, economical, and colloquial. The new style was particularly effective in recording the thoughts of the young, such as the brother and sister in *The Mountain Lion*; the inexperienced, such as Maggie Meriwether; or the intellectually limited, such as the woman in "The End of a Career" (1956) who devoted her life to being beautiful.

Unfortunately, style alone was not sufficient to maintain interest in Stafford's works. Compared to the exciting new experimental forms that began to appear in the 1970's, her realistic works seemed hopelessly old-fashioned. The result was that, for a decade and a half, Stafford was largely ignored. The first sign of a renewed interest in the author was Twayne's publication in 1985 of a biography of

Stafford written by Mary Ellen Williams Walsh. Over the next twenty years, major critical and biographical studies appeared at regular intervals. It was evident that Stafford had been rediscovered. Once again, it had been recognized that her unique voice, as well as her flawless style, should ensure her a permanent place in literary history.

BOSTON ADVENTURE

First published: 1944
Type of work: Novel

A poor girl, the daughter of immigrants, realizes her dream of penetrating Boston society, only to discover its falseness and its cruelty.

Boston Adventure, Stafford's first novel, was also her most popular work. Although critics do not consider it her best novel, they do point out how effectively Stafford presents the inner life of the protagonist, much in the manner of the nineteenth century novelists Henry James and Marcel Proust.

The story is divided into two parts, each of which has been given the title of a place. Book 1 is called "Hotel Barstow," after the summer place on the North Shore across from Boston, where Sonia Marburg, the poverty-stricken protagonist, sees the wealthy Bostonians whose lives she yearns to imitate. Book 2 is titled "Pinckney Street," after the exclusive area in Beacon Hill to which Sonia is taken by a benefactor.

Sonia has good reason to want to escape from the place of her birth. The daughter of two immigrants who have failed to achieve the American Dream, she spends her childhood in a drafty shack, listening to her parents' quarrels, which are interrupted only by their bouts of drunkenness. Her beautiful but bad-tempered Russian mother, who works as a chambermaid at Hotel Barstow, hates her husband, a German shoemaker she met on the boat trip to America, because he cannot give her the luxury he promised. From her earliest consciousness, Sonia feels unwanted; indeed, her father tells her that she should never have been born.

Sonia cannot help contrasting the chaotic atmosphere of her home with the order of the Hotel Barstow room occupied by an aristocratic Boston spinster, Lucy Pride. Because of her tranquil demeanor and her self-possession, Miss Pride becomes a symbol of an ideal way of life. When her father asks Sonia what she would like to be, she replies simply that she would like to live on Pinckney Street.

Ironically, it is the disintegration of Sonia's family that makes her dream a possibility. Her father walks out; her little brother, who is born shortly afterward, wanders away from home and dies in a snowstorm; and her mother, who has gradually declined into insanity, is institutionalized. At this point, Miss Pride, who has always taken an interest in Sonia, offers her a position as a secretary, tuition for the training she needs, and, most important, her own room in the mansion on Pinckney Street. The final sentence of this section has a significance that at the time Sonia does not grasp. Dropping in unexpectedly, Miss Pride has found her protégé reading the newspaper comic strips. Politely, she suggests that she does not expect to find such reading in her home. This comment should alert Sonia to the fact that whatever she gains by moving to Pinckney Street will be at the loss of her own identity.

In book 2, Sonia becomes the person Miss Pride wishes her to be, tailoring not only her reading habits but also her clothes and her conversation to her employer's pattern. Even though she is half in love with a young doctor, Philip McAllister, Sonia accepts the fact that Miss Pride has reserved him for her niece, the lovely, independent Hopestill ("Hope") Mather, whom Philip adores. Sonia soon becomes privy to this subtle society's secret codes, understanding what may be inferred from a word, a gesture, or a casual reference. This skill leads her to a shocking discovery: Hope is pregnant by a notorious philanderer and intends to maintain her respectability by marrying Philip. After the wedding, when it becomes evident that Philip, now undeceived, is taking a subtle revenge upon her, Hope deliberately causes her horse to throw her, losing both her baby and her own life. Now aware of the real viciousness beneath the surface of Beacon Hill society, Sonia sadly realizes that by promising to remain with Miss Pride until her death, she, too, has sold herself into bondage.

THE CATHERINE WHEEL

First published: 1952
Type of work: Novel

A middle-aged spinster and a twelve-year-old boy separately do battle with their selfish impulses.

As the epigraph indicates, the title of *The Catherine Wheel* was taken from a passage in *Murder in the Cathedral* (1935), a play by T. S. Eliot that compares the things of this world to children's pleasures, as ephemeral as firework displays. In her final novel, Stafford again shows the tragic results that occur when individuals become so intoxicated with their own imagined needs that they are willing to sacrifice other people, as well as their own integrities, in order to fulfill them.

The story is told alternately by two protagonists, Katharine Congreve, a wealthy, unmarried woman from Boston, and Andrew Shipley, a twelve-year-old boy, the son of John Shipley, the man whom Katherine loved and lost twenty years before. For years, Andrew and his older twin sisters have spent their summers at Katharine's country house in northern New England, never dreaming that their hostess is anything more than the longtime friend of both their parents and the first cousin of their mother, Maeve Maxwell Shipley. To the children, Katharine is the ultimate aunt, an understanding friend and confidant as well as a magician who can always suggest an exciting remedy for boredom.

This summer, however, both Andrew and Katharine are experiencing serious inner conflicts. After a difficult year at home, Andrew has looked forward to spending the summer with his best friend, Victor Smithwick, a fascinating local boy. This year, however, Victor is acting as nurse for his ailing older brother Charles, and he has no time for Andrew. Andrew feels betrayed, and out of hurt and anger he begins to pray for Charles's death. Meanwhile, Katharine is seriously considering betraying the children who trust her. Discovering in his middle years that he has done nothing with his talents, John Shipley has convinced himself that if he divorces his wife and marries Katharine, he can have a new beginning. Although she has lost her respect for John, Katharine is tempted to take him, not out of love but out of a desire for revenge.

Because both of these essentially decent and sensitive protagonists feel so deeply guilty about their thoughts, each of them mistakenly thinks that the other knows his or her secret. Because they are extremely fond of each other, the result is an intensification of their misery. Even Stafford admitted that the tragic ending of *The Catherine Wheel* was rather contrived. At a party modeled on a disastrous one of twenty years before, Katharine insists on a display of the spinning fireworks that spell out her name. When one of them sets Charles's clothing on fire, Katharine saves him, sacrificing her own life and begging the question of her love affair. At the end of the book, however, there is a moving scene in which Stafford has her protagonists realize, too late, that they have taken the wrong direction in their lives. The emotions that Katharine and Andrew should have cherished and nurtured were their deep feelings for each other.

"THE HEALTHIEST GIRL IN TOWN"

First published: 1951 (collected in *The Collected Stories of Jean Stafford,* 1969)
Type of work: Short story

An eight-year-old girl triumphs over a pair of sickly playmates who have made her believe that being healthy is somehow disgraceful.

"The Healthiest Girl in Town" is one of the stories based on Stafford's years in Colorado. It is set in 1924 in a Western town whose principal industry is "tuberculars," that is, people who have come there hoping for a cure for tuberculosis or, at least, for an extension of their lives. Naturally, the town is dominated by anecdotes of sickness and death. In this atmosphere, Jessie, the eight-year-old narrator, feels like an outsider. Blessed with a strong constitution and sensibly raised by her widowed mother, a practical nurse, Jessie cannot manage to get interestingly ill.

This problem becomes acute when she is thrown into the society of two spoiled, sickly girls, Laura and Ada Butler. Although she despises them on sight, Jessie is forced to play with them because her mother has a new position nursing the senile grandmother of the family.

The Butler girls seem to want Jessie at their home merely so that they can have someone to torment. They comment on her mother's inferior position and suggest that Jessie's own low status in society is proven by the fact that she has no ailments. Finally, they inquire into the death of Jessie's father. Although it was gangrene that killed him, Jessie is inspired to say that the cause of his death was leprosy. Immediately, she realizes that she is trapped. If she admits that she lied, the girls will never let her forget it, but if she sticks to her story, she is firmly convinced that both her mother and Jessie herself will be exiled to the Fiji Islands.

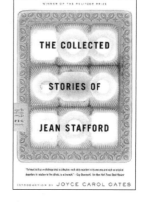

Following up their advantage, the Butler girls summon Jessie to take their nauseating "cure" for leprosy. She, however, has had enough. Defiantly, she insists that her father was shot, that he was as tall as the room they are standing in, and—the only truth in her tirade—that she has been called "the healthiest girl in town." She now has as much pride, or "vanity," in her health as the Butler girls do in their illness. Never again, in her visits to their home, does Jessie let them make her feel inferior.

Because it moves toward a discovery, in this case that health is not to be despised, "The Healthiest Girl in Town" is typical of Stafford's short stories. Not all of her stories, however, have the comic tone that is here evident. When she did choose to use comic irony, Stafford won high praise from critics, who did not hesitate to compare her to Mark Twain, America's greatest humorist.

Jean Stafford

"IN THE ZOO"

First published: 1955 (collected in *The Collected Stories of Jean Stafford*, 1969)
Type of work: Short story

Two sisters recall their childhood with a woman who derived her own happiness from destroying others.

"In the Zoo" is a story told within a frame. It begins and ends in the Denver, Colorado, zoo, where two middle-aged women are sitting on a bench, eating popcorn and watching the animals. Neither of them lives in Denver; Daisy has just come there to put her sister, the narrator, on a train heading east. After her departure, Daisy will return to her own home west of Denver. Neither sister has any intention of visiting Adams, Colorado, the nearby town where they spent their childhood. However, when Daisy observes that the blind polar bear reminds her of Mr. Murphy, the sisters are thrust back into a time and place they can never forget.

After the deaths of their parents, the two little girls were sent to Adams, where arrangements had been made for a Mrs. Placer to keep them in her boardinghouse. Mrs. Placer believed that everyone and everything in the world was a fraud. Aided by her embittered lodgers, she pursued her life's work, decoding conversations to reveal hidden insults and to ferret out evil intentions. She taught the girls to distrust everyone—their classmates, their teachers, even the tradesmen whom they encountered.

Their only friend was Mr. Murphy, an alcoholic with a collection of pets, including two capuchin monkeys. Mr. Murphy welcomed the girls' visits to his menagerie. One day, he gave them a puppy, which they named Laddy, and when they presented him as a future watchdog, Mrs. Placer let them keep him. Laddy was an exuberant, affectionate dog until Mrs. Placer decided to curb his freedom. She took him away from the girls, renamed him Caesar, abused and mistreated him, and turned him into a monster. When Mr. Murphy heard what had happened, he became furious. With one of his monkeys on his shoulder, he headed for the boardinghouse. As soon as Mrs. Placer saw him, she let

Caesar out, and the dog attacked Mr. Murphy and killed his monkey. The next day, Caesar died a horrible death; Mr. Murphy had poisoned him.

As soon as they were old enough, the sisters left Adams. They never went back. However, the author utilizes the frame to reveal a tragic truth: that they never recovered from what had been done to them in childhood. Given their history, their comments about the zoo animals are not as lighthearted as they at first appear to be; in fact, they show how deeply the sisters dislike the whole human race. At the train, both of them express sentiments that are worthy of Mrs. Placer. Daisy points out that someone else has snatched a redcap; the narrator suspects the porter of being a thief. Once the train begins to move, Daisy begins a letter to her sister detailing her suspicions of a priest and her certainty that the passing fields contain marijuana instead of alfalfa.

"In the Zoo" differs from many of Stafford's other stories in that, though it moves toward a revelation, the protagonists do not arrive at enlightenment; instead, only the author and the reader comprehend what has happened. As the title suggests, though the sisters think they are observers at the zoo, in fact they are as trapped as the animals in the zoo; their cages are just less visible.

SUMMARY

In her fiction, Stafford shows how the world looks from the perspective of those who feel alienated from it. Although her works range in tone from rollicking comedy and social satire to profound tragedy, they all move toward a revelation, knowledge that may bring new hope to the protagonist, who is usually female, but that more often destroys her peace of mind or even her life.

The rediscovery of Stafford's work is due in part to her insight into the inner lives of girls and young women. However, critics have also taken a new interest in her status as a woman writer from the American West, a section that has characteristically been thought of as a male domain, producing fiction in which women's interpretations of life there were not especially important. The fact that Stafford's fiction can sustain intense analysis from a number of different perspectives is an indication of her profound insight into the human condition.

Rosemary M. Canfield Reisman

BIBLIOGRAPHY

By the Author

SHORT FICTION:
Children Are Bored on Sunday, 1953
Bad Characters, 1964
Selected Stories of Jean Stafford, 1966
The Collected Stories of Jean Stafford, 1969

LONG FICTION:
Boston Adventure, 1944
The Mountain Lion, 1947
The Catherine Wheel, 1952
A Winter's Tale, 1954 (novella in *New Short Novels*; with others)

NONFICTION:
A Mother in History, 1966

CHILDREN'S LITERATURE:
Arabian Nights: The Lion and the Carpenter, and Other Tales from the Arabian Nights, Retold, 1959
Elephi: The Cat with the High I.Q., 1962

About the Author

Austenfeid, Thomas Carl. *American Women Writers and the Nazis: Ethics and Politics in Boyle, Porter, Stafford, and Hellman.* Charlottesville: University Press of Virginia, 2001.

Goodman, Charlotte Margolis. *Jean Stafford: The Savage Heart.* Austin: University of Texas Press, 1990.

Hulbert, Ann. *The Interior Castle: The Art and Life of Jean Stafford.* New York: Alfred A. Knopf, 1992.

Roberts, David. *Jean Stafford: A Biography.* Boston: Little, Brown, 1988.

Rosowski, Susan J. *Birthing a Nation: Gender, Creativity, and the West in American Literature.* Lincoln: University of Nebraska Press, 1999.

Ryan, Maureen. *Innocence and Estrangement in the Fiction of Jean Stafford.* Baton Rouge: Louisiana State University Press, 1987.

Walsh, Mary Ellen Williams. *Jean Stafford.* Boston: Twayne, 1985.

Wilson, Mary Ann. *Jean Stafford: A Study of the Short Fiction.* New York: Twayne, 1996.

DISCUSSION TOPICS

- How does the theme of isolation function in Jean Stafford's work?

- In her fictional works that are set in the West, Stafford is said to write about the West as it is seen by women rather than by men. What are some examples of this distinctive viewpoint?

- How does Stafford use humor in her fiction?

- Many of Stafford's works are about children or women who are victimized. Which of her characters seem totally helpless, and why?

- In which of Stafford's stories does a character's understanding of a situation have good results?

- In which of Stafford's stories does a revelation have unfortunate results?

- Do you see reflections in Stafford's fiction of her own battles with domestic violence, alcoholism, and insecurity?

Barbara Stafford

WILLIAM STAFFORD

Born: Hutchinson, Kansas
January 17, 1914
Died: Lake Oswego, Oregon
August 28, 1993

One of the most prolific and imaginative poets of his time, Stafford produced many poems of enduring value and greatly contributed to his readers' understanding of the creative process.

BIOGRAPHY

William Edgar Stafford was born in Hutchinson, Kansas, on January 17, 1914, the eldest of three children of Earl Ingersoll and Ruby Mayer Stafford. Though his family was relatively poor and had to move from town to town for his father to find work, Stafford's childhood seems to have been a happy one. His parents were enthusiastic readers and talkers, providing young William with a wealth of shared stories, poems, songs, gossip, and, especially in the case of his mother, a receptive listener to his own stories.

During their frequent moves during the Depression of the 1930's, Stafford took on odd jobs to help support the family: delivering papers, raising vegetables and selling them door to door, harvesting sugar beets, and working as an electrician's mate in an oil refinery. Even so, Stafford found time to roam the countryside, fishing and hunting with his father or camping alone. He developed a love of nature that was to sustain him in the years ahead.

After graduating from high school, he attended junior colleges briefly before enrolling at the University of Kansas, where he devoted himself more seriously to writing. While at the university, his lifelong political convictions also began to take shape.

Stafford joined a protest against segregation of the student cafeteria, defying campus rules by sitting with black students. It was at this time that Stafford took a further step that was to change the course of his life forever: He declared himself a pacifist opposed to U.S. involvement in World War II.

When the United States entered the war, Stafford applied for conscientious objector status and served four years in alternative service camps in Arkansas, Illinois, and California. Because the war was popular, maintaining pacifist principles required great courage. Few people could sympathize with conscientious objectors, and the experience for Stafford was isolating. (He describes this time in his first published work, 1947's *Down in My Heart*, a fictionalized memoir that he submitted for his master's thesis at the University of Kansas.) Stafford, though, enjoyed the work—firefighting, soil conservation, and other Forest Service tasks—and, if anything, this experience strengthened his belief in the pacifism and in the gentle, receptive, "listening" attitude that characterizes his best poetry. Moreover, the years in camp made Stafford more sharply attuned to the tensions between the demands of the external, social world and the distinctive inner life from which his poetry flowed.

In 1943, while still in the camps in California, Stafford met and married Dorothy Frantz, a schoolteacher and the daughter of a minister. After his release, Stafford taught high school briefly with his wife in San Francisco and then worked for Church World Service, a relief agency. In 1948, he took a position at the Lewis and Clark College in Portland, Oregon. During this time, Stafford wrote steadily and began to publish in important literary journals. From 1950 to 1952, he attended the University of Iowa, where he studied with some of the most significant writers of his generation, including Robert Penn Warren, Paul Engle, Randall Jarrell, and Karl Shapiro. After receiving his Ph.D., he returned to Portland and began a prolific and distinguished career as a poet, teacher, and lecturer.

Stafford's first volume of poetry, *West of Your City* (1960), did not appear until the poet was forty-six. The book met with immediate critical success, and thereafter the volumes followed in rapid succession, including *Traveling Through the Dark* (1962, winner of the National Book Award), *The Rescued Year* (1966), *Allegiances* (1970), *Someday, Maybe* (1973), *Stories That Could Be True: New and Collected Poems* (1977), *A Glass Face in the Rain: New Poems* (1982), *An Oregon Message* (1987), and *Passwords* (1991). Stafford also published two books of essays and interviews on the art of poetry as well as children's books and correspondence with the poet Marvin Bell. In addition, Stafford published more than twenty small-press books and chapbooks.

Stafford has been highly honored. In addition to the National Book Award, he won the Award in Literature of the American Academy of Arts and Letters, a Guggenheim Fellowship, and the Shelley Memorial Award. He served as a consultant in poetry for the Library of Congress and on the Literature Commission of the National Council of Teachers of English. He also lectured widely for the U.S. Information Service in Egypt, India, Pakistan, Iran, Nepal, Bangladesh, Singapore, and Thailand.

ANALYSIS

When once asked what made him start writing poetry, Stafford replied, "What made you stop?" This rather cagey answer reveals several of his most basic assumptions about poetry. First, for Stafford, poetry is not a specialized endeavor limited to an elite few. It is a natural activity available to anyone. Second, the value of poetry lies not in the success of the final product—which is no doubt why most people do stop writing—but rather in the creative process.

In *You Must Revise Your Life* (1986), Stafford speaks eloquently about trusting the creative process: "At times in my thinking I take my hands off

the handlebars and see what happens. In a poem I do that all the time. I let the total momentum of the experience dictate the direction the poem goes." Relinquishing control of the poem, letting it find its own direction, engenders a process of discovery that Stafford finds most valuable. Indeed, this openness to surprises is central to his poetry. To begin with a plan and then execute it would, in Stafford's view, kill the poem. Poetry comes alive in the readiness to accept whatever the imagination, the world, the language itself might offer.

Stafford's poems offer ample evidence of the worth of this approach. His work is full of surprises for writer and reader alike; when a Stafford poem begins one can never be sure where it will end. Nor is Stafford reluctant to break conventions. For example, nature is often humanized in his poetry: "The green of leaves calls out," "Trees hunch their shoulders," and "a bird says 'Hi!,'" for example.

Stafford ignores the strict modern censure of the pathetic fallacy with a childlike delight not to be found in other poets of his generation. That his work is so varied and unpredictable makes it difficult to generalize about him. His poetry does contain certain recurring themes, however, such as memory and the passing of time, concern about nuclear annihilation, the evocative power of the wilderness and its potential destruction, and, most prominently, a desire to be at home in the world, attentive and receptive both to the inner life and the outer environment, which Stafford once called the "two rivers of my life." Broadly stated, Stafford's most inclusive concern is "learning how to live."

For Stafford, learning how to live consists primarily of learning how to be receptive to the world and how to interpret its messages. Like William Wordsworth, Stafford views the world as charged with meaning. The poem "Sophocles Says" (1966) begins: "History is a story God is telling/ by means of hidden meanings written closely/ inside the skins of things." The poet's task is to penetrate the surfaces of things to discover their underlying meanings. In this sense, Stafford rejects the modernist view that nature is simply a nonhuman otherness with nothing to tell humans about themselves. Instead, he insists, "everything that happens is the message." In such a world, "everything counts," whether it is a nuclear bomb test, a snowstorm, or a cocktail party. The crucial point is to see the reality beneath the experience. Such "seeing" allows one to learn how to live in harmony with the world and, by implication, with God.

Stafford often expresses this harmony in images of home. Home for Stafford is not a specific place but an attitude of mind, a passive welcoming of process. Just as he believes that poems should unfold as they wish, without too much pressure from the poet, so too does he suggest that to live rightly is to let life unfold without trying to control or manipulate it. Images of wind and rivers, of going with rather than against their motions, embody the value he places on passive receptiveness.

The antithesis to this receptive, passive stance Stafford locates in its exact opposite: war. War is active, aggressive, and most often an attempt to manipulate the world rather than understand it. Fears of war, nuclear holocaust, and encroaching destruction of the wilderness appear throughout his poems. In "Cover Up" (1991), he writes: "don't worry about the mountains;/ and some trees even might survive, looking/ over a shoulder from places too cold for us." Because Stafford sees all life as having spirit—"there is a spirit abiding in everything"—destruction of the natural world, through war or development, appears as the most grotesque consequence of having failed to learn how to live harmoniously.

Still, Stafford's poetry as a whole is hopeful, playful, generous, sympathetic, and filled with a kind of wisdom rarely achieved and, even more rarely, so beautifully expressed. His style is colloquial but tight and quirky, full of sudden turns. His poems are always accessible and, indeed, inviting to the reader; he wishes to be understood. Clearly, too, Stafford's faith in the creative process has led him to many discoveries, and he is not reluctant to share those discoveries, or even, at times, to offer friendly advice. In "Freedom" (1973), he writes: "If you are oppressed, wake up about/ four in the morning: most places,/ you can usually be free some of the time/ if you wake up before other people." In "The Little Ways That Encourage Good Fortune" (1973), he warns: "If you have things right in your life/ but do not know why,/ you are just lucky, and you will not move/ in the little ways that encourage good fortune." Readers of Stafford will find themselves fortunate to follow the path of a poet who learned so well how to live.

"TRAVELING THROUGH THE DARK"

First published: 1962 (collected in *Traveling Through the Dark*, 1962)
Type of work: Poem

The poet finds a dead deer on a mountain road and faces a painful dilemma.

"Traveling Through the Dark" is Stafford's most famous, most often anthologized poem. It is somewhat atypical, as it tells a story about a real experience in a fairly straightforward way. Yet in its underlying concern with nature—in this case, a deer found dead in the road—with humans' invasion of the wilderness, and with the individual's responsibility to do what is right "for us all," the poem reveals some of Stafford's abiding themes.

"Traveling Through the Dark" achieves its power by subtly blending the symbolic and the real and by seeing underneath the surface event to its larger consequences. The title suggests not so much a drive on a mountain road as a spiritual journey through unknown territory. At the same time, something quite real has happened. Stafford has "found a deer/ dead on the edge of the Wilson River road." That he names the road specifically gives the poem the feel of authentic experience.

Roads and paths, for Stafford, often symbolize the ongoing process of life, and here he must confront a dilemma that involves his deepest relation to all of life. At first, he realizes that he should roll the deer into the canyon to protect other drivers who come after him; he notes that "to swerve might make more dead." When he examines the deer, however, he discovers that it is a pregnant doe; its fawn is still alive, waiting to be born. Suddenly, the choices are much more complicated. Should he try to save the fawn, or do as he originally intended?

He must act quickly, but the poem does allow the suspense to build. Where other writers might have treated this crisis sentimentally, Stafford shifts the focus from what he is feeling to a vivid, pulsing description of the scene:

The car aimed ahead its lowered parking lights;
under the hood purred the steady engine.
I stood in the glare of the warm exhaust turning
red;

around our group I could hear the wilderness listen.

The car lights point the way ahead, and the engine purrs as if it too were alive, waiting. The warm exhaust fumes "turning red" in the glow of the taillights suggest the blood that must now be flowing on the ground and cast a ghastly coloring over the whole scene. Most important, the poet can "hear the wilderness listen." To hear something listen is to listen carefully indeed. That it is the wilderness that is listening attributes an awareness of nature that is characteristic of Stafford's poetry; it also implies that his decision matters not only to the fawn and to the speaker but also to the whole of life, which waits to see what he will do.

The decision is not easy, nor does the speaker say how he arrives at it. He simply says that he "thought hard for us all—my only swerving—,/ then pushed her over the edge into the river." "For us all" here can mean the poet, the doe, the fawn, the wilderness, and, by implication, all living things. His thought swerves, as a car would have done, but he acts as he feels he must. By deliberately leaving out the precise nature of that thought, Stafford forces the reader to imagine the difficulty of the choice and thus puts the reader, retrospectively, into his dilemma.

"THINGS I LEARNED LAST WEEK"

First published: 1982 (collected in *A Glass Face in the Rain: New Poems,* 1982)
Type of work: Poem

A collection of random observations leads to an ominous reminder of death.

"Things I Learned Last Week" is a wonderfully odd, apparently random poem that illustrates a central element of Stafford's poetics. The poem at first seems remarkably offhand and unambitious, a simple disconnected listing of tidbits Stafford happened across during the week. Such an approach, lacking any grand intentions, reveals Stafford's willingness to follow his impulses wherever they might lead him.

The first two stanzas record observations that one would not usually expect to find in a poem: "Ants, when they meet each other,/ usually pass on the right," and "Sometimes you can open a sticky/ door with your elbow." Hardly stunning discoveries, these facts amuse partly because Stafford has put them in the poem. They are some of the things he learned last week and so must be included. Perhaps they imply that everyone learns something by paying attention to the small, daily events that are usually ignored.

The next stanza humorously depicts a "man in Boston" who "has dedicated himself/ to telling about injustice." It seems that the poem is about to take a more serious turn, but Stafford adds an element of irony to his description of the man by saying: "For three thousand dollars he will/ come to your town and tell you about it." Stafford gently obliterates the man's dedication simply by mentioning his lecture fees. The man has obviously dedicated himself to making a profit from injustice, making a career out of it, and so he himself commits a kind of injustice and a glaring hypocrisy. There is injustice in the world, no doubt, but Stafford sees that its opponents often participate in it, much as opponents of war often resort to violent protests.

Stafford has also learned some things about writers during the week, and he treats them, too, with a bemused irony. "Yeats, Pound, and Eliot saw art as/ growing from other art. They studied that." Here, Stafford implicitly rejects the poetics of three towering figures of modern literature. Because they believed that art grew from other art, they studied art, forming a closed, elitist circle and cutting themselves off from the soil of daily experience—the soil out of which Stafford's own poem grows.

The final two stanzas introduce a darker subject—death—but it is treated playfully at first. "If I ever die, I'd like it to be/ in the evening. That way, I'll have/ all the dark to go with me, and no one/ will see how I begin to hobble along." The use of the conditional "if" in reference to the one certain fact of existence, the preference for evening, and the hint of embarrassment at being seen hobbling along all make death seem hardly more than a clumsy problem of decorum. The final stanza, however, pushes the poem to a larger consciousness of death that is no joke:

> In The Pentagon one person's job is to
> take pins out towns, hills, and fields,
> and then save the pins for later.

It is one of the grim absurdities of modern life that one person's job would consist of taking pins, indicating targets, out of maps. That he saves the pins "for later" is an ominous reminder that there will be more wars, that death on a large scale will come again, without regard to the poet's preference for evening.

The poem begun so lightly thus leads to the inescapable knowledge of humanity's destructive power and the constant readiness for war that hovers over human existence. Everything that precedes the final stanza, however humorous, takes on a poignancy when seen in the light of the threat of nuclear annihilation. A poem that seems pointless and harmless at first thus sharpens itself at the end by reminding the reader of the dark current running beneath daily life.

"IT'S ALL RIGHT"

First published: 1991 (collected in *My Name Is William Tell,* 1992)

Type of work: Poem

Stafford sees that the natural world can console people for the difficulties they encounter in the social world.

"It's All Right" is one of Stafford's most charming poems. It is an example of his characteristic impulse to include the reader in the collaborative process of the poem's meaning. The poem's language and tone are simple and reassuring; it is as if the reader is being cheered up by an old friend or given some helpful counsel by a wise grandfather.

The poem speaks to the reader directly, as many Stafford poems do, addressing the reader as "you"

throughout. Stafford is concerned not only with the events of his own life but with the events of others' lives as well. The experiences he describes are ones that anyone can recognize. "Someone you trusted has treated you bad./ Someone has used you to vent their ill temper." Surely, all readers encountered such treatment. Yet Stafford knows that these difficulties are an inevitable consequence of social life: "Did you expect anything different?"

Stafford goes on to list, with sympathetic understanding, the failures and frustrations that, expected or not, can wear people down. "Your work—better than some others'—has languished,/ neglected. Or a job you tried was too hard,/ and you failed. Maybe weather or bad luck/ spoiled what you did." Stafford takes care to imagine types of disappointments in work that could apply to a wide variety of readers, from writers, who often feel unfairly overlooked, to farmers, whose best efforts may be ruined by the caprice of the weather.

Stafford knows, too, that personal relationships often cause pain. "That grudge, held against you/ for years after you patched up, has flared,/ and you've lost a friend for a time. Things/ at home aren't so good." In only ten lines, the poem has covered many of the sources of unhappiness that people experience in their daily encounters with the world, and the cumulative weight of the poem has become indeed heavy.

Having reached its low point, however, the poem suddenly turns. "But just when the worst bears down/ you find a pretty bubble in your soup at noon,/ and outside at work a bird says, 'Hi!'/ Slowly the sun creeps along the floor; it is coming your way. It touches your shoe." After such large disappointments, what can bring back happiness are the small things not usually noticed—"a pretty bubble"—and the steady, dependable forces of nature. If the social world is inevitably the source of frustration and disillusionment, the poem seems to say, the natural world is just as surely the source of contentment, consolation, and beauty.

SUMMARY

In a preface to *An Oregon Message,* Stafford said of his poetry that he must allow himself to be "willingly fallible" to deserve a place in the realm where "miracles happen." Whether his poems deal with home, memory, wilderness, fear of war, ordinary daily events, or the creative process itself, this quality of trust in the imagination and his ability to make, or let, miracles happen make Stafford so consistently engaging. Stafford's poems may not be perfect, but they do offer many surprises and provide a vivid picture of one man's quest to learn "how to live."

John Brehm

BIBLIOGRAPHY

By the Author

POETRY:

West of Your City, 1960
Traveling Through the Dark, 1962
The Rescued Year, 1966
Eleven Untitled Poems, 1968
Weather: Poems, 1969
Allegiances, 1970
Temporary Facts, 1970
Poems for Tennessee, 1971 (with Robert Bly and William Matthews)
Someday, Maybe, 1973
That Other Alone, 1973
In the Clock of Reason, 1973
Going Places: Poems, 1974
North by West, 1975 (with John Haines)
Braided Apart, 1976 (with Kim Robert Stafford)
Stories That Could Be True: New and Collected Poems, 1977
The Design in the Oriole, 1977
Two About Music, 1978
All About Light, 1978
Things That Happen Where There Aren't Any People, 1980
Sometimes Like a Legend, 1981
A Glass Face in the Rain: New Poems, 1982
Smoke's Way: Poems from Limited Editions, 1968-1981, 1983
Roving Across Fields: A Conversation and Uncollected Poems, 1942-1982, 1983
Segues: A Correspondence in Poetry, 1983 (with Marvin Bell)
Stories and Storms and Strangers, 1984
Listening Deep, 1984
Wyoming, 1985
Brother Wind, 1986
An Oregon Message, 1987
Fin, Feather, Fur, 1989
A Scripture of Leaves, 1989
How to Hold Your Arms When It Rains: Poems, 1990
Passwords, 1991
My Name Is William Tell, 1992
The Darkness Around Us Is Deep, 1993 (selected by Bly)
The Way It Is: New and Selected Poems, 1998

DISCUSSION TOPICS

- More than most poets, William Stafford saw himself in relation to his readers. How would you characterize this relationship?

- Are there any circumstances in which Stafford's receptiveness weakens his poetry?

- How does Stafford complicate the dilemma of "Traveling Through the Dark"?

- What convictions underlie Stafford's rejection of art "growing from other art"?

- Does destruction of the wilderness, in Stafford's view, do more harm to the wilderness or to the destroyer?

William Stafford

NONFICTION:

Down in My Heart, 1947
Friends to This Ground: A Statement for Readers, Teachers, and Writers of Literature, 1967
Leftovers, A Care Package: Two Lectures, 1973
Writing the Australian Crawl: Views on the Writer's Vocation, 1978
You Must Revise Your Life, 1986
Writing the World, 1988

EDITED TEXTS:

The Voices of Prose, 1966 (with Frederick Caudelaria)
The Achievement of Brother Antonius: A Comprehensive Selection of His Poems with a Critical Introduction, 1967
Poems and Perspectives, 1971 (with Robert H. Ross)
Modern Poetry of Western America, 1975 (with Clinton F. Larson)

About the Author

Andrews, Tom, ed. *On William Stafford: The Worth of Local Things.* Ann Arbor: University of Michigan Press, 1993.

Holden, Jonathan. *The Mark to Turn.* Lawrence: University Press of Kansas, 1976.

Kitchen, Judith. *Writing the World: Understanding William Stafford.* Corvallis: Oregon State University Press, 1999.

Pinsker, Sanford. "William Stafford: 'The Real Things We Live By.'" In *Three Pacific Northwest Poets.* Boston: Twayne, 1987.

Stafford, Kim. *Early Morning: Remembering My Father, William Stafford.* St. Paul, Minn.: Graywolf Press, 2002.

Stitt, Peter. "William Stafford's Wilderness Quest." In *The World: Hieroglyphic Beauty: Five American Poets.* Athens: University of Georgia Press, 1985.

WALLACE STEGNER

Born: Lake Mills, Iowa
February 18, 1909
Died: Santa Fe, New Mexico
April 13, 1993

Often called "the Dean of Western Letters," Stegner devoted his life to depicting the true West, as opposed to the "Wild West" sensationalized in popular fiction and motion pictures.

Library of Congress

BIOGRAPHY

Wallace Stegner was born in Lake Mills, Iowa, on February 18, 1909, the son of George and Hilda Paulson Stegner. His father was a dynamic but unstable dreamer who was always coming up with schemes to strike it rich in some new part of the West. Stegner's mother cherished culture, tradition, polite manners, and all the values of established civilization. She was mismatched to the rowdy, uncouth George Stegner but remained with him until her death from cancer in 1933.

Stegner had an unstable childhood because his family was always moving. They lived in Iowa, North Dakota, Saskatchewan, Montana, and Utah. This is the vast region that Stegner would write about for the rest of his life. He worshiped his mother but had mixed feelings about his improvident father, who sometimes provided the family with luxuries and sometimes led them to the brink of starvation.

Wallace, a sickly and timid boy, buried himself in books. He did so well in school that he was able to enter the University of Utah at the age of sixteen. During this time he began to conceive the possibility of becoming a professional writer, but he wisely continued with his academic work and remained a scholar and teacher throughout his life. He taught at a number of different colleges and universities, gradually building a reputation and achieving financial security. His salary as a professor enabled him to devote time to writing without financial anxiety, and his growing number of publication credits

made it easier for him to advance in the academic world. He became known as a distinguished American writer and one of the leading authorities on the American West.

Stegner projected his own psychological conflicts onto his fictitious characters. His mismatched parents had left him with problems about his personal identity. Wallace was so impressed by his own family history that he wrote thinly disguised versions of it in many novels and stories. Stegner was attracted to his father's adventurous spirit and his mother's high moral principles; he spent the rest of his life trying to reconcile these conflicting elements in his own nature through his writing. Perhaps his father's recklessness influenced him to select the risky career of a freelance writer, while his mother's conservative influence may have caused him to seek security by becoming a tenured college professor.

The combination was good for Stegner, who became a famous author and a revered teacher. He established one of the world's best creative writing programs at Stanford University in California and remained associated with it from 1945 until his retirement in 1971. He received many honors and awards during his lifetime, including election to the American Academy of Arts and Sciences and the National Academy of Arts and Letters.

Readers who first become acquainted with Stegner through his fiction often go on to read some of his equally well-written nonfiction, which includes such fine works as *Beyond the Hundredth Meridian: John Wesley Powell and the Second Opening of the West* (1954) and *The Gathering of Zion: The Story of the Mormon Trail* (1964). He was also a distinguished essayist as well as a biographer and historian. Many of his best essays were reprinted in *The Sound of Mountain Water* (1969).

Stegner died in 1993 as a result of injuries sustained in an automobile crash in New Mexico. He left behind a distinguished body of work in both fiction and nonfiction. His best memorial, though, may be Stanford University's Wallace Stegner Creative Writing Center, which he founded and directed for many years.

ANALYSIS

Stegner wrote in the great tradition of American realism. Other famous authors of this school were William Dean Howells, Theodore Dreiser, Sherwood Anderson, Stephen Crane, and William Faulkner, to name only a few. The distinguishing feature of realistic fiction is that it deals with ordinary events in the lives of ordinary people; the author's intention is to make the work resemble real life as most people experience it. Plots do not take spectacular turns but evolve slowly, the way most lives evolve. Changes do occur in people's lives, but they take place slowly and without any orderly pattern.

It was appropriate for Stegner to work in the tradition of realism because it was his lifelong purpose to depict what the American West was really like. For many years, popular fiction had been presenting a lurid picture of the West. The general public imagined a panorama of cowboys and Indians, the U.S. Cavalry riding to the rescue, shootouts on Main Street, masked bandits holding up stagecoaches, cattle stampedes, burning wagon trains, saloons full of drunken men and immoral women, and all the other stereotypes that are still perpetuated in motion pictures and on television. In his famous short story "The Blue Hotel" (1898), Stephen Crane highlighted the contrast between the real West and the Wild West of dime novels; this was what Stegner also wanted to do.

Stegner knew that, in reality, most of its people were quiet, hardworking pioneers trying to build homes and raise families. These were the people he admired, not legendary figures such as Billy the Kid or Jesse James. Many of Stegner's male characters carried guns, but they could not draw their weapons in a split second or shoot with superhuman accuracy.

The problem with literary realism is that it can be dull, as real life contains few dramatic events. Realism depends on sensitive description and close psychological analysis; the most important events take place inside characters' minds. Stegner was especially interested in how people change. In his novels, these changes may take place over lifetimes; in his short stories, the character changes often take place in a matter of minutes, as in "The Blue-Winged Teal."

Novelist James Joyce applied the word "epiphany" to fiction. An epiphany, in this sense, is like a miniature religious experience, a spiritual insight into the true nature of reality that brings about a change of character. These are not necessarily pleasant experiences but can be unpleasant or even terrifying; nevertheless, they are an essential part of growing up. Such epiphanies are integral to many of Stegner's short stories and novels.

In "The Blue-Winged Teal," for example, the whole point of the story is to be found in young Henry Lederer's sudden insight into his father's true nature—and, hence, into his own true nature as his father's son. In Stegner's best-known novel, *Angle of Repose* (1971), the hundreds of pages of narrative lead up to the final epiphany in which the narrator, Lyman Ward, understands his grandparents, their whole generation, their world, and his own nature as their descendant. He understands something that his contemporaries are in danger of forgetting: that it is important to learn to accept life with all of its limitations.

Although Stegner was a contemporary of many of America's most famous authors, including F. Scott Fitzgerald and Ernest Hemingway, he never achieved comparable popular success. His low-key approach to writing was not calculated to attract a mass audience. He supported himself and his family by teaching in colleges and consequently did not feel compelled to sensationalize his material. He is known to connoisseurs of good writing for his sensitive descriptions of people and places as well as for his crystal-clear, unaffected prose style. Readers who are looking for thrills may be disappointed with Stegner's fiction, but those who are looking for understanding of human nature will find his work satisfying.

Stegner preferred writing about the nineteenth century to the twentieth. He was appalled by the growing scorn of the work ethic, the loss of religious faith, the cynicism about morality, the use of drugs, and the sexual libertinism that he regarded as diseases of the modern world. His interest in the past led him to write history and biography as well as fiction.

Although Stegner is best known as a fiction writer, he left a large body of distinguished nonfiction behind when he died at the age of eighty-four. This versatility is the mark of keen intelligence and dedication to literature. He was also a college professor for much of his life, passing on to younger generations his love of learning, his love of literature, and his love for the American West.

THE BIG ROCK CANDY MOUNTAIN

First published: 1943
Type of work: Novel

A man drags his wife and two sons all over the West in search of riches but ends up penniless and disillusioned.

The Big Rock Candy Mountain was Stegner's first critical and popular success. The title derives from a popular song of the early twentieth century which describes "The Big Rock Candy Mountain" as a utopia where riches grow on bushes.

The book's protagonist, Harry "Bo" Mason, is one of the many dreamers who came West in search of riches. He tries many different occupations but fails to strike it rich. His wife, Elsa, wants security, respectability, and peace of mind, but she is tied to Bo. They have two children. Chet, the elder, inherits his father's temperament; Bruce inherits his mother's temperament, and he is considered a sissy by other boys and by his father.

Bo's best opportunity comes when the Volstead Act introduces Prohibition after World War I. He begins smuggling whiskey across the Canadian border in a car. For a time, he is making considerable money and lavishing it on his family. Then the same thing happens to him that happened repeatedly to freelance entrepreneurs during the growth

of the West: A group of better-organized, better-capitalized men drives the independent operators out of business.

Stegner uses a sophisticated format. His story is told from the points of view of all four family members. In the early chapters, the viewpoints of Bo and Elsa are featured, while those of Chet and Bruce become more prominent as the boys grow older. The story covers a period from 1906 to 1942. During that time, the family moves to North Dakota, Washington, Minnesota, Saskatchewan, Utah, and Nevada. Stegner describes the beauties of these places perhaps better than any other writer. He also describes the hardships of existence in regions where summer droughts kill crops and winter blizzards leave whole herds of sheep and cattle dead, standing in their tracks shrouded in ice.

Like most of Stegner's fiction, *The Big Rock Candy Mountain* is autobiographical, and Bruce Mason is a self-portrait. Bo and Elsa die in pursuit of the American Dream, the dream that the new land offers unlimited opportunities to everyone. The trouble is that Bo and his wife have different dreams and are hopelessly incompatible.

At the end of the novel, Bruce, who is now a college graduate, realizes that he must try to reconcile the values he has inherited from both parents. At the end, with both his parents and his older brother dead, Bruce reflects on what their tragedies mean to him:

Perhaps it took several generations to make a man, perhaps it took several combinations and re-creations of his mother's gentleness and resilience, his father's enormous energy and appetite for the new, a subtle blending of masculine and feminine, selfish and selfless, stubborn and yielding, before a proper man could be fashioned.

Wallace Stegner

"THE BLUE-WINGED TEAL"

First published: 1955 (collected in *Collected Stories of Wallace Stegner,* 1990)
Type of work: Short story

A young college student comes home to nurse his dying mother and struggles to cut himself free from a sordid, unhappy past.

Stegner is an acknowledged master of both the novel and short-story forms, and "The Blue-Winged Teal" is often cited as one of his best stories. "The Blue-Winged Teal" fits squarely into the tradition of American realism. It deals with ordinary events among ordinary people.

A young man named Henry Lederer who has returned home from college to be at his dying mother's bedside now feels out of place in his hometown. College has taught him to value culture and intellectual achievement; his father's ignorant cronies seem gross and absurd. Henry wants to get back to his college environment, but he has no money and is forced to share his father's hotel room and eat at his father's dingy, smelly poolroom. He finds that he despises his father for his lowbrow tastes and immoral behavior. His mother had kept his father on a higher plane, but as soon as his mother dies, his father returns to his old habits. After Henry's mother has been dead for only six weeks, his father is already consorting with loose women; he comes home smelling of cheap perfume.

Henry goes duck hunting and returns with nine ducks of assorted species. Later, one of his father's cronies cooks the ducks for a special feast. One of the ducks is a blue-winged teal; its beauty moves his father to tears, because he remembers how Henry's mother loved those birds.

Henry Lederer experiences an epiphany. He suddenly realizes that his father shares his grief but has a different way of expressing it. Perhaps more important, he realizes that his feelings are not unique but are shared by the whole human race. He realizes that he is young and self-centered; he also realizes that he is surrounded with quiet human suffering that is not often expressed. He becomes a different man as a result of this epiphany; its effect is to release him from psychological cap-

tivity in his hometown and to allow him to return to college, where he can pursue his career.

ANGLE OF REPOSE

First published: 1971
Type of work: Novel

A cultured woman with artistic talents shares her engineer husband's adventures in the West during the period following the Civil War.

Angle of Repose is generally considered to be Stegner's best novel. The narrator, Lyman Ward, a retired history professor, is writing a biography of his grandmother, Susan Burling Ward, and recounting her adventures in the West during the 1870's and 1880's. At the same time, the narrator is recording his own problems as a biographer and as a lonely, divorced retiree. This stylistic device allows Stegner to write about the past in the third-person voice and about the present in the first-person voice.

Stegner based his novel on a collection of letters written by Mary Hallock Foote to a woman friend in the East. His sophisticated novel is thus a combination of fact and fiction, of history and biography dramatized by his creative imagination.

Susan is a sensitive woman with artistic talents that find expression in writing, drawing, and painting. She loves culture and refinement and is subjected to a life of hardship and disillusionment when she falls in love with Oliver Ward, a mining engineer who takes her to the West.

Susan's sketches and written descriptions of the West prove to be in demand by Eastern publications. For years, she is the mainstay of the family; her husband, though intelligent and industrious, meets with one failure after another. Stegner describes their life in various mining communities. They have three children, and Susan struggles to make a home.

Susan and Oliver are essentially incompatible. She is verbally expressive, while he is taciturn, and she loves refinement and culture, while he loves the raw West. Yet they remain together throughout their long lives. Stegner's narrator says that his main purpose in writing Susan's biography is to try to determine why people such as his grandparents stayed married when people of his own time will separate on the merest whim.

Periodically, the narrator breaks into his story to tell about his day-to-day problems. His son thinks that the narrator is too old to be living alone and wants to put him in a nursing home. The young

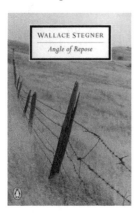

college girl he has hired as a secretary complicates his life with her personal problems, which involve drugs, sex, and a generally irresponsible lifestyle.

Past and present come together at the end of the novel. The narrator reveals that Oliver Ward develops a serious drinking problem because of his many disappointments in life. This leads to further marital estrangement because Susan had such high moral standards. The narrator has his own drinking problem, which he believes he has inherited from his grandfather.

Finally, the narrator describes Susan's illicit love affair with her husband's best friend, who is more sensitive and artistic than Oliver, and how that affair leads to tragedy. She and her lover, Frank Sargent, are so involved in a rendezvous that they do not realize that her five-year-old daughter has wandered off and drowned. Frank is so overwhelmed with remorse that he commits suicide.

Though the narrator's grandparents continue to live together for almost half a century, their relationship remains formal and distant. Stegner's narrator concludes that he is like his grandfather, and he is similarly unable to forgive his own wife, who has also been unfaithful. He chooses to remain alone for the rest of his life.

SUMMARY

Stegner loved the landscape and people of the West. He believed in the traditional American virtues of hard work, integrity, and fair play. Although he was as good a writer as any of his more famous contemporaries, he did not achieve spectacular commercial success because he avoided sensationalism. He wrote in the great tradition of American realism and wanted to depict the real West, which was vastly different from the violent West of the popular media. He taught literature and creative writing for much of his life and inspired many young writers.

Wallace was so impressed by his own family history that he wrote thinly disguised versions of it in many novels and stories. Stegner was attracted to his father's adventurous spirit and his mother's high moral principles; he spent the rest of his life trying to reconcile these conflicting elements in his own nature through his writing.

Bill Delaney

BIBLIOGRAPHY

By the Author

LONG FICTION:
Remembering Laughter, 1937
The Potter's House, 1938
On a Darkling Plain, 1940
Fire and Ice, 1941
The Big Rock Candy Mountain, 1943
Second Growth, 1947
The Preacher and the Slave, 1950
A Shooting Star, 1961
All the Little Live Things, 1967
Angle of Repose, 1971
The Spectator Bird, 1976
Recapitulation, 1979

Joe Hill, 1980
Crossing to Safety, 1987

SHORT FICTION:
The Women on the Wall, 1950
The City of the Living, and Other Stories, 1956
Collected Stories of Wallace Stegner, 1990

NONFICTION:
Mormon Country, 1942
One Nation, 1945 (with the editors of *Look*)
Look at America: The Central Northwest, 1947
The Writer in America, 1951
Beyond the Hundredth Meridian: John Wesley Powell and the Second Opening of the West, 1954
Wolf Willow: A History, a Story, and a Memory of the Last Plains Frontier, 1962
The Gathering of Zion: The Story of the Mormon Trail, 1964
The Sound of Mountain Water, 1969
The Uneasy Chair: A Biography of Bernard DeVoto, 1974
Ansel Adams: Images 1923-1974, 1974
One Way to Spell Man, 1982
American Places, 1983
Conversations with Wallace Stegner on Western History and Literature, 1983
The American West as Living Space, 1987
On the Teaching of Creative Writing: Responses to a Series of Questions, 1988 (Edward Connery Lathem, editor)
Conversations with Wallace Stegner, 1983, rev. 1990
Where the Bluebird Sings to the Lemonade Springs: Living and Writing in the West, 1992
Marking the Sparrow's Fall: Wallace Stegner's American West, 1998 (Page Stegner, editor)
Stealing Glances: Three Interviews with Wallace Stegner, 1998 (James R. Hepworth, editor)
On Teaching and Writing Fiction, 2002 (Lynn Stegner, editor)

EDITED TEXTS:
An Exposition Workshop, 1939
Readings for Citizens at War, 1941
Stanford Short Stories, 1946, 1947 (with Richard Scowcroft)
The Writer's Art: A Collection of Short Stories, 1950 (with Scowcroft and Boris Ilyin)
This Is Dinosaur: The Echo Park and Its Magic Rivers, 1955
The Exploration of the Colorado River of the West, 1957
Great American Short Stories, 1957 (with Mary Stegner)
Selected American Prose: The Realistic Movement, 1958
Report on the Lands of the Arid Region of the United States, 1962
Modern Composition, 1964 (4 volumes)
The American Novel: From Cooper to Faulkner, 1965
Twenty Years of Stanford Short Stories, 1966
The Letters of Bernard DeVoto, 1975

About the Author
Arthur, Anthony, ed. *Critical Essays on Wallace Stegner*. Boston: G. K. Hall, 1982.
Benson, Jackson J. *Wallace Stegner: His Life and Work*. New York: Viking Press, 1996.
_____, ed. *Down by the Lemonade Springs: Essays on Wallace Stegner*. Reno: University of Nevada Press, 2001.

DISCUSSION TOPICS
- What, according to Wallace Stegner, are the characteristics of the "true West"?
- Discuss Stegner's evocation of western landscape in *Angle of Repose*.
- In which of Stegner's short stories do problems of personal identity figure prominently?
- What is unusual about the point of view in *The Big Rock Candy Mountain*? What do the shifts in point of view accomplish?
- Stegner taught creative writing to Edward Abbey, Wendell Berry, Larry McMurtry, and Raymond Carver, among others. Do these writers share literary qualities that might be attributed to Stegner's influence?

Colberg, Nancy. *Wallace Stegner: A Descriptive Bibliography.* Lewiston, Idaho: Confluence Press, 1990.

Cook-Lynn, Elizabeth. *Why I Can't Read Wallace Stegner, and Other Essays.* Madison: University of Wisconsin Press, 1996.

Foote, Mary Hallock. *A Victorian Gentlewoman in the Far West: The Reminiscences of Mary Hallock Foote.* Edited by Rodman W. Paul. San Marino, Calif.: The Huntington Library, 1972.

Meine, Curt, ed. *Wallace Stegner and the Continental Vision: Essays on Literature, History, and Landscape.* Washington, D.C.: Island Press, 1997.

Nelson, Nancy Owne. "Land Lessons in an 'Unhistoried' West: Wallace Stegner's California." In *San Francisco in Fiction: Essays in a Regional Literature,* edited by David Fine and Paul Skenazy. Albuquerque: University of New Mexico Press, 1995.

Rankin, Charles E., ed. *Wallace Stegner: Man and Writer.* Albuquerque: University of New Mexico Press, 1996.

Robinson, Forrest Glen, and Margaret G. Robinson. *Wallace Stegner.* Boston: Twayne, 1977.

GERTRUDE STEIN

Born: Allegheny, Pennsylvania
February 3, 1874
Died: Neuilly-sur-Seine, France
July 27, 1946

American expatriate author Stein helped to reshape the sound of American prose.

Library of Congress

BIOGRAPHY

Gertrude Stein was born in Allegheny, Pennsylvania, on February 3, 1874, the youngest of five children in a well-to-do Jewish family of German descent. Before she was a year old, her family began a sojourn in Austria and France that would last five years. Stein's early exposure to the sound of English, German, and French may account for her conviction that words possess a weight and shape of their own.

Her childhood and adolescence were spent in Oakland, California, on a ten-acre farm where she grew up close to nature and the simple domestic objects that would make up the vocabulary of much of her later experimental writing. Her formal education was haphazard, but she read the works of William Shakespeare, Mark Twain, and Jules Verne and visited art galleries in San Francisco. The death of her parents by the time she was seventeen led her to form a close bond with her older brother Leo.

When Leo entered Harvard University to study history and aesthetics, Gertrude enrolled in Radcliffe College. There she attended the lectures of the philosopher William James and conducted research in automatic writing that later appeared in the *Harvard Psychological Review.* James considered

her one of his most brilliant students, and his lectures on the subconscious led her to experiment later with capturing the poetic quality of subconscious speech. After graduating summa cum laude from Harvard, she enrolled in The Johns Hopkins Medical School to prepare for a career in experimental psychology. After two years, however, she grew bored with her medical studies and joined Leo in Paris. Aside from a single visit to the United States in 1904, she would not return to her native country for thirty years.

Stein was twenty-nine when she arrived in Paris in 1903. Over the following forty-three years, she would produce some nine thousand pages of prose portraits, still lifes, geographies, plays, novels, and operas that would challenge the dominance of plot, character, and formal description in American literature. Her first important book, *Three Lives* (1909), about three working-class servant girls in Baltimore, was printed in a limited edition and admired by a number of appreciative readers. Her next undertaking, *The Making of Americans* (1925), was nearly a thousand pages long and traced the course of history in the lives of two American families.

Living in Paris during the decade when French cubists were transforming the definition of visual art, Stein filled copybook after copybook with sentences that employed words as if they were pieces in a verbal collage. The result was an evocative, nonrepresentational prose that provoked endless ridicule in contemporary reviewers but that continues to fascinate literary scholars to this day.

Gertrude and Leo Stein assembled a small collection of French abstract works. The paintings of

Paul Cezanne and Henri Matisse on the walls of the Steins' apartment at 27 rue de Fleurus gave their home the air of a private museum. The expatriate Spanish painter Pablo Picasso was a frequent visitor, and for several months in 1906 he painted Gertrude Stein's portrait while the two discussed the principles of cubism. The result for Stein was a series of word portraits, among them "Matisse" and "Picasso," and *Tender Buttons* (1914), a long cubist work. In *Tender Buttons*, Stein mixed wisdom and nonsense, accident and profundity in a series of meditations on food, rooms, and common household objects, such as: "Celery tastes tastes where in curled lashes and little bits and mostly in remains."

Jealous of his sister's growing reputation, Leo Stein broke off relations with her and moved to Florence, Italy. His place was taken by Alice B. Toklas, an American from California, who became Gertrude's lifelong companion and private secretary. During World War I, the two women became familiar figures far beyond Paris, as they delivered supplies in a large Ford truck to military hospitals all over France.

Paris by the 1920's was a literary mecca, and the apartment on rue de Fleurus became a gathering place for visiting writers such as Ernest Hemingway, Sherwood Anderson, and F. Scott Fitzgerald, who came to take tea with Toklas and discuss art and life with Stein. In her early fifties, with close-cropped hair, Stein was an imposing figure who preferred to dress in simple, homespun clothes. Her favorite topic of discussion concerned how a writer sees and how what is seen can be put down on paper. By this time, her own writing was appearing regularly in small literary magazines, although, outside certain literary circles, she was more talked about than read. Stein's name spread throughout the American avant-garde when Hemingway, in an epigram to his 1927 novel *The Sun Also Rises*, quoted her observation, "You are all a lost generation." When the novel became a best seller, Stein's remark became the label for an entire postwar generation.

By 1933, when *The Autobiography of Alice B. Toklas* was published, Paris and the "lost generation" had become part of literary nostalgia. There was a hunger on the opposite side of the Atlantic Ocean to hear about an earlier Parisian world that had launched modern art and modern literature. Stein's vivid memoir of that time, composed in the voice of her friend and companion, answered a popular need. She wrote the "autobiography" in six weeks, and it was an immediate success. Excerpts appeared in *The Atlantic Monthly*, a hardcover edition was chosen by the Literary Guild, and *Time* magazine did a cover story on her life and career.

In the following year, Stein and Toklas returned to the United States after an absence of thirty years. Together they traveled by plane from city to city, as Stein gave lectures to college audiences and gave numerous press and radio interviews. Her play *Four Saints in Three Acts* (1934) was produced as an opera with an all-black cast. The first lady, Eleanor Roosevelt, invited Stein to tea at the White House. Charlie Chaplin met her when she stopped in California. Random House became her publisher and began issuing editions of her more conventional works. Deprived of praise and recognition for two decades, Stein was finally a celebrity in her native country. Awareness of herself as a renowned author with a devoted audience temporarily disturbed her literary concentration, however, and she returned to France with a renewed commitment to carry her verbal explorations even further.

In the decades between World War I and World War II, Stein produced some of her most notable works. In her own mind, she divided her efforts of these years into "writing" (for a popular audience) and "really writing" (explorations conducted for herself). Her travels were confined to Europe and England. When Germany invaded France in 1939, she and Toklas withdrew to their country home in the Midi and later to a small town on the Swiss border, where the villagers sheltered them as elderly Jewish women during the Nazi occupation. They returned to Paris in late 1944 and opened their home to wandering American soldiers, who saw Stein and her celebrated apartment as a sort of literary shrine.

Until the end of her life, Stein continued to write every day with no diminution of her talent. *Brewsie and Willie* (1946) adroitly captured the flavor of GI slang and a new generation's wariness before an America grown powerful and self-satisfied.

Stein died of cancer on July 27, 1946, in the American Hospital outside Paris. Shortly before she was wheeled into the operating room to undergo an ultimately unsuccessful operation, she was heard to ask, "What is the question?" Receiving no reply, she concluded, "If there is no question then there is no answer." Her companion Toklas died twenty-one years later on March 7, 1967.

ANALYSIS

Stein believed that the struggle of thought to come to consciousness best revealed the shape and feel of human experience. In a career that spanned three decades, she sought to answer three questions: What is mind? What is writing? How are they connected? Her answers to these questions shattered the conventions of narrative writing and unsettled the reliance of fiction on character, description, and plot.

In her first book, *Three Lives*, about three working-class women in Baltimore, she endeavored to tell a traditional story with a beginning, middle, and end. She discovered, however, that by deliberately misplacing words she could evoke a continuous present in which the characters seemed to unfold before the reader's eyes. One of the book's stories, "Melanctha," was considered an almost perfect example of the modern short story. Typically, though, Stein never repeated the effort. She sought new literary territory that not even she had visited before.

In her next work, *The Making of Americans*, about two American families, she slowly expanded her chronicle until it became a history of the whole of human endeavor. Through repeated rewritings, she discovered that by beginning again and again she could weave the past and future into a continuous present. The book swelled to almost a thousand pages. In the meantime, she began composing word portraits of the people around her, using everything she could collect from their lives. She sought to encompass every fact and detail, until she saw that, with enough detail, all differences began to blur; every person was unique and yet not unique.

After her second book, she abandoned traditional subject matter to explore the working of language. Words, she reasoned, were related to one another just as the shapes and forms were related in a cubist canvas. There was no need for words to copy life, as words possessed a life of their own. She shunned ready-made sentences in order to create sentences that no one had heard before.

In Stein's view, words possessed an essential nature that was independent of their use in communication. Describing and explaining belonged to the nineteenth century; as a modernist, she wanted nothing to do with a past obsessed with class divisions, gentility, and linear reality.

She squeezed everything extraneous from her language and wrote in a deliberately primitive style that avoided any hint of history or place. She was not interested in finding her own voice; she wanted to be absent in her writing. She wanted a new prose that reached the limits of purity and innocence. She employed only simple nouns and verbs that had no associations other than their shape and sound on the page. By seeing words, she hoped, people could be made to see writing.

She employed a number of strategies to return words to their original purity. At Radcliffe, she had experimented with automatic writing, and she knew that sentences could be freed from the mind's will. Many people explored automatic writing in the wake of World War I, but Stein would continue her explorations for the rest of her life. Her explorations were not aimless; she wished not to dehumanize language but to free it. Speech, especially American speech, was clear and distinctive, and she looked for ways of catching the rhythm of speech in her sentences. She found that if she played with the arrangement of words, she could display shades of thought and feeling struggling to be heard. By repeating a phrase over and over in a slightly altered form, she forced the reader to see that rhythm was as much a part of prose as it was of poetry.

Through constant, deliberate repetition, she produced a ballet of words that surveyed everything while staying motionless. Stein demonstrated that prose could achieve a sense of a continuous present and that stories could be told from a central vantage point, without motion and without reliance on plot, character, or scene.

Her modernist explorations did not rely on ancient mythology or obscure academic references but came purely from the senses. Abstract painting taught her to see and write abstractly, without reference to past memory or present identity. Flying for the first time in an airplane in 1935 above the Great Plains, she saw that it was the limitless American landscape that allowed Americans to conceive of writing as cubist, without beginning, middle, or end. The geography of her homeland thus allowed her to envision a new kind of writing based solely on design and form.

The results were exciting but also bewildering and boring, and much of her early work was ridiculed and parodied by reviewers. Her most personal work never found a wide audience; the average reader was in a hurry to discover meaning, whereas what Stein offered was design. Each of her sentences was meant to be an object of contemplation.

Stein's writing falls into three groups. In the first are her relatively straightforward narratives and autobiographies: *Three Lives* (1909), *The Autobiography of Alice B. Toklas* (1933), *Everybody's Autobiography* (1937), and *Wars I Have Seen* (1945). In a second group belong her self-explanatory works that describe and defend her method of writing: *Composition as Explanation* (1926), *Lectures in America* (1935), *Narration: Four Lectures* (1935), and *What Are Masterpieces?* (1940). The final group consists of her personal explorations of sound and meaning in prose that make up her still lifes, geographies, word portraits, plays, novels, and operas. By the 1930's, she moved easily among all three.

Stein's literary influence was also as a celebrity; her salon in Paris was a meeting place for some of the most creative minds of the twentieth century. One of her earliest friends was the youthful painter Pablo Picasso, whose portrait of her hung above her writing desk. As Picasso's fame spread, so did Stein's; twice she wrote word portraits of him, and eventually she wrote a book for an exhibition of his work at the Museum of Modern Art. In championing modern art, Stein advertised herself. Modernism was the style and subject of her style, and as modernism spread to America after World War I, so did her fame and influence.

Perhaps her greatest influence was upon the prose of others. Many American and European writers sought her advice in the 1920's, but her most eager student was Ernest Hemingway. She corrected Hemingway's early manuscripts and urged him to abandon journalism to devote himself to fiction. From her, Hemingway learned the rhythms of modern prose and the truth that could be communicated in simple words. She became his teacher, and the cadence of her repetitive sentences echoes in some of Hemingway's finest writing. The two wrote about different worlds but in a kindred manner. Hers was the domestic world of the kitchen and garden, while his was the self-consciously masculine world of war, hunting, and travel. Later they would feud in public, but their recriminations spoke to the closeness of their creative marriage. If Hemingway is responsible for the new clarity that invaded literature after World War I, then the muted cadences of his teacher can be heard in American writing to this day.

"MELANCTHA"

First published: 1909 (collected in *Three Lives*, 1909)
Type of work: Short story

A restless woman seeks insight into her sensual nature through a series of love affairs.

"Melanctha," the central story in *Three Lives*, is considered one of the most original short stories of the twentieth century. By employing simple words to express complicated thoughts, Stein endowed ordinary people with a complex psychology that earlier writers had given only to characters of high social standing.

"Melanctha" tells the story of Melanctha Herbert, a beautiful, light-skinned black woman who struggles to comprehend her troubled, passionate nature. Melanctha's language, like her life, moves toward people, then away, then back again, in a spiral of acceptance and rejection.

Melanctha is a victim of her search for excitement and her barely controlled eroticism. In her affair with Jefferson Campbell, a young black doctor called in to attend her dying mother, Melanctha encounters a lover who is her exact opposite. Whereas Melanctha is vibrant, sensual, and committed to living in the present, Jeff Campbell is quiet and thoughtful, a man who recoils from physical passion.

The story describes in long stretches of dialogue their tormented debate over the virtues of their respective psychological natures. Slowly, Jeff learns to think less and to feel more deeply, until finally he is able to feel the glory of the physical world. Yet once Melanctha has taught him how to love as she does, she loses interest in him and enters into a series of love affairs that, in the end, leave her alone, facing death, in a home for impoverished consumptives.

To counter the bleakness of her tale, Stein invents a glowing, elemental language that evokes an eternal present. Vocabulary is pared to the bone, and syntax and diction are subtly distorted to echo common speech. Phrases are repeated over and over, with only minor changes, until they assume a hypnotic power. The story is about a love affair and the torture of two people trying to comprehend what they mean to each other.

The words they use to explain themselves entrap them. Language as a medium of expression both liberates and obscures emotion. The inner lives of two common people are revealed by the rhythms of their speech but can never be exactly known. Huge psychological spaces are suggested, while the story contains little plot or description. No character is treated as being more important than another. Absent entirely is the socially elevated tone of conventional fiction, and nowhere can the commanding presence of the author be found.

"Melanctha" was a breathtaking advance in short-story writing but one that Stein never repeated. It was read by few people when it was first published (partly at Stein's expense), but its influence was enormous on such writers as Hemingway, Anderson, and Richard Wright, who borrowed Stein's verbal rhythms to express the inner worlds of black people growing up in Chicago.

"PICASSO"

First published: 1912 (collected in *Matisse, Picasso, and Gertrude Stein, with Two Shorter Stories*, 1933)
Type of work: Word portrait

The artist Pablo Picasso doggedly struggles to create a new art that can be described but not named.

Stein's word portraits "Matisse" and "Picasso" appeared in a special issue of *Camera Work* in New York City in 1912. The publisher, Alfred Stieglitz, was an accomplished photographer who devoted his life to making photography a creative art. Stieglitz had not quite understood the pieces, which was why he immediately decided to publish them. In doing so, he introduced Stein's writing to the United States.

Stein was as much a historical figure as a celebrated writer. She and Picasso each created famous portraits of the other. Hers was in words. She had ample time to observe Picasso in the winter of 1906, when she posed for him some eighty times while he struggled to complete his portrait of her. Dissatisfied with his depiction of her head, Picasso departed for Spain. When he returned, he painted it in rapidly. When Stein cut her hair, friends worried that the famous portrait, which hung on the wall of her apartment, no longer resembled her. Picasso's reply was that he had painted Stein as she would come to look.

Stein's description of Picasso employs constant repetition to suggest the presence of someone doggedly moving forward. Picasso is portrayed as being ahead of others, and others are following his example, but he is not aware of his direction, only of the fact that he is moving. Stein's hypnotic, repetitious sentences suggest that Picasso is a man plodding along, his eyes on the work before him, working to bring something out of himself that cannot be described. Stein calls this something "a heavy thing, a solid thing and a complete thing."

She does not dehumanize Picasso, although his drive to paint and his need to paint are shown as almost machinelike. From the outset, she responds to him as a person and singles out his great charm as the hallmark of his nature. In the midst of this charm, she watches as Picasso struggles to bring out of himself something new and meaningful. All of his life, she thinks, something has been coming out of him that is lovely, interesting, disturbing, repellant, and very pretty.

He has always been working and will always be working, she sees. He seems to need to work, and his art is partly a way to satisfy his longing to work. Yet she concludes her portrait of Picasso with the tantalizing thought that even when he is working hardest, Picasso is never completely at work. She stops just short of saying how significant the ingredient play was to Picasso's art and life.

Later, Stein explained the extreme repetitive style of her portraits as a necessary technique that mimicked the continuous images of the cinema. Through a succession of hypnotic statements, she hoped to erase the distinction between sentences and to create a continuous thing called a portrait. Like Picasso's early canvases, Stein's portrait of the artist was a thing that might, by degrees, seem new, interesting, disturbing, and very pretty.

COMPOSITION AS EXPLANATION

First published: 1926
Type of work: Essay

The author lectures on the nature of composition, modernism, and the effect of World War I.

Composition as Explanation is an artful blend of literary theory, historical commentary, and personal confession. Delivered originally as a lecture to students at the University of Cambridge and the University of Oxford in 1926, it is one of the first attempts by Stein to explain her method of composition. The essay represents one of the most candid attempts by a writer to communicate the struggle to write to an audience of strangers. As in all of Stein's writing, her sentences refuse to be pinned down and yield new insights with each reading.

The essay begins haltingly, in the manner of a speaker searching for the precise location of her subject. Part of what Stein seeks to communicate, however, is the struggle to give voice to ideas; thus, her sentences echo this struggle. Thoughts are ungraspable, and Stein's halting manner of writing should not be mistaken for clumsiness. To express herself too coherently would be to make the subject of writing too simple and rational. Her words in this essay are best understood if read aloud, as they follow so closely the circular movements of her inner voice. The essential ideas of *Composition as Explanation*, like most of Stein's thinking, rest firmly in common sense and literary experience. Ideas, she suggests, can never be finished, and Stein gets greater range from her thoughts by playing with them, turning them around, and then starting them again from the beginning.

The world does not change, she argues; only the conception of things changes as each generation lives and thinks differently from the previous generation. Nothing changes between generations except the way in which things are seen, and this change leads to new works of art. Artists live on the outer edge of their time, and what they create often seems strange, even ugly, to contemporaries who lag a little behind. After enough time has elapsed for contemplation and study, new works of art are accepted by society, dubbed "classical," and declared to be beautiful. By the time a work of art has become an acknowledged classic, though, some of its thrill has disappeared, because it no longer challenges the viewer. Beauty, Stein argues, is most beautiful when it is new and disturbing. It would be better, she insists, if artists and their audiences could stand together at the same place in time.

Stein believes that artists exist in a continuous present when they write, compose, or paint, as the act of composition can take place only in the present. One result of World War I, she argues, was to push everyone forward in time by almost thirty years. Modernism had started earlier, but the whole world was brought up to the point of modernism by the war, with the result that artists and their contemporaries stood side by side, at the edge of understanding.

After establishing this foundation for her literary theories, Stein describes the course of her own career. Although she does not say as much openly, she suggests that her own works, which are considered strange and eccentric by her contemporaries, will someday qualify as classics.

THE AUTOBIOGRAPHY OF ALICE B. TOKLAS

First published: 1933
Type of work: Autobiography

A typical American woman describes artistic life in Paris in the first quarter of the twentieth century.

The Autobiography of Alice B. Toklas is Stein's inventive memoir of how she and her Parisian friends must have looked to Alice B. Toklas. The book was an immediate success in the United States and has remained in print. More conventional than any of Stein's previous books, it describes a crucial period in cultural history with a wit, charm, and mock-simplicity that disguised the book's brilliant inventiveness.

The subject presented a challenge to Stein's desire to live and write in a "continuous present." Like Picasso, Stein was willing to copy anyone but herself. How, then, was she to produce an autobiography that would be free of her past and of the laws of conventional identity?

Stein's answer was to write an "autobiography" of someone else and to construct a narrative of constant digression. *The Autobiography of Alice B. Toklas* became the impersonation of an age as seen through the eyes of an ordinary American woman who arrived in Paris in 1907. The years before World War I are described with wit and delight, the war and its aftermath more darkly. Like much of Stein's work, the writing hovers around a constant present by relying on the spoken word. The prose reads like dictation, as though Stein had merely transcribed the lilt and vocabulary of Toklas's voice. Part Stein, part Toklas, the prose is purely American. With its delight in irreverent gossip, the narrative resembles a novel of social history. Only at the end does Toklas reveal the true author, when she remarks that Stein has been threatening to write her autobiography and that this is it. The book thus holds onto a continuous present by ending at the moment of its beginning, as the reader is invited to reread the book as a work by Stein.

Throughout the book, chronology follows curiosity rather than linear time. The section "Gertrude Stein in Paris, 1903-1907" precedes "Gertrude Stein Before She Came to Paris." Although Toklas is seemingly the main character, she disappears on page 5 and does not reappear for many pages while Stein's story is told.

Indirection is at the heart of every observation. The painter Henri Matisse, for example, is first observed at three removes: Stein quotes a story told by Toklas about the cook Hélène's opinion of Matisse's dinner manners. Stein pretends to write about surface details, and yet she succeeds in revealing the nature of life underneath. She constantly digresses, only to return with what she wants to say.

Appraisals of character and talent are delivered from a female viewpoint that has little to do with the male world of professional success, education, and wealth. The long, brilliant section on the leading artists of the day concludes with a series of intimate anecdotes about their wives and mistresses. There is no upstairs or downstairs in Stein's world. Her vision of human personality is bold, irreverent, and thought-provoking. As a work of literary reminiscence, *The Autobiography of Alice B. Toklas* is one of the richest ever written.

SUMMARY

From the time of her arrival in Paris in 1903 until her death in 1946, Stein strove to be a central figure in modern literature. She directed a movement that broke with the past and sought fresh forms of literary expression. A bold explorer of prose, she broke away from the nineteenth century's reliance on plot, character, and conventional description to demonstrate how awareness and identity could be evoked through simple words. She deliberately chose an unliterary style and emphasized the power of words by arranging them in unusual ways.

Although her autobiographical works about France are best remembered, Stein left her mark on modern literature through her influence on writers such as Hemingway and Anderson. The cadence and artlessness of much contemporary writing echoes her early experiments in modern prose.

Philip Metcalfe

BIBLIOGRAPHY

By the Author

SHORT FICTION:
As Fine as Melanctha, 1954
Painted Lace, and Other Pieces, 1914-1937, 1955
Alphabets and Birthdays, 1957

POETRY:

Tender Buttons: Objects, Food, Rooms, 1914

Before the Flowers of Friendship Faded Friendship Faded, 1931

Two (Hitherto Unpublished) Poems, 1948

Bee Time Vine, and Other Pieces, 1913-1927, 1953

Stanzas in Meditation, and Other Poems, 1929-1933, 1956

LONG FICTION:

Three Lives, 1909

The Making of Americans, 1925

Lucy Church Amiably, 1930

A Long Gay Book, 1932

Ida, a Novel, 1941

Brewsie and Willie, 1946

Blood on the Dining-Room Floor, 1948

Things as They Are, 1950 (originally known as *Q.E.D.*)

Mrs. Reynolds and Five Earlier Novelettes, 1931-1942, 1952

A Novel of Thank You, 1958

DRAMA:

Geography and Plays, pb. 1922

Operas and Plays, pb. 1932

Four Saints in Three Acts, pr., pb. 1934

In Savoy: Or, Yes Is for a Very Young Man (A Play of the Resistance in France), pr., pb. 1946

The Mother of Us All, pr. 1947

Last Operas and Plays, pb. 1949

In a Garden: An Opera in One Act, pb. 1951

Lucretia Borgia, pb. 1968

Selected Operas and Plays, pb. 1970

NONFICTION:

Composition as Explanation, 1926

How to Write, 1931

The Autobiography of Alice B. Toklas, 1933

Matisse, Picasso, and Gertrude Stein, with Two Shorter Stories, 1933

Portraits and Prayers, 1934

Lectures in America, 1935

Narration: Four Lectures, 1935

The Geographical History of America, 1936

Everybody's Autobiography, 1937

Picasso, 1938

Paris, France, 1940

What Are Masterpieces?, 1940

Wars I Have Seen, 1945

Four in America, 1947

Reflections on the Atomic Bomb, 1973

How Writing Is Written, 1974

The Letters of Gertrude Stein and Thornton Wilder, 1996 (Edward Burns and Ulla E. Dydo, editors)

DISCUSSION TOPICS

- What did Gertrude Stein expect to accomplish by writing not her own autobiography but *The Autobiography of Alice B. Toklas*?

- Which of Stein's prose experiments seem most successful?

- What techniques are involved in Stein's word portraits?

- What is Stein's justification for the repetitious phrasing found in many of her writings?

- Probably no one ever learned to write by reading Stein's *How to Write*. If this book does not show people how to write, what can it do for them?

Baby Precious Always Shines: Selected Love Notes Between Gertrude Stein and Alice B. Toklas, 1999 (Kay Turner, editor)

CHILDREN'S LITERATURE:
The World Is Round, 1939

MISCELLANEOUS:
The Gertrude Stein First Reader and Three Plays, 1946
The Yale Edition of the Unpublished Writings of Gertrude Stein, 1951-1958 (8 volumes; Carl Van Vechten, editor)
Selected Writings of Gertrude Stein, 1962
The Yale Gertrude Stein, 1980

About the Author

Bloom, Harold, ed. *Modern Critical Views: Gertrude Stein.* New York: Chelsea House, 1986.

Bowers, Jane Palatini. *Gertrude Stein.* New York: St. Martin's Press, 1993.

Brinnin, John Malcom. *The Third Rose: Gertrude Stein and Her World.* Boston: Little, Brown, 1959.

Curnutt, Kirk, ed. *The Critical Response to Gertrude Stein.* Westport, Conn.: Greenwood Press, 2000.

DeKoven, Marianne. *A Different Language: Gertrude Stein's Experimental Writing.* Madison: University of Wisconsin Press, 1983.

Dubnick, Randa. *The Structure of Obscurity: Gertrude Stein, Language, and Cubism.* Urbana: University of Illinois Press, 1984.

Dydo, Ulla E. *Gertrude Stein: The Language That Rises: 1923-1934.* Evanston, Ill.: Northwestern University Press, 2003.

Hoffman, Michael J. *Gertrude Stein.* Boston: Twayne, 1976.

Kellner, Bruce, ed. *A Gertrude Stein Companion.* New York: Greenwood Press, 1988.

Knapp, Bettina. *Gertrude Stein.* New York: Continuum, 1990.

Pierpont, Claudia Roth. *Passionate Minds: Women Rewriting the World.* New York: Alfred A. Knopf, 2000.

Ruddick, Lisa. *Reading Gertrude Stein: Body, Text, Gnosis.* Ithaca, N.Y.: Cornell University Press, 1990.

Simon, Linda. *Gertrude Stein Remembered.* Lincoln: University of Nebraska Press, 1994.

Watson, Dana Cairns. *Gertrude Stein and the Essence of What Happens.* Nashville, Tenn.: Vanderbilt University Press, 2005.

Will, Barbara. *Gertrude Stein, Modernism, and the Problem of "Genius."* Edinburgh: Edinburgh University Press, 2000.

Romance Fiction

A Guide to the Genre

Second Edition

Kristin Ramsdell

California State University, East Bay

Genreflecting Advisory Series

Diana Tixier Herald, Series Editor

LIBRARIES UNLIMITED

AN IMPRINT OF ABC-CLIO, LLC

Santa Barbara, California • Denver, Colorado • Oxford, England

Library of Congress Cataloging-in-Publication Data

Ramsdell, Kristin, 1940–
　Romance fiction : a guide to the genre / Kristin Ramsdell. — 2nd ed.
　　p. cm. — (Genreflecting advisory series)
　Includes index.
　ISBN 978-1-59158-177-2 (hardcopy : acid-free paper) — ISBN 978-1-61069-235-9 (ebook)
　1. Love stories—Bibliography.
　2. Love stories—History and criticism.　I. Title.
　Z1231.L68R37　2012
　[PN3448.L67]
　016.80883'85—dc23　　　　2011045879

ISBN: 978-1-59158-177-2
EISBN: 978-1-61069-235-9

4773 5112 04/12

16　15　14　13　12　　1　2　3　4　5

This book is also available on the World Wide Web as an eBook.
Visit www.abc-clio.com for details.

Libraries Unlimited
An Imprint of ABC-CLIO, LLC

ABC-CLIO, LLC
130 Cremona Drive, P.O. Box 1911
Santa Barbara, California 93116–1911

This book is printed on acid-free paper ∞

Manufactured in the United States of America

Contents

Acknowledgments

Many people contributed in many different ways, knowingly or unknowingly, to both versions of this book. I am particularly indebted to my local public libraries, especially the Alameda County Public Library System, the Palo Alto Public Library, and the San Francisco Public Library for their endurance as I rummaged through their fiction sections; to the interlibrary loan department at California State University, East Bay, for obvious reasons; to my long-suffering colleagues and family for their patience and support; to my editor, Barbara Ittner, for her insight, literary skill, and incredible forbearance; to Lynn Coddington, Shelley Mosley, John Charles, Deborah Cloninger, Barbara Johnson, Stephanie Wells, Bette-Lee Fox, and Mary Kay Foss for their comments, suggestions, genre and author expertise, and generally unflagging support; to the Romance Writers of America (in particular my SFA-RWA chapter), the International Association for the Study of the Popular Romance, and the Romance Scholar Listserv for generously and most helpfully responding to my varied questions and requests; and to Mary K. Chelton, Joyce Saricks, and the late Betty Rosenberg, current and legendary leaders in the field of reader's advisory and popular fiction advocacy, for their initial ideas, encouragement, and support.

In spite of the input I have had from various sources, an effort like this is a highly subjective undertaking, and it is entirely possible that through ignorance, error, or chance, a favorite author or work has been omitted or miscategorized. I regret any errors and would appreciate any comments from readers that would aid in any future revisions of this work. Comments should be directed to me at kristin.ramsdell@csueastbay.edu or kristin.ramsdell@gmail.com.

Preface to the Second Edition

In the years since *Romance Fiction: A Guide to the Genre* was published in 1999, the Romance genre has seen some dramatic changes. As expected, of course, the number of titles published each year has increased markedly and a number of new authors have come onto the scene. In addition, however, the genre continues to expand and diversify, and while firmly clinging to its basic tenets, it has broadened its scope to include a wider variety of stories within its established subgenres, sometimes almost redefining the boundaries, as well as venturing into new territory. Characters, settings, themes, and plot situations have evolved with the times (e.g., more military heroes, GLBT and multicultural characters, comfortable, cozy communities) and sensuality levels and paranormal creativity continue to test the genre's limits. Technology is also changing the way in which romances, along with other genres, are written, published, acquired, and read, impacting everyone involved. Academic interest in the genre has finally born fruit, and although there is a long way to go, the recent number of articles, masters theses and doctoral dissertations, as well as the establishment of romance-dedicated journals, organizations, and grants, are definitely positive signs. It is clear that the Romance genre is evolving; and although much remains the same and many of the older authors and titles are still read, the genre of the 20th century is not that of the 21st. Obviously, a revision was needed to keep this guide useful, relevant, and up-to-date.

While nominally the second edition of *Romance Fiction: A Guide to the Genre*, this book is actually the third edition of *Happily Ever After: A Guide to Reading Interests in Romance Fiction* (1987), and as such, retains the same basic structure and organization as both its predecessors, deleting and adding new material and updates it as necessary. Two new chapters have been added ("Erotic Romance" and "Linked Romances") and one has been dropped ("Sagas"), reflecting the changing nature and format of the genre, as well as its popularity among readers.

The original subgenre chapters have all been updated, revised, and in a number of cases, reorganized. The definition, appeal, and readers advisory sections have been modified, as necessary; the history sections have been expanded to include events since the last edition, and the bibliographies have been reorganized to reflect subgenre changes and revised to include recent authors and titles. A section on "Chick Lit" has been added to the "Contemporary Romance" chapter, and "Urban Fantasy" is included in the greatly expanded "Alternative Reality Romance" chapter. Most of the other chapters, most notably "Inspirational Romance," have also grown, but the "Traditional Regency Romance" chapter has been reduced, acknowledging the dearth of recent publications in the subgenre. Representative recommended reading lists are included for most of the subgenre chapters in the new Take Five! side-bars, and brief subgenre definitions are also included in box formats.

The introductory chapters have been revised and updated. The history section has been expanded to include changes and events of the current century; and the appeal, readers' advisory, and collection development sections have been reworked to include new trends, issues, and concerns, including the impact of technology as appropriate. The chapters concerning Research Aids have also been revised and updated to include newer resources, both print and online, fixed and fluid. The "History and Criticism" chapter, as well as several others, has been expanded to allow for the growing academic interest in the field, and the "Publishers" chapter has been revised to include the recent consolidations within the industry, as well as the growing number of new, smaller presses.

Finally, for space reasons, many titles, and in some cases, authors, included in previous editions have been dropped from this edition—not because they were no longer valuable but simply because the space was needed to include the newer authors and titles. As a result, this edition is not cumulative and it is recommended that the earlier editions be retained for complete coverage.

Introduction

Love is life. And if you miss love, you miss life.

Leo Buscaglia

When I am attacked by gloomy thoughts, nothing helps me so much as running to my books. They quickly absorb me and banish the clouds from my mind.

Michel de Montaigne

Purpose and Scope

This guide attempts to organize the existing literature of romance fiction in such a way so that it will define the outlines of the genre and provide a useful resource for those interested in it, including those searching for reading material. Although its primary focus is librarians, especially those who are involved in readers' advisory service or collection development and may not be familiar with romance literature, it may be of interest to booksellers, romance readers, and writers, as well. Also, while it is not intended as a comprehensive research guide, it does contain a significant amount of research information and, therefore, may also be useful to scholars, researchers, and students of popular culture, literature, or women's studies.

The central focus of this book is on the romance literature itself, especially that currently available to American readers. Most of the materials listed, except for some prototypes or early examples, are currently available in either print or electronic format (check *Books in Print*, publishers' websites, Amazon.com, or similar sources for availability), or can be found in some of the larger libraries (check www.worldcat.org). Most are readily available in local public libraries that collect romance fiction in print or, increasingly, in downloadable e-book or audio formats. Except when of historical interest, materials not written in English will be excluded, although English translations of some foreign authors are included. Individual short stories and novellas are also generally excluded. Both male and female authors are represented. However, because the information is available elsewhere and because this guide takes a genre approach, biographical material relating to authors will not be included. Sources for this information are included in chapter 16, "Author Biography and Bibliography."

Organization

Although this guide begins with an introductory section that includes a definition of romance, a brief general history of the genre, sections on appeal, readers' advisory, and collection development, and concludes with a section on research aids that includes a wide-ranging assortment of research and reference sources, its basic focus is on the literature and the arrangement is by subgenre. Each broad subgenre has its own chapter, subdivided within as necessary, and each chapter includes sections devoted to the definition of the subgenre, the reasons for its appeal, specific hints for readers' advisory service, a brief history of the development of the particular subgenre, and pertinent bibliographies. A sample core collection bibliography and author/title and subject indices are also included at the end of the book.

Bibliographies

The bibliographies form the major part of this guide and are selective in both authors and titles included.

Authors Included

Authors have been selected for inclusion because they are writers of typical or classic examples in a particular subgenre, are exceptionally prolific or popular or both, are important from a historical point of view, or are in some way unique to Romance fiction. In addition, works by those included must be currently available to the American public, either because they are still in print, have been recently reprinted, are available in electronic format, or are still generally available in public library collections. As a rule, extremely new writers are not included because there has been insufficient time to assess their contributions to the genre, although an exception may be made for award winners. Also, unless they are exceptionally prolific and enduring, or write in other capacities, mass-market paperback series authors normally are not included separately. (The series themselves, however, are discussed.) Authors of single titles in mass-market, trade paperback, or hardcover format are included; e-book–only authors are not included unless they have also written works that have been published in hard copy.

Titles Included

Except in rare instances, only the authors' romance works will be listed. In general, a writer's works will be selectively listed and only in unusual circumstances will an author's entire writings be included. Because several print publications, as well as a growing number of online sources, that list relatively complete bibliographies for a number of romance writers are already in existence—see the "Author Biography and Bibliography" chapter for several suggestions—this should not present a problem. The books are chosen for inclusion because they are typical, unusual, particularly good, exceptionally popular, interesting, or important examples of the genre. In addition, a book will sometimes be included because it is the only, or one of the only, readily available books by the author. This is often the case with older writers or writers of genres that have gone out of favor.

Years Covered

Although there is an emphasis on recent books, especially those published since the first edition of *Romance Fiction: A Guide to the Genre* (Englewood, CO: Libraries Unlimited, 1999), both classic and contemporary romances (dating from 1740 to the present) are included and no effort has specifically been made to omit works from a particular time period. However, because of space considerations, a number of authors and/or their earlier works that were included in earlier versions of this guide have been omitted. The previous editions should be consulted for the earlier information.

Entries and Annotations

Original publication information (publisher and date) will be provided for most titles included; if the work was first published elsewhere and then later in the United States, the American publication information may also be given. In addition, if a work was published at some time under a different title, this will usually be mentioned. (Publication under different titles will occasionally happen if an older book is being reprinted, or if the same book is being released in both England and the United States. Interestingly, the same titles don't always appeal to both audiences—even though the stories do!) Title and imprint information in parentheses is usually British. Although the original publication date is always listed for the older and prototype novels, current publishing information may also be provided when useful.

Although every effort has been made to annotate all the entries, some are not. In cases where a major writer has a rather short list and all are important, all entries will be annotated. In other instances, especially if an author has a long list of relevant titles, entries will be annotated selectively because they are better, more important, typical, more interesting, unusual, or available. Prototypes and classic works will receive the most complete coverage. Other works will be annotated less thoroughly, and some will receive only brief comments. In some instances, books in series may receive an annotation for the series and not individual titles. Except in rare cases, no annotation provides a synopsis of the story, reveals the ending, or provides information that would otherwise spoil the story for the reader. Quotes appearing in the annotations are from publishers' promotional material, book jackets, book reviews, or, occasionally, the book itself. Unless otherwise noted, titles that are starred have won RWA's Rita award.

Cross-Indexing

When important, authors who write romance fiction under various names will be linked by notes under their names (e.g., Dreyer, Eileen [see also Kathleen Korbel in chapter 5, "Contemporary Romance"]).

In addition, *see also* references will be given for authors who write in various subgenres (e.g., see also chapter 6, "Romantic Mysteries"). Writers' entries will also be linked through the Author/Title Index.

Suggestions for Use

Although the arrangement of this guide is fairly straightforward and its use will be intuitive to many, not all readers will be using this book for the same purposes and, as a result, will not be accessing the information in the same ways. For example, students and scholars may be looking for academic materials as well as examples of the genre; librarians and booksellers may be looking for genre overviews and authors and titles to recommend; writers may be looking for information about important books and authors in particular subgenres; and readers may simply be looking for good books to read. The following suggestions may be helpful:

1. When looking for a specific title or author, consult the Author/Title Index in the back of the book to find out whether the author or title is included and, if it is, where the information is located.

2. When looking for authors or titles in a particular subgenre, use the Contents at the beginning of the book or the Subject Index to find the bibliography for that particular subgenre.

3. When looking for general information on a particular subgenre (history, definition, etc.) use the Contents, but when looking for more specific bits of information, the Subject Index at the back of the book may be more helpful.

4. When looking for scholarly materials and reference sources about the genre or a subgenre and its authors, consult the Research Aids section of this guide, as well as any Research Aids listings in the appropriate chapters.

5. When looking for books similar to known authors or titles, locate the entry(ies) for that known author or title and consider others in the bibliography that sound interesting or consider other books in the same subgenre. If the book is an award-winner or covers a specific subject that appeals to the reader, check the Subject Index.

6. When trying to get a feel for a particular subgenre, consider reading the books recommended in the "Take Five!" sidebars included in each subgenre chapter.

As alluded to earlier, this is something of a multipurpose book; so whether you are new to the Romance genre and just learning about it, seriously researching the genre, trying to help a reader find a good book, or simply looking for something to read yourself, I hope you will find this guide (as well as its predecessors) useful—and that you enjoy your foray into the world of the most popular, enduring, flexible, and resilient of all the fiction genres: Romance.

PART I

INTRODUCTION TO ROMANCE FICTION

Chapter 1

Definition and Brief History of Romance Fiction

Romance has been elegantly defined as the offspring of fiction and love.

Benjamin Disraeli, 1804–1881

The romance novel is a work of prose fiction that tells the story of the courtship and betrothal of one or more heroines.

Pamela Regis

Romance Has Arrived!

Jayne Ann Krentz

Jayne Ann Krentz is right: Romance *has* arrived. And the statement is even more true today than it was in 1996 when Krentz first dropped that bombshell and thrilled the audience with a speech at a Public Library Association (PLA) Conference. Romance is more on the literary radar than ever, and with the current interest being generated, it is likely to stay there for the foreseeable future. Naturally, there have been some changes in the genre in the last decade or so. Romances are sexier and hotter than ever before; the Inspirational Romance market has grown; the Traditional Sweet Regency Romance has been taken over, more or less, by the racier, more adventurous, Regency-set Historical; vampires, witches, demons, ghosts, fallen angels, ancient deities, shape-changers, dragons, and other supernatural characters abound as all things paranormal, fantastic, and futuristic fascinate fans; and the lines between the various fiction genres and subgenres continue to blur, blend, and change as Erotica, Urban Fantasy, Science Fiction, Women's Fiction, Chick Lit, and others impact Romance to varying degrees. Additionally, e-books and other electronic formats have taken the publishing industry—including Romance—by storm in a revolution that is fundamentally changing the publishing playing field as I write. There is no question that the outward trappings, the story packages that deliver the message, of the genre have changed and are changing. But the core of the genre has not. Its basic tenets and its message of the power of love remain the same—just as they have since the start.

Romance, as a part of the human experience, has existed since the first time a pair of lovers gazed at each other with love-blinded eyes and saw the world around them not as it was, but as they wanted it to be. The world has never been the same. Romance, as a literary form, has been around a somewhat shorter time, and while its impact can't compare with that of the real thing, the first heroine who ever agonized over the intentions of her beloved similarly ensured that the world of fiction would never be quite the same again. From the chilling tales of Ann Radcliffe and the witty novels of Jane Austen to the wide variety available today, romances have been written and published by the thousands and read by the millions. Maligned by their critics and adored by their readers, romances have definitely had an effect upon the literary world. But what, exactly, is this flourishing genre? Just what is a romance?

Definition

In the strictest literary sense, of course, "all popular fiction is romantic."[1] It portrays the world as it ought to be, not as it is, and is, therefore, unrealistic—or romantic. However, when today's readers refer to a romance, it is not usually fiction-in-general that they have in mind. On the contrary, the term *romance*, as it is used today, has a much more specific meaning and refers to a particular kind of fiction—the love story. *Webster's Ninth New Collegiate Dictionary* makes this clear when it states that one of the meanings of romance is "a love story [and/or] a class of such literature." And more recently, the latest edition of *Merriam-Webster Online* (www.merriam-webster.com/dictionary/romance?show=1&t=1303923664) clarifies the term even further by defining romance as "a love story especially in the form of a novel." Even Benjamin Disraeli agreed—although it is doubtful he had the current genre in mind—when he proclaimed that romance is a combination of love and fiction. In the simplest sense, of course, this definition is true. Romances *are* love stories, and they do apply a fictional treatment to the subject of love. But there is more to it than that. Not just any love story will do. Certain criteria must be met before a love story can qualify as a proper romance, at least by today's standards.

WHAT MAKES IT A ROMANCE?

1. The plot must focus on the developing love relationship or courtship between the protagonists.
2. There must be a satisfactory ending, usually called the "HEA—Happily Ever After" ending, although satisfactory can mean something other than an engagement or a wedding.
3. The story must engage readers emotionally, allowing them to participate in the courtship process.
4. Although there are often other things going on in a romance, some have said that if the romance is the last thing that is resolved (as opposed to the mystery, etc.), it is a romance.

To begin with, there is the matter of *focus*. In a romance the central (and occasionally the only) focus of the plot is on the love relationship and courtship process of the two main characters. Pamela Regis puts it succinctly, although she allows for multiple pairings, when she states that a romance novel "tells the story of the courtship and betrothal of one or more heroines."[2]

Of course, there are usually other complications and problems, such as mysteries to be solved, career goals or social successes to be achieved, and daring escapes to be made. Though these are always secondary to the love interest (from the reader's point of view, not necessarily the characters'), these subplots are often instrumental in the success of the love interest.

On the other hand, the primary plotline of a non-romance, even though it may contain a well-defined love story, revolves around something else entirely. Consider, for example, the myriad adventure stories, most of which contain a definite love interest. Although the love relationship is important and certainly adds to the story, the main emphasis is on the successful solution of the mystery or the outwitting of the villain by the hero and/or heroine. Compare the romantic suspense novels of Mary Stewart with the international espionage tales of Ian Fleming. Romantic relationships figure prominently in both authors' works. But in Stewart's novels, the romance drives the plot; in Fleming's works, it is merely peripheral—and seldom lasting. Of course, not all books lend themselves to such obvious analysis, and some are downright obscure, especially as romance authors have begun moving into other fiction genres. But, as a general rule, unless it is the resolution of the romantic entanglements that ultimately sustains the reader's interest in the story, the book is probably not a romance.

But it is not only subject matter and focus that determine a romance; a romance must also attempt to engage the reader's feelings. To put it simply, a romance must have a quality—whether it is achieved through character development, plot structure, point of view, style, or other means—that allows, almost demands, a certain emotional involvement on the part of the reader. In other words, a book cannot simply describe a love relationship; it must allow the reader to participate in it. As Janice Radway states in her reader's survey, "To qualify as a romance, the story must chronicle not merely the events of a courtship but *what it feels like* to the *object* of one."[3] Some books, of course, do this better than others, and how successfully it is done is a matter of opinion for individual readers. Although subjective and personal, this elusive quality is critical to the definition of the genre, because no matter how well a book conforms to the other criteria, unless it manages to connect with the reader's romantic emotions—even to a limited extent—the book will probably not be perceived as a romance; it will simply be a novel about love.

Another criterion for romance fiction is the *satisfactory ending*. Usually, but not always, this is the traditional happy one, with the protagonists overcoming whatever obstacles stand in their way and forming some kind of committed relationship (often betrothal or marriage) by the book's conclusion. Agreeing with this, the Romance Writers of America states that "an emotionally satisfying and optimistic ending" is one of the essential elements in a romance novel (www.rwanational.org), and Regis considers the "betrothal" essential to the genre. Other refinements, of course, may be added (e.g., no rape, no hero-against-heroine violence, honorable characters, monogamous relationships, heroines who "win"). But these are all extras, and while they may make the story better, they can't make it a true romance if the proper focus and emotional involvement aspects aren't already there.

With all the changes that have taken place in the Romance genre lately, it might be logical to assume that the definition of a romance has changed, as well. However, when you look closely, the basic premises, the core tenets, and the underlying message of the genre have remained stable throughout.

Obviously, it is possible to define a romance more narrowly—and many people do; however, because of the wide variance in public reading tastes and my desire to include as many of them as is reasonably possible, I have chosen to use a more all-encompassing definition. Therefore, for the purposes of this guide, a romance shall be defined as a love story in which the central focus is on the development and satisfactory resolution of the love relationship between the two main characters, written in such a way as to provide the reader with some degree of vicarious emotional participation in the courtship process.

A Brief History of the Romance Novel

Early Influences

Love stories have existed since the earliest times—first as part of the oral history tradition and then as recorded literature—as any quick glance through the Bible (Ruth and Boaz, David and Bathsheba, Sampson and Delilah, etc.) or a volume of early Greek myths will affirm. Stories of love and adventure (and usually war) were also popular throughout the Middle Ages, and it is from these epic tales of derring-do that our current term *romance* derives. Although the learned language of the period was still Latin, the people more commonly spoke in the derivative vernacular languages that were developing (those languages that would eventually become today's romance languages, such as French, Spanish, and Italian). As a result, the popular literature of the period was also being written in or translated into these languages and, subsequently, these works themselves became known as romances.

Eventually, the term came to include not only the language, but the subjects and the qualities of the literature itself. Thus, a romance came to be identified as a popular tale that centered on a theme of adventure and, sometimes, love. These romances of Medieval times, however, are not the popular romances of today, and except for the name they share, the larger-than-life heroic characters who overcome all odds, and the fact that love and adventure are sometimes components in both, they bear little relation to each other.

Other romantic stories and poems can be found throughout history, and for a brief, interesting attempt to trace the history of the romance from the fourth century AD, consult Annette Townend's "Historical Overview" section in *Words of Love: A Complete Guide to Romance Fiction* (New York: Garland, 1984) by Eileen Fallon.

Beginnings

Although bits and pieces of earlier types of love stories might have had an effect on the current romance genre, it is generally held that the direct antecedents of today's romances can be traced most successfully to the eighteenth century and the 1740 publication of Samuel Richardson's epistolary novel *Pamela: Or Virtue Rewarded*. This extremely popular novel in which a young servant girl resists repeated attempts on her virtue by "Mr. B—" and, as a result, ends up marrying him, was followed not too long after by Richardson's *Clarissa Harlowe* (1747) in which the heroine did not resist temptation and, therefore, in keeping with the fascinating logic of the time, dies. These stories spawned a host of imitations that were popular on both sides of the Atlantic until the end of the century. One of the most important of these was Susanna Haswell Rowson's classic seduction novel, *Charlotte Temple: A Tale of Truth,* first published in England in 1791 and in America in 1794, and considered by most to be America's first popular romantic novel.

At the same time that Pamela and her sisters were enjoying such favor, a new variety of romance, the Gothic, was being born. When Horace Walpole produced his macabre gothic tale of the supernatural, *The Castle of Otronto*, in 1764, primarily for the amusement of his female relatives, he had little idea what he was starting. Although some writers, such as Matthew Gregory "Monk" Lewis, developed the form into the true horror gothic, in the hands of Anne Radcliffe, Walpole's gothic mellowed into the less gruesome, but still truly terrifying, more romantic, yet always practically explained, sentimental gothic. By the end of the century, Radcliffe's *The Mysteries of Udolpho* (1794) and its successors, complete with threatened heroines and mysterious settings, had become the favorite "forbidden" reading material of young women in both England and America. These stories remained popular well into the Regency Period (1811–1820); even Jane Austen, whose works written during this decade would inspire the later Regency-type novels, acknowledged the Gothics in *Northanger Abbey*, a parody of the subgenre. (Incidentally, in today's Regencies, if the heroine is found reading a novel or other "unimproving" book, it often will be one by "Mrs. Radcliffe.") It is this same gothic thread that was picked up by the Brontës, most notably in *Wuthering Heights* and *Jane Eyre*, in the mid-1800s, almost a century after the Gothic's first appearance.

The Nineteenth Century

Although the sentimental gothic continued to be popular well into the first part of the nineteenth century, a new form, the Historical Romance, was beginning to spark the reading public's imagination. With the anonymous publication of *Waverley* in 1814, Sir Walter Scott ignited a movement that, while it would periodically be submerged in favor of what was currently popular, was never to completely die out. Scott was avidly read in both England and the United States, but following the War of 1812, the Americans began to favor novels with American settings. When James Fenimore Cooper produced *The Spy* (a romantic adventure of the American Revolution) in 1821, he was hailed enthusiastically as the "American Scott." The Historical Romance attracted numerous new practitioners, and for the next several decades it enjoyed widespread popularity.

About the same time, a group of women writers who would eventually become known as the Domestic Sentimentalists began to make their presence felt. Picking up the threads of both the earlier sentimental romance and the sentimental Gothic, these writers produced a wide variety of romances, some of which tended toward the Gothic, complete with adventure, suspense, and danger, and others which were of a more domestic and conventionally romantic bent. Many of these novels also made use of historical settings and some incorporated religious themes. The unifying factor in these works was one common to all romances: they dealt with the "relationships between men and women."[4] From about the 1820s on, influence of the Domestic Sentimentalists increased until their work completely dominated the market in1850s. Among the more popular Domestic Sentimentalists were Catharine Maria Sedgwick, E.D.E.N. Southworth, Elizabeth Wetherell (Susan Warner), Mary Jane Holmes, Caroline Lee Hentz, Maria Susanna Cummins, and Augusta Jane Evans Wilson. Once referred to by a frustrated Nathaniel Hawthorne as "a d—d mob of scribbling women," these novelists maintained their popularity until well after the Civil War.

Although a number of the novels written during the "Golden Age of the Sentimental Domestic Romance" had religious or inspirational aspects, during and just after the Civil War (perhaps somewhat predictably), novels that emphasized these principles were particularly popular. Augusta Jane Evans's *St. Elmo* (1867), and *The Gates Ajar* (1868) by Elizabeth Stuart Phelps are two especially popular examples of this type.

The decades that followed were host to a wide variety of romance types. The Sentimental Domestic novel continued to be widely read, but it was augmented by the highly popular weekly story papers and dime novel series. Of the numerous writers of the serialized story paper romances, Laura Jean Libbey was one of the most popular. Her works were published from the mid-1880s to the 1920s, and she remains one of the best remembered today. Bertha M. Clay, another popular name of the period, produced a dime novel series of Gothic Romances. Interestingly, Bertha M. Clay, a pseudonym used by English writer Charlotte M. Brame, particularly for her American releases until her death in 1884, was continued as a house name by her publisher, Street & Smith, after her death and a number of writers, including men, published romances under this pseudonym. (This idea surfaces once again in the next century when the Stratemeyer Syndicate began publication of series such as Nancy Drew and the Hardy Boys.) Unfortunately, because of the ephemeral nature of their physical formats (cheap paper, poor quality bindings), many of these works were not preserved, and, as a result, much of the literature from this period has been lost forever.

Following the American Centennial of 1876, there was a renewal of interest in Historical Romances, particularly those set in America; until the first decade of the new century, the Historical Romance in its myriad variations enjoyed great popularity. Religious novels with historical settings such as Lew Wallace's *Ben-Hur* (1880) or Henryk Sienkiewicz's *Quo Vadis?* (1896); novels with mythical settings such as Anthony Hope's *The Prisoner of Zenda* (1894); and novels with historical American settings such as Mary Johnston's *To Have and to Hold* (1900) and Helen Hunt Jackson's classic *Ramona* (1884) are just a few of the many variations on this type.

The Twentieth Century

Although the Historical Romance was by far the most popular type of romance written at the end of the nineteenth century, other varieties continued to be written. It was during the last part of the nineteenth century that Grace Livingston Hill began to produce her perennially popular contemporary, domestically oriented, inspirational novels. The Contemporary Romance, with and without inspirational overtones, continued into the new century and in later decades achieved new importance in the hands of such popular practitioners as Kathleen Norris, Faith Baldwin, and Emilie Loring, along with Hill. During the first part of this century, two other authors were also producing Contemporary Romances that today are considered the forerunners of the contemporary Young Adult (YA) Romance. Lucy Maud Montgomery's Anne of Green Gables series (first one in 1908) and Emily series (first one in 1923), along with Jean Webster's *Daddy-Long-Legs* (1912), were some of the first books to address the teenage concerns related to growing up and falling in love. Although they were originally intended for the adult market, they are now read primarily by young adults and are considered well within the YA Romance subgenre.

During this same time period, the earliest prototypes of the Saga were also being written. *A Man of Property*, the first volume in John Galsworthy's "The Forsyte Saga," appeared in 1906; by the 1920s and 1930s, with the start of Mazo De la Roche's Jalna series, Hugh Walpole's Herries series, and G. B. Stern's Matriarch series, the popularity of the Saga was guaranteed.

The 1920s saw a revival of interest in the Historical Romance with the advent of books such as Rafael Sabatini's *Scaramouche* (1921) and *Captain Blood* (1922). However, the real resurgence of interest in the Historical did not take place until the 1930s and 1940s when, to escape the realties of both the Great Depression and World War II, readers began to demand stories set in a more romantic and pleasant past. This was the time of *Anthony*

Adverse (1933) by Hervey Allen (a rollicking romp through the Napoleonic Era), *Gone With the Wind* (1936) by Margaret Mitchell (a sweeping view of the Civil War South through the eyes of a willful, beautiful, and not particularly "good" heroine), and *Forever Amber* (1944) by Kathleen Winsor (a slightly scandalous story of an English country girl who became the mistress to a king but could never forget the man who first loved her). A host of others soon joined the ranks; it is during this period that writers such as Samuel Shellabarger, Frank Yerby, and Anya Seton either began their careers or achieved their greatest popularity.

Not surprisingly, there was also a new interest in romances with religious or inspirational themes during this time period, and works such as Lloyd C. Douglas's *Magnificent Obsession* (1932) and *The Robe* (1942) were particularly popular.

This period also witnessed the birth of the modern prototype of the Gothic Romance, *Rebecca*, by Daphne Du Maurier, published in 1938. Although its roots are well established in the earlier works of the Brontës and even Ann Radcliffe, it is Du-Maurier's classic that solidified the mold and established the pattern for the modern Gothic, which would eventually dominate the romance fiction market during the 1960s.

The decade of the 1950s is one that is not particularly easy to define in terms of romance fiction. It was a time of relative quiet; although romances with historical settings were still popular, the emphasis was primarily in the traditional contemporary vein. The Canadian firm Harlequin had just begun to publish reprints of the British Mills and Boon light romances; the inspirational and traditional romances of Faith Baldwin, Grace Livingston Hill, and others were widely read; and the adolescent market, yet to be officially crowned "Young Adult" by the publishing industry (in the 1960s), was largely composed of light high school or early career romances written by popular authors such as Betty Cavanna and Rosamund Du Jardin. *The Price of Salt* (1952), a contemporary classic of lesbian literature by Claire Morgan, was acclaimed with some enthusiasm.

The 1960s—The Gothic Touch

With the advent of the 1960s, however, the atmosphere changed. Suddenly, brooding castles on windswept cliffs; distraught, threatened, but exceedingly curious, heroines; and dark, saturnine heroes with hooded eyes and sardonic expressions were everywhere. Books with covers displaying gloomy castles, glowing candles, and diaphanously clad, fleeing heroines lined the bookracks; readers haunted the libraries and bookstores, impatiently awaiting the next Victoria Holt, Barbara Michaels, or Phyllis Whitney title. The catalyst, of course, was the publication of Holt's classic, contemporary Gothic, *Mistress of Mellyn,* in 1960. Apparently ready for some mystery and excitement, the romance-reading public made this book an instant success, and the demand for more of the same type soared. The demand was not limited to the Gothic, however; readers were also devouring novels of Romantic Suspense with equal relish. Publishers reprinted suitable materials from their backlists and actively sought new writers. Older writers of Romantic Suspense and Gothic novels suddenly became popular, and the careers of numerous new authors were launched. Phyllis Whitney, Mary Stewart, Susan Howatch, Dorothy Eden, Barbara Michaels, and Victoria Holt are only a few of the writers who contributed in this field. In addition, the Regencies of Georgette Heyer were attracting a growing readership.

It was also during this decade that the term "young adult" was devised by the publishing industry as a sales device "to make it more convenient to market books to those who bring books and adolescent children together."[5] The term stuck, and today Young Adult Romance is a recognized subdivision of Romance.

During the late 1960s, two events resulted in a surge in popularity of two rather different types of romance literature, the Gay Romance and the Saga. The police raid on the Stonewall gay bar in 1969 launched the modern gay movement (which brought with it the publishing of gay and lesbian fiction, including romance), and the serialization of Galsworthy's The Forsyte Saga for television revived interest in the Saga.

The 1970s—The Hot Historical Explosion

Both the Saga and the Gay Romance gained in importance during the following the decade, but they were not alone. The decade of the 1970s saw the beginning of a new romance boom. With the introduction of the Sensual Historical in 1972 (*The Flame and the Flower* by Kathleen Woodiwiss) and the Sweet/Savage Historical in 1974 (*Sweet Savage Love* by Rosemary Rogers) the romance market exploded and Historicals were suddenly fashionable after a relative absence from the market of more than twenty years. These new Historicals, however, were not the innocent Historicals of the past. Flamboyant, adventuresome, and, above all, passionate and sexy, these highly romantic stories reached out to the new, contemporary reader—and sold beyond all expectations.

The spillover from this popularity, also, affected other types of Historicals. The Historical Novel and the Romantic Historical, both of which usually treated history quite seriously and often more sedately than the newer varieties, gained in readership; even the sweeter, more traditional varieties of Period Romance were widely read. As was mentioned earlier, the Saga (which was usually historical) also increased in popularity during this decade, due in part to the establishment of Book Creations by Lyle Kenyon Engel. This company literally created Saga series, first developing the ideas and then contracting with writers to realize them. Engel died in 1986, but many of these series, such as Wagons West and The Colonization of America/White Indian, continued on after his death.

The Historicals weren't the only game in town during the 1970s; light, innocent category (usually contemporary) romances were popular as well. The field was dominated by Harlequin, but by the beginning of the 1980s they had been joined by a number of publishers including Dell and Pocket.

The 1980s—The Romance Boom

The 1980s saw the romance movement expand and change directions, somewhat. Although Historicals were still published and read, interest was shifting away from them and toward Contemporary Romances—particularly those of the category or series variety. But the category romances themselves were changing. To be sure, the original innocent Harlequins and Silhouettes were still being published, but a number of new series were joining them. These new lines, reflecting the changing lifestyles and sexual mores of society, featured more aggressive and independent heroines and were much more sensual in nature; soon series with names such as Ecstasy, Desire, Rapture, Loveswept, and Temptation were appearing in the paperback racks. (Silhouette's Desire is one of these early series that survives as of this writing. Two other series, Bantam's Loveswept was discontinued in 1998 but was resurrected as an e-book imprint in 2011, and Harlequin's Temptation disappeared from the North American market in 2005.)

At the same time, other series, generally those of the innocent variety, were disappearing from the racks. One new series, Bantam's Circle of Love, a sweet, innocent series, was obsolete before it was even released, largely because of the rapidly changing tastes in romance fiction.[6] And this was not an isolated incident. Sensual series proliferated and the market exploded—and eventually, after a somewhat bloody battle, Silhouette and Harlequin merged and today are part of the same company. (This activity paralleled the merger and acquisition mania rampant in the larger corporate arena during the 1980s. The publishing world did not escape, and during that decade, a number of houses either merged or were acquired by larger companies.)

But society's more contemporary attitudes were not reflected exclusively in the category romances. Single-title romances were also becoming more realistic in their approaches; although the traditional romances of the sweeter variety were still read (and written by some), many of the new stories featured independent, career-minded heroines, high-powered settings, and more casual, but not necessarily promiscuous, attitudes toward sex. In addition, several trends that foreshadowed the phenomenon of "genreblending," so prevalent during the 1990s and beyond, were established within the Contemporary Romance of the 1980s. One was the growing tendency of the "sexy novel of the rich and famous [to fall] into a genre pattern."[7] eventually becoming the fast-paced, glitzy, and steamy novel of Glitz and Glamour variety. Another was the increased blurring of the lines between the Contemporary Romance, women's fiction, and the mainstream novel.

There was also activity in other romance areas during this decade. In 1980 Vincent Virga published *Gaywick*, a classic gay costume Gothic, and by the mid-1980s a small but growing number of gay and lesbian romances began to appear. Interest also increased in other genre varieties (e.g., mysteries, science fiction, fantasy) all with a gay orientation. Sagas, particularly those with American settings, continued to be extremely popular, attracting new readers and writers, some of whom were already well-known as writers in other romance subgenres. By the end of the decade, interest in Historicals was again on the rise, especially those with American settings—particularly those set in the American West. The Gothic, considered by many long dead, became a bit sexier and once more began to attract attention, as did Romantic Suspense. Regencies were holding their own, but the Inspirational, although it had profited earlier from the generally conservative and traditional atmosphere of the 1980s, was in decline. In addition, a number of romance authors were heading in a mainstream or non-genre direction.

But adult romance fiction wasn't the only arena of innovation during the 1980s. In 1980, noting the popularity of its light, innocent romances sold through its school book clubs, Scholastic launched its Wildfire Romance series, and in doing so, changed the way in which materials were marketed to young adults for the foreseeable future. Prior to this time, publishers had concentrated on reaching young adults indirectly through the schools and libraries; now they tried selling to them directly, with spectacular results. The series approach was as popular with young adults as it was with adults, and the young adult romance consumers soon added appreciably to the growing romance boom. By the mid 1980s the YA Romance market had grown to include original romance series, reprint series lines, and a variety of thematic and soap opera lines. Eventually, however, the market faltered, and, although YA Romance continued to be written and read during the late 1980s, sales declined and statistically remained low throughout much of the 1990s. Publishers began to be more optimistic during the late 1990s, convinced that despite societal and lifestyle changes ". . . one thing remains constant for teenagers: the allure of first romance."[8] However, the beginning decade of the twenty-first century proved to be mixed, with some series being canceled and other lines testing the waters. (See Carolyn Carpan,

Rocked by Romance: A Guide to Teen Romance Fiction [Westport, CT: Libraries Unlimited, 2004] for a complete overview.)

But the publishing industry is anything but static, and just as a correction comes in the stock market after a meteoric rise, a "shake down" came in the romance industry in the mid-1980s. Heavy competition, particularly in the Categories, resulted in cutbacks and the demise of a number of contemporary lines, and only Harlequin, Silhouette, and Bantam emerged relatively unscathed. This process was painful. However, given the earlier, relatively unchecked growth in the romance field, this fallout was not unexpected, and by the end of the decade, the genre was healthier, more sophisticated, and definitely on the upswing as it headed into the 1990s.

As the romance boom blossomed, a number of organizations, publications, and adjunct groups have developed to serve it. Best known, perhaps, is the Romance Writers of America (RWA), an organization established in 1980 for the purpose of supporting writers of romances and championing the cause of romance readers and writers, in general. Over the years it has evolved from a small group of founding writers who were focused primarily on perfecting their craft and nurturing fledgling writers into a sophisticated and influential organization, capable of fighting for its members' rights and for the romance genre as a whole. Currently RWA has more than 10,000 members and is the largest genre fiction organization in existence.

In addition, over the years a number of romance-related periodicals have sprung up. Some of the more important are: *Romantic Times* (*RT*), a periodical that provides reviews, biographical sketches, industry news, and a variety of other information for the romance reader; *Affaire de Coeur*, a similar publication but not so comprehensive as *RT*; and *Rendezvous*, a respected, review-only publication that ceased publication in 2006. Of historical note are: *Boy Meets Girl: A Weekly Review of Romance Authors, Agents, Publishers, and Fiction*, a specialized and pricey romance industry newsletter that was influential during the early 1980s but folded in 1986; *Heartland Critiques*, another newsletter that focused only on reviews and ceased publication sometime after the turn of the century; *The Gothic Journal*, a specialized publication that featured reviews of Gothics and Romantic Suspense, and ceased publication in 1998, now functioning only as a website; and *Romance Forever*, a promising magazine in the 1990s that never quite got off the ground. By their nature, most of these magazines are blatantly uncritical of romance and need to be regarded in that light. Nevertheless, those still published are widely read and do provide useful information about the romance industry and most of the books that are currently being released. By their very existence, they have contributed to the success of the romance market, simply by promoting the validity of the genre, as a whole.

The 1990s—A Decade of Diversity and Change

Characterized by diversity, growth, and change, the 1990s was anything but dull. The period began on an upbeat note, and except for the expected volatility and a few unexpected industry moves which shook things up a bit, continued in much the same vein for most of the decade. Interest was strong, sales increased, and the genre continued to evolve in new directions.

From a literary point of view, the genre became more diverse and inclusive, expanding to incorporate not only the traditional romance subgenres, but several newer ones, as well. Two of the more important of these are the Ethnic or Multicultural Romance, which features protagonists from various cultures and ethnic backgrounds, and the eclectic Alternative Reality Romance, which covers a wide range of love stories with paranormal, supernatural, fantasy, or science fiction themes. In addition, the growing phenomenon of genreblending, the migration of various elements across fiction genre boundaries—or across subgenres within genres—became one of the major trends of the decade. The results of cross-genre mergers were apparent everywhere, especially in many of the Alternative Reality Romance subtypes, Romantic Suspense, and more recently, Women's Romantic Fiction. The intra-genre blends were less flamboyant but no less innovative, as anyone who has read a vampire Regency or a psychic Futuristic romance knows. A side effect of this is that romance became harder and harder to categorize, causing problems for both marketers and librarians.

During the 1990s, Historicals accounted for approximately one-fourth to one-third of the titles published each year, and Contemporaries, always the market dominator responsible for well over half of the titles released each year, were busy adding to their market share. At least one publisher of Historicals branched out into the Contemporary single-title market with great success. In addition, during this decade Gothics as a separate subgenre briefly peaked and then plummeted almost out of existence, the Regency ranks solidified (although Regency Historicals grew in popularity), and Romantic Suspense expanded. The Ethnic Romance mentioned earlier gained in popularity (and diversity) and the Inspirational Romance, after losing readership earlier, ended the decade on the upswing. The 1990s also saw the rise of the anthology, and while collections of Christmas novellas were by far the favorite, other themes and holidays were also well represented. Linked books (especially trilogies) and limited series were also popular.

Although the standard romance themes were still the norm, several innovative (or recycled) trends attracted a fair amount of attention, and by the mid-1990s, stories featuring wounded or imperfect heroes (and sometimes heroines), bad boy heroes, older heroes and heroines, reunions or rekindled love, or serious social issues were commonplace. In addition, the Alternative Reality subgenre had made its mark, and while this group continued to have its ups and downs, the romances during this period were filled with angels, ghosts, vampires, reincarnated people, and time traveling characters. Humor in romance became increasingly important; a number of publishers either produced new "romantic comedy" lines or actively solicited humorous manuscripts. Many romances, especially those highlighting social issues, exhibited a new intensity, and a number of publishers and writers turned their attention toward erotica. In addition, various writers were pushing the romance envelope to the limit—crossing genre and subgenre boundaries, introducing elements traditionally excluded from the Romance, and producing books with definite mainstream or women's fiction elements. At the same time, in two not necessarily related trends, more romance writers were being published in hardcover and the overall quality of romance writing improved.

The publishing end of the genre also underwent a few changes. Cutbacks, startups, and regroupings were all part of the 1990s, and while numerous lines were discontinued and at least one romance publisher folded during the decade (Meteor/Kismet 1990–1994), a number of smaller and less traditional companies set up shop (e.g., Odyssey Books, Lionhearted, Red Sage, Hard Shell Word Factory). In addition, established publishers responded to reader demand by producing new, more focused lines (e.g., Pinnacle's Arabesque, Harlequin's Love and Laughter, Jove's Homespun, Silhouette's Shadows) or forming new partnerships (e.g., One World's Indigo Love Stories—a collaboration by Ballantine and Genesis Press).

Formats also evolved during this decade, and although neither audio nor video versions came close to replacing the printed romance—nor are they likely to do so in the near future—the 1990s saw increased experimentation with romance offerings in several new types of media. Building on early efforts begun during the 1980s and early 1990s (primarily on the part of smaller companies), the audio trend gradually gained wider acceptance, as evidenced in 1995 when Harlequin published unabridged audiotape versions of four romances by bestselling writers.

Romance also took to the television airways during this decade—with varying degrees of success—as a number of romances were made into television movies. Recently, cable TV has become important to the genre as Harlequin first joined forces with the Romantic Classics channel in 1997 to sponsor a series of romance author roundtable discussions on "Romantically Speaking—Harlequin Goes Primetime" and then linked up with Alliance Communications to produce television movies for The Movie Channel, with the first one airing on Valentine's Day 1998.[9]

Other format changes of the 1990s included more romances being published in hardcover, including the inauguration of Ballantine's innovative paperback-size hardcover in 1997 (which died a quick death soon after), and fledgling attempts at publishing romances in computerized formats or online. In addition, as the result of discussions held during the Public Library Association's Cluster Workshops in 1995, Harlequin also began providing romances in various language translations to American markets.

The 1990s also saw increased interest in the romance genre in a number of diverse areas, including universities, libraries, and on the Internet. The academic community was forced to take notice when *Dangerous Men and Adventurous Women: Romance Writers on the Appeal of the Romance*, edited by Jayne Ann Krentz, was published by the University of Pennsylvania Press in 1992. It subsequently became one of the publisher's best sellers, was reissued as a mass-market paperback in 1996, and received the American Popular Culture Association's Susan Brownmiller Award. Other indications of increased scholarly interest were the Internet presence of AIR: Academics in Libraries, a listserv for scholars interested in the romance (now defunct and replaced by RomanceScholar); an increase in the number of theses, dissertations, and articles on the romance genre (e.g., Kay Mussell, ed., "Where's Love Gone: Transformations in the Romance Genre" *Para*Doxa: Studies in World Literary Genres* 3 [1997]); and a number of professional conferences on the topic of romance fiction (e.g., "A Passionate Journey: Writing into the New Millennium" at Penn State in 1996, and a similar conference, "Rereading the Romance," at Bowling Green State University in June 1997).

There was also an increased interest in the romance within the library community during the 1990s. During that time romance fiction was the subject of professional workshops, programs at conferences for PLA, ALA (American Library Association), and a number of state and regional library associations, and several pre-conferences. In addition, in May 1994 *Library Journal* became the first mainstream publication to produce a romance review column on a regular basis. It now appears six times a year. *Publishers' Weekly* began attempting to give romances fairer review treatment, and in September 1998, *Booklist* began reviewing romances in a separate section, treating it the same way as the other fiction genres. There was also increased collaboration between RWA and the library world. For example, RWA maintained booths at a number of ALA conferences, librarians presented programs at several RWA conferences, and beginning in 1999, a Librarian's Day pre-conference has been held in conjunction with RWA's annual conference. In addition, since 1995 librarians have been honored by RWA's Librarian of the Year Award, presented at their annual conference.

The decade of the 1990s was the also decade of the Internet, and with large numbers of romance readers and writers already completely at home in cyberspace, usage exploded. A number of listservs sprang up to cater to these groups (e.g., RRA-L [Romance Readers Anonymous], rw-l [romance writers], AIR [Academics in Romance], and the various romance groups on the commercial services such as Genie, Prodigy, CompuServe, or AOL), irrevocably changing the way in which readers and writers communicated with each other and paving the way for the innovations to come in the new millennium. An interesting phenomenon during the 1990s was the increase in author involvement with promoting their books, especially in the online environment. Romance writers are savvy when it comes to marketing their own books, and with the growth of the Internet and the advent of the web, marketing took on a new dimension. By the end of the decade, most publishers and many writers had websites (complete with excerpts of works in progress, chat groups, and other reader-relevant offerings), and with more and more people going online, it was clear that this was just the beginning.

Other, more negative, things that affected the genre by the middle of the decade were the shrinking midlist and a consolidation of the distribution system.[10] Faced with a consolidation of the market and bottom-line concerns, publishers focused more attention and money on their bestselling authors and those they had newly acquired and hoped to propel to stardom, to the neglect of their solid, dependable, but not necessarily upward bound, midlist writers. They also reprinted and promoted the backlists of works by popular writers, leaving less shelf space for the midlist romances.

During this same time, there was massive consolidation in the mass-market distribution system, squeezing the independent distributors almost out of existence (an 89% reduction by some accounts) and resulting, once again, in fewer outlets, less shelf space, and lower sell-throughs.[11]

Although marked by industry consolidation, realignment, and the resulting turmoil, the 1990s were also years of growth and tremendous innovation as the romance genre created new subgenres, experimented with new ideas, and embraced the latest technologies and formats. This was a true decade of diversity and change, just the thing to catapult the romance genre into the new century.

A Brand New Century

Primed by the events of the 1990s, the genre surged into the new millennium, building upon past successes and exploring new directions. Much was the same as before, with romance continuing to dominate the genre fiction market, easily outpacing the rest of pack and accounting for nearly 2,300 releases and $1.2 billion in sales in 2004.[12] By 2010 the figures had climbed to 8,240 releases and $1.358 billion in sales, according to the latest figures from the Romance Writers of America.[13]

Contemporaries, both series and single titles, continued to account for the majority of romance titles released, with Historicals gradually slipping to account for only 21% of the total by 2004. Contemporary single titles were on the rise, as more writers broke out of category and new single-title lines were launched, and by 2004 the traditional one-third to two-thirds division between contemporary single titles and series romances had become a fifty-fifty split. The popularity of the sassy, urban chick lit stories, highlighted by the launching of Harlequin's Red Dress Ink in 2001, plus the move of seasoned writers toward the mainstream women's fiction market helped fuel this move, although both types skirt the edges of the romance genre.[14]

ROMANCE TRENDS FOR THE NEW CENTURY

1. Sexier, steamier romances.
2. The lines between erotica and super sexy romances edged closer and romance publishers created their own erotica lines.
3. Vampires were all the rage, Urban Romantic Fantasy became popular, and Paranormal, and other Alternative Realities romances skyrocketed.
4. Inspirational Romances (and other Christian fiction) took off upward.
5. Multicultural romance continued to be popular; African American imprints flourished and multicultural characters regularly appeared in mainstream romance.
6. Books linked by character or place became the only way to go.
7. Military, law enforcement, and fire fighting men and women were the heroes/ heroines of choice in Contemporary Romance.
8. Traditional Regency Romance bit the dust, but Regency-set Historicals were a top pick for the first decade of the new century.
9. Academics began to take serious notice of the Romance genre and actively study it.
10. Technology is changing the playing field with e-books and the various audio formats changing the way romances are "read," and publishers are offering more titles in digital format, some even moving to e-book-only publishing, and most others establishing e-only imprints.

A number of trends either gathered steam or began early in the decade, most notably the increase in hotter romance, in general, and the movement toward erotica, in particular; the stunning rise in popularity of paranormal romances; the explosion of the Christian fiction market, including Inspirational romances; the expansion of the multicultural romance market; and the prevalence of linked or related books.

By the end of the 1990s, romances generally were becoming more explicitly sexy, and romance publishers quickly took advantage of this new trend by launching new steamier lines, of which Kensington's Brava and Harlequin's Blaze (a spin-off from its Temptation line) lines, both launched in 2001, are only two examples. Red Sage continued to produce its sexually explicit Secrets anthologies and Ellora's Cave's Romantica line of erotic e-books proved to be so popular that by the middle of the decade they were selectively releasing titles in print format. As the popularity of these books grew, romance publishers saw another opportunity and launched lines with an erotic, not romantic, focus, for example, Berkley's Heat (2005), Kensington's Aphrodisia, Harlequin's Spice, and Avon Red (all 2006). Although erotica is not romance, as most of the lines will state, the cross-appeal between the two is obvious, and when a romance is also included, the lines between erotica and a sexually graphic romance can almost disappear.

Alternative Reality Romances, especially the Paranormal and Fantasy groups continued on their upward track during the first half of the decade and, as of this writing, are still going strong. Vampire romances, both dark and violent and light and funny, have been extremely popular, as have stories featuring other supernatural characters as diverse as werefolk of all kinds, psychics, immortals, and faeries, to name only a few. Once again, publishers rose to the challenge with the launch of new lines, including Tor Romance;

Harlequin's fantasy imprint, Luna; Silhouette's dark paranormal line, Nocturne; and Jove's Magical Love series. Futuristics and Time Travels, often with paranormal or fantasy elements, added more diversity to this group.

With the rise in the overall evangelical Christian publishing market, the Inspirational Romance has blossomed. New imprints and lines in mainstream publishing houses (e.g., Harlequin's Steeple Hill imprint, Dalton's Waterbrook Press and its recently acquired Multnomah Publishers) have joined the traditional ranks of conservative Christian publishing houses to produce a variety of religiously oriented romances that include Contemporary and Historical Romance, as well as Romantic Suspense. As of this writing, Romance featuring the Amish culture and religion are extremely popular. While not all would be considered Inspirational in the classic sense (the protagonists may not be Amish or particularly religious), some are and would appeal to this market.

Multicultural Romance, especially that focusing on African Americans, continues to grow, not only in dedicated lines, such as those of Genesis, Kensington's Dafina, or Harlequin's Kimani Arabesque (acquired from BET in 2005), but also as single-title releases from the general romance publishing houses.

Another trend that continues from the previous decade and has expanded beyond belief is romance's love affair with linked or related books. Lately, it seems as though every romance published is part of a trilogy, series, or other structure that connects the books in some way. Linked by family, place, object, or mission, these books hook readers in much the same way that sagas or soap operas do, and both readers and writers currently adore them.

Characters also are undergoing a subtle shift, and as terrorism, 9/11, and the wars in Iraq and Afghanistan became facts of life, military, law enforcement, firefighter, and similarly employed heroes fill the pages; physically fit, action-oriented heroines are suddenly all the rage, as well. At the same time, in an effort to remain relevant to the aging baby boomer population, heroes and heroines are getting older. And while mature characters appear in all types of romances and from all houses, certain lines, such as Harlequin's unfortunately shortlived Next and Everlasting, were aimed specifically at these readers.

As always, the industry continues to reposition itself to meet current needs. Harlequin, for example, always quick to move, reacted to poor North American sales figures in 2004 by trimming its staff and making major changes in its romance lineup, some of which are still playing out as of this writing.[15] Not unexpectedly, publishers continue to mine the backlists of their most popular writers for reprint potential, a practice that, while good for publishers' bottom lines, unfortunately results in fewer slots for midlist and beginning writers. The industry is also publishing more lines and individual titles in trade paperback and is experimenting with formats of various sizes, such as the taller mass-market version used for Harlequin's Next line.

Another victim of bottom line issues was the traditional Regency Romance. Always a niche market, the subgenre had fought to hold its own for years. But as readers demanded sexier books and Regency writers switched over to writing Regency-set Historicals, the lines between the two began to blur and the traditional Regency could no longer compete. In 2006, Signet, the last publisher to have a dedicated Regency Romance line, discontinued regular publication. However, one hopeful sign is Berkley/NAL's recently announced plans to resurrect the Signet Regency line as part of its new InterMix e-book imprint in early 2012.

On another positive note, academic awareness of the romance is increasing as more scholars are giving the genre serious consideration. Papers and dissertations are growing in number, college classes in romance fiction are springing up across the country, and the establishment of RWA's Research Grant Award in 2004 (made permanent in 2006) acknowledged the importance of the link between the genre and the academy.

Technology continues to make inroads, and although e-books were around earlier, they are rapidly coming into their own this century, along with audiobooks, which are now ubiquitous and downloadable to a variety of computers, iPods, MP3 players, and smartphones. Publishers are embracing e-books at a record pace, and as of this writing, most romance publishers offer titles in both print and e-book format; many major romance houses have established their own e-only imprints (e.g., Harlequin's Carina Press, Avon's Impulse, Grand Central's Forever Yours), and several have totally scrapped their mass-market print program in favor of e-books only. Television also continues to be important to the genre, as the airing of Nora Roberts's novel *Blue Smoke* as a TV film in early 2007 indicates.

Other miscellaneous items of interest this decade: romance began experimenting with graphic novels and manga; writers began seriously using the web and several literally marketed themselves to fame with their creative, compelling websites (e.g., Sherrilyn Kenyon); and Barbara Cartland, a writer whose name was synonymous—for good or ill—with romance, died in 2000.

As of this writing, the first decade of the twenty-first century has closed, and what lies ahead is coming at us rapidly and is anyone's guess. Except for the traditional Regency (which may surprise us all with a resurgence), most romance types are still available and holding their own. And although the favorites of the moment seem to be Contemporaries of all kinds, Paranormals (especially of the vampire/shapeshifter variety), Romantic Suspense, and Victorian, Scottish, and Regency-set Historicals—some of which display mainstream tendencies—reading tastes change so rapidly that it is difficult, if not impossible, to say exactly what will be popular in the future. But whether it is by returning to obsolete seduction novels, remaining with the status quo, or leaping ahead to some as yet unknown romance type, it is certain that the romance with its incredible flexibility will continue to survive in some form. The romance, after all, like love, has been around a long time, and it is, indeed, a most enduring genre.

NOTES

1. Kay J. Mussell, "Romantic Fiction," in *Handbook of American Popular Culture*, ed. M. Thomas Inge (Westport, CT: Greenwood, 1980), 317.

2. Pamela Regis, *A Natural History of the Romance Novel* (Philadelphia: University of Pennsylvania Press, 2003), 14.

3. Janice A. Radway, *Reading the Romance: Women, Patriarchy, and Popular Literature* (Chapel Hill: University of North Carolina Press, 1984), 64. Although Radway's study has received much recent criticism and reaches a number of flawed conclusions, this observation is not one of them.

4. Kay Mussell, *Women's Gothic and Romantic Fiction: A Reference Guide* (Westport, CT: Greenwood, 1981), 7.

5. Dorothy Briley, "Publishing for the Young Adult Market," in *Librarians and Young Adults: Media, Services, and Librarianship*, ed. JoAnn V. Rogers (Littleton, CO: Libraries Unlimited, 1979), 5–6.

6. Daisy Maryles, "Love Springs Eternal," *Publishers' Weekly*, January 14, 1983, 56.

7. Diana Tixier Herald, *Genreflecting: A Guide to Reading Interests in Genre Fiction*, 4th ed. (Englewood, CO: Libraries Unlimited, 1995), 168.

8. Heather Vogel Frederick, "The Future Looks Bright for Teen Romance," *Publishers' Weekly*, November 10, 1997, 47.

9. Lucinda Dyer and Robert Dahlin, "Birds Do It, Bees Do It; These Days Players on the Net Do It," *Publishers' Weekly*, November 10, 1997, 46.

10. Theresa Meyers, "Publish or Perish: Dissecting the Midlist Crisis—Part One," *RWR: Romance Writers' Report* 17 (1997): 12.

11. Ibid., 13.

12. Olivia Hall, "2004 ROMStat Report," *RWR: Romance Writers Report* 25 (2005): 20–22.

13. "Romance Literature Statistics: Overview," http://www.rwa.org/cs/the_romance_genre/romance_literature_statistics.

14. Recent statistics from RWA no longer break the subgenres down in the same way, but as of this writing Contemporary romances in all their forms continue to dominate the market and Historicals seem to have regained some of their popularity.

15. Edward Wyatt, "'Sorry, Harlequin,' She Sighed Tenderly 'I'm Reading Something Else,'" *New York Times*, August 17, 2004, E1–E6.

Chapter 2

The Appeal of Romance Fiction

Romance is the glamour which turns the dust of everyday life into a golden haze.

Amanda Cross (Carolyn Gold Heilbrun)

These books [romances] offer a vast reassurance that the world will come out right.

Gaye Tuchman, Sociologist

There's no denying that Romance fiction is popular. One only has to look at bookstore shelves, check out the collections and circulation statistics of public libraries, or glance over the recent bestsellers lists to get the point: the Romance genre of novels is undeniably popular and its appeal is stronger than ever. To a certain extent, this is nothing new. Persistent, pervasive, and omnipresent, romances and love stories have been around for a long time, charming and entertaining readers with an expanding assortment of romance fantasies, that vary with the current vogue (e.g., seduction, Gothic, sentimental, historical, romantic suspense, paranormal, erotic).

On the other hand, however, the level of this current, ongoing fascination with the Romance is somewhat unprecedented. Never before have so many writers written so many love stories for so many people—and never before have they been marketed so aggressively by publishers, acknowledged so proudly by writers, considered so seriously by scholars, or read so openly by fans. As quoted in chapter 1, "the Romance Has Arrived"[1] and the figures for the genre continue to be staggering. The latest statistics indicate that in 2009 romances generated $1.36 billion in sales, accounting for 13.2% of total consumer book sales (more than any other category) and 35.6% of fiction sales, when compared with Religion/Inspirational, Mystery, Science Fiction/Fantasy, and Literary Fiction.[2] The number of readers is also increasing—and diversifying in an interesting direction. According to the 2009 reader survey commissioned by RWA, the number of Americans who read at least one romance during the past year reached 74.8 million, up from the 64.6 million readers reported in the 2005 study; also the percentage of male readers came in at 9.5%, making it clear that Romance is not, and probably never has been, strictly a women's genre.[3]

Organizations and publications specifically aimed at readers and writers of Romance fiction are varied and thriving; romances continue to find their way into films (*Angels Fall* by Nora Roberts, Lifetime Original Movies, 2007, is only one example);[4] romance authors are regularly interviewed in a variety of media outlets; and major mainstream review sources such as *Library Journal* and *Booklist*, as well as several national newspapers, are critically reviewing romances on a regular basis. (See the section on organizations in chapter 19 and periodicals in chapter 17 of this guide.) In addition, the genre is at last receiving serious consideration by a growing number of scholars from within the academic community, something that was highlighted when McDaniel College, Westminster, Maryland, bestowed an honorary doctor of letters degree on romance author Nora Roberts in 2006, and when the International Association for the Study of Popular Romance (IASPR) was established in 2009 and launched its journal, *Journal of Popular Romance Studies*, in February 2010. The association also holds a conference each year. For more information on IASPR, see http://iaspr.org.

Obviously, romances are popular, and the lure of the love story is a given. But who are the romance readers, and just what is it that makes the Romance genre so appealing to so many people?

According to an early groundbreaking survey of 600 romance readers conducted by Carol Thurston, romance readers are essentially a cross-section of "the general population in age, education, and martial and socioeconomic status."[5] Thurston found that half the readers have attended college, most watch less television than the national average, 40% work full time outside the home, and 40% are firmly in the financial middle-class. Subsequent studies have generally confirmed her findings, and the latest data, as reported by the RWA based on a study it commissioned in 2009,[6] shows that 24.6% of those surveyed read at least one romance novel in 2008 (up from 21.8% in the 2005 survey); that people of all ages read romances, with 44% of readers being between the ages of thirty-one and forty-nine; and that 21.5 to 28.8% of the U.S. population reads romance—by region, the highest percentage is in the Midwest, the lowest is in the Northeast, and somewhere in-between are the West and South. Although the educational and financial information present in earlier studies was lacking in this latest one (which focused more on buying habits of readers), the 2005 survey found that 58% of all readers were married or widowed and 66% had attended college, with 42% having earned a bachelor's or an advanced degree (an increase over the previous survey); an earlier study put most readers firmly in the middle class economically. In addition, a 2002 study by Borders found that romance readers were older and more affluent than had been expected; something that is not surprising considering the educational levels of the readers.[7] Obviously, the average romance reader is not the undereducated, uninformed, frustrated housewife of recent mythology. Romances apparently appeal to a broad range of readers; the question is, "Why?"

The appeal of the Romance is straightforward, yet multifaceted, and the current definitive source on the subject is still *Dangerous Men and Adventurous Women: Romance Writers on the Appeal of the Romance* (Philadelphia: University of Pennsylvania Press, 1992), edited by Jayne Ann Krentz. This wide-ranging anthology is a groundbreaking effort and should be mandatory reading for anyone seriously interested in the topic. It would, of course, be tempting to simply refer everyone to this collection and consider the subject covered; however, that would not serve the purpose of those who want something more succinct. The discussion that follows is intended to be neither theoretical nor complete; it is merely an attempt to meet the needs of the reader who wants a few basic reasons for the appeal of the popular Romance.

The Romance genre novel appeals both generally and specifically. Its general appeal is that of all genre fiction—an escape fantasy that is predictable, enjoyable, and safe. Romance's specific appeal is more complex, attracting readers for diverse reasons that include, among others, emotional involvement, female empowerment, promotion of moral values, celebration of life, ultimate triumph of love, and a sense of unflagging optimism.

The General Appeal of the Romance

The fundamental general appeal of the Romance novel, like that of all genre fiction, is to our basic human desire and need for escape—from the routine and anxiety of everyday life into a fantasy where things are new, different, or exciting, and where everything will usually turn out "right." (Rarely do romances end with the protagonists separating, but when this does happen, it usually is the "right" ending.) The term *escape*, of course, can be defined in various ways, but whether identified as relaxation, time for myself, wish-fulfillment, enjoyment, refreshment, or fun, it all comes down to the same thing—the need to leave reality, however pleasant, behind and experience an alternative, if only for a brief time. A study done by Janice Radway confirms the interest in escape; she reports that a full 75% of the readers in her sample stated that they read romances primarily for the various escape qualities of the stories.[8] Note: The glow on this study has dimmed in recent years, but it is a seminal work and its conclusions still have value.

Escape is not used here as a negative concept. Escape is a part of everyday life and comes in forms that are acceptable (e.g., vacations, sports, reading, games, crafts, hobbies) and forms that are not (e.g., drug and alcohol abuse, suicide, certain types of mental illness). As Constance Casey satirically comments in her review of Radway's book, "Better . . . curled up by the hearth with *The Flame and the Flower* than popping Librium or downing vodka at midday."[9] Incidentally, reading as a means of escape is not limited to the female, romance-reading population. Adventure stories serve the same purpose for many male readers, and both sexes enjoy the escape attributes of mysteries, science fiction, fantasy, and, as noted above, romance, as well.

Romances are also generally appealing because they are predictable. Although the popular fiction genres, especially the Romance genre, are often criticized because they follow a type of pattern and adhere to certain genre conventions, it is this very predictability that is so attractive to most genre readers, including romance readers. They *know* that everything is going to work out right in the end. They may not know how, why, when, where, or, in some cases, even who, but the readers do know that by the time the last page is turned, all mysteries will be solved, all criminals brought to justice, all desperadoes dealt with, all new or alien worlds tamed or come to terms with, and all couples appropriately aligned. This predictable, satisfactory resolution to the story, or happy ending, if you will, is the promise of the genre writer to his or her reader, and the writer who breaks that promise ends up with a confused and disappointed audience.

Finally, romances appeal simply because they are enjoyable. As John Cawelti said about all the genres in general, "people choose to read certain stories because they enjoy them," and Sandra Brown said about the Romance in particular, "Romances are fun!" people read them because they like them and because they are fun. No better reason is needed.

The Specific Appeal of the Romance

Although romances are read and enjoyed for all of the generic reasons mentioned above, they are also read for elements that are specific to the Romance genre, itself.

One of the primary attractions of the Romance is that it is emotionally engaging. Romances are books about relationships, and they appeal directly to readers' feelings and emotions. They are compelling, and they make the reader care about the characters and what happens to them. Interestingly, this emotional appeal is also one of the reasons that Romance is so highly criticized. One can only wonder why it is assumed by some that if a book makes you feel, it cannot also make you think—or that thinking and logic are inherently preferable to intuition and feeling.

Another important, and perhaps the most controversial, of the attractions of Romance is the theme of female empowerment. Contrary to popular misconceptions, romances are not books about submissive heroines who give up everything for the hero. In fact, they are not stories about women giving up at all. They are stories of women who win, who get what they want, and who tame the hero in the process. As Krentz says, "With courage, intelligence, and gentleness she brings the most dangerous creature on earth, the human male, to his knees. More than that, she forces him to acknowledge her power as a woman."[10] This aspect of the Romance makes it one of the most subversive of all literature genres, because in affirming the empowerment of women, these novels invert the traditional patriarchal, male-dominated order and allow women to be heroes in their own right. (See various essays in Krentz, *Dangerous Men and Adventurous Women* for a more complete discussion of this idea.)

Although it is not always acknowledged openly, romances also appeal because they are sensual, sexual fantasies. Written primarily by women for women, the Romance describes relationships, romance, and sex in ways women can identify with; while this is not usually the primary reason for reading a romance or enjoying a particular author, it is a factor that is important and needs to be recognized. In fact, the rapid rise in the sizzle factor in romances of all types and the growing popularity of Erotic Romances and erotica leaves no doubt that this is an area of appeal for a number of readers.

Romances are also appealing because they promote the importance of moral values. Strong interpersonal relationships, family, fidelity, honor, caring, courage, compassion, dependability, tolerance, selflessness, and similar themes are all well-represented within the genre; and in a time when much literature rarely advocates such ideas and often dismisses or denigrates them, romances have an obvious appeal.

Closely linked to this moral advocacy aspect is the fact that romances also deal with important life changes and social issues, both inevitable and unexpected, such as aging, pregnancy, abandonment, spousal and child abuse, divorce, death, grief, alcoholism, racism, prejudice of all kinds, and mental and physical illness. While this might not seem to be appealing on the surface, it speaks to the needs of a great many readers; it allows them not only to confront real life problems through fiction, but also to envision healthy, hopeful, and successful solutions and outcomes.

Finally, one of the most basic reasons for the enduring appeal of the Romance genre is simply that it is the most optimistic and hopeful of all the fiction genres. It celebrates life and love with abandon and reaffirms one of the most basic of all fantasies—the triumph of true love against all odds. Of course, women know that all real-life endings are not happy, but that doesn't stop them from wanting everyone to live "happily ever after." The Romance genre allows readers to temporarily suspend reality and enjoy the fantasy without jeopardizing their lives in the real world. After all, most romance readers are firmly rooted in reality; and while they do enjoy building their dream fantasies, they are generally wise enough not to try, or even want to try, to live in them.

Obviously, romances attract readers for a variety of reasons, but whatever the reason, romance readers know exactly what they are reading and why. They are readers first and foremost, and although they may read both Faulkner and Mitchell, Shakespeare and Plaidy, or Eliot and Putney, few would confuse the two or think they serve the same purpose or accomplish the same goals.

Predictable, empowering, optimistic, and just plain fun, romances have something for everyone. Perhaps this is the greatest reason of all for the genre's broad popularity and enduring appeal.

NOTES

1. Jayne Ann Krentz, speech, Public Library Association Conference, March 27–30, 1996.

2. Romance Writers of America, "2009 ROMStat Report." http://www.rwanational.org/cs/the_romance_genre/romance_literature_statistics/industry_statistics.

3. InfoTrends, Inc. "2009 RWA Reader Survey," http://www.rwanational.org/cs/readership_stats.

4. PR Newswire, "Heather Locklear and Johnathon Schaech to Star in 'Angels Fall,' Third of Four Nora Roberts Best-Selling Novels Adapted Into Lifetime Original Movies Airing in February 2007," http://www.prnewswire.com/news-releases/heather-locklear-and-johnathon-schaech-to-star-in-angels-fall-third-of-four-nora-roberts-best-selling-novels-adapted-into-lifetime-original-movies-airing-in-february-2007-55961582.html.

5. Carol, Thurston, "The Liberation of Pulp Romances," *Psychology Today*, April 1983, 14.

6. InfoTrends, "2009 RWA Reader Survey," http://www.rwanational.org/cs/readership_stats.

7. "Research Reveals Romance Readers Are Richer Than Expected," *Book Publishing Report* 27, no. 4 (2002): 1.

8. Janice Radway. *Reading the Romance: Women, Patriarchy, and Popular Literature* (Chapel Hill, NC: University of North Carolina Press, 1984), 60–61.

9. Constance Casey, "The Great Escape: Better A Romance Novel than A Swig of Vodka," *San Jose Mercury News*, February 10, 1985, Arts and Books Section.

10. Jayne Ann Krentz, ed., *Dangerous Men and Adventurous Women: Romance Writers on the Appeal of the Romance* (Philadelphia: University of Pennsylvania Press, 1992), 5.

Chapter 3

Advising the Reader

Lady Peabury was in the morning room reading a novel; early training gave a guilty spice to this recreation, for she had been brought up to believe that to read a novel before luncheon was one of the gravest sins it was possible for a gentlewoman to commit.

Evelyn Waugh

Rosenberg's First Law of Reading: Never apologize for your reading tastes.

Betty Rosenberg

Readers' advisory service is essentially the process of putting the reader in touch with a book that he or she will enjoy reading. Romance readers' advisory service connects the romance reader with the proper romantic story. Unfortunately, this reference service for fiction is not always as simple to accomplish as it might seem, especially when it comes to romances. In the first place, reading tastes in fiction, particularly in the area of romances, are highly subjective, and a good deal of discussion is necessary to determine what the reader actually wants. Second, the variation in romances, both in subgenre and in the handling of such particulars such as sex, is extremely wide. Therefore, a good working knowledge of the literature is necessary—something that not all librarians have, or won't admit they have, particularly in the area of Romance fiction. Third, effective advisory service takes time, an almost nonexistent commodity in most libraries today.

Despite of these difficulties, it is still possible to give good readers' advisory service for romance readers. The ideal situation is to have a staff librarian who is an avid reader and connoisseur of all types of romances, who has annotated all romances he or she has read, maintains an extensive, easily searchable computerized database on them, and who has enough time to spend talking about romances in-depth with readers who need advice. Since this is all rather unlikely, alternative measures are necessary.

First, the two cardinal rules of reader's advisory service, know your literature and know your reader, cannot be ignored. Without them there is no service. Some suggestions for achieving both and putting them together in a practical way, specifically for the Romance genre, is the subject of the rest of this section.

Several books that will be of particular interest to romance readers' advisors include the following:

Adkins, Denice. "Romance Essay." In *Genreflecting: A Guide to Popular Reading Interests*. 6th ed., edited by Wayne A. Wiegand. Westport, CT: Libraries Unlimited, 2006.
Introducing the Romance section of the classic reference source, *Genreflecting*, this informative essay discusses the definition of romance and its particular appeal to women, the development of the genre, and the role book covers play in attracting readers. The entire chapter is an excellent romance-specific resource, as well. (See chapter 15, "History and Criticism.")

Bouricius, Ann. *The Romance Readers' Advisory: The Librarian's Guide to Love in the Stacks*. Chicago: American Library Association, 2000.
Written with humor and passion, this lively, informative guide offers good, practical suggestions for librarians needing help in making their libraries—and themselves—more "romance reader friendly." Her "Five Book Challenge" is particularly useful. Bouricius is a public librarian and a romance author.

Moyer, Jessica, ed. *Integrated Advisory Service: Breaking Through the book Boundary to Better Serve Library Users*. Santa Barbara, CA: Libraries Unlimited, 2010.
This groundbreaking guide takes a look at the many different formats materials now come in, and "is designed to assist librarians in making connections between all the different media in library collections and advising patrons." The section on Romance, written by Katie Dunneback and Mary Wilkes Towner, is especially useful for working with romance readers.

Saricks, Joyce G. *Readers' Advisory Service in the Public Library*, 3rd ed. Chicago: American Library Association, 2005.
Although not specifically focused on the Romance genre, the third edition of this classic volume should be required reading for anyone who intends to provide any kind of readers' advisory service. Overall, this is one of the best and most practical sources on the topic of readers' advisory available.

Saricks, Joyce G. *The Readers' Advisory Guide to Genre Fiction*, 2nd ed. Chicago: American Library Association, 2009.
Focusing on the various fiction genres, this eminently readable book provides excellent information and advice and should be on all readers' advisory librarians "must read" list. While all the chapters are useful, the sections on Romance and Romantic Suspense will be of particular interest. Note: The section on Literary Fiction (yes, it *is* a genre) is intriguing, enlightening, and may be of particular use to romance readers' advisors.

Know the Literature

Even though it is impossible to have read everything, most librarians who are responsible for providing readers' advisory service for Romance fiction should at least be conversant with the various subgenres and should have read several good, typical examples within each. (Actually, this is a necessary requirement for speaking the romance "language" when you begin to seek help in other places.) See *Readers' Advisory Service in the Public Library* mentioned above for hints on developing a reading plan. In addition, the suggestions listed in the "Take Five!" sidebar for each chapter might be a place to start.

Once familiar with the genre, you can then obtain help from a variety of outside sources. Begin by querying the library staff. Depending on the size of the library and system, you may find one or more romance readers. These people can be veritable gold mines of information, providing recommendations on authors and books, keeping you apprised of new entries in the field, and alerting you to other important trends and developments.

Library patrons who read romances are other good sources of information. Readers are usually more than happy to discuss their favorite books and writers, and once you have established yourself as a "romance-reader-friendly librarian," you may find yourself pleasantly inundated with readers who will love keeping you romantically informed. You might even consider having an online review wiki that readers could use to post reviews, if your system would support it.

In addition, colleagues in other libraries are wonderful resources. Many are successfully dealing with large romance-reading clienteles already and may have answers to many of your questions. Also, some of the online groups, such as RRA-L and Fiction-L (see "Organizations and Societies" chapter), include a number of librarians and can provide good recommendations for specific titles, particular authors, and other Romance fiction matters. As anyone knows who has put out a request to a list, people are usually more than willing to share opinions and information. Advice is often as near as your computer.

The Librarians' Day Event, which takes place just before the Romance Writers of America (RWA) annual conference in July, is another opportunity for librarians to learn more about the genre. This inexpensive, daylong workshop is filled with presentations from bestselling writers, librarians, booksellers, plus editors, agents, and other industry professionals, all aimed at helping librarians understand the Romance genre, alerting them to new trends, and providing them with practical insights for dealing with the genre and its readers in a library environment. It is an exceptional chance for librarians to meet authors and talk with other librarians interested in Romance fiction. Usually held the day before the RWA conference begins, this event, along with RWA's conference, changes location each year; check the RWA website (www.rwanational.org) for a listing of upcoming conference dates and places.

Don't neglect the bookstores, especially ones with large romance collections and buyers who understand the genre; they can be excellent sources of current genre information.

Reviews, bibliographies, and reading lists, both online and in print, are all obvious sources of Romance fiction information for the librarian and for the reader, as well. Reading lists are particularly useful, and some libraries, library systems, or library schools may have produced lists of Romance fiction, often arranged by subgenre, that they would be willing to share. A number of libraries are also making this information available online, so be sure to check their websites. Ask around; personal contacts can prove to be a valuable tool when seeking information of this sort.

Finally, romance-specific blogs, author and publisher websites, and even more general sites such as Amazon.com are becoming increasingly useful. Just remember that the usual caveats surrounding information on the web still apply.

(Note: Because of the role reviews play in the collection development process, romance reviews and their sources are discussed in the chapter 4, "Building the Collection." Bibliographies are discussed in the chapter 16, "Author Biography and Bibliography." See chapter 17, "Periodicals and Review Sources," for print and online sources.)

Know the Reader

In addition to knowing the literature, it is also important and necessary to know the readers and understand what types of romances they want to read. This is best accomplished by talking with them on a one-to-one basis. And while it is time consuming, it is still the most effective way of determining what the readers really want. But you don't have to do it all by yourself; other people can help. For example, if there is a romance fan on the staff, consider consulting or putting the reader in touch with this person.

Furthermore, because readers enjoy discussing books and authors with other readers, introducing romance-reading patrons to each other may indirectly provide them with readers' advisory service. In fact, you might want to consider something more formal, such as a romance readers' interest group. This group, in turn, might want to contribute to the general effort by producing bibliographies, writing reviews or commentaries, or maintaining various lists, online or in print, for other readers to consult. Personal contact and interest is very important to the success of readers' advisory service, and as both publishers and librarians know, a personal, word-of-mouth recommendation is probably the most effective form of advertising.

Finally, in addition to knowing what individual readers prefer to read, it is helpful for you to have an idea of the types of romances your library community reads as a whole. Does the clientele seem to prefer traditional Regencies or sexy Historicals? Do they strip the shelves of dark vampire-filled Paranormals and leave the light, funny angel stories gathering dust? Do they zero in on the contemporary paperbacks, or do they go for hardcover? If the romances in your collection are individually catalogued and your circulation system is automated, all of this information should be fairly easy to obtain. (This is a major argument for cataloging romances, by the way.) If not, you can still get a good idea by checking with those who work at the circulation desk and those who shelve books. Most of these people have a fairly accurate idea of what is popular because they watch the books circulate, checking them out and in and putting them away.

Connecting the Reader and the Romance

Although many readers do discuss their reading habits and wants with the library staff, an even larger number do not. This does not, however, mean they don't need help. They often need it more than those who ask, and it is important to provide some sort of readers' advisory service for these "silent readers." However, because they do not ask for it, the help and advice should be offered in a way that they can take advantage of on their own. Fortunately, there are several reference sources that can help. In addition to the classic *Genreflecting* (discussed in chapter 15, "History and Criticism"), the following sources might be of particular interest:

> *What Do I Read Next? A Reader's Guide to Current Genre Fiction.* Detroit: Gale Research, 1990–.
> Originally edited by Neil Barron, Wayne Barton, Kristin Ramsdell, and Steven A. Stilwell, and begun as an annual index, this readers' advisory source is now published biannually and features an expanded list of sections and contributors. Each year this index provides access to well over two thousand titles, most of which were published during the previous year, in the Mystery, Romance, Western, Fantasy, Horror, Science Fiction, Inspirational, Popular Fiction, and other genres. Entries provide bibliographic, character, time, and setting information, subject headings, a brief plot synopsis, lists of reviews and other works by the author, and a list of other titles the reader might like. Entries are arranged alphabetically by author within each genre section, which is prefaced by an overview for the year. Additional access is through nine indexes—Series, Time Period, Geographic, Genre, Subject, Character Name, Character Description, Author, and Title. Although this

is not a romance-specific resource, it does have a discrete romance section, and the fact that it also includes other genres that have stories with a strong romance emphasis is a definite plus. An interactive version including all editions is available online and two single retrospective volumes of the romance entries have been published, the latest in 1999, entitled *What Romance Do I Read Next? A Reader's Guide to Recent Romance Fiction*, 2nd edition.

Booklist Online (ALA), www.booklistonline.com.
This subscription resource provides access to articles and reviews in *Booklist* magazine from 1992 to the present. Blogs on a variety of topics and some other information is free of charge.

Books and Authors, booksandauthors.wiseto.com/bna.
Published by Gale Cengage Research, this subscription database source mines information from several of its existing sources (*What Do I Read Next?* and *Contemporary Authors*, in particular) and makes it accessible to readers, along with articles on fiction trends and related topics. A blog written by various genre authorities is also available.

NoveList. Ipswich, MA: Ebsco, 1994–.
The brainchild of Duncan Smith and originally published by the CARL Corporation, this online resource has since been acquired by Ebsco Publishing. This interactive database provides access to more than 135,000 fiction titles in all of the major fiction genres, including Romance; the majority of entries have annotations and full-text reviews. Readers can connect to titles through a wide variety of access points, and the list of more than 36,000 subject headings is impressive. Broader in scope than the online version of *What Do I Read Next?*, in addition to providing links to other books the reader might enjoy, *NoveList* carries readers' advisory service a step further, providing selected book discussion guides, book talks, first chapters, and various training and support materials.

Reader's Advisor Online. Westport, CT: Libraries Unlimited, 2006–.
Based on content from the books in the *Genreflecting* series, this interactive database allows readers to search through more than four hundred fiction genres, subgenres, and reading interest categories using a variety of access points. Books can be located by author, title, series, genre (broad or narrow), theme, time period, or location. Readers can also find books that have won awards or are similar in some way to others they have read. Definitions for each of the genres and subgenres are provided, and readers can print off lists of titles they have found, for future reference.

In addition to the commercial sources available, there are a number of other methods for providing a reader with information and connecting him or her to the appropriate book. One simple, low-tech, but extremely effective, way to accomplish this is by placing reviews or blurbs from the dustcover inside the books. This provides the browser with pertinent information directly at the point of need so he or she can make a better-informed decision then and there. After all, it is only rarely that a reader will go to the trouble of looking up a review of a book that is basically going to be read for pleasure.

Another way to provide this sort of passive readers' advisory service is to set up displays featuring various types of Romance fiction. Rather than displaying Romance fiction in general, focus on one particular type (e.g., Time Travels, Romantic Historicals, Classic Contemporaries, Romantic Suspense, Regencies, etc.). In the first place, it is easier; in the second, it is less misleading to the public since there is a big difference between, for example, Victoria Holt's Gothics and Susan Johnson's erotic historical romances.

A variation on the fiction display idea is to integrate both relevant nonfiction materials and romances within the display. For example, if the display is on Medieval Historicals, include some books on castles; the history of the period; social, costume, and food customs; contemporary art and artists (tapestries, stained glass, etc.); travel guides to the area (terrain is often somewhat the same and many castles, etc., have been preserved); or any other relevant materials that might interest the reader. The same idea works by displaying contemporary romances with pertinent travel or "place" information, biographies, or materials about particular industries, businesses, or careers.

Readers can also be reached by means of bibliographic bookmarks or flyers providing genre-specific lists of authors and titles—between ten and twenty is usually a good number. Although these lists can be either plain or annotated, a well-annotated bibliography is by far a more helpful tool than a simple listing of authors and titles. Incidentally, in addition to placing these near the reference desk or in other traditional places, consider locating them in the romance section of the stacks, and, of course, make them available on the library's website, where they can be easily updated and readers can download them, print them out, or even e-mail them to themselves and access them via their smartphones.

Another means of providing information to romance readers is to maintain files, binders, or databases of book reviews or annotations and have them available for public use. These can be arranged either by subgenre and cross-indexed according to author, title, topic, and the like, or by author and indexed according to subgenre, title, and topic. Whatever the method, good cross-indexing is a necessity. The physical format chosen for this resource can vary. However, it should be something that can be updated and added to easily. Card files or binders are low-tech, inexpensive, and familiar, but online databases are increasingly popular, and if the library has the facilities (hardware, software, public access space, etc.), the staff time and expertise, and the funding, a computer-based file, searchable by a variety of topics (genre, author, words in title, time period, place, etc.) would be another option. Adding a link to these on the library's webpage and having a mobile app for readers with smartphones would be a welcome plus for increasingly tech-savvy readers. Some libraries even have readers review books and make their reviews available for public use. (This might be something that would appeal to a romance reader's interest group, and a wiki or even a blog might be ideal in this situation, if it can be maintained regularly. It would be a great addition to the library's public website, as well.) In addition, some libraries might want to consider using annotations or reviews to create "shelf-talkers" to highlight a certain author, book, or subgenre.

Readers can also be reached en masse by such diverse means as a library romance review column published in the local paper, a romance review segment on a local radio or television station, book talk programs centering on various Romance subgenres, even a regular blog or Twitter account on the library's website that readers can follow or have fed to their homepages or phones. While these methods provide good advice to readers, they are also excellent promotional opportunities for the library, the collection, and the genre, and in the hands of an enthusiastic staff or readers' group, could yield rewarding and exciting results. Local author panels, open book discussions on current titles, or book groups that meet on a regular basis, Regency or Victorian teas, and genre workshops are only a few of the activities that already have been used successfully in libraries across the country—and the possibilities are endless. Many romance writers are willing to participate in library programs or present workshops on the genre, and your local chapter of RWA and

RWA's Speakers' Bureau should be excellent resources. Contact RWA headquarters in Houston (www.rwanational.org) for current names and contact information.

Selected Issues

Although many of the issues surrounding Romance fiction are purely theoretical or philosophical, and are the subject of some scholarly debate, there are a number that also have practical implications, particularly for the library and the readers' advisory staff. One that often comes up when discussing romance readers' advisory is the way in which sex and sensuality are handled in today's romances. Because these aspects vary so widely, and what is acceptable to one reader may not be acceptable to another, providing guidance for readers in this area is often helpful. (The irate patron who slammed *Sweet Savage Love* down on the reference desk exclaiming, "This isn't at all like Barbara Cartland!" may be something of an urban legend in library circles, but it does make the point.)

The category or series romances are the easiest to deal with in this respect because the sensuality levels, as well as other requirements of the various lines, are often clearly specified. A short list describing the various series posted near the collection is a help to readers and fairly easy to do. (Note: Writers' guidelines often indicate the level of sensuality, as well as other elements, expected for the various series and are usually available on the publishers' websites. See chapter 22, "Publishers," for contact information.)

Noncategory or single-title romances, however, present a different problem. Although most single titles have some degree of sensuality, the treatment and levels of explicitness vary widely—as do plot patterns, the handling of violence and social issues, and most other elements—and unless one knows the styles of particular writers or the "heat" level of certain imprints, it is not always easy to determine how sexually graphic a book really is. However, since many writers often handle sexuality in a similar manner from book to book, lists of authors arranged by sensuality level either posted or placed in binders near the romance area can be helpful, although not always foolproof. It might also be useful to include a list of imprints and/or publishers noted for treating sex in a particular way, such as Avalon (sweet romances) or Brava (steamy romances). The books could also be labeled symbolically with hearts, flowers, rising steam, fireworks, and the like, although this would demand intimate knowledge of the contents of the book on the part of the "labeler" and is labor intensive; however, if this is an issue for your library, it would be well worth the effort.

Genreblending (when elements from one fiction genre or Romance subgenre migrate into another) is another issue that can fluster the readers' advisory ranks. While this phenomenon has been around to varying degrees for years, it has expanded exponentially in the past decade or so and now readers' advisors are faced with paranormal romantic suspense, vampire chick lit, magic-laced historicals, and a host of other creative stories that expand the genre delightfully but defy easy categorization. It is sometimes hard to know where to put a particular book or how to recommend it, especially when it seems to belong in several slots. Specific issues will be addressed in the subgenre chapters, but in general, the key, as with all readers' advisory, would be to identify the underlying appeal elements of the books and then match them with the reader.

Perhaps the most important issue relating to advising the romance reader is one that is key to good readers' advisory service in general—librarian attitude. Closely linked to censorship (which will be addressed in chapter 4, "Building the Collection"), this issue has been the subject of several articles, including Mary K. Chelton's groundbreaking "Unrestricted Body Parts and Predictable Bliss: the Audience Appeal of Formula Romances" (*Library Journal* 116 [July 1991]: 44–49), "Exploring the World of Romance Novels" by Cathie Linz, Ann Bouricius, and Carole Byrnes (*Public Libraries* 34 [May/June 1995]: 144–151), and "The Librarian as Effete Snob: Why Romance?" by Shelley Mosley, John Charles, and Julie Havir (*Wilson Library Bulletin* 69 [May 1995]: 24–25), which received the RWA's 1995 Veritas Award for the best article that most positively represents the Romance genre. The more recent article discussing the results of a small scholarly study, "Relations Between Librarians and Romance Readers" (*Public Libraries* 45 [July/August 2006]: 54–64) by Denice Adkins, Linda Esser, and Diane Velasquez, indicated that this was still an issue, a fact confirmed when RWA awarded a grant to this research team to expand its study. However, the results of their latest study, discussed in "Promoting Romance Novels in American Public Libraries" *Public Libraries* 49 (July/August 2010): 41–48, which showed that about half of the libraries surveyed promote their romance collections actively through readers' advisory services and to a much lesser extent through other means, indicate that these attitudes gradually may be changing.

The "problem" alluded to above, of course, is the condescending attitude toward Romance fiction on the part of some librarians and the effect of this on the readers. Disparagement of the popular fiction genres in general, and romance in particular, is a time-honored tradition in many library circles. And although science fiction and mysteries have gained an aura of acceptability over the years, it is still considered permissible, even a professional duty by some, to denigrate the Romance. The historical roots of this practice are many and deep, and the current attitude is, in part, a holdover from the time when all fiction was considered suspect and beneath the regard of any person of intelligence. Add to that the vaguely Puritanical idea that anything enjoyable is bad, the elitist view that anything popular is substandard, the perceived superiority of logic and reason over emotion—and overlay it all with a bit of the hopeless pessimism of existentialism—and it's easy to see how attitudes toward romance—itself optimistic, highly popular, feelings-based, and relationship-oriented—have ended up where they have. It's also easy to see how librarians, teachers, and others charged with the educational and cultural enlightenment of society developed their bias. Nevertheless, tradition is no reason to continue bad practice, and comfortable, appealing, and noble though it may seem to set one's self up as an arbiter of good taste by criticizing the reading preferences of the masses, it is a luxury in which no librarian can indulge and remain true to the service ethic of the profession. Our job as librarians is to help readers find the books they want, not the books we think they should have. Whether we realize it or not, our attitude toward both the reader and the literature makes a difference. Fortunately, things appear to be changing for the better; nevertheless, this is still an issue in many libraries and needs to be addressed.

Although all five articles mentioned above should be required reading for anyone responsible for romance readers' advisory service, "The Librarian as Effete Snob: Why Romance?"—short, direct, succinct, and practical—is still applicable and is probably the place to start.

Finally, here are a few things to think about:

- You don't have to like romance to advise readers (although it helps), but you do have to know and understand it and be able to represent it fairly. If you truly dislike the genre and can't keep your feelings from showing, you'd be better off not advising readers about romance. Stick to a genre you like and let someone else take care of romance advising.

- Not all romances are equal; there are good romances and there are those that are not so good. It is fine to distinguish among them and make recommendations to readers based on quality. It is not productive, however, to criticize a romance for being a romance (e.g., for having a happy ending, a focus on the relationship between the two protagonists, or a belief in the power of love). That would be the same as criticizing a mystery for solving the crime.

- Romance fiction, like all genre fiction, is generally read for pleasure and relaxation; it is a recreational activity (much the same as going to the movies, listening to music, doing a puzzle, or watching football) and should be viewed as one. Reading a romance novel is as legitimate a recreational choice as any other.

- Your attitude is important and will affect readers more than you realize. While it is hard to believe that any librarian would deliberately discourage anyone from reading or make them feel that their choice of material was less than acceptable, a thoughtless remark, a raised eyebrow, or a dismissive gesture can have the same effect.

Effective readers' advisory service, then, is based on three things: knowing the literature, knowing the reader, and putting them in contact with each other. How this is done most effectively is up to the individual librarian and is largely dependent on the library, its staff, and its clientele. But whatever the situation, a librarian who reads, who cares, and who makes the effort will be amply rewarded in terms of satisfied readers.

Chapter 4

Building the Collection

Libraries are not made, they grow.

Augustine Birrell

In recent years library collections and collection development philosophies and procedures have undergone major changes. Print materials are no longer the only game in town, and they are sharing shelf space and financial resources with a rapidly increasing variety of formats and products. Audio and video CDs and DVDs, as well as online periodical databases, have long been standard fare, but these physical formats are now giving way to downloadable formats, just as print books and periodicals are being joined by e-books and online journals and articles. In addition, collection development is becoming more centralized, and in this impatient age of "I want it *now*," there is also increased emphasis on making materials available to patrons more quickly than ever. No question about it, a lot is changing in the acquisition and collection development world, and we do need to adapt.

Nevertheless, despite all the changes and innovations, the basic principles behind collecting romance, as well as other materials, remain the same. Ideally, romance fiction collections should be handled in much the same way as any other fiction collection—thoughtfully acquired, carefully catalogued, appropriately processed, attractively shelved, and systematically maintained. However, in practice this is rarely the case. Romances tend to be haphazardly acquired (often through gifts), minimally catalogued and processed (if at all), randomly tossed onto revolving paperback racks, and weeded without thought of replacement when they fall apart. In some libraries, of course, this is how all genre paperbacks are handled, and staffing limitations may preclude any other options. However, in other libraries, only romance is singled out for this "specialized" treatment, while mysteries and science fiction paperbacks receive the same attention as hardcover fiction. It goes without saying that all the genres should be handled in the same manner; not to do so instantly raises the issues of discrimination, sexism, and censorship—sins of which most librarians do not want to be guilty. It should be equally obvious that in order to provide the best service to romance readers, a useful, viable romance collection, appropriately developed and maintained, is essential.

Building a needs-based, reader-centered romance collection is not especially difficult, but it does take desire, commitment, creativity, and, upon occasion, a sense of adventure and a willingness to take risks. Like providing good readers' advisory service, good collection development is worth the effort, and the library that takes the time to do it well will be amply rewarded in terms of satisfied readers. The comments that follow are simply suggestions for achieving this goal.

Collection Building

Selection and Acquisition

Selection is key to the quality of any fiction collection—and it is doubly important to the popular genre collections. However, as alluded to above, it is often ignored or, at best, given only minimal attention. Perhaps this is not surprising considering the time constraints on librarians and the tendency to view the genres as trivial literature. This is unfortunate because building any popular fiction collection is not easy and creating a good romance collection is definitely more difficult and time consuming than it would seem. In the first place, the sheer volume of titles alone—currently almost seven hundred each month (according to RWA's latest statistics)[1]—makes it difficult to choose intelligently. And it goes without saying that these numbers effectively preclude purchasing everything in all but the most comprehensive of collections (not impossible in some of the less prolific genres). In addition, even though romances are rapidly increasing their hardcover, trade paperback, and e-book presence, most still are published as mass-market paperbacks, a format that is still subject to substandard treatment in a number of libraries and by some review sources. Finally, as with readers' advisors, selectors who understand and appreciate the romance genre are crucial—and equally hard to come by. (Note: Since the functions of choosing a book for the collection and recommending a book to a reader have much in common and require a similar expertise, many of the issues relevant to collection development have already been discussed in chapter 3, "Advising the Reader," and are not repeated here.)

This being said, how do you select for a romance collection? In addition to reading romances, becoming familiar with the genre, and enlisting the aid of knowledgeable readers, colleagues in other libraries, and staff members (all ideas discussed in chapter 3), consider the following if you oversee the selection process, but do not actively select materials.

1. Choose someone who likes, appreciates, and understands the genre to select romances or, failing that, a person who, at the very least, doesn't actively dislike the genre and is willing to learn about it;
2. Provide the selector with appropriate review materials, including print sources and online resources;
3. Consider relaxing the traditional "no purchase without a favorable review" requirement for the genre because, although the review situation has improved somewhat in recent years, most romances are not reviewed in traditional library sources and reliable reviews are still difficult to find—rely, instead, on the judgment of your selector;
4. Provide the selector with adequate time to do the job properly;
5. Give the selector the necessary authority to do the job properly. If you are also a romance reader, you may want to make suggestions, but the ultimate decisions should belong to the selector;

6. Provide a separate and adequate budget for romance materials, including individual purchases, series subscriptions, review sources, online costs, and miscellaneous book processing expenses; and

7. If you really want to endear yourself to the selector, provide time and funding for the selector to attend a conference, pre-conference, or workshop related to the genre. (Note: the annual Librarians' Day Pre-Conference at RWA's annual conference is one good choice, but PLA also often has romance-related programs, and the local RWA chapters have conferences, as well.)

Consider the following if you are responsible for selecting romances.

1. Become familiar with the romance genre and its various subgenres by
   - reading books and articles about the genre (reading this book and checking out some of the articles in the bibliographies is a good first step);
   - reading several titles in each subgenre (the Take Five! titles given for each chapter are a place to start);
   - spending time online looking at romance publisher's websites and/or subscribing to their various newsletters that alert you to upcoming titles;
   - exploring other romance-related websites, including RWA's; and
   - developing a network of people who like and understand the genre (consider subscribing to RRA-L, joining another online group, or regularly checking—or setting up an RSS or Twitter feed from—pertinent blogs or websites.

2. Become familiar with the romance-reading tastes of your library's clientele by
   - checking circulation statistics if your romances are catalogued or talk to those who staff the circ desk if they aren't;
   - talking with readers; and
   - observing the romance collection and how it is used.

3. Become familiar with the romance-reading habits of the community surrounding your library and learn what is popular by regularly
   - checking the paperback racks in local supermarkets and drug stores;
   - checking local newspapers for lists of local bestsellers; and
   - checking the shelves of your local bookstores and/or developing relationship with the store's romance selector.

4. Once reader preferences have been established, consider carrying a variety of romance types and a selection of titles within these types, monitoring them closely to see what is popular and what isn't. Also consider trying a few good "out of scope" titles periodically to see if tastes have changed, then adjust your selection accordingly.

5. Carry mass-market paperbacks, as well as hardcovers and trade paperbacks, and series romance lines, as well as single titles. (The majority of romances are still published in mass-market paperback and one-third of those are series lines.) If you don't carry the full range, your collection will be missing some of the best of the genre. Since many romances are now being released in a number of e-formats (and an increasing number of romance readers do read e-books and listen to downloadable audio versions), these are other formats that need to be considered.

6. Regularly consult appropriate review materials, including both print and online resources. (See section on reviews below.) Note: Because print romances have a very short shelf life (series, for example are often available for only four to six weeks and are rarely backlisted), keeping up with the literature is important. Online versions of backlisted titles may help with this, but e-formats won't satisfy all readers.

7. Develop a plan for systematic acquisition of romances, including budgeting for both hardcover and paperback purchases, regular subscriptions to selected romance series, and appropriate electronic versions.

Reviews

While Romance fiction is still rarely reviewed in many major review sources (e.g., *New York Times Book Review, Kirkus Reviews*), several important publications now are paying more attention to the Romance genre. For example, *Library Journal* has a bimonthly column exclusively devoted to romance reviews, *Booklist* regularly reviews romances in a separate section within its fiction review section, and *Publishers' Weekly* includes the occasional romance within the fiction and mass-market sections, but unfortunately does not provide romance with a separate section, as it does the other genres. In addition, a number of newspapers around the country (the *Chicago Tribune* is one of the more recent additions) have added romance review columns on a regular basis. (Check your local paper and if it doesn't include romance reviews; ask the review editor to consider it.)

Despite these advances, the majority of romance reviews still appear in genre-specific review sources, some of which are mentioned in chapter 17, "Periodicals and Review Sources," of this guide (e.g., Romantic *Times, Affaire de Coeur, The Romance Reader, Romance Reviews Today, Romance in Color*). While many of these sources are overly positive, they do review a large percentage of the romances published each month and are helpful in determining not only what is available but also what trends are developing for the future. For this reason alone, they are well worth the price of a subscription.

Collection Development Policy—Selected Issues

The following are all items that should be addressed in your library's collection development policy. If they aren't, or if your library doesn't have a written policy (as may be the case in some systems), this would be an excellent chance to get this critical job done while making sure romance is appropriately represented. Reviewing the policies of other libraries, talking with colleagues, and looking at any of the myriad books and growing number of websites available on collection development are good ways to begin this process. Just searching online for "Collection Development Policies" will give you a good list of useful websites.

One major concern for romance selectors is the issue of gifts and donations. Ideally, romances, both hardcover and paperback, should be purchased as part of a regular collection development plan, complete with budget allocation, systematic purchasing plan, regular buying trips, and monthly series subscriptions. But this is not always the case. In many libraries, gifts and donations often are responsible for much of the collection, and in some libraries, the romance collection is acquired exclusively in this way. On the surface this cheap and easy method of acquisition may sound appealing, but allowing your collection to be determined by readers' cast-offs has little to recommend it. This is especially true of the Romance genre, because romance readers are notorious for retaining their favorites, or "keepers," and discarding the ones they don't like, thus ensuring a library collection filled with the losers. However, this is not to say that gifts don't have a place in the romance collection. They do—but as a supplement to, not a substitute for, the regularly selected purchases. One other thing to consider: If the other fictions genres are not acquired primarily by donations, romance shouldn't be either.

Another issue that often plagues romance selection and acquisition is the relatively short shelf life (window of availability) of many of the titles. Series are notorious for this, often staying available for purchase for a mere month and then disappearing forever. Single-title paperback romances fare a little better, but older titles can still be hard to find, especially if they sold better than expected and the publisher was unprepared to do additional print runs. What this means is that titles need to be chosen and purchased quickly—often before reviews are available—or they can't be gotten at all. In the case of series, the best solution is to have ongoing subscriptions. This also alleviates the problem of going off to the vendor or bookstore each month to pick up the newest series titles, only to find that others were there ahead of you and the books that you wanted are gone. Hard-cover romances are available for a much longer period of time and can be treated in the same way as general fiction.[2]

A related issue is that of format. The vast majority of romances (80% in 2010)[3] are still published in either trade or mass-market paperback, and despite an improvement in the quality of paperback bindings, a bias against the format still exists. Because the format is seen as cheap and substandard (despite the obvious high prices attached to a number of trade paperbacks and the fact that some librarians swear that paperbacks last at least as long as some hardcovers), a bias also exists against the content of paperbacks. As a result, many periodicals don't review them (although this is gradually changing), and many libraries collect them quite selectively, catalogue them minimally, if at all, and shelve them randomly. Paperbacks are still viewed by many librarians as cheap and trivial and are treated accordingly. The effect of this on the romance genre is obvious and unfortunate. It is, however, a problem that can be remedied by an enlightened selector.

Another format issue concerns romance in audio and e-book formats. Books on cassette tape, CD, MP3, and other nonprint formats are rapidly gaining popularity, and as the technology improves and more people become comfortable with "reading" this way, libraries will face not only the issues of physical nonprint formats, but will also need to deal with the virtual world of downloadable books to both computers and audio players. Books on cassette and CD have been around for years and are a staple in almost all public library collections; downloadable books (in both audio and e-book formats), a topic of serious discussion in libraries everywhere, are quickly following, and in some cases are already showing signs of replacing the existing print and cassette/CD formats. The fact that Harlequin already offers books in both formats (print and e-book) is a good indication that this latest technological development is no longer just a techie trend. The idea has gone mainstream, the readers have already embraced it, and libraries will need to do the same—and be ready to meet the next technological challenge, which is surely already in the making.

Finally, there is the issue of censorship—not the overt kind where people march into the library and demand that a certain book be taken off the shelves, but censorship of a less obvious variety—the censorship of selection. By its very nature, all selection is a form of censorship. Each day librarians choose which materials will be in their collections and which won't, in effect "censoring" those that are excluded. Of course, choices must be made. No library can collect everything, and it is understandable that librarians will want only the best and most appropriate materials in the collection. However, "the best" is a highly subjective concept, and the individual taste and attitude of the selecting librarian can have an enormous impact on the collection, inadvertently skewing it so that it reflects the librarian's personal bias rather than patron demand. Most would agree that this is indefensible both professionally and fiscally. (See the related discussion of librarian attitude in chapter 3, "Advising the Reader.") Mosley, Charles, and Havir assert, "As librarians, our job is not to judge cultural relativity, but to provide a service relative to our culture."[4] And that service includes providing a collection that reflects the informational needs and reading interests of the library's clientele. If those needs and interests include Romance fiction, it should be provided.

Obviously, no responsible librarian would deliberately make selections solely on the basis of personal choice, and no conscientious librarian would purposely exclude materials requested or needed by the clientele. Nevertheless, there are still libraries that, regardless of user demand, do not collect subjects, formats, or genres that they consider to be "substandard," and that often includes Romance fiction. No library wants to be accused of prejudicial behavior. After all, freedom of information is an integral part of the professional code. However, when a library gives a genre short shrift, despite strong consumer demand, it skirts the edges of censorship. If a library elects to exclude or treat as inferior only the Romance genre, one largely written and read by women, it also opens itself up to accusations of sexism.

Collection Control and Display

Cataloging

Although more libraries are beginning to fully catalog their mass-market paperback romances (hardcovers, trade paperbacks, e-books, and various audio formats are routinely cataloged in most cases), the vast majority of libraries do not give them such treatment, opting, instead, to place romances into their collections with minimal, if any, cataloging. Cost, convenience, time, value, and perception are all factors in this decision, and the circumstances and reasons vary from library to library. Nevertheless, despite the fact that many libraries have legitimate reasons for not cataloging paperback romances, there are a number of equally compelling reasons for doing so. In "Exploring the World of Romance Novels" (*Public Libraries* 34 [May/June 1995]: 144–151), an older but still valid article, Cathie Linz, Ann Bouricius, and Carole Byrnes provide an excellent discussion of the subject and list several logical, well-thought-out reasons for cataloging romances. Each is important, but two stand out as especially critical—first, improved access to the collection (and with it improved circulation), and second, the positive implications for collection development and management.

Access to a collection is key to its usability, and without proper cataloging, neither reader nor librarian will know what materials are on hand. Even if romances are not fully catalogued, their mere presence in the catalog, accessible for searching by author and title (and series and subject, if possible), is a tremendous service to readers. More and more often, romance readers are requesting books by author and title, and while they may browse the shelves looking for interesting titles, if they are looking for a particular book, unless it is cataloged, they won't know if the library owns it or if it is available for check out, and they will only find it by luck. In addition, a side benefit of cataloging romances is an increase in circulation statistics, locally as well as through interlibrary loan.

Cataloging romances also makes selection and collection maintenance easier and more accurate. Many circulation systems have features that will allow statistics to be gathered and reported in a variety of ways. Knowing which authors, titles, and types of romance circulate best is invaluable to the selector when it comes to determining what to purchase, replace, or weed out in the collection. These statistics are also useful when it comes to budget allocation and may even surprise some skeptics into reevaluating their opinion of the importance of the genre.

Processing, Displaying, and Shelving

How romances are processed, displayed, and shelved depends upon the individual practices of each library or system, that library's specific physical arrangement, and the needs of the library's clientele. Nevertheless, there are a few common basics for libraries to consider.

- Treat all genres equally. If Mysteries and Science Fiction are shelved, processed, or promoted in some unique way, Romance, Westerns, Fantasy, and other genres should receive the same treatment.
- Consider separate genre sections, including a separate romance section. Fiction readers often read by genre and most appreciate having their particular specialties separated out; Romance readers are no exception. This separation allows readers to browse in a location where books that interest them are concentrated, allowing serendipity full reign. Also, consider shelving books in alphabetical order by author or by series. As mentioned earlier, most readers choose books either by author or by series. Using this information to create a user-friendly shelving arrangement can only benefit both users and librarians. A caveat: An increasing number of books so skillfully walk the line between the genres that it is not always easy to know where to shelve them. Once the decision is made, however, it could be useful to have signs in the various sections suggesting that readers check the other genre shelves if they can't locate the title or type of book they are looking for. Or perhaps one sign with a general message near the larger fiction section could take care of them all.
- Consider special processing. Placing some kind of identifying label on romances (and other genre fiction) is often helpful to readers. These labels can consist of anything from a simple-genre tag to more sophisticated indications of sensuality, violence levels, or other characteristics that are important to the particular group of readers.
- Consider special promotions or advertising. In her chapter "Promoting and Marketing Readers' Advisory Collections and Services" in *Readers Advisory Service in the Public Library* (Chicago: American Library Association, 2005), Joyce Saricks provides an excellent, practical discussion of promoting genre collections in general, suggesting a number of ideas that would work well for romance. Ann Bouricius's *The Romance Readers' Advisory* (Chicago: American Library Association, 1999) focuses solely on the romance genre and also has some creative ideas to offer.

Collection Maintenance

The counterpart to selection, de-selection—or weeding the collection—is an often-neglected part of the romance collection development process. The reason is that weeding is usually done by attrition and not by design (i.e., when the book falls apart, it is discarded). The problem with this method is that popular books circulate, disintegrate, and are weeded out while unpopular books remain pristine and on the shelves. The obvious solution to this problem is to replace books that circulate and eventually remove those that don't. Unfortunately, because romance titles often go out of print within a month or two (especially the series romances), replacing them is difficult. Suggestions for replacing popular books include the following.

- Contact the publisher or your vendor and try to reorder. Even if the book is out of print, it will send the message that there is a continuing demand for that title, author, or series.
- Consider downloadable e-books. A growing number of publishers are making their backlists available in e-book format and many romance readers are increasingly comfortable with that format.
- Check with large-print publishers. Often popular authors (including romance writers) are available from them.
- Check online sites, such as BookFinder.com, which searches "every major catalog online" for new and used titles available for purchase, or Amazon.com, which also sells used and hard-to-find books.
- Check with individual used bookstores. Not every bookstore has an online catalog that can be mined by search engines such as BookFinder, so this may be the only way to find some titles. If a book is out of print, going to the secondary market may be the only way to replenish the collection and meet reader demands.
- Keep a list of popular authors and titles you are looking for. That way if they ever come back into print, you will know which writers your clientele will be interested in. This is especially important now because publishers have discovered the appeal of keeping popular authors' backlists in print, and some titles you are looking for might be available in the future.
- Contact local authors and see if they have any extra copies of out-of-print books you can buy for the collection.
- Prevent the problem in the first place by buying multiple copies of popular writers while they are still available.

As mentioned above, weeding based on circulation (if it circulates, keep it; if it sits on the shelf, toss it) is common; it is also a practical and logical choice because it will be specific to your particular clientele. However, the hard part is to actually get rid of the books that aren't read. Nevertheless, a useful, viable reading collection is not filled with dead wood—and the books that don't circulate must be removed. Circulation statistics should help you determine which books should be weeded. Note: If your romances aren't catalogued, this is another excellent argument for seeing that they are.

Basic Resources

Basic collection development information is relatively easy to come by; it can be provided by several professional books on the topic. An LC subject search under Acquisitions or Collection Development should yield a number of choices, and while a number of these tend toward the theoretical or may be more comprehensive than necessary, they are a place to begin. However, information specific to genre fiction collection development in general, and romance fiction collection development in particular, is less prevalent and is usually confined to book chapters and articles, rather than being the subject of an entire book. Ann Bouricius clearly lays out the issues and provides useful solutions in "Romance v. 'Real' Books: The Controversy Lives On," her chapter on the topic in *The Romance Readers' Advisory: The Librarian's Guide to Love in the Stacks*, and Johanna Tuñon's "A Fine Romance: How to Select Romances For Your Collection" (*Wilson Library Bulletin* 69 [May

1995]: 31–34) is older, but still definitely worth reading. In addition, selected sections of "Exploring the World of Romance Novels" by Cathie Linz, Ann Bouricius, and Carole Byrnes (*Public Libraries* 34 [May/June 1995]: 144–151), "Reader's Advisory: Matching Mood and Material" (*Library Journal* 126 [February 2001]: 52–55) by Catherine Sheldrick Ross, and Mary K. Chelton's older, groundbreaking "Unrestricted Body Parts and Predictable Bliss: the Audience Appeal of Formula Romances" (*Library Journal* 116 [July 1991]: 44–49), as well as the annual romance segment in *Booklist*'s September 15 issue, will also provide useful information on this, as well as other topics. You may also wish to consult the Sample Core Collection in the Appendix of this book.

Research Collections

Although there are two broad types of fiction collections, reading and research, the vast majority of these are reading collections and are commonly found in public libraries. It is to these that the majority of the remarks in this chapter have been directed. Nevertheless, research collections that focus on Romance fiction do exist, and few though they are, these collections are critical to the academic study of the genre and shouldn't be ignored.

While romance reading and research collections have some obvious similarities (e.g., they are both collections of romance novels), there are some important differences that affect collection development and should be mentioned, if only briefly.

First, their purposes are different. Reading collections support the broad fiction reading interests of the library's clientele and are driven, primarily, by reader demand, often to the most recent popular books; research collections exist to support the scholarly interests of academics and, while they contain recent materials, they are usually retrospective and comprehensive for the areas they cover.

As a result, the selection criteria for these two types of collections are not the same. For their reading collections, public libraries generally buy the latest popular fiction, as well as replace older materials that are still in demand, with circulation statistics playing an important role in determining what is to be purchased. On the other hand, academic libraries select materials for their research collections based on the specialized requirements of the collections, which are usually spelled out in the collection development policies. In the case of Romance fiction, for example, there might be goals as general as collecting a broad selection of popular romances of all types (with over eight thousand titles published annually, rarely would a normal research library attempt to collect all the romances published) or as specific as collecting all the series romances of a particular publisher, all the works by particular authors, or all the romances in a particular subgenre (e.g., Regencies, Gothics, Time Travels) or time period. Whatever the particular focus, comprehensiveness is usually a primary goal.

Although books in research or special academic collections can be donated (in fact, many special research collections have been initiated by a large initial donation of a private collection), in the case of romance or any of the other popular fiction genres, materials will generally need to be purchased as they are in public library reading collections. As mentioned earlier, subscriptions and standing orders might be necessary to ensure getting all the needed titles before they go out of print, although academic libraries, unlike many public libraries, will often order out-of-print books for their specialized collections.

Once acquired, books in research collections should be completely cataloged to provide access, and processed as necessary, taking into account that the popular paperback, which is the most prevalent form for romance fiction, is often valued as an object (especially for the cover art) as well as for its content.

Reading and research collections also differ when it comes to use and circulation. Reading collections need to be able to stand up to heavy patron use because they circulate heavily; research collections, especially of the kind we are discussing, are often noncirculating for security as well as fragility concerns, and issues surrounding in-house access and photocopying will need to be addressed.

Finally, reading and research collections have different criteria when it comes to storage and shelving and collection maintenance. Storage and shelving of these items will often require specialized treatment and handling (e.g., climate control, acid-free boxes, etc.) because in addition to being in paperback format, many of these books were printed on acidic paper and are literally burning up on the shelves. The other difference between reading and research collections is in removing books from the collection (i.e., weeding or de-selection). Public libraries usually weed their collections heavily, based on the condition of the book, age, relevance, and circulation figures. On the other hand, specialized research collections, such as the ones we are discussing, are rarely weeded because their purpose is to collect, archive, and preserve the materials for future scholarly research, and the integrity and completeness of the collection is critical.

NOTES

1. Romance Writers of America, "Romance Literature Statistics: Overview," www.rwanational.org/cs/the_romance_genre/romance_literature_statistics.

2. The fact that publishers are now making many of their titles, new and old, available as e-books may eventually change these dynamics, but because of access and copyright concerns, libraries are often limited by what is available through their online e-book vendors (e.g., Overdrive).

3. "2010 ROMStat Report," *Romance Writers' Report* 31 (November 2011): 12–13.

4. Shelley Mosley, John Charles, and Julie Havir, "The Librarian as Effete Snob: Why Romance?" *Wilson Library Bulletin* 69 (May 1995): 24–25.

PART II

THE LITERATURE

Chapter 5

Contemporary Romance

The life of every woman is a romance!

Mme. de Genlis

Love is life. And if you miss love, you miss life.

Leo Buscaglia

Love is a game that two can play and both win.

Eva Gabor

Definition

> **Contemporary Romance**—Romance novels with contemporary settings (currently any time after World War II), these novels usually focus on the attempts of the characters to find success and fulfillment professionally, personally, and romantically.

The largest and possibly the most inclusive of all Romance subgenres, the Contemporary Romance is what most people have in mind when they refer to the generic Romance novel. Essentially love stories with contemporary settings (currently any time after World War II), these novels usually focus on the attempts of a woman to find success and fulfillment professionally, personally, and romantically. Usually by the end of the book, the heroine has happily attained these goals. Although there are certain exceptions, a committed, permanent, monogamous relationship—one that often includes marriage and possibly a family—is still the ultimate goal for this type of romance. However, in line with current social trends, many recent heroines do not retire to hearth and home but continue in their careers, not only after marriage, but after childbirth, as well. Novels written prior to 1970 often do not feature this particular trend, and in those written during the early part of the twentieth century, the heroine is typically not employed. Most likely she will be doing volunteer work, helping her family at home, or pursuing some other properly genteel occupation.

It is worth noting that the term "contemporary," as it is used in this book, is not merely a synonym for "modern-day." Although by far the majority of Contemporary Romances read today are both contemporary and modern-day, there are a number of novels of this kind written well before World War II that are still in print. These novels, while now exhibiting a historical flavor, were actually written as contemporary love stories and had as their purpose the telling of modern-day love relationships, relevant to the then-current times. Many works by prototypical authors such as Grace Livingston Hill and Faith Baldwin are examples of this. Eventually, of course, these works (if they remain in print) will be classified largely as Historicals, or as Inspirationals in the case of Hill, in much the same way as are the works by earlier writers of Contemporary Romances such as Jane Austen and Samuel Richardson.

It is also interesting to consider that the Contemporary Romances of today that survive may well become the Historicals of the future. Of course, romances written as Historicals and romances that endure to become historical are actually two different things, varying both in purpose and in the amount of background information supplied to the reader. Most Contemporaries will not make the transition; they will merely become dated and irrelevant and will eventually go out of print. Only those with exceptionally well-drawn, believable characters involved in basic human conflicts have even a chance for survival.

The settings used in Contemporary Romances are diverse and vary more widely than ever. Ranging from a peaceful Midwestern suburb, busy inner-city business district, or busy Texas ranch to a steamy tropical island, battle-torn third world country, or isolated mountain retreat, the choices for settings are endless and limited only by the real possibilities of the current time period. Typical settings include rural or small town domestic, social, or local business or ranch situations; urban work, business, apartment/condo, or community organizational settings (both upscale and inner city); suburban domestic, school, or social situations; and exotic foreign or romantic domestic vacation or job situations (e.g., isolated mountain retreat, beach house, cruise ship, ski resort, Mediterranean or Caribbean island).

The plots are also varied, dependent to a large extent upon the physical settings and occupations of the main characters; however, the basic boy-meets-girl, boy-misunderstands-and-therefore-loses-girl, boy-gets-girl structure (or its reverse) tends to remain more or less the same. In a typical plot, the heroine (either young and relatively innocent or older, independent, and more experienced—but always intelligent and attractive "in her own way") is trying to get on with her life, either by setting off to "seek her fortune," picking up the pieces of a broken past, or trying to accomplish some other goal. She soon encounters—or reencounters, if this is a reunion story—the hero (traditionally, but not always, handsome, self-assured—even arrogant—and successful or rich), to whom she takes an instant dislike; however, she is usually "strangely attracted" to him despite this initial aversion and can't understand why. Through a convenient set of circumstances (they share a common goal or interest, they must work together, they live next door to each other, they have children the same age, they are staying in the same resort, they are stranded together in the same jungle, etc.), they are thrown together and eventually fall in love. Inevitably, of course, conflicts arise and the lovers spend a good portion of the book trying to work things out. The conflict can be external (other people or situations keeping the protagonists apart) or internal (the feelings, values, and past histories of the hero and heroine causing the problems), and misunderstandings, both real and imagined, often play a large part in keeping the pair at odds. However, by the end of the story, all differences are resolved, the hero and heroine reconcile, and their happy future is generally assured. Although the main plot in all romances is the love story line dealing with the protagonists, subplots of various kinds appear in many of the longer romance works. These subplots are rarely as well-developed as is the main storyline, but they do add interest and depth to the story as a whole. Also, in the case of trilogies or other linked books, some type of subplot usually continues throughout the series and is resolved in the final volume.

While this basic romance plot pattern is relatively constant (just as the pattern for the Mystery genre will always revolve around the sleuth, the crime, and the solution), the past decade continues to bring new developments in the way in which it is applied. Situations and issues that were once seen as either taboo or too serious for Romance (e.g., substance abuse, child or spousal abuse, terminal illness, homosexuality, prostitution, illiteracy, infidelity, mental illness, impotence, interracial relationships) have become commonplace and characters who were considered unacceptable or too realistic for the genre (e.g., the hero or heroine deeply wounded by abuse, war, rape, torture, or other devastating tragedy; the ex-convict or alcoholic hero or heroine; the unwed mother heroine; the variously disabled hero or heroine; the bad girl heroine; the gay friend or couple) now rarely raise an eyebrow. This continuing trend toward more contemporary relevance, as well as more complex plotting and realistic characters, is no doubt one reason that the lines between the Romance and other types of more mainstream Women's Fiction are blurring. The boundaries between them are more fluid than ever and, while this continues to make it more difficult to neatly categorize the genres and the subgenres within them, it also is an indication that Contemporary Romance is coming of age and maturing into a genre that is socially pertinent, reflects current trends, and connects with today's readers.

Characters in Contemporaries will be as varied as the settings and the plots, and they will differ according to the type of romance. Nevertheless, most protagonists have several characteristics in common, whatever the romance style. Key among these are self-motivation, resilience, honesty, and above all, a highly developed sense of honor. The characters' actions may be suspect, but they are always performed for the "right" reasons—reasons that are usually selfless and have to do with helping or saving others (e.g., the hero kills his father because the father was molesting his sister or the heroine lies about her job qualifications so she can support her younger siblings). Approval of these characters is critical for reader identification, and while they have imperfections, they must be able to generate enough respect and admiration (along with likability, if possible) for the reader to care.

In addition, the Contemporary heroine often displays a high degree of independence, intelligence, initiative, and determination, relying more on herself to solve her problems than on the hero. She also may be wary of emotional relationships because of being hurt in the past. While at one point it could be generalized that the more daring heroines dominated the sensual romances and the less adventuresome women populated those romances of the innocent (or sweet) variety, this is no longer necessarily the case. Strong, independent, capable heroines appear in Contemporaries of all types, regardless of the sensuality levels. Heroines are also no longer necessarily pure and virginal. Changing societal patterns have paved the way for a more sexually experienced heroine—often one who has been widowed or divorced, but more recently, one who has simply had an earlier serious relationship that didn't work out (usually through no fault of her own). As a result, the sensuality levels of the Contemporary Romance have been rapidly rising, and while these vary widely and range from sweet to explicit, it is generally agreed that romances across the board are steamier and more sexually graphic than in the past. The innocent heroine, of course, still exists and is, in fact, practically mandatory in most traditional Regencies and Inspirationals as well as in the few remaining Innocent or Sweet category and single-title lines. However, the current trend in both publishing and in reader demand has been toward heroines of the more modern, sexually experienced variety.

Like heroines, heroes in Contemporaries come in all shapes and sizes. Often they are strong, take-charge men, handsome and possibly wealthy, who have already achieved success in their business or professional fields. However, this classic, dominant, alpha-male type hero is not the only choice available. The beta hero, who has a gentler, softer, more sensitive side has been part of the mix for some time, and while he currently takes a back seat to the more popular alpha hero—especially with the stellar success of action-oriented romances and their super alpha protagonists—his sympathetic nature and quiet strength has great appeal and is perfect for some situations. Although "pure" heroes of both types exist, the trend now is toward blending of some of these characteristics and in reality, the most successful heroes combine elements of both (e.g., the strong, take-charge hero with a well-hidden, surprisingly compassionate side or the unassuming, quiet, almost nerdy hero who takes on the town bully and wins). Whatever their types, heroes at first often appear reserved, even aloof, and somewhat mysterious, and are typically unwilling to become emotionally involved with anyone. Nevertheless, they are attracted to the heroine "in spite of themselves," and eventually must come to terms with the reasons for their feelings. (Typically, they have been hurt by a woman at some point in the past and assume that "women are all alike," or they have their own past or secret issues and consider themselves unworthy of love. The insightful, perceptive, caring heroine, of course, changes all that.) Of course, the reverse of this can also be true, with the heroine being the wary party and the hero knowing exactly how he feels.

Supporting characters also appear in these stories, and in the longer romances they are often described in a fair amount of detail. (The best friend, the other woman, the other man, the toxic boss, and the villain are examples of typical supporting characters.) Nevertheless, in these stories the emphasis is on the hero and heroine, and rarely are the additional characters developed more than is necessary to provide background for the main story line. The longer and more complex the story, of course, the more subplots there are and the greater the chance for more thorough development of the minor characters, especially if this story is part of a series and these characters will reappear in subsequent books. However, in most cases, these secondary characters are not as fully delineated as the protagonists.

Wide-ranging, and often murky, the Contemporary Romance subgenre essentially consists of two broad, primary groups—the Traditional Contemporary Romance, which is comprised primarily of single titles, and the Category, or Series, Contemporary Romance, all of which are part of the series lines. These are supplemented by several other separate, but closely related and often overlapping, fiction types—in particular, Women's Romantic Fiction, Chick Lit and its derivatives, and Soap Opera—all of which can further be blended or broken down into a number of diverse subsets of varying types.

Traditional Contemporary Romance

(Note: In earlier editions of this guide, Traditional Contemporary Romance was called Basic Contemporary Romance, primarily because the more appropriate term, "Traditional," had been used within the industry to indicate a sweet or innocent, usually category, romance. However, as times have changed and this is no longer the common perception, it now makes sense to make the switch.)

The most enduring and encompassing of all the Contemporary Romance sub-genres, the Traditional Contemporary Romance, is simply a nonformula love story with a contemporary setting. This subset includes within it most contemporary romances that are not subsumed within the other contemporary groups, and most are single-title romances, an industry term used to distinguish them from the various category romances and indicate the way in which they are published.

Unbound by certain restraints inherent in the other types of Contemporary Romances, especially the Category Series Romance, the Traditional Contemporary Romance makes use of a wide variety of characters and settings, occasionally employing plot patterns that are both unconventional and unpredictable. The way in which sex is handled also varies greatly in these stories, ranging from the innocent to the erotic, with the majority falling somewhere in between. As might be expected, older novels, especially those written prior to the 1970s, are generally of the more innocent variety, while many of those written in the decades since can contain much more sexually explicit material. Thanks to the influence of the Hot Historicals of the 1970s, the Traditional Contemporary steamed up in the 1980s, and with the advent of Erotic Romance, sensuality levels spiked even higher. The interest in Erotic Romance that began well over a decade ago, possibly with the release of Red Sage's first *Secrets* anthology in 1995, continues to flourish, gradually bleeding over into most other subgenres and ramping up the sizzle factor across the board. What began with several smaller print and online publishers (e.g., Red Sage Publishing, Ellora's Cave) now touches the entire industry and many of the major publishers have launched Erotic Romance lines of their own. (See chapter 14, "Erotic Romance.") The Traditional Contemporary Romance subgenre is, and always has been, one of the most popular and widely read of the Romance subgenres and is exemplified by the works of writers such as Nora Roberts, Debbie Macomber, Cathie Linz, Barbara Freethy, Jill Marie Landis, Jennifer Crusie, and Susan Elizabeth Phillips. However, popularity is not limited to just the *current* materials within the genre. Many bestselling authors of past decades are either still in print or have been reprinted (in either digital or hardcopy format) and are still read occasionally by today's romance readers. Among these authors are Grace Livingston Hill (now read primarily as an Inspirational writer), Faith Baldwin, Elizabeth Cadell, and, more recently, LaVyrle Spencer, who retired in 1997.

Category, or Numbered Series, Romance

The Category Romance, typified by the numbered series romance lines published by Harlequin and Silhouette, is essentially a love story written to a particular pattern. These patterns are determined by each publisher and are series-specific. Most series follow a variation of the boy-meets-girl, boy-loses-girl, boy-gets-girl plot pattern, with the specific requirements of each series being spelled out in the writing guidelines available online from the publisher. These guidelines outline the overall focus of the line, the degree of sensuality allowed or required, the acceptable word length, character types, and other information useful to the would-be author; however, they also help readers and librarians understand the differences among the lines. (As of this writing, guidelines for all the lines published by Harlequin Books, including both series and single titles, are available at eharlequin.com. Choose the "Writing Guidelines" link at the bottom of the page.) Although many category authors are well-known in their own right and are sought out by readers, most series are still marketed on the basis of their series appeal. Nevertheless, differences in writing styles ensure that these are not merely cookie-cutter books, and if some of them were published individually, they would be classified in the Traditional Contemporary Romance subgroup. Despite such variations in style, however, the books within a specific series all follow the same basic guidelines; the readers know, more or less, just what they are getting before they buy or check out the book.

While at one point in the past it was possible to neatly divide Category Romances into three basic types—the Innocent or Sweet, the Sensual, and the Young Adult—this is no longer the case. Category Romance has exploded and now includes a far more varied array of offerings. To be sure, the three mentioned above still continue, but there are also category lines for Romantic Suspense, the Paranormal, the Inspirational, African Americans, and Medical Romance to name only a few. In addition, lines have come and gone that specifically highlighted romantic comedy, written communication, action adventure, and a host of other themes. The Innocent or Sweet Category Romance, the most chaste of the categories, is exemplified by a warm emotional tone; engaging, charismatic characters; no explicit sex but usually a high degree of sexual tension; and relatively short length, 50,000–55,000 words. Harlequin Romance is the prime example of this type. Inspirational Category Romances are similar in tone, except that a relationship with God is key to the success of the romance. The other series are all more sensual in nature, and range in length and sexual explicitness from the short, sexy Harlequin Desire (formerly Silhouette Desire) or the slightly longer Harlequin Blaze to the more complex and somewhat longer Harlequin Special Edition (formerly Silhouette Special Edition) or Harlequin Intrigue. The longer category romances may also feature additional subplots, more fully realized secondary characters, a broader selection of themes and issues, and a wider range of sensuality levels than the shorter romances, depending upon the line. The Young Adult Category Romance is relatively short in length and similar in type to the Innocent Category, although the sensuality levels are more sophisticated than in the past. Its characters are younger—usually in high school and sometimes college—and most of these stories interweave typical problems of growing up with the romance plotline. (The Young Adult Romance is outside the scope of this book and is mentioned here only to indicate the range of the Category Romance. Consult *Rocked by Romance* by Carolyn Carpan [Englewood, CO: Libraries Unlimited, 2004] for a thorough discussion of the entire Young Adult Romance subgenre.)

Although most Category Romances are individual stories and definitely stand on their own, trilogies and other short series related by characters, theme, or place are increasing favorites of readers, writers, and publishers. Stories focusing on the romances of family members, especially sisters or brothers, or people in a particular locale continue to be especially popular. A longer vehicle, and one that has proved to have staying power, is the limited series. These generally consist of twelve books—one released each month and all written by different authors—are usually linked by place, and include some kind of running thread, often a mystery, that is eventually resolved in the final volume of the series.

Women's Romantic Fiction

Firmly straddling the line between the larger Women's Fiction genre, which focuses on the heroine's life journey and her various relationships, and romance, Women's Romantic Fiction is finally coming into its own, a fact acknowledged by RWA in 2004 when it established the Best Novel with Strong Romantic Elements category in its annual Rita Awards. These are generally longer, multilayered stories that feature a strong heroine, often with definite goals other than love and marriage, and yet they contain an important romance element.

Any number of plot patterns, characters, and locales are used, and while settings are most often contemporary, they can also be historical or Saga-like, spanning a number of years. In addition, writing style, tone, use of humor, and other technical aspects will vary widely. In fact, this category is so flexible that it might simply be considered "Women's Fiction with a satisfactory romantic ending." Obviously, this is a most inclusive subgenre, and its boundaries are blurry, evolving, and subjective. In fact, works of this type often are classified by publishers simply as "Fiction," and both readers and writers may disagree over the correct designation for a particular title. Writers working in this subgenre often currently write or previously have written romances. Barbara Delinsky, Barbara Samuel, and Kristin Hannah are only a few of the writers currently writing stories of this type. Stories that veer into the flashy, jet-setting world of the rich and famous, often known as Glitz and Glamour novels, can also fall within this subgroup if they meet the romantic criteria; more often, however, they are more properly classified as Women's Fiction or Fiction. (For a brief discussion and short bibliography of Glitz and Glamour, refer to the earlier edition of this book, *Romance Fiction: A Guide to the Genre* [Englewood, CO: Libraries Unlimited, 1999].)

Chick Lit

Another subgenre not totally within the confines of the Romance genre but vastly appealing to many younger romance fans is Chick Lit—and its more recent outgrowth, Mom Lit, or Mommy Lit. Sparked by the publication of Helen Fielding's *Bridget Jones's Diary* in 1996 and catapulted to wider fame when Candice Bushnell's *Sex and the City* (1997), a collection of essays she'd written as columns for *The New York Observer*, became a popular television series, Chick Lit typically features heroines (and friends) in their twenties and thirties (although some may focus on older characters), often living in an urban environment, dealing with work and interpersonal relationships of all kinds, and generally trying to sort out themselves and their lives. Unlike the Romance genres, in which the focus is on the romantic relationship between the two protagonists and a satisfactory ending is required, in Chick Lit and its many spin-offs (e.g., suspense Chick Lit, paranormal Chick Lit, teen Chick Lit, Christian Chick Lit), the focus is not necessarily on the romance and even when it is, the man involved may simply be Mr. Right Now, instead of Mr. Right. There is a certain growing up, learning to cope, coming-of-age flavor to many of these, similar to that associated with many Young Adult novels, and in spite of a slightly frivolous, often undeserved, reputation, many of them do deal with more serious issues than what shoes to buy or how to get a date for Saturday night. Cheeky, sexy, and upbeat, these light, often hilarious, stories are filled with witty dialogue and contemporary, realistic situations that resonate with their readers. In addition, these stories usually are told in the first person, most often from the heroine's point of view, a technique that guarantees a personal, intimate tone that tends to draw readers in and keep them engaged. Sophie Kinsella, Meg Cabot, Melissa Bank, and Lauren Weisberger are only a few of the many authors writing for this market. As of this writing, the chick lit output from the major publishers has declined somewhat and the market is not so robust as it once was. But whether that indicates that the characteristics of this subgenre simply have been adopted by others, which is happening, or there is a lack of interest, remains to be seen.

Soap Opera

Another fiction type falling more within the bounds of Women's Fiction than the Romance genre but appealing to some romance readers is the Soap Opera. With links to the family Saga and closely related to the popular radio and television serials from which the name is derived, it is a complex, relationship-driven, introspective type of romantic fiction that concentrates on the sins and sufferings of an individual, a family, or even a whole community. There are usually multiple plots in these often leisurely paced melodramas, and the action of the story often consists of interactions among the characters discussing their problems and their various reactions to events and situations. There is almost always a central "tent-pole" character (older, powerful), who, while not the protagonist, influences the lives of everyone else and generally provides coherence and stability to the complex plot line. Because of their overwhelming concentration on the vicissitudes of life, Soap Operas do not necessarily have happy endings (at least not for all the characters). Nevertheless, the reader is usually left with some feeling of hope for the future.

In the past several decades, the Soap Opera's appeal as a written form has declined, and while it is still quite popular in its television format and even adding new fans with some of the prime-time series offerings (viewers who often may not actually self-define as part of this subgenre), few pure books of this kind are currently being produced. However, with the genre lines blurring, sudsy elements do show up in other types of Contemporary Romance and fiction, and Danielle Steel and Eileen Goudge are examples of current authors who have written books that occasionally stray across the soapy border. Nevertheless, there is still a readership for these older books and many are still either in print or are available in many library collections. (For more complete coverage of the Soap Opera, including a history and selected bibliography, refer to the earlier edition of this book, *Romance Fiction* [1999].)

Medical Romance

Essentially a rather upbeat Soap Opera with a medical setting, the Medical Romance, like its parent Soap Opera, is in decline as a discrete type. Once quite popular, especially in England where there is still some interest (Harlequin/Mills & Boon has a Medical Romance series line), these stories derive much of their drama and tension from the highly charged atmosphere of a hospital setting. Focusing primarily on the personal and professional lives of the doctors, nurses, and other medical staff, these stories lead their characters through a series of disasters, critical illnesses, drug overdoses, epidemics, delicate and dangerous surgeries, and a host of everyday emergency situations that provide ample opportunity for a wide variety of plotlines, both simple and complex, complete with conflict, passion, and romance. A more innocent version of this type is the Nurse Romance, which is similar to a Contemporary Category Romance with a hospital setting and quite popular in earlier times. While the popularity of the Medical Romance as a separate type may be waning, this does not mean that medical personnel and hospital settings have actually lost their appeal. Doctors still show up as heroes and medical emergencies still play their parts in romantic crises. But today's heroines are more often doctors than nurses and the medical environment is likely to be tangential to the main plot, rather than the primary arena for the story's action. In other words, the elements of the Medical Romance are migrating to other Romance subtypes and are being incorporated within them. The boundaries are changing and the genres are blending, with interesting and often satisfactory results.

Although a number of these books still can be found in libraries and the subgenre is still popular in the United Kingdom, the Medical Romance as a separate subgenre is not a major influence in the current American romance market and is mentioned here only because of historical interest.

(For more complete coverage and a selected bibliography of prototypical and earlier Medical Romances, refer to an earlier version of this book, *Happily Ever After* [Littleton, CO: Libraries Unlimited, 1987].)

Contemporary Americana Romance

Contemporary Americana Romance, featuring rural or small town settings and focusing on the everyday lives of ordinary people and their "ordinary" problems, continues to attract readers. However, in the past decade these Americana elements have become so well-integrated into the broader Contemporary Romance subgenre that it seems unhelpful to separate romances with such settings from the larger groups. Relevant titles will be included in the following bibliographies as appropriate. (For additional coverage, refer to the previous edition of *Romance Fiction* [1999].)

***

As might be expected, there is a certain amount of crossover readership among the Contemporary Romance types. Those who enjoy the more sensual Category Contemporaries may also like Traditional Contemporaries or Women's Romantic Fiction, readers of the Innocent or Sweet Categories may find some early Traditional Contemporaries and some of the noncategory sweet titles interesting, and fans of humorous, lively paced Category Romance might also enjoy Chick Lit. In addition to crossover within the Contemporary grouping, there is also some degree of crossover reading among the Contemporary and other Romance subgenres. For example, because they're sweeter and less sexually explicit, some of the Innocent Categories or early Traditional Contemporaries may appeal to readers of Inspirational Romance or Traditional Regencies, and fans of Romantic Suspense may enjoy some of the suspense-oriented Category lines. Also, as might be expected, readers who enjoy longer, complex Contemporary Romances or Women's Romantic Fiction may also enjoy reading Women's Fiction or literary fiction, in general. Interestingly, there is less reader crossover between Contemporary and Historical Romances than one might expect. Readers, it seems, have definite preferences in this regard; they either like the present or the past, but usually not both..

Appeal

The specific appeal of the Contemporary Romance is twofold. First, the present is where we live; it is familiar, it grounds us, and we can identify with it. Second, and somewhat conversely, Contemporary Romance appeals to our basic desire to see the present as we wish it were or think it could be, not, necessarily, as it is. Just as some readers want to vicariously experience the novelty and excitement of the past without its attendant inconveniences, others want to do the same for the present—experience a new or romantically portrayed present without the mundane details of real, everyday life, and with a positive, hopeful outcome. Most of us occasionally indulge in playing the "What if . . ." game (e.g., What if I were an ad executive in New

York? What if I owned a coffee shop in a small town? What if I were rich/poor? What if I were on a Mediterranean cruise? What if I suddenly became a guardian for three children?). Contemporary Romances allow us not only to complete the question, but also to experience at least one author's version of the answer. The infinite variety of questions and possible answers accounts for the diversity within the subgenre.

Within the Contemporary subgenre, each type of format or story has its own particular appeal. The Category Romance offers consistency; the readers basically know what they are going to get before they open the book. On the other hand the Traditional Contemporary Romance provides more variety and, occasionally, the unexpected. Women's Romantic Fiction attracts those who enjoy a romance painted on a broader canvas with a slightly different brush. However, the overall appeal of the Contemporary Romance is to readers who prefer to venture briefly into a romantic version of a world they understand and perceive as a little closer to reality than those of some of the other subgenres—the world of the present.

Advising the Reader

While general readers' advisory information is provided in chapter 3, several points to consider specifically when advising Contemporary Romance readers are given below.

- Consider suggesting Contemporary subtypes in addition to the one the reader is currently reading. Innocent Categories might appeal to readers of some of the less racy Traditional Contemporaries and those who like Women's Romantic Fiction might also enjoy the more complex Traditional Contemporaries. Also, many popular authors write in more than one Contemporary Romance subgenre; if the reader likes books by a writer who does this, consider suggesting the author's titles from the other subgenres.
- Readers who enjoy older, classic Contemporary Romances, such as those by Grace Livingston Hill and others, may also like Inspirational Romances, and vice versa.
- Readers who like Soap Operas or multigenerational romances may find Sagas and Linked Books attractive, and Women's Fiction may appeal to readers of Women's Romantic Fiction. In addition, some readers of Innocent Category Romances may also enjoy Traditional Regencies or some of the less sexually explicit Historicals.
- Determine what particular kind of Contemporary Romance the reader prefers—sweet, sensual, erotic, complex, short, predictable, funny, dark, family-centered, filled with problem social issues, and so on. Keep in mind that lines and writers vary greatly—the sweet Harlequin Romances are quite different from the steamy Harlequin Blazes, and Susan Elizabeth Phillips is not Debbie Macomber. If the reader prefers sweet Innocent Categories, don't recommend *Peyton Place* or the Bad Boys anthologies. Likewise, don't suggest a short Category Romance to someone who wants a complex, intricately plotted story; try Women's Romantic Fiction or Traditional Contemporaries, instead. As always, common sense and a good knowledge of authors and types are your best allies in making successful recommendations.
- Readers who like upbeat Contemporary Romances with sassy humor and trendy urban settings might also enjoy Chick Lit. Although not necessarily romantically focused, Chick Lit does have some crossover appeal, and well-known titles such as Helen Fielding's *Bridget Jones's Diary* or Lauren Weisberger's *The Devil Wears Prada* would be solid recommendations for readers new to the type. Likewise, Chick Lit fans might enjoy funny, witty, fast-paced Contemporary Romances by writers such as Elizabeth Bevarly, Rachel Gibson, and Millie Criswell, to name only a few. Note: Imprints such as Red

Dress Ink, Strapless, and 5 Spot routinely publish chick lit titles. However, chick lit is published by more general imprints, as well.

- For the reader who is new to the Contemporary subgenre, recommend standard works by major authors in the field (e.g., Nora Roberts, Susan Elizabeth Phillips, Susan Wiggs, Stephanie Bond, Barbara Samuel, Kristin Hannah, Jennifer Greene, and Jennifer Crusie) and then branch out to others. That way, if the reader doesn't care for the book, it will be a judgment of the subgenre itself rather than the quality of the writing.

Brief History

When Samuel Richardson's epistolary tale *Pamela: Or Virtue Rewarded* was published in England in 1740, it helped launch what was generally considered to be a new form of literature—the novel. It is interesting that what is considered by many to be one of the earliest, if not the first, novel written in English was also a Contemporary Romance. To be sure, *Pamela*, as well as Richardson's other sentimental romances, had its roots in the past, especially in some of the long, fantastically exaggerated romances by earlier women writers such as Delarivière Manley, Aphra Behn, Madeleine de Scudéry, and Eliza Haywood, as well as in the introspective religious works of the previous century. However, it was the combination of the outward dramatic action with the inner emotional turmoil and reflection that made the novel something new and appealing (Martin C. Battestin, ed., *British Novelists, 1660–1800*, Dictionary of Literary Biography no. 39 [Detroit: Gale, 1985], 379). In addition, the fact that the story's situation (young, impoverished girl goes to work in wealthy home, only to be pursued with dishonorable intent by the son of the family) was a familiar one to many members of the working class and the heroine was spunky, determined, and nonaristocratic gave it an intense appeal for the newly rising, newly literate middle class. The book achieved tremendous popularity on both sides of the Atlantic, and although imported copies were available, Benjamin Franklin published it in the United States in 1744, only four years after it had first appeared in England (James D. Hart, *The Popular Book: A History of America's Literary Taste* [Westport, CT: Greenwood Press, 1950], 52).

The success of *Pamela* gave rise to a number of imitations, many of them copying not only the basic plot but also the letter/diary format. Until the end of the century, when the sentimental Gothics of Ann Radcliffe began to find favor with the reading public, the contemporary sentimental novel, or romance, reigned supreme. Among the most popular in the United States were *Charlotte Temple: A Tale of Truth* (1791) by Susanna Haswell Rowson and *The Coquette* (1797) by Mrs. Hannah Foster. Often considered the first American popular romantic novel (even though it was first published in England by a woman who moved to America soon after), *Charlotte Temple* (published in America in 1794) is a classic novel of seduction in which the heroine is seduced, impregnated, abandoned, and then left to die. Given the cautionary nature of the story and social mores of the time, Charlotte naturally had to pay for the sin of allowing herself to be seduced! Set in the United States and reputed to be based on fact (there is even a gravestone in New York with the name Charlotte Temple on it), this novel had immediate appeal for American readers; in all, more than two hundred editions of *Charlotte* have been produced. Popular through the first few years of the nineteenth century, seduction stories shared the spotlight with the sentimental

Gothics. Eventually, however, they gave way to a new wave of interest in Historical Romances, which peaked in the 1820s, and today the seduction story is remembered largely as a curiosity of the late eighteenth and early nineteenth centuries.

About the same time, the influence of a group of women writers, the Domestic Sentimentalists, was beginning to be felt. For the next few decades, their works grew in popularity, and by the 1850s, much to the dismay and mystification of more serious contemporary writers such as Nathaniel Hawthorne and Herman Melville, these writers completely dominated the romantic fiction market. Although many of these authors used historical settings or Gothic conventions, particularly during the 1820s, most of these novels were contemporary romances, intent on depicting the domestic here-and-now and the ways in which various women dealt with it.

Truly novels of the times, these domestic romances reflected the prevailing wisdom that held that while men might excel in worldly and business affairs, women were stronger in the moral, cultural, and domestic realms. Therefore, women had the duty to "improve" people (often the men in their lives), promote the cultural aspects of life, and see to the smooth running of the home and ensuring domestic tranquility, in general. Although the woman was definitely the ruling force within her domestic sphere, her place and influence was firmly within the home, and there was little for her to look forward to outside of marriage, home, and family. This attitude is reflected in most of these stories by the fact that the heroine, although she almost always overcomes numerous obstacles independently and becomes quite self-sufficient, is usually happily married by the end of the book.

Although a great number of women wrote contemporary domestic romances during this period, especially popular and prolific were E.D.E.N. Southworth, Mary Jane Holmes, Caroline Lee Hentz, and Elizabeth Oakes Smith. Several of the more popular books of this period were *The Lamplighter* (1854) by Maria Susanna Cummins, *Ruth Hall* (1855) by Fanny Fern (Sara Payson Willis), and *The Wide, Wide World* (1850) by Elizabeth Wetherell (Susan Warner).

Not surprisingly, domestic romances by English women writers were also popular in America during this period. One of the best known was *The Heir of Redclyffe* (1853) by Charlotte M. Yonge. Considered by some to be the book to which the beginnings of popular romantic fiction can be traced, according to Rachel Anderson, this books differs "from the 'didactic' novels of the times . . . [in] its combination of the important message [religious, in this case] with the author's own emotional involvement with her hero, her heroine, her theme, and her readers" (Rachel Anderson, *The Purple Heart Throbs: The Sub-Literature of Love* [London: Hodder & Stoughton, 1974], 25). It is this increased emotional intensity and involvement that Anderson feels makes this the forerunner of today's romance novels. It also is interesting to note that *The Heir of Redclyffe* additionally makes the point that love solves all problems, an underlying tenet of most romances today.

Following the Civil War, the works of the domestic sentimentalists continued to be popular, although romances of other types and in other formats were beginning to appear. Especially popular were the weekly story papers, which published serialized romance novels by numerous, now largely unremembered, writers. One of the most prolific and popular of these authors was Laura Jean Libbey. All of her more than eighty "working girl" novels, published from the mid-1880s to the mid-1920s, center around the plights of poor, virtuous girls forced to fend for themselves in the "wicked city." Eventually, of course, they are rescued from danger and drudgery by financially secure, upstanding heroes who whisk them off to futures of domestic wedded bliss. Unfortunately, although many of her serialized romances were reprinted in paperback as complete novels, few of Libbey's novels were hardbound. Her works are now dated and primarily of interest to students of popular culture, and while few have been reprinted recently, a large number have been preserved on microfilm and some original editions can be found in libraries throughout the country.

Toward the end of the nineteenth century Historical Romances became increasingly popular, and works by writers such as Mary Johnston and Amelia E. Barr were in vogue. Interest in Contemporary Romances, however, did not die out, and after the turn of the century, writers such as Grace Livingston Hill, Emilie Loring, Faith Baldwin, and Kathleen Norris continued the contemporary, domestic tradition with their individual styles.

Although the twentieth century has witnessed the rise in popularity of a number of romance types (e.g., the Historicals of the 1930s and 1940s, the Gothics of the 1960s, the Sensual Historical and Sweet-and-Savage Romances of the 1970s), Contemporary Romances have never lost their appeal for vast numbers of readers. Throughout the century, no matter what the current literary rage, Contemporary Romances have maintained a quiet, yet devoted audience.

With the decline of the erotic Historicals in the late 1970s, Contemporary Romances became increasingly popular with the public in general, and by the early 1980s, they were a dominant form. Exceptionally popular were Contemporary Category Romances, or stories written to conform to preset guidelines. Although romances of this type had been around for a number of years (Harlequin began publishing romances in 1949), it wasn't until the late 1970s that the market really exploded. Publishers, anxious to profit from the new surge of interest in romances, hurriedly launched new romance lines. During the first few years of the 1980s, most major paperback publishers were trying either to break into the romance field or to increase their existing business within it. The market burgeoned with new romance series.

But many of these new romances were not the Innocent Category fare of earlier years. To be sure, romances of the Innocent variety were still available and were supported by a loyal readership, but public taste was changing. The earlier success of the more sensual Historicals had shown that readers wanted a little more spice in their romances, and writers and publishers were more than happy to oblige. Many of these new series not only included more explicit sex scenes but also often featured independent, older heroines with definite career goals beyond the more traditional ones of marriage and a family. These romances were simply reflecting our changing society. With the median age of the population rising, more women entering the workforce at career levels, and sexual mores changing, these romances were merely attempting to do what Contemporary Romance novels have always done—romanticize the realities of everyday life.

Eventually, the excesses of the early 1980s resulted in a shakedown within the industry, and as Contemporaries came off their sales highs, competition was fierce, lines were cut back or discontinued, and a consolidation became a growing trend with publishers. (One of the more famous acquisitions of the decade was Harlequin Enterprise's purchase of Silhouette in 1984, which, together with the 1971 purchase of Mills & Boon, effectively consolidated the bulk of the Contemporary Series Romance market under the Harlequin umbrella.) However, Contemporaries have rarely been unpopular for long, and, despite a renewed interest in Sagas and Historicals, especially those with American settings, Contemporaries of all types continued to hold their own. Many even appeared on various bestseller lists.

Despite a few ups and downs, including the unfortunate 1993 demise of a promising new publishing house, Meteor, the Contemporary Romance continued to thrive during the 1990s, changing as necessary to meet the needs of an increasingly diverse and demanding readership. Change was rampant. New lines were established, houses that never published Contemporaries before were jumping into the fray (Avon, for one), a wide variety of relevant and sometimes controversial subjects were being addressed in the stories, and a number of established Contemporary writers broke with tradition and produced romances that crossed boundaries and linked genres in new and different ways. Late in the decade, a new subgenre emerged. Inspired by the phenomenal success of Fielding's *Bridget Jones's Diary* (1996), as well as driven by publishers' concerns about reaching twenty-something-plus readers, these funny, upbeat Chick Lit novels hit this target market dead on. Spurred on by the 2001 launch of Harlequin's trendy new imprint, Red Dress Ink, which was soon joined by a number of other similar imprints from other houses (e.g., Making It [Dorchester], Strapless [Kensington], Downtown Press [Pocket]), Chick Lit's popularity soared until the middle of the decade when interest began to settle down.

Contemporaries of all types continued to flourish into the 2000s, fluidly adapting to market changes as they came along. (Harlequin's major revision of a number of its lines in 2005, apparently in reaction to slumping North American category sales, is only one case in point.) The broader genre trends also impacted Contemporaries. Humor, whimsy, and upbeat action remained winners; subtle paranormal elements, as well as the occasional mild religious reference, tinged ordinary Contemporaries; and books linked by character, theme, or place were everywhere. The growing popularity of Erotica, ultimately acknowledged by the establishment of a variety of Erotic imprints by most of the large romance publishers, also ramped up the sensual levels in Contemporaries of all kinds. The graphic novel craze, however, has so far had little impact in the American market, although Harlequin, with its Ginger Blossom line of romantic manga, did experiment with the idea briefly in 2006 and early 2007. Only a few titles were released, although some Harlequin Violet (sensual) and Harlequin Pink (sweet and primarily for the YA market) titles can still be found.

Currently, Contemporary Romance accounts for nearly 50% of the titles published each year, and that doesn't include the other romance subgenres (e.g., Inspirational, Paranormal, Romantic Suspense) set in the present. Considering this, and given the historical longevity of the type (*Pamela*, after all, was a contemporary romance!), it continues to be safe to assume that the Contemporary Romance genre is here to stay. It may wax and wane in popularity and change with the current trends, but because it deals with the here and now, it will continue to appeal to the many readers who prefer their romances set in present times.

Traditional Contemporary Romance

The most inclusive of all Contemporary Romance types, the Traditional Contemporary Romance is essentially a noncategory romance with a contemporary setting. Thirty years ago it would have simply been called a love story; today, however, because of the plethora of romances and their many variations, it is now considered a distinct, although somewhat encompassing, type.

Because of its all-inclusive character, the Traditional Contemporary incorporates a wider variety of settings, plots, and characters than one might normally expect. For example, the settings for Traditional Contemporaries can vary from small town to big city, from the United States to all parts of the world, and from dingy tenement to elegant estate;

situations range from small town domesticity to the high-powered business world. Plot patterns differ tremendously, as well, and while the protagonists usually do find love and happiness in the end, unless there is some overriding practical need to find someone to marry, the heroines of today—unlike many in the past—are rarely on a husband hunt and are far more likely to find love by accident rather than by design. In general, although these are all basically love stories, because they do not adhere to a preset pattern, the plots of Traditional Contemporaries can take unpredictable twists and turns and the results are sometimes unexpected. The degree of sensuality in these novels can also vary greatly, but, although some of these are still quite mild, recent romances reflect the current trends and are much more sexually explicit than their predecessors. Characters, too, come in many shapes and flavors. Heroines may be innocent or experienced, beautiful or almost plain, aggressive or retiring, just out of high school or well into middle age; they all, however, tend to be smart, talented, and have "character," determination, common sense, and a sense of humor. Likewise, heroes can be reserved or outgoing, sophisticated or less than perfectly polished, handsome or charmingly homely, funny or serious; they are, however, most often intelligent, successful, strong, purposeful, capable, and honorable.

Early Classic Contemporary Romance Writers

Over the years, numerous writers have contributed to the Traditional Contemporary Romance subgenre. Several popular and prolific authors of early and prototypical works are listed below. Although many of their works are unavailable, many have been reprinted and copies of these and some originals may be available in large public libraries. (For more complete coverage and some selected titles, see the earlier versions of this guide.)

Ayres, Ruby M. (1883–1955)
Baldwin, Faith (1893–1978)
Bloom, Ursula (1893–1984)
Cadell, Elizabeth (1903–1989)
Dell, Ethel M. (1881–1939)
Gaskin, Catherine (1929–2009)
Loring, Emilie (1864–1951)
Norris, Kathleen (1880–1966)
Stevenson, D. E. (1892–1973)

Selected Traditional Contemporary Romance Bibliography

Contemporary Romance, including Traditional Contemporary Romance, continues to be a driving force in the Romance genre, and numerous writers produce titles in this vein.

The following authors are known for their Traditional Contemporary Romances, although they may also write and be noted for works in other subgenres. Only their Traditional Contemporaries are listed below. Any of their other romance works included in this book are discussed in the appropriate chapters.

Because many books published in the Contemporary Category series lines (see next section for more details) can easily qualify as stand-alone books, this bibliography includes both single titles and series line titles. Books related by character, place, or theme may also be discussed in chapter 13, "Linked Romances," although most will be included here, and books with a multicultural focus may be discussed in chapter 12, "Ethnic/Multicultural Romance." Earlier works by many of these writers may be found in the previous editions of this guide.

Andersen, Susan

Anderson's romances are typically funny, fast-paced, and sexy, often with a dash of suspense or danger and sometimes related by character.

Baby, I'm Yours. Avon, 1998.
A bounty hunter mistakes a teacher for her twin sister who has jumped bail and is on the run from a killer.

Baby, Don't Go. Avon, 2000.
Needing protection when he is threatened by thugs because of picture he took, a society photographer hires a woman from his romantic past as his bodyguard.

All Shook Up. Avon, 2001.
A single mom resents, but is attracted to, the former "bad boy" who inherits a share in her great aunt's lakeside resort.

Head Over Heels. Avon, 2002.
A woman returns to her small hometown when her sister is murdered to care for her young niece and must deal with the brother of her sister's husband who is trying to find the real killer and clear his brother of suspicion.

Hot and Bothered. Mira, 2004.
A detective is reunited with a woman with whom he'd had a brief, but memorable, fling in this story that features a murder, a runaway teenager, and a secret baby.

Skintight. Mira, 2005.
A recently widowed Las Vegas dancer falls for a professional gambler not knowing he is actually her late husband's estranged son and has an agenda of his own.

Just for Kicks. Mira, 2006.
A Las Vegas showgirl finds common ground with her difficult neighbor when he needs help caring for his teenage nephew.

Coming Undone. HQN, 2007.
The teenaged runaway from *Hot and Bothered* is all grown up and reconnects with a girl he met on the streets but is now a budding country music star when he is hired as her bodyguard.

Cutting Loose. HQN, 2008.
A woman falls for the man her friends hired to renovate an inherited mansion.

Bending the Rules. HQN, 2009.
A rigid detective hero clashes with a hippie-raised free-spirited heroine when it comes to dealing with a trio of young graffiti artists.

Burning Up. HQN, 2010.
A woman returns to the small town she left ten years earlier under an undeserved cloud of scandal and is attracted to the local fire chief.

Anderson, Catherine

Anderson is known for her insightful, heart-wrenching Contemporary and Historical Romances, many of which deal with abuse issues. (See also chapters 7 and 13, "Historical Romance" and "Linked Romances.")

Forever After. Avon, 1998.
In order to avoid losing her child to her cruel late husband's powerful father, Meredith Kenyon assumes a new identity and goes to Oregon and finds help and love in the arms of a local sheriff.

Seventh Heaven. Signet, 2000.
Former football star Joe Lakota takes his abused four-year-old son home to Oregon to leave the limelight and take a job as the high school coach—and reconnects with his high school sweetheart, Marilee Nelson, who has emotional problems of her own.

Always in My Heart. Signet, 2002.
Two young boys run away to the Oregon wilderness in hopes that their parents will reconsider their plans for divorce.

Only by Your Touch. Signet, 2003.
A woman escaping an abusive husband takes her young son and moves to the Oregon mountains and finds love and healing with a veterinarian who has issues of his own.

Andre, Bella (Pseudonym for Nyree Belleville)
See also chapter 14, "Erotic Romance."

Hot Shot Men of Fire Series
This sexy, action-oriented series with mystery elements focuses on the wilderness firefighters of the Sierra Nevada.

Wild Heat. Dell, 2009.
An arson investigator has a brief romantic encounter with a man she meets again six months later, when he turns out to be part of an elite forest firefighting crew and on her list of arson suspects, as well.

Hot as Sin. Dell, 2009.
A television host reconnects with a "hot shot" firefighter she ran away from ten years earlier when she is injured and her sister is kidnapped.

Never Too Hot. Dell, 2010.
A wounded firefighter returns to his family's old cabin and finds it already occupied for the rest of the summer by a woman in search of healing of her own.

Andrews, Beth
A Not-So-Perfect Past. Harlequin Superromance, 2009.
A divorced single mom seeks help from her ex-con renter when a car damages her bakery and finds unexpected attraction and romance.

His Secret Agenda. Harlequin Superromance, 2009.
A lawyer-turned-barkeeper is attracted to her new employee, unaware that he's been hired to find a runaway mom and her son, and he thinks she knows something about it.

Angell, Kate (Pseudonym for Roberta Brown)
Richmond Rogues, the Boys of Summer Series
This sexy, funny, lighthearted series focuses on the members of the Richmond Rogues baseball team. Note: Many of these books have more than one romantic pair.

Squeeze Play. Love Spell, 2006.
A baseball star returns to his Florida hometown, along with some of his teammates, and sets about winning the heart of the girl he thinks has always considered him her "rebound lover."

Curveball. Love Spell, 2007.
Three power hitters, suspended for thirteen games for fighting, find love during their "time out."

Strike Zone. Love Spell, 2008.
A pitcher reconnects with the woman who left him at the altar three years earlier when she returns to explain her actions.

Sliding Home. Love Spell, 2009.
Returning from spring training, an antisocial star left fielder, who likes his solitude, finds a homeless tomboy living in his old trailer and is surprised when he ultimately realizes he doesn't really want her to leave.

Arnold, Judith

Arnold is noted for touching, well-written, fast-paced books, with humorous flair and memorable characters.

Looking for Laura. Mira, 2001.
A packet of steamy love letters from someone named "Laura" in her late husband's belongings draws a widow and her late husband's best friend into an uneasy alliance as they work to solve the mystery.

Love in Bloom's. Mira, 2002.
Having carefully avoided working in her family's New York deli for years, Julia Bloom is named president and now must learn the business, deal with family members who think they should be running the show, and handle a persistent newspaper reporter doing a story on the famous deli.

Heart on the Line. Mira, 2003.
A talk-show producer and an attorney meet by chance on the train and watch their friendship turn to love in spite of a host of outside complications.

Blooming All Over. Mira, 2004.
Love blooms again in the popular Bloom deli.

The Fixer Upper. Mira, 2005.
A contractor offers to renovate an old fireplace for the attractive admissions director of the private school his son wants to attend, with problematic—and romantic—results.

The Marriage Bed. Harlequin Everlasting Love, 2007.
A medical emergency threatens the lives of a couple who never told their daughter who her real father was in this family-focused story that confronts some serious issues.

Meet Me in Manhattan. HCI, 2010.
High school sweethearts, who split up when Erika broke Ted's heart by heading off to college, meet again fifteen years later and struggle to balance their passionate feelings for each other against past hurts and Ted's current romantic involvement.

Banks, Leanne

Funny, sexy, feel-good romances are characteristic of Banks's work.

Sisters Trilogy
A loosely linked trilogy about three very different sisters.

Some Girls Do. Warner Forever, 2003.
A personal assistant and a security expert are charged with finding an appropriate husband for their wealthy boss's insecure daughter and fall in love as they deal with the runaway heiress who has fallen for a hog farmer in Texas.

When She's Bad. Warner Forever, 2003.
A baby left in her care changes the life of a brash, independent spa owner with a wild reputation and her wealthy, upper-crust neighbor in this romance that addresses social differences and self-esteem issues.

Trouble in High Heels. Forever, 2009.
An heiress who loves to give her money away and a CPA whose mission it is to protect her inheritance eventually find common ground in this fast-paced comedy.

Bellagio, Inc.
This trio of three romantic comedies focuses on three women who work for the international shoe company, Bellagio, Inc.

Feet First. HQN, 2005.
A fledgling shoe designer's "no strings" fling with the company VP turns into something more.

Underfoot. HQN, 2006.
A passionate night of "consolation" sex leads to a baby and plenty of complications for two friends and business associates.

Footloose. HQN, 2006.
Amelia goes with her temporary boss, Lillian Bellagio, to her Florida Keys estate and, thanks to a sexy venture capitalist, finds the trip is much more fun and romantic than she'd expected.

Becnel, Rexanne
Old Boyfriends. Harlequin Next, 2005.
Three women leave Los Angeles and head for New Orleans to reconnect with the old boyfriends they left behind.

The Payback Club. Harlequin Next, 2006.
Two women out to avenge themselves on their cheating husbands by dating each other's exes with ruinous intent are surprised with the results.

Blink of an Eye. Harlequin Next, 2007.
A depressed nurse finds a new purpose to life in the aftermath of Hurricane Katrina and in her relationship with a sympathetic doctor.

Betts, Heidi
Seven-Year Seduction. Silhouette Desire, 2006.
A pair meets again at a wedding after seven years apart in this passionate reunion story.

Christmas in His Royal Bed. Silhouette Desire, 2007.
An events planner with an undeserved sexy reputation is hard-pressed to fend off the manipulative, soon-to-be-married prince who hires her.

Tangled Up in Love. St. Martin's Paperbacks, 2009.
Two newspaper columnists compete in imaginative ways in this lively romp. Magic yarn plays a role in this and the two romances that follow.

Loves Me, Loves Me Knot. St. Martin's Paperbacks, 2009.
Interested in being a mom not a wife, a woman asks her ex-husband for a "favor" and ends up with a husband, as well in this knitting-linked romance.

Knock Me for a Loop. St. Martin's Paperbacks, 2010.
A heroine ends up helping her injured hockey star former fiancé pull his life back together in this knitting-themed romance.

Bevarly, Elizabeth
Bevarly is noted for lively, witty, often hilarious romps.

My Man Pendleton. Avon, 1998.
An heiress takes revenge on her family by resisting marriage until she falls for the man hired to find her after she runs off.

Her Man Friday. Avon, 1999.
A PI goes undercover as an auditor to track down a company's missing millions and ends up at the brilliant, eccentric CEO's estate, where he finds romance as he searches for answers.

How to Trap a Tycoon. Avon, 2000.
A PhD student who pseudonymously wrote a satirical book, *How to Trap a Tycoon*, in order to provide for her courtesan mother in her later years, risks exposure when her publisher wants her to go on tour.

He Could Be the One. Avon, 2001.
A high school reunion, an abduction threat, and cross country trips add up to sexy fun for two sisters and their bodyguards.

OPUS Series
Lively romantic cyber-romps involving OPUS (Office for Political Unity and Security), a top-secret security agency.

You've Got Male. HQN, 2005.
An ex-con agoraphobic computer whiz helps track down a criminal and begins to fall for the OPUS agent who is helping her.

Express Male. HQN, 2006.
A piano teacher is mistaken for an OPUS operative and is drawn into a plan to bring down a major criminal.

Overnight Male. HQN, 2008.
An OPUS agent goes undercover to smoke out a virus-creating criminal and falls for her partner in the process.

Derby Trilogy
Set against the background of the Kentucky Derby in Louisville.

Fast and Loose. Berkley Sensation, 2008.
A glass artist and a horse trainer fall for each other when he rents her Louisville house as he gets ready for the Derby.

Ready and Willing. Berkley Sensation, 2008.
A Louisville hat shop owner encounters the ghost of a riverboat captain who wants her to save the soul of his modern-day descendent.

Neck and Neck. Berkley Sensation, 2009.
A party planner needs to convince a celebrity millionaire to attend her Derby party but must deal with her target's hunky bodyguard in the process.

Blake, Jennifer
Blake is a veteran, multi-published author of Contemporary and Historical Romance. Her stories are usually set in the South and many have mystery or suspense elements. See also chapter 7, "Historical Romance."

Louisiana Gentlemen Series
This series focuses on the Benedict family of Turn-Coupe, Louisiana.

Kane. Mira, 1998.
Kane investigates a corrupt funeral services company that is trying to shut down the local funeral homes and falls for a woman being blackmailed into helping the crooks.

Luke. Mira, 1999.
Threatening phone calls reconnect Luke with a woman, now a romance author, he has never forgotten.

Roan. Mira, 2000.
Roan is attracted to a heroine on the run from her greedy stepfather and former fiancé who want her inheritance.

Clay. Mira, 2001.
Clay falls in love with the mother of a child with a serious renal disease in this story that involves the human organ black market.

"Adam" in With a Southern Touch. Mira, 2002.
Adam finds romance and a bit of danger with a witch.

Wade. Mira, 2002.
Sent to a Middle Eastern country to rescue a young woman in the "care" of her stepbrother, Wade inadvertently brings a jihad of sorts to Turn-Coupe.

Bond, Stephanie
Bond writes sexy, funny romances, often with a touch of mystery. See also chapter 6, "Romantic Mysteries."

*It Takes a Rebel. Harlequin Temptation, 2000.
Struggling to prove herself to her father, the head of the Tremont family department store empire, Alex clashes with the charming, former star athlete Jack Stillman, whose family's advertising firm is trying to win the Tremont account.

My Favorite Mistake. Harlequin Blaze, 2005.
After a tipsy Las Vegas wedding and a hasty annulment, a financial planner and a Marine reconnect during an IRS audit.

Cover Me. Harlequin Blaze, 2006.
A one-night stand with a small town veterinarian who turns out to be the cover model for her magazine's latest issue is just the beginning for a New York

assistant editor who is sent off to make sure the vet doesn't succumb to the "cover curse."

Just Dare Me. Harlequin Blaze, 2006.
An outdoor survival contest will determine the winner of a marketing account and quiet Gabrielle is determined not to let high-powered Dell win.

Sex for Beginners Trilogy

Letters that they wrote to themselves about their sexual fantasies ten years ago in a college sexuality class arrive in the mail and change the lives of three women in this spicy trilogy.

Watch and Learn. Harlequin Blaze, 2008.
A heroine who enjoys being watched gets more than she expected.

In a Bind. Harlequin Blaze, 2008.
A soon-to-be-married flight attendant's plans change when she indulges her secret desire for a bit of bondage with a sexy Australian.

No Peeking . . . Harlequin Blaze, 2008.
When the hunky playboy client of a personal concierge accidentally finds the concierge's "letter from the past," he decides to make those extreme fantasies she wrote about come true.

Seduction by the Book. Harlequin Blaze, 2009.
Four members of the Red Tote Book Club use their favorite passionate novels as guides to seduce the men of their dreams.

Her Sexy Valentine. Harlequin Blaze, 2010.
A wary woman, also a member of the Red Tote Book Club, learns to trust men in this sexy romance with a Ground Hog Day touch.

Brady, Mary

He Calls Her Doc. Harlequin Superromance, 2009.
Returning to her Montana mountain hometown to serve the community as a general practitioner, Dr. Maude DeVane is annoyed and wary when ER Dr. Guy Daley comes to town to manage his late brother's executive training business, fearing both loss of her practice and, maybe, her heart.

Brenna, Helen

Brenna is a popular, Rita Award–winning author, primarily of series romance. See also chapter 13, "Linked Books."

Treasure. Harlequin Superromance, 2007.
A marine archaeologist wanting to rid herself of a cursed artifact, and a treasure hunter searching for a sunken Spanish galleon find love in this debut novel.

Dad for Life. Harlequin Superromance, 2007.
A secret baby, a Mayan artifact, and a dangerous adventure eventually reunite an art gallery owner with her former husband.

Peak Performance. Harlequin NASCAR, 2008.
A racing mechanic with dreams of becoming a pit boss, and a sportscaster out for a story connect with romantic results.

Finding Mr. Right. Harlequin Superromance, 2008.
A computer business owner is attracted to the man she hires to negotiate a contract with the Greek government not realizing he has an agenda of his own.

From the Outside. Harlequin NASCAR, 2009.
A bad boy NASCAR driver and an actress with a good girl reputation agree to a "fake date" to shore up his playboy image and end up falling for each other instead.

Mirabelle Island Series
Peaceful, rustic Mirabelle Island in the Apostle Islands near Wisconsin's Lake Superior shore is the idyllic setting for this contemporary series.

First Come Twins. Harlequin Superromance, 2009.
A wounded photojournalist returns home to Mirabelle Island and finds that the woman he'd loved but who'd married his brother is now a widowed mother of twins and is as attractive as she ever was.

Next Comes Love. Harlequin Superromance, 2009.
A woman trying to protect her young nephew from his abusive cop father when her sister goes missing hides out on Mirabelle Island and attracts the attentions of the local police chief.

Then Comes Baby. Harlequin Superromance, 2009.
A social worker establishes a camp for at-risk kids and annoys (and attracts) the reclusive writer living next door.

Along Came a Husband. Harlequin Superromance, 2010.
Thinking her FBI agent husband died five years ago, Missy is stunned—and furious—when he shows up wounded, his cover blown, and on the run from the criminals he was after.

The Pursuit of Jesse. Harlequin Superromance, 2011.
An ex-con returns home to Mirabelle Island and finds romance with a single mom whose house he is hired to renovate.

Her Sure Thing. Harlequin Superromance, 2011.
A single doctor and a former cover model find romance on Mirabelle Island.

Redemption at Mirabelle. Harlequin Superromance, 2011.

Bretton, Barbara
Bretton's novels often explore interpersonal and family relationships with depth and compassion, as well as provide rewarding love stories.

At Last. Berkley, 2000.
Brutally separated when Noah's manipulative father gives Gracie a shocking bit of news just before the pair planned to elope, childhood friends Gracie and Noah return to tiny Idle Point, Maine, after eight years apart and finally learn the truth and come to terms with the past.

A Soft Place to Fall. Berkley, 2001.
Secrets, past hurts, and family pressure threaten to keep a young widow and her new neighbor in Shelter Cove, Maine, apart in spite of their attraction for each other.

Shore Lights. Berkley, 2003.
A bidding war over an antique Russian samovar brings an innkeeper and a barkeep—and their respective families—together in this romance that has a Christmas touch.

Girls of Summer. Berkley, 2003.
A doctor eventually finds love with her much-married-and-divorced partner and a new relationship with her hippie half-sister in this book set in the same town as *A Soft Place to Fall*.

Chances Are. Berkley, 2004.
The characters in *Shore Lights* prepare for their wedding in Paradise Point, New Jersey, amid plenty of family turmoil and old secrets.

Someone Like You. Berkley, 2005.
This story explores the relationship between two sisters and their rather fragile mother when they are reunited in Idle Point, Maine; more women's fiction than romance.

Just Like Heaven. Jove, 2007.
Two mature people, a divorced antique storeowner and a widowed Episcopalian priest, meet over a minor heart attack and find rewarding love, the second time around.

Just Desserts. Jove, 2008.
A small-town baker is hired to make a cake for a wealthy, aging rock star (unaware that she may be his daughter) and finds love with the attorney who came to town to check her out.

Britton, Pamela
See also chapter 7, "Historical Romances."

NASCAR Romances

These romances revolve around the lives of the people connected with the NASCAR racing circuit.

Dangerous Curves. HQN, 2005.
An FBI agent and the owner of a racecar team renew a teenage relationship when she is called in to investigate a fatal accident.

In the Groove, HQN, 2006.
A discredited kindergarten teacher gets a job driving a motor coach for a down-on-his-luck NASCAR driver and soon becomes his indispensible good luck charm. Note: This is the launch book for Harlequin's NASCAR series.

On the Edge. HQN, 2006.
A precocious ten-year-old is a determined matchmaker between her racecar driver dad and the owner of a racing team.

To The Limit. HQN, 2007.
A racecar designer is torn between a bad boy driver and the workaholic team owner who hired her.

"Miracle Season" in a NASCAR Holiday 2, HQN, 2007.
A single mom gets help with her love live from her young daughter when a former NASCAR driver comes in to their lives.

Total Control. HQN, 2007.
Goaded into action by a determined advocate for terminally ill children, a self-centered NASCAR star changes surprisingly when he meets the little boy whose wish was to meet the star.

On the Move. HQN, 2008.
A fledgling sports agent is assigned to teach a volatile bad boy driver how to behave in public and learns there's a reason for his anger; she just has to help him learn to control it.

Slow Burn. HQN, 2009.
Having dumped her abusive, underhanded fiancé right before the wedding, CPA Dana Johnson wins a date with Braden James, a star NASCAR driver, in a contest her friend had entered for her, and then must deal with her friend's jealousy, her ex's actions, and her growing feelings for Braden.

Brockway, Connie
See also chapter 7, "Historical Romance."

Hot Dish. Signet, 2006.
Returning to Fawn Creek, Minnesota, to participate in the town's sesquicentennial celebration along with sculptor Steve Jaax, rising TV star domestic goddess Jenn Lind suddenly finds things slipping out of control as an old sculpture (of Jenn!) carved from butter disappears and with it something that Steve will do anything to retrieve.

Skinny Dipping. Onyx, 2008.
A free-spirited psychic, determined not to let her wacky family sell its lakeside vacation estate, finds unexpected romance with the father of a brilliant teenager who lives in the neighboring property.

Brown, Carolyn
Brown has long been noted for her sweet, charming Contemporary and Historical Romances. See also chapter 7, "Historical Romance." Note: Many of her titles are published by Avalon, which markets primarily to libraries.

The PMS Club. Avalon, 2006.
A high school English teacher heads for a Florida vacation with no men only to be attracted to a college teacher who paints and sells T-shirts during the summer.

Broken Roads Series
All the roads lead to Oklahoma for various characters whose paths have changed or been broken along the way in this sweet series with a strong rural, down home feel; it takes its theme from the Rascal Flatts song "Bless the Broken Road."

To Trust. Avalon, 2007.
A woman returns to her small hometown after her disastrous marriage is annulled, and is reunited with a now wealthy childhood friend who had never forgotten her.

To Commit. Avalon, 2008.
A pair of divorced people, an innkeeper and a new rancher, are both attracted and repelled by each other because they remind each other or their respective exes.

To Believe. Avalon, 2009.
An expert tracker is sent into the hills to rescue her wealthy former husband who has been kidnapped in this reunion romance.

To Dream. Avalon, 2009.
A spoiled city girl finds romance with a small-town sheriff when she is forced to do community service for hitting and killing his bull.

To Hope. Avalon, 2009.
An injured female professional bull rider goes on the circuit as a judge in the company of a writer who has never been able to forget her.

Lucky Trilogy

The Luckadeau ranching men of the Oklahoma–Texas border country get lucky in love in this contemporary Western trilogy.

Lucky in Love. Sourcebooks Casablanca, 2009.
A single mom comes to help her grandfather on his ranch and recognizes her neighbor as Beau Luckadeau, the father of her young daughter. But Beau doesn't connect her with his alcohol-laced memories of their brief encounter two years earlier.

One Lucky Cowboy. Sourcebooks Casablanca, 2009.
An heiress on the run finds shelter at Nellie Luckadeau's ranch and love with grandson Slade.

Getting Lucky. Sourcebooks Casablanca, 2010.
A single mom schoolteacher and Griffin Luckadeau have daughters alike enough to be twins, but Griffin doesn't remember the one-night stand that is the reason for the similarity.

Honky Tonk Series

This Country-Western flavored series features the Honky Tonk bar, its various owners, and the locals from two counties (one wet and one dry) who consider it their place.

I Love This Bar. Sourcebooks Casablanca, 2010.
A happily single bar owner eventually agrees to a fake marriage with a rather judgmental rancher for the sake of his Alzheimer-stricken uncle who thinks they are married.

Hell, Yeah! Sourcebooks Casablanca, 2010.
A new bar owner and a sexy oilman in town on a short-term project set things ablaze in this lively, funny story with plenty of down home charm.

My Give a Damn's Busted. Sourcebooks Casablanca, 2010.
The relationship between the newest owner of the bar and a man with a hidden agenda gets off to a difficult start when he sends her car into a ditch as he swerves to avoid a deer.

Honky Tonk Christmas. Sourcebooks Casablanca, 2010.
The Honky Tonk bar's unconventional latest owner rethinks her plans never to marry when a handsome carpenter comes into her life.

Brown, Sandra

Most of Brown's recent titles are in the Romantic Suspense subgenre. However, her earlier titles are Contemporary Romances and many have been reissued or are available in large public libraries. See chapter 6, "Romantic Mysteries."

Cach, Lisa

Have Glass Slipper, Will Travel. Pocket Books, 2005.
Depressed and unemployed, a tech writer takes Oprah's advice, makes a "life map" and heads for England in search of a noble husband—which she finds after a few missteps in this modern Cinderella tale.

The Erotic Secrets of a French Maid. Pocket Books, 2006.
An unemployed architect takes a temporary job as a maid for a wealthy, workaholic entrepreneur, although she thinks she's been hired for more personal services in this sexy story that has an erotica bent.

Cameron, Stella
See also chapter 6, "Romantic Mysteries"; chapter 7, "Historical Romance"; and chapter 9, "Alternative Reality Romance."

Finding Ian. Kensington, 2001.
A father reconnects with the son he gave up for adoption thirteen years ago and finds romance as well in this emotionally complex story.

Tell Me Why. Kensington, 2001.
Shattered by a cruel divorce and the loss of custody of her daughter, a well-known jazz pianist fears that a new romantic relationship will jeopardize her chances to restore her relationship with her daughter.

Carr, Robyn
See also chapter 14, "Linked Books."

Blue Skies. Mira, 2004.
A widowed airline pilot moves to Las Vegas with her two children in search of a new life and finds a new love, as well.

Cates, Kimberly
See also chapter 9, "Alternative Reality Romance."

The Perfect Match. HQN, 2007.
A pet store owner with a slightly magical gift for matching the right pet with the right human finds love when she matches a huge dog to a lawman's wheelchair-bound daughter.

Child, Maureen
Child's many series romances are often witty, lively, and infused with family issues.

Marconi Sisters Trilogy
Set in Chandler, California, this trilogy focuses on the three Marconi sisters and their family construction business.

And Then Came You. St. Martin's paperbacks, 2004.
A divorce that was never finalized and a child Samantha Marconi thought had been given up for adoption brings Samantha and husband, Jeff, together, this time for good.

A Crazy Kind of Love. St. Martin's Paperbacks, 2004.
Sassy plumber Michaela "Mike" Marconi makes life difficult for the man who bought the land and house she had wanted for herself.

Turn My World Upside Down. St. Martin's Paperbacks, 2005.
Cash Hunter, whose love-making skills supposedly send women off into the world to do good deeds, intrigues Jo Marconi, but Cash resists the attraction because he wants to keep Jo around.

Baby Bonanza. Silhouette Desire, 2008.
A cruise line tycoon is shocked when his brief encounter with a woman he's never forgotten turns him into the father of twins in this family-centered romance.

Seduced into a Paper Marriage. Silhouette Desire, 2009.
A movie company CEO is shocked when his mild-mannered wife walks out on their loveless marriage and he is forced to woo her in order to get her back in this final volume in the jointly authored story that, while part of the Hudson Series, nevertheless stands on its own.

The Last Lone Wolf. Silhouette Desire, 2010.
A woman hires on at the ranch of the ex-military loner she considers responsible for her brother's death, with an unusual ulterior motive.

Craig, Christie

Craig's fun-loving, lively romances often include romantic suspense and mystery elements.

Divorced, Desperate, and D. . . . Trilogy

Three divorcées get over the issues and make better choices this time around in this funny, lighthearted, adventurous trilogy.

Divorced, Desperate, and Delicious. Love Spell, 2007.
Desperate to clear his name, a wounded detective takes refuge with a divorced photographer (and her dog and three cats), who eventually believes him and works to help him unmask the crooked cop who set him up.

Divorced, Desperate, and Dating. Love Spell, 2008.
A stalker brings a dating-averse mystery writer and a wary detective together—if only they can get over their pasts.

Divorced, Desperate, and Deceived. Love Spell, 2009.
A plumber who is really a government agent in the Witness Protection Program until he can testify against a major crook finds himself on the run with a gorgeous client when his cover is blown.

Weddings Can Be Murder. Love Spell, 2008.
A reluctant bride-to-be and a P.I. looking for missing brides give in to their mutual attraction when they are locked up together after a wedding planner is killed.

Gotcha! Love Spell, 2009.
A divorcée and a detective fall for each other as they try to keep a violent escaped killer (who chops off his victims' heads) from killing again.

Shut Up and Kiss Me. Love Spell, 2010.
A photojournalist's methods of attracting more tourist business for a small Texas town annoy the town sheriff, Sky Gomez, but when someone begins stalking the lovely Shala Winters, Sky must keep her safe.

Crandall, Susan

Crandall's Contemporary Romances often included suspense elements. See also chapter 6, "Romantic Mysteries."

Glens Crossing/Boudreau Family Series

Set in rural, traditional Glens Crossing, Indiana, this series realistically depicts small-town life.

Back Roads. Warner Forever, 2003.
A sheriff in Glens Crossing is attracted to a stranger who becomes a suspect when a young girl goes missing.

The Road Home. Warner Forever, 2004.
Divorced Lily Boudreau returns to Glens Crossing with her troubled teenage son and reconnects with a man from her past. Note: This and the two books that follow focus on members of the Beaudreau family.

Magnolia Sky. Warner Forever, 2004.
Luke Beaudreau goes to Mississippi to visit the family of a slain army buddy and meets a wife his friend never mentioned.

Promises to Keep. Warner Forever, 2005.
Dr. Molly Beaudreau returns to Glens Crossing to protect a baby that people assume is hers and is soon tracked down by the journalist brother of the baby's murdered mother who initially suspects Molly of involvement.

On Blue Falls Pond. Warner Forever, 2006.
A woman returns to her Tennessee hometown to care for her grandmother and reconnects with the firefighter who saved her life the night she lost her husband and unborn child. Autism, macular degeneration, amnesia, and abuse are part of this occasionally suspenseful story.

A Kiss in Winter. Warner Forever, 2007.
A photographer enlists the aid of a disillusioned psychiatrist when various local sites she has photographed for a new calendar are systematically vandalized.

Creighton, Kathleen

Creighton is a popular romance author and many of her earlier series romances [*Still Waters* (1986), *In Defense of* Love (1987), and *Winter's Daughter* (1988)] have been Rita Award winners. She is a member of RWA's exclusive Hall of Fame.

The Top Gun's Return. Silhouette Intimate Moments, 2003.
A prisoner of war's surprise return after eight years in an Iraqi prison impacts the lives of his wife and his daughter in unexpected ways as they all try to adjust to the "new normal."

Danger Signals. Silhouette Romantic Suspense, 2008.
A psychic called in to help with a serial killer investigation proves a valuable addition, in spite of the initial opinion of the detective in charge. This story is the first in Creighton's Taken series.

Criswell, Millie

Funny, upbeat, and full of Italian family charm, these stand-alone books are lightly linked by character.

The Trouble with Mary. Ivy, 2001.
Mary Russo, the owner of a new Italian restaurant, challenges the critic who panned her cuisine in this funny, lively family-filled romance.

What to Do about Annie? Ivy, 2001.
When Father Joe Russo decides to resign from the priesthood he hopes he can reconnect with Annie, his sister Mary's best friend in this book that follows *The Trouble with Mary*.

The Trials of Angela. Ivy, 2002.
Attorney Angela DeNero, single and pregnant by a cheating boyfriend, ends up on the opposite side of a custody case from a lawyer she's known, and been fascinated by, since high school.

Mad about Mia. Ivy, 2004.
An undercover FBI agent hires Mia DeNero to be his bodyguard in the hopes of taking advantage of her ties to the Russo family to investigate the family's supposed links to a crime ring.

Crusie, Jennifer

Crusie is noted for her sexy, hilarious, well-written romances filled with memorable characters (some of them animals, especially dogs) and plenty of zing and quirky, contemporary flair. Her early series romances are exceptional and several are included here. Many of her early titles have been reprinted.

Getting Rid of Bradley. Harlequin Temptation, 1994.
A cop and a schoolteacher are thrown together when someone is out to kill her; he suspects her ex in this absolutely hilarious romp—one of Crusie's best.

Charlie All Night. Harlequin Temptation, 1996.
A radio producer sets out to turn a temporary DJ into a nighttime success and ends up falling for her own "creation."

Anyone but You. Harlequin Love and Laughter, 1996.
This early series novel features a marvelous dog and an older heroine/younger hero relationship. It's one of Crusie's most memorable—a classic.

The Cinderella Deal. Bantam Loveswept, 1996.
A fake engagement results in the real thing for an uptight professor and his free spirited neighbor.

Tell Me Lies. St. Martin's, 1998.
A woman suspected of killing her cheating husband is "rescued" by her high school bad boy crush in this sexy, funny, character-rich romp.

Crazy for You. St. Martin's, 1999.
A high school teacher turns her life upside down for the better when she dumps her coach fiancé after he takes her new dog to the pound in this zany, hilarious story of love and sex in small town middle America.

Welcome to Temptation. St. Martin's, 2000.
A video photographer causes problems for the town mayor when she and her sister come to Temptation, Ohio, to shoot a video for an actress's audition for a porn producer in this funny, sexy romance.

Fast Women. St. Martin's, 2001.
A fiercely independent divorcée and a private detective clash when she becomes his secretary and totally disrupts his life.

Faking It. St. Martin's, 2002.
Everybody seems to be faking it in this madcap, secret-filled story that pairs an art forger with a con artist.

Bet Me. St. Martin's, 2004.
An outrageous bet and some major misunderstandings produce a delightful romance in which the heroine tries to turn the tables on the hero.

Maybe This Time. St. Martin's, 2010.
When Andie agrees to temporarily care for her ex-husband's two recently orphaned, very difficult wards, she ends up in a haunted house filled with unwanted guests, a suspicious fiancé, and an ex she can't quite forget.

Dahl, Victoria
Tumble Creek
The small town of Tumble Creek, Colorado, is the setting for these funny, racy, sex-filled romps.

Talk Me Down. HQN, 2009.
A closet erotica novelist with writers block returns home and reconnects with her teenage crush, now the police chief, who helps her with her problems, including a creepy stalker.

Start Me Up. HQN, 2009.
A mechanic who inherits her family auto shop when her father is injured and then dies finds hot romance with her best friend's brother—and mystery and danger when the police take another look at her father's case.

Lead Me On. HQN, 2010.
An outwardly proper office manager with a secret penchant for bad boys is attracted to a demolition expert.

Crazy for Love. HQN, 2010.
A woman publically humiliated when her fiancée fakes his own death to avoid marrying her heads for seclusion on a desert island and is attracted to the man next door.

Dailey, Janet
One of the most prolific and well-known romance novelists and the first American to write for the Harlequin (*No Quarter Asked*. Mills & Boon, 1974; Harlequin, 1976), Dailey's career took a tumble in 1997 when she was involved in a plagiarism suit. Since then she has added to her legendary Calder Saga and written several Contemporary Romances. A number of her earlier titles have been reissued. (See previous editions of this guide for more complete information and selected earlier titles.) See also chapter 13, "Linked Romances," for the Calder Saga Titles.

A Capitol Holiday. Zebra, 2001.
The president's daughter escapes for a bit of sweet holiday fun and meets a charming dog and his columnist owner.

Scrooge Wore Spurs. Zebra, 2002.
A bitter rancher finds love and healing when he becomes the guardian for his late sister's four children and needs help from a woman he once loved.

Something More. Kensington, 2007.
A skeleton found on a sprawling Wyoming ranch brings a Midwestern school teacher into the life of a widowed, and still grieving, rancher in this mainstream, low-key, treasure-touched story.

Dellin, Genell
Noted for her Historical Western and Native American Romances, this contemporary series has plenty of Western flavor.

Montana Series

This trilogy is linked by character, place, and horses.

Montana Blue. HQN, 2005.
A cowboy with near magical horse-taming skills and out for revenge is attracted to the step-daughter of the ruthless man he considers responsible for destroying his family.

Montana Gold. HQN, 2006.
A rodeo bullfighter/clown and a bronco rider must deal with their feelings when injury puts their careers on hold.

Montana Red. HQN, 2007.
A pampered, wealthy woman steals her beloved horse from her ex-husband and heads for Montana intending to live life on her own terms. But when her horse is lured into the wild by a legendary stallion, she and the wrangler next door head out to find her and find love along the way, as well.

Deveraux, Jude

Deveraux has written in a number of Romance subgenres and many of her stories have paranormal elements. She has also written Women's Fiction. A recent series, Edilean, includes books that are both Contemporary and Historical. See chapter 7, "Historical Romance"; and chapter 9, "Alternative Reality Romance."

Dimon, HelenKay

Dimon's romances are typically racy, witty, and sassy, and laced with mystery elements.

Viva Las Bad Boys. Brava, 2006.
A power outage in a Las Vegas hotel puts three unlikely couples together with sizzling results.

Your Mouth Drives Me Crazy. Brava, 2007.
A suspended police chief and a redhead on a mission deal with mystery and passion in this island-set romance.

Right Here, Right Now. Brava, 2008.
An undercover agent must win back the woman he dumped "for her own good," in this funny, sassy romp that is hot and sexy.

Hard as Nails. Brava, 2008.
Three couples find lust in a house under construction in this collection of novellas.

Hot as Hell. Brava, 2008.
A woman trying to figure out if her former fiancé is an embezzler goes to a spa to meet an informant and finds him dead and her "ex" claiming his innocence—with a passion.

It's Hotter in Hawaii. Brava, 2009.
The best friend and half-sister of a murder victim team up to find the truth, and find passion along the way.

Leave Me Breathless. Brava, 2010.
A hunky, ex-Marine judge resents being given a sexy female bodyguard when he is threatened in this sexy romance with dual love stories.

Eagle, Kathleen
    Most of Eagle's books feature Native American characters and sometimes focus on cultural issues. They will be of interest to readers of both Contemporary and Multicultural Romances. See chapter 12, "Multicultural Romance."

Evanick, Marcia
    Evanick has written earlier series romances but is best known recently for the series below.

Misty Harbor Series
    A small Maine coastal community is the setting for these heartwarming, sweet, character-rich novels. Several have a holiday theme and some have more than one love story.

    Catch of the Day. Zebra, 2002.
    A big city chef moves to town and opens Catch of the Day and is attracted to a carpenter with a tragic past.

    Christmas on Conrad Street. Zebra, 2002.
    Having sworn off love, a doctor is determined to find a fresh start in Misty Harbor but has a hard time resisting a persistent, gorgeous fisherman in this romance that has more than one love story.

    Blueberry Hill. Zebra, 2003.
    A disillusioned attorney joins her two sisters (heroines of two previous books) in Misty Harbor to reassess her life and takes a temporary job as a nanny to the three young children of the local sheriff.

    A Berry Merry Christmas. Zebra, 2004.
    A new widow comes to Misty Harbor to be part of her aunt's jam and jelly business and eventually finds new love with her late husband's business partner, once they stop feeling guilty.

    Harbor Nights. Zebra, 2005.
    A delicately built reporter, wary of men because of an abusive father and in need of emotional healing, is attracted to her handsome, brawny neighbor but fearful of his size.

    A Misty Harbor Wedding. Zebra, 2006.
    On a quiet mission to check out a new hotel site her family's hotel chain is considering, a single mom falls for a man who has planned for years to buy the land and the lighthouse that her company has in its sites.

    Mistletoe Bay. Zebra, 2007.
    Back in town to help care for his father, a UPS driver is drawn into the lives of a young widow running a home-based bath and beauty products business and her multigenerational family.

Foster, Lori
    Humor, a fast pace, and hot sex are some of the multi-published Foster's trademarks. Many of her stories are in series or loosely linked by character.

Visitation
    The small town of Visitation, North Carolina, is the setting for this series.

Say No to Joe? Zebra, 2003.
A sexy, self-confident former bounty hunter agrees to help a woman who's just inherited two children to fend off the townsfolk who don't want them around in this sometimes suspenseful story.

The Secret Life of Bryan. Brava, 2004.
A bounty hunter masquerading as a pastor in order to catch the person plaguing his clerical twin brother's safe house for hookers is attracted to a philanthropic woman he thinks is a prostitute.

When Bruce Met Cyn. Zebra, 2004.
A pastor (Bryan's twin) and an ex-prostitute find love in spite of a lot of obstacles.

Just a Hint: Clint. Brava, 2004.
A macho hero is determined to find out who's after the appealing woman he just rescued from kidnappers, even though she's engaged to someone else.

Jamie. Zebra, 2005.
A psychic loner and a woman with a similarly talented daughter connect in this story that adds a paranormal touch to the series.

Jude's Law. Zebra, 2006.
A bad boy celebrity hides out in a small town and is attracted to a shy art gallery owner with dangerous problems of her own.

Murphy's Law. Zebra, 2006.
A rich CEO pursues a custodian, but she has no intention of letting him distract her from achieving her goals in this slightly suspenseful story with links to *Jude's Law*.

SBC Fighters Series
This series focuses on the world of professional extreme fighting.

Causing Havoc. Berkley, 2007.
A fighter returns to his Kentucky hometown to help his sisters and finds love, as well, but he needs to make some changes along the way to make it all come together.

Simon Says. Berkley, 2007.
An abuse victim, who's also a P.I., connects with an SBC trainer when she is sent by his manipulative birth father (also the P.I.'s stepfather) to find him.

Hard to Handle. Berkley, 2008.
A fighter is determined to win a title, and his life coach landlady is intent on helping him find love—and there's a little danger along the way.

My Man Michael. Berkley, 2009.
An injured fighter is given a chance to be whole and save the race when a woman from the future makes a proposition in this story that is the one Futuristic in the series.

Back in Black. Berkley, 2010.
A PR expert is hired to clean up the image of the president of the SBC sports organization and falls for him in the process.

Fox, Roz Denny
Fox is particularly noted for her emotionally compelling, heart-tugging series romances.

Someone to Watch Over Me. Harlequin Superromance, 2003.
A woman consumed by bitterness and hatred when her abusive ex-husband kills their two children finally finds healing with a caring man who'd overcome a difficult past of his own.

On Angel Wings. Harlequin Superromance, 2006.
When the father of her unborn child is killed in an accident, a wounded smoke jumper has a hard time accepting help from a man who has always been attracted to her.

Looking for Sophie. Harlequin Superromance, 2007.
The search for an abducted child brings a Georgia detective and an Alaska mom together in this story with a fair amount of police procedural detail.

A Secret to Tell You. Harlequin Everlasting Love, 2007.
The discovery of a packet of old love letters during an old home remodel changes the lives of a number of people in this story that provides two love stories, one set during World War II and the other in the present.

More than a Memory. Harlequin Superromance, 2008.
A concert violinist who'd lost her memory in a car accident seven years earlier, discovers a past—and a love—she never knew about when she finds a box of puzzling high school memorabilia after her mother dies.

The Baby Album. Harlequin Superromance, 2009.
A photographer abandoned by her husband hides her pregnancy in order to get a job and then wonders how to tell the truth to her attractive boss, who lost his wife during an ectopic pregnancy, when they begin to develop a relationship.

The Cowboy Soldier. Harlequin Superromance, 2010.
A doctor who practices holistic medicine tries to resist falling for a wounded Native American veteran she treats.

Freethy, Barbara
Freethy's emotionally compelling romances often have a gentle hint of magic or the paranormal. See also chapter 9, "Alternative Reality Romance"; and chapter 6, "Romantic Mysteries."

Just the Way You Are. Avon, 2000.
Thinking her husband still loves her beautiful sister when she finds some old pictures among his things, a woman resigns herself to divorce—until her sister returns and they are forced to deal with the past, and the present.

Some Kind of Wonderful. Avon, 2001.
A journalist asks his neighbor for help—and finds romance—when his sister leaves her baby in his care.

Love Will Find a Way. Avon, 2002.
A woman learns that her late husband was living a double life when she and her husband's business partner look into the insurance company's claim that the car accident was a suicide.

Summer Secrets. Onyx, 2003.
An old sailing tragedy that has plagued the three McKenna sisters and their father for years is finally dealt with when a journalist comes to town with a hidden agenda.

Angel's Bay

Set in a small town on the Northern California coast where the townsfolk firmly believe in the town's legendary guardian angels, this series has subtle paranormal aspects and also includes a mystery in each book.

Suddenly One Summer. Pocket Star, 2009.
When her sister is killed by her abusive husband, Jenna takes her young niece and goes to ground in Angel's Bay, never thinking she will eventually attract the attention of a journalist in town to do a piece for a tabloid on the local angels.

On Shadow Beach. Pocket Star, 2010.
A woman reluctantly returns to town to care for her father and must face old memories and still haunting questions about her sister's murder, as well as her old boyfriend who is also back in town.

In Shelter Cove. Pocket Star, 2010.
A single mom returns to Angel's Bay and ends up living next door to the cop who was responsible for convicting her late husband of art theft.

At Hidden Falls. Pocket Star, 2011
A costume designer comes to Angel's Bay and is rescued from a near fatal car accident by a stranger who has been haunting her dreams.

Garden of Secrets. Pocket Star, 2011.
A doctor is torn between a pastor and a police chief in the final volume of this magical series that solves the ongoing mystery and nicely ties up all loose ends.

Gibson, Rachel

Gibson is noted for funny, nonstop romances, many of which involve players on the Seattle Chinooks ice hockey team.

*True Confessions. Avon A, 2001.
A tabloid reporter who writes sensational alien-type stories goes to tiny Gospel, Idaho, to stay out of the limelight temporarily and is charmed by the town and the hunky single dad sheriff, who has a secret of his own.

The Trouble with Valentine's Day. Avon, 2005.
After a disastrous, totally uncharacteristic flirtation attempt at a Sun Valley ski lodge, a P.I. in need of some rest and relaxation and on her way to her grandfather's in Gospel, Idaho, is shocked to learn that the man she approached owns the sports store next to her grandfather's grocery story, and now she must convince him that she's really not a loose woman. Serious issues humorously handled.

Sex, Lies, and Online Dating. Avon, 2006.
A thriller novelist uses the internet to research the online dating scene for her next novel and connects with a cop who is on the trail of a killer who uses the Internet to find his victims in this funny, relevant romance.

Tangled Up in You. Avon, 2007.
A true crime writer goes undercover to Truly, Idaho, to investigate her mother's long-ago murder and dredges up an old scandal that the sexy owner of the local bar would just as soon have stay in the past.

Not Another Bad Date. Avon, 2008.
A sci-fi/fantasy author goes to Texas to take care of her teenage niece while her sister is in the hospital and reconnects with her now-widowed college sweetheart in this story that has a gentle paranormal twist.

True Love and Other Disasters. Avon, 2009.
Having inherited a hockey team from her late husband, former playboy bunny Faith Duffy sets out to prove herself to everyone, especially the team captain, Ty Savage. If only they can ignore the sizzle that sparks between them.

Nothing but Trouble. Avon, 2010.
An injured ice hockey superstar and an aspiring actress set off sparks when Chelsea Ross is hired by the team to be Mark Bressler's home health aid in this hilarious romp.

Goodnight, Linda

Goodnight writes sweet contemporaries, as well as Inspirational Romances. See also chapter 11, "Inspirational Romance."

Married in a Month. Silhouette Romance, 2003.
A brief "convenient marriage" for the sake of a baby turns into a real one in this sweet story.

The Least Likely Groom. Silhouette Romance, 2004.
An injured rodeo cowboy and a fearful nurse who hates extreme sports find love despite their differences.

Married Under the Mistletoe. Harlequin Romance, 2006.
A wary restaurant manager with an abusive past agrees to let the owner's son temporarily share her apartment above the restaurant.

Winning the Single Mom's Heart. Harlequin Romance, 2008.
A single mom cake designer reconnects with one of her late husband's best friends at a wedding, with romantic results.

The Snow-Kissed Bride. Harlequin Romance, 2009.
Intrigued by solitary Melody Crawford and her search-and-rescue dogs and needing her expertise, John North works to win her trust in this suspenseful, secret-laced romance set in the Rockies.

Her Prince's Secret Son. Harlequin Romance, 2010.
A medical emergency for their son reconnects a book store owner and a prince who were treacherously separated years earlier.

Greene, Jennifer (Pseudonym for Alison Hart)

Greene's lively contemporaries are sexy, heartwarming, and filled with richly engaging characters and compelling situations. She is member of RWA's exclusive Hall of Fame.

Night of the Hunter. Silhouette Desire, 1989.
Set in the wild beauty of northern Minnesota, this romance brings two loners together in spite of their differences.

*Single Dad. Silhouette Desire, 1995.
A single dad contractor with three active children is forced into a relationship with an attractive store owner when his matchmaking six-year-old steals things from the store—on purpose!

*Nobody's Princess. Silhouette Desire, 1997.
A spirited, outgoing women's studies professor adds zing to the life of a quiet Southern gentleman who senses her deep vulnerability and teaches her that dreams can come true.

Where Is He Now? Avon, 2003.
A high school reunion provides answers to questions and second chances for former sweethearts.

Hot to the Touch. Silhouette Desire, 2005.
An infant massage therapist tries to help a wounded war veteran heal inside and out in this unusual, ultimately fulfilling romance.

Blame It on Chocolate. HQN, 2006.
A down-to-earth, serious botanist for a chocolate company and the sophisticated, chocolatier grandson of the company's owner are drawn to each other despite their major differences in this purely delicious romance.

Blame It on Cupid. HQN, 2007.
A woman becomes the guardian for the eleven-year-old daughter of a friend and finds help and unexpected love with the single dad of teenage twin boys who lives next door.

*"Born in My Heart" in Like Mother, Like Daughter. 2007.
A mother must deal with her feelings when her adopted teenage daughter locates her birth mom in this touching, well-written novella.

Blame It on Paris. HQN, 2008.
When a mugging at the Louvre throws two Americans (both from South Bend, Indiana!) together and it ends up in a Paris fling, Kelly knows it won't last—until Will follows after and, eventually, puts his life back in order.

Secretive Stranger. Silhouette Romantic Suspense, 2010.
Translator Sophie Campbell lives a quiet life in D.C. until her next door neighbor ends up murdered and his attractive academic brother comes to town to find out why. First in a projected series about the Campbell sisters.

Hailstock, Shirley
See chapter 12, "Multicultural Romance."

Harper, Julia (Pseudonym for Nancy M. Finney)
Harper writes Historical Romances as Elizabeth Hoyt.

Hot. Forever, 2008.
A librarian heroine swipes some documents in order to clear her late father's reputation of embezzlement and is pursued by a sexy FBI agent in this lively adventure.

For the Love of Pete. Forever, 2009.
The kidnapping of baby Pete sends the heroine and the FBI hero, plus a host of zany characters, on a wild chase through the Illinois countryside.

Higgins, Kristan
Higgins's stories are funny, fast-paced, and filled with small town ambience.

Catch of the Day. HQN, 2007.
The chatty owner of a diner in tiny Gideon's Cove, Maine, has a disastrous record with romance until a taciturn lobsterman comes into her life.

Just One of the Guys. HQN, 2008.
A newspaper editor heroine with a family filled with firefighters adores a firefighter who just thinks of her as a friend.

*Too Good to Be True. HQN, 2009.
A woman invents a perfect, always-out-of-town, boyfriend to keep her family and friends off her back and then falls for her neighbor, who is not quite so perfect.

The Next Best Thing. HQN, 2010.
A young widow finally decides she needs to find a man to marry, but her perfect person is her best-friend-with-benefits (and former brother-in-law), if only she'd realize it.

Hill, Teresa
Hill's stories are often family centered and emotionally compelling.

Twelve Days. Signet, 2000.
Three foster children who need a home over the holidays turn a couple's tottering marriage around.

The Edge of Heaven. Onyx, 2002.
A college student who is being stalked by her abusive boyfriend is helped by her adoptive father's long-lost brother.

Bed of Lies. Onyx, 2003.
Protagonists who have put their difficult pasts behind them meet unexpectedly and reassess their future.

Heard It Through the Grapevine. Silhouette Special Edition, 2003.
A pregnant woman agrees to marry a man she has always secretly loved when he offers his help.

A Little Bit Engaged. Silhouette Special Edition, 2006.
A young woman recovering from a broken engagement is attracted to the handsome parish pastor

Single Mom Seeks . . . Silhouette Special Edition, 2009.
A single mom who's sworn off men agrees to pretend to date her hunky neighbor to help him discourage unwanted attentions and ends up falling for him herself.

Runaway Las Vegas Bride. Silhouette Special Edition, 2010.
When her grandmother goes to Vegas to elope, a financial guru joins forces with the attorney whose elderly uncle is the intended groom, and they try to stop the wedding in his hilarious romp.

Countdown to the Wedding. Silhouette Special Edition, 2010.

Holm, Stef Ann
All That You Are. HQN, 2009.
A single mom and a construction company owner connect in Ketchikan, Alaska.

Howard, Linda (Pseudonym for Linda Howington)
   Although Howard is currently better known for her Romantic Suspense novels, she has written in a number of other subgenres, as well. Several of her more important early titles are listed below. See also chapter 6, "Romantic Mysteries."

Mackenzie Series
   This contemporary series focuses on members of the Mackenzie family and is a classic series that readers still talk about. Most of the titles have since been reissued in various editions and packages.

   Mackenzie's Mountain. Silhouette Intimate Moments, 1989.
   School teacher Mary Potter comes to tiny Ruth, Wyoming, and changes the life of Wolf Mackenzie—and the attitude of the town with her determination and belief.

   Mackenzie's Mission. Silhouette Intimate Moments, 1992.
   Air Force Colonel Joe Mackenzie is on the hunt for the insider who's sabotaging his test plane's new weapons system and his top suspect is beautiful weapons expert Caroline Evans.

   Mackenzie's Pleasure. Silhouette Intimate Moments, 1996.
   Navy SEAL Zane Mackenzie saves the ambassador's daughter, Barrie Lovejoy, from terrorists and finds a lifelong love, as well.

   "Mackenzie's Magic" in *Christmas Kisses*, Silhouette Books, 1996.
   Without a memory, horse trainer Maris Mackenzie must depend on FBI agent Alex MacNeil help her prove she's no horse thief, and keep her safe from the real crooks.

   A Game of Chance. Silhouette Intimate Moments, 2000.
   On an undercover mission to smoke out a terrorist, Chance Mackenzie decides to use the terrorist's daughter as bait, but his plan takes a different turn when he realizes she is in danger from her father, as well.

Hudson, Janis Reams
   All the Rooms of My Heart. Zebra, 2004.
   A New York professional woman in Texas to oversee the renovations to her late aunt's home gradually changes her cynical views about love and caring when she gets to know the her aunt's friends, and one carpenter in particular.

The Men of Cherokee Rose
   The Chisholm brothers find love in this contemporary trilogy.

   The Daddy Survey. Silhouette Special Edition, 2004.
   Two young girls decide that the rancher who rescued them and their mom from homelessness would make a perfect father.

   The Other Brother. Silhouette Special Edition, 2004.
   Two best friends find love in this warm romance that has a few unsavory characters.

   The Cowboy on Her Trail. Silhouette Special Edition, 2004.
   A soon-to-be dad chases down his baby's mother, who isn't sure she wants to get married.

Tribute, Texas
   Linked by place, these three stories have plenty of small town ambience.

Winning Dixie. Silhouette Special Edition, 2006.
A heart-transplant recipient goes to Tribute to look up his donor's family and finds love in a most unlikely place.

Finding Nick. Silhouette Special Edition, 2006.
A firefighter who survived 9/11 retreats to the quiet life in Tribute, Texas, but is followed by a persistent, attractive reporter.

Riley and His Girls. Silhouette Special Edition, 2006.
A Christmas visit to the husband and daughters of a military comrade who died in Iraq has heartwarming and heart-wrenching results for Sergeant Amy Galloway.

Hunter, Kelly
Exposed: Misbehaving with the Magnate. Harlequin Presents, 2010.
A young woman now living in Australia returns to France when her mother gets sick and renews a relationship with a man who was off limits for financial and class reasons in this romance that was first published in 2009 as a Mills & Boon Modern Heat title. Note: Linked by characters to the following title.

Revealed: A Prince and a Pregnancy. Harlequin Presents, 2010.
A French heiress goes to Australia for a wedding and reconnects with a man from her past in this sexy romance that was first released in 2009 as a Mills & Boon Modern Heat title.

Jacobs, Holly
Jacobs writes funny, witty, sweet romances often with small town settings (often Erie, PA) and plenty of family interaction. See also chapter 13, "Linked Romances."

The House on Briar Hill Road. Harlequin Everlasting Love, 2007.
Circumstances separate childhood friends and lovers, but they are reunited once again by tragedy in this decades-spanning heart-tugging romance.

Same Time Next Summer. Harlequin Superromance, 2008.
Two people have a second chance at love when a tragic accident occurs in this touching romance.

American Dads Series
Dads are highlighted in this publisher's series.

Once upon a Thanksgiving. Harlequin American Romance, 2008.
A single mom studying to be an RN finds romance with the temporary principal at her four children's school.

Once upon a Christmas. Harlequin American Romance, 2008.
When her nephew decides to find his birth father, his guardian aunt is concerned, until she meets the father, who is not quite what she expected.

Once upon a Valentine's. Harlequin American Romance, 2008.
A single mom of twin seventh graders who accidentally causes a fire is forced to teach fire safety classes, with the help of a handsome police chief, and finds unexpected romance.

One-of-a-Kind Family. Harlequin Superromance, 2010.
A life-skills coach for the developmentally disabled finds love—eventually—with the skeptical, somewhat over-protective twin brother of one of her clients.

Johnson, Susan

Johnson is noted for her lushly sensual, explicit, edgy romances. She writes both Historicals and Contemporaries. See also chapter 7, "Historical Romance."

Blonde Heat. Bantam, 2002.
A trio of friends returns to tiny Ely, Minnesota, for the summer and finds romance.

Hot Legs. Berkley, 2004.
An art curator and an expert art investigator are attracted to each other when a museum painting goes missing, but a meddling ex-wife stirs up trouble.

Hot Spot. Berkley Sensation, 2005.
A comic book store owner and a collector find passion and deal with a little mutual suspicion in this hot romp.

Hot Property. Berkley Sensation, 2008.
A researcher working on a an article about stolen Italian artifacts becomes the target of a wealthy collector and hires the former CIA interpreter next door to be her bodyguard—only someone is after him, as well.

Johnston, Joan

Johnston has written both Historical and Contemporary Romances, many of which are parts of series. (See previous editions of this guide for some earlier titles.) See chapter 13, "Linked Romances."

Kitt, Sandra

See chapter 12, "Multicultural Romance."

Kleypas, Lisa

Also noted for her Historical Period Romances. Note: The three titles below are all linked by character. See also chapter 7, "Historical Romance."

Sugar Daddy. St. Martin's Press, 2007.
Left to raise her young sister when her mother is killed in an accident, Liberty Jones attracts the fatherly attention of Churchill Travis and the suspicion and passion of son Gage. But when her first teenage cruse, comes on the scene, she must make some hard, practical choices in this story that is more Liberty's journey than a pure romance.

Blue-Eyed Devil. St. Martin's Press, 2008.
Haven Travis, a socialite victim of brutal spousal abuse, struggles to put her life back together and reconnects with wealthy oilman man Hardy Cates—a man from her past.

Smooth Talking Stranger. St. Martin's Press, 2009.
Suddenly responsible for her infant nephew, advice columnist Ella Varner sets out to find the unknown father, starting with sexy, wealthy Jack Travis.

Christmas Eve at Friday Harbor. St. Martin's Press, 2010.
A young widow afraid of loving again and a bachelor suddenly raising his young, orphaned niece are drawn to each other when Mark and Holly walk into Maggie's toy store in Friday Harbor—and Holly, mute since her mother's death, responds to Maggie and begins to talk. First of a projected series set in Friday Harbor.

Korbel, Kathleen (Pseudonym for Eileen Dreyer)

Korbel's works are poignant, emotionally compelling, and feature well-developed characters, and often a touch of suspense. She also writes Mystery Suspense and Historical

Romance under her own name. Korbel is a member of the RWA Hall of Fame. Her older titles (*Perchance to Dream* [1989], *The Ice Cream Man* [1989], *A Rose for Maggie* [1991], and *A Soldier's Heart* [1995]) were Rita Award winners. See also Korbel in chapter 9, "Alternative Reality Romance." and Dreyer in chapter 6, "Romantic Mysteries," and chapter 7, "Historical Romance."

> **Perchance to Dream*. Silhouette Intimate Moments, 1989.
> Danger stalks a psychologist and a man trying to deal with the death of his partner in this suspenseful tale.

> **The Ice Cream Man*. Silhouette Intimate Moments, 1989.
> A man, posing as an ice cream, is attracted to the young mother and potential criminal he has under surveillance—and she and the neighbors are suspicious of him.

> **A Rose for Maggie*. Silhouette Romance, 1991.
> A mother raising a child with Down syndrome and a heart condition finds love with a caring children's book author in this emotionally rich, hard-hitting classic.

> **A Soldier's Heart*. Silhouette Intimate Moments, 1995.
> A nurse suffering from PTSD after a stint in Vietnam is helped by a soldier she once saved on the battlefield.

> *Some Men's Dreams*. Silhouette Intimate Moments, 2003.
> A young doctor struggles with her romantic feelings for her boss, as well as the knowledge that his young daughter is starving herself.

Krentz, Jayne Ann

Krentz is a bestselling, popular writer in several romance subgenres, and she currently writes Historical Romances as Amanda Quick and Futuristic Romance as Jayne Caste. Most of her recent romances include mystery and romantic suspense elements in various degrees, as well as occasional paranormal elements, and could also be classified as Romantic Suspense (with an occasional paranormal touch). Her style is lively, upbeat, sexy, and laced with sassy humor. Her typical hero is a strong alpha male—successful, determined, protective, and used to being in charge—and her heroines are intelligent, intrepid, independent, and used to making their own decisions. Naturally, the sparks fly. Krentz often sets her Contemporary Romances in the Seattle area.

> *Eye of the Beholder*. Pocket, 1999.
> A hotel mogul goes to Arizona to investigate the suspicious death of his father, which happened over a decade ago, and connects with a woman who has her own reasons for helping him.

> *Soft Focus*. Putnam, 1999.
> A woman is forced to work with a man she dumped when a high-tech crystal is stolen and it's up to them to find it.

> *Lost and Found*. Putnam, 2001.
> Cady Briggs inherits an antiques business when her great aunt drowns, but Cady smells a rat and hires Mack Easton to investigate the death.

Eclipse Bay Trilogy

An old feud between the Hartes and the Madisons is at the heart of this lively, suspenseful trilogy.

Eclipse Bay. Jove, 2000.
An eight-year-old murder comes back to haunt Hannah Harte and Rafe Madison when they inherit equal shares of her aunt's house and a killer stalks again.

Dawn in Eclipse Bay. Jove, 2001.
Lillian Harte is forced to have one date—the last one on his contract—with new brother-in-law Gabe Madison when she closes her online dating business in Portland and heads home to Eclipse Bay to pursue her artistic calling.

Summer in Eclipse Bay. Jove, 2002.
Art gallery owner Olivia Brightwell comes to Eclipse Bay to fulfill her aunt's deathbed wish and make amends for starting the Harte/Madison feud. She plans to leave afterward, but her growing feelings for mystery writer Nick Harte—plus murder and an art theft— get in the way.

Smoke in Mirrors. Putnam, 2002.
The death of a woman who supposedly embezzled money from a college endowment fund brings an academic librarian and the brother of the fund manager together as they try to unravel a puzzling mystery that reaches back to the past.

Whispering Springs
Set in Whispering Springs, Arizona.

Light in Shadow. Putnam, 2003.
When a psychic interior decorator senses that one of her clients may have had something to do with his ex-wife's murder, Zoe Luce seeks the aid of P.I. Ethan Truax, whose own investigations threaten to uncover Zoe's own dark past.

Truth or Dare. Putnam, 2004.
Now married, Zoe and Ethan work on remodeling their home, but strange events and a friend from Zoe's past on the run from her murderous husband throw things into chaos in this story that is more mystery and suspense than romance.

Falling Awake. Putnam, 2004.
Paranormal elements add to this romantic thriller that involves a secret government dream research project and the search for a killer.

All Night Long. Putnam, 2006.
The supposed suicide of her childhood friend leads Irene Stensen and ex-military inn-keeper Luke Danner on a quest that may shed light on the deaths of Irene's parents years earlier—if they don't get killed first. Includes PTSD elements.

Landis, Jill Marie
Landis has also written a number of earlier Historical Romances. Her recent works are for the Inspirational market.

Twilight Cove Trilogy
Set in a tiny town along the California coast, the final story has a gentle paranormal touch.

Lover's Lane Ballantine, 2003.
An artist on the run to keep her young son out of her ex-in-laws' clutches changes her name and settles down in Twilight Cove, but when a P.I. sees her paintings, it threatens to blow her cover.

Heat Wave. Ballantine, 2004.
A wounded P.I., in Twilight Cove to heal as she house-sits for a fellow P.I., agrees to help a businessman try to find a teenage daughter he didn't know he had.

Heartbreak Hotel. Ballantine, 2005.
Suddenly widowed and left destitute, a young mother decides to renovate her dilapidated hotel in Twilight Cove and finds love with a burned-out writer whose muse is resurrected by the ghostly fisherman who haunts the hotel.

Langan, Ruth (also writes as Ruth Ryan Langan and R. C. Ryan)
Long-time romance writer Langan writes both Historical and Contemporary Romances, many of which have suspense elements. Some have been reprinted. See also chapter 7, "Historical Romance," and R. C. Ryan below.

The Wildes of Wyoming Trilogy
This series focuses on the wealthy Wilde brothers and incorporates romantic suspense elements, humor, and plenty of family interaction.

The Wildes of Wyoming: Chance. Silhouette Intimate Moments, 2000.
Business concerns are Chance's life until lovely, but slightly mysterious, Maggie Fuller is hired as a cook at the family ranch.

The Wildes of Wyoming: Hazard. Silhouette Intimate Moments, 2000.
When Hazard's herd begins dying off for no apparent reason, brilliant, but naive Dr. Erin Ryan steps in to help.

The Wildes of Wyoming: Ace. Silhouette Intimate Moments, 2000.
Pool shark Ally Brady hustles Ace Wilde out of enough money to pay her grandfather's medical bills and then learns Ace is her new boss. Family complications and danger follow.

The Lassiter Law Series
A publisher's series that involves the members of the Lassiter family.

By Honor Bound. Silhouette Intimate Moments, 2001.
A security expert is hired to protect the daughter of a wealthy software mogul without letting her know his mission, but when he begins to fall for her, he knows she'll never forgive the deception.

The Return of the Prodigal Son. Silhouette Intimate Moments, 2002.
A burned-out CIA operative returns home to rest and becomes involved in helping a young mother prove her late husband wasn't a criminal.

Banning's Woman. Silhouette Intimate Moments, 2002.
A new congresswoman and a police captain find romance, although they appear to be on opposite sides of a police corruption battle.

His Father's Son. Silhouette Intimate Moments, 2002.
An attorney is attracted to a social worker on the other side of a "cop killer" case he has taken on.

Law, Susan Kay
See also chapter 7, "Historical Romance."

Just Sex. Berkley, 2007.
A woman, told by her philandering CEO husband to have an affair to prove his point that his were "just sex," takes hold of her own destiny in this story that is more women's fiction with a chick lit feel than pure romance.

The Paper Marriage. Berkley Books, 2008.
When a former baseball player with a rebellious teenage daughter moves in next door, an architect whose husband has been in a coma for over a decade is forced to reassess her life and consider moving on.

Lee, Rachel (Pseudonym for Sue Civil-Brown)
See chapter 6, "Romantic Mysteries," and chapter 13, "Linked Romances."

Whisper Creek
Set in the small mining town of Whisper Creek, Colorado.

Snow in September. Mira, 2000.
A widow turns to her late husband's best friend when her teenager runs away in this story that is rife with complex emotions and dark family secrets.

A January Chill. Mira, 2001.
A father's bitter, unreasonable hatred of the man he blames for his daughter's death twelve years earlier threatens the growing love between his niece and the man (who was not guilty) in question.

July Thunder. Mira, 2002.
A deputy sheriff and a high school teacher, both hiding tragic pasts, find love and healing as a forest fire rushes toward their town.

Linz, Cathie (Pseudonym for Cathie L. Baumgardner)
Linz is a veteran writer of upbeat, funny, sexy series and single-title romances.

"Small Town" Pennsylvania Quartet
Set in the neighboring small towns of Serenity Springs and Rock Creek, Pennsylvania.

Good Girls Do. Berkley Sensation, 2006.
A "bad boy" returns to Serenity Springs, Pennsylvania, to run the family pub for six months or forfeit his inheritance and falls for the local librarian—and her kooky family.

Bad Girls Don't. Berkley Sensation, 2006.
The free-spirited sister from the previous title wins the lottery and decides to restore the theatre in Rock Creek, Pennsylvania. Romance comes in the form of the local sheriff.

Big Girls Don't Cry. Berkley Sensation, 2007.
A former plus-size model returns to Rock Creek and finds a job—and romance—with the local veterinarian, whom she once flattened when he teased her about her weight in school.

Smart Girls Think Twice. Berkley Sensation, 2009.
A smart researcher with surprising self-defense skills uses her trip home to Rock Creek for her sisters' weddings to do some research on the town's recent revitalization by talking to newcomers, including a handsome new bartender.

West Investigations

Mad, Bad, and Blonde. Berkley Sensation, 2010.
Jilted on her wedding day via text message, Faith West goes on her Italian honeymoon solo and becomes involved with a man who has a seductive agenda of his own—and a vendetta against her family.

Luck Be a Lady. Berkley Sensation, 2010.
An unconventional librarian and a sexy detective head into the Nevada desert on a wild, crazy hunt for the heroine's mother, a woman who was supposed to be dead!

Tempted Again. Berkley Sensation, 2012.

Lowell, Elizabeth (Pseudonym for Ann Maxwell)

Lowell has written in a number of romance subgenres but is currently best known for her Romantic Suspense novels. Many of her early Contemporary Series Romances have been republished and some have been updated. See chapter 6, "Romantic Mysteries."

Lucas, Jennie

The Christmas Love-Child. Harlequin Presents Extra, 2009.
An affair between a royal Russian playboy and a naive secretary has unintended consequences that change the lives of both parties.

Tamed: The Barbarian King. Harlequin Presents, 2010.
A barren woman engaged to be married is torn between love and duty when the man (now a king) she loved as a teenager begs her to reconsider.

Macomber, Debbie

Macomber writes sweet, heartwarming, family-centered romances that often have small town settings. Her holiday romances are especially popular (some of which feature her classic prayer ambassador angels), as are her recent women's romantic fiction series. Many of her early series titles have been reprinted. See also Women's Romantic Fiction Bibliography below and chapter 9, "Alternative Reality Romance."

Dakota Quartet

The people of slowly dying Buffalo Valley, North Dakota, set out to renew their town in this series that has a slightly old fashioned, historical feel.

Dakota Born. Mira, 2000.
Lynsay Snyder returns to town after her grandmother dies to consider her options and becomes the town's school teacher, and finds love with a rancher in the bargain.

Dakota Home. Mira, 2000.
Lynsay's friend Maddy Washburn comes to Buffalo Valley and finds romance with a solitary bison rancher.

Always Dakota. Mira, 2001.
Wealthy rancher Maggie Clemons sets her sites on landless cowboy Matt Eiler but must deal with a determined, duplicitous rival for his affections.

Buffalo Valley. Mira, 2001.
A returning vet, who now represents a large big-box chain, visits his parents who have relocated to North Dakota and ends up rethinking his life (and his love) when he realizes how the proposed store would change the town of Buffalo Valley.

The Christmas Basket. Mira, 2002.
A couple driven apart as teenagers by their mother's rivalry reconnect one Christmas in this story of holiday hope and reconciliation.

The Snow Bride. Mira, 2003.
A woman heading for Alaska to marry a man she met online has her plans changed by a man who knows the terrible reputation of her intended and takes her home with him, instead.

When Christmas Comes. Mira, 2004.
A house-swapping mix-up over the holidays results in romance between a widow and a Christmas-hating professor.

There's Something about Christmas. Mira, 2005.
A fruitcake-hating journalist who is assigned to do a story on the finalists in a fruitcake contest gains insight from three wise bakers and finds romance with the pilot who ferries her around.

Christmas Letters. Mira, 2006.
A woman who writes Christmas letters for other people finds unexpected romance with a psychologist who has no use for Christmas in this story that has links to the Blossom Street series.

A Cedar Cove Christmas. Mira, 2008.
A contemporary reworking of the Christmas Story, with a bit of a twist. Related to the Cedar Cove series.

The Perfect Christmas. Mira, 2009.
A woman looking for a perfect match (and a perfect Christmas) goes to a choosy matchmaker, who assigns her three tasks to complete before he introduces her to the "perfect" man.

Call Me Mrs. Miracle. Mira, 2010.
A single mom who works in a department store and her profit-oriented boss find love and a Christmas miracle during the holiday season.

McAllister, Anne
McAllister writes popular Contemporary Series Romances.

The Great Montana Cowboy Auction. Silhouette, 2002.
A Hollywood star returns to his Montana cowboy roots to be "auctioned off" at a fund-raiser and reconnects with a young widow from his past.

One-Night Love Child. Harlequin Presents, 2008.
When a footloose journalist returns to Ireland after five years away to take up his noble duties, he learns he is a father, heads for Montana where he meets his five-year-old son, and falls for the mother, as well. Links to *The Great Montana Cowboy Auction*.

One-Night Mistress . . . Convenient Wife. Harlequin Presents, 2009.
A young woman reconnects with a man she had a crush on years ago, and this time around, he's interested.

The Virgin's Proposition. Harlequin Presents, 2010.
A princess and a handsome Greek American actor are attracted when they meet at the Cannes Film Festival.

McCall, Dinah (pseudonym for Sharon Sala)

McCall's Contemporary Romances are typically dark andemotionally gripping, and are generally considered Romantic Suspense. Some have paranormal elements. An early classic is listed below. See also chapter 6, "Romantic Mysteries."

Jackson Rule. Mira, 1996.
Released after serving time for killing his abusive father, Jackson Rule works to put his life back together, help his emotionally disturbed sister, and resist his attraction to the woman who hired him to work in her nursery, preacher's daughter Rebecca Hill.

McNaught, Judith

McNaught is noted for her Historical Romances, as well. She also writes Romantic Suspense. The two early Contemporary titles listed below are classics, have links to *Every Breath You Take*, and are included in the earlier editions of this source. See also, chapter 6, "Romantic Mysteries."

Paradise. Pocket Books, 1991.
Perfect. Simon & Schuster, 1993.
Every Breath You Take. Ballantine, 2005.
While vacationing in Anguilla, Kate Donovan and wealthy Mitchell Wyatt meet and quickly fall for each other, only to be separated by the murder of Mitchell's father and a series of misunderstandings and suspicions. Note: The paperback version (2006) of this title was enhanced by the author to provide more detail.

Michaels, Fern

Although currently best noted for her popular Revenge of the Sisterhood series, Michaels has a number of Contemporary Romances and/or Women's Romantic Fiction novels to her credit; several recent examples follow. See also chapter 13, "Linked Romances."

The Nosy Neighbor. Pocket, 2005.
A woman, aided by her attractive neighbor (and his dog), tries to get to the bottom of things when she learns that the law is after her fiancé.

Mr. and Miss Anonymous. Kensington, 2009.
A couple that met years ago at a fertility clinic reconnect in this poignant reunion story.

Return to Sender. Kensington, 2010.
A woman sets out to ruin the now-wealthy man who left her pregnant as a teenager nineteen years ago.

Miller, Linda Lael

Miller has written in a variety of romance subgenres; many of her Contemporary and Historical Romances have a Western flavor and most are parts of family-linked series, many of which contain both Contemporary and Historical Romances. See chapter 13, "Linked Romances."

Nash, Joy

Nash also writes Paranormal Historical and Urban Fantasy Romances.

A Little Light Magic. Leisure, 2009.
A woman decides to turn an old seaside house into a new-age magic shop and is attracted to the contractor she hires for the job.

Palmer, Diana (Pseudonym for Susan Kyle)

Veteran romance writer Palmer has published in a number of subgenres, often setting her stories in the American West. Her ongoing Long, Tall Texans series (a few examples from which are below) is linked by place and character and is one of her more popular. Many of her books in this series, as well as other titles, have been reissued in various formats. Her stories can be sexy or sweet, emotionally compelling, often include an older hero and young, naive heroine, and may have elements of mystery and suspense. A few examples for her Long, Tall, Texans series follow.

Heartbreaker. Silhouette Desire, 2006.
A wealthy rancher's anger causes the young woman who adores him to have an accident that results in a temporary loss and forces him to rethink his feelings.

Fearless. HQN, 2008.
An attorney in Jacobsville, Texas, for her safety's sake is attracted to a farm manager who is working undercover for the DEA.

Heartless. HQN, 2009.
A woman's reluctant rejection of the man she loves sends him into the arms of a spiteful gold-digger, although they both do eventually get things right.

The Maverick. Silhouette Desire, 2009.
A trouble-prone cowboy is attracted to a woman who is investigating a murder that involves his family.

Dangerous. HQN, 2010.
An FBI Agent currently serving as a Jacobsville, Texas, police officer is attracted to a dispatcher as they work to bring down the person who killed his wife and child years earlier.

Tough to Tame. Harlequin Romance, 2010.
A difficult veterinarian's deep distrust of women puts his latest tech in danger when her violent, abusive ex-boyfriend shows up.

Perrin, Kayla

See chapter 12, "Ethnic/Multicultural Romance."

Phillips, Susan Elizabeth

Phillips writes funny, sexy, insightful Contemporary Romances with memorable characters (some of whom appear in subsequent novels) and is especially known for her books about a mythical football team, the Chicago Stars. (See earlier editions of this source for some previous titles.) Phillips is a member of the RWA Hall of Fame.

Chicago Stars Series

Phillips has gained both critical and popular acclaim with this series. Some previously published titles are annotated in the previous edition of this book. *It Had to Be You* (1994), *Nobody's Baby but Mine* (1997), and *Dream a Little Dream* (1998) are Rita Award winners.

This Heart of Mine. Morrow, 2001.
When she miscarries after she impulsively seduces and then marries resentful quarterback Kevin Tucker, children's author Molly Somerville becomes dangerously depressed; things change, however, when Kevin takes her to a camp-turned-family-B-and-B that he's inherited from his parents.

Match Me If You Can. Morrow, 2005.
A matchmaker takes on the job of finding a wife for a too-busy sports agent, and ends up being the only "match" he wants.

Natural Born Charmer. Morrow, 2007.
A charming quarterback takes pity on a down-on-her-luck artist and takes her to his newly acquired mansion, only to find his estranged mother overseeing the renovations in this funny, poignant, misfit-filled romp.

Lady Be Good. Avon, 1999.
A proper English schoolmarm is in Texas on a most unconventional mission to save her school by ruining her reputation. Unfortunately her chosen target, a noted golfing playboy, can't afford the bad press.

*First Lady. Avon, 2000.
Widowed when her husband is assassinated, the former first lady eludes her Secret Service bodyguards and ends up accompanying a journalist and his ex-wife's two daughters on a bizarre RV journey to their grandparents' Iowa farm.

Breathing Room. Morrow, 2002.
A self-help expert heads for Tuscany to reassess her shattered life and finds that the farmhouse she's rented for the season is owned by a film star with whom she was once very briefly involved.

Ain't She Sweet? Morrow, 2004.
High school queen and royal witch Sugar Beth Carey returns to town after three failed marriages in search of a valuable painting belonging to her late aunt, and finds a vengeful town and a teacher-turned-author she once caused to lose his job living in her aunt's old house.

What I Did for Love. Morrow, 2009.
When her personal life tanks and film star Georgie York ends up, through a bizarre set of mishaps, married to her childhood film series partner, Bram Shepard, the pair agree to pretend it's the real thing; surprisingly, it turns out that way in the end.

Call Me Irresistible. Morrow, 2011.
Meg Koranda comes to Wynette, Texas, to be in her best friend's wedding and connects (with plenty of sparks and passion) with the groom, Ted Beaudine, when the would-be bride, Lucy Jorik, leaves him standing at the altar. Links to *Glitter Baby* (1987), *Lady Be Good*, *First Lady*, and *What I Did for Love*.

Plumley, Lisa

Plumley's Contemporaries are lively, quirky, and filled with plenty of madcap humor. She also has written Western-set Historicals.

Reconsidering Riley. Zebra, 2002.
A heartbreak recovery expert takes a group of "heartbroken" women on an adventure tour and finds that the guide is the one man she herself has never gotten over.

Perfect Together. Zebra, 2003.
A single dad sportscaster forced to take part in a TV dating show in order to boost his ratings and an incognito TV series actress trying to revitalize her career are a match in this funny, screwball romp.

Perfect Switch. Zebra, 2004.
House sitting for her honeymooning celebrity twin (from *Perfect Together*), an advertising historian accepts an intriguing invitation meant for her sister, ends up trying to impersonate her for two weeks, and eventually finds romance with a man who's trying to save his film studio.

Josie Day Is Coming Home. Zebra, 2005.
A former Las Vegas showgirl returns to Donovan's Corner, Arizona, to open a dance school in an estate she's inherited, but her "enhanced" reputation makes things difficult; then there's the "handyman," who is really the owner of the estate.

Let's Misbehave. Zebra, 2007.
A recovering shopaholic is assigned a job as a nanny to the six-year-old triplets of a gorgeous football star.

Home for the Holidays. Zebra, 2008.
Home for the holidays in Kismet, Michigan, a currently disgraced celebrity stylist reconnects with a football star who is supposedly trying to match her up with his best friend.

My Favorite Witch. Zebra, 2009.
A young witch coming into her powers is compelled to return home to go through the "cusping" process with her peers in this romance that might appeal to the YA market, as well.

A Holiday Affair. Zebra, 2010.
A single mom takes her children to a Michigan B and B for Christmas, while also scoping out the place for another firm, and falls for a single dad world traveler who is part of the family that owns the inn.

Porter, Jane

Porter writes Contemporary Series Romances, primarily for Harlequin Presents, several of which are listed below; she also writes upbeat romances that will appeal to both chick lit and women's romantic fiction fans.

Hollywood Husband, Contract Wife. Harlequin Presents, 2006.
A country-bred film director and a sophisticated actor wed and then must work out their issues in this story that has a good amount of Hollywood detail.

At the Greek Boss's Bidding. Harlequin Presents, 2007.
A health-care worker is hired to convince a reclusive, disillusioned Greek playboy to accept the therapy he needs.

Sheikh's Chosen Queen. Harlequin Presents, 2008.
A school teacher is asked by a former love, a widowed Middle Eastern Sheikh, to come and help his daughters, and they rekindle the love they thought they had lost forever.

Duty, Desire, and the Desert King. Harlequin Presents, 2009.
When a dedicated playboy suddenly becomes the king of his family's desert kingdom, he goes to a matchmaker to find him a bride and is attracted to the matchmaker instead.

Putney, Mary Jo

Although Putney is noted primarily for her well-written Traditional Regency and Historical Romances, as well as some Paranormals, she has also written several Contemporary Romances that tackle serious issues. See also chapter 7, "Historical Romances."

The Burning Point. Ballantine, 2000.
Drawn home when her father is killed in a company-related demolition explosion, Kate Corsi must deal with her ex-husband when they are forced, by her father's will, to live in the same house for a year. Murder and abuse issues drive the plot of this intense story.

The Spiral Path. Berkley, 2002.
A film writer/director wants her almost-ex-husband actor to star in her film, but when it becomes clear that the script calls up such horrific memories that he may not be able to handle it mentally, she has some hard decisions to make.

Twist of Fate. Jove, 2003.
An attorney sets up her own practice and takes on a difficult death penalty pro bono case.

Quinn, Tara Taylor

Quinn writes both Contemporary Series Romances and single titles, some of which include romantic suspense elements. See also chapter 6, "Romantic Mysteries."

Just Around the Corner. Harlequin Superromance, 2001.
A professor and a psychologist are forced to rethink their ideas about long-term committed relationships when they learn a moment of passion is turning them into parents.

Where the Road Ends. Mira, 2003.
A woman goes undercover to locate her kidnapped son and the nanny she believes is responsible and is attracted to the P.I. she hired to help her.

Nothing Sacred. Harlequin Superromance, 2004.
When her daughter is raped by a stranger, bitter, divorced Martha Moore turns to the new pastor, who hides a secret past, for help. (One of Quinn's popular Shelter Valley Stories, as is the title below.)

Somebody's Baby. Harlequin Superromance, 2005.
Pregnant after an impulsive night of passion, a widow learns she may have a twin and heads for Shelter Valley to find her, and also to let the father of her baby know about the child.

Hidden. Mira, 2005.
After successfully hiding herself and her child from her abusive, influential husband for two years, Kate Whitehead comes out of hiding when her best friend goes missing, and her estranged husband is accused of killing her, as well as her friend.

A Daughter's Trust. Harlequin Superromance, 2009.
A foster mom falls in love with the uncle of one of her infant charges.

Ray, Francis

See chapter 12, "Ethnic/Multicultural Romance."

Ridgway, Christie

Ridgway's romances are sassy, sexy, unconventional, and often filled with hilarious dialogue.

> *Must Love Mistletoe*. Avon, 2006.
> After ten years away, a lawyer returns to help with the family Christmas shop and encounters her bad boy teenage love in this holiday-tinged romance.

> *I Still Do*. Silhouette Special Editions, 2009.
> A firefighter out to enjoy his bachelorhood and a quiet librarian who wants to live a little renew their school days friendship at a Las Vegas conference and end up married—and then must decide what to do about it.

Malibu and Ewe Trilogy

A knitting shop, Malibu and Ewe, attracts a surprisingly hip, interesting clientele in this series that features three half sisters (courtesy of the same sperm donor) and their unconventional extended family, and takes advantage of the current knitting craze.

> *How to Knit a Wild Bikini*. Berkley Sensation, 2008.
> A beleaguered men's magazine editor hires an unemployed chef to cook for him and keep women at arm's length by pretending to be his girlfriend in this story that has several romance lines.

> *Unravel Me*. Berkley Sensation, 2008.
> An older general's young widow finds friendship—and family—at the knitting shop and unexpected love with her late husband's aide

> *Dirty Sexy Knitting*. Berkley Sensation, 2009.
> The owner of the knitting shop finds love with a grieving man who seems bent on drinking himself to death in this final trilogy installment which also includes a mystery.

Three Kisses Trilogy

The three Baci sisters set out to save Tanti Baci (Italian for many kisses), their struggling family Napa Valley winery, by turning it into a wedding destination.

> *Crush on You*. Berkley Sensation, 2010.
> Alessandra's (Allie's) story.

> *Then He Kissed Me*. Berkley Sensation, 2011.
> Stephania's (Stevie's) story.

> *Drunk on Love*. Berkley Sensaion, 2011.
> Giuliana's (Jules's) story.

Roberts, Nora

Dubbed "America's most popular novelist" by the *New Yorker* (Lauren Collins, "Real Romance," June 22, 2009), award-winning, bestselling Roberts is arguably the Romance genre's best-known author. At the time of this writing, she has written just under two hundred novels, to say nothing of her numerous novellas and short stories, and has Contemporary Romance, both series and single-title, as well as Romantic Suspense and Fantasy, to her credit. (She also writes futuristic police procedurals, some with a touch of romance, as J. D. Robb.) Roberts's works are fast-paced, sexy, and well-written and feature engaging, believable characters, memorable dialogue, and clever plotting. She is a member of the RWA Hall of Fame. Typically, her Contemporary single titles are written as trilogies or other types of linked books. Her most recent examples, as of this writing, are included below.

See chapter 6, "Romantic Mysteries"; chapter 9, "Alternative Reality Romance"; and chapter 13, "Linked Romances."

Brides Quartet

Four childhood friends become partners in a wedding planning business called Vows.

> *Vision in White*. Berkley, 2009.
> The wedding photographer finds romance with the English teacher brother of one of Vows' clients, whom she knew in high school.

> *Bed of Roses*. Berkley, 2009.
> The wedding florist finds love with a commitment-shy man she has known for years.

> *Savor the Moment*. Berkley, 2010.
> The pastry chef and the older brother of one of her partners realize they are meant to be together.

> *Happy Ever After*. Berkley, 2010.
> Vows' manager gets her own, rather unexpected, happy ending.

BoonsBoro Inn Trilogy

The three Montgomery brothers, all involved with the family contracting business, restore a dilapidated historic—and haunted—inn in tiny Boonsboro, Maryland.

> *The Next Always*. Berkley, 2011.
> With a little help from the inn's resident ghost, architect/carpenter Beckett Montgomery finds love with an attractive war widow with three young sons.

Ross, JoAnn

Ross's contemporaries often feature a number of well-developed, likable characters, vividly realized settings, and some romantic suspense elements. See also chapter 6, "Romantic Mysteries."

> *Far Harbor*. Pocket Books, 2000.
> A divorcée returns to Coldwater Cove in Washington State to turn the town's lighthouse into an inn and finds romance with the uncle of a brain-damaged child.

> *Fair Haven*. Pocket Books, 2001.
> A world-traveling doctor goes to tiny Castlelough, Ireland, to help a dying friend with his medical practice and is attracted to a photographer who has recently learned he has an eight-year-old daughter. Slight paranormal elements.

> *Legends Lake*. Pocket Books, 2001.
> Concerned over his horse's dangerous behavior, a horse trainer seeks the help of the Irish beauty who bred the horse he intends to ready for the Kentucky Derby (and possibly the Triple Crown) and finds unexpected love in Castlelough. Follows *Fair Haven*.

Callahan Brothers

The heroes are the three Callahan brothers, Jack, Finn, and Nate, of Blue Bayou, Louisiana.

Blue Bayou. Pocket, 2002.
A divorced mom returns home to Blue Bayou and discovers her old family home, Beau Soleil, is now owned by her successful teenage love, who was driven away by her father, a now imprisoned judge.

River Road. Pocket, 2002.
A suspended FBI agent heads home to Blue Bayou and is put to work by his mayor brother as bodyguard to a TV star who is in town on location.

Magnolia Moon. Pocket, 2003.
An L.A. homicide detective comes to Blue Bayou to discover the truth of her heritage and is attracted to the town's mayor.

Shelter Bay Series
Set in a small town on the Oregon Coast, these romances feature returning Navy SEALS and include some suspense and mystery elements.

The Homecoming. Signet, 2010.
Navy SEAL Max Douchett returns to Shelter Bay and reconnects with a girl from his past, who is now a widowed single mom and the town's sheriff, when a human bone turns up on his land.

One Summer. Signet, 2011.

Ryan, R. C. (Pseudonym for Ruth Langan)
McCord Trilogy
Three estranged cousins are drawn back to the Montana ranch near Gold Fever where they grew up together to learn that they will inherit the extensive range equally if they continue their late grandfather's crazy quest for the legendary lost McCord gold.

Montana Legacy. Forever, 2010.
Jesse McCord has stayed on to help his grandfather with the ranch, but when his two far-flung cousins, as well as the love of his young life, Amy Parish, return to town and danger threatens, his life changes radically.

Montana Destiny. Forever, 2010.
Rodeo rider Wyatt McCord returns to town (and the treasure hunt) and finds romance with fiery emergency medic Marilee Trainor, as well as danger from an unknown source.

Montana Glory. Forever, 2010.
Documentary filmmaker Zane McCord has no intention of getting married, but when accountant and single mom Riley Mason walks into his life to sort out the ranch's books and accidents begin to threaten her and her daughter, Zane has second thoughts—now to convince Riley.

Seidel, Kathleen Gilles
Seidel writes complex, well-written romances filled with realistic, well-developed characters. Her recent works fall within the women's romantic fiction subgenre. Two older works (*After All These Years* and *Again*) are Rita Award winners.

Shalvis, Jill
Shalvis's romances are often adventurous, lively, and sprinkled with fun and sexy heat.

The Trouble with Paradise. Berkley Sensation, 2007.
After winning a singles cruise to Fiji, a clumsy heroine must deal with murder, a ship wreck, two attractive men—and a killer.

Wilder Trilogy
Featuring the three Wilder brothers and their wilderness adventure guide company, this series is set in the California Sierra Nevada mountains.

Instant Attraction. Brava, 2009.
An accountant and a former extreme-sports superstar find passionate adventure and healing, as well as new reasons to get on with their lives.

Instant Gratification. Brava, 2009.
A no-nonsense, big-city E.R. doctor comes to Wishful, California, to fill in at her father's clinic after he has surgery and finds romance with a sexy athlete and rescue worker.

Instant Temptation. Brava, 2010.
A biologist studying a rare coyote reluctantly takes T. J. Wilder with her when she heads into the mountains, knowing that she needs his experience but not the distraction he provides.

Lucky Harbor Series
A lively, laughter-laced series set in tiny Lucky Harbor on the Washington State coast.

The Sweetest Thing. Forever, 2011.
Simply Irresistible. Forever, 2011.
Head Over Heels. Forever 2011.

Shelley, Deborah
See also chapter 12, "Multicultural Romance."

Marriage 101. Avalon, 2008.
A new high school teacher who's a theoretical human relations expert and a coach who thinks all marriages in his family are genetically doomed find love despite their preconceptions in this sweet, funny romance with a realistic high school setting.

Spencer, LaVyrle
Spencer is a noted, Rita Award–winning writer of tender, insightful Contemporary and Historical Romances, particularly of the Americana variety. She is an RWA Hall of Fame member, and she retired from writing in 1997. See previous editions of this guide for complete bibliographies. Her Rita Awards, and its predecessor, the Golden Medallion, are listed in chapter 7, "Historical Romance."

Templeton, Karen
Wed in the West Series
Marriage is the focus in this series with a Western touch.

*A Mother's Wish. Silhouette Special Edition, 2008.
A woman who gave up her son for adoption under duress goes in search of him and finds romance with his widowed, adoptive father.

Reigning in the Rancher. Silhouette Special Edition, 2009.
A pregnant heroine resists marrying the man she loves in this poignant romance.

A Marriage-Minded Man. Silhouette Special Edition, 2009.
A single mom real estate agent and her old carpenter boyfriend reconnect and realize that they still might have a future together after all.

Welcome Home, Cowboy. Silhouette Special Edition, 2010.
A cowboy heading home to reconnect with an old friend finds romance with the friend's fiery, pregnant widow, instead.

Adding Up to Marriage. Silhouette Special Edition, 2010.

Thompson, Vicki Lewis
Thompson has a number of funny, quirky series romances to her credit, and is also well-known for her various single titles, including her Nerd series.

Nerd Series
These steamy, zany romances celebrate the delights of nerdy, intelligent heroes.

Nerd in Shining Armor. Dell, 2003.
A secretary ends up stranded on a desert island with a computer nerd and learns nerdy can be sexy.

The Nerd Who Loved Me. St. Martin's Paperbacks, 2004.
A Las Vegas single mom show girl and a nerdy accountant join forces to foil her ex-husband's plans.

Nerd Gone Wild. St. Martins Paperbacks, 2005.
A would-be wildlife photographer inherits her grandmother's nerdy personal assistant who is also has the undercover job of protecting her against a greedy relative.

Gone with the Nerd. St Martin's Paperbacks, 2005.
A gorgeous movie star takes her nerdy lawyer, also a Big Foot expert, with her into the woods to learn how to be a nerd for a role she is going to audition for.

Talk Nerdy to Me. St. Martin's Paperbacks, 2006.
A brainy inventor fashion model and a sexy, nerdy engineer have problems when someone tries to sabotage her invention.

Nerds Like It Hot. St. Martin's Paperbacks, 2006.
A witness to a murder assumes a sexy bombshell disguise and hides aboard a cruise ship full of nerds and falls for her sexy bodyguard.

My Nerdy Valentine. St. Martin's Press, 2007.
A psychology student plagued by a stalker finds romance with a stockbroker who volunteers to be her bodyguard.

Wax, Wendy
Wax's romances are funny, upbeat, modern, and often use relatively mature heroines. She also writes Women's Fiction.

7 Days and 7 Nights. Bantam, 2003.
Two talk show hosts, a feminist and a "man's man," agree to spend one week living together on camera to see which of their shows will survive based on their ratings.

Leave it to Cleavage. Bantam, 2004.
A former beauty queen puts her MBA and interpersonal skills to the test when she tries to convince the board of her family's lingerie company to take a chance on her ideas even as she covers up her thieving, cross-dressing husband's disappearance and works to avoid the hunky police chief's scrutiny.

Hostile Makeover. Bantam, 2005.
A woman must prove her business abilities to her archrival when he takes over the company after her father's heart attack in this book with a chick lit flair.

Single in Suburbia. Bantam, 2006.
Blindsided by a divorce, a suburban single mom who never quite fit in launches Maids for You (with the help of two friends) and begins working as an incognito housekeeper with hilarious and satisfactory romantic results in this insightful look at suburbia.

Wind, Ruth (Pseudonym for Barbara Samuel)

Wind's romances are touching and emotionally compelling. Recently, she has been concentrating on writing Women's Romantic Fiction under her own name, Barbara Samuel, as well as Barbara O'Neal. Her older book, *The Last Chance Ranch*, annotated in the previous edition of this book, was a Janet Dailey Award winner and a genre classic. Two other older titles, *Reckless* (1997) and *Meant to Be Married* (1998), were Rita Award winners.

In the Midnight Rain. Harper Torch, 2000.
A biographer goes to rural Texas to research a thirties jazz singer and finds romance as well as unexpected information about her past.

Woods, Sherryl

Woods is a veteran series and single-title romance author; many of her stories have an Americana feel. Her style is witty, warm, and lively.

Flamingo Diner. Mira, 2003.
A woman returns home to help with the family diner and finds love with the former bad boy police chief.

Destiny Unleashed. Mira, 2004.
A pair of former lovers reconnect when the hero challenges the heroine's family company in this romance featuring a pair of mature protagonists.

Flirting with Disaster. Mira, 2005.
Jilted at the altar, a woman returns home to volunteer her carpentry abilities for a charitable project and is attracted to the foreman who doesn't welcome her abilities.

Sweet Magnolias Series

Small Serenity, South Carolina, is the setting that ties this Americana-type women's fiction series together.

Stealing Home. Mira, 2007.
A divorced single mom becomes part owner in a women's gym and finds new love with her son's baseball coach.

A Slice of Heaven. Mira, 2007.
A woman who kicked her cheating husband out needs him to return for a variety of family and health reasons.

Feels Like Family. Mira, 2007.
A divorce attorney realizes that if she wants to have children, she needs to do something about it, but is a pastry chef with a difficult past the right father for her children?

Welcome to Serenity. Mira, 2008.
Two anti-Christmas protagonists find romance, as well as a new appreciation for the holidays, when they are forced to work together on the local Christmas festival.

Home in Carolina. Mira, 2010.
An injured single dad baseball player has difficulties convincing his former love that he's trustworthy, especially when his son's groupie mother starts causing trouble.

Sweet Tea at Sunrise. Mira, 2010.
A heroine still suffering from the emotional abuse of her former husband is reluctant to trust a former baseball player who is interested in her.

Honeysuckle Summer. Mira, 2010.
A divorced abuse victim who has become agoraphobic finds love with the new sheriff's deputy and hope for her illness.

Chesapeake Shores Series
Stories in this series are linked by characters and the small bayside town of Chesapeake Shores, Maryland.

The Inn at Eagle Point. Mira, 2009.
A New York stockbroker is called home to help rescue the family hotel and reconnects with a former love (now a loan manager), who insists she stay in town and assume the financial management of the hotel.

Flowers on Main. Mira, 2009.
An actress returns home and opens a flower shop but must deal with her former boyfriend, the only local flower supplier.

Harbor Lights. Mira, 2009.
A grieving paramedic single dad finally gets it together and finds romance with a local book store owner.

A Chesapeake Shores Christmas. Mira, 2010.
A couple ready to remarry is concerned that one of their children isn't in favor of their reunion.

Driftwood Cottage. Mira, 2011.
A single mom leaves the man she loves but who is wary of marriage and goes to live in his hometown, Chesapeake Shores.

Moonlight Cove. Mira, 2011.
Psychologist Will Lincoln loves innkeeper Jess O'Brien, but she thinks of him as a friend—until a kiss changes things.

Beach Lane. Mira, 2011.

Contemporary Category Romance

Contemporary Category Romances are basically stories written to conform to a specific pattern that has been established by the publisher. Usually produced in numbered series format, these romances tend to follow the classic boy-meets-girl, boy-loses-girl, boy-gets-girl pattern, varying, of course, within the proscribed guidelines of the individual series. However, while the plot patterns can be similar and the guidelines must be observed, these books are not carbon copies of one another, and will vary more than one might expect, even within the specific lines. Settings, style, characterization, dialogue, and quality of writing are all variables in the hands of the writer, and the differences can occasionally be startling. After all, a Harlequin Blaze by Stephanie Bond is not at all the same as one by Jo Leigh, and a Silhouette Desire by Merline Lovelace is quite different from one by Kasey Michaels. Each series has a particular emphasis or focus (e.g., mystery/intrigue, humor, adventure), and this, as well as the length of the story and the way in which sex is handled, will vary among lines. Series can range in length from 50,000 to 65,000 words or so, depending upon the line, with the shorter books (e.g., Silhouette Desire or Harlequin Romance) focusing primarily on the hero and heroine, and somewhat longer books (e.g., Silhouette Special Edition or Harlequin Superromance) often including additional subplots and peripheral characters.

A book can also be either Innocent (or Sweet) or Sensual. While the Innocent variety almost always includes a virginal (or at least not terribly experienced) heroine and concludes with a passionate kiss and usually a promise of marriage, the Sensuals can vary from lines that contain very little explicit sexual description (but lots of passionate imagery) to those that border on the erotic. As alluded to earlier, the individual books within a series are not identical; nevertheless, the parameters mentioned above are supposed to apply, and once the reader has found an acceptable series, he or she should be assured of getting something similar when it comes to length, theme, and level of sensuality in each succeeding volume of the series.

In many instances, writing guidelines detailing the particulars of the individual series are available to authors. In recent years publishers have become somewhat less prescriptive in these guidelines, opting for a more general approach and allowing the writer more latitude than in earlier years when the specifics were spelled in some detail. (For an example of one of these older versions, see the predecessor to this book, *Happily Ever After* [Littleton, CO: Libraries Unlimited, 1987], 44–45.) The current tip sheets or writing guidelines are much more succinct (listing word count, editorial contacts, and a short paragraph about the line's specific requirements) and can be found on the Harlequin website, eharlequin.com.

The early 1980s saw an explosion in the Contemporary Category Romance market and series proliferated exponentially. However, that quickly changed in the middle of the decade, and over the years, publishers consolidated and the series offerings dwindled so that today the only major publisher who is still producing pure Contemporary Category Romance is Harlequin under its Harlequin, Silhouette, and Mills & Boon imprints. (Harlequin Books' Kimani Arabesque line is discussed in chapter 12, "Ethnic and Multicultural Romance"; Harlequin Book's Steeple Hill's Love Inspired line is discussed in chapter 11, "Inspirational Romance"; and Silhouette's Nocturne line is discussed in chapter 9, "Alternative Realities Romance.") For space reasons individual authors and titles for Category Romance have not been included. However, a list of representative authors for specific series is included in the Sample Core Collection in the Appendix. A selected list of series currently being published or readily found in most libraries as of this writing is listed below. Note: The name "Silhouette" was replaced with "Harlequin" in 2011, but the content of the lines has remained the same.

Selected Category Romance Series

Harlequin American Romance

This series features mid-length, upbeat, "heartwarming stories about the pursuit of love, marriage and family in America," filled with likable characters and a good selection of supporting characters, and provides a well-defined sense of place.

Harlequin Blaze

Harlequin's sexiest series, a Blaze Romance is modern and passionate and can be light and funny or darkly erotic with the emphasis being on the developing physical relationship between the protagonists. Its mid-length allows room for some secondary characters, as well.

Harlequin Desire (Formerly Silhouette Desire)

Short, sensual contemporary romances that features modern, complex heroines, irresistible alpha-male heroes, and a plot with believable, strong, and dramatic emotional conflict.

Harlequin Intrigue

This series of mid-length, suspenseful contemporary romances combines a passionate love story with spine-tingling intrigue, taut suspense, and the unexpected.

Harlequin Presents (Mills & Boon Modern Romance)

A series of short, sensual "escapist romantic fantasies" in which characters are swept off to exotic, glamorous locales where they can blissfully give in to love.

Harlequin Romance (Mills & Boon Cherish Romance)

Replacing the original Harlequin Romance and Silhouette Romance lines, this series has more depth than its predecessors and features short, heartwarming romances overflowing with sexual tension and engaging, emotionally involved protagonists. International and inclusive in tone.

Harlequin Romantic Suspense (Formerly Silhouette Romantic Suspense)

Fast-paced suspenseful adventure provides the background for strong compelling romance between strong, complex protagonists in these mid-length, danger-filled stories that are rife with sexual tension and a high degree of sensuality (formerly called Silhouette Intimate Moments).

Harlequin Special Editions (Formerly Silhouette Special Editions)

These mid-length, sensual contemporary romances make use of high emotional tension, well-rounded characters, contemporary issues, and believable situations.

Harlequin Superromance

Harlequin's series for longer stories, these sophisticated, contemporary romances focus on "today's woman in today's world" and feature multidimensional characters, fairly complex storylines, and a high degree of sensuality.

Mills & Boon Medical Romance

Intense, gripping, highly emotional romances that focus on life-and-death issues in medical or hospital settings, these stories often feature doctors, nurses, and other health care professionals as protagonists and can range from sweet to passionate. British emphasis.

Women's Romantic Fiction

Essentially a blend between the Traditional Contemporary Romance (or occasionally Period Romance) and mainstream Women's Fiction, Women's Romantic Fiction has become increasingly popular in recent years, especially as more and more romance authors (e.g., Barbara Samuel, Kristin Hannah, Jude Deveraux, Kathleen Gilles Seidel, Patricia Gaffney) move toward the broader Women's Fiction and mainstream arenas. While these stories have strong romance plotlines, they also have definite mainstream tendencies and, like much of traditional Women's Fiction, are complex, multifaceted tales in which growth or triumph of the woman is more important than the development or success of the romantic relationship. Ideally, of course, both occur. Many books of this type span a number of years and have elements in common with certain types of sagas and some continuing or linked books. Not surprisingly, the boundaries of this evolving romance type are rather fluid and remain open to discussion.

Selected Women's Romantic Fiction Bibliography

The works and writers listed below are merely a sampling of those who fall within this designation.

Bostwick, Marie
Cobbled Court Series
This character-rich series is centered around the Cobbled Court Quilting Shop in historic New Bern, Connecticut.

A Single Thread. Kensington, 2008.
A recent divorcée moves from Texas to Connecticut, realizes her dream of opening a quilting shop, and attracts three women with whom she forms deep and important friendships. Illness plays a part in this book, as well.

A Thread of Truth. Kensington, 2009.
A woman fleeing an abusive husband goes to work at the quilting shop and gains the strength to stand up to her abuser when he tracks her down.

A Thread So Thin. Kensington, 2010.
A college senior is torn between her budding art career and marriage when she receives an unexpected proposal.

Bradford, Barbara Taylor
Bradford's novels often focus on the glamorous, sometimes exotic, world of the rich and famous, as well as the ambition, greed, betrayal, passion, and sometimes danger, that accompany it. Many of her works are linked by family and character. (See previous editions of this guide for earlier works.) See also chapter 13, "Linked Romances."

Where You Belong. Doubleday, 2000.
A photojournalist must deal with the death and betrayal of her lover, family, and career issues, and a new love interest in this story set against the devastation of the Balkan War.

Three Weeks in Paris. Doubleday, 2002.
Four artists are invited back to Paris for the eighty-fifth birthday of the head of their art school and must come to terms with a disagreement that broke up their friendship years ago.

Delinsky, Barbara

Although her earlier titles are Contemporary Romances, her current books are primarily mainstream Women's, sometimes romantic, Fiction. Her books are well-crafted, emotionally compelling, and often focus on family dynamics and include serious social issues. Recently, a number of her earlier works were reprinted. (See previous versions of this guide for earlier titles.)

Lake News. Pocket Books, 1999.
With her career and life devastated by malicious false media story, a musician heads home to Lake Henry, New Hampshire, to heal and reconnects with a man from her past who is now the small town's newspaper editor in this story that takes a hard look at the results of media excesses.

The Vineyard. Simon & Schuster, 2000.
The impending marriage of a widowed Rhode Island vineyard owner causes conflict among family members on both sides and puts the young mother hired to help with a family history project in a difficult position in this story that provides an insightful look back at life during the World War II years and the sacrifices many made.

The Woman Next Door. Simon & Schuster, 2001.
A widow's pregnancy causes three couples whose husbands have a history of cheating to reexamine their marriages.

The Accidental Woman. Simon & Schuster, 2002.
Lake Henry, New Hampshire, is the setting for this story that features a paraplegic heroine, Poppy Blake, who works to prove the innocence of her best friend who is accused of a fifteen-year-old murder. Intrigued by the story, an investigative reporter is attracted to Poppy, as well.

Flirting with Pete. Scribner, 2003.
When psychotherapist Casey Ellis inherits her psychologist father's Boston townhouse, complete with staff, she also discovers the diary of a young woman named Jenny, whose tragic story interweaves with Casey's in this intriguing story that has both mystery and romance.

The Summer I Dared. Scribner, 2004.
Surviving a deadly boating accident causes a woman to rethink her life, her future, and possibly a new love in this Maine-set story.

Looking for Peyton Place. Scribner, 2005.
A writer returns to Middle River, New Hampshire, a paper mill town, as well as the town that Grace Metalious based *Peyton Place* on, to find the truth about possible mercury poisoning—and runs into plenty of resistance.

Family Tree. Ballantine, 2007.
The birth of a child who looks African American causes problems for the marriage of a couple where the husband is from a heritage-proud New England family.

The Secret Between Us. Doubleday, 2008.
A doctor takes the responsibility when her daughter accidentally hits and injures a man one rainy night in a story that skillfully depicts the damage a lie can cause.

While My Sister Sleeps. Doubleday, 2009.
A runner's massive heart attack and subsequent coma causes her sister and the rest of the family to explore their relationships and make decisions about the future.

Not My Daughter. Doubleday, 2010.
Three college-bound high school seniors form a pact to get pregnant and raise their children together, and their mothers, including the high school principal and also a single mom, must deal with the judgmental small town fallout.

Duarte, Judy
Duarte also writes Contemporary Series Romances.

Fairbrook
The small town of Fairbrook is the setting for this mainstream, gently Inspirational romantic trilogy.

Mulberry Park. Zebra, 2008.
A child's letter to God draws a grieving young woman back into the world where she makes a difference in the lives of people around her.

Entertaining Angels. Zebra, 2009.
The lives of a single mom, a new pastor, and a host of others are transformed in any number of ways by a mysterious transient named Jesse.

The House on Sugar Plum Lane. Zebra, 2010.
A woman brings her young daughter to Fairbrook in search of her past and finds hope, healing, love, and second chances.

Gaffney, Patricia
Noted for her earlier Historical Romances, Gaffney now writes Women's Fiction.

The Saving Graces. Harper, 1999.
Four women who have supported each other though life's difficulties for years have the most difficult challenge when breast cancer targets one of them.

The Circle of Three. HarperCollins, 2000.
A woman gets a second chance at happiness after her husband dies when she helps a love from her past with a strange ark-building project in this multigenerational story with fascinating family dynamics.

Flight Lessons. HarperCollins, 2002.
Forced to come to terms with her past when her current existence shatters, a woman returns home to make peace with the aunt she thinks betrayed her and her mother years ago.

The Goodbye Summer. HarperCollins, 2004.
A woman raised by her grandmother learns to take charge of her future when her grandmother moves into a convalescent home.

Mad Dash. Shaye Areheart Books, 2007.
Told from two points of view, this lively story shows how a six-month separation affects the slightly stale twenty-year marriage of a couple who think they want something different.

Hannah, Kristin

Hannah's earliest titles are romances, but her current titles are primarily mainstream women's fiction that focus on family and interpersonal relationships. Several that include some romantic interest are listed below. (See earlier editions of this guide for previous works.)

On Mystic Lake. Ballantine, 2000.
A woman back home to heal from an unexpected divorce is reunited with the husband and young daughter of her late best friend who devastated her family by committing suicide.

Angel Falls. Crown, 2001.
Two men who love the same woman are drawn together when an accident puts her in a coma.

Summer Island. Crown, 2001.
In the San Juan Islands to recover from a broken leg and stay out of the limelight when her career is shattered by scandal, a popular advice guru is reunited with her estranged daughter, who has a vengeful agenda of her own, in this mother-daughter reconciliation story that includes a bit of romance, as well.

Distant Shores. Ballantine, 2002.
An artist whose marriage is unraveling reassesses her life when her husband accepts a new job and they end up living on opposite sides of the continent.

Between Sisters. Ballantine, 2003.
Two half-sisters reconnect when the elder, a troubled divorce attorney, heads for a mountain resort in Washington to check into her younger sister's upcoming marriage and finds unexpected romance as well as potential tragedy.

Comfort and Joy. Ballantine, 2005.
A woman betrayed by her ex-husband and her sister finds healing and love in this poignant holiday romance that has an unusual, supernatural twist.

Magic Hour. Ballantine, 2006.
A child psychiatrist returns to her small Pacific Northwest hometown to help with a young girl who appears to be feral, and is attracted to the town doctor in the process.

Kendrick, Beth

Kendrick's lively, modern tales slide between chick lit and women's fiction, and should appeal to fans of both.

My Favorite Mistake. Downtown Press, 2004.
A world-traveling culinary writer goes home to Minnesota to help her pregnant, abandoned little sister and reconnects with her former love.

Exes and Ohs. Downtown Press, 2005.
A child psychiatrist takes on a young patient who turns out to be the son that the current man in her life never knew he had, and now he must deal with the soap star mom who thinks they should reconcile in this nonstop, hilarious romp.

Fashionably Late. Downtown Press, 2006.
An aspiring fashion designer chucks her controlling fiancé and heads for Los Angeles in pursuit of her dreams in this funny, upbeat story.

Nearlyweds. Downtown Press, 2006.
Discovering that their new marriages weren't legal, three not especially satisfied women rethink things in this funny book.

The Pre-Nup. Bantam Discovery, 2008.
Pre-nups cause varied problems for three best friends in this story that focuses on friendship, loyalty, and love.

Second Time Around. Bantam, 2010.
Four college classmates are each left a quarter of a million dollars to pursue their dreams when one of their friends dies.

Keyes, Marian
Keyes's work, which can sometimes be considered chick lit, is current, lively, and darkly funny, and often deals with serious issues.

Walsh Sisters
The five Irish Walsh sisters are the focus of this lively series.

Watermelon. Avon, 1995.

Rachel's Holiday. William Morrow, 1998.
A bit into drugs, Rachel is taken off to a clinic and finds romance in the process.

Angels. William Morrow, 2002.
Maggie heads for glittery Los Angeles after she learns her husband has had an affair, and she must decide what she wants out of life.

Anybody Out There? William Morrow, 2006.
A seriously injured Anna Walsh goes home to recuperate at her parents' home in Ireland and then returns to reestablish her life at a New York cosmetics firm.

Last Chance Saloon. William Morrow, 1999.
Four friends deal with the difficulties of being in their thirties—until disaster strikes and nothing will ever be the same again.

Sushi for Beginners. William Morrow, 2003.
Three women with very different life situations connect in the Dublin magazine publishing world.

The Other Side of the Story. William Morrow, 2004.
The publishing world is the background for this story that involves three women and their entwined lives.

This Charming Man. William Morrow, 2008.
The effects of a charismatic, charming Irish politician—who is anything but—on the lives of four of the women with whom he interacted are stunningly described in this hard-hitting book.

Macomber, Debbie
A veteran writer of Contemporary Romances, Macomber's most recent works are more Women's Fiction than pure romance.

Cedar Cove Series
This series chronicles the lives of the residents of the mythical Cedar Cove, a town patterned on Macomber's hometown of Port Orchard, Washington, located on the Kitsap Peninsula in Puget Sound. Characters and issues continue from book to book, although each story is complete in itself. *1225 Christmas Tree Lane* is the last book in this series. (Note: The related *A Cedar Cove Christmas* is listed in the Contemporary Romance Bibliography above.)

16 Lighthouse Road. Mira, 2001.
204 Rosewood Lane. Mira, 2002.
311 Pelican Court. Mira, 2003.
44 Cranberry Point. Mira, 2004.
50 Harbor Street. Mira, 2005.
6 Rainier Drive. Mira, 2006.
74 Seaside Avenue. Mira, 2007.
8 Sandpiper Way. Mira, 2008.
92 Pacific Boulevard. Mira, 2009.
1022 Evergreen Place. Mira, 2010.
1105 Yakima Street. Mira, 2011.
1225 Christmas Tree Lane. Mira, 2011.

Blossom Street

The stories in this ongoing series revolve around the neighborhood shops (a yarn shop, in particular) on Blossom Street in Seattle and the people who frequent them. (Note: The related *Christmas Letters* is listed in the Contemporary Romance bibliography above.)

The Shop on Blossom Street. Mira, 2004.
A Good Yarn. Mira, 2005.
Susannah's Garden. Mira, 2006.
Back on Blossom Street. Mira, 2007.
Twenty Wishes. Mira, 2008.
Summer on Blossom Street. Mira, 2009.
Hannah's List. Mira, 2010.
A Turn in the Road. Mira, 2011.

Monroe, Mary Alice

The American South, especially South Carolina, strong women, interpersonal and family dynamics, and nature and environmental issues are often part of Monroe's novels which are known for providing readers with a good sense of time and place.

Girl in the Mirror. Mira, 1998.
A facially disfigured woman becomes beautiful after reconstructed plastic surgery—and then her body begins to reject the implants.

The Book Club. Mira, 1999.
A monthly book club forms the framework for this compelling story of five different suburban women at critical points in their lives.

The Four Seasons. Mira, 2001.
The three Season sisters fulfill the dying wish of their fourth sister, Merry—going on a cross-country search for the child she gave up as a teenager.

The Beach House. Mira, 2002.
A woman returns home to South Carolina when her mother becomes ill and soon becomes involved with protecting loggerhead sea turtles; she finds romance, as well.

Skyward. Mira, 2003.
A pediatric nurse is attracted to the naturalist who runs the birds-of-prey rehabilitation center when she becomes a nanny for his young diabetic daughter.

Sweetgrass. Mira, 2005.
A family struggles against increasing odds to hold on to its Southern Carolina plantation, and their way of life.

Swimming Lessons. Mira, 2007.
A single mom marine biologist who is active in loggerhead sea turtle rescue finds romance with a colleague—and then her young daughter's birth father shows up. Sequel to *The Beach House*.

Time Is a River. Pocket, 2008.
A cancer survivor takes up fly fishing in the North Carolina mountains and finds emotional healing, as well as an intriguing mystery.

Last Light over Carolina. Pocket, 2009.
A woman looks back over her thirty-three-year-long marriage while waiting for her husband, a shrimp boat captain, who is injured and alone at sea with a storm gathering.

The Butterfly's Daughter. Gallery, 2011.
This mother-and-daughter road-trip story highlights the plight of the monarch butterflies.

Morsi, Pamela
Morsi, an earlier writer of award-winning Period Americana Romances, now focuses more on women's fiction that features realistic, touching characters facing difficult, often believable situations—often witty and humorous.

Doing Good. Mira, 2002 (reprinted in 2010 as *The Social Climber of Davenport Heights*).
A self-centered, shallow real-estate agent, miraculously saved from a fatal car accident when she vows to do good if she survives, turns her life around with remarkable results.

Suburban Renewal. Mira, 2004.
A woman shocks her husband when she insists on renewing their vows on their twenty-fifth wedding anniversary or getting a divorce.

By Summer's End. Mira, 2005.
Two sisters get to know their paternal grandparents and learn about the father they never knew when their mother undergoes cancer treatment.

Bitsy's Bait and BBQ. Mira, 2007.
Ellen goes with her flighty younger sister, Katy, a divorced single mom, and ends up running a bait and BBQ restaurant in a quirky Ozark community—and then must deal with a custody battle when Katy's ex comes calling.

Last Dance at Jitterbug Lounge. Mira, 2008.
A driven, estranged pair rediscover the important things in life when they go back to rural Oklahoma after one of their grandfathers suffers a stroke in this story that has a lot of historical detail.

Red's Hot Honky Tonk Bar. Mira, 2009.
When she suddenly becomes responsible for her two grandchildren while their mom is in Afghanistan, bar owner Red Cullens learns there is a lot more to her young musician boyfriend than she ever expected.

The Bikini Car Wash. Mira, 2010.
Returning home to care for her ailing father, a woman reopens the family carwash, adds a bikini-clad female staff (which upsets the conservative townsfolk), and finds romance in the process.

O'Neal, Barbara (Pseudonym for Barbara Samuel)

*The Lost Recipe for Happiness. Bantam Discovery, 2009.
Hired by a charismatic film director and restaurateur to revitalize his restaurant in Aspen, Elena Alvarez deals with her past, her difficult staff, and her growing feelings for her boss in this touching story of a woman finding herself and love, as well.

Pilcher, Rosamunde

Although most noted for her elegant, complex Women's Fiction novels, many of Pilcher's earlier works were very much in the Romance tradition. (See the previous edition of this guide for Pilcher's earlier works.)

Winter Solstice. St. Martin's Press, 2000.
A woman who has already dealt with the loss of a significant other helps a good friend with the loss of his wife and daughter and finds new love in this heartwarming story set in rural England.

Rice, Luanne

Rice's books are often thoughtful and richly emotional. Many of her earlier Romances (not all are listed here) include more Romance; her most recent titles are primarily women's fiction. The seaside community of Hubbard's Point, Connecticut, is the setting for several of her novels.

Safe Harbor. Bantam, 2002.
An artist returns home to care for her two orphaned nieces and is attracted to a younger man.

That Perfect Summer. Bantam, 2003.
When her husband disappears leaving questions of embezzlement behind, a woman finds secrets, betrayal, and an old love.

Dance with Me. Bantam, 2004.
Returning home to help care for her failing mother, a woman sets out to find the daughter she was forced to give up years earlier and is attracted to her daughter's uncle.

Sand Castles. Bantam, 2006.
A daughter's impending marriage brings her estranged father back into the family circle, with miraculous healing and romantic results.

What Matters Most. Bantam, 2007.
In this story of love, separation, and miracles, two people raised in the same orphanage are reunited. Linked to *Sand Castles*.

Edge of Winter. Bantam, 2007.
A woman and her daughter put their lives back together in a small community on the Rhode Island coast and find love and romance in the process.

Light of the Moon. Bantam, 2008.
A woman goes to France to heal after the death of her mother and finds romance with a man who has a resentful daughter. Linked to *Edge of Winter*.

The Geometry of Sisters. Bantam, 2009.
A complex novel of sisters and family dynamics.

The Deep Blue Sea for Beginners. Bantam, 2009.
A young girl goes to Capri to find the mother who deserted her and her sister years earlier because of mental problems.

Richards, Emilie

Richards has written Contemporary Romance, both series and single-title, and most recently is writing Women's Fiction. She won a Rita in 1994 for her 1993 series title, *Dragonslayer*.

Whiskey Island. Mira, 2000.
Niccolo Andreani's delving into an old murder impacts the lives of the three Donaghue sisters, who own the struggling Whiskey Island Saloon.

Fox River. Mira, 2001.
A woman's hysterical blindness is linked to a forgotten tragedy in this family-oriented story full of mystery, heart-aching love, and long-hidden truths.

The Parting Glass. Berkley, 2003.
Peggy Donaghue and Nick Andreani deal with the destruction of the Whiskey Island Saloon, Peggy finds romance and mystery on Ireland, and all three sisters, including Casey, the youngest, finally sort out their confused heritage in this novel that is a continuation of *Whiskey Island*.

Shenandoah Album

Tom's Brook, Virginia, a tiny town in the Shenandoah Valley, is the setting for the stories in this touching, often romantic series that takes its titles from quilt names.

Wedding Ring. Mira, 2004.
Three generations of women are reunited when they come across a series of quilts as they help clean up the family matriarch's Shenandoah Valley cabin.

Endless Chain. Mira, 2005.
A small town activist pastor is attracted to his new church sexton, who has a hidden, dangerous past of her own.

Lover's Knot. Mira, 2006.
A city journalist who comes to restore herself and her husband's grandmother's cabin finds help for her troubled marriage, as well.

Touching Stars. Mira, 2007.
A woman brings her war-wounded ex-husband to stay at her B and B so he can reconnect with his three sons—and maybe her, as well.

Sister's Choice. Mira, 2008.
A woman agrees to become a surrogate mother for her sister and brother-in-law.

Happiness Key
Friendship and the relationships of women are the focus of this Florida-set series.

Happiness Key. 2009.
Taking over her incarcerated ex-husband's dilapidated Happiness Key development in Florida, Tracy DeLoche bonds with the diverse assortment of women who currently live on the property.

Fortunate Harbor. 2010.
The story continues as the women get on with their lives and the Tracy's husband gets a new trial.

Sunset Bridge. Mira, 2011.
A storm stirs things up as the story continues at Happiness Key.

Samuel, Barbara
Samuel's realistic, well-crafted stories feature fully developed characters and often deal with difficult, emotionally gripping issues. She also writes as Ruth Wind and Barbara O'Neal.

*No Place Like Home. Ballantine, 2000.
A woman and her teenage son return to Pueblo, Colorado, with a friend who is dying of AIDS and must deal with her past in this poignant story that also includes a satisfying romance.

A Piece of Heaven. Ballantine, 2003.
A divorced recovering alcoholic is drawn to a sympathetic adobe maker as she struggles with her addiction and reestablishing her relationship with her teenage daughter.

The Goddesses of Kitchen Avenue. Ballantine, 2004.
Four women at different places in their lives find the strength and courage to reach for their dreams—and for love.

*Lady Luck's Map of Vegas. Ballantine, 2005.
A forty-year-old web designer takes her mother on a trip to Las Vegas to revisit her youth and to try to find her missing schizophrenic twin sister, and learns some family secrets. She also makes some major decisions of her own in this main-stream women's fiction.

Madame Mirabou's School of Love. Ballantine, 2006.
The destruction of her old house propels a divorcée to take a chance on fulfilling her dreams and maybe finding a new love.

Seidel, Kathleen Gilles
Seidel excels in depicting the wide ranges and subtleties of family and emotional relationships.

Summer's End. HarperPaperbacks, 1999.
A newly married middle-aged couple invite their adult children and families to spend the summer with them in a cabin in Northern Minnesota in this story that beautifully depicts the range of family dynamics.

Please Remember This. Avon, 2002.
A woman who has ignored anything to do with her fantasy author mom and her mom's cult following returns to her late mother's home town to come to terms with her past and

finds love in the process. Interesting detail regarding a buried nineteenth-century steamboat.

Smith, Deborah

Smith's emotionally rich stories feature memorable characters, touches of humor, and plenty of Southern charm.

The Stone Flower Garden. Little Brown, 2002.
A wealthy, lonely girl and a stonecutter's son who fall for each other as children are separated by a murder, but they reconnect as adults when they finally uncover the truth as well as a number of devastating family secrets.

Charming Grace. Little, Brown, 2004.
The widow of a heroic Georgia Bureau of Investigation agent sets out to sabotage a film star's attempt to make her late husband's life into a brainless action flick but is attracted to the star's bodyguard despite their apparent opposing interests. Funny, heart-wrenching, and Southern.

The Crossroads Cafe. BelleBooks, 2006.
A beautiful celebrity, badly burned in a car accident, seeks solace in her grandmother's Appalachian cottage and meets a man who, having lost his family in 9/11, needs healing, as well.

A Gentle Rain. BelleBooks, 2007.
A woman's search for her birth parents takes her to a ranch in Florida that has become a haven for mentally and physically challenged people.

Snoe, Eboni

See chapter 12, "Multicultural Romance."

Steel, Danielle

Although a few of Steel's earlier novels are romances, the vast majority of what she writes now is Women's Fiction. Below is a recent title that does qualify as a romance.

H.R.H. Delacorte, 2006.
A princess falls in love with a doctor when they work together in Africa in this story that has its share of glitz, danger, and emotional angst but does deliver a happy ending.

Stone, Katherine

Another Man's Son. Mira, 2004.
A doctor falls in love with the son of her older friend and mentor who had agreed to father a child with her just before he dies.

Thomas, Jodi

Although best known for her award-winning Western Romances, Thomas brings contemporary Texas to life with empathetic characters, realistic interpersonal interactions, and good descriptive detail. (See also chapter 7, "Historical Romances.")

The Widows of Wichita County. Mira, 2003.
Five very different women bond after four of their husbands are killed and one is alive but burned beyond recognition in an oilrig accident that changes all of their lives forever.

Finding Mary Blaine. Mira, 2004.
The realization that she was the real target in a women's clinic bombing sends affluent, but insecure, Blaine Anderson fleeing to an alien, but strangely communal, life on the streets, where she gains personal strength as she struggles to avoid a killer, contact her husband who thinks she's dead, and protect the baby she just learned she is carrying.

The Secrets of Rosa Lee. Mira, 2005.
When reclusive Rosa Lee Altman leaves her estate to the town of Clifton Creek, Texas, the town must decide what to do with it and ends up unearthing surprising secrets that some don't want revealed.

Twisted Creek. Berkley, 2008.
Allie Daniels and her grandmother head for Texas and the property and small cafe she has surprisingly inherited from an uncle she is sure she didn't have and finds a new life and love with the undercover government drug agent who is investigating the suspicious events going on in the quiet resort community.

Rewriting Monday. Berkley, 2009.
A disgraced big-city reporter heads to her mom's old hometown in Texas and goes to work for the local paper. But when the threats start and things get violent, she and her boss must figure out which one of them is the target.

Welcome to Harmony. Berkley, 2010.
In an effort to belong somewhere, a young woman goes to Harmony, Texas, the hometown of an elderly woman she'd been friends with before the woman died, and pretends to be her granddaughter.

Somewhere Along the Way. Berkley, 2010.
After two years in town, Reagan Trent becomes more and more involved with the people around her.

Trollope, Joanna

Trollope's engaging, insightful, thought-provoking novels are usually set in rural or small town England, involve several families, and often focus on troubled relationships.

Marrying the Mistress. Viking, 2000.
A man's announcement that he is divorcing his wife to marry his mistress causes turmoil for all involved.

Second Honeymoon. Bloomsbury, 2006.
A lively pace and wry humor set the tone for this story of would-be empty-nesters and the complications that follow.

Friday Nights. Bloomsbury, 2008.
A man who comes into the life of one of the members of a close group of women friends throws everyone in the group off balance in a number of ways.

Wax, Wendy

The Accidental Best Seller. Berkley, 2009.
When Kendall Aims heads for the hills after she learns her publisher and her husband are both dropping her, her three long-time friends and writers rush to her aid to make sure that the final book in her contract is finished—and must deal with the scandal and fallout when the resulting literary collaboration, full of examples from the authors' own lives, becomes a best seller.

Magnolia Wednesdays. Berkley, 2010.
An investigative reporter learns what is really important in life when her career falls apart, she learns she is pregnant, and she moves to Atlanta—where she starts reporting pseudonymously on life in the South—to be with family.

Wiggs, Susan
Wiggs has written both Historical and Contemporary Romances. Many of her recent Contemporaries have a mainstream, as well as pure romance. See also chapter 13, "Linked Romances."

Summer by the Sea. Mira, 2004.
A couple from vastly different backgrounds are reunited years after they were abruptly torn apart and find that the passion is still there, and so are some old tensions.

The Ocean Between Us. Mira, 2004.
A Navy couple struggles to save their marriage.

Lakeside Cottage. Mira, 2005.
A single mom brings her young son to the family lakeside cabin for the summer and becomes involved with a military medic and an orphaned teenage runaway.

Table for Five. Mira, 2005.
When former golf pro and confirmed bachelor Sean Maguire becomes guardian to his brother's three orphaned children, he reluctantly accepts the help of Lily Robinson, the children's mother's best friend, as they struggle with grief, acceptance, and getting on with life—and love.

Just Breathe. Mira, 2008.
A cartoonist leaves her unfaithful husband, returns home, and renews an acquaintance with a boy she liked in high school, who is now a firefighter and single dad—and then she discovers she's pregnant.

Marrying Daisy Bellamy. Mira, 2011.

Chick Lit/Mom Lit and the Like

Spawned by Helen Fielding's groundbreaking *Bridget Jones's Diary* (1996) and propelled by Candice Bushnell's collection of newspaper column essays, *Sex and the City* (1997), which morphed into a startlingly popular HBO television series as well as a movie, this lively, sassy, irreverent subgroup deals with the life, loves, and varied troubles of women and often their assorted friends (generally in their twenties or thirties, but possible older, as well) as they try to get on with their lives. Funny, trendy, and often realistic, Chick Lit hovers between Romance and Women's Fiction and has generated a number of related "Lits," such as Mom (or Mommy) Lit, Hen Lit, Lady Lit, and so on. Chick Lit is one of the more recent fiction types to emerge and, while it was all the rage several years ago, as of this writing it is on the wane.

Selected Chick Lit/Mom Lit Bibliography

The works and writers listed below are merely a sampling of those who fall within this designation.

Alexander, Carly

Ghosts of Boyfriends Past. Strapless, 2003.
A woman in New York "celebrates" the holidays as she remembers her past loves.

The Eggnog Chronicles. Red Dress Ink, 2004.
Three women eventually get their lives together in three linked stories in this holiday-set story.

Banks, Melissa

The Girls' Guide to Hunting and Fishing. Viking, 1999.
A now classic collection of short stories in which the narrator, Jane Rosenal, describes what she learns from her observations of the romantic antics of her relatives and others as she grows from a teenager into adulthood.

Brown, Josie

True Hollywood Lies. Avon, 2005.
The daughter of a Hollywood actor struggles to stay afloat when her dad dies and she ends up destitute, thanks to one of her father's vindictive ex-wives.

Impossibly Tongue-Tied. Avon, 2006.
An aspiring actress works as a sex phone operator to give her husband a shot at a Hollywood acting career, but when he succeeds, everything changes.

Secret Lives of Husbands and Wives. Downtown Press, 2010.
A woman's efforts to help the husband in a difficult divorce become accepted by their neighbors has interesting results when the other wives in the neighborhood try to seduce him. (Note: This book is scheduled to become the basis for a series on network television in the 2012–2013 season.)

Browne, Hester

Funny, breezy, Brit chick lit.

The Little Lady Agency. Pocket, 2006.
A reserved British businesswoman creates a sexy alter ego and opens a highly successful escort agency (without the sex), and unexpectedly falls for an American client in this funny romp.

Little Lady, Big Apple. Pocket, 2007.
Our heroine ditches her alter ego and goes with her boyfriend to New York, and discovers a new market for her services in this sequel to *The Little Lady Agency*.

The Little Lady Agency and the Prince. Pocket, 2008.
Royalty mixes things up in this funny, fast-paced sequel to *Little Lady, Big Apple*.

The Finishing Touches. Pocket, 2009.
Left as a baby on the doorstep of a prestigious British finishing school and raised by the titled owners, Betsy Phillimore returns to use her modern expertise to keep the school from folding in this lively, funny romp.

Cabot, Meg

Well known for her Young Adult novels, in particular *The Princess Diaries*, Cabot also has written chick lit for the adult market.

The Boy Next Door. Avon, 2002.
A gossip columnist for the *New York Journal*, a photo-newspaper, takes over the care of her injured neighbor's pets and falls for the neighbor's nephew—who isn't exactly what he seems. Cabot uses e-mail entries to tell this story and the two that follow.

Boy Meets Girl. Avon, 2004.
Life at the *New York Journal* becomes more complicated than usual when Kate Mackenzie becomes involved in a firing that ends up in litigation.

Every Boy's Got One. Avon, 2004.
A comic-strip writer goes with her friends as they elope to Italy and has her hands full trying to keep the best man from stopping the wedding in this story that is told via e-mails and journal entries.

Queen of Babble

The adventures of overly talkative, chubby, fashion history major Lizzie Nichols are the focus of this lively trio.

Queen of Babble. William Morrow, 2006.
Lizzie goes to England, ends up in France, and meets handsome, and princely, charmer Luke—who has a greedy girlfriend.

Queen of Babble in the Big City. William Morrow, 2007.
Back in New York living with Luke and trying to finish up her degree, Lizzie juggles her legal receptionist and "volunteer" wedding dress specialist duties, her friend's difficulties, and a marriage-wary boyfriend.

Queen of Babble Gets Hitched. William Morrow, 2008.
Lizzie's wedding dress career takes off as she ponders her feelings about her own upcoming wedding.

Insatiable. William Morrow, 2010.
A psychically gifted (or cursed) dialogue writer for a TV soap with a new vampire plot thread becomes involved with a real vampire in this zingy chick lit take on the vampire theme.

Cach, Lisa
Dating without Novocaine. Red Dress Ink, 2002.
A seamstress pushing thirty puts a "plan" to snare a husband into action in this funny, earthy tale.

Curnyn, Lynda
Engaging Men. Red Dress Ink, 2003.
An aspiring actress struggles with both her career and her boyfriends, as one after another they leave her to become engaged to others.

Bombshell. Red Dress Ink, 2004.
A gorgeous, blonde heroine in her mid-thirties deals with potential job loss, lack of eligible men, and possible rejection by her biological mother in this upbeat story that will appeal to more mature readers.

Garcia, Eric

Cassandra French's Finishing School for Boys. Regan Books, 2005.
A wacky, over-the-top satiric spoof of the Chick Lit genre, complete with Hollywood glitz and a dash of crime.

Giffin, Emily

Giffin's stories of women and their choices are unconventional, lively, and sometimes unexpected. Many of the stories have characters in common, and her later novels drift into the larger women's fiction arena.

Something Borrowed. St. Martin's Griffin, 2005.
A woman ends up sleeping with—and eventually marrying—her spoiled best friend's fiancé in this unusual story that makes the betrayers sympathetic.

Something Blue. St. Martin's Griffin, 2006.
Pregnant and abandoned, a self-centered heroine leaves New York for England to stay with an old friend, who eventually forces her to change her selfish ways.

Baby Proof. St. Martin's Griffin, 2007.
A career woman who divorces her husband when he says he wants children (a dealbreaker in their childless-by-choice marriage) has second thoughts.

Love the One You're With. St. Martin's Griffin, 2008.
A married woman runs into an old flame and wonders how she can be happy with her husband when she still has feelings for her old love.

Heart of the Matter. St. Martin's Press, 2010.
An academic who gave up her career to raise her two children suspects that her doctor husband is attracted to the high-powered lawyer mother of one of his patients in this story that is told from the viewpoints of both women.

Green, Jane

Mr. Maybe. Broadway, 2002.
A London public relations worker who wants it all is caught between a poor writer and a rich banker.

Babyville. Broadway, 2003.
Three friends deal with different motherhood issues in this lively, breezily told story.

To Have and To Hold. Broadway, 2004.
A woman who "became" the woman her husband wanted her to be rethinks her choices when they move to the States and she realizes she needs to do something about her troubled marriage.

Swapping Lives. Viking, 2005.
A London magazine journalist and a Connecticut homemaker swap places for the sake of an article and gain needed insights into themselves and their lives.

The Other Woman. Viking, 2005.
A woman hoping for a good relationship with her husband's family finds problems with her manipulative mother-in-law.

Second Chances. Plume, 2007.
A group of former classmates are reunited by the death of a one of their own.

Dune Road. Viking, 2009.
A divorcée leaves her wealthy, diamond-studded life and moves to coastal Connecticut and a job with an author—and then new problems arise.

Green, Risa
Notes from the Underbelly. NAL, 2005.
A Bel Air high school guidance counselor tries to hide her pregnancy from her boss as she works to get one of her students into a prestigious school in a story that focuses on the physical aspects of pregnancy.

Tales from the Crib. NAL, 2006.
The heroin from the previous novel has her baby and discovers what it's *really* like to be a mom.

Halliday, Gemma
High Heels Mystery Series
The quirky, funny, murder-laced, madcap adventures of L.A. shoe designer Maddie Springer.

Spying in High Heels. Love Spell, 2006.
Maddie is drawn into a deadly mystery and the company of sexy detective Jack Ramirez when her boyfriend disappears along with a lot of money.

Killer in High Heels. Love Spell, 2007.
Maddie heads to Las Vegas to reconnect with her father and runs into an undercover Jack Ramirez, as well as a killer and a whole lot of shoe-smuggling trouble.

Undercover in High Heels. Love Spell, 2007.
Maddie takes a job as a TV show's wardrobe assistant to help Jack Ramirez get to the bottom of a stalking case that turns into murder.

Alibi in High Heels. Love Spell, 2008.
Fashion and murder with a Parisian flair.

Mayhem in High Heels. Love Spell, 2009.
Maddie and Jack prepare for their wedding, but murder gets in the way.

Scandal Sheet. Love Spell, 2009.
A young Los Angeles gossip columnist who lives in a retirement community finds romance with the bodyguard her boss hired to protect her when her life was threatened.

Holliday, Alesia
American Idle. Making It, 2004.
A television show production coordinator falls for a hunky carpenter in his funny romp that is perfect for fans of *American Idol*.

Nice Girls Finish First. Berkley Sensation, 2005.
The tough head of marketing has thirty days to get someone to call her "nice" or she forfeits a trip to Italy in this story that has links to *American Idle*.

Seven Ways to Lose Your Lover. Berkley Sensation, 2006.
A "break-up" expert starts her own business and begins dating a man who blames her for ruining his last romantic relationship.

Jump, Shirley

Jump also writes Contemporary Series Romances.

Boston Recipe Romance Quartet

The following delicious romances are set in Boston and all include recipes.

The Bride Wore Chocolate. Zebra, 2004.
A serious chocoholic begins to have doubts about her upcoming wedding when plans begin going awry and she is attracted to another.

The Devil Served Tortellini. Zebra, 2005.
A woman struggles to lose weight for her high school reunion, but a chef who thinks she is fine the way she is takes issue with her plan.

The Angel Craved Lobster. Zebra, 2005.
A small town girl heads for Boston to learn all about sex and passion and connects with a reformed bachelor who's sworn off casual sex.

The Bachelor Preferred Pastry. Zebra, 2006.
A pastry shop owner wins a wealthy bachelor in a charity auction and plans to use him in her ad campaign, but unexpected complications cause intriguing problems.

Kinsella, Sophie

Kinsella has written a number of British chick lit novels but is best known for the following series.

Shopaholic Series

Witty romps that all revolve around the shopping and spending habits of British financial "expert" Becky Bloomwood.

Confessions of a Shopaholic. Bantam, 2001.
Becky Bloomwood, a columnist for a financial magazine, has serious shopping and financial debt issues.

Shopaholic Takes Manhattan. Delta, 2002.
Becky heads for a shopping spree in New York City with advertising executive and boyfriend Luke.

Shopaholic Ties the Knot. Dial Press, 2003.
Having found her niche as a personal shopper, Becky gets engaged to boyfriend Luke and then must deal with two separate weddings planned by each of their mothers.

Shopaholic and Sister. Dial Press, 2004.
Back from her globe-trotting honeymoon, Becky is stunned to learn she has a half-sister—a very dowdy, frugal half-sister.

Shopaholic and Baby. Dial Press, 2007.
Becky struggles to balance a husband, a job, and pregnancy—along with the shopping, of course.

Mini-Shopaholic. Dial Press, 2010.
Becky faces the challenges of her two-year-old daughter who shows all the symptoms of becoming a bargain hunter like her mom.

Kwitney, Alisa

Does She or Doesn't She? Avon A, 2003.
An aspiring soap opera writer with an inattentive lawyer husband (and a daughter) is attracted to the sexy plumber who is a lot more than he seems.

On the Couch. Avon, 2004.
A mid-thirties psychologist is mistaken for a call girl by a detective when they meet as the result of a murder.

Mancusi, Marianne

A Connecticut Fashionista in King Arthur's Court. Love Spell, 2005.
The title says it all about this lighthearted, quirky time travel story that zaps a modern-day heroine back to the time of King Arthur.

What, No Roses? Love Spell, 2006.
A modern-day TV reporter is whisked back to Roaring Twenties Chicago to stop a massacre and finds love where she least expects it in this Chick Lit time travel story.

A Hoboken Hipster in Sherwood Forest. Love Spell, 2007.
With a little gypsy aid, a present-day woman goes back to medieval England and ends up showing Robin Hood and his merry men how the story *really* goes.

Markham, Wendy (Pseudonym for Wendy Corsi Staub)

Markham's romances are swift, witty, and modern.

Slightly Series

This lighthearted series follows the convoluted adventures of insecure, sometimes neurotic, Tracey Spadolini as she sorts her life out and eventually finds love, fulfillment, and happiness.

Slightly Single. Red Dress Ink, 2002.
Tracey "reinvents" herself during a summer in New York.

Slightly Settled. Red Dress Ink, 2004.
Tracey is attracted to Jack, who is her boss's roommate, but there are other men around, as well.

Slightly Engaged. Red Dress Ink, 2006.
Tracey is concerned that she and Jack have been together for a year-and-a-half and aren't engaged—yet.

Slightly Married. Red Dress Ink, 2007.
Tracey and Jack get married.

Slightly Suburban. Red Dress Ink, 2008.
Tracey and Jack try the suburban life.

Love, Suburban Style. Forever, 2007.
A single mom takes her teenage daughter back to her home town, moves into a supposedly haunted house, and reconnects with her high school flame, who is now a single dad and lives next door.

That's Amore. Forever, 2008.
A man's wedding plans change when he meets a pair of psychic sisters in this lively romantic comedy with a paranormal twist.

Messina, Lynn
Fashionistas. Red Dress Ink, 2003.
An associate magazine editor is caught up in battle between rivals at a glitzy magazine.

Mim Warner's Lost Her Cool. Red Dress Ink, 2005.
A teen trend forecaster, or "coolhunter," realizes her boss has some major problems when she begins making bizarre predictions that could sink their company.

Perrin, Kayla
See also chapter 12, "Multicultural Romance," and chapter 13, "Linked Romances."

Sweet Spot. Avon Trade, 2006.
A journalist ends up in one difficult spot after another, and then she goes to work for a tabloid and falls for a sports figure she is covering.

Porter, Jane
Flirting with Forty. 5 Spot, 2006.
A single mom celebrates her fortieth birthday in Hawaii and has a fling with a surfer in this growing-up story that has a lot in common with YA coming-of-age stories.

Odd Mom Out. 5 Spot, 2007.
A free-thinking biker, single mom, and advertising executive tries to fit in to the snobbish, super-rich circles she is inhabiting for the sake of her nine-year-old daughter, but is more successful in attracting the attentions of a handsome businessman.

Mrs. Perfect. 5 Spot, 2008.
A woman with everything loses it all and must learn to stand on her own, and gets help from the heroine in *Odd Mom Out.*

Easy on the Eyes. 5 Spot, 2009.
A thirty-something television journalist fears she'll lose her job if she doesn't get some plastic surgery and finds herself attracted to the surgeon.

She's Gone Country. 5 Spot, 2010.
With her marriage shattered, a top model takes her three teenage sons home to her family's Texas ranch and finally realizes she needs to let the past go and embrace her new present, and the love that might go along with it.

Sanders, Annie
Funny, lively, and very British. Note: Most of these titles have been also released in North America.

Goodbye, Jimmy Choo. Orion, 2004.
Two vastly different city women find friendship and salvation of an unlikely sort when they are forced to follow their husbands into the provincial English countryside in this hilarious, very British romp.

Busy Woman Seeks Wife. Orion, 2007.
A busy career woman hires a "wife" to help with the housekeeping when her mother moves in temporarily; things get interesting when the "wife's" brother, an out-of-work actor, takes over for his sister.

Getting Mad, Getting Even. Orion, 2009.
Revenge is sweet and funny when the owners of Domestic Angels, a women's household help agency, help wives get even with their straying husbands.

Senate, Melissa
See Jane Date. Red Dress Ink, 2003.
Jane embarks on a hilarious series of blind dates in order to find a real boyfriend (not the imaginary one she's been telling everyone about) in time for her cousin's wedding.

The Solomon Sisters Wise Up. Red Dress Ink, 2003.
A series of personal and family issues bring three sisters (two full and one half) together in this hilarious romp.

Whose Wedding Is It Anyway? Red Dress Ink, 2004.
A designer for *Wow Weddings* is having her wedding featured in (and paid for) by the magazine, but rethinks the whole thing when her boss takes over.

The Breakup Club. Red Dress Ink, 2006.
Four people dealing with various types of broken romantic relationships connect through family and work, and help each other with their problems.

Love You to Death. Red Dress Ink, 2007.
A columnist must work with a detective she liked in high school to clear herself of her boyfriend's murder.

Questions to Ask Before Marrying. Red Dress Ink, 2008.
Twin sisters go on a cross-country trip—one to find the father of her baby, the other to rethink her engagement—and learn unexpected things about their family and themselves.

Swain, Heather
Flawed, often likable characters struggle with realistic issues in these quirky, offbeat stories.

Eliot's Banana. Downtown Press, 2003.
A mid-twenties woman struggles with what—and who—she wants in life.

Luscious Lemon. Downtown Press, 2004.
The owner of a successful New York restaurant is determined not to let her unexpected pregnancy get in the way of her independence and career, but when she miscarries, her emotional recovery is more difficult than she expects.

Yardley, Cathy
L.A. Woman. Red Dress Ink, 2002.
A small town woman moves to Los Angeles because of a man and finds new friends, a new life, and a new lease on life.

TAKE FIVE!

Five Contemporary Romance Favorites:

- **Jennifer Crusie**—*Welcome to Temptation*
- **Rachel Gibson**—*True Confessions*
- **Susan Elizabeth Phillips**—*Call Me Irresistible*
- **Emilie Richards**—*Endless Chain*
- **Susan Wiggs**—*Table for Five*

Chapter 6

Romantic Mysteries

Mystery magnifies danger [in Romance] as the fog the sun.

Charles Caleb Colton (1925)

It is the dim haze of mystery that adds enchantment to pursuit.

Antoine de Rivarol, Comte de Rivarol

Definition

> **Romantic Mysteries**—Romance novels that include significant mystery, adventure, suspense, Gothic, or thriller elements, these stories usually combine separate Romance and Mystery/Suspense plotlines that are linked and become closely interwoven and resolved by the end of the book.

Romantic Mysteries, as their designation indicates, are combinations of Mystery-adventure and Romance. These stories usually employ two distinct plotlines—one Romance, one Mystery. The two plotlines may begin separately but are eventually linked in some way, most often through the heroine. As the story progresses, the story lines increasingly overlap and intertwine, ultimately arriving at the successful, nearly simultaneous, conclusion of both.

Because of the dual story lines, there is often a certain amount of difficulty in identifying the genre to which a book belongs—is it a Romance or is it a Mystery? The general rule is: If the emphasis is on the romance, the story is a Romantic Mystery; if the emphasis is on the mystery, the story is Mystery-Suspense. This is, however, a much simpler rule to say than to apply because many authors seem to have a foot in each camp. For example, the classic Cold War spy thrillers of Helen MacInnes often have a female protagonist and a strong romance storyline; they also have a hard-core espionage plotline. Similarly, Mary Stewart produces suspense stories with equally strong mystery and romance plotlines. There is, however, a difference between the two. Stewart uses the mystery to enhance the romance storyline; in MacInnes's work, the romance is generally secondary to the espionage aspects. Although both authors are read by Mystery and Romance fans alike, MacInnes's works are usually considered in the Spy/Espionage subgenre, while Stewart's are classed as Romantic Mysteries or Romantic Suspense. It is worth noting, incidentally, that such crossover in readership is not uncommon. Readers of Romantic Mysteries often read Mystery-Suspense stories as long as there is a strong love interest in the story, just as mystery fans will read Romantic Mysteries that contain effective suspense storylines. Gothic and Romantic Suspense novels and their authors are often claimed by both genres, as their inclusion in a number of mystery, crime, and suspense reference sources clearly demonstrates. The various editions of Allen J. Hubin's classic bibliographies, the most recent of which is *Crime Fiction IV: A Comprehensive Bibliography, 1749–2000.* (Shelburne, Ontario: Battered Silicon Dispatch Box, 2003); *Twentieth Century Crime and Mystery Writers* (New York: St. Martin's, 1985), and John Charles's *The Mystery Readers' Advisory: The Librarian's Clues to Murder and Mayhem* (Chicago: American Library Association, 2002) are only a few examples.

Included within the Romantic Mystery subgenre are two distinct, yet closely related types—the novel of Romantic Suspense and the Gothic Romance. Although the specific conventions, story lines, and geographical and historical settings can vary widely, the common denominator of both types is the threatened, vulnerable—although rarely helpless—heroine. Thrown, either by choice or chance, into a mysterious, puzzling, or frightening situation, she seeks to unravel the mystery, solve the crime, or catch the bad guy, thereby placing herself in danger. At the same time, she becomes romantically involved with the hero. Complications ensue, tensions mount, and at some point the heroine usually finds herself at the mercy of the villain(s) and often in fear for her life. Nevertheless, by the story's end, the mystery is properly solved, the villains get their comeuppance (often at the hands of the heroine in more recent stories), and the hero and heroine are safe in each other's arms.

In general, the difference between the two subtypes is one of setting, convention, and tone, rather than basic plot. Novels of Romantic Suspense are usually given a contemporary setting (hence today's common designation, Contemporary Romantic Suspense), although mysteries of this type set in the future or in the past, especially the Regency or Victorian periods, are currently creating some interest. Gothics are often, but certainly not always, set in the past, often during the Victorian period. In the novel of Romantic Suspense, the heroine is usually out and about, involved with people, and may travel to a number of far-flung, exotic places; in the Gothic, she usually travels to an isolated mansion, castle, or estate—and stays there. While ensconced in the castle, the Gothic heroine may witness mysterious, unexplained events, sometimes of a supernatural nature. Conversely, the heroine of Romantic Suspense rarely experiences anything that cannot be explained rationally. In addition, the pacing and style of the Romantic Suspense novel is usually lively, energetic, upbeat, proactive, and direct, whereas that of the Gothic is often measured and more circumspect. The two types may also differ when it comes to the mode of narration. Although both are typically told from the heroine's point of view, Gothics often employ the more intimate first-person mode, which also serves to increase the heroine's sense of isolation, whereas Romantic Suspense stories are usually narrated in the third-person subjective mode. While the heroine is usually the primary narrator, using additional viewpoints, especially the hero's or, more recently, the villain's, is a growing trend, especially in Romantic Suspense, where it adds depth to the plot and can heighten the suspense aspects.

The characters also vary between the types. The hero and the villain, of course, are common to both, but their typical personal characteristics may differ greatly. The sardonic, brooding hero of the classic Gothic is hardly the engaging, competent hero of the Romantic Suspense. However, while in the Romantic Suspense novel the heroine may interact with a large number of people, including friends, colleagues, fellow travelers, local natives, and even criminal types, in the Gothic she relates almost exclusively to a small, intimate group of assorted family members, acquaintances, servants, and, of course, to the house itself—which in the Gothic assumes the role of a major character. An obvious corollary of this is that in the novel of Romantic Suspense, the heroine is most often threatened by strangers (although the villain may eventually turn out to be someone she knows and even likes, as in Mary Stewart's *Wildfire at Midnight*); in the Gothic, her greatest danger comes from someone close to her. The atmosphere of the novel of Romantic Suspense is open, active, expansive, and dangerous; that of the Gothic is closed, secretive, and ingrown, but equally dangerous.

Obviously, all Romantic Mysteries do not divide themselves so easily along these rather arbitrary lines, and elements from one type have long been found in the other, often blurring their traditional distinctions. At the same time, some of these mystery, suspense, and Gothic elements are finding their way into other Romance subgenres, as well. In addition, the lines between the Romantic Mystery and the larger Mystery/Thriller genre and, in some cases, Action/Adventure, have become increasingly fuzzy, no doubt due, at least in part, to the large number of Romance writers crossing over into the popular Mystery/Thriller or Action-oriented genres, as well as the continuing tendency toward genreblending. Gothic elements, of course, are finding compatible homes within other genres, as well, especially some of the darker subsets of the Fantasy/Paranormal genre. While this cross-fertilization results in some amazingly creative and delightful new stories (and all genres and subgenres do need to evolve), it also makes it more difficult to relegate some of these books to a specific category. Fortunately, this is not always a problem because many readers do not consciously distinguish so narrowly among types, reading Romantic Suspense and mainstream thrillers and mysteries or Gothics and paranormal fantasies, all with a strong romance plotlines, with equal enjoyment. Nevertheless, defining the subgenre is becoming an increasingly subjective task, and when it comes right down to it, there is only way to be certain what category a particular book is in—read it and decide for yourself.

Note: By either accident or design, books of this type are often mislabeled. Romantic Suspense is occasionally labeled Mystery or Fiction and Gothics are sometimes designated as Romantic Suspense or even Fantasy or Paranormal. Once again, read for yourself and decide.

Appeal

The particular appeal of the Romantic Mystery is to our innate sense of adventure, excitement, and mystery. From our earliest games of peek-a-boo and hide-and-seek to the telling of ghost stories around the campfire or at a slumber party, we all have enjoyed the vicarious delight of being frightened in safety. Most of us, however, do not lead lives in which danger and adventure are everyday realities. Indeed, if we did, most likely we would find being stalked by methodical murderers, threatened by terrorists, or haunted by shimmering specters uncomfortable, unnerving, and not at all exciting or romantic. We want our excitement, mystery, and romance, but we want it without the danger. This is just what the Romantic Mystery provides—the thrill of adventure, mystery, and terror, together with the guarantee (usually) of a happy, romantic ending—all without risk!

Advising the Reader

While general readers' advisory information is provided in chapter 3, several points to consider specifically when advising Romantic Mystery readers are given below.

- Many readers of Romantic Suspense also read Mystery-Suspense or Thrillers. For example, a Mary Stewart fan might enjoy reading books by Helen MacInnes or Patricia Wentworth, and someone who likes Amanda Quick's lively, suspenseful Historicals may also enjoy books by Anne Perry, Rhys Bowen, or Robin Paige.
- Conversely, people who enjoy Mystery-Suspense may also like Romantic Mysteries. Evelyn Anthony, Elizabeth Peters, and Mary Stewart are often popular with both groups, as are some of the authors listed in the paragraph below.
- In addition, a number of Romance and Romantic Suspense writers have ventured into the Mystery-Suspense or Thriller genres (e.g., Iris Johansen, Tami Hoag, Eileen Dreyer, Nora Roberts as J. D. Robb, Tess Gerritsen, Lisa Gardner). Readers familiar with these writers' other works may like their Mysteries, as well.
- Readers who enjoy Gothics may also enjoy some of the Alternative Reality Romances, especially those within the Paranormal subgroup. For example, Christine Feehan's Carpathian vampire Romances have a definite Gothic feel, as do many by Amanda Ashley, Maggie Shayne, and Sherrilyn Kenyon.
- It is also important to determine whether a reader likes all types of Romantic Mysteries or is partial to a particular variety. A confirmed Gothic fan may not enjoy Mysteries by Elizabeth Peters (perhaps preferring to read her alter ego Barbara Michaels, instead), and a Romantic Suspense aficionado may detest Victoria Holt.
- For the reader who is completely new to the subgenre, recommend "tried and true" works by some of the major authors (e.g., early works by classic writers Mary Stewart, Phyllis Whitney, and Victoria Holt, and the more recent Romantic Suspense novels of Sandra Brown, Nora Roberts, Heather Graham, Linda Howard, Suzanne Brockmann, and Jayne Ann Krentz), and expand from there.

Brief History

Romantic Mysteries have their particular historical origins in the late-eighteenth-century literary Gothics (see discussions in the "Early Gothic Prototypes" and "Gothic Romance" sections). Inspired by Walpole's original Gothic novel, the chilling, supernatural *The Castle of Otronto* (1764), Ann Radcliffe in her popular works, including the classic *The Mysteries of Udolpho*, tempered the terror and horror with the elements of romance and sentimentality, at the same time explaining away the supernatural happenings as the deliberate, "natural" work of the villain. She also may have been influenced in some degree by the work of Clara Reeve who emphasized the past, using its unfamiliarity to create an atmosphere of mystery and terror. Radcliffe's works were tremendously popular during her lifetime (1764–1823), influencing not only contemporary writers, but those who followed her as well.

Although a variety of forms of the Gothic novel flourished in late-eighteenth- and early-nineteenth-century England, it was those of the Sentimental (à la Radcliffe) and Historical (à la Reeve) types that found the most favor in the United States. The other major type, the Terror Gothic (Walpole and a slightly later writer, Matthew "Monk" Lewis, were best known for this variety), held little appeal for the majority of Americans. Its elements were seen most often in the work of serious writers such as Edgar Allan Poe and Nathaniel Hawthorne. (Interestingly, it is the Terror Gothic, through its influence on the development of the mystery/thriller and novels of detection, that is indirectly responsible for many aspects of the modern-day novels of Romantic Suspense.) Most popular Gothic Romances read in America were of British origin, although there were some domestic writers successfully working in the genre, such as Sally Wood and Isaac Mitchell. Eventually, interest in the Gothic began to wane both here and abroad, and its various conventions drifted into other literary genres. (Mysteries, Science Fiction, Melodrama, and even the Western all reflect the Gothic influence.)

However, it was the works of the American women writers of the mid-nineteenth century that most closely carried on the Gothic tradition within the United States. (The Gothic tradition in England was being continued by a number of writers, including the Brontës.) Although many of their novels were domestic-romantic as opposed to Gothic, works by such popular writers as E.D.E.N. Southworth often employed a number of Gothic elements (e.g., orphaned heroines, lost inheritances, mistaken identities, isolated castles, lecherous villains, dashing heroes, and contrived coincidences). Another popular writer of the period was Bertha M. Clay, the pseudonym for English romance writer Charlott M. Brame, that was used after her death as a house name by her New York publisher for a group of people who produced Gothics for a popular dime novel series. Many of these novels still had European-type settings and characters (America obviously presented a problem in that it had no nobility and few castles). However, as time passed, local backgrounds and history began to be used more frequently, and by the end of the century, American history had achieved a validity of its own and its use in romantic novels was commonly accepted.

Although Gothic elements continued to be used in many popular romantic novels, it wasn't until the publication of *Rebecca* in 1938 by Britain's Daphne Du Maurier that the modern prototype for the contemporary Gothic novel appeared. *Rebecca* was popular and extensively read, but widespread interest in the Gothic Romance in general did not occur until the 1960s. Sparked by the 1960 publication of Victoria Holt's *Mistress of Mellyn* (an English Gothic Romance highly reminiscent of *Rebecca*), the demand for Gothic Romances and other Romantic Mysteries increased dramatically in both England and America. Writers, such as Mary Stewart, Phyllis Whitney, Dorothy Eden, and to some extent Anya Seton, who had already published novels of Romantic Suspense and Gothic Romance, found themselves caught up in this new wave of popularity. However, this movement not only renewed interest in the works of established authors, it also created a demand for new writers—launching the careers of a host of authors including Catherine Gaskin, Evelyn Anthony, and Susan Howatch.

After the 1960s, the popularity of Romantic Mysteries diminished somewhat, and by the mid-1970s many people were predicting the total demise of the subgenre. But the Romantic Mystery did not die, and by the mid-1980s the Gothic was on the rise once more, this time in the form of the new sensual Gothic. Classic Gothic heroines, for all their spunk and curiosity, are a fairly timid breed—and reference to sex, other than for kisses, chaste embraces, and unexplained feelings of euphoria and lightheadedness, is strictly forbidden. Zeroing in on the fact that a growing number of Romance readers enjoyed reading spicier books with more assertive heroines, Signet (New American Library) launched a new series of sexy Gothics in 1986. Romantic Suspense was also on the move, and by the end of the decade, interest was such that several publishers had added separate Romance lines that featured Romantic Suspense plotlines (e.g., Harlequin Intrigue, Avalon Mystery Romance).

Interest in both Romantic Mystery subtypes continued into the 1990s, with several publishers adding Gothic Romance lines and most houses actively seeking even more Romantic Suspense manuscripts. The Gothic reached a high point in 1993 with the launching of Silhouette Shadows, a line of Gothically tinged Romances. But the boom was short-lived and by the mid-1990s, interest had waned and most Gothic lines had been quietly discontinued. Romantic Suspense, on the other hand, continued to expand, and by the middle of the decade the trend was such that new writers were emerging, notable writers who had left the subgenre were returning (e.g., Mary Stewart), and a noticeable number of established Romance writers were either crossing over to the subgenre itself or incorporating dashes of mystery or suspense into the types of Romances they were already writing.

Romantic Suspense roared into the next decade and currently continues to be strong. While it might be tempting to say that the Romantic Suspense is hot and the Gothic is not, this would not be quite accurate, because despite the fact that the Gothic as a specific subgenre is still no longer being published in great numbers, many of its classic elements (e.g., isolated settings, old mysteries, family secrets, unexplained happenings, supernatural characters, a menacing or brooding atmosphere, a sense of impending doom) are alive and well—and living in almost any other Romance subgenre you can name. For example, Regencies have been known to play host to vampires, psychics are increasingly routine in Romantic Suspense (as are vampires and werewolves), ghosts and "unexplained happenings" appear in Paranormals, and isolated houses, brooding atmospheres, and other Gothic conventions are common in many Historical Romances, and are found increasingly in Romantic Suspense. Obviously, the Gothic has not lost its appeal—it has simply reinvented itself—either by changing form (or in some cases merely changing its label because currently "Paranormal" has much more cachet that "Gothic") or by spinning off various components and letting them migrate into other subgenres. With the recent rise of the Paranormal Fantasy Romances, especially the vampire, werewolf/shapeshifter, and "others-among-us" varieties (e.g., Christine Feehan's Dark [Carpathian] series, Kresley Cole's Immortals after Dark series), it could seem as though elements of the Gothic have been completely appropriated by the Paranormal subgenre. However, as of this writing, several new authors have appeared on the scene who seem to have a firm grip on the Gothic style, so the subgenre may yet survive. What happens next remains to be seen—however, whatever the result, the elements of the Gothic will always be there; they just might not always be where you might expect to find them.

Romantic Suspense

> **Romantic Suspense**—Romantic Mysteries, often with contemporary settings, are chilling, fast-paced, suspenseful stories that tend to be crime-oriented, sometimes gritty and gruesomely explicit, and can be set anywhere in the world

The novel of Romantic Suspense is in many ways the feminine counterpart of the male adventure story. Deriving directly from the mystery/detective and spy stories (which in turn had been influenced by the original horror Gothics), this subgenre is exemplified by fast-paced tales filled with action, mystery, suspense, and, of course, romance. A number of authors produced stories of this type during the first half of the twentieth century but it wasn't until the Romantic Mystery boom of the late 1960s that the type achieved general popularity. Although there are a number of highly competent authors of Romantic

Suspense, it is generally acknowledged that Mary Stewart set the standard for the subgenre. Even though the subgenre has evolved significantly since she first started writing, Stewart's works, especially the earlier ones, are considered classic examples of the type and are still the ones against which all others are judged.

In recent years, the Romantic Suspense subgenre has grown phenomenally, partly because of the overall surge of interest in Mysteries and Thrillers, and partly because an increasing number of both new and veteran Romance writers have moved in the Romantic Suspense direction. The significant number of publishers that have added dedicated Romantic Suspense lines to their offerings in the past decade is only one indication that interest is strong. The genre has grown in other ways, as well, adapting to current political and social situations and reader preferences with ease. Today's Romantic Suspense heroine is just as likely to be a lethal karate black belt tracking down drug lords or a military special ops agent infiltrating terrorist cells as she is to be a small town school teacher stalked by a serial killer or a woman on the run from an abusive spouse. This active, physically fit heroine, capable of taking care of herself and sometimes the hero, as well, is a new, additional model for the subgenre, and despite the short-lived success of the Silhouette Bombshell line in the mid-2000s, she seems to be here to stay. Romantic Suspense has been popular with both writers and readers for a number of years, and although the market will continue to have its ups and downs, the subgenre is important and is likely to remain in demand.

Classic Romantic Suspense Authors

(See previous editions of this guide for additional information.)

Eberhart, Mignon Good (1899–1996)
An early writer of atmospheric thrillers featuring female protagonists as sleuths, Eberhart wrote over fifty novels beginning with *The Patient in Room 18* (1929).

Gilbert, Anna—The Look of Innocence (1975) Romantic Novelists Association Major Award winner.

Elizabeth Peters (Barbara Mertz)—Jacqueline Kirby Series, Vicky Bliss Series, Amelia Peabody Series.

Mary Stewart—Madam, Will You Talk? (1955), **Wildfire at Midnight** (1956), **Thunder on the Right** (1957), **My Brother Michael** (1959), **The Ivy Tree** (1961), **The Moon-Spinners** (1962), **This Rough Magic** (1964), **Airs Above the Ground** (1965), **The Gabriel Hounds** (1967), **Wind off the Small Isles** (1968), **Thornyhold** (1988), **The Stormy Petrel** (1991), **Rose Cottage** (1997), and two Gothics Romances **Nine Coaches Waiting** (1958) and **Touch Not the Cat** (1976).

The writer who set the standards for the Romantic Suspense genre.

Selected Romantic Suspense Bibliography

The following authors are known for their contributions to Romantic Suspense, although they may also write in and be noted for works in other subgenres. Only their Romantic Suspense novels are listed below; any other Romance works included will be discussed in the appropriate chapters. Consult previous editions of this guide for authors, titles, or annotations that may have been dropped.

Adair, Cherry

Most of Adair's sexy Romantic thrillers are part of her globe-trotting T-FLAC (Terrorist Force Logistic Assault Command) series, which involve the members of a secret counterterrorist group. Her latest T-FLAC novels feature characters with supernatural powers.

Out of Sight. Ballantine, 2003.
A gorgeous T-FLAC sniper and the team leader set out to bring down a terrorist who has access to biochemical weapons.

On Thin Ice. Ballantine, 2004.
A veterinarian and her late husband's partner (also a secret T-FLAC agent) enter the Iditarod and become the target of terrorists.

Edge Trilogy

The three Edge brothers, all T-FLAC operatives with paranormal powers, in this trilogy that introduces Adair's new psi-T-FLAC group which is hush-hush even within the larger organization.

Edge of Danger. Ballantine, 2006.
Edge of Fear. Ballantine, 2006.
Edge of Darkness. Ballantine, 2006.

Night Trilogy

Three wizard foster brothers, who are psi-T-FLAC operatives, fight terrorists around the globe.

Night Fall. Ballantine, 2008.
Border wars, a mysterious deadly disease, and a diabolical villain bring a psi-T-FLAC operative and an impulsive, fearless publicist together in a tiny African country.

Night Secrets. Ballantine, 2008.
A psi-T-FLAC agent and a journalist meet in a Rio plastic surgery spa and uncover a number of deadly secrets.

Night Shadow. Ballantine, 2009.
Wizards of varying degrees, doppelgangers, and a host of other paranormal elements abound in this adventure that ties up Adair's latest trilogy within her larger series.

Alden, Jami

Alden writes steamy stories and also writes Erotic Romance.

Gemini Men Trilogy

Mystery, danger, and hot Romance swirl around the three Taggart brothers who run Gemini Security.

Caught. Brava, 2008.
Kept. Brava, 2009.
Unleashed. Brava, 2009.

Andersen, Jessica

Anderson also writes Contemporary Romance and Urban Fantasy. Interestingly, amnesia seems to play a critical part in many of her works.

Secret Witness. Harlequin Intrigue, 2004.
A forensic lab tech enlists the aid of a detective when she is threatened by a murderer who wants her to alter DNA evidence.

Rapid Fire. Harlequin Intrigue, 2006.
A criminal psychology expert, plagued by selective memory loss, must work with her former academy instructor in order to track down the criminals.

Classified Baby. Harlequin Intrigue, 2007.
A woman on the way to tell a former one-night stand that they are about to have a baby witnesses a bombing and becomes a killer's target.

Snowed in with the Boss. Harlequin Intrigue, 2009.
A secretary and her millionaire SEAL boss deal with a blizzard, as well as mob thugs, in this lively thriller.

Mountain Investigation. Harlequin Intrigue, 2009.
A woman needing protection from her terrorist ex-husband finds help from an FBI agent who lost family members in a terrorist bombing. Colorado Rockies setting.

Internal Affairs. Harlequin Intrigue, 2009.
An undercover detective, wounded and without memory, instinctively seeks out the woman he loves and brings danger along with him.

Anthony, Evelyn (Pseudonym for Evelyn Ward-Thomas)
Anthony's first books were historical fiction. Later she turned to Romantic Suspense of the thriller variety, specializing in well-crafted, compelling tales of international crime, espionage, and intrigue. Although love is a strong motivating factor in most of her works, the stories don't always end happily. Many of her novels are available in a variety of formats, and recently some of her older works have been reissued under different titles. (See the previous editions of this guide for a bibliography.) See also chapter 6, "Historical Romance."

Barton, Beverly (Pseudonym for Beverly Beaver)
Barton's chilling, often terrifying, thrillers often involve twisted stalkers or serial killers, some are linked by character or place, and most are set in the South. Some recent titles are listed below.

Cherokee Point Trilogy
Set in Cherokee Point, a small Tennessee town in the Smokey Mountains, and filled with sadistic murders, this trilogy is all the more frightening and unnerving because of its peaceful setting.

> *The Fifth Victim*. Zebra, 2003.
> *The Last to Die*. Zebra, 2004.
> *As Good as Dead*. Zebra, 2004.

Killing Her Softly. Zebra, 2005.
The prime suspect in a murder and the victim's cousin meet when they try to hire the same top-notch attorney.

Close Enough to Kill. Zebra, 2006.
A killer who woos, tortures, and kills his victims is causing problems for a pair of law enforcement officers in a small Southern town.

A Time to Die. HQN, 2007.
A woman who remembers nothing of a ten-year-old assassination she witnessed suddenly becomes the target of someone who wants to be sure she doesn't remember.

The Dying Game. HQN, 2007.
Beauty contest winners are targeted in a bizarre series of murders.

The Murder Game. HQN, 2008.
The partner of the killer in *The Dying Game* begins a new "game," with an FBI agent as his ultimate victim.

Dying for You. HQN, 2008.
When a female bodyguard to a South American heiress is accidentally kidnapped, her former boss comes to her rescue.

Silent Killer. Zebra, 2009.
A crazed killer targets pastors in the small Alabama town of Dunmore, and the detective on the case reconnects with his high school love, the widow of one of the victims.

Dead Trilogy

A trilogy linked by character, place, and the Powell Detective Agency, which plays a part in some of Barton's other novels.

Dead by Midnight. Zebra, 2010.
A serial killer stalks the high school sweetheart of the sheriff in this book that uses the same setting as *Silent Killer.*

Dead by Morning. Zebra, 2011.
A particularly vile serial killer is at the heart of this chiller.

Dead by Nightfall. Zebra, 2011.

Bond, Stephanie

Bond's Romantic Suspense tales are funny, quirky, and sometimes hover between the two subgenres. See also chapter 5, "Contemporary Romances."

I Think I Love You. St. Martin's Paperbacks, 2002
Three sisters at odds are reunited when their parents threaten to separate and the three need to help liquidate the family antique business in this offbeat story with more than a few complications.

Kill the Competition. Avon, 2003.
A divorcée moves to Atlanta for a fresh start and ends up suspected of killing her toxic boss when the body ends up in the trunk of her car.

Party Crashers. Avon, 2004.
A woman's search for her missing former boyfriend who is suspected of murder involves crashing some upper-crust parties and meeting a wealthy media mogul in this lively, complex suspenseful mystery.

Whole Lotta Trouble. Avon, 2004.
Three woman editors scheme to get back at a smarmy literary agent, but when he ends up dead, they are faced with difficult choices.

Finding Your Mojo. Avon, 2006.
An attorney, separated from her first love years ago by a witness protection program, hopes for a new life in Mojo, Louisiana, but finds danger and death, as well as her former love, who doesn't recognize her.

Body Movers

Carlotta Wren, series heroine, helps her brother transport corpses by night and works at a pricey department story during the day. This series is crime rather than Romantic Suspense, but it is being mentioned because it will appeal to some of her fans.

Body Movers. Mira, 2006.
2 Bodies for the Price of 1. Mira, 2007.
3 Men and a Body. Mira, 2008.

Charmed Killer Trilogy

These are three linked books within the Body Movers series that focus on a serial killer who leaves charm bracelets as "calling cards."

4 Bodies and a Funeral. Mira, 2009.
5 Bodies to Die For. Mira, 2009.
6 Killer Bodies. Mira, 2009.

Brady, Kate

*One Scream Away. Forever, 2009.
A woman struggles between trusting a former FBI agent and dealing with things on her own when the man who tried to kill her is released from prison.

The Last to Die. Forever, 2010.

Brant, Kylie
Mind Hunters

Raiker Forensics, a company headed by a former FBI profiler, provides the Mind Hunters, criminologists adept in psychological profiling and forensic investigation, to help solve assorted crimes across the country.

Waking Nightmare. Berkley Sensation, 2009.
A detective resents being partnered with a forensic psychologist as they work to bring down a serial killer in Savannah, Georgia.

Waking Evil. Berkley Sensation, 2009.
Myth and superstition add a paranormal twist to this thriller when a Mind Hunter is called to solve a murder in Buffalo Springs, Tennessee, and encounters a parapsychologist who both annoys and attracts her.

Waking the Dead. Berkley Sensation, 2009.
A forensic anthropologist joins forces with a wilderness guide to solve the mystery of seven headless skeletons discovered in an Oregon cave.

Brennan, Allison

Brennan creates some bizarre, quite frightening villains in her suspenseful thrillers. Currently, she is venturing into the Urban Fantasy arena.

Evil Trilogy

Sadistic killers and the Internet are players in this chilling trilogy.

Speak No Evil. Ballantine, 2007.
A Montana sheriff heads to San Diego to help his brother, who's been accused of murder, and helps track down a serial killer.

See No Evil. Ballantine, 2007.
Sexual abuse is at the core of this hard-hitting novel.

Fear No Evil. Ballantine, 2007.
FBI agent Kate Donovan goes it alone in her search for a killer she's been tracking online for years, but when he kidnaps a young woman and puts her "last hours"

on live video, the victim's forensic psychiatrist brother gets involved and needs to find Kate—fast.

Prison Break Trilogy

The title of the trilogy says it all in this series that involves killers who escape from San Quentin during an earthquake and continue with their violent, vindictive careers.

Killing Fear. Ballantine, 2008.
An escaped serial killer targets everyone who helped convict him, including a detective and the roommate of a supposed victim.

Tempting Evil. Ballantine, 2008.
A woman who is an escaped killer's obsession becomes a target in this thriller set in snowy Montana.

Playing Dead. Ballantine, 2008.
The estranged daughter of an escaped convict and an FBI agent work to prove the escapee's innocence despite a concerted, deadly effort to prove him guilty.

Fatal Secrets. Ballantine, 2009.
Sold into white slavery as a child, a woman joins forces with an FBI agent to bring the villain down.

Cutting Edge. Ballantine, 2009.
A security expert and an FBI agent work together to solve a series of biotech arsons.

Seven Deadly Sin Series

There promises to be plenty of suspense and action in Brennan's new Urban Fantasy series in which incarnations of the traditional seven deadly sins are loose to plague the world.

Original Sin. Ballantine, 2010.
Carnal Sin. Ballantine, 2010.

Brent, Madeleine (Pseudonym for Peter O'Donnell)

Brent specializes in strong, capable, and unusual heroines who are often in search of their identity or heritage; far-flung settings; and plots that incorporate both Gothic and Romantic Suspense elements—all in a Victorian setting and told in the first person. Brent won Britain's Romantic Novelists Association Major Award in 1978.

Brockmann, Suzanne

Brockmann's Navy SEAL series, Troubleshooter and Tall, Dark, and Dangerous, are filled with action, adventure, and danger. See chapter 13, "Linked Romances."

Brown, Sandra

Although she also writes Contemporary and Historical Romance, veteran writer Brown is best known for her passionate, riveting Romantic Mysteries. Taut suspense, violence, and murder are key elements in her latest tense, chilling tales. A selection of her recent works is listed below.

Envy. Warner, 2001.
An old crime and a victim's vengeful plan play out in two intertwined stories of envy and deceit.

The Crush. Warner, 2002.
A doctor becomes the romantic obsession of a hired killer, who will stop at nothing, even murder, to have her.

Hello, Darkness. Simon & Schuster, 2003.
A reclusive late-night talk show host becomes a target when a caller blames her for his romantic breakup.

Chill Factor. Simon & Schuster, 2005.
A blizzard strands a woman and a wounded stranger, who is suspected of being a serial killer, in a remote mountain cabin.

Ricochet. Simon & Schuster, 2006.
A detective is drawn into a morass of power, corruption, and murder when he investigates a shooting by the young wife of an influential Savannah judge.

Smoke Screen. Simon & Schuster, 2008.
An arson specialist and a reporter are caught up in an arson investigation in Savannah.

Smash Cut. Simon & Schuster, 2009.
The murder of an important Atlanta CEO has repercussions in unexpected directions in this fast-paced thriller that is enhanced with references to murder movies.

Butcher, Shannon K.
See also chapter 9, "Alternative Reality Romance."

Delta Force Series
Three Delta Force (DF) operatives are the heroes of the following three books.

No Regrets. Warner Forever, 2007.
A former DF operative is drawn back into service to protect a cryptologist from the same vicious terrorist group, the Swarm, that killed his wife.

No Control. Forever, 2008.
A former Swarm kidnap victim wants nothing to do with the CIA or the DF operative who saved her life, even though they are after her once again.

No Escape. Forever, 2008.
A former DF operative, now a security consultant, goes to the aid of a woman—whom he rescued as a teenager—when her old friends, all foster children, begin "committing suicide," and she fears it's murder.

Love You to Death. Forever, 2009.
A journalist and an ex-cop try to find the journalist's kidnapped sister before the sadistic killer slices her up. Gruesome detail.

Cameron, Stella
See also chapter 5, "Contemporary Romance," chapter 7, "Historical Romance," and chapter 9, "Alternative Reality Romance."

Bayou Series
A series of southern Louisiana–set romantic thrillers linked by character and place that often feature complicated plots and steamy sex.

French Quarter. Kensington, 1998.

Cold Day in July. Kensington, 2002.
The son of a wealthy family returns home to investigate his sister's murder and reconnects with a college love.

Kiss Them Goodbye. Mira, 2003.
A dead body on her family's old estate draws a young woman and a detective into a convoluted tale filled with secrets and danger.

Now You See Him. Mira, 2004.
Ice-pick murders resembling those in a popular thriller series, an eye witness with a secret past, a protective attorney, and an escaped convict add up to an intriguing tale of suspense.

A Grave Mistake. Mira, 2005.
A murder behind her bakery that may be linked to another killing draws a young woman and a New Orleans detective into a complex web of danger.

Body of Evidence. Mira, 2006.
A woman leaving her abusive politician husband fears she may be next when members of her support group are murdered.

A Marked Man. Mira, 2006.
A doctor suspected of murder and a woman wary of men because of an earlier rape find love as the murders mount.

Target. Mira, 2007.
A cult leader responsible for the deaths of his followers twenty years ago is on the hunt for the three children who escaped and now live in the Bayou.

A Cold Day in Hell. Mira, 2007.
Christmas loses its holiday feel when a teenager is shot in the Bayou while roaming through it with a friend who is in the witness protection program, and then other violence follows.

Cypress Nights. Mira, 2008.
A psychiatrist and a teacher try to unravel the murders connected with a proposed new school.

Carroll, Margaret

A Dark Love. Avon, 2009.
A woman fleeing from her controlling, psychopathic psychiatrist husband changes her name and appearance, and heads across the country where she finds a new life and love in the arms of a rugged outdoorsman—until her husband tracks her down.

Cassidy, Carla

Cassidy has written numerous Contemporary Series Somances, as well as single-title suspenseful romantic Thrillers. Several of her more recent titles are listed below.

The Perfect Family. Signet Eclipse, 2005.
A fireman's widow and her family are stalked by an insane killer who wants to claim them as his "perfect family."

Without a Sound. Signet Eclipse, 2006.
A woman returns home to care for her niece, who is mute after the murder of her mother, but the killer is still out there—waiting.

Every Move You Make. Signet Eclipse, 2008.
A doll-maker becomes the target of a killer who dresses his victims like some of the doll-making company's vintage dolls.

Broken Pieces. Signet Eclipse, 2008.
Having fled her small Missouri hometown after being raped and becoming pregnant, a single mom returns after sixteen years to sell her self-righteous parents' house and finds her attacker is still there.

Last Gasp. Signet Eclipse, 2009.
A woman orphaned when her mother and siblings were murdered is forced to rethink things when the killings start again after an attorney comes to town to prove her father, who was convicted of the murders, didn't do it.

Up Close and Personal. Signet Eclipse, 2009.
A cheerleader-turned-detective attends her fifteenth high school reunion, reconnects with an old flame, and is jolted into action when someone starts killing her friends.

Castillo, Linda

Castillo writes both series and single-title Romantic Suspense.

The Perfect Victim. Jove, 2002.
A woman decides to trace her roots after her adoptive parents are accidentally killed and fears she is in danger when she learns her birth mother has been murdered.

The Shadow Side. Berkley Sensation, 2003.
A research doctor and a burned-out cop are caught up in a deadly race to find a killer in a story that explores the darker side of medical research.

Fade to Red. Berkley Sensation, 2004.
A woman goes to Seattle in search of her missing sister and is drawn into a world of violence, drugs, and pornography.

Dead Reckoning. Berkley Sensation, 2005.
An assistant DA works with an emotionally damaged investigator to get to the bottom of a double murder that turns out to be far more deadly, and much more personal, than they expected.

A Whisper in the Dark. Berkley Sensation, 2006.
A preacher's daughter who secretly writes sexy novels becomes the target of a particularly twisted killer.

Overkill. Berkley Sensation, 2007.
Relieved of her job because she overreacted and beat up a child-killer and rapist, a single mom Chicago cop is given a second chance in a small town in Texas—but there's a killer on her trail.

Kate Burkholder Series

Kate Burkholder, who was raised in an Amish home but left the church when she turned eighteen, is the police chief in the Amish town of Painters Mill, Ohio. (Note: This series is Mystery/Suspense, rather than Romance but is included here because of the current interest in the Amish among Romance fans.)

Sworn to Silence. Minotaur, 2009.
Pray for Silence. Minotaur, 2010.
Breaking Silence. Minotaur, 2011.

Castle, Jayne (Jayne Ann Krentz)

Castle's futuristic Romantic Suspense novels are included in chapters 9 and 13, "Alternative Reality Romance" and "Linked Romances."

Cornelison, Beth

Cornelison's characters are often struggling with painful pasts.

In Protective Custody. Silhouette Intimate Moments, 2006.
Firefighter Max Caldwell and daycare worker Laura Dalton team up to protect his infant nephew from drug smuggling paternal relatives after Max's sister is shot.

Danger at Her Door. Silhouette Romantic Suspense, 2007.
A rape victim trying to keep the crime a secret and get on with her life finds her world threatened by the sexy investigative reporter who lives next door and the subsequent return of the rapist.

Tall, Dark Defender. Silhouette Romantic Suspense, 2009.
A single mom waitress is mugged on her way to deliver an envelop for her boss and is rescued by a protective undercover agent on the trail of a money-laundering scheme.

The Christmas Stranger. Silhouette Romantic Suspense, 2009.
A woman investigating her husband's murder is attracted to a homeless man she hires to do some renovation work on her home.

Coulter, Catherine

Coulter is a popular writer of a several types of Romance and is especially known for her numerous Historicals and Romantic Suspense, some of which are part of her FBI Thriller series and are often more Thriller than Romance. Some of her titles also have paranormal aspects. Two relatively recent Romantic Suspense titles are listed below.

The Eleventh Hour. Putnam, 2002.
A professor fleeing from a powerful, possibly lethal fiancé witnesses the murder of a priest and becomes involved with the priest's twin brother as they try to solve the mystery and avoid a killer. Part of Coulter's FBI Thriller series.

Born to Be Wild. Jove, 2007.
A TV soap star who returns to her Oregon hometown to recover after she is almost run down in Malibu is attracted to the sexy police chief, and must deal with a killer who has confused her with her bad-girl TV role.

Crandall, Susan

See also chapter 5, "Contemporary Romance."

Pitch Black. Forever, 2008.
When four teenagers go camping and the stepdad of one ends up dead, the newest kid in town, the adopted son of a journalist, is a prime suspect.

Seeing Red. Forever, 2009.
A recently paroled convict who is out for revenge on the woman who testified against him as a teenager drives the plot of this taut thriller that has its fair share of twists and a rewarding romance.

Sleep No More. Forever, 2010.
Fearing her deadly sleepwalking tendencies have returned when she wakes up in a crashed car and a young man is dead, a woman seeks help from the attractive local psychiatrist, hoping to learn the truth, despite the fact that someone doesn't want her to remember.

Cresswell, Jasmine

Cresswell is a long-time popular writer of Contemporary Romance and Romantic Suspense. Several recent titles are listed below.

Dead Ringer. Mira, 2003.
A missing husband who is a supposed IRA terrorist, a handsome French kidnapper, and a complex, quite twisted plot add up to a fascinating read.

Unit One (Melody Beecham) Trilogy

The romantic relationship between art gallery curator Melody Beecham and Nick Anwar, operatives for Unit One, a shadowy covert government organization, carries over throughout this action-packed trilogy.

Decoy. Mira, 2004.
Full Pursuit. Mira, 2004.
Final Justice. Mira, 2005.

Ravens Trilogy

The disappearance of billionaire and bigamist Ron Ravens affects his two families in various ways in this intriguing trilogy.

Missing. Mira, 2007.
Ron Raven's daughter Megan must deal with bank manager Adam Fairfax, the brother of her father's other wife, when she tries to convince him not to foreclose on their family's ranch.

Suspect. Mira, 2007.
Attorney Liam Raven, Ron's son, defends Chloe Hamilton against a murder charge and together they begin to uncover clues relating to Ron's missing dad.

Payback. Mira, 2007.
Assuming, as the police have, that her father, Ron Ravens, is dead, pastry chef Kate Fairfax is shocked when restaurateur Luke Savarini claims to have seen him. Together they try to get at the dangerous truth in this story that ties up all the loose threads in this trilogy.

Dees, Cindy
Medusa

The Medusa books are loosely linked and feature members of an all-female elite U.S. Special Forces team.

The Medusa Project. Silhouette Bombshell, 2005.
The Medusa team of six women is formed and they end up rescuing their trainer, who doesn't think women should be in Special Forces.

Medusa Rising. Silhouette Bombshell, 2005.
A Jamaican-born doctor on the Medusa team struggles with ethical issues and is attracted to a "terrorist" who insists he's an undercover agent.

The Medusa Game. Silhouette Bombshell, 2006.
The Winter Olympic Games are the setting for this thriller in which the life of a skater is in jeopardy.

The Medusa Prophecy. Silhouette Bombshell, 2007.
An arctic setting, drugs, and a super-strong heroine drive the action in this adventure.

The Medusa Affair. Silhouette Romantic Suspense, 2007.
A reconstructed Medusa beauty rescues a mysterious pilot and then must keep him from being killed.

The Medusa Seduction. Silhouette Intimate Moments, 2007.
A woman who can identify a terrorist trains to work with the Medusas.

Medusa's Master. Silhouette Romantic Suspense, 2009.
In the Caribbean on assignment, a Medusa captain proves herself to her sexy, skeptical supervisor.

The Medusa Proposition. Silhouette Romantic Suspense, 2010.
When a killer surfaces at an economic conference, a Medusa operative is assigned to be a bodyguard for a sexy billionaire who just happens to have a Special Forces background.

*The Soldier's Secret Daughter. Silhouette Romantic Suspense, 2009.
An undercover government agent is captured after a passionate encounter with a women he thinks has betrayed him and returns after two years in captivity to learn he has a daughter.

Dimon, HelenKay
See also chapter 5, "Contemporary Romance."

Under the Gun. Harlequin Intrigue, 2010.
A woman running from a murder accusation gets help from the one man who can help prove her innocence and keep her alive, her former fiancé.

Night Moves. Harlequin Intrigue, 2010.
A scientist, supposedly killed in an explosion, turns to her brother's best friend when she realizes she's being framed.

Dodd, Christina
Dodd is also a popular writer of Historical and, recently, Paranormal/Urban Fantasy Romance. See also chapter 7, "Historical Romance," and chapter 9, "Alternative Reality Romance."

Lost Texas Hearts Series
Separated when their parents disappear and are subsequently accused of embezzlement, the three Prescott sisters eventually find each other in this series that becomes more suspenseful as it progresses.

Just the Way You Are. Pocket Books, 2003.
Hope Prescott takes a job as Zach Given's secretary and they fall for each other even as she searches for her missing sisters.

Almost Like Being in Love. Pocket Books, 2004.
Landscaper Pepper Prescott flees after witnessing a murder and takes refuge at the Idaho ranch she once called home only to find Dan Graham, her old love and former Special Forces operative, living there.

Close to You. Pocket Star, 2005.
TV reporter Kate Montgomery (Caitlin Prescott) attracts a stalker and acquires a bodyguard, sexy Teague Ramos, in this story that gradually reveals the truth of the siblings' separation and reunites them once again.

Fortune Hunters Series

Trouble in High Heels. Signet, 2006.
An attorney decides to have a fling with a handsome Italian count only to learn he's a suspected jewel thief and she's been assigned to his case.

Tongue in Chic. Signet, 2007.
A woman fakes amnesia when she is caught breaking into her family's old mansion, but is caught off guard when the new owner claims her as his long lost wife.

Thigh High. Signet, 2008.
A banker is forced to work with the bank's sexy representative on a series of robberies not realizing she is under suspicion herself.

Danger in a Red Dress. Signet, 2009.
A home-care nurse flees for her life when her patient is murdered (possibly for her knowledge of a fortune), and she is the chief suspect in the story that ties up both the Fortune Hunters and the Lost Texas Hearts series.

Dreyer, Eileen

Dreyer also writes award-winning Contemporary Romances as Kathleen Korbel. Her hospital thrillers, while not necessarily Romances, are well-done and medically accurate, have an offbeat, quirky sense of humor, and may be of interest to readers who enjoy her Korbel books. See also chapter 7, "Historical Romance," and Kathleen Korbel in chapter 5, "Contemporary Romance."

*A Man to Die For. HarperPaperbacks, 1991.

With a Vengeance. St. Martin's Press, 2003.
A killer is methodically eliminating patients and Maggie O'Brien decides it's up to her to get to the bottom of things.

Head Games. St. Martin's Press, 2004.
A trauma nurse is targeted by a serial killer who may be the abused child she once tried to help in this dark, chilling story.

Saints and Sinners. St. Martin's Press, 2005.
A forensic nurse goes to New Orleans in search of her vanished sister, Faith, and finds murder and danger in this terrifying tale.

Forster, Suzanne

Forster's stories tend to be fast-paced, sexy, intense, and occasionally dark.

The Morning After. Jove, 2000.
A marketing director wakes up in a strange hotel room to learn she is married—and later pregnant—with no memory of any of it in this bizarre, suspenseful tale.

While She Was Sleeping. Berkley, 2003.
A detective must work with a sketch artist, who is his former fiancée, in order to bring down a killer.

The Arrangement. Mira, 2007.
A woman almost killed in a boating accident has partial amnesia and doesn't know whom to believe in this dark tale filled with a group of especially unlikable characters.

The Private Concierge. Mira, 2008.
A woman who needs help when someone seems out to destroy her blossoming concierge business is forced to work with an ex-cop who doesn't trust her.

Freethy, Barbara

Freethy writes fast-paced, compelling tales of Romantic Suspense, some of which have a touch of the paranormal. See also chapter 9, "Alternative Reality Romance," and chapter 5, "Contemporary Romance."

All She Ever Wanted. Signet, 2004.
A novel that seems to implicate her in her sorority sister's death sends a young medical resident to the victim's brother for help.

Golden Lies. Signet, 2004.
Danger, suspense, and mystery in San Francisco's China Town.

Don't Say a Word. Signet, 2005.
After seeing an old photograph of a Russian orphan, Julia DeMarco begins a dangerous search for her real identity with the help of photographer Alex Manning.

Taken. Signet, 2006.
Stained-glass artist Kayla Sheridan and engineer Nick Granville, who were taken advantage of by the same man, join forces to track the villain down and are pulled into a complicated mystery that goes back to Nick's college days and has links to Kayla's family.

Played. Signet, 2006.
The villain from *Taken* finally gets his comeuppance in this fast-paced story of diamonds, old secrets, and curses that brings a gem expert and the FBI agent together as they try to stop a heist and catch a wily con-artist.

Silent Run. Onyx, 2008.
A woman with no memory, a missing child, and an angry man who wants some answers drive the plot of this suspenseful, danger-filled mystery that has its characters searching for the truth—and a child—and trying to avoid a killer, as well.

Silent Fall. Onyx, 2008.
Lured into the woods, drugged, and then accused of murder, an investigative reporter (brother of the hero in *Silent Run*) turns to a psychic for help, not realizing that this is just what the villain wants—and that he has plans for them both.

Garwood, Julie

A Rita Award–winning Historical Romance writer, Garwood also writes Romantic Suspense. Humor and witty dialogue are often part of her books. Although not parts of an official series, many of her books have characters in common. See also chapter 7, "Historical Romance."

Heartbreaker. Pocket Books, 2001.

Mercy. Pocket, 2001.
An attorney goes to a small Louisiana town to renew his acquaintance with a lovely doctor who saved his life, and they both become caught up in a deadly web of murder, greed, and violence.

Killjoy. Ballantine Books, 2002.
FBI analyst Avery Delaney goes in search of her Aunt Carrie, who went missing on her way to a Colorado spa, and is joined by a Jean Paul Renard, a man who's been tracking the hit man who killed his sister and is now holding Carrie hostage.

Murder List. Ballantine Books, 2004.
A college assignment turns deadly when Regan Madison's "murder list" of people she despises ends up in the deadly hands of a psychopathic killer.

Slow Burn. Ballantine Books, 2005.
Kate McKenna wonders who is trying to kill her until she learns she is an heiress—with some greedy relatives.

Shadow Dance. Ballantine Books, 2007.
At the goading of FBI agent Noah Claybourne, math whiz Jordan Buchanan heads for Serenity, Texas, to discover more about the ancient feud between her family and the McKennas and finds that someone will do just about anything to keep the old secrets hidden.

Fire and Ice. Ballantine Books, 2009.
A reporter heads to Alaska, accompanied by a sexy FBI agent, to check out the story that a runner that she interviewed was supposedly killed by a polar bear.

Sizzle. Ballantine Books, 2010.
A college student's inadvertent find at a strange yard sale puts her on an inept killer's hit list—and under an FBI agent's protection—in this adventure that is lightened by Garwood's classic humor.

The Ideal Man. Dutton, 2011.

Gerard, Cindy
Gerard has also written Contemporary Series Romances, but recently has focused on hard-hitting, intense, edgy Romantic Suspense.

The Bodyguards Series
The men and women of Southern Florida's E.D.E.N. Securities, Inc., all with various skills honed in previous service to their country, are the major players in this edgy, intense, action-packed series.

To the Edge. St. Martin's Paperbacks, 2005.
To the Limit. St. Martin's Paperbacks, 2005.
To the Brink. St. Martin's Paperbacks, 2006.
Over the Line. St. Martin's Paperbacks, 2006.
Under the Wire. St. Martin's Paperbacks, 2006.
Into the Dark. St. Martin's Paperbacks, 2007.

Black Ops, Inc. Series
Linked to the Bodyguard series, the Black Ops, Inc. covert private security team is made up of tough, intense, talented operatives whose dangerous assignments take them around the globe.

Show No Mercy. Pocket Star, 2008.
A journalist becomes a terrorist target in this tense adventure that reunites her with a Black Ops operative she'd met years earlier.

*Take No Prisoners. Pocket Star, 2008.
An operative out to avenge his sister's death falls for a woman who can lead him to the murderer's Central American hideout in this exotic thriller.

Whisper No Lies. Pocket Star, 2009.
A casino dealer, who refuses a carte blanche offer from an Indonesian crime lord, is kidnapped and taken to Jakarta; it's up to the Black Ops men to bring her back in this adventure that touches on issues of human trafficking.

Feel the Heat. Pocket Star, 2009.
A Black Ops operative and an intelligence officer work against time to get the key to disabling a deadly bomb.

Risk No Secrets. Pocket Books, 2010.
A teacher in El Salvador turns to an old Black Ops friend when another little girl is kidnapped instead of her daughter.

Graham, Heather

Graham, a veteran writer of Contemporary Series and single-title Romances, Historicals, and Paranormals also writes as Heather Graham Pozzessere and Shannon Drake. Several of her recent stories of Romantic Suspense, some of which include paranormal elements, are listed below.

Picture Me Dead. Mira, 2003.
A forensic artist and a detective realize that their separate cases may be linked in this chilling thriller.

Haunted. Mira, 2003.
A sheriff and a psychic explore ghostly—and otherwise—occurrences at historic Melody House.

Ghost Walk. Mira, 2005.
A New Orleans ghost tour guide and a psychic investigator look into separate deaths and realize the deaths are connected.

The Island. Mira, 2006.
A human skull, an isolated island, a posh yacht club, and an enigmatic scuba diver add up to chilling danger for our heroine in this fast-paced thriller.

The Dead Room, Mira, 2007.
A woman who can connect with the dead investigates her fiancé's death.

The Last Noel. Mira, 2007.
A family gathering for Christmas gives shelter to a pair of thugs who turn out to be killers in this Holiday thriller.

Nightwalker. Mira, 2009.
P.I. Dillon Wolf comes to Las Vegas casino worker Jessie Sparhawk's aid when a stranger collapses on her and dies in this complex mystery that overflows with ghosts, some humor, and Native American legends.

Bone Island Trilogy

Ancient ghosts haunt Key West (Bone Island or Cayo Hueso [literally, bone key]) in search of vengeance, retribution, or sometimes to help and protect the living in this suspenseful trilogy introduced by an e-book prequel, *Ghost Memories*, that sets the stage for the mystery, violence, and terror that follows.

Ghost Shadow. Mira, 2010.
A photographer returns to Key West to investigate an old murder and is attracted to a woman who can see ghosts, including an intriguing privateer.

Ghost Night. Mira, 2010.
A writer investigating the two-year-old murders of two cast members of her slasher film connects with a documentary filmmaker who sees ghosts.

Ghost Moon. Mira, 2010.
A woman reluctantly returns to her late grandfather's "evil" house to dispose of the estate and reconnects with a man from her teenage past.

Gray, Ginna

The Witness. Mira, 2001.
When their plane goes down in the Rockies, an FBI witness and her protector deal with the elements, the bad guys, and fall in love along the way.

Pale Moon Rising. Mira, 2004.
An architect and an interior designer meet again in this reunion story that features a spooky mansion, a wicked, manipulative mother, and plenty of Southern atmosphere.

Fatal Flaw. Mira, 2005.
A homicide cop in charge of a series of murders is attracted to a plastic surgeon who was originally considered a suspect.

The Trophy Wife. Mira, 2006.
Class issues and murder are part of this contemporary marriage-of-convenience story.

The Prime Objective. Mira, 2009.
A CIA operative reconnects with his generally calm, self-sufficient ex-wife when she calls to say she needs his help.

Griffin, Laura
Borderline Duo

The heroines are best friends in this Texas-set duo.

One Last Breath. Pocket Star, 2007.
News reporter Feenie Malone and P.I. Marco Juarez join forces to gather information that will bring down Feenie's ex and the ex's drug lord friends and explain what happened to Marco's narcotics cop sister who went missing two years earlier.

One Wrong Step. Pocket Star, 2008.
When her ex is killed an hour after he comes to see her, Celie Wells's life is turned upside down by the FBI, the Mexican drug lords, and a sexy crime reporter.

Glass Sisters Duo
The heroines are sisters.

Thread of Fear. Pocket Star, 2008.
Forensic artist Fiona Glass reluctantly agrees to help a police chief in his search for a serial killer and ends up a target herself.

*Whisper of Warning. Pocket Star, 2009.
When a meeting with her married ex-boyfriend turns fatal, Courtney Glass is accused of the crime and her only help of avoiding prosecution—or the killer—is the attractive detective in charged of her case.

Tracers Series
The Tracers are a team of expert forensic scientists.

Untraceable. Pocket Star, 2009.
A P.I. suspects that her client has been killed by her abusive cop husband and works with a homicide detective and the Tracers to learn the truth.

Unspeakable. Pocket Star, 2010.
A true-crime writer and an investigator hoping to become an FBI profiler work with the Tracers to find a serial killer before he adds the heroine to his victims.

Heggan, Christiane
Blind Faith. Mira, 2001.
An investigative reporter and a sexy cop clash but eventually join forces to solve a pair of murders that are linked through the same casino.

Scent of a Killer. Mira, 2004.
When her ex-husband is killed right after he asks her for some old pictures she took for his company, a photographer enlists the aid of the P.I. who was working on a case for her ex and is swept into a morass of corporate crime and greed.

The Search. Mira, 2005.
An attorney investigates the kidnapping of a reporter friend, connects with a Special Forces agent who has suddenly become her neighbor, and is drawn into unexpected danger.

Now You Die. Mira, 2005.
A cartoonist's pictorial efforts to find out what happened to a body she saw in an alley attracts some very dangerous attention.

Where the Truth Lies. Mira, 2006.
When a woman begins taking inventory of an art gallery her murdered ex-fiancé willed to her, she discovers some irregularities that someone will do anything to keep hidden.

Hooper, Kay
See chapter 9, "Alternative Reality Romance."

Howard, Linda
Howard writes in a number of Romance subgenres. Her sexy stories can be dark and intense or laced with humor, and occasionally have a paranormal touch. A small selection of her recent works is listed below. See also chapter 5, "Contemporary Romance."

Mr. Perfect. Atria, 2000.
When three friends make up a list of qualifications for the "perfect man," they unknowingly set themselves up to be the target of a killer in this suspenseful story.

Cover of Night. Ballantine, 2006.
When thugs lay siege to a small Idaho town, it's up to the owner of a B and B and a handyman (who is much more than he seems) to save the town.

Up Close and Dangerous. Ballantine, 2007.
When their plane crashes in the Idaho wilderness, a young widow with greedy adult step-children and a sexy pilot manage to survive the elements—but evading a killer is another matter.

Burn. Ballantine, 2009.
Kidnapping, humor, and danger on the high seas are all part of this captive-in-love-with-captor Romance.

Veil of Night. Ballantine, 2010.
When a particularly difficult bride is murdered, the wedding planner is among the prime suspects—and she's also one of the killer's targets in this tale that blends humor, suspense, and romance.

Johansen, Iris
Now best known for her suspenseful thrillers, including her popular Eve Duncan forensic thriller series, Johansen also wrote Contemporary series and Historical Romances earlier in her career, a number of which have been reprinted. Several examples of her recent Romantic Suspense titles are listed below:

Killer Dreams. Bantam, 2006.
A doctor whose dream research discovery has been turned to deadly purposes joins forces with one of the victims to bring down the villain.

Pandora's Daughter. St. Martin's Press, 2007.
A gifted psychic doctor and a government agent are swept across Europe in a desperate search for a dangerous villain and an old ledger that contains her family's lineage and secrets.

Dark Summer. St. Martin's Press, 2008.
A vet on a search-and-rescue mission saves the life of a very special dog and becomes involved with an enigmatic stranger who will do anything to protect his "Dogs of Summer."

Deadlock. St. Martin's Press, 2009.
A CIA agent rescues an antiquities expert from vicious mercenaries in this fast-paced, vengeance-driven tale set in war-torn Afghanistan.

Kennedy, Elle
Silent Watch. Silhouette Romantic Suspense, 2009.
Now in a witness protection program, a woman who survived a serial killer attack has her cover blown by the media when she agrees to help an FBI agent.

Her Private Avenger. Silhouette Romantic Suspense, 2010.
A security expert goes on the hunt for his former fiancée when she escapes from a hospital after her supposed suicide attempt.

Krentz, Jayne Ann
Many of Krentz's Contemporary Romances hover between the Basic Contemporary and Romantic Suspense subgenres. See chapter 5, "Contemporary Romance," and chapter 13, "Linked Romances."

Lee, Rachel (Pseudonym for Sue Civil-Brown)
See also chapter 5, "Contemporary Romance," and chapter 13, "Linked Romances."

With Malice. Mira, 2003.
A U.S. senator and a detective are attracted to each other as they work to figure out who is out to ruin the senator by seeing him blamed for murder in this politically rich Romance.

Last Breath. Warner Forever, 2003.
A homicide detective, an attorney, and a parish priest try to unravel a current bizarre murder mystery that has roots in the priest's past.

Office 119
This international thriller series with a mystical touch follows the adventures of Tom Lawton (Lawton Caine) and Renata Bachle, operatives of the covert organization Office 119, as they try to thwart a shadowy group of people from taking over the world.

Wildcard. Mira, 2005.
A murder attempt on a political candidate brings Tom and Renata together as they try to figure out who shot at the candidate—and why—and wants them dead, as well.

The Crimson Code. Mira, 2006.
Deadly Christmas Eve cathedral bombings draw Renate and Lawton into a deadly politics-laced game that has global consequences.

The Jericho Pact. Mira, 2007.
An assassination and the resulting incarceration of all Muslims throws the European Union into chaos as Renate and Lawton look for answers, and a renegade priest continues his search for a powerful religious artifact.

The Hunted. Mira, 2008.
A journalist investigating the sex-slave trade becomes a target when she zeroes in on a large defense contractor and is aided by an FBI agent with a similar agenda.

London, Cait
London has also written a number of popular Contemporary Series Romances.

With Her Last Breath. Avon, 2003.
A woman flees from the man who destroyed her sister and tried to rape her and finds shelter with a warm Italian family in a small town on Lake Michigan—but her vengeful pursuer isn't about to let her escape.

What Memories Remain. Avon, 2004.
A successful boat-builder returns to Fairy Cove to solve the decades-old mystery of his parents' deaths and needs the help of a childhood friend, whose nightmares may hold the answers.

Silence the Whispers. Avon, 2006.
A woman returns to her childhood home to uncover the truth about her mother's death, but someone seems intent on driving her insane in this subtly paranormal Romance.

Psychic Triplets Trilogy

Inherited psychic abilities plague the Aisling-Bartel triplets in various ways in this compelling, suspenseful trilogy that has its beginnings in an ancient curse.

At the Edge. Avon, 2007.
Living alone to avoid other people's thoughts and feelings, empath Claire is befriended by her neighbor, Neil, when she is attacked.

A Stranger's Touch. Avon, 2008.
Sculptor Tempest's search for an ancient brooch connects her to Marcus Greystone, who needs her psychometric help to find his parents' murderer.

For Her Eyes Only. Avon, 2008.
Things come to a head and loose ends are tied up in this final volume of the trilogy that brings clairvoyant Leona and investor Owen Shaw together as they fight a psychic vampire.

Lovelace, Merline

Lovelace has written in a number of Romance subgenres, as well as Romantic Suspense.

Cleo North Trilogy

P.I. and security consultant Cleo North is thrown together with USAF special agent Jack Donovan in a variety of adventures in this fast-paced, sexy romantic trilogy.

The First Mistake. Mira, 2005.
Cleo and Jack meet when she is hired to protect a movie star from a killer and he is investigating some dangerous North Korean technology.

The Middle Sin. Mira, 2005.
Cleo and Jack head for Malta to stop a terrorist plot.

The Last Bullet. Mira, 2005.
Cleo and Jack go to England to investigate the murder of a USAF officer.

Code Name Danger Series

This ongoing series features the men and women of the covert government agency OMEGA. Each story is complete in itself; several recent titles are listed below.

Undercover Wife. Silhouette Romantic Suspense, 2008.
A pair of OMEGA agents fight their attraction in vane when the are sent to Hong Kong after an agent is murdered while investigating a potentially deadly virus.

Seduced by the Operative. Silhouette Romantic Suspense, 2009.
An OMEGA psychologist is reunited with a former love, a Central American ambassador, in an adventure that takes them to the Czech Republic and back.

Risky Engagement. Silhouette Romantic Suspense, 2010.
When her car breaks down near a Mexican hacienda that OMEGA agents have under surveillance, Dr. Nina Grant is swept up in a dangerous adventure and into the arms of agent Rafe Blackstone.

Danger in the Desert. Silhouette Romantic Suspense, 2011.

Lowell, Elizabeth (Pseudonym for Ann Maxwell)
Lowell has written in a number of Romance subgenres—most recently, Romantic Suspense. She also writes Mystery Suspense as Ann Maxwell. Each of her books is complete in itself, although some are linked by family or organization, with some links across series. Two of her more popular series are listed below.

Rarities Unlimited Trilogy
The agents of an exclusive art consulting firm find that art can be more dangerous and more mysterious than it seems.

> *Moving Target*. William Morrow, 2001.
> *Running Scared*. William Morrow, 2002.
> *Die in Plain Sight*. William Morrow, 2003.

St. Kilda Consulting
No job is too difficult for shadowy, no-holds-barred St. Kilda Consulting.

> *The Wrong Hostage*. William Morrow, 2006.
> When her teenage son is kidnapped by a Mexican gangster, Judge Grace Silva goes to the one person she knows can help, Joe Faroe of low profile, but most efficient, St. Kilda Consulting.

> *Innocent as Sin*. William Morrow, 2007.
> Realizing she's been set up as the scapegoat in a money laundering scheme, banker Kayla Shaw barely escapes death with the help of St Kilda operative Rand McCree, who is determined to bring down the international criminal who was responsible for Rand's twin brother's death.

> *Blue Smoke and Murder*. William Morrow, 2008.
> Unsigned paintings that are possibly the work of a major Western artist connect river guide Jill Breck with St. Kilda operative Zach Balfour when her life is threatened.

> *Death Echo*. William Morrow, 2010.
> St. Kilda operative Emma Cross heads for Seattle to check out a yacht that may be part of a terrorist plot and must deal with sexy, difficult transit captain MacKenzie Durand.

McCall, Dinah (Pseudonym for Sharon Sala)
McCall's thrillers are typically emotionally rich, dark, and compelling.

> *The Return*. Mira, 2000.
> A young woman returns to her Kentucky hometown to bury the woman who raised her and finds danger and superstition as she works, with the help of the sheriff, to uncover the secrets of her past.

> *Storm Warning*. Mira, 2001.
> A woman flees from a killer, who makes use of posthypnotic suggestion to systematically cause the suicides of her grade school classmates, and connects with an FBI agent who is on her trail.

> *White Mountain*. Mira, 2002.
> An FBI agent heads for Montana to investigate the death of a Russian scientist who supposedly died years earlier and finds a mysterious fertility clinic, a handful of wary scientists, the attractive daughter of the clinic's founder—and a killer.

The Perfect Lie. Mira, 2003.
Drugs, murder, kidnapping, and revenge are front and center in this gripping story that features both a secret baby and a reunion.

Bloodlines. Mira, 2005.
A child's skeleton found in the walls of a lakeside cottage causes a woman to question her own identity and a killer to make sure that his secrets never come to light.

The Survivors. Mira, 2007.
Deborah Sanborn's psychic gifts bring Mike O'Ryan into her life when she "sees" his son and another woman as survivors of a plane crash in this thriller that involves murder, as well.

McNaught, Judith
See also chapter 5, "Contemporary Romance."

Someone to Watch over Me. Atria, 2003.
A woman wakes up in the hospital after an accident to discover that her husband has been murdered—and she and one of his business partners are chief suspects in his complicated thriller that features a pair of romances.

Naughton, Elisabeth
Stolen Series
Linked characters and stolen artifacts loosely bind this steamy adventure series together.

Stolen Fury. Love Spell, 2009.
An archaeologist on the trail of a series of ancient Greek artifacts, the Three Furies, joins forces with a sexy thief in this fast-paced tale reminiscent of *Romancing the Stone*.

Stolen Heat. Love Spell, 2009.
A woman supposedly killed in Egypt runs into trouble—and her old love—when she retrieves an artifact that sets the bad guys on their trail.

Stolen Seduction. Love Spell, 2010.
Suspected of murder, a socialite heiress cop and the detective on her case (with whom she has a brief, but passionate, past) work to prove her innocence—and find the guilty party.

Neggers, Carla
Neggers's riveting, carefully plotted Romantic Suspense adventures are fast-paced, witty, and filled with sexual tension. Although many are parts of series and may have characters in common, all are stand-alone reads. Several of her recent titles are listed below.

BPD-FBI Series
These books are linked by character and move between Ireland, Boston, and Maine.

The Widow. Mira, 2006.
The widow of an FBI agent, now a detective, returns to Maine to investigate her husband's murder.

The Angel. Mira, 2008.
Artist Kiera Sullivan goes to Ireland to research a Celtic legend about a stone angel and is rescued by FBI agent Simon Cahill when she becomes trapped after she sees the angel in an ancient ruin—but the questions mount when the angel reappears in the United States.

The Mist. Mira, 2009.
When Lizzie Rush turns her psychopathic criminal boss in, she ends up on his hit list along with a number of others, including FBI agent Will Davenport.

The Whisper. Mira, 2010.
An archaeologist heroine left for dead in an Irish cave and a detective hero almost killed by an Irish bomb meet, are attracted but go their separate ways, and reconnect in Boston when her search for a missing Celtic treasure and his search for the bomber converge with potentially deadly results.

Black Falls Series
Murder mystery series set in Black Falls, Vermont.

Cold Pursuit. Mira, 2008.
The teenage daughter of a recently killed ambassador flees to New England and secret service agent Jo Harper and search-and-rescue expert Elijah Cameron are on the hunt to find her.

Cold River. Mira, 2009.
A firefighter sets out to discover the truth behind his father's death and thinks that Hannah Shay may have the answers—but she resists cooperating, which places everyone is serious danger.

Cold Dawn. Mira, 2010.
A smoke jumper and a search-and-rescue expert find passion and danger as they search for a killer arsonist.

Novak, Brenda
Novak's Romantic Suspense thrillers are well-plotted, sometimes humorous and witty, and filled with well-developed characters. A few of her recent titles are listed below.

Last Stand Series
This series centers on those involved with the Last Stand, an organization to help crime victims.

Trust Me. Mira, 2008.
An abuse victim must deal with the release of her sadistic attacker and his determination to kill her and is aided by the original detective on the case.

Stop Me. Mira, 2008.
When a psychological profiler receives her long-missing sister's bracelet in the mail, she heads for Louisiana to find a man whose daughter was murdered years earlier, possibly by the same killer.

Watch Me. Mira, 2008.
A social worker returns to Tennessee to check out a long-ago murder and is rescued from an attack by the brother of the victim in this chilling Romance.

The Perfect Couple. Mira, 2009.
When a teenage girl goes missing, her mom is aided by a P.I. who donates his time to the Last Stand, and they discover that the solution to the crime is closer than they'd thought.

The Perfect Liar. Mira, 2009.
When a victim's rights activist becomes involved in a rape accusation case, she ends up in serious danger when the accuser turns out to be a deeply disturbed pathological liar, fully capable of murder.

The Perfect Murder. Mira, 2009.
Believing that the man who killed his ex-wife and son faked his own suicide and is still alive, an investment banker follows a lead to Sacramento and connects with a victim's rights advocate who is working on a case that involves the man he is seeking.

Dept. 6 Hired Gun Series
White Heat. Mira, 2010.
A bizarre religious cult, the sizzling Arizona desert heat, and a pair of operatives sent to infiltrate the group are the ingredients for a hot, nonstop thriller.

Body Heat. Mira, 2010.
Killer Heat. Mira, 2010.

Pappano, Marilyn
Pappano's fast-paced suspenseful Romances are usually well-plotted and filled with mystery and danger, and sometimes a touch of the paranormal. She has written other types of Contemporary Romance, as well, and also writes as Rachel Butler. Several of her more recent titles are listed below, and while not a true series, many are set in Copper Lake, Georgia.

One Stormy Night. Silhouette Romantic Suspense, 2007.
A woman comes to a small Mississippi town disguised as her twin sister to find evidence that her twin's former husband, who is the police chief, is corrupt, and she attracts the attention of a sexy deputy.

Forbidden Stranger. Silhouette Romantic Suspense, 2008.
Missing strippers bring an undercover cop posing as a bartender to a strip club in Copper Lake and into the life of an exotic dancer who's turned over a new leaf and soon will be headed for a college teaching position.

Intimate Enemy. Silhouette Romantic Suspense, 2008.
An attorney and a construction company owner are reunited when a stalker threatens.

Scandal in Copper Lake. Silhouette Romantic Suspense, 2009.
A psychic heroine of mixed racial heritage returns to solve the mystery of her mother's death and attracts the attention and romantic interest of a lawyer, who is a member of one of the area's oldest and most influential families.

A Passion to Die For. Silhouette Romantic Suspense, 2009.
Ellie Chase's efforts to put her sordid past behind her and carve out a new life come to a halt when her estranged mother comes to town and is murdered—and all the evidence points to Ellie.

Criminal Deception. Silhouette Romanic Suspense, 2010.
Coffee-shop owner Joe Saldana is surprised when his twin's former girlfriend, Liz Dalton, comes to town looking for his brother, but the situation is not at all what Joe thinks.

Protector's Temptation. Silhouette Romantic Suspense, 2010.
A former big city cop and an attorney are reunited when she needs his protection.

Peters, Elizabeth (Barbara Mertz)

Also known for her Gothic Romances written as Barbara Michaels, Elizabeth Peters's works are marked by a sense of humor, intelligent writing, and a kind of lighthearted believability—all tied together by a strong mystery plotline and thorough research. Although she has written a number of stand-alone titles, most of her books feature one of three heroines (Amelia Peabody [Victorian archaeologist/adventurer], Vicky Bliss [art historian/museum curator], or Jacqueline Kirby [academic librarian]), and because in real life the author is an Egyptian scholar, a number of her novels are set in Egypt or the Middle East. More Mystery than Romance, Peters's novels appeal to readers in both genres. Most have been reprinted. For space reasons, only her most recent titles are listed below.

Vicky Bliss Series

Laughter of Dead Kings. Harper, 2008.
The theft of King Tut sends Vicky, her boss, Dr. Anton Schmidt, and John Tregarth (formerly Sir John Smythe) to Egypt and across continents in this story that reveals a number of fascinating secrets, ties up some loose ends, and resolves Vicky and John's relationship nicely. Possibly the last in the series.

Amelia Peabody Series

This entire series involves a marvelously anachronistic Victorian sleuth/heroine and her family and friends, and it pokes fun at Victorian novels and is something of a spoof of the entire Romantic Suspense subgenre. The independent and intrepid Amelia is generally considered to be Peters's most popular and best-known heroine. The series begins in the 1880s and has currently reached 1922, with the most recent book regressing back to 1910.

The Falcon at the Portal. Avon, 1999.
Bodies, accusations of forgery, romance, and cousin Percy's return, plus excerpts from Manuscript H and letters from Nefret.

He Shall Thunder in the Sky. William Morrow, 2000.
WWI, spies, and threats from the Ottoman Empire affect the family in Egypt in 1914.

Lord of the Silent. William Morrow, 2001.
The Emersons are back in Egypt dealing with mysteries in 1915.

The Golden One. William Morrow, 2002.
More bodies and mystery as Ramses is called back by British Intelligence in 1916.

Children of the Storm. William Morrow, 2003.
Three generations of the family are together in Egypt solving mysteries again in 1919.

Guardian of the Horizon. William Morrow, 2003.
A story from the recently discovered journal tells of the family lured into danger at the Lost Oasis in 1907/08.

Serpent on the Crown. William Morrow, 2005.
With the world at peace in 1922, the Emersons head back to the Valley of the Kings for more adventures.

Tomb of the Golden Bird. William Morrow, 2006.
King Tut's tomb is discovered and Amelia and Emerson deal with a whole new group of villains in 1922.

A River in the Sky. Harper Collins, 2010.
In 1910, Emerson and Amelia go to Palestine to help search for the Ark of the Covenant.

Potter, Patricia
Potter has also written a number of Historical Romances, as well as memorable Contemporaries and Romantic Suspense novels.

Twisted Shadows. Jove, 2003.
Shocked to learn she is the daughter of a notorious dying crime boss, an art dealer agrees to meet him and is plunged into a morass of greed, family conflict, and dangerous secrets.

Cold Target. Berkley Sensation, 2004.
Two sisters who never knew about each other face deadly attacks in this intricately plotted series that keeps readers enthralled.

Tangle of Lies. Berkley Sensation, 2005.
A woman, stunned when her mother is arrested for a thirty-year-old crime, joins forces with a cop whose dad was killed in the old crime in this nonstop thriller that will make readers think.

Tempting the Devil. Berkley Sensation, 2006.
A persistent journalist whose ethics won't let her reveal a source becomes a target of a crime network.

Catch a Shadow. Berkley Sensation, 2008.
A paramedic agrees to deliver a letter for a dying hit-and-run victim and ends up the target of a killer.

Behind the Shadows. Berkley Sensation, 2008.
A woman learns she was probably switched at birth, possibly for an heiress, and ends up in danger as a result.

Quinn, Tara Taylor
See also chapter 5, "Contemporary Romance."

Ivory Nation Trilogy
This suspenseful trio of stories focuses on the Ivory Nation, a powerful white supremacist group in Arizona.

In Plain Sight. Mira, 2006.
A prosecutor working on a dangerous case involving the Ivory Nation shares her fears for herself and her family with her next door neighbor, a former FBI agent.

Behind Closed Doors. Mira, 2007.
An interracial couple's marriage is almost destroyed when the wife is brutally raped and her husband takes matters into his own hands.

At Close Range. Mira, 2008.
A trial judge and a pediatrician are targeted by the Ivory Nation in this grim, suspenseful Romance.

The Chapman Files
These stories come from the varied files of psychologist and expert witness Kelly Chapman.

The First Wife. Harlequin Superromance, 2010.
The Second Lie. Mira, 2010.
The Third Secret. Mira, 2010.
The Fourth Victim. Mira, 2010.

Raybourn, Deanna
Lady Julia Grey Mysteries
This Victorian mystery series features the adventures of Julia Grey and inquiry agent Nicholas Brisbane.

Silent in the Grave. Mira, 2007.
The hunt for her husband's killer leads Lady Julia and Nicholas Brisbane into unexpected danger.

Silent in the Sanctuary. Mira, 2008.
Julia returns home from Italy for Christmas and must deal with a murder in the family chapel.

Silent on the Moor. Mira, 2009.
Julia goes with her sister to a remote Yorkshire estate that Nicholas has recently acquired and finds mysteries, mummies, and a poisoner.

The Dark Road to Darjeeling. Mira, 2010.
Julia and Nicholas, now married, journey to the Himalayan foothills to help a recently widowed, pregnant friend discover the truth about her husband's death.

Robards, Karen
Robards's stories are fast-paced, suspenseful, passionate, complex, sometimes funny, and occasionally dark. (See previous editions of this guide for a bibliography of her earlier works.) (See also chapter 7, "Historical Romance.")

Superstition. Putnam, 2005.
In an effort to boost the rating of her TV show, an investigative reporter arranges a séance at the site of a fifteen-year-old murder—with deadly results.

Vanished. Putnam, 2006.
An assistant DA is shot during a robbery, but her P.I. friend doesn't think it's an accident, and when she begins getting weird phone messages from her long-missing daughter, he's sure of it.

Obsession. Putnam, 2007.
Waking up in the hospital after being beaten and seeing her best friend murdered, a woman, unable to make her own shaky memories jibe with what people are telling her, flees—and is aided by her handsome neighbor, who is more than he seems.

Guilty. Putnam, 2008.
A prosecutor's teenage past resurfaces and threatens to ruin everything she has worked for in this taut thriller.

Pursuit. Putnam, 2009.
As the only survivor of a car accident that kills the First Lady, an attorney quickly changes her opinion of the crash when someone tries to kill her in the hospital, as well.

Shattered. Putnam, 2010.
An attorney discovers a photo of a woman who looks just like her in a thirty-year-old cold case file and decides to investigate—a decision that could get her killed.

Robb, J. D. (Pseudonym of Nora Roberts)
Robb's futuristic detective stories are included in the Alternative Reality Romance section.

Roberts, Nora
Award-winning, best-selling Roberts is one of the genre's luminaries; she writes both Contemporary Series and single-title Romances, some of which have fantasy and paranormal aspects. Her Romantic Suspense titles are chilling, suspenseful, appropriately atmospheric, and, like all her books, fast-paced, well-written, and feature well-developed, believable characters. Some of her older titles, such as *Public Secrets* (1990), *Private Scandals* (1993), and *Montana Sky* (1997), are Rita Award winners or classics. See also chapter 5, "Contemporary Romance," chapter 9, "Alternative Reality Romance," and chapter 13, "Linked Romances."

The Reef. Putnam, 1998.
Sunken treasure, murder, and a curse bring a marine archaeologist and a diver together as they work to find answers and outwit a wicked villain in this Caribbean-set Romance.

River's End. Putnam, 1999.
A young woman who has repressed the details of her movie-star mother's murder finds herself in danger when her father, who supposedly was the killer, returns to her life. Set on Washington's Olympia Peninsula.

Carolina Moon. Putnam, 2000.
A psychic "sees" the events of her best friend's rape and murder when they were both eight and ends up in the killer's sites when she returns home as an adult.

The Villa. Putnam, 2001.
A wine-country matriarch uses her will to force her granddaughter and step-grandson to work together in this suspenseful Romance that adds a dangerous threat from an unexpected source.

Three Fates. Putnam, 2002.
The three Sullivan siblings set out to reclaim a stolen statue and find its two mates (the Three Fates).

Birthright. Putnam, 2003.
A woman who was stolen as a baby and later adopted, finds her life in danger as she tries to get the facts.

Northern Lights. Putnam, 2004.
A big city cop becomes the police chief of a remote Alaskan town and is attracted to an intrepid bush pilot.

Blue Smoke. Putnam, 2005.
An arson cop is targeted by a killer with a grudge and finds help and love with her carpenter neighbor.

Angels Fall. Putnam, 2006.
An emotionally fragile newcomer to Angels Fist, Wyoming, knows she's witnessed a murder, but people are reluctant to believe her, especially when there's no evidence.

High Noon. Putnam, 2007.
A hostage negotiator finds romance with a local entrepreneur but is threatened by a killer with a vendetta against her.

*Tribute. Putnam, 2008.
A woman plans to renovate her late screen-star grandmother's Shenandoah Valley home and finds romance with a fascinating neighbor and a mystery that turns dangerous.

Black Hills. Putnam, 2009.
Summer vacation friends for years, an investigator and a wildlife biologist reconnect when Cooper Sullivan comes back to South Dakota, and he and Lil Chance are targeted by a serial killer who had them in his sites years earlier.

The Search. Putnam, 2010.
A woman who helped put a serial killer in prison is threatened by a copycat killer who wants to finish the job.

Chasing Fire. Putnam, 2011.
A killer causes deadly problems for Missoula smoke jumpers Rowan Tripp and Gulliver Curry as they fight wildfires in the blazing West.

Rose, Karen
Many of Rose's riveting thrillers feature twisted serial killers and are linked by character or place.

Don't Tell. Warner Forever, 2003.
After successfully escaping her abusive, corrupt cop husband by "being dead" for years, Caroline Stewart and her son are once again the target of his search—just as she is beginning to find love with her history professor boss.

Have You Seen Her? Warner Forever, 2004.
A special agent and a high school teacher are drawn together by a vicious killer who stalks teenage girls.

I'm Watching You. Warner Books, 2004.
An unbalanced admirer of a criminal prosecutor sets out to "take care of" the criminals who got off, creating a situation that quickly turns deadly for the prosecutor herself.

Nothing to Fear. Warner Books, 2005.
A women's shelter is threatened when a psychopathic killer and her young kidnap victim take refuge there.

You Can't Hide. Warner Vision, 2006.
A psychiatrist is being framed by a master killer when her patients begin committing suicide.

Count to Ten. Warner Vision, 2007.
A firefighter and a police detective, who is suffering from guilt over her partner's serious injury, try to stop a homicidal arsonist.

Die for Me. Grand Central Publishing, 2007.
An archaeologist works with a police detective to stop a killer from filling up the remaining empty graves in his "personal cemetery."

Scream for Me. Grand Central Publishing, 2008.
A special agent searches for a serial killer and becomes involved with a nurse who is being targeted by the current killer.

Kill for Me. Grand Central Publishing, 2009.
A woman returns to her small hometown to face her past and help bring down a sex slave ring with the help of a special state investigator and becomes the target of those who will stop at nothing to keep their evil secrets hidden.

I Can See You. Grand Central Publishing, 2009.
An emotionally and physically scarred grad student exploring the addictive nature of online communities joins forces with a homicide detective when her test subjects begin committing suicide and she suspects murder.

Silent Scream. Grand Central Publishing, 2010
A detective and a firefighter rekindle their long-ago romance as they try to outwit a killer who preys on teenagers.

Ross, JoAnn
See also chapter 5, "Contemporary Romance."

High Risk Series
Heroes recovering from a tragic mission in Afghanistan, and often suffering from PTSD, connect the stories in this intense, suspenseful series.

Free Fall. Signet, 2008.
A former Navy SEAL wounded mentally and physically returns home to South Carolina and reconnects with a young woman who is still recovering from a terrorist attack and together they must deal with a serial killer operating in the town.

Crossfire. Signet, 2008.
An FBI agent and a former Navy SEAL (with a very brief, passionate past) join forces to track down a serial killer.

Shattered. Signet, 2009.
A doctor (now working in a Central American clinic) and helicopter pilot (now with a prosthetic leg) who worked together in the Middle East reconnect when the doctor's partner is kidnapped and they both are part of the rescue mission.

Breakpoint. Signet, 2009.
A pair of former antagonists work together to solve a murder.

Sala, Sharon (Also Writes as Dinah McCall)

Sala is a veteran writer of Contemporary Romance and Romantic Suspense and writes riveting, suspenseful, often heart-wrenching stories.

Cat Duprée Series

Bounty hunter Cat Duprée tracks down the bad guys and finds romance with fellow hunter Wilson McKay.

> *Nine Lives*. Mira, 2006.
> *Cut Throat*. Mira, 2007.
> *Bounty Hunter*. Mira, 2008.

The Healer. Mira, 2008.
A mystical healer finds romance as he seeks to avoid a man who thinks the hero can help him live forever in this gently paranormal Romance.

The Warrior. Mira, 2009.
A woman flees when she learns her father is selling arms to terrorists and finds shelter with a man who has been on the track of her father for generations in this suspenseful tale tinged with touches of the paranormal.

Storm Front Trilogy

Storms and violent tornados set the scenes for this trio of suspenseful adventures, all with Louisiana settings.

Blown Away. Mira, 2010.
When a novelist surprises her ex-fiancé while he's digging a grave in the woods, she flees and takes on the identity of her look-alike cousin after the cousin is killed during a tornado.

Torn Apart. Mira, 2010.
Estranged parents reunite when their young son is kidnapped when a tornado blows through their small town.

Swept Aside. Mira, 2010.
A woman staying at an isolated Louisiana plantation is taken hostage by four prisoners who escaped during a violent storm, but finds help—and love—when one of the men turns out to be an undercover DEA agent.

Sawyer, Meryl

Sawyer's excels in gripping, complex, strongly plotted tales of romantic intrigue and suspense.

Lady Killer. Zebra, 2004.
The search for a serial killer targeting successful San Francisco women brings a columnist and an investigative reporter together.

Better Off Dead. HQN, 2005.
A dive shop owner with a top-secret life and a whistle blower in the Witness Protection Program find themselves targeted by the same villains in this Hawaii-set thriller

Half Past Dead. HQN, 2006.
A murder investigation has unexpected results for a reporter and a cop in this Romance steeped in Southern charm.

Kiss of Death. HQN, 2007.
Delightful dogs add charm to his chilling thriller that has more than its share of complex twists.

Death's Door. HQN, 2009.
A heroine on a serial killer's "to do" list and a retired detective join forces to solve the mystery and outwit the villains.

Play Dead. HQN, 2010.
An artist, targeted for murder and thought to be dead when her car explodes with her friend inside, works to solve the mystery—and stay alive—with the help of an FBI agent.

Shayne, Maggie (Pseudonym for Margaret Benson)
Shayne is a veteran, award-winning writer of Fantasy and Paranormal Romances, as well as Romantic Suspense. See also chapter 9, "Alternative Reality Romance."

Mordecai Young Series
Fanatical cult leader Mordecai Young impacts the lives of the characters in various ways in this series.

Thicker than Water. Mira, 2003.
When a popular newscaster's blackmailer ends up dead and her daughter is threatened, she turns to a shock-jock reporter for help.

Colder than Ice. Mira, 2004.
A government agent is sent to Vermont to protect a woman he thought he killed during a raid on Mordecai Young's cult seventeen years earlier.

Darker than Midnight. Mira, 2005.
A police officer and a wrongly incarcerated escaped murderer/mental patient find the real killer and fall in love at the same time. Some paranormal elements.

Secrets of Shadow Falls
This series is set in the quiet town of Shadow Falls, Vermont, and has character links to some of Shayne's earlier books.

Killing Me Softly. Mira, 2010.
A new series of murders makes the town wonder if the right man was convicted for the crimes of the Nightcap Strangler, who wreaked havoc on the town sixteen years ago, in the first of this trilogy that has character links to the Mordecai Young series.

Kill Me Again. Mira, 2010.
A wounded man with no memory and an English professor fall for each other as they work together to discover who is threatening them both.

Kiss Me, Kill Me. Mira, 2010.
A murder threatens to expose a doctor's long-kept secrets.

Skye, Christina (Pseudonym for Roberta Helmer)
See also chapter 9, "Alternative Reality Romances."

Code Name Series
High-tech combines with deadly thrills in this suspenseful action-packed series featuring paranormally enhanced operatives.

Code Name: Nanny. Dell, 2004.
An FBI agent and a Navy SEAL go undercover as a nanny and a gardener to safeguard the two children of an assistant DA, who is engaged to a presidential hopeful, from various threats.

Code Name Princess. Dell, 2004.
A stolen experimental koala bear brings an undercover hotel inspector (who is also the twin sister of the heroine in the previous novel) and a Navy SEAL together in a lively adventure.

Code Name: Baby. HQN, 2005.
A woman training biologically enhanced puppies becomes a target of an agent gone rogue.

Code Name: Blondie. HQN, 2006.
Rescued by a Navy SEAL when her plane goes down, a photographer is stranded on a remote island with a man who doesn't trust her, a man who is on their trail, and a wonderful dog—and there's a hurricane on the way.

Code Name Bikini. HQN, 2007.
Murder, sabotage, and romance plague a recovering Firefox operative and a pastry chef aboard a cruise ship. Includes some paranormal elements.

To Catch a Thief. HQN, 2008.
Includes characters from both the Skye's Code Name and Draycott Abbey series; included in chapter 9.

Spindler, Erica
Most of the Spindler's recently popular books are more Mystery than Romance. Several with some romantic elements are listed below.

Bone Cold. Mira, 2001.
A mystery writer has problems convincing a detective that her life is in danger—until he connects her with a series of murders in this Louisiana-set thriller.

Dead Run. Mira, 2002.
A woman goes to Key West to check into her sister's disappearance and joins forces with an ex-cop-turned-bar-owner when the murders start.

Blood Vines. St. Martin's Press, 2010.
A baby's remains unearthed in a Sonoma county vineyard throws a woman's life into chaos as she, with help of an attractive detective, discovers a lost past—and new danger.

Watch Me Die. Minotaur, 2011.

Staub, Wendy Corsi
Staub also writes Contemporary Romances and Chick Lit as Wendy Markham. Her well-plotted, complex, chillingly suspenseful tales are more Mystery than Romance, and some have paranormal aspects. Two recent titles with a dash of romance are listed below.

Dying Breath. Zebra, 2008.
A woman plagued her entire life by visions of children in danger finally takes action and ends up endangering her daughter in the process.

Dead before Dark. Zebra, 2009.
A psychic detective reconnects with a former flame when she becomes the target of a serial killer who has chosen her to be his grand finale.

Stewart, Mariah
Stewart combines clever plotting and taut suspense with just the right amount of romance in most of her suspenseful novels. Many of her books feature FBI agents and involve members of the Shields family.

Dead Series
Three inmates agree to murder people on each others' "to kill" lists, setting the stage for the perfect crimes, or so they think. The last book solves an ongoing mystery, as well.

Dead Wrong. Ballantine, 2004.
Dead Certain. Ballantine, 2004.
Dead Even. Ballantine, 2004.
Dead End. Ballantine, 2005.

Truth Series
The search for the truth about old serial killings drives the plot of most of the stories in this series.

Cold Truth. Ballantine, 2005.
A woman tries to learn the truth about a series of old killings her father was charged with and executed for when some current murders exhibit a striking resemblance to those for which her father was convicted.

Hard Truth. Ballantine, 2005.
A woman's search for the truth when the body of a supposed killer turns up on her land—dead for more than twenty years—threatens to unearth secrets the real killer would rather keep buried.

Dark Truth. Ballantine, 2005.
Recent murders make people think that the Bayside Strangler, who has supposedly died, has come back to tiny Bowers Inlet.

Final Truth. Ballantine, 2006.
A spate of killings after the release of a man who may be an unrelenting serial killer sends a true-crime writer and an FBI agent, who may have helped set him free, to North Carolina.

Last Series
The Shields family and the Mancini Task Force return in this trilogy.

Last Look. Ballantine, 2007.
The discovery of the body of a recently murdered woman who was thought to have been killed two decades earlier (and whose supposed killer has already been executed), sets off an investigation that could tear the town apart.

Last Words. Ballantine, 2007.
Police Chief Gabriel Beck and FBI Agent Mia Shields search for a serial killer.

Last Breath. Ballantine, 2007.
The search for some missing Middle Eastern artifacts brings an archaeologist and a special FBI agent together as the bodies and the danger mounts.

Mercy Street Foundation Series

This riveting series centers on the professionals who investigate cold cases for a privately endowed foundation dedicated to finding missing persons.

Mercy Street. Ballantine, 2008.
A crime writer and a detective take on the search for a pair of missing teens and the killer of two others.

Cry Mercy. Ballantine, 2009
A Mercy Street investigator's search for a missing college student leads her and the student's uncle/guardian to a fertility clinic and into unexpected danger.

Acts of Mercy. Ballantine, 2009.
A Mercy Street profiler and an FBI agent work against time to stop a clever serial killer who poses his victims to reenact the Seven Acts of Mercy.

Stewart, Mary

The writer who set the standards for the Romantic Suspense genre. See previous editions of this guide for earlier titles and annotations. The title listed below was not included in the earlier editions.

Rose Cottage. Morrow, 1997.
Sent back to her childhood home in northern England by her elderly grandmother to retrieve some family belongings, Kate Herrick, orphaned as a child and now widowed because of World War II, arrives at the closed-up Rose Cottage to find the place ransacked and the safe empty. Mystery, Romance, and a Gothic touch enhance this gently paced story.

Stuart, Anne (Pseudonym for Anne Kristine Stuart Ohlrogge)

Stuart is an award-winning, best-selling writer of Contemporary, Historical, and Paranormal Romances, as well as Romantic Suspense. Her stories are chilling, tense, and dark and may have a slightly paranormal cast.

Shadows at Sunset. Mira, 2000.
A haunted Hollywood mansion is the setting for this chilling, sometimes humorous, slightly paranormal Romance.

The Widow. Mira, 2001.
A woman returns to Tuscany to settle the estate of her much older artist/estranged husband and finds danger and love in this tale with a Gothic touch.

Still Lake. Mira, 2002.
A man returns to Colby, Vermont, to see who really killed the women he was originally convicted of murdering in this taut thriller.

Into the Fire. Mira, 2003.
A woman reconnects with a bad boy from her past who she considers responsible for leading her late cousin down the road to disaster.

Ice Series

This dark and dangerous series involves operatives of the shadowy, covert organization known as The Committee.

Black Ice. Mira, 2005.
Children's book translator Chloe Underwood accepts a job outside Paris, discovers she's working for an illegal arms cartel, and must depend on undercover Committee operative Bastian Toussaint to keep her safe.

Cold as Ice. Mira, 2006.
An attorney becomes ensnared in a terrorist plot and must work with an undercover Committee operative to stop the villain.

Ice Blue. Mira, 2007.
A museum curator, Summer Hawthorne's cherished blue ceramic bowl brings Committee operative Takahashi O'Brien into her life when her keepsake becomes the center of potentially destructive conflict.

Ice Storm. Mira, 2007.
The powerful Committee chairman, Isobel Lambert, must assure the safe passage of a terrorist who turns out to be a man she'd thought she killed years earlier.

Fire and Ice. Mira, 2008.
A grad student becomes the target of Russian hit men and becomes an "assignment" and an attraction for a Committee operative when she goes to Japan to visit her sister and sister's husband.

Silver Falls. Mira. 2009.
A freelance photographer single mom marries a college professor who turns out to be a serial killer—and she refuses to believe her husband's reporter brother who knows the truth.

Sutcliffe, Katherine
Sutcliffe also writes Historical Romances. Her stories are often dark, edgy, and gritty.

Darkling I Listen Jove. 2001.
A writer falsely convicted of rape and murder and now being stalked must decide if he can trust a tabloid reporter who volunteers to help him with his biography in this powerful, complex tale.

Bad Moon Rising. Jove, 2003.
A serial killer plagues New Orleans, threatening a former prostitute and an attorney who has his own reasons for wanting revenge in this dark thriller.

Taylor, Janelle
Taylor is also noted for her earlier Historical Romances. See also chapter 13, "Linked Books."

In Too Deep. Zebra, 2001.
A former cop protects a woman from an abusive ex-husband who might also be a killer.

Dying to Marry. Zebra, 2004.
A woman returns to her hometown for her cousin's wedding, reconnects with an old love, and is caught up in a dangerous mystery when she fears her cousin's life is in danger.

Sedgewick Daughters Trilogy
Three half-sisters must follow instructions left in letters by their late father in order to receive their inheritance in this suspenseful trilogy.

Watching Amanda. Zebra, 2005.
Amanda is saved from being killed when a bizarre requirement of her father's will that she sit in a window for an hour each day brings her "watcher" to her rescue.

Haunting Olivia. Zebra, 2006.
A woman reconnects with her high school love and discovers that he is raising the child she'd thought was stillborn.

Shadowing Ivy. Zebra, 2007.
Ivy Sedgewick may be in danger from the man she had planned to marry in the final volume of this trilogy.

White, Loreth Anne
Many of White's Romances are parts of publishers' series.

Seducing the Mercenary. Silhouette Romantic Suspense, 2007.
An undercover psychologist is attracted to the dictator she was sent to Africa to assess.

Heart of a Renegade. Silhouette Romantic Suspense, 2008.
A bodyguard and the investigative journalist he was hired to protect become targets of a violent band of Chinese criminals.

Her 24-Hour Protector. Silhouette Romantic Suspense, 2009.
Romance blossoms between the sister of a murder victim and the FBI agent who's heading up the murder investigation.

Cold Case Affair. Silhouette Romantic Suspense, 2009.
A woman returns to Alaska when her grandfather dies, reconnects with an old love, and becomes involved in solving the bombing mystery her grandfather was working on when he was murdered.

Whitney, Phyllis A.
See Gothic Romance bibliography.

Woods, Sherryl
See chapter 5, "Contemporary Romance," for Woods's current titles and previous editions of this guide for her Romantic Suspense novels.

York, Rebecca (Pseudonym for Ruth Glick)
See chapter 9, "Alternative Reality Romance."

Gothic Romance

Gothic Romance—Romantic Mysteries, often with historical settings, these stories feature isolated settings; relatively small groups of characters; brave, vulnerable heroines; enigmatic heroes; and a brooding, menacing atmosphere.

Early Gothic Prototypes

Several of the early literary Gothics have been reprinted and make fascinating reading. Written over two centuries ago in a different world for a very different group of readers, some of the characterizations, conventions, and assumptions implicit in them may seem alien to our contemporary culture. Essentially, these Gothic novels are not the Gothics of today. The study of psychology as we know it did not exist for Radcliffe and Walpole; the writers of today cannot remember when the ideas of Freud did not form the foundation for explaining every human thought, action, or reaction. Nevertheless, these works were extremely popular in their day and are still excellent examples of pure terror and suspense. The modern Romantic Mysteries owe them much, possibly their very existence.

These works have been reprinted in various editions and are all are in print as of this writing. The dates listed immediately following the title are those of original publication. (See previous editions of this guide for annotations.)

Lewis, Matthew Gregory. Ambrosio; or **The Monk** (1795).
Radcliffe, Ann. The Mysteries of Udolpho (1794).
Walpole, Horace. The Castle of Otranto (1764).

Modern Gothic Prototypes

Although the Gothic Novel can trace its roots from the late eighteenth century, it is in *Jane Eyre* by Charlotte Brontë and *Rebecca* by Daphne Du Maurier that the modern Gothic Romance has its true antecedents. (Note: This use of the term Gothic should not be confused with the Gothic time period of the late Middle Ages. This usage refers to works that have grotesque, macabre aspects and the typical novel often contained an abundance of castles or abbeys; specters; and other eerie, supernatural, or horrible [a la Monk Lewis] occurrences.) The basic plot patterns of both works have been widely adapted and their numerous variations form the frameworks for most contemporary Gothic Romances. *Jane Eyre* provides us with the poor-orphaned-governess-who-falls-in-love-with-the-man-of-the-house theme and *Rebecca* contributes the hasty-marriage-to-a-mysterious-man-who-has-a-terrible-secret plotline. *Rebecca* also gives us Manderley, the first house to become a truly memorable character in a Gothic novel.

While both works exude a properly Gothic atmosphere and include a number of archetypal Gothic characters (the resentful housekeeper; the insane relative; the moody, secretive hero; etc.), it is another work, *Wuthering Heights* by Emily Brontë, that provides us with some of the more chilling elements of the genre—revenge, violence, insidious evil, the supernatural, and the general sense of impending doom. In addition, its isolated setting and the wild and stormy atmosphere, as well as certain characteristics of the brooding, haunted hero, Heathcliffe, are widely imitated in many contemporary Gothics.

These three prototypes of the modern Gothic are now considered literary classics. All three are in print; all three have been made into major motion pictures; and all three make excellent reading.

Brontë, Charlotte. Jane Eyre (1847).
Brontë, Emily. Wuthering Heights (1847).
Du Maurier, Daphne. Rebecca (1938).

Although the Gothic Romance is currently less popular than its sister subgenre, Romantic Suspense, the Gothic is still around—and it is still being requested and read.

Older works are still in print and many works that are no longer being published are often still available in libraries or in individual private collections. Gothics by such classic luminaries as Victoria Holt, Phyllis Whitney, and Barbara Michaels have remained continuously in print, and there are several newer authors testing the Gothic waters. In addition, a number of recent Romances, particularly those of the Romantic Suspense and Paranormal varieties, make use of enough Gothic conventions that they may appeal to Gothic fans, as well.

Modern Classic Gothic Romance Authors

Coffman, Virginia (1914–2005) **Moura Series,** *Lucifer Cove Series*.
Wrote more than ninety novels that combined Gothic and detective conventions with historical, atmospheric settings.

Conway, Laura (Dorothy Phoebe Ansle)
Wrote more than two hundred Romances under a variety of pseudonyms.

Daniels, Dorothy
Wrote approximately 150 novels, primarily Gothic Romances with logically explained events. Her later books tended toward Romantic Suspense.

Victoria Holt (Eleanor Burford Hibbert) (1906–1993)—**Mistress of Mellyn** (1960), **Kirkland Revels** (1962), **Bride of Pendorric** (1963), **The Legend of the Seventh Virgin** (1965), **Menfreya in the Morning** (1966), **The King of the Castle** (1967), **The Shivering Sands** (1969).
Wrote Gothic and Historical Romances with Gothic elements under this pseudonym. These first seven are her best-known, most purely Gothic works.

Barbara Michaels (Barbara Mertz)—**The Master of Blacktower** (1966), **Ammie, Come Home** (1969), **Stitches in Time** (1995).

Whitney, Phyllis (1903–2008)
Whitney wrote more than seventy novels, most of which were well within the boundaries of the contemporary Gothic Romance.

Selected Gothic Romance Bibliography

The following authors are known for their contributions to Gothic Romance, although they may also write in and be noted for works in other subgenres. Only their Gothic Romance novels are listed below. A number of classic Gothic Romance authors are no longer writing, but their works may still be of interest. For space reasons, they could not be included here, but please see the previous editions of this guide for additional writers. In addition, earlier works by many of the writers listed below may be found in previous editions of this guide.

Aiken, Joan
Aiken is an imaginative, literate writer whose works are not always easy to categorize. However, Gothic elements are present in many of her novels.

Brandewyne, Rebecca
Brandewyne has written in a number of Romance subgenres, and many of her works make use of Gothic elements. Several of these are listed below.

The Love Knot. Mira, 2003.
A woman becomes a governess on an isolated Cornish estate and finds mystery, danger, and love in classic Gothic style.

The Ninefold Key. Mira, 2004.
The search for his father's killers involves Malcolm Ramsay and Ariana Levesque in a mystery that involves an ancient curse, a stolen Egyptian emerald, and danger.

From the Mists of Wolf Creek. Silhouette Nocturne, 2009.
A woman is saved from danger by a black wolf when she returns to Wolf Creek to restore her grandmother's farmhouse in this sweet Romance that has only hints of the paranormal.

Carr, Philippa (Eleanor Burford Hibbert—also writes as Victoria Holt and Jean Plaidy)

Carr's Daughters of England Saga, labeled Historical Gothics by Carr herself, takes the descendents of one family from the English Reformation to World War II. Carr's final book, published posthumously and titled *Daughters of England*, is not linked to this series. See the previous volumes of this guide for a bibliography of the series.

Chase, Allison (Pseudonym for Lisa Manuel)
See also chapter 7, "Historical Romance."

Blackheath Moor Series
A pair of 1830s Gothics with plenty of passion, a paranormal twist, and appropriately Gothic settings.

Dark Obsession. Signet Eclipse, 2008.
A pair of newlyweds try to get the bottom of a terrible mystery in a house haunted by ghosts.

Dark Temptation. Signet Eclipse, 2008.
A young woman and a troubled nobleman find love and danger when they investigate some unexplained lights in the harbor.

Eden, Dorothy
Eden is a renowned novelist in a number of fiction genres, including Romantic Suspense and Historical and Gothic Romance. Her writing career spanned over four decades and many of her earlier works were Gothic Romances or Romantic Suspense with Gothic elements.

Elgin, Mary
Elgin's few Gothics are well-written, appropriately set, and enhanced by a marvelous sense of whimsy and humor.

Erskine, Barbara
Erskine's Romances often contain supernatural, paranormal, or time travel elements. See chapter 9, "Alternative Reality Romance."

Heyer, Georgette
Noted for her Historical and classic Regency Romances, Heyer produced one true Regency Gothic. See also chapter 8, "Traditional Regency Romance."

Cousin Kate. Bodley Head, 1968 (Dutton, 1969).

Hill, Pamela
Hill writes Historical Romances, many of which have decidedly Gothic characteristics.

Holland, Isabelle

Holland's psychological Gothics occasionally include paranormal or psychic elements and several of her later novels have a number of characters in common.

Holt, Victoria (Eleanor Burford Hibbert)

Although a prolific writer in several Romance subgenres, her Gothic Romances are some of her best works. *Mistress of Mellyn* (1960), in particular, is a modern classic in the field, and aspiring writers of the Gothic have used her early Gothics as models of the genre. (After the first seven or so, her works were not so purely Gothic, even though they did contain many of the classic elements of the genre. In addition, her novels written toward the end of her career were not always up to her usual standard.) She also has written biographical Romantic Historicals as Jean Plaidy and Romantic Historicals with strong Gothic elements as Philippa Carr. See previous editions of this guide for earlier annotations. Titles listed below were not included and/or not annotated previously.

> *The Secret Woman.* Doubleday, 1970.
> Anna Brett's search for the "secret woman" leads her from Victorian England to the tropical island of Coralle—and into unexpected and deadly danger. Less Gothic than some.
>
> *Shadow of the Lynx.* Doubleday, 1971.
> This story of love and suspense sweeps Nora from England to Australia and back again, but she can never escape Lynx, the man who is her nemesis and her destiny. More Historical Romantic Suspense than pure Gothic.
>
> *Curse of the Kings.* Doubleday, 1973.
> An ancient Egyptian curse causes problems for the heroine.
>
> *The Pride of the Peacock.* Doubleday, 1976.
> An inheritance, a priceless opal, and a taste for adventure take Jessica Clavering halfway around the world to Australia—and excitement, danger, and love.
>
> *The Judas Kiss.* Doubleday, 1981.
> When Pippa sets out for Europe to discover the truth about her sister's whereabouts, she encounters frustration, deception, danger, and, eventually, love.
>
> *The Demon Lover.* Doubleday, 1982.
> An artist goes to a chateau to paint a nobleman's portrait and is taken advantage of by him in this story that is not up to Holt's usual standards.
>
> *The Time of the Hunter's Moon.* Doubleday, 1983.
> A young schoolmarm eventually finds love in this classic Gothic filled with old legends, a creepy, mysterious setting, and several handsome, enigmatic men.
>
> *Secret for a Nightingale.* Doubleday, 1986.
> A nurse goes to serve in the Crimea and falls for a doctor that she has long blamed for her husband's and child's deaths.
>
> *The Silk Vendetta.* Doubleday, 1987.
> The silk trade is the background for this story that overflows with family rivalries and mystery.
>
> *The India Fan.* Doubleday, 1988.
> A vicar's daughter goes to India to be a nanny and is caught in the Sepoy Rebellion.

Daughter of Deceit. HarperCollins, 1991.
The daughter of a noted actress suffers disillusionment and tragedy as she makes a life for herself in this Gothic tale set primarily in 1860s Victorian England and France.

Seven For a Secret. Doubleday, 1992.
The heroine finds mystery and romance in charming Harper's Green in this turn-of-the-century tale of suspense.

The Black Opal. Doubleday, 1993.
An orphan solves an old murder and finds love in Holt's last novel, published posthumously.

Hooper, Kay
See also chapter 9, "Alternative Reality Romance."

Haunting Rachel. Bantam, 1999.
A woman must unravel the mystery of her late father's mysterious loans and a stranger who looks a lot like her dead fiancé before she ends up dead, herself.

Howatch, Susan
A notable writer of historical and contemporary family sagas, Howatch wrote a number of modern Gothics early in her career.

James, Margaret (Pamela Bennetts)
Writes chilling Gothics that leave the reader guessing until the end. Some are more Thriller than Romance.

Johnston, Velda
Writes in both the Romantic Suspense and Gothic subgenres, using historical and contemporary settings.

Joyce, Lydia
Joyce writes steamy, emotionally involving Historical Romance with an abundance of Gothic atmosphere.

The Veil of Night. Signet Eclipse, 2005.
The heroine bravely takes on a reclusive noble hero and a mysterious ruined castle in this eerie, sensual historical Gothic.

The Music of the Night. Signet Eclipse, 2005.
Revenge, danger, and romance with a Venetian setting.

Whispers of the Night. Signet Eclipse, 2006.
A woman travels across Europe to marry a man she's never seen and is tricked into wedding another in his place.

Voices of the Night. Signet Eclipse, 2007.
A woman caring for a band of orphans agrees to "become" a lady in order to help a nobleman win a bet in this riff on *My Fair Lady* with a darker Dickensian touch.

Wicked Intentions. Signet Eclipse, 2010.
A nobleman considered responsible for his brother's death sets out to prove that a mysterious spiritualist is a fake, and falls in love with her, instead.

Kearsley, Susanna

Season of Storms. Jove, 2001.
An Italian villa is the setting for this mesmerizing story that merges the early-nineteenth-century past with the present as a modern-day actress agrees to play the role of a vanished woman (whose name she shares) in a play written by the woman's lover—the grandfather of the man who is producing the play.

Kurtz, Sylvie

Blackmailed Bride. Harlequin Intrigue, 2000.
A woman agrees to pose as the missing wife of a scientist, but once at his isolated mansion she questions her decision.

Under Lock and Key. Harlequin Intrigue, 2003.
Scarred in an accident and living in an isolated castle (in Texas!), a reclusive woman is attracted to the journalist her uncle sent to keep her safe and find out who wants to harm her.

LaForge, Emily (Pseudonym for Jill Jones)

Beneath the Raven's Moon. Pocket Books, 2005.
When her uncle's will stipulates that the heirs must live at the remote Ravenswood Castle in upstate New York and take part in a "game" to uncover its secrets, a young concert pianist finds long-sought answers as well as unexpected love in this chilling, evil-laced Gothic.

Shadow Haven. Pocket Books, 2005.
A woman returns with her young daughter to renovate her ancestral Louisiana home but must come to terms with her family's psychic heritage before she can overcome the danger and evil that still lurks.

Lee, Elsie

Although known primarily for her delightful Regencies, her earlier works include some well-crafted, modern Gothics, which are both more socially aware and somewhat more sensual than the norm of their time, perhaps foreshadowing the current more sensual Gothics.

Lisle, Holly

Midnight Rain. Onyx. 2004.
Fearing that her supposedly comatose, psychopathic ex-husband is stalking her and told to get help by a ghostly child, a woman goes to her neighbor who has also seen the child—his daughter who died five years ago. A chilling, creepy tale with a paranormal Gothic touch.

Night Echoes. Signet Eclipse, 2007.
A haunted farmhouse, a couple who feels an unexplained connection, a smattering of deaths, and insidious danger are all part of this brooding Southern Gothic thriller.

Marchant, Catherine (Pseudonym for Catherine Cookson)

Noted primarily for her historical sagas and single-volume stories featuring ordinary working-class protagonists, under the Marchant pseudonym, Cookson, wrote a number of quite Gothically inclined Romances.

Mallory, Anne (Pseudonym for Anne Hearn)

See also chapter 7, "Historical Romance."

The Viscount's Wicked Ways. Avon, 2006.
A young antiques expert goes to forbidding Blackfield Castle to catalog a collection of antiquities and is attracted to the mysterious Viscount Blackfield who suspects her of being a spy in this atmospheric Gothic with a humorous touch.

Maybury, Anne (Pseudonym for Anne Buxton)
Maybury's Gothic heroines are strong and independent, her settings are lavish (and deliciously described!), and the atmosphere is properly tense and threatening.

Michaels, Barbara (Pseudonym for Barbara Mertz)
This classic Gothic writer also writes Romantic Suspense as Elizabeth Peters. Many of her Gothics contain elements of the unexplained supernatural.

Stitches in Time. HarperCollins, 1995.
An old quilt is the key to this chilling story of possession that reprises two of the characters from her classic, *Ammie, Come Home*.

The Dancing Floor. HarperCollins, 1997.
A young woman helps the new owner of a neglected estate restore the grounds that were designed by a seventeenth-century gardener who shares her last name. Old legends of witchcraft enhance this spooky modern Gothic.

Other Worlds. HarperCollins, 1999.
Michaels retells two classic ghost stories, "The Bell Witch of Tennessee" and the "Phelps Haunting of Connecticut," and brings a group of fictional and actual sleuths and experts, including A. Conan Doyle and Harry Houdini, together to analyze the situations and come up with explanations.

Navin, Jacqueline
The Sleeping Beauty. Harlequin Historical, 2001.
A roguish gambler weds a reclusive heiress for her fortune and discovers love, as well as dark secrets and mystery, in this Gothic retelling of the classic fairy tale.

O'Grady, Rohan (Pseudonym for June O'Grady Skinner)
Highly reminiscent of the original literary Gothics, O'Grady's Gothic novels compellingly combine mystery, horror, and the supernatural.

Salisbury, Carola (Pseudonym for Michael Butterfield)
Salisbury wrote chilling period Gothics, most of which are set during the nineteenth century and feature well-developed plots, surprising twists, and intriguing characters. He also was a noted suspense writer under his own name.

Shannon, Colleen
Both of these Historical Gothics have Victorian settings.

The Wolf of Haskell Hall. Love Spell, 2001.
Delilah Haskell Trent and Ian Griffith must find a way to break the curse that causes the Haskell heiresses to be killed by wolves.

The Trelayne Inheritance. Love Spell, 2002.
A young American comes to her uncle's estate to research her mother's past and is attracted to her noble neighbor who might be responsible for the rumors of vampire killings in the area.

Silver, Eve

Silver's Gothic Romances are chilling, cleverly crafted, and sexy. Silver also writes Futuristics as Eve Kenin. See also chapter 9, "Alternative Reality Romance."

Dark Desires. Zebra, 2005.
An artist begins to wonder where her doctor employer gets the bodies he studies in this darkly sensual Gothic.

His Dark Kiss. Zebra, 2006.
A governess goes to a remote Welsh castle and falls for the enigmatic father of her young charge.

Dark Prince. Zebra, 2007.
A woman goes to work for the new owner of Trevisham House and is attracted to the mysterious man in this story filled with secrets and dangers.

His Wicked Sins. Zebra, 2008.
A young woman accepts a teaching position in a remote Yorkshire village only to learn that the former teachers have been murdered. Stalking, danger, and love follow in this mysterious tale.

St. Giles, Jennifer (Pseudonym for Jenni Leigh Grizzle)

St. Giles's Gothic's are reminiscent of the modern classic Gothics of the 1960s.

The Mistress of Trevelyan. Pocket, 2004.
A woman becomes a tutor to a pair of young boys and is attracted to the brooding, enigmatic master of the house in this San Francisco–set Gothic.

His Dark Desires. Pocket, 2005.
A woman whose husband disappeared with Confederate gold ten years earlier has forged a new life for herself, but when a San Francisco writer comes into her life, she wonders if he's just after the missing gold.

Midnight Secrets. Pocket, 2006.
Cassie Andrews poses as an estate chambermaid to find out what happened to her cousin and is attracted to Killdaren's owner, Sean Killdaren, in this dark, sexy Gothic.

Darkest Dreams. Berkley Sensation, 2006.
Cassie's sister Andromeda is attracted to Sean's twin brother, Alexander, as they work to solve a series of murders.

Stewart, Mary

Noted for her stories of Romantic Suspense, Stewart also wrote two novels that fall within the Gothic parameters, *Nine Coaches Waiting* (1958) and *Touch Not the Cat* (1976). (See the Romantic Suspense bibliography in this volume and previous editions of this guide for more complete information.)

Tanner, Janet

Morwennan House. Severn House, 2002.
Set on the Cornish Coast, this thrilling Gothic includes a governess heroine, an enigmatic hero, a brooding house, and plenty of mystery.

Tucker's Inn. Severn House, 2003.
Mystery, political intrigue, and murder keep things moving in this Gothic tale set in England during the French Revolution.

Forgotten Destiny. Severn House, 2004.
When a carriage accident leaves her with no memory, a woman considers marriage to a man she despises, until a chance encounter resurrects old memories and makes her life even more dangerous.

No Hiding Place. Severn House, 2004.
After an attorney questions her husband's business dealings, a woman's world begins falling apart in this modern-day Gothic.

The Penrose Treasure. Severn House, 2005.
Evil secrets abound in this darkly, brooding Gothic.

Tyrrel, Diane
On the Edge of the Woods: A Gothic Novel. Berkley Sensation, 2004.
A San Francisco architect buys an old estate in the Sierra foothills and must deal with her grouchy, but also mysterious, neighbor, as well as disturbing events that let her know that someone wants her to leave.

On Winding Hill Road: A Gothic Novel. Berkley Sensation, 2005.
A woman moves to an isolated home overlooking the San Francisco Bay and becomes a companion to a young teenager in this mysterious, romantic modern Gothic that recalls the early Gothics of Barbara Michaels and Phyllis Whitney.

Whitnell, Barbara
After Jodie. Severn House, 2005.
A woman learns that her friend's death wasn't an accident when she takes a job at Boscothey Manor and reconnects with an attorney friend in this contemporary Gothic.

Whitney, Phyllis
Although she did not necessarily consider her books Gothics, the majority of Whitney's works are well within the limits of the Contemporary Gothic Romance subgenre—and to many readers she is still the undisputed queen of that subgenre. Isolated mansions, family secrets, unprotected heroines, and, more recently, a bit of the unexplained supernatural are standard fare in these classics of the subgenre. Refer to previous editions of this book for lists of her titles.

Willman, Marianne
The Lost Bride. St. Martin's Paperbacks, 1998.
A fascinating painting, an ancient legend, and mysterious happenings drive the plot of this suspenseful, magical, richly crafted Gothic Romance.

Mistress of Rossmor. St. Martin's Paperbacks, 2002.
Brought together when Alastair McLean, master of Rossmor, becomes aware of Grace Templar's psychic, visionary powers, the pair marry and return to Rossmor—where mystery and danger awaits in this complex, spooky tale.

TAKE FIVE!

Five favorite Romantic Mysteries:

- **Suzanne Brockmann**—*The Unsung Hero*
- **Nora Roberts**—*Northern Lights*
- **Karen Rose**—*I'm Watching You*
- **Eve Silver**—*His Dark Kiss*
- **Lydia Joyce**—*Shadows of the Night*

Chapter 7

Historical Romances

History is a romance that is believed; romance, a history that is not believed.

Horace Walpole

Journalism allows its readers to witness history, fiction gives its readers an opportunity to live it.

John Hersey

A historical romance is the only kind of book where chastity really counts.

Barbara Cartland

Definition

> **Historical Romance**—Romance novels set at any time in the past, currently before the end of World War II, 1945, these novels usually focus on the attempts of the characters to find success and fulfillment, personally, romantically, and professionally, within the framework of the particular historical time and place.

One of the most diverse of the romance subgenres, the Historical Romance category includes everything from Georgette Heyer's exquisite Regencies through Jean Plaidy's embroidered biographies to the sassy, bawdy Georgians of Jo Beverly and Eloisa James or the steamy, Sweet/Savage romps of Rosemary Rogers and Bertrice Small. However, as disparate as many of these may seem, they are all, in essence, the same thing—love stories with historical settings. The design of the love story will vary slightly according to specific type, but it is the historical setting and how it is used that is the critical element in this subgenre.

In the first place, not just any historical setting will do. In order to qualify, the historical period must be properly romantic (i.e., it must be far enough removed in time and place so that its aura is tinged with unfamiliarity and mystery). Even though any time preceding our own can technically be considered historical, the current consensus is that any time before 1945, the end of World War II, is sufficiently remote to qualify as historical. Obviously, this deadline is both arbitrary and rolling, and books that were considered contemporary only a decade or two ago are now at least nominally within the historical camp. Although still comparatively rare, some recent romances have been set successfully during World War I, the Roaring Twenties, the Great Depression, and the World War II years, but the vast majority of Historicals still are set prior to World War I, usually no later than the Edwardian Period (1901–1910). This is partly because anything later than World War I is still too recent to be considered romantic—or even truly historical—by current readers, many of whom have actually lived through some of those decades. Most people are not likely to consider as "historical" a time period they can actually remember, nor are they likely to remember the difficult realities of those times as "romantic." In addition—and this is something that is critical to most Historical Romances, especially those of the Period variety—the Edwardian is the last period during which a good marriage was "officially" considered a woman's main objective in life and was her only practical choice. With the coming of World War I, the existing social structure began to crumble as women, moving from the home into the workplace in unprecedented numbers, learned to become self-sufficient and gradually gave up their total dependence on men. These changes in women's roles, options, and opportunities expanded during the decades that followed, altering the social landscape irrevocably and allowing a new, more modern heroine to emerge, one who had much more in common with those of today than she did with her Victorian and Edwardian sisters. However, now that we are firmly into the twenty-first century and more removed from the first half of the twentieth century, these years are taking on a more charming glow—and are beginning to lend themselves more easily to Historical Romance. The trends that emerge should be interesting.

On the other hand, the historical setting cannot be too unfamiliar or the reader will not be able to identify with the protagonists. It is for this reason that certain periods and settings, especially those that are pre-medieval or non-Western, are less popular than others with many of today's romance readers and writers. They are simply too alien to allow for the necessary identification. Nevertheless, there have been exceptions, such as the short-lived flurry of prehistoric romances in the early 1990s spawned by the popularity of Jean Auel's sexy, bestselling Earth's Children series, or the long-standing use of various British colonial or Middle Eastern desert settings, particularly during the Victorian Period and usually featuring English protagonists, for the occasional exotic romantic adventure. Recently, romances with various Asian settings have been popping up, and, while there are only a few to date, Jade Lee's Tigress series (China) and Mary Jo Putney's *The China Bride* (China) and *The Bartered Bride* (Macao) are excellent examples.

Given the stipulations, then, that Historical Romances need to be set in past time periods that are distant and unusual enough to be perceived as romantic, yet similar enough to our own to allow for easy identification, it is easy to see why certain historical periods and settings dominate this subgenre. Although the mix will change from time to time, medieval, Georgian, Regency, and Victorian England all continue to be long-time favorites. In addition, recently there has been a resurgence of interest in the nineteenth-century American West. With the expanding multicultural and international nature of the population, as well as the romance readership, preferences may shift; it will be interesting to watch what new directions they take.

The Historical Romance subgenre can be divided into two basic types: those in which actual historical events and characters are essential to the plot, Romantic Historicals; and those in which they serve primarily as a romantic background to the love story, Period Romances. Both types include well-written and diligently researched titles, as well as poorly crafted ones. While some readers may prefer one genre type over the other, the distinction is mainly structural and does not necessarily indicate quality. It is also worth noting that while many books clearly fall into one camp or the other, some are not so easily categorized and, depending on one's priorities, a good case could be made for their belonging in either group.

Romantic Historicals provide accurate historical settings, information, atmosphere, and characters that are essential to the story (i.e., the particular story could not [or probably would not] take place in another period in history). A number of fictionalized biographies fall into this category. However, in romances such as these, while the historical figures are central to the plot, the actual romantic interest often focuses on an invented, or real but lesser-known, hero and heroine.

In novels of this type, the love relationship is shaped, to a large extent, by the actual historical events of the period. For example, lovers are generally kept apart by wars or political circumstances rather than simple misunderstandings or romantic entanglements, although there may be those, as well. In addition, if the heroine is an actual historical figure, the story will not usually contradict *known* facts about her, although considerable liberty is usually taken with those areas of her life that have not been well-documented. For example, while it may be fact that a certain earl married a certain lady, the details of the courtship may be wholly at the discretion of the author, although these must accurately reflect the conventions of the times. Even if the important characters are not actual historical figures, they must behave in accordance with and must be subject to the historical events of the time. In general, romances of this type are well-researched and exhibit a relatively high quality of writing, although there are the inevitable exceptions.

The distinction between the Romantic Historical and the pure historical novel is a fuzzy one at best. Some have said that historical novels have more history and Romantic Historicals have more romance. Actually, this isn't far from the truth, although in this case, "romance" does not necessarily refer to a love interest. In general, although both types usually demonstrate a literary quality of writing and a high degree of historical research and accuracy, historical novels tend to be slightly more serious about presenting pure history, using less fictionalization and greater breadth of focus. This is, however, not always the case and, indeed, many Historicals could legitimately fall within either category.

Because of the similarities between the historical novel and the Romantic Historical, it is not surprising that there is significant crossover readership between the two types. Those who like historical novels will often read Romantic Historicals if the historical aspects are sufficiently important, accurate, and well-presented. Conversely, those readers who prefer Romantic Historicals will enjoy historical novels with interesting characters, lively dialogue, and intriguing plots.

The Period Romance, on the other hand, is essentially a generic love story in a historical setting, generally patterned on the boy-meets-girl, boy-and-girl-are-mutually-attracted-but-fight-it-or-are-kept-apart-by-misunderstandings, boy-gets-girl-at-last scenario. Although, like the Romantic Historical, this type provides genuine historical information, atmosphere, and even characters, the basic plot is not dependent on the historical background, and could be easily re-written with some modification into any number of historical periods. However, while the actual facts of the political, economic, and military history may not be overly important to readers of this genre, the historical atmosphere certainly is. They want to know exactly what it felt like to be living (and loving) during the particular period in history. In short, they want to actually *experience* the period. As a result, Period Romances abound in lengthy, usually quite accurate and often fascinating descriptions of the clothing, food, houses, countryside, entertainments, manners, customs, language, and numerous other details of everyday life during the selected period. Some of the best examples of this can be found in Georgette Heyer's Regencies. Her use of the language of the period is unequaled (despite a bit of twentieth-century slang), her research is impeccable, and her knowledge of the period and the British aristocracy is so extensive that, despite an occasional detractor, critics note that her novels "will probably be consulted by future scholars as the most detailed and accurate portrait of Regency life anywhere" ("Rakes and Nipcheeses," *Time*, February 21, 1964, 102). Although it has taken time, this prediction has come true, and Heyer's novels have not only been the subject of academic papers and dissertations (e.g., Helen Muriel Hughes, "Changes in Historical Romance: 1890s to the 1980s: The Development of the Genre from Stanley Weyman to Georgette Heyer and her Successors," PhD diss., University of Bradford, 1988; Karin E. Westman, "A Story of Her Weaving: The Self-Authoring Heroines of Georgette Heyer's Regency Romance," in *Double Plots: Romance and History*, edited by Susan Strehle and Mary Paniccia Carden [Jackson, MS: University Press of Mississippi, 2003]), but they are also assigned reading in a growing number of college courses that focus on the romance genre.

Diverse and abundant, Period Romances account for the vast majority of titles in the Historical Romance subgenre and can be organized in several, often overlapping, ways. The easiest and most typical division is by time period, with categories such as medieval, Georgian, Regency, or Victorian Romance being a few of the currently popular examples. Place is often a factor, as well. And while most Regency romances, for example, will be set in England (or occasionally on the continent, if the Napoleonic Wars are part of the plot), romances set during other periods can roam the world, and sometimes do. For example, Egypt is not an uncommon setting for Victorian romances featuring adventurous heroines, and medieval Period Romances set in Scotland are popular, as well. Period Romances can also be broken down by topic or cultural emphasis, resulting in a wide variety of specialized romances, including Indian (Native American), Western, Period Americana, and Period Inspirational, to name only a few of the many variations. The Period Romance can also be broken down by sensuality level. Although this is not so common as it once was, primarily because sensual romances are now the norm and, therefore, unremarkable, Period Romances currently range from the Innocent, or Sweet, through a sliding scale from the lightly sensual to the explicitly erotic, with the majority falling somewhere in between. Less a distinction than in the past and no longer a clear dividing line among Period Romances, sensuality levels were, nevertheless, originally extremely important and still matter to a majority of readers.

The Innocent or Sweet Period Romance, popularized by the late and legendary Barbara Cartland but refined and improved on by many subsequent writers, is usually a simple, straightforward love story complete with a spunky, resourceful, and virginal heroine; a strong, dashing, and wealthy or titled hero; and the usual assortment of ancient aunts, unscrupulous villains, faithful retainers, conniving other women, and simpering cousins—all in an historical setting. While they can be intensely romantic and often display a high degree of sexual tension, these stories are never sexually explicit, and the romantic high point of the plot is usually the passionate kiss at the end of the book. Although there are exceptions, Traditional Regency Romances (discussed in chapter 8), some Period Americanas, and Period Inspirationals (see chapter 11) are often of this type.

Prior to the early 1970s, Historical Romance of the innocent variety predominated. However, with the entry of Kathleen Woodiwiss and Rosemary Rogers onto the writing scene, Historicals with far more sensuality rapidly gained in popularity and soon accounted for the majority of new Historicals being published. In spite of the fact that there were and still are a number of Period Romances published that are merely gently sensual, for some readers today, and certainly the public at large, the phrase "Historical Romance" is still synonymous with a fast-paced, racy, adventurous romance filled with wild, explicit sex.

Historically, there is reason for this view. Early subsets within the Sensual Period Romance—most notably, the Sensual Historical, the Sweet/Savage Romance, and its close relative, the Plantation Romance—were all characterized by action, adventure, and sensuous, explicit, and occasionally brutal, sex. The settings were usually exotic and romantic, with pirate ships, medieval castles, Caribbean islands, and southern plantations being just a few of the favorites. Although characteristics of these novels can be found in current romances, these specific subtypes have generally met their demise, and few of these novels are being written today. Nevertheless, some of the earlier works have been recently reprinted or may still be available on library shelves or in private collections, and several writers associated with these subsets are still producing new material. For a more detailed discussion and selected bibliography of these earlier Sensual Historical and Sweet/Savage Romances, consult the first edition of this guide.

The Sensual Historical, popularized in 1972 by Woodiwiss's *The Flame and the Flower*, is typified by a heroine who remains faithful to the hero, even though he rapes her (usually by mistake toward the beginning of the story), ignores her, pursues her, and insults and humiliates her. She may also be the target of other men's sexual desires, but she always eludes them or is rescued from them, keeping herself for the hero only. In this type, as well as in the Sweet/Savage Romance, the heroine is often in hiding from someone (almost always a man) in her past who seeks revenge and threatens her present relationship with the hero. Eventually, of course, all problems are solved and the couple is blissfully united. It is from this type of romance, with its emphasis on monogamy, that today's Sensual Period Romance is most closely derived.

In the Sweet/Savage Romance, first written by Rogers (*Sweet Savage Love*, 1974), the heroine experiences rape, abuse, humiliation, and various kinds of sexual encounters with a number of men. She usually ends up with the hero, but he may or may not have been the first man in her life.

Strictly speaking, the Plantation Romance is a highly specialized type of Sweet/Savage Romance. Replete with slave uprisings, miscegenation, incest, family rivalries, long-kept secrets, and violence, these steamy romances can be set anywhere slavery existed (e.g., Lance Horner used ancient Rome in *Rogue Roman*, 1965). However, the large plantations of the American South and the Caribbean are the settings most often used. (The warmer the climate, it seems, the hotter the historical.)

Plantation Romances contain elements of both the Saga and the Soap Opera in that the characters often continue into sequels and the sins of the fathers (and mothers) usually return to haunt the children in full measure. Kyle Onstott launched this subgenre in 1959 with the publication of the now almost legendary *Mandingo*, and while novels of this type have long since fallen out of favor, their influence can be seen in some of the more exotic romances and Sagas today. For a selected bibliography of these classic Plantation Romances, consult *Happily Ever After: A Guide to Reading Interests in Romance Fiction* (Littleton: CO: Libraries Unlimited, 1987) by Kristin Ramsdell.

Unquestionably, the Sensual Period Romances of today owe much to their predecessors, particularly their increasingly frank treatment of sex and sensuality.

However, the rape, violence, and cruelty so common in the earlier novels are no longer acceptable (if, indeed, they ever really were), and a submissive, ineffective heroine is rare enough in Historicals today to cause comment. In addition, the current emphasis is on a monogamous love relationship rather than the polygamous or serially monogamous relationships so common in the original Sweet/Savage Romances.

Today's Sensual Period Romances are diverse in both content and sensuality levels. Incredibly varied in their handling of sex, they run the gamut from the sweetly sensual to the overtly erotic, with the majority falling somewhere in between, now most often toward the steamier end of the scale. Content and topic will vary with the historical setting of the romance, and several of the more popular periods and their key features will be discussed later in this section. Many of these settings and time periods are British in focus, but there are several types of Period Romance that are essentially American in setting (an interesting development in itself in that it has only been recently that the United States has been considered old enough to be interesting historically), and because of their current popularity and unique characteristics deserve to be mentioned separately.

The most distinctive of these is the Western or Frontier Period Romance. Set in the nineteenth-century American West (most often the last half), these stories revolve around the settling of America, usually west of the Mississippi, and can involve range wars, Westward treks, gold or silver strikes, "cowboys and Indians" and "lawmen and outlaws" scenarios, and a number of typically Western themes and events. Although they are often filled with fast-paced, violent, lawless action, they can also exhibit gentler tendencies where the focus is on homesteading, family building, community, and relationships, similar to the Americana Period Romance described below. Popular in earlier years but flagging until recently, the Western Romance is picking up steam once again and shows every sign of continuing the trend.

The Native American (or "Indian" as it often is called in the trade) Period Romance is generally considered a subset of the Western Period Romance and focuses on Native American culture and/or characters, often in relation to the settling of the West. However, not all Native American Period Romances are Western; a few focus on earlier time periods and other areas of the country. (See also "Ethnic or Multicultural Romance" bibliography.)

Americana Period Romance is the historical half of the Americana Romance subgenre and it focuses on everyday life in America, most often nineteenth-century rural or small towns in the eastern or Midwestern states, but occasionally in the far west. The characters are ordinary people, the plots usually revolve around commonplace, everyday events and interpersonal relationships, and the sensuality levels vary.

Although it is debatable whether or not to consider it a true Period Romance, one more romance type must be considered in this section—the Fantasy of Passion. Although few, if any, are being written today, the Sensual Period Romance and the Sweet/Savage Romance are direct descendants of these passionate, erotic stories that alternately enchanted and scandalized their avid readers. Although these books did not use historical backgrounds, their settings were so far removed from the experience of readers (mythical kingdoms, the Arabian Desert, etc.) that the appeal to the imagination was much the same as that of the Period Romance. The prototypes of this subgenre, *Three Weeks* (1907) by Elinor Glyn and *The Sheik* (1919) by Edith M. Hull, are read today primarily as Historicals.

***

Just as many readers selectively read both Historical Novels and Romantic Historicals, they may also read across the boundary between the Romantic Historical and the Period

Romance, especially if the Period Romance makes better than average use of the historical background and characters or the Romantic Historical features engaging characters and a compelling plot. Some readers will read novels of all historical types if they are set during a particular time period; others read across many periods as long as the pace, tone, style, or other critical element is to their liking. One area, however, where readers may be less flexible is in the area of sensuality. Although the lines between the romance types have blurred in recent years, the levels of sensuality are more extreme than ever, and readers often have definite ideas about the degree of sexual explicitness they want in their books. The reader who loves a lushly sensual Historical Regency may find a sweet classic Regency far too tame, while a fan of Avalon's sweet Historicals will be put off some of the Berkley Sensations titles. There is always the exception, of course: the reader who will read omnivorously.

Appeal

The specific appeal of the Historical Romance is to our basic fascination with life in past times and to our not-so-latent yearning to escape, if only for a moment, to a time when life was simpler, better defined (especially regarding roles and rules), infinitely more exciting, and much more romantic. From our earliest pleas of "Tell me about when you were a little girl, Mommy" or "What was it like in the olden days, Grandpa?" to our more adult interests in genealogy and family history, we have all enjoyed hearing about the past and wondering what it would have been like to have lived "way back then." Historical Romances allow us to do just that. With their ability to transport us to any chosen period in history and to allow us to become a part if it, if only temporarily, Historical Romances satisfy our curiosity in a way that history books never can. They allow us to experience history with our senses and emotions rather than to just understand it with our minds. However, like all romances, Historicals are not totally realistic. For example, while it is true that eighteenth-century London stank, medieval castles were cold and drafty, and the personal hygiene of most people prior to the twentieth century was appalling by today's American standards, these details are rarely dwelt on; most authors (and readers) prefer to consider the jewel-encrusted ball-gowns and the well-cut Weston coats rather than the unwashed bodies they covered.

Like memory, Historical Romances filter out the unpleasant, mundane, uncomfortable realities of everyday life and leave only the desirable, exciting, and romantic elements. Through them we are able to participate in the romance and adventure of the period without sharing in the inconvenient realities. As John W. Gardner states, "History . . . always looks confusing and messy, and it always feels uncomfortable" (*No Easy Victories* [New York: Harper and Row, 1968]). These stories allow us to have it both ways: to have our historical cake and eat it, too. Is it any wonder that Historical Romances exist?

Advising the Reader

While general readers' advisory information is provided in chapter 3, several points to consider specifically when advising Historical Romance readers are given below.

- Many readers of Historical Romances also read Historical novels, and vice versa. Rafael Sabatini and Dorothy Dunnett attract readers in both groups, and those who enjoy Jean Plaidy or Sara Donati may also like reading Margaret George or Rosemary Sutcliffe.
- Readers who enjoy Biographical Historical novels may also enjoy Jean Plaidy's many fictionalized biographical series or Anya Seton's well-researched Historical Romances. In addition, Georgette Heyer writes in and is read by those who enjoy both types of Historicals.
- Readers may also enjoy both Romantic Historicals and Period Romances, especially as the division between some of them continues to narrow. Also a number of authors write in several Historical subgenres and their fans may be either unaware or not care that they are reading in several different subgenres; they simply like the writer's work.
- Readers of all varieties of Historical Romance may also enjoy some Gothics, Romantic Suspense, or Time Travels with appealing historical settings. For example, Diana Gabaldon's Outlander series may attract fans of Scottish and American history, although the time travel elements may put off some readers.
- In such a diverse subgenre, determining what particular type of Historical Romance the reader prefers—lively or leisurely; humorous or serious; sweet, sensual, or erotic; political or social; light on the history or dense with detail; filled with real historical figures or totally fictional; and so on—is critical. After all, Pam Rosenthal is not Georgette Heyer and Julia Quinn is not Sir Walter Scott. If a reader enjoys sweet Historicals, *The Edge of Impropriety* would not be a good recommendation, just as *Ivanhoe* would not be a good choice for someone who wants a quick read.
- For the reader who is new to the Historical Romance subgenre, recommend some of the classic works by long-standing major authors (e.g., Georgette Heyer, Jean Plaidy, Anya Seton, Mary Balogh, Mary Jo Putney, Jo Beverley, and Loretta Chase) and then branch out to the many other excellent books that are available.

Brief History

Although elements of the Historical Romance can be found in earlier literary forms, it is generally considered that the genre achieved both definition and popularity with the novels of Sir Walter Scott. Already an acknowledged narrative poet, Scott turned to the newer and somewhat suspect form, the novel, and in 1814 anonymously published *Waverley*. Scott's anonymity lasted for only thirteen years, but his popularity endured well beyond his death in 1832 and continues, in a somewhat different form, into the present. Widely read on both sides of the Atlantic, Scott's imaginative and vigorous tales appealed directly to the current fascination for past times and vanished cultures, especially those of the Middle Ages. His works met the need admirably and, in many readers' opinions, satisfied public taste better than anything else currently available. In fact, as James D. Hart observes, "Uniting the attributes of prose and poetry, his [Scott's] historical romances presented the pageantry of the past, the adventure of heroic life, the beauty of spacious scenery, and a dramatic conception of human relations, all more exuberantly and firmly realized than in any other contemporary works of literature" (James D. Hart, *The Popular Book: A History of America's Literary Taste* [London: Oxford University Press, 1950; repr., Westport, CT.: Greenwood Press, 1976], 73).

Scott's success encouraged a number of younger writers to follow in his footsteps, and a few even achieved a certain degree of fame. Several of the most important were Edward George Bulwer-Lytton, G.P.R. James, and Alexandre Dumas. Although sometimes criticized for his scandalously immoral novels, Bulwer-Lytton was quite popular with the

fashionable readers of his time. He is best remembered today for his novel of ancient Rome, *The Last Days of Pompeii* (1834). While Bulwer-Lytton wrote in a number
of fictional styles (not all of them historical), the exceptionally prolific James chose
one and used it almost exclusively. Adventure, chivalry, and romance were all part
of his formula and his public loved it. The public also loved the works of another
writer of action adventures, Alexandre Dumas. *The Three Musketeers* (1844) and *The
Count of Monte Cristo* (1845) were widely read in America as well as in France and
England, and both works, along with a number of his other novels, remain popular
to this day.

Although American readers greatly enjoyed reading English, and some continental, authors, a spirit of nationalism developed following the War of 1812. People
began to want American-authored novels set in the American past. Of the many writers who subsequently began to publish American Historicals, James Fenimore Cooper was one of the first and probably remains the best-known. Considered by many
to be Scott's American counterpart, Cooper wrote more than thirty novels, often
using pre- and post–Revolutionary War settings. His first success, *The Spy*, a tale of
the American Revolution published in 1821, and his later Leatherstocking Tales (*The
Pioneers*, 1823; *The Last of the Mohicans*, 1826; *The Prairie*, 1827; *The Pathfinder*, 1840; and
The Deerslayer, 1841), are still considered American classics. Although his stories are
actually more historical adventure than romance, romance authors owe him a great
debt. By using American settings and history as a background for his highly popular stories, he firmly established the United States as an appropriate, acceptable, and
even desirable place in which to set a novel.

At the same time Cooper was beginning his publishing career and Scott was
enjoying extreme popularity, a group of romance writers, who eventually became
known as the Domestic Sentimentalists, were beginning to make their presence felt.
These women wrote many types of romance (domestic with Gothic overtones was a
prevalent variety) and a number of them used historical settings. Although the settings of these early Historicals were often European, readers and authors were beginning to find early American history, particularly the Puritan period, intriguing. Some
thirty novels set in this particular period appeared before the publication in 1850 of
The Scarlet Letter, Nathaniel Hawthorne's Puritan classic. Among the earliest of these
was *Hope Leslie* (1827) by Catharine Maria Sedgwick, whose works rivaled those of
Cooper in popularity.

Historical Romances continued to appear throughout the century, waxing and
waning in numbers and popularity as public taste dictated. By the 1840s, Historicals
in the vein of Cooper and Scott had been supplanted by novels of a more sentimental,
and in some instances sensational, nature. By the 1850s, romantic literature was almost completely dominated by the Domestic Sentimentalists. Following the centennial, in 1876, there was a renewed interest in the American past, and historical novels
and romances with American settings began to appear in greater numbers. In keeping with the general mood of the time, these novels tended to sentimentalize the past.
Unfortunately, in doing so they often sacrificed accuracy for the sake of romance,
creating a wealth of misconceptions that continued well into the next century. One of
the earliest and most enduring of these Historicals was Helen Hunt Jackson's *Ramona*
(1884), the classic story of love among the Native Americans of the early Southwest.
By the end of the century, a number of authors were producing romances with American historical settings. One of the most popular was Virginia-born Mary Johnston.
Of a number of romances set in early Virginia, *To Have and To Hold* (published in 1900

after serialization in *The Atlantic Monthly* in 1899) is considered to be her most significant and lasting work.

This historical resurgence, however, was not limited to American themes. Romances of all types and historical persuasions abounded, including a number of novels with mythical settings. Although Robert Louis Stevenson wrote an early novel of this type, *Prince Otto* (1885), it was Anthony Hope's *The Prisoner of Zenda* (1894) and the mythical kingdom of Ruritania that enchanted the reading public and set the form for the rest of the decade. In 1901, George Barr McCutcheon produced *Graustark*, adding the pièce de résistance, an American self-made hero who marries the princess. Graustarkian romances became the new rage. Eventually the form's popularity began to decline, and it might have totally died out had not Elinor Glyn added erotic sex to the basic formula and produced the sensational *Three Weeks* (1907). This fantasy of passion, along with *The Sheik* (1919) by Edith M. Hull, foreshadowed the sexier Historicals of the future. Indeed, *Forever Amber* (1944), the Sweet/Savage Romances of the 1970s, and the popular Erotic Romances of today might well trace their lineage to these pioneering works, although the current versions have taken sensuality to new heights.

Through the 1890s and into the first decade of the twentieth century, historical fiction continued to be popular. Although infinite in variety, it was singular in appeal. As James Hart observes:

> Sometimes the fiction dealt with wondrous far-off places of distant times where the reader might see knighthood in flower and ordinary Americans succeeding to the choicest blossoms; sometimes it dealt with a homely, happier, and simpler American day toward which the reader nostalgically turned backward glances. But whatever the subject, the mood was predominantly one of escape and the medium one of romance. (Hart, *The Popular Book*, 200)

The vogue for historical fiction declined somewhat during the second decade of the century but was revived during the 1920s by swashbuckling works such as *Scaramouche* (1921 and 1922) by Rafael Sabatini. However, Historical Romances achieved even greater popularity during the two decades that followed. Largely because of the social circumstances of the Great Depression, and later World War II, readers were once again attracted to stories of a more pleasant and light-hearted past so that "every year from 1930 to 1948 brought forth a new and extremely popular romance of the past, each one cut in the same pattern" (Hart, *The Popular Book*, 261). Of particular importance were *Anthony Adverse* (1933) by Hervey Allen, *Gone With the Wind* (1936) by Margaret Mitchell, and *Forever Amber* (1944) by Kathleen Winsor.

Although *Anthony Adverse* was a lusty adventure tale with historical trappings rather than a true romance, it set the stage for one of the most important Historical Romances of the century, *Gone With the Wind*. Not only did Mitchell create a sweeping historical panorama, as did many earlier historical novelists, but she also invented believable, if not necessarily admirable, characters and let them behave more realistically than most Historical Romance novelists had done before. The unprecedented success of Mitchell's work precipitated a deluge of Historical Romances, and for the next decade the success of anything "historical" was virtually assured. While the popularity of a number of these authors was transitory, many, including Samuel Shellabarger, Frank Yerby, Frances Parkinson Keyes, and Anya Seton, are still widely read today. Although many of these novels were patterned along traditional lines, the creation and public acceptance of a more "realistic" (i.e., egocentric, independent, and willful) heroine gave authors more latitude in their characterizations and gradually a new Historical heroine began to evolve. One of the most notorious, although not the most typical, heroines of the period can be found in Kathleen Winsor's *Forever Amber*. Chaste in comparison to the heroines in today's sexy and erotic Historical

Romances, Amber, nevertheless, defied conventions, behaved outrageously, and pursued her man in a manner quite unusual for the 1940s. The book was highly controversial and sold unbelievably well.

Despite *Forever Amber*'s popularity, the Historical Romances of the next two decades were generally much tamer (Barbara Cartland's works, for example) and were somewhat overshadowed by other romance types, most notably the Gothic and Romantic Suspense subgenres. It wasn't until 1972, with the publication of *The Flame and the Flower* by Kathleen Woodiwiss, that Historicals once again began to attract the attention of both readers and publishers. Two years later, Rosemary Rogers published *Sweet Savage Love* (1974) and the historical boom of the 1970s was on. These new novels, however, were not the Historicals of the immediate past. Appealing to the current, more open attitudes toward sexuality, these new Sensual Historicals offered their readers not only the adventure and romance of earlier Historicals, but also a high degree of sensuality and, in many cases, more explicit sex. Of course, other Historical Romance types, including Romantic Historicals and more innocent Period Romances, also benefited from this surge in reader interest, but it was clearly the sexier varieties of Historical Romance that were driving the market. Interest in Historicals peaked toward the end of the 1970s, and publishers and the reading public turned its attention in a more modern direction: the Contemporary Category Romance. Nevertheless, authors continued to write Historicals, readers continued to read them, and publishers continued not only to publish them, but also to keep popular older Historicals in print.

By the mid-1980s, interest in Historicals, particularly those with American settings, was once again on the rise. At the same time, American-set Sagas and series were also attracting some attention. This trend continued into the next decade, and despite a slight softening of the Historical market in general (some of which may have had more to do with the shrinking midlist, distribution, and other industry problems than it did with reader demand), Historicals of all types remained popular.

During the following decade, the subgenre bounced around a bit but continued to hold its own, often accounting for one-quarter to one-third of the romance titles published each year (according to statistics from various ROMStat Reports published annually in *RWR: Romance Writers' Report*, a publication of the Romance Writers of America.) American-set Historicals, particularly of the Western and Americana variety, were especially popular, and romances set in the British Isles continued to attract readers. Scotland roared to the top of the charts as a favorite locale, possibly due to the popularity of Gabaldon's Outlander series, with the favored time periods being the medieval, Georgian, Regency, and Victorian.

Historicals remained popular through the early years of the new century, but by the middle of the decade they were accounting for fewer than one-fifth of the titles published. Other subgenres were on the ascent, especially Paranormal and Speculative romances, and Historicals (including the Traditional Regency Romance which lost its last dedicated line in 2006) fell victim to publishers' bottom lines. Nevertheless, Historicals weren't down for long and as of this writing they are more popular than ever. Regency England is still the runaway favorite setting, but the neighboring Georgian and Victorian time periods have avid fans, as well. Medieval Scotland remains a popular setting, as always. Recently, the American West, which had slipped out of favor earlier in the decade, has been making a comeback, and once again ranchers, cowboys, homesteaders, and settlers are bringing the Old West back to life in new and different romantic ways.

As expected, the trend toward hotter romances has impacted Historicals, and while there are still some relatively sweet Historicals being published that aren't Inspirationals, writers across the board are elevating the steam factor to new limits and the vast majority of titles released today are more explicit than ever.

Another important development affecting Historical Romance, as well as the other subgenres, is the growing popularity of linked books. While there have always been some books related by family or character in the Historical Romance lineup, in the past most were individual, free-standing titles. Now the reverse is true, and most titles are connected to several others in some way, usually by character, family, or location, and are marketed as part of a series. There are a number of reasons for this, and since linked books are currently popular with readers, the trend is likely to continue. (For a more complete discussion of linked and related books, see chapter 13.)

This is where things stand in Historical Romance, as of this writing. However, things can change in publishing in the blink of an eye—and often do. Nevertheless, the Historical Romance has been around in some form for a long time, and given its remarkable ability to adapt and change with the times, it is likely to continue to happily entertain readers for years to come.

Historical Novel

The principal requirement of a Historical Novel is that it be a fictional work set at some time in the past. Beyond that, limits are not usually specified, and, as a result, there is no one typical plot pattern that dominates this subgenre. However, the protagonist (most often male, but occasionally female) usually will have a cause of some kind, which, in combination with the events of the period, will motivate the story (e.g., the quest for political, social, or material success; revenge; the righting of an old family wrong; the settling of old debts; the clearing of a family name; or the regaining of a rightful heritage). In addition, there will usually be some kind of romance plotline, which, though interesting, does not normally dominate the plot.

Just as there is not one mandatory plot type, neither is there a preferred historical time period. Historical novels have been set in almost any imaginable time and place, although certain time periods have been more popular than others. However, whatever the period, it is expected that the historical setting and events will be dealt with seriously and portrayed as accurately as possible.

Although straight historical novels are outside the scope of this guide, a number of them provide romance in sufficient amounts to appeal to many romance readers. Some selected examples are listed below. The older works listed first are still widely read and most are generally available in both hardcover and paperback. Many of these are now considered classics, and several are staples in high school and college literature courses.

Selected Bibliography of Classic Nineteenth-Century Historical Novels

Note: The dates listed are those of the original publication.

Cooper, James Fenimore
The Spy (1821). A tale of the Revolutionary war with a dash of romance.

The Pathfinder (1840). This is the only one of the five *Leatherstocking Tales* in which the protagonist, Natty Bumppo, actually falls in love. Not a true romance.

Dickens, Charles
Although most of Dickens's novels are read today as Historicals, he generally wrote about the Victorian times in which he lived and was, therefore, like Jane Austen, writing contemporary novels.

A Tale of Two Cities (1859). Story of love and self-sacrifice set during the French Revolution. One of Dickens's two true Historicals. The other was the less well-known *Barnaby Rudge: A Tale of the Riots of Eighty* (1841).

Dumas, Alexandre
The Three Musketeers (1844). Love, swashbuckling adventure, and espionage in seventeenth-century France during the time of Richelieu.

The Count of Monte Cristo (1845). Although not written as a true historical novel, it is read as such today. Dumas based his story on an actual incident that occurred during the first part of the nineteenth century.

Hugo, Victor
Les Misérables (1862). This classic French tale of law, justice, love, and redemption spans the time from Jean Valjean's release from prison in 1815 to the June Rebellion in 1832 and is considered one of the great novels of the nineteenth century.

Scott, Sir Walter
Often credited with beginning the historical novel, Scott published his early Historicals anonymously. His works were immensely popular in both England and the United States.

Waverley (1814). A tale or romance and adventure centering around the Jacobite Rebellion of 1745. It was Scott's first historical novel and is often considered the first historical novel published.

Rob Roy (1818). Action and adventure in the Highlands of Scotland just prior to the Jacobite Uprising of 1715.

Ivanhoe (1819). A story of love and romance, knights and their ladies, honor and challenge set in England during the late twelfth century, just after the end of the Third Crusade.

Selected Bibliography of Twentieth- and Twenty-First-Century Historical Novels

Note: For space reasons this bibliography is highly selective and has been abbreviated; for additional authors, titles, and more complete information consult the earlier editions of this guide.

Barnes, Margaret Campbell
Barnes's novels are noted for their exquisite blending of English history and romance; many of them have recently been reprinted.

My Lady of Cleves (1946).
Within the Hollow Crown (1947).
The Tudor Rose (1953).
Isabel the Fair (1957).
The King's Bed (1961).

Druon, Maurice

French novelist Druon is noted in particular for his The Accursed Kings (Le Rois Maudits) series detailing turmoil in the lives of the Capetian and Valois kings, from Philip IV (the Fair) to John II (the Good) during the fourteenth century. Note: The dates are for the French releases; in most cases, the English versions were released the year after.

The Accursed Kings (Le Rois Maudits) Series

The Iron King (Le Roi de Fer) (1955), *The Strangled Queen (La Reine Étragnlée)* (1955), *The Poisoned Crown (Les Poisones de la Couronne)* (1956), *The Royal Succession (La Loi des Mâles)* (1957), *The She-Wolf of France (La Louve de France)* (1959), *The Lily and the Lion (Le Lis et le Lion)* (1960), *When a King Loses France (Quand un Roi Perd la France)* (1977). (This last book was not part of the original six and does not appear to be available in English as of this writing.)

Dunnett, Dorothy

Dunnett is especially known for her Lymond and Niccolò historical series, which may appeal to readers who enjoy a little romance with a lot of fast-paced, swashbuckling action.

Lymond Chronicles (Crawford of Lymond)

Set in sixteenth-century Europe and Russia.

Game of Kings (1961), *Queen's Play* (1964), *Disorderly Knights* (1966), *Pawn in Frankincense* (1969), *The Ringed Castle* (1971), *Checkmate* (1975).

House of Niccolò Series

This lively series takes its late fifteenth-century hero from Bruges (Flanders) to Italy and other exotic places, many of which are around the Mediterranean. Note: This series is linked to the Lymond Chronicles and precedes it in time. However, the Lymond Chronicles should be read first.

Niccolò Rising (1986), *The Spring of the Ram* (1987), *Race of Scorpions* (1989), *Scales of Gold* (1991), *The Unicorn Hunt* (1993), *To Lie with Lions* (1995), *Caprice and Rondo* (1997), *Gemini* (2000).

King Hereafter (1982).

Set just prior to the coming of William the Conqueror, this is the majestic tale of Thorfinn, Earl of Orkney, whom Dunnett believed to be the historical MacBeth, uniting Scotland under his reign.

Fast, Howard

Fast was a popular, prolific novelist, producing numerous historical novels set in different time periods and writing mysteries as E. V. Cunningham. He also wrote multigenerational family sagas [e.g., The Immigrants (the Lavette Family Saga)] as well as television scripts.

Spartacus (1951).

Depicting the Roman slave revolt of 71 BC, this is probably Fast's most controversial novel. It was made into a film in 1960, and some credit it with helping to break the Hollywood blacklist.

Forester, C. S.

Although noted for his seafaring novels, in particular his Hornblower series, Forester is also remembered for a number of war-related stories, including the classic listed below.

The African Queen (1935).

The sister of a recently deceased Anglican missionary and the English captain of a launch, The African Queen, plot to destroy a German gunboat in this memorable World War I adventurous romance. Note: This was made into a film in 1951 starring Humphrey Bogart and Katherine Hepburn.

Gavin, Catherine
Gavin is noted for accurate historical portrayals and her ability to combine history with romance. Her World War II Trilogy is considered exceptional.

Second World War Trilogy
Traitor's Gate (1976), *None Dare Call It Treason* (1978), *How Sleep the Brave* (1980).

George, Margaret
Both a historian and a novelist, George writes serious, readable historical novels that immerse the readers in the lives and times of the characters.

The Autobiography of Henry VIII: With Notes by His Fool, Will Somers (1986).
Mary, Queen of Scotland and the Isles (1992).
The Memoirs of Cleopatra (1997).
Mary, Called Magdalene (2002).
Helen of Troy (2006).

Heyer, Georgette
Although best-known for her period Regencies, Heyer also wrote Historical novels. See also chapter 8, "Regency Romance," and chapter 7, "Historical Romance."

The Conqueror (1931).
The story of William the Conqueror, spanning the years from his illegitimate birth to his coronation as King of England in 1066.

My Lord John (1975).
Heyer's last novel, published posthumously, tells the story of British King Henry IV's life, reign, and mysterious death as seen through the eyes of his youngest son, John. Violent and intriguing.

Renault, Mary
Renault is noted for her well-done, highly readable stories about the ancient world, Greece, in particular. See also chapter 10, " Gay, Lesbian, Bisexual, and Transgendered Romance."

Theseus Series
Theseus was reputed to be the founder and king of Athens.

The King Must Die (1958), *The Bull from the Sea* (1962).
A retelling of the legend of Theseus and the love story of Theseus and Hippolyta.

Sabatini, Rafael
One of the most popular writers of historical fiction in the twentieth century, Sabatini wrote both Historical novels and Romantic Historicals, all of which are filled with swashbuckling adventure and romance.

Scaramouche: A Romance of the French Revolution (1922).
A tale of romance, adventure, and revenge set against the backdrop of the French Revolution. The hero is imaginary but the background is real.

Sutcliffe, Rosemary

Although most of her novels were written for children and young adults, her impeccable research, vivid descriptions, and graceful, readable style guarantees that these will be enjoyed by adults, as well. Many of her stories are set in ancient England, and her roman/British novels are considered especially well-done. The titles listed below are several that were written for the adult market.

Lady in Waiting (1956).
The story of Sir Walter Raleigh's wife, Bess Throckmorton, and the political intrigue, drama, and tragedy that surrounded her.

The Rider of the White Horse (1959) (***Rider on a White Horse*** [1960; American release]).
The story of Parliamentarian General Sir Thomas Fairfax and his wife, Anne, set during the time of the civil wars in seventeenth-century England.

The Sword at Sunset (1963).
An intriguing, well-conceived version of the beginnings of Britain—considered one of her best. Also part of her Arthurian Series.

Blood and Sand (1987).
Based on the life of Englishman Thomas Keith and his journey to becoming the Emir of Medina.

Undset, Sigrid

Undset received the Nobel Prize for Literature in 1928, primarily for the following work.

Kristin Lavransdatter Trilogy

Now usually published in a single volume, these three novels detail the harsh conditions that existed in fourteenth-century medieval Norway. Original Norwegian titles are in parentheses.

The Wreath—also published as ***The Bridal Wreath*** (*Kransen*) (1920), ***The Wife***—also published as ***The Mistress of Husaby*** (*Husfrue*) (1921), ***The Cross*** (*Korset*) (1922).

Romantic Historicals

Because the Romantic Historical has a history-dependent plot, many authors use this to their advantage, setting their novels during periods of change, turmoil, and general unrest. Revolutions, wars, and uprisings are especially popular, as are reigns of particularly controversial and flamboyant rulers. The idea, of course, is that exciting events make for exciting stories. While this is not always the case (we have all encountered at least one boring historical), it is generally true that dynamic stories more often than not have dynamic settings. Although most settings used have historical reality, occasionally, as in the case of several of the early examples listed below, the writer chooses to use an imaginary setting. Usually whole countries will not be invented (*The Prisoner of Zenda* is one exception), but nonexistent manor houses, castles, and families are commonplace in contemporary Romantic Historicals.

As with historical novels, there is not one particular plot pattern that is typical of Romantic Historicals. There are many and the possibilities are endless, ranging from quiet, pastoral English tales to swashbuckling adventures on the high seas. In most cases, however, the protagonist (male or female) is faced with a particular problem and the rest of the story describes the way in which he or she finds a solution to it. The historical circumstances, of course, play a large part both in what the problem is and in its inevitable solution. This is also one romance category in which the plot patterns can exhibit some inconsistency with the general definition of a romance. Although there is usually a strong romance line in most Romantic Historicals, it is not always the most important aspect of the plot. Sometimes that honor belongs to the solving of the original motivating problem, in other instances, the two plotlines are of equal importance. This is especially true of fictionalized biographies or family dynasty tales that often incorporate a large number of subplots, characters, and specific historical events. Admittedly, Romantic Historicals walk an uneasy line between the Historical Novel and the Period Romance, and many novels of this type legitimately fall into either category. While this kind of ambiguity drives some organized types to distraction, most readers won't care. For them, the designation is unimportant; it is the story that counts.

Selected Bibliography of Romantic Historical Prototypes

Most of the prototypes and/or important examples listed below are still read today.

Allen, Hervey—*Anthony Adverse* (1933).
Rollicking story of action and adventure set in Napoleonic times. A rambling tale, reminiscent of the Victorian three-decker (a novel published in three volumes).

Haggard, H. Rider—*She* (1887).
One of the original historical fantasy adventure stories involving an African sorceress, Ayesha, and a young Englishman who intends to avenge the death of an ancestor.

Hope, Anthony—*The Prisoner of Zenda* (1894).
Rudolf Rassendyll's resemblance to Rudolf, King of Ruritania, involves him in a dangerous scheme to outwit the king's half-brother, who would like to usurp the throne. This romantic adventure story established a form that is still popular today.

McCutcheon, George Barr—*Graustark* (1901).
This classic adds an American hero to the mythical romantic mix—and he ends up marrying the princess.

Mitchell, Margaret—*Gone With the Wind* (1936).
Beautiful, willful Scarlett O'Hara finds love, frustration, and tragedy in this classic romantic adventure set in Georgia during the Civil War and Reconstruction.

Orczy, Baroness—*The Scarlet Pimpernel* (1905).
Foppish, bored Sir Percy Blakeney was in actuality The Scarlet Pimpernel, the famed rescuer of numbers of French nobility slated for the guillotine.

"We seek him here, we seek him there,
Those Frenchies seek him everywhere.
Is he in heaven?—Is he in hell?
That demmed, elusive Pimpernel?"

The Scarlet Pimpernel

Winsor, Kathleen—*Forever Amber* (1944).
The lusty (for the times) story of an English country girl who eventually became the mistress of the king but couldn't forget the man she had first loved. This fast-paced romance has been criticized, condemned, and banned. Although it might have been scandalous in the 1940s, it is tame, but interesting, reading today.

Selected Romantic Historical Bibliography

Anthony, Evelyn (Pseudonym for Evelyn Ward-Thomas)
Although most recently known for her spy thrillers, Anthony wrote award-winning Historicals earlier in her career. Several titles not included in earlier editions of this guide are listed below. See also chapter 6, "Romantic Mysteries."

Imperial Highness. Museum Press, 1953—also published as **Rebel Princess** by Crowell, 1953.
A vivid portrayal of Catherine the Great of Russia.

Charles the King. Museum Press, 1961.
The story of Charles I and Henrietta set amidst a bloody Civil War.

Calandara. Hurst and Blackett, 1963.
A tale of love and war in the Highlands in 1745.

Bradshaw, Gillian
Island of Ghosts. Forge, 1998.
A Druid rebellion, a lovely Christian, and a Samartian prince find adventure in Roman Britain.

Dark North. Severn House, 2007.
War and love combine in this adventure with a third century Roman Briton setting.

Sun's Bride. Severn House, 2008.
Shipping, piracy, love, and adventure in the third century B.C. Eastern Mediterranean.

London in Chains. Severn House, 2009.
A young girl goes to London and gets a job in a print shop noted for printing treasonous literature in this adventure set during the English Civil War.

Donati, Sara
Wilderness Series
This series chronicles the lives and adventures of the Bonner family and their assorted friends as they carve out a life along the New York frontier during America's early years. The stories run approximately from 1792 to 1824 and are primarily set in the American and Canadian wilderness. The series has been compared with Diana Gabaldon's ongoing Outlander saga.

Into the Wilderness. Bantam, 1998.
Well-educated, gently born spinster Elizabeth Middleton leaves England to join her father in Paradise in Upstate New York and falls in love with frontiersman Nathaniel Bonner.

Dawn on a Distant Shore. Bantam, 2001.
This installment sweeps its characters into Canada and then on to conflict in Scotland.

Lake in the Clouds. Bantam, 2002.
Hannah, Nathaniel's half-Mohawk daughter, who wants to be a doctor, is at the center of this story that involves runaway slaves, bounty hunters, and deadly epidemics.

Fire Along the Sky. Bantam, 2004.
The War of 1812 affects the Bonner clan in various ways in this adventurous episode.

Queen of Swords. Bantam, 2006.
The action moves south to the French Antilles and New Orleans as Hannah and her brother rescue his fiancée, search for a child, and fight disease—all during a war.

The Endless Forest. Delacorte, 2010.
The Bonners' wicked nemesis, Jemima Southern, comes to town and threatens to destroy everything in this encompassing story that most satisfactorily concludes the saga.

Holland, Cecelia
Holland is a respected writer of well-researched Historicals that often feature strong, capable women and strong, unadorned writing.

An Ordinary Woman. Forge, 1999.
The true story, beautifully fictionalized, of one of the first women to cross the plains to California in the 1840s.

Lily Nevada. Forge, 2000.
An actress struggles to make a life for herself in 1877 California in this well-crafted story.

The Secret Eleanor: A Novel of Eleanor of Aquitaine. Berkley, 2010.
Although Eleanor, Duchess of Aquitaine, has been the subject of numerous novels, this one provides insight into feelings and motivations as she plans to free herself from Louis VII of France and marry Henry of Anjou.

Kaufman, Pamela
Lady Alix of Wanthwaite Trilogy
The adventures of a thirteenth-century English noblewoman.

Shield of Three Lions. Warner Books, 1984.
Banners of Gold. Crown, 1986.
Prince of Poison. Three Rivers Press, 2006.

The Book of Eleanor: A Novel of Eleanor of Aquitaine. Crown, 2002.
A fresh look at the life of this strong, passionate, legendary woman, who survived marriage to two kings (Louis VII and Henry II), political intrigue, and imprisonment.

King, Susan Fraser
King's works are well-researched and beautifully evocative of the times. She also has written earlier Historical Romances as Susan King and Sarah Gabriel.

Lady Macbeth: A Novel. Crown, 2008.
Based on current theory and historical evidence, this is a fictionalized account of the story of the Celtic warrior princess who became Lady Macbeth.

Queen Hereafter: A Novel of Margaret of Scotland. Crown, 2010.
The story of Margaret, a princess of the Saxon royal family and wife of Malcolm III, man King of Scots. She became St. Margaret when she was canonized in 1250.

Laker, Rosalind (Pseudonym for Barbara Ovstedal)
Laker is a respected, award-winning British historical novelist. She is noted for her strong, talented heroines, careful research, and vivid descriptions.

New World, New Love. Severn House, 2002.
A refugee from the French Revolution finds a new life and happiness in this rags-to-riches romance.

To Dream of Snow. Severn House, 2004.
An expert French needlewoman befriends the woman who will become Catherine the Great.

Brilliance. Severn House, 2007.
A young Parisienne's journey from traveling lanternist's assistant to star in the nascent film industry in the early twentieth century.

Garlands of Gold. Severn House, 2008.
Cosmetics, social class, and love in the seventeenth century.

The House by the Fjord. Severn House, 2011.
A woman goes to Norway after the end of World War II to connect with her late husband's family.

Penman, Sharon Kay
Eleanor of Aquitaine
This trilogy chronicles the events in the lives of Eleanor of Aquitaine and Henry II.

When Christ and His Saints Slept. H. Holt, 1994.
Time and Chance. Putnam's, 2002.
Devil's Brood. Putnam's, 2008.

Plaidy, Jean (Pseudonym for Eleanor Burford Hibbert)
(Also writes as Victoria Holt and Philippa Carr.) Jean Plaidy, the oldest and arguably the best known of Hibbert's pennames, is the one she used most often for her Historical novels of the lives of real people. She is especially known for her numerous series dealing with the various royal dynasties in England. Plaidy's work is well-researched, engaging and quite readable, and focuses on aspects of the characters and political situations that appeal to fans of social history and readers of romance fiction. The books in her series can be arranged in a number of ways, but her series generally break down as follows: Norman Trilogy, Plantagenet Saga, Tudor Series, Stuart Series, Georgian Series, French Revolution Series, Victorian Series, Queens of England, and a series on each of the following: Queen Victoria, Charles II, Mary, Queen of Scots, Catharine of Aragon, Catherine de'Medici, Lucrezia Borgia, and Ferdinand and Isabella. She has written other nonseries titles, as well. Many of her titles have been reprinted individually or as parts of collections, not always under the original titles, so readers will want to be sure to check the copyright dates and/or title information. Note: Hibbert died in early 1993; her last book, *The Black Opal* by Victoria Holt, was published posthumously. Two of her most recent Plaidy titles are listed below.

The Rose without a Thorn. London: Robert Hale, 1993.
The story of Katherine Howard, fifth wife of Henry VIII.

Madame du Barry. London: Robert Hale, 1994.
The story of the last mistress of King Louis XV of France.

Westin, Jeane
The Virgin's Daughters: In the Court of Elizabeth. I. NAL, 2009.
In a novel that is more history than romance, two of Elizabeth's ladies in waiting (Lady Katherine Grey and Mary Rogers) deal with their conflicting loyalties and romantic feelings in a treacherous court.

His Last Letter: Elizabeth I and the Earl of Leicester. NAL, 2010.
Details the classic, tempestuous romance between Robert Dudley and Elizabeth, focusing on the last three years of the relationship.

Period Romance

The Period Romance is basically a love story with an historical setting. It differs from the Romantic Historical and the Historical Novel in that, except for providing a few incidental historical characters and a compelling background against which to play out a traditional love story, the historical events of the period rarely affect the story line. The social history and customs of the time, however, have tremendous impact. Characteristically, a Period Romance recreates in great detail a romanticized version of a bygone era in which the readers can immerse themselves, experiencing along with the heroine (or hero) the everyday life in that particular time in history. As a result, the details of daily existence are of critical importance to the overall atmosphere of the story. There is a heavy emphasis on the description of clothes, food, houses and estates, entertainments, and manners. It is not unusual, for example, to be given exact descriptions of the clothes of all the important characters (male and female) in attendance at a particular ball, of the refreshments that were served, and of the dishes the late evening supper included.

Although there are numerous variations, the typical plot introduces an attractive, independent, usually unconventional heroine to a strong, purposeful, often wealthy, successful, or titled hero, places them in extreme opposition to each other, and then spends the rest of the book making sure, even though they fight it, that they fall in love and are altar-bound by the end of the book. It is important be aware that while these characters are always strong and honorable, they are not perfect by any means, and, particularly in recent years, there has been an emphasis on realistically flawed characters of many kinds (e.g., the alcoholic, the gambler, the "fallen woman," the physically or emotionally challenged, to name only a few). In fact, turning the villain from one story into the hero or heroine of another is a growing trend, especially in linked books. Typically, between the protagonists' initial, often fiery, meeting and their final embrace, any number of things will happen to keep them apart. But except for occasional historical interferences (e.g., the hero temporarily loses the heroine during the San Francisco earthquake and fire, or the hero is captured during the Peninsular wars), it is the interpersonal relationship between the protagonists and its inherent romantic tension as the two struggle with their many differences that keeps the plot moving and the story alive, not simply historical events.

Although Period Romances can be grouped in a number of ways, today they are most often divided simply by historical time period. (In the past, particularly following the rise of the Hot Historical of the 1970s, division by sensuality level was common; then romances were either sweet and innocent or sensual and sexy. However, today most Period Romances are sensual to varying degrees and the sweet/sensual distinction is less relevant than before. In fact, if anything, today's divisions lie more toward the sensual/erotic end of the scale, although except for the formal erotica lines, they are rarely broken out that way.) The descriptions that follow are for some of the most commonly used time periods as settings for Historical Period Romance.

Brief Historical Descriptions

Although it is theoretically possible for Period Romances to be set during any time in history, in actual practice most authors make use of only a few favored periods. Some of the political realities, social conditions, and customs of several of the most popular are briefly described below. Additional information can be found in most encyclopedias, by consulting the library catalog using official subject headings (e.g., Middle Ages—Social Life and Customs) or a combination of relevant terms (e.g. Scotland social life and customs) in a keyword search, or by searching the Internet.

Medieval Period

The Middle Ages, or the medieval period, lasted for approximately a millennium and filled the gap between the Classical Period and the Renaissance. Although the fifth through the fifteenth centuries are often given as the limiting dates, these are approximate at best, and the actual beginning and ending of the period are still being debated by scholars. It is, however, generally accepted that far from either beginning or ending abruptly, the medieval period grew and developed as the old Classical World declined, flourished throughout the eleventh through the thirteenth centuries, and gradually gave way to the Renaissance during the fourteenth and fifteenth centuries. By the time Columbus discovered the New World in 1492, only a few remnants of medieval society remained.

The Middle Ages are characterized, in general, by the rising power and influence of the Christian Church and the establishment, flowering, and decline of the feudal system. It was also the time of chivalry, courtly love, quests, the Crusades and other wars (including the Hundred Years War and the divisive War of the Roses), Viking raids, the development of trades and guilds, the building of many of Europe's greatest cathedrals, severe famines, and the devastating Black Death (by 1420, Europe had lost an estimated 30 to 60 percent of its population to the plague, which peaked between 1348 and 1350; see Suzanne Austin Alchon, *A Pest in the Land: New World Epidemics in a Global Perspective I* [Albuquerque: University of New Mexico Press, 2003], 21.). This was also the time of the legendary Robin Hood.

The social structure during this period was relatively simple; it consisted of three groups—the clergy, the peasantry, and the nobility—although a small, trade-centered middle class began to develop late in the period. In general, the nobles lived in castles surrounded by their lands on which the peasants worked. The peasants provided labor, loyalty, and taxes, and the nobles provided protection from outside harm.

For the nobleman, life consisted primarily of fighting and overseeing his estates, while noblewomen were concerned with managing the household affairs. However, household affairs of the Middle Ages were very different from those of today. In addition to supervising the creation and preparation of most of the food the people ate (cheese, flour, bread, cured meats, wine, ale, honey, etc.), the clothes they wore (which involved spinning, weaving, dying, etc.), and the herbs and medicines they needed to stay healthy, the medieval lady was also responsible for managing the estate when her husband was off doing battle—which was most of the time. This meant that she understood feudal law and legal matters, agriculture, and economics, and was able to deal well with the peasant subjects. She was also expected to be able to entertain beautifully, take care of all personnel problems, and keep the accounts in order. The Middle Ages produced some very capable and independent women.

However, even though she had social standing, independence, and a certain amount of control over her own wealth, the average noblewoman had little control over her love life. Infant betrothals and early teenage marriages (all arranged by parents) were common, and people usually married for political and social reasons, rarely for love. Occasionally, a woman would pay great sums of money for the right to choose her own husband, but this option was available only to the wealthy and influential.

Although the peasants far outnumbered the nobility, today's Period Romances generally deal with the upper levels of medieval society. The hero is most often a lord, laird (if in Scotland), or a knight—and if the heroine is not a lady at the beginning of the story, she usually has become one by its conclusion. The hero and the heroine are also together and in love by the end of the book, something that was rare during that actual time. These stories can be set at any time during the medieval period, although the High Middle Ages, the eleventh to the thirteenth centuries, are especially popular. Most reflect the violence and the general insecurity of the times and wars, sieges, and raids are common.

Magical and mystical elements can be part of romances set during the medieval period, and depending on the emphasis, treatment, or simply the marketing, these may be claimed by Historical Period Romance, Alternative Reality Romance (Fantasy or Paranormal, primarily), or both.

Sixteenth Century

This was the century of the Tudors, of Henry VIII and Elizabeth I, in particular. The War of the Roses was over, England was united, although somewhat uneasily, and the Renaissance, begun in Italy two centuries earlier, had finally reached the British Isles. Interest in the arts increased (Henry VIII was a noted patron), and luminaries such as Shakespeare, William Byrd, and Holbein (by way of Germany) were active during this period. Education and learning became important as people, in keeping with the humanistic thrust of the Renaissance, turned their attention to themselves and the world around them. This was also the era of the Reformation, the establishment of the Church of England, and the beginnings of British naval power. It was, in general, a time of growth and expansion, culturally and economically. It is often considered England's golden age.

Much of the activity during this period centered on the court of the reigning monarch, and many of the Period Romances set during this time take full advantage of this fact. Life at court was entertaining (Renaissance banquets and festivals are legendary), luxurious (by the day's standards), and often dangerous. It was a time when one accepted method of taking care of one's enemies was to kill them, and both Henry and Elizabeth had any number of people executed simply because they considered them threats or inconveniences. Plots of stories set in this period are filled with political intrigue, adventure, and romance—and arranged marriages, plots against political rivals, and clandestine affairs are typical elements.

It is interesting to note that in addition to being the setting for a number of Period Romances, the sixteenth century is also popular as a setting for Romantic Historicals, especially in the area of fictionalized biographies. Henry VIII and Elizabeth I both make excellent background or primary characters, and their courts were large and interesting enough to include any number of suitable heroes and heroines, real or imaginary.

Seventeenth Century

Although the change from the Tudor to the Stuart dynasties was accomplished peacefully when James I ascended the throne in 1603, the seventeenth century was marked by revolution and political and religious strife. This is the century of Oliver Cromwell and the Roundheads, the English civil wars, and the Restoration of the

Monarchy. Throughout most of the century the country was plagued by economic and political problems, but by its end, the power of Parliament had been firmly established and the role of the reigning monarch more clearly defined. Agricultural and commercial advances had resulted in a thriving economy and increasing international trade, and England had firmly established its naval supremacy.

Many of the Period Romances set during this period focus either on the clashes between the Royalist and Cromwellian (Roundhead) factions or on the Restoration. As might be expected, because most of these stories deal with life among the noble and wealthy, the heroes and heroines are usually Royalists or Royalist sympathizers. Although many express a more moderate view of the political situation, rarely are they supporters of the radical, moralistic Cromwell.

Cromwell did win, however, and Charles I was executed as a traitor to the Commonwealth in 1649. Under Cromwell, England entered a much more austere and Puritanical time and the social activities (to say nothing of the wealth and power) of the upper classes were severely limited. Not surprisingly, when Charles II was restored to the throne in 1660, there was a change in the mood of the country, and people once again began to enjoy themselves. In reaction to the extremely oppressive rule of Cromwell and the Puritans during the Interregnum, a number of highly restrictive laws were passed against the Puritans, and the Court of Charles II gained a reputation for being one of the more extravagant and immoral courts in English history.

The plots of those stories set before the Interregnum include much political intrigue and often center on outwitting the Cromwellians and saving a known Royalist (often the hero) from capture or death. Those set during the Restoration are usually lighter in nature, focusing on the social rather than the political aspects of the times. In general, most romances set during this period make some use of the varying political situations, and they are usually characterized by an abundance of action, adventure, and romance.

This was also the century of the early colonization of America, and a number of romances have been set during the early Puritan times. These stories tend to center on the difficulties of not only living under primitive colonial conditions, but also putting up with the numerous arbitrary strictures of Puritan society. Often the heroine is rebellious and spends most of her time fighting the system. Usually she wins, but she often must leave the colony as a result.

Georgian Period (1714–1830)

The Georgian Period, long and theoretically encompassing the reigns of the first four English kings named George (1714–1830), was marked by the Jacobite Rebellions, especially the "Forty-five" headed by Bonnie Prince Charlie (Prince Charles Edward, pretender to the English throne); the bloody Battle of Culloden; the French Revolution; the American Revolution; the war with France; and the beginnings of the Industrial Revolution. It was a transitional period from a more elegant, leisurely age into the faster-paced modern world of industry and democracy.

Although a number of Historicals have centered on the abortive attempt by Charles to take over the throne in 1745, many of the Reriod Romances known as Georgian are set in the Late Georgian Period, during the reign of George III (1760–1820). (The last nine years of his reign are known as the Regency Period and are discussed in the next chapter.) Some of these are quite similar in tone to the Regency Romance—light, diverting, and full of witty conversation—and except for the dates, could be classified as such. However, an increasing number are more typical of the eighteenth century, in general, and, accordingly, are fast-paced, adventurous, violent, licentious, and bawdy. Their plots usually deal with upper-class society; often focus on the French Revolution and rescuing French aristocrats from the guillotine; and often involve smuggling, robbery by highwaymen (and women), and other quite illegal, but highly intriguing, activities.

A number of romances set during this time also deal with the American Revolution. American in both setting and point of view, these stories feature spies, secret missions, hair-breadth escapes, and occasionally some battle action. The heroine is daring and independent and often becomes directly involved in the action. Although there is some mention of families divided against each other, this is not as important a feature in these stories as it is in the later stories of the Civil War. (See the Victorian description further on.)

Regency Period (1811–1820)

Because of the large number of romances set during this period and the fact that the Regency Romance is actually a separate subgenre, the Regency Period will be discussed in chapter 8.

Victorian Period (1837–1901)

The Victorian Period, named for the queen whose reign lasted from 1837 to 1901, is marked in England by increasing industrialization, rapid population and urban growth, the Crimean War, the Boer War, and world-wide colonization. The period was relatively peaceful, except for the Crimean War (1854–1856) and the Boer War (1899–1902), but those were fought far away and for relatively brief periods of time. For the English, it was an era of progress and achievement, and British power and world influence were at their height. In short, it was another golden age of the British Empire.

Because there were no major upheavals in Britain during this period, most of the romances set during this time center on society, family life, and the various effects of industrialization. One important event during Victoria's reign was the gradual shift in power from the landed gentry and nobility to the industrial magnates and the moneyed middle class. This new group could no longer be ignored, and, as a result, the *nouveau riche* came into increasing social contact with the old aristocracy. The newcomers, however, were not immediately recognized as true equals, and it often took several generations for a family to be truly accepted in all respects. These social position conflicts sometimes figure in Period Romances set during this time, and it is not unusual for a mother to deplore her titled daughter's wish to marry a man "in the trades."

Just as social position was important in this era, so was conduct and decorum. And although proper etiquette had been an issue in past times, never was behavior expected to be so prim and prudish as during Victoria's reign. Fortunately, most of today's Victorian romance heroines are exceptions to this rule, and much of the action in these stories occurs as they rebel valiantly against these arbitrary strictures.

Although some Victorian Historicals deal strongly with the many needed social reforms of the day, most current Period Romances set during this time concentrate on the social and family life of the upper classes. The heroine is attractive and can be sensible and capable, rebellious and occasionally improper, or sometimes is a bit of both. Plots usually center around marriage—to the "proper" man, of course, approved by Papa!—and can range from Regency-like novels of manners to more serious works that touch on a variety of current topics along with the strong romance line.

Although many of the same conditions that were prevalent in England during Victoria's reign existed in the United States, the major event of this period for America was the Civil War. This conflict killed more Americans than any war in history, divided families, radically changed society, and caused deep wounds that still have not healed. Novels set during this time often employ the same pattern as *Gone With the Wind*, beginning with the antebellum South, continuing through the violence and destruction of the war itself, and then finishing with the struggle of the Reconstruction Era. Plots will typically include a number of elements such as brother-fighting-brother and Southern-heroine-in-love-with-Northern-hero (or vice versa), and certain stereotypical characters (the faithful old slave, the lecherous carpetbagger, etc.) are rarely omitted. Heroines of novels of this type sometimes appear fragile and weak in the beginning (Scarlett not withstanding), but their hidden strength and resourcefulness appears just when it is needed, and they usually turn out to be very strong, capable women, indeed.

Another American event that has provided fertile background for romance novels is the Western Expansion movement. Novels set in the Old West make full use of devices such as Indian or outlaw raids, gunfights, severe weather conditions (e.g., a winter blizzard, a disastrous drought, or the summer desert heat), mutiny among the members of the wagon train, and numerous other hardships. The plots most often revolve around survival—either of the trip West or of the primitive and lawless conditions that the characters find once they get there. Success is usually achieved under extremely difficult conditions. The tone of these novels can range from violent and fast-paced to humorous and tender, and heroes and heroines alike are strong, determined individuals, capable of surviving and actually enjoying all the action that surrounds them. The American West, along with the Midwestern and Southern small town, is also popular as a setting for period versions of the Inspirational and Americana Romance subgenres.

Edwardian Period (1901–1910)

Situated between the death of Queen Victoria and the beginning of World War I, the Edwardian Period (roughly corresponding to the reign of Edward VII, 1901–1910) was a time of reaction, transition, and growing political uneasiness. It was also a time of luxury and leisure that was previously unknown in modern times, and the members of the upper classes, especially in England, were busy enjoying it. This small, privileged group, newly released from the moral and social constraints of the Victorian era and wealthy enough to be unconcerned about finances on a day-to-day basis, turned its attention to the pursuit of pleasure. And pursue it they did—methodically, consistently, and with great purpose. With productive labor increasingly considered unworthy and demeaning for the elite, it became their obligation to maintain a lifestyle of indulging in a constant variety of costly and elaborate entertainments.

Of all these numerous amusements, the Edwardian weekend house party was by far the most favored—and the most famous. Held in the large, old, elegantly furnished and beautifully landscaped homes of the upper classes, these gatherings could include as many as thirty guests, mostly members of society, but occasionally including a well-known author, political figure, or popular hero.

Food played an especially important role in these weekend affairs and, indeed, in all of Edwardian life. Food of all kinds was available at most hours of the day and night, and both lunch and dinner consisted of anywhere from eight to twelve courses. It is not surprising that this period is noted for its gourmands rather than its gourmets and that its members were inclined to vacation at the numerous continental spas to "take the waters" for their health.

Food, however, was not the only attraction at these weekend parties. It was an accepted fact that because of the strict behavioral code which absolutely forbade public scandal, these house parties were usually expected to provide numerous opportunities for discreet romantic interludes. The facilitation of these interludes was considered one of the most important jobs of the weekend's hostess. Indeed, the reputation of an Edwardian hostess could rise or fall on how perceptively she arranged her guests' sleeping accommodations.

Fashion was another important aspect of Edwardian life. Both men and women spent a great deal of time choosing and changing their clothes, often several times a day. Dandyism among the men was common and no Edwardian woman of consequence would travel anywhere for even a day without her assemblage of trunks and boxes, all containing clothes and accessories. This was the era of the S-shaped figure, the top hat, the pompadour, the walking stick, and the Gibson girl.

Although the reasons differ, the Edwardian period has much in common with both the Regency and Restoration periods. Social activity was at a high, leisure activities were all important, and the pursuit of pleasure was almost mandatory.

Like the Regencies, Edwardian Romances usually take full advantage of these aspects of the period with social behavior and manners being of paramount importance. Typically, the plots revolve around the social scene and marriage, and may include such elements as "upstairs-downstairs" situations. They may also include references to important historical events such as the sinking of the *Titanic* and the early incidents leading up to World War I. In general, however, although they can deal with serious issues, Edwardian romances are light, witty, and above all entertaining, true to their aim of depicting what has sometimes been called the last golden age.

Modern Historical Era (1911–1945)

Marked by violent conflict, great prosperity, dynamic social change, and severe economic hardship, these were the years of World War I (1914–1918), the Roaring Twenties, the Great Depression of the 1930s, and World War II (1939–1945). With the end of the Edwardian Era, the world began to change. Women of all classes were beginning to consider working outside the home, and the recruitment of nurses for the war effort fueled this trend. With the end of the war, countries began to rebuild and the mood became more optimistic. The 1920s heralded a period of social, cultural, and technological change; this was the age of jazz, prohibition (with the infamous speakeasies and bathtub gin), flappers, the Charleston, the Harlem Renaissance, Art Deco, women's suffrage achieved, and worldwide economic prosperity. It was a golden, euphoric age that came to an abrupt end when the American stock market crashed in October 1929 and ushered in the Great Depression. Characterized by massive unemployment, breadlines, bank failures, and the Dust Bowl and the resulting migrations, the 1930s brought bleak, hard times to most. Often credited with helping to end the Depression, World War II did improve the economy, but it did so at great cost and plunged the world into its second bloody conflict in less than thirty years.

Typically these romances take advantage of the important events that occur during the time frame of the story. Stories set around World War I often feature couples separated by war, heroines who want to serve as nurses or work in some other capacity but run up against family objections, returning wounded heroes, characters engaged in undercover work, and any number of other scenarios. Novels focusing on the World War II years can employ similar elements, although heroines working or joining the military would not be an issue and a spy heroine might be a definite option. A story set outside of America might also involve the characters in resistance efforts or actual warfare, as well. The 1920s provide a host of scenarios and plots can involve anything from bootlegging heroes and rebellious flapper heroines to crime bosses and business tycoons. Unlike the war years, this decade was flamboyant, outrageous, and daring, and the stories can reflect this with humor and sass, as well as deal with the more serious aspects of the times. Stories of the Depression years are often set on farms, ranches, or in small towns in middle America and focus on keeping the family together, saving the family farm/house/ranch from foreclosure, or simply living through the difficult times.

Although these years are now considered to be officially within the Historical camp and have served as the settings for a number of romances already, they are still too recent to have been the settings for many current ones. However, this is changing even as I write this; it's just a matter of time.

Selected Classic Period Romance Authors

Cartland, Barbara (1901–2000)
> A legend in her own time, Cartland was responsible for the writing of more than seven hundred light, sweet, period novels.

Eden, Dorothy (1912–1982)
> Noted for her Historical Romances, many of which have suspenseful, Gothic elements.

Rogers, Rosemary—*Sweet Savage Love* (1973).
> The novel that gave the Sweet/Savage genre its name.

Spencer, LaVyrle—*The Endearment* (1982), *Hummingbird* (1983), *Twice Loved* (1984), *The Gamble* (1987), *Morning Glory* (1989).
> A bestselling, Rita Award–winning author of classic, American-set Historical and Contemporary Romances and a member of RWA's Hall of Fame, Spencer retired from writing in 1997.

Woodiwiss, Kathleen (1939–2007)—*The Flame and the Flower* (1972).
> Credited with launching the Hot Historical craze of the 1970s.

Selected Period Romance Bibliography

The works listed here cover a variety of historical periods, exhibit a number of literary styles, and range in sensuality levels from the sweet and innocent to the sensual and sexually explicit. (Because they differ in several ways from Period fiction, in general, the Regency Period Romance is discussed in chapter 8 and the Period Inspirational Romance is discussed in chapter 11.) Many authors listed below also write other types of romantic fiction. Earlier works by many of these writers can be found in the previous editions of this guide.

Abe, Shana

Abe writes Historical Romance, some of which have paranormal and fantasy elements. See also chapter 9, "Alternative Reality."

> *A Rose in Winter*. Bantam, 1998.
> A woman forced to send the man she loves away and wed another is reunited with her first love as she plans to escape from her abusive marriage. Touching and satisfying.

> *The Truelove Bride*. Bantam, 1999.
> A beautiful heroine with the "sight" resists marrying a man she doesn't love just so he can break a family curse and becomes involved in political intrigue and unexpected passion.

Intimate Enemies. Bantam, 2000.
Although their families are old adversaries, a Scotswoman clan leader and an Englishman fight their attraction as they work together to save the Isle of Shot from Viking raiders—and then must outwit a traitor much closer to home in this exciting tale of twelfth-century Scotland.

The Secret Swan. Bantam, 2001.
Wed by family arrangement as teenagers and then separated by war and imprisonment, Tristan and Amiranth are reunited after eight bitter, difficult years—and must learn to trust each other, if they can.

Alexander, Victoria (Pseudonym for Cheryl Griffin)
Last Man Standing
Four men who know they must eventually marry and produce heirs wager a shilling each and a bottle of cognac to go to the man who remains unmarried the longest in this charmingly diverse Victorian quartet.

A Little Bit Wicked. Avon, 2007.
An abused widow with a slightly wicked reputation and a marriage-wary bachelor fall in love in spite of their good intentions.

What a Lady Wants. Avon, 2007.
When a notorious rake shows up in her garden just after she wished on a star for an exciting husband, our heroine decides that no one else will do in this hilarious romp.

Secrets of a Proper Lady. Avon, 2007.
Informed she must marry a wealthy American she's never met, a young woman seeks information from his "secretary," not realizing she is talking to her intended himself.

Seduction of a Proper Gentleman. Avon, 2008.
An ancient family curse, a heroine with amnesia, and a memorable hero combine in a clever, magical plot that nicely concludes this delightful quartet.

Harrington Family Trilogy
The Perfect Wife. Leisure, 1996.
The "perfect wife" is not so perfect in this complex story that nicely launches this trilogy.

The Virgin's Secret. Avon, 2009.
Discovered while trying to find a stolen artifact, a young woman finds unexpected allies and romance, as well.

Desires of a Perfect Lady. Avon, 2010.
A woman released from an abusive marriage by her husband's murder, is stunned to find that her eventual freedom from his control depends on her ability to find three artifacts.

Ashford, Jane (Pseudonym for Jane LeCompte)
A former traditional Regency writer, Ashford's more recent novels are lively, lightly humorous Regency-set Historicals with good historical detail and well-rounded characters.

The Marriage Wager. Bantam, 1996.
A reckless wager to save her brother from ruin brings healing and love to a gambler's widow and a disillusioned noble war veteran.

Charmed and Dangerous. Bantam, 1998.
A spy and a governess-turned-special-agent with a romantic past find passion and deadly danger in this tale of international intrigue amid the Congress of Vienna.

Bride to Be. Bantam, 1999.
Attempted murder amid the glitter of the Regency social swirl make this story of two aristocrats who are bored with the strictures of the *ton* a delightful read.

Ashley, Jennifer
Ashley also writes as Allyson James. See also chapter 9, "Alternative Realities."

Pirates
Pirates and outlaws abound in this lively, sexy trio.

The Pirate Next Door. Leisure, 2003.
A widow looking for a suitable husband is attracted to her totally unacceptable neighbor who, among other things, has a pirate past.

The Pirate Hunter. Leisure, 2004.
A pirate hunter is rescued by a woman he once kidnapped when he washes up on her beach.

The Care and Feeding of Pirates. Leisure, 2005.
A woman who married a pirate just before he was scheduled to be hung is shocked when he reappears years later—and turns her well-ordered life upside down.

Nvengaria
Set in the slightly magical kingdom of Nvengaria, this series combines lively, romantic historical romance with a dash of the paranormal.

Penelope and Prince Charming. Leisure, 2006.
A prophecy compels a prince to marry a romantic country girl in order to claim his throne.

The Mad, Bad Duke. Leisure, 2006.
A magic love-spell gone wrong results in a marriage that will eventually go right.

Highlander Ever After. Leisure, 2008.
A clairvoyant princess is sent to Scotland to escape her murderous husband and meets an attractive highlander.

Highland Pleasures
Sensual Victorian Romance with a dark edge featuring the four wealthy, powerful, wild, and eccentric Mackenzie brothers.

The Madness of Lord Ian Mackenzie. Leisure, 2009.
A supposedly mad nobleman who suffered an unspeakable childhood and is suspected of murder is attracted to a young widow who is strong enough to risk loving him.

Lady Isabella's Scandalous Marriage. Berkley Sensation, 2010.
An artistic nobleman who has reformed his wild ways is determined to get his estranged wife back.

The Many Sins of Lord Cameron. Berkley Sensation, 2011.
A widow on a secret mission for the queen tries to evade the advances of a rakish nobleman she was attracted to years ago—and still is.

The Duke's Perfect Wife. Berkley Sensation, 2012.

Ashworth, Adele (Pseudonym for Adele Budnick)
Several of Ashworth's books are linked by character and/or place.

*My Darling Caroline. Jove, 1998.
A forced "business" marriage between a budding botanist and a brooding nobleman becomes real in this engaging romance.

Winter Garden. Jove, 2000.
Spies, secrets, drug smugglers, and scandal are all part of this sensual, exceptionally well-plotted romance.

The Duke of Sin. Avon, 2004.
A woman agrees to become an infamous, reclusive duke's companion if he will sell her a manuscript she needs to retrieve in order to keep her scandalous past a secret. Mature characters.

The Duke of Scandal. Avon, 2006.
A French businesswoman confronts her larcenous husband at a ball and connects with his identical twin, instead, who is more than willing to help her track the villain down.

A Notorious Proposition. Avon, 2008.
A pair with a past join forces in the hunt for some missing jewels in this story that has setting links to *Winter Garden*.

The Duke's Captive. Avon, 2010.
A nobleman is out for revenge but jumps to some faulty conclusions in this rather dark Victorian tale, with character links to *A Notorious Proposition*.

Balogh, Mary
Balogh has written both Traditional Regencies and Historicals, some of which have recently been reprinted. Most of her recent books are linked or are parts of series. The two books listed below are loosely linked but definitely stand on their own. See also chapter 13, "Linked Romances."

One Night for Love. Dell, 1999.
Neville Wyatt, having seen his new bride killed in Spain, is planning to get on with his life when his wife, Lily, reappears, upsetting the family and jarring a murderer into action.

A Summer to Remember. Delacorte, 2002.
Viscount Ravensburg and Lauren Edgeworth, who was left standing at the altar in the previous book, agree to a fake engagement for the summer in order to keep the Viscount's father happy, planning to break things off later; naturally, fate has other ideas about their futures.

Barbieri, Elaine
Although many of Barbieri's Historicals are set in America, this is one of her few that is not.

The Rose and the Shield. Leisure, 2009.
A young woman dons male garb to help her mason father build a church and finds love with a Norman knight in this post-1066 medieval romance.

Barnett, Jill
Sentimental Journey. Pocket, 2001.

A touching, heart wrenching World War II saga that sweeps its characters from America and England to the African desert and provides an abundance of 1940s detail.

Basso, Adrienne

The Wedding Deception. Zebra, 2005.
A newly titled nobleman, Jasper Barrington, must deal with the fact that he is married to a young woman he's never met (thanks to the actions of his twin brother, Jason) when she shows up at his London home with the marriage lines to prove it.

The Christmas Heiress. Zebra, 2006.
An heiress is reunited at Christmas with a nobleman she kissed years earlier under the mistletoe in this light Holiday romance.

How to Enjoy a Scandal. Zebra, 2008.
A nobleman posing as his older, titled, newlywed twin to check out larcenous events on one of the family estates, finds romance in spite of his deception in this story that is the other half of *The Wedding Deception*.

How to Seduce a Sinner. Zebra, 2010.
A nobleman forced to wed learns that there's more to marriage than passion—there's love.

A Little Bit Sinful. 2011.
A nobleman bent on revenge falls in love with the woman he'd planned to use to accomplish his aims.

Benson, Jessica

See also chapter 8, "Regency Period Romance."

*Much Obliged. Zebra, 2001.
Betrothed as children, a prize fighter and a young woman who secretly writes a sports column for the *London Post* find love in this charming romp.

The Accidental Duchess. Pocket, 2004.
When the heroine marries the wrong twin, it takes the rest of the book to sort it all out.

Beverley, Jo

Beverly is a member Romance Writers of America Hall of Fame member and is noted for her Traditional Regencies and her Regency and Georgian Historicals. Many of her novels are linked and parts of series—in particular, The Company of Rogues and the Malloren Chronicles, and are included in the appropriate chapter. See chapter 13, "Linked Romances."

Blake, Jennifer (Pseudonym for Patricia Maxwell)

Blake is a veteran romance writer in a number of romance subgenres and won the Romance Writers of America Golden Treasure Award (now called the Lifetime Achievement Award) in 1987. Louisiana is one of her favorite settings. See chapter 5, "Contemporary Romance."

Master at Arms (Maitre D'Armes) Series

Master swordsmen are major players in this steamy, action-packed, New Orleans–set series.

Challenge to Honor. Mira, 2005.
A heroine bargains her virtue in exchange for her brother's safety.

Dawn Encounter. Mira, 2006.
Threats cause a widow to turn to the swordsman who killer her husband, in spite of the ensuing scandal.

Rogue's Salute. Mira, 2007.
A practical marriage turns into one of passion.

Guarded Heart. Mira, 2008.
A lady requests dueling lessons to be able to challenge an enemy.

Gallant Match. Mira, 2009.
A woman on her way to a forced marriage falls in love with her escort—who plans to kill the lady's intended, anyway.

Triumph in Arms. Mira, 2010.
A woman must consider marrying the new owner of her family's plantation when her father gambles it away.

Bourne, Joanna

Bourne's historical spy stories are witty, beautifully descriptive, cleverly plotted, and filled with sexual tension and smart, memorable characters.

The Spymaster's Lady. Berkley Sensation, 2008.
When British spymaster Robert Grey ends up in prison with Annique Villiers, the infamous spy he'd come to France to find, they strike a wary bargain and then must deal with their feelings and conflicting goals.

*My Lord and Spymaster. Berkley Sensation, 2008.
A spy's daughter out to prove her father isn't a notorious traitor gets help from the man she thinks might actually be the villain.

The Forbidden Rose. Berkley Sensation, 2010.
Set in Revolutionary France, an English master spy discovers a French aristocrat masquerading as an English servant and realizes she's the daughter of the murderous man he's hunting for in this sensual tale that overflows with deception and subterfuge.

Boyle, Elizabeth

Boyle writes lively, humorous, sexy Regency-set Historicals, many of which are linked by character. Note: A family character tree often accompanies these books to help readers sort things out. Her book *Brazen Angel* won the Rita Award in 1997.

Bachelor Chronicles

Something about Emmaline. Avon, 2005.
A nobleman is stunned when his "imaginary" wife suddenly appears.

This Rake of Mine. Avon, 2005.
A trio of schoolgirls makes sure that their starchy teacher and the rake she knew years ago finally make a match.

Love Letters from a Duke. Avon, 2007.
Newly returned from the war and informed that he is engaged to a woman he's never met, the Duke of Hollindrake plans to break the engagement—until his intended mistakes him for a servant and he decides to take the job.

Confessions of a Little Black Gown. Avon, 2009.
A pair of adventurous sisters, a pirate, and a spy drive the inventive plot of this lively, espionage-laced romp that involves a very special black dress.

Memoirs of a Scandalous Red Dress. Avon, 2009.
A pirate who's seen better days finds romance with a woman from his past—with the help of a memorable red dress.

The Bachelor Chronicles: Standon Widows

This is a trilogy within the larger Bachelor Chronicles series and involves the three widows of each Marquess of Standon and their subsequent happy marriages.

How I Met My Countess. Avon, 2010.
Separated by war and time, a couple is reunited when the Earl of Clifton asks Lucy to help him locate an old widowed noblewoman, never realizing that the widowed Lady Stanton (one of them) is Lucy herself.

Mad About the Duke. Avon, 2010.
Elinor, Lady Standon mistakes a duke for his solicitor brother in her search for a duke to marry in this comedy of mistaken identity.

Lord Langley is Back in Town. Avon, 2011.

Bradley, Celeste
See chapter 13, "Linked Romances."

Brisbin, Terri
Knights of Brittany Series
Set in Brittany and England in 1066.

A Night for Her Pleasure. Harlequin Historical, 2009.
A marriage of convenience becomes one in fact as a knight and his lady do fall in love.

Conqueror's Lady. Harlequin Historical, 2009.
A Norman knight is awarded a keep—and the keep's English owner as a bride, in this this classic Norman Conquest conflict tale.

The Mercenary's Bride. Harlequin Historical, 2010.
A knight has problems finding the lady he was given along with her lands.

Storm Series
Sexy passion and adventure in the eleventh century Scottish Isles with a paranormal touch.

A Storm of Passion. Brava, 2009.
A woman's plan of vengeance against the seer who caused her family's death crumbles when they fall in love.

A Storm of Pleasure. Brava, 2010.
A Norsewoman seeks the truthsayer who can clear her brother's name and finds love, and healing for the troubled psychic, in the process.

Mistress of the Storm. Brava, 2011.

Bristow, Gwen
Bristow's American Historicals are classics. (See earlier editions of this guide for bibliographies.)

Britton, Pamela
See also chapter 5, "Contemporary Romance."

Enchanted by Your Kisses. HarperTorch, 2001.
A nobleman decides to help a wary noblewoman with a tarnished reputation re-deem herself in society for his own purposes, but when she learns he is more than a mere nobleman and he takes her prisoner, things don't necessarily go as he expects.

Seduced. Warner Forever, 2003.
When a duke with a deadly and seductive reputation compromises a lady who has no use for him, the resulting marriage-in-name-only raises the stakes for them both as they fight their attraction in this steamy romance that adds a murder accusation to the mix.

Tempted. Warner Forever, 2004.
A smuggler's daughter takes a job as the nanny to the young daughter of a smug-gler-hunting marquess in this funny, animal-filled story.

Scandal. Warner Forever, 2004.
A nobleman who must live on the streets (and stay alive) for a month in order to in-herit is aided by a young woman who accidentally injures him in this sexy romance with a suspenseful twist and character links to *Tempted*.

Brockway, Connie

Strong, adventurous heroines and heroes worthy of them are characteristic of Brockway's humorous, sensual, well-crafted Historicals. See also chapter 5, "Contemporary Romance."

Bridal Favors. Dell, 2002.
A Victorian wedding planner calls in a ten-year-old debt when she convinces a no-bleman (also a secret spy) to let her use his family's estate for an upcoming wedding in this funny, sexy romp.

The Rose Hunters

Three young men saved by a man who died rescuing them from a French prison, promise to repay the debt by protecting the man's three daughters in this early-nineteenth-century trilogy.

My Seduction. Pocket Books, 2004.
Recently widowed Kate Nash Blackburn needs to provide for herself and her two sisters, but Kit MacNeill keeps getting in the way.

My Pleasure. Pocket Books, 2004.
Lady's companion Helena Nash is saved by master swordsman Ramsey Munroe when she attracts an unwanted suitor in Vauxhall.

My Surrender. Pocket Books, 2005.
Charlotte Nash and secret agent Dand Ross join forces in a bold deception to catch the man who caused Charlotte's father's death.

So Enchanting. Onyx, 2009.
A woman with paranormal abilities is not about to let the man who ruined her six years ago destroy her life in a small town in rural England. Wonderfully charming.

The Golden Season. Onyx, 2010.
An aristocratic *ton* leader who learns she is no longer wealthy sets out to find a rich husband only to fall in love with a man in similar straits.

Busbee, Shirley

One of the original "Avon Ladies," Busbee writes lively, fast-paced, sexy historical romances that often feature well-developed characters, humor, and complex plots

Scandal Becomes Her. Zebra, 2007.
Compromised when they seek shelter in the same isolated cottage, an unlikely couple is forced to wed in this romance with a good share of mystery and suspense, plus a dollop of the paranormal.

Seduction Becomes Her. Zebra, 2008.
Cornwall is the perfect setting for this Gothically tinged romance filled with danger, secrets, and passion; it follows *Scandal Becomes Her.*

Surrender Becomes Her. Zebra, 2009.
A nobleman and his wild young ward, who eloped to India ten years earlier, reconnect when she returns to England as a widow.

Passion Becomes Her. Zebra, 2010.
A young widow and a noble rake join forces to see that a despicable aristocratic villain gets his comeuppance.

Callen, Gayle

Many of Callen's adventurous, sensual Historicals are grouped into trilogies and often are set in the early days of Victoria's reign.

Sons of Scandal Trilogy

Three cousins with notorious parents and grandparents deal with their scandalous pasts in very different ways in this early Victorian trilogy.

Never Trust a Scoundrel. Avon, 2008
A woman whose mother wagers her away in a card game learns that the scoundrel who won her is not really the rake he seems.

Never Dare a Duke. Avon, 2008.
A journalist needing a scandalous story to save her family's paper agrees to a fake relationship with a duke that will keep the matchmaking mamas at bay and give her time to snoop.

Never Marry a Stranger. Avon, 2009.
A war hero, supposedly killed in India, returns home and finds his "wife" happily living with his family—only he knows he doesn't have a wife.

Scandalous Lady Trilogy

The identity of the heroine who was the model for a scandalous nude portrait is a mystery that continues throughout this trilogy. The stories continue with the sisters and/or cousins of the Sons of Scandal.

In Pursuit of a Scandalous Lady. Avon, 2010.
Three women claim to be the model for a scandalous portrait of a nude wearing a stunning red diamond in this adventure that has the Earl of Parkhurst chasing across the countryside after a woman seen wearing the diamond at a ball.

A Most Scandalous Engagement. Avon, 2010.
To avoid an unwanted marriage, a woman enters into a fake engagement with an old friend.

The Wedding Scandal. Avon, 2011.

Cameron, Stella

See also chapter 5, "Contemporary Romance," chapter 6, "Romantic Mysteries," and chapter 9, "Alternative Reality Romance."

Mayfair Square Quintet

The doings of the inhabitants of Mayfair Square, including the meddling ghost of Sir Septimus Spivey who tries his best to match-make his boarders into leaving, are the focus of this witty, intriguing, 1820s-set historical series.

More and More. Warner, 1999.
A viscount on a mission and an importer concerned about her kidnapped brother find love and adventure.

All Smiles. Mira, 2000.
An impoverished young woman falls in love with the royal brother of the spoiled young princess she has been hired to shape up for the upcoming season.

7B. Mira, 2001.
A modern young woman who wants a child, not a husband, decides a barrister whose partner has been kidnapped is just the person for the job.

The Orphan. Mira, 2002.
A young milliner needs rescuing from her wicked landlord and a daring rake is just the man for the job.

About Adam. 2003.
A reclusive artist with a secret past and the princess who loves him deal with dangerous enemies from the hero's past in the final book in this madcap series.

Camp, Candace (Pseudonym for Lisa Gregory)

Camp is a popular veteran romance writer. These are only a few of her recent novels.

Matchmaker Series

Lady Francesca Haughston, matchmaker par excellence, is key to each of these linked, but very different, mystery-enhanced romances.

The Marriage Wager. HQN, 2007.
A spinster chaperone is turned into the belle of the season in this lighthearted story with a Cinderella touch.

The Bridal Quest. HQN, 2008.
Knowing he must marry, the Earl of Radbourne, kidnapped as a child and raised on the streets, is taken in hand by Lady Francesca and falls for the nonconformist, no-nonsense Lady Irene Wyngate in this mystery-laced story.

The Wedding Challenge. HQN, 2008.
Saved from being accosted at a masked ball by her powerful brother's arch enemy, a woman goes to Lady Francesca for help when her brother forbids their relationship.

The Courtship Dance. HQN, 2009.
Lady Francesca makes a marvelous match—her own—in the fourth in this series.

Willowmere Trilogy

The four self-sufficient American Bascombe sisters come to England to find their grandfather, the Earl of Stewkesbury, after their mother dies.

A Lady Never Tells. Pocket Star, 2010.
Mary (aka Marigold) Bascombe is rescued by Sir Royce Winslow when she is attacked in this sexy romp that sets the stage for the stories to come.

A Gentleman Always Remembers. Pocket Star, 2010.
A widow takes the Bascombes to London for the season and finds love, as well as a bit of danger, herself.

Canham, Marsha

Midnight Honor. Island, 2001.
A couple has divided loyalties, but steadfast love, in this violent, passionate tale of betrayal and tragedy set during the Jacobite Rebellion before and after the bloody Battle of Culloden.

The Iron Rose. Signet, 2003.
A swashbuckling tale of passion, piracy, and treachery on the seventeenth-century high seas.

My Forever Love. Signet, 2004.
A violent, passionate tale of twelfth-century England during the time of the Crusades.

Carlyle, Liz

Carlyle's Historicals, many of which have families and characters in common and are occasionally grouped into trilogies by title characteristics, are adventurous, steamy, and sometimes full of secrets and mysteries.

The Devil You Know. Pocket Star, 2003.
When a passionate evening between longtime friends results in pregnancy, Freddie reluctantly agrees to marry Bentley and then must figure out how to help him resolve some old family issues if they want to make their marriage work.

A Deal with the Devil. Pocket Star, 2004.
In order to keep her young nephew safe, Aubrey Farquharson leaves Scotland and becomes a housekeeper at a remote castle in Somerset and the prime suspect when the absentee earl's uncle dies on her watch.

The Devil to Pay. Pocket Star, 2005.
A widowed teacher becomes the "Black Angel" at night in order to steal from wealthy womanizing cads and give to their victims, but when she steals from the wrong man and he becomes her neighbor, it's only a matter of time before her ruse is discovered.

One Little Sin. Pocket Star, 2005.
Certain that her toddler sister is the daughter of handsome, rakish Sir Alasdair MacLachlan, Esmée Hamilton goes to him for help and finds a future that neither had expected. Note: The heroes in this and the two books that follow were told by a gypsy that their past sins were going to catch up with them—soon.

Two Little Lies. Pocket Star, 2006.
A nobleman and a widowed Italian singer reconnect after ten years apart and find their immature feelings have grown into a love that is far more powerful.

Three Little Secrets. Pocket Star, 2006.

A widow and her son come to London and learn that the architect of the house is her first husband who disappeared during their honeymoon without a trace. Secrets abound in this sexy, mysterious tale.

Never Lie to a Lady. Pocket Books, 2007.
An unconventional, Barbados-bred heroine who manages her family's shipping company agrees to check out any possible links between the dashing nobleman she kissed one night at a ball and a smuggling ring, with dangerous, passionate results. Note: This and the two books that follow deal with the Neville family and friends.

Never Deceive a Duke. Pocket Books, 2007.
A twice-widowed duchess suspected of her last husband's death must deal with the long-lost heir, a self-made shipping magnate who wants nothing to do with the responsibilities he has inherited.

Never Romance a Rake. Pocket Books, 2008.
A beauty who needs to marry to inherit her grandfather's fortune is won by a notorious rake when her dissolute aristocratic father offers her as a prize.

Tempted All Night. Pocket Books, 2009.
A buttoned-up bluestocking on the hunt for a missing girl and a noble rake on the trail of a Russian spy ring find their goals mesh in dangerous and passionate ways.

Wicked All Day. Pocket Books, 2009.
When a public consoling kiss requires that Zoe Armstrong wed Lord Robert Rowland to save her reputation, Robert's brother, the Marquess of Mercer, is forced to acknowledge his feelings for Zoe.

One Touch of Scandal. Pocket Books, 2010.
A governess suspected of killing her employer turns to an enigmatic nobleman for help in this spy-laced Victorian romance that is the first book in a trilogy linked by the shadowy Fraternitas Aurea Crucis society.

Caskie, Kathryn
Caskie's engrossing Historicals are primarily grouped into series. See chapter 13, "Linked Romances."

Cates, Kimberly (Pseudonym for Kim Ostrum Bush)
The Virgin Queen's Daughter. Crown, 2009.
Based on the premise that Elizabeth I gave birth to an illegitimate daughter before she became queen, this Historical Romance is brings country-bred Lady Elinor de Lacey to court where she must face intrigue, politics, and jealousy—and where she also finds love.

Chase, Allison (Pseudonym for Lisa Manuel)
Her Majesties Secret Servants
Four orphaned sisters, childhood friends of Princess Victoria, are asked by Victoria to secretly investigate threats to the crown. The sisters' past holds secrets, as well, adding a continuing mystery to the series.

Most Eagerly Yours. Signet Eclipse, 2010.
Laurel Sutherland poses as a widow to investigate the queen's cousin, George Fizclarence, and is suspected of being in league with him by an attractive agent, Aidan Philips, who is also on George's trail.

Outrageously Yours. Signet Eclipse, 2010.
Ivy Sutherland goes outrageously undercover as a Cambridge student in order to recover a stolen gem from a nobleman scientist.

Recklessly Yours. Signet Eclipse, 2011.
Holly Sutherland's story.

Chase, Loretta (Pseudonym for Loretta Chekani)

Rapier wit, clever dialogue, well-crafted plots, a delicious sense of irony, and unique, memorable characters are hallmarks of Chase's works.

*Lord of Scoundrels. Avon, 1995.
A spinster and an infamous nobleman spar charmingly in the unusual, beautifully done post-Regency (1828) romance laced with suspense and evil. This exquisitely written novel is still considered one of the best Historicals written and is often used as an example of excellence.

Carsington Family

The Carsington brothers and other members of their family are the main characters in this continuing series.

Miss Wonderful. Berkley Sensation, 2004.
Alistair Carsington and Mirabel Oldridge clash spectacularly when he accompanies a friend to Derbyshire to convince the locals to let him build a canal through the area.

Mr. Impossible. Berkley Sensation, 2005.
The theft of an ancient Egyptian papyrus and a kidnapping send Daphne Pembroke, secretly a hieroglyphics expert, and Darius Carsington, who is more than he seems, down the Nile on a wild adventure.

Lord Perfect. Avon, 2006.
A "perfect" gentleman and a lady from a totally disreputable family are drawn together when her daughter and his nephew go running off in search of buried treasure.

Not Quite a Lady. Avon, 2007.
A secretly ruined lady successfully avoids marriage until a jaded, but scientifically inclined, rake moves into the adjoining estate and becomes intrigued by the lady and her clever schemes.

Last Night's Scandal. Avon, 2010.
Peregrine and Olivia, the two irresistible children in *Lord Perfect*, reappear as the hero and heroine as Olivia once again leads Perry on a funny, madcap adventure.

Your Scandalous Ways. Avon, 2008.
A British spy heads for Venice to wrest some politically dangerous letters from one of the most celebrated courtesans in Europe and falls victim to her charms in this rather dangerous adventure.

Dressmakers Trilogy

Three sisters work to establish themselves as sought-after dressmakers in this cleverly conceived projected trilogy.

Silk is for Seduction. Avon, 2011.
Fashion designer Marceline Noirot sets out to convince the Duke of Clevedon that she and her sisters would be the best people to "dress" his bride-to-be and ends up falling for him in the process.

Cornick, Nicola
Cornick has written a number of popular Regency and Regency-set Historical Romances. A few of the more recent titles are listed below.

Unmasked. July 2008.
A heroine formerly involved with a Robin Hood–like group of women falls for a man who will not approve of her past in this prequel to the Brides of Fortune Trilogy.

The Brides of Fortune Trilogy
The tiny village of Fortune's Folly is the setting for this lively trilogy.

The Confessions of a Duchess. HQN, 2009.
An old tax law requiring women to marry or hand over half of their wealth brings hoards of bachelors to town—and an old love into the life of a dowager duchess.

The Scandals of an Innocent. HQN, 2009.
A maid who inherited a substantial bequest deals with a handsome rake who tries to blackmail her into marriage.

The Undoing of a Lady. HQN, 2009.
A woman kidnaps a man to keep him from marrying a woman he doesn't love and ends up compromised herself in this secret-filled story.

Scandalous Women of the *Ton*
Three women tarnished by scandal are unusual, intriguing heroines.

Whisper of Scandal. HQN, 2010.
A woman travels to the Arctic with her late husband's best friend and fellow explorer in order to find her husband's illegitimate child.

One Wicked Sin. HQN, 2010.
A society beauty ruined by divorce agrees to become an Irish baron's mistress—unaware of his true motives.

Mistress by Midnight. HQN, 2010.
A bluestocking sets out to avenge her family's ruin and ends up forced to marry the man she holds responsible.

Coulter, Catherine
Although recently more noted for her novels of contemporary romantic suspense, earlier in her career she wrote a number of popular Historical Romances. (See also chapter 6, "Romantic Mysteries.") See previous editions of this guide for earlier bibliographies.

The Valcourt Heiress. Putnam, 2010.
In this medieval adventure a new earl returns to find his castle home in shambles after the "Black Demon" tore the place apart looking for a fortune in silver and is aided by an outspoken healer who is a bit more than she seems.

Dain, Claudia (Pseudonym for Claudia Welch)
Courtesan Chronicles
> Legendary courtesan-turned-matchmaker Lady Sophia Dalby works her marital magic to help various couples connect in this sensual series.

> *The Courtesan's Daughter*. Berkley, 2007.
> *The Courtesan's Secret*. Berkley, 2008.
> *The Courtesan's Wager*. Berkley, 2009.
> *How to Dazzle a Duke*. Berkley, 2009.
> *Daring a Duke*. Berkley Sensation, 2010.

Dare, Tessa
> See chapter 13, "Linked Romances."

Day, Sylvia
> Day writes hot romances filled with plenty of passion and steamy sensuality. See also chapter 14, "Erotic Romance."

> *Ask for It*. Brava, 2006.
> A cryptographer is assigned to protect a woman from his past, a widow whose husband was killed for the secrets he possessed, and she is now in danger herself. A dangerous, sexy Georgian adventure.

> *The Stranger I Married*. Brava, 2007.
> A couple who marry for convenience and are then separated unexpectedly for four years must decide what kind of marriage they really want when they are reunited in this passionate Regency affair.

> *A Passion for the Game*. Brava, 2007.
> A noblewoman with a Black Widow reputation and a notorious pirate use their seductive wiles and crafty skills on each other to learn each other's secrets—or suffer deadly consequences in this spy-laded, sexy Georgian adventure.

> *A Passion for Him*. Brava, 2007.
> A young woman (sister of the previous book's heroine) is attracted to a masked stranger who reminds her of a man she loved, but who died for her—or so she thought—in this sequel to *A Passion for the Game*.

> *Don't Tempt Me*. Brava, 2008.
> A rake is alternately attracted and confused when he reconnects with a woman he loved years earlier, and with good reason: there are two women—identical twins.

DeHart, Robyn
The Ladies' Amateur Sleuth Society Series
> The name says it all for this Victorian-set series.

> *A Study in Scandal*. Avon, 2006.
> A missing statue of Nefertiti unites Lady Amelia Watersfield and inspector Colin Brindley in this dangerous, but fascinating, adventure.

> *Deliciously Wicked*. Avon, 2006.
> When proving the hero's innocence in the theft of some chocolate boxes would result in her social ruin, a woman turns to the Ladies' Amateur Sleuth Society to find the real thief.

Tempted at Every Turn. Avon, 2007.
An amateur sleuth and a Scotland Yard detective clash their way to love—and the solution to a murder—in this lively romance.

Legend Hunters Series
Treasure hunters abound in this gently paranormal, always adventurous series.

Seduce Me. Forever, 2009.
The hunt for Pandora's box is the focus of this sexy Historical.

Desire Me. Forever, 2010.
A map of Atlantis and a prophecy that needs to be decoded is at the heart of this dangerous, sexy adventure.

Delacroix, Claire (Pseudonym for Deborah Cooke)
Jewels of Kinfairlie Trilogy
Alexander, the laird of Kinfairlie, finds husbands for his sisters in this engaging, fantasy-laced series set in fifteenth-century Scotland.

The Beauty Bride. Warner, 2005.
A bride bolts when her brother decides to auction her off, but a warrior who wants her goes in pursuit.

The Rose Red Bride. Warner, 2005.
A woman wakes to find the man she made love to in her dreams is real—but can he actually become the "man of her dreams"?

The Snow White Bride. Warner, 2005.
It's Alexander's turn to find love when a lady seeks sanctuary at Kinfairlie.

Deveraux, Jude
Deveraux has been a popular romance writer since the 1970s when she wrote some of her best-remembered sexy and adventurous Historicals. Many of her more recent works have included paranormal elements. (See also chapter 9, "Alternative Reality Romance.") The series below is a combination of Contemporary and Historical Romance.

Edilean Series
A multigenerational series that spans centuries and continents.

Lavender Morning. Atria, 2009.
Jocelyn Minton returns to Edilean, Virginia, when she inherits a manor house and other things from the woman who raised her, Edilean Harcourt, and finds plenty of secrets, as well as romance, in this story that alternates between the years of World War II and the present.

Days of Gold. Atria, 2010.
A Scottish laird finds love, heartache, and fulfillment with beautiful Edilean Talbot in a gold-driven adventure that takes the pair from Scotland to America in the last part of the eighteenth century.

Scarlet Nights. Atria, 2010.
Detective Mike Newland goes undercover to Edilean, Virginia, to smoke out Greg Anders, a criminal with an unsavory past, but must convince the now-missing Greg's fiancée, Sara Shaw, to trust him.

Devine, Thea

Veteran writer Devine is known for her hot, erotically explicit, earthy, mystery-laced romances. Many of her works could have been included in the "Erotic Romance" chapter of this book.

Bliss River. Brava, 2002.
Sex, murder, and betrayal in a late Victorian South African setting.

The Forever Kiss. Brava, 2003.
A man masquerades as another in order to infiltrate a mysterious manor house and find a killer in this late Victorian Gothic mix of treachery, sin, and secrets.

Satisfaction. Brava, 2004.
A dark, twisted tale of betrayal and revenge that pits father against son.

Sensation. Brava, 2004.
Murder, mystery, and diabolical evil abound in this steamy, but chilling, Victorian romance.

Dodd, Christina

Dodd's Historicals are well-written, action-packed, sensual, and filled with well-developed characters. They are also often funny, tender, and may be a bit Gothic.

Governess Bride Series (Distinguished Academy of Governesses)

Begun as a trilogy, this series has definitely evolved and expanded.

Rules of Surrender. Avon, 2000.
A noblewoman hires a governess for her two grandchildren, but she really hopes her son who's been living in the Middle Eastern desert for a large part of his life will be civilized by the woman.

Rules of Engagement. Avon, 2000.
In order to gain favor with Queen Victoria, a nobleman wants the co-owner of the Distinguished Academy of Governesses to find him a governess and a child to adopt; she agrees, but on her own deceptive terms.

Rules of Attraction. Avon, 2001.
The former co-owner of the Distinguished Academy of Governesses accepts a companion position only to find the lady's son is the husband she once ran from years earlier.

In My Wildest Dreams. Avon, 2001.
A gardener's daughter becomes a governess to the daughter of a nobleman she'd long adored, but his brother has other ideas for her.

Lost in Your Arms. Avon, 2002.
A woman nurses her long-lost husband back to health after he was wounded in this amnesia story filled with espionage and spies—and a surprising ending.

My Favorite Bride. Avon, 2002.
An unconventional governess is banished to the Lake District where she captivates the attention of six girls and their military dad.

My Fair Temptress. Avon, 2005.
A governess with a past to overcome is hired to teach a young bachelor how to go on in society, but he's not quite the idiot he seems.

In Bed with the Duke. Avon, Signet, 2010.
Dismissed from her position as companion, Emma is rescued while lost in the forests of Moricadia by the legendary Reaper, who is much more than he seems.

Taken by the Prince. Signet Select, 2011.

Drake, Shannon (Pseudonym for Heather Graham Pozzessere)
Wicked. HQN, 2005.
A dark Beauty-and-the-Beast tale with a Victorian Gothic setting.

Reckless. HQN, 2005.
Thrilled at the chance to go to Egypt because the man she's interested in is there, a lady is less thrilled to be forced into a fake engagement with a handsome archaeologist—which she'll have to do if she wants to make the trip.

Beguiled. HQN, 2006.
The murder of anti-royal journalists causes concern for our secret journalist heroine, who is surprised to learn that her proper fiancé may be far more dashing than she'd thought.

The Queen's Lady. HQN, 2007.
A friend and advisor to Mary, Queen of Scots, finds love and danger as she tries to help the young queen.

The Pirate Bride. HQN, 2008.
A fierce woman pirate seeking the villain who sold her into slavery as a child is aided by a sea captain who is after the same man.

Dreyer, Eileen
Dreyer writes mysteries and paranormals, as well as contemporary romances. See also chapter 6, "Romantic Mysteries."

Drake's Rakes Series
Elegant, sophisticated bachelor rakes have secret lives in service to the crown.

Barely a Lady. Forever, 2010.
A woman ruined by a scandalous divorce five years earlier finds her unconscious ex-husband on the Waterloo battlefield dressed in a French uniform and tries to protect him from his enemies until he regains his memory of the past five years.

Never a Gentleman. Forever, 2011.
Forced to marry when they wake up in bed together with no memory of how they got there, an urbane, sought-after rake and an unpolished, socially unskilled woman find love, even as they are targeted by traitors.

Always the Temptress. Forever, 2011.
Anger and passion sizzle between a pair of long-standing antagonists when Sir Harry Lidge is assigned to keep the young Dowager Duchess of Murther safe from traitors.

Duran, Meredith
Duke of Shadows. Pocket Star, 2008.
Betrayed by her fiancé when she arrives in India, Emmaline Martin turns to Julian Sinclair, a nobleman caught between two worlds because of his mixed blood, for help during the Sepoy Rebellion in this insightful romance.

Bound by Your Touch. Pocket, 2009.
Counterfeit Egyptian antiquities and a quest to find the villain unite an antagonistic pair in this lively adventure.

Written on Your Skin. Pocket, 2009.
A British spy and a woman who saved his life reconnect four years later when she needs his help in this sequel to *Bound by Your Touch*.

Wicked Becomes You. Pocket, 2010.
Jilted again, Gwen Maudsley decides its time to stop living up to her "nice" reputation and start being naughty. But she runs into trouble when Alex Ramsay, her late brother's best friend, decides to honor a deathbed promise to look after Gwen and keep her safe.

Farrell, Marjorie
Red, Red Rose. Topaz, 1999.
The bastard son of an earl saves the life of a young woman during the Peninsular Wars but considers himself unworthy of her—until she gets him to see reason in this exceptional romance.

Feather, Jane
Feather is a multi-published, veteran romance writer of sensual, lively, descriptive Historicals that feature adventurous heroines in intriguing, often dark and dangerous, situations, with heroes to match. A few of her more recent titles are listed below.

Almost a Bride. Bantam, 2005.
A woman is reluctant to marry the ruthless man who ruined her brother.

Almost a Lady. Bantam, 2006.
A woman poses as a look-alike spy and joins forces with a privateer in a dangerous game of espionage.

Cavendish Square
Three women inherit a London home in this adventurous trilogy laden with spies and secrets and set in the early years of the nineteenth century.

A Wicked Gentleman. Pocket Star, 2007.
A war widow with two young children is attracted to an undercover spy.

To Wed a Wicked Prince. Pocket Star, 2008.
An independent London deb impulsively marries a Russian prince and then begins to learn his secrets.

A Husband's Wicked Ways. Pocket Star, 2009.
A widow learns the truth about her husband's death and agrees to help a spy for the crown ferret out some "social-climbing" spies by means of a fake courtship.

Blackwater Brides Trilogy
The Blackwater brothers must each save and marry a fallen woman before their wealthy uncle dies in order to inherit in this bawdy Georgina trilogy.

Rushed to the Altar. Pocket, 2010.
The Earl of Blackwater mistakes an unaccompanied young gentlewoman searching for her brother in Covent Gardens for a prostitute and decides she's perfect for his plans.

Garwood, Julie
Garwood is known for her lively, witty, often funny romances which are filled with appealing characters. Her favorite settings are the British medieval and Regency periods

and Victorian America and the American West. (Consult the previous edition of this guide for a bibliography of her earlier works, such as 1989 Rita Award winner *The Bride*.) See also chapter 6, "Romantic Mysteries."

Ransom. Pocket Books, 1999.
An Englishwoman, whose home and family were wrenched from her when she was a child by a ruthless nobleman, reclaims her heritage and finds unexpected love with a fierce Highland Laird in this medieval novel set during the violent reign of King John.

Shadow Music. Ballantine Books, 2008.
When her husband-to-be is murdered just before the wedding and she is denounced in a jealous plot and cruelly banished, Lady Gabrielle of St. Biel is rescued by Highland Laird Colm MacHugh in this lively, often funny, cleverly plotted adventure that has links to Garwood's contemporary *Shadow Dance* and her Historical *Ramsom*, and is her first Historical Romance since *Ransom*.

Gellis, Roberta
Although Gellis's earlier works were primarily Historical romances, and her classic Roselynde Chronicles are still popular with readers, her more recent books have been in the Mystery, Fantasy, and Science Fiction genres. See chapter 13, "Linked Romances."

Givens, Kathleen
Givens's novels are exceptionally well-researched, historically accurate, and compelling.

On a Highland Shore. Pocket, 2006.
Viking raiders destroy a woman's world, but a half-Irish, half-Norse warrior soon becomes the only man she can trust in this exquisitely written, beautifully descriptive romance that captures the violence and political treachery rampant in thirteenth-century Scotland.

Rivals for the Crown. Pocket, 2007.
Two women and the highlanders who befriend them are caught up in Scotland's struggle against English rule in thirteenth-century Scotland.

Goodger, Jane
Gifts from the Sea. Signet, 2002.
A woman whose husband is lost at sea rescues the lone survivor, the captain, of a whaler in this poignant, touching romance with plenty of New England ambience.

Christmas Series
Character and the holidays link these stories that move from England to America and back.

Marry Christmas. Zebra, 2008.
A marriage of convenience turns real in this Holiday-set Victorian.

A Christmas Scandal. Zebra, 2009.
A couple is reunited but must overcome scandal and secrets in this story that has links to *Marry Christmas*.

A Christmas Waltz. Zebra, 2010.
A noblewoman leaves England for Texas to surprise her fiancé and then must turn to his responsible brother when the lying cad rejects her.

Goodman, Jo (Pseudonym for Joanne Dobrzanski)
See also the Period Americana bibliography in this chapter.

Compass Club Quartet
Three schoolboy friends, each of whom has a name that ties loosely into the four points of the compass, find love in this often suspenseful, engaging series.

Let Me Be the One. Zebra, 2002.
The Earl of Northam (north) finds love with the crippled Libby Penrose.

Everything I Ever Wanted. Zebra, 2003.
On the trail of a killer, the Earl of Southerton (south) kidnaps the lovely actress, India Parr, in order to learn her secrets and keep her safe at the same time.

All I Ever Needed. Zebra, 2003.
Marquess of Eastlyn (east) and Lady Sophie Colley eventually make a match but have greedy relatives and a bit of intrigue to contend with in the process.

Beyond a Wicked Kiss. Zebra, 2004.
Unexpectedly becoming the Duke of Westphal (west), Evan Marchman is doubly shocked to have acquired a ward, Ria Ashby, who involves him in a dangerous adventure that has links back to the boys' school-day adversaries.

A Season to be Sinful. Zebra, 2005.
A nobleman becomes responsible for a woman caring for three street-wise orphans when she saves his life in Covent Garden.

The Price of Desire. Zebra, 2008.
A gentlewoman is "given" to the owner of a gaming hell as debt collateral and ends up finding romance in this rather dark Regency that also involves issues of child abuse.

Gracie, Anne
Devil Riders
Former comrades in arms, former Devil Riders, are the heroes of these romantic adventures.

The Stolen Princess. Berkley Sensation, 2008.
A princess running to keep her son safe from an assassin is aided by a nobleman who has just returned from war.

His Captive Lady. Berkley Sensation, 2008.
A hero who just wants to settle down and breed horses finds love with the impoverished daughter of the former owner of the estate he just bought.

To Catch a Bride. Berkley Sensation, 2009.
A nobleman goes to Cairo in search of a missing heiress to escape an unwanted marriage and finds a street-smart urchin instead.

The Accidental Wedding. Berkley Sensation, 2010.
A man with no memory and the woman who takes him in as he recovers are forced to marry for propriety's sake.

Greiman, Lois
Witches of Mayfair
The women of Lavender House each have special abilities in this romantic trilogy that has a healthy dose of suspense.

> *Under Your Spell*. Avon, 2008.
> *Seduced by Your Spell*. Avon 2009.
> *Charming the Devil*. Avon, 2010.

An Accidental Seduction. Avon, 2010.
An actress posing as the newly married spouse of an abuser attracts the attentions of a man on an undercover mission in this light, sensual Regency-set Historical.

Grey, Amelia (Pseudonym for Gloria Dale Skinner)
A Taste of Temptation. Berkley Sensation, 2005.
While hunting for a ghost, a couple ends up compromised—and weds, in this gently paranormal tale.

Rogues' Dynasty Trilogy
Three bachelor cousins find love in spite of themselves in this Regency-set trilogy filled with humor, sensuality, and danger.

A Duke to Die For. Sourcebooks Casablanca, 2009.
A duke becomes the guardian for a young woman who thinks she's a curse to her guardians, four of whom have already died.

A Marquess to Marry. Sourcebooks Casablanca, 2009.
Two determined people vie over a valuable pearl necklace but must join forces when the necklace is stolen.

An Earl to Enchant. Sourcebooks Casablanca, 2010.
An earl returns to the country and mistakes a young lady visiting his estate for a courtesan he'd arranged for in this funny, sensual conclusion to the trilogy.

Guhrke, Laura Lee
Humor, witty dialogue, and compelling characters are hallmarks of Guhrke's romances.

Guilty Pleasures. Avon, 2004.
Faced with the possibility of losing his valuable art restorer when she thinks of finding a husband, a nobleman working on a Roman villa on his estate sets out to convince her, in some very creative ways, to stay.

His Every Kiss. Avon, 2004.
Years after violinist Grace Cheval keeps depressed, disillusioned composer Dylan Moore from committing suicide, he needs her help again—this time as governess to his young daughter. Insightful characterizations.

The Marriage Bed. Avon, 2005.
A married couple that has lived apart for seven years reconnects most satisfactorily when an heir needs to be produced.

She's No Princess. Avon, 2006.
A nobleman charged with finding a husband for a charmingly difficult royal bastard ends up attracted to her in the process.

And Then He Kissed Her. Avon, 2007.
A secretary and etiquette writer leaves her newspaper editor in a lurch when she learns that he has been rejecting her pseudonymously written stories without reading them, and he decides he needs to get her back—whatever it takes.

Girl-Bachelor Chronicles
Independent women in the late Victorian period.

Secret Desires of A Gentleman. Avon, 2008.
A cook's daughter whose puppy-love elopement was thwarted by her beloved's elder brother goes to France, returns home as a talented pastry chef, and attracts the attentions of the nobleman who ruined her teenage dreams.

The Wicked Ways of a Duke. Avon, 2008.
A seamstress who becomes an heiress if she weds within a year and an aristocratic rogue who must marry for money find love—eventually.

With Seduction in Mind. Avon, 2009.
A critic who wants to get her own book published and a playwright with writer's block end up working together in a country setting that sets a variety of sparks flying in this lively romance.

Abandoned at the Altar Trilogy
Wedding of the Season. Avon, 2010.
After abandoning her to pursue his dream six years earlier, William Mallory returns from Egypt to find Lady Beatrix about to wed another—unless he can stop it.

Scandal of the Year. Avon, 2011.
Twice jilted and his reputation tarnished by scandal, the Duke of Trathen sets out to find a new bride—only to have his life turned upside down when the woman from his scandalous past returns.

Hawkins, Karen
Many of Hawkins's humorous, sexy romances, many of which are linked by character, feature Scottish settings and characters.

The Abduction of Julia. Avon, 2000.
A nobleman abducts the wrong bride in this funny, touching, sensual romance.

Lady in Red. Avon, 2005.
An heirloom ring with legendary matchmaking powers sets the sparks flying between a pair of aristocratic antiques experts.

How to Abduct a Highland Laird. Pocket, 2007.
An abduction and marriage in order to stave off a bitter feud between warring clans gets this book, the first in a loosely connected series, off to a rousing start.

Sleepless in Scotland. Pocket, 2009.
Compromised in a mix-up of mistaken identity when trying to stop their respective siblings from getting married, Catriona Hurst and Hugh MacLean end up wed.

The Laird Who Loved Me. Pocket, 2009.
Now it's Caitlyn's, Catriona's hoyden twin sister, turn to find love—if she can ever convince Alexander MacLean to forgive her.

Heath, Lorraine (Pseudonym for Jan Nowasky)

Heath writes Historicals and Contemporary romances; many of her earlier works were set in the American West. Her works are emotionally compelling and memorable, and her 1996 *Always to Remember* won a Rita Award.

The Scoundrels of St. James

With a nod to Dickens's *Oliver Twist*, this series follows the fortunes of those rescued from Fagin's band.

In Bed with the Devil. Avon, 2008.
Catherine enlists the aid of the one person who can save her from her wicked guardian, the dangerous Devil Earl, Lucian Langdon, who may have killed his uncle.

Between the Devil and Desire. Avon, 2009.
The owner of a gentleman's club, Jack Dodger (the Artful Dodger), is named guardian of the Duke of Lovingdon's young heir, which puts him in conflict with the four-year-old's attractive mother.

Surrender to the Devil. Avon, 2009.
Frannie Darling, another of the rescued band, attracts the attentions of the Earl of Greystone in this romance that takes them back to the slums and into danger.

Midnight Pleasures with a Scoundrel. Avon, 2009.
A woman determined to avenge her sister's death is rescued by a man who intends to keep her in his sites.

London's Greatest Lovers Series

Legendary lovers meet their matches.

Passions of a Wicked Earl. Avon, 2010.
A woman sets out to seduce the now notorious husband who banished her to the country years earlier for supposedly betraying him with his brother.

Pleasures of a Notorious Gentleman. Avon, 2010.
A rake-turned-soldier is home recovering from his wounds and is stunned when a woman shows up at the door with baby in his tale of deception and love.

Waking up with the Duke. Avon, 2011.
A nobleman agrees to provide his wheelchair-bound cousin with an heir by sleeping with the cousin's wife but falls in love in the process.

Hern, Candice

See Also chapter 13, "Linked Romances."

The Bride Sale. Avon, 2002.
Lord James Harkness, appalled that a bride sale is taking place in his town, bids for Verity Osborne in order to save her in this touching, emotionally compelling story, with a slightly Gothic touch.

Heyer, Georgette

Although primarily noted for her delightful, standard-setting Regency romances, Heyer also wrote Historical novels, Period Romances, and mysteries. (See previous editions of this guide for a bibliography of her Period Romances that were set outside the strict Regency time period.) See also chapter 8, "Regency Romance."

Hill, Sandra

Hill writes in a number of romance subgenres; her books, most of which are grouped into series, are usually sexy and filled with laugh-out-loud humor. See chapter 13, "Linked Romances."

Viking in Love. Avon, 2010.
Fleeing after killing her sister Vana's abusive husband, Princess Breanne of Stoneheim and her four sisters turn Lord Caedmon's keep—and life—upside down, but there are more life-changing surprises in store for them both.

Viking Takes a Knight. Avon, 2010.
A Viking king's daughter and her young orphan charges seek shelter from an English knight when a Saxon warrior comes looking for the king's illegitimate son. Tenth-century Britain.

Dark Viking. Berkley Sensation, 2010.
A modern-day stunt woman is hired by the Navy SEALs and ends up captured by Vikings in this intriguing time travel.

Hoyt, Elizabeth

See chapter 13, "Linked Romances."

Hunter, Madeline

See chapter 13, "Linked Romances."

Ivie, Jackie

Lady of the Knight. Zebra, 2004.
A young woman on a mission of vengeance disguises herself as a boy and ends up as a squire to (and attracted to) the youngest son in the clan she intends to destroy.

The Knight before Christmas. Zebra, 2006.
A winter storm brings two people together in this tale of hidden identities in fifteenth-century Scotland.

A Knight Well Spent. Zebra, 2008.
A healer and a knight find love, eventually, in twelfth-century Scotland.

Ivory, Judith (Pseudonym for Judy Cuevas)

The Proposition. Avon, 2000.
A reverse Pygmalion tale in which a lady linguist turns a rat catcher into the toast of the *ton*.

The Indiscretion. Avon, 2001.
A Texas millionaire and a proper Victorian Englishwoman are stranded together in a coach accident and are surprised by mutual attraction as they make their way back to civilization.

Untie My Heart. Avon, 2002.
A nobleman coerces a sheep farmer into helping him get some stolen things back from a relative, with lively and romantic results.

James, Eloisa

See chapter 13, "Linked Romances."

James, Samantha (Pseudonym for Sandra Keinschmit)

McBride Family Trilogy

Wounded heroes find healing and love in a Victorian setting.

The Secret Passion of Simon Blackwell. Avon, 2007.
Compromised by a kiss, deeply wounded Simon Blackwell and fiercely passionate Annabel McBride have a lot to work through in this emotionally intense romance with a slightly Gothic touch.

The Seduction of an Unknown Lady. Avon, 2008.
On her late night walks, bookstore owner and secret horror novelist Fionna Hawkes attracts the attention of Lord Aiden McBride, who thinks she needs protection.

The Bride of a Wicked Scotsman. Avon, 2009.
Maura O'Donnell tricks Alec McBride into marriage in order to reclaim an ancient Celtic artifact, not planning to fall in love along the way.

Jeffries, Sabrina
See chapter 13, "Linked Romances."

Jensen, Emma
Jensen has also written award-winning traditional Regencies. Members of the infamous "Ten" group of spies are heroes in a number of her romances.

Fallen. Ivy, 2001.
Slowly sinking into a dissolute life of gambling and drink because of guilt, a former spy is sent to the Isle of Skye to find and kill a traitor, but finds love and healing, as well. Follows *Entwined* (1997).

Moonlit. Ivy, 2002.
In England to settle an old score, a young Irish widow assumes the guise of a courtesan in search of a new protector and ends up involved with a physically and emotionally scarred viscount, another of the infamous "Ten."

Jewel, Carolyn
See also chapters 9 and 13, "Alternative Realities Romances" and "Linked Romances."

Scandal. Berkley Sensation, 2009.
A rake falls in love with his friend's wife who fears losing her independence even in widowhood in this sensual Regency.

Indiscreet. Berkley Sensation, 2009.
A gentlewoman traveling in the Middle East with her uncle escapes from a pasha's harem with the help of an English nobleman.

Johansen, Iris
Now noted for her popular mystery thrillers, Johansen wrote a number of Historical Romances early in her career. *Lyon's Bride* is included below because it is the predecessor to her recent, long-awaited by some, Historical Adventure. See also chapter 5, "Romantic Mysteries," and chapter 13, "Linked Romances."

Lyon's Bride. Bantam Books, 1996.
A twelfth-century tale of runaway weaver Thea and a mercenary, Lord Ware, who find a new life for themselves despite their separate enemies. Passionate, picaresque, and exotic.

The Treasure. Bantam Books, 2008.
Picking up where *Lyon's Bride* leaves off, Lady Selene Ware follows reformed assassin Kadar back to Syria when he is tricked into returning by a power-hungry Nasim and the pair become pawns in Nasim's insane quest in this sexy story of good and evil.

Johnson, Alissa

Johnson writes lively, humorous Regency-set Historicals that often have a dash of mystery and adventure.

As Luck Would Have It. Leisure, 2008.
A nobleman is charmed by the woman he is supposed to be keeping an eye on for the crown while she is engaged in a spy mission of her own.

Tempting Fate. Leisure, 2009.
A pair who fought as children become neighbors once again and continue their sparing—all the way to the altar in this light hearted romp that follows *As Luck Would Have It*.

McAlistair's Fortune. Leisure, 2009.
A young woman falls in love with the retired assassin who's been hired to protect her after she receives a threatening letter in this story that features a pair of perfectly imperfect protagonists.

Destined to Last. Leisure, 2010.
A clumsy heroine and a wealthy government agent fall in love as they try to uncover a smuggling plot.

Johnson, Susan

Johnson has long been noted for strong, independent heroines and steamy, lushly hot, explicit romances, some of which set a standard in the field. She writes both Contemporary and Historical Romance. See previous editions of this guide for bibliographies of her earlier work. See also chapter 5, "Contemporary Romance."

Darley Series

The various Marquises of Darley are front and center in this time-spanning, sexy series.

When You Love Someone. Brava, 2006.
An affair turns into something else when a notorious rake and a "virgin" wife fall in love in this Georgian Romp.

When Someone Loves You. Brava, 2006.
A Waterloo veteran retired to the country to breed horses and a notable actress caring for her late sister's child fight their attraction and agree on friendship—for a while.

At Her Service. Brava, 2008.
A pair of spies meet and find love while on separate missions in the Crimea.

Gorgeous as Sin. Berkley Sensation, 2009.
A nobleman decides to seduce the owner of a property he wants and falls in love in the process.

Sexy as Hell. Berkley Sensation, 2010.
A marriage of convenience to avoid the heroine's unwanted match has the expected romantic results in this late Victorian tale.

Jordan, Sophie

Once upon a Wedding Night. Avon, 2006.
Lady Meredith Brookshire, desperate to assure that her family and retainers can remain on her late husband's estate when her husband's half-brother returns, pretends to be pregnant in this funny, lively tale full of deceptions, passion, and memorable characters.

Surrender to Me. Avon, 2008.
Texan Griffin Shaw is in Scotland to find his family; the last thing he expects is to save a desperate duchess from danger twice, or to fall in love with her in the process.

Sins of a Wicked Duke. Avon, 2009.
Unable to keep a servant's job because of her rejection of men's advances, beautiful, orphaned Fallon O'Rourke disguises herself as a boy and becomes a footman for the Duke of Damon.

In Scandal They Wed. Avon, 2010.
A woman claims her sister's illegitimate child as her own to save him from the orphanage, but must deal with the deception when the cousin of the child's late father offers marriage for the sake of the child.

Wicked Nights with a Lover. Avon, 2010.

Joyce, Brenda
De Warrene Dynasty Saga
Follows the fortunes of the De Warrene family from the eleventh century to more recent times.

The Conqueror. Dell 1990.
Promise of the Rose. Avon, 1993.
The Game. Avon, 1995.

House of Dreams. St. Martin's Paperbacks, 2000.
A vindictive ghost stalks her descendants in this darkly paranormal Gothic romance that pairs historical novelist Cassandra de Warrene with Professor Antonio de la Barca and sweeps its characters to a sinister castle in Spain.

The Masquerade. Mira, 2005.
Lizzie Fitzgerald claims her selfish, beautiful sister's illegitimate child as her own and eventually finds love with Tyrell de Warrene, the baby's father.

Stolen Bride. HQN, 2006.
Eleanor de Warrene is stolen on the eve of her wedding by Sean O'Neill, her first love, who is now running from the law.

A Lady at Last. HQN, 2006.
Amanda Carre, raised by a pirate, is taught the ways of polite society by privateer Cliff de Warrene, who falls in love with her in the process.

The Perfect Bride. HQN, 2007.
Reclusive Rex de Warrene and Lady Blanche Harrington help each other deal with the past as they come to realize their love for each other.

A Dangerous Love. HQN, 2008.
Free-thinking Ariella de Warrene falls in love with a half-gypsy nobleman who is also her neighbor in this unusual pre-Victorian romance.

An Impossible Attraction. HQN, 2010.
Alexandra Bolton knows she must marry an elderly squire in order to rescue her family from financial ruin—and then Stephen de Warrene, Duke of Clarewood, sets out to make her his mistress.

The Promise. HQN, 2010.
Elysse vows to make her fake marriage one in fact when her long-absent husband, Alexi de Warrene, returns from the sea again in this early Victorian romance.

Justiss, Julia

Justiss's knowledge of Regency times and society and her deft handling of the language and historical detail comes through clearly in her exceptional, well-written Historicals.

My Lady's Trust. Harlequin Historical, 2002.
A gentlewoman living quietly in the country to avoid her abusive husband attracts the attention of a nobleman when she tends to his brother's injury.

My Lady's Pleasure. Harlequin Historical, 2002.
A widow who'd never experienced passion and an experienced rake agree to a short, no-strings affair, and then they fall in love.

The Courtesan. HQN, 2005.
When courtesan and expert swordswoman Lady Belle wounds Captain Jack Carrington in a duel, she agrees to care for him, and he begins to see her in a new light.

The Untamed Heiress. HQN, 2006.
Freed from her isolated existence by her father's death, a young woman goes to London with her mother's friend to take her place in Society in this funny, tender charmer.

A Most Unconventional Match. Harlequin Historical, 2008.
An artist and mother, now widowed, Elizabeth Lowery is at a loss when it comes to the family finances and is more than happy when quiet, awkward Hal Waterman comes to her aid in this tender, touching, realistic romance.

Kelly, Carla

Noted for her award-winning Regency Romances, Kelly has recently begun writing Regency-set Historicals.

Beau Crusoe. Harlequin Historical, 2007.
A shipwrecked survivor (à la Robinson Crusoe) is helped to readjust to civilization by a disgraced widow with a child.

Marrying the Captain. Harlequin Historical, 2009.
A woman with a distrust of naval men and helping her grandmother keep their old inn going is attracted to a handsome sea captain who has never married for fear of leaving a widow.

The Surgeon's Lady. Harlequin Historical, 2009.
A widow and a military surgeon connect romantically during the Napoleonic Wars.

Marrying the Royal Marine. Harlequin Historical, 2010.
Realistic romance during the Peninsular Wars.

The Admiral's Penniless Bride. Harlequin Historical, 2011.

Kerstan, Lynn
Jungle Cat Series

Golden Leopard. Onyx, 2002.
The search for a jeweled leopard sets off an Indiana Jones–type search in this lively romance.

Heart of the Tiger. Onyx, 2003.
The hero and heroine both have reasons to want the evil Duke of Tallant dead, but when he is killed, the question is, who did it?

The Silver Lion. Onyx, 2004.
A social activist on a mission and nobleman with a grudge find each other—and love—in this romance that doesn't reveal all its secrets until the end.

Black Phoenix
Evil, danger, and secret societies are at the heart of this darkly thrilling, chilling Regency-set series. As of this writing, book three is still in progress.

Dangerous Deceptions. Signet, 2004.
Dangerous secrets abound at Paradise, an exclusive Lake District resort, and actress Kate Fanshaw and spy Jarrett Dering are just the people to uncover them.

Dangerous Passions. Signet Eclipse, 2005.
Revenge drives the plot of this dark and dangerous novel as the hero targets a killer, with the help of a society lady.

Kinsale, Laura (Pseudonym for Amanda Moor Jay)
Kinsale's romances are touching, poignant, and often feature flawed and/or wounded characters. *Prince of Midnight* (1990) is a Rita Award winter, and *Flowers from the Storm* (1992) has become a classic with readers.

Shadow Heart. Berkley, 2004.
The assassin from *For My Lady's Heart* (1993) becomes the hero in this captor-in-love-with-captive romance.

Lessons in French. Sourcebooks Casablanca, 2010.
In a break with her past style, Kinsale has produced a lighthearted, whimsical, well-plotted romance that reunites an independent spinster heroine (who breeds prize bulls) and her childhood love (who was banished by her father) with plenty of humorous flair.

Kleypas, Lisa
Kleypas's works are lively, sensual, and charmingly laced with humor. Often they are connected by character. See also chapter 5, "Contemporary Romance."

The Wallflowers Series
Four young women, wallflowers for assorted reasons, set out to find husbands in this sensual, lighthearted, early Victorian series.

Secrets of a Summer Night. Avon, 2004.
Poor but noble Annabelle Peyton tries to resist falling for a wealthy businessman, Simon Hunt.

It Happened One Autumn. Avon, 2005.
Outspoken American heiress Lillian Bowman clashes with the snobbish Earl of Westcliff.

The Devil in Winter. Avon, 2006.
Shy, wealthy Evie Jenner proposes a platonic marriage to a rake in order to safeguard her inheritance.

Scandal in Spring. Avon, 2006.
Daisy Bowman, Lillian's younger sister, must make a match of her own choosing or marry a man she thinks she hates, businessman Mathew Swift.

A Wallflower Christmas. St. Martin's Press, 2008.
An American rake comes to England to meet his prospective bride and is charmed by her cousin, instead, in this holiday story that reprises characters from the original four Wallflower titles.

Hathaway Family Series

An open-minded, eccentric group of siblings inherits a crumbling country estate (along with the title for the eldest brother) and makes often unconventional matches in this Victorian quintet.

Mine Till Midnight. St. Martin's Paperbacks, 2007.
The story of Amelia Hathaway and half-gypsy club owner Cam Rohan (met in *The Devil in Winter*).

Seduce Me at Sunrise. St. Martin's Paperbacks, 2008.
The story of Winnifred Hathaway and Kev Merripen, a Romany gypsy who was taken in by the Hathaways as a boy.

Tempt Me at Twilight. St. Martin's Paperbacks, 2009.
The story of Poppy Hathaway and mysterious, rather wicked hotel owner Harry Rutledge.

Married by Morning. St. Martin's Paperbacks, 2010.
The story of Leo Hathaway, Viscount Ramsay, and governess Catherine Marks.

Love in the Afternoon. St. Martin's Paperbacks, 2010.
The story of animal lover Beatrix Hathaway and Captain Christopher Phelan.

Krahn, Betina

Multidimensional characters, clever plotting, witty humor, and sensuality are hallmarks of Krahn's work.

Brides of Virtue

The heroines are all connected in various ways to the French Convent of the Brides of Virtue in this medieval trilogy.

The Husband Test. Bantam, 2001.
A knight who needs a worthy bride to break the curse on his lands is sent back to his estate with the independent Sister Eloise, a novitiate, who will judge his matrimonial fitness by administering The Husband Test, and finds himself attracted to a "nun."

The Wife Test. Berkley, 2003.
A woman, raised in the convent and wanting for answers about her parentage, masquerades as a nun and accompanies a group of potential brides to England, and finds love and danger, as well as the answers she seeks.

The Marriage Test. Berkley, 2004.
The convent's cook's culinary reputation attracts the notice of a nobleman who arranges for her to cook for him for a year, not realizing that the cook will soon attract him as much as her delicious food.

The Book of Seven Delights. Jove, 2005.
An American librarian makes a surprising discovery in the bowels of the British Museum and heads to North Africa to find the lost Great Library of Alexandria, acquiring the company of a sexy, and often useful, adventurer along the way.

The Book of True Desires. Jove, 2006.
An adventurous woman's crafty old grandfather will only fund her expedition to Mexico if she first finds a series of Mayan artifacts and takes his condescending "butler" with her to validate her findings, in this exotic, occasionally dangerous adventure. Late Victorian setting.

Make Me Yours. Harlequin Blaze, 2009.
Charged with finding an agreeable husband for innkeeper Mariah Eller so the Prince of Wales can take her as his mistress, Jack St. Lawrence falls for the lovely widow, creating a dilemma for all concerned.

Landis, Jill Marie
See also chapter 5, "Contemporary Romance."

Blue Moon. Jove, 1999.
A woman struggling to get home to Illinois after escaping captivity in New Orleans is aided by a scarred, haunted man from the bayou.

The Orchid Hunter. Jove, 2000.
A woman raised in Africa learns she has an identical twin in England, but when her sister's brother takes her back to England with him, her unconventional, free-spirited ways turn everyone's proper Victorian lives upside down.

Summer Moon. Jove, 2001.
An orphaned school teacher agrees to become a mail-order bride, only to arrive in Texas and learn her groom is as surprised as she and that his father, who had engineered the match, is dead.

Magnolia Creek. Jove, 2002.
Returning home with her young child after being deserted by her Yankee lover, a Southern woman learns that the husband she thought was dead is very much alive in this story of difficult choices and second chances.

Langan, Ruth Ryan (Also Writes as Ruth Langan and R. C. Ryan)
See also chapter 5, "Contemporary Romance."

Paradise Falls. Berkley Sensation, 2004.
Orphaned when her father dies, a woman accepts a teaching post in rural Michigan and finds love with a local famer.

Ashes of Dreams. Berkley Sensation, 2005.
A widow struggling to keep her family's Kentucky horse farm intact hires an Irish immigrant to help her.

Duchess of Fifth Avenue. Berkley Sensation, 2006.
A duke turns an immigrant woman into a lady so she can gain custody of her late friend's son in this a New York version of *My Fair Lady*, with a twist.

Heart's Delight. Berkley Sensation, 2007.
Running a dairy farm and caring for her nieces and several other children, Molly O'Brien is resigned to a quiet life, until she discovers two wounded men in her field: one a killer and one the lawman, but which is which?

Laurens, Stephanie
Laurens's adventurous historical romances typically feature strong, protective heroes, fiery, independent heroines, and steamy sex. Most of them are parts of se-

ries and are set in the years during or surrounding the English Regency period. See chapter 13, "Linked Romances."

Law, Susan Kay
See also chapter 5, "Contemporary Romance."

Marrying Miss Bright
The three impoverished Philadelphia-bred Bright sisters head West to seek new lives in this popular trilogy.

The Bad Man's Bride. Avon 2001.
Anthea becomes a teacher in Kansas and finds love with the "bad man" hero.

Marry Me. Avon, 2002.
Emily goes to Montana to stake her homestead claim and runs into trouble when the man who originally owned the land wants it back.

A Wedding Story. Avon, 2003.
Widowed Kate enters the Centennial Race and hopes to win the $50,000 prize with the help of her late husband's explorer friend, a British nobleman.

A Wanted Man. Avon, 2004.
Hardened gunslinger Sam Duncan pretends to be a bodyguard hired by Laura Hamilton's father in order to gain access to the Silver Spur Ranch, the last place his missing friend was seen alive.

Layton, Edith (Pseudonym for Edith Felber)
Empathetic, well-matched characters, exceptional plotting, witty humor, and skillful writing are characteristics of Layton's works.

The Devil's Bargain. Harper, 2002.
A nobleman out for revenge plans to use a young woman who helped him avoid a marriage trap to accomplish his goals.

To Wed a Stranger. Avon, 2003.
A society belle agrees to wed a man she hardly knows, but when she falls ill and loses her beauty, her stranger husband helps her realize what is really important in life.

Gypsy Lover. Avon, 2005.
A prim gentlewoman and a part-gypsy nobleman search for the same missing girl, and risk ruin and fall in love along the way.

For the Love of a Pirate. Avon, 2006.
A nobleman is surprised to learn that he is engaged to a woman he's never met, thanks to an old agreement between their fathers.

His Dark and Dangerous Ways. Avon, 2008.
A gentlewoman who gives dancing lessons to children of the wealthy is hired by a handsome spy to keep tabs on the movements of the brother of one of his colleagues in this danger-filled adventure.

A Bride for His Convenience. Avon, 2008.
A couple turn their marriage of convenience into something more, in spite of efforts to drive them apart.

To Love a Wicked Lord. Avon, 2009.
A woman is attracted to the man commissioned to find her missing fiancé.

Lin, Jeannie
     See chapter 12, "Ethnic/Multicultural Romance."

Linden, Caroline
     Linden's Regency-set Historicals are steamy and often include elements of danger, adventure, and, sometimes, espionage.

What a Woman Needs. Zebra, 2005.
A fortune hunter falls for the attractive guardian of the heiress he is pursuing.

What a Gentleman Wants. Zebra, 2006.
A couple married by proxy in a deception arranged by the hero's rogue twin brother agree to give the marriage a try and end up falling in love. Note: This and the two books that follow have some characters in common.

What a Rogue Desires. Zebra, 2007.
The bad boy twin of the previous story is determined to reform his wicked ways and falls for a totally unacceptable woman, the thief who stole his family's signet ring.

A Rake's Guide to Seduction. Zebra, 2008.
A noble rake sets out to woo the now-widowed woman he was attracted to before she was married.

A View to a Kiss. Avon, 2009.
A world-traveled earl's daughter is bored with the eligible men of the *ton* and is attracted to the mysterious man who is actually a spy investigating rumors of treason.

For Your Arms Only. Avon, 2009.
Falsely accused of treason and working to vindicate himself, a soldier-turned-government-spy goes in search of a missing soldier and finds romance with the missing man's daughter.

You Only Love Once. Avon, 2010.
A trained assassin is paired with an American businessman in order to track down an embezzler in this Regency caper.

Lindsey, Johanna
     One of the original "Avon Ladies," writers of sexy Historical romances during the 1970s, Lindsey's adventurous love stories still attract fans today. See also chapter 14, "Linked Books."

A Man to Call My Own. Pocket, 2003.
Identical twins—selfish, spoiled Amanda and sweet-tempered, self-effacing Marian—can't inherit until they marry and are sent to life with their aunt in Texas after their father dies, where Marian attracts the attention of a local rancher.

Marriage Most Scandalous. Pocket, 2005.
A romance filled with attempted murder, sinister plots, and plenty of poignant humor.

The Devil Who Tamed Her. Pocket, 2007.
A nobleman accepts the challenge of turning a hoyden into a delightful lady—and is captivated by his results. Links to *The Heir* (2000).

A Rogue of My Own. Pocket, 2009.
A spy and a maid to Queen Victoria are caught up in a web of intrigue and danger that sends them off to France in this lively romantic adventure. Links to *The Devil Who Tamed Her*.

When Passion Rules. Gallery, 2011.
An infant princess saved from murder by her would-be assassin returns to her country to reclaim her heritage.

Lindsey, Sara
Weston Family Chronicles
The romantic adventures of the often improper Westons, seven siblings named after Shakespearean characters.

Promise Me Tonight. Signet Eclipse, 2010.
Isabella Weston is determined to marry her childhood love and her brother's good friend James Sheffield—if only she can make him see that falling in love is really worth the risk.

Tempting the Marquis. Signet Eclipse, 2010.
Romantic Olivia Weston wants an adventure before she settles down and a brooding, widowed marquis she meets while spending Christmas in Wales is the perfect challenge.

A Rogue for All Seasons. Signet Eclipse, 2011.

London, Julia (Pseudonym for Dinah Dinwiddie)
Desperate Debutantes
The well-born Fairchild girls struggle to keep up appearances when they learn their unscrupulous stepfather has stolen their fortune.

The Hazards of Hunting a Duke. Pocket Star, 2006.
Ava marries a duke and then must figure out how to keep him.

The Perils of Pursuing a Prince. Pocket Star, 2007.
Greer goes to Wales when she learns of an inheritance and finds a prince of her own—eventually—in this Gothicly tinged tale.

The Dangers of Deceiving a Viscount. Pocket Books, 2007.
Phoebe secretly designs gowns as Madame Duprée and is attracted to a nobleman when she travels to his home to outfit his sisters.

Scandalous Trilogy
The Book of Scandal. Pocket Books, 2008.
Princess Caroline's infamous *Book of Scandal* is the impetus for reuniting an estranged couple in this Regency-set romance.

Highland Scandal. Pocket Books, 2009.
Scandal drives the hero from England and into a handfasted marriage in Scotland.

A Courtesan's Scandal. Pocket Books, 2009.
A courtesan who's caught the attention of the prince and the nobleman charged with pretending to be the lady's latest conquest actually fall in love—a dangerous prospect, indeed.

Secrets of Hadley Green Series
A projected three-book series.

The Year of Living Scandalously. Pocket, 2010.
At the request of her cousin Lily Boudine, Kiera Hannigan goes from Ireland to Hadley Green in England to set Lily's inherited estate to rights, but her decision to let everyone think she is Lily soon causes problems when an old friend, Declan O'Connor, recognizes her in this mystery-laced Regency-set Historical.

Long, Julie Anne
To Love a Thief. Warner Forever, 2005.
A nobleman decides to make a charming pickpocket he captured into a lady to make a woman he's interested in jealous in this story with a Pygmalion plot.

Pennyroyal Green
The Eversea and Redmond families are the focus of this series.

The Perils of Pleasure. Avon, 2008.
Rescued from the hangman by mercenary Madeline Greenway, notorious Colin Eversea joins forces with her when it becomes clear that someone wants her dead.

Like No Other Lover. Avon, 2008.
Cynthia Brightly attracts the attention of Miles Redmond, even though he is supposedly interested in someone else in this funny story that has its share of creepy, crawly critters.

Since the Surrender. Avon, 2009.
When her sister is falsely imprisoned, Rosalind March has no choice but to ask Chase Eversea, a man with whom she shares a past, for help.

I Kissed an Earl. Avon, 2010.
Violet Redmond is conflicted when the sea captain she is attracted to sets out to find her missing brother, a man he thinks is a notorious pirate.

What I Did for a Duke. Avon, 2011.

Lord, Sasha
Wild Series
Sexy medieval romance focusing on the O'Bannon family with an occasional touch of fantasy magic.

Under a Wild Sky. Signet, 2004.
In a Wild Wood. Signet, 2004.
Across a Wild Sea. Signet Eclipse, 2005.
Beyond the Wild Wind. Signet Eclipse, 2006.
In My Wild Dream. Signet Eclipse, 2007.
Wild Angel. Signet Eclipse, 2008.

Lowell, Elizabeth (Pseudonym for Ann Maxwell)
Lowell has written in a number of romance subgenres but is currently best-known for her Romantic Suspense novels. She wrote only a few Historical Romances, but some have become classics in the subgenre and have been reprinted and/or are available electronically. See earlier editions of this guide for bibliographies. See chapter 6, "Romantic Mysteries."

MacLean, Julianne
Pembroke Palace
> The Sinclair noblemen are heroes in this Victorian series.

> ***In My wildest Fantasies***. Avon, 2007.
> Needing to marry to retain his inheritance, Devon Sinclair easily convinces Rebecca Newland to marry him, but then must convince her to love him.

> ***The Mistress Diaries***. Avon, 2008.
> Thinking she is dying, disgraced widow Cassandra Montrose takes her child to her noble father, Vincent Sinclair, but must change her plans when she doesn't die and the father wants to be part of his daughter's life.

> ***When a Stranger Loves Me***. Avon, 2009.
> A woman discovers Blake Sinclair washed up on her Jersey beach and decides that he's the solution to her unwanted marriage and family inheritance problems—she just needs to accomplish her goals before Blake gets his memory back.

MacLean, Sarah
> ***Nine Rules to Break When Romancing a Rake***. Avon, 2010.
> A twenty-eight-year-old spinster bargains with a nobleman for his help in completing a list of adventurous, daringly scandalous tasks in return for chaperoning his half-sister in this steamy romance.

> ***Ten Ways to Be Adored When Landing a Lord***. Avon, 2010.
> A young noblewoman struggles to save her young brother's inheritance by selling a collection of Grecian statues and to keep her sanctuary for desperate young women secret from the handsome lord who may buy her marbles.

> ***Eleven Scandals to Start to Win a Duke's Heart***. Avon, 2011.
> A very proper duke and an impulsive, scandal-prone society miss set out to teach each other lessons in behavior and passion, respectively, and find love in the process.

Maguire, Margo (Pseudonym for Margo Wilder)
> *The Bride Hunt*. Avon, 2006.
> Kidnapped by a band of Scots, an English noblewoman is rescued by a bold knight and together they fight their way to safety in this classic medieval historical set in eleventh-century Scotland and England.

> *The Perfect Seduction*. Avon, 2006.
> A Norman lady is saved from being ravished by a band of Scots by a dispossessed Saxon lord in this passionate medieval adventure.

> *Wild*. Avon, 2009.
> Found in Africa after being thought dead for twenty years, Anthony Maddox, the new Earl of Sutton, wants to return to his African life—until he meets the lovely woman who's been assigned to civilize him.

> *Taken by the Laird*. Avon, 2009.
> Running from her wicked guardian and an evil fiancé, Brianna Munro heads for Scotland and ends up taking shelter in Hugh Christie's crumbling Castle Glenloch.

> *The Rogue Prince*. Avon, 2010.
> A man falsely convicted of a crime plans to avenge himself by seducing the sister of his enemy.

Mallory, Anne (Pseudonym for Anne Hearn)
See also chapter 6, "Romantic Mysteries," and chapter 13, "Linked Romances." Spies, intrigue, and mysteries are often part of Mallory's sensual, Regency-set Historicals.

Masquerading the Marquess. Avon, 2004.
A caricaturist disguised as a courtesan ends up working with her latest noble "victim" when a mutual friend disappears in this spy-laced romantic mystery.

Daring the Duke. Avon, 2005.
A noble spy and a reluctant thief play a lively cat-and-mouse game as they come to love and respect each other.

The Earl of Her Dreams. Avon, 2006.
Disguised as a boy and running from her brother and wicked fiancé, the heroine is stranded at an inn with a mysterious nobleman posing as a Bow Street runner, who quickly sees through her deception.

What Isabella Desires. Avon, 2007.
Tired of being a proper widow, the heroine sets out to seduce the man (and friend) she's always loved, unaware he knows a secret that could keep them apart.

Three Nights of Sin. Avon, 2008.
An impoverished woman falls in love with the mysterious man who requires "three favors" of her to help her recently arrested brother.

The Bride Price. Avon, 2008.
A third and illegitimate son of a duke is torn between love and his desire to win the competition that will grant him wealth and a title.

Seven Secrets of Seduction. Avon, 2010.
A bookish young woman intrigues a jaded rake who engages her to catalog his library in this sensual story with a few fascinating twists.

Mallory, Margaret
All the King's Men
Set during the turbulent years of the early fifteenth century.

Knight of Desire. Forever, 2009.
Lady Catherine Rayburn has no choice but to marry William FitzAlan when King Henry gives all her lands to him in this medieval romance filled with treachery and danger.

Knight of Pleasure. Forever, 2009.
Although engaged to a French aristocrat for political reasons, Lady Isobel Hume is attracted to the Sir Stephen Carleton, the English spy who is also her guardian until she weds.

Knight of Passion. Forever, 2010.
A noblewoman who once chose vengeance over love is given a second chance—if she has the courage and the will to take it.

Martin, Kat
Necklace Trilogy

These Regency tales are tied together by characters and a diamond-and-pearl heirloom necklace thought to bestow either great happiness or great tragedy.

The Bride's Necklace. Mira, 2005.
A young woman protects her sister's virtue by bashing the villain; then, taking an heirloom necklace (with a legendary curse) to finance their escape, they both head for London and find work in the home of the notorious Earl of Brant.

The Devil's Necklace. Mira, 2005.
A privateer seeks vengeance against a woman, now the owner of the necklace, he blames for his false imprisonment by kidnapping her.

The Handmaiden's Necklace. Mira, 2006.
A nobleman convinces his former fiancée to marry him, but it is some time before they solve a number of problems and have a real marriage.

Heart Trilogy

Three Victorian journalists find love, adventure, and mystery in this often humorous, suspenseful trilogy.

Heart of Honor. Mira, 2007.
Publisher Krista Hart is drawn to a man, who is really more Viking than Victorian, from the remote mythical isle of Draugr.

Heart of Fire. Mira, 2008.
A journalist goes undercover to investigate her sister's death and falls in love with the man who might have been the killer.

Heart of Courage. Mira, 2009.
A journalist investigates a murder and is assigned a macho, very annoying Norse bodyguard.

Brides Trilogy

A sexy Victorian series featuring the aristocratic Dewar men.

Royal's Bride. Mira, 2009.
Royal Dewar, Duke of Bransford, agrees to marry for money but is attracted to his prospective bride's cousin, instead.

Reese's Bride. Mira, 2010.
The Countess of Aldridge seeks help from dangerous, greedy relatives from a man she betrayed years earlier, Major Reese Dewar.

Rule's Bride. Mira, 2010.
High-living London businessman Rule Dewar is shocked when an American he married as a teenager and then left arrives seeking an annulment—which he now doesn't want.

McCabe, Amanda

McCabe also has written Traditional Regency Romances.

Lady Midnight. Signet Eclipse, 2005.
When a shipwreck allows a courtesan's daughter to start a new life, she becomes a governess and attracts the notice of her noble employer.

A Notorious Woman. Harlequin Historical, 2007.
A woman's hopes of creating a peaceful new life for herself are threatened when an irresistible sea captain arrives in Venice.

A Sinful Alliance. Harlequin Historical, 2008.
A beautiful assassin must trust the man she plans to kill in this intriguing adventure set during the time of Henry VIII.

High Seas Stowaway. Harlequin Historical, 2009.
A woman changes her mind about revenge when she helps a pirate recover from his wounds in this sixteenth-century high seas adventure.

The Winter Queen. Harlequin Historical, 2009.
Romance and intrigue during the Christmas holidays at Elizabeth's court.

Chase Muses Trilogy
Three women from a family intrigued by antiquities, and each named for a Greek muse, find love in this mystery-laced, Regency-set trilogy.

To Catch a Rogue. Mira, 2010
Calliope Chase's story.

To Deceive a Duke. Mira, 2010.
Clio Chase's story.

To Kiss a Count. Mira, 2010.
Thalia Chase's story.

McCarty, Monica
Campbell (Highland) Trilogy
Feuds, clan rivalries, and deception and intrigue abound in this adventurous seventeenth-century trilogy.

Highland Warrior. Ballantine, 2009.
Jamie Campbell and Caitrina Lamont are attracted to each other, but when Jamie's clan kills Caitrina's family, their relationship seems doomed.

Highland Outlaw. Ballantine, 2009.
Elizabeth Campbell is attracted to a man who helps her more than once, not realizing that he is a member of an outlawed clan.

Highland Scoundrel. Ballantine, 2009.
Duncan Campbell returns to Scotland after ten years of exile in France, but in order to clear his name of treason, he needs the help of a woman he has never forgotten.

Highland Guard
Robert the Bruce chooses ten warriors to be his secret "special ops force" in his fight to free Scotland in this highly detailed, scrupulously researched trilogy set in early-fourteenth-century Scotland.

The Chief. Ballantine, 2010.
Christina Fraser marries fierce Highland warlord Tor MacLeod in place of her less fiery sister, but Tor resists his feelings for her—for a while.

The Hawk. Ballantine, 2010.
Erik MacSorley, expert seafarer and member of Bruce's Guard, rescues a woman from the sea, not realizing she is the daughter of an Irish nobleman and ally of King Edward.

The Ranger. Ballantine, 2011.
A top spy infiltrates the clan responsible for his father's death but is attracted to the chieftain's daughter.

Maxwell, Cathy

Maxwell's romances are lively, filled with humor, and peopled with memorable characters. Most of her books are set in and around the Regency Period.

Cameron Sisters

The Temptation of a Proper Governess. Avon, 2004.
Falsely accused of murder, a man vows vengeance but never plans on having the illegitimate daughter of the nobleman concerned end up in his arms.

The Price of Indiscretion. Avon, 2005.
The granddaughter of an earl raised in America agrees to travel to England to marry well and help her sisters make suitable matches but is kidnapped by a privateer, who turns out to be her first love, on the way.

In the Bed of a Duke. Avon, 2006.
A coach ride to Scotland makes a couple realize they don't hate each other after all, but danger awaits in this lively tale.

Bedding the Heiress. Avon, 2007.
A Scottish blacksmith who's just found out he's a duke and a beautiful, unconventional heiress connect with sparkling results.

In the Highlander's Bed. Avon, 2008.
Constance Cameron's plans to leave Scotland and go back to America are foiled when she is kidnapped by a fierce Scot who wants her brother-in-law to return the Sword of MacKenna.

Scandals and Seductions

The title says it all for this Regency-set series linked by character and filled with scandals, seductions, adventure, and love.

A Seduction at Christmas. Avon. 2008.
A caper gone wrong lands penniless Fiona Lachlan and the Duke of Holborn in an adventure together as they sort out the mystery of a missing family ring and try to stay alive in the process.

The Earl Claims His Wife. Avon, 2009.
A nobleman who left his new wife to be with his mistress before going to war has returned home to find his wife wants a divorce and a lover—but he wants her.

The Marriage Ring. Avon, 2010.
A woman out to prove her father innocent of earlier embezzlement charges blackmails the men she thinks were involved and attracts the attentions of one of their sons, who ends up working with her to uncover the truth.

His Christmas Pleasure. Avon, 2010.
In order to avoid an unwanted marriage, a young woman elopes with a noble rake in this classic marriage-of-convenience romance with a holiday touch.

Medeiros, Teresa

One Night of Scandal. Avon, 2003.
A curious young miss is mistaken for a courtesan and ends up compromised and wed to the supposedly dangerous marquis who moved in next door in this funny, romantic tale.

Kincaid Highland

The loves and adventures of the Kincaid clan.

Some Like It Wicked. Avon, 2008.
In order to avoid an undesirable suitor and return to Scotland and restore honor to her clan, Catriona Kincaid enlists the help of her childhood hero, but she needs to get him out of Newgate first.

Some Like It Wild. Avon, 2009.
A homeless pair of sisters join with a highwayman in a scheme to earn the reward for finding a duke's missing heir in this lively story with many intriguing twists.

The Devil Wears Plaid. Avon, 2010.
Fiery Emmaline Marlowe is abducted from her wedding to a Hepburn laird by the Hepburn clan's sworn enemy, Jamie Sinclair, but the results surprise them both.

Metzger, Barbara

Metzger is an acclaimed writer of Traditional Regency Romances. Her recent works are primarily witty, humorous, charming, well-crafted Regency-set Historicals.

Wedded Bliss. Signet, 2004.
An absent father is called to account by the resourceful widow who is raising his younger son in this charming Regency Era romance.

A Perfect Gentleman. Signet, 2004.
A poor nobleman making ends meet by escorting women to parties and routs meets a woman who wants to hire him for access to various social events so she can search for her missing sister.

The Duel. Signet, 2005.
When his bullet accidentally hits a young boy, the Earl of Marden takes him home and sends for the boy's sister, never thinking that marriage will be the result.

The Hour Glass. Signet, 2007.
A ruthless knight from the Crusades ends up as a grim reaper at Waterloo looking for a magical hourglass and finds love with an outcast widow in this romance with a healthy dollop of the paranormal.

Yours Truly. Signet Eclipse, 2007.
A heroine suspected of killing her wicked stepfather is rescued by a hero who has the innate ability to know when someone is lying, and together they solve a mystery in this sweet tale. (Hero sees truth and lies in colors.)

The Scandalous Life of a True Lady. Signet Eclipse, 2008.
A smart, well-bred, impoverished heroine desperate enough to consider becoming a courtesan is hired by a hero on a secret mission and who needs a social cover in this romantic mystery adventure that is linked to *Yours Truly* by the hero's ability to know when someone is telling the truth. (Hero tastes the truth.)

The Wicked Ways of a True Hero. Signet Eclipse, 2009.
A military officer with the ability to discern the enemy's lies takes some time off but ends up helping his sister make her debut—and reconnecting with a woman from his past. (Hero gets a rash when he hears lies.)

The Bargain Bride. Signet Eclipse, 2009.
Penny Goldthwaite and Viscount Westfield marry after being engaged—and mostly apart—for thirteen years but must deal with some unexpected dangers, as well as the expected ones, on their way to a true marriage.

Michaels, Kasey
See chapter 13, "Linked Romances."

Miller, Linda Lael
See chapter 13, "Linked Romances."

Moore, Kate
See chapter 13, "Linked Romances."

Nash, Sophia
Nash also wrote several earlier Traditional Regency Romances.

Widows Club Series
The unconventional dowager Duchess of Helston forms a "ladies club" for widows in this Regency-set series.

A Dangerous Beauty. Avon, 2007.
Almost socially ruined and now widowed, Rosamunde Baird accepts the dowager duchess's invitation and is surprised to be attracted to the new Duke of Helston, even though she has sworn off passion and love.

The Kiss. Avon, 2008.
Georgiana Wilde, widow of the Marquis of Ellsmere who died on their wedding night, is reunited with a man from her past when the new Marquis of Ellsmere comes to Cornwall to convince Georgiana to leave.

Love with the Perfect Scoundrel. Avon, 2009.
A snowstorm strands Countess Grace Sheffield at the farmhouse of blacksmith Michael Rainer in this poignant, tender romance.

Secrets of a Scandalous Bride. Avon, 2010.
A pretend widow, Elizabeth Ashburton, runs from a suitor she thinks is a murderer and ends up in the carriage—and the life—of an infamous rake, the illegitimate son of the Earl of Wallace.

Noble, Kate
Compromised. Berkley Sensation, 2009.
A nobleman needing to get married or be disinherited becomes engaged to the sweet Evangeline but ends up drawn to her opinionated, witty sister, instead.

Revealed. Berkley Sensation, 2009.
An aristocratic young widow helps the notorious spy the Blue Raven gain access to critical *ton* affairs in return for being able to reveal him to society at one of her balls and falls in love with him in the process.

The Summer of You. Berkley, 2010.
A young society miss reluctantly accompanies her increasingly senile father, the Duke of Rayne, and irresponsible younger brother to their cottage in the Lake District and finds romance with a reclusive war hero who's thought by the townsfolk to be a highwayman.

Osborne, Maggie
Osborne's Western romances are poignant, humorous, and filled with compelling characters, and often take on serious issues.

Silver Lining. Ivy, 2000.
When a woman nurses a group of prospectors back to health during a pox epidemic, they agree to give her anything she wants, but when she says she wants a baby, but not a husband, things get complicated, indeed.

I Do, I Do, I Do. Ivy, 2000.
A woman goes West in search of her husband and finds two other wives along the way in this funny, unusual story.

The Bride of Willow Creek. Ivy, 2001.
Married as teens, separated by family, but never divorced, a couple reconnect after ten years and decide to stay together until they can save enough money to end their marriage—but by then they don't want to. Set primarily in the 1920s.

Prairie Moon. Ivy, 2002.
A lawman and former soldier fulfills a promise to a fallen comrade years after the fact when he visits the comrade's widow on her Texas farm in this story that addresses issues of grief and healing.

Shotgun Wedding. Ivy, 2003.
A free-thinking, single woman's decision to keep her baby in a small, judgmental Kansas town has repercussions when the town decides that the sheriff is the baby's father in this romance set during the early twentieth century.

Plumley, Lisa
Plumley's Historicals are most often set in 1880s Arizona. See also chapter 5, "Contemporary Romance."

The Drifter. Harlequin Historical, 2002.
A journalist wanting to become a magazine columnist needs to marry to get her inheritance, so she targets an illiterate bounty hunter who needs reading lessons and wants to settle down. Obviously, their goals clash.

The Matchmaker. Harlequin Historical, 2003.
A "women's rights" matchmaker is at work in town, much to the dismay of the confirmed bachelors, and timber mill owner Marcus Copeland thinks baker Molly Crabtree might be responsible.

The Scoundrel. Harlequin Historical, 2006.
A marriage of convenience turns into one in fact when the bride demands her marital rights and the groom decides on seduction.

The Rascal. Harlequin Historical, 2006.
A suffragist and a saloon owner find love, eventually.

Potter, Patricia
Potter has written a number of Historical romances and also writes Romantic Suspense. See previous editions of this guide for bibliographies. See also chapter 6, "Romantic Suspense."

Dancing with a Rogue. Berkley, 2003.
When actress Merry Anders and Gabriel Manning, Marquess of Manchester, meet, they have no idea that they are out to destroy the same man, the Earl of Stanhope, and his nefarious group.

Scottish Highland Trilogy

Clan feuds and warfare combine with an ancient curse that predicts that no MacLean bride will ever be happy or live long and that the whole clan will suffer if a MacLean marries in this sensual, adventurous sixteenth-century trilogy.

Beloved Imposter. Berkley Sensation, 2004.
Felicia Campbell is mistaken for the laird's daughter Janet, kidnapped, and brought to Rory MacLean as a bride, but he is wary of wedding because of the curse.

Beloved Stranger. Berkley Sensation, 2006.
Wounded and left on the battlefield for dead, Lachlan MacLean is rescued by English-woman Kimbra Charleston, even though he is a stranger and a Scot—like the men who killed her husband—and is suffering from amnesia, as well.

Beloved Warrior. Berkley Sensation, 2007.
Engineering a mutiny aboard a Spanish slave ship after yeas of servitude, Patrick Mac-Lean heads for Scotland, bringing with him the captain's daughter, who is supposed to marry a cruel English nobleman.

Putney, Mary Jo

See chapter 5, "Contemporary Romance," and chapter 13, "Linked Romances."

Quick, Amanda (Pseudonym for Jayne Ann Krentz)

Quick is noted for her sassy, funny, Historical Romances and her strong alpha-male heroes and smart, intrepid, adventuresome heroines. See previous editions of this guide for bibliographies of earlier works. (See chapter 13, "Linked Romances," under Jayne Ann Krentz)

I Thee Wed. Bantam, 1999.
A psychic heroine and a hero in search in an ancient book of elixirs meet when they are trapped together in a wardrobe during a country house-party in this funny, sexy Regency-set romp.

Wicked Widow. Bantam, 2000.
A woman plagued by her late husband's ghost seeks the help of an exorcist in this suspenseful story with an intriguing twist.

The Paid Companion. Putnam, 2004.
An impoverished gentlewoman agrees to pose as the fiancée of a nobleman to stave off the matchmaking mothers and give him time to investigate his uncle's murder.

Wait Until Midnight. Putnam, 2005.
A popular mystery writer and a wealthy gentleman join forces to find the killer of a medium and find a missing diary in this lively romance that is the first of Quick's stories to be set in the Victorian period.

Lie by Moonlight. Putnam, 2005.
A governess and her four female charges wreak havoc on a crime lord's castle and are given shelter by a gentleman detective who is investigating the same villain.

The River Knows. Putnam, 2007.
Louisa Bryce fakes her own death when she accidentally kills a nobleman who broke into her house, reinvents herself as a pseudonymous journalist investigating a rash of "suicide drownings," and eventually joins forces with a man who's certain his fiancée didn't jump to her death in the river.

Quinn, Julia

See chapter 13, "Linked Romances."

Ranney, Karen

Ranney's romances are adventurous, sexy, and passionate. These are some of her more recent titles.

Autumn in Scotland. Avon, 2006.
A woman married and left by her Scottish earl turns his crumbling castle into a girls' school—and then he returns—or is it his cousin, instead?

The Scottish Companion. Avon, 2007.
Spurred into marriage by the mysterious deaths of his brothers, the Earl of Straithern selects a local doctor's daughter but is drawn to her intelligent companion instead in this passionate, dangerous, Victorian tale.

Scotsman in Love. Avon, 2009.
A woman unfairly disgraced and a nobleman grief stricken after the deaths of his wife and daughter meet on his remote Scottish estate and eventually connect emotionally as they begin to heal.

Sold to a Laird. Avon, 2009.
A marriage of convenience turns into a real one in this Victorian romance.

A Highland Duchess. Avon, 2010.
A noblewoman trapped in a cruel marriage discovers freedom and love when she is abducted by a highland laird in this suspenseful adventure.

Rice, Patricia

Rice's romances are often humorous, whimsical, and entertaining. She has written in a number of subgenres.

Magic

The psychically gifted Malcolm women and Ives men find love in this slightly magical series.

Merely Magic. Signet, 2000.
A local legend predicts disaster for the town if a Malcolm witch and an Ives devil ever be involved, so when herbalist Ninian Malcolm Siddons and Drogo Ives meet, everyone expects the worst.

Must Be Magic. Signet, 2002.
A Malcolm widow herbalist who can also smell emotions is attracted to an Ives male who is reputed to have killed his wife.

The Trouble with Magic. Signet, 2003.
A woman who "reads" people by touch seeks the help of Ewen Ives in finding a book of spells to help solve her problems.

This Magic Moment. Signet, 2004.
A heroine who can see ghosts and auras is concerned when her love's aura turns dark in this charming romance with a malicious villain.

Much Ado about Magic. Signet Eclipse, 2005.
A heroine whose paintings are said to predict the future captures the hero's attention when one of her paintings has everyone thinking he killed his cousin.

Magic Man. Signet Eclipse, 2006.
A heroine helps a fiery Scot research his heritage and they both discover unexpected talents in this satisfying conclusion to the Magic series.

The Wicked Wyckerly. Signet Eclipse, 2010.
A fast-living nobleman (with a lively, young, illegitimate daughter) who never expected to be an earl and needs to marry for money and a woman who needs to wed to gain custody of her four siblings are attracted to each other, in spite of a number of obstacles. First of a projected series.

Robards, Karen

Noted primarily for her riveting tales of Contemporary Romantic Suspense, Robards has also dipped her toes into the Historical Romance waters. See previous editions of this guide for her earlier works. See also chapter 6, "Romantic Mysteries."

Banning Sisters Trilogy

Three orphaned sisters find love and adventure during the British Regency period.

Scandalous. Pocket Star, 2001.
A woman determined to give her sister a London season hides the news of their long-absent half-brother's death—but then who is the man who claims to be their brother when they come to London?

Irresistible. Pocket Star, 2002.
A noblewoman is abducted by a man who thinks she is a spy for the French.

Shameless. Gallery, 2010.
Spies, kidnappings, and abductions abound in this lively story that winds up the Banning Sisters Trilogy in fine style.

Rogers, Rosemary

Rogers, another of the original "Avon Ladies," founded the Sweet/Savage subgenre with the publication of *Sweet Savage Love* in 1973. These novels are characterized by plenty of action, colorful historical settings, occasional rape, and violent sex that is not necessarily monogamous. Several of her recent titles are listed below.

Savage Desire. Mira, 2000.
Ginny and Steve from the original *Sweet Savage Love* (and others), are reunited when Ginny goes to London to convince Steve to reconcile.

An Honorable Man. Mira, 2002.
When her brother kills her senator father over his decision to release his slaves and help President Lincoln, Cameron Campbell enlists the aid of Union undercover agent Jackson Logan.

Return to Me. Mira, 2003.
Danger threatens in the lawless Reconstruction Era South as Cameron Campbell Logan heads to the Mississippi plantation to have her baby over the objections of her Union captain husband Jackson. Follows *An Honorable Man*.

A Daring Passion. HQN, 2007.
A cross-dressing heroine pretending to be her highwayman father is kidnapped by a man who intends to use her to get his brother freed from prison in this story that sweeps from England to France.

Scandalous Deception. HQN, 2008.
Russian political schemes, assassination attempts, assorted villains, an intrepid heroine, and aristocratic twins trading places are all in the mix in this sexy adventure.

Bound by Love. HQN, 2009.
The other twin gets his girl in this spin-off of *Scandalous Deception*.

Scoundrel's Honor. HQN, 2010.
An innkeeper turns to the infamous, powerful Beggar Czar of the St. Petersburg underworld for help when her sister runs off with a pair of men and is swept up in a passionate, country-hopping adventure.

Rolls, Elizabeth
Note: Several of these titles were earlier published in the United Kingdom by Mills & Boon.

The Unexpected Bride. Harlequin Historical, 2004.
Mystery and romance combine in this intriguing Regency.

The Unruly Chaperone. Harlequin Historical, 2005.
A nobleman who must marry falls for his quarry's widowed cousin and chaperone, instead.

His Lady Mistress. Harlequin Historical, 2005.
Orphaned and now working as a maid, a young woman is offered carte blanche by a nobleman she knew years earlier but who doesn't recognize her; when he does, the playing field changes.

The Chivalrous Rake. Harlequin Historical, 2006.
The hero and heroine bicker their way to love in this romance laced with secrets and misunderstandings.

The Compromised Lady. Harlequin Historical, 2007.
A heroine with a terrible secret and a hero strong enough to help her overcome the past find love in this story that is a sequel to *His Lady Mistress*.

Lord Braybrook's Penniless Bride. Harlequin Historical, 2009.
A nobleman who puts a premium on money and an aristocratic heritage falls in love with a woman with neither.

Rosenthal, Pam
Rosenthal's Historicals, which have a literary quality about them, are insightful, beautifully written, feature intelligent, bold heroines and worthy heroes, and are often erotic and sexually explicit.

Almost a Gentleman. Brava, 2003.
The Earl of Linseley is most relieved when the elegant, trendsetting "gentleman" he is strangely attracted to turns out to be a woman who is reinventing herself after a disastrous marriage and determined to live life on her own terms. Threats and danger add to the mix.

The Bookseller's Daughter. Brava, 2004.
Becoming a servant after her father dies in order to save up to buy her own bookstore, an educated young woman soon realizes that she knew of the aristocrats she

now works for as a book smuggler during the dangerous times leading up to the French Revolution.

The Slightest Provocation. Signet Eclipse, 2006.
Married young but separated for years because of differences in lifestyles and desires, a couple meet again and consider divorce—until a plot against the government forces them to work together, and they renew their relationship.

*The Edge of Impropriety. Signet Eclipse, 2008.
An aristocratic widow uses her scandalous reputation to increase sales of her popular romance novels, but when the studious, art appraiser uncle (who is actually the father) of a young nobleman who is actually just her friend arrives to "save" the boy, he ends up fascinated by the lady himself.

Ross, Julia (Pseudonym for Jean Ross Ewing)
Ross wrote Traditional Regency Romances earlier in her career. Lyrical writing, lush sensuality, and well-developed characters are typical of her work, which often contains elements of suspense.

Wyldshay Trilogy
Two brothers and a cousin are the adventurous heroes in this intriguing Regency-set trilogy.

Night of Sin. Berkley Sensation, 2005.
A "dragon's fang" fossil tossed into her shopping basket by a thief just before he dies lands Anne Marsh in a dangerous and passionate adventure when she is whisked off to Wyldshay Castle by Wild Lord Jack (Jonathan St. George), a world-traveling nobleman.

Games of Pleasure. Berkley Sensation, 2005.
Knowing there can be no future for the heir to a dukedom and a courtesan and carrying a deadly secret and after Lord Ryderbourne (Laurence St. George) rescues a battered Miracle Heather from a foundering dinghy and they share a night of passion, Miracle runs—but Ryder is not about to let her go in this sensual, suspenseful story.

Clandestine. Berkley Sensation, 2006.
A widow needs a gentleman's help in locating her cousin, but secrets and mysteries abound in this final volume of the Wyldshay Trilogy.

Ryan, Nan
Ryan's romances, set primarily in the West and South, are filled with action and are sexually explicit with Sweet/Savage elements. See previous editions of this guide for earlier works. A brief selection of her recent works follows.

Naughty Marietta. Mira, 2003.
Confederate officer Cole Helflin is saved from the hangman only to learn that the price he must pay is to bring a dying man's spitfire granddaughter back home.

Chieftain. Mira, 2004.
A gritty, fast-paced, violent, sometimes crude tale of the Old West that deals with the overt racism the Native Americans faced

Dearest Enemy. Mira, 2006.
A Southern belle spy will do anything to make sure the South wins the war, even sacrifice the Union Naval officer she loves in this dangerous, sexy, story of passion and vengeance.

Schone, Robin

Schone's explicitly sexy stories sometimes border on erotica, and often take a hard look at women's issues and the lack of legal power women had, particularly during the Victorian Period.

The Lady's Tutor. Zebra, 1999.
A lady seeks instruction in pleasing her husband from a bastard nobleman and falls in love with her tutor. A groundbreaking, passionately erotic story that deals with cultural, gay, and women's power issues.

The Lover. Zebra, 2000.
In return for his services, a wealthy woman agrees to help a man renown for giving women pleasure find the man responsible for his career-stopping burns and scars in this tale of revenge, passion, and love.

Gabriel's Woman. Brava, 2001.
Linked to *The Lover*, this story of golden, tormented Gabriel and a woman so desperate she's auctioning off her virginity features seriously wounded protagonists and truly evil villains—and is darker and more intense than some.

Awaken, My Love. Brava, 2001.
Through the mysteries of time travel, a modern-day computer geek whose husband isn't interested in sex and a nineteenth-century nobleman with a frigid wife have their needs met when she ends up in his wife's body. But danger and evil lurk in this unusual story and they need to be dealt with. Note: This is the author's preferred version of her first novel which was first published by Avon in 1995.

Scandalous Lovers. Berkley Sensation, 2007.
A country-bred widow comes to London, attends the Men and Women's Club—an organization that intellectually studies sensuality—and attracts the attention of a handsome attorney in a book that confronts double-standards, hypocrisy, and scandal, as well as women's rights issues.

Cry for Passion. Berkley Sensation, 2009.
A woman, whose husband is sterile and an alcoholic because of it, seeks a divorce and intrigues the lawyer she retains in this extremely sexually explicit story that explores the inhumane Victorian marriage laws and is based on a real case that actually changed the British marriage laws. Follows *Scandalous Lovers*.

Scott, Amanda (Pseudonym for Lynne Scott-Drennan)

Scott also has written and won a Rita Award for her Traditional Regency Romances. Most often set in medieval Scotland, Scott's Historicals are adventurous, well-plotted, filled with engaging characters, historically accurate, and evocative of time and place. A small sampling of her recent titles is listed below.

Scottish Borders

Romance, danger, and conflict along the Scottish/English border during the late fourteenth century.

Border Wedding. Forever, 2008.
A man faced with hanging or marrying a plain woman chooses life—and finds love and happiness in the bargain.

Border Lass. Forever. 2008.
When a woman overhears plans for treason, the knight who saves her from discovery must also keep her safe from the villains.

Border Moonlight. Forever, 2009.
A man saves a woman and child from drowning only to realize that he's saved the woman who rejected him several years earlier.

Tamed by a Laird. Forever, 2009.
A woman seeking one last adventure before she is married to a stranger becomes part of a traveling group of minstrels and gets more than she'd bargained for.

Seduced by a Rogue. Forever, 2010.
When a clan war begins to brew over a tax debt, Rob Maxwell kidnaps Lady Mairi in a complicated scheme to force her father to pay up. But the plan falls apart, the pair fall in love, and the situation threatens to spin out of control.

Tempted by a Warrior. Forever. 2010.
A woman who fears she's killed her cruel husband because he can't be found and she can't remember what happened is aided by her husband's cousin to discover what took place.

Highland Master. Forever, 2011.
The daughter and granddaughter of powerful chieftains takes a wounded man home with her, not realizing that the man she rescued is not only a political mission but has a deadly goal of his own.

Small, Bertrice

Another of the original "Avon Ladies," Small continues to write lively, sexy stories of a variety of historical types. She is especially known for her O'Malley series, which started in 1980 with the legendary *Skye O'Malley*, a story in the Sweet/Savage vein. See previous editions of this guide for earlier works. A small sampling of her more recent titles is listed below.

Border Chronicles

A sextet (so far) of diverse romances involving the Scottish/English order conflicts during the fifteenth and sixteenth centuries.

A Dangerous Love. NAL, 2006.
The Border Lord's Bride. NAL, 2007.
The Captive Heart. NAL, 2008.
The Border Lord and the Lady. NAL, 2009.
The Border Vixen. NAL, 2010.
Bond of Passion. NAL, 2011.

Squires, Susan

Two romances set during a particularly cruel, violent period with a touch of myth and magic.

Danegeld. Leisure, 2001.
A woman raped by a cruel Saxon leader heals a Viking warrior who suffered a similar fate and needs his sense of self restored.

Danelaw. Leisure, 2003.
A Saxon healer and priestess who communicates with animals waits for the man who will become her destiny in this battle-filled ninth-century romance.

Stuart, Anne

Stuart is a multi-published member of RWA's Hall of Fame, and she writes in a number of Romance subgenres. She excels in intense, tortured heroes and her Historicals are often darker than most.

Hidden Honor. Mira, 2004.
A woman planning to devote her life to Christ travels to a shrine with a group of monks and knights, and is attracted to King John's very sinful bastard son.

The Devil's Waltz. Mira, 2006.
A spinster is determined to guard her young charge from the advances of a fortune-hunting rake, but intrigues the man herself.

House of Rohan Series

This wickedly dark Georgian series about a decadent family and the secret Heavenly Host society where aristocrats indulge their most depraved desires was introduced by an e-book prequel, *The Wicked House of Rohan*.

Ruthless. Mira, 2010.
The Viscount Rohan encounters a naive woman who won't be lured by his seductive talents, even though she is tempted.

Reckless. Mira, 2010.
Another member of the Rohan clan falls victim to a woman who won't be charmed.

Breathless. Mira, 2010.
A ruined Rohan woman is trapped into marriage by a man who plans to use her in his quest for vengeance.

Shameless. Mira, 2011.
Lord Benedick Rohan meets his match in outspoken crusader Lady Melisande Carstairs when she seeks his help when one of her reclaimed "soiled doves" goes missing.

Sundell, Joanne

Matchmaker, Matchmaker. Five Star, 2006.
A Jewish woman doctor faces difficulties and cultural concerns when she moves to Colorado and is attracted to a saloon owner.

A . . . My Name's Amelia. Five Star, 2007.
A woman deaf since childhood answers an ad for a mail-order bride, but doesn't tell her husband that she's deaf.

The Parlor House Daughter, Five Star, 2008.
A girl chastely raised in a brothel wants to find the person who killed her mother in this realistic look at life of prostitutes in the Old West.

Taylor, Janelle

Noted for her Native American romances, Taylor has recently been writing Contemporary Romantic Suspense. See previous editions of this guide for her earlier Historical titles. (See also chapter 6, "Romantic Mysteries," and chapter 13, "Multicultural Romance.")

Thomas, Sherry

Lyrical, eloquent writing, complex characters, and intriguing, often uncommon plots are hallmarks of Thomas's Victorian Era Historical Romances.

Private Arrangements. Bantam, 2008.
Things come to a head for a proper Victorian couple who've lived apart for a decade when Gigi files for divorce and Camden demands an heir in this unusual, emotionally compelling romance.

Delicious. Bantam, 2008.
The quiet, secure life of a sought-after chef is threatened when her long-time employer dies and his politician brother, with whom she had a long-ago incognito affair, inherits the estate.

*Not Quite a Husband. Bantam, 2009.
Leaving England to avoid the scandal of a broken, annulled marriage and to pursue her medical dreams, Bryony ends up on the dangerous, disease-ridden Indian frontier, where Leo finally finds her, intending to bring her home because her father is ill.

*His at Night. Bantam, 2010.
A razor-sharp undercover agent of the crown who moves in society as a feckless, harmless nobleman and a woman desperate to escape her cruel, sadistic uncle are compromised and forced into an uneasy marriage in this secret-laden romance.

Thornton, Elizabeth (Pseudonym for Mary George)

Thornton is noted for her adventurous, fast-paced stories that feature intelligent protagonists and are often laced with humor and mystery. See previous editions of this guide for a selection of her earlier works.

Trap Trilogy

A lively Regency Era series that focuses on three fast friends, Jack Riggs, Brand Hamilton, and Ash Denison.

The Marriage Trap. Bantam, 2005.
A mathematical wizard who is a dowdy companion by day and the alluring, mysterious gambler Aurora, by night, Ellie is compromised and ends up in a marriage of convenience with Lord Jack Riggs, a cynical aristocrat and jaded soldier she knew as a boy.

The Bachelor Trap. Dell, 2006.
Concerned when he receives a letter from his late mentor concerning a mysterious twenty-year-old disappearance of her younger sister and the current danger to her niece, Lady Marion Dane, Brand Hamilton, a duke's illegitimate son and self-made newspaper tycoon and aspiring politician, seeks Marion in this story that has a roaring good mystery, as well as a sweet romance.

Pleasure Trap. Bantam, 2007.
A clairvoyant writer of Gothic romances and a nobleman looking for the author of scandalous gossip columns have already caused one murder and must deal with a wicked step-mother, an ancient curse, an insane villain, and their growing attraction for each other—and stay alive.

Seers of Grampian Trilogy

In an unusual twist, the heroes are the ones with the psychic abilities in this Victorian trilogy that is the late Thornton's final series.

The Runaway McBride. Berkley Sensation, 2009.
When his grandmother passes her clairvoyant gift to him on her death, widower James Burnett "sees" Faith McBride, his old love, in deadly danger and knows he has to find her.

The Scot and I. Berkley Sensation, 2009.
A psychic spy tracks down a courier (now disguised as a boy) who foils an assassination plot against the queen and together they work to bring down a deadly group of anti-Royalists.

A Bewitching Bride. Berkley Sensation, 2010.
A pair of psychically gifted protagonists join their talents to investigate a murder and end up compromised—and wed—in the process.

Veryan, Patricia
Veryan writes well-researched, carefully plotted Regency and Georgian Era romances filled with realistic characters and situations. (See chapter 8, "Regency Romance.") See previous editions of this guide for bibliographies of some of her earlier works.

Wiggs, Susan
Wiggs wrote a number of Historical romances earlier in her career but is currently focusing on Contemporaries. See also chapter 13, "Linked Romances."

Calhoun Chronicles
Politics, intrigue, and romance drive the plots of most of these late Victorian stories that involve the Calhoun family members and feature unconventional, strong heroines and heroes who love them.

The Charm School. Mira, 1999.
A bright, but awkward, young Bostonian woman stows away aboard a Rio-bound ship and charms the crew, enchants the captain, and gains a tremendous amount of self-confidence on the voyage.

The Horsemaster's Daughter. Mira, 1999.
A skillful, island-raised horsemaster and a society plantation owner fall in love in this story that deals with class, among other issues.

Halfway to Heaven. Mira, 2001.
A physically impaired, brilliant astronomer finds love in a rather unexpected place in this politics-laced book.

An Enchanted Afternoon. Mira, 2002.
Spousal abuse and illiteracy are issues in this late Victorian American romance.

A Summer Affair. Mira, 2003.
An adventurous woman on the run and wounded is rescued by a widowed doctor who spends his nights trolling the San Francisco streets in search of those who need help in this story set in the 1880s.

Willig, Lauren
See chapter 13, "Linked Romances."

Willingham, Michelle
MacEgan Brothers Series
An adventurous twelfth-century series featuring the MacEgan brothers. These titles are listed in the author's recommended reading order.

Her Warrior Slave. Harlequin Historical, 2008.
Although written after some of the other books in the series, this is a prequel to the MacEgan brothers series.

Her Warrior King. Harlequin Historical, 2008.
Blackmailed into marriage with a Norman noblewoman, Patrick MacEgan resists his feelings for his lovely bride.

Her Irish Warrior. Harlequin Historical, 2007.
An Irish warrior feels compelled to rescue a Norman lady from her brutish fiancé even though he has good reason to hate the Normans.

The Warrior's Touch. Harlequin Historical, 2007.
A healer reconnects with the man she loved as a boy when she finds him wounded and near death.

Taming Her Irish Warrior. Harlequin Historical, 2009.
Although intending to wed for money, an Irish lord is attracted to his fiancée's warrior sister, instead.

Surrender to an Irish Warrior. Harlequin Historical, 2010.
Two troubled souls find healing and love in this story that solves a mystery and ties up the loose ends of this series.

The Accidental Countess. Harlequin Historical, 2010.
A husband with amnesia can't remember his marriage which presents problems for his wife.

The Accidental Princess. Harlequin Historical, 2010.
A noblewoman is attracted to a soldier who is on a quest to learn the truth of his heritage.

Wolf, Joan

Wolf has written a number of well-crafted romances in several subgenres, but focuses primarily on Historicals. Her most recent titles have been set during the Regency Period. See previous editions of this guide for bibliographies of her earlier works.

Someday Soon. Warner, 2000.
A woman must marry the seventh Earl of Wilton in order to inherit, but when a Scotsman turns out to be the heir instead of the man everyone expects, things become dangerous and a little wild.

Royal Bride. Mira, 2001.
A woman marries a prince when her sister jilts him for another in this story with a fair amount of danger and political intrigue.

White Horses. Mira, 2004.
A woman inherits her late father's circus as well as his undercover job transporting money to the troops for the crown but is forced into take a military escort—and pretend to be married—when she takes a shipment of gold to Wellington.

To the Castle. Mira, 2005.
A political marriage and a battle over hereditary rights keep the action lively in this medieval romance.

His Lordship's Desire. Mira, 2006.
Teenage sweethearts are reunited when the Earl of Standish returns from the war planning to wed Diana Sherwood, but Diana is still resentful that he chose the military over her.

Woodiwiss, Kathleen

With the publication of *The Flame and the Flower* in 1972, Woodiwiss is credited with launching the boom in sensual historical fiction. Note: Woodiwiss's earlier books are considered to be among her best, and readers should be aware that all of her titles are products of their times and will read very differently from today's Historicals. Her most recent titles are listed below.

The Elusive Flame. Avon, 1998.
Heather and Brandon's son Beau protects lovely Cerynise from a greedy villain by marrying her and taking her on his ship to America in this sequel to *The Flame and the Flower*.

A Season beyond a Kiss. Avon, 2000.
Following *The Flame and the Flower* and *The Elusive Flame*, this is the story of Brandon's younger brother Jeff and his wife, Raelynn.

The Reluctant Suitor. Avon, 2003.
A hero returns from the war to assume his hereditary title and is attracted to the woman his late father wanted him to marry, in spite of his wishes to the contrary—but the lady in question isn't so sure she's interested in a man who broke her heart years earlier.

Everlasting. Morrow, 2007.
Abrielle is attracted to a virile Scottish ambassador, Raven, but is promised to another in this twelfth-century tale that is the late Woodiwiss's final book.

Woods, Janet

Woods is an award-winning, multi-published writer of Historical Romance, Contemporary Romance, and mainstream fiction. A small selection of her titles is listed below.

Daughter of Darkness. Robert Hale, 2001.
A woman must deal with the fall-out from her family's less-than-pristine reputation in this slightly Gothic story.

Amaranth Moon. Severn House, 2005.
A young woman, relegated to nanny duties for her cousins, is hired by a neighboring nobleman as his social secretary in this Traditional Regency Romance.

Cinnamon Sky. Severn House, 2006.
Shocked to find that he has not only inherited an estate but also the responsibility for five young women, Kynan Trent is soon at odds with the eldest of the group, Alexis, and attracted to her, as well.

Salting the Wound. Severn House, 2009.
A young woman tries to mend the family fences when her sister jilts the sea captain who expected to marry her but ends up compromised and wed, instead.

Straw in the Wind. Severn House, 2010.
A sea captain learns his illegitimate daughter is alive and sends a detective to look for her in this romantic story that holds a few surprises and follows *Salting the Wound*.

Paper Doll. Severn House, 2010.
A woman is caught between a disastrous marriage and the man she loves in this 1920s novel.

Western Period Romance and Selected Bibliography

Set in the American West, usually west of the Mississippi and during the second half of the nineteenth century, these stories are the Romance genre's version of The Western. Plots are wide-ranging and focus on survival and the "taming of the West," and can include trail drives, homesteading, bank robberies, showdowns, chases, range and Indian Wars, and anything else appropriately Western. Characters will vary with the story, but gunslingers, ranchers, outlaws, lawmen, saloon hostesses, schoolmarms, pioneers, and other assorted people of the frontier are favorites. Styles can be rough and fast-paced or gentle and tender, and all levels of sensuality are represented. (Note: Some romances of this type, especially the gentler ones with small town settings, could also fall within the Period Americana subgenre discussed below.) The books listed below are merely examples of the many romances of this variety.

Anderson, Catherine

Anderson's touching Historicals combine aspects of both the Western and Americana Period Romances. See also chapters 5 and 13, "Contemporary Romance" and "Linked Romances."

Simply Love. Avon, 1997.
A naive young woman wins the heart and respect of a wealthy cynic and changes his life in this romance with a Colorado mining town setting.

Cherish. Avon, 1998.
A former gunslinger, now a rancher, falls in love with a young woman he rescues after outlaws destroy her Quaker wagon train.

Barbieri, Elaine
Texas Trilogy

A sweeping Reconstruction Era saga of the offspring of Buck Star, who must deal with the disastrous fallout of his past indiscretions.

Texas Star. Leisure, 2003.
Cal Star returns home to find his father sick and married to a woman whose mission it is to destroy everything the Stars hold dear. Darker than some.

Texas Glory. Leisure, 2004.
Honor Gannon goes to Texas to confront her father, Buck, and finds love where she least expects it.

Texas Triumph. Leisure, 2005.
Pinkerton agent Taylor Star and his partner, Vida Malone, go to Texas to investigate a murder and end up solving the trilogy's ongoing mystery and falling in love at the same time.

Sign of the Wolf

After hearing the "cry of the wolf," which always foretells tragedy, Letty Wolf, estranged from her three daughters, dispatches detectives to find them before it's too late in this gently paranormal trilogy that brings the West of the 1880s vividly to life.

Sign of the Wolf. Leisure, 2007.
Eldest daughter Meredith falls in love with the detective sent to find her in this Texas-set romance.

Night of the Wolf. Leisure, 2007.
Johanna also hears the cry of the wolf, knows she is in danger on her way to Arizona, and is saved from attack by a man who is on the run from the law.

Cry of the Wolf. Leisure, 2008.
Justine, desperate and clueless in the kitchen, takes a job as a ranch cook in Oklahoma and falls for a man who's been hired to teach her to cook but is also looking for a missing heiress, not realizing she is the woman he seeks.

Getting Lucky. Leisure, 2009.
A woman who loses everything on the way out west connects with a gambler in San Francisco in this vividly descriptive tale of California during the Gold Rush days.

Renegade. Leisure, 2010.
A woman heads for Texas to avenge her father's murder, becomes a saloon girl, and is attracted to the man she thinks is the killer.

Bittner, Rosanne
America West Trilogy
With accurate historical details and vivid descriptions, Bittner chronicles the events in the lives of the fictitious Wilde family from the 1750s in Pennsylvania to Ohio in the early 1800s.

Into the Wilderness: The Long Hunters. Forge, 2002.
A realistic, sometimes violent tale set during the time of the French and Indian War.

Into the Valley: The Settlers. Forge, 2003.
The Revolutionary War affects the lives of the Wilde family in unexpected ways.

Into the Prairie: The Pioneers. Forge, 2004.
A young mother marries a Native American to save her young son when her husband goes missing and then must make some decisions when he reappears.

Dellin, Genell
See chapter 12, "Ethnic/Multicultural Romance."

Gentry, Georgina
Gentry's name is synonymous with gritty, realistic, well-researched, sometimes funny, fast-paced Westerns that feature strong, often wounded, alpha-male heroes and the equally strong, resourceful heroines who love them. Many of her romances feature multicultural characters and her early romances focused on Native Americans. Several of her more recent titles are listed below. See also chapter 12, "Ethnic/Multicultural Romance."

To Tame a Savage. Zebra, 2002.
The half-Cheyenne son of a Boston-bred cavalry officer is captured and sent "home" to Boston and must deal with the family he's never known and a young governess who steals his heart.

To Tame a Texan. Zebra, 2003.
A suffragette disguises herself as a boy and joins a cattle drive in order to get to a women's rights conference in Dodge City.

To Tame a Rebel. Zebra, 2004.
Civil War rivalries and revenge motivate this adventure story that focuses on the Native American involvement in the conflict.

To Tempt a Texan. Zebra, 2005.
An activist newspaper owner and Northern sympathizer and a saloon owner and Southern loyalist square off against each other over a number of issues in this funny Western romp.

To Tease a Texan. Zebra, 2006.
A barmaid fleeing the law answers an ad for a mail-order bride, impersonates her suffragist twin, and ends up wed to the man who got her into trouble in the first place—or is he someone else? Deception reigns in this hilarious romp.

To Love a Texan. Zebra, 2007.
A bordello and saloon co-owner leaves her half of the business to her straight-laced, spinster niece, who decides to clean the place up, much to the annoyance of gambler Brad O'Neal, the other coowner of the business.

To Wed a Texan. Zebra, 2008.
An upcoming boxing match pits the fight's promoter and an activist librarian against each other in this sassy, hilarious battle of the sexes.

To Seduce a Texan. Zebra, 2009.
A group of loyal Texans, needing money for the Confederate cause, kidnap a Kansas banker's stepdaughter and hold her for ransom, not realizing that the slimy, evil banker has no intention of paying to get her back.

Texans
Adventure, violence, and passion in a late nineteenth-century setting.

Diablo. Zebra, 2010.
A half-Sioux gunslinger sets out on a mission of vengeance on the man who scarred and sexually abused him as a boy and falls in love with the villain's fiancée in this Beauty-and-the-Beast tale.

Rio. Zebra, 2011.
A woman is caught between a powerful Texas politician and the cowboy she loves in this riveting adventure.

Greenwood, Leigh (Pseudonym for Harold Lowry)
Greenwood is a veteran writer of fast-paced Historical Western romances. His earlier Seven Brides series is among his most memorable.

Night Riders
The remaining members of the Night Riders, a top group of Confederate raiders, seek revenge against the evil traitor who sold out their unit, Laveau deViere, in this series set in the post–Civil War era.

Texas Homecoming. Leisure, 2002.
A Texas rancher falls in love with the sister of the man he and the Night Riders are after.

Texas Bride. Leisure, 2002.
A handsome hero and a plain heroine come to terms with their internal self-perception issues in this romance that explores the effect and importance of physical appearance.

Born to Love. Leisure, 2003.
Alcoholism, vengeance, and healing, both physical and mental, are themes in this story about a doctor who doesn't want to practice after enduring the horrors of battlefield medicine.

Someone Like You. Leisure, 2009.
A former soldier reluctantly returns to California when he inherits his father's ranch but must deal with his treacherous, selfish young stepmother as well as his growing feelings for her sister.

When Love Comes. Leisure, 2010.
A handsome hero, who was scarred facially during the war and now believes he is unlovable, and a beautiful heroine who thinks no man sees beyond her beauty find love and understanding.

No One but You. Leisure, 2011.
A marriage of convenience in order to save the heroine's ranch becomes a real relationship—until the past and outside forces try to make trouble. Slightly connected to the earlier Seven Brides series.

Parra, Nancy J.
Morgan Family Series
Strong, capable protagonists drive the plots of this sweet Western series that is graced with humor, charm, and a dash of adventure.

Saving Samantha. Avalon, 2002.
A Wanted Man. Avalon, 2002.
Loving Lana. Avalon, 2003.
Wyoming Wedding. Avalon, 2004.
The Marryin' Kind. Avalon, 2004.
The Bettin' Kind. Avalon, 2005.
The Lovin' Kind. Avalon, 2006.

Thomas, Jodi
Thomas's Western romances are tender, touching, sensual, often laced with humor, and filled with wounded characters. She is unofficially called the Queen of Texas Romance and is a member of the RWA Hall of Fame for her three Rita Awards in the Historical Romance category. *The Tender Texan* (1991) and *To Tame a Texan's Heart* (1994) are two of her early Rita winners.

Wife Lottery Series
Three women, Bailee, Sarah, and Lacy, convinced they'd killed a man who'd attacked them after they'd been abandoned by their wagon train, turn themselves in to the crafty sheriff who raffles them off as brides to men willing to pay the women's fines. Note: The last book is a character spin-off of the original trilogy and the heroine is not part of the original wife lottery.

The Texan's Wager. Jove, 2002.
Bailee Moore is won by reclusive, silent Carter McKoy, a man with a tragic past, but before they can be happy, they must sort out their pasts and deal with present dangers.

When a Texan Gambles. Jove, 2003.
Widowed Sarah Andrews and feared and hated bounty hunter Sam Gatlin find danger, adventure, and eventually love in this lively romance.

A Texan's Luck. Jove, 2004.
Lacy and army Captain Walker Larson, married by proxy when Walker's father wins Lacy in the lottery, are forced to live together for Lacy's protection when the man the women originally thought they'd killed returns and is out for revenge.

*The Texan's Reward. Berkley, 2006.
A wounded rancher realizes she needs to find a husband to help her manage her lands, but when a man she has loved all her life applies for the "position," she balks at becoming a burden to him.

Whispering Mountain Series

Featuring the orphaned McMurray siblings, this series is named after their ranch, Whispering Mountain.

Texas Rain. Berkley, 2006.
Fleeing from an arranged marriage, Rainey Adams steals Texas Ranger Travis McMurray's horse, but when she feels guilty after he is wounded in an ambush, she writes to him, beginning a correspondence that eventually draws them together as trouble stalks them both.

Texas Princess. Berkley, 2007.
Reclusive horse breeder Tobin McMurray befriends vulnerable Liberty Mayfield when he finds her hiding in the barn from her cruel greedy fiancé. And when someone tries to kill her senator father, Tobin takes her to his Apache grandfather's people for safety.

Tall, Dark, and Texan. Jove, 2008.
Trusting that Teagan McMurray will be as kind as his letters to her late husband sound, Jessie Barton takes her three young daughters to Whispering Mountain in a effort to keep her avaricious in-laws from taking the girls—and ends up married to, and falling in love with, the lonely rancher.

The Lone Texan. Berkley, 2009.
Widowed doctor Sage McMurray returns to Texas but is taken hostage during a robbery and then auctioned off to the highest bidder—a tall cowboy who is actually working undercover with the Texas Rangers.

Texas Blue. Berkley, 2011.
Gambler Lewton Paterson has his work cut out for him when he decides to woo Texas Ranger Duncan McMurray's cousin Emily in this adventurous romance.

Native American or "Indian" Romance

A subset of both the Western Period Romance and the Ethnic Romance, these stories generally focus on Native American characters in the Old West. The hero, heroine, or both, may be full- or half-blooded Native Americans, and the stories often revolve around cultural difference issues, prejudice, and the destruction of the tribal way of life. Although most of these stories take place in the American West, these romances can also be set in other times and in other parts of America. For example, Colonial New England, eighteenth-century Minnesota, and so on.

Books of this type are included in the bibliography in chapter 12, "Ethnic and Multicultural Romance," in the Native American section. The authors listed below are examples of those included.

Anderson, Catherine
Baker, Madeline
Barbieri, Elaine
Bittner, Rosanne
Dailey, Janet
Dellin, Gennell
Gentry, Georgina
Johnson, Susan
Kay, Karen
Lindsey, Johanna
Smith, Deborah
Taylor, Janelle

Period Americana Romance and Selected Bibliography

Part of the larger Americana Romance subgenre, these stories essentially focus on everyday life in the American past. Often making use of small town or rural settings in all areas of the country, these stories feature down-to-earth characters involved in ordinary situations and are generally driven by the interpersonal relationships of the characters. This is not a subgenre of violence, wild adventure, or fast-paced action, although there may be a mystery or disaster that needs to be taken care of. Rather, these stories focus on the everyday and the ordinary. The domestic side of life—family, children, and marriage—is important and often highlighted. They can be both practical and charmingly nostalgic, and warm and humorous—and sensuality levels range from sweet to sexy. (Note: Romances of this type set in the West, particularly during the last part of the nineteenth century, could also fall within the Western Period Romance subgenre discussed above.) Many Period Americana authors write in other romance subgenres, as well. The authors and books below are selectively listed and are merely examples of those available.

Brown, Carolyn
Brown has long been noted for her sweet, charming Contemporary and Historical romances. See also chapter 5, "Contemporary Romance." Note: Many of her titles are published by Avalon, which markets primarily to libraries.

Drifters and Dreamers
Set during the oil boom days of 1917—a not-so-popular time period for romance—in Healdton, Oklahoma, this trilogy has plenty of historical flavor and an abundance of down-home charm.

Morning Glory. Avalon, 2007.
A spinster innkeeper and a roustabout in town because of the oil boom eventually find common, romantic ground.

Sweet Tilly. Avalon, 2007.
A heroine from a long line of moonshine runners is not about to let a handsome lawman interfere with her business.

Evening Star. Avalon, 2007.
A doctor hired by an oil company and then rejected because she's a woman, connects with Tilly (*Sweet Tilly*) and ends up setting a grouchy, confirmed bachelor farmer's broken leg and caring for him until he heals.

The Dove. Avalon, 2008.
A zealous, interfering, holier-than-thou preacher breaks up his son's teenage relationship with Katy, the daughter of the town drunk. But when Joshua returns as the new pastor, Katy has become the owner of a successful Saloon, The Soiled Dove—and now they just have to get over their attraction for each other.

Black Swan Trilogy
The O'Shea Sisters of the Black Swan Inn of Hutting, Arkansas, in the years following World War I and the flu epidemic of 1918.

Pushin' Up Daisies. Avalon, 2009.
A detective in town investigating the disappearance of a mob figure is suspicious of the O'Sheas but is attracted to Catherine.

From Thin Air. Avalon, 2009.
A man thought killed in action returns to Hutting and is hired to work at the Black Swan Inn by Alice, a woman that the town considers to be something of a dimwit.

Come High Water. Avalon, 2010.
With her two sisters married, Bridget now runs the inn, but when she hires a poor soldier, she has no idea he is not at all what he appears to be in this story that imports a few characters from the Drifters and Dreamers series.

Angels and Outlaws
Three outlaw cousins and three sisters (not actually nuns) are the focus of this lively and sweet series.

From Wine to Water. Avalon, 2011.

Garlock, Dorothy
Garlock writes gritty, realistic Historicals that are occasionally dark and dangerous, often filled with violence and murder, sometime lightened with flashes of humor, and generally set in the American West, Midwest, and parts of the South. She has used both the late nineteenth century and the first part of the twentieth century as settings and is particularly noted for her romances set during the 1920s and 1930s. A small selection of her recent titles is listed below.

High On a Hill. Warner, 2002.
Prohibition, bootlegging, and small town life in Missouri in the Roaring Twenties.

Mother Road. Warner, 2003.
Murder, abuse, gossip, and love abound in a small Oklahoma town on the legendary Route 66.

A Place Called Rainwater. Warner, 2003.
A woman runs a hotel in an Oklahoma town full of rowdy oilmen in the early days of the oil boom.

Train from Marietta. Warner, 2006.
Kidnapped and taken to the outlaws' hideout in Texas, a nurse is rescued but must keep her Texas Ranger hero alive until they get back to civilization in this Depression Era romance.

A Week from Sunday. Grand Central, 2007.
A woman flees from an unwanted marriage and ends up in a car accident that lands her in a tiny Louisiana town playing in a bar to work off her debt in this romance that beautifully captures the flavor of 1930s, Depression Era America.

Leaving Whiskey Bend. Grand Central, 2008.
Two women rescue another from abuse and go on the run in this gritty, hard-hitting, realistic romance that is typical of Garlock's work.

The Moon Looked Down. Grand Central, 2009.
A Jewish family is tormented by bigots in the small Midwestern town of Victory, Illinois, during World War II, and a crippled young man comes to the family's aid.

Stay a Little Longer. Grand Central, 2010.
A midwife assumes the care of her young niece, Charlotte, after Charlotte's mother dies in childbirth, and befriends a sick man, who appears to be a stranger, in this post–World War I romance.

Keep a Little Secret. Grand Central, 2011.
Charlotte, now a teacher, heads to Oklahoma Follows *Stay a Little Longer* and becomes involved with a man who has a vengeful agenda of his own.

Goodman, Jo (Pseudonym for Joanne Dobrzanski)
These two stories are set in the small mountain town of Reidsville, Colorado, in the 1880s.

Never Love a Lawman. Zebra, 2009.
A woman inherits the control of a critical railroad spur line, but only if she marries the sheriff.

Marry Me. Zebra, 2010.
A doctor takes a position in Reidsville, thanks to his interfering younger sister, and falls in love with an abused young woman—who has been living as a boy.

Harte, Amanda (Pseudonym for Christine B. Tayntor)
See chapter 13, "Linked Romances."

Morsi, Pamela
Morsi wrote a number of funny, charming historical Americana romances early in her career. See previous editions of this guide for her earlier titles. (See also chapter 5, "Contemporary Romance.")

Sealed with a Kiss. Avon, 1998.
Gidry Chavis returns to town years after he jilted Prudence Belmont and now must deal with the fiercely independent woman with an agenda of her own, as well as his feelings for her—which haven't died.

The Sweetwood Bride. Harper, 1999.
A desperate woman traps a kind man into marriage in this touching Tennessee tale.

Here Comes the Bride. Avon, 2000.
A spinster decides it's time to marry and ends up attracting the man she's using to make her quarry jealous in this turn-of-the-century Texas romance.

TAKE FIVE!

Five favorite historical romances:

- **Connie Brockway**—*The Golden Season*
- **Loretta Chase**—*Lord of Scoundrels*
- **Eileen Dreyer**—*Barely a Lady*
- **Kathleen Givens**—*On a Highland Shore*
- **LaVyrle Spencer**—*Morning Glory*

Chapter **8**

Traditional Regency Romance

A lady's imagination is very rapid; it jumps from admiration to love, from love to matrimony in a moment.

Jane Austen

Definition

> **Traditional Regency Romance**—The Traditional Regency Romance (primarily set during the English Regency, 1811–1820, or closely adjacent years) is essentially a novel of manners and social custom that focuses on the characters and their relationships to each other and to the strictly structured, upper-class Society.

Considered by many to be the most elite and intellectually appealing of the romance subgenres, the Traditional Regency Romance (primarily set during 1811–1820 or closely adjacent years) is essentially a novel of manners and social custom. The emphasis is on the characters, their relationships, and their places within the confines of a highly structured society where social position and consequence are all important. And in a true Regency, society itself functions as a character. Set within the limited sphere of London High Society, these charming confections describe a glittering, aristocratic world in which one's place in society and acceptance by the *ton* are *everything*. Indeed, an aspiring young lady's career can be left in ruins by a chance remark, an objectionable manner, or even her choice of gowns. (The heroine is rarely one of these unfortunate damsels, but if she is, through a combination of spunk, charm, and strength of character, she usually manages to have both the hero and the rest of the socially elite at her feet by the end of the story.) These stories typically take place in London during the season (that is, the "social season," which lasted from when the Parliament came into session until late spring and was aimed at marrying off eligible daughters), on lavish country estates, and at fashionable resorts such as Brighton or Bath. And the social whirl, including clothes, food, surroundings, and customs, is described in great detail. Overflowing with aristocrats, royalty, and the wealthy, most of these stories make at least passing reference to a number of actual historical figures. Prinny (the Prince Regent), Beau Brummel, Napoleon, Byron, and the Patronesses of Almack's (especially the Ladies Jersey, Cowper, Sefton, and Castlereagh) are particular favorites. Also, current events of the time (e.g., Waterloo, Peninsular Wars, politics, scandals) can be topics of conversation and are occasionally integral to the plot.

Although high levels of skill in accomplishments such as curricle racing, horseback riding, or boxing are admired in the Regency hero, these are not novels of action. In spite of the fact that a "race to Gretna Green" (usually with the hero in hot pursuit of the villain who has abducted the heroine) is a fairly commonplace event in these stories, most of the real action is verbal and takes place at the numerous social functions—balls, routs, country weekends, nights at the opera, dinner parties, picnics, holiday festivities—where the characters have a chance to engage in the verbal repartee so characteristic of and important to this subgenre. The language is one of the delights of the Regency, and readers who are addicted to them occasionally report that phrases such as "It doesn't signify!" or "How Gothick!" accidentally creep into their everyday vocabularies. In addition, classic Regencies contain no explicit sex, and sensuality in general is often totally ignored.

The Traditional Regency plot typically revolves around a young lady's entrance into Society, her adventures therein, and her courtship and eventual engagement to the hero. The heroine can be sprightly and impulsive or reserved and capable, but she is usually unconventional and is always independent with a mind of her own. The hero— usually titled, wealthy, and extremely eligible—is initially captivated or repelled by the heroine and spends the rest of the story either convincing her that she is the only woman in the world for him or coming to that conclusion himself. The heroine, however, is not just sitting idly by. On the contrary, she has problems of her own, often, but not always, related to the social whirl into which she has been thrown. Sometimes she is busy trying to decide how to avoid marrying someone just to save the family finances. Sometimes she must extricate a younger brother or cousin from the clutches of the moneylenders or creditors. Sometimes she must try to save a younger sister's reputation. As a result, she often gets into situations from which she is either rescued by the hero or, more recently, escapes through her own efforts. In the end, of course, all wrongs are righted, all villains punished, all misunderstandings explained, and all couples properly aligned. Interestingly, the predictability of these plots does not detract from the Regency's overall charm. But then, classic Regencies are not read for their plots; they are read for their style, humor, wit, characterizations, and, especially, for their delightful use of language.

The Evolving Regency

The Traditional Regency as described above still exists and is the focus of this chapter. However, for the past several decades its style has been gradually changing. Regency writers have been pushing at the edges of the genre both sexually and socially, and while traditional youthful debutantes and dashing noblemen are still the norm, older, more experienced heroines and less-than-perfect heroes have made their way into the subgenre. Darker, more realistic plots, often focusing on social abuses of the period, are much in evidence. In addition, despite the traditional taboos against it, Regencies have become much more sensual and occasionally are overtly sexual.

These trends have caused some confusion. As the subgenre has begun to incorporate more and more changes, the lines defining the subgenre have blurred, and a question being asked more and more frequently is: What is the difference between a Regency and a Historical set during the Regency period? Despite the growing tendency of some to call any romance set during the Regency period a "Regency," most readers and writers agree that there is a difference. Basically, it is a difference in focus. As mentioned above, Regencies concentrate on the manners, language, customs, and social doings of the period, essentially recreating the period in minute detail for the reader. The action is verbal and social rather than adventurous, and the emphasis is on the characters, society, and their interrelationships rather than physical action or plot. Social consequence and outward appearance are all important, often driving the plot and determining the course of action. For all intents and purposes, Society functions as a character in these stories, perhaps in much the same way that the setting (often a house or estate) functions as a character in a Gothic.

Historicals, on the other hand, tend to be more action-oriented, concerned with larger issues than societal acceptance. Although some Historical writers are quite good with period detail, the focus is more on the plot and action rather than on recreating the period. While it would be simple to say that Historicals are plot driven and Regencies are character or period driven, it would not be accurate; there are too many Historicals with wonderful characters and too many Regencies with interesting plots to make that generalization.

In addition, there are the "space" considerations—both physical and social. The world of the Regency is small, focusing primarily on friends, family, and the social milieu of the period; the scope of the Historical can be global. A typical Regency could easily take place within the confines of a single house or estate, and in fact, in some the characters never set a foot outside, unless it is to walk in the garden! However, it would be a rare Historical that did not require a much larger theatre for its activities.

And then there's the matter of sex. In the past, one could just say that Traditional Regencies didn't have sex and Historicals did. Now, it is not so easy. In fact, some current Regencies have more sex in them than some Historicals, and almost all Regencies (with a few chaste exceptions) have much more sensuality and sexual tension in them than ever before. Regencies are now on a continuum in regard to sex—none to some—and while this is still an issue for purists, for a growing number of readers, it is no longer the defining feature it once was.

Clearly the genre has changed during the past decade, and, while it would be tempting to say it has morphed into what we know today as the Regency-set Historical, that wouldn't be accurate. As discussed above, these are two separate genres, and while they share a time period, setting, and social culture, they aren't interchangeable. However, the decline of one can be linked to the rise in popularity of the other because as the Traditional Regency lines were discontinued (the last, Signet Regency, ceased regular production in 2006 but is slated to be resurrected as part of Berkley/NAL's new InterMix e-book imprint in 2012) a number of Regency writers began switching to Historicals, bringing their in-depth knowledge of the period and carefully honed dialogue, descriptive, and characterization skills along with them. They brought their fans to this new genre, as well, swelling the ranks of the Regency-set Historicals as the Traditional Regency met its demise.

The Regency Period

The Regency Period began in 1811 (February 5) when George III was declared insane and the Prince of Wales (Prinny) became Prince Regent. The Regency lasted until the death of George III in 1820, and Prinny was crowned George IV on January 31 of that year. Although the official period lasted for only nine years, the flavor of the Regency is evident in works set both before and after these dates. While most Regencies are set within the traditional nine-year parameters, it is really the *tone* of the novel that defines it as a Regency, and a number of novels of this type (including many classics by Georgette Heyer) have been set either before or after the official Regency decade. (Novels of this kind are sometimes referred to as "Regency-type" romances.)

Politically, the period saw a number of conflicts, including the War of 1812 and the Battle of Waterloo. These wars, however, did not take place on English soil and except for a few casual references (and an occasional book) they are not of critical importance to the storyline of most Regencies. Occasionally, a book with a definite Regency flavor will be set outside the boundaries of the period (e.g., *The Scarlet Pimpernel* set during the French Revolution) and will include more specific references to the hostilities, but in general, wars and other political realities simply act as background and are peripheral to the Regency Romance.

The social climate of the period was educated, permissive, and dissolute, at least for the upper class. People of the aristocracy had a great deal of leisure time, and their major task seemed to be to entertain themselves. They succeeded admirably. (There is a striking similarity between the Edwardian and the Regency periods in this respect.) Gambling was a great pastime among the men, and bets were routinely placed on everything from the results of a horse race to the sex of the next child of a local peeress. Visiting their private clubs, attending sporting events (including illegal prize fights), and hunting were all popular among men. Women planned social events, gambled occasionally (but usually only at a game called silver loo), and also had discreet affairs, but, in general, women did not enjoy the freedoms men did, especially before they were married. Both sexes enjoyed playing cards, horseback riding, and dancing. The high point of the Regency social calendar was the Season, which took place during the winter months, and dances (especially those tedious affairs held at Almack's under the sponsorship of the Patronesses every Wednesday night), routs, balls, and dinner parties were extremely popular. It was during this Season that a young lady was first introduced into Society and expected to "make a match." If she didn't "take" her first Season, she returned to enjoy several more. However, if she were not married by her early to mid-twenties, she was considered to be a spinster and "on the shelf."

Social standing was always a consideration, whether in composing guest lists or in deciding which suitor to marry. It was always thought better to marry "up," so young women were always "setting their caps" for men with titles or fortunes superior to their own. People engaged in commerce or the trades were rarely admitted to the social circles of the elite, and even though these "cits" were becoming an economic force in Regency England, the aristocracy ignored them for as long as they could.

Manners and language were of particular importance. Indeed, the way in which something was said was often more important than the actual content, and being able to converse wittily was imperative to social success. In the same vein, a proper outward image was more important than what one actually did—for example, affairs were tolerated so long as the participants were discreet.

In general, the primary activity of the Regency aristocracy was to enjoy itself, and this it did with abandon. It is this carefree, luxurious, lifestyle that is the basis for today's Regency Romances.

Although research abounds and many books have been written about Regency England, the two cited below might be of particular interest to Regency readers, especially fans of Georgette Heyer.

Chris, Teresa. *Georgette Heyer's Regency England*. London: Sidgwick & Jackson, 1989.
Filled with liberal references to Heyer's stories and characters, this readable work takes Regency fans on a delightful tour of the England depicted in Georgette Heyer's Regency Romances. A number of walking tours are included, complete with commentary, and topics and places are covered in chapters with such intriguing titles as "Male Preserves: The St. James's Area," "Where Not To Live: The Fringes of Society," "Pleasure Jaunts: Escaping from the Heart of London," and "Pump and Circumstance: South-East Bath." Most useful to travelers in England, but interesting to all readers. Includes illustrations by Arthur Barbosa.

Kloester, Jennifer. *Georgette Heyer's Regency World*. London: Heinemann, 2005.
Using twenty-six of Heyer's novels as a basis, this resource discusses Regency life as depicted in these books. Topics are wide ranging and chapters entitled "Up and Down the Social Ladder," "The Pleasure Haunts of London," "Shopping," and "Eat, Drink and Be Merry" are only the tip of the iceberg. An index and six useful appendices (e.g., "Glossary of Cant and Common Regency Phrases") conclude this specialized source.

Readers interested in Regency society from the male point of view might enjoy the latest of the many editions of the memoirs of Captain Rees Howell Gronow.

Gronow, R. H., and Christopher Summerville, eds. *Regency Recollections: Captain Gronow's Guide to Life in London and Paris*. Welwyn Garden City, U.K.: Ravenhall Books, 2006.
A Regency dandy, duelist, and a military officer who survived the Battle of Waterloo, Gronow moved in the highest circles of Regency society. His acquaintances included the Prince Regent, Beau Brummell, and other luminaries of the time, and although he wrote these accounts years after the fact while in debt and living in Paris, his observations and recollections provide one of the most fascinating accounts of Regency society available.

The web also is a good source of information on the Regency; one of the better sites is listed below.

Good Ton: A Resource for Readers of Regency Romance Novels (www.the nonesuch.com)
Extensive listings of Regency Romances arranged by author, title, theme/subject/plot, or publication date; a lexicon of terms commonly found in the genre; and links to related sites are among the resources available on this site.

Appeal

The general appeal of the Regency Romance is the same as for any historical or period romance: It indulges our fascination with life in past times and allows the reader to experience what life was like "back then." However, the specific appeal of the Regency is more focused. Sparkling language, witty repartee, meticulous historical detail, and good writing are hallmarks of the subgenre and attract many readers. It is also a comfortable subgenre for its fans. That is, because the Regency time period is so limited (less than a decade), fans are familiar with the conventions and details of the period. As a result, reading a Regency is a bit like coming home: It is a comfortable, familiar, predictable setting in which only the plots and characters change. It is also the world of Jane Austen, a fact that appeals to many readers.

Advising the Reader

Although readers' advisors should consult both the general advisory section and the specific advisory section for Historical Romances, there are a few points that might be helpful for advising Regency readers.

- Readers who enjoy Jane Austen might also like some of the better contemporary Regency authors, and vice versa.
- Readers who particularly enjoy the Regency Period might also appreciate Period Romances set during the same time, and vice versa.
- Readers who have favorite Regency authors might also enjoy these writers' Period romances (e.g., Candice Hern, Mary Balogh, Jo Beverley, Loretta Chase, Mary Jo Putney).
- Be aware that some Regencies are more sensual than others, and make recommendations accordingly.

Origins and Brief History of the Regency Romance

The origins of the Regency Romance are often traced to Jane Austen, who, in writing about the life and people she knew, set the style for the Regencies of today. However, several of her near-contemporaries also influenced the direction of today's Regency genre, and while they are no longer often read, their contributions cannot be ignored. A generation earlier, Fanny Burney in her *Evelina: Or, The History of a Young Lady's Entrance into the World* (1778) captured a quality and described a social scene that was decidedly Regency in flavor if not in fact, and Edward Bulwer-Lytton, who wrote after the Regency, achieved a properly scandalous tone in his *Pelham: Or, Adventures of a Gentleman.* (1828).

Although Austen is widely read today and for a decade or more has enjoyed a popular revival (due, perhaps in part, to impeccably done, well-received film and television versions of several of her novels and bestselling books, such as Stephanie Barron's Jane Austen Mystery series, Karen Joy Fowler's *The Jane Austen Book Club,* the numerous continuations (e.g., *His Cunning or Hers: A Postscript to Persuasion* [1993] by June Menzies, *Sanditon, Jane Austen's Unfinished Masterpiece* [2009] by Juliette Shapiro), the explosion of recent "sequels," such as *Mr. Darcy's Daughters* (2003) by Elizabeth Aston, Pamela Aidan's Fitzwilliam Darcy, Gentleman Trilogy (2003–2004), *Seducing Mr. Darcy* (2008) by Gwyn Cready, or the various Darcy books published by Sourcebooks by writers such as Linda Berdoll, Amanda Grange, and Sharon Lathan, and the latest rash of Jane Austen paranormal parodies and mash-ups, such as *Pride & Promiscuity: The Lost Sex Scenes of Jane Austen* (2001) by Arielle Eckstut and Dennis Ashton, and *Pride and Prejudice and Zombies* (2009) by Jane Austen and Seth Grahame-Smith, it is Georgette Heyer who, despite an occasional purist detractor, is the acknowledged doyenne of the modern Traditional Regency. Influenced by turn-of-the-century writer Jeffery Farnol as well as the earlier Regency writers, Heyer employs exquisite language, attention to detail, knowledge of the period and its society, and her ability to create a vivid sense of place to set the standard for the modern Regency. While she has many imitators, she has few equals, and her books, most of which are currently in print, are still widely read today.

Dedicated, knowledgeable, and highly critical, Regency readers are quite serious about their books, often demanding more of their subgenre than readers of any of the other romance types. Historical accuracy and strict attention to detail are essential, and because many readers are near-experts on the period, discrepancies are quickly noted—and rarely forgiven. The authors have responded, and many recent Traditional Regencies are some of the best-written, most carefully crafted stories in the romance genre. Despite this, the subgenre has been treading water for years, struggling against bottom line issues, largely resulting from the perception that the niche nature of the genre and the finite number of readers would result in slow or no growth, something that has become much more of an issue since publishing's merger-and-acquisition mania of recent years.

Despite the launching of a new Super Regency line by Signet in 2003, things reached a new low when the two remaining dedicated Traditional Regency lines, Zebra Regency and Signet Regency, ceased publication in 2005 and 2006, respectively. This is not to say, however, that no Traditional Regencies are being published—there are a few originals, as well as reprints, being published within regular historical and e-book lines, and tech-savvy authors are connecting directly with readers and reissuing their backlists, as well as new titles, as e-books—or that the Regency should be dismissed as a viable subgenre. In fact, Berkley/NAL just announced that it will be including the old Signet Regency line in its new e-book imprint, InterMix, which should launch in January 2012, certainly a positive sign for the subgenre. The Regency readership is there—stable, committed, and militant—and fans will still be looking for books—if not for new ones on the bookstore shelves or online, certainly for tried-and-true titles on the shelves or databases of the local libraries. Finally, although for the moment the Traditional Regency is slightly underwater, given its long history, amazing resilience, and lasting popularity, as well as the creative persistence of its authors and remarkable ability of the publishing industry to seize opportunity, there is the hope—and expectation—that the subgenre is on its way to resurfacing once again.

Early Regency Prototypes

The prototypes cited below (expect for those by Farnol) are not actually Historical Romance; they are, instead, contemporary romances written during a historical period. Their authors were not writing about a distant romantic past; they were writing about the world they knew and lived in. For them, the setting was the reality of the here and now, not the romance of there and then. Although Jane Austen's novels are the only ones actually written during the Regency, the others exhibit the characteristic Regency flavor of elegance, wit, and licentiousness. (Consult earlier editions of this guide for more detailed information.)

Austen, Jane. *Sense and Sensibility* (1811), *Pride and Prejudice* (1813), *Mansfield Park* (1814), *Emma* (1814), *Northanger Abbey* (1818), *Persuasion* (1818).
Bulwer-Lytton, **Edward**. *Pelham: Or, Adventures of a Gentleman* (1828).

Burney, Fanny. *Evelina: Or, The History of a Young Lady's Entrance into the World* (1778).

Farnol, Jeffery. *The Broad Highway* (1910), *The Amateur Gentleman* (1913).

Modern Regency Classics

Heyer, Georgette

In a class by herself, Heyer set the standard for the modern Traditional Regency subgenre. For annotations and additional publishing information, please consult the earlier editions of this guide. (Note: The two annotated titles below were not included in the previous editions.)

Powder and Patch: The Transformation of Philip Jettan (1930).
Devil's Cub (1934)
Regency Buck (1935).
An Infamous Army. Heinemann, 1937.
Romance blossoms between Lady Barbara Childe and Colonel Charles Audley, aide-de-camp to Wellington, in this story that has character links to several other books, including *Regency Buck* and *Devil's Cub*, and is notable for its exceptionally well-depicted Battle of Waterloo. Set in Belgium in 1815.

The Spanish Bride. Heinemann, 1940.
Based on the true story of Sir Harry Smith, a brigade major under Wellington (Wellesley), and his young wife, Juana, this battle-rich romance focuses on their early marriage during the Napoleonic Wars.

The Corinthian (1940).
Faro's Daughter (1941).
Friday's Child (1944).
The Reluctant Widow (1946).
The Foundling (1948).
Arabella (1949).
The Grand Sophy (1950).
The Quiet Gentleman (1951).
Cotillion (1953).
The Toll-Gate (1954).
Bath Tangle (1955).
Sprig Muslin (1956).
Sylvester, or the Wicked Uncle (1957).
April Lady (1957).
Venetia (1958).
The Unknown Ajax (1959).
A Civil Contract (1961).
The Nonesuch (1962).
False Colours (1963).
Frederica (1965).
Black Sheep (1966).
Charity Girl (1970).
Lady of Quality (1972).

Although the titles by these authors are listed selectively, almost all of the works by these modern classic writers are good examples of the genre and are worth tracking down.

Balogh, Mary—*Promise of Spring* (1990), *The Secret Pearl* (1991), *Dancing With Clara* (1994), *Lord Carew's Bride* (1995), *The Famous Heroine* (1996), *The Temporary Wife* (1997), *The Last Waltz* (1998), *Unforgiven* (1998).

Beverley, Jo—*Emily and the Dark Angel* (1991), *An Unwilling Bride* (1992), *Deirdre and Don Juan* (1993).

Carroll, Susan—*Sugar Rose* (1987), *Brighton Road* (1988).

Chase, Loretta—*The Sandalwood Princess* (1990).

Chesney, Marion—Six Sisters Saga (1982–1985), **A House for the Season Series** (1986–1989), **School for Manners Series** (1988–1990), **Daughters of Mannerling Series** (1995–1997).

Cummings, Monette—*The Beauty's Daughter* (1985).

Darcy, Clare—*Georgina* (1971), *Cecily: or A Young Lady of Quality* (1972), *Lydia: or Love in Town* (1973), *Victoire* (1974), *Allegra* (1975), *Lady Pamela* (1975), *Regina* (1976), *Elyza* (1977), *Cressida* (1977), *Eugenia* (1977), *Gwendolen* (1978), *Rolande* (1978), *Letty* (1980), *Caroline and Julia* (1982).

Dolan, Charlotte Louise—*The Substitute Bridegroom* (1991), *Three Lords for Lady Anne* (1991), *The Resolute Runaway* (1992), *The Unofficial Suitor* (1992), *The Black Widow* (1992), *Fallen Angel* (1993), *The Counterfeit Gentleman* (1994).

Dunn, Carola—*The Miser's Sister* (1984), *The Lady and the Rake* (1995), *The Tudor Secret* (1995), *Scandal's Daughter* (1996), *The Babe and the Baron* (1997), *The Improper Governess* (1998), *Crossed Quills* (1998).

Kelly, Carla—*Summer Campaign* (1989), *Miss Chartley's Guided Tour* (1989), *Marian's Christmas Wish* (1989), *Mrs. McVinnie's London Season* (1990), *Libby's London Merchant* (1991), *Miss Grimsley's Oxford Creer* (1992), *Miss Billings Treads the Boards* (1993), *Miss Whittier Makes a List* (1994), *Mrs. Drew Plays Her Hand* (1994), *Reforming Lord Ragsdale* (1995), *The Lady's Companion* (1996), *With This Ring* (1997), *Miss Milton Speaks Her Mind* (1998), *One Good Turn* (2001), *The Wedding Journey* (2002).

Metzger, Barbara—*Lady in Green* (1993), *A Loyal Companion* (1993), *The Primrose Path* (1997), *A Worthy Wife* (2000), *Saved by Scandal* (2000), *Miss Westlake's Windfall* (2001), *A Debt to Delia* (2002), *Lady Sparrow* (2002), *The Diamond Key* (2003).

Michaels, Kasey—*The Lurid Lady Lockport* (1984).

Putney, Mary Jo—*The Controversial Countess* (1988) (rewritten as *Petals in the Storm*), *The Would-Be Widow* (1988) (rewritten as *The Bargain*), *Lady of Fortune* (1988), *The Rake and the Reformer* (1989) (rewritten as *The Rake*), *The Rogue and the Runaway* (1990) (rewritten as *Angel Rogue*).

Scott, Amanda—*Lord Abberley's Nemesis* (1986).

Smith, Joan—*An Affair of the Heart* (1977), *Talk of the Town* (1979), *Love's Way* (1982), *Lady Madeleine's Folly* (1983), *Memoirs of a Hoyden* (1988), *The Kissing Bough* (1994), *A Tall, Dark Stranger* (1996), **Berkley Brigade Series** (1996–1999).

Veryan, Patricia—Sanguinet Saga (1981–1987), **Golden Chronicles Series** (Georgian) (1985–1989), **Tales of the Jewelled Men Series** (Georgian) (1990–1995), **Riddle Saga** (1997–2002).

Walsh, Sheila—*The Golden Songbird* (1975), *Kate and the Marquess* (1997), *The Lady from Lisbon* (2001).

Selected Traditional Regency Romance Bibliography

Following are some contemporary examples of the Traditional Regency Romance. Many of the older titles are now out of print but are well worth finding. Fortunately, an increasing number of these are being made available in e-book format. Note that Historical romances set during the Regency period are included in the chapter on Historical Romance in the Period Romance Section. Because new Traditional Regencies are being published only rarely, this bibliography has been severely trimmed. Please consult previous editions of this guide for the many authors, titles, and annotations that have been dropped from this edition.

Baldwin, Kathleen

Generally, light, charming Regencies.

Lady Fiasco. Zebra, 2004.
A trouble-prone lady is dogged by a very real villain in this lively, humorous Regency.

Mistaken Kiss. Zebra, 2005.
Kissing the wrong brother causes a nearsighted heroine to rethink her marriage plans.

Cut from the Same Cloth. Zebra, 2005.
A young woman's plan to attract a husband with her fashion sense is scuttled by a handsome aristocrat on a mission of his own.

Bancroft, Blair

The Indifferent Earl. Signet, 2003.
A young American woman is compelled to join forces with a British nobleman in order to inherit a cottage left to her by a distant relative—with romantic results.

The Major Meets His Match. Signet, 2003.
A noblewoman and a military engineer find love despite their differences.

A Season for Love. Signet, 2004.
Warned against the *ton* by her late mother, a young woman goes to London when her father announces his remarriage and finds herself falling for the very type of man her mother told her to avoid.

The Lady and the Cit. Signet, 2005.
A young noblewoman marries a London "cit" in order to save her heritage and ultimately—and surprisingly—finds love in the marriage of convenience.

Lady Silence. Signet, 2005
A military nobleman returns home to find that a mute waif he had taken into his employ had turned into a fascinating young woman—with a hidden past.

Barbour, Anne (Barbara Yirka)

Classic well-written, witty, intriguing Regencies.

A Man of Affairs. Signet, 1999.
In search of a wife for the legitimate son of his noble employer and adopted father, a young man of affairs is unexpectedly attracted to the elder sister of the young debutante he was considering for his foster brother.

Miss Prestwick's Crusade. Signet, 2003.
The heroine's quest to prove that her nephew is the heir to a British earldom is complicated by her attraction to the current holder of the title.

Benson, Jessica
*Much Obliged. Zebra, 2001
A carefree nobleman, promised to a young miss since childhood, seeks to extricate himself from the obligation, but soon realizes that's not what he wants at all in this light-hearted charmer that was reissued in 2006.

Bergin, Louise
The Spinster and the Wastrel. Signet, 2004.
An inheritance allows the heroine to start a school, but she has to deal with her benefactor's handsome nephew who is after her funds.

A Worthy Opponent. Signet, 2004.
A young woman, who needs to marry well to provide for her siblings, meets her match in the hero who wants to keep her from snagging his wealthy best friend—and falls in love himself.

The Winter Duke. Signet, 2005.
A case of mistaken identity threatens the developing romance between a young country gentlewoman and a duke.

Bishop, Laurie
The Best Laid Plans. Signet, 2003.
An American heiress in search of a titled husband finds love with the man who is helping her in her quest.

Deceiving Miss Dearborn. Signet, 2004.
A hero with amnesia and a gentlewoman trying to save her manor house find love while struggling with her financial and his identity issues.

When Horses Fly. Signet, 2005.
A heroine faces a dilemma when an elderly cousin asks her to marry him, and then she falls in love with his son.

Lord Ryburn's Apprentice. Signet, 2006.
A nobleman, suspicious of the intentions of a young woman his aunt has taken under her wing, agrees to tutor her in the ways of the *ton* and ends up falling in love with his pupil.

Blair, Catherine
Lively, often humorous, somewhat unusual Regencies.

A Family for Gillian. Zebra, 2001.
A ruined heroine and a widowed father make a marriage of convenience work in this Irish-set Regency.

A Scholarly Gentleman. Zebra, 2003.
A widow and a noble scholar find love, even though she rejected him in the past.

A Viscount for Christmas. Zebra, 2003.
A careless viscount and the outspoken daughter of his estate manager find love when he comes to take charge of the estate.

A Notorious Lady. Zebra, 2004.
A ruined young mother seeks refuge and anonymity in Cambridge and finds love instead.

Blayne, Sara
Powell Sisters Quartet
The noble Powell sisters find love in this sweet, lively quartet of Regencies.

A Noble Deception. Zebra, 1995.
A Noble Pursuit. Zebra, 1997.
A Noble Resolve. Zebra, 1998.
A Noble Heart. Zebra, 2000.

An Improper Bride. Zebra, 2001.
A heroine who can see the future heads off to London to protect the man who is her soul mate in this mystery-laden romance of star-crossed lovers.

Blayney, Mary
Braedon Family Series
The members of the infamous, scandalous Braedon family find love in this quartet of Regencies.

His Heart's Delight. Zebra, 2002
A gambling nobleman in search of a sham fiancée finds true love, instead.

His Last Lover. Zebra, 2002.
Love-wary James Braedon falls for a French émigré hired to care for his crazy dad.

The Pleasure of His Company. Zebra, 2003.
A widow comes to London for the season and finds love.

The Captain's Mermaid. Zebra, 2004
An aquatically inclined heroine and a rigid sea captain eventually find romance in this country-set story that overflows with children.

Buck, Gayle
Buck began writing Regencies in the 1980s and is noted for lively, funny, quirky Regencies. These are a few of her more recent ones.

Cassandra's Deception. Signet, 2000.
When twins Cassandra and Belle switch places, romance becomes complicated.

Lord Darlington's Darling. Signet, 2002.
A handsome, arrogant lord falls in love with a shy, retiring woman in this heartwarming story of two people who see beyond the surface to the real person beneath.

The Fleeing Heiress. Signet, 2003.
A kidnapped heroine, a gallant rescue, and some stubborn, interfering relatives to stir the pot nicely season this funny, off-beat tale.

Butler, Nancy
Keeper of the Swans. Signet, 1998.
When a young woman's boat breaks away and races downstream, she lands on an island where she decides to stay—with the man who rescued her and cares for the swans. Lyrical and unusual.

The Rake's Retreat. Signet, 1999.
A mature heroine and a flawed hero with a dark past find love in this witty, tightly plotted Regency.

The Prodigal Hero. Signet, 2000.
A wounded hero overhears a plot to kidnap his boss's daughter and ends up abducting her himself to save her. Wonderfully romantic.

The Ramshackle Suitor. Signet, 2000.
A dream of a crying child sends the heroine to the Isle of Man and into the arms of the hero.

Prospero's Daughter. Signet, 2003.
Rendered an invalid as the result of a tragic carriage accident, Miranda Runyon is wasting away until Morgan Pearce arrives to help Miranda's uncle with his memoirs and ends up giving Miranda a new lease on life—and love—as well.

The Kindness of a Rogue. Signet, 2004.
A governess and a rogue find love and danger as they try to discover why young women are disappearing in this gothic Regency with a Cornwall setting.

Castaway Hearts. Signet, 2004.
Shipwrecked on the coast of Brittany when a freak storm blows them off course, Lydia and the captain (a notorious spy) are captured by brigands, with deadly and adventurous results. This is a Signet Super Regency and is longer and has more action than is typical of the Traditional Regency subgenre.

Cartland, Barbara
Some of Cartland's more than five hundred romances are set during the Regency period. For a fairly complete listing of Cartland's works, see the third edition of *Twentieth Century Romance and Historical Writers* (London: St. James, 1994), edited by Aruna Vasudevan and Lesley Henderson. This reference source is discussed in chapter 16, "Author Biography and Bibliography."

Carleton, Susannah
The Marriage Campaign. Signet, 2003.
A young woman who is considered a threat by her stepmother and forced to "become" a governess to her younger step-siblings finds love and romance with a marquess.

A Twist of Fate. Signet, 2003.
A snowstorm brings two love-wary people together.

A Rake's Redemption. Signet, 2004.
A scandalous situation and a faux engagement result in love.

Twin Peril. Signet, 2005.
Twin sisters cause problems for a duke in search of a bride who loves him for himself.

Counts, Wilma
Willed to Wed. Zebra, 1999.
A well-done marriage-of-convenience romance.

My Lady Governess. Zebra, 2000.
A young noblewoman goes underground as a governess to avoid a distasteful marriage and finds love with the father of her charges.

The Willful Miss Winthrop. Zebra, 2000.
An independent young woman finds romance on the Peninsula during the final campaign of the war.

The Wagered Wife. Zebra, 2001.
An immature couple forced into marriage by an ill-advised wager and separated by meddling relatives, grow up and reconcile happily when they are reunited after five years apart.

The Trouble with Harriet. Zebra, 2001.
A crusading heroine who writes anonymous political essays stirs things up and finds love in the process.

The Lady and the Footman. Zebra, 2004.
A lively romp filled with mystery, deception, and ghosts.

Devon, Marian
On the Way to Gretna Green. Fawcett Crest, 1998.
A race to Gretna Green to stop an elopement brings love to the pursuers, a jilted spinster, and a handsome lord.

Eastwood, Gail
Lady from Spain. Signet, 1997.
An enigmatic lady from Spain stirs things up in a small English village in this dark, occasionally violent Regency.

The Magnificent Marquess. Signet, 1998.
A nobleman's deadly past threatens the heroine in this funny, suspenseful romance.

The Rake's Mistake. Signet, 2002
An artist's daughter with an undeserved scandalous reputation and a noble rake find love.

Ewing, Jean R.
Ewing's Regencies feature compelling characters and thought-provoking, multilayered plots. She has written Historical Romances as Jean Ross Ewing and, most recently, as Julia Ross.

*Love's Reward. Zebra, 1997.
A confirmed rake and an intelligent artist avoid a scandal and end up wed.

Fairchild, Elisabeth (Donna Gimarc)
Beautifully written, intelligent, thoughtful, generally well-researched Regencies.

Miss Dornton's Hero. Signet, 1995.
A returning war hero is plagued by horrifying nightmares of the war but finds love with a heroine who has tragic memories of her own in this realistic, romantic story.

The Holly and the Ivy. Signet, 1999.
A cheerful young woman visits her grandmother in London for the Holidays and meets Gran's thorny, Christmas-hating neighbor, Lord Balfour in a poignant story that confronts grief, loneliness, and betrayal with sensitivity and understanding.

Breach of Promise. Signet, 2000.
An impoverished beekeeper and the mysterious nobleman she rents her manor house to find love in spite of their past separate breach-of-promise experiences in an emotionally rich, thought-provoking story.

Captain Cupid Calls the Shots. Signet, 2000.
A returning war hero and a young woman with a ruined reputation find love and healing in this deeply emotional story.

Sugarplum Surprises. Signet, 2001.
A duke and a nobly born dressmaker find unexpected love in spite of past disappointments in this holiday-tinged romance.

A Game of Patience. Signet, 2002.
Friends with Pip and Richard since childhood, Patience sets her cap for one, but discovers that character is more important than surface appeal. A poignant story of love, friendship, and growing up.

Valentine's Change of Heart. Signet, 2003.
A falsely disgraced teacher finds love with the once dissolute father of one of her students when she is hired as governess to her young charge. A heartwarming, thoughtful sequel to *Captain Cupid Calls the Shots*.

Farr, Diane
Well-written, insightful Regencies.

The Nobody. Signet, 1999.
A country-bred heroine in town for the Season attracts the attentions of a young noble who is engaged to a spiteful beauty in this well-written debut novel that has a touch of mystery, as well.

Fair Game. Signet, 1999.
The daughter of a famed courtesan does not intend to follow in her mother's footsteps, much to the shock of the man to whom she has been "given."

Falling for Chloe. Signet, 2000.
A compromising situation results in an unwanted engagement between two good friends who eventually realize that marriage is just what they want, after all.

Once Upon a Christmas. Signet, 2000.
A young orphan and a confirmed bachelor fall victim to the matchmaking plans of the Duchess of Arnsford in this charming Regency with a country Christmas setting.

Duel of Hearts. Signet, 2002.
An argumentative, not always likable, pair join forces to dissuade her father and his young cousin from marrying and end up falling in love themselves—eventually.

The Fortune Hunter. Signet, 2002.
An impoverished nobleman determined to marry for money in order to save his estate falls for an independent lady who is determined never to cede control of her life to anyone.

Under the Wishing Star. Signet, 2003.
A nobleman wants to make a young gently born woman his daughter's governess, but society won't allow this unless they wed—something that Lord Malcolm is willing to do. The problem? Lord Malcolm doesn't believe in love and Natalie won't marry without it. First in the projected Star trilogy.

Under a Lucky Star. Signet, 2004.
A young gentleman and the daughter of an earl whose "duty" it is to marry wealth must chart their own course in this gentle, character-driven Regency. Second in the Star trilogy.

Gaston, Diane

Has written Regency-set Historicals as Diane Perkins and also as Diane Gaston.

The Mysterious Miss M. Mills & Boon, 2004 (Harlequin Historical, 2005).
An aristocratic Waterloo veteran becomes responsible for a young woman and her child and is caught in the classic dilemma—marry appropriately or lose his inheritance.

The Wagering Widow. Mills & Boon, 2005 (Harlequin Historical, 2006).
When a man needing to restore the family fortune elopes with a woman he mistakenly thinks is an heiress, they both turn to the gambling tables as their way out in this compelling story that immerses its characters in some of the less savory aspects of the period. Follows *The Mysterious Miss M.*

*A Reputable Rake. Mills & Boon, 2005 (Harlequin Historical, 2006).
A rake determined to become respectable and a gentlewoman who secretly is running a school for runaway courtesans fall in love as they struggle to keep the *ton* from discovering her project, something that would ruin them both. Follows *The Wagering Widow*.

Heath, Sandra

Noted for exceptionally well-written books steeped in the traditions and history of the British Isles. See also chapter 9, "Alternative Reality Romance."

Counterfeit Kisses. Signet, 2000.
A young widow determined to recover a stolen family tiara finds love with an old, but brief, acquaintance when she attempts to recover the heirloom in this story that is filled with exotic characters and plenty of action.

Hide and Seek. Signet, 2001.
A brother who would steal her inheritance forces the heroine to link up with a dangerous rake in order to find a missing codicil in this tale that delves into the darker side of the Regency Period.

An Easy Conquest. Signet, 2001.
A woman who agrees to a financially desirable marriage for the sake of her family falls for an exotic stranger who has been sent (unknown to her) to save her.

Playing with Fire. Signet, 2002.
A cruel, spoiled beauty and her gentle cousin fall for the same nobleman; may the best woman win in this enchanting story that is filled with exotic adventure, Egyptian artifacts, and even a dash of magic.

False Steps. Signet, 2003.
Mistaken identity proves intriguing in this lively tale of a banished lord and a young commoner.

Lavender Blue. Signet, 2003.
More Gothic than Regency, this fast-paced, intricate tale makes good use of old myths to spin a tale of riddles, romance, and love.

Winter Dreams. Signet, 2004.
Spies, espionage, and psychic connections are part of this fast-paced adventure set during the Napoleonic wars.

Diamond Dreams. Signet, 2005.
A young woman, orphaned and impoverished, heads for Wales where she is attracted to a nobleman who is already engaged.

Hendrickson, Emily

Hendrickson is a prolific author of light Traditional Regencies, many of which have been reprinted. Only several of her most recent titles are listed below.

The Ivory Dragon. Signet, 2002.
A storm sends the heroine into a barn where she encounters the hero, as well as a stolen ivory pin and a lot of mystery. Links to *Lord Nick's Folly*.

Herberts Series

A series about the six children of a country clergyman.

Lord Nick's Folly. Signet, 2002.
A carriage ride results in an unlikely romantic relationship between a rector's daughter and the noble brother of the man she once loved in a romance with a bit of a mystery.

Druscilla's Downfall. Signet, 2003.
A handsome lord, suspicious that his mother's young vicarage-bred companion is after her money, is charmed, as well as scolded, by the lady in question in this "house-party" tale that features a number of additional romantic threads.

Pursuing Priscilla. Signet, 2003.
A curate's daughter goes to London for the Season and captures the heart of a scandal-ridden nobleman who's out to wed a proper lady—and then he finds her at the gaming tables!

Tabitha's Tangle. Signet, 2004.
A lively rector's daughter attracts and is attracted by the nobleman whose books she has been hired to catalog even though they are both promised to others. Third in the Herberts series.

The Madcap Heiress. Signet, 2004.
Pursued by her obnoxious cousin, an independent, impulsive heiress falls for an adventure-seeking rector's son even though she is wary of his motives.

My Lady Faire. Signet, 2005.
An artistic lady who paints the fairies she sees in her garden finds love with her stepson's guardian in a heartwarming, family-centered story.

Hern, Candice

Hern is noted for exceptionally well-written and researched Traditional Regencies; she now writes Regency-set Historical Romances.

The Best Intentions. Signet, 1999.
A widowed lord must choose between a beautiful widow and her unconventional sister in this well-crafted tale.

Miss Lacey's Last Fling. Signet, 2001.
A shy, quiet woman, who thinks she has only a short time to live, goes to London and recreates herself as a fun-loving socialite and finds love in the arms of a jaded aristocrat.

Hinshaw, Victoria

The Fontainebleau Fan. Zebra, 2002.
A young artist seeks to make amends for a counterfeit fan sold to an aristocrat and ends up painting a mural in his house, instead.

Cordelia's Corinthian. Zebra, 2004.
An idyllic summer turns chaotic and quite romantic for Cordelia when a war hero and his friends come to the country for some rest and relaxation.

An Ideal Match. Zebra, 2004.
A fake engagement to thwart the matchmaking efforts of their various relatives turns romantic for a pair of independent widowed friends.

Least Likely Lovers. Zebra 2005.
A resourceful young woman and a recovering war hero join forces to change the poisonous atmosphere in the house where they are both staying, and find mystery and romance in the process.

Huntington, Kate

Lady Diana's Darlings. Zebra, 2000.
A nobleman disapproves of his late cousin's wife's unsuitable behavior, but finds she is not what he'd thought when she ends up sponsoring his unofficial fiancée during her first Season.

Mistletoe Mayhem. Zebra, 2000.
A lady and a country gentleman are reunited at a Christmas house party four years after their romance fell apart; this time the results are different.

A Rogue for Christmas. Zebra, 2001.
A disinherited, gambling lord is attracted by a young woman who believes in him and is determined to set things to rights.

The Merchant Prince. Zebra, 2002.
A young woman traveling in Italy is aided by a charming priest who, she discovers years later, turns out to be a nobleman who secretly heads up Venice's resistance against Austria.

His Lordship's Holiday Surprise. Zebra, 2003.
An independent, intelligent young woman left in charge of three young children when her widowed sister abruptly leaves, finds love with the man who'd planned to marry her sister.

The General's Daughter. Zebra, 2004.
An officer ordered to escort his general's bastard daughter back to England after the army doctor she thought was her father dies finds he prefers her to the legitimate daughter to whom he has been engaged since childhood.

A Hero's Homecoming. Zebra, 2004.
Follows *The General's Daughter*.

To Tempt a Gentleman. Zebra, 2005.
A solitary widower finds his life turned upside down by a charming young woman who was "willed" to him by her cousin to put his house in order and find him a wife. Funny and romantic.

Jensen, Emma

Lively, funny, heartwarming, and well-written Regencies. Jensen has also written Regency-set Historicals.

Best Laid Schemes. Fawcett, 1998.
A childhood friend disrupts an earl's plans to select a proper bride at a house party he holds for that purpose when she is invited by his mother, as well.

His Grace Endures. Fawcett, 1998.
A young widow chaperones her sister-in-law for the Season and encounters a nobleman she jilted years earlier.

The Irish Rogue. Signet, 1999.
An Irish nobleman finds himself competing with his secret folk-hero alter ego in his wooing of an artistic lady. Dublin setting is a refreshing change from London.

A Grand Design. 2000.
Secretly the true architect in her family's firm, a talented, outspoken young woman finds love with the scandal-ridden Marquess whose home she is renovating.

Kelly, Carla
Kelly produces well-crafted, realistic, carefully researched, emotionally involving Regencies that are considered classics in the subgenre. She is a Rita Award winner in the Regency category (*Mrs. Drew Plays Her Hand* [1994], *The Lady's Companion* [1996]) and many of her titles have been reprinted, some of which are collector's items.

With This Ring. Signet, 1997.
Cruelly treated by her mother and sister, a heroine who spends her time ministering to wounded soldiers agrees to marry a nobleman Major who needs a bride and goes with him to Northumberland—and a totally new life.

Miss Milton Speaks Her Mind. Signet, 1998.
A down-trodden, "poor relation" heroine who has cared for her twelve-year-old nephew since birth is concerned and spurred to action when relatives begin to question the boy's paternity and right to inherit his late father's title in this romance that is darker than some.

One Good Turn. Signet, 2001.
Desperate when his young niece and butler come down with the chicken pox on the way to his estate, a disillusioned nobleman enlists the aid of a young Spanish woman who has secrets of her own in this poignant romance.

The Wedding Journey. Signet, 2002.
A captain and military surgeon marries a young woman he secretly loves to keep her from the clutches of a lecherous officer and then must figure out how to lead the mobile hospital to safety when they are wickedly left behind by the thwarted officer in this Peninsula-set story. A remarkable journey.

Kerstan, Lynn
Kerstan also writes Historical Romances and is a Rita Award winner in the Regency Category. See also chapter 9, "Alternative Reality Romance."

A Midnight Clear. Fawcett, 1997.
A scandalous book and a snowstorm bring a nobleman and the author's secretary together in this story with a Christmas twist.

Francesca's Rake. Fawcett Crest, 1997.

Marry in Haste. Fawcett, 1998.
A blow to the hero's head—deftly administered by the heroine and her skillet—results in a forced marriage that eventually becomes a union of love.

Celia's Grand Passion. Fawcett, 1998.
A young widow wanting to experience love and passion, but not remarriage, targets a widower she admires.

Lucy in Disguise. Fawcett, 1998.
A young woman rescues a smuggler from the quicksand and finds a noble hero, as well.

Lord Dragoner's Wife. Signet, 1999.
An undercover military spy returns planning to divorce the wife he married and deserted six years earlier, but his wife has other ideas.

Kihlstrom, April
Kihlstrom has written nearly thirty Regency Romances, many of which feature linked characters.

Langford Brothers Trilogy
The Reckless Barrister. Signet, 1999.
A new attorney reluctantly agrees to help a young reformer in her efforts to improve the lot of factory workers and becomes more involved with her than he'd planned.

The Wily Wastrel. Signet, 1999.
A smart, mechanically inclined heroine and an inventor hero find they have much in common.

The Sentimental Soldier. Signet, 2000.
On a mission in France, an English spy rescues a peace activist heroine from the sea and then feels responsible for getting her to safety.

Barlow Sisters Trilogy
Three impoverished, orphaned sisters eventually make happy marriages when they see the faces of their future husbands in a "magic" locket.

The Ambitious Baronet. Signet, 2001.
A young woman who is secretly "stealing" and caring for abused children becomes the housekeeper in what used to be her home and captures the heart of the new owner.

The Widower's Folly. Signet, 2001.
A shy children's book author who has vowed to stay single helps the hero's young daughter recover from her mother's tragic death and rethinks her resolve when he comes to her aid when a scandal threatens her career.

The Soldier's Bride. Signet, 2002.
A hasty marriage and a separation by war combine with cruel family treatment and charges of infidelity to add complications to the eventual reunion of the protagonists.

King, Valerie
King is a multi-published Regency Romance author with over thirty Regencies to her credit.

Pamberley Sisters Series
A Country Flirtation. Zebra, 1998.
A pair of carriage accidents places two lords in the care of a spinster who falls for one of them as she nurses him back to health.

A London Flirtation. Zebra, 2000.
A lady goes to London to make a match and discovers love is much closer to home.

A Brighton Flirtation. Zebra, 2000.
A plot to assassinate the Prince Regent adds adventure and romance to a lady's stay in Brighton.

My Lord Highwayman. Zebra, 2001.
A mysterious highwayman's romantic kiss causes problems for a governess who is also attracted to a disgraced lord in this action-packed, multilayered Regency.

My Lady Valiant. Zebra, 2002.
An intrepid lady kidnaps an undercover spy to coerce him into marrying her cousin and ends up involved with the adventurer herself.

A Rogue's Deception. Zebra, 2002.
An impersonation deception aimed at putting a bothersome lady in her place has unintended consequences when the duplicitous earl falls for the lady, instead.

A Rogue's Embrace. Zebra, 2002.
A lady and a rake who shared a passionate kiss years ago (although he was too drunk to remember) spend two weeks together collecting items for a charity auction.

A Rogue's Wager. Zebra, 2003.
Still hurt and angry by her former fiancé's apparent betrayal seven years earlier, a lady reunites with him and finally learns the truth.

A Daring Courtship. Zebra, 2003.
An English lady threatened with poverty helps a Scotsman, who has bought and is renovating a castle, be accepted by the local English country society.

A Rogue's Revenge. Zebra, 2004.
Furious that his life was apparently the model for a popular book, a nobleman plans revenge but finds love, eventually, instead.

An Adventurous Lady. Zebra, 2004.
When an old map leads her to the neighboring estate in her search for a smuggler's buried treasure, a wealthy lady must convince a grouchy, difficult earl to let her continue.

Garden of Dreams. Zebra, 2005.
A lady helps restore an estate's gardens to their former beauty and finds love with the resistant owner in the process.

Wicked and Wonderful. Zebra, 2005.
A rake bent on seduction meets his match in a smart, independent singer who is much more than she seems.

Kingsley, Mary
Kingsley also writes Historical Romance and Historical Romantic Suspense.

Marrying Miss Bumblebroth. Zebra, 2002.
A clumsy heroine marries a lord who agrees with her that friendship is the goal of their union only to find that love has somehow become involved.

The Reluctant Hero. Zebra, 2003.
A marriage-averse lady is rescued from would-be kidnappers and decides the kind, noble hero is worthy of consideration.

Kirkland, Martha

Kirkland is a multi-published author of charming, witty, well-written Regencies often with humor and a touch of mystery. A selection of her more recent titles is listed below.

That Scandalous Heiress. Zebra, 2000.
A single woman inherits a house but runs into village prejudice when she plans to live there unchaperoned until a neighboring nobleman lends a hand.

An Uncommon Courtship. Signet, 2000.
A hero who has done nothing but cause trouble for the heroine since childhood redeems himself in her opinion when he helps locate her kidnapped brother.

His Lordship's Swan. Zebra, 2001.
When a nobleman's flip of a coin results in a marriage proposal to the wrong sister, the pair agree to a mock engagement with surprising—at least to them—results.

The Rake's Fiancée. Signet, 2001.
A young woman who once rejected the man she loved because of a misunderstanding is stranded with him in his newly inherited home during a snowstorm.

Mr. Montgomery's Quest. Signet, 2001.
An unconventional heroine who gains a contract to lead a walking tour by using a man's name is attracted to a mysterious man who joins her tour.

Miss Wilson's Reputation. Signet, 2002.
When a nobleman confuses her with the notorious courtesan of a similar name, jewelry designer Harriet Wilson, who helped him escape a band of thieves, is swept up in a lively, funny, deception-filled adventure.

An Inconvenient Heir. Signet, 2003.
A lady caring for her late best-friend's baby and the baby's uncle suspect each other's motives in this story that also involves a murder mystery and a bit of political intrigue.

The Secret Diary. Signet, 2003.
A young woman in London to arrange for the publication of her late cousin's beautiful love poems meets a dashing wounded war veteran whom she thinks might be her late cousin's love interest.

A Perfect Scoundrel. Signet, 2004.
A young nobleman agrees to briefly take his irresponsible twin brother's place at a house party his grandfather is hosting and encounters the one person who has always been able to tell the twins apart, a charming, but illegitimate, young woman who has loved him since childhood.

Lane, Allison

Unusual characters and situations add interest to these Regencies that can be darker than some and are laced with mystery and intrigue.

Devall's Angel. Signet, 1998.
A young debutante attracts the attentions of a notorious rake who thinks she is a fortune hunter.

A Clandestine Courtship. Signet, 1999.
A nobleman returns home to discover who killed his twin and finds hostility and mystery, as well as romance and help with an old friend, in this rather dark Regency.

A Bird in Hand. Signet, 1999.
An independent heroine who refuses to marry just to oblige her father, a noble hero who wants to be loved for himself, and a case of mistaken identity add up to a charming story.

The Beleaguered Earl. Signet, 2000.
A woman loses her home in a wager.

Birds of a Feather. Signet, 2000.
A fashionable nobleman and a smart, but rather dowdy lady end up in a forced marriage and learn they have a lot in common. Links to *A Bird in Hand*.

<u>The Seabrook Trilogy</u>
   The Notorious Widow. Signet, 2000.
   An earl is asked by an old school friend to see what he can learn about a campaign to tarnish his widowed sister's reputation and finds romance, as well as a malevolent sociopathic villain, in this dark suspenseful Regency.

   The Rake and the Wallflower. Signet, 2001.
   A quiet, intelligent lady is forced to go with her self-centered sister to London and ends up attracting a notorious nobleman and helping him find a would-be killer.

   The Purloined Papers. Signet, 2002.
   When her father, who was secretly working to bring some scoundrels to justice, ends up dead, a lady and her childhood friend set out to solve the mystery and find love, as well.

Kindred Spirits. Signet, 2002.
A shy heiress whose guardian controls her by telling everyone she is insane and a wounded veteran depressed at being considered a traitor meet when she saves him from throwing himself over a cliff and they renew an old acquaintance, helping each other take control of their feelings and their lives.

Emily's Beau. Signet, 2003.
A young woman's romantic hopes are thwarted, for a time, by the hero's ward, a vicious, destructive chit who will stop at nothing to get what she wants.

The Madcap Marriage. Signet, 2004.
Alcohol and a concussion contribute to the impulsive marriage between two people who want to avoid wedding others and then must deal with the results of their actions.

Lansdowne, Judith A
Lansdowne's tales feature lively, engaging characters and much humor.

Amelia's Intrigue. Zebra, 1995.
A nobleman's unusual, sometimes mysterious, behavior intrigues a lovely lady in this stunning debut.

The Bedeviled Duke. Zebra, 1996.
A widowed duke returns from exile to make a home for his eight children and to complete a secret mission, as well.

Legion's Ladies. Zebra, 1996.

Camilla's Fate. Zebra, 1997.
A lady falls for an illiterate highwayman who claims to be a nobleman's missing grandson.

A Devilish Dilemma. Zebra, 1998.

Balmorrow's Bride. Zebra, 1998.
To save the family from poverty, a young woman marries a widowed nobleman she's never met and finds conspiracy as well as love.

A Season of Virtues. Zebra, 1999.
An earl who studies killers and who is currently investigating a murder and a bright young miss are involved in danger and mystery in this busy romp.

Annabella's Diamond. Zebra, 1999.
A duke determines that his shy childhood friend will have a marvelous Season and ends up falling for her as she blossoms.

Mutiny at Almack's. Zebra, 1999.
Finding his young brother seriously ill after fighting a duel over a debutante, a nobleman is drawn to the young woman who has attracted his brother.

Lord Nightingale Series
A parrot, Lord Nightingale, is intricately involved in all four books in this series that, although each contains a complete romance, are best read in order.

Lord Nightingale's Debut. Zebra, 2000.
Lord Nightingale's Love Song. Zebra, 2000.
Lord Nightingale's Triumph. Zebra, 2000.
Lord Nightingale's Christmas. Zebra, 2000.

Layton, Edith
Layton wrote numerous Traditional Regency Romances early in her career, some of which have been reprinted. More recently she has written novellas for Traditional Regency collections and Regency-set Historicals. (See chapter 7, Historical Romance.)

Ley, Alice Chetwynd
Although not so well-known as some, Ley's work is reminiscent of Heyer's and features well-developed characters and skillful recreations of the historical periods. Several of her novels take place during the Georgian Period, but they all share the Regency flavor.

Mack, Dorothy
Mack is a popular veteran Regency author; some of her more recent titles are included below.

The Gamester's Daughter. Signet, 1998.
Determined to fulfill her father's dying wish that she leave Paris for England and return some property that his partner stole, a young woman ends up at the estate of a snobbish nobleman she once saw at her father's gaming establishment—a man who considers her somewhat disreputable.

The Gold Scent Bottle. Signet, 2000.
When the effort to retrieve her cherished scent bottle that her twin brother had gambled away goes awry, a young woman agrees to pose as a nobleman's fiancée in exchange for the return for the bottle.

The Abducted Bride. Signet, 2005.
A nobleman drugs and kidnaps a woman he thinks is his runaway bride—but she's not.

Manning, Jo
The Reluctant Guardian. Regency Press, 1999.
A confirmed bachelor finds himself in charge of two marriageable misses who don't think they need a guardian and ends up falling for one of them.

Seducing Mr. Heywood. Five Star, 2002.
A notorious widow (the "other woman" in *The Reluctant Guardian*) who arrives in a Yorkshire village to see her children and generally get her life in order ends up making a match with their vicar guardian. Follows *The Reluctant Guardian*.

McCabe, Amanda
Noted for witty dialogue and well-drawn characters, McCabe also writes Historical Romance.

The Spanish Bride. Signet, 2001.
A nobleman who believes his wife was a traitor and was killed during the war encounters her at a London ball when she comes to town to track down a blackmailer.

Lady Rogue. Signet, 2002.
A wealthy artist and an impoverished nobleman are attracted to each other, but pride gets in the way.

The Errant Earl. Signet, 2002.
A new earl returns home after four years away to find his stepsister hosting a rehearsing troupe of traveling actors whom he believes, thanks to the lady's quick thinking, are household servants.

The Golden Feather. Signet, 2002.
A gently bred widow, who now is living quietly at Wycombe-on-Sea but once ran an inherited London gambling house incognito, attracts the attentions of a nobleman she encountered in her former life.

A Loving Spirit. Signet, 2003.
A young Jamaican-raised woman and a bookish, no-nonsense nobleman find romance in a Cornish castle with the help of its friendly ghosts.

One Touch of Magic. Signet, 2003.
A widow who wants to fulfill her late husband's dream of excavating a "cursed" Viking Village and the new property owner who wants to farm the land resolve their differences and solve a murder, as well.

Lady in Disguise. Signet, 2003.
A lady dresses as a servant in order to freely wander about London and encounters an intelligence officer who thinks she may be a spy.

The Rules of Love. Signet, 2004.
A widowed schoolmistress who is the anonymous author of a popular etiquette book and is a stickler for the "rules," meets her match when she locks horns with a noble rake.

The Star of India. Signet, 2004.
A fabled sapphire and a treacherous deception add tension to this sweet reunion story.

A Tangled Web. Signet, 2006.
A country house party planned by a matchmaking dowager viscountess reunites a young widow and her childhood sweetheart in spite some outside interference.

Metzger, Barbara

Metzger's highly popular Regencies are generally light, witty, and often liberally laced with humor and lovable animals. However, they can address some very serious social issues, as well. She also writes Regency-set Historical Romance.

The Primrose Path. Fawcett Crest, 1997.
A lord whose aunt left her cottage to her many dogs finds love with the woman responsible for the animals' care.

A Worthy Wife. Signet, 2000.
A couple married under a misconception survive numerous difficulties on their way to discovering love.

Saved by Scandal. Signet, 2000.
A jilted lord offers marriage to a gently born singer who accepts his offer when he agrees to protect her and her young, newly titled brother from the schemes of a greedy uncle.

Miss Westlake's Windfall. Signet, 2001.
A frustrated nobleman plants a small fortune in gold in his neighbor's orchard hoping that when she finds it and is no longer poor, she will accept his marriage proposal—but his plans take an unexpected turn.

The Painted Lady. Signet, 2001.

*A Debt to Delia. Signet, 2002.
An honorable major offers marriage to the sister of the man who saved his life, but despite her difficult situation, she only wants to marry for love.

Lady Sparrow. Signet, 2002.
A young widow tracks down her late husband's many illegitimate children and finds love and danger in this rather serious Regency.

The Diamond Key. Signet, 2003.
A noblewoman trapped in a dress shop fire vows to marry the man who saves her, but her "savior" turns out to be a dog and his wealthy, but scandal-ridden, owner has no intention of getting married.

Mindel, Jenna

Miranda's Mistake. Signet, 2003.
A widow encounters the man she jilted years earlier and they find that there is still a spark between them.

Kiss of the Highwayman. Signet, 2004.
A nobleman who wants to avenge his brother's death and a lady who wants to get a prized ring back join forces in tracking down an unusual band of highwaymen.

Miss Whitlow's Turn. Zebra, 2005.
Seeking to redeem himself in the eyes of the *ton* so he can marry well and settle down, a former rake pays court to a well-respected woman whose reputation might rub off on him, with unexpected results. Light and funny.

Lord Grafton's Promise. Signet, 2005.
When the carriage crash that killed her wealthy husband turns out to be no accident, Lucinda is forced to accept aid from Lord Grafton, who suspects her of fortune hunting. Mystery and attempted murder enliven this Regency.

Moore, Kate
Moore's Regencies are exceptionally well-researched and well-written. She has also written Historical and Contemporary romances. See also chapter 7, "Historical Romance."

Nash, Sophia
Nash produces refreshing, well-crafted Regencies that are more sensual than some; she also writes Regency-set Historicals.

A Secret Passion. Signet, 2004.
Fleeing London and an unacceptable marriage arranged by her debt-ridden father, a widow goes to the country and encounters a bad tempered, but intriguing earl.

*A Passionate Endeavor. Signet, 2004.
A heroine nurses a wounded war veteran who has vowed to never marry, but when he proposes a marriage in name only, she decides she wants to marry for love.

Lord Will and Her Grace. Signet, 2005.
Escaping to the seaside to lick their separate social wounds, a lady and a gentleman bet that they can teach each other to attract members of the opposite sex; whoever does it first, wins.

Oliver, Patricia
A popular, much-admired Regency writer of well-written romances.

An Inconvenient Wife. Signet, 1998.
Compromised and forced to marry the daughter of an enemy of his late father's, a nobleman banishes the woman to a distant estate only to have his plans foiled when he is drawn back for family reasons.

The Lady in Gray. Signet, 1999.
Ruined by a botched elopement, a lady-turned-portrait-painter repairs to Cornwall and the home of an eccentric aunt and finds love and suspense with a mysteriously widowed lord.

Scandalous Secrets. Signet, 1999.
A wealthy divorced woman rescues a little girl from a thief and begins a rocky acquaintance with the child's uptight military father with—ultimately—romantic results.

Lady Jane's Nemesis. Signet, 2000.
A young bride wins the love and admiration of her husband in spite of the machinations of his former mistress.

Broken Promises. Signet, 2001.
A nobleman plans to avenge himself on the woman who jilted him ten years earlier, but things don't work out as he plans.

Daphne's Diary. Signet, 2002.
A beautiful woman who was traumatized as a teenager when she sees her sister's husband dallying with another woman secludes herself on her grandfather's estate and vows never to marry—until a determined nobleman arrives on the scene.

Lady in Disguise. Signet, 2003.
A lady dons a maid's disguise to explore London on her own and finds romance with a nobleman who suspects her of being a spy in this book that helped launch Signet's Super Regency line.

Overfield, Joan
Many of Overfield's Regencies have a dash of the paranormal.

Parks, Julia
The Devil and Miss Webster. Zebra, 2001.
Sparks fly between a spinster companion and governess (also a competent estate manager) and the brother-in-law of her friend and employer when he returns home to take over the estate in this tale with its share of secrets and blackmail plots.

His Saving Grace. Zebra, 2002.
A lady running a progressive girls' school and a priggish vicar find love in spite of their differences.

A Gift for a Rogue. Zebra, 2002.
When his scandalous lifestyle renders him "unsuitable," a nobleman is aided by a family friend who helps him improve himself so he can find a proper wife. Follows *His Saving Grace*.

To Marry an Heiress. Zebra, 2003.
Having lost his fortune at the gaming tables, a nobleman sends his three sons to London to marry money

Fortune's Fools. Zebra, 2004.
A pair of brothers go in search of wealthy wives for the sake of the family cash flow in this sequel to *To Marry an Heiress*.

Lady Olivia to the Rescue. Zebra, 2005.
An optimistic lady decides to help a dour widower find romance and they discover they have more in common than they'd thought.

Marriage Minded. Zebra, 2005.
A happily single lady meets a captain who changes her mind.

Pickens, Andrea (Andrea DaRif)
The Defiant Governess. Signet, 1998.
Faced with an intolerable marriage, a duke's daughter runs away and becomes a governess to an absent nobleman's ward.

Code of Honor. Signet, 1998.
A scholarly miss who brings her brother to London for the Season finds her unconventional behavior makes her the object of an outrageous bet.

The Hired Hero. Signet, 1999.
A lady acting as a secret courier hires a nobleman to escort her to London and keep her safe.

Second Chances. Signet, 2000.
A nobleman is irate when he learns that his son has hired a woman as a tutor—a woman who has an ulterior motive, as well.

The Major's Mistake. Signet, 2000.
A military man believing his wife to be unfaithful goes to war and years later discovers he may have been too hasty in his judgment.

A Lady of Letters. Signet, 2000.
A reformer and a rake find a common bond in anonymous correspondence but spar in person.

A Diamond in the Rough. Signet, 2001.
A desperate nobleman who knows nothing of golf accepts a wager that could wipe out all his father's debts and save his engagement and ends up playing at St. Andrew's with a caddie who turns out to be an outspoken society miss.

The Banished Bride. Signet, 2002.
A nobleman sent to find a spy mistakenly accosts his wife, now a feminist activist, who he hasn't seen since they were wed years earlier.

The Storybook Hero. Signet, 2002.
A pair of English nationals in Russia find romance in unusual circumstances.

A Stroke of Luck. Signet, 2003.
An artistic English lady who thinks little of aristocrats rescues a nobleman from the Mediterranean and finds romance with him in spite of society's strictures.

Rasley, Alicia
Rasley is a Rita Award–winning writer. See also chapter 9, "Alternative Reality Romance."

The Reluctant Lady. Kappa Books, 1997.
A widowed lady finds romantic excitement with a notorious duke while planning marriage to a safer man, but she reckons without the power of love.

Richardson, Evelyn (Pseudonym for Cynthia Johnson)
Warm, intelligently written Regencies with mature characters and realistic issues are hallmarks of Richardson's work. Some of her titles have been reprinted and many are available in e-book format.

Lady Alex's Gamble. Signet, 1995.
The Reluctant Heiress. Signet, 1996.
My Wayward Lady. Signet, 1997.
The Gallant Guardian. Signet, 1998.

My Lady Nightingale. Signet, 1999.
A nobleman furthers the singing career of a French émigré and falls in love in the process.

Lord Harry's Daughter. Signet, 2001.
A famed officer's daughter who has spent much of her life among soldiers finds friendship and love with a man who is more than he seems.

Fortune's Lady. Signet, 2002.
Thinking they have nothing in common, a reserved lady and a dashing lord find they are of like minds on a number of things, including their approach to cards.

A Foreign Affair. Signet, 2003.
Set during the Congress of Vienna of 1814–1815, this historically rich tale is filled with treachery, intrigue, politics, and features a mature, reserved heroine and a dashing hero who find they have much in common.

The Scandalous Widow. Signet, 2004.
A widow who starts a school for young women over her family's objections encounters a nobleman who betrayed her years earlier and is now thinking of enrolling his niece in the school—and checking things out at the same time.

A Lady of Talent. Signet, 2005.
Enchanted by a woman's portrait he had bought years earlier, a nobleman is shocked to learn that the woman is the artist who has been hired to paint a portrait of his bride-to-be.

Robens, Myretta

Once Upon a Sofa. Zebra, 2005.
A chance kiss results in a widow's marriage to the friend of the nobleman she was targeting.

Just Say Yes. Zebra, 2005.
The heir to a dukedom pretends to be the steward of his brother-in-law's estate in order to learn the ropes, falls for the vicar's daughter, and must deal with objections from both their families.

Savery, Jeanne

Savery's Regencies are generally well-researched and detailed and can deal with more serious social issues. May include some mystery and suspense.

The Six

This series focuses on the lives and loves of six friends. A delightful tiger plays an occasional role.

Taming Lord Renwick. Zebra, 1999.
A tiger acts as matchmaker to his nearly blind master and a lively spinster who comes to help him with his memoirs.

Lady Serena's Surrender. Zebra, 2000.
A lady planning to make a marriage of convenience to escape the cruel control of her father marries the brother of her intended when her fiancé unexpectedly dies.

The Christmas Gift. Zebra, 2000.
A depressed, wounded veteran finds healing and love, thanks to his friends and a perceptive heroine.

The Perfect Husband. Zebra, 2001.
A lady from a financially impaired family seeks to marry the perfect husband and compromises the wrong man.

A Perfect Match. Zebra, 2001.
The opposing political views of her father and the man she loves threaten to keep a lady from marrying until her father's life is in danger and her suitor comes to the rescue.

Smuggler's Heart. Zebra, 2002.
A French aristocratic smuggler is forced to marry an Englishman in order to be safe from her cousin.

Miss Seldon's Suitors. Zebra, 2002.
A lady cheated of her inheritance is taken in by a clever, eccentric noblewoman and soon has a surfeit of men asking for her hand.

An Independent Lady. Zebra, 2003.
A nobleman thinks to court a lady who jilted him years earlier but finds he prefers the friend who took her in when she left home, instead.

The Family Matchmaker. Zebra, 2003.
A nobleman falls in love with the young woman he asks to help him avoid the matchmaking ploys of her aunt.

The Reluctant Rake. Zebra, 2003.
A lady needs to feign an engagement to a rake she has long adored.

My Lady Housekeeper. Zebra, 2004.
A lady, practically disinherited unless she either marries within a year or can break her father's will, poses as a housekeeper at her late father's remote estate and attracts the attentions of a lord she admired years ago. Mystery elements.

The Christmas Matchmaker. Zebra, 2004.
A gentleman rescues a war widow and her child and takes them with him to a house party where his matchmaking cousin has plans of her own.

The House Party. Zebra, 2005.
A nobleman hosts a lengthy theatrical house party and discovers that one of the actresses is a woman he loved years ago and the woman his son is interested in.

Scott, Regina (Pseudonym for Regina Lundgren)
Light, enjoyable stories. See also chapter 11, "Inspsirational Romance."

The Twelve Days of Christmas. Zebra, 1998.
A financially strapped lady is wooed by a man she loves when he presents her with the Twelve Days of Christmas gifts without spending a penny.

The Bluestocking on His Knee. Zebra, 1999.
A fortune hunter tries to convince a bluestocking that he would be the perfect husband for her.

A Dangerous Dalliance. Zebra, 2000.
An American inherits an earldom and is attracted to a quiet schoolmarm instead of the beauty the late earl's greedy, malicious widow wants him to wed.

The Incomparable Miss Compton. Zebra, 2001.
A lord needs a political wife but the lady wants to marry for love, not business reasons.

The Irredeemable Miss Renfield. Zebra, 2001.
A lady tired of her family's matchmaking efforts strikes a bargain with the latest suitor that should get her off the hook very nicely—then, of course, they fall in love.

Lord Borin's Secret Love. Zebra, 2002.
A lady's plan to spy on the man she thinks her sister should marry backfires when he catches her and is attracted to her instead.

Utterly Devoted. Zebra, 2002.
A rake must apologize to all the women he's wronged if he is to inherit; all goes well until the last lady decides he needs to perform three tasks to prove his sincerity.

Simonson, Sheila

Simonson's Regencies are gems, true to the form and sparkling with humor and authentic, witty dialog. She also wrote a mystery series.

Simpson, Donna

A Rake's Redemption. Zebra, 2002.
A high-living, rakish earl, attacked by highwaymen and left for dead, is cared for by a vicar's daughter who has no idea who he is—and the earl is reluctant to tell her.

A Country Courtship. Zebra, 2002.
To avoid an arranged marriage, a lady heads to the country and takes on a new identity and falls in love with a farmer who is not what he seems.

A Matchmaker's Christmas. Zebra, 2002.
Triple matches result from the merry making in this lively house party holiday romp that highlights the efforts of a lady to forge a match between her companion and her godson not realizing that they had a rather disastrous prior acquaintance.

Pamela's Second Season. Zebra, 2003.
A spirited lady tries to reform in order to win the man she's loved since childhood but finds that her natural, less ladylike behavior attracts the admiration of another. Follows *A Country Courtship*.

Rachel's Change of Heart. Zebra, 2003.
A successfully engaged lady can't forget her childhood friend. Follows *Pamela's Second Season*.

Lord Pierson Reforms. Zebra, 2004.
A reforming rake is attracted by a young, spoiled noblewoman's beauty but eventually falls in love with her levelheaded, compassionate chaperone, instead.

The Duke and Mrs. Douglas. Zebra, 2004.
A disillusioned duke is attracted to his aunt's companion, but is wary of being betrayed by another woman.

Gilded Knight. Zebra, 2005.
A widowed noblewoman and her fragile child are saved from eviction by the new viscount's brother, who is not the coldhearted wastrel he seems.

Smith, Joan

Smith writes witty, amusing Regencies, highly derivative of Georgette Heyer and filled with interesting characters and bright, verbally quick protagonists. Her earliest works are among her best and a number are being reissued in print and in e-book format.

Veryan, Patricia

Veryan writes intriguing and somewhat action-filled Regency and Georgian Period Romances. Her linked books are especially popular. (See previous editions of this guide for some earlier titles.)

Riddle Saga

The Riddle of Alabaster Royal. St. Martin's Press, 1997.
A war veteran returns to his haunted manor and finds a beautiful woman living there.

The Riddle of the Lost Lover. St. Martin's Press, 1998.
The protagonists from the previous story engage in a chase across France.

The Riddle of the Reluctant Rake. St. Martin's Press, 1999.
A dishonorably discharged officer seeks the villain who arranged for him to be falsely accused of compromising a lady.

The Riddle of the Shipwrecked Spinster. St. Martin's Press, 2001.
A shipwrecked lady returns to England to learn she is no longer engaged.

The Riddle of the Deplorable Dandy. St. Martin's Press, 2002.
A woman hopes to save her brother but must rely on a difficult dandy, who turns out to be remarkably attractive.

Walsh, Sheila
Walsh is a veteran writer who has penned numerous Traditional Regencies featuring self-reliant, resilient heroines and cynical heroes who evolve into caring, loving men.

The Lady from Lisbon. Signet, 2001.
An intelligent, self-assured young woman irritates and attracts a nobleman who was wounded by love and isn't looking for a match.

Woodward, Rhonda
A Spinster's Luck. Signet, 2002.
An orphaned vicar's daughter can't believe that a duke would be attracted to her, even though she is now wealthy and has been accepted by the *ton*.

A Hint of Scandal. Signet, 2003.
Compromised and forced to wed a rakish duke she had nursed back to health after he was shot by highwaymen, a young woman is dogged by scandal and danger as she makes her way in society.

The Wagered Heart. Signet, 2003.
With her Season in shreds when a duke kisses her on a public street, a young lady retires to the country to plot her revenge, but when she meets the duke again in Bath, things do not go as planned.

Moonlight and Mischief. Signet, 2004.
An ambitious mother and an aristocratic rake cause problems for an independent heroine in this lively house party romp.

Lady Emma's Dilemma. Signet, 2005.
After thirteen years apart, a couple reconnects in London, each with differing memories about why they never married but equally determined to resist their mutual attraction.

Selected Anthologies

The following examples demonstrate the wide diversity of Regency anthologies available.

His Eternal Kiss. Zebra, 2002.
Vampires and all things supernatural make this trilogy a good one for Halloween. Included are: Karla Hocker's, "A Lady of the Night," Judith A. Lansdowne's "The Cossack," and "Dark Seduction" by Jeanne Savery.

A Kiss for Papa. Zebra, 2002.
An unusual Father's Day collection that focuses on children out to find the perfect women for their dads includes "The Best Father in England" by Jo Ann Ferguson, "A Father's Love" by Valerie King, and "A Father's Duty" by Jeanne Savery.

A Match for Mother. Zebra, 1999.
Matchmaking children make sure their mothers are happily wed in this trilogy of novellas. Included are: "A Match for Mama" by Mona Gedney, "Lady Radcliffe's Ruse" by Kathryn Kirkwood, and "Sweeter Than Candy" by Regina Scott.

Magical Kittens. Zebra, 2000.
Kittens, witches, and all things magical abound in this trilogy of tales perfect for Halloween. Includes Donna Bell's "The Reluctant Warlock," Catherine Blair's "The Black Kitten," and Joy Reed's "A Cat by Any Other Name."

Once Upon a Waltz. Zebra, 2001.
Inspired by various fairy tales, this anthology includes Carola Dunn's "The Firebird," Karla Hocker's "The Dancing Shoes," and Judith A. Lansdowne's "The Thrushbeard."

Regency Christmas Spirits. Signet, 2001
Ghosts, fairies, and magic of all kinds add sparkle to the Christmas season in this quintet of short stories that includes Nancy Butler's "The Merry Wanderer," Emma Jensen's "The Wexford Carol," Edith Layton's "High Spirits," Barbara Metzger's "The Christmas Curse," and Andrea Pickens' "A Gathering of Gifts."

Regency Christmas Wishes. Signet, 2003.
Five charming Holiday short stories from some of the best Regency writers in the field. Included are: Sandra Heath's "The Merry Magpie," Emma Jensen's "Following Yonder Star," Carla Kelly's "Let Nothing You Dismay," Edith Layton's "Best Wishes," and Barbara Metzger's "The Lucky Coin."

Valentine Kittens. Zebra, 2005.
Matchmaking kittens enliven this trio of novellas. Included are: Jo Ann Ferguson's "Belling the Kitten," Valerie King's "A Tangle of Kittens," and Cynthia Pratt's "The Birthday Kitten."

A Valentine Waltz. Zebra, 2004.
Celebrating Valentine's Day, this anthology includes Jo Ann Ferguson's "My Dearest Daisy," Maria Greene's "Cupid's Challenge," and Kate Huntington's "My Wicked Valentine."

Waltz with a Rogue. Zebra, 2006.
Waltzing brings love to the protagonists in these three charming Regencies: Kathleen Baldwin's "The Highwayman Came Waltzing," "The Rebel and the Rogue" by Mona Gedney," and "Dance with Me" by Lisa Noeli.

Wedding Belles. Signet, 2004.
Romance and weddings are the focus of this trio of novellas from three of the subgenre's best. Included are: Allison Lane's "For Richer or Poorer," Edith Layton's "A Marriage of True Minds," and Lynn Kerstan's "The Marriage Scheme."

With This Ring. Zebra, 2004.
Marriage and courtship are the links in the stories in this Regency anthology. Included are: Shannon Donnelly's "Stolen Away," Jennifer Malin's "A Perfect Duet," and Donna Simpson's "Sorrow's Wedding."

TAKE FIVE!

Five favorite Traditional Regency Romances:

- **Mary Balogh**—*Dancing with Clara*
- **Georgette Heyer**—*Venetia*
- **Carla Kelly**—*Mrs. Drew Plays Her Hand*
- **Barbara Metzger**—*A Debt to Delia*
- **Mary Jo Putney**—*The Rake and the Reformer*

1

2

3

4

5

6

7

8

Chapter 9

Alternative Reality Romance

Imagination is more important than knowledge.

Albert Einstein

Love is a canvas furnished by Nature and embroidered by imagination.

Voltaire

Definition

> **Alternative Reality Romance**—Romance novels that include supernatural, fantasy, paranormal, science fiction, time travel, magic, or other elements that may be labeled as "unreal."

Of all the romance subgenres, Alternative Reality is arguably the most diverse and, possibly, the most fluid. This is true, most likely, because it is not a single subgenre but rather a collection of separate mini-subgenres linked by the common thread of the supernatural, fantasy, or "unreality." Including everything from darkly sensual Gothically tinged vampire tales and action-packed "the-others-among-us" or "guardian" Contemporary adventures to upbeat stories of disoriented time travelers, quirky modern-day witches, questing princess warriors, or shape-changing dragons, these romances fall into several broad categories—Fantasy, Paranormal, Futuristic, and Time Travel. Sometimes these will be labeled differently, blended in various ways, or broken down even further. For example, currently, the term Paranormal is often used to refer to the whole group, and, as of this writing, Urban Fantasy Romance, a fascinating blend, is taking the genre by storm and is well on the way to becoming it's own subgenre. (Note: Definitions and brief discussions of these individual subgroups will be provided in the appropriate bibliography sections below.)

Just as the Romantic Mystery subgenre is strongly related to the larger Mystery/Suspense fiction genre, many of the specific types included under the Alternative

9

Reality umbrella have direct counterparts in genres outside Romance, in particular, the Fantastic Fiction (sometimes called Speculative Fiction) genres. Compare, for example, Futuristics with Science Fiction, Romance Fantasy with Fantasy, the Paranormal with Horror, and Urban Fantasy Romance with Urban Fantasy. The similarities are obvious. The element that distinguishes them from one another, however, is the same as that which separates Romantic Mysteries from the Mystery/Suspense genre—focus. As in all of Romance, in all the Alternative Reality Romance types, the primary focus of the story is on the developing love relationship between the two main characters. In the other genres, even though there may be a strong romantic relationship, the main emphasis is on other elements of the plot. Straight forward though this distinction appears to be, in practice it is often not so easy to make a choice. Many writers hover between types, and as genreblending or genre-blurring (the migration of elements from one genre into another, resulting in stories with characteristics of both) continues to make inroads across the fiction genres, the lines between the genres are becoming increasingly muddied and less well-defined, making it more and more difficult to decide what, exactly, the story's basic type is.

Disconcerting though this may be for those who like to have things categorized and neatly arranged (especially along library shelves), this is not necessarily bad and even may not be so much of a problem for readers as we think. It might even be a plus. In the first place, many readers will read across genre lines, for example, enjoying both Science Fiction and Futuristics or Fantasy or Horror and Urban Fantasy Romance. For these readers, the problem of categorization may be a nonissue; in fact, some may even appreciate the closer links. In other cases, this may result in readers' exposure to a genre or a writer they might never have tried otherwise.

Appeal

The essential appeal of the Alternative Reality Romance is to our imagination and inborn sense of wonder. Most of us have been fascinated from childhood by stories of fairies, elves, dragons, and other tales of myth and magic. As we grew older, ghosts, witches, vampires, and creatures both deliciously macabre and gruesome joined the list. By the time most of use had reached our teens, stories of aliens, space travel, interplanetary exploration, and intergalactic wars had caught our interest and fired our imaginations. Although we grew up and, of necessity, became more practical and realistic, most of us are still fascinated with the magical, the mystical, the supernatural, the futuristic, and the unexplained. It is to this basic interest that both the Fantastic Fiction genres and the Alternative Reality Romance directly appeal. But the Alternative Reality Romance, much like the Romantic Mystery, provides something its counterpart Fantastic Fiction genres generally do not—a satisfactory love story. It is this double appeal that many romance readers find so attractive.

Advising the Reader

While general readers' advisory information is provided in chapter 3, several points to consider specifically when advising for this particular subgenre are given below.

10

11

12

13

14

15

16

- Increasingly, readers are reading across genre and subgenre lines, a trend that is particularly relevant when advising readers in this subgenre.
- Many readers of Futuristics also read Science Fiction. A fan of Susan Grant's or Robin D. Owens' Futuristics might also enjoy books by C. J. Cherryh, Lois McMaster Bujold, Sheri Tepper, Andre Norton, or Catherine Asaro. Anne McCaffrey and Marion Zimmer Bradley are classic writers often popular with both groups.
- Readers may also read both Fantasy and Fantasy Romance and would be open to recommendations of either type. Additionally, there are a number of writers who have produced Science Fiction works that read enough like Fantasy (e.g., Anne McCaffrey's Dragonriders of Pern series and Marion Zimmer Bradley's Darkover novels) that they can be easily recommended to Fantasy Romance readers. The same is true of some mystical, most often Medieval, Historicals.
- The large, inclusive Paranormal grouping provides a wealth of crossover options. Readers who prefer the darker, edgier Paranormals may also enjoy Gothics, some Mysteries, and Horror, while Fantasy may appeal to fans of the lighter, whimsical Paranormals.
- Stories in any of these subgenres can have a religious slant, and readers who enjoy these may also like certain Inspirationals (particularly of the "angelic" or "miraculous" variety) or classic Christian Fiction works such as the Ransom Trilogy by C. S. Lewis.
- Readers who enjoy Urban Fantasy Romance may also enjoy Urban Fantasy as well as Paranormal Romances.
- Time Travels often have much in common with Historicals, and fans may also enjoy a regular Historical set during a favorite time period. Rarely, Time Travels involve a visit to the future; in this case, Futuristics might be recommended. Readers who particularly enjoy the dynamics of the character's dilemma of being in an unfamiliar situation may also enjoy stories that involve similar "out of place" situations (e.g., an American heiress comes to England and must deal with the strictures of the British elite) but don't involve time travel.
- Because this is a particularly complex and diverse group, it is important to determine exactly what the reader is looking for. In addition to the obvious differences among the subgenres, length, pacing, style, tone, and sensuality levels vary widely within each group. Does the reader prefer fast-paced, quirky, sexy Futuristics (e.g., Jayne Castle); sassy, funny, vampire stories (e.g., MaryJanice Davidson's Undead series or Lynsay Sands' Argeneau series); darkly magical Fantasies (e.g., Susan Krinard's Fane series); or violent, intense vampire or shapeshifter tales (e.g., Christine Feehan's Dark series or J. R. Ward's Black Dagger Brotherhood series)? These books are not the same and appeal to readers for different reasons.
- For the reader who is completely new to these subgenres, recommend standard works by major authors.

Brief History

The roots of the various broader fiction types that make up the Alternative Reality Romance genre reach far into the past.

The seeds of both Science Fiction and Fantasy were present in the myths and legends of the earliest peoples as they wove stories that attempted to explain both the world around them and universe beyond. The Middle Eastern and Classical worlds added to the traditions with tales both earthly and divine, even producing a second-century Greek satire that included an imaginary voyage to the moon (Marshall B. Tymn, "Science Fiction," in

Handbook of American Popular Literature, edited by M. Thomas Inge [New York: Greenwood Press, 1988), 274]).

The Scandinavian and Germanic mythologies added a somewhat darker influence to the Fantasy tradition, and the folktales, heroic epics, legends, and Christian fantasies (e.g., Dante's *Divine Comedy* [1307–1321]) of the Middle Ages all made their contributions. Occasional stories of things unreal continued to appear from time to time, including David Russen's *Iter Lunare: or, A Voyage to the Moon* (1703) and Jonathan Swift's still popular social and political satire, *Gulliver's Travels* (1726). Then, in the mid-eighteenth century, Horace Walpole wrote his classic Gothic, *The Castle of Otranto* (1764), a story that is often cited as the first Gothic novel, and a work whose influence is still felt within the various Fantasy, Horror, and Paranormal genres today.

Scholars are often reluctant to pinpoint the exact beginnings of the Fantasy genre or to name the first fantasy novel, although Edmund Spenser's epic poem, *The Faerie Queene* (1590–1596), is considered by many to be the earliest fantasy written in English (Charlotte Spivack, *Merlin's Daughters: Contemporary Women Writers of Fantasy* [New York: Greenwood Press, 1987] 5). On the other hand, there seems to be general agreement that Mary Shelley's *Frankenstein: or, The Modern Prometheus* (1818), was probably the first Science Fiction novel and was certainly "the prototypical work of science fiction" ([Karl Kroeber, *Romantic Fantasy and Science Fiction* [New Haven: Yale University Press, 1988] 1), replacing the supernatural with the scientific and establishing the early parameters of the genre.

The latter half of the eighteenth century saw the beginnings of the Industrial Revolution, and with it, an increased interest in science and technology. By the middle of the nineteenth century, the Industrial Age was in full swing, and the overall optimism of the period, largely based on the potential of the new technologies and the limitless possibilities of the future, was beginning to be reflected in the literature. Many writers, including Nathaniel Hawthorne, Edgar Allan Poe, and Mark Twain, tried their hands at writing fiction incorporating these new themes, but it was Jules Verne, with his inventive adventures, (e.g., *From the Earth to the Moon* (1865), *Twenty Thousand Leagues Under the Sea* [1870]) who was the genre's first major popular success and, guaranteed its survival (Tymn, "Science Fiction," 275).

Although this new scientific fiction was attracting much attention, the fantasy and Gothic threads that would also eventually become part of Alternative Reality continued to appear in the works of a number of writers, including the fairytales and fantasies of George MacDonald (e.g., *Phantastes* [1858], *The Princess and the Goblin* [1872]), *Alice's Adventures in Wonderland* (1865) by Lewis Carroll, the interesting early time-travel by Mark Twain, *A Connecticut Yankee in King Arthur's Court* (1889), and the various Gothically tinged stories of Poe (e.g., "The Fall of the House of Usher"). Of particular note is Robert Louis Stevenson's short story "The Strange Case of Dr. Jekyll and Mr. Hyde" (1886) which, while somewhat in the Science Fiction camp, contains a fair amount of the fantastic and also has links to the modern werewolf stories.

These trends persisted into the 1890s with the publication of two classic, but very different, stories, both of which had definite implications for the Alternative Reality Romance. In 1895, H. G. Wells's novella "The Time Machine" sparked an interest in the concept of time travel that continues to this day, and Bram Stoker's *Dracula*, an epistolary novel published in 1897, while not the first vampire story published [e.g., John Polidori's "The Vampyre" (1819)], it is the best known and provided the inspiration for the many vampire tales that followed. It is an intriguing twist that that while

Count Dracula was actually the villain of the piece, the vampires in many of today's Paranormal Romances are often the heroes.

The fantastic fiction genres continued into the twentieth century with the rising popularity of series books. The Oz stories (1900–1920) of L. Frank Baum and the fantastic adventure series of Edgar Rice Burroughs (including Tarzan—beginning with *Tarzan of the Apes* in 1914—and the various space series) were particularly popular. The publication of the pulp magazine *Amazing Stories* in 1926 precipitated the rapid expansion of the Science Fiction magazine market during the next decade and set the stage for the Golden Age of the genre which lasted roughly from 1938 to 1950. Note: It is interesting that the genre wasn't officially labeled until 1929 when Hugo Gernsback, publisher of *Amazing Stories*, did so in his editorial in the inaugural issue of *Science Wonder Stories* (June 1929) (Tymn, "Science Fiction," 292).

Although much of the attention was on Science Fiction, Fantasy was still being written, and it was during this time that academic and lay theologian C. S. Lewis produced his classic space (or Ransom) trilogy of good, evil, and redemption (*Out of the Silent Planet* [1938], *Perelandra* [1938], *That Hideous Strength* [1945]) which is still read and studied. The 1950s produced several more fantasy classics, including C.S. Lewis's *The Chronicles of Narnia* (1950–1956), J.R.R. Tolkien's *The Lord of the Rings* (1954–1955), and T. H. White's *The Once and Future King* (1958). Tolkien's works are especially important because, as Ann Swinfen observed, "Tolkien made fantasy 'respectable.' " (*Defence of Fantasy: A Study of the Genre in English and American Literature since 1945* [London: Routledge & Kegan Paul, 1984], 1), and White's Arthurian stories have obvious links to the Romance.

While some of these early antecedents of the Alternative Reality Romance did contain love interests, few, if any, would qualify as romances by today's standards. Nevertheless, changes were occurring in these genres that eventually would impact the Romance and encourage the development of various subgenres within Alternative Reality Romance. One of the most important was the growing presence of women writers. In their hands, these traditionally male dominated stories began to develop a "feminine perspective on plot, character, theme, structure, and imagery." (Spivack, *Merlin's Daughters*, 8–9). They featured female protagonists who were both strong and aggressive, yet caring and sensitive; plots that valued relationships and feelings over conquest and dominance; and a point of view that was feminine as opposed to masculine. A few writers, such as Anne McCaffrey, wrote stories such as *Restorée* (1967) and The Dragonriders of Pern series (*Dragonflight* [1968], *Dragonquest* [1970], *The White Dragon* [1978]) with enough sensual appeal to still attract both Science Fiction and Romance readers today. Other favorite works of Romance readers are *Beauty: A Retelling of the Story of Beauty and the Beast* (1978), *Rose Daughter* (1997), and *Spindle's End* (2000), all by fantasy writer Robin McKinley. Also worth reading, but for totally different reasons, is William Goldman's charming spoof *The Princess Bride* (1973). Also of note is Historical Romance writer Anya Seton's *Green Darkness* (1972) which includes elements of reincarnation. The Gothic Romances soared to popularity during the 1960s, providing the suspense and horror elements that have become standard in darker varieties of the Paranormals.

One of the earliest of the true Alternative Reality Romances was *Journey to Yesterday* (1979), a time travel by veteran romance writer June Lund Shiplett. She followed it with *Return to Yesterday* (1983), and gradually a few more romance writers began to experiment with their own versions of the genre (e.g., Jayne Ann Krentz with *Sweet Starfire* [1986] and *Crystal Flame* [1986], Maura Seger with *Golden Chimera* [1985] and other "Atlantis" books, Lori Copeland with *Out of this World* [1986], Constance O'Day-Flannery with *Timeswept Lovers* [1987]). By the end of the decade, other writers had joined in, including veterans such as Jude

Deveraux (*Wishes* [1989] and her groundbreaking *A Knight in Shining Armor* [1989]), Johanna Lindsey (*Warrior's Woman* [1989]), and Rebecca Brandewyne (*Passion Moon Rising* [1988]). Interest skyrocketed, and with the publication of Diana Gabaldon's *The Outlander* (first of her now classic time travel series) in 1991 and the official recognition of the subgenre in 1992 when the Romance Writers of America added a separate "Futuristic/Fantasy/Paranormal" category to its annual Rita and Golden Heart Awards, the Alternative Reality subgenre was firmly established. The years that followed were big ones for Alternative Reality Romance with several publishers establishing dedicated lines (e.g., Leisure Love Spell, Topaz Dreamspun, Silhouette Shadows) and "unreal" elements appearing regularly in romances of all types. Vampires, angels, time traveling heroes and heroines, ghosts, faeries, werewolves, space travelers, and other fantastic characters populated an ever-growing variety of romances that included everything from New Age Paranormals, angel-filled Fantasies, and fast-paced Time Travels to the darker stories of the supernatural, mystical tales of magic and legend, and innovative Futuristic romantic adventures. As a whole, the subgenre continued to be popular through the mid-1990s, but except for Time Travels, which retained some popularity, the group took a dip toward the end of the decade.

The turn of the millennium heralded a turnaround for subgenre, as well, and by the middle of the decade, all things otherworldly—although often more sensual and much darker and intense—were back in style. Once again vampires, immortal guardians, shapeshifters, mentally and physically enhanced humans, visiting aliens, intergalactic travelers, faeries, sorcerers, and demonic-types were everywhere—and while many of these stories were set in distant galaxies, alternate universes, or mythical lands, the newly recognized Urban Fantasy Romance, with its mix of contemporary, familiar settings and paranormal characters was topping the charts and garnering rave reviews from fascinated fans. The market was being supplied both by Fantasy and Science Fiction writers who were turning toward romance and by romance writers who were adding Fantasy, Paranormal, and Science Fiction aspects to their works, attracting readers from both groups and increasing new interest in both genres. Alternative Reality Romance continued strong for the next few years, and, as of this writing, except for Time Travels, which have waned in popularity, most segments of the subgenre continue to prosper. Not surprisingly, Urban Fantasy Romance is a current favorite and, at the moment, shows no intention of giving up its position. The Alternative Reality Romance has always been one of the more volatile subgenres. However, while there will always be fluctuations within the individual categories and an eventual leveling out of interest, this subgenre has succeeded in capturing the imagination of its readers and shows every intention of continuing to do so.

***

The Alternative Reality Romance is a fragmented, inclusive subgenre, and while there is an increasing amount of overlap among the types (e.g., Fantasy and Paranormal, Paranormal and Futuristic, and so on), the major subtypes listed below are currently popular and are discretely described. The subgenre's growing fluidity also means that elements from one subtype can often be found in another, resulting in stories that are not easily categorized. The same is true of some of the authors listed below. For example, Lynn Kurland writes both Fantasies and Time Travels; Susan Krinard writes Paranormals, Fantasies, and Futuristics; and Christine Feehan writes Vampire Paranormals and several varieties of Urban Fantasy Romance, to name only a few. In addition, many of the authors included also regularly write in a number of other romance subgenres or the other broader fiction genres. Writers and works included below are merely examples of the many relatively recent romances available within these subtypes. See previous editions of this guide for authors or titles that have been dropped from this edition.

Selected Modern Classics

Bujold, Lois McMaster—*Shards of Honor* (1986).
Deveraux, Jude—*A Knight in Shining Armor* (1989).
Gabaldon, Diana—*Outlander* (1991).
Kerstan, Lynn and Alicia Rasley—*Gwen's Christmas Ghost* (1995).
Krentz, Jayne Ann—*Sweet Starfire* (1986), *Crystal Flame* (1986), *Shield's Lady* (1989).
Kurland, Lynn—*Stardust of Yesterday* (1996).
Lindsey, Johanna—*Until Forever* (1995).
Stuart, Anne—*Fallen Angel* (1993).

Fantasy Romance

> **Fantasy Romance**—A combination of romance and fantasy, these stories draw heavily from myth, legend, and fairytales (just as the larger Fantasy genre does) and often include magical and mystical elements and characters such as witches, sorcerers, fairies, angels, and other powerful beings.

Drawing heavily from myth, legend, and fairytales, this category corresponds roughly to the larger Fantasy subgenre. However, as with all Romance types, it is the love story that is the primary focus, not the fulfillment of a quest, the defeat of dark forces, battles, or any of the other emphases of the traditional fantasy novel. Magic can play a big part in these romances, and they are often highly mystical and lyrically written. The tone can be light and humorous or dark and intense, and if they become too dark, there may be some confusion with the Paranormal subgroup. All manner of characters people these stories and fairies, elves, leprechauns, dragons, unicorns, and other fantastic creatures, as well as witches, sorcerers, and other powerful beings, are commonplace among their pages. Fantasies can be both contemporary and historical, with Historical Fantasies being the more common by far since Contemporary Fantasy Romance often falls within the Urban Fantasy Romance subgroup. Depending on the treatment, Historicals incorporating magical elements can fall within this type.

Selected Fantasy Romance Bibliography

Asaro, Catherine
The Lost Continent
This engaging romantic fantasy series, set in the magical world of Aronsdale and the surrounding kingdoms, will appeal to both fantasy and romance fans.

"Moonglow" in *Charmed Destinies*. (Luna, 2003).

The Charmed Sphere. Luna, 2004.
A shape-mage and a prince find disappointment and love in a world where shape-mages use colors and shapes to work their magic.

The Misted Cliffs. Luna, 2005.
A brave young woman marries a man with a cruel heritage in order to avoid a war and discovers there's more to her husband than she'd thought.

The Dawn Star. Luna, 2006.
More political intrigue, magic, and romance.

The Fire Opal. Luna, 2007.
A young priestess breaks a taboo and heals a stranger with her fire opal with devastating results.

The Night Bird. Luna, 2008.
Allegra Linseed is kidnapped in Aronsdale by nomads and taken to the desert where she attracts the powerful warrior Markus Onyx.

Dare, Justine (Justine Davis)
Hawk Trilogy
This trilogy follows the fortunes of the Hawk family and the mysterious book that appears whenever the family is in danger of dying out.

Wild Hawk. Topaz, 1996.
Heart of the Hawk. Topaz, 1996.
*Fire Hawk. Topaz, 1997.
When their peaceful glen is invaded by a violent warlord, Jenna Hawk goes in search of a champion to save her people in this magical conclusion to the trilogy. A Rita Award winner.

Davis, Kathryn Lynn
Many of Davis's historical works have mystical and fantasy-like elements.

Jones, Linda Winstead
These Fantasy Romances that follow are primarily set in an alternate medieval world in the kingdom of Columbyana.

Fyne Sisters (Sisters of the Sun)
Three magically gifted sisters are under a curse that brings early death to anyone who loves them in this trilogy.

The Sun Witch. Berkley Sensation, 2004.
Sophie Fyne nurses wounded warrior Kane back to health, seduces him, and then disappears, but when Kane finds her again and learns they have a daughter, he insists they marry.

The Moon Witch. Berkley Sensation, 2005.
Juliet, who has the gift of sight, is kidnapped by Anwyn shapeshifter Ryn, and discovers love, as well as secrets about herself she never knew.

The Star Witch. Berkley Sensation, 2006.
Isadora, the eldest of the three sisters, captured by the evil emperor, clashes with warrior Lucan in this final story of this fiery trilogy.

Children of the Sun
Continues the adventures begun in the Fyne Sisters trilogy with the stories of their first-born children and their quest to fulfill a prophecy.

Prince of Magic. Berkley Sensation, 2007.
Ariana's story—the daughter of Sophie and Kane.

Prince of Fire. Berkley Sensation, 2007.
Keelia's story—the daughter of Juliet and Ryn.

Prince of Swords. Berkley Sensationb, 2007.
Rayne's story—the daughter of Isadora and Lucan.

Emperor's Bride Trilogy

Emperor Jahn of Columbyanan seeks a bride.

Untouchable. Berkley Sensation, 2008.
Alix, the emperor's twin brother, is attracted to a beautiful slave with exotic, dangerous powers when he is sent to escort six potential brides to the palace.

22 Nights. Berkley Sensation, 2008.
Shocked to learn that he was drugged and bound in marriage to Belavalari six years earlier, Merin reconnects with Bela when he is to take her to the Emperor. They agree to divorce, but that means being bound together by a short tether for twenty-two days and nights.

Bride by Command. Berkley Sensation, 2009.
When Lady Morgana is forced by her father to wed a lowly palace guard, Jahn Devlyn, she has no idea that Jahn is really the Emperor in disguise in this intrigue-laced adventure that concludes this trilogy.

Korbel, Kathleen (Pseudonym for Eileen Dreyer)

See also chapter 5, "Contemporary Romance."

Daughters of Myth

The three very different daughters of the Fairy Queen, Mab, deal with conflict, treachery, seduction, and love in this darkly romantic Fantasy series that effortless moves between the human and faery worlds.

Dangerous Temptation. Silhouette Nocturne, 2006.
Nuala falls in love with an anthropologist who tumbles into her world even knowing he can't stay.

Dark Seduction. Silhouette Nocturne, 2008.
Sorcha is sent to the human world to find a magical stone that will restore springtime to her fey world and falls in love with a nobleman who has a hard time believing in magic or faeries.

Deadly Redemption. Silhouette Nocturne, 2008.
In punishment for her reckless behavior, seductive Orla is forced to wed the prince of a rival faery clan and try to restore the balance to her world.

Krinard, Susan

Fane Series

This historical fantasy series, set during the nineteenth century, revolves around the relationship between the Fane, an ancient race, and humans.

The Forest Lord. Berkley, 2002.
The Forest Lord, one of the Fane, sets out to reclaim the child he sired with a human woman to save his dying race.

Lord of the Beasts. HQN, 2006.
A veterinarian and son of the legendary Forest Lord is attracted to a human, who also loves animals, but can he forsake his heritage to marry her?

Lord of Legends. HQN, 2009.
A new bride deserted by her husband finds a man imprisoned on the estate and sets out to help him, not realizing at first that he is really Arion, King of the Unicorns.

Lord of Sin. HQN, 2009.
A new widow descended from a magical family bound to help others find love, is attracted to a nobleman who thinks she has something to hide—and she does.

Kurland, Lynn
See also Paranormal and Time Travel bibliographies in this chapter.

Nine Kingdoms
Archmage Miach and shieldmaiden Morgan struggle to stop the evil dark mage that is attacking and gradually destroying the kingdom of Neroche and find love along the way in the first three books of this richly described fantasy series that includes a strong, ongoing romance thread.

Star of the Morning. Berkley Sensation, 2006.
A powerful sword, a bit of magic, and the quest for the source of evil begins.

The Mage's Daughter. Berkley Sensation, 2008.
Morgan learns her true identity and finds the source of the evil.

Princess of the Sword. Berkley Sensation, 2009.
Miach and Morgan battle the evil—and win.

A Tapestry of Spells. Berkley, 2010.
Sarah is desperate to stop her evil brother from destroying the Nine Kingdoms but needs the help of a mage who has renounced his powers. This book begins a new Nine Kingdoms trilogy set during the same time as the first.

Lackey, Mercedes
Five Hundred Kingdoms
In a world where everyone has a prescripted role to play, the Tradition tries to keep everyone on track, but doesn't always succeed, in this generally funny, light-hearted, magical series that takes its cue from fairy and folk tales—and gives them an inspired twist.

The Fairy Godmother. Luna, 2004.
When Elena can't fulfill her destiny as Cinderella in the tradition-bound kingdom of Otraria because the prince is way too young, she ends up becoming a Fairy Godmother, instead.

One Good Knight. Luna, 2006.
A princess chosen to be the virgin sacrifice to stop dragon attacks goes with her "champion" to find the dragon in his lair.

Fortune's Fool. Luna, 2007.
Sent to scope out the situation in the Drylands, the daughter of the Sea King falls for the prince, but is kidnapped by an evil djinn who hopes to steal her magic.

The Snow Queen. Luna, 2008.
The Queen of the Northern Lights must stop an enemy from harming her people in this story that is a bit darker that the rest, much as the original "The Snow Queen" fairy tale is.

McDonald, L. J.
Sylph
Brought into the kingdom of Eferem from another dimension through a closely guarded magical gate and bound to serve individual human masters, sylphs are empathic spirit creatures from a hive society with supernatural abilities linked to earth, water, air, fire, and healing. Battle sylphs are the aggressive males of the species and usually only bound to strong, violent men.

The Battle Sylph. Leisure Books, 2010.
A young girl intended for sacrifice accidentally binds a powerful battle sylph, who considers her his queen and will do anything to protect her, and changes the dynamics in Eferem forever.

The Shattered Sylph. Leisure Books, 2010.
Kidnapped and carried off to a diabolical fate and a distant, dissolute land, a young woman is saved by her father, the man who loves her, and a battered, tired battle sylph.

Queen of the Sylphs. Leisure Books, 2011.

Roberts, Nora
See also chapter 5, "Contemporary Romance," and chapter 6, "Romantic Mysteries."

Circle Trilogy
When the evil vampire queen turns his brother, Cian, into a vampire and he is unable to save him, twelfth-century sorcerer Hoyt Mac Cionaoith is charged by the goddess Morrigan with gathering the Circle of Six, a diverse assortment of talented people from a wide variety of times and places, in order to defeat the vampire queen's plan to destroy humanity and take over the world. This trilogy is a classic fantasy struggle between good and evil (but with Roberts's unique twists) and will appeal to both Fantasy and Romance fans.

Morrigan's Cross. Jove, 2006.
Hoyt is transported to modern-day New York and then back to Ireland, picking up the various members of the Circle, including his "lost" vampire brother, Cian, along the way. Romance flares between Hoyt and witch Glenna Ward as they prepare for battle.

Dance of the Gods. Jove, 2006.
The battle preparation continues and romance blossoms between shapeshifter Larkin and demon hunter Blair.

Valley of Silence. Jove, 2006.
Warrior Queen Moira leads the band into battle and she and vampire Cian struggle with their passionate feelings for each other in their star-crossed relationship.

Sign of Seven Trilogy
Three ten-year-olds, Caleb, Fox, and Gage, unwittingly release an ancient evil entity when they spill their blood on the Pagan stone; twenty-one years later it is up to them and the three women who are also involved, Quinn, Layla, and Cybil, to set things to rights. Although each book completes one couple's romantic journey, the overall story builds with each book and they should be read in order. Contains strong, dark fantasy elements.

Blood Brothers. Jove, 2007.
Quinn and Caleb's story.

The Hollow. Jove, 2008.
Layla and Fox's story.

The Pagan Stone. Jove, 2008.
Cybil and Gage's story.

Shayne, Maggie
   Shayne writes in a number of Alternative Reality subgenres; the titles below are some of her classics that have a definite fantasy feel.

Immortal High Witch Trilogy
   Immortal protagonists battle dark forces to fulfill their centuries-spanning romantic destinies in this series of reincarnation, vengeance, magic, and the classic struggle between good and evil.

Eternity. Jove, 1998.
Infinity. Jove, 1999.
Destiny. Jove, 2001.

Futuristic Romance

> **Futuristic**—A combination of romance and science fiction, these stories are set in the future, often in other galaxies or on an altered Earth.

This category is the Romance's version of Science Fiction. The settings are almost always in the future and often involve other planets, space travel, alien cultures, or an alternate or post-Apocalyptic Earth. Futuristics differ from Fantasies in much the same way as the Science Fiction and Fantasy genres differ from each other (i.e., Science Fiction extrapolates from what we know is logically possible in the future, whereas Fantasy allows for the creation of entire imaginary environments with no restrictions as long as the rules established by the writer are not violated). As with all romance types, the developing romantic relationship between the protagonists is the primary focus of the plot.

Selected Futuristic Romance Bibliography

Bujold, Lois McMaster
   Although Bujold is known primarily for her Science Fiction novels, especially her Vorkosigan series, some of her works include a strong enough romance plotline to be considered within the Romance genre, such as her classic, *Shards of Honor*, listed above.

Castle, Jayne (Jayne Ann Krentz)
   Castle's Futuristic Romances are clever, creative, funny, and sexy with sassy, intrepid, sma... heroines and intelligent, take-charge heroes. See also Krentz, Jayne Ann, in chapter 6, "Romantic Mysteries," and chapter 13, "Linked Romance."

Harmony (Ghost Hunters) Series
   Originally settled by explorers from Earth who were cut off from Earth when the energy curtain that had opened to allow space travel suddenly closed, Harmony

is a mysterious place, featuring dangerous ruins of a former civilization, intriguing flora and fauna, and a population that exhibits a wide variety of psychic abilities.

"Bridal Jitters" in *Charmed*. Jove, 1999.

After Dark. Jove, 2000.
Para-archaeologist Lydia Smith is hired by wealthy, powerful Emmett London to find a missing family heirloom and finds dead bodies, ghosts, and dangerous illusion traps—and completely inappropriate romantic sparks, as well.

After Glow. Jove, 2004.
Now a pair, Lydia and Emmett must deal with more dead bodies, an ex-fiancé, more ghosts, a new, dangerous job, and a marriage of convenience in this lively, funny story that nicely continues the series.

Ghost Hunter. Jove, 2006.
Thinking her ghost hunter fiancé is marrying her for all the wrong reasons, academic Elly St. Claire gives him back his ring and leaves town, never realizing that she would soon need his help finding her missing friend in the dangerous catacombs.

Silver Master. Jove, 2007.
On the hunt for a stolen relic that was bought by an amazingly talented matchmaker, Celina Ingram, as a toy for her dust bunny, P.I. Davis Oakes fights the attraction that sizzles between them as the search for the artifact becomes more dangerous than either had expected.

Dark Light. Jove, 2008.
Tabloid investigative reporter Sierra McIntyre and guild boss John Fontana agree to put their differences aside and work together to find out what the relationship is between a new drug and some missing older ghost hunters, never expecting their temporary marriage of convenience (so John can better protect Sierra) to turn romantic.

Obsidian Prey. Jove, 2009.
Although there were mentions of the ancient Arcane Society in *Silver Master* and *Dark Light*, this is the first book that is officially part of the Arcane Society series, which includes titles written under each of Krentz's three publishing names.

Davis, Justine (Justine Dare)

Justine Dare Davis is a Romance Writers of America Hall of Fame member and writes in a number of Romance subgenres. Both of the classic Futuristics listed below make use of the captor/captive plot pattern.

*Lord of the Storm. Topaz, 1994.
A Rita Award winner.

The Skypirate. Topaz, 1995.

Grant, Susan
Star Series
Set in the worlds of a distant galaxy and also on Earth, this series follows the personal and political lives of Jas and Rom and their offspring.

The Star King. Love Spell, 2000.
A young Air Force pilot, Jas, and a royal interplanetary traveler, Rom, who saved each others lives after crashing in the desert years earlier, meet again when a delegation from our hero's home world visits Earth twenty years later.

The Star Prince. Love Spell, 2001.
Jas's son, Ian Hamilton, now a prince of the realm, and Vash Princess Tee'ah Dar are at the center of this galaxy-spanning, identity-concealing tale as Ian tries to prove himself and bring peace to all the warring factions and Tee'ah rebels against the severe Vash behavioral restrictions, swipes a starship, and ends up as a pilot for Ian's ship.

The Star Princess. Love Spell, 2003.
Ilana Hamilton, Hollywood filmmaker and sister to Prince Ian, finds love when Vash Prince Che Vedia comes to Earth for a little fun before he is forced to marry.

Contact. Love Spell, 2002.
A jetliner and all its passengers and crew are "rescued" by aliens in this well-plotted story of fierce interstellar politics and unexpected personal revelations. A Rita Award winner.

Joy, Dara
Ritual of Proof. William Morrow, 2001.
In an alternate futuristic Regency-style world (set on the inhabitable moon, Forus, of the distant planet Arkeus) where women rule and men are property, a noblewoman buys and marries an attractive man but must fight a vicious rival as well as society's intriguing conventions. Although Joy considers this Futuristic, many would label it Fantasy.

Kenin, Eve (Eve Silver)
Set in a post-apocalyptic, late-twenty-first-century future in the frozen Northern Waste and linked by character, these two gritty, action-packed adventures feature compelling, fearless protagonists, often with enhanced abilities; a creative mixture of supporting characters; heart-stopping danger; clever, thought-provoking plotting; and steamy romance. See Eve Silver in chapter 6, "Romantic Mysteries."

Driven. Love Spell, 2007.
A trucker heroine, determined to win a harrowing race in order to get the money to save her sister, picks up a mysterious passenger who has as many secrets as she does.

Hidden. Love Spell, 2008.
While hunting for a plague that was created with her DNA and could destroy the world, Tatiana and a puzzling stranger, Tristan, end up trapped in the underground lab where the plague was born, facing danger, desire, and a desperate need to escape and stop the villain responsible.

Knight, Deidre
Midnight Warriors
An alternate world, parallel timelines, and paranormal elements form the basis for this inventive, action-packed series in which the fate of the Earth, naturally, is in jeopardy.

Parallel Attraction. Signet Eclipse, 2006.
A shapeshifting alien Refarian king and a human geologist meet briefly and then reconnect several years later when wounded Jared needs Kelsey's help.

Parallel Heat. Signet Eclipse, 2006.
A Refarian warrior sent to Earth to guard the newly wed royal protagonists from the first novel is attracted to a woman he'd known in another dimension in this complex adventure.

Parallel Seduction. Signet Eclipse, 2007.
A time-traveling warrior is caught in a time not his own and is drawn to a vision-impaired linguist.

Parallel Desire. Signet Eclipse, 2007.
A time traveler bent on revenge for the loss of his wife finds healing and love with a medic sent to return him to the Refarian king in the final book in the series.

Krinard, Susan

Kinsman's Oath. Berkley Sensation, 2004.
A spaceship captain heroine from a planet where women are not valued and a hero raised by alien cat-like warriors and taught to hate humans connect telepathically and otherwise in this adventure that is rich with political intrigue, laced with a bit of mystery, and is a spinoff of the short story, "Kinsman," from the anthology *Out of This World* (Jove, 2001).

Lindsey, Johanna
Ly-San-Ter Series
This Futuristic Romance series features strong, uber-alpha heroes and independent, outspoken heroines that clash their way to happiness in these sexy stories.

Warrior's Woman. Avon, 1989.
Keeper of the Heart. Avon, 1993.
Heart of a Warrior. William Morrow, 2001.
Dalden Ly-San-Ter comes to Earth to find a villain planning to take over the planet and connects with Brittany Callaghan, who helps him and ends up being his life-mate.

Morgan, Kathleen

Morgan was an early writer of Futuristic and Paranormal romances. (See the previous edition of this guide for Morgan's titles.)

Owens, Robin D
Celta's Heartmates Series
This creative series is set on the planet Celta, a planet originally settled by Wiccans and where a hierarchical, family-centric social structure now dominates, psychic powers, or Flair, are taken for granted, and discovering one's predestined "heartmate" is a life-changing, sometimes surprising, event.

*Heart Mate. Jove, 2001.
A man who survives the murder of his family and rebuilds the family fortune and restores the power of the GreatHouse T'Ash discovers his heartmate in a young orphan with latent Flair gifts of her own. A Rita Award winner.

Heart Thief. Berkley Sensation, 2003.
A disenfranchised hero without psionic talents finds love with an empath.

Heart Duel. Berkley Sensation, 2004.
A pair from warring families find love in spite of opposition.

Heart Choice. Berkley Sensation, 2005.
A nobleman who must provide an heir for his line and a commoner who is sterile find love despite all odds.

Heart Quest. Berkley Sensation, 2006.
A guardsman is reluctant to claim his much younger heartmate because he fears he will die early.

Heart Dance. Berkley Sensation, 2007.
A woman trying to redeem her scientist father's discredited reputation is wooed by a man from the family that ruined her father.

Heart Fate. Berkley Sensation, 2008.
A young woman repudiates her marriage to an abusive husband, takes refuge in the sacred FirstGrove, and meets a man who needs healing, as well.

Heart Change. Berkley, 2009.
A troubled heroine helps a young woman through her psychic "passage" and finds her own gifts—and love—as a result.

Heart Journey. Berkley 2010.
An independent cartographer and an aspiring actor resist the fact that they are each others' heartmates.

Heart Search. Berkley, 2011.
A nobleman burned by a greedy, duplicitous spouse he believed to be his heartmate is wary of acknowledging the independent woman who is his true heartmates—and isn't about to trust him, either. Note: This story takes place more than a decade after some of the earlier stories in the series and introduces several characters in the "new" generation.

Robb, J. D. (Pseudonym for Nora Roberts)
Eve Dallas Series
Although more mystery/suspense than romance, Roberts does a good job of keeping the romantic relationship alive in these gritty, realistic, fast-paced police-procedural detective stories that are set in twenty-first-century New York City and depict the adventures of police detective Eve Dallas and her husband, business tycoon Roarke. For brief annotations of these titles, consult www.jdrobb.com/jdbooks.htm.

Naked in Death. Berkley, 1995.
Glory in Death. Berkley, 1995.
Immortal in Death. Berkley, 1996.
Rapture in Death. Berkley, 1996.
Ceremony in Death. Berkley, 1997.
Vengeance in Death. Berkley, 1997.
Holiday in Death. Berkley, 1998.
"Midnight in Death" in *Silent Night*. Jove, 1998.
Conspiracy in Death. Berkley, 1999.
Loyalty in Death. Berkley, 1999.
Witness in Death. Berkley, 2000.
Judgment in Death. Berkley, 2000.
Betrayal in Death. Berkley, 2001.
"Interlude in Death" in *Out of This World*. Jove, 2001.
Seduction in Death. Berkley, 2001.
Reunion in Death. Berkley, 2002.
Purity in Death. Berkley, 2002.

Portrait in Death. Berkley, 2003.
Imitation in Death. Berkley, 2003.
Remember When. G. P. Putnam's Sons, 2003.
Written in conjunction with Nora Roberts, J. D. Robb's alter ego, this story of jewel theft and con men alternates between the present and the future.

Divided in Death. G. P. Putnam's Sons, 2004.
Visions in Death. G. P. Putnam's Sons, 2004.
Survivor in Death. G. P. Putnam's Sons, 2005.
Origin in Death. G. P. Putnam's Sons, 2005.
Memory in Death. G. P. Putnam's Sons, 2006.
"Haunted in Death" in *Bump in the Night*. Jove, 2006.
Born in Death. G. P. Putnam's Sons, 2006.
Innocent in Death. G. P. Putnam's Sons, 2007.
"Eternity in Death" in *Dead of Night*. Jove, 2007.
Creation in Death. G. P. Putnam's Sons, 2007.
Strangers in Death. G. P. Putnam's Sons, 2008.
Salvation in Death. G. P. Putnam's Sons, 2008.
"Ritual in Death" in *Suite 606*. Berkley, 2008.
Promises in Death. G. P. Putnam's Sons, 2009.
Kindred in Death. G. P. Putnam's Sons, 2009.
"Missing in Death" in *The Lost*. Jove, 2009.
Fantasy in Death. G. P. Putnam's Sons, 2010.
Indulgence in Death. G. P. Putnam's Sons, 2010.
Treachery in Death, G. P. Putnam's Sons, 2011.

Shinn, Sharon

Shinn writes Science Fiction and Fantasy novels, often laced with romance, some of which will also appeal to romance fans.

Jenna Starborn. Ace, 2002.
Orphaned, rejected, and working on a remote estate, nuclear generator technician Jenna finds belonging and love—after some major disappointments—in this futuristic retelling of *Jane Eyre*.

Sinclair, Linnea

Sinclair skillfully blends hard Science Fiction with Romance in her suspenseful, action-oriented stories.

Finders Keepers. Bantam Spectra, 2005.
A space trader captain becomes involved with stranger and swept up in a dangerous adventure when his ship crashes on the isolated planet where she is repairing her space ship.

An Accidental Goddess. Bantam Spectra, 2006.
A Special Forces captain is attacked and wakes up more than three hundred years later only to learn that the people consider her a goddess.

Games of Command. Bantam Spectra, 2007 (c. 2002).
Two former adversaries, a spaceship captain and an admiral, thwart a plot and find love in this sexy space opera adventure.

Down Home Zombie Blues. Bantam, Spectra, 2007.
A space commander and a homicide detective join forces in order to keep the Earth from being used as a breeding ground for biomechanical organisms run amok—and to keep Earth's people unaware of intergalactic life.

Dock Five Universe
An adventurous, intergalactic space opera series with various character links. (Dock Five is a dangerous, infamous outpost.)

*Gabriel's Ghost. Bantam Spectra, 2005.
Court-martialed and imprisoned for a crime she didn't commit, Imperial spaceship captain Chaz Bergren is rescued by Gabriel Sullivan, a man with super psychic gifts and who is supposedly dead, and helps him foil a diabolical plot with serious political ramifications. A Rita Award winner.

Shades of Dark. Bantam, 2008.
Chaz and Sully continue their fight to save the Empire and keep the enemies from breeding jukors, vicious war creatures.

Hope's Folly. Bantam, 2009.
Admiral Philip Guthrie, Chaz's ex-husband and member of a powerful family, reconnects with a girl (now a woman) from his past as he works to repair a rundown ship he will command as part of the rebel Alliance.

Rebels and Lovers. Bantam, 2010.
Devin Guthrie, Philip's youngest brother, joins forces with Captain Makaiden Griggs to find his teenage nephew when he disappears after his bodyguard is killed.

Ware, Joss
See chapter 13, "Linked Romances."

Paranormal Romance

> **Paranormal Romance**—A combination of romance and many things supernatural or unexplained by "natural causes," these stories can include vampires, werewolves, and other shapeshifters, ghosts, demons, succubi, psychics, and any number of other such beings, and many could be claimed by either this or the Urban Fantasy Romance subgroup.

This category is one of the most eclectic of the Alternative Reality Subgenres, basically incorporating everything not otherwise defined. Unless it falls within the new Urban Fantasy Romance parameters (and many stories previously included in this subgroup would), almost anything supernatural or unexplained by "natural causes" might be included here. Settings can be either historical or contemporary, and as with all romances, the love story drives the plot. Occasionally, aspects of the Paranormal will blend with another subtype, resulting in stories, for example, about time traveling vampires or futuristic psychics.

Selected Paranormal Romance Bibliography

Abé, Shana
Drakon Series
A powerful, magical race of shapeshifting, jewel-prizing dragon-people struggle to maintain their secret existence by allowing no one to leave Darkfrith without permission.

The Smoke Thief. Bantam, 2005.
The mysterious Smoke Thief is confounding the London authorities, but Christoff (Kit), Marquess of Langford and Drakon Alpha leader, knows it is a Drakon "runner," but he never expects it to be Clarissa Rue Hawthorne, a woman and a halfling (half human/half Drakon), at that.

The Dream Thief. Bantam, 2006.
A human jewel thief and Rue and Kit's clairvoyant daughter, Amalia, go on a dangerous quest for a fabled diamond that could prove disastrous to the Drakon in the wrong hands.

Queen of Dragons. Bantam, 2008.
Maricara, a princess from another Drakon tribe infiltrates Darkfrith and finds love with the Earl of Chasen, his clan's Alpha, as they realize they must join forces if they are to protect their kind from the hunters.

The Treasure Keeper. Bantam, 2009.
A young Drakon seamstress with the powers of invisibility and empathy ends up saving the imprisoned Rhys from a dangerous group of hunters and together they unmask a traitor.

The Time Weaver. Bantam, 2010.
A young Drakon woman has the dangerous ability to weave across time, but her relationship with the "man of her dreams" could fulfill the prophesy that could bring disaster to them all.

Bretton, Barbara
See also chapter 5, "Contemporary Romance."

Sugar Maple Series
Set in the enchanted town of Sugar Maple, Vermont, home to a variety of magical creatures, this series of stories revolves around knitting and has a large dose of the paranormal.

Casting Spells. Berkley Trade, 2008.
Chloe Hobbs, the half-witch owner of the local knitting shop, needs to find love in order to come into her magical powers so she can renew the deteriorating spell that protects the town. But will love with human Luke MacKenzie do the trick?

Laced with Magic. Berkley Trade, 2009.
Chloe continues to work on her relationship with Luke, deal with the townsfolk, and battle ghosts and a wicked Fae.

Spun by Sorcery. Berkley Trade, 2010.
When the entire town disappears, Chloe heads for Salem to get some answers.

Brown, Laurie
Hundreds of Years to Reform a Rake. Sourcebooks Casablanca, 2007.
A modern-day paranormal investigator goes back to Regency England to help a ghost reclaim his family's fortune.

What Would Jane Austen Do? Sourcebooks Casablanca, 2009.
A modern-day costume designer is swept back to 1814 on a mission to prevent a duel in this lively time travel romance with spy thriller overtones.

Cates, Kimberly
See also chapter 5, "Contemporary Romance."

Magic. Pocket, 1998.
When Fallon uses a magic brooch to summon warrior Ciaran out of the past to save Ireland from the ruthless English, she is faced with more than a legendary hero—she now has a man on her hands. Charming, sensual, and romantic.

Carroll, Susan
The Bride Finder (St. Leger) Trilogy
This haunting, magical, slightly Gothic trilogy focuses on the St. Leger family, in which the legendary Bride Finder selects appropriate brides for the men, and their matrimonial, paranormal, and lingering family issues.

The Bride Finder. Fawcett Columbine, 1998.
A delightful Beauty-and-the-Beast tale.

The Night Drifter. Fawcett Columbine, 1999.
A heroine thinks her night drifting hero is a ghost, only to discover he really can go through walls.

The Midnight Bride. Ballantine, 2001.
A vengeful plot turns into one of healing in the final volume of this memorable trilogy.

Cole, Kresley
Cole writes both Historical and Paranormal Romance.

Immortals after Dark Series
Inhabiting a world they call The Lore, creatures of myth and legend, immortal and powerful, walk among humans but fight for supremacy among themselves in this hot, creative series.

A Hunger Like No Other. Pocket Star, 2006.
Lachlan, leader of a werewolf clan, goes in search of his one true mate, Emmaline, only to discover she is a vampire—and vampires and werewolves are ancient enemies.

No Rest for the Wicked. Pocket Star, 2006.
An emotionless Valkyrie who ruthlessly kills vampires begins to feel again when she meets vampire Sebastian Wroth, but her quest for a prize in a race (the Talisman's Hie) that will change history and save her sisters may cost her that growing love.

Wicked Deeds on a Winter's Night. Pocket Star, 2007.
A werewolf still grieving after losing his mate competes in the Talisman's Hie for a prize that will change the past but can't resist the sizzling attraction he feels for a witch he is competing against.

Dark Needs at Night's Edge. Pocket, 2008.
The ghost of murdered ballerina Neomi Laress haunts the mansion where a nearly insane vampire, Conrad Wroth, has been imprisoned for his own safety and is as surprised that he can see her as he is that his attraction to her makes him want to control his anger.

Dark Desires after Dusk. Pocket, 2008.
Math grad student Holly Ashwin has no idea she's a halfling until a lightning strike awakens her Valkyrie tendencies and she's told she's to be a Vessel and give birth to a special child. Fortunately, she has rage demon Cadeon Woede to help her manage.

"Untouchable" A novella in *Deep Kiss of Winter*. Pocket, 2009.
A vampire and an ice fey-Valkyrie are passionately attracted to each other but her icy skin can't stand his touch.

Kiss of a Demon King. Pocket, 2009.
A powerful sorceress captures a demon king and together they find love and fulfill a prophecy. A Rita Award winner.

Pleasure of a Dark Prince. Pocket, 2010.
This prequel to some of the earlier books in this series takes the hero and heroine on an Amazon adventure as they try to find a way to defeat an evil god.

Demon from the Dark. Pocket, 2010.

Dreams of a Dark Warrior. Pocket, 2011.
Declan, killed before he could wed his love, Regin, is reincarnated but doomed to die when he remembers his past.

Davis, Justine

Davis also writes Futuristics and Contemporary Series Romances and also writes as Justine Dare. The following story is a memorable classic.

Angel for Hire. Silhouette Desire, 1991.
A guardian angel sent to Earth falls for the woman he has come to help in this contemporary romance that won the first Rita Award (1992) in the Futuristic/Fantasy/Paranormal category.

Deveraux, Jude

Deveraux writes romances of many types, many of which have paranormal or time travel elements. Her books about the Montgomery family (more than twenty as of this writing) span centuries and are some of her most popular.

An Angel for Emily. Pocket, 1998.
When Emily hits her guardian angel with her car, knocking him out and leaving him with no memory, she does what any helpful, small town librarian would do, she takes him home with her—and therein lies the story.

Forever Trilogy

A psychic heroine and a man delving into the mysteries of his past find love, separation, and sinister danger in this paranormal trilogy that features members of the Montgomery clan.

> *Forever*. Pocket, 2002.
> *Forever and Always*. Pocket, 2003.
> *Always*. Pocket, 2004.

Wild Orchids. Atria, 2003.
An author in search of inspiration after the death of his wife and a young storyteller go to rural North Carolina on the trail of the same bizarre "devil" story and realize that it might all be true.

Someone to Love. Atria, 2007.
Trying to solve the mystery of his fiancée's supposed suicide three years earlier, Jace Montgomery buys a haunted British estate and finds a persistent ghost who might have some of the answers and a beautiful journalist willing to help.

9

Erskine, Barbara

Erksine's gothically inclined books lean toward mainstream and often make use of reincarnation themes and other paranormal elements through which the past affects and often parallels the future. Many of her earlier works have been reprinted.

Whispers in the Sand. HarperCollins, 2000.
A recently single woman retraces her Victorian great-grandmother's Nile adventure and through her diary learns the terrifying truth about a mysterious scent bottle and the dangers it poses.

10

Hiding from the Light. HarperCollins, 2002.
A woman moves to an English village and becomes involved, along with the local rector, in the battle between seventeenth-century witch and witch finder ghosts that are beginning to have a disastrous affect on the town.

Feehan, Christine

11

Feehan is a best known for her Dark, Sea Haven novels (Drake Sisters and Sisters of the Heart), GhostWalker series. See also chapter 13, "Linked Romances."

The Scarletti Curse. Love Spell, 2001.
A healer summoned by the Scarlettis to care for a child is claimed by Don Giovanni Scarletti as his bride, even though Nicoletta has no wish to marry a man who carries the "Scarletti Curse." Note: This story is not part of the Dark series, but one of Giovanni and Nicoletta's descendants is the heroine in *Dark Symphony* (2003).

12

Freethy, Barbara

These warm, compelling contemporary romances have a dash of the paranormal. See also chapter 6, "Romantic Mysteries," and chapter 5, "Contemporary Romance."

*Daniel's Gift. Avon, 1996.
A boy hovering between life and death and his curmudgeonly guardian angel bring his long-estranged parents together. A Rita Award winner and one of her most memorable.

13

Ryan's Return. Avon, 1996.
Teenage sweethearts are reunited with a little ghostly help.

Graham, Heather

14

One of the most prolific writers in the Romance genre, Graham writes Contemporary, Historical, Romantic Suspense, as well as Paranormal Romance. She also writes as Shannon Drake and Heather Graham Pozzessere. Below are several of her more recent novels with paranormal elements.

15

Haunted. Mira, 2003.
The highly skeptical owner of a pre–Revolutionary Era estate that is said to be haunted calls in an investigation firm noted for its work with the supernatural, and is both irritated and attracted by the lovely psychic investigator who discovers that not all the threats are from the dead, and that someone very much alive wants to keep the secrets of Melody House hidden.

Ghost Walk. Mira, 2005.
Brent Blackhawk, an FBI psychic investigator brought in to check on the death of a fellow agent connects the dots and realizes that tour guide Nikki DuMonde might be in danger in this atmospheric New Orleans–set mystery with a paranormal bent.

16

The Vision. Mira, 2006.
A doubting hero and a heroine who sees ghosts combine with a real killer in this ghostly thriller.

Kiss of Darkness. Mira. 2006.
Believing a dark cult is once again at work when some grad students disappear in the forests of Transylvania, ancients Bryan McAllister and Jessica Fraser join forces to stop the evil—if they can.

The Dead Room. Mira, 2007.
After her fiancé is killed in an explosion and archaeologist Leslie MacIntyre suddenly has the ability to talk to ghosts, she returns to the site of the explosion and, with some ghostly help, learns that the explosion might not have been an accident. Although not really a romance, the romantic touches are still there.

The Death Dealer. Mira, 2008.
A social worker and a P.I. join forces to figure out if there is a link between the deaths of two members of an Edgar Allan Poe society in this thriller with a number of ghostly elements.

Nightwalker. Mira, 2009.
A whispered word from a dying man is enough to have Jessy Sparhawk seeing ghosts and P.I. Dillon Wolf and his ghostly sidekick on the trail of an old mystery and a modern-day killer.

Unhallowed Ground. Mira, 2009.
Ghosts, as well as a very real killer, are at work in this spooky story of a woman who is restoring an old mansion and makes a horrifying discovery and the P.I. who's investigating a missing person case.

Night of the Wolves. HQN, 2009.
Vampires and vampire slayers kick up the action and the romance in an Old West Texas setting.

Flynn Brothers Trilogy
Three P.I. brothers find love as they work to solve mysteries and murders with paranormal elements.

Deadly Night. Mira, 2008.
Aiden Flynn and psychic Kendall Montgomery find mysteries on the Flynn's inherited Louisiana plantation and links to a current serial killer.

Deadly Harvest. Mira, 2008.
Jeremy Flynn and psychic Rowena Cavanaugh find love and a killer in this chilling thriller set in witchy Salem, Massachusetts.

Deadly Gift. Mira, 2008.
Nurse Caer Cavannaugh, who is more than she seems, accompanies Sean Riley back from Dublin and attracts the interest and suspicion of Zach Flynn.

Prophecy Series
Characters rush to find a way to stop the destruction of the world in this projected four book series.

Dust to Dust. Mira, 2009
A graphic artist and a dog trainer share disastrous visions and head for Rome in search of the mysterious Oracle.

Guhrke, Laura Lee
  Not So Innocent. Pocket, 2003.
  A clairvoyant young woman warns a Scotland Yard detective that he may be in danger, but when an officer is killed, he begins to take notice in this Victorian Historical.

Handeland, Lori
Nightcreature Series
  Werewolves fill the night in Handeland's creative, compelling series.

  Blue Moon. St. Martin's Paperbacks, 2004.
  Hunter's Moon. St. Martin's Paperbacks, 2005.
  Dark Moon. St. Martin's Paperbacks, 2005.
  Crescent Moon. St. Martin's Paperbacks, 2006.
  Midnight Moon. St. Martin's Paperbacks, 2006.
  Rising Moon. St. Martin's Paperbacks, 2007.
  Hidden Moon. St. Martin's Paperbacks, 2007.
  Thunder Moon. St. Martin's Paperbacks, 2008.
  Marked by the Moon. St. Martin's Paperbacks, 2010.
  Moon Cursed. St. Martin's Paperbacks, 2011.
  Crave the Moon. St. Martin's Paperbacks, 2011.

Harbaugh, Karen
  See pervious editions of this guide for earlier titles, some of which have been reprinted. See also chapter 8, "Regency Romance."

De la Fer Family Series
  Night Fires. Dell, 2003.
  An immortal, Simone de la Fer, who avenges her family and then helps people escape from Revolutionary France finds unexpected love with an English spy.

  Dark Enchantment. Dell, 2004.
  An English nobleman saves a "boy" from a street fight and learns she is Catherine de la Fer, a noblewoman with secrets of her own, in this dark paranormal historical romance with Links to *Night Fires.*

Heath, Sandra
  Noted for exceptionally well-written Traditional Regencies steeped in the traditions and history of the British Isles, many with light paranormal elements. See also chapter 8, "Traditional Regency Romance."

  Mistletoe Mischief. Signet, 2000.
  A nobleman who distrusts "companions" finds himself falling for one in this funny, lively holiday tale that includes a matchmaking Lady and a meddling ghost.

  Breaking the Rules. Signet, 2001.
  Mismatched lovers, an inheritance, a delightful white wolfhound, and some magical interference add up to a funny, romantic Regency romp.

  Second Thoughts. Signet, 2002.
  A young widow applies to be a governess and receives a proposal of marriage from her potential employer, instead, in this Regency romance with an animal-linked paranormal twist.

Holly, Emma

Holly is noted for her steamy, sexually explicit romances. See also chapter 14, "Erotic Romance."

Midnight (Upyr) Series

Shapeshifting immortal Upyrs and other supernatural beings populate the pages of this diverse, generally loosely linked series.

"Luisa's Desire" in *Fantasy*. Jove, 2002.

Catching Midnight. Jove, 2003.

To learn more about the human world, Gillian, once human herself, transforms into a falcon and leaves her Upyr family in the Scottish woods and is captured by master falconer Aimery Fitz Clare in this fourteenth-century-set story.

Hunting Midnight. Berkley Sensation, 2003.

Crushed that Gillian has left him for a mortal, clan leader Ulric takes temporary solace in the arms of mortal women—and then he meets Juliana and things become much more complicated.

"The Night Owl" in *Hot Blooded*. Jove, 2004.

Courting Midnight. Berkley Sensation, 2005.

When ancient vampire Lucius takes the place of a dying man who looks exactly like him, he is tossed into a Regency social whirl and finds a woman who steals his heart, if she will still love him when she learns what he really is.

Kissing Midnight. Berkley Sensation, 2009,

A war with rogue vampires threatens to expose Edmund Fitz Clare's vampire identity to his family and Estelle, the woman he loves, in this cliff-hanger romance set in 1933 London. This and the two titles that follow came out in consecutive months and are closely linked stories that revolve around Edmund Fitz Clare.

Breaking Midnight. Berkley Sensation, 2009.

Edmund is kidnapped in the continuing battle among the vampires and it's up to his family to save him.

Saving Midnight. Berkley Sensation, 2009.

The members of the Fitz Clare clan continue to evolve beautifully in the final book of this series.

Demon World Series

This super sexy series is set in an alternate Victorian world where aristocratic demons (Yamas) are superior to humans.

The Demon's Daughter. Berkley, 2004.

A half-demon woman and a human police inspector enhanced by demon implants find romance when she finds him wounded on her doorstep.

Prince of Ice. Berkley, 2006.

A royal courtesan and a demon prince who knew each other as children are reunited when he buys her to be his "pillow girl."

Demon's Fire. Berkley Sensation, 2008.

A naive young woman and her cousin become part of an archaeological dig near the Yaman city of Bhamjran and, with a Prince who thought to never find love again, explore their desires in this story that includes characters from the first two books in the series.

Hooper, Kay

Hooper has written Contemporary series romances, as well as some contemporary Gothics and Romantic Suspense. Her recent suspenseful thrillers involve characters with psychic paranormal abilities, often a touch of romance, and are part of a single, overarching series.

Noah Bishop/Special Crimes Unit Series

Psychic FBI Profiler Noah Bishop is a key figure in these thrillers, even though the protagonists often vary in each story. The books within each trilogy are loosely linked in some way and may have continuing elements, but each story generally stands on its own.

Shadows Trilogy
Stealing Shadows. Bantam, 2000.
A psychic heroine who can tap into the heads of killers unsuccessfully tries to convince the law enforcement locals—until her prediction comes true.

Hiding in Shadows. Bantam, 2000.
When an accident victim, Faith, wakes from a coma, her journalist friend Dinah vanishes—and then Faith begins having strange visions she doesn't understand.

Out of the Shadows. Bantam, 2000.
Noah Bishop reconnects with psychic sheriff Miranda Knight when a demented, sadistic killer strikes in her small Tennessee town.

Evil Trilogy
Touching Evil. Bantam, 2001.
A Seattle psychic police sketch artist who can recreate the faces of killers is called in to help with a series of violent rapes that appear to be mimicking some that occurred during the 1930s.

Whisper of Evil. Bantam, 2002.
A psychic returns home and reconnects with her old flame to solve a rash of murders.

Sense of Evil. Bantam, 2003.
A psychic Special Crimes Unit operative who fits the killers' victim modus operandi becomes bait, much to the local police chief's distress in the "tie-up" book in this trilogy.

Fear Trilogy
Hunting Fear. Bantam, 2004.
A carnival psychic and a Special Crimes Unit operative join forces to outwit a psychopathic killer who has it in for the hero.

Chill of Fear. Bantam, 2005.
A psychic agent and a medium work together to solve the mystery of the evil that has infected a resort for years.

Sleeping with Fear. Bantam, 2006.
A psychic heroine, who's an occult expert, loses her recent memory and her mental powers and must rely on help from others in bringing down a murderer.

Blood Trilogy

This trilogy features the members of the Haven, a civilian "sister" organization to the Special Crimes Unit, as well as characters from earlier books in the series.

Blood Dreams. Bantam, 2008.
A psychic whose dreams often come true is caught up in the hunt for a serial killer.

Blood Sins. Bantam, 2008.
A Haven operative poses as a recent widow to infiltrate the Church of the Everlasting Sin in order to bring down a deranged preacher with lethal psychic powers.

Blood Ties. Bantam, 2010.
A serial killer has the entire Special Crimes Unit in his sites in this chilling final book in the trilogy that brings in a number of operatives.

Kenyon, Sherrilyn

Kenyon is noted for her numerous dark, sexy paranormals, many of which are part of or linked to her popular ongoing and ever-expanding Dark Hunter Series, which features strong men and women who give their souls to Artemis when they die in return for immortality, supernatural powers, and the chance for vengeance, and have an eternal mission to hunt soulless Daimons (vampires who kill people). An intriguing blend of ancient mythology and paranormal elements. Selected titles are listed below.

Fantasy Lover. St. Martin's Paperbacks, 2002.
A sex therapist summons a Greek love slave from the pages of a book where he has been trapped for two millennia.

Night Pleasures. St. Martin's Paperbacks, 2002.
Ancient Dark Hunter Kyrian of Thrace is on the hunt for a particularly evil Daimon and ends up magically handcuffed to Amanda Devereaux, a modern-day woman who wants nothing to do with the paranormal.

Night Embrace. St. Martin's Paperbacks, 2003.
When Sunshine Runningwolf saves Dark Hunter Talon from being killed during Mardi Gras, they are attracted to each other without realizing that they have been set up by some vengeful gods.

Night Play. St.Martin's Paperbacks, 2004.
Wolf Were-Hunter Vane Kattalakis and Bride McTierney unexpectedly end up mated when they spend the night together.

Seize the Night. St. Martin's Paperbacks, 2005.
When vampire hunter Tabitha Deveraux accidentally wounds Dark Hunter Valerius Magnus, she helps him, even though he is an enemy of her sister's husband.

Unleash the Night. St. Martin's Paperbacks, 2006.
Were-cat Wren Tigarian and human Maggie Goudeau find love in spite of their differences.

Devil May Cry. St. Martin's Press, 2007.
Ex-god Dark Hunter Sin joins forces with a woman who's been sent to kill him in order to thwart some demons who want to destroy the world.

Acheron. St. Martin's Press, 2008.
Dark Hunter leader, Acheron, finally gets his chance at love with Tory in this lengthy book that does fill in some gaps in Acheron's history.

Bad Moon Rising. St. Martin's Press, 2009.
Aimee Peltier must take on Daimons in order to save the life of were-hunter wolf Fang. Kattalakis

Retribution. St. Martin's Press, 2011.
A Dark Hunter and a human who's been protecting vampires by killing off Dark Hunters in revenge for her parents' deaths must work together or be killed by those who want both races to die.

Krinard, Susan
Krinard's sensual werewolf and vampire stories provide a gentler and more lyrical interpretation of these legends than most.

19th Century Werewolves
Traces the history and origins of the werewolf clans introduced in earlier stories. The first three books have been called the Forster Trilogy.

Touch of the Wolf. Bantam, 1999.
A werewolf determined to ensure the continuation of his race finds love with a young American werewolf seeking her heritage.

Once a Wolf. Bantam, 2000.
Revenge and treachery abound in this story that features reluctant werewolf Rowena Forster and Tomas Alejandro Randall.

Secret of the Wolf. Berkley, 2001.
When psychiatrist Dr. Johanna Schell finds Quentin Forster unconscious near her home, she takes him in to her establishment and eventually learns the truth about the demons that have been haunting him.

To Catch a Wolf. Berkley Sensation, 2003.
Crippled Athena Munroe and circus "wolfman" Morgan Holt learn of their similar werewolf heritage in this romance set in 1880s Denver.

To Tame a Wolf. HQN, 2005.
While searching for her brother, a young woman learns that the man she has hired to help her is a werewolf.

Bride of the Wolf. HQN, 2010.
A mail-order bride arrives at her future husband's ranch to find him missing (and ultimately dead) and is attracted to the ranch foreman, who is more than he seems.

Luck of the Wolf. HQN, 2010.
Estranged from his werewolf clan, Cort Renier wins a young woman in a San Francisco poker game who is not what she seems.

Roaring Twenties Vampires
Fast-paced adventure during a fascinating time period with the added panache of vampires.

Chasing Midnight. HQN, 2007.
Dark of the Moon. HQN, 2008.
Come the Night. HQN, 2008.

Kurland, Lynn
Kurland writes Fantasy, Paranormal, and Time Travel romances, some of which fall into more than one of these subcategories. Most of her books are part of the De

Piaget or MacLeod series. (See also the Fantasy and Time Travel bibliographies in this chapter.)

My Heart Stood Still. Berkley, 2001.
A businessman buys a ruined English keep and falls in love with the thirteenth-century ghost who claims it is hers. (MacLeod)

Much Ado in the Moonlight. Jove, 2006.
A play director and a bad tempered eight-hundred-year-old ghost find love, eventually, when Victoria MacKinnon comes to Thorpewood Castle to use it to stage *Hamlet*. (MacLeod)

Macomber, Debbie
Christmas Angel Series
These Christmas fantasies feature the wacky and unconventional doings of heavenly prayer ambassadors Shirley, Goodness, and Mercy as they try their best to obey the Archangel Gabriel and answer the prayers of a diverse group of people. (Note: These stories have been repackaged and reprinted multiple times.)

A Season of Angels. Harper, 1993.
The Trouble with Angels. Harper, 1994.
Touched By Angels. Harper, 1995.
Shirley, Goodness, and Mercy. Mira, 1999.
Those Christmas Angels. Harlequin Superromance, 2003.
Where Angels Go. Mira, 2007.

Mallory, Anne
See also chapter 7, "Historical Romances."

For the Earl's Pleasure. Avon, 2009.
A woman's paranormal abilities allow her to communicate with a badly wounded, unconscious nobleman she is attracted to but wary of because of his wild ways.

McCoy, Judi
McCoy's paranormal fantasies are often light-hearted, witty, sexy, and funny. Some of her recent titles follow.

I Dream of You. Zebra, 2001.
A recently jilted woman with a troubled graphic design firm finds a genii in a bottle with hilarious, romantic results.

Angel Trilogy
Angels at work in the human world generally achieve their goals in this lively, sometimes hilarious series.

Heaven in Your Eyes. Zebra, 2003.
A bit of angelic blackmail "encourages" Tom McAllister (deceased) to make sure his widow finds love in this funny, witty, sometimes suspenseful romp.

Heaven Sent. Zebra, 2003.
An angel sent to Earth as a mortal to learn a few virtues bonds with a young girl and falls for her widowed father.

Match Made in Heaven. Zebra, 2004.
A school teacher needing financial help for her foundering school and a wealthy man get a romantic nudge from above in this story of seductive wagers, tropical vacations, and blossoming love.

Goddesses Trilogy

Zeus sends three of his muse daughters to Earth for a year to prove they're effective, and, incidentally, they can't fall in love with mortals, or they'll lose their place on Olympus.

Almost a Goddess. Avon, 2006.
In a Las Vegas casino to prove to Zeus that humans can still believe in luck, Kyra, muse of Good Fortune, attracts the attention of a professional gambler sent to check into the casino's recent losses.

One Night with a Goddess. Avon, 2007.
Chloe, the Muse of Happiness, needs to show Zeus she's doing her job, but when her employer's doctor son returns from a disheartening stint in the third world, things become dicey.

Making over Mr. Right. Avon, 2008.
Zoe, Muse of Beauty, is up to the challenge of making over a computer genius—and then she falls for him.

Meyer, Stephenie
Twilight Saga

Seventeen-year-old Isabella (Bella) Swan moves to Forks, Washington, an isolated small town on the Olympic Peninsula and becomes involved with Edward Cullen and his family, a group of vampires that has sworn off drinking human blood, Jacob Black, part of a werewolf clan, and other assorted characters (good, bad, human, and otherwise) in an action-packed, blood-thirsty, angst-filled story that is told in the first person from Bella's point of view. Although intended for the YA market, which is not the target audience of this guide, this romantic paranormal series has been so popular with adults that it only made sense to include it.

Twilight. Little, Brown, 2005.
New to the high school, Bella is attracted to Edward and must come to terms with his vampiric nature, as well as danger from an evil, vindictive vampire.

New Moon. Little, Brown, 2006.
Edward leaves Bella when he realizes his family poses a threat to her and Bella teams up with Jacob and his protective clan and is somewhat torn between her feelings for both Edward and Jake.

Eclipse. Little, Brown, 2007.
The romantic tension and the danger ramps up as Jake and Edward compete for Bella's affections, but put their jealousies on hold, forego their long-standing clan feuds, and join forces to protect her from a pack of vengeful vampires.

Breaking Dawn. Little, Brown, 2008.
Bella and Edward finally tie the knot and get on with their lives together (as do others) in this final volume that ties up a number of loose ends.

Miller, Linda Lael
Vampire Series

These popular early vampire tales have been reprinted in two collections, *Out of the Shadows* (Berkley, 2002) and *Into the Night* (Berkley, 2002).

Forever and the Night. Berkley, 1993.
For All Eternity. Berkley, 1994.

Time without End. Berkley, 1995.
Tonight and Always. Berkley, 1996.

Moning, Karen Marie
Fever Series
The magical world of the Fae is the backdrop for this darker, erotic Paranormal series that is rich in Celtic lore and features a heroine on a quest and a pair of seductive men to tempt her. More dark fantasy than romance and would be equally at home within the Urban Fantasy Romance group.

> *Darkfever*. Delacorte, 2006.
> Seeking information about her sister's murder, MacKayla goes to Dublin and learns that she is able to see the *sidhe*, or Fae, something that most mortals can't do and an ability that could get her destroyed by the Fae. Enter mentor and potential romantic interest, Jericho Barrons.

> *Bloodfever*. Delacorte, 2007.
> *Sidhe*-seer and slayer Mac vows to avenge her sister's death in a world where the boundaries between the Faery and mortal worlds are becoming thinner.

> *Faefever*. Delacorte, 2008.
> Mac gains power and the quest continues, getting darker as it goes along.

> *Dreamfever*. Delacorte, 2009.
> The danger and sensuality levels increase as Mac learns more about herself and the *sidhe*, but more questions remain.

> *Shadowfever*. Delacorte, 2011.
> The stakes are raised, the action intensifies, and a number of secrets are finally revealed in the final installment of Moning's series.

O'Day-Flannery, Constance
O'Day-Flannery also writes Time Travel romances. (See previous edition of this book for additional earlier paranormal works.)

The Foundation
A secret society dedicated to bringing the world back into enlightened balance is the backdrop for this pair of paranormal romances.

> *Shifting Love*. Tor, 2004.
> A bookstore owner shapeshifter working for the shadowy Foundation and dedicated to healing men's hearts finds love, herself, with a widowed businessman.

> *Colliding Forces*. Tor, 2005.
> A TV news anchor is attracted to a man who is not quite what he seems and may well be involved in a conspiracy involving her TV station.

Yellow Brick Road Gang
Six friends support each other as they get their lives together and find love and spiritual answers in this paranormal trio filled with angels, sensuality, feminist ideas, and a healthy dose of metaphysics.

> *Best-Laid Plans*. Tor, 2006.
> *Twice in a Lifetime*. Tor, 2006.
> *Old Friends*. Tor, 2007.

9

Overfield, Joan

The Shadowing. Love Spell, 2002.
Under an ancient curse that he feels will result in his madness and wanting to provide for his clan, Laird Ruairdh McCairn plans to sell the family keep, but when he falls in love with appraiser Anne Garthwicke, the pair set out to make sure he doesn't fall victim to the Shadowing.

Putney, Mary Jo

Putney also writes Historicals, as well as an occasional Contemporary.

Kiss of Fate. Ballantine, 2004.
A heroine from a powerful Guardian family thinks she is giftless until a kiss from a powerful weather mage proves her wrong.

Stolen Magic. Del Rey, 2005.
Imprisoned in a unicorn's body by rogue Guardian Drayton, Simon is set free (and changed back) by Drayton's enchanted slave, Meg, and together they set out to stop Drayton's diabolical plans.

The Marriage Spell. Ballantine, 2006.
A woman with healing powers demands marriage as the price of saving the life of a nobleman; the results have much to say about society and prejudice.

A Distant Magic. Del Rey, 2007.
Nicolai, a pirate with untrained powers, kidnaps Jean, a Scottish Guardian weather mage, in the mistaken belief that he was betrayed and left to slavers by her father, but finds healing, understanding, and love as they work together to battle slavery in this wide ranging story that involves both magic and time travel.

Riley, Eugenia

The Phantom of the Bathtub. Love Spell, 2006.
A woman moves into a haunted house in 1896 Savannah, is haunted (in the bathtub) by the ghost of the house's original owner, and is annoyed by and attracted to her handsome next door neighbor.

Roberts, Nora

Many of Roberts's single titles are parts of trilogies or quartets, some of which, such as this one, have paranormal or fantasy elements. See also Fantasy bibliography above. See also chapter 5, "Contemporary Romance," chapter 6, "Romantic Mysteries," and chapter 13, "Linked Romances."

In the Garden

A troubled ghost, thought to be the "Harper bride," haunts the people and the grounds of the old Harper mansion and its gardens in Memphis. The titles refer to rare or nonexistent colors for each flower.

Blue Dahlia. Jove, 2004.
A widowed mom with a nursery management degree gets a job on the Harper estates in the Garden Nursery and clashes with as landscape architect.

Black Rose. Jove, 2005.
The owner of the Harper mansion hires a genealogy expert to look into the background of the mansion's ghost and falls in love with him, in spite of ghost's anger and trouble from other sources.

Red Lily. Jove, 2005.
A young single mom is attracted to the son of the mansion's owner in this story that finally unravels an old mystery and finds the truth that will allow the ghost to rest in peace.

Shayne, Maggie
Wings in the Night Series
This continuing vampire series remains one of Shayne's most popular and is a classic in the genre.

Twilight Phantasies. Silhouette, 1993.
Vampire Eric Marquand saved Tamara Dey's life when she was a child, but now she needs him again as they work to outwit the DPI and make sense of their feelings.

Twilight Memories. Silhouette, 1994.
Roland and Rhiannon, after being apart for centuries, finally come together when danger threatens.

Twilight Illusions. Silhouette Shadows, 1994.
P.I. Shannon Mallory, afflicted with a deadly blood disease, wants to find her friend's killer before she dies, and when she goes to vampire Damien with her questions, he feels compelled to protect her.

"Beyond Twilight" in *Strangers in the Night*. Silhouette, 1995.

Born in Twilight. Silhouette, 1997.
A novitiate who is attacked and turned into a vampire almost starves herself until Jameson Bryant saves her with his own blood—and then the bad guys from the vampire-hunting DPI come.

"Twilight Vows" in *Brides of the Night*. Silhouette Intimate Moments, 1998.

Twilight Hunger. Mira, 2002.
A writer who uses old journals describing the life of the vampire Dante, who earlier lived in the house of family friend, as the basis for a screenplay, is startled when Dante appears.

Embrace the Twilight. Mira, 2003.

"Run from Twilight" in *Two by Twilight*. Silhouette, 2003.
Edge of Twilight. Mira, 2004.
Vampire Edge and halfling Amber are hunting the evil Frank Stiles—but for very different purposes.

Blue Twilight. Mira, 2005.
P.I. Maxine and ex-cop Lou Malone become involved in a mysterious disappearance that seems to have paranormal aspects in this story that closely follows *Edge of Twilight*.

Prince of Twilight. Mira, 2006.
Vlad Dracul is forced to choose between his lost love and her reincarnation.

Demon's Kiss. Mira, 2007,
Loner vampire Reaper is suddenly part of a team hunting down renegade vamp Gregor, and he's not sure he likes it.

Lover's Bite. Mira, 2008.
Topaz decides to do some sleuthing into her mother's unsolved murder and is aided by Jack Heart, a vamp she thinks she can never trust again.

Angel's Pain. Mira, 2008.
Telling herself it's only to settle a score with bad vamp Gregor and her abusive step-father, Briar joins Reaper's gang and discovers she and Reaper share a lot more than she'd thought.

Silver, Eve
Otherkin Series
A prequel to this trilogy, *Sin's Daughter* (HQN, 2010), is available in download-able e-book format.

Sins of the Heart. HQN, 2010.
Dagan Krayl, a powerful soul reaper of the Underworld and son of Sutekh, and Roxy Tam, a Daughter of Aset (Otherkin) and sworn to protect humankind, find themselves working together in spite of the fact that they serve gods who are arch enemies.

Sins of the Soul. HQN, 2010.
Alastor Krayl, another soul reaper and son of the evil Underworld god, vows ven-geance for the death of one of his brothers, and secretive Underworld enforcer Naphré Kurata is the key to his quest.

Sins of the Flesh. HQN, 2010.
Soul reaper Malthus Krayl joins forces with Calliope Kane, a daughter of Aset and his supposed enemy, to avenge the death of his brother, Lokan, in a story that ties up the trilogy but leaves room for more.

Body of Sin. HQN, 2011.
Resurrected by his brothers but still trapped in the Underworld, Lokan needs the help of Bryn Carr, his daughter Dana's mother, to guide him out safely.

Simpson, Patricia
Ghosts and mysticism play important parts in many of Simpson's paranormal romances.

Forbidden Tarot
A deck of cursed tarot cards and an ancient power that threatens the present is at the heart of this dark, paranormal series.

The Dark Lord. Tor, 2005.
A professor inherits half a house from her mentor when he is killed, but needs to share it with her benefactor's difficult son in this story in which a chance action by a willful woman unleashes an ancient evil bent on revenge.

The Dark Horse. Tor, 2005.
The deck of cursed tarot cards turns up again in this story of linguistics expert Claire Coulter, who, to save her brother's life, agrees to go with her boss as he searches for the fountain of youth in the California desert, but is aided by enigmatic guide Jack Hughes when the evil erupts once again.

Spellbound. Lucky Publishing, 2009.
While on her way to her wedding in Scotland, Tara Lewis ends up in a crypt and ac-cidentally releases Hugh Lachlan, an enchanted medieval knight, who changes her life in a number of unexpected ways.

Skye, Christina
Draycott Abbey Series
This series overflows with ghosts, reincarnated people, mystery, and magic. Many have been reprinted.

"Enchantment" in *Haunting Love Stories*. Avon, 1991.

"What Dreams May Come" in *Bewitching Love Stories*. Avon, 1992.

Hour of the Rose. Avon, 1994.

Bridge of Dreams. Avon, 1995.

Bride of the Mist. Avon, 1996.
A psychic magazine publisher in Scotland trying to convince Duncan MacKinnon to allow her to use Dunraven Castle in her latest photo shoot finds far more than she expected when her psychic instincts kick in and Duncan's insane twin brother, Kyle, returns.

Key to Forever. Avon, 1997.
The search for an ancient family sword brings former lovers Alexei Cameron and Joanna Russell together.

Season of Wishes. Avon, 1997.
Ian McCall is hired to keep heiress Jamee Knight from being kidnapped and ends up falling for her in the process.

The Christmas Knight. Avon, 1998.
Medieval knight Ronan MacLeod comes into the present to help Hope O'Hara save her home in this holiday-linked romance.

The Perfect Gift. Avon, 1999.
A jewelry designer and a spy learn that they were involved in an ill-fated love affair in the past; this time they mean to get things right.

To Catch a Thief. HQN, 2008.
A Navy SEAL instructed to keep his eye on art expert Nell MacInnes sends her to Draycott Abbey for safekeeping when she is almost kidnapped in this complicated thriller that includes characters from both the Dracott Abbey and Code Name series.

Bound by Dreams. HQN, 2009.
Kiera Morissey is honoring a deathbed promise when she returns to Dracott Abbey, but when she enters the estate, she is attacked by thugs and rescued by a wolf, who just may have some connection to Calan MacKay.

Thompson, Vicki Lewis
See also chapter 5, "Contemporary Romance."

Hex Series
A pair of paranormal matchmakers, banished to Big Knob, Indiana, to deal with the resident dragon, decide to do a little human matchmaking as long as they are there.

Over Hexed. Onyx, 2007.
A gorgeous hunk has his sex appeal hexed away and is forced to convince the woman of his dreams to fall in love with him.

Wild & Hexy. Onyx, 2008.
A little matchmaking magic helps a beauty queen and a computer geek get together.

9

Casual Hex. Onyx, 2009.
A little magic causes problems when a fairy prince vies with a mortal for a woman's affections.

<u>Babes on Brooms Series</u>
Witches, magic, and romance.

Blonde with a Wand. Signet, 2010.
A witch is stripped of her powers when she turns her date into a cat for lying, but she needs him to undo the hex.

10

Chick with a Charm. Signet Eclipse, 2010.
A witch gives a sexy lawyer a love potion but then must wonder if his feelings for her are real.

Webber, Minda
Webber's stories, many of which are "fractured fairytales," are funny, witty, and lightly paranormal.

11

The Remarkable Miss Frankenstein. Love Spell, 2005.
Determined to win the Discovery of the Decade science award, Claire Frankenstein sets out to prove that vampires exist in this story that is filled with literary references and plenty of humor.

The Reluctant Miss Van Helsing. Love Spell, 2006.
A reluctant vampire slayer sets out to prove her worth by killing a powerful vampire only to end up married to him, instead.

12

Bustin'. Love Spell, 2007.
A hero and heroine from rival ghostbusting families fall for each other as the families battle for supremacy.

The Reinvented Miss Bluebeard. Love Spell, 2007.
For the sake of propriety, Eve Bluebeard, who runs an asylum for the paranormally insane, invents a husband—and then he shows up.

13

The Sisters Grimm. Love Spell, 2008.
A desperate mother sends her two daughters to Prussia—and the land of the vampires—to find husbands.

14

York, Rebecca (Pseudonym for Ruth Glick)
Many of York's Romantic Suspense stories have paranormal or supernatural elements. Her Moon series is one of her most popular and most enduring.

<u>Moon</u>
The books in this series, which have character links to the Marshall werewolf clan, have evolved from pure werewolf stories to include a parallel universe where paranormal powers are taken for granted.

15

Killing Moon. Berkley Sensation, 2003.
A researcher and a werewolf P.I. bring a serial killer to justice and find love in the bargain.

Edge of the Moon. Berkley Sensation, 2003.
A graphic designer and a detective become pawns in a magical battle between a magician and a demon.

16

Witching Moon. Berkley Sensation, 2003.
Vengeful witches cause problems for a werewolf swamp ranger and a psychic scientist in this fast-paced conclusion to this trilogy.

Crimson Moon. Berkley Sensation, 2005.
A werewolf who steals from those who harm the land is attracted to a wealthy lumberman's daughter, a woman who has secrets of her own.

Shadow of the Moon. Berkley Sensation, 2006.
A private club in Washington, D.C., leads its characters into deadly danger from a mind-draining creature from a parallel universe.

New Moon. Berkley Sensation, 2007.
A werewolf and an escapee from the parallel universe first introduced in *Shadow of the Moon* bond as they try to escape an evil that has followed the heroine into our world.

Ghost Moon. Berkley Sensation, 2008.
A woman from the other world comes through the veil and meets the ghostly werewolf who takes over the body of a murder victim with knowledge of a terrorist plot.

Eternal Moon. Berkley Sensation, 2009.
A pair of lovers who are meant to be together and who have met and been separated by demon interference over the centuries have another chance when they join forces, this time as a werewolf and a P.I., to track down a serial killer.

Dragon Moon. Berkley Sensation, 2009.
A slave sent across the veil to get things ready for her evil master's invasion of Earth encounters a werewolf, and while she wants to ask him for help, painful mental blocks stop her whenever she tries.

Day of the Dragon. Berkley Sensation, 2010.
First introduced in *Dragon Moon*, Ramsay Gallagher connects with an archaeologist who is in danger because of her current Italian dig in this thriller that is possibly the start of a new series.

Dark Warrior. Berkley Sensation, 2011.

Time Travel Romance

> **Time Travel**—Romance novels in which the characters are transported between/ among two or more time periods.

Traditionally, one of the more popular of the Alternative Reality Romance subgenres (although not the case as of this writing), the Time Travel romance features protagonists who are transported from one time period to another. The exchange is usually between the present and some time in the past, but other options are possible. Conflicts usually result because of time-based cultural differences (e.g., most often when a modern heroine ends up in the male-dominated past) or the fact that the hero and heroine are usually from different time periods and must make major sacrifices in order to stay together. Occasionally, a specific character is literally dropped into the body of someone in the time into which he or she has been transported. However, this is different from the typical reincarnation romance in which a person from the past is "reborn" as a person in a later time period.

Selected Time Travel Romance Bibliography

Cready, Gwyn

*Seducing Mr. Darcy. Pocket, 2008.
When a "therapeutic" massage sends modern day ornithologist Flip Allison into Mr. Darcy's arms for one fantasy night in Regency England, she is shocked to realize she has changed Austen's story and needs to fix it fast—if only she can convince the arrogant academic, Magnus Knightly, to help her. A Rita Award winner.

Gabaldon, Diana

Noted for her Outlander Series, a classic time travel romance series that is still in progress.
See chapter 13, "Linked Romances."

Graham, Heather

Home in Time for Christmas. Mira, 2009.
Jake Mallory, a Revolutionary War patriot about to be hanged, is suddenly swept into the twentieth century and the life of a surprised Melody Tarleton.

Heath, Sandra

Heath is a well-known writer of Regency romances, some of which have paranormal and time travel elements.

Magic at Midnight. Signet, 1998.
An unhappy modern-day wife changes places with an equally miserable Regency bride with the hope that happiness will come to both.

Hill, Sandra

See chapter 13, "Linked Romances."

Joy, Dara

Rejar. Love Spell, 1999.
Following *Knight of a Trillion Stars* (1995), this tale takes a time traveling "cat" shapechanger, sets him down in Regency England where he becomes the most eligible bachelor in the *ton*, and pairs him with the one woman he has to fight to win.

Krinard, Susan

Twice a Hero. Bantam, 1997.
A young woman goes to the Mayan jungle to fulfill her grandfather's dying wish that she return a stolen artifact and is swept back to 1884 and into the life of her adventurer great-great grandfather's handsome partner.

Kurland, Lynn

Kurland writes Fantasy, Paranormal, and Time Travel romances, some of which fall into more than one of these subcategories. Most of her books are loosely linked and are part of the De Piaget and/or MacLeod series. (See also Fantasy and Paranormal romance bibliographies in this chapter.)

A Dance Through Time. Jove, 1996.
A romance writer ends up in Medieval Scotland, but when she saves the hero's life, she changes the future—and she and the hero must go to the future to fix things. (MacLeod)

The Very Thought of You. Jove, 1998.
A woman determined to protect her estate and avoid marriage to a vile suitor, sets out to kidnap the suitor's brother and ends up with time traveler Alex Smith, instead. (MacLeod)

The More I See You. Jove, 1999.
A woman transported to the thirteenth century falls in love with her chivalrous knight but returns to the present so he can marry as the King decrees and save his lands. (De Piaget)

A Garden in the Rain. Berkley, 2003.
A woman vacationing in Scotland after being betrayed by her partner and fiancé is attracted to Patrick MacLeod, a man from the thirteenth century who prefers life in the present day. (MacLeod)

Dreams of Stardust. Jove, 2005.
A gemologist finds himself back in the thirteenth century, attracted to a noblewoman and frustrated with his lack of wealth to win her. If only he could return home—and come back with the gold he has there. (De Piaget)

When I Fall in Love. Jove, 2007.
Violinist Jennifer McKinnon despairs of finding the right man until she falls through a time portal and ends up with Nicholas De Piaget, a true life-saving hero, in the thirteenth century. (De Piaget and MacLeod)

With Every Breath. Jove, 2008.
When she moves into the ancient witch's cottage on the MacLeod estate, Sunny Phillips is shocked when Robert Cameron comes seeking the MacLeod witch to save his brother and drags her into the past with him. (MacLeod)

Till There Was You. Jove, 2009.
When time traveling Zachary Smith ends up in a thirteenth-century dungeon with Mary de Piaget, he knows he can't disrupt the past. And then Mary is poisoned and he must do something to save her. (De Piaget)

One Enchanted Evening. Jove, 2010.
Montgomery De Piaget and Pippa Alexander find danger and love in a dilapidated English Castle in this lively, magical story. (De Piaget)

One Magic Moment. Jove, 2011.
Tess Alexander finds more that medieval research to intrigue her when she moves into a restored castle and meets sexy John De Piaget, a mechanic with a strong resemblance to a man who married her sister—centuries earlier. (De Piaget)

MacAlister, Katie

Steamed: A Steampunk Romance. Signet, 2010.
A lab explosion sends a scientist and his sister into the steam-powered quasi-Victorian world of his favorite novel and onto the airship of a fierce, but lovely, Aerocorps captain.

Markham, Wendy

If Only in My Dreams. Signet Eclipse, 2006.
Diagnosed with breast cancer, a film star suddenly ends up in 1941and falls in love with a soldier doomed to die at Normandy.

The Best Gift. Signet Eclipse, 2009.
Picking up where *If Only in My Dreams* leaves off, our heroine, now happily married to a reincarnated version of her soldier, is celebrating Christmas by telling her husband she is pregnant, when an earthquake strikes and she ends up in 2012—alone.

Maverick, Liz

These two related stories creatively combine romance, suspense, cyberpunk, and time travel.

Wired. Dorchester Shomi, 2007.
A computer programmer is caught between two men and their ambitions in this cyperpunk romance.

Irreversible. Dorchester Shomi, 2008.
A woman relives a perfect week, over and over, never realizing it is not real until she is rescued by a time anomaly expert.

Moning, Karen Marie
Highlander Series

This darkly magical series featuring an assortment of virile Scottish heroes with differing abilities is sexy, lively, compelling, and graced with occasional flashes of humor.

Beyond the Highland Mist. Dell, 1999.
In a vengeful pique, the Queen of the Fairies sends modern-day Adrienne de Simone back to the sixteenth century and into the life of an arrogant Scottish laird—as his bride.

To Tame a Highland Warrior. Dell, 1999.
A powerful warrior afraid of his berserker tendencies resists love but is eventually healed by the woman who has adored him for years in this Historical with only minimal paranormal elements.

The Highlander's Touch. Dell, 2000.
After touching a magical flask, the heroine ends up in the bathroom of a fourteenth century warrior in this romance that deals with a serious medical issue.

Kiss of the Highlander. Dell, 2001.
An American tourist accidentally wakens an enchanted sixteenth-century Scottish nobleman when she slides down a hill and into the cave where he's lying.

The Dark Highlander. Dell, 2002.
A druid, plagued by a baker's dozen of evil druid spirits, knows that art historian Chloe Zanders is the one person who can help rid him of his demons.

The Immortal Highlander. Delacorte, 2004.
Punished for his constant interference by the Queen of the Fae, immortal Adam Black, now powerless and invisible to humans, goes to America to find his son and ask for help and meets *sidhe*-seer Gabby O'Callaghan, who wants nothing to do with the dangerous Fae.

Spell of the Highlander. Delacorte, 2005.
A druid bound into a mirror ends up in the possession of a Chicago grad student, who ends up being his soul mate.

O'Day-Flannery, Constance

O'Day-Flannery was one of the earlier writers of time travel romances. (See previous edition of this guide for additional earlier works, some of which have been reprinted.)

Anywhere You Are. Avon, 1999
A woman skydives (courtesy of a government experimental glitch) into the arms of a former Civil War veteran on a vision quest, and finds a plant that might cure her brother's cancer, if only they can get it back to the future.

Once and Forever. Avon, 1999.
While wandering through a maze at a Renaissance Faire, a woman ends up in the sixteenth century, involved in a political plot, and in love with a man she doesn't want to leave.

Heaven on Earth. Avon, 2000.
A heroine is zapped by lightening back to 1878 Santa Fe and meets another time traveler with romantic results. Good detail about Hispanic American culture of the period.

Time after Time. Avon, 2001.
A woman is swept back a hundred years into post–Civil War Louisiana and finds love with a widower who looks just like her late husband.

Here and Now. Avon, 2001.
A man from the 1920s and a woman from the present, both betrayed and disillusioned, find healing and love when the hero jumps into a river and is rescued by the heroine.

Riley, Eugenia
Many of Riley's Time Travel romances have Southern or Western settings. (See previous edition of this guide for additional earlier works, some of which have been reprinted.)

Phantom in Time. Avon, 1996.
A modern-day chorus girl finds love—and a bit of danger—with a Victorian opera tenor.

Waltz in Time. Avon, 1997.
A time traveling matchmaker finds a match of her own in the Old South. A Holt Medallion Award winner.

Embers of Time. Love Spell, 2000.
Time travel with a Charleston setting.

Bushwacked Bride. Love Spell, 2004.
While on an academic excursion to a ghost town, Jessica Garrett's coach is attacked by robbers and suddenly she is back in the real Old West with the four Recklaw brothers vying for her hand in marriage.

Bushwacked Groom. Love Spell, 2004.
A contemporary cowboy goes off a cliff and ends up in a marriage of convenience to Molly Recklaw in the Old West. Follows *Bushwacked Bride*.

Sizemore, Susan
Sizemore is best known for her Historical, Time Travel, and Paranormal Romances.

A Kind of Magic. Cerridwen, 2007.
A modern-day engineer is zapped back to thirteenth-century Scotland where she ends up being handfasted to the autocratic Laird of the Murray clan.

Speer, Flora M.
Timestruck. Love Spell, 2000.
A twentieth-century heroine working on a Y2K project is zapped back to eighth-century Francia and Charlemagne's politically complex reign and into the life of handsome, heroic Dominick. This historically detailed story is linked to *A Time to Love Again* (1993) and *A Love Beyond Time* (1994), which were reprinted in 2000 and 1999, respectively.

Stover, Deb

Although some of Stover's earlier romances were light and funny (see the earlier edition of this guide), the title below is a fast-paced thriller with chilling paranormal aspects.

The Gift. Love Spell, 2009.
Driven to drink by her empathic ability to experience a murder victim's last memories, ex-homicide detective Beth Dearborn, now a recovering alcoholic and insurance investigator, goes to rural Tennessee to investigate a seven-year-old missing person/death claim and finds mystery, love, and a spirit who needs to be heard.

Urban Fantasy Romance

Urban Fantasy Romance—Romance novels, usually with contemporary settings, that feature preternatural beings living among and interacting, often openly, with humans.

One of the more recent subgroups within the Alternative Reality subgenre, Urban Fantasy Romance is an outgrowth of the larger Urban Fantasy subgenre, which features preternatural beings living among and interacting, often openly, with humans. Like the parent subgenre, these stories usually feature suspenseful, action-oriented plots and often involve violent, life-and-death struggles among the various powerful factions; they also employ a wide variety of contemporary settings, ranging from gritty urban environments to bucolic rural, small town, or ranch settings. Although the tone is often dark and intense, lighter, fun-filled stories are not uncommon, and the sensuality levels, as do character types, range across the board. Modern-day vampires, shape-changers, witches, demons, and immortals of various types (immortals charged with keeping humanity safe are especially popular at the moment) are only a few of the myriad characters that are part of this inclusive, flexible subgroup that often merges with others within the larger Alternative Reality/Paranormal/Speculative Fiction subgenre. In many cases, these stories could be claimed by more than one genre or subgenre at the same time.

Selected Urban Fantasy Romance Bibliography

Ashley, Jennifer
Shifters Unbound

Shifters of various types face discrimination (e.g., forced to live in Shiftertown, wear aggression-controlling collars) in this gritty, sexy series that is filled with mystery and adventure.

Pride Mates. Leisure, 2010.
A human attorney must depend on her dangerously attractive lion shifter client when a feral shifter targets them both.

Primal Bonds. Leisure, 2011.
A half wolf shifter/half Fae woman comes to Shiftertown to escape an aggressive would-be mate and agrees to a "mating-in-name-only" to Siftertown Guardian Sean Morrissey so she can stay.

Bast, Anya
Elemental Witch Series

Witches with various "elemental" gifts and talents fight demons, warlocks, and others who would destroy them in this sensual series.

Witch Fire. Berkley Sensation, 2007.
Gifted with the ability to control fire, Jack McAllister is assigned by the Coven to guard Mira Hoskins, who has no idea she is an air witch, from a group of wicked witches out to steal her power.

Witch Blood. Berkley Sensation, 2008.
Water witch Isabelle Novak and earth witch Thomas Monahan join forces to fight a demon.

Witch Heart. Berkley Sensation, 2009.
Claire is rescued by handsome playboy fire witch Adam Tyrell, who is assigned to keep her safe from demons who will kill for the power her demon master "gave" her before he thrust her out of Eudae.

Witch Fury. Berkley Sensation, 2009.
A fire witch who has no idea of her nature is kidnapped by a powerful earth witch who thinks she is in cahoots with the evil warlocks in this rousing finish to the series.

Briggs, Patricia
River Marked. Ace, 2011.
Part of her ongoing Mercy Thompson Urban Fantasy series, this episode has more romance than some and may appeal to romance fans, as well as introduce them to a new fantasy genre.

Butcher, Shannon K.
See also chapter 6, "Romantic Mysteries."

The Sentinel Wars Series

Immortal Theronai warriors, who need soul mates to drain off toxic energy so they don't lose their souls, struggle to protect humanity from the Synestryn demons in this gripping Urban Fantasy Romance series.

Burning Alive. Onyx, 2009.
A woman meets the man (actually a Theronai warrior) she has seen watching her burn alive in her nightmares, and is attracted to him in spite of her fears.

Finding the Lost. Onyx, 2009.
A woman struggling to save children, including her sister, from the Synestryn, meets a Theronai warrior who may be able to help but who needs her, as well.

Running Scared. Onyx, 2010.
A woman, fearing and hating the Theronai, rethinks her involvement in a plot to destroy them when she realizes the truth of the situation.

Living Nightmare. Signet, 2010.
Nika, a Sentinel woman determined to find her kidnapped sister and Mardoc, a Theronai warrior who's on the verge of losing his soul, work against tremendous odds to accomplish their goals.

Blood Hunt. Signet, 2011.
Hope, a woman with no past but with a strange power in her blood is caught between a cruel lord who would steal her power and a Sanguinar demon-slayer who needs her blood to survive.

Cameron, Stella
See also chapter 5, "Contemporary Romance," chapter 6, "Romance Mysteries," and chapter 7, "Historical Romance."

Court of Angels Series
This New Orleans–set Paranormal Romantic Suspense trilogy focuses on the Millets, an ancient family of clairvoyants, and their battle with the underworld Embran race. Rich with French Quarter atmosphere.

Out of Body. Mira, 2010.
Marley Millet sees women being tortured and killed and teams up with a former cop (now a journalist) to stop the murders.

Out of Mind. Mira, 2010.
Willow Millet tries to deny her psychic heritage but is forced to reconsider when her clients start dying.

Out of Sight. Mira, 2010.
Artist Sykes Millet and Poppy Fortune must work together to stop the evil Embrans.

Davidson, MaryJanice
Davidson's Undead (Vampire Queen Betsy) and Wyndham Werewolf series are two of her most popular. See chapter 13, "Linked Romances."

Dodd, Christina
Darkness Chosen Series
A deal with the Devil defied a millennium ago visits vengeance on the Wilder family in this shapeshifting paranormal family saga in which the pieces of an icon must be found in order to save their souls.

Scent of Darkness. Signet, 2007.
Seeing her boss change from a wolf into a man, Ann Smith ultimately learns his family history and knows it must be up to her to break the curse.

Touch of Darkness. Signet, 2007.
Archaeologist Rurik Wilder and journalist Tasya Hunnicutt meet and discover they are looking for the same artifact, but for different reasons.

Into the Shadow. Signet, 2008.
Warlord Adrik Wilder and businesswoman Karen Sonnet connect passionately in Nepal, but even though he sends her away for her safety, he finds her again.

Into the Flame. Signet, 2008.
Firebird Wilder learns she's not the biological child of her parents and her college love, Doug Black, learns he *is* a Wilder in this story that nicely—and violently—resolves all issues and ties up the series.

The Chosen Ones Series
In the dawn of time, twins, born and cast aside because of imperfections, were rescued and came into their gifts—one would bring light to the world, the other

would bring darkness and destruction. As they gathered similarly gifted others around them, the lines between good and evil were drawn and their descendents became known as the Chosen, or the Others, and the fight extends to this day.

> *Storm of Visions*. Signet, 2009.
> Seer Jacqueline Vargha denies her gift until a disaster, and Caleb D'Angelo, make her acknowledge her true destiny.

> *Storm of Shadows*. Signet, 2009.
> Picking up where *Storm of Visions* ends, librarian Rosamund Hill thinks the legend of the Chosen ones is simply a myth—until Aaron Eagle arrives and convinces her otherwise.

> *Chains of Ice*. Signet Select, 2010.
> While on a wildlife expedition to Russia, Genny Valente is charged with also locating John Powell, who has been secluded in the Ural Mountains, and convince him to return home because he and his gifts are needed.

> *Chains of Fire*. Signet Select, 2010.
> A Chosen mind-control expert and a healer are trapped in an avalanche, deliberately arranged by the Others, when they go to rescue a child.

Feehan, Christine

Feehan's GhostWalker series includes Urban Fantasy elements and will appeal to fans of that subgenre. See chapter 13, "Linked Romances."

Frost, Jeaniene
Night Huntress Series

Written in the first person, this nonstop series focuses on the hair-raising adventures and intense interpersonal relationships of half-human/half-vampire vampire slayer heroine Cat Crawfield and her star-crossed love relationship with vampire hunter, Bones.

> *Halfway to the Grave*. Avon, 2007.
> Cat has been killing the un-dead quite successfully until she runs into Bones, who eventually convinces her to team up with him.

> *One Foot in the Grave*. Avon, 2008.
> Four years later, Cat goes after rogue vamps for the government and is no longer with Bones—until she becomes an assassination target and he's the only one who can save her.

> *At Grave's End*. Avon, 2009.
> Now married, Cat and Bones are both members of the government team but must deal with assassins and a potentially deadly political plot.

> *Destined for an Early Grave*. Avon, 2009.
> Just when Cat thinks things have calmed down, the hidden past returns to turn her world upside down.

> *This Side of the Grave*. Avon, 2011.
> Cat and Bones face new challenges as tensions increase between the ghouls and the vampires.

Night Huntress World

Cat's world expands to focus on other characters.

> *First Drop of Crimson*. Avon, 2010
> Cat's best friend, Denise, contacts vampire Spade when her relatives are killed by demons and she realizes she needs help.

Eternal Kiss of Darkness. Avon, 2010.
Private investigator Kira Graceling goes to the aid of someone who needs help and is drawn into the dangerous world of vampire Mencheres.

Gay, Kelly
The Better Part of Darkness. Pocket Books, 2009.
Single mom, cop Charlie Madigan, killed and subsequently resurrected with strange new powers, works with her gorgeous alien siren partner Hank Williams to track down a dangerous new drug that has been brought to Atlanta through the portals that lead to two parallel worlds, Elysia and Charbydon.

Havens, Candace
Noted for her witty, sassy urban fantasies with a chick lit flair.

Bronwyn the Witch
The adventures of Bronwyn, high witch, protector, and undercover agent for the British Prime Minister, and her struggle to combine her demanding career with her personal life.

Charmed and Dangerous. Berkley, 2005.
In addition to fighting the bad guys and staying alive, a handsome sheik and a gorgeous doctor (who's also a warlock) pose romantic problems for Bronwyn, who never dates clients or warlocks.

Charmed and Ready. Berkley, 2006.
Bronwyn takes on demons and the paparazzi in this latest romp.

Charmed and Deadly. Berkley, 2007.
An evil ex-boyfriend who has it in for Bronwyn is the villain in this fast-paced story.

Caruthers Sisters
This series features four wealthy, socialite sisters with paranormal abilities and, as the Guardian Keys, they have a mission to keep the world safe.

The Demon King and I. Berkley, 2008.
Gillian Caruthers, assassin of demons, is surprised when the new Demon King calls for a truce to fight a common enemy; she's even more surprised to be attracted to him.

Dragons Prefer Blondes. Berkley, 2009.
When an enemy dragon warrior decides Alex Caruthers is the woman for him, dragon slayer Alex Caruthers convinces the head of Caruthers security to pretend to be her boyfriend.

James, Allyson
Dragon Master Series
This paranormal series has good splashes of humor and suspense.

Dragon Heat. Berkley Sensation, 2007.
A young woman inherits her grandmother's apartment—complete with shape-changing dragon.

The Black Dragon. Berkley Sensation, 2007.
A powerful young witch and a bad boy dragon work to save his dwindling race.

The Dragon Master. Berkley Sensation, 2008.
Fire dragon Seth blazes into the life of restaurateur Carol who has no idea of her dragon master powers until dark forces bring Seth into her life.

Jewel, Carolyn

My Wicked Enemy. Grand Central, 2008.
An orphaned heroine comes into her own—and her true powers—when she flees her duplicitous mentor and meets a demon lord who has killing her on his To Do list.

My Forbidden Desire. Grand Central, 2009.
A witch, a demon bodyguard, and a magical amulet are part of this adventure that follows *My Wicked Enemy*.

Knight, Deidre
Gods of Midnight Series

Greek mythology and an alternate world form the basis for this action-packed series full of adventure and immortal Spartan warriors.

Red Fire. Signet Eclipse, 2008.
Ajax and Shay must solve a prophecy if they are to be together.

Red Kiss. Signet Eclipse, 2009
Emma Lowery draws blood with an enchanted dagger only to have it transformed into Spartan slave River.

Red Demon. Signet Eclipse, 2010.
A bargain with a djinn brings passion and problems for Aristos and his long-lost love Juliana.

Red Mortal. Signet Eclipse, 2011.
Daphne, the Oracle of Delphi, and Leonidas battle Ares in the final book in the quartet.

Liu, Marjorie M.
Dirk & Steele

Focusing on members of an organization of people who have various special psychic abilities, these paranormal thrillers use a wide variety of settings, many in the Far East.

Tiger Eye. Love Spell, 2005.
When Dela opens a Chinese puzzle box, she releases a virile ancient warrior and is swept up in an adventure that involves drug rings, the evil Magi, and a love she'd never imagined.

Shadow Touch. Love Spell, 2006.
A psychic healer saves the life of a Dirk & Steele operative when they are both kidnapped by the same evil consortium, and in doing so they are linked telepathically.

Red Heart of Jade. Love Spell, 2006.
On the hunt for a serial killer, who appears to be a shapeshifting dragon, Dean Campbell is shocked to meet a woman from his teenage past, a woman he was certain had died years earlier.

Eye of Heaven. Leisure, 2006.
Blue Perrineau's search for a stepbrother he never knew about takes him to a Las Vegas circus and lovely shapeshifter Iris McGillis—and into a whole lot of danger.

Soul Song. Leisure, 2007.
A violinist who can foresee death and an enchanted merman forced to steal mortal souls with his songs find an unexpected bond as they fight the deadly forces that are after them.

The Last Twilight. Leisure, 2008.
The evil Consortium is up to its wicked ways and this time the adventure takes Dr. Rikki Kinn to virus-plagued Africa and into the life of Dirk & Steele operative Amiri.

The Wild Road. Leisure, 2008.
A woman, waking in a bloody, body-strewn hotel room with no memory, takes a cryptic note's advice and runs—straight into Lannes Hannelore, a gargoyle who can sense her thoughts and who sets out to help her.

The Fire King. Leisure, 2009.
A wounded language expert and a three-thousand-year-old chimera who is on someone's hit list are the leads in this taut, treachery-laced thriller.

MacAlister, Katie

MacAlister's books tend to be funny, sexy, inventive with zany plots, and laced with angst.

Dark Ones Series

Dark Ones (vampires without souls) stalk the night in the quirky stories in this Contemporary Urban Fantasy series.

A Girl's Guide to Vampires. Love Spell, 2003.
Skeptic Joy Randall takes on vampires—and others—in the Czech Republic.

Sex and the Single Vampire. Love Spell, 2004.
A vampire hero looking for love and a heroine who summons ghosts, demons, and assorted spirits find the romantic road a bit rocky.

Sex, Lies, and Vampires. Love Spell, 2005.
A heroine who can charm away curses is sent to find and save a hero cursed to betray his fellow vampires.

Even Vampires Get the Blues. Signet, 2006.
A vampire in search of a relic to save his mother from losing her soul is attracted to the half-elf P.I. he hires to help him in his quest.

Last of the Red-Hot Vampires. Signet, 2007.
A magical gift, a not-quite-human champion, and some difficult faery tests are challenges for the heroine.

Zen and the Art of Vampires. 2008.
Pia, giving up on her dream of marriage, goes on a trip to Iceland and ends up with a husband—and more—in this story that is continued in the next book.

Crouching Vampire, Hidden Fang. Signet, 2009.
Pia, now alone, heads to Seattle where she eventually decides to make her marriage work, even though the odds seem against it since she's someone's target and her husband doesn't seem to want her around.

Aisling Grey Series
    This funny, sassy series features the adventures of apprentice Guardian and sleuth Aisling Grey and wyvern Drake Vireo, leader of the green dragons and Aisling's "assigned" mate, as they deal with murders, wars, demons, mages, and other assorted creatures and events.

> *You Slay Me*. Onyx, 2004.
> Aisling and Drake meet over a dead body and before long Aisling is the chief suspect and is heading into the underworld after Drake to clear herself of the crime.

> *Fire Me Up*. Signet, 2005.
> Murder, romance, and danger in Budapest.

> *Light My Fire*. Signet, 2006.
> Still learning to be a Guardian, Aisling must deal with Drake, imps, and other dangers while studying in London.

> *Holy Smokes*. Signet, 2007.
> Aisling goes after Drake when he disappears before their wedding.

Silver Dragons
    Torn between her demon boss, Magoth, and her silver dragon lover, Gabriel, doppelganger shadow twin Mayling Northcott has her hands full in this adventurous series.

> *Playing with Fire*. Signet, 2008.
> May and Gabriel meet when she is sent on a burglary mission to his estate and he realizes she is his intended mate and decides to claim her.

> *Up in Smoke*. Signet, 2008.
> Gabriel has his own reasons for advising a wary May to go through with the consort ceremony with her evil demon boss.

> *Me and My Shadow*. Signet, 2009.
> Life becomes even more complicated for May as a dragon war seems to be brewing and she must deal with her love for Gabriel and life with Magoth.

Michelle, Patrice
    See also chapter 14, "Erotic Romance."

Scions Series
    An ancient prophecy links the stories in this vampire and werewolf-rich Urban Fantasy series.

> *Scions: Resurrection*. Silhouette Nocturne, 2008.
> A new author inadvertently resurrects the supposedly extinct vampire race when she writes about a legendary vampire prediction.

> *Scions: Insurrection*. Silhouette Nocturne, 2008.
> A police officer and a P.I. are caught up in a battle between vampires and werewolves.

> *Scions: Perception*. Silhouette Nocturne Bites, 2008.
> This is a linked novella available in e-book format only.

> *Scions: Revelation*. Silhouette Nocturne, 2008.
> A woman wanting to find her kidnapped aunt joins forces with a werewolf who eventually needs her help to save his clan, as well.

Morgan, Alexis (Pseudonym for Pat Pritchard)
Paladins of Darkness Series

A race of immortal warriors, who die over and over again but lose a bit of their humanity and sanity each time it happens, battle the Others in an ongoing effort to save humankind.

Dark Protector. Pocket, 2006.
Paladin Devlin Bane, fearing he is losing his struggle to keep his humanity, falls in love with Dr. Laurel Young, his mortal Handler, who revives him each time he dies.

Dark Defender. Pocket Star, 2006.
Paladin Blake Trahain tracks down a traitor among their ranks and struggles to keep the woman he has loved since he was a teen safe.

In Darkness Reborn. Pocket Star, 2007.
Barak, an exiled Other, works with the Paladins to discover who is benefiting from this constant conflict between the two races and is attracted to geologist Lacey Sebastian.

Redeemed in Darkness. Pocket Star, 2007.
Paladin Cullin Finley, trapped in the Other world while carrying a message, is sheltered by Lusahn, and he learns of the desperate plight of the Others.

Darkness Unknown. Pocket Star, 2009.
Jarvis is torn between his growing love for Gwen and the knowledge that her young brother is an incipient Paladin and the part he must play in introducing the teenager to his dangerous future.

Defeat the Darkness. Pocket Star, 2010.
Wounded and near breaking, Paladin Hunter Fitzsimon is sent to monitor the thinning barrier between the worlds and try to unmask profiteering traitors on both sides and is attracted by his lovely landlady, Tate Justice.

Palmer, Pamela

Palmer's urban fantasies are sexy and unusually creative.

The Dark Gate. Silhouette Nocturne, 2007.
A psychic and a police detective struggle to keep the evil Esri from opening the gate between the two worlds and enslaving humanity.

Dark Deceiver. Silhouette Nocturne, 2008.
A half-human/half-Esri hero on a mission to find the means to keep the gate between the worlds open falls in love with a human and rethinks his goals.

Feral Warriors

This series focuses on group of immortal shapeshifting warriors whose mission is to save the world from evil.

Desire Untamed. Avon, 2009.
Kara is kidnapped by Lyon and told she is also immortal and is their Radiant, their source of power.

Obsession Untamed. Avon, 2009.
Warrior Tighe needs the help of FBI agent Delaney Randall to regain the part of his soul claimed by his clone and stop a reign of violence.

Passion Untamed. Avon, 2009.
Kidnapped as a child and abused for years by the evil Mage Birik who wants to use her power, Mage witch Skye is forced to capture the Feral Warrior Paenther and keep him as a sexual slave—until Paenther turns the tables and seduces her in this story that has much to say about the power of trust and love.

Rapture Untamed. Avon, 2010.

Pineiro, Caridad
See also Latino Bibliography in chapter 12, "Ethnic/Multicultural Romance."

The Calling Series
A passionate, fast-paced, dark, edgy vampire series set in New York that includes a number of Latino characters.

Darkness Calls. Silhouette Intimate Moments, 2004.
FBI Agent Diana Reyes investigates a series of killings that are linked to The Lair, a club belonging to mysterious Ryder Latimer.

Danger Calls. Silhouette Intimate Moments, 2005.
Dr. Melissa Danvers searches for the cure to Ryder's illness with the help of Diana's brother, Sebastian.

Temptation Calls. Silhouette Intimate Moments, 2005.
A vampire running a women's shelter in Spanish Harlem works with a detective to get to the bottom of a series of crimes aimed at vampires.

Death Calls. Silhouette Nocturne, 2006.
Diana's investigations and her affair with Ryder draw her more deeply into the Manhattan vampire culture.

Devotion Calls. Silhouette Nocturne, 2007.
Nurse Sara Martinez is wary of healer Ricardo Hernandez but will try anything to save her mother.

Desire Calls. Harlequin.com, 2007.
A free e-book novella at Harlequin.com.

Blood Calls. Silhouette Nocturne, 2007.
A dying artist learns she's inadvertently copied a painting that her client plans to sell as the real thing and goes to a gallery-owner friend (and secret vampire) for help.

"Honor Calls." Silhouette Nocturne Bite. An e-book that is also in *Awakening the Beast* (2009).

Fury Calls. Silhouette Nocturne, 2009.
Vampire Blake Richards goes to work in the restaurant of the woman he turned, chef Meghan Thomas, in a effort to win her love.

Ardor Calls. Silhouette Nocturne, 2012.
Vengeance Calls. Silhouette Nocturne, 2012.

Rowan, Michelle

Angel with an Attitude. Forever, 2006
An angel sent back to earth on a mission has a hard time resisting her Temptor Demon in this funny, zany romance.

Immortality Bites Series
Turned into a vampire when a blind date bites her on the neck, Sarah Dearly is forced to learn the ways of the vamps and survive in this sassy chick lit series that treats the fantasy vampire world with plenty of humor.

Bitten & Smitten. Forever, 2006.
Sarah flees vampire hunters, is taken under the wing of vampire master Thierry de Bennicour—a most melancholy hero—and ends up with the dangerous nickname, Slayer of Slayers.

Fanged & Fabulous. Forever, 2007.
Still trying to adjust to her new "life," Sarah is caught up in a war between crazy hunters and vamps and must also deal with the cold shoulder from Thierry.

Lady & the Vamp. Forever, 2008.
This story leaves Sarah for the moment and focuses on a conflicted vampire-hunter–turned-vampire and an assassin in search of a magical, wish-granting artifact who find love along the way.

Stakes & Stilettos. Forever, 2009.
Among other disasters, Sarah is cursed by an evil witch to become the vilest of vampires, a Nightwalker—now to find a way to keep the worst of the curse under control.

Tall, Dark, & Fangsome. Forever, 2009.
Sarah struggles against the Nightwalker curse and must deal with a vampire hunter who wants her to turn him into a vamp.

Singh, Nalini
Singh writes some contemporary series romance as well as intense, creative urban fantasies.

Psy-Changeling Series
Two opposite races, the emotionless Psy class linked mentally via the PsyNet and the shapshifting Changelings, who thrive on touch and emotion, coexist, not always peacefully, on the futuristic Earth of this highly charged series.

Slave to Sensation. Berkley Sensation, 2006.
The hunt for a crazed Psy serial killer brings changeling Lucas Hunter and Sasha Duncan, a Psy who has emotions she has always concealed, together in a passionate, conflicted relationship.

Visions of Heat. Berkley Sensation, 2007.
A Psy whose visions often foretell the future is plagued by dangerous visions and sensations of forbidden pleasure that could destroy her.

Caressed by Ice. Berkley Sensation, 2007.
Judd, a renegade Psy assassin, is the only one who can help Brenna, a Changeling whose mind has been all but destroyed by a serial killer—but she has things to teach him, as well.

Mine to Possess. Berkley Sensation, 2008.
Two changelings reconnect after twenty years apart and deal with their passionate feelings as they continue to fight against the increasingly ruthless Psy.

Hostage to Pleasure. Berkley Sensation, 2008.
A brilliant Psy scientist anxious to keep her child safe finds love with a Changeling sniper.

Branded by Fire. Berkley Sensation, 2009.
A pair of Changelings with wildly different personalities from recently allied packs strike sparks of many kinds—many of them passionate.

Blaze of Memory. Berkley Sensation, 2009.
An amnesiac heroine is programmed to kill the hero in this fast-paced adventure.

Bonds of Justice. Berkley Sensation, 2010.
A human cop with natural Psy-proof mental shields and a Justice Psy who reads the minds of criminals and is on the verge of a mental breakdown are attracted as they work to find a murderer.

Kiss of Snow. Berkley Sensation, 2011.
A Psy refugee, accepted into the pack as a child, finally finds love with the Snow-Dancer wolf pack's leader as they battle enemies determined to destroy the rebellious Changelings.

Guild Hunter Series
A fast-paced, rather dark Urban Fantasy series set in a world where angels hold sway over vampires.

Angel's Blood. Berkley, 2009.
Vampire hunter Elena is sent by Archangel Raphael to find a deadly rogue archangel and falls for Raphael in the process.

Archangel's Kiss. Berkley, 2010.
Transformed into an angel, former vampire hunter Elena and her lover, Archangel Raphael, are faced with a formidable enemy when Elena is invited to a treacherous ball.

Archangel's Consort. Berkley, 2011.
Another evil immortal is out to cause trouble for Elena and Raphael—his mother!

Archangel's Blade. Berkley, 2011.

Ward, J. R. (Pseudonym for Jessica Bird)
The Black Dagger Brotherhood Series
Vampires are being dogged by slayers from the Lessening Society and the Black Dagger Brotherhood, a band of six special vampires, is sworn to defend their race in this fierce, dark, erotically sensual series.

Dark Lover. Signet, 2005.
Wrath, the only pureblood vampire of the group, finds love with half-vampire, Beth.

Lover Eternal. Signet, 2006.
Rhage, a member of the brotherhood fueled by violence and sex, finds peace and healing with Mary.

Lover Awakened. Signet, 2006.
Tormented Zsadist finds healing and self-acceptance with Bella.

Lover Revealed. Signet, 2007.
Ex-cop Butch, who is more than he seems, finds love with vampire Marissa.

Lover Unbound. Signet, 2007.
Vishous (V) avoids relationships until Dr. Jane Whitcomb saves his life.

Lover Enshrined. Signet, 2008.
Phury has problems accepting his role as Primale in this volume that takes the series in a less romantic direction.

Lover Avenged. New American Library, 2009.
Rehvenge, a secret sympath vampire, finds love and acceptance with nurse Ehlena.

Lover Mine. New American Library, 2010.
John (aka Darius) comes to terms with his past, fights to protect his race, and finds an unexpected soul mate in sympath assassin Xhex.

Lover Unleashed. New American Library, 2011.
Payne, Vishous's warrior twin sister, finds love with the skeptical human doctor who helps her when she is injured.

Fallen Angels Series

Angels and Demons battle for souls—seven battles for seven souls—in this world-fate-determining series featuring Harley-riding angels.

Covet. Signet, 2009.
Fallen angel Jim Heron must help a businessman make the right choice for himself and his love in the first battle of this series.

Crave. Signet, 2010.
Directly following Covet, former XOps operative Isaac Rothe, on the run and eventually arrested, finds love with lawyer Grier Childe as they join the deadly battle.

Envy. Signet, 2011.

Wilks, Eileen
World of the Lupi

This werewolf Urban Fantasy saga focuses on Lily Yu and Rule Turner in a world that is undergoing a number of magical changes.

Tempting Danger. Berkley Sensation, 2004.
Detective Lily Yu works with the leader of the Nikolai clan, Rule Turner, to discover who is trying to frame him for murder, never realizing that they are life mates.

Mortal Danger. Berkley Sensation, 2005.
Danger stalks Lily (now of the FBI Magical Crimes Unit) and Rule as they are pulled into another dimension, leaving part of Lily in the human plane.

Blood lines. Berkley Sensation, 2007.
A werewolf sorcerer, Cullen Seabourne, and finder, Cynna Weaver, and Lily's powerful grandmother join the FBI in discovering who is attacking the werewolves.

Night Season. Berkley Sensation, 2008.
Cynna, Cullen, and several others are drawn into another magical world by gnomes who want Cynna's help finding an important artifact.

Mortal Sins. Berkley Sensation, 2009.
Lily becomes involved in a serial murder case with magical overtones in this installment that nicely balances the paranormal aspects with practical police investigative procedures.

Blood Magic. Berkley Sensation, 2010.
Secrets are revealed and old enmities come to the fore as Lily investigates an attempted murder.

Blood Challenge. Berkley Sensation, 2011.
Threats and danger continue, but the romantic focus in this installment is on Benedict Turner and part-*sidhe* Arjenie.

Death Magic. Berkley Sensation, 2011.

TAKE FIVE!

Five favorite Alternative Reality Romances:

- **Lynn Kurland**—*With Every Breath*
- **Debbie Macomber**—*A Season of Angels*
- **Robin D. Owens**—*Heart Mate*
- **Nalini Singh**—*Slave to Sensation*
- **J. R. Ward**—*Dark Lover*

Chapter 10

Gay, Lesbian, Bisexual, and Transgendered Romance

Definition

> **GLBT Romance**—Romance novels in which the main characters are gay, lesbian, bisexual, or transgendered.

Gay, Lesbian, Bisexual, and Transgendered (GLBT) Romances are love stories in which the romantic interest centers on gay, lesbian, or bisexual couples. Except for this one basic difference, these novels are much like other romances (i.e., their plots revolve around the love relationship of the two main characters, they allow the reader to become emotionally involved in the courtship process, and they come in a variety of types; e.g., Gothic, Romantic Suspense, Historical, Contemporary, Paranormal, Young Adult). As in all romances, there is a wide assortment of problems that the characters must work out before they can be happily united; however, while the Gay, Lesbian, Bisexual, and Transgendered Romance shares them all, there can also be additional issues related to the sexuality of the protagonists. For example, one of the main characters may have difficulty accepting his or her sexual orientation or is dealing with coming-out issues, or outside prejudice against homosexuality may threaten the relationship. Nevertheless, as long as the love relationship between the two protagonists is the focus of the story, these are not considered "problem novels"; they are romances.

However, in the past, GLBT Romances aimed at the young adult (YA) market ran a greater risk of being labeled problem novels than those appealing to other segments of the population. This was largely because the YA novel by its nature tends to focus on the concerns of growing up and coming of age. Choosing values, making friends, dealing with feelings and emotions, becoming independent, and coming to terms with one's sexuality are all examples of the issues the YA novel treats. During the 1970s, the emphasis in these books expanded to include more serious, often taboo, social questions (e.g., drugs, alcoholism, pregnancy, abortion, divorce, death, suicide, mental illness, abuse, sexual orientation) and the problem novel was born. In recent years, however, the world has moved on and the trend away from the darker novels of this type has been marked. Of course, serious issues are still common to the typical YA story, but these stories have changed with the times, and the issues and the characters, including GLBT teens (and sometimes adults), are portrayed in a much more positive, realistic light than before. There were, of course some early YA GLBT novels, such as *Annie on My Mind* (1982) by Nancy Garden, that played down the "gayness as a problem" aspects of the plot and focused on the first-love storyline. However, they were the exception; today's teens have many more choices. *Call Me by Your Name* (2008) by André Aciman, *My Most Excellent Year* (2008) by Steve Kluger, and *Keeping You a Secret* (2005) by Julie Ann Peters are only three of the many excellent examples of GLBT first-love novels. Novels of this type are definitely within the Romance genre. (For more in-depth coverage of this topic, see pages 114 through120 in Carolyn Carpan's *Rocked by Romance: a Guide to Teen Romance Fiction* [Westport, CT: Libraries Unlimited, 2004] and Carlisle K. Webber's *Gay, Lesbian, Bisexual, Transgender and Questioning Teen Literature: A Guide to Reading Interests* [Santa Barbara, CA: Libraries Unlimited, 2010]).)

As with other romances, sexual explicitness in GLBT Romances can vary, and while sex is often an important aspect in these stories, its treatment can range from relatively innocent through steamily erotic to nearly pornographic.

The plot patterns and characters in GLBT Romances can be (and often are) as varied as those found in heterosexual romances and many could also fall into other categories—for example, Historical Romance or Romantic Suspense subgenres. For instance, a tall, arrogant, mysterious hero is tamed by an innocent, large-eyed young man in a typical gay Gothic; a pair of teenagers discover love and bring a rapist to justice in a classic YA lesbian romance; and a divorcee comes to terms with her own sexuality and finds love with younger woman in a contemporary lesbian romance. Plots can include untold secrets, mysteries, betrayals, and numerous misunderstandings on the part of the lovers—all of which, of course, are cleared up by the end of the book. In addition, certain stereotypical characters, both gay and straight (e.g., the other man/woman, villain, loyal friend/servant, meddling friends or relatives), appear with great regularity. It is also worth noting that just as straight secondary characters appear in GLBT Romances, gay and lesbian characters also show up in supporting roles in straight romances—and in recent years this trend has increased.

Appeal

The primary appeal of the Gay, Lesbian, or Bisexual Romance is to the homosexual reader who is interested in reading a love story with which he or she can more easily identify. Most readers enjoy a book more when they have something in common with the characters and situations it describes; when they can empathize with the characters and relate to their experiences. However, the gay or lesbian reader has not always been able to do this, particularly in the area of romance fiction, simply because, for these readers, the basic premise of the average love story (i.e., boy loves girl, girl loves boy) is invalid. The Gay or Lesbian Romance offers an alternative to the heterosexual status quo—a love story that assumes the validity of the gay or lesbian lifestyle and proceeds from there.

Although GLBT Romance is a very small and highly specialized niche market, the appeal of these books is not necessarily limited to members of the GLBT community; these stories may also be of interest to heterosexuals who have an understanding of or an interest in the gay lifestyle. Consider, for example, the general popularity of the groundbreaking film *Brokeback Mountain* (based on Annie Proulx's short story of the same name) and the subsequent attempts of some publishers (e.g., Running Press) and/or authors to target the heterosexual market with gay-oriented romances. The likelihood of this kind of crossover readership is especially enhanced by well-written books that contain both gay and straight characters and portray them all with realism, openness, and warmth.

Advising the Reader

General readers' advisory information is provided in chapter 3; several points to consider when advising gay, lesbian, and bisexual readers are listed below.

- Readers who enjoy GLBT Romances may also enjoy other types of gay or lesbian fiction—short stories, essays, poetry, biographies, mysteries, science fiction, and so on. *Gay, Lesbian, Bisexual and Transgendered Literature: A Genre Guide* (Westport, CT: Libraries Unlimited, 2008) by Ellen Bosman, John P. Bradford, and Robert Ridinger is a good resource to start with.
- Readers of GLBT Romances might also be interested in works that, while not exclusively gay, do describe cultures in which the homosexual lifestyle is a valid and accepted option. Many of these are in the science fiction or fantasy categories and are exemplified by works such as Marion Zimmer Bradley's Darkover novels and Tanith Lee's *Biting the Sun* (novellas originally published separately as *Don't Bite the Sun* and *Drinking Sapphire Wine*). For a decade or more, sensitively treated gay or lesbian secondary characters have been included in romance novels, as well. *Hot Target* by Suzanne Brockmann (see chapter 13, "Linked Romances") and *Measure of a Man* by Adrianne Byrd (see chapter 11, "Ethnic/Multicultural Romance") are only two of the more recent examples.
- Sexual explicitness varies within the GLBT Romance subgenre, just as it does in other romance subgenres, and the same caveats apply to both.
- Occasionally, a reader new to gay or lesbian fiction will ask for advice on what to read first. Although a lot depends on the situation, in general, classics or particularly well-done works such as *Patience and Sarah* by Isabel Miller, *The Ladies* by Doris Grumbach, *Curious Wine* by Katherine V. Forrest, or *Annie on My Mind* by Nancy Garden are good choices.
- Although it is important for advising readers in all romance subgenres, the reference interview is especially important in the area of Gay, Lesbian, Bisexual, and Transgendered Romance. Unless they live in an urban or university setting where there are likely to be bookstores that specialize in books targeting the gay community or generic bookstores that carry a good variety of similar materials, many homosexuals will be dependent on the library (Alyson, Sasha. "What Librarians Should Know About Gay and Lesbian Publishing," Collection Building [Spring 1984]: 22–23). A sensitive librarian, skilled in the art of the reference interview and aware of the wide variety of available resources, in addition to a progressive collection development policy that ensures a comprehensive collection, can be invaluable in putting readers in touch with relevant and appropriate materials.
- Take advantage of the growing amount of relevant information available on the web. Websites for publishers (see below) and organizations such as the Gay, Lesbian, Bisexual, and Transgendered Round Table (GLBTRT) of the American Library

Association (www.ala.org/ala/glbtrt/welcomeglbtround.htm) might be especially useful. Some public libraries also include relevant booklists on their websites.

Selected Reference Sources

Although the amount of information online continues to grow, reference sources focusing on literature and library services for the Gay, Lesbian, and Bisexual community continue to appear in print. Several of the more general reference works are listed below and may be helpful to those wanting additional information.

Betz, Phyllis M.
Lesbian Romance Novels: A History and Critical Analysis. Jefferson, NC: McFarland, 2009.
"A history of the lesbian romance novel is followed by analyses of both individual works by authors writing in the genre as well as the ways in which lesbian romance novels reflect and transform the techniques of heterosexual romance novels."

Bosman, Ellen, John P. Bradford, and Robert B. Marks Ridinger
Gay, Lesbian, Bisexual and Transgendered Literature: A Genre Guide. Westport, CT: Libraries Unlimited, 2008.
This introduction to twentieth-century gay, lesbian, bisexual, and transgendered literature has a readers' advisory focus and provides access to more than eight hundred relevant titles in a wide variety of genres and subgenres.

Buschman, John E., and Gloria J. Leckie, eds.
The Library as Place: History, Community, and Culture. Westport, CT: Libraries Unlimited, 2007.
The chapter "Locating the Library as Place among Lesbian, Gay, Bisexual, and Queer Patrons" by Paulette Rothbauer may be of interest.

Cart, Michael and Christine A. Jenkins
The Heart Has Its Reasons: Young Adult Literature with Gay/Lesbian/Queer Content, 1969–2004. Lanham, MD: Scarecrow Press, 2006.
This well-organized resource takes a historical approach and analyzes GLBT-themed YA literature over thirty-five years, discussing landmark books and providing annotated bibliographies, a chronological listing, and relevant references.

Day, Francis Ann
Lesbian and Gay Voices: An Annotated Bibliography and Guide to Literature for Children and Young Adults. Westport, CT: Greenwood, 2000.
Primarily of interest to school and public children's and young adult librarians, this is useful for both collection development and readers' advisory.

Gough, Cal, and Greenblatt, Ellen, eds.
Gay and Lesbian Library Service. Jefferson, NC: McFarland, 1990.
Primarily of interest to librarians, or possibly booksellers who serve the GLBT community. Limited discussion of genre fiction.

Malinowski, Sharon, ed.
Gay and Lesbian Literature. vol. 1. Detroit: St. James Press, 1994.
This bio-bibliographic source covers more than two hundred writers, including some who have written romance.

Martin, Hillias J., and James R. Murdock
Serving Lesbian, Gay, Bisexual, Transgender, and Questioning Teens: A How-To-Do-It Manual for Librarians. New York: Neal-Schuman, 2007.
This useful, well-designed handbook provides a wealth of information on collection development, access, readers' advisory, programming, and other relevant topics for librarians who serve the LGBTQ population. This resource also may also be of interest to librarians who work with gay and lesbian adults.

Pendergast, Tom, and Sara Pendergast, eds.
Gay and Lesbian Literature. vol. 2. Detroit: St. James Press, 1998.
The two volumes of this older bio-bibliographic source includes biographical, bibliographic, and critical information on several hundred writers who focus on gay, lesbian, or bisexual themes, including some who have written romance.

Summers, Claude J., ed.
The Gay and Lesbian Literary Heritage: A Reader's Companion to the Writers and Their Works, from Antiquity to the Present. rev. ed. New York: Routledge, 2002.
A revised edition of the 1995 version, this classic companion is alphabetically arranged by subject and provides over 380 essays on a variety of topics and authors. Bibliographies are provided for most entries.

Webber, Carlisle K.
Gay, Lesbian, Bisexual, Transgender and Questioning Teen Literature: A Guide to Reading Interests. Santa Barbara, CA: Libraries Unlimited, 2010.
Well-arranged, and insightful, this guide (with six thematically subdivided chapters of annotated titles and a final section addressing practical issues) provides up-to-date, useful information for YA readers' advisory and collection development librarians. The sections on "First Love" and "Teen Romance" may be of particular interest.

Woods, Gregory
A History of Gay Literature: The Male Tradition. New Haven, CT: Yale University Press, 1998.
A wide-ranging, informative history of gay literature from the classics to the present.

The following older works may also still be of interest.

Cruikshank, Margaret. *Lesbian Studies: Present and Future*. New York: The Feminist Press, 1982.

Young, Ian. *The Male Homosexual in Literature: A Bibliography*. 2nd ed. Metuchen, NJ: Scarecrow, 1982.

Publishers

Although a number of major publishers do produce an occasional GLBT Romance, most are published by smaller firms, often those specializing in GLBT materials. Several of these are listed below. For more complete information, refer to chapter 22, "Publishers."

Alyson Publications	www.alyson.com
Bella Books	www.bellabooks.com
Bold Strokes	www.boldstrokesbooks.com

Cleis	www.cleispress.com/index.php
Firebrand Books	www.firebrandbooks.com
Intaglio Publications	www.intagliopub.com
New Victoria	newvictoria.com
Running Press	www.perseusbooksgroup.com/perseus/home.jsp
Seal Press	www.sealpress.com/home.php
Spinsters Ink	www.spinsters-ink.com
Torquere Press	www.torquerepress.com

Brief History

Although homosexual literature has existed since antiquity, the Gay, Lesbian, Bisexual, and Transgendered Romance, as we know it today, is a relatively new phenomenon. Prior to the birth of the modern gay movement in 1969 (precipitated by the police raid on the Stonewall gay bar), the availability of GLBT literature was relatively limited. There were, of course, a few isolated novels, such as Radclyffe Hall's *The Well of Loneliness* (1928), which was banned on both sides of the Atlantic, and Claire Morgan's *The Price of Salt* (1952), which achieved a certain amount of acclaim and general exposure. However, except for the lesbian pulps popular during the late 1950s and early 1960s, gay and lesbian literature was more or less dormant and definitely underground.

The 1969 Stonewall raid changed all that. By the mid-1970s GLBT publishing of all types was in full swing. Some earlier works were being republished, newer materials, such as *Rubyfruit Jungle* (1973) by Rita Mae Brown, were appearing in print, and small presses, such as Naiad in 1971, were testing the waters. Late in the decade a number of major publishers tried to appeal to the gay market, contracting with writers not only for serious materials, but also for light fiction, such as *Gaywick* (1980) by Vincent Virga. Unfortunately, the endeavor was not successful from the larger publishers' point of view, and much GLBT publishing became concentrated in the smaller, specialized publishing houses.

Although serious GLBT materials continued to be published, the first half of the 1980s saw a new trend—a growing interest in gay fiction of the genre variety. Mystery series, science fiction, and romances, all with homosexual orientations, began to appear in the market. Older works of this type that had been neglected were reprinted and/or remarketed and new genre authors were actively being sought. In spite of society's conservative swing over the past decades, this trend has endured, and despite the expected ups and downs, the gay genre market, particularly mystery, science fiction, and fantasy, continues to expand and to provide a definite crossover appeal to the reading community in general. Romance has also benefited from this renewed interest, and recently the genre seems to have taken on new life as established authors continue to please their fans, new authors begin to attract readers, new publishers appear and older ones reinvent themselves, the Internet provides access and connects readers in ways impossible before, and the Romance Writers of America has recently added a special interest chapter, Rainbow Romance Writers, for writers of GLBT Romance. Although it is still a niche market with a specialized readership, the improving quality and variety of the books should guarantee a growing readership, possibly with some crossover potential.

Note: Readers interested the state of the GLBT publishing market may wish to read Michael Bronski's "The Paradox of Gay Publishing," *Publishers' Weekly* 249 (August 26, 2002):

27–28, 30–31; "Making It, Gay & Lesbian" *Publishers' Weekly* 252 (April 25, 2005): 29–30 by Robert Dahlin; or other more recent ones published in this trade journal.

9

Classic Gay, Lesbian, Bisexual, and Transgendered Romances

Aldridge, Sarah (Anyda Marchant)

One of the first lesbian writers to give lesbian romances girl-gets-girl happy endings. After she retired from practicing law, she founded Naiad Press and then A&M Books. She died in 2006; her titles are all currently available from A&M Books. (P.O. Box 283, Rehoboth Beach, DE 19971, www.sarahaldridge.com).

The Latecomer (1974), *Tottie: A Tale of the Sixties* (1975), *Cytherea's Breath* (1976), *All True Lovers* (1978), *The Nesting Place* (1982), *Madame Aurora* (1983), *Misfortune's Friend* (1985), *Magdalena* (1987), *Keep to Me Stranger* (1989), *A Flight of Angels* (1992), *Michaela* (1994), *Amantha* (1995), *Nina in the Wilderness* (1997), *O, Mistress Mine* (2003).

10

11

Bannon, Ann

One of the classic pulp writers of the 1950s.

Beebo Brinker Series

The following books are all part of the legendary Beebo Brinker series, which provides a glimpse into lesbian life in Greenwich Village during the 1950s. They have been reprinted several times over the years, most recently by Cleis Press (2001–2003). Note: The first four books are written in chronological order; the last is a prequel to the series.

Odd Girl Out (1957), *I Am a Woman* (1959), *Women in Shadows* (1959), *Journey to a Woman* (1960), *Beebo Brinker* (1962).

12

13

Grumbach, Doris

The Ladies (1984).

A classic, fictionalized account of two eighteenth-century women, Eleanor Butler and Sarah Ponsonby, who defied convention and chose to live as a married couple.

Hall, Radclyffe

The Well of Loneliness (1928).

A classic in lesbian fiction, not actually romance, set in the Paris during the 1920s.

14

Miller, Isabel (Alma Routsong)

A Gradual Joy (1953), *A Round Shape* (1959), *Patience and Sarah* (1972) (originally published in 1969 as *A Place for Us*), *The Love of a Good Woman* (1986), *Side by Side* (1990), *Laurel* (1996).

Morgan, Claire

The Price of Salt (1952).

Classic lesbian romance, considered one of the finest examples of the genre.

15

Renault, Mary

Many of her classic historical novels deal with gay relationships, although they would not properly be called gay romances.

The Last of the Wine (1956), *Fire from Heaven* (1959), *The Persian Boy* (1972), *Funeral Games* (1981).

16

Taylor, Valerie

Taylor is a well-known early lesbian pulp fiction writer. Some of her works have been reprinted and are now the object of academic study.

> **Erika Frohmann Series** (*Journey to Fulfillment* [1964], *World without Men* [1963], *Stranger on Lesbos* [1960], *Return to Lesbos* [1963], *Ripening: The Conclusion to the Erika Frohmann Series* [1988]), *The Girls in 3-B* (1959).

Virga, Vincent

> *Gaywick*. (1980)
> A classic groundbreaking gothic gay historical romance.

Selected Gay, Lesbian, Bisexual, and Transgendered Romance Bibliography

The following are merely a few examples of the wide variety of materials, from classics to contemporaries, currently available. Many authors will also have other titles of interest to GLBT Romance readers. When applicable, the year a work was originally published appears in parentheses following current publication information. See previous editions of this guide for some authors or titles that have been dropped from this edition.

Beecroft, Alex

> *False Colors*. Running Press, 2009.
> Two naval officers deal with piracy, violence, and their own feelings in this Georgian Era Romance that is one of Running Presses M/M Historical Romances written by women authors for women romance readers.

> *Shining in the Sun*. Samhain Press, 2011.
> A wealthy, closeted man meets a handsome surfer when his car breaks down along the Cornish coast.

Bennett, Saxon

Lively, light-hearted stories that combine a sense of fun with often serious themes are typical of Bennett's work.

> *The Wish List*. Naiad, 1996.
> A funny, poignant reunion story that spans thirty years.

> *Old Ties*. Naiad, 1997.
> A young woman struggles to put her past behind her and get on with her life, but finds it difficult.

> *Both Sides*. Naiad, 1999.
> Polar opposite lesbian twins learn about themselves, each other, and love in this lively romance.

> *Sweet Fire*. Bella Books, 2000.
> A small Arizona town with an abundance of lesbian residents heats up when an artist's former lover comes back to town.

> *A Question of Love?* Bella Books, 2003.
> Love with an academic twist.

Talk of the Town. Bella Books, 2003.
Gigi and Mallory come of age along with their friends in this funny, lively contemporary tale.

Talk of the Town Too. Bella Books, 2004.
Sequel to *Talk of the Town*.

Higher Ground. Bella Books, 2004.
Date Night Club. Bella, 2007.
An eclectic group of women decide to take a proactive, systematic approach to looking for love in this funny, heartwarming story.

Family Affair. Bella Books, 2009.
A mistake at the gynecologist office results in a pregnancy for the heroine in this funny, family-oriented story.

Black, Ronica
Writes sexually explicit, well-plotted, fast-paced, contemporary lesbian romances, often with an adventurous touch.

In Too Deep. Bold Strokes, 2005.
Homicide cop Erin McKenzie investigates a suspected serial killer, but needs help from a lesbian colleague because the suspect is lesbian. Golden Crown Literary Society Debut Author winner.

Wild Abandon. Bold Strokes, 2006.
A clinical psychologist who loves her speedy bike connects with a cop who's into control. Golden Crown Literary Society winner for Best Erotica.

Hearts Aflame. Bold Strokes, 2007.
A neophyte ranch owner needs the help of a local vet in this Arizona-set sizzler.

Deeper. Bold Strokes, 2008.
Past suspicions resurface leaving Erin McKenzie in a quandary. Follows *In Too Deep*.

The Seeker. Bold Strokes, 2009.
The search for an attempted murderer puts the life of an FBI profiler and her family in danger.

Chasing Love. Bold Strokes, 2010.
A woman on a futile quest for love finally finds it when and where she least expects it.

Boulter, Amanda
Around the Houses. Serpent's Tale, 2002.
Follow the lives of the inhabitants of Madrigal Close in this funny, offbeat English romp that features a quirky cast of gay, lesbian, and straight characters.

Back Around the Houses. Serpent's Tale, 2003.
The quixotic lies of the folks of Madrigal Close continue with hilarious abandon in this sequel to *Around the Houses*.

Bradley, Marion Zimmer
Although her novels are not really gay romance, some of her science fiction Darkover novels deal with gay relationships—and may appeal to readers of gay romances. The following Darkover titles focus on the Renunciates, a guild of Free Amazons

oath-bound to each other and their guild rather than the more traditional family or clan. Note: These have been reprinted in a single volume as *The Saga of the Renunciates* (DAW, 2002).

> *The Shattered Chain.* DAW, 1976.
> *Thendara House.* DAW, 1983.
> *City of Sorcery.* DAW, 1984.

Braund, Diana Tremain

Lesbian romances set in rural and small town Maine. Many of the stories have an environmental slant.

> *Bold Coast Love.* Bella Books, 2000.
> Two women and false sexual harassment charges cause a doctor problems in a small Maine town.

> *Wicked Good Time.* Bella Books, 2005 (1999).
> A cop seeking peace in rural Maine finds romance with a forest ranger.

> *The Way Life Should Be.* Bella Books, 2004 (1998).
> An attorney who's sworn off love heads for a tiny Maine town and finds romance in spite of her intentions.

> *Finest Kind of Love.* Bella Books, 2004.
> Murder adds a sinister touch to this romance that brings a Bar Harbor lawyer to tiny Gin Cove, Maine, for vacation where she meets a lovely lobster fisherman.

> *The Tides of Passion.* Bella Books, 2005.
> A woman with intriguing ideas for the island arrives on Bath Island, Maine, and finds romance, as well as problems.

> *Aspen's Embers.* Bella Books, 2007.
> A woman's plan to revitalize the town of Codyville Plantation, Maine, causes problems for a local teacher and environmentalist.

Brockmann, Suzanne

> *All Through the Night: A Troubleshooter Christmas.* Ballantine, 2007.
> The Boston wedding of a federal troubleshooter, Jules Cassidy, and his actor partner, Robin Chadwick, attracts unwanted and sometimes dangerous attention in this latest addition to Brockmann's Troubleshooter series.

> *Force of Nature.* Ballantine, 2007.
> Plenty of action and espionage propel this Troubleshooter story that highlights two romantic relationships, one heterosexual, the other gay.

Brown, Rita Mae

Noted for her groundbreaking lesbian novels, especially her now-classic coming-of-age novel, *The Rubyfruit Jungle* (1973), Brown is also the author of several mystery series.

> *Alma Mater.* Ballantine, 2001.
> A college student realizes she's a lesbian and in love with another coed to the shock of her fiancé and very Southern mother in this coming-of-age tale.

Calhoun, Jackie

Calhoun's novels often feature middle-aged women, many of whom have left their husbands for another woman, coming to terms with their relationships; infidelity is often, but not always, involved. A number of her older titles have been reprinted.

By Reservation Only. Naiad Press, 1998.
Birds of a Feather. Naiad Press, 1999.
Off Season. Bella Books, 2000.
Tamarack Creek. Bella Books, 2001.
Outside the Flock. Bella Books, 2002.
Crossing the Center Line. Windstorm Creative, 2003.
A partially autobiographical novel about Calhoun's own experience told in a fictional way using a husband who realizes he is gay and the ultimate results of this revelation.

Woman in the Mirror. Bella Books, 2004.
Breast cancer adds a serious dimension to this complex family story.

Abby's Passion. Bella Books, 2005.
Abby's bipolar sister is a focus of this story with more than one romantic relationship.

Obsession. Bella Books, 2006.
A married woman must come to terms with her new feelings and make some hard choices.

The Education of Ellie. Bella Books, 2007.
Now each divorced and with grown children, two old friends meet again in the town where they grew up and deal with the past as they explore their feelings for each other.

Roommates. Bella Books, 2008.
Freshman college roommates from very different backgrounds are drawn to each other as they face serious challenges.

Looking for Julie. Bella Books, 2011.
"A fast-paced, tangled story of passion and romance from the structured halls of academia to the wild, challenging trails of cross-country skiing."

Chambers, Jane
An award-winning author and playwright.

Burning. T'n'T Classics, 1998 (c.1978).
The spirits of two women from an earlier time seek to control two modern-day women and live out their love through them. A lesbian Gothic Romance of passion and possession.

Christian, Paula
Christian is a writer of pulps from the 1950s and 1960s. Some of her books are considered classics and a number are available as reprints, most recently from Kensington.

This Side of Love. Avon, 1963.

Another Kind of Love. Kensington, 2003
Includes *Another Kind of Love* (1961) and *Love Is Where You Find It* (1961).

Twilight Girls. Kensington, 2003.
Includes *Edge of Twilight* (1959) and *This Side of Love* (1963).

The Other Side of Desire. Kensington, 2004.
Includes *Amanda* (1965) and *The Other Side of Desire* (1965).

Clevenger, Jaime

All Bets Off. Spinsters Ink, 2006.
Two women, one rich and one poor, experience the San Francisco Earthquake of 1906 and develop a romantic relationship.

Cohen, Celia

Smokey O: A Romance. Naiad, 1994.
An old pro and a young rookie find romance on the baseball field.

Payback. Naiad. 1995.
Two women who run afoul of a powerful, corrupt senator get their revenge.

Courted. Naiad, 1997.
A policewoman reminisces about her past and finds love with a tennis player she is assigned to protect.

Conn, Nicole

Claire of the Moon. Naiad Press, 1993.
Book based on the classic lesbian movie of the same name.

Passion's Shadow. Simon & Schuster, 1995.
A romance with a mystery that includes a variety of straight, gay, and lesbian couples.

She Walks in Beauty. Naiad Press, 2001.

Dunne, Nann

The War Between the Hearts. Intaglio, 2005.
A cross-dressing Union spy is wounded and falls in love with the Southern woman who saves her life but betrays her.

Erastes

Frost Fair. Linden Bay Romance, 2008.
A printer/engraver and his wealthy client connect during the unusually cold winter of 1814, the year the Thames froze over.

Transgressions. Running Press, 2009.
Set in seventeenth-century Cromwellian England, two men who met as teenagers are separated by war and witch hunts in this romance that is one of Running Press's M/M Historical Romances, written by women authors and aimed at women romance readers.

Forrest, Katherine V.

Forrest has written romances, many of which have been reprinted, as well as created the popular Kate Delafield Mystery series. She is a Lambda Pioneer Award winner.

Curious Wine. Allyson Books, 2002 (1983).
A classic lesbian romance.

Daughters Trilogy

Daughters of a Coral Dawn. Naiad Press. 1984.
An erotic lesbian science fiction romance in which a group of women flee Earth and colonize the planet Maternas.

Daughters of an Amber Noon. Alyson Books, 2002.
Sequel to *Daughters of a Coral Dawn* that follows the fates of the women left behind on earth in an increasingly repressive society.

Daughters of an Emerald Dusk. Alyson Books, 2005.
Follows *Daughters of an Amber Noon* and reunites the women of both societies.

Dreams and Swords. Bywater Books, 2007 (1987).
Short story collection.

Kate Delafield Mystery series
A lesbian sleuth is the heroine of this popular series.

Amateur City. Naiad Press, 1984.
Murder at the Nightwood Bar. Naiad, 1987.
The Beverly Malibu. Naiad, 1989.
Murder by Tradition. Naiad, 1991.
Liberty Square. Berkley Prime Crime, 1996.
Apparition Alley. Berkley Prime Crime, 1997.
Sleeping Bones. Berkley Prime Crime, 1999.
Hancock Park. Berkley Prime Crime, 2004.

Frances, Jane
Lively, contemporary stories filled with the ups and downs of careers, friendship, and romance.

Reunion. Bella Books, 2006.
Three women struggle to find love from three different emotional places in life.

Reality Bytes. Bella Books, 2007.
A fourth woman joins the friends from *Reunion* as they deal with life and assorted love relationships.

Training Days. Bella Books, 2008.
A travel-show reporter is attracted to a French backpacker while on a cross-country trip in Australia.

Futcher, Jane
Dream Lover. Alyson, 1997.
Love blooms when two women meet again after twenty years apart. Northern California (Marin County) setting.

Garden, Nancy
Although she has written for all age levels, this multi-published, award-winning author of lesbian-oriented books is best-known for her classic novels for young adults.

Annie on My Mind. Farrar, Straus, & Giroux, 2007 (1982).
A classic, lyrical love story that should appeal to gay and straight young adults alike, this story has been banned in a number of places and burned in Kansas City.

*Good Moon Rising. Farrar, Straus & Giroux, 1995.
Two high school students connect during the production of *The Crucible* in this Lambda Award–winning romance.

Nora and Liz. Bella Books, 2002.
Two women meet when a flat tire sends Liz to Nora's farm to borrow a jack in Garden's first romance novel for adults.

Guy, Rosa
Ruby. Just Us Books, 2005 (Bantam, 1976).
A YA classic dealing with the lesbian relationship of two young black women.

Hayes, Penny

Omaha's Bell. Naiad. 1999.
This Historical Romance focuses on a church bell and the relationship between a local activist and a woman who is attached to another.

City Lights, Country Candles. Bella Books, 2003 (Naiad, 1998).
A story-within-a-story romance that is notable for its historical aspects rather than the romance.

The Tomstown Incident. Bella Books, 2004.
A happily married woman discovers a link to the past and a lover that she is increasingly drawn to in this Paranormal Romance.

Herendeen, Ann

Phyllida and the Brotherhood of Philander: A Bisexual Regency Romance. Authorhouse, 2005.
A gay aristocrat marries the intrepid, independent, but impoverished, Phyllida for convenience, and then meets the man of his dreams. Blackmail adds dangerous intrigue to this unique romance by a writer who is hoping to start a new subgenre, the bisexual Historical Romance.

Hill, Gerri

Hill's popular lesbian romances often use mountain and wilderness settings.

One Summer Night. Rising Tide, 2000.
A college professor resists falling for a flirtatious woman.

Gulf Breeze. Bella Books, 2004.
A wildlife photographer and a biologist find romance when they become involved in trying to save the Texas Coast wetlands.

Sierra City. Bella Books, 2004.
A woman returns to her tiny Sierra Nevada mountain hometown to deal with her past—and her mother—and finds love with a search-and-rescue expert.

Artist's Dream. Bella Books, 2005.
A pastor's daughter denies her own feelings until she meets a woman she is attracted to.

Hunter's Way. Bella Books, 2005.
Homicide cop partners struggle with their mutual attraction.

Dawn of Change. Bella Books, 2005.
An unhappily married woman finds love with another woman amid a lot of family interference.

The Killing Room. Bella Books, 2006.
An openly lesbian cop and a closeted domestic violence psychologist track down a serial killer while fighting their feelings for each other.

Coyote Sky. Bella Books, 2006.
An author with writer's block accepts a friend's invitation to spend the summer in New Mexico and finds love with the local sheriff.

Behind the Pine Curtain. Bella Books, 2006.
A young woman returns to the home she left as a teenager and finds she is still attracted to a woman from her past.

The Target. Bella Books, 2007.
A senator's daughter and the undercover detective hired to protect her find love amid danger in the Rocky Mountain wilderness.

The Cottage. Bella Books, 2007.
Two married women find friendship and love with each other.

The Rainbow Cedar. Bella Books, 2008.
An interior designer and a landscape designer are attracted to each other.

Partners. Bella Books, 2008.
A detective sets out to find a killer targeting single women who live alone.

No Strings. Bella Books, 2009.
A sheriff is sent to quiet Lake City, Colorado, but hesitates to become involved with a lovely forest ranger because she's not going to stay in Lake City very long.

The Scorpion. Bella Books, 2009.
Life becomes dangerous for an investigative reporter who specializes in cold cases.

Love Waits. Bella Books, 2010.
High school sweethearts are reunited when they attend a school reunion.

Devil's Rock. Bella Books, 2010.
The heroine tracks down a serial killer with the help of an FBI agent.

Storms. Bella Books, 2011.

Kallmaker, Karin
Many of the titles of this popular, enduring romance writer connect have been reprinted. She also writes romances with fantasy and paranormal elements as Laura Adams.

Wild Things. (1996). Bella Books, 2004.
A pair of independent women, one struggling with family and church coming-out issues and the other considering a political career find love in what some consider one of Kallmaker's best romances.

One Degree of Separation. Bella Books, 2003.
A big city girl finds unexpected romance with an Iowa City librarian in this funny romance with plenty of small town atmosphere.

Unforgettable. (2001) Bella Books, 2004.
A singer deals with the ups and downs of the entertainment world and finds new love when she goes home for a high school reunion.

Substitute for Love. (2001) Bella Books, 2004.
A math genius leads a prosaic married life until she realizes that she wants and needs something more.

Sugar. Bella Books, 2004.
A baker has three women to choose from in this romance of growth and self-discovery.

Just Like That. Bella Books, 2005.
The Napa vineyards are the setting for this fast-paced romance in which a winery owner and a Manhattan corporate turnaround specialist find love in spite of their initial antagonism.

18th and Castro. Bella Books, 2006.
A collection of erotic short stories.

Finders Keepers. Bella Books, 2007.
When a shipwreck lands Linda and Marissa on an island, they explore their love for each other and learn something about themselves in the process.

In Deep Waters: Cruising the Seas. Bella Books, 2007 (coauthor, Radclyffe).
This story of romance on a Mediterranean cruise is the first collaboration between these two popular authors.

Cristabel. Bella Books, 2008.
This much revised version of a 1998 title originally published under the pseudonym Laura Adams is a gothic tale with a touch of pure evil that weaves its magic between two time periods.

The Kiss that Counted. Bella Books, 2008.
A woman finds it hard to keep her secrets when she begins to fall in love.

Night Vision. Bella Books, 2008.
A group of women join forces to discover the cause of their nightmares.

Warming Trend. Bella Books, 2009.
A woman who fled to Florida from Alaska has a chance to redeem herself and her research when the glaciers begin to melt.

Stepping Stone. Bella Books, 2009.
A movie producer is wary of love and relationships after being burned.

Above Temptation. Bella Books, 2010.
An investigator searches for an embezzler that may be someone within the company, Sterling Proof, which is noted for its highly ethical, unblemished reputation.

LaFontaine, Kimberly

Picking Up the Pace. Intaglio, 2005.
Investigative reporter Angie Mitchell finds danger on the Fort Worth streets and surprising love with singer Lauren Lucelli.

Preying on Generosity. Intaglio, 2007.
Following *Picking Up the Pace*, this story takes Angie on a hunt for a dangerous story that causes tensions with her lover, Lauren.

Lynch, Lee

A long-time lesbian writer, Lynch often focuses on working-class butch and femme issues. She received the Alice B. Reader's for Lesbian Fiction in 2007 and was inducted into the Saints & Sinners Literary Hall of Fame in 2006.

Rafferty Street. New Victoria, 1998.
New York City cab driver Annie Heaphy (first met in *Toothpick House* [1986]) moves to tiny Morton River Valley looking for peace and finds challenges.

Sweet Creek. Bold Strokes, 2006.
Set in rural Waterfall Falls, Oregon, a town with an abundance of lesbians and small town ambience, this story revolves around the Natural Woman Foods store, its older hippie proprietors, and the amazingly diverse group of people who inhabit the town. One of Book Marks Top Ten Fiction list for 2006 by Richard La Bonte.

Beggar of Love. Bold Strokes, 2009.
This story follows a woman from youth to middle age as she looks for love in all the wrong places.

Mann, William J.
Provincetown Series
Set in Provincetown, Massachusetts, these sexy novels chronicle the lives and loves of Jeff O'Brien and Lloyd Griffith and their friends and acquaintances.

The Men from the Boys. Dutton, 1997.
A debut, coming-of-age novel that is riveting and realistic and focuses on Jeff O'Brien and Lloyd Griffith.

Where the Boys Are. Kensington, 2003.
Jeff and Lloyd meet again but circumstances keep them apart.

Men Who Love Men. Kensington, 2007.
Henry Weiner, a friend of Jeff"s, is the focus of this Provincetown story.

All American Boy. Kensington, 2005.
An actor returns to Brown's Mill to deal with his family and his past.

Object of Desire. Kensington, 2009.
A Hollywood golden boy who has everything he needs to confront his past and reclaim what he'd lost.

Martin, Marianne K.
Many of these books have characters in common or other links to each other. Many of these have recently been reprinted.

Love in the Balance. Bywater Books, 2010 (1998).
A woman burned by love eventually finds romance, but must deal with violent prejudice, as well.

Legacy of Love. Bywater Books, 2002 (rev. ed.; 1998).
New Yorker Sage moves to a small town in Michigan to establish a retirement home with her grandmother's legacy and meets Deanne, who is wary of Sage's reputation as a player.

Dawn of the Dance. Bywater Books, 2005 (1999).
Classic coming-of-age romance.

Mirrors. Bella Books, 2001.
This coming-out story is linked to *Dawn of the Dance* and is set in a small town in Michigan.

Never Ending. Bywater Books, 2006 (1999).
This sequel to *Legacy of Love* explores the continuing relationship of Sage and Deanne.

Under the Witness Tree. Bywater Books, 2003.
Surprised to inherit an old Southern mansion from a relative she didn't know she had, Dhari Weston heads for Georgia to dispose of the property and becomes involved with the history of the house and its secrets instead. Romance and mystery flavor this relatively short read. A Lambda Literary Award finalist.

Dance in the Key of Love. Bywater Books, 2006.
A woman on the run encounters a woman from her past in this sequel to *Dawn of the Dance*.

For Now, for Always. Bywater Books, 2007.
A young woman struggles to care and provide for her younger siblings and find fulfilling love, despite a social worker's homophobic bias.

Martinac, Paula

Out of Time: a Novel. Seal Press, 1999.
Ghosts and mystery combine in this time-hopping romance that moves between the Roaring Twenties and the present.

Merrick, Gordon

Unusual for the time period when most gay relationships were portrayed negatively, Merrick's often overly romantic stories end happily and feature well-adjusted gay characters. Most are sexually explicit and shocking for the times; they were written in a pre-AIDS era.

Peter & Charlie Trilogy

This trilogy focuses on Peter and Charlie, lovers since college days.

The Lord Won't Mind. Alyson Books, 1995 (1970).
One for the Gods. Allyson, 1996 (1971).
Forth Into Light. Alyson Books, 1996 (1974).

An Idol for Others. Alyson Books, 1998 (1977).
A Broadway star in a perfect marriage is not quite what he seems.

The Quirk. Alyson Books, 1998 (1978).
A rich boy is attracted to a bohemian model.

Perfect Freedom. Alyson Books, 1999 (1982).
The Cosling family acquires great wealth, lives well during the 1930s, and then declines during WWII.

The Great Urge Downward. Alyson Books, 2000 (1984).
A man escapes a failed marriage in a small Central American town and finds a variety of amusements.

A Measure of Madness. Alyson Books, 2001 (1986).
Romance on romantic Crete is tainted by jealousy.

The Good Life. Allyson, 1997 (coauthor, Charles G. Hulse; posthumous publication; Merrick died in 1988).
Murder adds intrigue to this story about rich, young, gay men.

Meyer, JLee

First Instinct. Bold Strokes, 2006.
Securities fraud, murder, and intrigue add up to a fast-paced adventure as a financial genius and a software expert/investigator find love along with danger in this 2007 golden Crown Literary Society Award winner.

Forever Found: A Love Story. Bold Strokes, 2006.
Separated as children, friends Dana and Kerri are reunited years later but must deal with past issues before they can find happiness.

Rising Storm. Bold Strokes, 2007.
A kidnapping in Pakistan sends Conn and Leigh on a desperate journey in this thriller that is a sequel to *First Instinct.*

Hotel Liaison. Bold Strokes, 2008.
A professor needs access to some papers recently discovered in a hotel, but clashes initially with the hotel owner.

High Risk. Bold Strokes, 2010.
A top actress and an agent reconnect in this Hollywood-tinged romance.

Proulx, Annie
"Brokeback Mountain."
First published in the *New Yorker* magazine on October 13, 1997, and later expanded and published as part of a collection, *Close Range: Wyoming Stories*, this short story about two men who fall in love and then meet over the years on brief camping trips is not a romance, but it is an important piece of writing and will be of interest to some readers. The film version (2005) sparked a lot of popular interest and it won several Oscars.

Radclyffe (Len Barot)
Prolific writer Radclyffe is a double Lambda Literary Award winner and was the 2003 and 2004 recipient of the Alice B. Readers' Award.

The Provincetown Tales
These romances are set in Provincetown and are linked by local characters that continue from story to story.

Safe Harbor. Bold Strokes, 2004 (2001).
Beyond the Breakwater. Bold Strokes, 2004 (2003).
Distant Shores, Silent Thunder. Bold Strokes, 2005.
Storms of Change. Bold Strokes, 2006.
Winds of Fortune. Bold Strokes, 2007.
Returning Tides. Bold Strokes 2009.

The Honor Series
Secret Service Agent Cameron Roberts and President's daughter Blair Powell are the romantic twosome in this adventurous series.

Above All, Honor. Bold Strokes, 2004 (2002).
Honor Bound. Bold Strokes, 2005 (2002).
Love & Honor. Bold Strokes, 2004 (2002).
Honor Guards. Bold Strokes, 2004.
Honor Reclaimed. Bold Strokes, 2005.
Honor under Siege. Bold Strokes, 2007.
Word of Honor. Bold Strokes, 2008.

The Justice Series
Detective Rebecca Frye and Dr. Catherine Rawlings pair up romantically and solve crimes, as well, in this series.

Shield of Justice. Bold Strokes, 2005 (2002).
In Pursuit of Justice. Quest Books, 2003.
*Justice in the Shadows. Bold Strokes, 2004 (2003) (GCLS Award Winner).
*Justice Served. Bold Strokes, 2005 (GCLS Award Winner).
Justice for All. Bold Strokes, 2009.

Fated Love. Bold Strokes, 2004.
A pair of doctors, each with troubles of their own, find love amid the tension of the ER room in this 2005 GCLS Award winner.

Love's Masquerade. Bold Strokes, 2004 (2003).
Set in the publishing world, this tender romance deals with some serious life issues.

Love's Melody Lost. Bold Strokes, 2004 (2001).
A pair of lost souls find love and healing when they find each other in this romance with a slight gothic feel.

Shadowland. Bold Strokes, 2004 (2003).
Dominance and submission are part of this nontraditional romance.

Tomorrow's Promise. Bold Strokes, 2004 (2002).
An isolated island provides the setting for two women in need of healing to find the love they both need.

Innocent Hearts. New Ed. Bold Strokes, 2005 (2002).
A young woman from Boston falls in love with a tough rancher in this 1860s Montana-set romance.

Promising Hearts. Bold Strokes, 2006.
A doctor who lost everything in the Civil War and New Hope's madam find love in rural Montana in this novel of the Old West. Follows *Innocent Hearts*.

Turn Back Time. Bold Strokes, 2006.
A pair of ambitious women who have no time for romance are caught up short by their feelings. The 2006 Independent Publishers Silver Award for Romance.

When Dreams Tremble. Bold Strokes, 2007.
A high-powered New York attorney returns to her family home in upstate New York and learns she can't avoid the past in the form of biologist Devon Weber.

The Lonely Hearts Club. Bold Strokes, 2008.
Three friends sort out their lives and find love and romance in this upbeat, sexy tale.

Secrets in the Stone. Bold Strokes, 2009.
A headstone carver in a small Pennsylvania town finds love when two new women enter her life.

First Responders Series
The title says it all for this series that involves those who are the first on the scene of traumatic events.

Trauma Alert. Bold Strokes, 2010.
A trauma doctor and a firefighter connect during an emergency.

Firestorm. Bold Strokes, 2011.
A cool, by-the-book firefirghter/paramedic and a rebellious smoke jumper find love as they work together.

Rowan, Lee (J. M. Lindner)
Royal Navy Series
Same-sex romances set amid the vivid pageantry of His Majesty's Royal Navy during the late 1700s and early 1800s.

Ransom. Linden Bay Romance, 2006.
Two British Naval officers, William Marshall and David Archer, discover love when they are kidnapped by a sadistic pirate who enjoys tormenting his captives in this late-eighteenth-century tale.

Winds of Change. Linden Bay Romance, 2007.
The command to pretend an illicit relationship presents an interesting, and dangerous, dilemma for David and William.

Eye of the Storm. Linden Bay Romance, 2009.
A covert mission, deception, misunderstandings, and danger add zing to the next in this popular series.

Home is the Sailor. Cheyenne Publishing, 2010.
Will and Davy are sent into hiding at David's Devon home and end up dealing with family issues, as well as a mystery.

Walking Wounded. Linden Bay Romance, 2007.
Two gay military men are separated, reunited, and then forced to deal with a villain from the past in this contemporary romance.

Tangled Web. Running Press, 2009.
A man seeks to help his best friend, who is being blackmailed, and finds unexpected help and love.

Rule, Jane
An award-winning, groundbreaking novelist of both fiction and nonfiction. Rule's final two romances, *Memory Board* (1987) and *After the Fire* (1989), were nominated for the Ethel Wilson Fiction Prize.

Saint-Clair, C. C.
Labeled the "thinking woman's lesbian romance novelist," Saint-Clair raises a number of social issues in her works. Many of her works have been reprinted.

Silent Goodbyes. 1st Books, 2002.
A romantic sea voyage, passion, and separation

Risking-Me. 1st Books, 2002.
This story explores aspects of lesbian domestic violence.

Far from Maddy. Bookmakers Ink, 2003.
Homeless lesbian youth are the focus of this realistic story.

Jagged Dreams. Bookmakers Ink, 2003.
This story deals with the abuse of women, how it affects them, and how they deal with it.

Morgan in the Mirror. Lazy Moon Productions, 2nd ed., 2007 (Bookmakers Ink, 2004).
Taking on the issues of transgendered romance—female to male transversion—the first edition of this book targeted a juvenile audience.

Stewart, Jean

Emerald City Blues. Rising Tide Press, 1996.
A pair of teenage lesbian runaways struggle with life on the Seattle streets and become involved with Chris Olson and Jenifer Hart in this realistic romance that touches on many serious issues.

Isis Series

Featuring a futuristic world destroyed by plague and now divided into the uninhabitable Wilderness, the male-dominated, rigid, elitist, right wing Elysium, and the female-controlled Freeland with a series of democratic colony-cities, this series focuses on the women Freeland Warriors of Isis. Many of these have been reprinted.

Return to Isis. Rising Tide, 1992.
Freeland Warrior Whit is rescued by Amelia, a farmer in Elysium, and together they escape and discover who betrayed Isis ten years earlier, as they fall in love.

Isis Rising. Rising Tide, 1993.
The women struggle to rebuild their colony of Isis.

Warriors of Isis. Rising Tide, 1995.
The warriors battle an evil, genetically engineered woman who is out to destroy Isis.

Winged Isis. Bella Books, 2001.
Failing satellites that maintain the critical border and political rivalries threaten Isis unless the Warriors can save the day.

Wizard of Isis. Bella Books, 2004.
Whit and her life partner end up in a part of Elysium that is controlled by Amazon Outlaws, a resistance group that has regressed and may be controlled by an evil Whit has met before.

Virga, Vincent

Vadriel Vail. Alyson Books, 2001.
Vadriel Vail and Armand de Guise struggle against numerous social, religious, and legal odds to find happiness in early-twentieth-century New York.

Waters, Sarah

Waters is noted for her Lesbian Victoriana novels, many of which have a decidedly Gothic touch.

Tipping the Velvet. Riverhead Trade, 2000.
Oyster girl Nancy Astley and male impersonator Kitty Butler explore their passions in this erotic late Victorian tale that does an exceptional job of recreating the London scene. A debut novel.

Affinity. Riverhead Trade, 2002.
Darker than her first novel, this Victorian Era mystery is also something of a romance with paranormal and gothic touches.

Fingersmith. Riverhead Books, 2002.
With a hint of *Oliver Twist*, this is another dark, sexy trip into the seamier side of Victorian London.

TAKE FIVE!

Five favorite GLBT romances:

- **Saxon Bennett**—*Family Affair*
- **Suzanne Brockmann**—*All through the Night: A Troubleshooter Christmas*
- **Ann Herendeen**—*Phyllida and the Brotherhood of Philander: A Bisexual Regency Romance*
- **Karin Kallmaker**—*Warming Trend*
- **Annie Proulx**—"Brokeback Mountain" (in *Close Range*)

9

10

11

12

13

14

15

16

Chapter 11

Inspirational Romance

So Jacob served seven years to get Rachel, but they seemed like only a few days to him because of his love for her.

Genesis 29:20

There is no more lovely, friendly and charming relationship, communion or company than a good marriage.

Martin Luther

Definition

> **Inspirational Romance**—Romance novels in which spiritual or religious beliefs play a major role in the protagonists' romantic relationship.

The Inspirational Romance is essentially a love story infused with religious (most often conservative Christian) values and beliefs. These stories usually employ one of the basic romance storylines, most often of the Innocent or Sweet Romance variety, but as the love relationship progresses, the characters also grow spiritually. They come to grips with their inner feelings regarding some basic tenet of religious faith as they learn to deal with their romantic feelings, and usually need to resolve things with God before their love relationship can work out. This combination of romantic and spiritual growth is the distinguishing characteristic of the Inspirational Romance subgenre. (Note: By definition, Inspirational Romances can focus on any spiritual belief system. However, the vast majority of Inspirationals on the market as of this writing are Christian Romances.)

Settings for Inspirationals can be either contemporary, historical, or in rare instances set in the future or a fantasy environment of some kind. A decade ago the market was relatively evenly divided between modern day and historical settings (Shirley Hailstock, "ROMSTAT: 1996 Romance Statistics," *Romance Writers' Report* 17 [June 1997]: 12–15). However, in the mid-2000s that changed. With Harlequin's Steeple Hill greatly expanding its contemporary lineup and other publishers coming on board, the balance shifted, and as a glance at the current offerings of the major Inspirational publishers shows, contemporary settings now dominate the market.

Inspirationals are as varied as other Romance types and while most are still sensually sweet and rarely sexually explicit, their diversity has increased in recent years. Religiously tinged tales of mystery and suspense, love stories with paranormal or futuristic (often End Time) elements, and Chick Lit, YA, and Women's Fiction Romances have joined the classic Historicals and Contemporaries to create a subgenre that essentially parallels the broader romance market and broadens the Inspirational's overall appeal. Styles can range from the cheerily upbeat or sweetly nostalgic, to the violent and adventurous, to the hard-hitting and emotionally wrenching; characters can be rich and polished, poor and unsophisticated, sassy and in your face, living an alternative lifestyle, or firmly middle-class; and settings run the gamut from futuristic or imaginary worlds, through modern urban America, to the ancient Middle East— and any time and place in-between. All settings have their fans; currently, however, romances set in contemporary America, often in a small town, seem to have the edge.

Typically, the Inspirational Romance plot introduces a religiously oriented heroine to a worldly, wounded, or alienated hero (or vice versa), arranges for them to be attracted to each other, and then provides numerous obstacles, often in the form of conflicting religious values, to their relationship. Eventually, of course, they are allowed to live "happily ever after," but not before both characters have done much soul-searching and have reconciled most of their differences, religious and otherwise. Although the less religious member of the couple usually comes to accept the beliefs of the other, the changes are not all one-sided. In fact, occasionally it is the "religious" one who experiences the most spiritual growth. Sometimes this happens in situations where that individual has been especially rigid in his or her beliefs or intolerant and judgmental of nonbelievers. The plot pattern outlined above as well as the themes of forgiveness, redemption, and spiritual awakening have been staples of the subgenre for years. However, other variations exist, and as the subgenre has expanded and some publishers are becoming less rigid and allowing writers more freedom in a effort to reach a broader audience, Inspirationals featuring realistic, sensitive treatment of themes popular with the chick lit and YA markets (e.g., lifestyle, peer pressure, behavioral choices); contemporaries that consider other relevant thorny social issues; and paranormals and futuristics that deal with epic themes, (e.g., good-against-evil) are appearing. Considering the new directions and current popularity of this market, there will likely be more innovations to come.

In most cases the Inspirational Romance is nondenominational, expressing generic, rather than denomination-specific, beliefs. (Occasionally, a particular religious group will publish romances that promote its own denomination, but this is the exception rather than the rule.) However, while the views expressed in these stories are not denomination-related, as a whole, the general slant of the Inspirational Romance is in a single direction—toward the conservative. There will, of course, be some exceptions, but, in general, these romances express basic fundamentalist rather than more liberal religious views.

Appeal

The appeal of the Inspirational Romance is primarily to those who espouse the various religious views presented in the stories. Readers enjoy reading stories about people who share their beliefs; it lends a certain validity to their own views. In fact, reading about how someone successfully deals with problems similar to one's own and within a similar frame of reference can be quite helpful, sometimes even "inspirational."

Because of their selective focus, Inspirational Romances, unlike some Romance sub-genres, do not have a broad, general appeal. For their target audience, however, they do fulfill a definite need, and, their popularity, as well as that of all Christian and religious fiction and nonfiction, has grown over the past decade as statistics from RWA's various RomSTAT reports show: There has been an increase from 6% to 7.56% of total Inspirational Romance titles between 1998 and 2009. Fueled largely by the country's generally conservative mood of the recent past and the visibility and influence of Christian fundamentalist groups and churches, Inspirationals have been published, marketed, and read in record numbers. And while things seem to be leveling off a bit in the current economy, it is still an important and influential subgenre in many communities.

Advising the Reader

General readers' advisory information is provided in chapter 3; several points to consider when advising Inspirational Romance readers are listed below.

- Religious fiction is not new. Many Inspirational Romance fans may also enjoy reading some of the older religious historical novels such as Henryk Sienkiewicz's *Quo Vadis?*, Lloyd C. Douglas's *The Robe*, or *The Silver Chalice* by Thomas Costain. Also consider recommending novels that present fictionalized accounts of Biblical characters' lives, such as *Two From Galilee: The Story of Mary and Joseph* and its sequels by Marjorie Holmes, or *The Road to Bithynia: A Novel of Luke, the Beloved Physician* or *The Song of Ruth: A Love Story from the Old Testament* both by Frank G. Slaughter.
- Readers who like Inspirational Romances might also like other types of inspirational literature. For example, religious poetry, inspirational guides to daily life, testimonials, or biographies of popular religious figures.
- Readers of Inspirational Romances may also enjoy some romances of the non-Inspirational variety, especially some in the sweet Traditional Contemporary Category lines that tend to be relatively conservative in their approach to love and marriage and are not sexually explicit. Traditional Regency Romances might also appeal, even though faith or religion is rarely mentioned. Note: Explicit sex is not part of most Inspirationals, so be sure your non-Inspirational recommendations are innocent rather than sensual.
- Although the religious emphasis in most of these romances is nondenominational, some publishing houses are church related and their romances do reflect a specific religious doctrine. It is important, therefore, to be aware of this during the reference interview and to try to match the reader with the appropriate book. For example, some conservative Christians might not find Inspirationals expressing certain Mormon principles acceptable, and vice versa. Simply knowing which publishers are aligned with which denominations (and what some of their beliefs and practices are) will help with this.
- The reference interview is particularly important in the area of Inspirational Romance. Religious convictions are personal and often deeply felt, and many people have very strong opinions concerning them. Therefore, it may be necessary to spend a bit more time than usual determining the specific type of romance the reader wants.

(Note: Those who want more information on Inspirational Romances may find the periodic review columns on Christian Fiction in *Library Journal*, the occasional updates or spotlights in *Booklist* and *Publishers' Weekly* or Lyn Cote's article "Christian Inspirational Romance Market 2005," in the October 2005 issue of *Romance Writers' Report* helpful.)

Publishers

Although Harlequin's Love Inspired (formerly Steeple Hill) imprint currently publishes a large percentage of popular Inspirational Romances and several mainstream houses have added Inspirational lines, many Inspirationals are produced by a number of smaller religious publishing houses. Several of these are listed below. (For more complete information refer to chapter 22, "Publishers.")

Baker Publishing Group (Includes Bethany House and Revell)
Barbour and Company
    Publishes Heartsong Presents lines of Historical and Contemporary Romances.
Bethany House (Division of Baker Publishing Group)
Cedar Fort
Doubleday Religious Publishing Group (Includes WaterBrook Multnomah)
FaithWords (Division of Hachette)
Harvest House Publishers
Thomas Nelson Publishers
Steeple Hill (Division of Harlequin Books)
Tyndale House Publishers
WaterBrook Multnomah (Division of Doubleday Religious Publishing Group)
Westbow Press (Division of Thomas Nelson Publishers)
Zondervan Publishing House (Division of HarperCollins)

Brief History

Although the Inspirational Romance in its current form is a relatively recent addition to the romance market, novels that express religious principles, promote certain religious beliefs and behaviors, or depict religious events have been around for years. Some, of course, weren't even religious by design; they simply reflected the customs and widely held beliefs of the times. For example, the highly successful mid-nineteenth-century novel *The Wide, Wide World* (1850) by Elizabeth Wetherell (Susan Warner) was not a religious book per se. Nevertheless, in addition to having a universally appealing plot situation—an orphaned heroine in the care of a singularly unsympathetic relative—it also managed incidentally to promote the desirability of a Christian home situation and lifestyle by featuring the children of a local clergyman as important characters in the story. A number of other writers during the same general period, however, intentionally used religious themes in their works. Novels of this type were extremely popular during and just after the Civil War, and many of the favorites were written by women who were part of the most active writing group of the period, the Domestic Sentimentalists. Two particularly popular works of this kind were *St. Elmo* (1867) by Augusta Jane Evans and *The Gates Ajar* (1868) by Elizabeth Stuart Phelps.

Following the 1860s, the popularity of the religious novel declined. However, it was renewed in the mid-1880s with the belated popularity of Lew Wallace's *Ben-Hur* (1880) and firmly reestablished by the next decade with a host of *Ben-Hur* imitations and a number of other religious Historicals including the perennial favorite *Quo Vadis?* (1896) by Henryk Sienkiewicz. By the turn of the century, interest in religious romances had waned in favor of other types, in particular, the nationalistic historical. There are a few were isolated exceptions, such as the extremely popular *The Rosary* (1910) by the English writer Florence Barclay, and the perennially popular inspirational love stories by Grace Livingston Hill. However, it wasn't until the decades of the 1930s and 1940s, with the grim realities of the Great Depression and World War II, that religious novels once again began to appear on the bestsellers list. Works such as *Magnificent Obsession* (1932) and *The Robe* (1942) by Lloyd C. Douglas, *The Keys to the Kingdom* (1941) by A. J. Cronin, and Sholem Asch's *The Nazarene* (1939) were some of the more popular.

The next few decades saw a leveling off in popularity of religious materials, except, interestingly, for sudden surge of interest during the 1950s in large-scale religious motion pictures (Cecil B. DeMille's *The Ten Commandments, Ben-Hur, Quo Vadis?*, etc.). However, from the late 1970s and into the mid-1980s, in keeping with the general feeling of the times, there was renewed interest in romantic novels with a specific religious message. The movement was strong, and both the adult and young adult markets were targeted. Earlier religious writers were reprinted, established writers experimented with the Inspirational genre, and new Inspirational Romance writers appeared in print. In the late 1980s, interest slumped. Series were canceled (among them, Silhouette's Inspirations line) and in 1987 the RWA discontinued the Inspirational Romance category in its Rita (then known as the Golden Medallion) and Golden Heart Awards. Eventually, the market rebounded and new publishers and lines came on the scene (e.g., Questar with Palisades/Palisades Presents lines, Barbour with Heartsong Presents), and by 1995 the subgenre had recovered to the extent that the RWA reinstated the Inspirational Romance category of their Rita and Golden Heart Awards. In 1997 Harlequin got on board with the September launch of the Steeple Hill Love Inspired line and in 1998 Bantam/Doubleday/Dell began publishing romances under its Christian books imprint, WaterBrook Press. Since then the subgenre has been on a roll, moving from under 0.5% of all romances published in 1996 (Hailstock, "ROMSTAT:1996 Romance Statistics," 12–15.) to more than 7% in 2007 (Romance Writers of America. *Romance Literature Statistics: Overview*, www.rwanational.org/cs/the_romance_genre/romance_literature_statistics). There have been mergers and acquisitions (e.g., Multnomah and WaterBrook, HarperCollins and Zondervan), existing lines have been expanded, and new lines have been launched. Love Inspired is the most notable example, adding another title each month to its original Inspirational Romance line and launching Love Inspired Cafe, a Chick Lit line, and a new women's single-title line—all in 2004; this was quickly followed by the inauguration of Love Inspired Suspense in 2005, and three years later Love Inspired Historical joined the group, with even more changes being planned (Recently, as part of Harlequin's standardization program, the Steeple Hill imprint has been replaced by Love Inspired.). Other publishers were adding lines, as well, and Avon Inspire, which features both Contemporary and Historical Romances, was launched in 2007. The Young Adult market has also been a target, and both Zondervan and FaithWords began publishing YA Inspirationals in 2008 and 2007, respectively.

Inspirational Romance has come a long way since the 1990s, and although it is still a specialized market, the genre is becoming more inclusive, a lot more savvy, and is reaching a broader audience than ever before. Clearly, the age-old combination of faith, hope, and love still resonates with readers and, at the moment, that doesn't seem likely to change.

Classic Inspirational Romance Writers

Bacher, June Masters

A noted writer of inspirational nonfiction, Bacher also wrote Inspirational Romance Fiction, primarily of the pioneer or Period Americana variety. She died in 1993, but many of her works are still available library collections. Please consult the first edition of this guide for individual series/title information.

Hill, Grace Livingston

A prolific and extremely popular novelist for more than half a century, Hill wrote more than a hundred religious romances filled with adventure, conflict, and domesticity. In spite of the fact that her stories are quite dated (especially in regard to ethnic, racial, and sexist references), evangelistic, and fairly predictable, her works strike a chord with many of today's readers, and many are still popular and in print to this day. Many of her works can still be found in their original editions in many older public libraries, but many have been repackaged and reissued in various formats in recent years. A complete list of her books, in addition to other information, can be found at www.gracelivingstonhill.com.

Holmes, Marjorie—*Two from Galilee* (1972), *Three from Galilee* (1985), *The Messiah* (1987).
Karon, Jan—*At Home in Mitford* (1994), *A Light in the Window* (1995).
Karr, Kathleen— **From This Day Forward* (1985). A Rita Award winner.

MacDonald, George

A nineteenth-century author, known for his children's stories and fantasies, MacDonald also produced a number of religious novels and some romances, many of which have been rewritten, retitled, and republished individually or in collections numerous times by various houses. Many titles have been "edited for today's readers" by Michael R. Phillips.

Marshall, Catherine—*Christy* (1967), *Julie* (1984).

A writer of inspirational materials and best known for her biography of her husband, Peter Marshall, *A Man Called Peter* (which is a love story itself), Marshall has also written young adult classics that can be considered within the Inspirational Romance subgenre.

Nichols, Charlotte—**For the Love of Mike* (1984). A Rita Award winner.
Oke, Janette—**Love Comes Softly Series** (1979–1989), **Seasons of the Heart Series** (1981–1989), **Canadian West Series** (1983–2001), **Women of the West Series** (1990–1996).

Rivers, Francine—*A Voice in the Wind* (1993), **An Echo in the Darkness* (1994), *Redeeming Love* (1994), **As Sure as the Dawn* (1995), **The Scarlet Thread* (1996), *The Atonement Child* (1997). Rivers is an RWA Hall of Fame member with three Rita Awards.

Wells, Marian—*When Love is Not Enough* (1979), *The Wedding Dress* (1982), *With This Ring* (1984).

Selected Inspirational Romance Bibliography

A number of writers who are no longer writing, as well as older titles of others, have been removed from this list. Please see previous editions of this guide for authors or titles that have been dropped from this edition.

Alexander, Tamera

Most of the books by this award-winning author are set in the Colorado Territory in the decades following the Civil War.

Fountain Creek Chronicles

A Western Historical setting.

Rekindled. Bethany House, 2006.
A mismatched couple struggle to make their marriage work and ultimately are faced with a challenge and must decide if they can rekindle their love and learn to trust each other.

*Revealed. Bethany House, 2006.
A young widow expecting a child advertises for a driver to take her to her land in Idaho and ends up hiring a man who blames her for her husband's death—his brother. A Rita Award winner.

Remembered. Bethany House, 2007.
A young woman leaves Paris to find her father in the mining towns of Colorado and finds love with a widower who is just beginning to get on with his life in this Christy Award winner.

Timber Ridge Reflections

Set in Timber Ridge, Colorado, during the late nineteenth century.

From a Distance. Bethany House, 2008.
Photographer Elizabeth Westerbrook comes to the Colorado Territory in 1875 to take pictures and recover her health and finds love with a war-weary former Confederate soldier as well as danger when she takes an incriminating photograph.

Beyond this Moment. Bethany House, 2009.
A college professor heads west to become a school teacher, but her past eventually catches up with her and her budding romance with the town sheriff.

Within My Heart. Bethany House, 2010.
A young widow resists falling for the town doctor (her doctor father always put his work ahead of his family) as she tries to manage her ranch and her two young boys.

*The Inheritance. Thomas Nelson, 2009.
A woman relocates to Copper Creek, Colorado, attracts the interest of the sheriff as she struggles to raise her young niece, be a parent to her rebellious, wayward brother, and keep the family together.

Baer, Judy

Baer is a popular, multi-published writer and is also noted for her Inspirational YA Romances.

The Whitney Chronicles. Steeple Hill Cafe, 2004.
In this lively chick lit romp, Whitney Blake, thirty, slightly chubby, and unattached, sets out to lose weight and find an appropriate Christian man—who turns out to be her best friend's doctor.

Be My Neat-Heart. Steeple Hill Cafe, 2006.
A neatnik organizer finds romance with the brother of a client in this funny, delightful read.

9

The Baby Chronicles. Steeple Hill Cafe, 2007.
Now married to Dr. Chase Andrews, Whitney's focus, and that of her two friends, turns to the ups and downs of pregnancy. Sequel to *The Whitney Chronicles*.

Oh, Baby! Steeple Hill Cafe, 2008.
Molly Cassidy, a dedicated doula (professional birthing coach), has professional conflicts with hard-nosed obstetrician Clay Reynolds but finds her way to his heart, as well.

10

The Cinderella List. Steeple Hill Love Inspired, 2010.
A caterer with a special-needs nephew and an architect who breeds horses connect over a riding program for developmentally challenged children.

11

Ball, Karen
The Breaking Point. Multnomah, 2003.
A marriage at risk is saved when a couple is stranded in the Oregon wilderness during a blizzard.

Family Honor Series
This series focuses on the lives of the Justice siblings, Avidan (Dan), Annie, and Kyla.

12

Shattered Justice. Multnomah, 2005.
A widowed police officer with a strong sense of justice struggles to put his life back together in a small Oregon town in spite of continuing difficulties.

Kaleidoscope Eyes. Multnomah, 2006.
An artist heroine "gifted" with synesthesia and on a search-and-rescue mission to find a lost child is aided by a TV producer, and targeted by an unknown assailant in a story that addresses issues of belonging.

13

What Lies Within. Multnomah, 2007.
A Christian contractor works against tremendous odds, including pressure from her fiancé, to turn an inner city church into a youth center.

14

Bateman, Tracey
Second Chance. Barbour, 2005
A young woman flees false accusations and finds love in a small California mining town. One of a series by various authors about the Chance brothers.

15

Mahoney Sisters Series
An Inspirational Romantic Suspense series.

Reasonable Doubt. Steeple Hill, 2005.
A widowed father trying to prove he didn't kill his wife takes refuge in his old cabin and finds love, as well as a bit of suspicion, with his childhood sweetheart, who is now a police officer.

16

Suspicion of Guilt. Steeple Hill, 2005.
A reporter uncovers dangerous secrets as she investigates a story involving her former fiancé.

Betrayal of Trust. Steeple Hill, 2005.
A TV reporter renews a friendship with a politician to get a story and then must choose between him and her job.

The Penbrook Diaries Series

Old secrets and racial prejudice are at the heart of these Historical Inspirational novels that are best read as a pair. Set in the 1940 with links to the past.

The Color of the Soul. Barbour, 2005.
A young African American reporter interviews a dying Southern novelist and finds, through her diaries, that they are linked in ways he never expected.

The Freedom of the Soul. Barbour, 2006.
A young woman discovers family diaries that lead her on a dangerous quest to reclaim her heritage and what is rightfully hers.

Westward Hearts Series

Faith and romance blossom as the characters in this series head west on the same wagon train in this Historical Inspirational series.

Defiant Heart. Avon, 2007
An orphaned young woman escapes servitude with her two young siblings and joins a wagon train heading west but runs into trouble with the wagon master, who doesn't want single women in his group.

Distant Heart. Avon, 2008.
A reformed prostitute finds a haven on the wagon train and the beginnings of a new life as she heads west, but she despairs of ever finding love because of her sinful past.

Dangerous Heart. Avon, 2008
A young woman struggles between revenge and faith in the conclusion to this trilogy.

Drama Queen Series

A lively, funny Christian chick lit series about three New York roommates—all in their thirties.

Catch a Rising Star. Faithwords, 2007.
A "killed-off" soap opera star returns to her former role and faces many of the same problems that she had to deal with before.

You Had Me at Goodbye. Faithwords, 2008.
An editor plots revenge by submitting a scathing novel proposal under an assumed name to the new senior editor who just fired her but needs to deal with her attraction for him, as well.

That's (Not Exactly) Amore. Faithwords, 2008.
A young woman is attracted to a man whose family may have mob connections in the final book in this funny trilogy.

Bates, Shelley

Bates also writes Contemporary Series Romance.

Elect Trilogy

A gripping, emotionally wrenching trilogy that focuses on religious cults and "toxic churches" and their effects on those directly or peripherally involved. The fictional "Elect" is the particular cult in this series.

Grounds to Believe. Steeple Hill, 2004.
A crime investigator, whose infant daughter was taken by a cult and now works to find her and keep other children from harm, infiltrates a cult under suspicion and is attracted to one of the members.

A Pocketful of Pearls. Warner Faith, 2005.
Rescued, in Good Samaritan fashion, by a woman literally enslaved by the demands of a cult, a robbed, slandered, and then fired college professor hires on as her handyman. As their relationship grows, he helps her see the truth as they both come to terms with their pasts.

A Sounding Brass. Warner Faith, 2006.
A young woman who grew up in the cult (The Elect) must choose between a charismatic radio evangelist and a non-Elect police investigator in the final book in the trilogy.

Benson, Angela

Benson has also written sweet Contemporary Romances, as well as Inspirational Women's Fiction, including the popular *Amen Sisters* (2005) and *Up Pops the Devil* (2008). Some of her earlier works have been reprinted.

Awakening Mercy. Tyndale House, 2000.
A single mom assigned to do community service for not paying parking tickets attracts the attention of the director of social services in this touching African American Inspirational Romance.

Abiding Hope. Tyndale House, 2001.
A couple struggles through a tragedy and the aftermath to renew their marriage in this sequel to *Awakening Mercy.*

Bittner, Rosanne

Western Historical writer Bittner sets these Inspirationals in the last half of the nineteenth century during the Alaskan gold rush, in Alaska, during the gold rush of the 1890s, on a wagon train to Montana, and on the Nebraska plains during the coming of the railroad, respectively.

Where Heaven Begins. Steeple Hill, 2004.
A young woman goes in search of her pastor brother in Alaska and falls in love with a hardened bounty hunter who rescues her along the way.

Walk by Faith. Steeple Hill, 2005.
A single mom finds unexpected love with an ex-soldier when she and her young daughter head west to Montana.

Follow Your Heart. Steeple Hill, 2005.
The railroad barons clash with the Nebraska farmers in this Inspirational that brings the son of a wealthy family together with farm owner Ingrid Svensson, first in friendship but then in love.

Blackstock, Terri

Blackstock's recent novels are more Inspirational Mystery/Suspense than Romance, but many will still appeal to romance readers.

Cape Refuge Series

Suspenseful mysteries with a touch of romance set on a small barrier island off the coast near Savannah, Georgia.

Cape Refuge. Zondervan, 2002.
Sisters Blair and Morgan Owens struggle to keep Hanover House, their murdered parents' halfway house, open and find a killer before he kills again.

Southern Storm. Zondervan, 2003.
When Chief Matthew Cade disappears while working on a murder case, Blair Owens smells a rat and sets out to find him.

River's Edge. Zondervan, 2004.
More danger and mysterious disappearances in this fast-paced mystery.

Breaker's Reef. Zondervan, 2005.
Chief Cade comes under suspicion as he investigates murders mimicking scenes in a mystery writer's novels.

Restoration Series (Futuristic/Post-Apocalyptic)

In this futuristic series, a catastrophe cuts off all electricity, taking modern society back decades and forcing people to learn to live in harmony with God and each other. Mostly Christian Science Fiction, but there is plenty of mystery suspense and some romance. Members of the well-to-do Banning family of suburban Birmingham, Alabama, are the main characters in this series.

Last Light. Zondervan, 2005.
When an unexplained event wipes out all electronics, Americans are left helpless and must go back to the basics.

Night Light. Zondervan, 2006.
People begin to pull together to make the best of things even as crime increases and winter—and the cold—is coming soon.

True Light. Zondervan, 2007.
The Bannings continue to work to establish order but the lawlessness continues.

Dawn's Light. Zondervan, 2008.
The blackout comes to an end but the Bannings still have plenty of soul-searching to do to make sense of it all.

Blackwell, Lawana

Blackwell focuses on Inspirationals set in nineteenth-century England but also writes for the contemporary Inspirational Women's Fiction market.

The Gresham Chronicles

The first three stories in this charming Victorian series set in the village of Gresham Green, England, were reprinted in 2007/2008 just prior to the publication of the final volume in the series.

The Widow at Larkspur Inn. Bethany House, 1997.
After her husband's death a young widow and her three children leave London for tiny Gresham Green, where she restores an old inn and, with the help of the vicar, begins to build a new life.

The Courtship of the Vicar's Daughter. Bethany House, 1998.
A young woman is torn between her feelings for a young curate and a former love who has returned to convince her of his worthiness.

The Dowry of Miss Lydia Clark. Bethany House, 1999.
A spinster schoolmarm finds unexpected love when an archaeologist comes to her for literary help in order to attract another woman.

The Jewel of Gresham Green. Bethany House, 2008.
A single mother leaves the city to protect her young daughter and moves to Gresham Green where she becomes indispensable to the vicar's family and the town, at large. A touch of evil and danger, as well a look at real social issues, are part of this book that is set approximately fifteen years after the first three in the series.

Tales of London
Inspirational tales set in Victorian England.

The Maiden of Mayfair. Bethany House, 2000.
An orphan is taken in by a rich woman who thinks the child may be her late son's illegitimate daughter.

Catherine's Heart. Bethany House, 2002.
A sheltered, naive young woman goes off to college and falls for a rake before she learns to tell the difference between real affection and love, and simple infatuation.

Leading Lady. Bethany House, 2004.
When a London theatre wardrobe mistress spurns the advances of a suitor and inadvertently causes his death, the man's actress sister plots revenge that yields unexpected results.

A Table by the Window. Bethany House, 2005.
A successful young woman leaves San Francisco and goes to Tallulah, Mississippi, when she inherits a house and a fortune and finds mystery and danger, along with love.

Brownley, Margaret
Rocky Creek Series
Rocky Creek, Texas, 1880s.

A Lady like Sarah. Thomas Nelson, 2009.
An outlaw with a price on her head connects with a disgraced preacher on their way west in this funny, touching romance.

A Suitor for Jenny. Thomas Nelson, 2010.
A woman with strict ideas about what makes a good husband tries to avoid falling for the sheriff as she looks for proper mates for her sisters.

Brunstetter, Wanda E.
Many of Brunstetter's books focus on the various Amish communities in the United States.

The Daughters of Lancaster County
A kidnapping ties these stories together in a years-spanning trilogy.

The Storekeeper's Daughter. Barbour, 2005.
A young woman, burdened with caring for her younger siblings and helping in the family story after her mother dies, flees to the city with an Englisher friend when her baby brother is kidnapped and she is feeling guilty.

The Quilter's Daughter. Barbour, 2005.
A young woman leaves her quilting shop in Ohio to help her mother in Pennsylvania during her pregnancy, only to have her fiancé die when her shop burns down.

The Bishop's Daughter. Barbour, 2006.
An Englisher comes to Pennsylvania to find his birth family and is attracted to the school teaching daughter of an Amish bishop.

The Brides of Webster County

Set among the Amish in Missouri, this quartet of romances features heroines who struggle with acceptance and knowing God's will.

Going Home. Barbour, 2005.
Now a widowed single parent, a young woman who left the Amish community for a career outside, returns home, reconnects with her roots, and finds love as well.

On Her Own. Barbour, 2005.
Left with four boys to raise and a harness shop to run when her husband is killed, a young widow is courted by two very different men.

Dear to Me. Barbour, 2005.
A heroine's love of animals earns her family criticism and could possibly cost her the love of her life.

Allison's Journey. Barbour, 2006.
A young woman with a terrible self-image comes into her own and finds love in the final volume of this series.

The Sisters of Holmes County

This Romantic Suspense trilogy focuses on the loves and difficulties of the three Hostettler sisters and includes an ongoing mystery.

A Sister's Secret. Barbour, 2007.
The eldest sister, Grace, is preparing for her wedding when a man she dated during her rumspringa (when the young people leave to live among the Englishers before joining the community or leaving it altogether) returns to cause problems for her and the community.

A Sister's Test. Barbour, 2008.
Attacks continue on the family and Ruth, recently wed, must deal with unexpected tragedy.

A Sister's Hope. Barbour, 2008.
Martha sets out to learn who is behind the attacks on the family in order to clear the name of the man she loves in this final volume that finally clears up the mystery.

Indiana Cousins Series

Set in the Amish country of Indiana, this series focuses on a group of cousins who all have problems to solve.

A Cousin's Promise. Barbour, 2009
A crippling car accident causes problems for a couple when the hero doesn't want to become a burden to his fiancée—and then an old boyfriend complicates things.

A Cousin's Prayer. Barbour, 2009.
When her boyfriend is killed in a car accident, a young woman struggles with depression and the fear of loving and trusting again.

A Cousin's Challenge. Barbour, 2010.
Tragedy and confusion abound in this story that continues this series.

Burkard, Linore Rose
Before the Season Ends. Harvest House, 2008.
A Regency miss who wants to marry a man who shares her faith goes to London for the Season and is attracted by a popular rake. A debut book.

Capshaw, Carla
Roman Series
This Historical Inspirational series is set in Ancient Rome during the early days of Christianity.

The Gladiator. Steeple Hill Love Inspired Historical, 2009.
A Roman gladiator buys a young Christian slave who changes his life in a number of ways.

The Protector. Love Inspired Historical, 2010.
A Christian gladiator slave becomes a bodyguard for a wealthy socialite.

The Champion. Love Inspired Historical, 2011.
A Christian noblewoman and a gladiator defy family and custom for freedom and their faith.

The Duke's Redemption. Love Inspired Historical, 2010.
An English duke comes to South Carolina in search of the person who killed his brother and falls in love with an American colonial spy.

Carlson, Melody
Carlson currently writes Inspirational Fiction for the young adult, chick lit, children's, and women's fiction markets.

*Homeward. Multnomah, 1997.
A young woman returns home to reconnect with her family after years away and discovers long-buried secrets that cause her to reassess her ideas and rediscover God, in the process. A Rita Award winner.

Copeland, Lori.
Copeland's books are usually lively, fast-paced, humorous stories that are considered faith-filled but not preachy.

Monday Morning Faith. Zondervan, 2006.
Humor and faith help a new "older" bride deal with the realities of the mission field as she goes with her doctor husband to New Guinea.

Yellow Rose Bride. Steeple Hill, 2006.
Married briefly as teenagers, but forced apart by their fear and their feuding families, Vonnie and Adam had their marriage annulled. Now, seven years later, the landscape has changed, and as old secrets come to light, there may be hope for them, yet.

Bluebonnet Belle. Steeple Hill, 2007.
Determined to teach the local women about their health, a woman herbalist clashes with a doctor who doesn't agree with her ideas.

Belles of Timber Creek
Set in a small town in post–Civil War Texas, this Historical Inspirational series focuses on three school teachers who band together to survive in the aftermath of the war.

Twice Loved. Avon Inspire, 2008.
A young woman is faced with a choice between marrying for the good of others and marrying for love.

Three Times Blessed. Avon Inspire, 2009.
Love blooms for a young woman and a widower as they work to save the town from illness and a treacherous flood.

One True Love. Avon Inspire, 2010.
A teacher badly wounded in a fire must depend on a man she can't get along with during the long journey to get medical help.

Western Sky Series
These Western Historicals are all Inspirational rewrites of previously published titles.

Outlaw's Bride. Harvest House, 2009.
A man falsely accused of murder gets a second chance, but focuses on revenge until he meets a woman and a town that can change his mind in this 1999 book that was originally published by Avon as *The Bride of Johnny McAllister*.

A Kiss for Cade. Harvest House, 2010.
A town decides that the gunslinger uncle of four orphans and the woman who is caring for the children should marry in this 1997 book that was originally published by Avon as *The Courtship of Cade Kolby*.

Walker's Wedding. Harvest House, 2010.
A man in need of an heir advertises for a mail-order bride, but the bride he ends up with is not the one he "ordered" in this 2000 book that was originally published by Avon as *Marrying Walker McKay*.

Cote, Lyn
Cote is a popular, most prolific Inspirational Romance writer.

Northern Intrigue Series
Mystery, romance, and faith in rural Northern Wisconsin.

Winter's Secret. Tyndale House, 2002.
A county sheriff and a home nurse find romance as they try to stop a burglar who is preying on the elderly.

Autumn's Shadow. Tyndale House, 2003.
Teenage pranks at the school bring a high school principal and a deputy sheriff together as they work to find the culprit before something really dangerous happens.

Summer's End. Tyndale House, 2003.
A new doctor scheduled to repay her medical school loans by working at the local clinic intends to pay the money, find a replacement, and leave, but God has other plans.

9

Sisters of the Heart
Three good friends find love while dealing with various problems in this Illinois-based trilogy.

10

His Saving Grace. Steeple Hill, 2004.
A computer expert and his assistant go in search of a hacker and find love along the way.

Testing His Patience. Steeple Hill, 2004.
A teacher and a DA clash over a robbery conviction, but find love, and the true culprit, in the end.

11

Loving Constance. Steeple Hill, 2004.
An attorney joins forces with a police detective to find her friend's missing husband and finds romance in the process.

Harbor Intrigue Series
Mystery, danger, and romance abound in a Wisconsin lakeside resort town, Winfield, in this Romantic Suspense series that also addresses serious social issues from a faith-based point of view.

12

Dangerous Season. Steeple Hill, 2007.
An arsonist brings the town lawman and a cafe owner together as they work to find the culprit.

13

Dangerous Game. Steeple Hill, 2007.
Convicted of a fatal hit-and-run years earlier, our hero returns home and finds love and redemption with a law enforcement officer.

Dangerous Secrets. Steeple Hill, 2007.
Looking for the answer to her cousin's death, the heroine finds love with the state detective who's been sent to Winfield to help sort things out.

14

Texas: Star of Destiny Series
Spanning three generations and twenty-five years of Texas history, these historical stories provide adventure and love for their faith-oriented characters.

15

The Desires of Her Heart. Avon Inspire, 2009.
A frontier scout and a New Orleans woman find romance and challenges on the Texas frontier of 1821.

His Inheritance Forever. Avon Inspire, 2009.
A proud Mexican rancher and a Texas cowboy find love despite Comanche raids, greedy relatives, and the growing tensions of the Texas Rebellion and the Battle of the Alamo in 1836.

16

Her Abundant Joy. Avon Inspire, 2010.
A young German immigrant widow and a Texas Ranger find love in 1846 Texas.

Duarte, Judy (See chapter 5, "Contemporary Romance.")

Gist, Deeanne
Gist's Historical Inspirational stories are vivid, refreshing, well-plotted, and filled with appealing characters.

Deep in the Heart of Trouble. Bethany House, 2008.
The outrageous, headstrong spinster head of an oil company catches the eye of one of her new employees, who is actually the disenfranchised son of an oil tycoon.

A Bride in the Bargain. Bethany House, 2009.
A woman travels from Massachusetts to Seattle to become a cook for a lumberjack only to learn he wants a wife, instead.

Maid to Match. Bethany House, 2010.
A housemaid and a reluctant footman find love while working at the opulent Biltmore Estate in the late nineteenth century.

Goodnight, Linda
Goodnight also writes sweet non-Inspirational Contemporary Romances.

In the Spirit of . . . Christmas. Steeple Hill, 2005
A Christmas tree farm owner and a single dad find love even though secrets could threaten their budding relationship.

A Very Special Delivery. Steeple Hill, 2006.
A woman who panics around children because her nephew died while she was caring for him and a single dad paramedic with a baby daughter are trapped by the weather with romantic results.

Brothers Bond Series
Three brothers separated as children come together as adults after years apart.

A Season of Grace. Steeple Hill, 2006.
A social worker enlists the aid of a police officer to help with a troubled teen in this story with a holiday slant.

*A Touch of Grace. Steeple Hill, 2007. (Love Inspired)
A reporter investigating group homes finds love and truth with the pastor of one of the homes in this Rita Award winner.

The Heart of Grace. Steeple Hill, 2007.
A wounded war photographer finds healing and love when he reconnects with his estranged wife.

Missionary Daddy. Steeple Hill, 2007.
A model meets a missionary building an orphanage during a shoot in Africa and reconnects with him when he becomes the assistant director at a local adoption agency.

A Time to Heal. Steeple Hill, 2008.
A burned-out doctor goes home to rest and reconnects with her high school sweetheart, but he is concerned about her workaholic tendencies.

Home to Crossroads Ranch. Steeple Hill, 2009.
A single woman who adores her foster children is attracted to a rancher who doesn't want kids—until they all set out to convince him otherwise.

The Baby Bond. Steeple Hill, 2009.
A single firefighter bonds with a baby he rescues and must convince the child's attractive aunt, now the child's guardian, that they are meant to be a family.

9

Redemption River Series
Redemption, Oklahoma, is the setting for this series.

Finding Her Way Home. Steeple Hill, 2010.
A woman looking for a new start finds one with a single dad and his young daughter.

10

The Wedding Garden. Steeple Hill, 2010.
A former bad boy returns when his beloved aunt is dying and renews his love with the girl he was forced to leave.

Gunn, Robin Jones
Gunn is a multi-published author of Inspirational YA, chick lit, and women's fiction.

11

Sisterchicks Series
This fun-loving, world-hopping, Inspirational series featuring heroines in mid-life is less romance and more about friends and relationships. Christian chick lit for grownups

12

Sisterchicks on the Loose! 2003.
A homemaker goes to Finland with her long-time friend who is looking for her relatives.

Sisterchicks Do the Hula. Multnomah, 2004.
Two friends celebrate their fortieth birthdays in Hawaii.

13

Sisterchicks in Sombreros. Multnomah, 2004.
Two sisters go to Mexico to take a look at their inherited property and reconnect as sisters.

Sisterchicks Down Under. Multnomah, 2005.
A woman goes to New Zealand with her husband when he accepts a three-month film job and meets a woman who becomes an instant sisterchick.

14

Sisterchicks Say Ooh La La! Multnomah, 2005.
Best friends from childhood but estranged as teenagers and then reunited as adults, two sisterchicks fulfill a long-time dream and go to Paris.

15

*Sisterchicks in Gondolas. Multnomah, 2006.
Sisters-in-law go to stay in a restored palace in Venice and end up being cooks for a retreat group in this Christy Award winner.

Sisterchicks Go Brit! Multnomah, 2008.
Two long-time friends escort an elderly neighbor to England to visit her sister and fulfill dreams of their own, as well.

16

Sisterchicks in Wooden Shoes. Multnomah, 2009.
A disturbing medical test result sends a woman to the Netherlands to meet her long-time pen pal for a wonderful vacation and salutary heart-to-heart talks.

Father Christmas Series

A duet of novellas that tell of a young woman's search for her biological father, and her own sense of family, as well.

Finding Father Christmas. Faithwords, 2007.
Miranda Carson leaves the States to search for her biological father in London during the holidays.

Engaging Father Christmas. Faithwords, 2008.
Family, belonging, and romance come to the fore in this sequel to *Finding Father Christmas*.

Hannon, Irene

It Had to Be You. Steeple Hill, 1999.
A woman who gave up love to raise her sister's children finds happiness—at last—with the man she let go.

The Way Home. Steeple Hill, 2000.
A career-oriented broadcast journalist begins to reassess her values and goals when she first clashes with and then begins to admire a faith-filled attorney.

*Never Say Goodbye. Steeple Hill, 2002
A man who caused the accident that killed his daughter finds the Lord in prison and returns home hoping to win his wife's trust and forgiveness and help her overcome the loss that his behavior had caused in this Rita Award winner.

Crossroads. Steeple Hill, 2003.
A high school principal helps a single mother with her troubled teenage son, but when they fall in love, they must deal with their own pasts as well as the teenager's feelings.

Sisters & Brides Series

Three sisters inherit different gifts from their beloved great aunt—if they do what she specifies for half a year—in this popular series.

The Best Gift. Steeple Hill, 2005.
A bookstore manager and the woman who inherits the store find love in spite of their differences in this engaging story.

Gift from the Heart. Steeple Hill, 2005.
A young woman volunteers as a nanny to a pre-teen-ager and finds love and a family, as well.

The Unexpected Gift. Steeple Hill, 2005.
A workaholic woman shares a New England cabin with a man whose mother was devoted to her career and finds out what is truly important in life.

All Our Tomorrows. Steeple Hill, 2006.
A newspaper editor finds unexpected love with the brother of her dead fiancé.

Rainbow's End. Steeple Hill, 2007.
Two scarred people, one physically, the other emotionally, find love when a rainstorm changes the course of three lives.

Heartland Homecoming Series

Newcomers and current residents of small Oak Hill, Missouri, find healing and love in this trilogy.

From this Day Forward. Steeple Hill, 2007.
A former surgeon is called in to help his estranged wife deal with PTSD after she witnesses a murder.

A Dream to Share. Steeple Hill, 2008.
The *Oak Hill Gazette* editor clashes with the urban playboy publisher who has his own ideas about the future of the paper.

Where Love Abides. Steeple Hill, 2008.
A badly damaged heroine finds healing and love—and a family—in this heart-warming Inspirational.

Apprentice Father. Steeple Hill, 2009.
A wary bachelor suddenly becomes a dad when his sister dies but gets help from a physically handicapped Christian.

Lighthouse Lane
A series of stories set in Nantucket.

Tides of Hope. Love Inspired, 2009.
A single mom struggles to resist her attraction to the new Coast Guard commander.

The Hero Next Door. Love Inspired, 2009.
A big-city cop comes to Nantucket and ends up making a difference in the lives of a troubled teen and his attractive aunt.

The Doctor's Perfect Match. Love Inspired, 2010.
A wary doctor and a waitress in need of healing find love.

A Father for Zach. Love Inspired, 2010.
A young widow and her young son get a new lease on life when a carpenter, with issues of his own, comes into their lives.

Heroes of Quantico
Members of the FBI Hostage Rescue Team based at the Marine Corps base in Quantico are the heroes of this suspenseful, Inspirational Romance series.

Against All Odds. Revell, 2009.
A hostage rescue team member falls in love with the very difficult woman he is sworn to protect.

An Eye for an Eye. Revell, 2009.
A member of an FBI Hostage Rescue Team reconnects with an old love and then must track down a sniper who's either targeting him or the woman he is falling in love with once again.

In Harm's Way. Revell, 2010.
A Raggedy Ann doll leads a psychic and a skeptical FBI agent into danger in this romantic, suspenseful tale.

Hatcher, Robin Lee
Hatcher also wrote popular non-Inspirational Romances earlier in her career, some of which she has rewritten for the Inspirational market.

Patterns of Love. HarperPaperbacks, 1998.
A young Swedish woman agrees to a marriage of convenience, but will it be the right thing? This book was originally written as a non-Inspirational Historical Romance and is second in Hatcher's Coming to America series.

The Forgiving Hour. WaterBrook, 1999.
Issues of infidelity and forgiveness are part of this gripping contemporary Inspirational.

The Shepherd's Voice. WaterBrook, 2000.
Returning to Idaho after an undeserved ten-year prison stint, Gabe is rejected by his wealthy father and is taken in by the owner of a sheep ranch where he finds healing, forgiveness, and love in this Depression Era Historical.

Ribbon of Years. Tyndale, 2001.
A woman gains insight into how she needs to change her life when she attends the estate sale of a woman whose own struggles provide insight.

Speak to Me of Love. Tyndale, 2003.
A woman puts her acting career on temporary hold because of her daughter's illness and takes a job as a housekeeper to a crusty reclusive rancher in this Inspirational that is a rewritten version of one of Hatcher's secular Historical titles, *Chances Are* (1996).

Catching Katie. Tyndale, 2004.
A suffragist and a newspaperman clash as they find love in this lively romance set in 1916 Idaho; this is a revised version of Hatcher's earlier non-Inspirational *Kiss Me, Katie* (1996).

Loving Libby. Zondervan, 2005.
Escaping from her wealthy past, Libby is happy (and hidden) on her Idaho sheep ranch, but her happiness is threatened by a stranger on a vengeful mission of his own in this revised version of Hatcher's earlier non-Inspirational Historical Romance, *Liberty Blue* (1995).

Diamond Place. Revell, 2006.
A preteen matchmaker's efforts work for her mother and her coach—and then she changes her mind in this light Inspirational Romance.

Trouble in Paradise. Steeple Hill, 2007.
A woman feels called to become a writer, moves to a cabin in rural Idaho, and finds love with the neighboring widower.

Wagered Heart. Zondervan, 2008.
An innocent bet lands a sweet pastor's daughter in trouble when an unscrupulous rancher with gubernatorial ambitions decides to get rid of the competition for her affections in this Montana-set Historical.

When Love Blooms. Zondervan, 2009.
A refined, educated woman takes a job teaching two children on a remote Idaho ranch and finds romance with the skeptical rancher in this Historical.

Sisters of Bethlehem Springs Series
Spunky sisters make forays into the traditional "man's world," in this series that is set in rural Bethlehem Springs, Idaho, in the 1910s. Historical Inspirational Romance.

A Vote of Confidence. Zondervan, 2009.
An independent woman falls in love with her opponent in a mayoral race in this lively, humorous romance.

Fit to Be Tied. Zondervan, 2009.
A rancher tries to turn an English aristocrat into a cowboy in this funny, heartwarming romance.

A Matter of Character. Zondervan, 2010.
The grandson of a man being portrayed in a negative light in the heroine's pseudonymous dime novels sets out to clear his grandfather's name.

Henderson, Dee
Henderson's Inspirational Romances make good use of mystery and suspense. Many of her books have been republished.

*Danger in the Shadows. Multnomah, 1999.
A reclusive, bestselling writer who endured a horrible childhood kidnapping and the resulting death of her twin sister finds her anonymity—and her safety—jeopardized when a well-known former football star comes into her life in this Rita Award Winner that is the prequel to the O'Malley series.

O'Malley Series
Seven orphans band together to become a family, choosing O'Malley as their common surname, in this popular Inspirational Romantic Suspense series.

The Negotiator. Multnomah, 1999.
An expert hostage negotiator and an FBI agent are attracted to each other but the heroine's lack of belief is a problem for the hero in this story that also connects the heroine (one of the O'Malley siblings) with a brother she didn't know existed.

The Guardian. Multnomah, 2001.
A U.S. Marshal must find a judge's killer, keep the attractive eyewitness safe, and deal with his O'Malley siblings' various issues, including one of his sister's battle with cancer.

The Truth Seeker. Multnomah, 2001.
A forensic pathologist deals with injury and struggles with the conflict between science and belief as she and a U.S. Marshal work to learn the identity of an arsonist before he kills again.

The Protector. Multnomah, 2001.
A firefighter on the trail of an arsonist is attracted to the only witness to the crime.

The Healer. Multnomah, 2002.
A Red Cross psychologist trained to help disaster victims work through their traumas and a firefighter find romance even as personal and community tragedies strike.

The Rescuer. Multnomah, 2003.
A paramedic struggling with the death of his sister and people's sufferings, in general, comes to the aid of a blind friend when she suspects someone has been in her house, and finds healing as well as love.

Uncommon Heroes Series
Taut, suspenseful thrillers featuring a variety of strong, capable heroes,

True Devotion. Multnomah, 2000.
A life-threatening rescue of a teenager at sea causes a lifeguard and Navy SEAL widow to reassesses her fears of loving another SEAL, little realizing that they both may be the next targets of her husband's killer.

True Valor. Multnomah, 2002.
When a Navy combat pilot goes down behind enemy lines in the Middle East, she must rely on the Air Force rescue expert she loves to get her out.

True Honor. Multnomah, 2002.
A retired CIA spy is pulled out of retirement to go after a man who knew about 9/11 beforehand and becomes a terrorist target herself. She also falls in love with a handsome Navy SEAL.

True Courage. Multnomah, 2004.
An FBI agent on the trail of a woman who's been kidnapped and held for ransom falls in love with her sister, who trades places with her sister and ramps up the stakes for the hero. Republished by Tyndale as *Kidnapped* in 2008.

The Witness. Tyndale, 2006.
A woman on the run from a man who wants her dead and a sheriff determined to save her find love in this suspenseful romance.

Before I Wake. Tyndale, 2006.
Women are dying in a small town and the evidence points to drug testing in this fast-paced Inspirational Romantic Suspense.

Hickman, Patricia

Katrina's Wings. WaterBrook, 2000.
A touching coming-of-age novel about two sisters combined with a sweet romance with a Deep South 1970s setting.

Hudson-Smith, Linda

A Silver Season. Kimani New Spirit, 2006.
A widow moves to a new town to put her life back together and struggles with her feelings for her late husband when meets an attractive widower.

Hunt, Angela Elwell

Hunt is a multi-published Inspirational author of Contemporary and Historical fiction and nonfiction; her Historicals often include a romance thread.

Heirs of Cahira O'Connor

This series is based on the legend of Cahira O'Connor, the fiercely independent daughter of a thirteenth-century Irish king, who begged God as she lay dying to send future women who would carry on her mission to break down barriers for women.

The Silver Sword. WaterBrook 1998.
Although considering the tale of Cahira a mere myth, when Kathleen O'Connor realizes she has Cahira's mark, a mark that appears on one of Cahira's descendants every two hundred years, she sets out to learn more about the "heirs" who followed Cahira. A fifteenth-century woman who yearns to be a knight is the focus of this story.

The Golden Cross. WaterBrook 1998.
Raised on the streets of Indonesia, a cross-dressing heroine with a gift for drawing goes to sea with a mapmaker and ends up finding love as well as a new life in the seventeenth century.

The Velvet Shadow. WaterBrook 1999.
A young Southern medical student caught in transit between the North and South as the Civil War begins, pretends to be a soldier and begins to treat the wounded.

The Emerald Isle. WaterBrook 1999.
Kathleen O'Connor learns more about Cahira and also the role she is to play as the twenty-first-century "heir" in this romantic tale set in Ireland.

Kingsbury, Karen
Kingsbury's recent Inspirationals listed below have a romance thread.

Just Beyond the Clouds. Center Street, 2007.
A rodeo man retires to do something that might help people like his Down Syndrome brother and finds fulfillment and love, as well.

Between Sundays. Zondervan, 2007.
A foster parent with a child who thinks a pro football player is his father meets the star with romantic results.

Klassen, Julie
The Lady of Milkweed Manor. 2008.
A pregnant young woman disowned by her judgmental clerical father finds healing and love in this Historical Inspirational Romance that also includes a fair amount of relevant historical data.

The Silent Governess. Bethany House, 2009.
A nobleman hires a woman who may have overheard a devastating secret as a governess so he can keep an eye on her, but he is attracted to her in this nineteenth-century historical.

The Girl in the Gatehouse. Bethany House, 2011.
A socially ruined woman goes to live in an abandoned gatehouse, supports herself by writing pseudonymous novels, and attracts the attentions of a wealthy returning war veteran in this Regency Era Inspirational.

Landis, Jill Marie
Many of Landis's Inspirationals are set in the fictional town of Glory, Texas, in the 1870s. See also chapter 5, "Contemporary Romance," and chapter 7, "Historical Romance."

Homecoming. Steeple Hill, 2008.
A young woman taken by Comanches is restored to the white world but struggles to fit in.

The Accidental Lawman. Steeple Hill, 2009.
When he accidentally foils a bank robbery, journalist Hank Larson is drafted as town sheriff and now must find the robber who got away, a situation that poses a dilemma for Amelia Hawthorne, the town healer, who knows that the missing robber is her young brother.

Irish Angel Series
Irish orphaned sisters separated as children by cruel, selfish relatives come into their own in this Western Americana series.

Heart of Stone. Zondervan, 2010.
A young widow and a pastor, both with serious past issues, eventually find peace and love.

Heart of Lies. Zondervan, 2011.
A young woman, raised on the New Orleans streets, is forced into a kidnapping caper by her "brothers," but is attracted to the Pinkerton agent assigned to the case.

Heart of Glass. Zondervan, 2012.

Lewis, Beverly
Lewis is noted for her highly descriptive, sensitive Inspirational stories of Amish society.

Annie's People
Annie Zook struggles with her love of art and for the Englisher, Ben, in this descriptive, multifaceted series that is typical of Lewis's work.

The Preacher's Daughter. Bethany, 2005.
Annie finds joy in her art but it is forbidden by the strict laws of the Old Order, and Annie is torn between her love of art and her family.

The Englisher. Bethany, 2006.
Annie tries to please her father by giving up her art but it's as hard to do as giving up her feelings for the forbidden Englisher, Ben.

The Brethren. Bethany, 2006.
Many things come to a head and secrets are revealed that could change Annie's and Ben's lives in the final volume of the trilogy.

The Courtship of Nellie Fisher Trilogy
The conflict between the Old Order and New Order Amish belief are part of this trilogy set during the 1960s.

The Parting. Bethany, 2007.
Still grieving over the drowning death of her young sister, Nellie Mae Fisher is happy when Caleb asks to court her, but things don't work out as she'd planned.

The Forbidden. Bethany, 2008.
Caleb and Nellie are torn apart by their families' differing Amish beliefs.

The Longing. Bethany, 2008.
Nellie loves Caleb but wishes he could understand her new beliefs—and then a young Mennonite comes to town.

The Rose Trilogy
Set in 1985 in Lancaster County, the heart of Pennsylvania Amish country, this trilogy deals with the two very different Kauffman sisters, their choices, and their loves.

The Thorn. Bethany House, 2010.
Hen Kauffman, who left the community and married an Englischer, wants to return to the community with her young daughter, and her sister, Rose Ann, who never left, has attracted the attentions of the bishop's foster son, who is not Amish.

The Judgment. Bethany House, 2011.
Engaged to an Amish man, Rose Ann still pines for another, while Hen and her husband are at odds.

Mason, Felicia
Sweet Devotion. Steeple Hill, 2004.
A caterer escaping an abusive marriage begins again in a small town in Oregon but clashes with the local police chief who brings to mind her battered past.

Morris, Gilbert
A retired pastor and English professor, Morris has written well over two hundred faith-based novels, some of which are romances. His novels are primarily historical, ranging from early Biblical times to WWII, and are often grouped into series, some of which are coauthored with others. He is a Christy Award winner. A sampling of his works is below.

House of Winslow Series
This series includes forty books that track the Winslows from their arrival on the Mayflower (1620) through 1942 and World War II. Not all are romances, but the series will appeal to Inspirational Romance fans. A small sampling of this series is listed below.

The Honorable Imposter: 1620. Bethany House, 1986.
The patriarch of the Winslow family is forced to become a clergyman for the Church of England and ends up as a spy in the story that launches this series.

The Glorious Prodigal: 1917. Bethany House, 2000.
A man finds God in prison but must convince his wife and family that he has reformed his profligate ways.

The Amazon Quest: 1918. Bethany House, 2001.
A writer goes with her photographer brother to the Amazon and encounters the man who betrayed her and broke her heart.

The Golden Angel: 1922. Bethany House, 2001.
An adventurous female stunt pilot deals with romance and tragedy as her life sweeps her from Africa to Hollywood.

The Fiery Ring: 1928. Bethany House, 2002.
A young woman becomes a circus animal trainer but struggles with her conflicting desires for love and family loyalty and revenge.

The Beloved Enemy: 1931. Bethany House, 2003.
An ex-con goes to Egypt on an archaeological dig and finds love with a young Jewish woman.

The Shining Badge: 1931. Bethany House, 2004.
Forced by the Depression to earn a living, a privileged woman becomes a sheriff in the South and ends up dealing with moonshiners and those who don't want a woman as their lawman.

The Royal Handmaid: 1935. Bethany House, 2004.
A would-be missionary sets off for the South Seas and ends up shipwrecked on an island with a handsome man.

The Silent Harp: 1935. Bethany House, 2004.
A wealthy socialite who swears off love after her fiancé is killed in WWI is attracted to a man not of her social class.

The Gypsy Moon: 1940. Bethany House, 2005.
A woman working with the Holland underground to help Jews escape is reunited with a German OSS officer from her past.

The Unlikely Allies: 1940. Bethany House, 2005.
A missionary to the Lapps is caught in Norway at the beginning of WWII, joins the Resistance, and ends up as a spy in the German camp and attracted to the enemy.

The High Calling: 1940. Bethany House, 2006.
A woman thinking she's been called to be a missionary reassesses her goals when a former boyfriend, an RAF, pilot goes missing.

The Hesitant Hero: 1940. Bethany House, 2006.
An American returning home is caught in France as the war breaks out and he helps a friend help three Jewish children escape.

The Widow's Choice: 1941. Bethany House, 2006.
A widow with children to raise marries for convenience and then is attracted to another man.

The White Knight: 1942. Bethany House, 2007.
A military pilot devastated when his girlfriend's family is killed gives in to alcohol and causes the death of a friend. However, when he falls in love with his friend's sister, who doesn't know the situation, problems arise—and then Pearl Harbor occurs and the landscape shifts.

Cheney Duvall, M.D. Series

Co-authored with daughter Lynn Morris, this series tells of the struggles of one of the first women doctors in America; set following the Civil War. A romance builds throughout this faith-based series.

The Stars for a Light. Bethany House, 1994.
Cheney's first job as a real doctor is as a doctor aboard a ship transporting two hundred women from New York to Washington Territory.

Shadow of the Mountains. Bethany House, 1994.
Cheney answers a pregnant friend's plea to come to the Ozarks and finds resentment, suspicion, and surprising danger in the backwoods community.

A City Not Forsaken. Bethany House, 1995.
A potential cholera outbreak in New York causes Cheney, who is currently working with the elite and being courted by a handsome doctor, to question her priorities.

Toward the Sunrising. Bethany House, 1996.
Cheney and her male nurse, Shiloh Irons, stop in Charleston en route to New Orleans and become embroiled in social and economic conflicts that ultimately threaten their lives.

Secret Place of Thunder. Bethany House, 1996.
Told by a West Indian cult that they must leave their indigo plantation or be cursed, Cheney's elderly aunts are aided by Cheney and Shiloh, who try to get to the bottom of what the cult really wants.

In the Twilight, in the Evening. Bethany House, 1997.
Cheney is working in San Francisco during the 1906 earthquake.

Island of the Innocent. Bethany House, 1998.
Cheney goes to Hawaii where Shiloh is trying to find his long-lost family, the Winslows, and in addition to the mystery that surrounds Shiloh's origins, they must deal with an active volcano.

Driven with the Wind. Bethany House, 2000.
Cheney refuses Shiloh's proposal because he's not a Christian but circumstances change when someone sets out to ruin Cheney's medical reputation.

Cheney and Shiloh: The Inheritance Series
Coauthored with daughter Lynn Morris, this Historical Inspirational series continues the Cheney Duvall, M.D. series.

Where Two Seas Met. Bethany House, 2001.
Shiloh and Cheney's shipboard honeymoon is interrupted by a storm that strands the ship on an island wracked by a highly contagious illness.

The Moon by Night. Bethany House, 2004.
Back in New York, Cheney is faced with uncovering the villain behind some surgical disasters and unexplained new illnesses at the new hospital, and Shiloh is running the Winslow Brothers Shipping Company, but their relationship soon suffers.

There Is a Season. Bethany House, 2005.
Hoping for a warm escape from the cold New York winter, Cheney and Shiloh go to Florida and find a dead body, instead.

Spirit of Appalachia Series
Coauthored with Aaron McCarver, this five-book Historical Inspirational series describes early American frontier life in the Appalachian Mountains.

Over the Misty Mountains. Bethany House, 1996.
Two people are united by separate tragedies and come together to form a family on the Tennessee frontier.

Beyond the Quiet Hills. Bethany House, 1997.
Two stepbrothers pursue the same young woman and rivalry escalates.

Among the King's Soldiers. Bethany House, 1998.
The American Revolution causes plenty of conflict and loyalty issues abound when a young man takes his stepsister back to Williamsburg to visit relatives and she is attracted to a Scot fighting for the British.

Beneath the Mockingbird's Wings. Bethany House, 2000.
Fox Carter, half-Cherokee, and his mother head for the Appalachian frontier where they are caught up in the increasing conflicts between the settlers and the Cherokees.

Around the River's Bend. Bethany House, 2002.
A young Englishwoman inherits property in the American frontier and, accompanied by her indentured servant, she sets off to start a new life.

*Edge of Honor. Zondervan, 2000.
A Civil War doctor falls in love with the widow of an enemy soldier he killed in this novel of love and forgiveness. A Christy Award winner.

Heaven Sent Husband. Steeple Hill, 2005.
A nurse with missionary plans is guided by God to find love with an intern she knew back in high school but thinks it is an impossible dream.

The Creole Series

This Historical Inspirational series, cowritten with daughter Lynn Morris, tells of four Ursuline Convent–educated girlfriends and their journeys to faith and love in nineteenth-century Louisiana.

The Exiles. Thomas Nelson, 2003.
Chantel Fontaine endures the death of her mother, neglect by her father, betrayal by a greedy suitor, and a host of other difficulties before giving up her Catholic faith and finding true love with a Protestant friend.

The Immortelles. Thomas Nelson, 2004.
Damita DeSalvado's family falls on hard times and struggles to keep its plantation while Rissa, a slave girl Damita had once owned but abused, is now a free woman and wealthy, as well.

The Alchemy. Thomas Nelson, 2004.
Socialite Simone d'Or is attracted to a young opera singer of humble beginnings but her brother's debts may mean she must marry another to save the family name.

The Tapestry. Thomas Nelson, 2005.
Leonie Vernay, abandoned at the Ursuline Convent at birth and now working as a seamstress, has a chance to discover her roots—and gain a family she's always yearned for.

Singing River Series

A story of love, faith, and the Freeman siblings set in the South during the Great Depression.

The Homeplace. Zondervan, 2005.
With her mother dead, her father falsely imprisoned, and the depression looming, a young teenager's dreams are put on hold as she struggles to care for her younger siblings and keep their home.

The Dream. Zondervan, 2006.
The attentions of a wealthy young man and the arrival of a bike-riding young minister who causes a bit of community conflict add to Lanie Freeman's problems.

The Miracle. Zondervan, 2007.
Lanie still dreams of becoming a writer in this story that has its share of tragedies that could derail her hopes.

The Courtship. Zondervan, 2007.
Lanie's on the road to achieving her dreams in this story that see's her father vindicated and her romantic future assured.

Wagon Wheel Series

Three women find love along three different trails in the mid-nineteenth-century American West.

Santa Fe Woman. B&H Books, 2006.
A young woman heads along the Santa Fe Trail with her family after a depression wipes out their fortune and falls in love with their rough Western guide.

A Man for Temperance. B&H Books, 2007.
A spinster raised in a repressive religious Oregon colony takes a group of orphans back to relatives after a cholera epidemic devastates the community and finds love with the hard-drinking drifter who guides them along the trail east.

Joelle's Secret. B&H Books, 2008.
A young woman flees her stepfather's lecherous advances, poses as a boy, and ends up on a wagon trail heading for the California gold fields.

Angel Train. B&H Fiction, 2009.
A young woman's Pennsylvania religious community plans to go to Oregon but the best people to lead them are a group of prison inmates who will be granted parole once the job is safely accomplished.

Oke, Janette
A Prairie Legacy Series
Sequel to the Love Comes Softly series, this Historical Inspirational series follows the loves and lives of the descendents of Marty and Clark Davis.

The Tender Years. Bethany, 1997.
A Christian-raised young woman, teenage Virginia Simpson, rebels against family expectations and is tempted by a new friend to make other choices.

A Searching Heart. Bethany, 1998.
Virginia must deal with unexpected family and romantic issues as she comes of age.

A Quiet Strength. Bethany, 1999.
Virginia marries former boyfriend Jonathan and learns to adjust to marriage and parenthood.

Like Gold Refined. Bethany, 2000.
Virginia and Jonathan face difficult family issues, including the fact that Virginia's grandparents can no longer live on their farm on their own, in this last volume of the series.

Song of Acadia
This Historical series, cowritten with T. Davis Bunn, that begins in the mid-eighteenth century in Acadia, the modern-day Nova Scotia and New Brunswick areas of Canada, but sweeps its characters to the Louisiana bayous, England, and the American Colonies.

The Meeting Place. Bethany, 1999.
Two young women—one French, one English—from villages separated by hostilities meet as they gather flowers for their weddings.

The Sacred Shore. Bethany, 2000.
Two young women, purposely switched by their parents at birth, find each other and their respective families.

The Birthright. Bethany, 2001.
A young woman goes to England to claim her birthright and finds love, as well.

The Distant Beacon. Bethany, 2002.
Although with her happily married "sister" in England, a young woman is still searching for her identity and heads for the American Colonies as the Revolution looms.

The Beloved Land. Bethany, 2002.
Both women and their husbands are caught up in the turmoil and danger of the American Revolution.

Acts of Faith

This Historical series, coauthored by Davis Bunn and Janette Oke, focuses on the early days of the Christian church and the struggles its members endured. These books often end with unresolved issues.

The Centurion's Wife. Bethany House, 2009.
An intriguing look at the crucifixion of Christ and the aftermath from an unexpected viewpoint.

The Hidden Flame. Bethany House, 2010.
A young Christian woman is pursued by two very different men, but is attracted to Stephen, who ends up being the first martyr.

The Damascus Way. Bethany House, 2011.
Two couriers who pass messages among the far flung Christian communities are attracted to each other.

Page, Carole Gift
Heartland Memories Series

This Historical series spans four decades in the lives of the Reed and Herrick families of Willowbrook.

The House on Honeysuckle Lane. Thomas Nelson, 1994.
In the early 1930s two young girls, Cath Herrick and Annie Reed, promise to always be friends but events draw them apart.

Home to Willowbrook. Thomas Nelson, 1995.
Gradually regaining her memory after being in a coma after a car crash, Cath must come to terms with anger and heartbreak in this story set following WWII.

The Hope of Herrick House. Thomas Nelson, 1996.
When her mother dies in a fire, Bethany moves in with Cath, the half-sister she didn't know she had, but must deal with the fact that her mother was murdered, maybe by someone in the family.

Storms over Willowbrook. Thomas Nelson, 1998.
Alice Reed deals with grief, a pregnancy, and a new love on a life-threatening quest tracking down Nazis.

A Rose for Jenny. Thomas Nelson, 1999.
A young woman and her boyfriend go with their rock band around the country in the early 1960s and deal with the civil rights movement, JFKs assassination, and other era-defining events.

A Locket for Maggie. Thomas Nelson, 2000.
Maggie Herrick has mixed feelings as her fiancé goes off to the Vietnam War.

In Search of Her Own. Steeple Hill, 1997.
A woman searches for her birth son after his adoptive parents are killed and finds romance with the P.I. she hires to help her. Originally published as *To Chase a Shadow* (Accent, 1985).

Rachel's Hope. Steeple Hill, 1998.
A woman hopes the birth of an unexpected child will restore her family to its former happy state.

A Family to Cherish. Steeple Hill, 2000.
A couple still grieving over the loss of their daughter find healing and love when they reach out to help another young girl.

Minister's Daughters Trilogy
A widowed pastor's three grown daughters find love in vastly different places, and their dad remarries, as well, in this heartwarming trilogy.

Cassandra's Song. Steeple Hill, 2001.
A woman falls for the son of the woman she thinks is the perfect match for her widowed father.

A Child Shall Lead Them. Steeple Hill, 2001.
A marriage of convenience for the sake of a child becomes a love match.

A Bungalow for Two. Steeple Hill, 2001.
An artist needing to regain her perspective moves into a beach house and is attracted to her handsome neighbor.

Beguiling Masquerade. Barbour, 2003.
A grad student masquerades as an elderly woman for research purposes and while in disguise falls for a young sociology professor.

Palmer, Catherine
Treasures of the Heart Series
This lively series is set in Africa and details the adventures and romances of the four Thornton siblings.

A Kiss of Adventure. Tyndale, 2008.
Tillie, engaged but bored with her life, is caught up in a dangerous, adventurous game when she joins forces with handsome Graeme McLeod in the hunt for a treasure. Originally published in 1998 by Tyndale as *Treasure of Kilimanjaro*.

A Whisper of Danger. Tyndale, 2008.
Jessica and her son move to Zanzibar to start a new life when she inherits a house on the island and find death, danger, and, worst of all, the husband who walked out on Jessica before her son was born. Originally published in 1997 by Tyndale as *The Treasure of Timbuktu*.

A Touch of Betrayal. Tyndale, 2000.
A fashion designer's world falls apart and when her life is threatened she goes to anthropologist Grant Thornton for help.

Sunrise Song. Tyndale, 2003.
While studying a herd of elephants in Kenya, Fiona's blissfully solitary life is turned upside down by a businessman who zooms into her site with plans of his own.

A Town Called Hope Series
Newcomers and residents alike find love in Hope, Kansas, in the years after the Civil War.

Prairie Rose. Tyndale, 1997.
Orphaned and illegitimate, Rosie goes west to Kansas with Seth Hunter and his young son to be their housekeeper—and eventually more—in this sometimes humorous romance.

Prairie Fire. Tyndale, 1998.

Having lost everything, Jack Cornwall moves to Hope and finds love with Caitrin Murphy, although the townsfolk, who are primarily Irish immigrants, have problems with his Cornish ancestry.

Prairie Storm. Tyndale, 1999.

When the medicine show that Lily Nolan works with arrives in Hope, she meets Pastor Elijah Book and agrees to stay and help him care for an orphaned baby. She is attracted to him but has problems with his profession because her abusive father was also a clergyman.

A Dangerous Silence. Tyndale, 2001.

A pediatrician returns home to Kansas because her father needs help and finds mystery and danger, as well as love, in this intriguing Contemporary Inspirational.

Love's Proof. Tyndale House, 2003.

A heroine who doubts God's existence is involved in a race to find information that will keep her father from the gallows in this Regency Romance.

Wild Heather. Tyndale, 2004.

A Regency Era Romance that deals with some rather serious issues.

Sweet Violet. Tyndale, 2005.

An English woman raised in India resists returning to England for an arranged marriage in this early-nineteenth-century Inspirational.

Miss Pickworth Series

Sweet, Inspirational Regency Romances with comments by a society gossip columnist.

The Affectionate Adversary. Tyndale, 2006.

Wealthy Sarah Carlyle, who wants to be rid of her fortune, and Charles Locke, who is seeking his, meet and are attracted to each other when he is attacked by pirates and she nurses him back to health. Now Charles must figure out how to convince Sarah he's not after her fortune.

The Bachelor's Bargain. Tyndale, 2006.

Fearing she will die and leave her family penniless, housemaid Anne Webster accepts the Marquess of Blackthorne's mock proposal so he will care for them when she is gone; then, of course, she lives.

The Heart's Treasure. Steeple Hill, 2007.

An estranged couple work on saving their marriage.

The Briton. Steeple Hill, 2008.

A widowed Briton noblewoman and a Norman knight find love amid adversity in this twelfth-century historical romance.

Thread of Deceit. Steeple Hill, 2008.

Lead paint and troubled kids bring the journalist heroine and community activist together—with sparks.

The Maverick's Bride. Steeple Hill, 2009.

A young woman finds love with a rancher in the late Victorian Period in East Africa.

The Outlaw's Bride. Steeple Hill, 2010.

A woman who witnessed a murder has become a target and is saved by a hasty marriage to a cowboy she barely knows in this Western Historical Inspirational.

The Gunman's Bride. Steeple Hill, 2011.
A reformed gunslinger tries to make amends with the woman he loves in this Historical Inspirational Romance.

Pattillo, Beth

*Heavens to Betsy. WaterBrook, 2005.
A woman pastor deals with the trials and tribulations of her parish and finds love in the process in this funny, touching story.

Earth to Betsy. WaterBrook, 2006.
Betsy's ministry takes her to an old church in downtown Nashville and she is faced with the decision of moving the congregation to the wealthier suburbs or staying put—and making her own wedding plans at the same time. Follows *Heavens to Betsy*.

Pella, Judith

Beloved Stranger. Bethany, 1998.
An impulsive marriage to a near stranger causes problems for the heroine.

Texas Angel. Bethany, 1999.
A racial outcast and a holier-than-thou pastor find forgiveness and healing in this 1830s Western Romance.

Heaven's Road. Bethany, 2000.
A preacher's teenaged son, wild and bitter, escapes hanging by agreeing to become a Texas Ranger and finds healing, forgiveness, and love, but not without a lot of soul searching. Sequel to *Texas Angel*.

Daughters of Fortune Series
The three daughters of newspaper mogul Keegan Hayes find adventure and romance in this Historical World War II series.

Written on the Wind. Bethany, 2002.
Journalist Cameron Hayes goes to Russia and bonds with a Russian surgeon from America who was forced to go back to Russia for political reasons.

Somewhere a Song. Bethany, 2002.
Pearl Harbor finds each sister in different circumstances—Cameron is still in Russia covering the war, Jackie has fallen in love with a Japanese American man in California, and Blair is in Manila looking for her military husband with mixed results. Difficulties plague them all but Blair's story is the focus of this book.

Toward the Sunrise. Bethany, 2003.
Jackie and Sam Okuda struggle against racism when they marry and eventually he enlists.

Homeward My Heart. Bethany, 2004.
With the war over, the sisters are putting their lives back together, but when their mother tells them she has a son, and they have a half-brother, in Russia, they set off to find him, even though the Cold War makes things difficult. Cameron and her Russian doctor, Alex, are highlighted in this story that ties up most loose ends nicely.

Patchwork Circle Series
A series set in 1880s Maintown, Oregon, with a focus on quilting and the women involved.

Bachelor's Puzzle. Bethany, 2007.
A new bachelor pastor has the young women's hearts aflutter, but he has secrets that might change their opinions of him if they were revealed. A pattern for the Bachelor's Puzzle quilt is included.

Sister's Choice. Bethany, 2008.
Maggie struggles to be the best quilter in order to please the difficult mother of Colby, a boy she likes, but when a beautiful girl comes to town and attracts the attention of all the men, including her Colby, she begins to question her judgment as well as her feelings for the long-time friend, Evan, who has always been there for her.

Raney, Deborah

*Beneath a Southern Sky. WaterBrook, 2001.
A missionary loses her husband in Columbia and eventually finds love with a man who'd also lost his wife in this heart-wrenching novel.

After the Rains. WaterBrook, 2002.
A rebellious young woman goes to Columbia to find her birth father in this story that follows *Beneath a Southern Sky*.

Playing by Heart. Barbour, 2003.
A woman needing a quiet place to write uses a professor's house during the day and finds love where they both least expect it in this funny romance.

Nest of Sparrows. WaterBrook, 2004.
Custody and insurance issues drive the plot of this emotionally involving story.

Over the Waters. WaterBrook, 2005.
Missionaries to Haiti find friendship and romance.

Clayburn Series

Heartwarming stories of love and faith set in tiny, rural, out-of-the-way Clayburn, Kansas.

Remember to Forget. Howard, 2007.
A woman comes to Kansas to escape an abusive boyfriend and changes her name and starts a new life—but what about the truth?

Leaving November. Howard, 2008.
A woman comes to Kansas to take over her ill mother's coffee shop and finds romance with an artist just out of rehab.

Yesterday's Embers. Howard, 2009.
A widower with five children to raise and a daycare provider rush into marriage and then must figure out how to make it all work.

Roper, Gayle
The Amish Trilogy

Mystery, Suspense, and romance with an Amish setting, the Zook's farm near Bird-in-Hand, Lancaster County, Pennsylvania

The Key. Multnomah, 1998.
A chance meeting in an emergency room leaves teacher Kristie Matthews with a mysterious key, a host of problems, and a romance, as well.

The Document. Multnomah, 1998.
A novelist comes to Bird-in-Hand to discover her roots and finds more than she expected.

The Decision. Multnomah, 1999.
A heroine who can't forgive herself and a wheelchair-bound hero who's not sure about God's grace find love and forgiveness in this romance with a suspenseful edge.

Seaside Seasons Series
Set in small Seaside, New Jersey, these stories have an element of mystery about them, as well.

Spring Rain. Multnomah, 2001.
A teacher and single mother reconnects with her son's father (who doesn't want to acknowledge him) in this reunion story that deals with a situation rarely encountered in conservative Christian fiction, a character who has AIDS.

Summer Shadows. Multnomah, 2002.
A woman moves to the shore to recover from the car accident that killed her husband and daughter and injured her, as well, and finds romance with her landlord.

*Autumn Dreams. Multnomah, 2003.
A single bed and breakfast owner caring for her parents and niece and nephew must deal with a hurricane—with the help of a visiting finance specialist.

Winter Winds. Multnomah, 2004.
A pastor and his estranged wife rekindle their love in the conclusion to this series.

See No Evil. Steeple Hill, 2007.
The target of a killer after she witnesses a murder, an art teacher sparks the protective instincts of a contractor in this funny, suspenseful romance that briefly introduces reporter Merry Kramer, a character in the Amhearst Mystery Series.

Amhearst Mystery Series
This Inspirational Romantic Suspense series follows the adventures of newspaper reporter Merry Kramer and the love of her life, artist Curtis Carlyle. The first three volumes were republished by Steeple Hill in 2007.

Caught in the Middle. Zondervan, 1997.
A reporter can't figure out who or why someone is trying to kill her in this suspenseful romance.

Caught in the Act. Zondervan, 1998.
With a good share of humor and sass, reporter Merry Kamer goes to her estranged husband's home and finds a body in this lively romantic mystery.

Caught in a Bind. Zondervan, 2000.
Merry goes on a hunt for a coworker's missing husband suspected of theft and also must deal with an aggressive female gallery owner who has designs on her artist boyfriend.

Caught Redhanded. Steeple Hill, 2007.
After finding a murdered woman on her morning run and then doing some sleuthing, Merry must decide if finding a killer is worth the threat to her life.

Fatal Deduction. Multnomah, 2008.
Twins must share a house for half a year in order to inherit, but a body, a crossword puzzle, and other mysteries make things difficult.

Amish Farm Trilogy
A contemporary Amish trilogy set in Lancaster County, Pennsylvania.

A Stranger's Wish. Harvest House, 2010.
A young Englisher woman living in an Amish community is given a key by a stranger and is caught up in a dangerous mystery, as well as a romantic quandary.

A Secret Identity. Harvest House, 2010.
A woman goes to Lancaster County to learn the truth of her birth and is met with resistance.

A Rose Revealed. Harvest House, 2011.
A murder sets the ball rolling in this story that unearths old family secrets and forces a young nurse and a wheel-bound man to confront their pasts and their true feelings.

Scott, Regina
See also chapter 8, "Traditional Regency Romance."

The Irresistible Earl. Love Inspired Historical, 2011.
Meredee Price rescues a young woman from drowning and is distressed to learn that the young woman's brother, the Earl of Allyndale, is her irresponsible stepbrother's nemesis in this lightly religious Traditional Regency Romance.

Snelling, Lauraine
Red River of the North Series
The historical saga of Roald and Ingeborg Bjorklund as they leave Norway, come to America, and build a new life for themselves and their family in the Dakota Territory. These were reprinted by Bethany House in 2006 and 2007.

An Untamed Land. Bethany, 1996.
Roald and Ingeborg come to America, go to the Dakota Territory, and realize that very little is as they thought it would be.

A New Day Rising. Bethany, 1996.
A widowed Ingeborg struggles with the difficult life and finds love once again.

A Land to Call Home. Bethany, 1997.
The town grows up and gets a name, Blessing, as the railroad arrives in this installment that features a number of family changes.

The Reapers' Song. Bethany, 1998.
A man on the run because he accidentally killed someone takes a pair of orphans into his care as they head for Blessing, where they will cause problems for the Bjorklunds.

Tender Mercies. Bethany, 1999.
A young pastor in Blessing is attracted to a lovely young woman who must go back to the South to care for her mother.

Blessing in Disguise. Bethany, 1999.
A young Norwegian woman who understands no English takes the wrong train and finds love as the mail-order bride for a handsome rancher.

Return to Red River Series

This Historical series picks up where the Red River of the North Series left off and reprises a number of characters. It is essentially the story of Thorliff Bjorklund and his pursuit of his education, career, and dreams, and the love he finds in the process.

A Dream to Follow. Bethany, 2001.
Thorliff Bjorklund heads off to college and yearns to be a journalist but struggles with his feeling of responsibility to take over the family farm; at the same time, Elizabeth Rogers, who wants to be a doctor, faces discrimination issues.

Believing the Dream. Bethany, 2002.
Thorliff is still committed to being a journalist but his relationship with Anji, the girl he left behind, is failing.

More than a Dream. Bethany, 2003.
Thorliff resolves his issues as he is called home to help rebuild the town of Blessing, North Dakota, after a flood causes chaos in the town.

Dakotah Treasures Series

Dove House, a former brothel but now a hotel, is the setting for this romantic series that features the Torvald sisters and is set in the 1880s in the Dakota Territory.

Ruby. Bethany, 2003.
Ruby inherits the Dove House and changes it—and its inhabitants—dramatically.

Pearl. Bethany, 2004.
A woman flees an unwanted marriage and comes to the Dakota Territory to be a teacher. Her romance is threatened when her father demands she return home.

Opal. Bethany, 2005.
After Dove House is destroyed in a fire, Ruby and her sister Opal move to Rand's (Ruby's husband) ranch. Opal is thrilled, but her love of ranching is a barrier when a young pastor falls for her.

Amethyst. Bethany, 2005.
Sent by her domineering father to bring a nephew home from the Dakota Territory, Amethyst meets a retired army major and is torn between duty to her father and her heart.

Breaking Free. Faithwords, 2007.
A program that rehabilitates horses gives a woman convict a chance at a new life and a new love when she is finally released.

Daughters of Blessing

Heartwarming historical stories of love and faith set among the descendants of the Norwegians of Blessing in rural North Dakota around the turn of the nineteenth century.

A Promise for Ellie. Bethany, 2006.
Old rivalries cause problems for Andrew and Ellie Bjorklund when an embittered man causes Andrew to go back on his nonviolent promises.

Sophie's Dilemma. Bethany, 2007.
A young woman who eloped against her family's wishes returns home pregnant after tragedy strikes.

A Touch of Grace. Bethany, 2008.
Grace, serious-minded sister of Sophie, must choose between two very different men.

Rebecca's Reward. Bethany, 2008.
Rebecca has serious problems with an undesirable man who has been saying she's engaged to him, and when she confronts and contradicts him, the situation gets worse.

Home to Blessing
Set in North Dakota circa 1903.

Measure of Mercy. Bethany House, 2009.
A young woman who's always wanted to be a doctor must choose between her education and her love.

No Distance Too Far. Bethany House, 2010.
A young would-be medical missionary struggles to figure out where she is really called to be.

Thoene, Bodie, and Brock Thoene
The Thoenes are noted popular authors in the general Inspirational Fiction arena. They have a number of series to their credit, such as The Galway Chronicles, The Zion Chronicles, The Zion Legacy Series, and the A.D. Chronicles. Their stories are not necessarily romances, but they may appeal to many Inspirational fans; several of their recent titles are listed below.

Love Finds You in Lahaina, Hawaii. Summerside, 2010.
The wife of an MIA soldier goes to Hawaii as part of a historical research project and thanks to the journals of the royal family of Hawaii, comes to terms with her feelings and her future.

The Gathering Storm. Summerside, 2010.
A young woman leaves Germany to go to work in London with war refugees in this World War II tale that is the first in the Zion Diaries series.

Tronstad, Janet
Dry Creek Series
This popular, continuing contemporary series is set in small town Dry Creek, Montana.

An Angel for Dry Creek. Steeple Hill, 1999.
A police artist on the run from a hit man ends up in Dry Creek and turns around the lives of a disillusioned widowed pastor and his two sons in this holiday-centered story with a suspenseful twist.

Gentleman for Dry Creek. Steeple Hill, 2000.
A rancher has his work cut out for him when he falls for the wary victim of an abusive marriage and must prove he's worthy of trust.

A Bride for Dry Creek. Steeple Hill, 2001.
Francis Elkton and Flint Harris learn that their impulsive Las Vegas marriage as teenagers twenty years ago was not invalid, as they had been told, and now must deal with the fact that they are still married and that Francis's life is in danger.

A Rich Man for Dry Creek. Steeple Hill, 2002.
Wealthy playboy Robert Buckwalter III, tired of his superficial life and looking for a simpler one, wants a woman to share it with and sets his sights on his family's personal chef, Jenny Black.

A Hero for Dry Creek. Steeple Hill, 2003.
The whole town gets into the act when trucker Garrett Hamilton is attracted to rancher Nicki Redfern in this Cinderella romance with a Thanksgiving emphasis.

A Baby for Dry Creek. Steeple Hill, 2004.
A single mom and a rancher find love in this funny, tender story.

A Dry Creek Christmas. Steeple Hill, 2004.
A Christmas gift delivery goes wrong when Millie Corwin is seen sneaking into the town cafe and is tagged a thief by Brad Parker in this funny heartwarming story that brings everyone a little closer for Christmas.

Sugar Plums for Dry Creek. Steeple Hill, 2005.
An amateur performance of *The Nutcracker* brings the ballet instructor and the guardian of two of her students together in this holiday-themed romance.

At Home in Dry Creek. Steeple Hill, 2006.
A sheriff determined to protect a newly arrived young mother from unwanted visitors, especially friends of her imprisoned ex-husband, is attracted to her and her two children.

A Match Made in Dry Creek. Steeple Hill, 2007.
A matchmaking mom engineers a difficult reunion between a pair of high school sweethearts who haven't spoken since their elopement went awry years earlier.

Shepherds Abiding in Dry Creek. Steeple Hill, 2007.
A Latino widow moves to town to keep her eleven-year-old son from becoming a gang member only to have him suspected of stealing the shepherd from the town's plastic Christmas creche, an event that introduces her to a caring, handsome lawman.

Dry Creek Sweethearts. Steeple Hill, 2008.
The town bad-boy-turned-singing-star comes back to Dry Creek for some peace and quiet and renews his relationship with his teenage sweetheart who turned him down years ago because of family responsibilities.

A Dry Creek Courtship. Steeple Hill, 2008.
A widow and her widowed best friend, Charley, separately realize that they love each other but can't figure out to let the other one know without damaging their decades-long friendship.

Snowbound in Dry Creek. Steeple Hill, 2008.
A rodeo champion agrees to do the Christmas Eve mail run (in a Santa suit) and ends up snowbound on an isolated farm with a widow and her two children in this touching holiday romance.

Silent Night at Dry Creek. Steeple Hill, 2009.
A P.I. is attracted to a lovely woman with a shadowed past who may be in danger.

Wife Wanted in Dry Creek. Steeple Hill, 2010.
A mechanic is stunned when the very woman he described as the "perfect wife" shows up in town.

Dry Creek Historical Series
Set in the early days of Dry Creek in the last half of the nineteenth century.

Calico Christmas at Dry Creek. Steeple Hill, 2008.
After losing her infant daughter and husband to the flu, Elizabeth O'Brian agrees to act as a wet nurse to the youngest of Jake Hargrove's two half-Sioux nieces and, for propriety's sake, to a marriage in name only, never expecting the problems or the love that waits for her in Dry Creek.

Sisterhood Series (Love Inspired Café)
Cancer survivors who first met as teens find life, love, and faith in this Pasadena, California, series that is more Women's Fiction than Romance.

Sisterhood of Dropped Stitches Series. Steeple Hill, 2007.
Marilee Davidson struggles with her reluctance to date and finds romance where she least expects it.

A Dropped Stitches Christmas. Steeple Hill, 2007.
Carly Winston fears to reveal her long-kept secret (she is poor but everyone thinks she's rich because of where she lives), but knows she has to get the courage to do this, even if it means losing people she cares about.

A Heart for the Dropped Stitches. Steeple Hill, 2008.
Becca Snyder, always wary of showing emotions, finally opens her heart to love when she falls for the wealthy director of the shelter for homeless teens where she volunteers.

A Dropped Stitches Wedding. Steeple Hill, 2009.
Wedding planner Lizabett McDonald plans to get her brother's best friend to see her in a new, more romantic light.

Warren, Susan May
Deep Haven Series
This series centers on the sleepy town of Deep Haven, Minnesota, and the people who live and visit there.

Happily Ever After. Tyndale, 2003.
An author posing as a handyman finds romance with a bookstore owner as they deal with their own issues, as well as someone who wants the store to fail.

Tying the Knot. Tyndale, 2003.
A wounded EMT ends up in a Minnesota camp for inner city kids and finds love and healing with a Native American former gang member.

The Perfect Match. Tyndale, 2004.
An interim fire chief and a pastor-cum-volunteer-firefighter find romance and arson in this charming romance.

Mission: Russia Series
Russians and Americans come together to solve crimes and help people in this contemporary series that has some Cold War elements.

In Sheep's Clothing. Steeple Hill, 2005.
A missionary to Russia becomes involved in a murder and works with a Russian agent to solve the crime.

Sands of Time. Steeple Hill, 2006.
An American medical missionary is helped by a Russian rebel agent, with whom she has a romantic past, to deal with a deadly epidemic and escape the dangers posed by the current government.

Wiser than Serpents. Steeple Hill, 2008.
A Russian agent in search of her sister infiltrates a sex-trade ring but needs help from an American undercover agent who's after the head of the ring.

Josey Series
Chronicles the Russian adventures of Josey.

Everything's Coming Up Josey. Steeple Hill, 2006.
Josey heeds the missionary call and heads for Russia to spend a chilly year in Siberia.

Chill Out, Josey! Steeple Hill, 2007.
Now married and dreaming of small town Minnesota, Josey is appalled when her new husband's job takes him—and her—to Russia.

Get Cozy, Josey! Steeple Hill, 2008.
Josey, now the mother of twins, gets on with her life in Russia.

Noble Legacy Series
This contemporary series focuses on the Noble siblings and their Silver Buckle Ranch.

Reclaiming Nick. Tyndale, 2007.
A prodigal son returns home to try to keep the family ranch from falling into "enemy" hands.

Taming Rafe. Tyndale, 2008.
A woman's efforts to save her mother's charitable foundation end up saving a troubled man whose actions almost destroyed it.

Finding Stefanie. Tyndale, 2008.
A rancher and a Hollywood star clash when he wants to turn his ranch into a magnet for the rich and famous, but disasters plague his efforts and they begin to wonder if someone wants him to fail.

P. J. Sugar Series
This Inspirational Romantic Suspense series features private investigator P. J. Sugar.

Nothing but Trouble. Tyndale, 2009.
A woman returns home for her sister's wedding and reconnects with her high school flame when someone is killed.

Double Trouble. Tyldale, 2010.
House sitting for witnesses in custody proves more dangerous than P. J. had expected.

Nightingale. Summerside, 2010.
A romantic triangle amid the conflict and confusion of World War II.

Point of No Return. Steeple Hill, 2011.

Wick, Lori
Although she has written several Contemporary Romances, as well as stand-alone novels, Wick is noted for her historical series, set primarily in England during various time periods and in various locales throughout the nineteenth-century American West. Many have been reprinted.

The Princess. Harvest House, 1999.
In this Contemporary Romance a young woman enters an arranged marriage with a widowed prince but wonders if he will ever come to love her. Something of a Cinderella story.

Yellow Rose Trilogy
The Rawlings men find love in 1880s Texas.

Every Little Thing about You. Harvest House, 1999.
When former Texas Ranger Slater Rawlings finds himself arrested, the only thing that shocks him more is that the person doing the deed is acting deputy Liberty Drake, a woman who attracts him as no other.

A Texas Sky. Harvest House, 2000.
Texas Ranger Dakota Rawlings rescues adventurous Darvi Wingate from scrape after scrape, but when she gets kidnapped, things become a lot more complicated.

City Girl. Harvest House, 2001.
Disillusioned by love, city girl Reagan Sullivan takes a job in Texas to start afresh and is attracted by rancher Cash Rawlings, in spite of her intentions to never love and trust again.

English Garden Series
This series puts a religious twist on the classic English Regency Romance and was reprinted in 2009.

The Proposal. Harvest House, 2002.
An aristocratic bachelor suddenly becomes the guardian to three young cousins, and he finds help, and love, from his sister's lovely neighbor.

The Rescue. Harvest House, 2002.
When a gentleman rescues a young woman from a fall, her mentally challenged father insists that they wed in this interesting marriage-of-convenience story that takes a hard look at gossip and the damage it can cause.

The Visitor. Harvest House, 2003.
A gentleman whose sight has been damaged by a fall from horseback falls in love with a young woman who reads to him while he recovers, but he wonders how he can court her if he might end up blind.

The Pursuit. Harvest House, 2003.
A gentleman who aids a widow on his way back from Africa, encounters her once again when he reaches home and they renew their acquaintance—with romantic results.

Tucker Mills Trilogy
Set in Tucker Mills, Massachusetts, in the late 1830s.

Moonlight on the Millpond. Harvest House, 2005.
An interfering woman meddles in her brother's life and tries to quash a budding romance.

Just Above a Whisper. Harvest House, 2005.
A young bond servant, released from her contract when her owner dies, takes a job as a housekeeper to the young man who arranged for her release and finds love with her employer in early Victorian Massachusetts.

Leave a Candle Burning. Harvest House, 2006.
A bachelor doctor becomes a "father" when he assumes guardianship of his three-year-old niece and also struggles with his feelings for a married woman.

Big Sky Dreams Series
Set in Token Creek, Montana Territory, in the 1880s, this series focuses on second chances, redemption, and forgiveness.

Cassidy. Harvest House, 2007.
A young woman has secrets about her past that she fears will keep her from true happiness as a wife and mother.

Sabrina. Harvest House, 2007.
A reformed prostitute finds a new life in Montana.

Jessie. Harvest House, 2008.
A husband returns to his wife and children after eight years and must convince his wife that he has changed for the good; a sweet reunion story.

Windsor, Linda
Windsor's stories often have a humorous, adventurous flair.

Honey, I'm Home. Multnomah, 1999.
A terrorist prisoner thought dead returns home to his wife (whom he was in the process of divorcing) and sons and wants his family back in this touching, funny story.

Not Exactly Eden. Multnomah, 2000.
A woman looking for her birth father ends up in the Peruvian rainforest and finds romance with one of his partners.

It Had to Be You. Multnomah, 2001.
Love, fun, and a dash of mystery aboard a cruise ship.

Fires of Gleannmara Series
This adventurous Historical Inspirationalseries focuses on the Christian Celts in seventh-century Ireland.

Maire. Multnomah, 2000.
Irish warrior queen Maire finds love and new life with Rowan, a man she takes hostage.

Riona. Multnomah, 2001.
A young woman weds a noble warrior in order to provide a home for three orphans and finds love in the process.

Deirdre. Multnomah, 2002.
A Saxon pirate claims an Irish princess he captures at sea, thinking that she may be the key to regaining his birthright, and finds love and redemption, as well.

Along Came Jones. Multnomah, 2003.
A woman on the run from the law and the mob after being framed for embezzlement finds help and healing in the arms of a Montana rancher in this suspenseful romance.

Moonstruck Series
Romance and faith connect in Mexico in this adventurous, contemporary, often humorous, series.

Paper Moon. Westbow, 2005.
Two single parents go with their teenage daughters to Mexico and must deal with their daughters' kidnapping and their growing feelings for each other, as well.

Fiesta Moon. Westbow, 2005.
An American social worker and a profligate engineer in need of redemption work to turn an old, possibly haunted, hacienda into an orphanage and find love and respect along the way.

Blue Moon. Westbow, 2006.
A marine archaeologist searching off the coast of Yucatan for the fabled Luna Azul with its treasure cargo is drawn to the captain of the boat she hires for an expedition that is threatened by an unscrupulous thief who is after their sunken treasure rights.

Piper Cove Chronicles
Set on the Maryland Eastern Shore this projected contemporary series follows the lives of four high school friends.

Wedding Bell Blues. Avon Inspire, 2007.
A divorced interior decorator finds she still loves her ex when he returns home to be the best man in her sister's wedding.

For Pete's Sake. Avon Inspire, 2008.
A motorcycle-riding landscape designer is attracted to her single parent neighbor who is engaged to a totally wrong woman in this funny, intriguing story with a dash of mystery.

Brides of Alba Series
Set during the time of King Arthur in the region of Alba.

The Healer. David C. Cook, 2010.
A reclusive healer finds love with a wounded man she rescues.

The Thief. David C. Cook, 2011.

Worth, Lenora
His Brother's Wife. Steeple Hill, 1999.
A young widow is required to marry her late husband's brother by a stipulation in the will.

In the Garden Series
Set in the Louisiana bayous, this series follows the lives and loves of the Dorsettes.

When Love Came to Town. Steeple Hill, 2001.
Lorna Dorsette comes to Louisiana to restore her aunt's plantation after tornado damage and is attracted to handsome tree expert Mick Love, who lends a hand.

Something Beautiful. Steeple Hill, 2002.
Lucas Dorsette finds love with Willa O'Connor as they both work to understand what God wants of them.

Lacey's Retreat. Steeple Hill, 2002.
A widow searching for happiness shelters a man who's wanted by the law and finds that her trust is rewarded.

Easter Blessings: The Lily Field. Steeple Hill, 2003.
A woman goes home to Louisiana to be with her grandmother and is attracted to the manager of the lily field that has always been part of her life.

Sunset Island Series
The Dempsey men, Rock, Stone, and Clay, find love on tiny Sunset Island.

The Carpenter's Wife. Steeple Hill, 2003.
A down-to-earth pastor/carpenter despairs of finding the right woman until he meets the equally pragmatic owner of a local tearoom.

Heart of Stone. Steeple Hill, 2003.
Sparks fly and eventually romance flares between a determined widow and a stubborn businessman who wants her land.

A Tender Touch. Steeple Hill, 2004.
A widowed veterinarian whose husband was a police officer and an injured K-9 officer and his companion meet on Sunset Island and must learn to trust again before they can find happiness.

After the Storm. Steeple Hill, 2004.
An abused woman taking refuge in the Georgia mountains is attracted to the man who helped deliver her baby during a storm, but she's not sure she can trust him.

Texas Hearts Series
Three city girls return to their small town Texas roots for various reasons in this contemporary trilogy.

A Certain Hope. Steeple Hill, 2005.
A New York career woman returns to her Texas ranch when her father falls ill and must sort things out with the man she left behind.

A Perfect Love. Steeple Hill, 2005.
A young woman from the city visits her family's small town for the summer and finds everything she's looking for when she meets a handsome landscaper.

Leap of Faith. Steeple Hill, 2006.
Returning home to Texas, a young accountant clashes with the man her father hired to deal with the family financial firm.

Secret Agent Minister. Steeple Hill, 2007.
A pastor's secret agent past puts him and his secretary in danger in this suspenseful story.

Deadly Texas Rose. Steeple Hill, 2008.
When a single mother is almost abducted, the sheriff is intrigued and attracted to her but wants to know what she is running from.

Mountain Sanctuary. Steeple Hill, 2008.
A single mom running a rustic Arkansas B&B is attracted to one of her guests, a cop in need of a rest.

Heart of the Night. Steeple Hill, 2009.
A father comes to claim the son he's just learned about because he fears they are all in danger.

Gift of Wonder. Steeple Hill, 2009.
A reported has a hard time trusting an attractive newcomer, especially when she does some investigating.

Hometown Princess. Steeple Hill, 2010.
A woman battles a wicked stepmother as she tries to make a success of her business.

Risky Reunion. Steeple Hiss, 2010.
A woman in the witness protection Witness program is endangered by a leak, as well as the fact that she witnessed another murder, this time by a cop.

Y'Barbo, Kathleen
Fairweather Keys
This Historical Inspirational trilogy is set in the tropical Fairweather Keys.

Beloved Castaway. Barbour, 2007.
A runaway mixed-race slave from New Orleans finds romance with a ship's captain when she escapes aboard his ship.

Beloved Captive. Barbour, 2008.
A school teacher and a naval officer struggle with her mixed-race heritage and his past in order to find love.

Beloved Counterfeit. Barbour 2009.
A woman determined to start all over again is plagued when a villain from her past threatens her new love and her carefully crafted present.

The Confidential Life of Eugenia Cooper. WaterBrook, 2009.
A book-loving socialite heroine who wants to have adventures before she settles down gets more than she bargained for when she poses as a governess and heads to Colorado in this adventurous Historical Inspirational.

Anna Finch and the Hired Gun. WaterBrook, 2010.
Determined to become a newspaper reporter but heading for trouble, the heroine eventually finds love with the Pinkerton agent hired to protect her in this Western Historical Inspirational.

9

10

TAKE FIVE!

Five favorite Inspirational Romances:

- **Tamera Alexander**—*The Inheritance*
- **Deeanne Gist**—*A Bride in the Bargain*
- **Dee Henderson**—*Danger in the Shadows*
- **Beverly Lewis**—*The Preacher's Daughter*
- **Francine Rivers**—*The Scarlet Thread*

11

12

13

14

15

16

Chapter 12

Ethnic/Multicultural Romance

We are enriched by our reciprocate differences.

Paul Valery

Definition

> **Ethnic/Multicultural Romance**—Romance novels in which the cultural, racial, or ethnic background of one or more of the characters plays a major role in the story and in the protagonists' romantic relationship.

In its simplest, narrowest form, the Ethnic, or Multicultural, Romance is a love story in which one or both of the protagonists are African American, Latino, Native American, Asian, Pacific Islander, Middle Eastern, or have a heritage other than the more traditional Anglo Saxon. More broadly, romances focusing on the Amish, Cajun, or other culturally distinct groups could also be included within this subgenre, although this is rarely the practice. In fact, given the European immigrant origins of the United States and to some extent, Canada, there are many romances in which the characters' cultural backgrounds (e.g., Italian, Irish, Jewish, Polish, Swedish, French Canadian) are an integral part of the story. Theoretically, these could be considered as part of this subgenre, but as a matter of practice, possibly because most Americans have ancestral roots elsewhere, they usually are not.

Additionally, in these romances the ethnicity and/or cultural background of the characters is both important and acknowledged, lending a culturally authentic flavor to the book and providing a realistic setting for the story. Obviously, this aspect varies in degree from story to story—in some cases the characters' ethnicity or culture is critical to the plot; in others, it merely provides the background. But whatever the situation, these are not "plug and play" romances into which one can drop characters of any ethnic origin and have the story ring true.

Multicultural Romances employ contemporary, historical, and, occasionally, futuristic and/or fantasy settings, which will vary with the story and the particular ethnic group being portrayed. For example, the historical American West is a traditional setting for stories featuring Native American characters, while many of the recent romances featuring African American protagonists are set in contemporary urban environments or, occasionally, the rural South. By the same token, stories featuring Latino and Asian characters often use contemporary settings in the Southwest, Florida, the West Coast, or Hawaii.

However, these are only generalizations, and on the flip side, Native American characters continue to grace the pages of Contemporary novels by bestselling author Kathleen Eagle, African American characters find love and adventure in the Historical Romances of popular writers such as Anita Richmond Bunkley and Beverly Jenkins, and Latino protagonists are part of any number of Historical Romances set in the Old West or early California. Obviously, nothing can be taken for granted in this dynamic subgenre, and with the growing mobility of our population, the settings and the characters that populate these stories, especially the Contemporaries, are bound to reflect this transition.

Similarly, the plot patterns used in Multicultural Romances are neither predictable nor one-dimensional. Diverse, wide-ranging, and increasingly varied, they mirror much of what is found in the broader romance arena, and although many are straightforward, man-meets-woman love stories, a growing number are action-packed tales of romantic suspense; family-oriented, multilayered stories in the women's fiction mode; or, more recently, an intriguing selection of inventive paranormal romances. By definition, race and culture are integral parts of these stories, and while issues involving prejudice and discrimination occasionally add their own complications, they rarely overshadow the developing romantic relationship between the protagonists, keeping these stories well away from the realm of the classic "problem novel."

Multicultural Romance encompasses a wide variety of ethnicities and cultural groups, and while romances featuring characters from many backgrounds do exist, at the time of this writing the African American segment is by far the largest, the most visible, and the most easily found. This is partly due to several well-established lines and series devoted to African American Romance, currently including Harlequin's Kimani Press Arabesque and Kimani Romance, Kensington's Dafina, and Genesis Press's four Indigo lines. In addition, a number of popular African American writers have broken out of series into the broader romance stream, taking their fans with them and expanding their general readership, as well. Romances featuring characters of other cultures and ethnicities do, of course, exist and are increasing in number and popularity, However, in spite of several attempts at establishing dedicated lines (e.g., Kensington's Encanto), most other Multicultural Romances remain part of the general mix of lines and series. Although this makes them more difficult to find as a group, the fact that most readers are increasingly choosing books by author makes this less of an issue than in the past.

Appeal

The basic appeal of the Ethnic or Multicultural Romance is to the readers who are part of the particular cultural group portrayed in the story. Readers enjoy reading about characters and situations with which they can identify—that they can connect with. Although historically there have been fewer opportunities for romance readers from many ethnic groups to do this, this has been changing rapidly in recent years, and the increasing number of Multicultural Romances now available is providing that opportunity for a large number of long-neglected readers, including a growing number of bi- and multiracial fans. This is not to say, however, that other readers will not read and enjoy books about ethnic groups and cultures other than their own. (It is, after all, what many African American, Latino, Asian, Native American, biracial, and Multiracial Romance readers have been doing from the other side for years.) But, in general, the attraction is greatest for readers who see themselves and their cultures reflected in the story and can identify with characters who share a similar heritage.

Advising the Reader

General readers' advisory information is provided in chapter 3, but there are several specific points that might be helpful when advising Ethnic and Multicultural Romance fans.

- Readers who enjoy Ethnic or Multicultural Romance may also enjoy non-ethnically oriented romances of a similar type. A reader who enjoys some of the sexy, passion-filled stories in the Kimani Press series line, Kimani Romance, might also be interested in a Silhouette Desire or, possibly, a Harlequin Blaze; readers who like their ethnic romances with a bit of mystery or suspense, might also enjoy a Silhouette Romantic Suspense or thrillers by writers such as Karen Harper, Beverly Barton, and Linda Howard; those who want their Multicultural Romances on the paranormal or futuristic side might also enjoy a Silhouette Nocturne or a romance from Dorchester's edgy Shomi line; and readers who appreciate Historical Romances by writers such as Beverly Jenkins might like other romances with American Civil War settings.
- Readers who like Ethnic or Multicultural Romances may also enjoy nonfiction or fiction other than romance that focuses on a particular cultural group. Consider recommending well-known writers such as Amy Tan, Maya Angelou, Terri MacMillan, Sandra Cisneros, and Alice Walker as well as other newer, cutting-edge authors.
- Although this is merely standard good reference interview technique, don't assume that you know what readers want before they tell you. Don't assume that readers want to read African American Romances simply because they are black, are interested only in books related to Asians because they are Japanese, or, for that matter, aren't interested in Ethnic Romances because they don't *look* "ethnic." In other words, don't assume anything. Ask—and by asking questions, making suggestions, and evaluating readers' reaction, let them tell you what they really want.
- Finally, as always, be sensitive and aware. Whatever your own ethnic background, it is easy to offend without intending to, and offending readers will defeat your primary purpose, which is to put the reader in touch with good books they will enjoy.

Brief History

Although the Ethnic or Multicultural Romance as we think of it today is a relatively recent phenomenon, love stories that feature characters from a variety of cultural and ethnic backgrounds are not new. One only has to look at something as obvious as Shakespeare's

Othello or even *Anthony and Cleopatra* (albeit these are not your average uplifting romances) to see that protagonists of diverse ethnicities have been falling in and out of love for years. In America, stories set in the South or along the frontier were fertile ground for secondary, if not primary, romantic plotlines involving African American, Native American, or Latino (primarily Mexican) characters. And while most of these are not essentially romances and were written for other purposes (e.g., Harriett Beecher Stowe's *Uncle Tom's Cabin* [1852]), a few, such as *Ramona* (1884) by Helen Hunt Jackson or Edna Ferber's *Show Boat* (1926), have strong romantic themes.

By the late 1950s, ethnic characters, primarily African American or Caribbean, were playing important roles in the lusty, violent Plantation Romances. Launched in 1957 by Kyle Onstott's *Mandingo*, these steamy, often brutal tales of sex and slavery remained popular for several decades, eventually even lending some of their characteristics (but not necessarily their ethnic characters) to the Sweet/Savage Romances of the 1970s. With the advent of the 1980s came the publication of Rosalind Welles's *Entwined Destinies* (Dell Candlelight, 1980), one of the earliest Category Romances with African American characters, and things ever so slowly began to change. Ethnic heroes and heroines were still few and far between, and they were not emphasized, but they were there. Native American heroes (and occasionally heroines) began to appear in Historicals set in the West (e.g., *Savage Ecstasy* [Zebra, 1981] by Janelle Taylor) and by the end of the decade, "Indian" Romances were an accepted fact. But other ethnic characters were still facing an uphill struggle. Even though there were a number of African American and Latino writers producing romances during the 1980s, they were mainly writing about white characters. Things took a new turn in 1990 when Leticia Peoples launched Odyssey Books and began publishing romances with African American heroes and heroines. Several other small houses established their own lines with varying success, including Genesis Press which was established in 1993 and released its first Indigo imprint romance in 1995. However, it wasn't until July 1994, when Kensington Publishing launched Pinnacle's Arabesque line of Multicultural Romances with *Serenade* by Sandra Kitt and *Forever Yours* by Francis Ray that things really took off. The line proved highly successful and by 1997 had doubled its releases, from two to four each month. In 1998 BET (Black Entertainment Television) Holdings bought the Arabesque line, and in 2000 Kensington launched its own African American trade paperback imprint, Dafina. Arabesque changed hands again in 2005 when Harlequin Enterprises acquired it, along with Sepia (general single-title fiction) and New Spirit (inspirational), from BET to form the basis for Kimani Press, Harlequin's new program featuring a number of lines focusing on African American characters and culture. As of this writing, Kimani Press houses four imprints, Kimani Press (mainstream), Kimani Press Arabesque Romance (single-title romance), plus TRU (Young Adult) and Kimani Press Romance (category series romance). In addition, Kensington's Dafina remains a viable player in the market, and in keeping with the current interest in the young adult market, has added a YA line to the Dafina imprint. Genesis Press, which has had its ups and downs over the years, currently publishes four Indigo Romance imprints: Indigo (classic romance), Indigo after Dark (sensual romance), Indigo Love Spectrum (cross-cultural romance), and Indigo Vibe (romance for the urban, twenty-five-and-under crowd). In addition to these specialized lines and imprints, African American Romances also can be found on the lists of most of the major romance publishers.

Although African American Romance is the most visible and well-represented segment of the Ethnic and Multicultural Romance market, and has been for some years, efforts have been made to establish similar lines for other cultural groups. One of the most successful was Kensington's Encanto Romance line, a bilingual Spanish/English line that highlighted Latino characters and cultures. Launched with high hopes in 1999, the line unfortunately ceased publication in 2002. Other attempts came and went, and as of this writing there are no major lines or series, other than those for the African American Market, dedicated to publishing Multicultural Romances. It is worth noting that there are a number of romances available in translation, primarily thanks to Harlequin (e.g., the Spanish language Deseo and Bianca series), but for the most part these are simply translations of the series romances and are not Multicultural Romances.

A recent phenomenon that is not Romance and beyond the scope of this guide, but that may be of interest to readers because of the multicultural (originally and most often African American but more recently Latino, as well) and erotica elements, is the development and rise of Urban Lit or Street Lit. This gritty, no-hold-barred genre zeroes in on the underside of urban life and the sex, violence, crime, and language are explicit and realistic. Born in the Black Power days of the 1970s, it declined only to resurface in the late 1990s, sparked by interest in titles such as *Coldest Winter* by Sister Souljah, and has been evolving and gaining popularity ever since. Urban erotica also is part of the larger Urban Lit scene, and writers such as Zane, who were originally self-published but subsequently picked up by larger houses, have definitely made an impact and may appeal to some romance fans. For more information on this popular genre, consult *Urban Grit: A Guide to Street Lit* (Santa Barbara, CA: Libraries Unlimited, 2010) by Megan Honig.

Despite the lack of specific lines dedicated to particular ethnic groups or cultures, the number of romances that include multicultural characters seems to be on the rise. It is no longer that unusual for a hero or heroine to be bi- or multiracial, to have a heritage that is totally or partially non–Northern European, or to have a culturally diverse group of friends and acquaintances. (In fact, for settings in many parts of the country, it would be unrealistic if that weren't the case.) It's just that a growing number of these books are not currently being singled out for publication on this basis. These stories are simply mirroring our culture's changing demographics and lifestyles, and the fact that many of these romances are slipping into the mainstream and being published as part of general romance lines says a lot about the maturing of the subgenre and may say even more about the expectations of the readers.

Publishers

Most romance publishers include some Multicultural Romance titles. However, the following publishers have dedicated African American Romance lines. For additional information refer to chapter 22, "Publishers."

The Genesis Press
Indigo line
Indigo
Indigo after Dark
Indigo Love Spectrum
Indigo Vibe

Harlequin Enterprises
Kimani Press
Kimani Press

Arabesque Romance
Kimani Romance
TRU

Kensington Books
Dafina imprint
Dafina Trade Paperbacks
Dafina Young Adult Trade Paperbacks

Classic Ethnic and Multicultural Romance Writers

Anderson, Catherine—**Comanche Series** (*Comanche Moon* [1991], *Comanche Heart* [1991], *Indigo Blue* [1992], *Comanche Magic* [1994]).
This classic series spans generations and deals with physical handicaps and abuse issues.

Dailey, Janet—*Night Way* (1981), *The Pride of Hannah Wade* (1985), *The Proud and the Free* (1994).
The Apache, Navajo, and Cherokee cultures are the foci of these three classic Historical Romances, respectively.

De Blasis, Celeste—*The Proud Breed* (1978).
A three-generational California-set classic featuring a Latino biracial heroine.

Eagle, Kathleen—*Sunrise Song* (1996).
An unusual, touching romance infused with Lakota culture that features parallel romances from the 1930s and 1970s.

Johnson, Susan—**Braddock-Black Absarokee Series** (*Blaze* [1986], *Silver Flame* [1988], *Forbidden* [1991], *Brazen* [1995]), *Pure Sin* (1994).
Sensual, erotic romances with strong heroines and heroes to match.

Kitt, Sandra—*Adam and Eva* (1984).
An island setting brings romance and love to two very deserving people in this story that was Harlequin's first romance by a black author to feature African American character.

Kitt, Sandra—*Serenade* (1994), *Sincerely* (1995), *The Color of Love* (1995), *Significant Others* (1996), *Suddenly* (1996), *Between Friends* (1998).

Stone, Katherine—*Pearl Moon* (1995).
An emotionally involving exotic classic.

Taylor, Janelle—**Gray Eagle/Alisha Series** (*Savage Ecstasy* [1981], *Defiant Ecstasy* [1982], *Forbidden Ecstasy* [1982], *Brazen Ecstasy* [1983], *Tender Ecstasy* [1983], *Stolen Ecstasy* [1985], *Bittersweet Ecstasy* [1987], *Forever Ecstasy* [1991]).
This classic three-generational series follows the lives of Lakota Warrior Gray Eagle and Alisha Williams and their offspring. Note: Like a number of Historical Romances of the 1970s and 1980s, this series includes sweet/savage elements and will not read like many of the Historical Romances of today.

Welles, Rosalind (Elsie B. Washington)—*Entwined Destinies* (1980).
One of the earliest series romances featuring African American characters, this sweet traditional takes a capable magazine reporter and an arrogant oil company executive, sets them down in England, and lets them fall in love.

Wind, Ruth (Barbara Samuel)—*The Last Chance Ranch* (1995).
This Janet Dailey Award winner focuses on abuse issues and features a Latino hero.

Selected Ethnic and Multicultural Romance Bibliography

This selective bibliography is not comprehensive; the titles listed below are merely examples of the growing number of Ethnic/Multicultural Romances being produced. Contemporary, Historical, and romances of other types will be included within each cultural grouping, as appropriate. (See previous editions of this guide for any authors or titles that may have been dropped from this edition.)

African American

Alers, Rochelle
Alers writes fast-paced, suspenseful romances, Women's Fiction, and Contemporary Romance, often with flashes of humor. Her best known books are part of the Hideaway series which is included in chapter 13. See also chapter 13, "Linked Romances."

Secrets Never Told. Pocket, 2003.
A betrayed woman goes home to rural Georgia to heal and learns many secrets about her family's past and finds the strength to deal with the future.

Lessons of a Low Country Summer. Pocket, 2004.
Three people go to a South Carolina barrier island for the summer and find healing, peace, a new lease on life in this ambience-rich, mainstream story that includes a romance, as well.

Whitfield Brides Trilogy
Three independent New York businesswomen (a cousin and two sisters) find love in this upbeat trilogy.

Long Time Coming. Kimani Arabesque, 2008.
A DA and a wedding planner thrown together during a blackout fall for each other but are wary of commitments.

The Sweetest Temptation. Kimani Arabesque, 2008.
A pastry chef afraid to trust finds love with a former air force pilot.

Taken By Storm. Kimani Arabesque, 2008.
A floral designer who witnessed a murder is assigned a live-in bodyguard, with the expected romantic results.

Best Men
Three childhood friends share ownership in a charming brownstone in Harlem.

Man of Fate. Kimani Arabesque, 2009.
A car crash brings a responsible attorney who believes in fate into the life of a woman who doesn't see things his way.

Man of Fortune. Kimani Arabesque, 2009.
Trapped in an elevator together, a wealthy man who lost his fiancée in 9/11 and a doctor whose marriage went on the rocks, find common ground—eventually.

Man of Fantasy. Kimani Arabesque, 2009.
A wary psychotherapist and a career-minded photographer find love despite their individual issues.

Butterfly. Kimani Arabesque, 2010.
A strong, talented woman navigates the dangerous waters of the high-profile modeling industry.

Wainwright Legacy

Focuses on the wealthy, powerful Wainwright family, some of whom were introduced in previous books.

Because of You. Kimani Arabesque, 2010.
Attorney Jordan Wainwright helps a fellow lawyer with her sexual harassment lawsuit and helps her learn to trust again.

Here I Am. Kimani Arabesque, 2011.

Bunkley, Anita Richmond

Bunkley's earlier novels were primarily Historicals; her recent ones are Contemporaries. See previous editions of this guide for her earlier works.

Relative Interest. Dafina, 2003.
A woman who returns from an assignment in Africa finds a wealthy white couple planning to adopt her young niece in this story filled with racial politics and social issues.

Silent Wager. Dafina, 2006.
Multiple tragedies afflict Camille and Max Granville in this story that is a combination of suspense and women's fiction.

Between Goodbyes. Dafina, 2008.
A young Afro-Cuban émigrée achieves Broadway stardom but can't decide which of three men to marry.

Spotlight on Desire. Kimani Romance, 2009.
A soap opera star has problems keeping her own life and her on-screen persona separate.

Vote for Love. Kimani Romance, 2010.
A senate candidate and an image consultant are attracted to each other but wary of the others' motives.

First Class Seduction. Kimani Romance, 2010.
A flight attendant and a security expert meet in Acapulco and then again on the flight home, and then again when her home is vandalized in this fast-paced sexy story with a hint of danger.

Byrd, Adrianne

Byrd's many novels usually provide good descriptions and are quite varied. Some of her titles have been reprinted.

Comfort of a Man. BET Arabesque, 2003.
An impulsive one-night stand becomes something more.

Unforgettable. BET Arabesque, 2004 (Kimani Press, 2011).
A ladies' man never dates his coworkers, but when he goes to a masked ball, he connects with his secretary with unforgettable results. A bit of a Cinderella story.

Measure of a Man. BET Arabesque, 2005.
Confusion and hilarity reign in this story of mistaken identities and sexual orientations that features a firefighter/sculptor hero and an art expert heroine.

The Beautiful Ones. BET Arabesque, 2005.
A man regrets not telling his long-time friend he loves her when she becomes engaged to her current boyfriend. Character links to *Unforgettable*.

Blue Skies. Kimani Arabesque, 2007.
Impulsively wed, the career military protagonists separate and then are reunited under dangerous circumstances.

To Love a Stranger. Kimani Romance, 2007.
Thrilled when her husband and his mistress are supposedly killed in a plane crash, a woman carves out a happy life for herself and her child—until her husband returns, a changed man and unable to remember anything.

When Valentine's Collide. Kimani Romance, 2008.
After ten years of marriage, the relationship experts, the Valentines, are about to split, unless they can reconcile their vast differences.

Forget Me Not. Kimani Arabesque, 2008.
A detective trying to discover who killed her partner seeks help from an FBI agent when she realizes she is being set up by someone who doesn't want her to learn the truth.

Her Lover's Legacy. Kimani Romance, 2008.
Politics and romance Texas-style.

Sinful Chocolate. Kimani Romance, 2009.
A chocolatier meets a notorious playboy whose world is falling apart when she bakes his birthday cake.

Heart's Secret. Kimani Arabesque, 2010.
A former model and banker meet as a result of a matchmaking set up, but their relationship may fizzle if the hero finds out the truth. Part of a publisher's multiauthored series with titles linked by a matchmaker. (Part of Kimani Arabesque's Match Made series that includes stories by various authors.)

Body Heat. Kimani Romance, 2010.
Playright Nikki Jamison's plan to hole up in a villa in St. Lucia that the owner rarely visits takes an interesting twist when the owner shows up and learns that Nikki has told the locals that she is his wife.

Castoro, Laura

Crossing the Line. Berkley, 2002.
A young light-skinned African American widow with a teenage daughter returns home to Dallas and finds love with an activist, much to the disapproval of her family and friends.

Love on the Line. Avon A, 2009.
A young college student, the daughter in *Crossing the Line*, must deal with her mixed heritage in this story that focuses on race, color, and society's expectations.

Craft, Francine

The Best of Everything. BET Arabesque, 2004.
Suspense, mystery, and healing are part of this emotionally involving romance.

Dream of Ecstasy. BET Arabesque, 2005.
Good friends eventually become something more in this intense story.

Never Without You . . . Again. Kimani Romance, 2007.
A pair of college sweethearts are reunited after years in a romantic story that has a few villains who try to make trouble.

The Way You Make Me Feel. Kimani Romance, 2007.
Murder, amnesia, and the music scene are part of this light read.

Designed for Passion. Kimani Romance, 2008.
A plus-sized mother of twins who owns a boutique finds love—and a better self-image—with the detective who is looking into her cheating husband's death.

Esdaile, Leslie

Esdaile writes lively, upbeat, often funny, romances. She also writes mysteries as Leslie Esdaile Banks and paranormals as L. A. Banks.

Love Potions. BET Arabesque, 2002.
A P.I. comes to Nicole for a psychic reading and gets a love potion that really works in this funny story of four women trying to make the best of their lives.

Though the Storm. BET Arabesque, 2002.
A woman recovering from divorce and a single dad with two daughters meet on a blind date and realize that there might be something good in the future, after all.

Sister Got Game. Dafina, 2004.
With no options left, a smart, beautiful, jobless woman accepts a job offered by the man who came to collect her car—a job that takes her from Philadelphia to Macon and into the life of a businessman who's sworn off women—or so he thinks. Funny and lively.

Better Than. Dafina, 2008.
Bent on self-improvement, a biracial (half-black/half-Cherokee) heroine meets a reclusive art teacher, and as they become friends and search for self-fulfillment, they also find love.

Ford, Bette

When a Man Loves a Woman. BET Arabesque, 2002.
A fearful woman who wants to dissolve her fledgling marriage is convinced to try it for a year; the results are rewarding.

Prescott Sports Series
This series is loosely linked by character.

Unforgettable. HarperTorch, 2003.
A football star finally realizes his best friend's little sister, Anna Prescott, has finally grown up.

An Everlasting Love. Avon, 2005.
A rape victim tries to ascertain the identity of the father of her child and must deal with her former boyfriend's (Devin Prescott) hurt and anger.

Can't Say No. Avon, 2008.
Ralph Prescott, an NBA player with a reputation for being a "player," must convince a skeptic that he really has reformed.

Can't Get Enough of You. Avon, 2010.
A woman, adopted as a child and separated from her siblings, returns to teach in her home town and look for her family, and reconnects with her former fiancé.

Forster, Gwynne

Forster writes both romance and mainstream women's fiction that deal with serious issues. A number of her earlier works have been reprinted.

Beyond Desire. BET Arabesque, 1999.
A pregnant school principal and a father who needs funds for his daughter's operation agree to a marriage of convenience in this emotionally intense romance.

Scarlet Woman. BET Arabesque, 2001.
The widow of an older man learns that she must establish a literacy foundation and marry within a year or lose her inheritance.

Harrington Series

The three wealthy Harrington brothers find love in this series.

Once in a Lifetime. Arabesque, 2002 (Kimani Arabesque, 2010).
A former college teacher with past secrets accepts a housekeeping position and falls in love with one of her employers.

After the Loving. BET Arabesque, 2005.
A plus-size woman with low self-esteem tries to slim down to attract her man, but what she really needs to work on is her self-confidence.

Love Me or Leave Me. BET Arabesque, 2005.
A man wanting to establish himself career-wise and a professional woman whose biological clock is ticking must come to terms with what they really want.

Love Me Tonight. Kimani Arabesque, 2010.
An adopted lawyer learns he has links to the Harrington family.

Blues from Down Deep. Dafina, 2003.
A hotel manager leaves Hawaii to discover her roots and a family to love in North Carolina and discovers a dysfunctional family and plenty of secrets, instead. Music and romance lighten the mix.

When You Dance with the Devil. Dafina, 2006.
A woman learning how to cope on her own and a man struggling with heartbreak move into the same boarding house.

Getting Some of Her Own. Dafina, 2007.
A woman who has had a hysterectomy rejects a man she could love because she cannot have children.

What Matters Most. Kimani Arabesque, 2008.
A doctor expected by his socially prominent family to marry money finds himself falling for a nursing school student who works in his office, instead. This romance is one of a series that highlights St. Jude's Children's Research Hospital.

A Different Kind of Blues. Dafina, 2008.
A woman who thinks she is dying tries to right all her past wrongs and finds love as she does so.

Holiday Kisses. Kimani Romance, 2009.
A dentist and a news anchor aspiring to a national spot must deal with trust issues before their hearts can heal enough to fall in love.

Destination Love. Kimani Romance, 2010.
A famous author plans to get back at the professor who interfered with his timely graduation (and doesn't recognize him) by seducing and then dumping her while they are on the same cruise.

Guillaume, Geri

A Perfect Pair. BET Arabesque, 2001.
A woman on her way to an interview and a workaholic for his family business meet when he saves her life, but their relationship becomes more serious when she goes to work for his company.

Hearts of Steel. BET Arabesque, 2002.
A woman home for her grandparents' anniversary celebration and a football player she met on the plane become the matchmaking targets of her family in the first of the Family Reunion trilogy (also includes *A Family Affair* [2002] by Shirley Hailstock and *Ties That Bind* [2002] by Eboni Snoe).

Winter Fires. BET, Arabesque, 2003.
Childhood friends meet again years later and must sort out current relationships as well as their growing romantic feelings for each other.

Her Brother's Keeper. Kimani Arabesque, 2006,
An unusual, compelling holiday story with a dash of the supernatural.

Kiss Me Twice. Kimani Romance, 2009.
A man reluctantly takes over his family business and is attracted to the consultant he hires to help him improve the safety and working conditions. Character links to *A Perfect Pair*.

Hailstock, Shirley
Many of Hailstock's romances have action and suspense elements, as well as emotional depth, and feature heroines whose lives have taken unexpected turns.

More than Gold. BET, 2000.
The hero and heroine are on the run from a killer after the heroine's best friend is murdered by mistake.

A Family Affair. BET Arabesque, 2002.
Second in the Family Reunion trilogy (*Hearts of Steel* [2002] by Geri Guillaume and *Ties That Bind* [2002] by Eboni Snoe) in which cousins are reunited at a family event.

Clayton Sibling Series
This series focuses on the children who were adopted by Devon and Reuben Clayton.

A Father's Fortune. Silhouette Special Edition, 2003.
A teacher and a carpenter learn to put their past hurts behind them and build a new life together.

9

10

11

12

13

14

15

16

Love on Call. Silhouette Special Edition, 2004.
A pair of medical doctors are attracted to each other even they know it's not a good idea.

The Secret. Dafina, 2006.
An interior decorator searching for her true identity falls in love with one of the adopted sons of her birth family.

On My Terms. Dafina, 2008.
A movie producer and a woman who owns the property the film crew is using clash but can't deny their mutual attraction.

Last Night's Kiss. Dafina, 2008.
A model and a former TV journalist come to Montana for a taste of simplicity and find unexpected love.

You Made Me Love You. Dafina, 2005.
After nine years in a Federal Witness Protection Program and sick of law enforcement types, Rachel Wells returns home to take her life back, only to find herself in danger once more and attracted to the chief of police.

My Lover, My Friend. Kimani Romance, 2006.
A doctor and a political speechwriter suffer tragic losses and return home to rural Maine to heal and renew their teenage friendship.

Wrong Dress, Right Guy. Kimani Romance, 2008.
A wedding dress delivered by mistake results in romance for the accidental recipient and a journalist who has no intention of marrying.

Nine Months with Thomas. Kimani Romance, 2009.
A widower falls in love with the woman who has agreed to be the surrogate mother for his and his late wife's last fertilized egg.

The Right Wedding Gown. Kimani Romance, 2009.
A woman who doesn't believe in marriage, a man who does, and an antique wedding dress are all part of this romance with character links to *Wrong Dress, Right Guy*.

Harrison, Shirley

Harrison's romances often include suspense elements.

Picture Perfect. BET Arabesque, 1999.
A woman's desire to reclaim her father's paintings puts her in conflict with a man she is attracted to in this mystery-laced, fast-paced debut romance.

Dangerous Fortune. BET Arabesque, 2001.
A young woman in a psychic family swears off love when several of her boyfriends die accidentally, a decision that causes problems for an architect who is attracted to her.

The Pleasure Principle. BET Arabesque, 2004.
A pair of former lovers gradually renew their relationship and deal with shady financial dealings at the accountant heroine's work in this light romantic suspense.

Sweet Justice. BET Arabesque, 2004.
A murder investigation places pressure on the protagonists' romantic relationships.

Hill, Donna

Hill's books explore serious relationship issues and writes both mainstream and romance.

A Scandalous Affair. BET Arabesque, 2000.
An activist and an attorney meet and are attracted to each other during a Civil Rights case, but the fact that the heroine's sister had a secret affair with the hero years earlier causes a few problems in this intense, passionate romance.

If I Could. Dafina, 2000.
A mismatched pair sort their relationship out in this story that is fiction rather than romance.

Say Yes. Dafina, 2004.
The new-found happiness of Regina Everette and Parker Heywood is put to the test when her ex-husband wants her back and his teenage daughter wants Regina out of the picture. Follows *If I Could*.

Pause for Men Series
Four friends go into business together and open a spa for men.

Love Becomes Her. Kimani Romance, 2006.
One of the spa partners finds romance with a younger man.

Saving All My Loving. Kimani Romance, 2006.
A woman thinks her life is on the right track until her ex returns and says he wants her back.

If I Were Your Woman. Kimani Romance, 2007.
A once-burned-twice-shy public relations manager has second thoughts when she is attracted to a man she thinks is married.

After Dark. Kimani Romance, 2007.
An ex-husband and the hero's Black Panther past threaten a couple's new relationship.

TLC Series
Focuses on the members of The Ladies Cartel (TLC), a secret women's crime-fighting organization that masquerades as a cosmetics company.

Sex and Lies. Kimani Romance, 2008.
An architect husband and a secret crime operative wife suspect each other of having affairs in this fast-paced TLC romance.

Seduction and Lies. Kimani Romance, 2008.
An operative on her first assignment has a hard time keeping the truth from a man she's interested in.

Temptation and Lies. Kimani Romance, 2009.
A TLC operative out to expose a sex scandal causes the man in her life to be suspicious.

Longing and Lies. Kimani Romance, 2010.
A TLC operative and an FBI undercover agent pose as a married couple in order to expose a baby-trafficking operation.

Heart's Reward. Kimani Arabesque, 2010.
The matchmaker is attracted to one of her clients, which is something she can't allow to happen. (Part of Kimani Arabesque's Match Made series which includes stories by various authors.)

Hudson-Smith, Linda
See also chapter 11, "Inspirational Romance."

Sass. BET Arabesque, 2003.
A woman plans vengeance on the man who betrayed her only to find herself falling in love all over again.

Above the Clouds. BET Arabesque, 2005.
A flight attendant and a pilot find the path to love is a bit bumpy and somewhat long.

Secrets and Silence. BET Arabesque, 2006.
A parole officer resists his feelings for the sign language teacher he needs to work with so he can communicate with one of his parolees but is won over by her genuine caring and love.

Sweeter than Temptation. Kimani Arabesque, 2006.
This romance between a substance abuse counselor and a pastor has some Christian Inspirational aspects.

Forsaking All Others. Kimani Romance, 2007.
Jessica Harrington and Wes Chamberlain are shocked to find themselves attracted to each other after years of fighting their parents' plans to bring them together.

Indiscriminate Attraction. Kimani Romance, 2008.
A journalist heroine meets and is attracted to a homeless man at the shelter where she volunteers, not realizing he is looking for his twin and is only pretending to be destitute.

Destiny Calls. Kimani Romance, 2009.
A woman struggling to care for her ill sister and put herself through college becomes a phone-sex operator and strikes up a friendship with a man working on a book about the phone-sex industry.

Kissed by a Carrington. Kimani Romance, 2010.
A sports doctor is signed by the team of a pro basketball star with whom she has a brief, but sizzling, past.

Jenkins, Beverly
Although more noted for Historical Romances, Jenkins also writes Contemporaries.

A Chance at Love. Avon, 2002.
A woman hitching a ride on a wagon train headed to California has no intention of getting married, until she falls for a Kansas farmer's twin daughters—and then the father, himself.

The Edge of Midnight. HarperTorch, 2004.
A desperate woman, a man determined to get crime off the streets, and some stolen diamonds drive the plot of this lively romance that is a Contemporary offering from a noted Historical Romance writer.

The Edge of Dawn. HarperTorch, 2004.
A kidnapping victim has a hard time trusting her rescuer in this lively suspenseful romance.

Winds of the Storm. Avon, 2006.
Set in New Orleans after the Civil War, this story takes a secret government agent posing as an infamous madame, pairs her with a handsome hotelier, and lets the danger and the adventure begin.

Sexy/Dangerous. Avon, 2006.
A brilliant scientist is distracted by the gorgeous security agent assigned to keep him safe.

Deadly Sexy. Avon, 2007.
A trucker, who is much more than he seems, rescues a noted sports agent when her car breaks down and the romance takes off from there.

Wild Sweet Love. Avon, 2007.
An infamous Black Seminole outlaw, Teresa July, has been pardoned and released into the custody a Philadelphia socialite who hopes to turn Teresa into a proper lady. However, things take an intriguing turn when she realizes that independent Teresa and her buttoned-up son, Madison, are just what the other needs—if only they would realize it.

Jewel. Avon, 2008.
Jewel reluctantly agrees to pretend to be Eli Grayson's wife when he needs one to convince a visiting newspaper owner to back his newspaper, but when the town learns of their "marriage," they end up married—and then must deal with the fall out.

Captured. Avon, 2009.
An eighteenth-century high seas adventure in which a woman bargains her virtue for her passage home; naturally, it doesn't work out the way they had intended.

Midnight. Avon, 2010.
An adventurer seeking revenge for the death of his father connects with the infamous rebel spy, Lady Midnight, who is not at all what anyone would suspect in this Revolutionary Era romance.

King-Gamble, Marcia
Illusions of Love. BET, Arabesque, 2000.
A reporter is charged with interviewing an illusionist (and a former high school classmate) thought to be responsible for the disappearances of several women when he returns to his home town.

All about Me. Kimani Romance, 2007.
A mouthy, brash, self-serving, overweight secretary eventually becomes a decent, professional person with a lot of help from her personal trainer who has issues of his own.

Down and Out in Flamingo Beach. Kimani Romance, 2007.

Sex on Flamingo Beach. Kimani Romance, 2007.
A young woman falls for a man whose race will be unacceptable to her father in this modern romance.

Meet Phoenix. Kimani Romance, 2008.
An art expert must deal with her attractive ex-husband when she sets out to recover a valuable statue.

The Way He Moves. Harlequin, 2008.
A magical pendant brings romance to a wary Argentinean heiress when she meets a man who is a dead ringer for her former lover in this mystery-tinged, exotic romance.

Tempting the Mogul. Kimani Romance, 2008.
A spoiled son is jolted into reality when his father's health appears to be failing and his life coach takes him in hand.

Kitt, Sandra
One of the best-known writers of African American Romance, Kitt was the first African American writer to sign with Harlequin. She also launched Pinnacle's Arabesque line in 1994 along with Frances Ray. Sensitively handled interpersonal relationships, complex family dynamics, and multidimensional characters are hallmarks of her work.

Suddenly. Pinnacle, 1996.
A model falls for a doctor who is wary of superficial women.

Family Affairs. Signet, 1999.
A woman's past returns with a vengeance when her daughter's father (totally unaware he is a father) returns to town and her ex-con brother comes to display his art work at her gallery.

Close Encounters. Signet, 2000.
A woman inadvertently shot during a sting operation is befriended by one of the men responsible.

She's the One. Signet, 2001.
An upwardly mobile professional woman becomes the guardian of a six-year-old biracial child over the objections of a concerned firefighter and gradually learns about responsibility, parenting, and love.

Southern Comfort. BET Arabesque, 2004.
A joint inheritance of a beach cottage brings a jewelry designer and a musical attorney together in a relationship that eventually ends in love.

The Next Best Thing. BET Arabesque, 2005.

Celluloid Memories. Kimani Arabesque, 2007.
A young woman gains a new appreciation of her actor father and his struggles when she comes to L.A. to care for him and meets many who knew him. Good historical descriptions of the early Hollywood scene.

For All We Know. Kimani Arabesque, 2008.
Michaela Landry's house-sitting stint in Memphis takes an intriguing turn when she finds a sick, runaway teenager in her shed in this emotionally involving and educational romance; it is one of several romances written to call attention to and benefit St. Jude's Children's Research Hospital in Memphis.

RSVP with Love. Kimani Romance, 2009.
An events planner reconnects with a college classmate when she checks out his nightclub as a possible reunion site in this romance with suspense elements.

Promises in Paradise. Kimani Romance, 2010.
Past resentments get in the way of their relationship when an attorney reconnects with the daughter of the man who took him in as a teenager on a holiday trip to the Virgin Islands.

Mason, Felicia
See also chapter 11, "Inspirational Romance."

Heart Family Series
This Contemporary series centers on the Heart family and their department store chain.

Foolish Heart. Arabesque, 1998.
Coleman Heart III risks everything to save his family's stores and is aided by business consultant Sonja Pride, a woman with her own agenda.

Forbidden Heart. BET Arabesque, 2000.
Mallory Heart is determined to succeed in building her own company on her own, but when her brusque manner alienates people, she is forced to ask Ellis Carson for help.

Enchanted Heart. Dafina, 2004.
A lingerie boutique owner tries to keep her relationship with her playboy partner on a business-only level with mixed results.

Norfleet, Celeste O.
Norfleet also writes for the Young Adult market.

A Christmas Wish. BET Arabesque, 2002.
A matchmaking teen sets up her uncle with her school counselor in this heartwarming holiday romance.

Mamma Lou Series
Features matchmaking grandmother, Mamma Lou, and friends.

Priceless Gift. BET Arabesque, 2002.
Mamma Lou decides her relationship-wary grandson and a teacher recovering from a cheating boyfriend and is renovating an old house as therapy are perfect for each other; of course they have to agree, as well.

One Sure Thing. BET Arabesque, 2003.
Mamma Lou brings a pair of doctors together in this humorous romance.

Irresistible You. BET Arabesque, 2004.
An executive can't forget a ballerina he had a fling with, but she doesn't want anything permanent.

The Fine Art of Love. BET Arabesque, 2005.
A Harley-riding museum curator tries to avoid Mamma Lou's matchmaking attempts but she is attracted to the FBI agent sent to investigate a recent theft.

When Love Calls. Kimani Arabesque, 2008.
When a political activist tries to connect with an important senator, things don't go as planned—for either of them.

Only You. BET Arabesque, 2005.
When the media blows an argument into a lovers' quarrel, a fashion buyer and a football star who barely know each other suddenly become the latest hot couple—and attract a stalker.

Following Love. Kimani Arabesque, 2007.
Two independent people who've sworn off love are targeted by a matchmaking aunt in this sexy romance.

Love After All. Kimani Arabesque, 2007.
A con-artist's daughter and a former cop meet on a plane and discover that they are both looking for the same person in this suspenseful page-turner.

Sultry Storm. Kimani Romance, 2009.
A deputy sheriff and a woman he has admired from afar are stranded together during a tropical storm.

Heart's Choice. Kimani Arabesque, 2010.
An NFL star seeks help from matchmaker Melanie Harte and finds love with entertainer Jazzelle Richardson.

Perrin, Kayla
See also chapter 13, "Linked Romances."

Midnight Dreams. BET Arabesque, 1999.
Love, forgiveness, and second chances are key elements in the passionate, emotional romance.

Sweet Honesty. BET Arabesque, 1999.
A heroine framed for murder finds love with an undercover cop in this intriguing romance.

Holiday of Love. BET Arabesque, 2000.
A heroine searching for her mother reconnects with her college love who helps her. Kwanzaa is featured.

Flirting With Danger. BET Arabesque, 2001.
A woman trying to find her mother's killer finds her own life is in danger in this suspenseful tale.

If You Want Me. HarperTorch, 2001.
A successful movie star returns home to make peace with her mother and deal with those who were mean to her when she was a quiet, overweight teenager.

The Sisters of Theta Phi. St Martin's, 2001.
A secret from four sorority sisters' college days threatens the present in this passionate romantic suspense.

If You Need Me. HarperTorch, 2002.
Mistaken identity causes problems for the hero in this lively romp.

In a Heartbeat. BET Arabesque, 2003.
A car accident brings a talk show host fearing a murderous fan and an ex-cop grieving over past losses together in a relationship that helps them deal with the present and heal from the past.

Tell Me You Love Me. Harper Torch, 2003.
When the boyfriend who disappeared a year ago comes back into her life claiming to have been undercover, Tyanna Montgomery has a very hard time believing him in this lively romantic suspense tale.

Fool for Love. BET Arabesque, 2003.
A couple that split abruptly reconnects after ten years in this sexy reunion story.

Gimme an O! Avon Trade, 2005.
A pro football player caught in a media scandal and a celebrity sex therapist are caught up in a hunt for his missing wife who created the problems in the first place.

Love, Lies, and Videotape. Kimani Arabesque, 2007.
A betrayed Hollywood star and a man recovering from divorce meet on magical St. Lucia and begin to heal, trust, and find love again.

We'll Never Tell. St. Martin's Griffin, 2007.
African American sorority sisters deal with murder, revenge, and love in this mainstream story.

Single Mama Drama. Mira, 2008.
Single mom Vanessa's life is turned upside down when her cheating fiancé is murdered as she tries to deal with the scandal, a vengeful ex-wife, a budding romance, and doing well in her job.

Single Mama's Got More Drama. Mira, 2009.
The drama continues.

Island Fantasy. Kimani Romance, 2010.
Catching her fiancé cheating the night before the wedding, a woman jilts him, goes on her Jamaican honeymoon alone, and finds unexpected romance.

Poarch, Candice
Tender Escape. BET Arabesque, 2000.
A widow finds romance with the P.I. she hires to find a blackmailer.

The Last Dance. BET Arabesque, 2001.
A man-shy computer nerd and a detective with a womanizing reputation join forces to solve a crime and find love as well.

Coree Island Series
This small North Carolina barrier island is the setting for this romantic, occasionally suspenseful series.

Shattered Illusions. BET Arabesque, 2000.
A retired Navy SEAL goes to Coree Island to investigate his brother's murder and is attracted to the widowed campground director who had a relationship with his brother.

Lighthouse Magic. BET Arabesque, 2003.
A woman inherits a lighthouse on Coree Island, goes there to learn the truth of her heritage and to solve an old crime, and finds love with a local campground owner.

Loving Delilah. BET Arabesque, 2004.
A woman heads for Coree Island after being fired by her two-timing boss, finds love with the local doctor, and becomes a killer's target.

Bittersweet. Dafina, 2006.
Desiree Prescott leaves her fast-paced New York life (including a fiancé) and goes to Atlanta to become the guardian to her late long-lost brother's three children and finds support and eventually romance with the baseball player next door.

Sweet Southern Comfort. Kimani Romance, 2006.
A young businesswoman known for her good interpersonal advice clashes with a betrayed husband when she tries to help him get his life back on track.

His Tempest. Kimani Romance, 2007.
Humor enlivens this flirty story that provides the hero and heroine with a few challenges before their love jells.

Loving Spoonful. Kimani Romance, 2009.
A couple rebuilds their marriage that has crumbled because of insecurity and communication issues.

Safe in His Embrace. Kimani Romance, 2010.
A victim of spousal abuse flees her powerful ex, changes her name, and relocates to Alaska but fights her attraction to a sexy engineer, who suspects who she is and why she is so fearful of relationships.

Quest for the Golden Bowl Quartet
This romantic suspense series focuses on the community on tiny Paradise Island, Virginia, and involves the Claxton family's legendary golden bowl and tales of the people who first settled the area in the seventeenth century.

Golden Night. Dafina, 2007.
Gabrielle Claxton thinks she is responsible for the death of one of her B and B guests and seeks help from Cornell Price, a man her family hates.

Long Hot Nights. Dafina, 2008.
Danger stalks detective Alyssa Claxton and attractive club owner Jordan Ellis as she investigates a pair of murders.

Island of Deceit. Dafina, 2010.
Barbara Turner returns to Paradise Island to find her grandmother's killer and attracts the attention of Harper Porter, the local sheriff.

Deadly Intentions. Dafina, 2011.
A dead body and a sexy Navy SEAL complicate things for Lisa Claxton as she searches for her family's legendary heirloom.

Rainey, Doreen
Foundation for Love. BET Arabesque, 2002.
Deeply scarred protagonists, although successful business-wise, need love and healing and find it with each other. Debut novel.

The Game of Love. Kimani Arabesque, 2006.
A district attorney proves to be a romantic challenge for a football star in this lively romance.

Will to Love. Kimani Arabesque, 2007.
A confirmed bachelor playboy meets his match with a businesswoman who doesn't do long-term relationships either.

Ray, Francis
Ray pens emotionally involving, compassionate romances that explore a wide range of human emotions. Many of her stories are family oriented and involve continuing characters. See previous editions of this guide for some of her earlier titles.

Heart of the Falcon. Arabesque, 1998.
Daniel Falcon, a relationship-wary, powerful businessman, has a hard time coming to terms with his feelings for Madelyn Taggart, who is pregnant with his child, in this emotionally compelling romance.

The Turning Point. St. Martin's Paperbacks, 2001.
A recently divorced woman and a blind man help each other heal in this heartwarming story of renewed trust and love.

I Know Who Holds Tomorrow. St. Martin's Press, 2002.
A television celebrity takes in her husband's infant illegitimate child when he is killed in an accident in this emotionally wrenching romance.

Someone's Knocking at My Door. St. Martin's Griffin, 2003.
Although the primary romance is between art historian Kristen Wakefield and carpenter Rafe Crawford, the two other romances in this story add depth and complexity to this well-crafted romance.

Graysons of New Mexico Series
The members of the successful Grayson family drive the plots of these high-energy romances.

Until There Was You. BET Arabesque, 1999.
Luke Grayson meets his match in a gorgeous gun-toting stranger at his mountain retreat in this lively romance.

You and No Other. St. Martin's Paperbacks, 2005.
Mom Grayson matches her lawyer son, Morgan, with a lovely, independent artist, Phoenix Bannister, in this realistic story.

Dreaming of You. St. Martin's Paperbacks, 2006.
Mom Grayson does it again, this time with restaurateur son Brandon and his best friend, hotel manager Faith McBride.

Irresistible You. St. Martin's Paperbacks, 2007.
The youngest Grayson son, Pierce, falls victim to actress Sabra Raineau's charms, much to the delight of his matchmaking mother, Ruth.

Only You. St. Martin's Paperbacks, 2007.
Real estate agent Sierra Grayson lands a plum job in Dallas and ends up falling for her ruthless boss, Blade Navarone.

Grayson Friends Series
Friends of the Graysons get their own stories in this series that sometimes reprises characters from the Graysons of New Mexico series.

The Way You Love Me. St. Martin's Paperbacks, 2008.
Hired to pose as a houseguest and check out the boyfriend of wealthy heiress Paige Albright, tough, competent Shane Elliott finds himself falling for Paige himself, and she doesn't even know what his real role is.

Nobody but You. St. Martin's Paperbacks, 2009.
A NASCAR driver and his former love meet again with life-changing results.

One Night with You. St. Martin's Paperbacks, 2009.
An archaeologist researching cave paintings and a Montana rancher find love in spite of their differing goals.

It Had to Be You. St. Martin's Paperbacks, 2010.
Annoyed that a beautiful classical violinist refuses to work with him because of his reputation, producer Zach Wilder sets out to charm her without revealing his identity.

Invincible Women Series
The Invincible Sisterhood is a group of widows who meet for support and friendship.

Like the First Time. St. Martin's Griffin, 2004.
Three women use their individual talents to form a business and reform their lives in this satisfying story that is both romance and women's fiction.

Any Rich Man Will Do. St. Martin's Griffin, 2005.
A destitute socialite finds redemption and love in the arms of a computer expert when she walks into his sister's shop and collapses.

In Another Man's Bed. St. Martin's Griffin, 2007.
A woman tied to a cheating husband, who is now in a coma, discovers love with an old flame—and then must make some difficult decisions.

Not Even If You Begged. St. Martin's Griffin, 2008.
Two widows, neighbors and members of the Sisterhood, each find unexpected romance when one of their homes is broken into.

And Mistress Makes Three. St. Martin's Griffin, 2009.
A single mom struggling to put her life back on track finds a man she can love and respect—and then her cheating ex comes back to the delight of the children.

If You Were My Man. St. Martin's Griffin, 2010.
A hostage negotiator who feels he will never have a permanent relationship because of the dangers of his job is attracted to a widowed restaurant owner with a secret past.

Rutland, Eva
No Crystal Stair. Mira, 2000.
With gentle humor and sensitivity this saga-like story sweeps its characters from genteel Atlanta into the rigors of WWII and then into the struggle against prejudice and the Civil Rights movement of the sixties and seventies.

Savoy, Deirdre
Always. BET Arabesque, 2000.
Humor adds to this touching reunion story.

Midnight Magic. BET Arabesque, 2001.
A couple finally learns how to communicate and save their marriage in this realistic romance.

Holding Out for a Hero. BET Arabesque, 2002.
A cop is assigned to coach an attractive actress for an upcoming role, but also suspects that the accident that killed his brother, and the actress's former fiancé, wasn't an accident.

Could It Be Magic? BET Arabesque, 2003.
Humor and plenty of misunderstandings keep this romance simmering.

Lady in Red. BET Arabesque, 2004.
A P.I. agrees to protect a young woman whose mother thinks she is in danger, even though the girl wants nothing to do with him.

Looking for Love in All the Wrong Places. BET Romance, 2005.
A woman reluctantly enlists the aid of a photographer/playboy in finding her biological father, but things don't turn out as expected.

Body of Truth. Dafina, 2005.
A drive-by shooting victim confronts the police with their inaction and is attracted to a homicide detective in spite of her anger about the situation.

An Innocent Man. Dafina, 2006.
The hunt for the real killer targeting female athletes at a Georgia school turns dangerous and romantic for P.I. Nelson Santiago and determined Frankie Hairston.

Body of Lies. Dafina, 2006.
A cop, a psychologist, and a serial killer combine in this riveting romantic thriller.

Forbidden Games. Kimani Romance, 2009.
New York cop Zaria Fuentes agrees to a dangerous assignment to help the FBI bring down a prostitution ring, but when a fellow cop, who wants to protect her, interferes, the sparks fly.

Schuster, Melanie
Schuster's romances are often touching and gently humorous.

Let It Be Me. BET Arabesque, 2004.
An older heroine finds love with a younger hero in this romance about two long-time friends.

Something to Talk About. BET Arabesque, 2005.
A pair of architect friends who agree that romance will never ruin their friendship are hard pressed to keep things platonic.

Working Man. Kimani Romance, 2007.
An independent true crime writer and a self-made, take-charge man clash as they fall in love in this story that has a funny, memorable cat.

Model Perfect Passion. Kimani Romance, 2008.
A former model and a real estate mogul clash in this witty, funny romance.

Trust in Me. Kimani Romance, 2008.
A handsome, sexy man must convince a woman who doesn't trust good looking men and has been dating dullards that he's the one for her in this story with a post-Katrina New Orleans setting.

A Case for Romance. Kimani Romance, 2009.
A young woman raising her nephews is pursued by a high-powered lawyer who has decided she is the one.

Picture Perfect Christmas. Kimani Romance, 2009.
An artist is surprised when her childhood love walks into her first exhibit—but not so surprised as he is when he sees some of her pictures.

Snoe, Eboni
Snoe often makes use of mystery elements and somewhat exotic settings. Her latest works are mainstream African American women's fiction, not romance.

Tell Me I'm Dreamin'. Avon, 1998.
A collection of magnificent art treasures, an earthquake, and mystical legends add a touch of magic and the paranormal to this exotic Caribbean Island–set romance.

A Chance on Lovin' You. Avon, 1999.
A young woman inherits property on the Florida Keys and clashes with a handsome man who claims ownership of the same lands in this romance tinged with magic and curses.

9

10

11

12

13

14

15

16

Wishin' on a Star. Avon, 2000.
A woman accompanies a compelling stranger to a small island near Grenada to be part of a mystical rite that will help her nephew with a rare blood disease in this exotic romance.

Ties That Bind. BET Arabesque, 2002.
Matters come to a head when a young woman who has learned that a noted politician is her birth father shows up at the family reunion in this powerful, romantic story. Third in the Family Reunion Series (other titles are *Hearts of Steel* [2002] by Geri Guillaume and *Family Reunion* [2002] by Shirley Hailstock).

When Everything's Said & Done. BET Sepia, 2004.
Three sisters fall for the same man with devastating results in this complicated story; this is Snoe's first mainstream novel.

Taylor, Simona
Exotic, tropical settings are part of many of Taylor's touching romances.

Love Me All the Way. BET Arabesque, 2003.
A marine biologist takes a daring chance to help her husband, also a marine biologist, save a tropical reef and their marriage at the same time in this touching romance with an exotic setting.

Wonderful and Wild. BET Arabesque, 2004.
A Fantasy novelist and an artist collaborate on a graphic novel and find love along the way.

Then I Found You. BET Arabesque, 2005.
An actress under attack from someone out to destroy her and her family falls in love with the former football player assigned to protect her while she is in Trinidad.

Dear Rita. Kimani Romance, 2008.
An advice columnist and a divorce attorney set the sparks flying when they act as a "double date" for some friends, only to realize that the sparks had some sizzle in them. A mystery adds intrigue to this funny story.

Meet Me in Paris. Kimani Romance, 2009.
A woman agrees to work off a debt by becoming a housekeeper for her former boss, but romance changes their relationship.

White, Kimberley
Ballantyne Family Trilogy
This trilogy focuses on the smart, sexy Ballantyne men.

Only in My Dreams. BET Arabesque, 2003.
An attorney sets out to convince his childhood friend, who swore off men after her philandering husband was killed, that they have a romantic future together.

To Love a Ballantyne. BET Arabesque, 2005.
This heartwarming story makes good use of the older woman/younger man plot device.

Ballantyne's Destiny. Kimani Arabesque, 2006.
A reclusive mountain man and a sexy, independent librarian find unexpected love although the sparks fly.

Forever After. BET Arabesque, 2004.
A heroine still recovering from her last terrible relationship is wary of beginning another, but when her salon business is threatened (evil schemes and wicked doings abound), she turns to a man who is actually worthy of her trust, if she can only believe it.

Conquering Dr. Wexler's Heart. Genesis Indigo Sensual Love Stories, 2005.
A doctor involved in a medical scandal goes to work at a clinic in rural Tennessee and is attracted to the owner of the clinic.

All the Way. Dafina, 2008.
A murder witness running for her life carjacks a reporter's van and learns he's investigating the people who are after her. They join forces, dodge bullets, and fall in love in this action-packed thriller.

I Need More. Dafina, 2009.
A doctor must choose between her estranged husband, who is battling cancer, and a man she was dating in this mainstream novel.

White-Owens, Karen

As Long As There Is Love. BET Arabesque, 2002.
A chance encounter at the hospital reunites a daycare center owner and a doctor, who is surprised to learn he has a daughter.

Circles of Love. BET Arabesque, 2004.
When a pregnancy results in a marriage proposal, long-time lovers must come to terms with what they each want in the relationship—and in life.

Love Changes Everything. BET Arabesque, 2005.
A veteran teacher in a new school ends up working with—and eventually falling in love with—one of her former students, who is now a teacher, as well.

Someone to Love. Kimani Romance, 2006.
A sports agent lets other things get in the way of his romantic relationship with a nurse in this Chicago-set story.

The Way You Aren't. Dafina, 2007.
A man accepts a bet to remake a dowdy, socially inept, but razor-sharp smart computer geek into a bombshell—with romantic results.

I Can Make You Love Me. Dafina, 2009.
The owner of a nursing company reconnects with a boy she used to babysit with in this older heroine/younger hero romance.

You're All I Need. Dafina, 2010.
A French lawyer and an administrative assistant fall in love when he comes from her company's home office in Paris in this story where the interracial romance is a theme.

Winters, Angela

Saving Grace. BET, 2003.
A woman seeking vengeance in an old discrimination case hires an arrogant lawyer who has sworn off women after his fiancée is killed in a car crash and turns his life around.

A Class Apart. BET, 2004.
A socially well-connected writer witnesses a crime when she rides along with a police officer for research purposes and ends up needing his protection in this suspenseful story laced with class issues.

High Stakes. BET, 2004.
A woman heads for Las Vegas when she hears that the man who's been wooing her is only interested in her wealth—of course he quickly follows.

A Capitol Affair. BET, 2005.
The murder of a congressional candidate casts suspicion on both his fiancée and his opponent in this story that takes "opposites–attract" to a whole new level.

View Park series

Although there is some romance involved, this relatively mainstream Los Angeles–set series chronicles the life, loves, and intrigues of the wealthy, often dysfunctional African American Chase family of cosmetics fame. Should be read in order.

View Park. Dafina, 2006.
Never Enough. Dafina, 2007.
No More Good. Dafina, 2008.
A Price to Pay. Dafina, 2009.
Gone Too Far. Dafina, 2010.

Wootson, Alice

To Love Again. BET Arabesque, 2002.
A pair of matchmaking mothers decide their two adult children would be perfect for each other, except that they have both been badly betrayed and aren't about to trust anyone.

Kindred Spirits. BET Arabesque, 2004.
A pair who met earlier in a brief airport encounter meet again when they are both trying to uncover the same conspiracy in a Florida company.

Aloha Love. BET Arabesque, 2005.
A helicopter crash leads to questions about replacement parts in this lively romantic mystery.

Perfect Wedding. BET, Arabesque, 2005.
A high school teacher wanting to go to Hawaii convinces a fellow teacher to pretend to be her fiancé so they can enter a reality show and win the perfect wedding and honeymoon—to Hawaii.

Wright, Courtni

The Last Christmas Gift. BET Arabesque, 2003.
The logistics of love are difficult for a driven career woman and the man she loves.

Windswept Love. BET Arabesque, 2005.
A couple is faced with separation and decisions when she heads for flight school and he for submarine training after they graduate from the Naval Academy.

Love Under Construction. BET Arabesque, 2006.
The co-owner of a construction and renovation company is attracted to a client, an attorney who just bought an old Victorian.

Asian and Asian American

Ali, Thalassa
Paradise Trilogy

Adventurous Englishwoman Mariana Givens and Muslim nobleman Hassan Ali Khan find conflict and love in this trilogy set in mid-nineteenth-century India and Afghanistan. Good cultural detail. Note: These stories need to be read in order, much like an old Victorian "triple decker."

A Singular Hostage. Bantam, 2002.
Mariana risks her life to rescue a miraculously gifted Indian orphan, Saboor, and marries Hassan Ali Khan, Saboor's father, an act that scandalizes the English.

A Beggar at the Gate. Bantam, 2004.
Mariana and Hassan are often separated and she considers divorcing him and returning to English society, all as they are caught up in an increasingly violent civil war between various factions.

Companions of Paradise. Bantam, 2007.
Mariana continues to struggle with her decisions and ends up in the English cantonment in Kabul just before the first Afghan war begins in this story that nicely completes the trilogy.

Brockmann, Suzanne
Into the Storm. Bantam, 2006.
During a raid-and-rescue training session in the New Hampshire winter wilderness, the "victim" goes missing, sending Navy SEAL Mark Jenkins and Troubleshooter Lindsay Fontaine and the rest of the team into the storm on the trail of a killer. The heroine's grandmother was born in Japan.

Donovan, Marie
Her Book of Pleasure. Harlequin, 2007.
An impulsive bedroom romp and a Japanese "pillow" book bring Japanese art expert Megan Michiko O'Malley and P.I. Rick Sokol together in this sexy Harlequin Blaze.

Feehan, Christine
Mind Game. Jove, 2004.
A hardened telepathic sharpshooter goes to the Louisiana Bayous to find a psychically gifted and quite lethal young woman in this sexy, action-packed military-type thriller that is second in Feehan's Ghostwalker series and features a half-Japanese hero and an Asian heroine.

Fox, Roz Denny
She Walks the Line. Harlequin, 2005.
A Chinese police lieutenant who is concerned that her family may be involved in an antiques theft and murder case is attracted to the insurance investigator on the case.

Hall, Jessica
White Tiger Swords Trilogy

Asian mobsters and a legendary sword collection link the stories in this trilogy.

The Deepest Edge. Signet, 2003.
An art expert becomes involved with son of a Chinese tong leader who wants his son back in the tong or dead.

9

10

11

12

13

14

15

16

The Steel Caress. Signet, 2003.
Note: The protagonists are not multicultural in this undercover adventure that ventures deep into the Chinese underworld.

The Kissing Blades. Signet, 2003.
A Japanese American jewelry designer suspected in her shop assistant's disappearance enlists the aid of he man who kidnapped her in the previous novel.

James, Allyson
Dragon Master Series
A Contemporary Fantasy Romance series with dragon heroes and some multicultural heroines.

Dragon Heat. Berkley Sensation, 2007.
Lisa Singleton has inherited her grandmother's apartment which contains a dragon, Caleb, charged with protecting her, and a portal to Dragonspace.

The Black Dragon. Berkley Sensation, 2007.
Powerful witch Saba Watanabe and black dragon Malcolm, who formerly held her captive, reconnect when she is attacked by a white dragon.

The Dragon Master. Berkley Sensation, 2008.
Although dim sum restaurateur Carol Juan considered her grandmother's dragon tales just old legends, when she runs into a fire dragon named Seth and learns that there is evil afoot and that her own powers have suddenly been awakened, she rethinks her original position.

Jeffrey, Anna
The Love of a Cowboy. Onyx, 2003.
A half-Filipino heroine trying to come to terms with her cheating husband's death and a divorced rancher with ex-wife and child custody issues find healing and love in spite of family interference.

Lee, Jade
Tigress Series
An erotic series set in pre-revolutionary China that features Chinese and English protagonists who explore the spiritual path to immortality through the sensual practices of the mysterious Dragon/Tigress religious sect.

White Tigress. Leisure, 2005.
Hungry Tigress. Leisure, 2005.
Desperate Tigress. Leisure, 2005.
Burning Tigress. Leisure, 2006.
Cornered Tigress. Leisure, 2007.
Tempted Tigress. Leisure, 2007.

Seduced by Crimson. Love Spell, 2006.
A Cambodian healer and a Druidic botany professor find love as they work to send the demons back where they belong in this fifth book in the Crimson City series.

Lin, Jeannie
Butterfly Swords. Harlequin Historical, 2010.

A betrayed princess flees to avoid a political marriage and finds help and love with a barbarian warrior in ancient China.

The Dragon and the Pearl. Harlequin Historical, 2011.
A former royal consort and a fierce warlord find romance amid the political turmoil during the Tang Dynasty. Follows *Butterfly Swords*; the hero in this novel is the villain in the former story.

Liu, Marjorie M.
The Red Heart of Jade. Love Spell, 2006.
Archaeologist Miribelle Lee and Dirk & Steele operative Dean Campbell meet again after twenty years, each having thought the other had died, when they are thrown into the hunt for a killer in this suspenseful thriller with paranormal aspects. (This is Dirk & Steele, book 3.)

Low, Gennita
Facing Fear. Avon, 2004.
In the second of Low's Shadowy Assassins (S.A.S.S.) series, a government agent heroine is sent to investigate a CIA hero and falls in love with him as they try to uncover the villain in a national security case. Heroine has a Chinese grandmother.

Lowell, Elizabeth
Jade Island. Avon, 1999.
Jade expert and bastard daughter of a powerful Chinese trading family, Lianne Blakely works with Kyle Donovan to track down a dangerous thief and avoid an international incident in the sexy second book in the Donovan Brothers trilogy.

Mahon, Annette
Mahon's sweet romances are set in the Hawaiian Islands and often feature characters with Hawaiian, Pacific Islander, and/or other Asian heritages.

Secret Series
These books are set in the small fictional town of Malino on the big island, Hawaii. Townsfolk are ever present matchmakers in this sweet series.

The Secret Admirer. Avalon, 2001.
The heroine begins receiving flowers from a secret admirer.

The Secret Wedding. Avalon, 2002.
A wedding coordinator at an island resort is attracted to a client who's planning his sister's wedding.

The Secret Santa. Avalon, 2003.
A college student is attracted to a handsome rancher, even though she has an aversion to cowboys because her mother does.

The Secret Beau. Avalon, 2004.
A bridesmaid needs a date for a wedding and a veterinarian who's just returned to the island fills the bill.

The Secret Wish. Avalon, 2006.
An offbeat hair stylist and a handsome firefighter find love when she comes back to town and renovates a beauty salon.

The Secret Correspondence. Avalon, 2008.
A health-care professional secretly contacts her neighbor's CPA son when the neighbor breaks a leg and refuses to do so, saying that he's too busy and she doesn't want to bother him.

Matchmaker Quilt Series
A quilt guaranteeing true love links these romances.

Dolphin Dreams, Avalon, 2007.
A marine biologist spars with a businessman, and then her grandmother gives her "the quilt."

Holiday Dreams. Avalon, 2009.
"The quilt" works its magic once again, this time for a librarian and her apartment manager/owner.

Massey, Sujata
Rei Shimura Mysteries
Mystery blends with romance in these cross-cultural adventures featuring biracial Rei Shimura. More mystery than romance.

The Salaryman's Wife. HarperPaperbacks, 1997.
When the beautiful wife of a successful Japanese businessman is murdered at a historic Japanese resort, bi-racial Rei Shimura and Scottish Hugh Glendinning find themselves caught in a web of suspicion and danger as they try to unravel the mystery that is the first of this intriguing series.

Zen Attitude. HarperPaperbacks, 1998.
The Flower Master. HarperCollins, 1999.
The Floating Girl. HarperCollins, 2000.
The Bride's Kimono. HarperCollins, 2001.
One of the more romantic of the series.
The Samurai's Daughter. HarperCollins, 2003.
The Pearl Diver. HarperCollins, 2004.
The Typhoon Lover. HarperCollins, 2005.
Girl in a Box. HarperCollins, 2006.
Shimura Trouble. Severn House, 2008.
The final book in the series.

Putney, Mary Jo
The China Bride. Ballentine, 2000.
A Eurasian woman (Scottish and Chinese), well-educated and trained in the martial arts, and an English nobleman find danger and love in this nineteenth-century story that alternates between England and China. Sequel to *The Wild Child* (1999).

Reese, Jenn
Jade Tiger. Juno Books, 2006.
An Amerasian crime fighting heroine searches for a jade crane in her effort to complete the ancient mystical Jade Circle and finds danger and love with an archaeologist in this action-packed romantic adventure. A debut novel.

Smith, Deborah
When Venus Fell. Bantam, 1999.

A free-spirited singer of Japanese and Italian heritage and a secret service agent who met as children, come together in a stormy relationship to guarantee her inheritance and save his family's inn.

Stuart, Anne

Ice Blue. Mira, 2007.
This chilling thriller pairs art scholar Summer Hawthorne, the owner of a priceless blue bowl that a dangerous cult will kill to get, with Takashi O'Brien, a member of the Japanese mafia (Yakuza), who needs to keep the bowl out of the cult's hands at any price. This is part of Stuart's suspenseful "Ice" adventures, featuring members of the Committee.

Fire and Ice. Mira, 2008.
Brainy Jilly Hawthorne comes to Tokyo to spend time with her sister, Summer, and husband, Taka, only to be saved from a murderous attack by bike-riding Reno, Taka's fierce Yakuza cousin, who has been sent to protect her. Also part of the "Ice" series.

Tan, Maureen

A Perfect Cover. Silhouette Bombshell, 2004.
A special agent, whose Vietnamese and African American heritage provides her with the "perfect cover," looks for a killer in New Orleans and finds love, as well as more danger than she expects.

Wilks, Eileen

See also chapter 9, "Alternative Realities Romance."

Tempting Danger. Berkley, 2004.
Cop Lily Yu searches for a werewolf killer and is attracted to a powerful lupus leader in the process. First in the World of the Lupi series.

Yip, Mingmei

Song of the Silk Road. Kensington, 2011.
A struggling writer sets out to travel the legendary Silk Road and accomplish some unusual tasks in order to receive some money from a previously unknown aunt and finds more than she expected in this unusual romance.

Anthologies

Playing with Matches. Signet, 2003.
Contemporary matchmaking is the theme of this anthology by four Asian American authors who draw on their individual cultures to craft modern, appealing, often funny stories that highlight issues faced by Asian American women in today's society. Included are "Romancing Rose" by Kathy Yardley, "Dragon for Dinner" by Katherine Greyle, "The Spice Bazaar" by Sabeeha Johnson, and "Love.com" by Karen Harbaugh, which focus on Vietnamese, Chinese, Indian, and Japanese cultures, respectively. The first anthology of Asian American romances written by Asian American writers.

Latino

Alers, Rochelle

Many of her stories include Latino, often biracial, characters. See the African American bibliography in this chapter.

Castillo, Mary

Hot Tamara. Avon A, 2005.
A twenty-six-year-old Latina, who asserts her independence, dumps her comfy boyfriend, and leaves home to make it on her own, reconnects with her high school bad-boy-turned-firefighter crush in this sexy romance.

In Between Men. Avon A, 2006.
Jarred into action after being named the most un-sexy teacher in the school, enduring the on-air insults of her ex, and then accidentally being knocked unconscious by a hunky soccer coach, divorced single mom and high school ESL teacher Isa Avellan decides on a total sexy makeover, with funny, heartwarming results.

Switchcraft. Avon A, 2007
In this fun chica lit romp with a paranormal twist, two friends literally switch lives (and bodies) and learn the grass isn't necessarily greener.

Ferrer, Caridad

Adios to My Old Life. MTV, 2006.
A young Cuban American musician is caught up in the fast pace of success (think *American Idol*) and must learn to sort out what is really important in life. YA appeal.

It's Not About the Accent. MTV, 2007.
A college-bound freshman decides to play up her distant Cuban heritage and ends up in more trouble than she expects. YA appeal.

When the Stars Go Blue. St. Martin's Griffin, 2010.
A young dancer heading for a professional career risks it all when she spends the summer traveling with a competitive drum and bugle corps, playing Carmen, and finding romance with the lead horn player.

Montoya, Tracy

Montoya's award-winning chilling, suspenseful romances often feature Latino and sometimes Native American protagonists. Some of these stories are linked by character.

Maximum Security. Harlequin Intrigue, 2004.
A man out to avenge his sister's rape and murder connects with a woman who'd been similarly attacked.

House of Secrets. Harlequin Intrigue, 2005.
Someone is willing to kill to make sure that P.I. Joe Lopez doesn't remember what happened in Emma Reese's Victorian House that keeps appearing in his dreams.

Shadow Guardian. Harlequin Intrigue, 2005.
An actress turns to a bodyguard for help when she picks up a stalker.

Next of Kin. Harlequin Intrigue, 2005.
A librarian and a detective reconnect when her life is threatened.

Telling Secrets. Harlequin Intrigue, 2007.
Psychic Sophie Brennan knows that danger from the past lurks for Lakota search-and-rescue tracker Alex Gray, and her, as well, as they try to solve a rash of murders.

Finding His Child. Harlequin Intrigue, 2007.
A tracker works with a detective, whose daughter disappeared half a year earlier, when a serial killer begins attacking women in the park; they think the cases may be related.

I'll Be Watching You. Harlequin Intrigue, 2008.
A yoga instructor is stalked by the man who killed her fiancé.

Pineiro, Caridad
Many of Pineiro's Paranormal and Suspense romances also have Latino characters; she also wrote for the short-lived Encanto line as Caridad Scordato. The books
below are lively, funny chick lit romps filled with plenty of Miami's South Beach culture, Cuban American style. See also chapter 6, "Romantic Mystery," and chapter 9,
"Alternative Reality."

Sex and the South Beach Chicas. Downtown Press, 2006.
Four successful friends decide something is missing in their lives and they set out to
change that in this funny, sassy romp.

South Beach Chicas Get Their Man. Downtown Press, 2007.
A journalist and a cop are attracted but clash over her investigation of a fellow cop's
death.

Platas, Berta
Lively, Contemporary Latina romances.

Cinderella Lopez. St. Martin's Griffin, 2006.
Cyn Lopez begins a romantic relationship with Eric Sandoval unaware that he is
the CEO of a company that has just bought the studio where she and her glamorous
stepsisters work in this funny fairy tale.

Lucky Chica. St. Martin's Griffin, 2009.
Winning a $600 million lottery changes Rosie's life in drastic ways.

Richards, Emilie
Endless Chain. Mira, 2005.
A pastor in a rural Virginia community is attracted to his new Guatemalan church
sexton, a woman who has a dangerous past she is afraid to reveal. Second in Richards's Shenandoah Album series.

Rios, Lara
Becoming Latina in 10 Easy Steps. Berkley Trade, 2006.
A young woman who isn't Latina enough for her family (career-oriented, unmarried, can't cook, only half-Mexican) sets out to out-Latina them all, in this funny,
heartwarming, realistic Contemporary.

Becoming Americana. Berkley Trade, 2006.
A former at-risk teen, first introduced in the novel above, comes of age in college
and must make some difficult, life-changing decisions as she tries to keep her life on
track. Deals with some of the darker realities facing today's Latinas.

Samuel, Barbara
Dancing Moon. Harper, 1996.
Irish immigrant Tess escapes her cruel husband and heads west with the pregnant
slave, Sonia, and is aided by Joaquin Morales, a biracial Native American/Latino hero.

A Piece of Heaven. Ballantine, 2003.
Luna McGraw, a recovering alcoholic and mother to a teenager, and Thomas Coyote, a divorced person with serious issues of his own, find healing in this story that
his more women's fiction than romance.

Sandoval, Lynda
Sandoval writes for the YA market, as well, and also wrote for the short-lived Encanto romance line. Many of her romances include Latino characters.

One Perfect Man. Silhouette, 2004.
A single father determined to give his daughter the best Quinceañera ever is attracted to the marriage-averse events planning heroine.

Unsettling. HarperCollins Rayo, 2004.
Believing her family is the victim of a "marriage curse," Lucy Olivera runs away after the wedding and heads off with three friends in search of some answers. More about friendship and self-discovery than romance.

Troublesome Gulch Series
A long-ago prom night accident continues to affect the lives of the townsfolk of Troublesome Gulch.

The Other Sister. Silhouette Special Edition, 2007.
Years after a prom night accident killed several students, including his best friend, Brody Austin returns to Colorado to come to terms with his feelings and reconnects with Faith Montsantos, the younger sister of his friend, who also lost her older sister in the crash.

You, and No Other. Silhouette Special Edition, 2008.
A poor boy having made millions returns to town and reconnects with the girl he'd always loved.

Deja You. Silhouete Special Edition, 2009.
An impulsive one night stands results in a pregnancy for firefighter Erin DeLuca, who is doubly surprised when Nate Walker, the baby's father, suddenly turns up wanting to be a dad.

Lexy's Little Matchmaker. Silhouette Special Edition, 2009.
Wheelchair-bound Lexy Cabrera and widowed single dad Drew Kimball are attracted to each other but have many issues that must be resolved.

Shelley, Deborah
See also chapter 5, "Contemporary Romance."

It's in His Kiss. Kensington Precious Gems, 1999.
Cultures and personalities clash with sparks and wit when a New England architect and a Latina construction manager square off over the designs of an Arizona building project.

Simpson, Patricia
The Dark Horse. Tor Paranormal Romance, 2005.
A Latina heroine language specialist in possession of a cursed deck of Tarot cards finds love with a horse rancher and together they confront an ancient evil. Second in the Forbidden Tarot series.

Valdes-Rodriguez, Alisa
The Dirty Girls Social Club. St. Martin's Press, 2003.
A group of Latina college chums get together six years after graduation and catch up in this funny, sexy, zingy romp that some consider a Latina take on Terry McMillan's *Waiting to Exhale*.

Playing with Boys. St. Martin's Press, 2004.
An agent and publicist finds romance with a sexy Cuban rocker in this witty story that is filled with good cultural detail.

Make Him Look Good. St. Martin's Griffin, 2007.
Latin pop star Ricky Biscayne and the various women in his life are the focus of this relationship-rich Miami-set chica lit.

Dirty Girls on Top. St. Martin's Griffin, 2008.
Five years after their initial reunion, the members of *The Dirty Girls Social Club* get together again to catch up at a New Mexico resort.

Wind, Ruth (Barbara Samuel)
Wind's romances often deal with Native American or Latino characters and cultures. See also the Native American bibliography in this chapter.

Beautiful Stranger. Silhouette Intimate Moments, 2007.
Teacher Marissa Pearce struggles with weight and self-esteem issues but attracts the attention of Robert Martinez, the uncle of one of her students.

Native American

Many of the writers listed below also write Western Romances that do not necessarily feature Native American characters. As in the other sections, romances of various types and with a variety of settings are included. Stories in this section may include some older "Indian captive"–type stories as well as those with paranormal or mystery aspects and contemporary social issues.

Aitken, Judie
A Love Beyond Time. Jove, 2000.
An anthropologist sent to a dig at the site of the Little Big Horn is tossed back to the past to find a thief and finds love with a Native American lawyer who has ended up in the past, as well.

A Place Called Home. Jove, 2001.
Land and heritage are at the heart of the conflict between a Wyoming rancher who may be forced to sell and a city lawyer for the other side in this Contemporary Romance.

Distant Echoes. Berkley Sensation, 2003.
A documentary about the Indian Schools of the late nineteenth century throws Jesse Spotted Horse and Kathleen Prescott back to 1886 in this heart-wrenching time travel that will remind readers of Kathleen Eagle's more modern *Sunrise Song* (1996).

Secret Shadows. Berkley Sensation, 2004.
An undercover Lakota FBI agent falsely imprisoned for his young sister's murder and the doctor who testified against him come together after his release on a technicality and are attracted to each other as they work together to find the drug dealers plaguing the reservation. Some mystical aspects.

Baker, Madeline
Baker's Historical, Contemporary, and Time Travel Romances usually feature Native American characters.

Apache Flame. Signet, 1999.
Alisha's life is turned upside down when the man she loves, Mitch Garrett, returns for her and later when her wicked, meddling preacher father admits her son is still alive and living with Apaches.

Spirit's Song. Leisure, 1999.
A bounty hunter falls in love with the woman he is supposed to return to her abusive husband.

Lakota Love Song. Signet, 2002.
A woman who saved the life of a Lakota warrior eventually marries him, but must deal with her own family and culture, as well.

Dude Ranch Bride. Silhouette, 2003.
A wealthy heroine bolts from her own wedding and takes refuge on a dude ranch and finds love with a man she'd known as a teenager in this Contemporary Romance.

Wolf Shadow. Signet, 2003.
A tracker falls in love with the woman, kidnapped ten years ago and living with the Sioux, whom he has been hired to find.

Under Apache Skies. Signet, 2004.
A rancher and a half-Apache cowboy find love as they travel to rescue the heroine's sister from Apache captivity.

Every Inch a Cowboy. Silhouette, 2005.
A jilted heroine, in Montana to regain her perspective, rescues a wounded cowboy and is drawn into his world in spite of her intentions to the contrary in this Contemporary Romance.

Dakota Dreams. Signet, 2006.
Rancher Catherine Lyons shelters escaped prisoner Nathan Chasing Elk and accompanies him on his mission to avenge his wife's death.

Bittner, Rosanne

Noted for her Western Romances, many of which feature Native American characters, Bittner also writes Inspirational Romances. See also chapter 7, "Historical Romance."

Mystic Indian Series

This trilogy includes elements of Magical Realism and focuses on the lives of the Lakota and their efforts to save their people and land. Good cultural detail but violent.

Mystic Dreamers. Forge, 1999.
Mystic Visions. Forge, 2000.
Mystic Warriors. Forge, 2001.

Dellin, Genell

Over the years, Dellin has written a number of Native American Romances, many of which have been grouped into trilogies or series (i.e., Comanche Trilogy, Cherokee Trilogy, Choctaw Trilogy).

Cherokee Warriors

Members of the powerful Sixkiller family and others find love and adventure in the Cherokee Nation, Texas, and the environs in 1870s.

The Lover. Avon, 2002.
A wealthy Cherokee rogue and a desperate rancher pose as husband and wife on a long trail drive with romantic results.

The Loner. Avon, 2003.
A Cherokee cavalryman tracks down an elusive thief with Robin Hood tendencies only to find his quarry is an attractive woman on a mission.

The Captive. Avon, 2004.
A young woman and the proud man she refused to marry years earlier because of his Cherokee blood are thrown together as they search for her brother.

Eagle, Kathleen
Eagle pens emotionally involving romances and is noted for her sensitive portrayal of contemporary Native American culture and issues. (See previous editions of this guide for earlier titles.)

The Last True Cowboy. Avon, 1998.
When her grandson rancher suddenly dies, Judge Sally Weslin coerces the veteran horse trainer who has come to take charge of a herd of wild mustangs into saving the family ranch. Horses, at-risk kids, and a pair of delightful romances add to this "Horse Whisperer" tale.

What the Heart Knows. Avon, 1999.
A former basketball star returns to the reservation when his father is killed and reconnects with an old love as they work to solve the murder and root out casino corruption at the same time.

The Last Good Man. William Morrow, 2000.
A former model returns home to rural Wyoming in an air of mystery and finds healing, understanding, and love with an old friend in this hard-hitting, heart-wrenching romance.

You Never Can Tell. William Morrow, 2001.
A journalist goes in search of a reclusive legendary Native American activist and finds an emotionally wounded man in need of healing and love.

Once upon a Wedding. William Morrow, 2002.
A family wedding is the setting for this poignant reunion story.

Night Falls like Silk. William Morrow, 2003.
Opposites attract in this gripping tale that follows *The Night Remembers* (1997).

A View of the River. Mira, 2005.
An Ojibwe shaman and the skeptical manager of a B&B find romance, unexpected secrets, and understanding in this mystical, mysterious tale.

Ride a Painted Pony. Mira, 2006.
A badly beaten woman running for her life is rescued on a lonely highway by a wary Lakota rancher and ends up working on his ranch as a horse trainer. Horse-racing, crime, and hidden agendas add to this satisfying romance.

Mystic Horseman. Mira, 2008.
Dillon Black agrees to let his new horse camp for at-risk Lakota teens be the object of a TV reality show and finds romance with a woman who is having a hard time coming to terms with her own heritage. Follows *Ride a Painted Pony*.

476 12—Ethnic/Multicultural Romance

Beaudry/Drexler Trilogy
Linked by character, these three stories feature Native American cowboy heroes.

In Care of Sam Beaudry. Silhouette Special Edition, 2009.
Sheriff Sam Beaudry's life—and developing romance with single mom and nurse Maggie Whiteside—takes a troubled turn when a seven-year-old, who may be his daughter, arrives in town bringing mystery and danger in her wake.

One Cowboy, One Christmas. Silhouette Special Edition, 2009.
Rodeo cowboy Zach Beaudry, caught in a South Dakota blizzard, is attracted to the lovely "angel," Ann Drexler, who rescued him, not realizing that they'd met briefly, and passionately, years earlier.

Cool Hand Hank. Silhouette Special Edition, 2010.
Living with multiple sclerosis has taught rancher Sally Drexler to get the most out of life while she can, but when she meets rodeo physician's assistant Hank Night Horse, a temporary fling just might become something more.

Gentry, Georgina
Gentry's early Historical Romances often focused on Native American characters. Her most recent novels are listed in the Western Romance bibliography of chapter 7, "Historical Romance."

Apache Tears. Zebra, 1999.
Libbie Winters is attracted to Indian scout Cougar, but a lot of turmoil, violence, and prejudice must be endured before they can find happiness together; Arizona Territory setting.

Warrior's Honor. Zebra, 2000.
A Choctaw lawman is honor-bound to hunt down Lusa's brother, a runaway brave convicted of murder, but Lusa is sure he's innocent in this mid-nineteenth-century adventure.

Warrior's Heart. Zebra, 2001.
This "wagon train" romance focuses on a woman with a biracial child and Shoshoni outcast

Harrington, Kathleen
Dreamcatcher. Avon, 1996.
Fly with the Eagle. Avon, 1997.
Enchanted by You. Avon, 1998.
Juliette, one of Strong Elk and Rachel's twin daughters, saves the life of a laird while she's in Scotland and finds love in this charming, funny tale.

Kay, Karen
Lost Clan Series
A village that angered the Thunder god is banished to a shadow existence. The clan's only hope is in the hands of a warrior chosen each generation to complete a quest and lift the curse. Each warrior does so with the help of a special woman.

The Angel and the Warrior. Berkley Sensation, 2005.
Spirit Hawk begins the quest in 1816.

The Spirit of the Wolf. Berkley Sensation, 2006.
This time it is Grey Coyote's turn to complete the quest in 1835.

Red Hawk's Woman. Berkley Sensation, 2007.
Red Hawk picks up the challenge in 1867.

The Last Warrior. Berkley Sensation, 2008.
Black Lion completes the quest and lifts the curse in 1892.

Lee, Rachel
Lee's popular Conard County books often have Native American and/or Latino characters. See chapter 13, "Linked Romances."

McCall, Dinah (Pseudonym for Sharon Sala)
Legend. HarperPaperbacks, 1998.
Raine Beaumont and Joseph Colorado meet again when she returns to give their stillborn son a proper burial in this story that is filled with magic and mysticism.

Touchstone. HarperPaperbacks, 1999.
A beautiful half-Cherokee model learns that fame and fortune have drawbacks and dangers.

McKenna, Lindsay
Many of McKenna's adventurous books include Native American or Latino characters, display exceptionally well-integrated cultural detail, and include mystical or paranormal aspects. Many of her books are part of her popular Morgan's Mercenaries series (begun in 1988) and the miniseries within them. A small sampling is listed below.

Heart Miniseries
A paranormal, mystical adventure series set in Peru.

Heart of the Jaguar. Silhouette, 1999.
Danger, good cultural detail, and native mysticism add to this romantic adventure.

Heart of the Warrior. Silhouette, 2000.
A grieving mercenary finds love and healing when he comes to know Inca, an environmentalist with some mystical skills.

Heart of Stone. Silhouette, 2001.
A hero with a bias against women combat pilots must work with the woman who almost ruined his career.

Maverick Hearts Miniseries
Man of Passion. Silhouette, 2000.
A wary Brazilian ranger takes on the task of helping an artist find orchids, but the jungle is more dangerous than it seems in this romance that is part of Morgan's Mercenaries.

A Man Alone. Silhouette, 2000.
A hardened Marine is wounded and sent home to heal, which he does with the help of a kind and caring nurse in this romance that is part of Morgan's Mercenaries.

Man with a Mission. Silhouette, 2001.
The search for the hero's missing sister brings a Peruvian helicopter pilot into his life in this jungle adventure that is part of Morgan's Mercenaries.

First Born. Silhouette, 2004.
Helicopter pilot Apache Annie Dazen is given the job of bringing hot shot Jason Traherne into line and making him part of her team before they head for Afghanistan in this military romance with good Apache cultural detail. Part of Morgan's Mercenaries.

Beyond the Limit. HQN, 2006.
A construction supervisor and a Marine major clash and then find love amid the violence of Afghanistan. A Morgan's Mercenaries story.

Heart of the Storm. HQN, 2007.
Knowing she must recover the sacred medicine pipe before the thief can use it to mystically murder someone else, Dana Thunder Eagle needs help becoming stronger, and it comes in the form of soldier and psychic warrior Chase Iron Hand in this romance with paranormal aspects.

Shelley, Deborah
Talk about Love. Zebra Precious Gems, 1999.
A librarian leaves her Phoenix family of overprotective law enforcement brothers and heads for rural Kansas where she finds romance with a half-Cherokee sheriff in this funny, fast-paced Contemporary.

Smith, Deborah
Several of Smith's early works, some of which have been reprinted, focused on Cherokee characters. See previous editions of this guide for some earlier works.

Silk and Stone. Bantam, 1994.
Samantha Vanderveer and Jake Raincrow are determined to be together in spite of family objections in this slightly paranormal romance that centers on the destructive influences of the famed Pandora Ruby.

Taylor, Janelle
Most of Taylor's romances feature Native American Characters; her most memorable work is the Gray Eagle/Alisha Series. (See the Classic Ethnic/Multicultural Romance bibliography in this chapter.)

Cherokee Storm. Zebra, 2010.
Cherokee warrior Storm Dancer and Shannon O'Shea cling to their love for each other amid war and violence in this mid-eighteenth-century romance. This is Taylor's first Native American Romance in a number of years.

Thurlo, Aimee
Thurlo's suspenseful romances, which she writes with husband David under her own name and several pseudonyms, focus on contemporary Navaho culture. They have also written several Navaho-set mystery series (Ella Clah, Sister Agatha, and Lee Nez) and have published them under both of their names together. A sampling of their more than fifty novels is listed here.

Christmas Witness. Harlequin Intrigue, 1999.
Twin brothers, Jake and Nick Black Raven, work with widowed and pregnant Annie Sandusky to solve their father's murder two weeks before Christmas.

Black Raven's Pride. Harlequin Intrigue, 2000.
Tribal cop Nick Black Raven is reunited with a former love and gains a son, as well, in this story that is the sequel to *Christmas Witness*.

Brothers of Rockridge Duo
Two brothers, Ashe and Travis Redhawk, are the heroes in this pair of suspenseful romances.

Redhawk's Heart. Harlequin Intrigue, 1999.
Navajo lawman Ashe Redhawk works with attractive FBI agent Casey Feist to find his foster parents' killers.

Redhawk's Return. Harlequin Intrigue, 1999.
Travis Redhawk must protect Katrina Johnson, who is going to testify against her parents' murderer, because someone has betrayed her and her life is in danger.

9

Brotherhood of Warriors
Mystical powers infuse this series.

Council of Fire. Harlequin Intrigue, 2007.
A P.I. needs the help of the man her father said she can trust in her quest of a Navajo dagger that will clear her late father's reputation.

10

Restless Wind. Harlequin Intrigue, 2007.
An Anglo school teacher who was abducted and a Navaho bound to protect his people work together for a just solution.

Stargazer's Woman. Harlequin Intrigue, 2008.
A former Marine intelligence officer seeks to find her sister's killer with the help of a Navaho police officer who is also the tribe's Stargazer.

11

Whitefeather, Sheri
Many of Whitefeather's series romances feature Native American characters. She writes edgier Erotic Romance as Cherie Feather. A sampling of titles is listed here.

12

Cherokee Dad. Silhouette Desire, 2003.
Michael Elk is stunned when Heather Richmond, a woman who had run out on him a year earlier, shows up with a baby she says is her brother's and needs protection from the mob.

Cherokee Stranger. Silhouette Desire, 2004.
A bad boy hero in the Witness Protection Program and a good girl heroine with skin cancer are an odd pair in this sexy romance.

13

Apache Nights. Silhouette Desire, 2005.
The romantic tension begins to sizzle between detective Joyce Riggs and activist and former Special Forces operative Kyle Prescott when she goes to him for physical training.

Always Look Twice. Silhouette Bombshell, 2005.
A Native American psychic uses her gifts to unmask a serial slasher in this suspenseful story that is linked to *Never Look Back*.

14

Betrayed Birthright. Silhouette Desire, 2005.
At the request of his sister, a man reluctantly searches for his birth mother and finds something totally unexpected.

Never Look Back. Silhouette Bombshell, 2006.
A shaman artist unexpectedly summons a man cursed by her great-grandmother in this romance rich with Native American mythology.

15

Mob Mistress. Silhouette Romantic Suspense, 2007.
When a woman pretends to be the mistress of the secret heir to a mob empire, they end up in a situation that is both dangerous and romantic.

16

Imminent Affair. Silhouette Romantic Suspense, 2009.
When her home is vandalized, artist Allie Whirlwind goes to Daniel Running Deer, the man who saved her once before but has amnesia as a result, for help. Psychic and some paranormal elements add to this suspenseful story.

Wind, Ruth (Barbara Samuel)

Wind's beautifully descriptive romances often deal with Native American, Indigenous, or Latino characters and cultures. See also the Latino bibliography in this chapter.

Sisters of the Mountain Trilogy

Features the three Rousseau sisters and a murder mystery that is solved in the third volume.

Juliet's Law. Silhouette Intimate Moments, 2006.
A young woman whose sister is accused of murder finds help and love in the arms of single dad, tribal cop Joshua Mad Calf.

Desi's Rescue. Silhouette Intimate Moments, 2007.
Under suspicion for her ex-husband's murder, veterinarian Desi Rousseau is wary of becoming more than friends with half-Maori New Zealander Tam Neville, even though the attraction is mutual.

Miranda's Revenge. Silhouette Intimate Moments, 2007.
This mystery is finally solved and Miranda, the third sister, finds love with P.I. James Marquez in the process.

Other Multicultural Romances

Gates, Olivia
Throne of Judar

This trio of passionate, modern-day sheikh romances featuring three royal brothers from the fictional kingdom of Judar and the women who win their hearts is highlighted by poetic language, strong characters, and an exotic, well-depicted setting.

The Desert Lord's Baby. Silhouette Desire, 2008.
Prince Farooq Aal Masood will let nothing stop him from marrying Carmen and claiming his child, but he has to find her first.

The Desert Lord's Bride. Silhouette Desire, 2008.
For the sake of peace in the region, Crown Prince Shehab Aal Masood needs to marry Farah Beaumont, a woman he has never met, but she wants no part of the deal—so he woos her without telling her who he really is.

The Desert King. Silhouette Desire, 2008.
Kamal Aal Masood rejected Aliyah seven years earlier because he believed she was a drug addict, but now he must marry her to avert a war.

TAKE FIVE!

Five favorite Ethnic/Multicultural Romances:

- **Kathleen Eagle**—*Sunrise Song*
- **Sandra Kitt**—*The Color of Love*
- **Jeannie Lin**—*Butterfly Swords*
- **Eva Rutland**—*No Crystal Stair*
- *Playing with Matches* **anthology**

Chapter 13

Linked Romances

Call it a clan, call it a network, call it a tribe, call it a family. Whatever you call it, whoever you are, you need one.

Jane Howard, *Families*

It takes a thousand voices to tell a single story.

Native American Proverb

Definition

> **Linked Romances**—Groups of individual Romance titles connected in some specific way—usually character, place, theme, or artifact—and often marketed as a group or a series.

Linked Romances are groups of individual Romance titles connected in some specific way and are often marketed as a group or a series. As few as two titles (e.g., Julia Quinn's *The Lost Duke of Wyndham* and *Mr. Cavendish, I Presume*) or as many as fifteen or more (e.g., Stephanie Laurens's Cynster Series) can make up one of these Linked Romances. Most, however, fall somewhere in between, with trilogies or quartets being two of the more common formats at the moment.

The books within the series are related most often by characters, place, or theme or artifact, with the character connection being the current favorite. Brothers, sisters, cousins, and variously mixed sibling and family groups are common, as are groups of friends (e.g., childhood, school, military) and, occasionally, people linked in other ways. Although each character will normally have his or her own story, which will be the romantic focus of one of the books in the series, the other members of the group will usually be present to some degree as supporting characters, depending on the circumstances. As a general rule, the characters are equally important. However, occasionally there may be one character in the group who ties things together or dominates in some way (e.g., Bey Malloren in Jo Beverley's Malloren Chronicles). If this character is not married, his or her courtship story is usually told last. Occasionally, a series is linked by a character who is not a romantic lead, at least not at first, but facilitates the relationships in each of the books (e.g., Nana Vancy in Holly Jacob's Everything but . . . series and Lady Sophia Dalbey in Claudia Dain's Courtesan books).

Linked Romances are also often connected by place. Small towns in all areas of the country and Western rural and ranch settings are by far the most common, but estates, schools, hotels, apartments, alien worlds, and other less-expected locations can also be used. Often these stories feature characters who are returning, for various reasons, to the places where they grew up, but others focus on the locals who live there. Many combine both elements. Robyn Carr's Virgin River, California; Holly Jacob's Erie, Pennsylvania; and Marcia Evanick's Misty Harbor, Maine; are typical examples. Linked Romances can also be related by both town and character, such as Linda Lael Miller's Creeds trilogy (three brothers return to their family ranch). Books may also be linked by theme or artifact, with the latter being the most-often used. Clothing, jewelry, objet d'art, and other heirlooms, usually with magical characteristics or superstitions attached, are typical of the items that have been used effectively. A pearl and diamond necklace in Kat Martin's Necklace trilogy, a quilt in Annette Mahon's Matchmaker Quilt series, and a small statue of the legendary Pegasus in Iris Johansen's Wind Dancer trilogy are only a few of the many examples.

Regardless of the way in which they are linked, the first book in the series usually sets the scene for those to come, but enough information is usually repeated in the books that follow to allow readers joining the series in midstream to understand what is going on. So while most books in these series can stand on their own, it usually makes sense to read them in order because of possible references to earlier events. Also, if there is a continuing mystery element, as in the case of the anonymous benefactor in Sabrina Jeffries's School for Heiresses series, reading the books out of sequence would be a definite spoiler.

These books are most often chronologically arranged, with the events in one following after the other. However, in a recent trend, in some of these stories the action happens concurrently, providing an alternate view of the action in the preceding book. Linked Romances are often conceived of as a finite series, usually based on the number of characters in the original group. However, occasionally, especially if the stories are particular popular and readers ask for more, writers will extend the series beyond its original length with spinoffs of various kinds.

While most Linked Romances are written by a single writer, the continuity series typically is not. Popularized by Harlequin, this type of series commonly consists of twelve books linked by place or family, usually written by twelve different authors, and scheduled so that one is released each month over the course of a year. Each book, of course, has a completed romance, yet there is usually a thread of mystery or other unresolved element that lasts throughout the series. In addition, theme/character-based miniseries of fewer books (often four or so) are common within many of Harlequin's series lines and several multiauthored shorter series have been published by nonseries houses, as well.

Although continuity series are usually released in consecutive months, most Linked Romances are not—or at least not until recently. In the past few years it has become popular for authors to publish these books in back-to-back months, to the delight of both publishers and readers, if not always the writers. However, this is not the norm, and whether it remains a viable timetable remains to be seen.

Linked Romances versus Publishers' Series

Finally, a word about the difference between Linked Romances and Romance series. Linked Romances are not the same as what many people think of as "Series" Romances.

Those Category or numbered Series Romances are actually publisher lines (e.g., Harlequin's family of lines, primarily) that have books that conform to specific guidelines and aren't necessarily linked by anything other than that. Silhouette Desire, Harlequin Intrigue, and Kimani Romance, are several examples. Linked Romances, as the term is used in this guide, have much in common with the old Sagas in that they make use of continuing places, characters, families, and so on in books that are each individual but share elements. In some respects, this is a format or an organizational tool, but it is also a way of telling a much longer, complex story by breaking it up into shorter, stand-alone parts.

Note: As alluded to above, Linked Romances are actually an outgrowth of the Saga and could be considered one of its modern incarnations (the Soap Opera is another). For a further discussion of the Saga and a bibliography of earlier series, consult the earlier edition of this guide.

Appeal

The primary appeal of the Linked Romance is that it creates a community, invites the reader in, and then continues, at least for a little while. While not so sweeping in scope as the Saga nor so unending as the television Soap Opera, the Linked Romance, nevertheless, does have some of the same attraction in that it allows readers to satisfy some of their curiosity about "what happens next." Readers no longer need to wonder whether or not Arabella's brainy, bluestocking sister will ever be lured to he altar—and by whom?; if Steve's bad boy, irresponsible brother will finally get his act together and redeem himself; or if the last bachelor in a group of friends will ever tie the knot. If they're part of the group, their stories will be told, and so will bits and pieces of the continuing stories of the characters in the earlier books.

The Linked Romance also provides readers with a greater sense of community than most individual novels typically provide. Whether the series allows readers to revisit a particular family to be sure all the brothers find brides or spend time in a town they find charming, getting to know more of the townsfolk, these books will appeal to those who appreciate reading stories set in a familiar world and want to experience more of it. This, combined with the ongoing nature of these series, makes it easy to understand why the Linked Romance is appealing to so many readers.

Advising the Reader

General readers' advisory information in provided in chapter 3. However, several additional points specifically relating to Linked Romances are discussed below.

- Some people who like Historical Linked Romances may also enjoy Sagas, especially those set during a favorite time period. By the same token, consider recommending Historical Linked Romances to Saga fans.
- Many people who enjoy Linked Romances began reading them *accidentally* when they discovered that a book they had read and liked was actually part of a series. Since they didn't necessarily start out to read a series of related books, it is important to discover why the reader likes that particular set of stories.

- Maybe it really is the linked nature of the stories that appeals. If so, consider recommending other Linked Romances, series in other fiction genres, or Sagas.
- However, if it is the subgenre (Contemporary, Historical, Paranormal, Fantasy, etc.) that they primarily enjoy, then suggest individual titles, as well as other Linked Romances, in those areas.
- If it is the setting or the characters that appeal, books with similar settings or characters, regardless of subgenre, might be good suggestions. For example, a reader who likes reading about groups of sisters might not care if the setting is either historical (in any period) or contemporary, or a fan who likes stories with ranch settings may read Western Romances set in the Old West as well as those with Contemporary settings.
- Finally, for the reader new to Linked Romances, recommend standard works by some of the major authors (e.g., Jo Beverley, Nora Roberts, Mary Balogh, Christine Feehan) and then branch out to others.

Brief History

Linked Romances, as we know them today, are a relatively recent phenomenon, but they have much in common with the older romantic Saga (not the early Anglo-Saxon and Nordic epic sagas) and can trace their origins to that form. (For a more detailed discussion of the Saga, see the earlier edition of this guide.)

Although not popular when first published early in the twentieth century, John Galsworthy's memorable classic, *The Forsyte Saga*, sparked a renewed interest in the form when it was made into a BBC television program in the 1960s, and soon a number of writers began producing sagas of their own. During the 1970s, book packager Lyle Kenyon Engel began developing and commissioning a variety of saga-like series that became exceptionally popular with readers. Roberta Gellis's Rosalynde Chronicles (1978–1983), today considered a classic series by most Romance fans, was one of these. Sagas of all varieties blossomed and remained popular throughout the 1980s but began to slip from favor during the 1990s.

However, as the formal Saga declined, books with remarkably similar characteristics were on the ascent. Continuity series, trilogies, and other kinds of Linked Romances attracted readers with their variously related characters and ongoing storylines and soon became staples within the industry. Clearly, readers still wanted to know "what happened next," and authors and publishers were more than willing to accommodate them. Linked Romances soared after the turn of the millennium and still haven't come back to earth. Generally, except for the monthly continuity series, which are not normally written by one writer, most Linked Romances are released on a normal publishing timetable (i.e., one, two, or three a year, depending on the writer's pace and the publisher's schedule), much as they would be if they were individual books by the author. Recently, however, several of these series—most often trilogies or quartets—have come out as monthly back-to-back releases, although whether this is a harbinger of the future or merely a trial balloon remains to be seen. But however they're released, Linked Romances are hot and, as of the moment, seem to be the norm rather than the exception.

Classic Linked Romances

Building on the earlier romantic Saga and series prototypes (e.g., Galsworthy's Forsyte Saga, Mazo De la Roche's Jalna series, Philippa Carr's Daughters of England series, Dorothy Dunnett's Crawford of Lymond adventure series), the following series helped establish the form for Linked Romances and are considered classics today.

Carr, Philippa (Pseudonym for Eleanor Burford Hibbert; also writes as Victoria Holt and Jean Plaidy)

Daughters of England Saga

Labeled Historical Gothics by Carr herself, take the descendants of one family from the English Reformation to World War II. Carr's final book, published posthumously and titled *Daughters of England*, is not linked to this series. See the previous volumes of this guide for a bibliography of the series.

Dailey, Janet

See also chapter 5, "Contemporary Romance."

The Calder Series (*This Calder Sky* [1981], *This Calder Range* [1982], *Stands a Calder Man* [1983], *Calder Born, Calder Bred* [1983]).

A contemporary western saga centering on the lives and fortunes of the Calder family. The wide-open spaces of Montana (and occasionally Texas), the rugged individualism of the characters, and the timeless quality of ranching life all combine to give these generally modern-day stories (except for the prequels to the series, *This Calder Range* and *Stands a Calder Man*) a vaguely historical quality.

Note: The four titles above are the original books in the series and are classics; those following are included for the sake of continuity.

Calder Pride. HarperTorch, 1999.

Cat Calder's proud, grief-stricken decision to prosecute the drunk driver who killed her fiancé eventually reaps vengeful rewards that put the lives of her son, herself, and the man she now loves, Echohawk, in danger.

Green Calder Grass. Kensington, 2002.

A manipulative first wife threatens the happiness of Ty and Jessy Calder in this bittersweet Romance.

Shifting Calder Wind. Kensington, 2003.

Attacked and left without a memory, Chase Calder is rescued and hidden until he can remember who wants to kill him in this story with a double romance.

Calder Promise. Kensington, 2004.

Laura Calder (Ty and Jessy's daughter) is wooed by two very different men, but one has an ulterior motive in this story that moves between Europe and Montana.

Lone Calder Star. Kensington, 2005.

In Texas to check up on the family's Cee Bar ranch, Quint Echohawk battles a greedy, ruthless billionaire, Max Rutledge, but finds love in the process.

Calder Storm. Kensington, 2006.

Max Rutledge is out for vengeance and causes plenty of grief in this occasionally tragic story.

Santa in Montana. Zebra, 2010.

Chase Calder decides his widowed daughter, Cat, needs a new romance in her life in this holiday-set story.

Gellis, Roberta

The Roselynde Chronicles (*Roselynde* [1978], *Alinor* [1978], *Joanna* [1978], *Gilliane* [1979], *Rhiannon* [1982], *Sybelle* [1983], *Desirèe* 2005]).

These well-researched Romances of medieval England (and sometimes France), detail the lives and loves of the women who are connected to the powerful keep Roselynde. Political intrigue, battles, Crusades, and passionate adventure are all part of this classic, richly historical series that spans the years roughly from 1189 to 1230. The first six of these have been reprinted. Although written later, *Desirèe* chronologically fits between *Roselynde* and *Alinor*.

Heaven, Constance

Kuragin Trilogy (*The House of Kuragin* [1972], *The Astrov Legacy* [1973] [also published as *The Astrov Inheritance*, 1973], *Heir to Kuragin* [1979]).

These three novels are a series of related stories set amidst the glitter and wealth of tsarist Russia. The first was the Romantic Novel of the Year winner for 1973, Romantic Novelists' Association.

Lindsey, Johanna

Malory Family Series (*Love Only Once* [1985], *Tender Rebel* [1988], *Gentle Rogue* [1990], *The Magic of You* [1993], *Say You Love Me* [1996], *The Present* [1999], *A Loving Scoundrel* [2004], *Captive of My Desires* [2006], *No Choice but Seduction* [2008], *That Perfect Someone* [2010]).

One of Lindsey's most beloved series, this adventurous series follows the loves and fortunes of the Malorys (and also the Andersons) during the first part of the 19th century.

Roberts, Nora

Born in . . . Trilogy (Concannon Trilogy) (*Born in Fire* [1994], *Born in Ice* [1995], *Born in Shame* [1996]).

Set primarily in Western Ireland, this is one of Roberts's earliest and most memorable "sisters" trilogies.

Selected Linked Romances Bibliography

Many of the authors listed below also write "un-linked" Romances. The following are only a few examples of the wide variety of Linked Romances available. Linked Romances may also be included in the subgenre chapters along with the authors' relevant bibliographies. (Note: Inspirational Romances are typically published as series and will not be listed here; consult chapter 11, "Inspirational Romance.")

Alers, Rochelle
Hideaway Series

This series of suspenseful stories features the multicultural Cole/Delgado family, and their friends, relatives, and descendents. The first three stories in this series have been reprinted as the collection *Hideaway Saga* (BET, 2004).

Hideaway First Generation
Hideaway. Pinnacle, 1995.
Parris Simmons and Martin Cole's story that reunites two lovers and helps them put the past to rest.

Hidden Agenda. Pinnacle, 1997.
In a desperate attempt to get her son back, Eve Blackwell agrees to marry Matt Sterling, a man she hardly knows and who has a deadly agenda of his own, with passionate and dangerous results. Mexican setting.

Vows. Pinnacle, 1997.
Vanessa Blanchard can't forget Josh Kirkland, the man who stole her heart—and her hand—on a vacation in Mexico, and then disappeared after the wedding.

Heaven Sent. Pinnacle, 1998.
In Costa Rica to help her politically influential stepfather free her half-brother from false imprisonment, Serena Morris-Vega is attracted to badly wounded David Cole, an enigmatic stranger with plenty of dangerous secrets.

Hideaway Daughters and Sisters Trilogy
Harvest Moon. BET, 1999.
Newly widowed Regina Cole-Spencer finds unexpected love with her late husband's son, Aaron,

Just Before Dawn. BET, 2000.
A weary federal prosecutor goes to the family New Mexico ranch and finds love with a neighboring veterinarian unaware that she is being targeted by a killer.

Private Passions. BET, 2001.
A secret marriage causes potential danger for a candidate for governor of New Mexico and a journalist who is covering his opponent in this secret-filled romance that features biracial (African American/Latino) protagonists.

Hideaway Sons and Brothers Trilogy
No Compromise. BET, 2002.
A woman is both stalked by her murderous ex-brother-in-law and targeted for death by a powerful politician in this riveting page-turner.

Homecoming. BET, 2002.
Fearful of being abused, Jolene Walker has difficulty trusting men until strong, protective Michael Kirkland changes her mind.

Renegade. BET, 2003.
Undercover as a drama teacher, driven, focused DEA agent Summer Montgomery trusts no one, until she meets attractive musician Gabriel Cole.

Best Kept Secrets. Kimani Sepia, 2006.
Prequel to the Hideaway series.

Stranger in My Arms. Kimani Arabesque, 2007.
CIA agent Merrick Grayslake and grad student Alexandra Cole meet at a family wedding and agree to be just friends; Merrick, however, has other ideas.

Secret Agenda. Kimani Arabesque, 2009.
Widowed when her politician husband is killed, Vivienne Neal becomes an assistant to the wealthy businessman Diego Cole-Thomas and finds romance in the present but deadly danger from the past.

Breakaway. Kimani Arabesque, 2010.
A grieving doctor meets an FBI agent while she is healing in her mountain cabin.

Anderson, Catherine
See also chapters 5 and 7, "Contemporary Romance" and "Historical Romance."

Kendrick/Coulter/Harrigan Series
Generally set in Oregon ranch country, this series follows the loves and fortunes of several important families.

Baby Love. Avon, 1999.
Taking her young son and running from an abusive stepfather, Maggie Stanley hops aboard train and ends up being rescued by a disillusioned, hard-drinking widower, Rafe Kendrick, and inadvertently giving him a reason to live.

Phantom Waltz. Onyx, 2001.
Wealthy rancher Ryan Kendrick loves wheelchair-bound Bethany Coulter, but he needs to convince her that they are meant to be together.

Sweet Nothings. Onyx, 2002.
Horse trainer Jake Coulter agrees to help cruelly abused stallion Sonora Sunset if Molly Wells, a woman in need of healing herself, agrees to work as the ranch's cook and housekeeper.

Blue Skies. Signet, 2004.
An impulsive one night stand with rancher Hank Coulter results in a pregnancy that may threaten the newly restored sight of Carly Adams in this heartwarming marriage-of-convenience story.

Bright Eyes. Signet, 2004.
The destructive actions of a rebellious twelve-year-old brings rancher Zeke Coulter and singer and supper club owner Natalie Patterson together in this gently humorous, touching story.

My Sunshine. Signet, 2005.
Veterinarian Isaiah Coulter hires Laura Townsend, a victim of aphasia as a result of a head injury, as his kennel keeper and is attracted to her at the same time he realizes someone doesn't want her to succeed.

Summer Breeze. Signet, 2006.
Tucker Coulter discovers his great-great-grandmother's journal and learns the story of her family's brutal massacre and the love that develops between her and rancher Joseph Paxton. This is one of the few Historical Romances in this series

Sun Kissed. Signet, 2007.
When veterinarian Tucker Coulter ends up with a broken nose when he comes to the aid of Samantha Harrigan when she defends an abused horse, the stage is set for a romance that is tinged with a dash of danger.

Morning Light. Signet, 2008.
Clairvoyant Lori MacEwen and rancher Clint Harrigan head into the wilderness to rescue a young boy who Lori senses is Clint's son but who is supposedly the son of an important politician.

Star Bright. Signet, 2009.
Faking her own death to escape a psychotic husband, Rainie Danning takes a job as an accountant and office manager for Parker Harrigan's horse breeding ranch and finds a man—and a family—who can keep her safe when her spouse finally locates her.

Early Dawn. Signet, 2010.
Run out of San Francisco by a vindictive former fiancé, Eden Paxton is rescued from kidnappers by Matthew Coulter, who is still grieving from the brutal murder of his wife, in this Historical that fills in more of the backstory of this popular series.

Balogh, Mary
Many of Balogh's Historicals and Regencies are in series or linked in some way. Several of her more recent series are listed below. Some of these have been reprinted.

Mistress Trilogy
The Duke of Thresham and his siblings are featured in this heartwarming trilogy.

More Than a Mistress. Delacorte, 2000.
When Jane Ingleby's attempt to stop a duel results in the Duke of Thresham's leg injury, he takes his revenge by hiring her as his nurse, not realizing that Jane is not quite what she seems nor that they will be attracted to each other.

No Man's Mistress. Delacorte, 2001.
Lord Ferdinand Dudley arrives in a country town to claim an estate he won in a card game and finds it inhabited by the lovely, determined Viola Thornhill, who claims she has inherited it and she's not about to leave.

The Secret Mistress. Delacorte, 2011.
Flamboyant, unconventional Lady Angeline Dudley is not about to marry a rake like the men in her family, but the quiet, civilized man she sets her sites on isn't so sure she's the right woman for him.

Slightly Series
The six aristocratic Bedwyn siblings, first introduced in *A Summer to Remember*, a book not part of this series, are the main players in this popular series.

Slightly Married. Dell, 2003.
Having promised to protect a dying officer's sister, Colonel Aidan Bedwyn and Eve Morris agree to a brief marriage of convenience to save her home, inheritance, and household only to have their hand forced by Aidan's family who now consider Eve one of their own.

Slightly Wicked. Dell, 2003.
Anticipating a loveless lifetime as a poor relation, parson's daughter Judith Law poses as an actress when a carriage accident strands her and engages in a passionate tryst with a Rannulf Bedwyn, never thinking she will meet him again when he comes courting her spoiled cousin.

Slightly Scandalous. Dell, 2003.
Independent Freya Bedwyn and the Marquess of Hallmere agree to a fake betrothal to foil his greedy aunt's matrimonial plotting and fall victim to passion in the process.

Slightly Tempted. Dell, 2004.
Young Morgan Bedwyn is in Brussels searching for her diplomat brother after the Battle of Waterloo and accepts help from the Earl of Rosthorn, who has devious goals of his own.

Slightly Sinful. Dell, 2004.
After being wounded and thrown from his horse, Alleyne Bedwyn wakes up with no memory in a Belgian brothel being tended by gently bred Rachel York and eventually poses as her husband to help her gain her inheritance and help a villain get his comeuppance.

Slightly Dangerous. Delacorte, 2004.
Wulfric Bedwyn, the powerful, unemotional Duke of Bewcastle, after avoiding marriage for years, unexpectedly falls for an irrepressible young widow whose unconventional background and lively behavior is just what the chilly duke needs.

Simply Quartet

The heroines of these books are all teachers at Miss Martin's School for Girls in Bath. Characters, primarily Bedwyn siblings and spouses, from the Slightly series often appear in these stories, and some of those from the Simply series were first introduced in the Slightly series.

Simply Unforgettable. Delacorte, 2005.
Schoolmarm Frances Allard is trapped with Lucius Marshall, Viscount Sinclair, at an isolated inn during a violent snowstorm and they begin a romantic relationship that is fraught with social difficulties.

Simply Love. Delacorte, 2006.
Anne Jewell, a teacher and unwed mother, is invited to spend part of the summer at a Cornwall estate with her son and finds love with an emotionally wounded, scarred war hero, who needs healing and understanding as much as Anne.

Simply Magic. Delacorte, 2007.
On her own after her gentleman father's suicide when she was twelve, Susanna Osborne is satisfied with her life until she meets charming Peter Edgeworth, a man who has a dark connection to her past.

Simply Perfect. Delacorte, 2008.
In this final volume of the series, the school owner, Claudia Martin, finds the man of her dreams in the Marquess of Attingsborough, while spending the summer at a country estate with some of the school's "charity girls."

Huxtable Quintet

An unexpected inheritance, complete with title, comes to teenage Stephen and changes the lives of the four Huxtable siblings, as well as that of their somewhat mysterious second cousin, in this Regency-set Historical series.

First Comes Marriage. Dell, 2009.
Thinking never to marry again, widowed Vanessa Dew stops her elder sister, who loves another, from sacrificing for the family once again and offers herself to the top-lofty Viscount Lyngate, instead.

Then Comes Seduction. Dell, 2009.
Young Katherine Huxtable and the notorious Jasper Finley meet again after a disastrous first meeting three years earlier, are still attracted, and make a wager that neither will be able to keep—that neither will fall in love with the other.

At Last Comes Love. Dell, 2009.
The notorious Earl of Sheringford has only two weeks to convince Margaret Huxtable to marry him and with her skepticism and his reputation it won't be easy.

Seducing an Angel. Delacorte, 2009.
No longer a mere stripling, Stephen Huxtable, Earl of Merton, accepts scandal-ridden Cassandra Belmont's offer to become her protector but chooses to say nothing of their relationship, instead protecting her from more scandal and redeeming her reputation in society.

A Secret Affair. Delacorte, 2010.
Enigmatic Cousin Constantine finds love in the final volume of this quintet.

Beverley, Jo
The Company of Rogues
This Regency-set series focuses on twelve men who met as boys at Harrow and formed a "brotherhood of protection" in order to survive the anarchy and abuse typical of schools of the day.

Some of the early books were Traditional Regencies and not all books feature rogues as heroes. Many have been reprinted.

An Arranged Marriage. Zebra Regency, 1991.
An Unwilling Bride. Zebra Regency, 1992.
Christmas Angel. Zebra Regency, 1992.
Forbidden. Zebra, 1994.
Dangerous Joy. Zebra, 1995.

Three Georges Trilogy
"The Demon's Mistress." (a novella in *In Praise of Younger Men*) Signet, 2001.
In this trilogy set within the Company of Rogues world, a debt-ridden, disillusioned soldier almost kills himself but is rescued by a widow who will pay him handsomely to pretend to be her fiancé for six weeks.

The Dragon's Bride. Signet, 2001.
A rogue returning from battle inherits the Earldom of Wyvern, and the bizarre mansion that goes with it, and reconnects with a woman with whom he has a difficult past.

The Devil's Heiress. Signet, 2001.
In an effort to save his home, a gentleman needs to prove a woman had a hand in a nobleman's violent death; the problem is that he begins to care for her.

Hazard. NAL Signet, 2002.
A marriage-wary, crippled heroine finds love with an adventurous former soldier in this gently mysterious Romance.

St. Raven. NAL Signet, 2003.
A nobleman pretending to be a highwayman to save another from the gallows holds up a coach and ends up rescuing a young woman and becoming involved in her quest to regain her family's fortune.

Skylark. NAL Signet, 2004.
A single mother afraid that her son is in danger from his uncle's determination to secure the title and fortune for his own son enlists the aid of a man she has once rejected.

The Rogue's Return. NAL Signet, 2006.
An aristocratic rogue plans to return to England after fighting in the War of 1812 in Canada but in defending a young woman's honor, he ends up marrying her, despite the differences in their social position.

To Rescue a Rogue. NAL Signet, 2006.
A rogue struggles with depression and laudanum addiction when he returns from war but is saved by the young woman who has adored him since her childhood.

Lady Beware. NAL Signet, 2007.
Another fake engagement turns into a real love match in this story that revolves around family and personal honor.

Malloren Chronicles

This funny, bawdy, action-packed series chronicles the lives of the Malloren siblings, as well as expands to include other friends and relatives. The first six titles have all been reissued, and the first two are being republished in the United Kingdom by Everlyn, the first under a modified title, *Lady Notorious*.

My Lady Notorious. Avon, 1993.
Trying the help her sister and infant nephew elude their wicked father, Lady Chastity Ware dons men's clothes, holds up a coach, and captures Lord Cynric Malloren who becomes part of the cause in this funny, cross-dressing story.

Tempting Fortune. Zebra, 1995.
There's nothing like being held at gunpoint by a lovely lady to intrigue a jaded nobleman, as Arcenbryght Malloren discovers when Portia St. Claire gets the drop on him.

Something Wicked. Topaz, 1997.
A daring masquerade and an overheard treasonous plot lands bored, almost on-the-shelf Lady Elfled Malloren (Cynric's twin) in the "care" of the hated Earl of Walgrave in this adventurous romp.

Secrets of the Night. Topaz, 1999.
Brand Malloren is rescued and then held captive by Rosamunde Overton, a facially scarred woman determined to provide her impotent husband with an heir.

Devilish. Signet, 2000.
Beowulf Malloren, the confirmed bachelor Duke of Rothgar, and the happily single, very independent Diana Westmount, Countess of Arradale, are forced together by the King and eventually fall in love in this story that finally sees all the Malloren siblings wed.

Winter Fire. Signet, 2003.
When a compromising situation forces Genova Smith and the Marquess of Ashart into a pretend betrothal at the winter festivities at Rothgar Abbey, love eventually follows in this story that includes a mystery, a baby, and the Malloren clan.

A Most Unsuitable Man. Signet, 2005.
Damaris Myddleton, the jilted beauty from the previous story, finds love with Octavius Fitzroger, the man she's asked to help her find a suitable husband.

Georgian Secrets (or the Rakish Trilogy)
Characters from the Malloren series are involved in these stories, as well.

A Lady's Secret. Signet, 2008.
Disguised as a nun, Petra d'Averio heads for England to find her unknown father and is aided by the Earl of Huntersdown in this dangerous adventure.

The Secret Wedding. Signet, 2009.
A couple wed ten years earlier and then separated in this story filled with deceptions find each other once again when Caro Hill wants to remarry, but needs to be sure she is a widow.

The Secret Duke. Signet, 2010.
A woman seeks out a notorious sea captain who once rescued her, not knowing that he is really a nobleman in this complicated Romance that rounds out Beverley's Rakish Trilogy.

Bradford, Barbara Taylor
See also chapter 5, "Contemporary Romance."

Harte Family Saga
This century-spanning series follows the fortunes of the Harte dynasty, beginning with Yorkshire serving girl Emma Harte, who founds a retail empire, and is the one for which Bradford is best known. Although more Women's Fiction than Romance, there are any number of important romantic relationships throughout the series. Many of the titles in the series have been reprinted.

A Woman of Substance. Doubleday, 1979.
Hold the Dream. Doubleday, 1985.
To Be the Best. Doubleday, 1988.

Emma's Secret. St. Martin's Press, 2004.
Three decades after Emma's death and the beginning of the twenty-first century, the arrival of American fashion designer Evan Hughes (female), prompts Paula to read her grandmother's wartime diaries, where she uncovers a remarkable secret.

Unexpected Blessings. St. Martin's Press, 2005.
Evan goes to work for the Harte department store, discovers something about her heritage, and falls in love in this story that follows the lives of Paula's two daughters, as well.

Just Rewards. St. Martin's Press, 2006.
Emma's grand and great-grandchildren are now running the Harte empire, but they must fight off the continuing threat from wicked uncle Jonathan Ainsley in this installment that sees a number of couples happily wed.

Breaking the Rules. St. Martin's Press, 2009.
A top model's past comes back to threaten her and her family, but "M" (Emma's great-granddaughter) is not about to let a psychopathic killer destroy everything she holds dear.

Bradley, Celeste
Bradley's Historicals are usually humorous, passionate, and broader and more realistic in social scope than some.

Liar's Club

The characters in this series are members of a renegade organization of undercover, "unofficial," spies for the crown, most often working against Napoleon.

The Pretender. St. Martin's Paperbacks, 2003.
A young woman looking for her brother in London needs a "husband" to pull off her married woman disguise and unwittingly enlists the aide of a spy who thinks her brother is a traitor.

The Imposter. St. Martin's Paperbacks, 2003.
When political cartoons by the pseudonymous Sir Thorogood endanger the security of the crown, a master spy pretends to be the artist in order to unmask him and finds himself in the sites of the real cartoonist, a young widow who is out to do some unmasking of her own.

The Spy. St. Martin's Paperbacks, 2004.
Disguised as a male tutor, the daughter of a famous code-master who has been captured in Spain, goes to work in the home of the Liars Club member who is searching for her.

The Charmer. St. Martin's Paperbacks, 2004.
Sparks fly between a charming "Liar" and the first woman Liars Club member as they are forced to work together on a dangerous mission.

The Rogue. St. Martin's Paperbacks, 2005.
A noted gambler is sent by the Liars Club to flush out an aristocratic traitor and discovers that he already knows, and is attracted to, the man's niece—who may also be a traitor.

The Royal Four

The heroes of this adventurous quart are four aristocratic spies—the Cobra, the Lion, the Fox, and the Falcon—who report only to the Prince Regent.

To Wed a Scandalous Spy. St. Martin's Paperbacks, 2005.
Accidentally compromised, a young, well-born woman marries a near-stranger who is thought to be a traitor but is on the real traitor's trail.

Surrender to a Wicked Spy. St. Martin's Paperbacks, 2005.
A young wife wonders about the true nature of her new husband's affairs in this sexy romp.

One Night with a Spy. St. Martin's Paperbacks, 2006.
A spy-in-training to become one of the Royal Four is assigned to see if the widow of one of the Royal Four, who has been acting in her late husband's stead for the past three years, is actually qualified to take his place.

Seducing the Spy. St. Martin's Paperbacks, 2006.
A young woman agrees to pose as mistress to one of the Royal Four in order to foil a plot in the final book in the series.

Heiress Brides

Three cousins compete to be the first to marry a duke in order to inherit their grandfather's fortune.

Desperately Seeking a Duke. St. Martin's Paperbacks, 2008.
A vicar's daughter accepts a proposal and then realizes she has accidentally accepted the wrong man.

The Duke Next Door. St. Martin's Paperbacks, 2008.
A young beauty marries a man in line for a dukedom and then is out for revenge when he reveals a rather important secret.

Duke Most Wanted. St. Martin's Paperbacks, 2008.
An intelligent, witty heroine resigns herself to her cousin's winning the inheritance but strikes up a friendship with a man who suddenly inherits a dukedom but must find an heiress to wed.

Runaway Brides
The possibility that any one of them could have fathered a charming three-year-old, Melody, links the three aristocratic bachelors in this trilogy.

Devil in My Bed. St. Martin's Paperbacks, 2009.
A woman running from her abusive, crazed husband and needing a place to hide allows an old flame to think she may be Melody's mother.

Rogue in My Arms. St. Martin's Paperbacks, 2010.
While pursuing the actress he thinks may be Melody's mother, a nobleman falls for the woman who is helping him.

Scoundrel of My Dreams. St. Martin's Paperbacks, 2010.
A nobleman learns that the woman he thinks might be Melody's mother is not the woman with whom he spent a passionate night three years ago.

Brenna, Helen
See chapter 5, "Contemporary Romance."

Britton, Pamela
See chapter 5, "Contemporary Romance."

Brockmann, Suzanne
Brockmann writes fast-paced, action-packed stories usually featuring U.S. Navy SEALs.

Troubleshooter Series
This series focuses on members of U.S. Navy SEAL Team Sixteen.

The Unsung Hero. Ivy, 2000.
Navy Seal officer Tom Paoletti foils a terrorist plot by putting together his own counter-terrorist team and finds love with pediatrician Kelly Ashton in his Massachusetts hometown.

The Defiant Hero. Ivy, 2001.
After her daughter and grandmother are kidnapped by extremists, translator Meg Moore takes the Kazbekistani ambassador hostage and demands to negotiate with Navy SEAL John Nilsson.

Over the Edge. Ivy, 2001.
Helicopter pilot Teri Howe and Senior Chief Petty Officer, part of a SEAL team charged with rescuing a senator's daughter from a plane hijacked and taken to Kazbekistan, find love, as well as adventure.

Out of Control. Ballantine, 2002.
Savannah von Hopf enlists the aid of a college classmate, military operative Wild-Card Karmody, to save her uncle from terrorists, but things spin "out of control" when they both end up in an alien jungle in fear of their lives.

Into the Night. Ballantine, 2002.
Joan Da Costa and Lt. Mike Muldoon find romance as they try to keep the president from becoming a terrorist target while at the Coronado Naval Base in San Diego.

Gone Too Far. Ballantine, 2003.
Navy SEAL Sam Starrett becomes a murder suspect when he finds a body in his ex-wife's house and his young daughter is missing and is reunited with a woman from his past, FBI agent Alyssa Locke.

Flashpoint. Ballantine, 2004.
Sent as undercover spies to unstable Kazbekistan, Tess Bailey and Diego Nash pose as newlyweds on a mission to help after an earthquake.

Hot Target. Ballantine, 2004.
Movie producer Jane Chadwick lands in hot water and attracts threats from all sides when she makes a film about a real life gay World War II hero, and it takes vacationing Navy SEAL Cosmo Richter to make sure she stays safe.

Breaking Point. Ballantine, 2005.
When it turns out that Gina Vitagliano was not killed in a bombing in Germany but has been kidnapped, Max Bhagat sets out to find her in this intricately plotted thriller.

Into the Storm. Ballantine, 2006.
While engaged in winter training exercises, a woman goes missing and SEAL Mark Jenkins and Troubleshooter Lindsey Fontaine become involved in solving the complicated crime.

Force of Nature. Ballantine, 2007.
A simple missing-person case turns into something far more dangerous for P.I. Ric Alvarado and his office assistant Annie Dugan—and then the FBI asks for their help with a terrorist plot.

All Through the Night: A Troubleshooter Christmas. Ballantine, 2007.
A stalker, a former lover, and a pushy reporter liven things up at the wedding of FBI agent Jules Cassidy and his partner actor, Robin Chadwick.

Into the Fire. Ballantine, 2008.
Still suffering from the violent loss of his wife for which he blames a neo-Nazi group, Vinh Murphy seeks out his old friend Hannah Whitfield only to eventually fear she may be in danger and he may lose the woman he loves once again.

Dark of Night. Ballantine, 2009.
When a Toubleshooters, Inc., agent is kidnapped by the evil Agency while trying to locate a Troubleshooter-in-hiding, the action spikes in this thriller that features several romantic duos.

Hot Pursuit. Ballantine, 2009.
Troubleshooter Alyssa Locke's latest assignment, to teach a new politician self-defense techniques, turns dangerous when the murders start and she ends up kidnapped by a serial killer who's targeted her for years.

Carr, Robyn

See also chapter 5, "Contemporary Romance."

Grace Valley Trilogy

This quiet series set in the outwardly peaceful town of Grace Valley, California, is filled with quirky characters and plenty of small-town charm; it should be read in order.

Deep in the Valley. Mira, 2000.
Dr. June Hudson is torn between love and ethics when an undercover DEA agent comes to town.

Just over the Mountain. Mira, 2002.
June must deal with many issues when her high school love comes home with fourteen-year-old boys while her DEA agent is away on assignment.

Down by the River. Mira, 2003.
June's pregnancy causes talk as danger looms in this story that wraps up this gentle series.

Virgin River Series
Set in the hamlet of Virgin River amid the Redwoods of Northern California, this series, sometimes subdivided into trilogies, includes a number of recurring characters and often features military heroes.

Virgin River. Mira, 2007.
A baby on the doorstep helps a nurse practitioner/midwife decide to stay in Virgin River, where she recovers from her husband's murder and finds a new love of her own.

Shelter Mountain. Mira, 2007.
An ex-Marine-turned-cook finds love with a victim of domestic violence.

Whispering Rock. Mira, 2007.
Date rape is a theme in this hard-hitting Romance that ties up the first trilogy in this series.

A Virgin River Christmas. Mira, 2008.
A woman on a mission of thanks finds an Iraq vet who needs healing, closure, and love.

Second Chance Pass. Mira, 2009.
A woman's second chance at love with the best friend of her late husband is derailed temporarily by another's unexpected pregnancy.

Temptation Ridge. Mira, 2009.
A young woman moves to Virgin River to care for her uncle while she tries to get her life in order and falls in love with a jaded former Blackhawk pilot, even though they are totally wrong for each other.

Paradise Valley. Mira, 2009.
The fiancé of a seriously wounded Iraq vet is not about to give up on him in this story with more than one romance.

Forbidden Falls. Mira, 2010.
A widowed pastor buys Virgin River's abandoned church and finds a calling and a most unexpected love.

Angel's Peak. Mira, 2010.
A pair of former lovers are reunited in this Romance that includes a secret baby element.

Moonlight Road. Mira, 2010.
A divorced Navy doctor roughing it and a woman finally on her own after raising her siblings sort out their futures separately—and eventually together—in this heartwarming Romance.

Caskie, Kathryn
Featherton Series

This funny, enchanting series focuses on the matchmaking efforts of the spinster Featherton sisters.

Rules of Engagement. Forever, 2004.
Intent on being an artist, Eliza Merriweather foils her great aunts' plans to get her married off by striking a bargain with Magnus MacKinnon, Lord Somerton, to fake a courtship which, eventually, turns into the real thing.

Lady in Waiting. Forever, 2005.
A young lady's maid who pretends to be a Lady when she is caught trying out a carriage by its noble owner is aided, surprisingly, in maintaining her pretense by the Feathertons.

Lady's Guide to Rakes. Forever, 2005.
A woman researching London rakes for her forthcoming books for young women on dealing with rakes is caught up short by a rake who has supposedly reformed.

Love Is in the Heir. Forever, 2006.
A pair of noble twins in search of their inheritance cause problems for Hannah Chilton in this lively tale filled with deception.

Royle Sisters Trilogy

Triplet sisters learn that they may actually be the illegitimate daughters of the Prince of Wales.

How to Seduce a Duke. Avon, 2006.
Intent on keeping his brother out of the clutches of Mary Royle, the Duke of Blackstone falls in love with her, instead.

How to Engage an Earl. Avon, 2007.
Hunting for some letters that might prove the triplets' royal birth, Anne Royle ends up compromised by the Earl of MacLaren and announces they are engaged.

How to Propose to a Prince. Avon, 2008.
Elizabeth Royle just knows she's going to marry a prince; what she doesn't know is that the man she thinks is the unfortunately engaged prince is actually his cousin, who has no such encumbrances.

Seven Deadly Sins

Known as the Seven Deadly Sins throughout society, the seven Sinclair siblings, each of whom exhibits a particular "sinful" flaw, must mend their wild ways or be forced to fend for themselves and forfeit their inheritance in this lively series.

To Sin with a Stranger. Avon, 2008.
Sterling Sinclair tries to provide for his family by prize fighting, but when Isobel Caringston tries to break up a fight and the *ton* takes notice, he sees another way to get what he wants. Sin: Greed.

The Most Wicked of Sins. Avon, 2009.
When Lady Ivy decides to make her intended suitor jealous, she hires a handsome actor to pretend to be the new Marquess of Counterton, not realizing that she has actually hired the real marquess, himself! Sin: Envy.

The Duke's Night of Sin. Avon, 2010.
Vulnerable and still mourning her fiancé's death, Lady Siusan gives in to passion with an unknown man one night, never realizing that he would reappear in her life one day as the Duke of Exeter, the father of one of her students. Sin: Sloth.

Craig, Christie
See chapter 5, "Contemporary Romance."

Dare, Tessa
Regency Trilogy
Set during the Regency period and linked by characters, these books were published in successive months and are the author's debut works.

Goddess of the Hunt. Ballantine, 2009.
Naïve Lucy Waltham plans to seduce Toby Aldridge, the man of her youthful dreams, but falls in love with Jeremy Trescott, the good friend she's talked into helping her practice her amorous technique.

Surrender of the Siren. Ballantine, 2009.
Tired of her constrained, boring life and wanting freedom and adventure, wealthy, well-bred Sophia Hathaway jilts Toby Aldridge, "becomes" governess Jane Turner, and boards a ship for Tortuga, never expecting to find romance with Benedict Grayson, who is trying his best to reform his rakish reputation.

A Lady of Persuasion. Ballantine, 2009.
Toby Aldridge finds love, at last, in the arms of Benedict Grayson's sister, Isabella, in this story that is enhanced by appearances of characters from previous books.

The Stud Club Trilogy
Mystery and suspicion link three men from diverse social backgrounds, all joint owners of a valuable racehorse, when the club's owner is killed.

One Dance with a Duke. Ballantine, 2010.
Twice Tempted by a Rogue. Ballantine, 2010.
Three Nights with a Scoundrel. Ballantine, 2010.

Davidson, MaryJanice
Davidson writes in a number of Romance subgenres and has several other series, including several books about the Wyndham Werewolves, that are related to the series below, but the Undead series is the one for which she is currently the best-known.

Royal Series
This funny series with an alternate world twist deals with the royal family of the independent country of Alaska.

The Royal Treatment. Brava, 2004.
Christina Krabbe, a visiting American tourist, is targeted as the bride for his son by the King of Alaska.

The Royal Pain. Brava, 2005.
Princess Alexandria of Alaska goes to North Dakota to help open the new Institute of Sea Life and is attracted to her marine biologist guide.

The Royal Mess. Brava, 2007.
A reluctant illegitimate princess and a hunky bodyguard find love in the last volume in this funny, offbeat series.

Undead Series

The contemporary vampire world of Minneapolis is the primary setting for this hilarious, irreverent series that focuses on shoe-obsessed Betsy Taylor, Queen of the Vampires, and is a cross between Paranormal Romance and Chick Lit.

Undead and Unwed. Berkley Sensation, 2004.
Leveled by an SUV and returning as a vampire, shoe fanatic Betsy Taylor is shocked to learn that she is destined to become the Queen of the Vampires—and a conflict with a major villain, Nostro, and the attentions of sexy Eric Sinclair just add to her problems.

Undead and Unemployed. Berkley Sensation, 2004.
Betsy, now having gotten a job at Macy's to support her shoe habit, is on the trail of a serial vampire killer, as well as dealing with the unwanted attentions of Vampire King Eric Sinclair.

Undead and Unappreciated. Berkley Sensation, 2005.
Betsy learns that she has a Satan-sired half-sister with whom, according to an ancient prophecy, she is destined to rule the world, but she faces a dilemma when the "Devil's spawn" turns out to be a sweet, naive pastor's daughter.

Undead and Unreturnable. Berkley Sensation, 2005.
Betsy has her hands full with needy ghosts, a serial killer, and assorted problems as she plans her wedding to sexy Eric Sinclair.

Undead and Unpopular. Berkley Sensation, 2006.
Betsy deals in her typical off-the-wall fashion with her upcoming birthday, a group of visiting European vamp dignitaries, and a friend's possible illness—and she still doesn't have her wedding planned.

Undead and Uneasy. Berkley, 2007.
Problems compound as Betsy's fiancé becomes difficult and her friends are sick or otherwise unavailable to help, although the Wyndham wolves do come and add a dash of hilarity, as she continues to get ready for her wedding, more or less on her own.

Undead and Unworthy. Berkley, 2008.
Finally married and back from the honeymoon, Betsy is plagued by feral vampires (Fiends), ghosts, and numerous other problems.

Undead and Unwelcome. Berkley, 2009.
Betsy goes to return a body to the Wyndham werewolves and is unwelcome, to say the least, as problems continue to arise at home.

Undead and Unfinished. Berkley, 2010.
A deal with the devil is in the works for Betsy in this story that continues to take the series in a darker direction.

Undead and Undermined. Berkley, 2011.

Duarte, Judy

See chapter 5, "Contemporary Romance."

Evanick, Marcia

Evanick has written earlier series Romances but is best known recently for the series below.

Misty Harbor Series

A small Maine coastal community is the setting for these heartwarming, sweet, character-rich novels. Several have a holiday theme and some have more than one love story.

Catch of the Day. Zebra, 2002.
A big city chef moves to town and opens Catch of the Day and is attracted to a carpenter with a tragic past.

Christmas on Conrad Street. Zebra, 2002.
Having sworn off love, a doctor is determined to find a fresh start in Misty Harbor but has a hard time resisting a persistent, gorgeous fisherman in this romance that has more than one love story.

Blueberry Hill. Zebra, 2003.
A disillusioned attorney joins her two sisters (heroines of two previous books) in Misty Harbor to reassess her life and takes a temporary job as a nanny to the three young children of the local sheriff.

A Berry Merry Christmas. Zebra, 2004.
A new widow comes to Misty Harbor to be part of her aunt's jam and jelly business and eventually finds new love with her late husband's business partner, once they stop feeling guilty.

Harbor Nights. Zebra, 2005.
A delicately built reporter, wary of men because of an abusive father and in need of emotional healing, is attracted to her handsome, brawny neighbor but fearful of his size.

A Misty Harbor Wedding. Zebra, 2006.
On a quiet mission to check out a new hotel site her family's hotel chain is considering, a single mom falls for a man who has planned for years to buy the land and the lighthouse that her company has in its sites.

Mistletoe Bay. Zebra, 2007.
Back in town to help care for his father, a UPS driver is drawn into the lives of a young widow running a home-based bath and beauty products business and her multigenerational family.

Feehan, Christine

Feehan's paranormal works, most of which are grouped into series, are diverse, creative, and combine a number of fantasy and, sometimes science fiction, elements. Three of her most popular series are listed below.

Dark (Carpathian) Series

This erotically sensual, darkly compelling series revolves around the Carpathians, an ancient race of blood-drinking, supernaturally gifted, shape-shifters (not to be confused with the evil vampires who are their enemies) and their struggle to preserve their slowing dwindling species, including staving off attacks from those who would hasten their demise.

Dark Prince. Love Spell, 1999.
Dark Desire. Love Spell, 1999.
Dark Gold. Love Spell, 2000.
Dark Magic. Love Spell, 2000.
Dark Challenge. Love Spell, 2000.
Dark Fire. Love Spell, 2001.
"Dark Dream." (a novella in *After Twilight*) Love Spell, 2001.
Dark Legend. Leisure, 2002.
Dark Guardian. Leisure, 2002.
Dark Symphony. Jove, 2003.
"Dark Descent." (a novella in *The Only One*) Leisure, 2003.
Dark Melody. Leisure, 2003.
Dark Destiny. Leisure, 2004.
"Dark Hunger." (a novella in *Hot Blooded*) Jove, 2004.
Dark Secret. Jove, 2005.
Dark Demon. Jove, 2006.
Dark Celebration: A Carpathian Reunion. Berkley, 2006.
> The Carpathian clan gather during the holidays and enjoy good fellowship, fight vampires, deal with danger from a dark mage, and work to solve their low birthrate problem. Slightly lighter in tone than some of the others, this is the first in the series to be in hardcover, and includes recipes for "Dark Desserts."

Dark Possession. Jove, 2007.
Dark Curse. Berkley, 2008.
Dark Slayer. Jove, 2009.
Dark Peril. Berkley, 2010.
Dark Predator. Berkley, 2011.

Drake Sisters

Seven sisters with vastly different magical gifts work to fulfill their destinies and find love along the way in this series set primarily in Sea Haven, a fictional town on the Northern California coast.

Magic in the Wind. Berkley, 2005 (originally released as a novella in the *Lover Beware* anthology,Berkley, 2003.).
Defense system genius Damon Wilder takes refuge from a killer in Sea Haven and finds his destiny with Sarah Drake, the eldest of the magically gifted Drake sisters, who is also his guardian.

The Twilight before Christmas. Pocket Star, 2003.
Author and bookstore owner Kate Drake finds love with former Army-Ranger-turned-contractor Matt Granite when they are confronted with a newly released evil and a malevolent fog that threatens the town over the Christmas holidays.

Oceans of Fire. Jove, 2005.
Dolphin expert Abigail Drake witnesses a murder and ends up rescuing an Interpol agent, Alexandr Volstov, a man from her past.

Dangerous Tides. Jove, 2006.
Healer Dr. Libby Drake uses her magical abilities to rescue brilliant, but skeptical, reclusive Tyson Derrick when he risks his life in a rescue operation.

Safe Harbor. Jove, 2007.
After a variety of dangerous situations, gorgeous model and magically gifted Hannah Drake and family friend Sheriff Jonas Herrington realize they are meant to be together.

The Turbulent Sea. Jove, 2008.
Plagued by a stalker, rock star Joley Drake needs help from Ilya Prakenskii, who is more than he seems.

Hidden Currents. Jove, 2009.
Seventh Drake sister Elle is caught in a violent situation on a private island, owned by monumentally depraved Stavros Gratsos, from which Deputy Sheriff Jackson Deveau and her sisters eventually rescue her.

GhostWalkers Series
The lives of two groups of psychically gifted, genetically enhanced, but also at-risk, people—a group of elite military men with enhanced physical and psychic abilities, the GhostWalkers, and a group of women, all named after flowers, who were psychically abused as children by the same brilliant scientist who created the GhostWalkers—are woven together in the thrillers in this sexy, paranormal science fiction adventure series.

Shadow Game. Jove, 2003.
Knowing he will be the next of his fellow GhostWalkers to die if he doesn't escape his underground "prison," Ryland Miller escapes with the aid of Dr. Lily Whitney, daughter of the GhostWalkers' creator.

Mind Game. Jove, 2004.
GhostWalker Nico Trevane is sent to the Louisiana bayous to find a reclusive young woman, Dahlia LeBlanc, who Lily Whitney believes is one of her father's "flower" experiments.

Night Game. Jove, 2005.
GhostWalker Gator Fontenot heads for New Orleans to rescue the dangerously enhanced Iris "Flame" Johnson before she can cause problems—or be killed by the assassin who is after her as well.

Conspiracy Game. Jove, 2006.
A young trapeze artist, Briony Jenkins, becomes pregnant after a brief affair with GhostWalker Jack Norton and needs to find him in order to save her baby and herself.

Deadly Game. Jove, 2007.
GhostWalker Marigold "Mari" Smith is taken captive by Ghostwalker Ken Norton and falls for him in this story with a "twin" theme and a twist.

Predatory Game. Jove, 2008.
A radio personality and a wounded ex–Navy SEAL, both GhostWalkers and both on somebody's hit list, guard their secrets warily, even as they fall in love.

Murder Game. Jove, 2009.
GhostWalker Kadan Montague needs the help of psychic wildlife photographer Tansy Meadows to find out who is killing people and then blaming the GhostWalkers for it.

Street Game. Jove, 2010.
A GhostWalker with a gift for urban warfare reconnects with a past flame who is now a spy and desperately needs his help.

Ruthless Game. Jove, 2011.
The safety of an unborn child is at risk in this perilous story that nicely continues the series.

Sisters of the Heart
Set in Sea Haven, the same town as the Drake Sisters series, the two series have some characters in common. But Sisters focuses on a group of six unrelated, magically talented, deeply wounded women who bonded during counseling and now live, each in separate houses, on a large farming community they bought with their combined resources.

Water Bound. Jove, 2010.
A mildly autistic diver saves a stranger from drowning and finds danger and love in the process.

Spirit Bound. Jove, 2012.
Deadly danger follows an undercover agent when he comes to Sea Haven looking for his brother, as well connecting with a beautiful artist he has been sent to find.

Gabaldon, Diana
Outlander Series
Featuring the improbable, enduring romance between a time traveling twentieth-century army nurse and an eighteenth-century Scotsman, this now-classic Time Travel Romance series is taking on saga-like dimensions as it continues to spin the stories of Jamie Fraser and Claire Randall and their offspring. Note: There are more books to come in this series.

*Outlander. Delacorte Press, 1991.
On holiday in Scotland with her husband, Frank, WWII army nurse Claire Randall is thrust back into eighteenth-century Scotland, where she meets and falls in love with Jamie Fraser.

Dragonfly in Amber. Delacorte Press, 1992.
Twenty-two years later, Claire, now widowed, returns to Scotland with her daughter, Briana, to discover what happened to her beloved Jamie.

Voyager. Delacorte Press, 1994.
Returning to Scotland in the eighteenth century, Claire is reunited with Jamie and they set out for a new life and find danger as well as hope for the future.

Drums of Autumn. Delacorte Press, 1997.
Now in eighteenth-century Charleston, Claire and Jamie deal with colonial America and the story begins to focus on their daughter, Briana, and the man she loves, Roger.

The Fiery Cross. Delacorte Press, 2001.
Claire and Jamie continue to build their lives in pre-Revolutionary North Carolina along with their daughter, Briana, her husband, Roger, and their son, Jemmy, in this character-driven installment.

A Breath of Snow and Ashes. Delacorte Press, 2005.
Set right before the American Revolution, this story continues the adventures of Claire and Jamie and Briana and Roger.

An Echo in the Bone. Delacorte Press, 2009.
The American Revolution comes to life through Claire and Jamie's experiences as Roger and Briana search for their own answers in their lives in the twentieth century.

Harte, Amanda (Pseudonym for Christine B. Tayntor)
Hidden Falls Series
Class conflicts and family disagreements abound in this sweet, unusual series that is set in the factory town of Hidden Falls, New York, in the early 1900s and the present.

Painted Ponies. Avalon, 2006.
Anne Moreland is thwarted by her brother when she wants to establish a childcare center for the workers at her family's mill but is aided by the woodcarver who is working on a carousel for her.

The Brass Ring. Avalon, 2007.
Jane Moreland returns to town to discover that the man she had once loved is now an attorney for the mill workers at her family's mill.

Dream Weaver. Avalon, 2007.
Hidden Falls is dwindling in numbers and vitality until John Moreland returns to take a hand in this Romance that brings the town into the present.

Stargazer. Avalon, 2008.
An artist hired to restore the ponies on an antique carousel comes to Hidden Falls and finds resentment, love, and a bit of danger.

The Golden Thread. Avalon, 2008.
A New York heiress avoids an unwanted marriage by taking a job at the mill in Hidden Falls, but is surprised to be attracted to the town newspaper owner in this story that returns the series to the past.

Hern, Candice
Hern is noted for impeccably crafted, witty, historically accurate Regency and Regency-set Romances. Two of her series are listed here. See also chapter 7, "Historical Romance."

The Ladies Fashionable Cabinet Trilogy
The action in this series revolves around the people involved with a popular women's magazine, *The Ladies Fashionable Cabinet*.

Once a Dreamer. Avon, 2003.
A nobleman who writes an advice column, "The Busybody," as an anonymous female is forced to go with the aunt of a young girl who took his "advice" and ran off with a rake to help find the young couple before the girl is totally ruined.

Once a Scoundrel. Avon, 2003.
A gentleman who wins *The Ladies Fashionable Cabinet* in a card game is shocked to find that the magazine's editor is his childhood adversary, a girl who won every bet

they made; now they make another, with delightful results for them both. A group of ladies of the night add humor to this lively romp.

Once a Gentleman. Avon, 2004.
Forced into marriage by her irate family when she falls asleep at her desk—which is located in the townhouse of the magazine's co-owner, Nicholas Parrish—and stays there all night, assistant editor Prudence Armitage and Nicholas agree to a friendly marriage—until the shy, hardworking Prudence begins to bloom.

Merry Widows Series

A group of widowed gentlewomen, the Merry Widows, agree not to marry but to take lovers instead in this sensual, often funny, series.

In the Thrill of the Night. Signet Eclipse, 2006.
A widow asks an old friend (and notorious rake) to help her find a suitable lover, but they fall for each other, instead.

Just One of Those Flings. Signet Eclipse, 2006.
Intent on taking care of her two daughters and overseeing her niece's society debut, a widow is surprised into an affair with one of the *ton*'s most eligible noblemen.

Lady Be Bad. Signet Eclipse, 2007.
One of the *ton*'s most eligible noble rakes agrees to a wager that he can seduce any woman in the *ton*, little realizing that his challenger will name a notoriously proper bishop's widow, but secret member of the Merry Widows, as his target.

Hill, Sandra

Hill writes in a number of Romance subgenres; her books, many of which are grouped into series, are usually sexy and filled with laugh-out-loud humor. Some of her most recent series are listed below.

Viking Series II

This multigenerational series begins when the three Viking Ericsson brothers separately find their ways from the late tenth century to the present.

The Last Viking. Love Spell, 1998.
A tenth-century Viking Geirolf ends up in modern-day Maine and finds the longboat he needs to get home is only half done and is owned by a skeptical medieval historian.

Truly, Madly Viking. Love Spell, 2000.
While hunting at sea for his missing brother, Jorund is taken by a killer whale into Orcaland in the twenty-first century, where a psychologist sends him off for evaluation.

The Very Virile Viking. Leisure, 2003.
Setting out from the Norselands with most of his eleven children for a better life in Vinland, Magnus, a very virile tenth-century Viking ends up on a film set in present-day California and attracted to a woman vintner.

Wet and Wild. Leisure, 2004.
An eleventh-century Viking lands in a twenty-first-century Navy SEALs training camp and falls for a very attractive superior officer.

Hot and Heavy. Leisure, 2005.
A woman from the eleventh century ends up in an Iraq desert and is captured by a group of Navy SEALS in search of terrorists.

Rough and Ready. Berkley Sensation, 2006.
An eleventh-century Viking turned Navy SEAL heads back in time to take care of a villain, and, along with a group of SEALs who went with him, lands in a women's sanctuary.

Down and Dirty. Berkley Sensation, 2007.
While planning to fake her own death to avoid marriage, an eleventh-century Viking woman warrior ends up in a feminine version of the Navy SEALS training program and is reunited with a man she'd met before.

Viking Unchained. Berkley Sensation, 2008.
An eleventh-century Viking lands in modern times and meets a grieving Navy SEAL widow who looks like his former wife in this story with a touch of reincarnation.

Viking Heat. Berkley Sensation, 2009.
A contemporary psychologist in the women's Navy SEAL training program ends up auctioned off to a Viking lord in the tenth century.

Cajun Series

Linked by character and place (New Orleans and the Louisiana bayous), this series introduces Tante Lulu and is related to the Jinx series. Several of these have been reissued.

The Love Potion. Love Spell, 1999.
A very proper Creole chemist creates an experimental "love potion" in the form of jelly beans and then must deal with the effects when a sexy bayou attorney, who has plagued her since childhood, eats one by mistake.

Tall, Dark, and Cajun. Warner, 2003.
An interior decorator fleeing a broken relationship heads for the bayou and finds a fascinating birth grandmother and love with a pilot wounded during Desert Storm.

The Cajun Cowboy. Warner, 2004.
A much-married former beauty queen swears off men only to have her first husband return with the proof they are still married and have inherited a ranch together.

The Red-Hot Cajun. Warner, 2005.
A Creole TV celebrity heroine and a Cajun environmental lobbyist hero clash in this lively romp that involves kidnapping, as well as serious environmental issues.

Jinx Series

This funny, offbeat series centers on the doings of treasure-hunting company Jinx, Inc. and is related to Hill's Cajun series. Matchmaking grandmother Tante Lulu is featured throughout.

Pink Jinx. Warner Vision, 2006.
A Boston attorney ends up in charge of her grandfather's treasure-hunting company and in search of a lost ship and some missing diamonds, and dealing with the Mafia and the man she can't live with—or without.

Pearl Jinx. Warner Vision, 2007.
An ex–Navy SEAL and a skeptical archaeologist find romance in their search for some legendary "cave pearls."

Wild Jinx. Forever, 2008.
A reporter's story endangers an undercover cop with whom she has a past and leads to plenty of danger, sexy sparks, and, eventually, love.

Howard, Linda
See chapter 5, "Contemporary Romance," for her Mackenzie series titles.

Hoyt, Elizabeth
Prince Trilogy
This loosely linked Georgian Era trilogy is set in 1760.

The Raven Prince. Forever, 2006.
A rather plain, smart widow takes a position as a secretary to a difficult, unattractive nobleman and ends up becoming his anonymous lover in this unusual Romance.

The Leopard Prince. Forever 2007.
A noblewoman falls in love with the steward she's hired to help manage her large estate in this Romance that is enhanced by a touch of mystery.

The Serpent Prince. Forever, 2007
A young woman rescues a wounded nobleman on a mission of revenge, but their growing attachment is threatened by his overwhelming passion for vengeance.

Legend of Four Soldiers Quartet
Four former military men search for a traitor in this Georgian Era series.

To Taste Temptation. Forever, 2008.
A Boston businessman comes to England to track down the man who betrayed his regiment into a massacre by the Indians and is attracted to the frosty sister of one of his comrades who was killed.

To Seduce a Sinner. Forever, 2008.
When a nobleman who really needs to marry is jilted, he accepts a surprise proposal from a shy wallflower who secretly has loved him for years, and finds unexpected passion.

To Beguile a Beast. Forever, 2009.
A woman who needs a home for herself and her two children convinces a reclusive naturalist and former soldier to let her become his housekeeper in this Beauty-and-the-Beast Romance.

To Desire a Devil. Grand Central Vision, 2009.
A nobleman, thought to been burned at the stake in the colonies seven years earlier, survives to return home to reclaim his heritage and find healing in love in this story that finally solves the treasonous mystery.

Maiden Lane Series
Set in Georgian London at the height of the gin craze, the books in this series are linked by Maiden Lane, a fictional street in the dangerous, squalid stews of St. Giles.

Wicked Intentions. Grand Central Publishing, 2010.
First in this projected series, this story pairs the head of the Home for Unfortunate Infants and Foundling Children with a nobleman who needs her help to find a killer.

Hunter, Madeline
Hunter's sexy Historicals are noted for their lush detail, accuracy, and ability to bring the past to life.

Medieval Series

Set in fourteenth-century London, the books in these series were not written in chronological order. They are listed below in the proper order and the first three and the last three can be considered trilogies of a sort within the series.

By Possession. Bantam, 2000.
A nobleman returning from the Crusades and the freed bondswoman who's been caring for his son find love, in spite of numerous obstacles.

By Design. Bantam. 2001.
A well-born sculptor and her Freemason protector find love amid much confusion in this complex tale.

Stealing Heaven. Bantam, 2002.
A man loyal to the English King becomes attracted to the rebellious, rather scandalous sister of the Welshwoman to whom he has been betrothed.

By Arrangement. Bantam, 2000.
A pair betrothed by command of the King find love in spite of their preconceived ideas.

The Protector. Bantam, 2001.
The Black Plague drives much of the action in this lively tale.

Lord of a Thousand Nights. Bantam, 2002.
An intrepid noblewoman, determined to save her home and her people, is drawn into a dangerous game of wealth, power, and intrigue when she meets a seductive rake.

Seducers Series

Although each book stands on its own, this series, which spans the years from 1818 to 1833, is linked by characters who are members of the London Dueling Society.

The Seducer. Bantam, 2003.
A man bent on revenge plans to use his lovely young ward as bait but falls in love with her, instead.

The Saint. Bantam, 2003.
A nobleman striving to be proper is at his wits end when he discovers his young American ward wants to be an opera singer, a totally inappropriate occupation for an English lady.

The Charmer. Bantam, 2003.
An English nobleman is attracted to the independent duchess he is sent to France to retrieve for the King's political purposes.

The Sinner. Bantam, 2004.
An unusual marriage of convenience between a debt-ridden nobleman and a woman running from her stepfather's controlling plans turns into the real thing.

The Romantic. Bantam, 2004.
A woman finds love with the solicitor who is helping her rid herself of an abusive husband in a legally tinged romantic adventure.

Rothwell Series

Set in the 1820s, this series revolves around the three aristocratic Rothwell brothers and the Longworth family.

Rules of Seduction. Dell, 2006.
Alexia Longworth, financially ruined by a massive bank failure, and Lord Hayden Rothwell, whom she blames, are attracted in spite of the circumstances, which are not quite what Alexia believes.

Lessons of Desire. Dell, 2007.
Elliot Rothwell rescues publisher Phaedra Blair from prison on the condition that she not publish her late father's memoirs, some of which could harm his family.

Secrets of Surrender. Dell, 2008.
Forced by poverty and her thieving brother's perfidy to become a nobleman's mistress, Roselyn Longworth ends up "sold" to an architect who offers marriage.

The Sins of Lord Easterbrook. Dell, 2009.
Shipping company owner Leona Montgomery and Christian Rothwell, Lord Easterbrook, renew a former relationship and solve some mysteries in the final book of this series.

Rarest Blooms Quartet

A group of women with diverse secret pasts live together in the country and support themselves by raising flowers.

Ravishing in Red. Jove, 2010.
A woman intent on clearing her late father's name and one of his aristocratic accusers meet at gunpoint and then must deal with the scandal when the gun goes off in this lively adventure.

Provocative in Pearls. Jove, 2010.
Finally locating the wife who fled after being forced into marriage by her wicked cousin, the Earl of Hawkeswell ends up negotiating a provocative bargain with his wife, Verity, that doesn't end as she expects.

Sinful in Satin. Jove, 2010.
Pleased when she inherits a small London house from her courtesan mother, a young woman is shocked to find she has inherited a handsome tenant, as well.

Dangerous in Diamonds. Jove, 2011.
The proprietor of The Rarest Blooms attracts the attentions of the dissolute duke who has inherited the property that houses her flower shop.

Jacobs, Holly

Jacobs writes funny, lively Contemporary Romances, many of which are set in Erie, Pennsylvania. Several of her most popular series are listed here. See also chapter 5, "Contemporary Romance."

Perry Square

This series focuses on Perry Square, a small park in Erie, Pennsylvania.

Do You Hear What I Hear? Silhouette Romance, 2002.
A hair salon owner with a hearing-impaired daughter clashes with a new doctor in town, but when he strikes up a relationship with the daughter, things change.

A Day Late and a Bride Short. Silhouette Romance, 2003.
A businesswoman who needs legal help and a lawyer who needs a fiancée to make partner strike a bargain in this sweet, funny story that is part of the loosely linked Perry Square series.

Dad Today, Groom Tomorrow. Silhouette Romance, 2003.
A man returns to town and discovers the girl who ran from him eight years before and a son he didn't know he had.

Be My Baby. Silhouette Romance, 2004.
A baby brings a receptionist and an attorney together.

Perry Square Royals
Royalty comes to Perry Square in this series within a series.

Once upon a Princess. Silhouette Romance, 2005.
Once upon a Prince. Silhouette Romance, 2005.
Once upon a King. Silhouette Romance, 2005.

Here with Me. Silhouette Romance, 2006.
A big-city bachelor becomes his infant niece's guardian and moves home for a month to see if he can handle the responsibility and reconnects with a childhood friend.

WLVH Series
A radio station dedicated to love, WLVH, in Erie, Pennsylvania, is the focus of this funny, sweet series.

Pickup Lines. Avalon, 2005.
A teacher and businessman who want to win the pickup truck that the radio station is offering, agree to sit in the truck until one of the two gives up in this funny story that is the first in this series.

Lovehandles. Avalon, 2005.
The station's "Punch and Judy in the Morning" partners, who have been long-time friends, find that opposites really do attract.

Night Calls. Avalon, 2006.
A nighttime DJ who's given up on love and a divorce lawyer become friends—and eventually more.

Laugh Lines. Avon, 2007.
Dani Sinclair, CEO of an academic publishing firm intent on updating its image, makes contact with the owner of a local comedy club, sexy Luke Miller, in more ways than one.

Everything but . . . Series
With Jacobs's typical setting, Erie, Pennsylvania, as the backdrop, this funny, sweet, heartwarming series features a Hungarian grandmother who blames herself for the Salo Family wedding curse, and takes it upon herself to make things right for her three unmarried grandchildren. She expands her matchmaking efforts to friends and acquaintances in the fourth book in the series.

Everything but a Groom. Avalon, 2007.
When her intended dumps her and the press is after her because of the wedding curse story, Vancy Salo hides out as a nanny and finds love with the uncle of her charges.

Everything but a Bride. Avalon, 2008.
Jilted just before the wedding, Noah Salo eventually finds love with his long-time friend—and step-sister of his former fiancée.

Everything but a Wedding. Avalon, 2008.
Contractor Dori Salo has sworn off men until she ends up working with an interior designer who is not at all he is pretending to be.

Everything but a Christmas Eve. Avalon, 2009.
Bored because the wedding curse has finally been broken, Nana Vancy tries her hand at matchmaking and reconnects two wary people with a schooldays past.

James, Eloisa (Pseudonym for Mary Bly)

James is noted for her quick-witted, well-written, carefully researched Regency and Georgian Historical Romances.

Pleasures Trilogy

This trio of pre-Regency Romances is linked by character; some have been reprinted.

Potent Pleasures. Delacorte, 2000.
Alex Foakes falls in love with Charlotte Calverstill, a woman he ravished at a masked ball years earlier, but doesn't recognize—a situation that causes a few problems for their relationship.

Midnight Pleasures. Delacorte, 2000.
A secretly brilliant young woman set to marry a dull nobleman in order to avoid an unhappy marriage with a philandering husband, ends up marrying a rake she has always loved but might not trust, instead.

Enchanting Pleasures. Delacorte, 2001.
An unconventional young woman is drawn to the brother of her fiancé, who has a migraine-linked sexual disability that apparently precludes a relationship.

Duchess Quartet

Flawed characters find love in this Regency series that focuses on women's friendships and includes a fascinating character, Esme, who continues from book to book.

Duchess in Love. Avon, 2002.
A woman seeking an annulment from a man she wed as a child twelve years ago is wooed by her husband who realizes he doesn't want to let her go.

Fool for Love. Avon, 2003.
A confirmed spinster who mistakenly thinks she will never have children because of a physical disorder finds love in the arms of an urban dandy who can't resist her charms.

A Wild Pursuit. Avon, 2004.
Tainted by scandal, Lady Beatrix decides her reputation can't suffer any more, so she decides to pursue the man she really wants, Stephen Fairfax-Lacy.

Your Wicked Ways. Avon, 2004.
Agreeing to move back into her estranged husband's house (with his mistress in residence!) in exchange for his agreeing to father a child, a proper society matron rekindles a love that was all but lost in this story that introduces a memorable rake who will become a major player in the Essex Sisters Quartet.

Essex Sisters Quartet

Four Scottish sisters become the wards of an English duke in this sexy series that makes good use of the author's Shakespearean scholar background.

Much Ado about You. Avon, 2005.
Realizing that their alcoholic guardian will not be much help on the matrimonial mart, Tessa Essex sets out to attract the attentions of one eligible nobleman, but falls for another, instead.

Kiss Me, Annabel. Avon, 2005.
Determined to marry a wealthy Englishman, Annabel resists her attraction to the Earl of Armor, ostensibly a poor Scot, until fate decrees otherwise.

The Taming of the Duke. Avon, 2006.
Widowed Imogen Essex Maitland decides to take a lover but is drawn to her troubled guardian, Rafe Jourdain, in spite of her plans to the contrary.

Pleasure for Pleasure. Avon, 2006.
Nicknamed "the Scottish Sausage" because of her tightly corseted voluptuous figure by a rejected suitor, Josie Essex decides she needs seduction lessons and turns to the Earl of Mayne, the rake her eldest sister left standing at the altar, for instruction, which works better than either had expected.

Desperate Duchesses Series

A group of independent, often unconventional, noblewomen enjoy romantic relationships and find love in this sexy Georgian series that is set primarily during the 1780s, a more licentious, less restrictive time than the later Regency and Victorian periods. Although each book resolves at least one romantic dilemma, multiple storylines are present in each.

Desperate Duchesses. Avon, 2007.
Thinking she's fallen in love with the dangerous Duke of Villiers, young Roberta St. Giles sets out to win him but falls in love with Damon Reeves, the man who's helping her in her mission, instead.

An Affair Before Christmas. Avon, 2007.
The Duke and Duchess of Fletcher finally resolve their communication and sex issues in this book that flashes back and forth between two time periods.

Duchess by Night. Avon, 2008.
Bored with her proper life and wanting adventure, Harriet, Duchess of Berrow, goes to a scandalous party disguised as a boy and attracts the attention of the party's host, Lord Justinian Strange.

When the Duke Returns. Avon, 2008.
Wed by proxy as a child, Isadore has waited eleven years to finally meet her husband, Simeon Jermyn, Duke of Cosway. But when Simeon asks for an annulment, Isadore is determined to change his mind—whatever the cost.

This Duchess of Mine. Avon, 2009.
Separating immediately after their wedding nine years ago, Jemma and Elijah, Duke and Duchess of Beaumont, have lived apart. Now the Duke needs an heir—and Jemma wants to be the one woman her husband loves.

A Duke of Her Own. Avon, 2009.
The notorious Duke of Villiers, a character who develops nicely throughout the series, becomes engaged to smart, capable Lady Eleanor and then becomes distracted by a less conventional woman.

Fairy Tale Series

Classic fairy tales get a new look.

A Kiss at Midnight. Avon, 2010.
Forced to attend a ball when her stepsister can't, Kate meets the prince in this witty, very clever twist on the Cinderella tale.

When Beauty Tamed the Beast. Avon, 2011.
A jilted beauty agrees to an engagement in order to save her reputation and finds her difficult hero is more of a challenge than she'd expected in this delightfully revised Beauty-and-the-Beast tale.

The Duke Is Mine. Avon, 2012.
This funny, lively adventure puts a remarkably creative spin on *The Princess and the Pea*.

Jeffries, Sabrina (Pseudonym for Deborah Gonzales)

Jeffries is noted for her Regency-set sensual, laughter-laced Historicals, most of which are grouped into series. These are a few of her recent series.

Royal Brotherhood

This trilogy features three bastard sons of the Prince of Wales who pool their separate skills and resources to make something of their lives.

In the Prince's Bed. Pocket Star, 2004.
The Earl of Iversley has a title but needs a wealthy wife; so he sets his sites on Katherine Merivale, who thinks the Earl is rich and is only helping her to make another man jealous.

To Pleasure a Prince. Pocket Star, 2005.
Reclusive Viscount Draker agrees to let Lady Regina's brother court his half-sister if Lady Regina will let him court her in this classic Beauty-and-the-Beast tale.

One Night with a Prince. Pocket Star, 2005.
A gaming club owner agrees to help a noblewoman regain some damaging letters in return for a barony (and to avenge himself on his father, the prince), and finds love and intrigue in the process.

School for Heiresses

An exclusive English school for wealthy girls is the connecting point for this lively historical series set during and just after the Regency Period. A thread of mystery about the school's mysterious benefactor, Cousin Michael, is not resolved until the final book in the series.

Never Seduce a Scoundrel. Pocket, 2006.
An adventurous young heiress gives English deportment lessons to a dashing American soldier who secretly is in England to find a crook.

Only a Duke Will Do. Pocket, 2006.
When a wealthy noblewoman discovers that her former suitor is courting her to enhance his political career, she plots her own brand of revenge.

Beware a Scot's Revenge. Pocket, 2007.
Kidnapped by a man she knew as a child but who is out to avenge himself on her father, Lady Venetia Campbell finds herself falling for her Scottish captor.

Let Sleeping Rogues Lie. Pocket, 2008.
A young teacher falls for an aristocratic rake who agrees to give her wealthy young charges lessons in how to avoid being taken advantage of by a rake.

Don't Bargain with the Devil. Pocket, 2009.
When Miss Harris's school is threatened by a neighbor's plans to turn his estate into a pleasure garden, instructor Lucinda Seton sets out to stop mesmerizing magician Diego Montalvo's plans.

Wed Him Before You Bed Him. Pocket, 2009.
Charlotte Harris learns the identity of her benefactor, Cousin Michael, and finds a love of her own in the final volume of this series.

The Hellions of Halstead Hall Series
Wild, rebellious, and slightly scandalous, the five Sharpe siblings are given an ultimatum by their grandmother: get their lives together and marry within a year or forfeit their inheritance.

The Truth about Lord Stoneville. Pocket, 2010.
The eldest son, Oliver, plans to derail his grandmother's plans by bringing home a "ladybird" as his fiancé but changes his plans when he comes to the aid of the lovely Maria Butterfield, an American who needs help finding her missing fiancé.

A Hellion in Her Bed. Pocket, 2010.
Jarret, the gambler of the group, makes a deal with his grandmother to run the family brewery for a year in exchange for being absolved of having to marry. He doesn't count on the enchanting brewster Annabel Lake—or her outrageous wager.

How to Woo a Reluctant Lady. Pocket, 2011.
Minerva's plan to become engaged to an unacceptable rogue backfires when she falls for the rakehell barrister who is the model for a spy in the gothic novels she writes.

To Wed a Wild Lord. Pocket Star, 2011.
A reckless lord meets his match when he strikes a daring bargain with a fearless heroine, who thinks she has every reason to hate him.

Johnston, Joan
Bitter Creek Series
The roots of this modern-day rivalry between the Blackthornes and the Creeds, Texas ranchers, dates to the Civil War. Many of these stories contain mystery elements and may fall within the Romantic Suspense subgenre.

The Cowboy. Dell, 2000.
The Texan. Island, 2001.
The Loner. Dell, 2002.
The Price. Pocket Star, 2003.
The Rivals. Pocket, 2004.
The Next Mrs. Blackthorne. Pocket, 2005.
A Stranger's Game. Pocket, 2008.
Shattered. Mira, 2010.

Krentz, Jayne Ann/Amanda Quick/Jayne Castle

Krentz has written a number of related books under her various pseudonyms. This is her most recent and one of the most creative. See also Jayne Castle in chapter 9, "Alternative Reality Romance."

Arcane Society Series

This unusual series is written under Krentz's various pseudonyms and follows the fortunes of the psychically gifted members of the Arcane Society over a number of centuries. Danger, mystery, passion, and humor are hallmarks of the books in this series. Note: Krentz writes Historicals as Quick, Contemporaries as Krentz, and Futuristics as Castle.

Second Sight. Putnam, 2006. (Quick)
Devastated when the death of a man who had employed her to photograph some rare Arcane Society artifacts—and with whom she had spent one glorious night—is announced in the papers, psychically gifted Venetia Milton adopts his last name and, as the respectable, widowed Mrs. Jones, launches her London photographic career. But when Gabriel Jones shows up alive and Venetia becomes a murder witness, they are forced to deal with a killer that only Venetia, with her aura-reading abilities, can identify.

White Lies. Putnam, 2007. (Krentz)
A pair of "unmatchable" Level Ten para-sensitives (she's a human lie detector and he's a psychic hunter) work together to find a diabolical villain in a story riddled with secrets, humor, and passion.

Sizzle and Burn. Putnam, 2008. (Krentz)
A psychic heroine who reads human emotions from inanimate objects by touch becomes the target of a witch hunter and is forced to trust a man her family has reason to hate.

The Third Circle. Putnam, 2008. (Quick)
Separately on the hunt for the legendary Aurora stone, a psychic crystal reader and a mesmerist realize they must work together to defeat a sadistic killer and a group of power-hungry psychics who want the stone for themselves.

Running Hot. Putnam, 2008. (Krentz)
A former cop and a librarian who zeroes in on auras are sent to Maui as honeymooners on a routine mission and find there's a lot more going on, including Nightshade involvement, than they expected.

The Perfect Poison. Putnam, 2009. (Quick)
A botanist with expertise in rare plant poisons hires a fellow member of the Arcane society to help her find the real killer of a man she is suspected of poisoning.

Dreamlight Trilogy

Thanks to the insane meddling of their long-ago Arcane Society ancestor, the male members of the Winters family run the risk of developing multiple talents and, thus, going mad—unless the Burning Lamp and a powerful dreamlight reader can be found to work its mind-saving energy. The Dreamlight Trilogy is a series within the Arcane Society series that includes titles written in each of Krentz's writing names.

Fired Up. Putnam, 2010 (Krentz)
Fearing he will become a victim of the Winters's curse of madness, Jack Winters hires P.I. and dreamlight reader Chloe Harper to find the Burning Lamp and work its energy so he won't fall victim to the curse.

Burning Lamp. Putnam, 2010 (Quick)
A social activist dreamlight reader and a crime boss who has already achieved his second talent and is afraid of going mad, finally strike a deal that will satisfy them both in the shadowy stews of Victorian London.

9

Midnight Crystal. Jove, 2010. (Castle)
The dreamlight curse is taken care of on the planet of Harmony when the head of the ghost hunters guild and a master dreamlight reader solve its mystery.

10

Looking Glass Trilogy
Deadly, beautifully crafted clockwork toys that were created by gifted Victorian inventor, Millicent Bridewell, turn lethal in this lively series that includes three stories, each written under a different one of Krentz's writing names.

In Too Deep. Putnam, 2010. (Krentz)
A woman on the run and a powerful chaos-theory talent finds plenty of paranormal trouble and unexpected love in tiny Scargill Cove.

11

Quicksilver. Putnam, 2011. (Quick)
Beautiful, lethal clockwork toys, mirrors, and murder are the order of the day in this fast-paced tale.

Canyons of Night. Putnam, 2011. (Castle)
The dangerous and mysterious preserve on Rainshadow Island holds secrets, answers, and dangers for an antique expert and a psychic hunter in the final volume of this trilogy, which also presages another futuristic series to come.

12

Laurens, Stephanie
Laurens is noted for her sexy historical adventures, most of which are grouped into several interrelated series. Many of these have been reprinted.

13

Cynster Family Series
Following the doings of the rather notorious Cynster family during the years of and following the English Regency, this ongoing series currently includes fifteen novels. The first six books in the series are about the Cynster cousins, or Bar Cynster. The remainder focus on extended family and friends of the Cynsters. The last three are a trilogy about the Cynster sisters.

14

Devil's Bride. Avon, 1998.
A Rake's Vow. Avon, 1998.
Scandal's Bride. Avon, 1999.
A Rogue's Proposal. Avon, 1999.
A Secret Love. Avon, 2000.
All about Love. Avon, 2001.
All about Passion. Avon, 2001.

15

The Promise in a Kiss. Avon, 2001.
This is a special Christmas book about the Cynster couple that began it all, the Duke and Duchess of St. Ives. It is a prequel and is not one of the numbered Cynster books.

16

On a Wild Night. Avon, 2002.
On a Wicked Dawn. Avon, 2002.
The Perfect Lover. Avon, 2003.
The Ideal Bride. Avon, 2004.

The Truth about Love. Avon, 2005.
What Price Love? Avon, 2006.
The Taste of Innocence. Avon, 2007.
Temptation and Surrender. Avon, 2009.
Viscount Breckenridge to the Rescue. Avon, 2011.
In Pursuit of Eliza Cynster. Avon, 2011.
The Capture of the Earl of Glencrae. Avon, 2012.

The Bastion Club

A group of seven highly eligible bachelors, who were part of the Secret Service of the Crown, form a club dedicated to their right to determine their own marital futures.

Captain Jack's Woman. Avon, 1997.
Series prequel.

The Lady Chosen. Avon, 2003.
Agreeing to keep an eye on the renovation of the Bastion Club's new house, the Earl of Trenton is attracted to the woman who lives next door, Leonora Carling, in the first official book in the series.

A Gentleman's Honor. Avon, 2003.
Posing as a widow, "Mrs. Carrington," in order to launch her lovely young sister into society, Alicia's plans run into trouble when she is suspected of murder and Viscount Torrington takes over the investigation.

A Lady of His Own. Avon, 2004.
While investigating smuggling operations near his home in Cornwall, Charles St. Austell renews a relationship with Lady Penelope Selborne and finds secrets and deception in the bargain.

A Fine Passion. Avon, 2005.
Baron Warnefleet is puzzled when he finds a beautiful, most eligible young woman rusticating in the country—and then he learns the dangerous reason for her presence.

To Distraction. Avon, 2006.
In need of a wife, Viscount Paignton takes his aunt's advice and charms vibrant Phoebe Malleson, a woman with a cause, and a woman who is in danger, and a woman who has no wish to marry.

Beyond Seduction. Avon, 2007.
A nobleman bows to his sisters' desires and agrees to marry a suitable local woman, if one can be found in Cornwall, and ends up falling for the lovely Madeline Gascoigne, in spite of his efforts to prove that they are totally incompatible.

The Edge of Desire. Avon, 2008.
A woman who married another while the hero was away at war asks him for help; he agrees, but has his own plans for revenge in this story that highlights the importance of communication.

Mastered by Love. Avon, 2009.
The mysterious leader of the Bastion Club, "Dalziel" Royce Varisey, Tenth Duke of Wolverstone, meets his fate in the arms of none other than his castle's chatelaine, Minerva Chesterton.

Black Cobra Quartet

A group of fearless, heroic military officers of the Crown who served together in India before they resigned their commissions, set out to stop a diabolical villain known as the Black Cobra, the head of a cult that has been ravaging India and threatens England, as well, in this series that combines political intrigue, adventure, and fiery, earthy sex.

The Untamed Bride. Avon, 2009.
Heading home to England after planning with his three comrades to take separate routes home to throw the enemy off, Colonel Derek "Del" Delborough is thrown together with the impossible, irresistible Deliah Duncannon as they try to elude the cultists who have followed them.

The Elusive Bride. Avon, 2010.
When a brief meeting with handsome Major Gareth Hamilton causes Emily Ensworth, the niece of the Governor of Bombay, to follow him on his way to England, a cultist attack forces them to stay together for their own safety.

The Brazen Bride. Avon, 2010.
Shipwrecked, wounded, and with no memory, Logan Monteith is rescued by Linnet Trevisson, who eventually accompanies him on his mission to deliver information to England.

The Reckless Bride. Avon, 2010.
Various characters from previous novels make an appearance and Rafe Carstairs and Loretta Michelmarsh find romance as this quartet is wrapped up with a few surprises.

Lee, Rachel (Pseudonym for Sue Civil-Brown)

Lee is a veteran writer of many Contemporary Romances, including her enduringly popular Conard County series. Her Romances often include suspense and mystery aspects, feature Native American characters, and may have a touch of the paranormal.

Conard County (Wyoming) Series

A popular contemporary series of interrelated stories set in the wide, open spaces of Conard County, Wyoming. (Many of these have been reprinted.)

Exile's End. Silhouette Intimate Moments, 1992.
Cherokee Thunder. Silhouette Intimate Moments, 1992.
Miss Emmaline and the Archangel. Silhouette Intimate Moments, 1993.
Ironheart. Silhouette Intimate Moments, 1993.
Lost Warriors. Silhouette Intimate Moments, 1993.
Point of No Return. Silhouette Intimate Moments, 1994.
Thunder Mountain. Silhouette Shadows, 1994.
A Question of Justice. Silhouette Intimate Moments, 1994.
A Conard County Reckoning. Silhouette, 1996.
Nighthawk. Silhouette Intimate Moments, 1997.
Cowboy Comes Home. Silhouette Intimate Moments, 1998.
The Catch of Conard County. Silhouette, 1998.
Conard County: Boots and Badges. Silhouette, 1999.
A collection of four novellas.
Involuntary Daddy. Silhouette Intimate Moments, 1999.

"The Dream Marine," (a novella in *The Hearts Command*) Silhouette, 2002.
A Marine returns from the Middle East and considers giving up his military career but is reminded of what it means to be a true hero.

"I'll Be Home." (A novella in *A Soldier's Christmas*) HQN, 2004.
A Navy SEAL resigned to being alone finds love waiting for him in the middle of a blizzard.

A Soldier for All Seasons. (published as part of a duet: *Holiday Heroes*) Silhouette Romantic Suspense, 2007.
A park ranger and a Marine who is home for the holidays are snowed in during a blizzard and find love, as well as the peace each is hoping to find.

A Soldier's Homecoming. Silhouette Romantic Suspense, 2008.
A disillusioned soldier comes to town to connect with his roots and finds healing and love with a sheriff's deputy and her young daughter, and a bit of suspense, as well.

Protector of One. Silhouette Romantic Suspense, 2009.
A woman ends up as a killer's target when an accident leaves her with psychic abilities.

The Unexpected Hero. Silhouette Romantic Suspense, 2009.
A doctor is attracted to a nurse practitioner who is suspected of murder when patients begin to die.

The Man from Nowhere. Silhouette Romantic Suspense, 2010.
Having failed to act on a premonition, with disastrous results, Grant Wolfe is determined to save accountant Trish Devlin from a similar fate—if only she will take him seriously.

Her Hero in Hiding. Silhouette Romantic Suspense, 2010.
Running from a lethally abusive boyfriend, Kay Young is rescued by writer and former soldier Clint Ardmore who shelters her at his isolated ranch and is determined to protect her when danger threatens once again.

No Ordinary Hero. Silhouette Romantic Suspense, 2011.
A Native American veterinarian caught between science and his cultural beliefs finds romance when he agrees to help a widow get to the bottom of the strange things going on at her house.

Mahon, Annette

Mahon writes sweet, Hawaiian-set Romances, some of which are Linked Romances. See chapter 12, "Ethnic/Multicultural Romance."

Michaels, Fern

Although Michaels is now best-known for her popular Revenge of the Sisterhood series, the Kentucky series below continues the stories begun in her earlier Vegas and Texas series about the Thornton and the Coleman families. (See the previous edition of this book for title information on the earlier series.) See also chapter 5, "Contemporary Romance."

Kentucky

Set amid the rarified horseracing world, this series continues the sagas of the Coleman families and focuses on independent, resilient Nealy Coleman Diamond.

Kentucky Rich. Zebra, 2001.
Kentucky Heat. Zebra, 2002.
Kentucky Sunrise. Zebra, 2002.

Michaels, Kasey

Michaels has written in a wide variety of Romance subgenres; these are some of her more recent Romance series.

Romney Marsh

This Regency Era series chronicles the lives, loves, and various adventures of the Becket siblings (adopted and otherwise) of Romney Marsh.

A Gentleman by Any Other Name. HQN, 2006.
Chance Becket needs a nanny for his daughter while he tracks the smugglers along the coast for the War Office and engages lovely Julia Carruthers to do the job.

The Dangerous Debutante, HQN, 2006.
Beautiful, independent Morgan Becket heads for the season in London and meets her fate in arms of the wild, dangerous Earl of Aylesford in this story that is dark and filled with secrets and misunderstandings.

Beware of Virtuous Women. HQN, 2006.
Confirmed spinster Eleanor Becket attracts the attention of a man who sees her worth, Jack Eastwood.

A Most Unsuitable Groom. HQN, 2007.
Wounded in the War of 1812, Spencer Becket returns home and is forced to marry Mariah Rutledge, who is pregnant with a child he's not sure is his.

A Reckless Beauty. HQN, 2007.
Fanny Becket follows her brother to Waterloo dressed as a man and is rescued by the Earl of Brede.

Return of the Prodigal. HQN, 2007.
Rain Becket is nursed back to health after a Waterloo wound by a lovely woman who is working for someone who wants to destroy the Beckets.

Becket's Last Stand. HQN, 2007.
Cassandra Becket and her adopted brother, Courtland, find love in this final volume that answers the lingering questions of the series.

Daughtry Family Series

Featuring a special e-book prequel, *How to Woo a Spinster* (2009), this Regency era series focuses on the loves and adventures of the Daughtry family.

How to Tempt a Duke. HQN, 2009.
A pair of childhood friends find love when the hero returns from war as a duke in this lively story that also features a bit of a mystery.

How to Tame a Lady. HQN, 2009.
Treachery and deception are part of this lively Romance that links a lady who's given up on love and a nobleman who is out for revenge.

How to Beguile a Beauty. HQN, 2010.
A nobleman tries to honor his battlefield promise to a friend to take care of the friend's sweetheart by finding a suitable husband for her—but it's hard when he really wants her for himself.

How to Wed a Baron. HQN, 2010.
When the Prince Regent commands, one usually obeys, which results in the marriage of a noted rake to a fiery beauty—and a bit of a mystery that the unwilling bride vows to solve.

Miller, Linda Lael

Miller has written in a variety of Romance subgenres; many of her Contemporary and Historical Romances have a Western flavor and most are parts of family-linked series, many of which contain both Contemporary and Historical Romances and several examples are listed below.

McKettrick Family Series

This series focuses on the many generations of the McKettrick ranching family of the Triple M Ranch near Indian Rock, Arizona, and later Blue River, Texas. Note: Although this series began as a trilogy, it quickly took on a life of its own and includes several trilogies within the larger series.

High Country Bride. Pocket, 2002.
When he and his two brothers, Kade and Jeb, are told by their father, Angus, that the first one to marry and have a baby will inherit the ranch, Rafe McKettrick sends for a mail-order bride—Emmaline Harding, who grew up, innocently, in her aunt's brothel.

Shotgun Bride. Pocket Star, 2003.
Marshall Kade McKettrick has an abundance of mail-order brides at his disposal, but he's dealing with an outlaw gang and is attracted to the step-daughter of the leader of said gang.

Secondhand Bride. Pocket, 2004.
Jeb McKettrick quickly marries school teacher Chloe Wakefield, only to learn she supposedly has a husband—or does she?

McKettrick's Choice. HQN, 2006.
Holt McKettrick drops everything to go to Texas to keep Gabe McKettrick from being hanged and falls for independent Lorelei Fellows, the owner of the neighboring ranch.

Sierra's Homecoming. HQN, 2006.
Sierra McKettrick takes her asthmatic son to live on the old McKettrick ranch and is attracted to handsome Travis Reid in this Romance that juxtaposes this modern-day romance with a parallel love story set in 1919.

McKettrick's Luck. HQN, 2007.
Cheyenne Bridges comes to Indian Rock to convince Jesse McKettrick to sell some land for a condo development and falls in love with both Jesse and the town.

McKettrick's Pride. HQN, 2007.
Still mourning his wife's death, single dad Rance McKettrick has no wish to remarry, until he meets bookstore owner Echo Wells, who is nothing like his former wife.

McKettrick's Heart. HQN, 2007.
Keegan McKettrick is suspicious of Molly Shields when she comes to town at the request of the dying woman who adopted her son, but he is attracted to her, as well.

The McKettrick Way. Silhouette Special Edition, 2007.
Meg McKettrick wants Brad O'Ballivan to be the father of her baby, but she's not interested in marriage; Brad has other ideas.

A McKettrick Christmas. HQN, 2008.
When an avalanche strands Lizzie McKettrick's train on her way home for Christmas, the resulting crisis—and how her citified-fiancé handles things—causes her to rethink her future marriage plans in this Historical Romance with slight paranormal elements.

9

McKettricks of Texas: Tate. HQN, 2010.
Divorced dad Tate McKettrick and Libby Remington have their lives full enough without having to deal with each other, but Tate blew their relationship once before, and nothing is going to stop him from claiming Libby's love this time.

10

McKettricks of Texas: Garrett. HQN, 2010.
Fast-living Garrett McKettrick returns home to reassess his life and is drawn to a divorced mom teacher he knew in high school.

McKettricks of Texas: Austin. HQN, 2010.

11

Montana Creeds
Three cowboy brothers, estranged since their father's funeral, return to the neglected family ranch and reconcile their differences. Note: The brothers are cousins to the McKettrick clan.

Logan. HQN, 2009.
Former rodeo star and wealthy attorney Logan comes home to restore the ranch and meets a divorced mom and her two sons who are living in one of his brother's houses on the ranch.

12

Dylan. HQN, 2009.
When former rodeo rider Dylan finds his two-year-old daughter left by her irresponsible mom in his truck in Las Vegas one night, he takes young Bonnie and heads for the ranch, eventually reconnecting a woman from his past, now the town librarian.

13

Tyler. HQN, 2009.
Rodeo star Tyler returns to the ranch, finds a teenaged boy taking refuge in his deserted house, and eventually is reunited with his high school love.

A Creed Country Christmas. HQN, 2009.
This historical prequel to the contemporary series pairs single dad rancher Lincoln Creed with school teacher Juliana Mitchell in a warm, holiday Romance.

14

Moore, Kate
Moore also wrote well-crafted traditional Regency Romances.

Sons of Sin
The three sons of a noted London courtesan are the heroes in this creative, sensual trilogy that provides a new look at the Regency Period and tantalizes readers with an ongoing mystery, as well.

15

To Tempt a Saint. Berkley Sensation, 2010.
A man who dreams of lighting up the rookery of St. Giles and getting rid of crime and a woman who must wed to gain her inheritance marry, never thinking that this will be more than a convenience to them both. Naturally, they are wrong.

16

To Save the Devil. Berkley Sensation, 2010.
A former Bow Street runner buys lovely, terrified "Helen of Troy" to save her virtue, but keeping her safe, especially since they are both after the same wicked blackmailer, will be harder than he expects.

To Seduce an Angel. Berkley Sensation, 2011.
Danger awaits the youngest of the three brothers when he becomes heir to a dukedom and hires a young woman to teach the young boys in his care.

Owens, Robin D.
See chapter 9, "Alternative Reality Romance."

Putney, Mary Jo
A noted writer of various kinds of Romances, Putney is best known for her exquisite Regency-set Historicals.

Silk Trilogy
This trilogy makes use of a number of exotic settings during the 1840s. All of these have been reprinted.

Silk and Shadows. New American Library, 1991.
Silk and Secrets. Onyx, 1992.
Veils of Silk. Onyx, 1992.

Fallen Angels Series
Featuring brave, dangerous spies, this is one of Putney's most popular series; many of these novels are in the process of being reprinted.

Thunder and Roses. Topaz, 1993. (Republished as *Fallen Angel*, 2009.)
Petals in the Storm. Topaz, 1993. (A revision of the traditional Regency *The Controversial Countess*.)
Dancing on the Wind. Topaz, 1994.
Angel Rogue. Topaz, 1995. (A revision of the traditional Regency *The Rogue and the Runaway*.)
Shattered Rainbows. Topaz, 1996.
River of Fire. Signet, 1996.
One Perfect Rose. Fawcett Columbine, 1997.

The Bride Trilogy
Linked by character, this exotic trilogy is set primarily in the 1830s.

The Wild Child. Ballantine, 1999.
A nobleman stands in for his absent twin in a marriage to a mentally withdrawn woman and finds love with the Lady in spite of himself.

The China Bride. Ballantine, 2000.
A Eurasian woman poses as a man so she can work as a translator and finds love with an English nobleman in search of a forbidden temple.

The Bartered Bride. Ballantine, 2002.
A British shipping magnate rescues an enslaved Englishwoman through combat with a wily island ruler and finds danger, as well as love, as they return to England.

Lost Lords Series
This Regency-set series is linked by boys, now men, who bonded while at school. (Note: *One Perfect Rose* has links to this series, as well.)

Loving a Lost Lord. Zebra, 2009.
When a man with no memory washes up on her shore, Mariah Clarke claims his as her long-lost husband (and the answer to her prayers so she can avoid marriage to a totally

undesirable man), not knowing that he is actually the Duke of Ashton, presumed lost at sea when his steamship exploded.

Never Less than a Lady. Zebra, 2010.
A woman blamed by her father-in-law, the Earl of Daventry, for the murder of her first husband escapes and lives quietly in the country until circumstances bring the new heir to the title into her life with all the attendant problems and joys.

No Where Near Respectable. Zebra, 2011.
A spirited half-Hindu/half-English princess and a gaming club owner find love when they work together to foil a plot against the crown.

Quinn, Julia

Quinn is a popular writer of light, often gently humorous, Historicals set during and near the time of the English Regency. Note: Many of her characters make repeat performances in various books, although they are not necessarily parts of official series.

Bridgerton Series

This, her most popular series, focuses on the eight Bridgerton siblings and is set during the English Regency period.

The Duke and I. Avon, 2000.
Daphne Bridgerton and Simon Bassett, Duke of Hastings, agree to a pretend courtship in order to avoid the manipulations of matchmakers and are surprised when they fall in love.

The Viscount Who Loved Me. Avon, 2000.
Anthony Bridgerton has decided to marry young Edwina Sheffield, but he reckons with her older sister, Kate, who is not about to let her little sister marry such a disreputable rake.

An Offer from a Gentleman. Avon, 2001.
Forced into a Cinderella-like existence by her stepmother and stepsisters, Sophie Beckett, with the help of sympathetic servants, attends a masquerade ball and attracts the attention of Benedict Bridgerton—and then disappears.

Romancing Mr. Bridgerton. Avon, 2002.
Penelope Featherington has loved the older Colin Bridgerton since she was a girl, but now, at twenty-eight, she is resigned to spinsterhood—until Colin returns from traveling and sees her in a very different light.

To Sir Phillip, with Love. Avon, 2003.
Eloise Bridgerton, another confirmed spinster, impulsively heads to London to meet her pen pal, botanist Sir Phillip Crane, who has just proposed marriage only to learn he is the father of twins and is nothing like she had imagined.

When He Was Wicked. Avon, 2004.
After mourning her husband for four years, Francesca Bridgerton rejoins the polite world and finds love with the man who has loved her in silence for years, Michael Stirling. This book is darker and more intense than Quinn's usual romps.

It's in His Kiss. Avon, 2005.
Brainy, headstrong Hyacinth Bridgerton agrees to help Gareth St. Clair translate his Italian grandmother's diary, an activity that leads to adventurous escapades, as well as love.

On the Way to the Wedding. Avon, 2006.
Gregory Bridgerton, who wants to marry only for love, sets his sites on a woman who loves someone else. But when her best friend, Lucy Abernathy, agrees to help him in his quest, he finds love where he least expected.

The Lost Duke of Wyndham Duo

The same events are seen from two different perspectives in this clever Regency tale.

The Lost Duke of Wyndham. Avon, 2008.
A highwayman is identified as the possible Lost Duke of Wyndham throws everyone's lives into chaos.

Mr. Cavendish, I Presume. Avon, 2009.
The man who thought he'd inherit the title has his life changed in fascinating, but ultimately satisfactory, ways.

Bevelstoke Series

This series focuses on various Bevelstoke family members, assorted relations, and friends.

The Secret Diaries of Miss Miranda Cheever. Avon, 2007.
A young woman sets out to claim the love of the now bitter, disillusioned man she fell in love with as a ten-year-old.

What Happens in London. Avon, 2009.
A curious debutante watching from her window attracts the attention of the nobleman next door, who is then charged by the War Office to keep an eye on her because she is being courted by a Russian prince suspected of being a spy.

Ten Things I Love About You. Avon, 2010.
Expected to marry a repulsive elderly earl for her family's sake, Annabel Winslow is drawn to Sebastian Grey, a closet Romance author and the earl's heir, instead, creating a volatile situation for everyone.

Roberts, Nora

In addition to her numerous individual titles, Roberts has produced numerous groups of linked books. Three favorites are listed here. See also chapter 6, "Romantic Mysteries," chapter 5, "Contemporary Romance," and chapter 9, "Alternative Reality Romance."

Born in . . . Trilogy (Concannon Trilogy)

Set primarily in Western Ireland, this is one of Roberts's most memorable "sisters" trilogies.

Born in Fire. Jove, 1994.
Born in Ice. Jove, 1995.
Born in Shame. Jove, 1996.

Chesapeake Bay Saga

This series features the Quinn family. The first three were originally known as the Quinn Brothers Trilogy.

Sea Swept. Jove, 1998.
Champion boat racer Cameron Quinn is called home by his dying father to provide a home for young Seth, a boy his father has taken in, just as he and his wife took Cameron and his brothers in years earlier.

Rising Tides. Jove, 1998.
Fisherman Ethan Quinn relies on single parent Grace Monroe to help him with Seth when Cameron is on his honeymoon in this story that brings two wounded characters together with love and healing.

Inner Harbor. Jove, 1999.
Businessman Phillip Quinn is attracted to writer/psychologist Sybil Griffin who claims she's researching their family for a book—and then he learns she's Seth's biological aunt and could destroy their family.

Chesapeake Blue. G. P. Putnam's Sons, 2002.
Seth, now a world-famous artist, returns from Europe and falls for florist Dru Banks.

Three Sisters Island Trilogy
Three powerful women come together on Three Sisters Island to destroy the ancient evil that threatens the magically protected island in this paranormal trilogy.

Dance upon the Air. Jove, 2001.
Arriving at Three Sisters Island after faking her own death to escape a violent, abusive husband, Nell Channing gradually settles in, attracts the attentions of Sheriff Zach Todd, and comes to realize that she has a part to play breaking the island's ancient curse.

Heaven and Earth. Jove, 2001.
Deputy Ripley Todd rejected her powers years ago, but when researcher MacAllister Booke arrives to explore the rumors of witchcraft on the island, she realizes she must accept who she is, if she is to help the others save the island and have a future with the man she has come to love.

Face the Fire. Jove, 2002.
Sam Devlin returns to the island to find the woman he's never forgotten, Mia Devlin, and is caught up in the final battle that will decide the fate of the island and its inhabitants forever.

Sands, Lynsay
Argeneau and Rogue Hunter Series
Focusing on the vampire members of the Argeneau Family, this lively series with chick lit flair is one of the first to treat vampires with humor and sass. The Rogue Hunter books are a series within a series and focus on rogue hunters (vampires who hunt down murderous rogue vampires) but are linked to the Argeneau vampire world.

Argeneau Family Series
Single White Vampire. Love Spell, 2003.
When reclusive vampire Lucern Argeneau pens his family's history, the books become bestsellers as Paranormal Romances, and now he must deal with a very pushy, attractive editor, Kate Leever, who insists he meet his public at a Romantic Times Conference.

Love Bites. Love Spell, 2004.
Coroner Rachel Garrett takes a hit meant for vampire Etienne Argeneau and ends up immortal when he "turns" her to save her.

Tall, Dark, and Hungry. Love Spell, 2004.
Terri Simpson comes to England to be in Kate's wedding and ends up staying in the family penthouse with Bastien Argeneau; the results are funny and romantic.

A Quick Bite. Avon, 2005.
Lissianna Argeneau's mom hopes that psychologist Greg Hewitt can help her with her blood phobia but things don't go as expected in this sexy story that, according to the author, should have been the first book in the series.

A Bite to Remember. Avon, 2006.
Human P.I. Jackie Morrisey intends to keep vampire Vincent Argeneau safe from an assailant who would turn him back to dust, but when she accidentally swallows some vampire blood, she begins to turn, herself.

Bite Me, if You Can. Avon, 2007.
When jaded Lucian Argeneau rescues Leigh Gerard from a rogue vampire who has already bitten her, he realizes he must help her learn to live as an immortal—and then he realizes he's no longer bored.

The Accidental Vampire. Avon, 2008.
Elvi Black is having a hard time learning the ways of the vamp world ever since she was accidentally turned—and then she meets Victor Argeneau, a man who can teach her everything she needs to know, as well as keep her safe.

Vampires Are Forever. Avon, 2008.
Thomas Argeneau is tapped to search for the missing family matriarch, Marguerite, and he is aided by Inez Urso, an Argeneau Enterprises vice president, who turns out to be his life-mate.

Vampire Interrupted. Avon, 2008.
It's Marguerite Argeneau's turn to find a life-mate, and although a bad five-hundred-year marriage has made her wary, Julius Notte may just be the one in this story that features older, more mature characters with plenty of past issues.

Rogue Hunter Series

The Rogue Hunter. Avon, 2008.
Decompressing from her workaholic life in a cottage in the country, lawyer Samantha Willan is attracted to her sexy neighbor, rogue hunter Garrett Mortimer, who has some very odd habits.

The Immortal Hunter. Avon, 2009.
Rogue hunter Decker Argeneau saves Dr. Danielle McGill from rogues and realizes he's saved his life-mate.

The Renegade Hunter. Avon, 2009.
Once a hunter but now a renegade, Nicholas Argeneau saves Josephine Willan from a rogue and finds a woman willing to fight for him in this story that begs for a sequel to answer a number of questions.

Taylor, Janelle
Taylor is best known for her early Gray Eagle/Alisha series (or Ecstasy series) of historical Native American Romances. See chapter 12, "Ethnic/Multicultural Romance."

Ware, Joss
Awakening Heroes Series
The Earth as we know it has been destroyed and reordered though violent earthquakes that were caused by a group of power-hungry people who wanted immortality. Now, after fifty years, a group of men who were protected in a cave in Sedona, Arizona, awake into this post-apocalyptic world and find they have mysterious powers. Envy is

the popular name for N.V. or New Vegas, the city that was Las Vegas and houses the survivors but is now located on the Pacific Ocean. This is a dark, fascinating series.

Beyond the Night. Avon 2010.
A doctor who awoke to this strange new world to find that he has an enhanced ability to heal is attracted to a woman, Jade, who was brutally held by the "immortals" and is bent on revenge.

Embrace the Night Eternal. Avon, 2010.
A man with a violent past enters the "new world" and learns he has the power to become invisible, a talent that will help him save both a town and Sage Corrigan, the woman who loves him despite his unsavory past.

Abandon the Night. Avon, 2010.
A pair on a mission of vengeance learn the truth about the devastation and the people responsible.

Wiggs, Susan
Lakeshore Chronicles
Tiny Avalon on the shores of Willow Lake in the Catskills is the setting for the varied stories in this touching, compelling, often wise, series that revolves around members and friends of the wealthy Bellamy family.

Summer at Willow Lake. Mira, 2006.
A woman returns to Willow Lake to prepare her family's Camp Kioga for her grandmother's fiftieth wedding anniversary and reconnects with a man from her past.

The Winter Lodge. Mira, 2007.
When her grandmother dies and her home burns down, a food columnist temporarily moves in with the police chief to sort things out. Food, romance, and a bit of mystery add to the mix.

Dockside. Mira, 2007.
A single mom who'd wanted to buy the old inn at Willow Lake herself reluctantly agrees to manage it for the wealthy single dad who owns it. A reunion story with realistic complications.

Snowfall at Willow Lake. Mira, 2008.
A high-powered lawyer reconsiders her life after almost being killed and heads to Willow Lake in order to reconnect with her two children where she finds unexpected romance with a man who's younger than she is.

Fireside. Mira, 2009.
A celebrity sports publicist helps a baseball player on the verge of a breakout polish up his image as he learns he's a father to a son he's just met.

Lakeshore Christmas. Mira, 2009.
A librarian who adores Christmas is forced to work as codirector of the annual pageant with a former celebrity who hates the holiday in this gently mystical Romance that overflows with small town charm.

The Summer Hideaway. Mira, 2010.
Suffering from a brain tumor, George Bellamy returns to Willow Lake to make peace with his brother Charles before he dies, and, in addition, engineers a match

between his grandson Ross and his private-duty nurse, Claire Turner, a woman with secrets of her own.

Marrying Daisy Bellamy. Mira, 2011.
Daisy's world—and marriage—is is thrown into chaos when the man she's always loved but thought dead returns from captivity.

Willig, Lauren
The Pink Carnation Series

This engaging series follows the loves and adventures of those connected to "England's most elusive spy," the Pink Carnation, and their efforts to thwart Napoleon and his deadly "bouquet" of spies, in particular the Black Tulip. Researcher Eloise Kelly is the contemporary anchor for this lively series that alternates between the adventures of the historical characters and Eloise's modern-day life and relationship with English aristocrat Colin Selwick.

The Secret History of the Pink Carnation. Dutton, 2005.
Eloise finds the stash of letters about the Pink Carnation and readers are swept into their story.

The Masque of the Black Tulip. Dutton, 2006.
Henrietta Selway and Miles Dorrington go in search of a deadly French spy who's targeting the Pink Carnation.

The Deception of the Emerald Ring. Dutton, 2006.
Letty Alsworthy jumps into the fray when her new husband, Geoffrey Pinchingdale-Snipe, heads for Ireland to deal with an uprising and a deadly plot.

The Seduction of the Crimson Rose. Dutton, 2008.
Mary Alsworthy turns seductive spy and catches the romantic attentions of her mentor, English Lord Vaughn.

The Temptation of the Night Jasmine. Dutton, 2009.
The Duke of Dovedale and Lady Charlotte Landsowne find love and adventure as he searches for a killer.

The Betrayal of the Blood Lily. Dutton, 2010.
Forced into marriage and sent off to India, Penelope Staines, not trusting her husband, bonds with Captain Alex Reid as they are drawn into the search for a dangerous spy called Marigold.

*The Mischief of Mistletoe: A Pink Carnation Christmas. Dutton, 2010.
Inept Turnip Fitzhugh visits his sister at her boarding school and finds danger, adventure, and love with schoolmistress Arabella Dempsey in this holiday romp that is set between *The Seduction of Crimson Rose* and *The Temptation of the Night Jasmine*.

Multiauthored Series

While most series are written by a single author, some series are developed by either publishers or groups of writers and include books written by a number of writers. Several recent examples are listed below.

2176

This five-book Futuristic series involves time travel and features capable, take-charge heroines who struggle to bring democracy back to the repressive world in which they find themselves and find love in the process.

Grant, Susan. *The Legend of Banzai Maguire*. Love Spell, 2004.
Fighter pilot Banzai Maguire and her wingman, Cam, are shot down over North Korea, put in suspended animation by a crazed scientist, and wake up in 2176 to a world of limited freedoms and great technological advances.

Nance, Kathleen. *Day of Fire*. Love Spell, 2004.
Canada, now free of the viruses that terrorists unleashed on it years earlier, is ready to open its borders once more when a new small pox virus is discovered and a Mountie and a plague hunter must team up to stop it from becoming another epidemic.

Maverick, Liz. *The Shadow Runners*. Love Spell, 2004.
The dumping ground for criminals, dissidents, and toxic waste, Australia is also the home of the Shadow Voice (think Voice of America), but when the voice goes silent, Deck convinces Jenny Red, one of the few to ever escape that prison, to help him get in and then to the Outback so he can complete his mission for the Shadow Runners.

O'Shea, Patti. *The Power of Two*. Love Spell, 2004.
A Special Forces operative, Jake Tucker, is stunned to learn that the "computer" he has been mentally linked to for years is actually a woman, Cai Randolph.

Grant, Susan. *The Scarlet Empress*. Love Spell, 2004.
Cam Tucker, Banzai's wingman, searches for Banzai but finds love with a most unexpected person in the final installment of this series which neatly ties everything up.

Bridesmaids Chronicles
A funny, occasionally serious, quartet that focuses on one wedding as seen through different eyes.

Kendall, Karen. *First Date*. Signet, 2005.
A woman heads to Texas to stop her younger sister from marrying a man she hardly knows and is attracted to the prospective groom's best friend.

Adams, Kylie. *First Kiss*. Signet, 2005.
Caught in a compromising situation, an employed actress takes refuge from the paparazzi in a rather notorious hotel and finds love with the owner.

Kendall, Karen. *First Dance*. Signet, 2005.
In Texas to make sure her friend gets a pre-nup, a tough New York lawyer reunites with her ex-lover, who is the groom's attorney and best friend.

Kenner, Julie. *First Love*. Signet, 2005.
Family members descend and planning disasters plague the wedding, but all is sorted out in the end.

Crimson City
In the city that was once Los Angeles, a variety of beings (werewolves, vampires, demons, humans, and otherwise) coexist uneasily, trying to maintain peace in the face of various threats. This series combines Romance, Science Fiction, and Fantasy, with a bit of cyberpunk thrown in for good measure.

Maverick, Liz. *Crimson City*. Love Spell, 2005.
Liu, Marjorie M. *A Taste of Crimson*. Love Spell, 2005.

O'Shea, Patti. *Through a Crimson Veil*. Love Spell, 2005.
Jewel, Carolyn. *A Darker Crimson*. Love Spell, 2005.
Lee, Jade. *Seduced by Crimson*. Love Spell, 2006.

Maverick, Liz. *Crimson Rogue*. Love Spell, 2006.
Shards of Crimson. Love Spell, 2007.
This anthology includes stories by Liz Maverick, Patti O'Shea, Carolyn Jewel, and Jade Lee.

Maverick, Liz. *Crimson & Steam*. Love Spell, 2010.
A deadly virus that is killing vampires leads journalist Jill to the research of a Victorian scientist in this story that adds a steam punk element as it switches back and forth between Jill's issues and relationships in Crimson City and rose engineer Charlotte's in 1850s England.

TAKE FIVE!

Five favorite Linked Romances:

- **Mary Balogh**—The Simply Quartet
- **Rachel Lee**—Conard County (Wyoming)
- **Kate Moore**—Sons of Sin Trilogy
- **Nora Roberts**—Born in . . . Trilogy: *Born in Fire, Born in Ice, Born in Shame*
- **Crimson City** (a multiauthored series)

Chapter 14

Erotic Romance

Definition

> **Erotic Romance**—Romance novels—complete with happy endings—in which the love relationship between the protagonists develops through and is inextricably linked to sexual interaction which is explicitly described.

Erotic Romance is one of the newest, or at least one of the most newly recognized, of the Romance subgenres and, as of this writing, there is a struggle to correct some popular misconceptions about it. Although often labeled and marketed as such, Erotic Romance is not Erotica. Neither is it pornography of any kind, which solely intends to sexually arouse the reader, nor is it necessarily just "sexy romance," which, according to some, is romance with explicit sex that is not critical to the plotline. All these types of stories are sexually explicit, but there is where most similarities end. There has been plenty of discussion on the topic, particularly among writers and librarians, and while there are slight differences of opinion, most agree that *Erotic Romance* is essentially a romance—complete with happy ending—in which the love relationship between the protagonists develops through and is inextricably linked to sexual interaction which is explicitly described.

Erotica, on the other hand, focuses on the individual sexual journeys of the characters, and neither a romantic relationship nor a happy ending is required. As more than one person has commented, "Erotic Romance is about the romantic relationship; Erotica is about the sex." Obviously, it's not quite that simple, but it does make the point. There are numerous variations of these definitions of terms and there will continue to be discussion, especially when it comes to sorting out any differences that may exist between very sexy Romance and Erotic Romance. However, Sylvia Day's explanations of Erotic Romance, Erotica, Porn, and Sexy Romance are exceptionally clear and potentially helpful and are available on her website: www.sylviaday.com (Sylvia Day, *What is Erotic Romance?*, http://www.sylviaday.com/extras/erotic-romance).

Romantica is a term trademarked by Ellora's Cave Publishing and refers to its line of Erotic Romance novels which they define as "any work of literature that is both romantic and sexually explicit. . . . [in which] the main protagonists develop 'in love' feelings for one another that culminate in a monogamous relationship." Many of the books in this line fall within the definition of Erotic Romance; the company also publishes Erotica for women under its EXOTIKA (also trademarked) line. (See the Ellora's Cave website for more information: www.jasminejade.com/t-romantica.aspx.)

Because the Erotic Romance subgenre is defined primarily by its sexual explicitness and creativity, as well as its frank language, the characters and settings are not usually limited in other ways. Erotic Romance readers are just as likely to encounter a contemporary, high-powered CEO or special ops agent heroine as they are a wickedly seductive eighteenth-century courtesan, a mesmerizing vampire queen, or a resourceful captive on an intergalactic starship. In other words, the characters and settings in these stories can be similar to those found in many of the other Romance subgenres; it's the role and treatment of sex and how it impacts the characters that makes the difference

As noted above, Erotic Romance, as well as ordinary explicit, sexy romance, is often labeled and marketed as Erotica. Whatever the reason—ignorance, unfamiliarity with the subgenre, a hard-to-classify title, or a desire to cash in on the cachet of the term "Erotica,"—this practice causes confusion for readers, writers, bookstore owners, and librarians, alike. Readers may be mislead, choosing to read or not read a book based on faulty labeling; writers may not connect with their target audiences for the same reason; bookstore owners may miss sales because customers won't find books because of improper labeling; and librarians may make the wrong collection development decisions simply because of incorrect designations. All of this means that publishers' labeling cannot necessarily be relied on to indicate what kind of book one is looking at and other measures are necessary. Authors' names can be helpful and so can publishers' imprints, although many authors write various kinds of romances (however, some use pseudonyms to distinguish among the types) and an imprint doesn't necessarily guarantee similarity. As usual, reading the book and deciding for one's self is probably the best solution. However, there is one final caveat: Even with the current definitions at hand, some of these books hover so close to the rather blurry borders that they might legitimately fall into either camp, making the decision difficult and somewhat arbitrary, at best.

For an excellent, much longer discussion of this topic, see Toni Blake's article "Erotic Romance vs. Erotica: What are the Differences and Why Is It Important?" in the June 2007 issue of *RWR: Romance Writers Report*.

Appeal

The specific appeal of the Erotic Romance is to readers who not only enjoy Romances with a high level of explicitly described sex, but who also want a story in which sex plays an important part in the character growth and in the development of the romantic relationship between the two main characters. These stories take readers on a romantic, emotional journey as the protagonists explore their feelings and sexuality within a romantic relationship that culminates with Romance's traditional happy ending. In most of these stories, sex is not just incidental to the plot; it is key, and it cannot be omitted without affecting the overall story.

Although some traditional ultra-sexy romances may also appeal to fans of the Erotic Romance, because of the difference in focus and lack of a true romantic relationship, Erotica or Erotic Fiction will probably not. On the other hand, if a reader enjoys Erotic Romance primarily for the sex, there may be some crossover appeal.

Advising the Reader

9

General readers' advisory information is provided in chapter 3. However, several points that might be specifically helpful in advising readers of Erotic Romance are listed below.

- For a number of reasons, readers may not tell you specifically that they are looking for Erotic Romance. However, asking what authors they like or what titles they have enjoyed may give you some clues and help you make suggestions.
- There are important differences between Erotic Romance and pure Erotica or Erotic fiction, and fans of one won't necessarily enjoy the other. Unless the reader is willing to discuss the topic, the best solution is the same as above—to use the reader's favorite authors and titles to help make suggestions.
- Because Erotic Romance and very sexy traditional Romance have a lot in common (e.g., romantic relationship focus, happy ending, steamy sex), there is often some crossover readership. However, style, language, and sexual activities vary widely among these books, with Erotic Romance, in general, being edgier, riskier, and much more like Erotica in tone and terminology. Because of this, it will be important to be intimately familiar with the works of any authors recommended.
- Becoming familiar with Erotic Romance publishers and the kinds of books and e-books they publish, as well as some of their better-known authors, will give you a head start.

10

11

12

Brief History

Although the classic form of Erotica can be traced to antiquity, and because through history any number of books have been written with explicit detail about sexual interactions of varying kinds, it hasn't been until recently that what we now call Erotic Romance has come to the fore. Although there was likely some activity earlier, it was the 1990s when the genre began to make its presence felt. In 1992, the British publisher Virgin Books launched Black Lace books (Erotica and), and the following year, Alexandra Kendall founded Red Sage Publishing. Red Sage's first *Secrets* anthology of Erotic Romance novellas was published in late 1995, beginning a successful trade paperback series that continues to this day. (Note: Red Sage has recently begun publishing individual titles of various lengths in e-book format, as well as the *Secrets* anthologies.)

13

14

The mid-1990s was not an easy time for aspiring romance writers, especially for those whose stories were too hot for the major New York/Toronto romance publishers to handle. But help was on the horizon. Taking advantage of the rapid advances in technology and the can-do euphoria of the dot-com boom, the fledgling e-publishing industry took off. Small e-publishing companies popped up everywhere (Hard Shell Word Factory, New Concepts Publishing, Liquid Silver, to name only a few), offering an alternative to writers of all kinds, including Erotic Romance writers. However, it wasn't until 2000, around the time that Tina M. Engler (who writes as Jaid Black) founded her e-publishing company, Ellora's Cave, and began publishing super steamy Erotic Romance that things began to change noticeably. Sex was beginning to get hotter across the entire Romance industry, and with the inauguration of Jove's Seduction line in 2000 (short-lived though it proved to be), the 2001 launches of

15

16

Kensington's Brava—a trade paperback imprint that guaranteed "the best in erotic romantic fiction"—and Harlequin's Blaze books spinning off from Temptation to become its own line, several of the major houses were now, at least part way, in the game.

These lines, however, were, for the most part, not Erotic Romance; that continued to be the domain of Ellora's Cave, Red Sage, and similar houses. In 2002, Ellora's Cave expanded its horizons and began adding print books (often titles that were also published as e-books) to its inventory, and in 2003, the publisher met RWA's requirements for being a recognized commercial publisher, a critical step for the writers, as well as the publishing house. Erotic Romance continued to attract readers and by the middle of the decade, a number of small new publishers, both print and e-book, had joined the ranks. Then New York and Toronto decided to get in on the action, quickly launching four new erotically focused imprints: Heat (Berkley) in 2005, and Aphrodisia (Kensington), Spice (Harlequin), and Avon Red, all in 2006. Most of the books in these lines are spicier and more focused on sex than those in other lines. However, as mentioned earlier, there is a range of opinion on what is considered Erotic Romance, and not all editors think alike, so some titles may not fit the definition.

One relatively recent fiction genre that may be worth mentioning because of its erotica content is Urban Lit or Street Lit. (See also chapter 12, "Ethnic and Multicultural Romance.") Erotica writers such as Zane have done much to popularize what is often known as Urban Erotica, and while these stories are usually not Erotic Romance, there will be some crossover appeal between the two types. For more information on Urban or Street Lit, in general, consult *Urban Grit: A Guide to Street Lit* (Santa Barbara, CA: Libraries Unlimited, 2010) by Megan Honig.

For the past several years, the big houses also have been experimenting with e-book and audio formats, as well, and many of these titles are now available. Although the technology still needs some improvement, many readers are already familiar with the e-book format, thanks to the e-publishers like Ellora's Cave who paved the way, and are happily embracing these new offerings. At the moment, most of the major publishers offer titles (backlist and current) in both electronic and print formats, and most have established e-only Romance imprints, as well. One dedicated Erotic Romance line that is e-only is Harlequin's short-story line, Spice Briefs. As of this writing, Erotic Romances and super sexy-romances are still hot (although there are recent rumblings that things have gone a little too far for some dedicated fans tastes and indications that the heat is lessening slightly in some of the non–Erotic Romance subgenres), many writers who began with the e-publishers have moved into print and are becoming bestsellers, writers are jumping on the self-publishing bandwagon and publishing their own erotic titles in both e-book and print formats with phenomenal success, and the subgenre's influence continues to affect the rest of the market. How long they remain popular remains to be seen, but if the past is any guide, once the sensual genii is out of the bottle, it may be tempered, but it's probably here to stay.

Publishers

Several of the major publishers of Erotic Romance are listed below. For more complete information, see chapter 22, "Publishers."

Aphrodisia (Kensington)
Avon Red
Black Lace (Virgin Publishing)
Ellora's Cave Publishing
Heat (Berkley)

Imajinn
Liquid Silver (Atlantic Bridge Publishing)
Red Sage Publishers
Samhain Publishing
Spice (Harlequin)

9

Selected Erotic Romance Bibliography

10

This selective bibliography is not comprehensive; the titles listed below are merely examples of the growing number of Erotic Romance novels being produced.

Alden, Jami

Delicious. Aphrodisia, 2006.
A TV chef hires a man she once made passionate love to be her bodyguard when she fears a stalker.

11

A Taste of Honey. Aphrodisia, 2007.
A trio of sexy novellas featuring the Donovan brothers and their reunions with women from their pasts.

Private Party. Aphrodisia, 2007.
A betrayed bride finds passion with the groom's brother on her "wedding night" and follows him to the Caribbean in this sizzler.

12

Andre, Bella

See also chapter 5, "Contemporary Romance."

Take Me. Pocket, 2005.
A voluptuous, plus-size heroine leads the hero on a sexy chase, all the way to Italy.

13

Tempt Me, Taste Me, Touch Me. Pocket, 2007
A linked trio of novellas set in the Napa wine country.

Bad Boys of Football—San Francisco Outlaws
Steamy stories with gridiron heroes.

14

Game for Anything. Pocket, 2008
A star quarterback reconnects with the girl whose virginity he took in high school when she (now a top image consultant) is charged with cleaning up his image.

Game for Seduction. Pocket, 2008.
A sexy wide receiver comes to the rescue of his agent's attractive daughter when she ventures into the wrong bar.

15

Game for Love. CreateSpace, 2010.
In order to fulfill his grandmother's dying wish that he marry a good girl, a football player and a school teacher make a temporary marriage bargain, but end up falling in love.

Love Me. CreateSpace, 2010.
A trauma surgeon and a fashion designer find love in this sexy story that follows *Take Me* and features the brother and sister of the hero and heroine, respectively.

16

Bast, Anya

Bast also has written a number of Erotic Romances, most with paranormal or futuristic elements, that are available in e-book format. See also chapter 9, "Alternative Reality."

Water Crystal. Ellora's Cave, 2005.
Toxic rain, poisoned water, and a crystal that can clean it all up bring the crystal thief and her captor together with sizzling passion for each other and a determination to heal the world in this erotic Futuristic.

The Chosen Sin. Heat, 2008.
A vengeance-driven woman becomes a vampire in order to bring down the villain who almost destroyed her and finds love with the man whose bite "turned" her in this lust-laden futuristic world of the Chosen.

Black, Jaid (Tina M. Engler)
Engler, who writes primarily as Jaid Black, is the founder of Ellora's Cave Publishing and Cerridwen Press. She is a multi-published author and many of her works were first published in e-book form.

Trek Mi Q'an Series
Seven-foot-tall warriors claim their Sacred Mates in this futuristic/fantasy Erotic Romance series that is one of Engler's most popular.

The Empress' New Clothes. Ellora's Cave, 2001.
An Earth woman is captured by her alien warrior, wed, and taken to his home planet.

No Mercy. Ellora's Cave, 2001.
A frustrated warrior comes to Earth and finds his Sacred Mate, a woman who looks like a goddess he worships.

Enslaved. Ellora's Cave, 2001.
A sixties feminist becomes a Sacred Mate.

No Escape. Ellora's Cave, 2001.
A woman scheduled to be wed flees to a female-dominated planet in search of a little freedom but is tracked down by her determined warrior.

No Fear. Ellora's Cave, 2001.
A fatally ill librarian is claimed by her sexy warrior.

Seized. Ellora's Cave, 2002.
A woman goes after her best friend when the friend is kidnapped by a warrior and ends up being claimed herself in this story that is linked to *The Empress' New Clothes.*

One Dark Night. Berkley Sensations, 2004; Berkley Heat, 2006.
A doctor barely escapes from a serial killer she'd connected with online and finds help—and more—with the detective working on the case.

Deep, Dark, & Dangerous. Pocket, 2006.
A starlet and her sister escape to Alaska only to end up in a strange underground medieval Viking society called New Sweden.

After the Storm. Ellora's Cave, 2008.
Written under Engler's Tia Isabella pseudonym, this Erotic Romance with a time travel twist, sweeps its very modern heroine back to medieval Scotland and into the arms of a very demanding laird.

Black, Nikita (Nina Bruhns)
Also writes Contemporary Romance as Nina Bruhns.

Cajun Hot. Cajun Hot Press, 2006.
Two Cajun brothers fall in love with a photographer in the steamy Louisiana swamps.

Slave to Love. Cajun Hot Press, 2007.
The search for a vicious killer adds excitement to this erotic thriller.

Blake, Toni

Swept Away. Avon Red, 2006.
A woman on the verge of matrimony reconnects with a man she's never forgotten when he arrives on her family's island pursued by smugglers.

Tempt Me Tonight. Avon Red, 2007.
A woman revisits her hometown determined to seduce—and then leave—the boy, now a man, who broke her heart but finds she still loves him.

Bradley, Eden

The Dark Garden. Bantam, 2007.
A mistress in a San Francisco BDSM club accepts a challenge to resist submission for thirty days in this story of passion, bondage, and submission.

Forbidden Fruit. Delta, 2008
An alternative sexuality professor learns first hand about all the things she's been teaching from one of her sexy students.

Burton, Jaci

Burton is a veteran writer of Erotic Romance and has dozens of titles to her credit. She also has written for Ellora's Cave.

Rescue Me. Samhain, 2006.
A pair of wary, wounded people light up the sky with sparks and passion in this story of a rancher who needs an investor to keep things afloat.

Unwrapped. Samhain, 2007. (Also included in **Holiday Seduction**. Samhain, 2008.)
A high-powered attorney experiences her fantasy in a ménage a trois arranged by a coworker who had read her online journal. A Romance Reviews Today 2007 award winner.

Show Me. Samhain, 2007.
Taking a chance on indulging her fantasies could put a woman's future in jeopardy.

Nothing Personal. Samhain, 2008.
A multimillionaire marries his assistant in order to retain control of his company, but they must also have a child in order to fulfill the terms of his grandfather's will.

Wild Riders
A special ops group of bad boy bikers melt asphalt and hearts—and find unexpected love—as they as they ride to the rescue in this lively series.

Riding Wild. Heat, 2008.
Riding Temptation. Heat, 2008.
Riding on Instinct. Heat, 2009.
Riding the Night. Heat, 2010.

Burton, Louisa

Burton's Erotic Romances are noted for their exceptional writing, attention to historical detail, refreshing creativity, and hot, explicit sex scenes.

Hidden Grotto

Set in the idyllic French countryside in the Chateau de la Grotte Cachée, a remarkable castle inhabited by an assortment of sexually insatiable and adept paranormal beings that continue throughout the series, each book in this erotic series interweaves several stories, usually widely separated by time. An intriguing blend of mythology and Erotic Romance.

House of Dark Delights. Bantam, 2007.
One of the HellFire club's notorious black masses leads a woman into an adventure involving bondage and discipline, and a contemporary tennis pro is seduced by Elic, a shape-changing immortal.

Bound in Moonlight. Bantam, 2007.
A naïve heiress learns the art of love, a rector's daughter agrees to be auctioned off as a sex slave for a week, and the daughter of the Chateau's administrator returns to Grotte Cachée after years away—and gets some surprises.

Whispers of the Flesh. Bantam, 2008.
A young priest disguises himself to investigate the dark secrets of the Chateau and gets in touch with who he really is in the process, and the daughter of the dying Chateau administrator is faced with a dilemma in a story that continues from the previous book and includes flashbacks.

In the Garden of Sin. Bantam, 2009.
A scarred nobleman tutors a would-be courtesan, who has a hidden agenda, in the arts of love, and a pair of insatiable vampires tangle with Elic and a beautiful succubus, Lili, in a contemporary romp that includes a memorable Renaissance festival.

Croft, Sydney (Larissa Ione and Stephanie Tyler)
ACRO Series

An erotic action/adventure series in which operatives of ACRO (Agency for Covert Rare Operatives) fight against the evil Itor Corporation which wants to take over America—and the free world. Romantic, erotic passion of varying kinds blossoms in these fast-paced novels.

Riding the Storm. Delta, 2007.
Unleashing the Storm. Delta, 2008.
Seduced by the Storm. Delta, 2008.
Taming the Fire. Delta, 2009.

Dane, Lauren
Witches Knot Series

Focuses on the powerful witches of the Chavez family; New Orleans setting.

Triad. Ellora's Cave, 2005.
A witch dreamer and a vampire find passion—and then another man comes on the scene.

A Touch of Fae. Ellora's Cave, 2006.
A scholarly witch on the hunt for a magical book meets a faerie warrior sent by his queen to keep the book from falling into dangerous hands.

Vengeance Due. Ellora's Cave, 2007.
A man whose family was killed by vampires tries to ignore his attraction to a witch who has a vampire in the family.

Thrice United. Ellora's Cave, 2007.
A woman discovers her latent talents while reading the tarot and attracts two vampires who claim she is their mate.

Undercover. Heat, 2008.
A futuristic adventure of a woman who must pose as a concubine for two men as part of a covert military operation.

Day, Sylvia
See also chapter 7, "Historical Romance."

Dream Guardian Series
In the world of Twilight, Dream Guardian warriors bring erotic dream fantasies to mortal women, protect humans from dreaded Nightmares, fight the increasingly violent battle between the Dream Guardians and the Nightmares, deal with the Elders, and sometimes enter the mortal world and fall in love in this paranormal Erotic Romance series.

Pleasures of the Night. Avon Red, 2007.
A Dream Guardian unexpectedly falls in love with woman who may be the Key, a woman who legend decrees must be destroyed.

Heat of the Night. Avon Red, 2008.
A wary single mom and a Dream Guardian find passion and love when he comes to Earth on a dangerous mission.

Hart, Megan
Hart is especially noted for deep exploration of her characters' emotions, their feelings about the past, and how that affects their sex lives.

Stranger. Spice, 2009.
A funeral director, who leads a secret life with an escort service, mistakenly connects with the wrong—but, oh, so right—man and is forced to confront her repressed feelings when she tries to forget him, but can't. Intense and emotional.

Holly, Emma
See also chapter 9, "Alternative Realities."

Personal Assets. Venus Book Club of Bookspan, 2001; Berkley, 2004, 2005.
Two best friends find love and passion separately in the fast-paced boutique-business world.

In the Flesh. Cheek, 2004.
A Japanese American businessman falls for the woman who is the model for one of the characters in his company's computer game.

Strange Attractions. Berkley Sensation, 2004.
A woman receives an erotic education at the estate of a wealthy physicist who manipulates people as if they were Barbie and Ken dolls.

Cooking Up a Storm. Cheek, 2004.
Delicious delights, both culinary and sexual, await a restaurant owner and her new chef in this engaging story.

Fairyville. Berkley Sensation, 2007.
A psychic, who has feelings for her landlord, who doesn't know she's alive, decides to use her old high school love to make him jealous, with unexpected results.

James, Allyson
See also chapter 9, "Alternative Realities."

Mortal Series
Gods, demi-gods, and mortals interact in this erotic fantasy series that involves multiple partners.

Mortal Temptations. Heat, 2009.
A psychic antique store owner joins forces with a winged demi-god and a were-leopard, both cursed by Hera, and sets out to break the enchantment. They experience a wide variety of erotic encounters in their adventures.

Mortal Seductions. Heat, 2009.
A former vengeance demon in service to Aphrodite who slips up is given a chance to redeem, but she needs help in this millennia-spanning story.

Lee, Deanna
Holman Art Gallery Series
The characters in these books are linked by their varying relationships to the Holman Art Gallery in Boston.

Undressing Mercy. Aphrodisia, 2006.
Mercy is on target to becoming the director of an art gallery but is tricked into being a model for an artist if she wants his exhibition. First published as an e-book by Liquid Silver in 2005.

Bare-Naked Jane. Aphrodisia, 2007.
An interracial Erotic Romance told from the heroine's first-person point of view.

Exposing Casey. Aphrodisia, 2008.
"Watching Casey" and "Seducing Lisa" are the two linked novellas that conclude this series.

Leigh, Lora
One of the best-known writers in this area, Leigh also writes steamy books in several other subgenres, and many of them could easily be considered Erotic Romance, as well. Many of her earlier books were released as e-books. This is only a small sampling of her works.

The Breeds Series
This popular erotic paranormal series focuses on humans who were genetically bred to become killers by the evil Genetics Council with DNA from various animal breeds (big cats, coyotes, wolves, etc.). The breeds are often dangerous and sexually driven. As of this writing there are at least a dozen books and a number of novellas in this ongoing series (sometimes divided into various breed types), published by various houses and variously classified. However, these stories are universally extremely hot and erotic in nature. They are selectively listed.

Tempting the Beast. Ellora's Cave, 2003.
This first book lays out the premise for the series discussed above.

The Man Within. Ellora's Cave, 2004.
A woman must deal with the discovery that her mate is one of the genetically altered feline Breeds.

Elizabeth's Wolf. Ellora's Cave, 2005.
A military wolf breed refuses to believe that a young girl he'd corresponded with while in the Middle East and her mother are dead, and when he learns they are alive and on the run, he knows he will do everything in his power to save the child and the woman he believes was meant for him.

Kiss of Heat. Ellora's Cave, 2004.
A tale of misunderstanding, betrayal, and revenge.

Soul Deep. Ellora's Cave, 2004.
A Breed is assigned to protect the president's daughter.

Megan's Mark. Berkley Sensation, 2006.
When Breeds begin dying in rural New Mexico, an empathetic sheriff's deputy joins forces with a fierce Feline Breed to find the killers.

Harmony's Way. Berkley Sensation, 2006.
A deadly Lion Breed huntress is paired with a sheriff who works to temper her fierce nature and keep her safe.

Tanner's Scheme. Berkley Sensation, 2007.
A revenge kidnapping has unexpected results.

Jacob's Faith. Ellora's Cave, 2003.
Faith and Jacob are reunited after six years apart.

Aiden's Charity. Ellora's Cave, 2007.
Charity and Aiden struggle with conflicting values and instincts.

Dawn's Awakening. Berkley Sensation, 2008.
A Feline Breed must overcome her devastating childhood in order to be emotionally ready to mate, as well as fight a killer who is after the human who is destined be her mate.

Mercury's War. Berkley Sensation, 2008.
Ria Rodriguez poses as a clerk to uncover the traitor who's been passing Breed secrets to a pharmaceutical company.

Coyote's Mate. Berkley Sensation, 2009.
A Coyote Breed works with a human supporter to rescue a group of imprisoned Coyote Breeds from a Russian lab, but when he betrays her trust and they are swept up by an unexpected mating heat, they are forced to deal with the consequences.

Bengal's Heart. Berkley Sensation, 2009.
A reporter whose husband was responsible for the slaughter of some Bengal Breeds is captured by a survivor in retribution.

Lion's Heat. Berkley Sensation, 2010.
Jonas Wyatt finally claims his love in this fast-paced adventure that has a baby to ramp up the interest.

Styx's Storm. Berkley Sensation, 2010.
An emotionally damaged heroine with a hatred of Breeds finds healing and love.

Navarro's Promise. Berkley Sensation, 2011.
Wolf Breed Navarro struggles to claim Micah Toler as his mate, but she doesn't want to be claimed.

Lawe's Justice. Berkley Sensation, 2011.

Nauti Series
The first three books form a trilogy focusing on the wickedly sexy Mackay cousins; those that follow are linked to the family in this wild and sensual series.

Nauti Boy. Heat, 2007.
Nauti Nights. Heat, 2007.
Nauti Dreams. Berkley Sensation, 2008.
Nauti Intentions. Berkley Sensation, 2009.
Nauti Deceptions. Berkley Sensation, 2010.

Lyons, Susan
Awesome Foursome Series
Four girlfriends (Suzanne Brennan, Jenny Yuen, Ann Montgomery, Rina Goldberg) find passion and love in this erotic quartet.

Champagne Rules. Aphrodisia, 2006.
An interracial couple eventually finds that sex isn't all they want their relationship to be about.

Hot in Here. Aphrodisia, 2006.
A Chinese Canadian journalist covers a firefighter calendar competition and finds passion with Mr. February.

Touch Me. Aphrodisia, 2007.
An uptight attorney finds release with her talented massage therapist.

She's on Top. Aphrodisia, 2008.
A classical musician can't forget the love of her life, now a world-famous creator of music videos, and when he comes back to town they reconnect.

McCarty, Sarah
Noted for her alpha heroes and sexy cowboys, among other things.

Promises Series
An series of Erotic Western Romances.

Promises Linger. Ellora's Cave, 2004.
A woman marries a gunslinger in order to save her ranch in this sizzler that is a revised version of a book published in 2001 under a different title and pseudonym.

Promises Keep. Ellora's Cave, 2005.
A woman escapes her bordello past and finds love with a lawman.

Promises Prevail. Ellora's Cave, 2005.
A young widow suffering from years of emotional abuse adopts a half–Native American baby left on her doorstep and marries a hardened lawman in order to be able to keep the child.

Promises Reveal. Berkley Sensation, 2008.
A shotgun wedding between an outlaw-turned-pastor and a feminist sets the sparks a-flying

Hell's Eight Series
Eight friends are orphaned by a massacre and become the wild, sexy Hell's Eight in this erotic Western series.

Caine's Reckoning. Spice, 2007.
A Texas Ranger rescues a woman and then marries her to protect her from her guardian.

Sam's Creed. Spice, 2008.
A Texas Ranger is drawn into danger when he finds the sole survivor of a brutal attack, then must escort her home to her family's ranch.

Tucker's Claim. Spice, 2009.
A widowed Quaker nurse finds passion and love with a Texas Ranger.

Tracker's Sin. Spice, 2010.
Tracker searches for a kidnapped heiress and ends up marrying her in order to protect her and her child.

McKeever, Gracie C.
McKeever writes intriguing, interracial Erotic Romance.

In Plain Sight. Siren, 2006.
A ghost and a human, bent on revenge as they search for a murderer, are romantically attracted to the same man.

Between Darkness and Daylight. Siren, 2007.
A psychic has a hard time convincing a social worker that he's in danger in his taut, complex erotic story of romantic suspense.

Eternal Designs. Siren, 2008.
A marriage counselor is reincarnated into the body of the late husband of one of his client's.

McKenna, Shannon
McKenna's erotic thrillers have fans in both the Romantic Suspense and Erotic Romance subgenres.

McCloud Brothers Series
This contemporary series focuses on the crime-fighting McCloud clan.

Behind Closed Doors. Brava, 2002.
Two people out for revenge on the same person connect passionately as they pursue their goals.

Standing in the Shadows. Brava, 2003.
A former FBI agent protects the daughter of a traitorous agent when a killer comes after her.

Out of Control. Brava, 2006.
Margot Vetter, a woman on the run after being framed for murder, connects with P.I. Davy McCloud.

Edge of Midnight. Brava, 2006.
Sean McCloud, still reeling from the death of his twin, Kevin, reconnects with his long-lost love, Olivia Endicott.

Extreme Danger. Brava, 2008.
A midnight swim plunges Becca Cattrell into deadly danger and threatens Nick Ward's undercover operation.

Ultimate Weapon. Brava, 2008.
Val Janos, an undercover agent for the villain, falls for the woman, Tamara Steele, he is supposed to abduct.

Fade to Midnight. Brava, 2010.
Kevin McCloud's search for his lost memory leads him to Edie Parrish, an artist who draws a character who resembles Kev.

Return to Me. Brava, 2004.
A bad boy photojournalist returns home to look into his uncle's suspicious death and reconnects with the woman he has always loved. Dangerous, suspenseful, and erotic.

Mellor, P. J.

Give Me More. Aphrodisia, 2007.
Romantic vacation settings serve as the backgrounds for this trio of erotic novellas.

Make Me Scream. Aphrodisia, 2008.
A woman on the run from an ex-boyfriend finds passion with the manager of the Florida beach apartment where she takes refuge.

Drive Me Wild. Aphrodisia, 2009.
This sexy, funny trio of character-linked novellas focuses on two sets of twins and their amorous adventures.

Michelle, Patrice
Bad in Boots Series
Linked by character and place (Texas) all these sexy cowboy stories were first published earlier in e-book format by Ellora's Cave.

Hunger and Temptation. Ellora's Cave, 2006.
Includes "Harm's Hunger" and "Ty's Temptation." Jenna Hudson finds love when she heads for Texas to sell her great-aunt's property in the first novella, and her brother, Ty, is surprised to find romance with a sexy cowgirl in the second story.

Colt's Choice. Ellora's Cave, 2008.
Coowners of a Texas ranch are attracted to each other, in spite of their conflicts.

Hearts are Wild. Ellora's Cave, 2005.
This anthology includes "Hearts Afire," a novella that is the third in this series.

Parks, Lydia
Addicted. Aphrodisia, 2008.
Two erotic vampire novellas, "Once Bitten" and "Bite Me Again," feature strong vampire heroes who follow their own compassionate, considerate codes of ethics in their dealings with the smart, sassy heroines.

Perrin, Kayla

Getting Even. Spice, 2007.
Three ill-used women decide to get even with the men involved in this sexy sometimes funny story of creative revenge.

Obsession. Spice, 2008.
Sex used as revenge is a theme in this sizzler.

Raine, Ashleigh
Talisman Bay Series
This dark, erotic, paranormal suspense series focuses on the Shadow Walkers
who protect the town from harm. Originally published as e-books, the first has been
reprinted.

Forsaken Talisman. Ellora's Cave, 2004.
A kidnapped woman must learn to trust the Shadow Walkers who rescue her.

Lover's Talisman. Samhain, 2008.
A Shadow Walker endangers everyone when he falls in love in his story that was
originally published by Ellora's Cave in 2003.

Driven to Distraction. Samhain, 2008.
A daring stuntwoman connects with a man who turns out to be her boss in this story
that is all fast cars, fast living, and hot sex, Hollywood-style.

Rice, Lisa Marie
Rice's sexy Romantic Suspense stories often feature strong, protective heroes
and threatened, feminine heroines.

Dangerous Lover. Avon Red, 2007.
A formerly wealthy woman finds love with a hardened military man who's admired
her since childhood; only he is now wealthy and has a killer on his trail.

Dangerous Secrets. Avon Red, 2008.
A librarian, and undercover government agent, and an obsessed Russian terrorist
keep things hopping in this erotic thriller.

Dangerous Passion. Avon Red, 2009.
A powerful underworld arms dealer actually becomes the hero in this unusual story.

Into the Crossfire. Avon Red, 2010.
A former Navy SEAL and a former U.N. translator caring for her father are attracted
to each other, but must deal with threats and a kidnapping.

Roycraft, Jaye

Dance with Me, My Lovely. Imajinn, 2007.
Seeking help to control his violent vampire nature, an exotic dancer seeks help from
a shaman skilled in spiritual healing, a woman who has seen him dance, fantasized
about him, and had a vision that leads her to believe he is a killer.

Schone, Robin
Many of Schone's Historicals could be considered Erotic Romance and will appeal to the same readers. See chapter 7, "Historical Romance."

Skully, J. B.
To the Max Series
   This chilling, erotic mystery series follows the passions and adventures of psychic, vision-seeing Max Star (who's haunted by her murdered husband's ghost on occasion) and Detective DeWitt Long and is set in San Francisco. (All are available as e-books.)

   Dead to the Max. www.liquidsilverbooks.com, 2003.
   Max's dreams of a woman being murdered help her track down the killer.

   Evil to the Max. www.liquidsilverbooks.com, 2004.
   Detective De Witt Long is skeptical of Max's abilities, even though he's seen them at work, but he becomes convinced, eventually.

   Desperate to the Max. www.liquidsilverbooks.com, 2005.
   Another murder, this time next door to DeWitt's mom, ramps up the action.

   Power to the Max. www.liquidsilverbooks.com, 2005.
   Another murder that connects to one of Max's visions gets the pair, and a few others, on the trail of a killer.

   Vengeance to the Max. www.liquidsilverbooks.com, 2005.
   Max learns the truth about her husband's murder, as well as his past, in this story that answers a lot of questions from previous books in the series.

Tabke, Karin
   Skin. Pocket, 2007.
   A mob boss's daughter and an undercover cop find passion in the midst of a murder investigation.

   Good Girl Gone Bad. Pocket, 2007.
   A fashionable strip club is the setting for this steamy story of a pair of undercover cops on the trail of some missing women.

   Jaded. Pocket, 2008.
   A tough, suspicious cop suspects the beautiful, frosty manager of a gentlemen's club of multiple murders and finds unexpected passion and love, instead.

   Have Yourself a Naughty Little Santa. Pocket Star, 2008.
   The interests of a workaholic in lovely Evergreen, California, to seal a development deal conflict with those of the man she is attracted to in this holiday sizzler.

Terry, Kimberly Kaye
   Get Your Sexy On. Aphrodisia, 2008.
   A stripper who is working only to pay off debts and doesn't want emotional entanglements is caught off guard by a passionate encounter with a sexy P.I.; she leaves only to meet him again several years later, when she needs his help.

Walker, Shiloh
Hunters Series
   This series focuses on paranormal warriors whose job it is to find and weed out the rogues among them. Most of these stories in Walker's popular Hunters series were previously published in e-format and have since been combined into print volumes.

Hunters: The Beginning. Ellora's Cave, 2004.
Tori is turned into a vampire and goes to police officer Declan for help in the first story and ancient vampire Eli is attracted to fiery witch Sarel in this collection that includes the first two stories in the series, "Declan and Tori" and "Eli and Sarel."

Hunters: Interlude. Ellora's Cave, 2005.
Byron doesn't expect to fall for the woman he has promised to care for and a hunter resists his attraction to the lovely healer because he feels unworthy in stories three and four in the series, "Byron and Kit" and "Jonathan and Lori."

Ben and Shadoe. Ellora's Cave, 2005.
Ben finally finds the lost child who'd disappeared from the pack years earlier, and is attracted to her in spite of himself.

Rafe and Sheila. Ellora's Cave, 2005.
Rafe finally realizes he's in love with Sheila when she leaves in this story of jealousy and danger.

Hunting the Hunter. Berkley Sensation, 2006.
This novel stands alone but is linked to the Hunters series.

Hunters: Heart and Soul. Heat, 2007.
Includes "Soul of a Hunter" and "Heart of a Hunter."

Hunter's Salvation. Berkley Sensation, 2007.
A hero with magical powers born to destroy the evil beings who prey on humans comes to the aid of a psychic heroine on the trail of the evil villain who killed her sister.

Zane
Dubbed by some the "Queen of Erotica," Zane is a *New York Times* bestselling writer of contemporary African American Erotic Romance and erotica and the publisher of Strebor Books, an imprint of Atria/Simon & Schuster.

Shame on It All. Strebor Books International, 2002.
Three close women friends get their lives and loves in order in this sexy romp.

Total Eclipse of the Heart. Atria, 2009.
A waitress with self-esteem issues in an abusive relationship and a successful businessman in an unhappy marriage are thrown together by tragedy and examine the realities of their lives.

9

10

11

12

13

14

15

16

PART III

RESEARCH AIDS

Chapter 15

History and Criticism

There is growing evidence that scholars are finally beginning to realize what popular fiction readers and writers have known all along—that Romance Fiction (like Mysteries, Science Fiction, Fantasy, and all the other genres before it that have gained a certain respectability) bears serious consideration. Although few will argue its merits as great literature (indeed, most genre fiction rarely aspires to such a designation despite the fact that a number of popular fiction writers from the past are now considered part of the literary canon), the appeal of Romance fFction is well-documented. A genre that has achieved and retained such long-term popularity can no longer be ignored, and researchers in the fields of literature, women's studies, library and information science, and popular culture have begun to show serious interest. "Begun," of course, is still the operative word. Although the scholarly material available for Romance Fiction is a mere trickle compared to that for the other genres,[1] the situation has improved markedly during the past few years and shows every sign of continuing. More books and articles are being published, more graduate theses and dissertations are appearing, and the scholarship that is being presented is, in general, more thoughtful, insightful, and objective than in the past. Likely, there is not just one reason for this increased interest, but the fact that Romances are both read and written by members of the academic community—and this now is being publicly acknowledged—plus the fact that college courses that focus on or incorporate Popular Romance—and therefore, need supporting scholarship—are popping up everywhere, might have something to do with it. Granted, we don't have the whole library, yet, but we're making progress and are definitely farther along than we were a few years ago in building the body of critical, historical, and reference literature necessary for this long-neglected area of study.

Though many of the sources listed below are books, much critical, historical, and state-of-the-art information available on the Romance Genre, particularly the recent research, is in the form of magazine or journal articles. Certain publications, such as *Publishers' Weekly*, *The Writer*, *Journal of Popular Culture*, *RWR: Romance Writers' Report*, *Journal of Popular Romance Studies* (a new online journal specifically for the study of the Popular Romance novel, published by the International Association for the Study of Popular Romance), *Booklist*, or *Library Journal*, tend to carry the bulk of such information, but consulting the major indexes is also recommended. Expanded Academic ASAP, Academic Search Premier, *Readers' Guide to Periodical Literature*, ProQuest Newspapers, LEXIS/NEXIS, and other general periodical indexes are useful in locating materials that appear in popular magazines and newspapers—and in the case of Expanded Academic ASAP and Academic Search Premier, some scholarly publications—while *Library Literature, LISTA,* the *Humanities Index,* and the *MLA Bibliography* are helpful for locating materials in the professional or scholarly journals. In addition, depending on the focus of the research, *Psychological Abstracts/PsycINFO, ERIC, Sociological Abstracts,* or any of the myriad subject-specific databases available will be useful, as well. Also, Digital Dissertations, a full-text database, is a good source for theses and dissertations. While most research materials still are available through subscription databases such those mentioned above, the open web is an increasingly valuable source of both popular and scholarly materials.

Although it is still largely hit-and-miss, occasional articles and theses and dissertations can be found in full text versions on the open web, and when searching this way, Scholar Google (www.scholar.google.com) is one place to start.

Note: In any sources that make use of Library of Congress Subject Headings (including many library catalogs), the primary heading "Love Stories" is useful in retrieving materials on romantic fiction. For a keyword approach, which is useful for most databases and the web, try using various combinations of the words "romance," "popular," "novel," "fiction" (e.g., "romance fiction," "popular romance novel"), as well as the term "love stories."

General

Although works that provide a broad historical overview or a survey of the Romance Genre are still few and far between, the publication of Pamela Regis's *A Natural History of the Romance Novel* in 2003 (listed below) helps fill in the gap and does much to remedy the situation. In addition, critical and historical information on the genre can be gleaned from several of the excellent older general surveys and studies that are still available. Three of the sources listed below (Cawelti, Hart, and Nye) are classics in the area of popular fiction and, in addition to providing relevant information, are fun to read. (Consult earlier editions of this guide for annotations and titles that have been dropped.)

Cawelti, John G. *Adventure, Mystery, and Romance: Formula Stories as Art and Popular Culture.* Chicago: University of Chicago Press, 1976.

Flesch, Juliet. *From Australia with Love: A History of Modern Australian Popular Romance Novels.* Freemantle, Western Australia: Curtin University Books, 2004.
In a lively, readable style, this book unflinchingly takes on critics and scholars and delivers a fresh look at Australian Romance Novels published during the last half of the twentieth century from the viewpoint of both their writers and readers. Although the primary focus is on Australia, because of the international character of publishing and the Romance Genre, this book will appeal beyond the Australian readership.

Hart, James D. *The Popular Book: A History of America's Literary Taste.* New York: Oxford University Press, 1950; Westport, CT: Greenwood Press, 1976.

Nye, Russel B. *The Unembarrassed Muse: The Popular Arts in America.* New York: Dial Press, 1970.

Regis, Pamela. *A Natural History of the Romance Novel.* Philadelphia: University of Pennsylvania Press, 2003.
Defining the Romance Novel as "a work of prose fiction that tells the story of the courtship and betrothal of one or more heroines," Regis traces the development of the Romance Novel from Richardson's *Pamela* through the works of Jane Austen, the Brontës,

and other classic writers into the present day and the works of authors such as Nora Roberts and Jayne Ann Krentz, showing how each adheres to the core requirements of the genre while adapting to its own particular time period. Her "eight essential elements of the romance novel" are particularly intriguing and her thoughtful defense of the genre is exceptionally well done. Note: Regis is currently working on an American-focused Romance history.

Guides to the Literature

As interest in the Romance Genre has grown and the amount of literature available on it has increased, books that function as guides to the literature have slowly begun to appear. Several of the more recent examples are listed below. (See previous editions of this guide for earlier titles.)

Baym, Nina. *Women's Fiction: A Guide to Novels By and About Women in America, 1820–1870*. Ithaca, NY: Cornell University Press, 1978.

Carpan, Carolyn. *Rocked by Romance: A Guide to Teen Romance Fiction*. Westport, CT: Libraries Unlimited, 2004.
This long-needed, well-done guide focuses on the literature of teenage Romance, breaking the materials down by subgenre and discussing them in separate chapters. In addition, separate sections on relevant research materials and practical ways in which librarians can provide services to teenage readers are also included. Appendices include a "Sample Core Collection" of teen Romance and "Romance Readers' Advisor Resources."

Fallon, Eileen. *Words of Love: A Complete Guide to Romance Fiction*. New York: Garland Publishing, 1984.
Now dated, this is one of the first attempts at providing an overview of the popular Romance Genre and is primarily of historical interest.

Mussell, Kay. *Women's Gothic and Romantic Fiction: A Reference Guide*. Westport, CT: Greenwood Press, 1981.
Concentrating primarily on the scholarly literature of interest to researchers, this is the first (now classic) guide to begin the process of organizing the widely scattered materials on Romance Fiction.
The following are sections of books that act as "Guides to the Literature."

Hoffman, Frank W. "Romance." In *American Popular Culture: A Guide to the Reference Literature*, 73–74. Englewood, CO: Libraries Unlimited, 1995.
This too brief, but competently done and most welcome, section on Romance reference sources includes six annotated entries and divides them into the following categories: Bibliographies, Biographies, Guides to the Literature, and Handbooks.

Herald, Diana Tixier, and Denice Adkins. "Romance." In *Genreflecting: A Guide to Popular Reading Interests*, 6th ed., by Diana Tixier Herald, edited by Wayne A. Wiegand, 253–312. Westport, CT: Libraries Unlimited, 2006.
The Romance section of this classic guide to popular fiction begins with an introductory essay by Denice Adkins (253–260) which briefly outlines the development of the genre, discusses reasons for its longstanding appeal, and touches on the ever-popular issue of "the cover." "Themes and Types" by Diana Tixier Herald makes up

the rest of the chapter, describing the various Romance subgenres (complete with author lists), and providing information on reference sources, publishers, book clubs, periodicals, and authors' associations. Although, of necessity, too short to be comprehensive, this chapter does provide a good place to start for those unfamiliar with the current Romance Genre. Since the Romance genre is continually changing and subsequent editions of *Genreflecting* are not necessarily cumulative, readers may also find the earlier editions, the first two of which were written by the late Betty Rosenberg, of interest.

History, Surveys, and Criticism

Of all the areas of interest within the Romance Fiction Genre, the works of the original Gothic novelists and the American Domestic Sentimentalists have received the most attention and are, therefore, the best documented. Although much of this research appears in the dozens of articles that pepper the literature, a number of relevant books do exist. In addition to Baym's book (mentioned above), two of the more important and useful ones are listed below. Both are considered classics in the field and have been reprinted. (Consult previous editions of this guide for annotations or titles that have not been included in this edition.)

Classic Overviews

Brown, Herbert Ross. *The Sentimental Novel in America, 1789–1860.* Durham, NC: Duke University Press, 1940.
A standard in the field.

Papashvily, Helen Waite. *All the Happy Endings: A Study of the Domestic Novel in America, the Women Who Wrote it, the Women Who Read it, in the Nineteenth Century.* New York: Harper, 1956.
Interesting discussion of the domestic novels of the nineteenth century.

Classic Gothic Overviews

Those especially interested in the early Gothics, might wish to consult the following bibliography:

Frank, Frederick, S. *Guide to the Gothic: An Annotated Bibliography of Criticism.* Metuchen, NJ: Scarecrow Press, 1984.
Concerned primarily with the original literary Gothics. Updated by *Guide to the Gothic II: An Annotated Bibliography of Criticism, 1983–1993* (Lanham, MD: Scarecrow Press, 1995), and *Guide to the Gothic III an Annotated Bibliography of Criticism, 1994–2003* (Lanham, MD: Scarecrow Press, 2005).

Frank, Frederick S. *Through the Pale Door: A Guide to and Through the American Gothic.* New York: Greenwood, 1990.
A scholarly look at the Gothic on the American side of the Atlantic.

Thomson, Douglass H., Jack G. Voller, and Frederick S. Frank, eds. *Gothic Writers: A Critical and Bibliographical Guide.* Westport, CT: Greenwood Press, 2002.
This source includes entries on over fifty authors ranging from the classic Gothic writers of the eighteenth century, such as Horace Walpole and Ann Radcliffe, to present-day writers, such as Stephen King and Margaret Atwood, and includes some authors and works

not previously included within the Gothic "canon." Each entry includes an analytical essay, a list of the author's Gothic works, and a selected bibliography of criticism. Several thematic entries, a time line of authors and works, a list of reference sources, and a pair of indexes round out this eclectic resource that is intended for scholars but would be useful to anyone interested in the Gothic.

British Perspectives

Those interested in the British point of view might enjoy the following surveys. Both are popular, rather than scholarly, in style and are highly readable.

Anderson, Rachel. *The Purple Heart Throbs: The Sub-Literature of Love*. London: Hodder and Stoughton, 1974.
An entertaining survey of nineteenth- and twentieth-century romantic fiction, primarily British.

Cadogan, Mary. *And Then Their Hearts Stood Still: An Exuberant Look at Romantic Fiction Past and Present*. London: Macmillan, 1994.
Similar in tone and style to *The Purple Heart Throbs*, this lively survey is "an appreciative assessment of twentieth-century romance fiction" and covers everything from Gothics to glitz, with the notable exception of some of the more recent Romance subgenres.

Research Articles, Studies, and Books

In addition to the more general and comprehensive studies listed above, many books and articles have been written about specific aspects of romantic fiction. Many of these can be found by consulting the guides and bibliographies listed above and in the following chapter or the various bibliographies and reading lists included in the works listed below. The list that follows is intended to demonstrate the current level of scholarly interest in the Romance genre and to provide a brief sketch of the way the discussion has progressed over the past four decades; it is not intended to be exhaustive. For more comprehensive coverage of earlier works, please consult Johanna Tuñon's bibliography included in *North American Romance Writers* (Metuchen, NJ: Scarecrow Press, 1999). For an evolving online scholarly bibliography, see *Romance Scholarship: An On-Line Bibliography* (www.romancewiki.com/Romance_Scholarship). Also, the newly establish *Journal of Popular Romance Studies* focuses exclusively on research on the Popular Romance and is an excellent resource, as well. Note: While not all authors dealt with in the following studies fall strictly within the Romance Genre, many of them produced prototypes of Romance forms that are used today. (Consult previous editions of this guide for older titles and annotations which may have been dropped.)

Adams, Lisa, and John Heath. *Why We Read What We Read: A Delightfully Opinionated Journey Through Contemporary Bestsellers*. Naperville, IL: Sourcebooks, 2007.
The chapter "Hopefully Ever After: Love, Romance and Relationships" may be of particular interest.

Barrett, Rebecca Kay. "Higher Love: What Women Gain from Christian Romance Novels." *Journal of Religion and Popular Culture* 4 (summer 2003), www.usask.ca/relst/jrpc/art4-higherlove.html

This article discusses the role that Christian Inspirational fiction plays in the lives of its readers. *The Journal of Religion and Popular Culture* is one of the growing number of scholarly online journals.

Brackett, Kim Pettigrew. "Facework Strategies among Romance Fiction Readers." *Social Science Journal* 37, no. 3 (2000): 347–360.
Using Goffman's concepts of face and facework as a theoretical framework, this study uses interviews with twelve women who read Romances and analyzes their use of two types of strategies (corrective and preventative) in dealing with the stigma of reading Romances that can arise in social situations.

Brown, Sonya C. "Does This Book Make Me Look Fat?" *Journal of Popular Romance Studies* 1, no. 2 (2011).
Romances with plus-size heroines are the focus of this insightful article.

Bryce, Jane, and Kari Dako. "Textual Deviancy and Cultural Syncretism: Romantic Fiction as a Subversive Strain in Black Women's Writing." *Matatu: Journal for African Culture and Society* 21–22 (2000): 155–164.
Focusing on West Africa, this article analyzes a number of Popular Romance novels by writers such as Ama Ata Aidoo (especially her novel *Changes*) and shows how they subvert the social and sexual norms of power.

Calhoun-French, Diane M. "Of Love and Death: Murder and Mayhem Meet the Romance." *Clues: A Journal of Detection* 21 (spring/summer 2000): 1–16.
This article examines murder mysteries that feature Romance writers as characters and explores the intersection of the Romance and Mystery genres and the varied ways in which the authors portray and deal with both genres.

Coles, Claire D., and M. Johnna Shamp. "Some Sexual, Personality, and Demographic Characteristics of Women Readers of Erotic Romances." *Archives of Sexual Behavior* 13 (1984): 187–209.
An older, but often referenced, study detailing various characteristics of women Romance readers.

Crane, Lynda L. "Romance Novel Readers: In Search of Feminist Change?" *Women's Studies* 23 (1994): 257–269.

Darbyshire, Peter. "Romancing the World: Harlequin Romances, the Capitalist Dream, and the Conquest of Europe and Asia." *Studies in Popular Culture* 23 (October 2000): 1–10.

Darbyshire, Peter. "The Politics of Love: Harlequin Romances and the Christian Right." *Journal of Popular Culture* 35 (spring 2002): 75–88.
This article discusses how the growth of the fundamentalist Christian political right influenced American society during the 1990s and how this is reflected in women's Popular Romance Fiction, particularly Harlequin's Love Inspired Line.

Ebert, Teresa L. "Chick Lit: 'Not Your Mother's Romance Novels.' " In *The Task of Cultural Critique*, 97–117. Urbana: University of Illinois, 2009.
A detailed discussion of Chick Lit that includes an analysis of Romance Fiction, in general.

Engler, Sandra *"A Career's Wonderful, but Love Is More Wonderful Still": Femininity and Masculinity in the Fiction of Mills & Boon*. Tubingen: Francke, 2005.
This recent study explores the ways in which gender stereotypes are represented in the Mills & Boon Romances published between 1930 and 1995. The author acknowledges

that the books respond to numerous societal changes, but concludes that "the absolute centrality of love and marriage in a woman's life" is still a core tenet of the genre.

Ferriss, Suzanne, and Mallory Young, eds. *Chick Lit: The New Woman's Fiction.* New York: Routledge, 2006.
This collection of informative, readable, scholarly essays explores the origins, nature, and complexities of one of the newest fiction genres.

Frantz, Sarah S. G. " 'Expressing' Herself: The Romance Novel and the Feminine Will to Power." In *Scorned Literature: Essays on the History and Criticism of Popular Mass-Produced Fiction in America*, edited by Lydia Cushman Schurman and Deidre Johnson, 17–36. Westport, CT: Greenwood Press, 2002.
This article examines the power of the Romance and the "feminine economy of exchange" through previous scholarship and commentary and the texts of various Romances. Although only part of the article, Frantz's discussion of the heroine's breast milk as a source of power is unusual and intriguing.

Frantz, Sarah S. G. " 'I've Tried My Entire Life to Be a Good Man': *Suzanne Brockmann*'s Sam Starrett, Ideal Romance Hero." In *Women Constructing Men: Female Novelists and their Male Characters, 1750–2000*, edited by Sarah S. G. Frantz and Katharina Rennhak, 227–247. Lanham, MD: Lexington, 2009.

Frenier, Mariam Darce. *Goodbye Heathcliffe: Changing Heroes, Heroines, Roles, and Values in Women's Category Romances.* New York: Greenwood Press, 1988.
Of particular interest—primarily because it is often ignored—is the chapter detailing the differences between American and British Romances, "Silhouettes aren't Harlequins."

Gill, Rosalind, and Elena Herdieckerhoff. "Rewriting the Romance." *Feminist Media Studies* 6 (December 2006): 487–504.
A discussion of the ways in which chick lit is influencing current Romance Fiction based on the analysis of feminist writings about the Popular Romance and twenty chick lit novels written between 1997 and 2004. British emphasis.

Goade, Sally Ann, ed. *Empowerment versus Oppression: Twenty-First Century Views of Popular Romance Novels.* Newcastle, UK: Cambridge Scholars, 2007.
This eclectic anthology attempts to shed new light on the long-standing question, are readers and writers oppressed or empowered by the romance narrative? Articles such as "Becoming Both Poet and Poem: Feminists Repossess the Romance" (Mary Beth Tegan), "How Dare a Black Woman Make Love to a White Man! Black Women Novelists and the Taboos of Interracial Desire" (Guy Mark Foster), "Romance: The Perfect Creative Industry? A Case Study of Harlequin-Mills and Boon Australia" (Glen Thomas), "Bound to Love: Captivity in Harlequin's Sheikh Novels" (Emily A. Haddad), "Forming a Local Identity: Romance Novels in Hong Kong" (Amy Lee), and "The Romance Genre Blues or Who We Don't Get No Respect" (Candice Procter) illustrate the work's wide-ranging diversity.

Goris, An. "Romance the World Over." In *Global Cultures*, 59–72. Newcastle-upon-Tyne: Cambridge Scholars, 2009.
A discussion of Harlequin's immense worldwide marketing, translation, and distribution operation.

Graybill, Beth. "Chasing the Bonnet: The Premise and Popularity of Writing Amish Women." *Journal of the Center for Mennonite Writing* 2, no. 4 (July 15, 2010): 1–6.
A relevant, readable discussion of the recent popularity of Romances and other genres featuring Amish characters and focusing on the Amish/Mennonite cultures.

Grescoe, Paul. *The Merchants of Venus: Inside Harlequin and the Empire of Romance.* Vancouver: Raincoast Books, 1996.
A readable, highly informative story of the origins and rise of the Harlequin publishing empire.

Hall, Glinda Fountain. "Inverting the Southern Belle: Romance Writers Redefine Gender Myths." *Journal of Popular Culture* 41, no. 1 (February 2008): 37–55.

Hall, Glinda F. *The Creators of Women's Popular Romance: The Authors Who Gave to Women a Genre of Their Own.* Lewiston, NY: Edwin Mellen Press, 2009.
This work examines the role of popular women's fiction in "constructing gender and revealing power structures," and is notable for "Hall's analysis of sexuality's meaning within the genre."

Hebard, Andrew. "Romantic Sovereignty: Popular Romances and the American Imperial State in the Philippines." *American Quarterly* 57 (September 2005): 805–830.
Examines the relationship between the Popular Romance and American imperialism in the Philippines.

Hughes, Helen. *The Historical Romance.* London: Routledge, 1993.
Essentially a revamping of her doctoral dissertation, Hughes surveys historical novels published between 1890 and 1990 in order to study "the ways in which an artificial 'past' can gain 'mythical' significance, confirming attitudes or highlighting fears and hopes which arise from the nature of contemporary society." Although primarily British in focus, many of the authors discussed (e.g., Sabatini, Heyer, Farnol, Orczy, Conan Doyle, Cartland, Dunnett) will be familiar to most American readers. Includes notes, a bibliography, and an index.

Jarmakani, Amira. "'The Sheik Who Loved Me': Romancing the War on Terror.'" *Signs* 35, no. 4 (summer 2010): 993–1017.
This article reexamines the ever-popular sheik-themed Romances in the context of today's global political situation.

Juhasz, Suzanne. *Reading From the Heart: Women, Literature, and the Search for True Love.* New York: Viking, 1994.
Written by an academic for "real people" (as opposed to scholars) this study proposes that the reason women read Romance Fiction is to "replicate the facilitating environment of the mother-infant bond." Although her selections are often literary classics (e.g., Austen, the Brontës, Alcott), and not Popular Romance, her ideas and observations may interest some readers. Includes notes, a bibliography, an index, and an appendix detailing the psychoanalytic theories used or mentioned.

Kaler, Anne K. "Dysfunctional Detectives and Romantic P.I.s: Impediments to the Happy Marriage of Mystery and Romance." *Clues: A Journal of Detection* 21 (spring/summer 2000): 61–72.
Using various examples of popular suspense and romantic suspense novels, Kaler argues that a mystery featuring a female detective heroine cannot be successful as Romantic Suspense because the necessary elements from Romance (e.g., emotion, inward quest toward enlightenment) are in direct opposition to the requirements of the mystery hero(ine) (e.g., reason, logic, outward heroic quest) and cannot be reconciled satisfactorily.

Kaler, Anne K. and Rosemary E. Johnson-Kurek, ed. *Romantic Conventions.* Bowling Green, OH: Bowling Green State University Popular Press, 1998.
This collection of essays focuses on the various literary conventions common to the Romance Genre. Contributing scholars include several who are also Romance writers (e.g., Jennifer Crusie Smith and Julie Tetel Andresen). The essays are divided among three sections, "Archetypes and Stereotypes," "Conventions of Time and Place," and "Language and Love," and discuss a wide variety of topics that range from the Jungian shadow archetype, captivity, and the Cinderella myth through Fabio, time travel, and witchcraft.

Keller, Yvonne. " 'Was It Right to Love Her Brother's Wife So Passionately?': Lesbian Pulp Novels and U.S. Lesbian Identity, 1950–1965." *American Quarterly* 57 (June 2005): 385–410.
Discusses the importance of the lesbian pulp novels so popular during the 1950s and much of the 1960s and their role in the formation of lesbian identity and the rise of the gay liberation movement in the 1970s.

Kloester, Jennifer. "Georgette Heyer and the Great Jane." *Sensibilities* 32 (June 2006): 101–117.
Using much of the information from Heyer's private papers she accessed during her dissertation research, Kloester explores the admiring connection between Heyer and her favorite author, Jane Austen.

Kramer, Kyra. "Raising Veils and other Bold Acts: The Heroine's Agency in Female Gothic Novels." *Studies in Gothic Fiction* 1, no. 2 (2011): 24–37.
Among other things, the author posits that some novels labeled "romance" or "romantic suspense" were actually Female Gothics.

Krentz, Jayne Ann, Editor. *Dangerous Men and Adventurous Women: Romance Writers on the Appeal of the Romance.* Philadelphia: University of Pennsylvania Press, 1992.
This groundbreaking collection of essays provides insights from published Romance writers on the appeal of and the rationale behind the Romance Genre. This diverse collection includs articles both long and short and popular and scholarly in tone; all are well-written and provocative. Includes a brief bibliography and an index. Note: This was a bestselling book for the University of Pennsylvania Press and was reissued in mass-market format in 1996. It also received the American Popular Culture Association's Susan Brownmiller Award.

Leavenworth, Maria Lindgren. "Lover Revamped: Sexualities and Romance in the Black Dagger Brotherhood and Slash Fan Fiction." *Extrapolation: A Journal of Science Fiction and Fantasy* 50, no. 3 (2009): 442–462.

Lutz, Deborah. *The Dangerous Lover: Gothic Villains, Byronism, and the Nineteenth-Century Seduction Narrative.* Columbus: Ohio State University Press, 2006.
This discussion of classic heroes of the dark and dangerous variety examines heroes in the literature of the nineteenth and twentieth centuries and is the first full-length study of the topic. Based on Lutz's Ph.D. dissertation.

Maher, Jennifer. "Ripping the Bodice: Eating, Reading, and Revolt." *College Literature* 28 (winter 2001): 64–83.
Focusing on Alisa Kwitney's 1992 novel, *Till the Fat Lady Sings*, this article explores the possible parallels between overeating and Romance reading.

Mann, Peter H. *The Romantic Novel: A Survey of Reading Habits*. London: Mills & Boon, 1969.
One of the earliest Romance reader surveys, this was commissioned by Mills & Boon and conducted in 1968. The results indicate that Romance readers are a less homogeneous and more literate group of women than previously supposed.

McAleer, Joseph. *Passion's Fortune: The Story of Mills & Boon*. Oxford: Oxford University Press, 1999.
A well-researched, clearly documented account of the development, growth, and editorial policies of a major British publisher of Popular Romance Fiction. Mills & Boon merged with Harlequin in 1971 but Romances are still produced under this imprint.

McCafferty, Kate. "Palimpsest of Desire: The Re-Emergence of the American Captivity Narrative as Pulp Romance." *Journal of Popular Culture* 27 (spring 1994): 43–56.
McCafferty uses several of Zebra's captivity narrative Romances from the 1980s to show how the captivity narrative, dating from the 1680s but losing popularity in the 1930s, has changed and resurfaced as mass-market Romance. She also discusses the reasons for the recent popularity and what it means for the genre.

McClain, Lee Tobin. "Paranormal Romance: Secrets of the Female Fantastic." *Journal of the Fantastic in the Arts* 11, no. 3 (2000): 294–306.
Discusses the appeal of the Paranormal Romance and suggests that these stories function at two levels for the reader and, more than any subset of fantastic fiction, provide insights into the "real fears and secret desires of women now."

McClain, Lee Tobin. "Sweet, Savage Academe: True Confessions of a Pulp Professor." *The Chronicle of Higher Education* 49 (August 15, 2003): 19.
A Romance writer and an academic, McClain discusses her dual career and gives advice on making the two work together.

McClain, Lee Tobin. "When Love Is Divine: The Christian Romance Novel." *The Chronicle of Higher Education* 48 (February 15, 2002): 14.
This article discusses the current popularity of Inspirational Romance and examines the inherent tensions that exist between two key elements of the subgenre: the empowerment of women and the Christian fundamentalist antifeminist stance, and the struggle between the secular and the divine, or the flesh and the spirit.

McDonald, Nicola. *Pulp Fictions of Medieval England: Essays in Popular Romance*. Manchester: Manchester University Press, 2004.
Each of the ten essays in this collection discusses one of the less-well-known Medieval Romances that were exceptionally popular at the time, but have not received much serious study by the academic community. Provides insights into medieval culture and values and how these are reflected in these Romances. It will appeal to those interested in both Romance and popular culture. A unique collection.

McKnight-Trontz, Jennifer. *The Look of Love: The Art of the Romance Novel*. New York: Princeton Architectural Press, 2002.
Chronicling the development of the cover art of the Romance novel from the 1940s to the 1980s, this entertaining and informative compilation features an introductory overview, a brief bibliography, and an abundance of cover art illustrations arranged by theme.

Meyer, Basil. "Till Death Do Us Part: The Consumptive Victorian Heroine in Popular Romance Fiction." *Journal of Popular Culture* 37 (Fall 2003): 287–309.
Using the works of Georgiana Fullerton and Rhoda Broughton, this study explores the role of the consumptive heroine (who usually dies) in the popular Romance fiction of the Victorian period.

Moore, Michael, and Daniela Kramer. "Satir for Beginners: Incongruent Communication Patterns in Romantic Fiction." *ETC: A Review of General Sematics* 56 (Winter 1999–2000): 429–437.
This study uses excerpts from popular Romance novels to illustrate some of Virginia Satir's theories of interpersonal communication.

Morgan, Paula. "Like Bush Fire in My Arms: Interrogating the World of Caribbean Romance." *Journal of Popular Culture* 36 (Spring 2003): 804–828.
Using several 1993 books from Harlequin's Caribbean Caresses series and a 1988 title (*Ti Marie*) by one of the series authors, Morgan analyzes their potential to present an accurate and empowering view of Caribbean culture and people.

Mussell, Kay J. "Beautiful and Damned: The Sexual Woman in Gothic Fiction." *Journal of Popular Culture* 9 (Summer 1975): 84–89.
One of the earlier works on the subject and something of a classic.

Mussell, Kay, ed. "Where's Love Gone: Transformations in the Romance Genre." *PARA*DOXA: Studies in World Literary Genres* 3, nos. 1–2 (1997).
Coordinated and edited by Kay Mussell, this groundbreaking issue of *PARA*DOXA* examines important changes within the Popular Romance Genre. It contains twenty relevant research articles, a bibliography of Romance reference sources, a discussion of online resources, a book review essay, and interviews with Romance writers Jayne Ann Krentz, Nora Roberts, Barbara G. Mertz, and Janet Dailey. This publication adds immeasurably to the research in the field, and although it is not widely held and possibly difficult to locate, it is well worth the effort. Contributors include: Kay Mussell, Tania Modleski, Beth Rapp Young, Lynn Coddington, Barbara Samuel, Jennifer Crusie Smith, Sandra Marie Booth, Deborah K. Chappel, Harriet Margolis, Pamela Regis, Sylvia Kelso, Julia Bettinotti, Marie-Francoise Truel, Gabriele Linke, Patricia Koski, Lori Holyfield, Marcella Thompson, Sara Webster Goodwin, Victoria Badik, Kathleen Gilles Seidel, Norbert Spehner, Robert Ellrich, and Darby Lewes. A provocative, well-done collection of scholarly criticism by researchers who understand the genre.

Neal, Lynn S. *Romancing God: Evangelical Women and Inspirational Fiction*. Chapel Hill: University of North Carolina Press, 2006.
Based on Neal's dissertation in which she interviews readers and writers of Inspirational Romance, this readable book examines why evangelical women read Inspirational Romances and the complex role the books play in their daily lives.

Nyquist, Mary. "Romance in the Forbidden Zone." In *Reimagining Women: Representations of Women in Culture*, edited by Shirley Neuman and Glennis Stephenson, 160–181. Toronto: University of Toronto Press, 1993.
Using Peter Rutter's *Sex in the Forbidden Zone: When Men in Power—Therapists, Doctors, Clergy, Teachers, and Others—Betray Women's Trust* (New York: HarperCollins, 1995) as well as well-known Romance studies, Nyquist discusses the traditional role of male mentorship of women and how it is perpetuated in modern Romance Fiction, and incorporates relevant racial, sexual, and gender orientation topics.

O'Connell, Lisa. "Dislocating Literature: The Novel and the Gretna Green Romance, 1770–1850." *Novel: A Forum on Fiction* 35 (Fall 2001): 5–23.
This study discusses the role of Gretna Green in the Romances of the late-eighteenth century and the first half of the nineteenth century and will be of particular interest to modern fans of the Regency Romance.

Paizis, George. *Love and the Novel: The Poetics and Politics of Romantic Fiction.* New York: St. Martin's Press, 1998.
Linking the ancient narrative roots of the romantic novel and elements of the realist bourgeois novel, Paizis shows that the Romance Novel combines fantasy and reality, tradition and collective and individual experience, resulting in works that reflect a woman's desires for individual achievement, recognition, and a better life, yet at the same time indicate that these conditions are absent in their real lives.

Palmer, Paulina. *Lesbian Gothic: Transgressive Fictions.* London: Cassell, 1999.
Focusing on the ways in which lesbian Gothic fiction has evolved since the 1970s, this study examines the recent use of classic Gothic characters and motifs (e.g., vampires, witches, ghosts) to explore and express the transgressive nature of lesbian existence.

Parameswaran, Radhika. "Reading Fictions of Romance: Gender, Sexuality, and Nationalism in Postcolonial India." *Journal of Communication* 52 (December 2002): 832–852.
This intriguing study discusses how reading Romance Fiction has benefited a group of well-educated, middle- and upper-class young Indian women. It is linked to the study listed below.

Parameswaran, Radhika. "Western Romance Fiction as English-Language Media in Postcolonial India." *Journal of Communication* 49 (Summer 1999): 84–105.
This ethnographic study analyzes the reception and function of Western Romance fiction, primarily Mills & Boon publications, by socially and educationally elite English-educated women in modern-day, postcolonial India. The implications of the study for future research were also addressed.

Pattee, Amy S. *Reading the Adolescent Romance: Sweet Valley High and the Popular Young Adult Romance Novel.* New York: Routledge, 2011.
This study examines the development of young adult literature since the early 1980s with a focus on Francine Pascal's popular paperback series, Sweet Valley High.

Pearce, Lynne. "Popular Romance and Its Readers." In *A Companion to Romance: From Classical to Contemporary.* Malden, MA: Blackwell, 2004.

Pearce, Lynne, and Gina Wisker. *Fatal Attractions: Re-Scripting Romance in Contemporary Literature and Film.* London: Pluto Press, 1998.
This collection of essays by various scholars acknowledges the common belief that love can changes the lives of those it touches and goes a step farther to ask, "Can love, itself *be transformed*?" Various films and novels serve to illustrate the authors' views.

Pearce, Lynne, and Jackie Stacey, eds. *Romance Revisited.* New York: New York University Press, 1995.
Originating from a conference hosted by the Centre for Women's Studies at Lancaster University in March 1993, this older anthology of original scholarly essays takes a critical look at romance in the lives of women and examines subjects as diverse as interracial and lesbian relationships, Popular Romance Fiction, Valentine's Day, Futuristic Romances,

resistance to romance, and romance and the family. Rosalynn Voaden's "The Language of Love: Medieval Erotic Vision and Modern Romance Fiction," Bridget Fowler's "Literature Beyond Modernism: Middlebrow and Popular Romance," and Jenny Wolmark's "The Postmodern Romances of Feminist Science Fiction" may be of particular interest. Contributors are primarily British.

Radway, Janice. *Reading the Romance: Women, Patriarchy, and Popular Literature*. Chapel Hill: University of North Carolina Press, 1984. (Reprinted with a new introduction by the author in 1991.)
In this fascinating survey, Radway details the Romance reading preferences of forty-two women (all from one Midwestern town and primarily patrons of one book store), describes her methodology (including providing sample questionnaires), analyzes the results (largely in terms of the theories advanced in Nancy Chodorow's *The Reproduction of Mothering: Psychoanalysis and the Sociology of Gender*. Berkeley: University of California Press, 1978.), and draws a number of both expected and unexpected conclusions. An often-mentioned, often-criticized classic.

Rapp, Adrian, Lynda Dodgen, and Anne K. Kaler. "A Romance Writer Gets Away with Murder." *Clues: A Journal of Detection* 21 (Spring/Summer 2000): 17–21.
This article in this special issue of *Clues* focuses on the works of romantic suspense writer Sandra Brown.

Raub, Patricia. "Issues of Passion and Power in E. M. Hull's *The Sheik*." *Women's Studies* 21 (1992): 119–128.
Noting that Carol Thurston considers *The Sheik* to be "the first romance of the twentieth century," Raub takes a fresh look at this infamous book and concludes that it is "a significant work in the development of popular women's fiction."

Regis, Pamela. "Female Genre Fiction in the Twentieth Century." In *The Cambridge History of the American Novel*. Cambridge: Cambridge University Press, 2011.
This chapter offers a definition of the Romance Novel, discusses its place in literary history, and analyzes seven twentieth-century Romance novels.

Roach, Catherine. "Getting a Good Man to Love: Popular Romance Fiction and the Problem of Patriarchy." *Journal of Popular Romance Studies* 1, no. 1 (August 4, 2010), jprstudies.org/2010/08/getting-a-good-man-to-love-popular-romance-fiction-and-the-problem-of-patriarchy-by-catherine-roach.
Roach discusses the Christian and mythic roots and redemptive nature of the romance narrative and how the narrative allows women readers to "engage in a reparation fantasy of healing in regard to male/female relations. . . . and deal with the paradoxical relationship toward men within a culture still marked by patriarchy and threats of violence."

Roberts, Sherron Killingsworth. "Twenty-Five Years and Counting of Sweet Valley: Jessica and Elizabeth in Romance Novels for Young Children?" *Journal of Research in Childhood Education* 24, no. 2 (April 2010): 123–139.
The author's analysis shows that the same marketing techniques are used to reach both the Sweet Valley series readers (including young grade school children targeted by Sweet Valley Kids) and the adult Romance market.

Ross, Catherine Sheldrick. "Reader on Top: Public Libraries, Pleasure Reading, and Models of Reading." *Library Trends* 57, no. 4 (Spring 2009): 632–656.
Using series book readers and Romance readers as test cases, this study explores two "competing models that have been available for librarians to use in their discourse and policy making about pleasure reading. . . . 'Reading with a Purpose' and 'Only the Best.' "

Ryder, Mary Ellen. "Smoke and Mirrors: Event Patterns in the Discourse Structure of a Romance Novel." *Journal of Pragmatics: An Interdisciplinary Journal of Language Studies* 31 (August 1999): 1067–1080.
An amazing study that considers one 1953 novel by Barbara Cartland typical of the entire Romance Genre, analyzes the climax of the novel, implies that Romance heroines are uniformly passive, and draws the conclusion that the goal of Romance writers is to "sell their audience dreams without substance."

Saunders, Corinne, ed. *A Companion to Romance: From Classical to Contemporary*. Malden, MA: Blackwell, 2004.
This series of essays on romance in literature by various scholars casts a broad net and includes chapters on everything from Ancient Romance and Arthurian Romance to Quest romance in Science Fiction and Popular Romance and Its Readers. Poetry, prose, and drama are all included in this critical anthology.

Scott, Alison M. "Romance in the Stacks; or, Popular Romance Fiction Imperiled." In *Scorned Literature: Essays on the History and Criticism of Popular Mass-Produced Fiction in America*, edited by Lydia Cushman Schurman and Deidre Johnson, 213–231. Westport, CT: Greenwood Press, 2002.
This article discusses the lack of research access to Popular Romance Novels, especially the series, because they are not deemed worthy of collection by most academic libraries.

Stein, Atara. *The Byronic Hero in Film, Fiction, and Television*. Carbondale: Southern Illinois University, 2004.
This readable study traces the history of the classic Byronic hero (ambitious, aggressive, individualistic, creative) and explores his modern-day manifestations in current fiction and media. Some attention is paid to the Byronic heroine, as well.

Strehle, Susan, and Mary Paniccia Garden, eds. *Doubled Plots: Romance and History*. Jackson: University Press of Mississippi, 2003.
Challenging the assumption that the history and Romance genres are diametrically opposed, the ten essays in this collection argue that the two genres actually parallel and reflect each other and share expectations in numerous ways. An exceptionally wide-ranging collection.

Sullivan, Larry E., and Lydia Cushman Schurman, eds. *Pioneers, Passionate Ladies, and Private Eyes: Dime Novels, Series Books, and Paperbacks*. New York: Haworth Press, 1996.
An illuminating collection of essays on the development and significance of series books, dime novels, and paperbacks, their relationship to each other, and their cultural importance. " 'The Bride of the Tomb' of The Story Paper Debut of Mrs. Alex. McVeigh Miller" by Angela J. Farkas and "Romancing the Reader: From Laura Jean Libbey to Harlequin Romance and Beyond" by Jean Carwile Masteller are particularly relevant.

Thompson, Anne B. "Rereading Fifties Teen Romances: Reflections on Janet Lambert." *Lion and the Unicorn: A Critical Journal of Children's Literature* 29 (September 2005): 373–396
This article revisits Lambert's Tippy Parrish series and compares it with other romances of the time, as well as with *Jane Eyre* and today's Sweet Valley series.

Thurston, Carol. *The Romance Revolution: Erotic Novels for Women and the Quest for a New Sexual Identity.* Urbana: University of Illinois Press, 1987.
Still useful and often referenced.

Tsagaris, Ellen M. *The Subversion of Romance in the Novels of Barbara Pym.* Bowling Green, OH: Bowling Green State University Popular Press, 1998.
This study explores the relationship between Barbara Pym's novels and the Popular Romance and concludes that in subverting a number of classic elements of Romance, Pym shows that the true "happy ending" for her heroines is living and enjoying "life on their own terms, without looking over their shoulder to see if society approves." An interesting, thought-provoking study.

"Special Issue on American Romance Authors." *Teaching American Literature: A Journal of Theory and Practice* 2, nos. 2–3 (Spring/Summer 2008).
This special issue of this open-access online journal includes articles on "Suzanne Brockmann" (Sarah S. G. Frantz), "Anita Richmond Bunkley" (Fahamisha Patricia Brown), "Jennifer Crusie" (Wendy Wagner), "Janet Evanovich" (Leslie Haynsworth), "Beverly Jenkins" (Fahamisha Patricia Brown), "LaVyrle Spencer" (Lee Anna Maynard), "Nora Roberts" (Wylene Rholetter), "Rosemary Rogers" (Gillian Mason), and "Danielle (Fernande) Steel" (Suzanne Milton).

Wardrop, Stephanie. "The Heroine is Being Beaten: Freud, Sadomasochism, and Reading the Romance." *Style* 29 (fall 1995): 459–473.

Whelehan, Imelda. *The Feminist Bestseller: From Sex and the Single Girl to Sex and the City.* New York: Palgrave Macmillan, 2005.
Although not strictly about the Romance Genre, this study reexamines the effect of feminism on women's fiction from the classics of the late sixties to the chick lit of today and concludes that today's popular women's fiction bears the imprint of feminist ideas and that feminism must become more open to popular culture if it is to survive.

Wikborg, Eleanor. *The Lover as Father Figure in Eighteenth-Century Women's Fiction.* Gainesville: University of Florida Press, 2002.
An intriguing examination of the ways in which women authors of the period reconciled the contradiction that women would be happy and satisfied in marriage with the inequality of power that actually existed between husband and wife. An illuminating study of novels that the author says could serve as "conduct books for men."

Wood, Helen. "What *Reading the Romance* Did for Us." *European Journal of Cultural Studies* 7 (May 2004): 147–154.
Discusses the far-reaching effects of Janet Radway's *Reading the Romance*, which she approached from a literary background, on a number of sociological disciplines, such as anthropology, librarianship, sociology, communication, history, and cultural studies.

Young, Erin S. "Escaping the 'Time Bind': Negotiations of Love and Work in Jayne Ann Krentz's 'Corporate Romances.'" *Journal of American Culture* 33 (June 2010): 92–106.
Using Krentz's *Sharp Edges* as an example of the "corporate romance," and comparing it initially to older "conventional romances," Young seeks to "unpack the corporate romance's generic implications and contribute to a new understanding of romance's social significance in the era of flexible global capitalism."

Zinberg, Marsha. *The Art of Romance: 30 Postcards: A Century of Romance Art*. Don Mills, Ontario: Harlequin Enterprises, 1999.
Drawing on the back-files of Mills & Boon and Harlequin, this novelty collection of thirty postcards provides examples of Romance book cover art for the past hundred years. Not a scholarly resource, but useful and informative.

Governesses and Ladies' Maids

As any reader of Historical Romances knows, household employees (particularly the governess, the companion, or the abigail/lady's maid) often play a prominent part in these stories—either as the heroine (a particularly popular convention in Gothics) or as a supporting character. The following studies provide a serious, yet entertaining, look at the English governess and abigail of fact and fiction. Unfortunately the Stuart and the West books are currently out of print, but they should be available in larger libraries.

Hughes, Kathryn. *The Victorian Governess*. London: Hambledon Press, 1993. (Reprinted by Hambledon & London, 2003.)
Meticulously documented and nicely illustrated, this study uses both primary and secondary sources to examine the role of the governess in Victorian society. Serious, well-researched, and readable.

Stuart, Dorothy Margaret. *The English Abigail*. London: Macmillan, 1946.
This fascinating study covers the English abigail as she existed in history and is portrayed in literature for six centuries. Especially interesting for its pre-nineteenth-century coverage.

Thomson, Patricia. *The Victorian Heroine: A Changing Ideal, 1837–1873*. New York: Greenwood Press, 1956. (Reprinted by Greenwood Press, 1978.)
The section on governesses is exceptionally well-done.

West, Katharine. *Chapter of Governesses: A Study of the Governess in English Fiction, 1800–1949*. London: Cohen and West, 1949. (Reprinted by Norwood Editions, 1978.)
An excellent survey of English "literary governesses" from the Regency Period to just after World War II.

Dissertations and Theses

One indication of a subject's legitimacy, at least within the academic community, is the number of doctoral dissertations and masters theses it generates. Although Romance Fiction has been minimally represented in this literature, the last two decades have seen an exponential increase in scholarly studies of this type. A small selection of recent and relevant older examples are listed below. Consult previous editions of this guide for titles and annotations that may have been dropped, and for an ongoing online scholarly bibliography, see *Romance Scholarship: An On-Line Bibliography* (www.romancewiki. com/Romance_Scholarship).

Adams, Kathleen Barzun. "Thirty Years of Change: Heroes, Heroines, and the Popular Romance." Master's Thesis. Trinity College, 2003.

Anderton, Gretchen E. "Excitement, Adventure, Indifference: Romance Readers' Perceptions of How Romance Reading Impacts Their Sex Lives." EdD diss., Widener University, 2009.

Araujo, Gail. "Living to Read Romance: The Transformative Potential of Interpretive Practice in Romance Reading." master's thesis, California State University, Fullerton, 2009.
Using data gathered from extensive interviews with nine women, Araujo demonstrates that "romance reading serves as a crucial resistive practice for women. . . . and counters the argument that romances negatively influence women readers."

Bryson, Mary. "Public Library Services to the Romance Reader: an Online Survey of Romance Readers." master's thesis, University of North Carolina at Chapel Hill, 2004.
Using an online questionnaire to determine the needs of Romance readers and analyze how well these needs were being met by public libraries, this study points out ways in which libraries are not meeting the needs of Romance readers and makes suggestions for improved services.

Burley, Stephanie Carol. "Hearts of Darkness: The Racial Politics of Popular Romance." PhD diss., University of Maryland, College Park, 2003.
Examines the ways in which the codes of whiteness (feminine/purity) and darkness (male/danger and sensuality) function in various Romance subgenres by analyzing a Silhouette miniseries, Western Romances, and the works of Dara Joy and Sandra Kitt. "Playing in the Dark" by Toni Morrison informs the study.

Chappel, Deborah Kaye. "American Romances: Narratives of Culture and Identity." PhD diss., Duke University, Durham, North Carolina, 1991.
This wide-ranging study examines the relationship between the American Popular Romance and American feminism through the works of Jude Deveraux, LaVyrle Spencer, Janet Dailey, Kathleen Winsor, Margaret Mitchell, Edna Ferber, and E.D.E.N. Southworth. An important dissertation.

Coddington, Lynn. "Romance and Power: Writing Romance Novels as a Women's Writing Practice." PhD diss., University of California, Berkeley, 1997.
Uses a "critical theory interpretive framework and an ethnographic case study approach [to] analyze the ways in which a small group of professional and aspiring Romance writers create and negotiate identity and community through their writing practices." Unique and informative.

DiVisconte, Jessica. "The Recession and Its Effect on the Romance Genre." master's thesis, Pace University, 2009.
Examines the reasons for the success of the Romance Genre in the midst of a major economic recession.

Faust, Meredith S. " 'Love of the Purest Kind': Heteronormative Rigidity in the Homoerotic Fiction of Ann Herendeen." master's thesis, DePaul University, 2010.
Examines the ménage relationships in Herendeen's *Phyllida and the Brotherhood of Philander* and *Pride and Prejudice* to determine whether "heteronormative desires

15

16

17

18

19

20

21

22

and structures are subverted, maintained, or reconfigured entirely creating multiple and complicated representations of sexuality."

Fletcher, Lisa. "I Love You: Historical Romance Fiction and Heterosexuality." PhD thesis, University of Melbourne, 2002.

Funderburk, Amy. "Romance Collections in North Carolina Public Libraries: Are All Genres Treated Equally?" M.S.L.S. Thesis. University of North Carolina at Chapel Hill, 2004.
Compares the numbers of award-winning genre fiction books held in public libraries in North Carolina with the availability of reviews in major review sources and concludes that there is a direct correlation between the two (i.e., books that have been reviewed are more likely to be in public library collections than those that have not).

Goade, Sally Ann. "'And with the Land, Our Spirits So Blended': Interrelated Frontier Quests of Self in Contemporary Historical Romance: A Study of Rosanne Bittner's 'Savage Destiny' Series." DA diss., Idaho State University, Pocatello, 1999.
Examines Bittner's seven-book Savage Destiny series, drawing parallels between the interpersonal relationship of the half-Cheyenne hero and white heroine within their domestic sphere and the events in the public sphere of the larger world.

Gregor, Theresa Lynn. "From Captors to Captives: American Indian Responses to Popular American Narrative Forms." PhD thesis, University of Southern California, 2010.
This broad study "examines the metamorphosis of the American Indian captivity narrative" in several forms, including the role it plays in the popular American/Indian Romance. Includes a discussion of the works of Cassie Edwards and Janet Wellington.

Griffin, Linda Coleman. "An Analysis of Meaning Creation through the Integration of Sociology and Literature: A Critical Ethnography of a Romance Reading Group." EdD diss., University of Houston, Texas, 1999.
Analyzes the social structure of Romance reading groups to determine how women use Romances to construct meaning and to understand the tension between the literary critics and those who read Popular Romances.

Harzewski, Stephanie. "The New Novel of Manners: Chicklit and Postfeminist Sexual Politics." PhD diss., University of Pennsylvania, 2006.
An analysis of "chicklit as a genre as well as an overlooked source of sociocultural commentary."

Henderson, Courtney R. "Ladies and Loners: A Comparative Gender Study of the Romance and Popular Western." master's thesis, University of Texas, Arlington, 2007.
This study seeks to discover the reasons for these two genres' popularity through and analysis of the gender-specific fantasies provided by them.

Hurley, Frances Kay. "In the Words of Girls: the Reading of Adolescent Romance Fiction." EdD diss., Harvard University, 1999.
Using the premise from an earlier study (Brown and Gilligan, 1992) that described the "perfect girl" as passive, selfless, and thin by "white" standards, Hurley uses a sample of twenty young adolescent, middle-class girls to determine the effect of the Sweet Valley High series on their perceptions of what the "perfect girl" should be.

15

Jagodzinski, Mallory Diane. "Of Bustles and Breeches: Cross-Dressing Romance Novel Heroines and the Performance of Gender Ideology." master's thesis, Bowling Green State University, 2010.
Using the theories of Stella Bruzzi and Lisa Fletcher to examine *The Spy* by Celeste Bradley, *Duchess by Night* by Eloisa James, and *Almost a Gentleman* by Pam Rosenthal, the author shows that the cross-dressing heroine plot device aids the "heroine in her discovery of self."

16

Johnson, Naomi Ruth. "Consuming Desires: A Feminist Analysis of Bestselling Teen Romance Novels." PhD diss., University of North Carolina, Chapel Hill, 2007.
The author argues, through an examination of three Young Adult Romance series lines, that the "novels' central focus is not romance at all, but rather how an idealized femininity may be established through consumption."

17

Kamble, Jayashree. "Uncovering and Recovering the Popular Romance Novel." PhD diss., University of Minnesota, 2008.
An in-depth analysis of the development and perception of the Popular Romance novel that "proves the genre's struggle with an economic, political, and social ideology that has gathered force over the last hundred years." Also includes a study of Romance reading in India.

18

Kinard, Amanda Marette. "Forbidden Pleasures: The Romance and Its Readers." PhD diss., Vanderbilt University, 1998.
Using a wide range of Romance texts, nonliterary sources, and interviews, this study takes a serious, open approach to the genre, tracing the development of its structure and conventions and examining a variety of its aspects of the genre (e.g., the constructive relationship of the writer, the reader, and the heroine; the often unacknowledged articulation of feminist principles; women's quest for fulfillment in a variety of areas; and issues of gender, class, and capitalism).

19

Kloester, Jennifer V. "Georgette Heyer; Writing the Regency; History in Fiction from *Regency Buck* to *Lady of Quality* 1935–1972." PhD diss., University of Melbourne, 2004.

20

Kolko, Beth E. "Writing the Romance: Cultural Studies, Community, and the Teaching of Writing." PhD diss. University of Texas at Austin, 1994. Abstract in *Dissertation Abstracts International* 55 (December 1994): 1561A.
Kolko uses a three-year study of the Romance Writers of America to illustrate her contention that "adopting a postmodern feminist perspective and subsequently focusing on sites and acts of cultural production is an effective mode of inquiry." An important, unusual study that focuses on the writers, the act of writing, and the resulting community.

21

Lohmann, Jennifer. "'Beauty and the Beast' Themes in Romance Novels." master's thesis, University of North Carolina, Chapel Hill, 2006.

22

Moffitt, Mary Anne Smeltzer. "Understanding Middle-Class Adolescent Leisure: A Cultural Studies Approach to Romance Novel Reading." PhD diss., University of Illinois at Urbana-Champaign, 1990.
A series of three studies that examine the popularity of adolescent leisure reading, the Romance reading habits of teenage girls, and differences and similarities between adult and adolescent readers. Findings indicate that "reading romance novels holds significant importance . . . because it is leisure, it is adolescent leisure, and it is fun."

Morrisey, Katherine. "Fanning the Flames of Romance: An Exploration of Fan Fiction and the Romance Novel." master's thesis, Georgetown University, 2009.
An analysis of romantic fan fiction and Romance novels through examining texts and publisher's writing guidelines and surveying of fiction readers.

Mussell, Kay Johnson. "The World of Modern Gothic Fiction: American Women and Their Social Myths." PhD diss., University of Iowa, 1973.
One of the earliest dissertations to treat modern Romance Fiction seriously.

Pearce, Elizabeth Florence. "Reading the Lesbian Romance: Re-Imagining Love, Sex, Relationships, and Community." PhD diss., University of Iowa, 2004.
Examines the development of mainstream and lesbian Romance novels through twenty-five lesbian Romances and interviews and conversations with readers.

Secrease, Cassandra L. "A Comparative Analysis of Lesbian Romance Novels and Heterosexual Romance Novel Themes." March 2000. master's thesis, Central Missouri State University, Warrensburg, 2000.
Compares the plot patterns and protagonists of five lesbian novels with their stereotypical counterparts in heterosexual romance and concludes that the romance "formula" is fundamental to both types of Romance, even though there are some differences.

Tennenhouse, Tracy. "Female Fantasies in Women's Popular Fiction." June 1996. PhD diss., University of California, Santa Barbara, 1996.
Comparing the current Romance novel with the American domestic novel of the nineteenth century, Tennenhouse concludes that although the novel and its heroine have evolved and adapted (ethnically, sexually, culturally) as society has changed, they still reflect women's basic concerns about their societal roles as shown through the escapist fantasies these novels provide.

Therrien, Kathleen Mary. "Trembling at Her Own Response: Resistance and Reconciliation in Mass-Market Romance Novels." 1997. PhD diss., University of Delaware, Newark, 1998.
Explores the works of Julie Garwood, Jayne Ann Krentz/Amanda Quick, and Susan Wiggs focusing on inconsistencies that could cause the collapse of the internal logic of the novels and the various ways in which these are negotiated and resolved.

White, Ann Yvonne. "Genesis Press: Cultural Representation and Production of African American Romance Novels." PhD diss., University of Iowa, 2008.
Focuses on Genesis Press, an early publisher of African American Romance Novels.

Young, Beth Rapp. "But Are They Any Good?: Women Readers, Formula Fiction, and the Sacralization of the Literary Canon." PhD diss., University of Southern California, 1995.
Tracing the bias against popular fiction to the sacralization of the literary canon in the late nineteenth century which "privileged 'vertical' reading . . . over 'horizontal' reading" (which she likens to reading hypertext and also rereading), Young argues that popular genre novels, which must be read horizontally (reading many books of the same type instead of only one in depth) in order to understand the complexities of the genre, cannot be legitimately evaluated or appreciated unless this basic difference, as well as the specific needs and practices of the individual reader, are taken into account.

Young, Erin. S. "Corporate Heroines and Utopian Individualism: A Study of the Romance Novel in Global Capitalism." PhD diss., University of Oregon, 2010.

Using the "corporate" novels of Jayne Ann Krentz, Elizabeth Lowell, Nora Roberts, and Katherine Stone, and the paranormal Romances of Laurel K. Hamilton, Carrie Vaughn, Charlaine Harris, and Kelley Armstrong, Young contrasts the ways in which the heroines in the two subgenres deal with the tension between work and home.

Trade and Library Publication Articles

The primary source of articles on the topic of the Romance, particularly for writers, is *RWR: Romance Writers' Report* (see chapter 17, "Periodicals and Review Sources"), but articles on Romance do appear in more general publications. A limited selection of these, both older and more recent, is listed below.

Adkins, Denice, Linda Esser, and Diane Velasquez. "Relations Between Librarians and Romance Readers." *Public Libraries* 45 (July/August 2006): 54–64.
This article reports on a survey of Missouri public librarians' attitudes toward romance fiction and its readers. The authors are in the process of conducting a similar study on a nationwide basis.

Adkins, Denice, Linda R. Esser, and Diane Velasquez. "Promoting Romance Novels in American Public Libraries." *Public Libraries* 49 (July/August 2010): 41–48.
This article reports on a nationwide survey that asked "*If* libraries were promoting the Romance genre, and if they were, *how* they were going about that promotion." Results indicated that half of the libraries provided readers' advisory services for Romance, four in ten used displays, and only 5% to 10% provided any type of Romance programming.

Charles, John, and Shelley Mosley. "Getting Serious about Romances: Adult Series Romances for Teens." *Voice of Youth Advocates* 25 (June 2002): 87–93.
This article takes a look at the adult series Romance lines and focuses on those titles that might appeal to and be appropriate for teens. Includes a useful bibliography of reference sources (both print and online) and a delightfully long list of recommended series Romance titles.

Charles, John, and Shelley Mosley. "Core Collection: Cowboys in Love." *Booklist* 106 (August 1, 2010): 43.
A short, highly relevant annotated bibliography of recent, popular Western Romances.

Charles, John, and Shelley Mosley. "Core Collection: The New Stars of Historical Romance." *Booklist* 107 (September 15, 2010): 40.
A short, highly relevant annotated bibliography of recent, popular Fistorical Romances.

Charles, John, Shelley Mosley, and Ann Bouricius. "Romancing the YA Reader: Romance Novels Recommended for Young Adults." *Voice of Youth Advocates* 21 (February 1999): 414–419.
Providing a brief overview and positive discussion of the adult Romance genre and its relevance to teenage readers, this well-crafted article includes useful lists of selected reference resources and recommended Romances. Winner of the 2000 Romance Writers of America Veritas Award for the article best representing Romance Fiction published in 1999.

Charles, John, and Cathie Linz. "Romancing Your Readers: How Public Libraries Can Become More Romance-Reader Friendly." *Public Libraries* 44 (January/February 2005): 43–48.
Takes a creative look at ways of providing better service to Romance readers.

Chelton, Mary K. "Readers' Advisory 101." *Library Journal* 128 (November 1, 2003): 38–39.
A survey by library school students seeking help in local public libraries are discussed in this enlightening survey that describes some incredibly bad examples of readers' advisory service, including some examples of totally inappropriate read-a-likes.

Chelton, Mary K. "Unrestricted Body Parts and Predictable Bliss: The Audience Appeal of Formula Romances." *Library Journal* 116 (July 1991): 44–49.
A lively, groundbreaking article on the appeal of the popular Romance, its conventions, its place in libraries, and how to select and handle material and advise readers. Includes a useful grid analysis of the various Romance lines. A classic in the field.

Chelton, Mary K., Cathie Linz, Joyce Saricks, Lynne Welch, and Ann Bouricius. "What Kind of Romance Are You in the Mood For?: A Recommended Reading List." *Booklist* 98 (September 15, 2001): 210–212.
Takes an insightful look at the importance of matching Romance novels to the readers' moods and offers readers' advisory tips for accomplishing this. Includes a good bibliography.

Danford, Natalie, Lucinda Dyer, Suzanne Mantell, and Judith Rosen. "Love For Sale." *Publishers Weekly* 251 (July 5, 2004): 20–24.
A category close-up segment that focuses on the business side of Romance and what the various houses are doing to expand their markets.

Danford, Natalie. "Seducing the Reader." *Publishers' Weekly* 241 (May 30, 1994): 28–30.
Overview of Romance promotion, including covers, contests, and TV campaigns.

Danford, Natalie, Lucinda Dyer, Karen Holt, and Judith Rosen. "Toujours l'Amour: Publishers Are Seeking to Increase Readership by Diversifying Subgenres and Adding New Category Niches." *Publishers Weekly* 250 (December 1, 2003): 26–36.
One of *Publishers Weekly*'s regular close-up features on the Romance Genre, this article focuses on the genre's new directions.

Dyer, Lucinda, and Robert Dahlin. "Roundup on Romance: Birds Do It, Bees Do It." *Publishers' Weekly* 244 (November 10, 1997): 40–50.
One of *Publishers Weekly*'s periodic reviews of the state of Popular Romance Fiction, this lively article won the 1998 Romance Writers of America's Veritas award for the article best representing Romance Fiction published in 1997.

Kloberdanz, Kristin. "Don't Write Off Romance: Thought You Could Dismiss It? Think Again: Meet Nora Roberts, the Queen of the Genre, Who Reigns Over a Changed Landscape." *Book* (March/April 2002): 46–52.
The title says it all in this well-done article that focuses on Nora Roberts and the evolving Romance industry.

Krentz, Jayne Ann. "All the Right Reasons: Romance Fiction in the Public Library." *Public Libraries* 36 (May/June 1997): 162–166.
Originally presented as a speech at the Public Libraries Association Conference in Portland, Oregon, in March 1996, this powerful article discusses the evolution of the Popular

Romance novel from dime store paperback to bestselling hardcover and its eventual recognition as a legitimate literary genre, worthy in its own right because, like all the popular fiction genres, it "preserves the heroic traditions and affirms our core values and beliefs."

Krentz, Jayne Ann. "The Alpha Male." *Romance Writers' Report* 10 (January/February 1990): 26–28.
This seminal article defines and discusses one of the basic Romance hero types.

Mantell, Suzanne. "Online Romance: A Little-Known Author Courts Fans with a Website That Propels Her Career to New Heights." *Publishers Weekly* 249 (August 12, 2002): 246.
This article highlights Romance and Fantasy author Sherrilyn Kenyon/Kinley MacGregor's use of the web to increase her name recognition and reach current and countless new fans. Exceptional example of the power of the web.

Maxwell, Ann, and Jayne Ann Krentz. "The Wellsprings of Romance." *Romance Writers' Report* 9 (September 1989): 21–22.
Excellent discussion of basic myths and archetypes on which Romance is based.

Mosley, Shelley, John Charles, and Julie Havir. "The Librarian as Effete Snob: Why Romance?" *Wilson Library Bulletin* 69 (May 1995): 24–25+.
A hard-hitting, articulate article that takes librarians to task for the profession's traditional superior attitude toward the Romance Genre. Destroys the time-honored excuses librarians use for keeping Romances out of their collections and then provides credible reasons for collecting Romances. Winner of RWA's 1995 Veritas Award, given for the publication that best represents the Romance Genre. Another required read.

Osborne, Gwendolyn. "How Black Romance—Novels That Is—Came to Be." *Black Issues Book Review* 4 (January/February 2002): 50–51.
This short, informative article traces the origins of the African American Romance novels from the years after WWII (includes mention of Frank Yerby, Elsie B. Washington, and Sandra Kitt as groundbreakers) through the establishment of the Arabesque (Kensington) line in the mid-1990s.

Ramsdell, Kristin. "Young Adult Publishing: A Blossoming Market." *Top of the News* 39 (winter 1983): 173–181.
An early discussion of book publishing for young adults and the beginning of the series Romance market aimed at teen readers.

Ross, Catherine Sheldrick, and Mary K. Chelton. "Reader's Advisory: Matching Mood and Material." *Library Journal* 126 (February 1, 2001): 52–55.
Examines the results of Ross's survey of avid, experienced readers to determine "how they chose books for pleasure reading and what elements they sought," which concludes that the reader's mood is one of the most important factors, and relates the findings to helping readers' advisory librarians more effectively serve the reading public. The analysis of readers' book selection strategies is especially interesting and helpful.

Tuñon, Johanna. "A Fine Romance: How to Select Romances For Your Collection." *Wilson Library Bulletin* 69 (May 1995): 31–34.
A concise, still-relevant article that gives librarians more than enough information to begin the occasionally difficult process of building a good Romance collection.

Wyatt, Neal, ed. "Core Collections in Genre Studies: Romance Fiction 101." *Reference and User Services Quarterly* 47 (Winter 2007): 120–125.
Five librarians who study and/or deal with popular fiction (Georgine Olson, Kristin Ramsdell, Joyce Saricks, Lynne Welch, and Neal Wyatt) pool their expertise to provide suggestions for core collections in the various fiction genres.

Wyatt, Neal, ed. "A Selection of Core Resources for Readers' Advisory Services." *Reference & User Services Quarterly* 49 (Fall 2010): 5–10.
An exceptionally well-thought-out list of readers' advisory sources including books, articles, various websites, blogs, and databases put together by a stellar cast of readers' advisory librarians (Jen Baker, John Charles, Mary K. Chelton, Sarah Statz Cords, Lisa Fraser, Neil Hollands, Teresa L. "Terry" Jacobsen, Cindy Orr, Joyce Saricks, Jacqueline Sasaki, Kaite Mediatore Stover, Barry Trott, Kimberly Wells, and David Wright).

Popular Press Articles

Over the years, the Popular Romance has garnered a bit of coverage in the popular press—most often negative. Recently, however, the coverage has been less condescending and more evenhanded. And although there is still a fair amount of Romance-bashing around, the debate is not nearly as one-sided as in the past. Perhaps the public has finally begun to see the genre for what it really is—and they are liking what they see.

Athitakis, Mark. "That Secret Shame." *SF Weekly*, July 25, 2001.
An insightful, in-depth article based on interviews primarily with Romance writers who live in the San Francisco Bay Area and are members of the San Francisco Bay Area chapter of the RWA.

Babineau, Guy. "The Business of Romance." *Georgia Strait*, February 12, 2004.
This largely positive article focuses on interviews with several popular authors. (The *Georgia Straight* is "Canada's largest urban weekly paper," and serves Vancouver.)

Bly, Mary. "A Fine Romance." *New York Times*, February 12, 2005, A17.
This op-ed piece by academic Mary Bly is the winner of the 2006 Romance Writers of America Veritas Award for the article best representing Romance Fiction published in 2005. Bly, a professor of English at Fordham University, writes Romances as Eloisa James.

Carpenter, Betsy. "Living the Fantasy: Romance Writers Get Some Respect, Scholarly Interest and Tons of Readers." *U.S. News & World Report* 119 (November 16, 1995): 78–81.
A well-done, evenhanded article on the current situation in Romance Fiction. Winner of the 1996 Romance Writers of America Veritas Award.

Cohen, Sarah. "Romance, Chapter & Verse: Sex Flavors the Genre's Heady Brew, but a Context of Commitment is Essential." *Indianapolis Star*, May 29, 2001.
This generally positive, upbeat article is based on interviews with Romance writers, readers, and scholars.

Collins, Lauren. "Real Romance." *The New Yorker*, June 22, 2009, 60–69.
An informative profile of Nora Roberts's life, her books, and their influence.

Graham, Ellen. "Romances, Long Denied Reviews, Get Some Respect." *Wall Street Journal*, June 28, 1995, B1.
Short, evenhanded commentary on the Romance Genre and the reviews (and the new respect) the books are now getting in mainstream publications.

Grossman, Lev. "Rewriting the Romance." *Time* 161 (February 3, 2003): 64.
This short, funny, somewhat flip article is primarily an interview with historical author Julia Quinn.

McLaughlin, Patricia. "Love and Hisses: Go Ahead, Make Jokes. We'll be Here with Our Fans." *Washington Post*, July 23, 2000, B01.
This article features comments by a number of Romance writers and is the winner of the 2001 RWA Veritas Award for the article best representing Romance fiction published in 2000. McLaughlin writes Romances as Patricia McLinn.

O'Briant, Don. "Romantic Encounters—Romance Diversifies, Expands." *Atlanta Journal-Constitution*, February 13, 2004, B1.
This short article was the winner of the 2005 Romance Writers of America Veritas Award for the article best representing Romance Fiction published in 2004.

Ogunnaike, Lola. "With Trembling Hand, She Reached Out and Caressed the Autograph." *New York Times*, July 21, 2003, E1.
This article covers the annual RWA Conference (in 2003 is was in New York) and includes an interview with author Suzanne Brockmann.

Riggs, Doug. "Romance by the Book." *Providence Sunday Journal*, February 24, 1999, Arts Week, K1.
Five Rhode Island authors discuss the genre, their participation in it, and the joys and difficulties involved.

Schoenberg, Nara. "Romancing the Classroom—Purple Passion Hits Campus as Bodice Rippers Become a Focus of Serious Study." *Chicago Tribune*, February 13. 2001, 1.
Winner of the 2002 Romance Writers of America Veritas Award for the article best representing Romance Fiction published in 2001, this article discusses the growing presence of college courses that teach the Romance Novel.

Senior, Jennifer. "The Dream Girl." *New York* (August 21, 2000): 34–39.
An in-depth article that focuses on Harlequin's no-nonsense editorial chief, Isabel Swift, and the publisher's plans for reaching new readers.

Sprackland, Teri. "Romancing Readers Worth billions." *National Desk*, July 29, 2002.
This article by UPI Wire correspondent Sprackland won the 2003 Romance Writers of America Veritas Award for the article best representing Romance Fiction published in 2002.

"True Love Returns: the Romance Novel." *The Economist* 364 (July 27, 2002): 31.
This short, unsigned article is an example of coverage of the genre in a rather unexpected source.

Vidimos, Robin. "Embracing No-Pulp Fiction." *Denver Post*, April 29, 2001, I03.
Covering the Romancing the Rockies Conference in Denver, this article features interviews with Romance writers Catherine Coulter and Robin Lee Hatcher.

White, Pamela. "Romancing Society." *Boulder Weekly*, July 15–22, 2002.
Based on interviews with writers and other industry professionals gathered during RWA's Annual Conference in Denver, this article discusses the state of the genre and some common misconceptions about it.

NOTE

1. The Mystery/Detective, Science Fiction, and Fntasy genres, in particular, boast numerous reference sources and critical and historical materials. Although many individual guides exist for these genres, *Genreflecting: A Guide to Reading Interests in Genre Fiction*, 6th ed., by Wayne Wiegand and Diana Tixier Herald (Westport, CT: Libraries Unlimited, 2006) covers many of the basic sources in a single volume.

Chapter 16

Author Biography and Bibliography

Biographical and bibliographical information for those writers whose romantic novels have been deemed worthy of the appellation "literature" is abundant and readily available. This is particularly true for authors of historical importance, such as Jane Austen and the Brontës. However, although the situation is improving, this same kind of information for less well-known historical authors or current writers of Romance is not so easily located.

Of course, the Internet and the web have made searching for this kind of information much simpler than in the past. Today most of us try online sources first, and then head for print, if we don't have any luck finding what we were looking for online. To be sure, there are any number of excellent resources to help us with our online searches, such as subscription databases (e.g., Gale's Literature Resource Center), author and publisher websites, and a host of other freely available websites. And while much of what is currently available is actually in print, as well—or at least started life that way—it is also true that less information is making its way into books than before and a lot more is going directly online.

Yes, the web and its resources are wonderful—however, they are not always enough. For example, while information on older, "read and dead" authors is plentiful online (consider the plethora of relatively accurate data freely available on Jane Austen or the Brontë sisters), information on less popular writers is not so easily come by. To be sure, author websites for current authors abound and they are often filled with personal reflections, some biographical information, and almost always plenty of information about their upcoming books. (The purpose of most of these sites, entertaining though many of them may be, is to sell books, after all.) The best sites are excellent and often provide detailed bibliographies, complete with character links and publishing information. However, even these may not always give you what you need. (How often have you tried to figure out where an author lived and couldn't? Or tried to find an author's website only to learn he or she didn't have one—or that it was last updated in 2008?) The open web is truly wonderful and filled with all kinds of good information, but it is also uncontrolled, changeable, and accountable to no one.

The fee-based resources, often electronic versions of print sources, are more reliable, although because they all aren't retrospective, they may be incomplete, as well. The point is, sometimes you may need more than the web can provide—and you just might have to go to print. Fortunately, there are plenty of resources available, especially for older, sometimes hard-to-find information.

Publications that include biographical articles on current Romance writers are among those listed in the "Periodicals" section of chapter 17, "Periodicals and Review Sources." In addition, particularly popular current authors may be profiled in certain general interest magazines, many of which are indexed in tools such as *Readers' Guide to Periodical Literature, Biography Index, Expanded Academic ASAP, Academic Search Premier,* and other periodical databases. Standard author biography sources, such as *Contemporary Authors* will list brief biographical and bibliographical information for a number of authors, including some relatively well-established Romance writers. In addition, a number of sources that provide information on specific types of nonromance authors may also include writers of romantic fiction. For example, *American Women Writers: A Critical Reference Guide From Colonial Times to the Present* (New York: Frederick Ungar, 2000), second edition, includes among its entries a number of not-quite-so-well-known early Romance writers in addition to more recent ones. Although older, some of the following books in the St. James or Twentieth Century Writers series are still worth consulting. The *St. James Guide to Crime and Mystery Writers* (Detroit: Gale, 1996), fourth edition, (previous editions were entitled *Twentieth Century Crime and Mystery Writers*), a source similar in format and coverage to *Twentieth-Century Romance and Historical Writers* listed below, contains entries for a number of writers in the romantic suspense genre. The other "siblings," *Twentieth-Century Western Writers* (Chicago: St. James, 1991), second edition; *St. James Guide to Science Fiction Writers* (Detroit: St. James, 1995), fourth edition; and *St. James Guide to Fantasy Writers* (New York: St. James, 1996), may also yield information on Romance writers whose works cross over into these other genres. Another source worth considering is Gale's Dictionary of Literary Biography series. With approximately 360 volumes to date, this wide ranging series currently includes volumes on Western Romance (*Twentieth Century Western Writers,* 1999 [first and second series], 2002 [third series]), mysteries (*American Mystery and Detective* Writers, 2005), and Canadian and British fantasy and science fiction writers (*Canadian Fantasy and Science Fiction Writers,* 2002, and *British Fantasy and Science Fiction Writers,* 2002), as well as earlier genre fiction authors. Unfortunately, as of this writing, a volume on Romance Fiction Writers has not been produced. A basic general author biography index that covers a wide variety of sources and might be worth consulting is the *Author Biographies Master Index* (Detroit, Gale, 1997), fifth edition, which contains references to sources for biographical information on more than one million authors, including a number of past and present Romance writers. The "mother" index for this source, *Biography and Genealogy Master Index* is also useful, particularly in its online version. Note: Many of the Gale sources mentioned above, as well as the other indexes, are available online, and are most easily used in this format.

Author Biographical Sources

Over the past several decades, works in a variety of formats and, more recently, websites that specifically target Romance authors have begun to appear; several are listed below.

Charles, John, and Shelley Mosley. *Romance Today: An A-to-Z Guide to Contemporary American Romance Writers.* Westport, CT: Greenwood, 2007.
One of the newest of these sources, this well-done reference work includes entries on more than a hundred important American Romance writers, providing biographical and bibliographical

information for each, updating and expanding on earlier works of this type. Informative essays and complete bibliographies arranged by pseudonym enhance this useful resource.

Fallon, Eileen. *Words of Love: A Complete Guide to Romance Fiction*. New York: Garland, 1984.
Dated and limited, this was an early attempt to collect and publish Romance author information.

Mussell, Kay and Tuñon, Johanna, eds. *North American Romance Writers*. Metuchen, NJ: Scarecrow, 1999.
Focusing on North American Romance authors and how they have shaped the genre during the last twenty years, this source features essays by almost fifty influential writers and provides biographical and bibliographical information for each. This work is introduced by an informative and readable essay on the development of the Romance genre since 1950 by Kay Mussell and is concluded by comprehensive bibliography of materials on the subject of the Popular Romance by Johanna Tuñon. Although dated at this point, this is a well-done and most useful and resource.

Sheehan, Sarah E. *Romance Authors: A Reseach Guide*. Santa Barbara, CA: Libraries Unlimited, 2010.
Covering fifty American and international Romance authors, primarily of the twentieth and twenty-first centuries, this alphabetically arranged guide provides biographical information, a list of works, and citations for research sources for each author. A good, recent resource.

Vasudevan, Aruna, and Henderson, Lesley, eds. *Twentieth-Century Romance and Historical Writers*. 3rd ed. London: St. James, 1994.
This and its predecessors are classics in the field.

Biographies, Autobiographies, and Other Single Author Sources

Although volumes of bio-bibliographical materials are readily available for "historically classic" Romance writers, whole books devoted to one current Romance author are fairly rare. Articles, of course, exist in abundance and can be located by searching the appropriate indexes. Below are several examples of the books that do exist.

Cartland, Barbara. *I Reach for the Stars: An Autobiography*. London: Robson, 1994.
The autobiography of one of the legends in the Romance field, complete with pictures and portraits.

Dailey, Janet. *The Janet Dailey Companion: A Comprehensive Guide to Her Life and Her Novels*. New York: Harper Collins, 1996.
A recent guide to Dailey's life and works, featuring interviews and other commentary.

Fahnestock-Thomas, Mary. *Georgette Heyer: A Critical Retrospective*. Saraland, AL: PrinnyWorld Press, 2001.
This eclectic collection of materials by and about the works of Georgette Heyer includes: three short stories and three essays by Heyer, reviews of her books, obituary

notices, a bibliographic essay discussing her inclusion in various reference sources, a bibliography of articles, books, and book chapters—scholarly and otherwise—that discuss Heyer, and dramatizations of her books and accompanying reviews. A chronological and an alphabetical list of her works are also included.

Friedman, Lenemaja. *Mary Stewart*. Boston: Twayne Publishers, 1990.
Part of the Twayne English Authors series and aimed primarily at students, this is one of the few bio-critical sources that focus on this classic Romance writer. Her Romantic Suspense novels, as well as her Arthurian trilogy, are discussed.

Kloester, Jennifer. *Georgette Heyer's Regency World*. London: Heinemann, 2005.
Discussed in the chapter on the Traditional Regency Romance, this resource discusses Regency life as depicted in 26 of Georgette Heyer's Regency novels.

Little, Denise, and Laura Hayden, eds. *The Official Nora Roberts Companion*. New York: Berkley, 2003.
Introduced by Nora, herself, and with a forward by author Julie Garwood, this eclectic compendium includes everything from biographical essays, interviews, and travel commentaries to a complete listing of Roberts's books, complete with bibliographic data, summary, and cover photos. A useful, enjoyable resource.

Robyns, Gwen. *Barbara Cartland: An Authorized Biography*. New York: Doubleday, 1985.
A spirited account by the biographer of Princess Grace and Agatha Christie.

Snodgrass, Mary Ellen. *Reading Nora Roberts*. Santa Barbara, CA: Greenwood Press, 2010.
This reader's guide includes a biography and an in-depth discussion of Roberts's remarkable body of work and her evolving place within the literary field.

From time to time various serial publications appear devoted to one particular writer. Most of these are short-lived and have limited circulation. *The Dailey Report* (Janet Dailey) and *The Friends of Elizabeth Peters Newsletter* (Elizabeth Peters) are two examples. However, with the increasing popularity of the web and e-mail, things have changed radically, and now author websites provide biographical and bibliographic details, chat space, blogs, online newsletters, and a host of other features for fans.

Bibliographies

The works listed above include both biographical and bibliographical information in varying degrees; those that follow are strictly bibliographical. Books devoted solely to the Romance genre and/or its divisions and books that target other genres but include various Romance Subgenres are included. Note: An obvious, but often incomplete and sometimes messy, source of author bibliographies is one of the large online databases, such as OCLC's World Cat or RLIN, or even *Books in Print*. Amazon or other retail websites are also possibilities, especially for current titles, and if the author in question has a website, it will probably include a list of titles, although the bibliographic information may not be complete. In addition, websites such as Fantastic Fiction (www.fantasticfiction.co.uk) and FictionDB (www.fictiondb.com) are becoming quite comprehensive (although there are occasional mistakes in them) and can be useful, as well.

Adamson, Lynda G. *American Historical Fiction: An Annotated Guide to Novels for Adults and Young Adults*. Phoenix, AZ: Oryx Press, 1999.
Includes over three thousand titles of fiction works set in North America, many of which are Romances. The briefly annotated entries are organized by time period, and five indexes (author, title, genre, geographic, and subject) aid access. Note: The genre index has divisions for Love Story and Romance, among other relevant headings.

Adamson, Lynda G. *World Historical Fiction: An Annotated Guide to Novels for Adults and Young Adults*. Phoenix, AZ: Oryx Press, 1998.
Includes more than six thousand titles of fiction works set outside North America, a number of which are Romances. The briefly annotated entries are organized by setting and time period, and five indexes (author, title, genre, place and time, and subject) provide good access. Note: The genre index has divisions for Love Story, Regency Novel, and Romance, to name a few relevant headings. Effectively updates McGarry and White's *World Historical Fiction Guide* listed below.

Hubin, Allen J. *Crime Fiction IV: A Comprehensive Bibliography, 1749–2000*. Shelburne, Ontario: Battered Silicon Dispatch Box, 2003.
This well organized and indexed tool updates Hubin's earlier works and includes listings for various important romantic suspense and gothic writers. A good source, but not widely available.

Husband, Janet, and Jonathan F. Husband. *Sequels: an Annotated Guide to Novels in Series*. 4th ed. Chicago: American Library Association, 2009.
Including series begun since 1989 and updated through 2007, this classic resource includes a number of the items in the Romance or Saga genres and should be of interest to Romance readers. Note: Earlier editions may be of interest as well.

Jaegly, Peggy J., ed. *Romantic Hearts: A Personal Reference for Romance Readers*. 3rd ed. Lanham, MD: Scarecrow, 1997.
Now dated, this would be useful for identifying older titles.

Johnson, Sarah L. *Historical Fiction: A Guide to the Genre*. Westport, CT: Libraries Unlimited, 2005.
Although the primary focus of both titles is on Historical Fiction (set prior to 1950), Johnson includes a chapter on Historical Romance, "Romancing the Past," that should be of interest to Romance readers. This volume includes titles published between 1995 and 2004.

Johnson, Sarah L. *Historical Fiction II: A Guide to the Genre*. Westport, CT: Libraries Unlimited, 2009.
This updates the original volume with over twenty-seven hundred books published from 2004 through mid-2008 and supplements, rather than replaces, it.

Kay, Mary June. *The Romantic Spirit: A Romance Bibliography of Authors and Titles*. San Antonio, TX: MJK Enterprises, 1982 (1983–1984 Update, 1984; 1985–1986 Update, 1986; 1987–1988 Update, 1988).
Now dated, this source is of historical importance because it was one of the earliest attempts at organizing this data.

Ramsdell, Kristin. *What Romance Do I Read Next?* 2nd ed. Detroit: Gale Research, 1999.
A spin-off of the larger *What Do I Read Next?*, this bibliography contains over twenty-seven hundred Romance entries from earlier editions of *What Do I Read Next?*. Numerous indexes provide easy access.

15

16

17

18

19

20

21

22

The Internet

The Internet is also a source of biographical and bibliographical information on Romance authors. In addition to the various lists mentioned in chapter 19, "Societies and Organizations," which often discuss authors and have a number of writers as participants, the web is now burgeoning with websites that focus on Romance authors and their works. Most Romance authors have their own promotional websites, as do the publishers, which will provide bio-bib information in varying degrees. A number of group sites hosting groups of writers exist, as well. In addition to various other amenities (blogs, chat groups, interviews, newsletters, etc.) these may also provide links to the writer's home pages. The Lipstick Chronicles (http://thelipstickchronicles. typepad.com), and Romance Divas (http://romancedivas.com) are only two of the many examples. In addition, RWA (www.rwanational.org) maintains an extensive list of links to members' websites. If you don't have a particular URL, authors websites can usually be located by a simple name search on Google or other search engine, and a number of publishers' websites are listed in chapter 22, "Publishers." A number of websites focus on particular Romance subgenres: Rakehell.com (www.rakehell.com), a Regency-focused site, and The Internet Speculative Fiction Database (www.isfdb.org), an excellent author and title database for all varieties of speculative fiction, are only two examples listed in chapter 17, "Periodicals and Review Sources." Finally, be aware that the web is always a work in progress, and while some websites are quite stable, others come and go quickly, and addresses change. What is there today may not be there tomorrow—but there might be something even better.

Chapter 17

Periodicals and Review Sources

Periodicals

Although Romance Fiction may be discussed, analyzed, or reviewed in a number of general professional periodicals such as *Publishers Weekly*, *The Writer*, *The Writer's Digest*, *Booklist*, *Public Libraries*, or *Library Journal*, the publications listed below are exclusively devoted to Romance Genre Fiction. These vary in method of presentation and may be available in print, online, or both.

Affaire de Coeur

Louise Sneed, Publisher/Editor
3976 Oak Hill Road
Oakland, CA 94605–4931
(510) 569–5675; FAX (510) 632–8868
Website: www.affairedecoeur.com
Published bimonthly.

This publication is available online and in print and provides a selection of ranked reviews, articles, short stories by their short-story contest winners, author interviews, agent profiles, author pseudonyms, information on publishing trends, and other items of interest to Romance readers and writers.

The Gothic Journal

Website: gothicjournal.com

Features reviews and information about the Gothic Romance subgenre. Note: Ceased publication with the October/November 1998 issue. It now functions primarily as a website with reading recommendations and other information about Gothic Romances and links to the Gothic Romance Lending Library and the Gothic Journal Amazon Bookstore.

Journal of Popular Romance Studies

International Association for the Study of Popular Romance (IASPR)
Website: http://iaspr.org
Journal website: http://jprstudies.org

A scholarly online journal published by the International Association for the Study of Popular Romance that was launched in August 2010 and is dedicated to the study of Popular Romance.

The Literary Times

Website: www.tlt.com

Established in 1986, this publication is now online and provides articles, reviews, and other information for fans. Note: at the moment the site is off line and in transition.

PANdora's Box

Romance Writers of America
14615 Benfer Road
Houston, TX 77069
(832) 717–5200

Originally published by the Published Authors Network (PAN) of RWA, this newsletter has been incorporated into RWA's primary publication, *RWR: Romance Writers' Report*, and the PAN portion of RWA's website.

The Regency Reader Newsletter

Website: www.thebeaumonde.com/regencyreader

Published by the Beau Monde, the Regency Special Interest Chapter of RWA, this free monthly online newsletter is aimed at alerting librarians and booksellers to the upcoming crop of Regency Romances being published. Books are summarized rather than critically reviewed, and Regency type (e.g., traditional, romp, sensual, paranormal) is indicated. Some articles are included. Subscribe at the website above.

Rendezvous: A Monthly Review of Contemporary and Historical Romances, Mysteries, and Women's Fiction

Love Designers Writers' Club
1507 Burnham Avenue
Calumet City, IL 60409
(708) 862–9797

This simply presented source includes reviews for most Romances published each month. No advertising is accepted and books do not receive ratings. A credible review source. Its reviews are also available in NoveList, a database available in many public libraries (see Chapter 3, "Advising the Reader"). Ceased publication with the September 2006 issue.

Romance Forever Magazine

This short-lived publication is now defunct.

RWR: Romance Writers Report

Romance Writers of America
14615 Benfer Road
Houston, TX 77069
(832) 717–5200
Website: www.rwanational.org

Available at no cost to members of Romance Writers of America, this monthly (bi-monthly prior to March 1996) publication provides readers with information on market trends, surveys, interviews with writers, agents, editors, and publishers, how-to articles by practicing writers, organizational news, contest and conference announcements, and a wealth of other features of interest to Romance writers and readers.

Romance Sells

Romance Writers of America
14615 Benfer Road
Houston, TX 77069
(832) 717–5200
Website: www.storyforu.com/romancesellsnew.htm

This quarterly publication is available free to booksellers and librarians and includes upcoming Romance releases and relevant articles. See the website listed above for more information.

RT Book Reviews (Romantic Times Book Club Magazine)

Romantic Times Publishing Group
55 Bergen Street
Brooklyn, New York 11201
(718) 237–1097; FAX (718) 624–4231
Website: www.rtbookreviews.com

The best known and most comprehensive periodical in the field, *RT* includes ranked reviews of most Romances published each month, publishing news, author sketches, interviews, articles, and other items of interest to Romance fans and professionals, alike. Even though the reviews tend to be overly positive, the amount of advertising occasionally overwhelming, and the style flamboyant, *RT* currently provides the best overall coverage of the genre. And if you could only subscribe to one Romance periodical, this would probably be it. Note: *RT*'s name changed from *Romantic Times* to *Romantic Times Book Club Magazine* mid-year in 2002, and more recently to RT Book Reviews.

Romantics at Heart

Romance Readers Association

This publication and its supporting organization are no longer in existence.

The SFR Newsletter (Science Fiction Romance)

This source is no longer being published.

Book Review Sources

When looking for Romance reviews, in addition to consulting those periodicals listed above that include reviews, readers may find the following sources helpful. Note: These indexes are most useful in locating reviews of specific Romances by major, established Romance authors. Both print and online sources are included.

Indexes/Databases

These sources are available on a subscription basis and can be found in most public libraries.

Academic Search Premier

This online database lists citations to articles in a variety of popular and scholarly magazines and journals. Romance novels reviewed in the periodicals indexed in this source may be included. Many of the articles are in full text.

Book Review Digest

Arranged by author and indexed by title, this annually cumulated source provides a brief synopsis of the book, excerpts from various reviews, and bibliographic citations for those and others not quoted. Only the most widely read and reviewed Romance authors are found in this tool since a book must receive at least four reviews to be included. It is the oldest source of this type (since 1905) and is available as an online database.

Book Review Index

More comprehensive than *Book Review Digest*, this annually cumulated source provides brief citations of book reviews in various journals. Romance novels reviewed in the periodicals indexed by this source will be included. Available in print and online.

Expanded Academic ASAP

Similar to Academic Search Premier listed above, this online database lists citations to articles in a variety of popular and scholarly magazines and journals. Romance novels reviewed in the periodicals indexed in this source may be included. Many of the articles are in full text.

Lexis/Nexis

The Nexis portion of this full-text resource can be a source of reviews too recent to be included in other indexes. Nexis includes a wide variety of newspapers and popular magazines, many of which are updated on a daily basis.

Proquest Newspapers

This online full-text database lists citations to articles in more than three hundred U.S., International, and regional newspapers. Romance novels reviewed in the newspapers indexed in this source will be included.

Readers' Guide to Periodical Literature (Book Review Section)

The Book Review section at the back of each volume contains an alphabetical listing, by author, of the book reviews included in the magazines and journals indexed in *Readers' Guide*. It is also available online.

Review Columns

In addition to the reviews in the Romance periodicals discussed above, Romance reviews and review columns appear in a number of more general and mainstream sources. Although these come and go, Romance review columns are showing up in newspapers across the country (e.g., *Chicago Tribune*/John Charles) and in the professional journals—*Publishers' Weekly* is reviewing Romances a bit more often, *Library Journal* has increased the frequency of its regular Romance review column to every other month, and *Booklist* now has separate Romance reviews within the general fiction section of each issue.

"Fiction: Romance" in Booklist

Website: www.BooklistOnline.com
Although it had previously included Romance reviews in its General Fiction section, beginning with the September 15, 1998, issue, *Booklist* gave Romance its own column within the broader Fiction section. A variety of Romances are reviewed in each issue. In addition, each September their "Spotlight" feature focuses on Romance.

"Romance" in Library Journal

Website: www.libraryjournal.com
In the May 15, 1994, issue, *LJ* inaugurated the first Romance review column to appear regularly in a major publishing trade or library publication. It was published three times a year until 1996, when it became a quarterly column, with occasional extra mini-columns. In 2006, it became bimonthly and now appears in the February 15, April 15, June 15, August, October 15, and December issues. Although all types of Romances may be reviewed in any one column, most columns focus on a particular type of Romance, theme, or issue and include a definition and brief discussion of the theme. Most reviews are for print materials, although some e-original Romances are now being reviewed. Romance is also reviewed in the online Xpress Reviews. Note: Use the "LJ in Print" link to get to the columns in the various issues or choose the Xpress Reviews link under the Reviews menu to get to the Xpress online column.

Internet Sites

Not surprisingly, the Internet is also a source of Romance reviews and commentary, and it is growing in importance. The various lists mentioned in chapter 19, "Societies and Organizations," often discuss specific Romances, sometimes on a scheduled "book chat" basis, and in addition to the websites of the organizations and publications mentioned above, there are a number of private and commercial websites that also publish formal reviews. Several of those available as of this writing are listed below. However, the web being what it is, if these sites don't work for you, you can find others yourself—simply use a good search engine and toss in a few well-chosen words. It's surprising what you can find that way.

All about Romance (www.likesbooks.com)
Calling itself "The Back Fence for Lovers of Romance Novels," this site has over six thousand reviews as of this writing, as well a host of other features for fans of the genre.

Eye on Romance (www.eyeonromance.com)
An online fiction community for Readers and Authors that includes a wide variety of information, including reviews.

Amazon.com (www.amazon.com)
Familiar to most people, this online bookstore includes publisher comments and editorial and customer reviews for most of the books it lists. *Publishers Weekly* and *Booklist* are among the critical review sources regularly included.

Barnes & Noble.com (www.barnesandnoble.com)
The online counterpart to the brick-and-mortar Barnes & Noble stores, this website includes publisher comments and reviews from both critics and customers, when available. *Publishers Weekly* and *Library Journal* are among the critical review sources regularly included.

MrsGiggles.com (www.mrsgiggles.com)
An often-mentioned, but not always respected, website featuring rather thorough reviews that can be cutting and sarcastic.

The Internet Speculative Fiction Database (www.isfdb.org)
An excellent, detailed resource for book and author information related to any of the Alternative Realities subgenres—paranormal, fantasy, futuristic, and time travel. This is primarily a database and, as of this writing, does not include reviews.

Rakehell.com (www.rakehell.com)
This Regency-focused site features reviews of both Traditional Regencies and Historicals with Regency settings.

Reader's Advisor Online Blog (www.readersadvisoronline.com/blog)
This free blog is provided by Libraries Unlimited and provides a weekly update of author news, booklists, award announcements, relevant links and articles, and more.

Romance in Color (www.romanceincolor.com)
This site focuses on African American Romance and provides reviews as well as author profiles, reading lists, and other information of interest to readers.

The Romance Reader (theromancereader.com)
One of the original online Romance review sites, this source lists a well-organized collection of ranked reviews. Includes archives.

A Romance Review (www.aromancereview.com/news)
In addition to a newsletter, articles, and other features of interest to readers, this site includes a large (more than eighty-four hundred reviews as of this writing), diverse database of ranked reviews.

Romance Reviews Today (www.romrevtoday.com)
Each monthly "issue" includes a good selection of reviews arranged by subgenre, as well as author interviews and other features.

Smart Bitches Love Trashy Books (www.smartbitchestrashybooks.com)
Features sassy, no-holds-barred reviews that "give it to you straight."

Chapter 18

Miscellaneous Romance Reference Sources

Romance Authorship Aids

For anyone contemplating a career as a Romance writer, the obvious and best first resource is the Romance Writers of America (RWA). (See chapter 19, "Societies and Organizations.") With its broad network of local chapters, wide array of professional services, and "prime directive" to help Romance writers succeed, RWA can provide much of what the beginning writer needs, and it is definitely a good place to start. However, help also exists in print—abundantly. From the classics of basic fiction writing to the handbooks specifically tailored to the Romance genre, books that attempt to guide the writer from "plot to print" abound and can be readily found in most local libraries or bookstores. The selective list that follows is a mere sampling of the many works that exist.

Beard, Julie. *The Complete Idiot's Guide to Getting Your Romance Published*. Indianapolis: Alpha Books, 2000.
This simple, straightforward guide by a published Romance writer offers interesting insights and practical, clear, step-by-step suggestions for the fledgling Romance writer.

Erotic Writer's Market Guide, The. Cambridge, MA: Circlet Press, 2006.
Put together by the Circlet Press Collective, this eclectic guide to the erotic fiction market includes a wealth of useful information for budding writers of erotica. Topics in the Advice section range from "Overcoming Your Inhibitions," "Care and Feeding of Pseudonyms," and "Telling the World What You Do" to the more mundane "The Business of Writing" and "Rights and Contracts." Sections on Market Listings and Resources and References round out the book.

Estrada, Rita Clay, and Rita Gallagher, eds. *Writing Romances: A Handbook by the Romance Writers of America*. Cincinnati: Writer's Digest Books, 1997.
This informative anthology includes twenty-five essays on the craft and business of Romance writing by a number of editors, agents, and bestselling Romance authors (e.g., Kate Duffy, Richard Curtis, Janet Dailey, Roberta Gellis, Kathleen Eagle, Jo Beverley).

Estrada, Rita Clay, and Rita Gallagher. *You Can Write a Romance.* Cincinnati: Writer's Digest Books, 1999.
This short volume (120 pages) does a credible job of briefly covering the basics of writing a Romance and dealing with the business end of publishing. The writers are a mother-daughter team; Estrada was the first president of the RWA.

Falk, Kathryn. *How to Write a Romance for the New Markets and Get Published.* Columbus, MS: Genesis Press, 2000.
Billed as a sequel to Falk's earlier book, *How to Write a Romance and Get It Published: With Intimate Advice from the World's Most Popular Romantic Writers,* rev. ed. (New York: NAL-Dutton, 1989), this is an updated collection of essays providing advice to beginning Romance writers and targeting some of the "newer" Romance subgenres. Contributors are writers and other professionals in the Romance field.

Kent, Alison. *The Complete Idiot's Guide to Writing Erotic Romance.* New York: Alpha, 2006.
Bestselling author Kent pens a useful resource that provides a wealth of detailed information on plotting, characterization, writing good sex scenes, and ramping up the emotional tension. The forward by the late Kate Duffy, the editor who launched the Brava line at Kensington, adds to this book's cachet.

Knight, Angela. *Passionate Ink: A Guide to Writing Erotic Romance.* San Francisco: Loose ID, 2007.
A frank, candid guide to writing Erotic Romance.

Lanigan, Catherine. *Writing the Great American Romance Novel.* New York: Allworth Press, 2006.
A multi-published author provides step-by-step instructions for writing and publishing a Romance novel.

MacManus, Yvonne. *You Can Write a Romance and Get it Published.* rev. ed. Laceyville, MD: Toad Hall Press, 1996.
A revised, expanded edition of her 1983 guide, filled with practical, step-by-step information for getting published, including tips from Romance novelists and publishers. Out of print, but should be available on the secondary market and in libraries.

Michaels, Leigh. *On Writing Romance: How to Craft a Novel that Sells.* Cincinnati: Writer's Digest Books, 2007.
After explaining the various aspects and subgenres within Romance, Michaels discusses all aspects of crafting a compelling love story, as well as provides a practical guide to getting published.

O'Conner, Patricia T. *Woe is I.* 2nd ed. New York: Riverhead Books, 2003.
A revised and expanded version of her popular 1996 book, this eminently readable grammar book provides clear, concise advice on all things grammatical—including e-mail language—and should be within easy reach on every writer's desk. An invaluable resource.

Orr, Alice. *No More Rejections: 50 Secrets to Writing a Manuscript that Sells.* Cincinnati: Writer's Digest Books, 2004.
Filled with practical, common-sense insights and advice for all budding writers, this book also includes a number of "secrets" of particular interest to Romance writers. Orr is a noted literary agent, editor, novelist, and writing teacher.

Pianka, Phyllis Taylor. *How to Write Romances*. rev. ed. New York: Writer's Digest Books, 1998.
A revised, updated version of her 1988 classic, this well-done basic text by Romance writer and writing teacher Pianka provides fledgling writers with practical, no-nonsense information on writing and publishing Romances.

Swain, Dwight V. *Techniques of the Selling Writer*. Norman, Oklahoma: University of Oklahoma Press, 1965.
Practical, no-nonsense advice on writing fiction that sells. This book has been reprinted numerous times, is still available, and is considered one of the best by many fiction writers, including those who write Romance.

Vinyard, Rebecca. *The Romance Writer's Handbook: How to Write Romantic Fiction & Get It Published*. Waukesha, WI: Writer Books, 2004.
Supplemented with brief interviews with various popular Romance authors (e.g., Susan Elizabeth Phillips, Lorraine Heath, Suzanne Brockmann), this recent, readable handbook features short chapters and provides an abundance of useful advice on crafting and promoting Romances.

Wainger, Leslie. *Writing a Romance Novel for Dummies*. Hoboken, NJ: Wiley Publications, 2004.
Helpful hints for writing and publishing a Romance novel from an executive editor at Harlequin Books. Clear and well-organized.

Historical Background Sources

Although most Historical Romance writers logically head for the special collections or history sections of their libraries or trusted historical sites on the web when they need to do serious research for their books, there are a number of handbooks out there that attempt to simplify the process. A few of these are listed below. Nothing, of course, can take the place of doing your own research, and the books that follow must be used with care. Nevertheless, they may prove useful, and they are definitely fun to read.

Laudermilk, Sharon H., and Theresa L. Hamlin. *The Regency Companion*. New York: Garland, 1989.
This handy volume provides detailed information about the English Regency Period (1811–1820) and would be useful to readers and writers, alike. Includes an extensive bibliography.

Pool, Daniel. *What Jane Austen Ate and Charles Dickens Knew: From Fox Hunting to Whist—the Facts of Daily Life in 19th-Century England*. New York: Simon & Schuster, 1993.
Similar in purpose to the McCutcheon, this source focuses on nineteenth-century England. Delightful reading with some illustrations.

The Writer's Guide to Everyday Life Series
This series from Writer's Digest Books covers time periods ranging from the Middle Ages to World War II. Most volumes offer a wide variety of information on everything from dress, food, household management, social life, courtship, and

marriage to government, warfare, transportation, and architecture—and everything in between. Although enjoyable reading and filled with intriguing details, the depth of coverage varies greatly and they are most appropriate as starting points for research. Readers will appreciate the many references that most include. Several examples are listed below.

> Hughes, Kristine. *The Writer's Guide to Everyday Life in Regency and Victorian England from 1811 to 1901.* Cincinnati: Writer's Digest Books, 1998.
>
> Kenyon, Sherrilyn. *The Writer's Guide to Everyday Life in the Middle Ages: The British Isles, 500 to 1500.* Cincinnati: Writer's Digest Books, 1995. (A paperback edition was published in 2000.)
>
> McCutcheon, Marc. *The Writer's Guide to Everyday Life in the 1800s.* Cincinnati: Writer's Digest Books, 1993. (A paperback edition was published in 2001.)
>
> Moulton, Candy. *The Writer's Guide to Everyday Life in the Wild West from 1840–1900.* Cincinnati: Writer's Digest Books, 2002.

Word Books, Recipe Books, Spell Books, and Other Miscellany

The following items do not easily fall into any of the more serious research-aid categories included in this guide. They are, however, potentially useful and fun to read. This selective list includes only a fraction of the many titles of this type.

> Brown, Diane. *The Seduction Cookbook: Culinary Creations for Lovers.* rev. ed. New York: Innova, 2005.
> The clear, simple recipes in this delightful collection are gathered into chapters that range from "Seductive Starters: Getting Warmed Up" to "Sweet Seduction: Desserts for Debauchery" and include tips on menu planning, basic culinary techniques, and growing an herb garden.
>
> Cartland, Barbara. *Barbara Cartland's Book of Love and Lovers.* New York: Ballantine, 1978.
>
> Cartland, Barbara. *Recipes for Lovers.* New York: Bantam, 1978.
>
> Friedman, Gil, comp. *A Dictionary of Love.* Arcata, CA: Yara Press, 1990
> Accessible through a detailed Table of Contents that functions more like a subject index, this collection of more than six hundred quotes (grouped into 191 categories) on the topic of love runs the gamut from Shaw to Socrates and includes verbal gems from people as diverse as Phyllis Diller, Napoleon Hill, and Mother Theresa.
>
> Guiley, Rosemary. *LoveLines: A Romance Reader's Guide to Printed Pleasures.* New York: Facts on File, 1983.
> A dated, but delightful, collection of anecdotes, interviews, and fascinating tidbits, both historical and contemporary, from the wonderful world of Romance.
>
> Johnson, Victoria M. *All I Need to Know in Life I Learned from Romance Novels.* Santa Monica: General Publishing Group, 1998.
> Introduced by Romance author and writing instructor Phyllis Taylor Pianka, this easily read, enjoyable book consists of a series of very short chapters that tell readers how to improve their lives courtesy of the truths that Romance novels have to offer. Chapter titles include: "Real Heroes Do Not Wear Suits of Armor These Days," "No One Is Going

to Rescue You—You Have to Rescue Yourself," and "Communication Is the Key to a Healthy Relationship."

Kemp, Gillian. *The Love Magic Book: Potions for Passion and Recipes for Romance.* New York: Little, Brown, 2003.
Spells and advice for all aspects of one's love life from a popular British clairvoyant medium.

Kent, Jean, and Candace, Shelton. *The Romance Writer's Phrase Book.* New York: Putnam, 1984.
Still in print and available, this source contains lists of descriptive phrases the authors consider useful for Romance writers. More than thirty years out of date and generally irrelevant to today's Romances, many of the suggestions in this slim volume now make for hilarious reading.

Kipfer, Barbara Ann, comp. *Bartlett's Book of Love Quotations.* Boston: Little, Brown, 1994.
Containing almost a thousand quotations on love and romance gleaned from the venerable *Bartlett's Familiar Quotations*, this source is divided into five broad sections ("Romance," "Passion," "Marriage," "Family and Friendship," and "God, Country, The World"). Quotes are arranged alphabetically by author within each section; there is no Index. Good for skimming, but the larger *Bartlett's Familiar Quotations* is more useful if looking for a particular quote.

18

Ravenwolf, Silver. *Silver's Spells for Love.* St. Paul: Llewellyn, 2001.
A collection of over a hundred spells for bringing love of many kinds into your life by a popular author of books on Wicca.

Reed, Tina, ed. *Words of Love II . . . The Romance Continues.* New York: Perigee, 1994.
This pocket-sized book of love quotations follows Reed's earlier *Words of Love* and provides an eclectic collection of serious and humorous quotes from a diverse group of people that includes, among others, Bette Midler, Edgar Allan Poe, and Napoleon Bonaparte. No Index or Table of Contents.

Sodamin, Rudolf. *Seduction and Spice: 130 Recipes for Romance.* New York: Rizzoli, 2000.
An elegantly presented collection of "aphrodisiac" recipes for serious cooks that is also fun to read.

Tabori, Lena, and Natasha Tabori Fried. *The Little Big Book of Love.* New York: William Morrow, 1999.
This charmingly done, nicely illustrated anthology includes everything from excerpts from romantic novels by Jane Austen and D. H. Lawrence, letters between historic couples such as Elizabeth and Robert Browning, and love-laced poems by Byron and Yeats to recipes with a romantic flair, lyrics from classic love songs, and retold romantic myths. A surfeit of love and romance.

Wendell, Sarah, and Candy Tan. *Beyond Heaving Bosoms: The Smart Bitches Guide to Romance Novels.* New York: Fireside, 2009.
The creators of the popular blog *Smart Bitches, Trashy Books* have penned a witty, snarky, sassy, over-the-top hilarious book that, while not a true guide to the Romance

genre, is too much fun to be missed. Chapter titles such as "Chapter Secret Cowboy Baby: Cringe-worthy Plot Devices We Know and Love" and "Chapter WTF: Defending the Genre (No, It's Not Chick Porn. Dammit.)" are typical and demonstrate the overall, delightfully irreverent tone of the book, which is similar to that of the blog.

Websites

The Internet is an easily accessible source of information of all kinds, and many writers have already discovered that whether their story requires photographs of Jupiter's moons, a map of the Loire Valley, the text of the president's latest speech, current stock prices, or a recipe for tarte tatin, they probably can find it somewhere in cyberspace. Increasingly, for the savvy searcher, the Internet is also a gold mine of Romance-specific resources, including book reviews, chapters of books in progress, blogs and chat sites, detailed lists of reference resources, websites for authors, publishers, and various organizations—and this is just the tip of the iceberg.

Romance writers and readers were early users of the Internet (one of the first LIST-SERVs was RRA-L, established well before web browsers made much of the Internet easily accessible), and as such, they have created and/or contributed substantially to the web's current content. Over the past decade, the amount of information available online has increased dramatically, and while what is available online is still only a fraction of the information that exists, the Internet is a rich source of information that no one can ignore. Naturally, the usual caveats apply to all information found on the web (e.g., Is it accurate? Is it current? What is the source? Who is responsible for the information? Is there a bias? Is it what you need?), and sites and addresses can change without notice. However, with the new, improved search engines (as of this writing Google is still one of the best) and some well-honed evaluation skills, if what you are looking for actually exists online, finding it should not be too hard. To search, simply use a good search engine, a few specific names (e.g., Romance Writers of America, Nora Roberts home page) or thoughtful terms (e.g., Romance paperback sales statistics, Romance writers resources) and see where you end up. In many cases, the sites you find will provide links, in true web-like fashion, to other pages of interest.

Note: There is a lot of outdated material on the web by now, so it's important to check how current the information is. The websites listed below are simply a few examples of the thousands that exist. See also a few additional sites listed in the other chapters in the "Research Aids" section of this book.

Charlotte Dillon's Resources for Romance Writers
www.charlottedillon.com/WritingRomance.html
A good place to get started with a number of links to other useful sites.

Romance Writers of America (RWA)
http://www.rwanational.org
An excellent source of information for aspiring and published Romance writers, this site provides membership information, industry statistics, lists of award winners, and much more.

Romance Wiki
www.romancewiki.com
This rapidly developing wiki focuses on the Popular Romance genre and is worth a look. Contains good links to other academic sites and resources such as the following two.

Teach Me Tonight Blog—http://teachmetonight.blogspot.com

Romance Scholarship Bibliography—www.romancewiki.com/Romance_Scholarship

Writing Links and Links for Writers: Fiction
http://www.internet-resources.com/writers/wrlinks-fiction.htm
An eclectic assortment of potentially useful links for all fiction writers, but pick and choose carefully.

Chapter 19

Societies and Organizations

A number of useful organizations for readers, writers, and, most recently, scholars of Romance fiction currently exist. Some of these are quite formally organized, with constitutions, by-laws, and all the accoutrements of serious enterprise; others are less rigidly structured; and still others exist primarily in the virtual world of the Internet. Note: Although these organizations for readers and writers have been categorized separately, in many cases the distinction between the two is rather fluid, and many of the groups would be of equal interest to both parties.

Writers' Organizations

Although writing is a solitary occupation, writers are not necessarily solitary people. Most find it important, if not absolutely essential, to communicate not only with the world in general but also with fellow writers in particular—especially those who write within the same genre. While this is often done on an informal basis, a number of official organizations also have been established to meet this need. These groups offer a variety of services for their constituencies. However, one of their primary membership benefits is the network of shared interests and information and personal contact that they provide. The organizations listed below are only a few of the many that Romance writers might want to consider joining. Several also welcome readers of genre fiction in addition to writers.

Romance Writers of America (RWA) Established 1980

14615 Benfer Road
Houston, TX 77069
(832) 717–5200
www.rwanational.org

Founded for the purpose of supporting writers of Romance fiction and to encourage the recognition of the Romance genre as a valid literary form, RWA sponsors competitions, workshops, and conferences, distributes an email newsletter, hosts various lists, and publishes the monthly *RWR: Romance Writer's Report*. RWA also presents a number of annual awards, including the Rita and Golden Heart Awards, at its yearly conference in July. It also sponsors an annual Research Grant Program to encourage research and scholarship in the area of Romance fiction. RWA has a number of subgenre-specific interest groups as well as the Published Authors Network (PAN) and PRO, a group for writers who have completed and submitted a full-length Romance manuscript. Unpublished as well as published writers are welcome, as are agents, publishers, librarians, and others interested in the genre. Since the entire focus of this organization is on Romance fiction, writers of all varieties of Romance fiction should find this association of interest.

International Thriller Writers (ITW) Established 2004

P.O. Box 311
Eureka, CA 95502
www.thrillerwriters.org

Founded for the purpose of promoting the thriller genre and providing "opportunities for collegiality among thriller authors and industry professionals," ITW publishes a monthly webzine, *The Big Thrill*, holds an annual ThrillerFest conference, as well as a workshop program, CraftFest, and sponsors several awards. Several classes of membership are offered, including Active for commercially published writers, and Associate for industry professionals and others. While the primary focus of this organization is on the thriller genre, it may be of interest to writers who include these elements in their Romances.

Mystery Writers of America (MWA) Established 1945

1140 Broadway, Suite 1507
New York NY 10001
(212) 888–8171
www.mysterywriters.org

Aimed at fostering and promoting the causes and interests of writers of mystery fiction, MWA supports various legislation, provides contract advice, offers a scholarship for mystery writing, sponsors the annual Edgars Week Symposium, maintains various email lists, and publishes an annual anthology of short stories by MWA members and *The Third Degree*, a newsletter for members. MWA also sponsors the Edgar Allan Poe Awards, as well as several others, which are presented at their annual awards banquet in New York City each spring during Edgars Week. Several classes of membership are offered, including: Active, for published writers in the mystery field,: Associate, for professionals in related fields (e.g., publishers, agents, librarians, writers of other genres, paid reviewers.); Affiliate, for unpublished mystery writers; and Corresponding, for those living outside the United States. Although the focus of this organization is on the mystery genre, it may be of interest to writers of Romantic Suspense, Gothics, and other Romances that include mystery and suspense elements.

Novelists, Inc. Established 1989

P O. Box 2037
Manhattan, Kansas 66505
www.ninc.com

Open to any writer who has published two or more novels in print format, one within the last five years, Novelists publishes a newsletter, hosts an annual conference, maintains an active email list, and provides a variety of useful information, including an Agents List, for published writers in all genres.

Science Fiction and Fantasy Workshop (SF&FW) Established 1980

This organization is now defunct. The last issue of its *Science Fiction and Fantasy Workshop Newsletter* was October 2006; newsletter archives are available at userpages.burgoyne.com/workshop/. Science Fiction and Fantasy writers interested in an online forum are directed to the Hatrack River Writers Workshop at www.hatrack.com/writers/index.shtml.

Science Fiction and Fantasy Writers of America (SFWA) Established 1965

www.sfwa.org

Formerly known as Science Fiction Writers of America, this organization of professional Science Fiction and Fantasy writers promotes public interest in the genre, maintains a speakers' bureau, conducts seminars and lectures, and encourages the production of high quality Science Fiction and Fantasy literature. SFWA sponsors the Nebula Awards, as well as several others, which are presented at a banquet during the Nebula Awards Weekend in the spring. SFWA also publishes the bimonthly *Bulletin*.

Sisters in Crime (SinC) Established 1987

Sisters in Crime
P. O. Box 442124
Lawrence, Kansas 66044
(785) 842–1325
www.sistersincrime.org

Similar to RWA in purpose (but focusing on mystery rather than romance), this worldwide organization seeks "to promote the professional development and advancement of women crime writers to achieve equality in the industry." The organization sponsors various grants, workshops, conferences, and other events that further these goals.

Western Writers of America (WWA) Established 1953

(505) 277–5234
www.westernwriters.org

This organization welcomes freelance writers of many types of Western fiction and nonfiction, including Romance. Membership levels and requirements vary. WWA sponsors various competitions, issues *Roundup Magazine* (now available electronically), and presents the Spur Awards in a wide variety of fiction and nonfiction categories, as well as several others. The focus of this organization is primarily on "all things Western," so writers of Romances set in the American West may find this group useful.

Romantic Novelists Association (RNA) Established 1960

www.romanticnovelistsassociation.org

This British counterpart to the RWA may be of interest to some. The RNA offers various services to its membership, holds several meetings and seminars each year, maintains an online forum, ROMNA, and publishes *Matters*, a quarterly magazine, and the e-newsletter, RNA News, especially for librarians. RNA presents a number of annual awards which are described in the "Awards" chapter of this book.

Readers' Organizations, Lists, and Websites

The following may be of particular interest to Romance readers.

All about Romance
www.likesbooks.com
This is just one example of the many websites aimed at Romance readers.

Fiction-L
www.webrary.org/rs/flbklistmenu.html
Sponsored by the Morton Grove Public Library, this very active general fiction list of readers and librarians often discusses Romance.

Romance Readers Association Established 1995
This short-lived organization, which published the Romantics at Heart newsletter and was mentioned in the previous edition of this guide, is now defunct.

RRA-L (Romance Readers Anonymous LISTSERV) Established 1992
http://groups.yahoo.com/group/rra-l
Established in 1992 by Leslie Haas and Kara Robinson, this list is probably the oldest in existence and discusses Romance novels, authors, publishers, and a wide variety of Romance-related topics. An archive of past discussions, as well as the lists of annual RRA-L Romance Awards (as of this writing, these are no longer given), is maintained on the website. Subscription instructions are also available on the website. Readers and writers are welcome.

Academic and Scholarly Organizations, Lists, Blogs, and Websites

Recent interest among scholars for whom popular Romance fiction is the focus of their research and teaching has resulted the establishment of several websites and lists. Several of particular interest are listed below.

International Association for the Study of Popular Romance (IASPR), Established 2009
iaspr.org
Established in response to the academic community's growing interest in the study and teaching of popular Romance fiction, IASPR fosters and promotes "the scholarly exploration of all popular representations of romantic love." The association sponsors an annual international conference and publishes an online journal, *Journal of Popular Romance Studies*, as well as a quarterly newsletter for members only. For membership information see the website listed above.

Romance Scholars LISTSERV Established 2006
mailman.depaul.edu/mailman/listinfo/romancescholar
Begun in 2006 by Eric Selenger of DePaul University, this active list serves as "an on-line forum for the academic study of popular Romance novels and related works of literature, film, and popular culture." The list is private; subscription information is on the website listed above.

Teach Me Tonight: Musings on Romance Fiction from an Academic Perspective
teachmetonight.blogspot.com
This blog concerns itself with various aspects of teaching popular Romance fiction in higher education and provides links to a wide variety of related, useful websites (e.g., Resources for Teaching Popular Romance Fiction, Romance Scholarship: an On-Line Bibliography, The Romance Wiki).

Chapter **20**

Awards

Awards for American romance fiction have existed since the early 1980s, but compared with those for other literary genres (e.g., the Edgar [1946–], Spur [1953–], and Nebula [1965–]), they are a relatively recent phenomenon. They continue to evolve, reflecting the dynamic nature of the genre, and in recent years new awards have been established and existing awards have disappeared, changed names, modified categories, or redefined themselves in any number of ways. Most of these awards are for individual novels and are based on the style and quality of writing. However, some publisher's awards are given strictly on the basis of sales. In addition, a few awards are given in recognition of an outstanding career or for other contributions to romance fiction. Many of these awards, including the prestigious Ritas, are presented by the Romance Writers of America as a whole, but a growing number are also presented by unrelated organizations, as well as the specialized sections or individual local chapters within RWA, often in conjunction with a contest (e.g., Maggie, Silver Heart, Golden Quill, Holt Medallion). Romance writers are also recognized by various publications, including two of the oldest romance review sources, *Romantic Times* and *Affaire de Coeur*. Romance is also honored by several mainstream professional journals including *Booklist*, which includes its Top Ten Romances in the September 15 issue, which highlights romance, and *Library Journal*, which lists the ten best romances of the year in the December issue along with the rest of its annual "best" books.

The list that follows is highly selective and lists only a portion of the major national awards given. (Note: Lists of many of the individual award winners can be found in the publications or on the websites of the organizations presenting the awards. The semi-annual volumes of *What Do I Read Next?* [Gale, 1980–] also include some current award winners.)

Affaire de Coeur Reader/Writer Poll Awards

Selected by popular vote of the *Affaire de Coeur* magazine readership, these awards are given in a wide variety of categories, which may vary from year to year. (www. affairedecoeur.com)

Romance Writers of America Awards

Each year RWA presents a number of awards, honoring romance writers for their works and others for significant contributions to the genre. Considered by many to be the most prestigious in the genre, most of these awards are based on excellence in writing rather than popularity or sales. The names of some of the awards have changed over the years. Although many of the service awards are announced earlier, all, except for the Research Grant Award, which is handled separately, are presented at the annual RWA Conference in July. Selected awards of several special-interest chapters are also listed below. (www.rwanational.org)

Golden Heart Awards

These annual awards are presented annually at the RWA Conference to unpublished writers for book-length romance fiction manuscripts. Golden Hearts are awarded in a number of categories which have varied over the years and most recently included the following: Regency Historical Romance, Historical Romance, Inspirational Romance, Young Adult Romance, Contemporary Series Romance, Contemporary Series Romance: Suspense/Adventure, Romantic Suspense, Paranormal Romance, Contemporary Single Title Romance, and Novel with Strong Romantic Elements. All entrants must be members of RWA.

Rita Awards

Formerly known as the Golden Medallion Awards, these awards are named for RWA's first president, Rita Clay Estrada, and are presented to published writers of romance fiction. Ritas are awarded in a number of categories that have varied over the years and most recently included the following: Regency Historical Romance, Historical Romance, Inspirational Romance, Young Adult Romance, Contemporary Series Romance, Contemporary Series Romance: Suspense/Adventure, Romance Novella, Romantic Suspense, Paranormal Romance, Contemporary Single Title Romance, Novel with Strong Romantic Elements, and Best First Book.

RWA Service Awards

These awards are given to the RWA members who have made major volunteer contributions to the organization. Nominations are made by the membership at large; the final decisions are the responsibility of the national RWA board. Several of these awards are given each year.

RWA Emma Merritt National Service Award

Named for a past president of RWA, this award is presented to the RWA member who has made the most significant contribution to the organization at the national level. Nominations are made by the membership at large; the final decision is the responsibility of the national RWA board.

Lifetime Achievement Award

Formerly known as the Golden Treasure Award, this award is presented "to a living writer whose career in romantic fiction dates back at least 15 years." This award of excellence recognizes long-term contributions to the romance genre.

Hall of Fame Award

This honor is given to those writers who have won at least three Ritas in the same romance category. Nora Roberts was the first member, inducted in 1986.

Favorite Book of the Year

Selected by a popular vote of the RWA membership at large, this award was last given for books published in 2003 and has been discontinued.

Janet Dailey Award

This award was presented at the annual RWA Conference for the romance novel that best raises public consciousness about an important social issue and included a $10,000 prize. This award was last presented in 1997 and has been discontinued.

Veritas Award

This award is presented for "print articles that best depict the romance genre in a positive light."

Librarian of the Year

Established in 1995, this award honors librarians who "go above and beyond in their support of the romance genre, its authors, and readers."

Steffie Walker Bookseller of the Year

Established in 1995, and renamed in 1999 to honor a late former recipient, this award recognizes the bookseller who "loves romances and romance readers and demonstrates notable support of romance authors and the romance genre."

Vivian Stephens Industry Award

Formerly known simply as the Industry Award, the name of this award was changed in 2006 to honor one of RWA's founders. It is presented to professionals in the romance publishing industry and related fields for outstanding contributions to RWA or the genre as a whole. Recipients have included publishers, agents, editors, executives, booksellers, attorneys, and writers.

ARTemis Awards

Chosen by popular vote at the annual RWA Conference, these awards were presented for excellence in cover art in various categories. These awards were last given in 2004 (for books published in 2003) and have since been discontinued.

RWA Research Grant Program

This program supports "academic research devoted to genre romance novels, writers and readers" with an annual grant competition that is open to qualified scholars and researchers and provides an award of up to $5,000. The program was established in 2004, made its first award in 2005, and was made permanent by the RWA board in 2006.

RWA Special Interest Chapter Awards

Royal Ascot Award

These awards are presented by the Beau Monde Chapter (Regency England) for the best Long Regency-set Historical and the best Short/Traditional Regency Romances.

Prism Award

These awards are presented by the Futuristic, Fantasy, and Paranormal Chapter for the best in supernatural romance fiction in a variety of categories.

Daphne Du Maurier Award

These awards are presented by the Kiss of Death Chapter (Mystery & Suspense) for the best in published and unpublished romantic mystery/suspense in a number of categories.

RT Book Reviews Magazine Awards

Sponsored by *RT Book Reviews Magazine* (formerly *Romantic Times Magazine*), these awards are presented at the annual RT Booklovers' Convention. Although originally this publication and awards were primarily for romance titles, over the years other fiction genres have gradually been included. (www.rtbookreviews.com)

Reviewers' Choice Awards

Presented primarily for outstanding romances, these awards are made in a wide variety of categories that may vary from year to year. Selection is done by the appropriate RT romance reviewer and a committee.

Career Achievement Awards

Presented primarily to romance writers in recognition of outstanding career achievement in the various categories of romance fiction.

Sapphire Awards

Presented by *The SFR Newsletter* this award honored "readers' choices for the year's best speculative romance in both novel and short story formats" and were given from 1996 to 2006.

Quill Book Awards

Established in 2005 by a joint venture between Reed Business Information (RBI), the parent of *Library Journal* and *Publishers Weekly,* and NBC Universal Television Stations in an effort to promote literacy, reading, and recognize authors of important books, this award honored writing and publishing excellence in a number of diverse categories, one of which was romance fiction. Books were nominated by a panel of over six thousand booksellers, librarians, and other literary professionals; winners were selected by public vote. Awards were presented at a televised gala ceremony in the fall. Note: These awards were discontinued in 2008.

Borders/Walden Bestselling Romance Awards

Presented by Borders and Waldenbooks, these awards are based on sales and are awarded in a number of categories which many vary annually and most recently included: Historical Romance, Contemporary Romance, Multicultural Romance, Paranormal Romance, Romantic Suspense, and Greatest Sales Growth Achievement. Borders filed for bankruptcy in 2011 and eventually ceased all operations. These awards were last given in 2010 for books published in 2009.

Romance Readers Anonymous LISTSERV (RRA-L) Awards

These awards were selected annually by the members of the RRA-L electronic mailing list and were presented in a number of categories, most recently Best Romance Novel, Best Romance Novella, Best Debut Romance Novel, and Best Non-Romance-Genre Romantic Novel. Note: As of this writing, these awards are no longer given.

Romantic Novelists' Association (RNA) Awards

Because there is so much crossover between the American and British romance market, readers may find the following British awards of interest. Both the names and purposes of some of these awards have changed over the years and a major change, the introduction of the RoNAs, is planned for 2012. Most of these awards are presented at the annual RNA Awards Lunch in the spring. Details and entry forms may be found on the organization's website (http:// www.romanticnovelistsassocia tion.org).

RoNA (Romantic Novel) Awards

Presented by the RNA for the best romantic novels in each of five different categories, these works must first have been published in the United Kingdom and must have been published in paperback during the year under consideration. RoNAs will be given in the following categories: Contemporary Romantic Novel, Epic Romantic Novel, Historical Romantic Novel, Romantic Comedy Novel, and Young Adult Romantic Novel. (Note: The RNA Historical Award was discontinued in 1974, reestablished in 2011, and is now one of the RoNAs categories.)

RoNA Rose Award

Previously known as the "Love Story of the Year Award" and earlier RNA Romance Prize, this award is for excellence in writing category romance (defined as a novel in which the central romantic love relationship is the main focus) and is open to members of RNA. Details and entry forms can be found on RNA's website, listed above.

Romantic Novel of the Year Award

Chosen by a panel of judges from among the winners of the five RoNA Awards, this overall award is presented at the RNA Summer Party in May.

Member Awards

Only members of RNA are eligible for the following awards for published and unpublished work.

Katie Fforde Bursary

Established by Katie Fforde, this award is presented to the writer in the New Writers' Scheme "who Katie feels has the greatest potential."

Joan Hessayon New Writers' Scheme Award

Established in 1960 and presented by RNA, this award is open to writers who are probationary members of RNA and are unpublished in the romance novel genre. Manuscripts for consideration are submitted in September under the New Writers' Scheme for critique. Manuscripts that pass through the New Writers' Scheme and are accepted by a publisher for publication are eligible for this award. A cash prize is associated with this award. Details and entry forms can be found on RNA's website, listed above.

Elizabeth Goudge Trophy

This award is a silver bowl presented for a three-thousand-word chapter or short work. Attendees at the annual RNA Conference are eligible. Details can be found on RNA's website, listed above.

Georgette Heyer Prize

Established in 1977 by Bodley Head and Corgi Books but now discontinued, this award was presented for an outstanding full-length historical novel and commemorated Heyer's contribution to the serious historical novel genre. Although this award is no longer given, readers may find references to it in the literature and it is listed here for that reason.

Betty Trask Prize and Awards

Established in 1983 and presented by The Society of Authors, these awards are given to authors under age thirty-five for a published or unpublished first novel of "a romantic or traditional nature." Applicants must be Commonwealth citizens. The prize monies for the Betty Trask Prize and Betty Trask Awards total £20,000, and the number of awards given each year may vary. Further information can be had from The Society of Authors, 84 Drayton Gardens, London SW10 9SB or the website (www.societyofauthors.net).

Chapter 21

Collections

Romance fiction can be found in two basic types of library collections throughout the United States: the general or recreational reading collection and the research collection. While both may contain items of interest to readers and researchers alike, in general, researchers will want to explore the academic research collections and romance readers will want to make use of the recreational reading collections appropriate to their reading interests. Note: For material not available locally, consider an interlibrary loan. This has generally been an option for students and researchers affiliated with an academic library and is becoming a possibility in a growing number of public library systems.

Reading Collections

Most often located in public libraries, general or recreational reading collections do an excellent job of providing access to current romance novels. Although fiction in public libraries, especially those using the Dewey Decimal Classification System, is usually arranged in a single alphabet by author's last name, many libraries have established separate genre collections in which books of certain types (e.g., mysteries, Westerns, fantasies, horror) are grouped together. Romances are often shelved in this fashion. While such an arrangement can be helpful, with the increasing tendency toward genreblending in recent years, a book may legitimately fall into more than one category, and it is important to remember that novels of Romantic Suspense often find their way into the mystery section, Gothics and some darker Paranormals may lurk among the horror novels, many Futuristics and Fantasy romances are equally at home on the Science Fiction and Fantasy shelves, and romances of other varieties can occasionally be found among the general fiction. Check to be sure.

Most public libraries will have some romances in their collections. However, the number and the type will generally depend on the demands of the local clientele (unless the library maintains a retrospective romance collection for archival purposes, either as a part of a large library system or for other reasons). In many large metropolitan library systems, the largest fiction collection is often kept in the main branch. However, this might *not* be the best source for romances. For example, if a branch library has a greater demand for romances or a librarian particularly interested in the genre, it may have a larger, more diverse, and more current collection than the main library. To find out, either ask the local library staff or, if there is a system-wide online catalog, check that by searching for a few romance authors to see which branch has the largest holdings.

Perhaps the best way to find out where the prime romance collections are located in your area is simply to ask other people interested in the genre. As with other types of fiction, some of the best sources of information about books, authors, and collections are often satisfied, interested fans and readers. A few minutes of discussion with a knowledgeable reader can often provide the best and most practical answers in the shortest amount of time. Note: This includes online discussion, too. LISTSERVs and chat groups, while often worldwide in membership, often have participants living in your local area who would be more than happy to help.

Finally, although library collections are by far the most common way for most readers to access romance fiction, some readers are busy building up their own collections. Some do this by intent; others do it simply because they prefer to buy books rather than borrow them. Either way, there are some rather extensive private romance collections in existence. Since these are personal collections, knowledge of them is usually by word of mouth, and access, of course, is strictly by invitation. But just knowing of their existence and learning something of their strengths and weaknesses can be helpful and valuable information in its own right.

Research Collections

Anyone interested in doing research in romance fiction would do well to begin by consulting Lee Ash's classic reference work, *Subject Collections: A Guide to Special Book Collections and Emphases as Reported by University, College, Public, and Special Libraries and Museums in the United States and Canada*, 7th ed. (New Providence, NJ: Bowker, 1993) and sections of several works by Kay Mussell—Appendix I, "Collections and Research Facilities" in her *Women's Gothic and Romantic Fiction: A Reference Guide* (Westport, CT: Greenwood Press, 1981) and the sections on research collections in her essays on "Gothic Novels" and "Romantic Fiction" in *Handbook of American Popular Literature*, edited by M. Thomas Inge (New York: Greenwood Press, 1988). Although all these sources are relatively old, special collections in libraries are remarkably stable and the basic information should still be useful as a starting point. Ash's guide is the most recent edition available and provides comprehensive listings for a large number of specialized collections. It is arranged by subject. However, since there is no one subject heading that covers all American romance fiction and authors, several headings will need to be consulted to be sure of finding all relevant sources. Mussell's works are less current but more to the point, and the brief bibliographic essays provide good overviews of research collections in the United States that contain examples of romantic and gothic fiction. Although useful beginning points, these sources should be supplemented, at the very least, by online searches. Subscription databases, as well as the nonsubscription WorldCat, are especially useful in locating materials specific to particular writers in library collections around the world, and search engines such as Google may lead researchers to other materials of interest.

Librarians and researchers might find these two older, but still relevant, articles interesting reading—Robert G. Sewell, "Trash or Treasure? Pop Fiction in Academic and Research Libraries," *College and Research Libraries* 45 (November 1984): 450–461, and A. Ellis, "Popular culture and Acquisitions," *Acquisitions Librarian* no. 8 (1993): 1–146. Danianne Mizzy's more recent article, "Adventure, Romance, Mystery, and LCSH" (*College and Research Libraries News* 64, no. 1 [January 2003]: 14–15) discusses the practical issues of working with materials and patrons in the Popular Culture Library at Bowling Green State

University. For those interested in developing a research collection of romance fiction, there are any number of books devoted to creating and maintaining special collections, in general, and several focus on popular culture collections, in particular. Two relevant examples are listed below.

> Ellis, Allen. *Popular Culture and Acquisitions*. New York: Haworth Press, 1992. Nancy L. Buchanan's "Selection Tools for Popular Romances" in this useful collection of essays is of particular interest.

> Sudduth, Elizabeth A., Nancy B. Newins, and William E. Sudduth, comps. *Special Collections in College and University Libraries*. Chicago: American Library Association, 2004.

> Compiled by the College Library Section of the Association of College and Research Libraries, a division of the American Library Association, this source contains a diverse collection of sample mission statements, collection development policies, and other useful documents and forms.

Several notable collections are listed below. This list is not comprehensive, and does not include the many manuscript collections that exist hidden in the archives of smaller academic and public libraries, local historical societies and museums, and private collections. It merely serves as an example of the variety of resources available to the researcher in the romance fiction field. Many of these collections provide some online access. Note: An additional resource worth checking out is the list of academic libraries with Romance collections on the Romance Wiki (http://www.romancewiki.com/Romance_Resources_for_Academics).

Boston University

Collects papers, manuscripts, and works by and about twentieth-century authors, including writers of popular fiction. Among the romance authors represented are Norah Lofts, Catherine Cookson, Dorothy Eden, Faith Baldwin, Barbara Cartland, Margaret Mitchell, Anya Seton, and Phyllis Whitney.

Bowling Green State University

The Pat and Ray Browne Library for Popular Culture Studies at Bowling Green actively collects and maintains a large, catalogued collection of popular fiction, much of which is romance. In addition to more than ten thousand series romance titles (including many in now-defunct lines) and a large collection of single-title mass-market romances, the library also collects relevant supporting materials, reference works, and periodicals. The collection also includes some young adult romances, both series and single title. Since January 1996 the library has been the official archive for the RWA and the romance genre—and as such, collects papers and manuscripts of current romance writers, reviewers, and scholars as well as book covers and other materials of interest to romance scholars. Materials do not circulate. One of the largest and best collections available. The University library catalog, BGLINK, provides online access. See the library's Romance Collection web page, www.bgsu.edu/colleges/library/pcl/pcl13.html for further information.

Brown University

This university houses a small collection of the novels and papers of romance novelists who are Brown University and Pembroke College alumnae and/or who live in

Rhode Island. Barbara Keilor, Jo Ann Ferguson, Patricia Coughlin, and Sylvia Rosen Baumgarten are among the authors included. Materials are part of the Romance Novels by Brown and Rhode Island Authors Collection and are available for research purposes but do not circulate.

California State University, Fullerton (CSUF)

CSUF maintains a small Romance Genre Collection consisting of more than five hundred volumes of older series and single-title romances, as well as number of manuscripts pertaining to romance publishing and criticism. The university is no longer actively collecting in this area, although it will accept sample copies of newer series as gifts.

Michigan State University

The Women's/Romance Fiction section of the Russel B. Nye Popular Culture Collection includes some four thousand romance novels (three thousand of which are Harlequins) and nearly fifteen hundred issues of related periodicals dating from the 1920s through 1995. The Juvenile Series Fiction section includes titles from several young adult series romances popular the 1980s. The library is no longer actively acquiring in the romance area.

Stanford University

Stanford's Dime Novel and Story Paper Collection contains more than eight thousand items, including a number of romances, and was one of the earliest of its type.

University of Virginia

This university houses a three hundred thousand volume collection of American fiction published between 1775 and 1980. The collection purports to be complete for the period 1775 to 1875, and very nearly complete for those that follow. The collection includes the works of over a thousand authors, five hundred of which are considered major. Because of its comprehensiveness, this collection should be of particular interest to researchers of the women writers of the nineteenth century. The papers of various authors are also available, including those of Frances Parkinson Keyes, Mary Johnston, and early writer Susanna Rowson. The one thousand–plus volume Sadleir-Black Gothic Collection, a major source of Gothic novels (primarily English), and the nineteen hundred volume Lillian Gary Taylor Collection of Popular American Fiction, a collection of bestselling fiction from 1800 to 1950 with some recent additions, are also located here.

Library of Congress (LC)

Because it is the copyright depository, LC is one of the primary sources of hardcover and, more recently, paperback, romances novels published in the United States during the twentieth century. Since romance novels are usually not catalogued by subject, primary access is by author. Of particular interest to researchers of earlier women's fiction is LC's forty thousand volume Dime Novel Collection (Rare Books and Special Collections Division) which includes a number of romances by popular women writers. The Pulp Fiction Collection (Serial and Government Publications Division) includes some romance comic books and magazines and may also be of interest to researchers.

New York Public Library (NYPL)

NYPL is both a public and a research library. Included within the various collections of this vast resource are materials on a number of American romance authors such as

Susanna Rowson, Catharine Maria Sedgwick, Jean Webster, Elizabeth Oakes Smith, E.D.E.N. Southworth, Grace Livingston Hill, Mary Johnston, and Mary Roberts Rinehart. Early romance fiction can also be found in the Beadle Collection of Dime Novels and the Arents Collections of Books in Parts. Works by current popular romance authors are also available.

***

The majority of romance writers included within research collections are of early or historical importance. However, materials on an increasing number of popular contemporary authors are appearing, and with the continuing popularity of women's studies and literatures, along with the rapidly growing interest in popular romance fiction among scholars (the establishment of RWA's Research Grant Award in 2004 is only one indication of this), it can be hoped that the number of current romance writers represented will continue to increase. The 1996 establishment of the archive for the romance genre and the RWA at the Popular Culture Library at Bowling Green State University was a milestone for the romance genre. Not only does this validate the genre from both a popular culture and a literary point of view, but it also ensures that this often ephemeral material now will be collected and preserved as it is being generated and will be available for future researchers and historians to use.

Chapter 22

Publishers

Romances are published in a variety of formats: mass-market paperback; trade paperback; hardcover; large-print hardcover; and several nonprint formats, with audio (cassette, CD, and, recently, digital) and e-books currently being the most prevalent of these increasingly popular nonprint formats. Traditionally, most romance fiction has been published in mass-market paperback—and the vast majority still is. However, an increasing number of houses are now publishing new romances in hardcover, and more recently trade paperback, with good results. In addition, a number of original paperback romances are currently being reprinted in hardcover, and many romances (both paperback and hardcover originals) are routinely reprinted in large-print hardcover editions, primarily for the library market. In the past decade, the market has exploded with audio versions of romances available on tape cassette, on CD, and in digital versions that can be downloaded directly to computers, MP3 players, or iPods. E-books are also making their mark, and while many of these are "e-originals," romances first published in print are also available in this form. (A quick glance at the Fictionwise.com website or a similar source will give you an idea of what is available.) It is interesting to note that some publishers who began as e-publishers exclusively (e.g., Ellora's Cave) are now releasing some of their e-titles in print, as well.

A number of houses, both large and small, publish romance fiction; however, Torstar's Harlequin Enterprises (Harlequin/Silhouette/Mira/HQN/Luna/Mills & Boon/Red Dress Ink/Steeple Hill/Spice/Kimani Press) is still by far the largest player in the game, primarily because of its large number of series titles published each month, as well as its popular single-title releases. Several of the larger houses and conglomerates with healthy numbers are Kensington (Brava/Dafina/Kensington/Pinnacle/Strapless/Zebra), Pearson (Berkley/Dutton/Jove/NAL/Putman/Signet/Topaz/Viking), Bertelsmann (Ballantine/Bantam/Broadway/Crown/Delacorte/Dell/Doubleday/Fawcett/Knopf/Ivy/Random House/Waterbrook), HarperCollins (Harper, Avon, William Morrow, Thomas Nelson), and Dorchester (Leisure/Love Spell). Several of these reflect the merger and acquisition activity of recent years.

(Note: Although the information below was the most current available as of this writing, the publishing industry is not static and is adjusting to the recent digital revolution as I write. Please consult publishers websites for the latest information.)

Alyson Publications

P.O. Box 4371
Los Angeles, CA 90078
www.alyson.com

Gay/lesbian/bisexual/transgender fiction and nonfiction, including romance and erotica. Lace Publications is among Alyson's imprints.

Avalon Books

A division of Thomas Bouregy.

160 Madison Avenue
New York, NY 10016
www.avalonbooks.com

Hardcover, single-title Contemporary Romance, Historical Romance, Career Romance, Mysteries, and Westerns. Short (40,000–70,000 words), sweet, secular, "wholesome" books. Focus is library market.

Avon Books

A division of HarperCollins.

10 E. 53rd Street
New York, NY 10022
www.avonromance.com

A wide variety of Historical and Contemporary Romance. Avon Inspire is its e-original imprint.

Baker Publishing Group

P.O. Box 6287
Grand Rapids, MI 49516
www.bakerpublishinggroup.com

Publishes evangelical Christian fiction and nonfiction, including contemporary and historical romances through its Bethany House division.

Ballantine Publishing Group

A division of the Random House Publishing Group.

1745 Broadway
New York, NY 10019
http://ballantine.atrandom.com/

Bantam Dell Publishing Group

A division of the Random House Publishing Group.

1745 Broadway
New York, NY 10019
www.randomhouse.com/bantamdell/sf.html

Publishes a wide variety of fiction and nonfiction, including some contemporary, historical, suspense, and alternative reality romances.

Barbour Publishing

P.O. Box 719
1810 Barbour Drive
Uhrichsville, OH 44683
www.barbourbooks.com

Evangelical Christian publisher of fiction and nonfiction, including contemporary and historical romances under its Heartsong Presents imprint.

Bella Books

P.O. Box 10543
Tallahassee, FL 32302
www.bellabooks.com

A lesbian feminist press that now includes Naiad Press, one of the early publishers in the field. Publishes fiction and nonfiction titles, including romance. Bella After Dark (B.A.D.) is its erotic romance line. Handles distribution for a number of other lesbian publishers.

Belle Books

P.O. Box 300921
Memphis, TN 38130
www.bellebooks.com

Publishes women's fiction with a Southern flavor (Southern Fried Fiction), including some romance. Bell Bridge is its new e-book imprint.

The Berkley Publishing Group

A division of the Penguin Group, owned by Pearson.

375 Hudson Street
New York, NY 10014
http://us.penguingroup.com/static/pages/publishers/adult/berkley.html

Publishes Historical, Contemporary, Romantic Suspense, and Alternative Reality Romances under both Jove and Berkley Imprints

Bold Strokes Books

P.O. Box 249
Valley Falls, NY 12185
www.boldstrokesbooks.com

Publishes a wide variety of Lesbian/Gay/Bisexual/Transgendered/Queer books, primarily fiction, including romance and erotica, along with other genre fiction.

Blush

c/o Ellora's Cave Publishing
1056 Home Avenue
Akron, OH 44310
www.jasminejade.com/t-blush.aspx

"The Ellora's Cave line of great romance stories without erotic content" (formerly known as Cerridwen Press). These e-romances have three levels of sensuality: sweet, suggestive, and sensual, none of which are at the erotic level.

Cedar Fort

2373 W 700 S
Springville, UT 84663
www.cedarfort.com

Publishes fiction and nonfiction materials with a Mormon emphasis (Church of the Latter Day Saints/LDS), including some romance.

Cerridwen Press

A division of Jasmine-Jade Enterprises. As of January 2011 this line has changed its name to Blush. See above.

Cleis Press

2246 Sixth Street
Berkeley, CA 94710
www.cleispress.com

Publishes a wide variety of books on sexuality, gender, and gay and lesbian studies, including erotica and fiction.

Dorchester Publishing

200 Madison Avenue, Suite 2000
New York, NY 10016
www.dorchesterpub.com

Publishes Historical, Contemporary, Romantic Suspense, and Alternative Reality romances under its Leisure and Love Spell imprints, contemporary teen romance under the Smooch imprint, and chick lit under the Making It imprint. In 2010 the company announced that its mass-market titles would be released in e-book format only.

Ellora's Cave Publishing

1056 Home Avenue
Akron, OH 44310–3502
www.elorascave.com (or www.jasminejade.com/default.aspx?skinid=11)

An e-publisher of erotic romances of all types and coined the term "Romantica." Publishes some books in print. Mainstream e-fiction is published by Blush (formerly Cerridwen Press). See entry above for additional information and website address.

FaithWords

A division of Hachette.

Two Creek Crossing
10 Cadillac Drive, Suite 220
Brentwood, TN 37027
www.hachettebookgroup.com/publishing_faith-words.aspx

Publishes inspirational Christian materials.

Firebrand Books

2232 South Main Street #272
Ann Arbor, MI 48103
www.firebrandbooks.com

Publishes feminist and lesbian books, including some romance.

Five Star Publishing

An imprint of Thomson Gale.

10 Water Street, Suite 310
Waterville, ME 04901
www.gale.cengage.com/fivestar

Publishes original genre fiction, including romance. Targets the library market.

Grand Central Publishing

A part of the Hachette Book Group USA.

c/o Hachette Book Group USA
3 Center Plaza
Boston, MA 02108
www.hachettebookgroup.com/publishing_grand-central-publishing.aspx

Formerly Warner Books, this company was acquired by Hachette Livre and changed its name in 2007. It publishes romance under its Forever imprint and "fresh, original voices in women's fiction and nonfiction" under its 5 Spot trade paperback imprint.

Robert Hale

Clerkenwell House
45–47 Clerkenwell Green
London, EC1R 0HT
www.halebooks.com/index.asp?TAG=&CID=

Light, short, British Contemporary and Historical Romances.

Harlequin Enterprises

A division of Torstar.

225 Duncan Mill Road
Don Mills, Ontario, Canada M3B 3K9
www.eharlequin.com

The book-publishing arm of the Canadian media giant Torstar, Harlequin Enterprises publishes series romances in a number of lines and single-title romances and women's fiction under several different imprints. Note: Harlequin purchased Mills & Boon in 1971 and took over Silhouette in 1984. Harlequin originally established its romance reputation during the 1950s and early 1960s by reprinting Mill & Boon's hardcover romances. Also note: Harlequin's imprints and various series within them can change quickly; please check the publisher's website for the most current information.

Harlequin Series

Series romances, primarily contemporary, some with elements of intrigue, adventure, or suspense. Major lines current as of this writing are listed below. Note: In 2011 Harlequin renamed its Silhouette lines (e.g., Silhouette Desire became Harlequin Desire).

Harlequin American
Sensual romance with an American flair.

Harlequin Blaze
The hottest, steamiest of Harlequin's series.

Harlequin Desire (Formerly Silhouette Desire)
Short, sexy, intense romances feature arrogant, powerful, alpha-male heroes; smart, complex heroines; and dramatic storylines.

Harlequin Everlasting
Launched in 2007, this now defunct series features romances that often span decades as they follow the relationships of one couple through the years

Harlequin Ginger Blossom
Classic Harlequins retold manga-style. Harlequin Pink is aimed at teens; Harlequin Violet targets adults (ceased publication in early 2007).

Harlequin Historical/Mills & Boon Historical
Historical romances with settings that range from ancient civilizations to World War II.

Harlequin Intrigue
A blend of romance, mystery, and suspense.

Harlequin Medical Romance/Mills & Boon Medical Romance
Romances with a medical focus.

Harlequin Next
More women's fiction than romance, these stories feature older heroines and the unexpected choices and opportunities that can change their lives. No longer being published.

Harlequin Nocturne (Formerly Silhouette Nocturne)

This new dark, sexy, contemporary paranormal line (launched 2006) features fast-paced action and powerful, mission-driven characters struggling with serious issues in a complex, believable, supernatural world. Also includes Nocturne Cravings, a new short-story format with strong erotic and dangerous paranormal elements, currently available only in e-book format. Nocturne Cravings now also includes the less erotic e-book short stories, Nocturne Bites.

Harlequin Presents/Mills & Boon Modern

Provocative, fast-paced, contemporary romantic fantasies featuring wealthy, alpha-male heroes; fiery, independent heroines; and glamorous, dramatic settings.

Harlequin Presents Extra/Mills & Boon Riva

Originally Harlequin Temptation, this short, sexy, upbeat, urban-set series focuses on the lively, passionate relationship of its young, modern protagonists.

Harlequin Romance/Mills & Boon Cherish

This new short, character-driven series aims for emotional depth and good sexual tension (not explicit sex), and replaced both the Harlequin Romance and Silhouette Romance lines in 2007.

Harlequin Romantic Suspense (Formerly Silhouette Romantic Suspense)

A line of fast-paced, adventurous suspense stories laced with glamour and intrigue. Prior to 2007, this series was Silhouette Intimate Moments.

Harlequin Special Edition (Formerly Silhouette Special Edition)

Character-driven, sophisticated, romantic stories that focus on the development of the emotional relationship between the protagonists.

Harlequin Superromance

Complex, well-rounded, relationship-filled romances with a mainstream flair.

Harlequin Bianca

Sweet romances in Spanish.

Harlequin Deseo

Passionate romances in Spanish.

Silhouette Series

Series romances, primarily contemporary, some with elements of intrigue, adventure, suspense, or the paranormal. The series that are currently being published have been renamed and are listed above in the Harlequin Series section.

Silhouette Bombshell

This female action series was discontinued in 2007.

Silhouette Romance

(see Harlequin Romance)

Silhouette Romantic Suspense

Formerly Silhouette Intimate Moments; now Harlequin Romantic suspense.

Mira Books

Harlequin's first single-title imprint focuses on women's fiction of all types, including romantic suspense, paranormal, romantic comedy, relationship stories, and thrillers.

HQN

Single title romances of all varieties.

15

Kimani Press

Harlequin's African American romance program.

Kimani Press Arabesque

Single-title romances. In 2006 this line was added to Harlequin's lineup when it was purchased from BET.

16

Kimani Press Romance

Sexy, entertaining, realistic series romances

Kimani Press Kimani TRU

Teen Romances.

17

Kimani Press Special Releases

"Special releases from your favorite Kimani Press authors."

Luna

Romantic fantasy single-title line.

18

Red Dress Ink

Modern, witty, sexy contemporary single-title line. Chick lit with attitude.

Spice

Harlequin's new single-title line of erotica and ultra sexy women's fiction. Also includes Spice Briefs, a new short-story format currently available only in e-book format.

19

Love Inspired (Formerly Steeple Hill)

Harlequin's Evangelical Christian Inspirational romance imprint. "Women's fiction that inspires."

20

Love Inspired

Inspirational series romances.

Love Inspired Historical

Inspirational historical series romances.

21

Love Inspired Suspense

A faith-laced romantic suspense series.

HarperCollins

10 E 53rd Street
New York, NY 10022

22

Publishes a wide variety of romances under its Avon imprints, as well as some under its William Morrow, and numerous Harper imprints.

Harvest House Publisher

990 Owen Loop North
Eugene, OR 97402–9173
www.harvesthousepublishers.com

An Evangelical Christian publisher of fiction and nonfiction, including some romances.

Hodder & Stoughton

A Hachette UK Company.

338 Euston Road
London, NW1 3BH
www.hodder.co.uk

Publishes a wide variety of fiction and nonfiction through its various imprints, including some Contemporary and Historical romances under the Hodder & Stoughton imprint.

ImaJinn Books

P.O. Box 74274
Phoenix, AZ 85087
www.imajinnbooks.com

Publishes fantasy, paranormal, Regency, and erotica romances in print and e-book formats.

Intaglio Publications

P.O. Box 794
Walker, LA 70785
www.intagliopub.com

Publishes a variety of lesbian literature, including romance.

Kensington Publishing Corporation

119 West 40th Street
New York, NY 10018
www.kensingtonbooks.com

Publishes Contemporary, Historical, Alternative Reality, and Multicultural Romances, and Chick Lit, Erotica, and Women's Romantic Fiction in mass-market, trade, and hardcover under its Brava, Dafina, Zebra, Pinnacle, Aphrodisia, Strapless, and Kensington imprints. Precious Gems and Zebra Regencies are no longer being published and Arabesque is now part of Harlequin's Kimani Romances.

Liquid Silver

An imprint of Atlantic Bridge Publishing.

10509 Sedgegrass Drive
Indianapolis, IN 46235
www.liquidsilverbooks.com

Publishes Erotic Romance, primarily in e-book format, with occasional print releases of previously published titles.

Medallion Press

1020 Cedar Avenue, Suite 216
St. Charles, IL 60174
www.medallionpress.com

A publisher of genre and mainstream fiction, including Contemporary, Historical, Alternative Reality, and Romantic Suspense.

William Morrow

An imprint of HarperCollins.

10 East 53rd Street
New York, NY 10022
www.harpercollins.com/imprints/index.aspx?imprintid=518003

Selective imprint of quality fiction; publishes some romances.

Multnomah Publishers

See Waterbrook/Multnomah.

Naiad Press, Inc.

See Bella Books.

Thomas Nelson Publishers

Box 141000
Nashville, TN 37214
www.thomasnelson.com

Publishes Evangelical Christian Inspirational materials and some romances. Westbow Press is an imprint. Thomas Nelson is scheduled to be acquired by Harper-Collins by the end of 2011.

New American Library (NAL)

A division of the Penguin Group, owned by Pearson.

375 Hudson Street
New York, NY 10014
http://us.penguingroup.com/static/pages/publishers/adult/nal.html

Publishes a wide variety of Historical, Contemporary, Romantic Suspense, Alternative Reality Romances, and erotica under its various imprints including: Signet, Signet Eclipse, Onyx, and NAL trade paperbacks. Note: NAL no longer publishes Topaz Romances but Berkley/NAL announced plans to resurrect the Signet Regency line, which had ceased regular publication in 2006, as part of its new InterMix e-book line in early 2012.

New Victoria

www.newvictoria.com

Publishes lesbian feminist books, including romance, mystery, and speculative fiction.

Random House Publishing Group

1745 Broadway
New York, NY 10019
atrandom.com

Publishes fiction and nonfiction, including romances, in a number of formats under a variety of imprints, some of which are: Ballantine, Bantam, Broadway, Crown, Delacorte, Dell, Doubleday, Ivy, Knopf, Random House, and Waterbrook.

Red Sage Publishing

P.O. Box 4844
Seminole, FL 33775
www.redsagepub.com

Publishes sexy, erotic romance as single titles and as novellas in the *Secrets* anthologies. Also has a line of single-title erotic romances ranging from very short stories to saga-length books available in e-book format.

Running Press

2300 Chestnut Street, Suite 200
Philadelphia, PA 19103
(215) 567–5080
www.perseusbooksgroup.com/runningpress/home.jsp

A member of the Perseus Book Group, Running Press publishes a wide variety of titles, including some gay fiction, within which is an experimental M/M Historical Romance series written by women for women romance readers.

St. Martin's Press

The U.S. publishing arm of Pan Macmillan.

175 Fifth Avenue
New York, NY 10010
us.macmillan.com/SMP.aspx

Publishes Contemporary, Historical, and Alternative Reality Romances, women's fiction, and erotica.

Samhain Publishing

577 Mulberry Street, Suite 1520
Macon, GA 31201
www.samhainpublishing.com

Publishes a wide variety of Romances, Erotic Romance, Erotica, and GLBT romance in print, and, primarily, e-book format.

Seal Press

1700 4th Street
Berkeley, CA 94710
www.sealpress.com/

Publishes fiction and nonfiction of interest to women; some lesbian romance and erotica.

Simon & Schuster

1230 Avenue of the Americas
New York, NY 10020
www.simonandschuster.com (also romance.simonandschuster.com)

Publishes Contemporary, Historical, and Alternative Reality Romances, Gothic and Romantic Suspense, and women's fiction under a variety of imprints including Atria, Gallery, Pocket, Pocket Star, Strebor.

Siren Publishing

2500 S. Lamar Boulevard
Austin, TX 78704
www.sirenpublishing.com

Erotic Romance of many types.

Spinsters Ink

P.O. Box 242
Midway, FL 32343
www.spinstersink.com

Publishes primarily lesbian women's fiction and nonfiction; books are distributed through Bella Books.

Thorndike Press

Part of Cengage Learning.

10 Water Street, Suite 310
Waterville, ME 04901
www.gale.com/thorndike

Publishes large-print hardcover editions of most romance subgenres, primarily for the library market.

Tor/Forge

An imprint of Tom Doherty Associates, part of Pan Macmillan.

175 Fifth Avenue
New York, NY 10010
us.macmillan.com/torforge.aspx

Publishes Science Fiction, Fantasy, and mainstream fiction as well as Alternative Reality Romance and chick lit under the Tor imprint.

Torquere Press

P.O. Box 2545
Round Rock, TX78680
www.torquerepress.com

Publishes a large variety of GLBT fiction in e-book format; selected titles are also published as paperbacks.

Tyndale House Publishers

351 Executive Drive
Carol Stream, IL 60188
www.tyndale.com

Publishes Evangelical Christian fiction and nonfiction, including Contemporary and Historical Inspirational Romances.

Virgin Books

An independent imprint of Ebury Press within the Random House Group.

Thames Wharf Studios
Rainville Road
London, W6 9HA
www.virginbooks.com

It has published paranormal, contemporary, and, occasionally, historical erotic novels in its Black Lace line.

Warner Books

See Grand Central Publishing.

Waterbrook Multnomah

Evangelical/Christian division of Random House.

12265 Oracle Boulevard, Suite 200
Colorado Springs, CO 80921
waterbrookmultnomah.com

Publishes Evangelical Christian fiction and nonfiction, including romances and women's fiction under the Waterbrook and Multnomah imprints.

Zondervan Publishing House

Affiliated with HarperCollins.

5300 Patterson Avenues S.E.
Grand Rapids, MI 49530
www.Zondervan.com

Publishes a wide variety of Christian fiction, including some romance and suspense, much of which is part of various series, including some for the YA market.

15

16

17

18

19

20

21

22

Appendix

Sample Core Collection

Despite the fact that each romance collection must be developed with its unique target audience in mind, there are, nevertheless, some works that may be appropriate for most collections. The following list contains a number of such works and provides recommendations for the beginnings of a basic romance collection. However, because the list is in no way comprehensive, it should be used only as a guide to the possibilities that exist and should be adapted and expanded to fit the needs of each situation. Note: For reasons of age or current publishing practices, some of these works may be out of print temporarily and, therefore, difficult to add. However, with the increasing prevalence of e-formats and the number of publishers making their backlists available electronically, the many public domain books now online, and the improving library-related technologies, it may be easier to provide access to these than ever before.

Literary and Early Romance Classics

Some of the works that follow are not strictly romances, but they had an impact on the development of the genre and deserve a place in any collection that takes a serious approach to romance fiction. Note: This list does not include anything earlier than *Pamela*. However, some libraries may wish to include relevant earlier materials such as the Greek sensual romances, medieval romances, or works by some of the late seventeenth-century and early eighteenth-century women writers.

Richardson, Samuel. *Pamela: or Virtue Rewarded* (1740)
Richardson, Samuel. *Clarissa Harlowe* (1747)
Walpole, Horace. *The Castle of Otronto* (1764)
Burney, Fanny. *Evelina: Or, the History of a Young Lady's Entrance into the World* (1778)
Rowson, Susanna Haswell. *Charlotte Temple: A Tale of Truth* (1791, England; 1794, United States)
Radcliffe, Anne. *The Mysteries of Udolpho* (1794)
Foster, Hannah. *The Coquette* (1797)
Austen, Jane. *Sense and Sensibility* (1811), *Pride and Prejudice* (1813), *Mansfield Park* (1814), *Emma* (1814), *Northanger Abbey* (1818), *Persuasion* (1818)
Scott, Sir Walter. *Waverley* (1814), *Rob Roy* (1818), *Ivanhoe* (1819)

Shelley, Mary. *Frankenstein* (1817 or 1818)

Cooper, James Fenimore. *The Spy* (1821); The Leatherstocking Tales, especially *The Pathfinder* (1840)

Sedgwick, Catharine Maria. *Hope Leslie* (1827)

Dumas, Alexandre. *The Three Musketeers* (1844), *The Count of Monte Cristo* (1845), *Man In the Iron Mask* (1850, third section of *Le Vicomte de Bragelonne*, usually published in English in three separate volumes—*Le Vicomte de Bragelonne, Louise de la Vallière, The Man in the Iron Mask*)

Brontë, Charlotte. *Jane Eyre* (1847)

Brontë, Emily. *Wuthering Heights* (1847)

Wetherell, Elizabeth (Susan Warner). *The Wide, Wide World* (1850)

Hentz, Caroline Lee. *Linda: or The Young Pilot of the Belle Creole* (1850), *The Planter's Northern Bride* (1854)

Yonge, Charlotte M. *The Heir of Redclyffe* (1853) (Some trace the roots of romance from this book because of its emotional intensity, the author's own emotional involvement with the characters and readers, and its premise that love solves all the problems.)

Cummins, Maria Susanna. *The Lamplighter* (1854)

Fern, Fanny (Sara Payson Willis). *Ruth Hall: A Domestic Tale of the Present Time* (1855)

Holmes, Mary Jane. *Tempest and Sunshine* (1854), *Lena Rivers* (1856)

Dickens, Charles. *A Tale of Two Cities* (1859), *David Copperfield* (May 1849–November 1850, twenty-part serial)

Southworth, E. D. E. N. *The Hidden Hand* (1859)

Evans, Augusta Jane. *St. Elmo* (1867)

Phelps, Elizabeth Stuart. *The Gates Ajar* (1868)

Libbey, Laura Jean. Any of her story papers (mid-1880s–1920s)

Clay, Bertha M. (Pseudonym for Charlotte M. Brame and after her death in 1884 for a group of dime novel Gothic writers). 1870s—early twentieth century

Jackson, Helen Hunt. *Ramona* (1884)

Stevenson, Robert Louis. "The Strange Case of Dr. Jekyll and Mr. Hyde" (1886, short story)

Hope, Anthony. *The Prisoner of Zenda* (1894)

Stoker, Bram. *Dracula* (1895)

Johnston, Mary. *To Have and To Hold* (1900)

McCutcheon, George Barr. *Graustark* (1901)

Galsworthy, John. The Forsyte Saga (First volume: *A Man of Property* [1906]; published as a unit (three books) in 1922)

Glyn, Elinor. *Three Weeks* (1907)

Montgomery, Lucy Maud. Anne of Green Gables series (First volume: *Anne of Green Gables* [1908]; eight titles in all)

Webster, Jean. *Daddy-Long-Legs* (1912)

Hull, Edith M. *The Sheik* (1919)

Sabatini, Rafael. *Scaramouche: A Romance of the French Revolution* (1921)

Norris, Kathleen. *Certain People of Importance* (1922), *The American Flaggs* (1936)

Prouty, Olive Higgins. *Stella Dallas* (1923), *Now, Voyager* (1941)

De La Roche, Mazo. Jalna Series (first volume: *Jalna* [1927]; sixteen titles in all)

Douglas, Lloyd C. *Magnificent Obsession* (1932), *The Robe* (1942)

Allen, Hervey. *Anthony Adverse* (1933)

Hill, Grace Livingston. *Matched Pearls* (1933)

Baldwin, Faith. All works, especially *The High Road* (1939), *Blaze of Sunlight* (1959)

Seton, Anya. All works, especially *Dragonwyck* (1944), *Katherine* (1954)

Shellabarger, Samuel. *Prince of Foxes* (1947)

Golon, Sergeanne. *Angelique* (1958), plus others in series

White, T.H. *The Once and Future King* (1958, some parts published earlier)

Dunnett, Dorothy. The Crawford of Lymond Chronicles (1961–1975), the House of Niccolò Series (1986–2000)

Cadell, Elizabeth. *Honey for Tea* (1961, in England; 1962, United States), *Canary Yellow* (1965), plus others

Modern Romance Classics

The works and writers listed below either have provided innovation, set a standard, defined a prototype, or have otherwise influenced the development of the modern romance genre. While some of these are quite recent, many are older but are still widely read. A number of these classics have managed to hold up quite well, but because the genre has changed with the times, others have not and should definitely be read with their historical context in mind.

Anderson, Katherine. *Coming Up Roses* (1993), *Cheyenne Amber* (1994), and others

Auel, Jean. *The Clan of the Cave Bear* (1980)

Balogh, Mary. All works, especially *The Secret Pearl* (1991), *Tangled* (1994)

Bannon, Ann. The Beebo Brinker series (*Odd Girl Out* [1957], *I Am a Woman* [1959], *Women in Shadows* [1959], *Journey to a Woman* [1960], *Beebo Brinker* [1963])

Beverley, Jo. *My Lady Notorious* (1993); first of Beverley's classic Malloren Chronicles

Brandewyne, Rebecca. *No Gentle Love* (1980)

Bujold, Lois McMaster. *Shards of Honor* (1986)

Cartland, Barbara. *Jig-Saw* (1925), *The Black Panther* (1939; reissued as *Lost Love*, 1970)

Castle, Jayne (Jayne Ann Krentz). *Gentle Pirate* (1980)

Chase, Loretta. *Lord of Scoundrels* (1995)

Dailey, Janet. *No Quarter Asked* (1974, England; 1976, United States), *Ivory Cane* (1977, England; 1978, United States), the Calder series (*This Calder Sky* [1981], *This Calder Range* [1982], *Stands a Calder Man* [1982], *Calder Born, Calder Bred* [1983]), *The Pride of Hannah Wade* (1985)

Deveraux, Jude. *The Black Lyon* (1980), the Velvet series (*The Velvet Promise* [1981], *Highland Velvet* [1982], *Velvet Angel* [1983], *Velvet Song* [1983]), *A Knight in Shining Armor* (1989)

Du Maurier, Daphne. *Rebecca* (1938)

Eagle, Kathleen. *Sunrise Song* (1996)

Fielding, Helen. *Bridget Jones's Diary* (1996)

Forrest, Katherine V. *Curious Wine* (1983)

Gabaldon, Diana. The Outlander Series (*The Outlander* [*Cross-Stitch* in the United Kingdom, 1991], *Dragonfly in Amber* [1991], *Voyager* [1994], *Drums of Autumn* [1996], *The Fiery Cross* [2001], *A Breath of Snow and Ashes* [2005], *An Echo in the Bone* [2009])

Garwood, Julie. *The Bride* (1989), *Saving Grace* (1993)

Gellis, Roberta. *Bond of Blood* (1965), the Roselynde Chronicles (*Roselynde* [1978], *Alinor* [1978], *Joanna* [1978], *Gilliane* [1979], *Rhiannon* [1982], *Sybelle* [1983], and others)

Heyer, Georgette. All works, but in particular, *These Old Shades* (1926), *An Infamous Army* (1937), *Sylvester, or the Wicked Uncle* (1957), *Venetia* (1958), *Frederica* (1965)

Holt, Victoria. Most early works, but in particular, *Mistress of Mellyn* (1960)

Johnson, Susan. *Love Storm* (1981), *Golden Paradise* (1990), and others

Kelly, Carla. All works, especially *Mrs. Drew Plays Her Hand* (1994)

Kinsale, Laura. *Uncertain Magic* (1987), *Prince of Midnight* (1990), *Flowers from the Storm* (1992), *For My Lady's Heart* (1993), and others

Kitt, Sandra. *Serenade* (1994), *The Color of Love* (1995), and others

Korbel, Kathleen. *A Rose for Maggie* (1991), *A Soldier's Heart* (1994), and others

Krentz, Jayne Ann. *Gift of Gold* (1988), *Gift of Fire* (1989), *Sweet Starfire* (1986), and others

Lindsey, Johanna. *Captive Bride* (1977) and others

McCaffrey, Anne. The Dragonriders of Pern series (*Dragonflight* [1968], *Dragonquest* [1970], *The White Dragon* [1978]), *Restorée* (1967), and others

McNaught, Judith. *Whitney, My Love* (1985)

Metalious, Grace. *Peyton Place* (1956)

Michaels, Barbara. All works, but in particular *Ammie, Come Home* (1968)

Miller, Isabel. *Patience and Sarah* (1972)

Mitchell, Margaret. *Gone With the Wind* (1936)

Morgan, Claire. *The Price of Salt* (1952)

Orczy, Baroness. *The Scarlet Pimpernel* (1905)

Plaidy, Jean. All works (1945–1993)

Peters, Elizabeth. All, but in particular *Crocodile on the Sandbank* (1975)

Putney, Mary Jo. *The Rake and the Reformer* (1989)

Ray, Francis. *Forever Yours* (1994)

Roberts, Nora. All, but especially the Born in … (Concannon Sisters) Trilogy (*Born in Fire* [1994], *Born in Ice* [1995], *Born in Shame* [1996])

Rogers, Rosemary. *Sweet Savage Love* (1974)

Shiplett, June Lund. *Journey to Yesterday* (1979), *Return to Yesterday* (1983)

Small, Bertrice. *Skye O'Malley* (1980)

Spencer, LaVyrle. All, but especially *The Fulfillment* (1979), *The Gamble* (1987), *Morning Glory* (1989)

Stewart, Mary. All, but in particular *Nine Coaches Waiting* (1958), *My Brother Michael* (1960)

Taylor, Janelle. The Gray Eagle/Alisha (Ecstasy) Series (*Savage Ecstasy* [1981], *Defiant Ecstasy* [1982], *Forbidden Ecstasy* [1982], *Brazen Ecstasy* [1983], *Tender Ecstasy* [1983], *Stolen Ecstasy* [1985], *Bittersweet Ecstasy* [1987], *Forever Ecstasy* [1991])

Veryan, Patricia. Any works, but especially the Golden Chronicles series (1985–1989), the Sanguinet Saga (1981–1987), Tales of the Jewelled Men series (1990–1995)

Virga, Vincent. *Gaywick* (1980)

Welles, Rosalind. *Entwined Destinies* (1980)

Whitney, Phyllis. All works, but in particular *Window on the Square* (1962), *Spindrift* (1975)

Winsor, Kathleen. *Forever Amber* (1944)

Woodiwiss, Kathleen. *The Flame and the Flower* (1972), *The Wolf and the Dove* (1974)

Current Romances

The following list includes a selection of currently popular romance writers and, in a few cases, some of their more important or more popular titles. Highly selective, it is intended to serve only as a sampling of the writers and titles available and to suggest several representative authors for each of the various romance subgenres. The switch was made from titles (as in the first two sections) to authors at this point because, while there are any number of excellent titles that could be singled out for special mention, in many cases it is still too early to tell which ones will become classics. Those titles that have already achieved that status are listed in the previous section. In addition, since most readers make selections by author rather than specific title, a recommended list of current writers who consistently produce well-written romances would seem to be the better, more logical, choice. Note: Many authors write and have written in a number of subgenres and sometimes their works include elements of more than one subgenre. In addition, many who are currently writing single-title releases began by writing category (series) romances, and some writers continue to do both.

Contemporary

Series

Collectively accounting for the largest number of titles of any of the subgenres, the contemporary series are popular with readers and should be represented in any core romance collection. The selection of specific series will vary from library to library, but several different types of lines (e.g., a sweet, innocent line; a short, sexy line; a longer, more complex line; a "specialty" line) should be included. Each series has a number of authors, some of whom write for more than one line. A few of the current writers in each series are included here as examples. (Note: While some series lines have been stable for years, others will come and go as the market dictates. Those listed below are some of those in existence as of this writing.)

Harlequin American—Laura Altom, Jacqueline Diamond, Marie Ferrarella, Tanya Michaels, Pamela Stone, Cathy Gillen Thacker, Rebecca Winters

Harlequin Blaze—Tori Carrington, Elle Kennedy, Jo Leigh, Julie Leto, Joanne Rock, Isabel, Sharpe, Vicki Lewis Thompson

Harlequin (Silhouette) Desire—Kate Carlisle, Michelle Celmer, Maureen Child, Barbara Dunlop, Katherine Garbera, Ann Major

Harlequin Intrigue— Carla Cassidy, B. J. Daniels, HelenKay Dimon, Cassie Miles, Jenna Ryan, Alice Sharpe, Gayle Wilson

Harlequin Medical Romance—Caroline Anderson, Amy Andrews, Marion Lennox, Wendy S. Marcus, Joanna Neil, Alison Roberts

Harlequin Presents—Sara Craven, Robyn Donald, Lynne Graham, Abby Green, Kelly Hunter, Sharon Kendrick, Jane Porter, Annie West

Harlequin Romance—Lucy Gordon, Fiona Harper, Shirley Jump, Barbara McMahon, Diana Palmer, Patricia Thayer, Barbara Wallace

Harlequin (Silhouette) Romantic Suspense—Beth Cornelison, Cindy Dees, Rachel Lee, Merline Lovelace, Marilyn Pappano, Kimberly Van Meter

Harlequin (Silhouette) Special Edition—Teresa Hill, Beth Kery, Allison Leigh, Victoria Pade, Christine Rimmer, Karen Rose Smith, Wendy Warren

Harlequin Superromance—Beth Andrews, Helen Brenna, Holly Jacobs, Janice Kay Johnson, Valerie Parv, Tara Taylor Quinn, Tracy Wolff

Single Title

Susan Andersen, Catherine Anderson, Leanne Banks, Elizabeth Bevarly, Jennifer Blake, Barbara Bretton, Pamela Britton, Connie Brockway, Carolyn Brown, Robyn Carr, Christie Craig, Jennifer Crusie, Janet Dailey, HelenKay Dimon, Kathleen Eagle, Lori Foster, Barbara Freethy, Rachel Gibson, Jennifer Greene, Kristan Higgins, Teresa Hill, Linda Howard (Mackenzie series), Holly Jacobs, Joan Johnston, Lisa Kleypas, Jayne Ann Krentz, Ruth Langan/R. C. Ryan, Cathie Linz, Debbie Macomber, Linda Lael Miller, Susan Elizabeth Phillips, Heather Graham Pozzessere, Nora Roberts, JoAnn Ross, Jill Shalvis, Wendy Wax, Susan Wiggs, Ruth Wind, Sherryl Woods

Women's Romantic Fiction

Barbara Taylor Bradford, Robyn Carr, Barbara Delinsky, Judy Duarte, Patricia Gaffney, Kristin Hannah, Debbie Macomber, Mary Alice Monroe, Pamela Morsi, Luanne Rice, Emilie Richards, Barbara Samuel/Barbara O'Neal, Kathleen Gilles Seidel, Deborah Smith, Jodi, Thomas, Susan Wiggs

Chick Lit

Josie Brown, Meg Cabot, Helen Fielding, Emily Giffin, Jane Green, Gemma Halliday, Alessia Holliday, Sophie Kinsella, Wendy Markham, Lynn Messina, Jane Porter, Annie Sanders

Historical

Victoria Alexander, Catherine Anderson, Mary Balogh, Elaine Barbieri, Jo Beverley, Jennifer Blake, Joanna Bourne, Elizabeth Boyle, Celeste Bradley, Terri Brisbin, Connie Brockway, Shirley Busbee, Candace Camp, Liz Carlyle, Kathryn Caskie, Loretta Chase, Nicola Cornick, Claudia Dain, Jude Deveraux, Christina Dodd, Sara Donati, Shannon Drake, Eileen Dreyer, Jane Feather, Dorothy Garlock, Julie Garwood, Georgina Gentry, Jo Goodman, Anne Gracie, Leigh Greenwood, Laura Lee Guhrke, Karen Hawkins, Lorraine Heath, Candice Hern, Sandra Hill, Madeline Hunter, Judith Ivory, Eloisa James, Sabrina Jeffries, Susan Johnson, Joan Johnston, Brenda Joyce, Laura Kinsale, Lisa Kleypas, Betina Krahn, Rosalind Laker, Stephanie Laurens, Edith Layton, Johanna Lindsey, Julia London, Julie Anne Long, Sarah MacLean, Margo Maguire, Anne Mallory, Kat Martin, Cathy Maxwell, Monica McCarty, Teresa Medeiros, Barbara Metzger, Kasey Michaels, Linda Lael Miller, Kate Moore, Sophia Nash, Maggie Osborne, Patricia Potter, Mary Jo Putney, Amanda Quick, Julia Quinn, Patricia Rice, Pam Rosenthal, Amanda Scott, Bertrice Small, Jodi Thomas, Sherry Thomas, Elizabeth Thornton, Lauren Willig, Joan Wolf

Romantic Mysteries

Romantic Suspense

Cherry Adair, Beverly Barton, Stephanie Bond, Allison Brennan, Suzanne Brockmann, Sandra Brown, Shannon K. Butcher, Stella Cameron, Linda Castillo, Catherine Coulter, Christina Dodd, Eileen Dreyer, Julie Garwood, Cindy Gerard, Heather Graham, Laura Griffin, Karen Harper, Linda Howard, Iris Johansen, Jayne Ann Krentz, Rachel Lee, Cait London, Elizabeth Lowell, Carla Neggers, Brenda Novak, Elizabeth Peters, Patricia Potter, Tara Taylor Quinn, Deanna Raybourn, Karen Robards, J. D. Robb, Nora

Roberts, Karen Rose, Sharon Sala, Meryl Sawyer, Maggie Shayne, Christina Skye, Erica Spindler, Wendy Corsi Staub, Mariah Stewart, Anne Stuart, Janelle Taylor

Gothic

Classic works by Victoria Holt, Barbara Michaels, Phyllis Whitney; also selected works by Allison Chase, Lydia Joyce, Eve Silver, Jennifer St. Giles, Janet Tanner

Alternative Reality

Fantasy

Catherine Asaro, Linda Winstead Jones, Kathleen Korbel (Daughters of Myth trilogy), Susan Krinard (Fane series), Lynn Kurland, L. J. McDonald, Nora Roberts, Maggie Shayne

Futuristic

Jayne Castle, Susan Grant, Eve Kenin, Deidre Knight, Susan Krinard, Kathleen Morgan, Robin D. Owens, J. D. Robb, Linnea Sinclair, Joss Ware

Paranormal

Shana Abè, Barbara Bretton, Kresley Cole, Christine Feehan, Heather Graham, Lori Handeland, Emma Holly, Kay Hooper, Sherrilyn Kenyon, Susan Krinard, Debbie Macomber, Judi McCoy, Karen Marie Moning, Constance O'Day-Flannery, Mary Jo Putney, Nora Roberts, Maggie Shayne, Eve Silver, Christina Skye, Vicki Lewis Thompson, Rebecca York

Time Travel

Jude Deveraux, Diana Gabaldon, Sandra Hill, Lynn Kurland, Karen Marie Moning, Constance O'Day-Flannery, Deb Stover

Urban Fantasy

Jennifer Ashley, Anya Bast, Shannon K. Butcher, Stella Cameron, MaryJanice Davidson, Christina Dodd, Jeaniene Frost, Deidre Knight, Marjorie M. Liu, Katie MacAlister, Pamela Palmer, Caridad Pineiro, Michelle Rowan, Nalini Singh, J. R. Ward, Eileen Wilks

Regencies

Note: Traditional Regency Romances are being published on a limited basis as of this writing. However, a good core collection should contain the older, Traditional Regencies by writers such as the following: Mary Balogh, Blair Bancroft, Anne Barbour, Jo Beverley, Sara Blayne, Mary Blayney, Nancy Butler, Loretta Chase, Marion Chesney, Wilma Counts, Clare Darcy, Carola Dunn, Gail Eastwood, Jean R. Ewing, Elisabeth Fairchild, Diane Farr, Diane Gaston, Sandra Heath, Emily Hendrickson, Candice Hern, Georgette Heyer, Kate Huntington, Emma Jensen, Carla Kelly, Lynn Kerstan, April Kihlstrom, Valerie King, Mary Kingsley, Martha Kirkland, Allison Lane, Judith A. Lansdowne, Edith Layton, Amanda McCabe, Barbara Metzger, Kate Moore, Sophia Nash, Patricia Oliver, Joan Overfield, Julia Parks, Andrea Pickens, Mary Jo Putney, Evelyn Richardson, Jeanne Savery, Regina Scott, Joan Smith, Patricia Veryan, Rhonda Woodward. Note: Many of these older titles are now available in e-book format and some have been re-issued in print.

Inspirational

Tamera Alexander, Judy Baer, Tracey V. Bateman, Shelley Bates, Terri Blackstock, Lawanna Blackwell, Lori Copeland, Lyn Cote, Deeanne Gist, Linda Goodnight, Robin Jones Gunn, Irene Hannon, Robin Lee Hatcher, Dee Henderson, Jill Marie Landis, Beverly Lewis, Gilbert Morris, Janette Oke, Carole Gift Page, Catherine Palmer, Judith Pella, Deborah Raney, Francine Rivers, Lauraine Snelling, Janet Tronstad, Susan May Warren, Lori Wick, Kathleen Y'Barbo

Ethnic/Multicultural

African American

Rochelle Alers, Anita Richmond Bunkley, Adrianne Byrd, Laura Castoro, Francine Craft, Bette Ford, Gwynne Forster, Shirley Hailstock, Donna Hill, Linda Hudson-Smith, Beverly Jenkins, Marcia King-Gamble, Sandra Kitt, Celeste O. Norfleet, Kayla Perrin, Candice Poarch, Francis Ray, Melanie Schuster, Kimberley White, Karen White-Owens, Angela Winters

Asian

Thalassa Ali, Christine Feehan (*Mind Game*), Jessica Hall (White Tiger Swords trilogy), Allison James (Dragon Master Series), Jade Lee, Jeannie Lin, Marjorie M. Liu, Annette Mahon, Sujata Massey, Mary Jo Putney (*The China Bride*), Jenn Reese (*Jade Tiger*), Anne Stuart (*Blue Ice, Fire and Ice*), Mingmei Yip

Latino

Caridad Ferrer, Tracy Montoya, Caridad Pineiro, Berta Platas, Emilie Richards (*Endless Chain*), Barbara Samuel, Lynda Sandoval, Alisa Valdes-Rodriguez, Ruth Wind

Native American (sometimes called "Indian" in the trade)

Judie Aitken, Madeline Baker, Rosanne Bittner, Genell Dellin, Kathleen Eagle, Georgina Gentry, Karen Kay, Rachel Lee, Johanna Lindsey, Lindsey McKenna, Deborah Shelley, Janelle Taylor, Aimee Thurlo, Sheri Whitefeather, Ruth Wind

Sagas

Consult earlier versions of this guide for classic saga recommendations.

Linked Romance

Catherine Anderson (Kendrick/Coulter/Harrigan series), Rochelle Alers (Hideaway Series), Mary Balogh, Jo Beverley (Company of Rogues & Malloren Chronicles), Celeste Bradley, Suzanne Brockmann (Troubleshooter Series), Robyn Carr (Virgin River Series) Kathryn Caskie, Janet Dailey (Calder series), MaryJanice Davidson, Christine Feehan, Diana Gabaldon (Outlander series), Roberta Gellis (The Roselynde Chronicles), Candice Hern, Sandra Hill, Madeline Hunter, Holly Jacobs, Eloisa James, Sabrina Jeffries, Joan Johnston (Bitter Creek Series), Jayne Ann Krentz/Amanda Quick/Jayne Castle (Arcane Society Series), Stephanie Laurens (Cynster Family Series, Bastion Club Series), Rachel Lee (Conard County Series), Liz Maverick, et al. (Crimson City Series), Kasey Michaels (Romney Marsh Series), Linda Lael Miller, Robin D. Owens (Celta's Heartmates Series), Mary Jo Putney, Julia Quinn

(Bridgerton Series), Francis Ray (Grayson Series), Nora Roberts, Lynsay Sands (Argeneau and Rogue Hunter Series), Susan Wiggs (Lakeshore Chronicles), Lauren Willig (Pink Carnation series),

Gay/Lesbian

Alex Beecroft, Saxon Bennett, Ronica Black, Suzanne Brockmann (*All Through the Night*, *Force of Nature*), Katherine V. Forrest, Nancy Garden, Ann Herendeen, Gerri Hill, Karin Kallmaker, Lee Lynch, Annie Proulx ("Brokeback Mountain"), Radclyffe, Lee Rowan, Jane Rule, Sarah Waters

Erotic Romance

Jaci Burton, Louisa Burton, Sylvia Day, Emma Holly, Lora Leigh, Sarah McCarty, Robin Schone, J. B. Skully

Author/Title Index

Subject Index

Note: In most cases topics included in the Table of Contents will not be duplicated in this index.

About the Author

Photo by Jesse Cantley

KRISTIN RAMSDELL has been a romance reader since she discovered Betty Cavanna and Maureen Daly in her junior high library and a science fiction fan since she discovered Robert Heinlein and Ray Bradbury in the same place. She is also the romance columnist for *Library Journal*; the editor of the romance fiction section of the readers' advisory reference source *What Do I Read Next?*; a regular contributor to Gale's Books and Authors blog; the author of the previous edition of *Romance Fiction: A Guide to the Genre* and its predecessor, *Happily Ever After*; a frequent speaker and panelist on the romance genre; and a Librarian Emerita at California State University, East Bay. She received the Romance Writers of America Librarian of the Year Award in 1996 and the Melinda Helfer Fairy Godmother Award from *Romantic Times* in 2007.